McGraw-Hill Encyclopedia of World Drama

4

O-S

4
O-S

An international
reference work
in 5 volumes

McGraw-Hill Book Company

New York   Madrid
St. Louis   Mexico
San Francisco   Montreal
                New Delhi
                Panama
Auckland   Paris
Bogotá   San Juan
Guatemala   São Paulo
Hamburg   Singapore
Johannesburg   Sydney
Lisbon   Tokyo
London   Toronto

McGraw-Hill Encyclopedia of World Drama

Stanley Hochman

EDITOR IN CHIEF

McGraw-Hill Encyclopedia of World Drama, *Second Edition*

1 2 3 4 5 6 7 8 9 0   DODO   8 9 2 1 0 9 8 7 6 5 4 3

ISBN 0-07-079169-4

Library of Congress Cataloging in Publication Data

McGraw-Hill encyclopedia of world drama.

   Bibliography: p.
   Includes index.
   1. Drama—Dictionaries. 2. Theater—Dictionaries.
3. Drama—Bio-Bibliography. I. Hochman, Stanley.
II. McGraw-Hill, inc.
PN1625.M3   1983   809.2   83-9919
ISBN 0-07-079169-4

McGraw-Hill Encyclopedia of World Drama

4

O-S

O

Obaldia, René de (1918–)

French dramatist and novelist. Born of a Panamanian father and French mother in Hong Kong, he came to France when very young and studied in Paris. During World War II, he was a prisoner in Germany. He was first noticed for his novel *Fugue à Waterloo* (1956), for which he received the prize for *humour noir*, after which he won another prize, the *Prix Combat*, for his second novel, *Le centenaire* (1959).

Chronologically, however, his first literary activity was devoted to the theatre. As assistant to the director of the Centre International de Culture of Royaumont from 1949 to 1952, to amuse his guests he wrote impromptus, which have been gathered, with others written later, under the title *Seven Impromptus at Leisure (Sept impromptus à loisir,* 1957). They present strong surrealistic elements; their dialogue and invention recall the intermezzos of Cervantes and won him a place among avant-garde authors.

His play *Génousie* (1960) revealed his talent to the public and established him as a playwright. In this play he goes so far as to invent a new language, "génousian"; hence Irene says "gouroulougiliou" to the young poet with whom she has fallen in love, as if to say "I love you." "What do we care about others since we've found each other?" retorts Christian the poet. This inventive image, product of the two lovers' imagination, adds to the comical dialogue an acceleration of rhythm like that in Feydeau's plays.

The La Villette Satyr (Le Satyre de la Villette, 1963) recalls the plays of boulevard theatre. *The Unknown General (Le général inconnu,* 1964) is a parody of the Resistance movement and espionage dramas. *The Agricultural Cosmonaut (Le cosmonaute agricole,* 1965) and especially *Wind*

Annie Sinigalia and Michel Bouquet in *Monsieur Klebs et Rosalie* as directed by Jacques Rosny at the Théâtre de l'Oeuvre in 1975. [Agence de Presse Bernand]

Monique Mauclair, Jacques Mauclair, and Marc de Jonge in *Le Cosmonaute Agricole* at the Théâtre du Marais in 1977. [Agence de Presse Bernand]

in the Sassafras Branches (*Du vent dans les branches de sassafras*, 1965) have been performed all over the world. The latter, subtitled "A Chamber Western," still grants a large part to parody, but adds an intrigue similar to that of a far-western movie. The Rockefellers, poor Kentucky settlers, their daughter Pamela, and an alcoholic doctor are besieged on their farm by Indians. A warmhearted whore, a hoodlum son, and the Apache chief, who is on the palefaces' side, fight the Comanches and are saved at the end by a rescue column.

In the End the Bang (*A la fin était le bang*, 1968) deals with the supersonic bang that destroys Oscar—a young *illuminée* who has been living for three years as a stylite in order to dialogue with heaven—while tourists and rubbernecks scurry in the constant presence of the guide. Two plays were produced in 1971: *The Baby-sitter (La baby-sitter)*, in which Obaldia uncovers the inanities and hidden lies of life and treats them as wholly logical; and *Two Women for a Ghost (Deux femmes pour un fantôme)*, in which the two women are Brigitte and Viviane, respectively wife and mistress of Pierre who, unknown to them, has just been killed in a car accident; this makes their dialogue unreal and painfully comical.

His play *Mr. Klebs and Rosalie (Monsieur Klebs et Rosalie*, 1975) is a futurist comedy. Rosalie, the computer with monstrous knowledge, converses, argues, or jokes with Klebs, her inventor, who dreams of engendering through her a world in which man will no longer be a machine but human again. "Since humans have become machines, I Klebs am inventing the machine to fabricate humans." But Klebs fails in his Faustian undertaking. No machine is perfect: Rosalie lisps, and out of gear, she chokes her inventor to death.   JOSEPH E. GARREAU

Oberammergau

Village in southern Bavaria, famous for its performances of a Passion play every ten years since 1634. Since religious plays depicting the Passion of Christ developed in the Middle Ages and enjoyed their heyday in the fifteenth century, the Oberammergau Passion play, though a relative latecomer, is distinguished for being the only Passion play performed regularly up to the present; moreover, it is presented exclusively by the permanent residents of the village.

In 1633 the surviving inhabitants of Oberammergau vowed to perform the Passion of Christ every ten years in perpetuity out of gratitude for having been saved from the plague that had ravaged the village for several months. The play was first staged in 1634 and performed every ten years until 1674. From 1680 on, the Passion has been presented every ten years, excepting those rare occasions when war or government decree has prohibited performance of the play.

No text of the original play survives. The earliest extant version, written in 1662, is largely plagiarized from three different sources, the earliest from the mid-fifteenth century. This version was performed until Ferdinand Rosner, a Benedictine friar, composed a totally new Passion play, which was staged in 1750 and 1760. These early versions had many medieval and baroque elements. On the one hand, the sufferings of Jesus, Mary and their followers were depicted in a naive but genuinely moving manner; on the other, there were many scenes of the type that delighted baroque audiences, with spectacular visual and sound effects (thunder, lightning, and earthquakes), clowning, and gruesome imagery (for example, the devils ate the entrails of the dead Judas). Stylistically these plays employed the forms of medieval and baroque mystery plays, such as spoken verse, solo and choral songs, Biblical passages, pantomime, and tableaux vivants.

In 1770, when the Enlightenment took hold of the Bavarian state and church hierarchy, the Passion play was banned because it was considered blasphemous to depict the sufferings of Christ on stage, especially in the putatively gross manner of Oberammergau. The village was, however, able to regain permission to perform a decade later, and from 1780 to 1800, a "cleaned-up" version of the Rosner play, including only half of the original lines, was performed.

In 1811 the Benedictine Otmar Weis wrote a totally new version of the play. This served as the basis for the text by Josef Alois Daisenberger, a local priest, which was performed in 1850 and has been repeated up to the present. The Weis-Daisenberger version definitely eliminated all elements of baroque theatricality, such as the supernatural effects and the devilry of the earlier versions; instead, Jesus was portrayed as a divine actor in a fully human environment. In its current state, the Daisenberger play consists of a prologue, a series of tableaux vivants depicting scenes from the Old Testament, followed by sixteen scenes describing the Passion of Christ, which are separated by other tableaux vivants. The seven-hour performance employs sixty soloists and about seven hundred supernumeraries.

In the 1960s the Passion play came under heavy criticism on account of the blatant anti-Semitism of the text, and since 1970 the relevant passages have been omitted.

A representation of the Last Supper from the 1960 production of the Passion play at Oberammergau. [German Information Center]

At the same time many villagers and spectators have opposed the Daisenberger version in general because of the stiltedness and coldness of the language; they would prefer to return to a modified version of Rosner's much warmer and more baroque text, which is closer to the original Passion play tradition. Despite these persistent protests, the majority of the Oberammergau population has elected to retain the 1850 version.

Ever since the mid-nineteenth century the Oberammergau Passion play has been an international tourist attraction, and the community has reaped great financial rewards from the performances. This has understandably led to protests against the commercialism and tourism associated with the venture. Although there is some truth in these accusations, it must be said in defense of the villagers that they have steadfastly resisted suggestions to perform the Passion more frequently, and they have also turned down lucrative contract offers to film their performance.

PETER JELAVICH

Obey, André (1892–1975)

French dramatist. Born on May 8, 1892, in Douai, he began his career as a dramatist in 1921, collaborating with Denys Amiel on *The Wife with a Smile (La souriante Madame Beudet)*. After writing a second play with Amiel in 1926, Obey met Jacques Copeau, who was then forming the Compagnie des Quinze at the Vieux-Colombier. Between 1931 and 1933 Obey wrote four plays for the troupe, winning the Brieux Prize for *The Battle of the Marne (La bataille de la Marne*, 1931). During the next few years Obey wrote plays of his own and adapted works by Shakespeare, Aeschylus, and Sophocles for presentation on the French stage. *See* AMIEL, DENYS.

Interested in experimentation, he wrote in 1941 a verse drama, *Eight Hundred Meters (Huit cents mètres)*, combining dramatic and sporting elements. The work was produced at the Roland Garros Stadium in Paris under the unfavorable circumstances of the Nazi occupation. In 1946 Obey was made director of the Comédie-Française, but he resigned the following year after carrying out a reorganization in the course of which the Odéon was added to the Comédie-Française setup and reserved for the presentation of modern plays. Obey wrote dialogue for several films, and his adaptation of his own first play was a significant event in the early avant-garde cinema. He died on April 14, 1975.

André Obey.

Rosy Varte and Bernard Blier in *Maria*. [French Cultural Services]

Katharine Cornell and Brian Aherne in *Lucrece.* New York, Belasco Theater, 1932. [Photograph by Vandamm. Theatre Collection, The New York Public Library at Lincoln Center, Astor, Lenox and Tilden Foundations]

WORK

André Obey's first play, written in collaboration with Denys Amiel, was a rather uncharacteristic conventional drama, *The Wife with a Smile* (1921), in which a bored provincial wife makes an unsuccessful attempt to kill her boorish husband. Afterward, however, Obey came under the influence of Jacques Copeau and his Compagnie des Quinze, and his fourth play, *Noah* (*Noé*, 1931), is in the experimental, poetic vein that is the basis of his reputation today. In this modern-language retelling of the story of the Flood, Obey chose a free comic format to present the tragedy of man's incorrigible attraction to vice, contrasting the simple faith of Noah and the animals with the rebellious discontent of the other passengers on the ark. Later critics saw in the play a parable foreshadowing the tragedy of World War II, but Obey himself stoutly denied this.

Obey continued working with Les Quinze, and his next play, *Lucrece* (*Le viol de Lucrèce*, 1931), was a one-act adaptation of Shakespeare's poem *The Rape of Lucrece*. In this work, which shows the influence of Jean Cocteau's *The Eiffel Tower Wedding Party*, much of the dialogue is replaced by a commentary by two narrators on action mimed by the actors. It proved an excellent vehicle for Copeau's stylized and ballet-oriented approach to the theatre, but many contemporary critics find that the alternation between lyrical prose and harsh modern slang detracts from the overall effect. Obey's *The Battle of the Marne* (1931) introduced additional dramatic innovations and tells of this historic moment in 1914 by using a nar-

Scene from an American Conservatory Theatre production of *Noah*, Pittsburgh, 1965. [Courtesy of the American Conservatory Theatre, San Francisco, Calif.]

rator who serves as a variation on the Greek chorus, an allegorical figure representing France, and music and songs that both support and advance the action. The author himself is said to have thought that Copeau's spectacular production was superior to his own text.

After a dramatic adaptation of Shakespeare's *Venus and Adonis* in 1932, Obey returned to the allegorical epic spectacular in *Loire* (1933), in which the flooding river and its tributaries are personified and once more we are treated to the talking animals that aroused such delight in *Noah*. In 1934 Brussels and London saw Obey's *Don Juan*, which was subsequently revised and staged by Copeau as *The Deceiver of Seville* (*Le trompeur de Séville*, 1937) and eventually entered the Comédie-Française repertoire as *The Man of Ashes* (*L'homme de cendres*, 1949). *Eight Hundred Meters* (1941), presented during the Occupation, is a strange work combining sports and dramatic poetry. In *Lazarus* (*Lazare*, 1951), Obey gives us a man resentful of being brought back to life and torn from the comforting earth; and in *A Girl in Exchange for Wind* (*Une fille pour du vent*, 1953), he presents an antiwar satire by recasting the Greek tale of the sacrifice of Iphigenia.

In addition to his original stage plays, Obey wrote film scenarios and radio plays, and he was responsible for a highly esteemed adaptation of Shakespeare's *Richard III* (1933) as well as for translations of Aeschylus and Euripides.

Noah (*Noé*, 1931). Modern, somewhat slangy transposition of the Biblical story of Noah. Though bewildered by God's command, Noah awkwardly sets about building an ark that he then shows to his contemptuous family, who scoff at his tale of the forthcoming flood, though eventually all but his rationalist son Ham come to accept it. Three children God intends as wives for Noah's three sons appear, as do the animals, and the rain begins even as the village representative jeers at the ark. The calm that follows the storm brings joy, but as the days pass and land fails to appear, the cynical Ham raises doubts that poison the atmosphere. Only the animals remain submissive to the will of God. Just as Noah's children turn on him, the dove appears with the olive branch and the ark at last comes to rest. Abandoned by his children, who go forth to seek their separate destinies, and berated by his wife, whose mind has become unhinged, Noah, though unable to understand the ways of the Lord, begins to rebuild a home. A reassuring rainbow appears in the sky.

Lucrece (*Le viol de Lucrèce*, 1931). Poetic tragedy based on the poem by Shakespeare. The events surrounding the rape of Lucrece are largely recounted by two narrators, a man who relates the inner struggles of Tarquin and a woman who describes the character and spirit of Lucrece, while the characters mime their parts. Brutus inadvertently tells Tarquin, a defiant soldier in the Roman Army, of the beauty and domestic virtues of Lucrece, wife of Collatine. Tarquin, stimulated by Brutus's description, steals from camp and proceeds to her house, where in her husband's absence she welcomes him as a guest. Her appeals to his sense of morality fail to thwart his advances, and he rapes her. When Collatine arrives home accompanied by Brutus, Lucrece tells them what has happened; she then kills herself. Brutus swears to avenge her death.

[JOSEPH E. GARREAU]

All were first performed in Paris.

1. (With Denys Amiel). *La souriante Madame Beudet** (*The Wife with a Smile*). Play, 2 acts. Published 1921. Produced Nouveau-Théâtre, Apr. 16, 1921.

2. *Les amis de la dernière heure* (*Friends of the Last Hour*). Play, 2 acts. Produced Théâtre Albert I, Dec. 22, 1924.

3. (With Amiel). *La carcasse* (*The Carcass*). Play, 2 acts. Published 1926. Produced Comédie-Française, Apr. 16, 1926.

4. *Noé** (*Noah*). Play. Published 1931. Produced Théâtre du Vieux-Colombier, Jan. 5, 1931.

5. *Le viol de Lucrèce** (*Lucrece*). Play. Published 1932. Produced Théâtre du Vieux-Colombier, Mar. 12, 1931. Based on William Shakespeare's poem *The Rape of Lucrece*.

6. *La bataille de la Marne* (*The Battle of the Marne*). Play. Published 1932. Produced Théâtre du Vieux-Colombier, Dec. 5, 1931.

7. *Vénus et Adonis** (*Venus and Adonis*). Play. Published 1948. Produced Théâtre de l'Atelier, Dec. 5, 1932. Based on Shakespeare's poem.

8. *Loire*. Play. Published 1933. Produced Théâtre de l'Atelier, Apr. 28, 1933.

9. *Le trompeur de Séville* (*The Deceiver of Seville*). Play. Produced Théâtre de la Porte-Saint-Martin, Jan. 28, 1937. Revision of an earlier work presented in Brussels and London under the title *Don Juan* (1934).

10. *Introduction au Cid* (*Indroduction to "Le Cid"*). Play. Produced Théâtre de la Comédie, Nov. 11, 1940.

11. *Huit cents mètres* (*Eight Hundred Meters*). Play. Produced Roland Garros Stadium, July 5, 1941.

12. *Maria*. Play. Produced Comédie des Champs-Élysées, Mar. 24, 1946.

13. *Revenu de l'étoile* (*Back from the Star*). Play, 2 acts. Produced Baden-Baden, 1947.

14. *L'homme de cendres* (*The Man of Ashes*). Play. Produced Théâtre de la Comédie, Dec. 21, 1949. Revision of *The Deceiver of Seville*.

15. *Lazare* (*Lazarus*). Play. Produced Théâtre Marigny, Nov. 22, 1951.

16. *Une fille pour du vent* (*A Girl in Exchange for Wind*). Play, 3 acts. Produced Comédie-Francaise, Apr. 15, 1953.

17. *Les trois coups de minuit* (*The Three Strokes of Midnight*). Play. Produced Théâtre de l'Oeuvre, Nov. 18, 1958.

18. *La fenêtre* (*The Window*). Play, 1 act. Produced 1959.

19. *Le jour du retour* (*The Day of Return*). Comedy. Produced Comédie-Française, Jan. 21, 1972.

20. *L'Ascension du Sinaï* (*The Climb of the Sinaï*). Play. Produced Radio Lausanne, 1977.

21. *Douze hommes eu colère* (*Twelve Angry Men*). Drama. Produced Théâtre de la Louvière, Oct. 21, 1978.

EDITIONS

Noah. Published in *Twenty Best European Plays on the American Stage,* ed. by J. Gassner and tr. by A. Wilmurt, New York, 1957.

Venus and Adonis. Published in *From the Modern Repertoire*, ed. by E. R. Bentley and tr. by W. Becker, ser. 2, Bloomington, Ind., 1949–1956.

O'Casey, Sean (1880–1964)

Irish dramatist. He was born John Casey on March 30, 1880, in Dublin, the thirteenth child of Michael Casey, a proselytizing Protestant clerk from Limerick, and Susan Archer Casey from Wicklow. Before his birth eight Casey children had died, and when he was six, his father died of a spinal injury, leaving the family near destitution in the Dublin slums. The young O'Casey contracted a chronic eye disease that blinded his left eye and damaged his right, making it impossible for him to stay at school for more than three years. At the age of fourteen, with a dictionary and books left over from the family's schooling, O'Casey taught himself to read and write. He also took his first job, as a stock boy, and began spending small sums for secondhand books.

To please his mother and out of friendship for the fatherly Reverend Edward Martin Griffin of St. Barnabas Church, O'Casey was confirmed at seventeen in the Church of Ireland. He sang in the choir and taught Sunday school, becoming well versed in the Bible and the Book of Common Prayer. At eighteen he became a com-

Sean O'Casey.
[Irish Tourist Board]

mon laborer, and until he was forty-five, when he decided that he could devote himself wholly to writing, he worked among hod carriers, dockers, and construction gangs. In his twenties O'Casey became a militant "lapsed" Protestant, taking a stand against both Irish puritanism and Catholic clericalism. In a search for new values, he sketched and painted and helped found the St. Lawrence O'Toole Club, which sponsored musical and dramatic activities. He liked to perform scenes from Shakespeare and Dion Boucicault. He learned Gaelic, changed his name from John Casey to Sean O'Cathasaigh (pronounced O'Casey), and steeped himself in Celtic mythology.

In 1909 O'Casey joined with James Larkin, the charismatic prophet of Irish labor, to help organize the Irish Transport and General Workers Union. In 1914 he became secretary of the Irish Citizen Army organized in self-defense by the union. He also took part in the anti-British Easter Rebellion of 1916. Soon after, however, he became disillusioned by the lack of constructive action in the Citizen Army and withdrew. In 1918 he buried his beloved mother in a pauper's grave.

By 1919, after having written only short articles chiefly for the labor movement, O'Casey finished his first book, *The Story of the Irish Citizen Army*, which earned him £15. He then involved himself seriously in writing and began submitting plays to the Abbey Theatre. Although his first three plays were rejected, the Abbey directors William Butler Yeats and Lady Augusta Gregory wrote him encouraging letters, and in 1923 they accepted his first full-length play, *The Shadow of a Gunman*. It played three nights to full houses, earning the author, renamed Sean O'Casey, a £4 royalty. *See* GREGORY, LADY AUGUSTA; IRISH DRAMA; YEATS, WILLIAM BUTLER.

The next year the Abbey production of O'Casey's *Juno and the Paycock* had a record run of two weeks and saved the Abbey from bankruptcy. On the strength of this success, from which he earned £25, O'Casey quit his laborer's job to try to make his way as a dramatist. In 1926 the Abbey mounted *The Plough and the Stars*, which because of its unsentimental and even antiheroic portrayal of Irish freedom fighters offended many in the audience; riots broke out at the second performance. Attacked by the press as a "betrayer," O'Casey became convinced that he could never achieve artistic freedom in Ireland, and after a brief visit to London in 1926 to receive the Hawthornden Prize of £100 for *Juno and the Paycock*, he moved to London, never again to return to his native land. In 1927 he married Eileen Reynolds, an Irish actress who used the name Carey as leading lady of the London production of *The Plough and the Stars*.

O'Casey's exile seemed justified when in 1928 Yeats, who had defended him during the riots, but whose experimentation with the traditions of the Nō drama had blinded him to the value of other experimentation, turned down *The Silver Tassie*, an antiwar play that O'Casey had sent him. It was first produced in London in 1929, after a bitter exchange between the two over the experimental theme. This incident interrupted O'Casey's close association with Yeats and the Abbey for several years. Later he and Yeats were reconciled, and in 1935 *The Silver Tassie* was produced at the Abbey.

In 1934 O'Casey went to New York to oversee the production of *Within the Gates*. In 1939 he moved his family, which had increased by two sons and a daughter, from London to Totnes, Devon, where they lived until 1955, when they moved to St. Marychurch, near Torquay. During the years in southwestern England, O'Casey wrote his autobiography (more than half a million words), in which he refers to himself in the third person and often employs dialogue. The six volumes are a vivid and moving recounting of his life: *I Knock at the Door* (1939) and *Pictures in the Hallway* (1942) are about his childhood and youth; *Drums under the Window* (1946) focuses on his activities from 1905 to 1916; *Inishfallen, Fare Thee Well* (1949) describes the death of his mother and his move into self-exile; *Rose and Crown* (1952) covers the period from 1926 to 1934; and *Sunset and Evening Star* (1954) brings his life up to 1953.

Other published works by O'Casey include *Windfalls* (1934), a collection of poems, short stories, and one-act plays; *The Flying Wasp* (1937), a collection of essays attacking the popular London plays of the 1930s; and *The Green Crow* (1956), a short self-portrait.

In 1957, *The Drums of Father Ned* was chosen as one of the plays to be given at the 1958 Dublin Tostal Festival. By January of that year the program had been threatened by the objections of the Archbishop of Dublin to both the O'Casey and Joyce selections, and in February both were dropped from the program. Soon after, Samuel Beckett announced in Paris that he was withdrawing his plays as well. After the festival incident O'Casey refused, save for rare exceptions, to permit his plays to be produced in Ireland. At Torquay, despite his failing vision, he continued to write essays until his death there on September 18, 1964.

WORK

O'Casey's first three plays, on which his fame rests, deal with historical events of the Irish War of Independence

(1916–1922) in Dublin. There is a sharp tone of outrage in his Swiftian portraits of life in the slums of a beleaguered city. The women, who are the victims of war, rise to become its heroines. They are realists, while their men, impotent dreamers, can do little but brag and drink. As wives and mothers they realize there can be no victory in war for them if they lose their men and homes. O'Casey mocks all illusions by looking at the brutality of war through the eyes of working-class Irish women instead of through the haze of sentimental patriotism. Yet there is nothing solemn about O'Casey. When the tragic events of war and poverty become most poignant, he will counterbalance them with low comedy—a music hall turn or a raucous ballad. For example, while everyone awaits a raid by the Black and Tans in *The Shadow of a Gunman*, Dolphie Grigson parades into the house spouting songs and Biblical rhetoric in drunken bravado. Just when Mrs. Tancred is on her way to bury her son in *Juno and the Paycock*, the Boyles have launched their wild drinking party. While the streets ring with patriotic speeches about heroism in *The Plough and the Stars*, the tenement women get into a fight about respectability.

O'Casey's talent lay in mixing elements of tragedy and comedy, realism and expressionism, poetry and prose, idealism and irony. Having spent his first forty-four years among slum dwellers and laborers, O'Casey brought to the stage characters drawn from the Dublin he knew during the first quarter of this century: nationalists, union leaders, drunks, poets, armchair patriots, gunslingers, and their women. His own participation in the Irish struggle for independence from England gives his major works the vitality and clarity of truth.

He felt keenly the injustice of the existing economic and political system, but he believed that even in a chaotic world man could retain his individuality. Consequently, many of his plays are works of social protest leavened with the now tragic, now comic reactions of his characters. The objects of his enmity include capitalism, war, Catholicism, puritanism, and British rule over Ireland.

O'Casey's move away from realism began in *The Silver Tassie* (1929), the experimental, expressionistic play over which he quarreled with Yeats. Although the first and third acts are realistic, the second act is symbolic. This was followed by *Within the Gates* (1934), which is totally antirealistic, being a "morality" play in which the characters—the Poet Dreamer, the Atheist, the Young Whore—are abstractions. The struggle is for the soul of the Young Whore; institutional religion, as represented by the Bishop, is shown as impotent vis-à-vis the love and joy of the Poet Dreamer.

His comedies express the same dissatisfaction with the world as in his other works. *Purple Dust* (1944), although set in Ireland, lampoons the ways of the English and exalts the spirit and humor of the Irish. A more serious comedy with a rural Irish setting is *Cock-a-Doodle-Dandy* (1949), in which fantasy and reality intermingle with trenchant criticism of Irish puritanism and clericalism.

Scenes from an Abbey Theatre production of *The Shadow of a Gunman:* (above) Pat Laffan and Philip O'Flynn; (right) Bernadette McKenna and Pat Laffan. [Dermot Barry photographs]

Other noteworthy plays are *Bedtime Story* (1952), a farce about a clerk who nervously carries on an affair in a friend's apartment; *The Star Turns Red* (1940), an unsatisfactory piece that has been called straight propaganda, about striking workers and the forces that oppose them; *Oak Leaves and Lavender, or A World on Wallpaper* (1947), an unsuccessful antiwar play with a masquelike prelude and epilogue; *Hall of Healing* (1952), an ironic farce set in a dispensary; and *The Drums of Father Ned* (1959), a good-natured satire dealing with preparations for a Tostal celebration which O'Casey withdrew from the 1958 Tostal Festival when the Archbishop of Dublin expressed objections.

The Shadow of a Gunman (1923). Tragedy of the inadvertent involvement in war of a poet and a peddler, set in Dublin in 1920 during the guerrilla warfare between the insurgent Irish Republican Army (IRA) and the British forces. The peddler, Seumas Shields, takes into his tenement quarters Donal Davoren, a struggling self-proclaimed poet whom the neighbors mistake for a brave IRA fighter. Davoren enjoys his newfound notoriety, especially when Minnie Powell falls in love with the image of him as the romantic poet-gunman. Meanwhile, a real patriot, Shields's friend Maguire, secretly hides a bagful of homemade bombs in the unsuspecting Shields's room and then goes off to an ambush that

proves fatal. Afterward, during the resulting curfew, the Auxiliary Guard descends on the tenement. Having discovered Maguire's bombs, both Shields and Davoren panic, but Minnie retrieves the bag and hides it in her room. As a result, she is arrested and in trying to escape is shot to death. It is the shock of Minnie's death that reveals to Davoren his cowardly self-deception and the fact that he is really only a "shadow" of a gunman.

Juno and the Paycock (1924). Tragicomedy of the tenement dwellers in Dublin of 1922, a world invaded by the cruelties of war. While "Captain" Jack Boyle struts about from pub to pub like a "paycock," his long-suffering wife Juno struggles to make ends meet in their meager home. Their daughter Mary, having joined the workers' strike, is no longer providing money for food, and their son Johnny, armless and lame as a result of his part in the battle for independence, has become timid and afraid, especially when he hears of the violence in the street. It appears that the bullet-ridden body of Robbie Tancred, a young neighbor with whom Johnny vehemently denies any friendship, has been found. Although Juno and the Captain try to comfort Mrs. Tancred, they are not deeply affected by her tragedy. However, the news brought by Mary's new suitor, the lawyer Charlie Bentham, that they have inherited half the property of a rich relative, sets them to animated rejoicing. The Captain promises to change his ways, to stop drinking, at last to get a job, and to give up his drinking companion Joxer. Now the Boyles begin to accumulate on credit the garish trappings of prosperity. But the will, ineptly phrased by Bentham, proves litigious, Charlie secretly skips off to England, and creditors begin to appear to take possession of the Boyles's new things. Meanwhile, two months have passed with no word from Bentham, and Mary has discovered she is pregnant, a fact that her other suitor, Jerry Devine, cannot accept although he still loves her. As men arrive to take back the new furniture, Irish irregulars also arrive to take away Johnny, who they have discovered was the one who betrayed Robbie Tancred. When police arrive to tell Juno that her son has been killed, she goes off with Mary to identify the body, now echoing Mrs. Tancred's lamentations and enduring the burden of her fate. The Captain is left with Joxer, both of them extremely drunk and maudlin. ''Th' whole worl','' says the Captain, '''s in a terrible state o' chassis!''

The Plough and the Stars (1926). Tragicomedy set in a Dublin tenement district late in 1915 and early in 1916, before and during the Easter Rebellion, whose participants fight under the banner of Irish independence, the plough and the stars. Peace-loving Nora Clitheroe, a pregnant young bride, tries to prevent her husband Jack from becoming a commandant in the Irish Citizen Army. Their boarders and neighbors include Peter Flynn, an old Irish Patriot; ''the Covey,'' an ineffectual Communist; Fluther Good, an easygoing Catholic; Bessie Burgess, a hymn-singing drunk who is loyal to the Crown; and Rosie Redmond, a tart. Jack leaves to take command of

his troops, and Bessie, having surveyed the battle, reports that the city is full of looters. Loyalty to the cause of Irish independence seems to vanish when all the neighbors join in the plundering. Meanwhile, Nora frantically searches for Jack. He returns, only to leave her again to help a dying comrade-in-arms. With much of Dublin in flames, word comes of Jack's heroic death, but Nora, whose mind has given way, cannot be told. The rebels are surrounded, and all who are not fighting are to be herded into churches to prevent further sniping. Nora, having lost her baby, goes mad with anxiety, and while trying to shield her from stray bullets, Bessie Burgess is shot fatally. Nora, unable to move, cries for Jack's help, still unaware of her husband's death.

Two scenes from *Juno and the Paycock*. **(Right)** Barry Keegan and Dermot Kelly. **(Below; l. to r.)** Niall Buggy, Barry Keegan, Angela Newman, John Kavanagh, and Bernadette McKenna. Abbey Theatre, Dublin. [Dermot Barry photograph]

The Silver Tassie (1929). Expressionistic tragicomedy about World War I containing a bitter indictment of war. Harry Heegan, a football hero who has won a coveted silver cup, the Silver Tassie, which for him symbolizes victorious youth, loves beautiful Jessie Taite. Harry and Jessie drink the heady wine of love and victory from the cup before Harry must go back to the front. An expressionistic second act shows the horrors of the battlefield, and the succeeding two acts reveal the realistic consequences of that horror. The war kills and injures many who are dear to Harry, and he returns from it a wheelchair invalid whom Jessie drops for his healthy friend Barney. At a celebration of the Avondale Football Club after the war, the disabled wear their medals. Harry, symbolic of all soldiers, bitterly resents his lot, and in a moment of high ceremony he drinks wine, which resembles the blood shed in battle, from his old silver cup.

Within the Gates (1934). Religious parable resembling an old morality play and taking place in a beautiful park resembling London's Hyde Park, a microcosm of the world of the 1930s. Ranging through four seasons starting with the regeneration of spring, symbolic characters oppose each other for the soul of Jannice, a whore. Jannice attempts to save herself from sin and death and to identify herself with the spirit of life. Abandoned by the Atheist, who cannot save her, rejected by the Gardener, whom she offers to marry, and fearing hell's fire, she desperately asks help of a Bishop, who, recognizing her as his own illegitimate child, guiltily offers her a religious life in a hostel under the supervision of nuns. She rejects his offer. The Poet Dreamer represents the good

David Renton and Phyllis Malcolm Stewart in a 1967 Canadian production of *Juno and the Paycock*. [Neptune Theatre, Halifax, Nova Scotia]

life, joy, and love. He emphasizes the celebration of life through God and joy and tries to win Jannice over. But her choice of the Poet Dreamer's way of life comes too late, for she is dying of heart trouble. As she dies and the park gates close, she reconciles the Bishop's God and the Poet Dreamer's, bringing the two, God and joy, closer together.

The Star Turns Red (1940). A propaganda drama showing an Irish family on Christmas Eve as a microcosm of world division. The Old Man is content with little; the Old Woman lives for her religion; one son, Jack, is a Communist; and another, Kian, a Fascist. When Jack is threatened by storm troopers, his fiancé Julia strikes their leader and as a result is led away to be whipped. In his attempt to rescue his daughter, Julia's father is shot by Kian, leaving Jack to fight for the Communist cause. Meanwhile, attempts are made by priests and union leaders to sabotage the impending strike. Inevitably, war between Fascists and Communists breaks out, Jack is killed, and symbolically the star of Bethlehem turns red while the workers sing "The Internationale."

Purple Dust (1944). A farce about two English buffoons, Cyril Poges, rich and self-made, and Basil Stokes, a middle-aged, Oxford-educated fool, who bring their young Irish mistresses, Souhaun and Avril, to a dilapidated Tudor mansion, planning to restore it and enjoy Irish country life. The builder's foreman, O'Killigain, and a poetic workman, O'Dempsey, flirt with the two girls. Both English and Irish are tested by amateur farming, wretched telephone service, a lack of modern heating and toilet facilities, and a disastrous flood caused by a

Barry Fitzgerald and Eileen Crowe in an Abbey Theatre production of *Juno and the Paycock*. [Theatre Collection, The New York Public Library at Lincoln Center, Astor, Lenox and Tilden Foundations]

spell of Irish rainfall. Having used the Englishmen to gain financial independence, the girls leave them the "purple dust" of Tudor Ireland and go off with their homespun Irish lovers.

Red Roses for Me (1943). Morality play, autobiographical in content, centering on Ayamonn Breydon, a young Protestant laborer with poetic aspirations. He works in the Dublin railroad yards and is one of the leaders in the union's attempt to win a shilling increase in wages. The workers fear their demands will be rejected and are planning a strike. Ayamonn's Catholic sweetheart Sheila is against the strike. She begs him to give up his foolish songs and his dreams for a better Ireland.

Ayamonn is forced to choose between Sheila and his ideals of religion, nationalism, and labor. He decides he must fight for his dream of a better world. The strike is called, and in the riot that follows, Ayamonn is killed by the police. Sheila painfully realizes that his death is an inspiration for others to carry on the fight for a better life.

Oak Leaves and Lavender, or A World on Wallpaper (1947). Patriotic drama celebrating the indomitable spirit

Jenny Egan (standing) and Jenny Hecht in the Phoenix Theatre's 1960 production of *The Plough and the Stars*. [Courtesy of Phoenix Theatre. Photograph by Henry Grossman]

Kieron Moore and Maureen Prior in a London production of *Red Roses for Me*, 1946. [Raymond Mander and Joe Mitchenson Theatre Collection]

of the British people during the early days of World War II. Making liberal use of music, the play successfully integrates fantasy and realism. O'Casey's characters are representative of various types: the old, doomed to sorrow; the young men, fated to die; the young girls, bound to grieve; the cowards; and the ordinary people who face the future courageously and optimistically. The Hatherleighs' only son Edgar and their Irish butler's only son Drishogue, young fighter pilots with short life expectancies, love their sweethearts, to their parents' dismay, through blackouts, alerts, bombings, and home-guard drills. Drishogue's sweetheart is left happily pregnant and secretly married. The young men are brought home in flag-draped coffins, but freedom and new life survive.

Cock-a-Doodle-Dandy (1949). Comic fantasy in which an enchanted cock is O'Casey's symbol for man's freedom and love of life: the life force. The Cock-a-Doodle-Dandy, a life-size dancing bird, is turned loose in a joyless little Irish town where the priest warns the people that the cock is an incarnation of the devil. The main question is whether the cock represents the forces of good or the forces of evil. The women in Michael Marthtaun's life—his daughter, his young second wife Lorna, and Marion, the maid—are not afraid of the cock. But they are eventually driven from the town into exile by the forces of fear and superstition, and Michael is left to face a bitter old age alone.

The Bishop's Bonfire (1955). Comedy of protest with a melodramatic conclusion centering on a Bishop's visit to his native village of Ballyoonagh. Preparations are being made in the home of the richest man in town, Councillor Reiligan, who has just been made a papal count. The festival atmosphere conveyed by the bumbling but joyous workmen contrasts with solemn ritual preparations that are to culminate in a huge bonfire of "evil" literature. The pietism of Councillor Reiligan is reflected in his domination of his children's lives. He forces his daughter Keelin to give up her lower-class suitor and arranges a match for her with a wealthy old farmer. He wants his other daughter, Fooraun, to keep her vows of perpetual chastity despite the fact she loves Manus Moanroe. A sympathetic young curate urges Fooraun to break her vows and marry Manus. Manus then breaks into Reiligan's house and steals the church funds. When Fooraun tries to stop him, he shoots her. Dying, she signs a suicide note to absolve him from the crime. At the play's end, the Bishop's bonfire, the town's welcome, is seen burning brightly, the symbol of sham morality.

The Drums of Father Ned (1959). Comic fantasy dealing with an ancient family feud between Mayor Bennington and Deputy Mayor McGilligan while a Tostal, a national arts festival, is being held in Doonavale. Michael Bennington and Nora McGilligan of the two feuding families are in love and represent the only hope for Doonavale and Ireland. In the background Father Ned, who does not appear onstage, is often heard beating his drum, a symbolic reminder of the joy of life. He has a miraculous influence upon the young people of Doonavale, who organize the Tostal their own way and bring friendly cooperation to Doonavale.   [CAROL GELDERMAN]

PLAYS

1. *The Shadow of a Gunman.* Tragedy, 2 acts. Published 1925. Produced Dublin, Abbey Theatre, Apr. 9, 1923.
2. *Cathleen Listens In.* Comic fantasy, 1 act. Produced Dublin, Abbey Theatre, Oct. 1, 1923.
3. *Juno and the Paycock.* Tragedy, 3 acts. Published 1925. Produced Dublin, Abbey Theatre, Mar. 3, 1924.
4. *Nannie's Night Out.* Farce, 1 act. Produced Dublin, Abbey Theatre, Sept. 29, 1924.
5. *The Plough and the Stars.* Tragedy, 4 acts. Published 1926. Produced Dublin, Abbey Theatre, Feb. 8, 1926.
6. *The Silver Tassie.* Tragicomedy, 4 acts. Published 1928. Produced London, Apollo Theatre, Oct. 11, 1929.
7. *Within the Gates.* Morality play, 4 scenes. Published 1933. Produced London, Royalty Theatre, Feb. 7, 1934.
8. *The End of the Beginning.* Farce, 1 act. Published 1935. Produced Dublin, Abbey Theatre, Feb. 8, 1937.
9. *The Star Turns Red.* Morality play, 1 act. Published 1940. Produced London, Unity Theatre, Mar. 20, 1940.
10. *Purple Dust.* Wayward comedy, 3 acts. Published 1940. Produced Boston, Boston Tributary Theatre, Dec. 6, 1944.
11. *Red Roses for Me.* Play, 4 acts. Published 1942. Produced Dublin, Olympia Theatre, April, 1943
12. *Oak Leaves and Lavender, or A World on Wallpaper.* Morality play. Published 1946. Produced London, Lyric Theatre, Hammersmith, May 13, 1947.
13. *Pound on Demand.* Farce, 1 act. Published 1951. Produced New York, American Repertory Theatre, January, 1947.
14. *Cock-a-Doodle-Dandy.* Comic fantasy. Published 1949. Produced Newcastle on Tyne, People's Theatre, Dec. 11, 1949.
15. *Hall of Healing.* Farce, 1 act. Published 1951. Produced New York, Yugoslav-American Hall, May 7, 1952.
16. *Bedtime Story.* An Anatole burlesque, 1 act. Published 1951. Pro-

duced New York, Yugoslav-American Hall, May 7, 1952.
17. *Time to Go.* Morality comedy, 1 act. Published 1951. Produced New York, Yugoslav-American Hall, May 7, 1952.
18. *The Bishop's Bonfire.* Comedy. Written 1954. Published 1955. Produced Dublin, Gaiety Theatre, Feb. 28, 1955.
19. *The Drums of Father Ned.* Comic fantasy. Written 1958. Produced Lafayette, Ind., 1959; Toronto, 1962.
20. *The Moon Shines on Kylenamoe.* Comedy. Published 1961. Produced New York, Theatre de Lys, 1962.
21. *Behind the Green Curtains.* Drama. Published 1961. Produced Rochester, N.Y., University of Rochester, 1962.
22. *Figure in the Night.* Comedy. Published 1961. Produced New York, Theatre de Lys, 1962.

EDITIONS

Collections
Collected Plays, 4 vols., London, New York, 1949–1951. Vol. 1 (1949): *Juno and the Paycock, The Shadow of a Gunman, The Plough and the Stars, The End of the Beginning, A Pound on Demand;* vol. 2 (1949): *The Silver Tassie, Within The Gates, The Star Turns Red;* vol. 3 (1951): *Purple Dust, Red Roses for Me, Hall of Healing;* vol. 4 (1951): *Oak Leaves and Lavender, Cock-a-Doodle-Dandy, Bedtime Story, Time To Go.*
Mirror in My House: The Autobiographies of Sean O'Casey, 2 vols., New York, 1956, London, 1963. Contains six volumes of autobiography: vol. 1, *I Knock at the Door;* vol. 2, *Pictures in the Hallway;* vol. 3, *Drums under the Windows;* vol. 4, *Irishfallen, Fare Thee Well;* vol. 5, *Rose and Crown;* vol. 6, *Sunset and Evening Star.*
The Letters of Sean O'Casey, ed. by D. Krause, New York, 1975–1978: vol. 1, 1910–1941 (1975); vol. 2, 1942–1954 (1977); vol. 3, 1955–1964 (1978).
Miscellaneous
Songs of the Wren, 1st and 2d ser., 1918; *More Wren Songs,* 1918; *The Story of Thomas Ashe,* 1918; *The Sacrifice of Thomas Ashe,* 1918; *The Story of the Irish Citizen Army,* 1919; *Windfalls,* 1934; *The Flying Wasp,* 1937; *The Green Crow,* 1956; *Feathers from the Green Crow: Sean O'Casey 1905–1925,* ed. by R. Hogan, 1962; *Under a Colored Cap,* 1963; *Blasts and Benedictions,* 1967.

CRITICISM

R. Hogan, *The Experiments of Sean O'Casey,* New York, 1960; D. Krause, *Sean O'Casey: The Man and His Work,* New York, 1960 (rev. ed., 1975); S. Cowasjee, *Sean O'Casey, the Man Behind the Plays,* New York, 1963 (rev. ed., 1966); G. Fallon, *Sean O'Casey, the Man I Knew,* London, 1965; *The World of Sean O'Casey,* ed. by S. McCann, London, 1966; W. Armstrong, *Sean O'Casey,* London, 1967; D. Krause, *A Self-Portrait of the Artist As a Man: Sean O'Casey's Letters,* Dublin, 1968; M. Malone, *The Plays of Sean O'Casey,* Carbondale, Ill., 1969; M. Margulies, *The Early Life of Sean O'Casey,* Dublin, 1970; B. Bernstock, *Sean O'Casey,* Lewisburg, Pa., 1971; E. O'Casey, *Sean,* New York, 1971; J. O'Riordan and E. H. Mikhail, *The Sting and the Twinkle, Conversations With Sean O'Casey,* London, 1974; *Sean O'Casey, A Collection of Critical Essays,* ed. by T. Kilroy, 20th Century Views Series, Englewood Cliffs, N.J., 1975; *Sean O'Casey Review,* ed. by R. Lowery, from 1975.

Odets, Clifford   (1906–1963)

American dramatist and screenwriter. He was born in Philadelphia on July 18, 1906, the son of Lithuanian Jewish immigrants. Two years later, the family moved to New York, where Odets's father became a successful printer. Clifford, having attended high school from 1921 to 1923, left in his third year to write poetry. When his father violently opposed his choice of a career, Odets turned to the theatre, acting on radio programs and in stock companies. Beginning in 1928, he played bit parts for the Theatre Guild, an organization formed to present superior noncommercial plays to the American public, and later joined its offspring, the Group Theatre, a troupe that in general devoted its repertory to plays of social significance. In 1933 Odets wrote *Awake and Sing* but found no producer for it. His first successful play, the one-act *Waiting for Lefty,* was written in three days as an entry to a New York Theatre League contest. It won the award and was produced by the league in 1935.

Elia Kazan (with both hands raised) as Agate Keller in *Waiting for Lefty*. New York, Longacre Theatre, 1935. [Photograph by Vandamm. Theatre Collection, The New York Public Library at Lincoln Center, Astor, Lenox and Tilden Foundations]

The Group Theatre then began to stage Odets's plays. *Till the Day I Die* (1935), an anti-Nazi drama, won acclaim and became the group's mainstay; the same year the group also presented *Awake and Sing* and *Paradise Lost*.

Both the Group Theatre and Odets were significantly affected by the Depression; political sympathies veered toward the left, and Odets criticized the tenets of capitalism and the bourgeoisie in many of his plays. When, in 1952, he was called to testify before the House of Representatives Committee on Un-American Activities investigating Communist influence in the arts, Odets explained that he joined the Communist party in 1934, when he was "living on ten cents a day," but had dissociated himself from the party within a year because it had tried to make him conform to ideological formulas in his writings.

In 1936, to aid the financially faltering Group Theatre, Odets began working in Hollywood as a writer and producer, and for a year and a half he earned a salary of $2,500 a week. He returned to New York with a new play, *Golden Boy* (1937), which became his biggest hit. After that he worked mainly in Hollywood as a writer and director; periodically he wrote plays that met with only mild approval. His last Broadway success was *The Country Girl* (1950). Two marriages, one to Luise Rainer and the other to Betty Grayson, ended in divorce.

Odets died of cancer in Los Angeles on August 14, 1963.

WORK

The leading dramatist of the Group Theatre, Odets is the most important of the American social dramatists of the 1930s whose concern focused on the working-class man, his aspirations, and his place in modern society. Less didactic and self-consciously proletarian than many of his fellow writers of the left, Odets in his more successful earlier plays fused the zeal of militant social reform with insight into human behavior. Thus, whereas proletarian dramatists generally tended to rail against the social order and the inequities of the class structure in broad gestures, Odets chose to concentrate on the daily problems and aspirations of ordinary individuals living within a complex industrial society. Although his work transcends the social problems of the 1930s and yields characters of wider psychological and social validity, Odets's plays, particularly the early ones, reflect an attachment to his times that precludes true universality. His later plays, such as *The Big Knife* (1949), *The Flowering Peach* (1954), and particularly *The Country Girl* (1950), reveal a broader understanding of American life than the earlier works, but they lack their kinetic energy.

Odets's first four plays, all produced in 1935, are social dramas. In *Awake and Sing*, youths struggle to escape from the frustrations of a lower-middle-class Jewish home in New York; in *Paradise Lost* a "good" man watches his business and family fall to ruin; *Waiting for Lefty* is a short, episodic staging of events leading to a strike of taxicab drivers; and *Till the Day I Die* depicts the conflict of a young proletarian who, caught working in the anti-Nazi underground, commits suicide to avoid exposing his comrades.

Golden Boy (1937), frequently regarded as Odets's most successful play, concerns the American quest for success. It was followed by *Rocket to the Moon* (1938), in which the central character, a dentist, learns the truth of his bleak life but cannot change it; *Night Music* (1940), a hopeful drama about a Hollywood messenger boy's trip to New York; *Clash by Night* (1941), a tight drama of a husband's revenge; and *The Russian People* (1942), based on the drama by Konstantin Simonov, concerning the Russian people in their fight to save their motherland during the Nazi invasion. *See* SIMONOV, KONSTANTIN.

After years in Hollywood, Odets wrote *The Big Knife*, a portrait of the life he observed there; and *The Country Girl*, a great success, in which a seedy actor makes his comeback. His next play, *The Flowering Peach*, updates the Biblical story of Noah. *The Silent Partner* and *The Law of Flight*, his last plays, have not been produced.

Awake and Sing (1935). Social drama set in the Berger household in the Bronx. The Berger children, Ralph and Hennie, dream of breaking away from their bourgeois environment. Dominating the household is their mother Bessie, stifling their complaints, deriding her weak husband Myron, and mocking her father Jacob, who finds solace in his Enrico Caruso records. Hennie discovers she is pregnant, but when the father cannot be found, Bessie arranges a match with Sam Feinschreiber, a timid and unsuspecting clerk. The following year,

Frances Farmer and Elia Kazan as they appeared in *Golden Boy*. New York, Belasco Theatre, 1937. [Theatre Collection, The New York Public Library at Lincoln Center, Astor, Lenox and Tilden Foundations]

John Garfield and Morris Carnovsky in the Group Theatre production of *Awake and Sing*. New York, Belasco Theatre, 1935. [Photograph by Vandamm. Theatre Collection, The New York Public Library at Lincoln Center, Astor, Lenox and Tilden Foundations]

Ralph discovers that the baby born to his sister after her marriage is not Sam's. Appalled by his mother's role in snaring the unsuspecting Sam and frustrated by Bessie's refusal to countenance the girl he loves, he turns on his mother and father. In the furor that follows, Bessie breaks her father's records. Jacob leaves to walk the dog on the roof, and moments later the janitor reports that he has fallen from the roof and been killed. Now Bessie and Uncle Morty conspire to keep the insurance money from Ralph, who is the beneficiary of Jacob's policy. But their roomer Moe Axelrod, a one-legged, cynical veteran, claims to have found a suicide note under Jacob's pillow and threatens, if they cheat Ralph of his claim, to disclose that the death was not accidental. Axelrod, having loved Hennie secretly for years, now persuades her to risk a new life with him. She leaves the baby in her mother's care, and together they leave the Berger household. With the shock of Jacob's death, Ralph's energy and hope return; he decides to stay and build a new future.

Waiting for Lefty (1935). One-act drama in which the theatre becomes a meeting hall of the taxi drivers' union, which is about to take a strike vote. Union officers are onstage, and the members are dispersed among the audience. Since Lefty, the members' militant representative, has not arrived at the meeting, Fatt, the union secretary, and other officers and racketeers have taken the time to belittle the membership's strike talk. The members jeer as Fatt angrily asks where Lefty is, insinuating that he has run out. In order to vouch for Lefty and assure the membership that the strike is justified, several members of the committee come forward to speak. As they talk, flashes of their lives appear behind them. Joe speaks of his wife Edna, their financial difficulties, and their final resolve to take a stand in favor of the strike despite the hardship it will entail. A scene that depicts a warmongering industrialist is followed by another in which a young driver and his girl bitterly agree that they cannot afford to marry on his wages. Finally, aroused by the discovery of the presence in the hall of a management spy and by the news that Lefty has been killed by an unknown assailant, the members vote to strike, shouting with increasing fervor: "Strike! Strike! Strike!"

Golden Boy (1937). Drama in which an overactive drive for material success corrupts Joe Bonaparte, a talented young violinist who discovers that he can earn more money from prizefighting than from music. At first, Joe is reluctant to box because he fears injuring his hands; but Tom Moody, the boy's manager, and Lorna, Moody's girl friend, recognizing Joe's great skill and moneymaking capability, try to persuade him to devote himself to fighting. Propelled by his passion for expensive cars and a growing love for Lorna, Joe abandons music and takes on a series of twenty-six matches throughout the Midwest, returning to New York a potential champion. Although he and Lorna admit their mutual love, she is unable to tell Moody of it for fear of

Night Music, **with Jane Wyatt, Morris Carnovsky, (standing), and Elia Kazan. New York, Broadhurst Theatre, 1940. [Theatre Collection, The New York Public Library at Lincoln Center, Astor, Lenox and Tilden Foundations]**

John Garfield and Joan McCracken in *The Big Knife.* **New York, National Theatre, 1949. [Photograph by Vandamm. Theatre Collection, The New York Public Library at Lincoln Center, Astor, Lenox and Tilden Foundations]**

hurting him. This infuriates Joe, and, breaking with Lorna, he becomes a deadly fighter. Despite a flashy exterior, Joe, affecting silk shirts and driving fast sports cars, is morose over Lorna's impending marriage to Moody. In this frame of mind he delivers an embittered punch to an opponent, accidentally killing him. As Lorna attempts to comfort him, she admits her love for him. Following an agonized confession of mutual love, Joe and Lorna go for a drive in his car and are killed in a crash.

The Flowering Peach (1954). Drama retelling the story of Noah's Ark in the accents of a homely Jewish family. When old Noah tells Esther, his wife, that God has instructed him to build an ark to save his family and the animal kingdom from a flood, she scolds him for drinking too much. Noah's two married sons, practical Shem and philistine Ham, deride their father's vision, but his son Japheth, a rational and philosophical bachelor, is appalled by the prospect of the earth's annihilation. Although Japheth labors to construct the ark, he refuses to take a wife and says he will not join the others when the deluge comes. To please his parents, however, he introduces easygoing Goldie to them. Goldie bores Japheth, but Ham, who ignores his wife Rachel, woos her. The family's doubts about Noah's authority are dispelled when he is miraculously transformed into a robust man of fifty, and as the storm begins, everyone but Japheth boards the vessel. Confessing to Rachel that he loves her, Japheth says he would rather die protesting God's brutality than be saved; but Noah knocks him unconscious and takes him aboard. During the journey the ailing Esther observes the young couples and concludes that Japheth should marry Rachel and Ham should marry Goldie.

Meanwhile, Noah finds himself in perpetual conflict with Japheth, who believes man should shape his own destiny. Esther dies, leaving Noah smitten with remorse for having refused her final wish that the couples be married; he therefore performs the weddings. At length the ark lands by a flowering peach tree, and Noah's children debark with their mates, planning new lives. Noah, once again an old man, tells God that during the journey he has learned to be humble and to see that the welfare of the world is man's responsibility.

[EDWARD MURRAY]

PLAYS

All were first performed in New York.

1. *Awake and Sing*. Drama, 3 acts. Written 1933. Published 1935. Produced Belasco Theatre (Group Theatre), Feb. 19, 1935.

2. *Waiting for Lefty*. Play, 5 episodes. Published 1935. Produced Longacre Theatre (Group Theatre), Mar. 26, 1935.

3. *Till the Day I Die*. Play, 7 scenes. Published 1935. Produced Longacre Theatre (Group Theatre), Mar. 26, 1935.

4. *Paradise Lost*. Play, 3 acts. Published 1936. Produced Longacre Theatre (Group Theatre), Dec. 9, 1935.

5. *Golden Boy*. Play, 3 acts. Published 1937. Produced Belasco Theatre (Group Theatre), Nov. 4, 1937.

6. *Rocket to the Moon*. Drama, 3 acts. Published 1939. Produced Belasco Theatre (Group Theatre), Nov. 24, 1938.

7. *Night Music*. Drama, 3 acts. Published 1940. Produced Broadhurst Theatre (Group Theatre), Feb. 22, 1940.

8. *Clash by Night*. Drama, 2 acts. Published 1942. Produced Belasco Theatre, Dec. 27, 1941.

9. (Adaptation). *The Russian People*. Drama, 3 acts. Published 1946.

Produced Guild Theatre, Dec. 29, 1942. Based on the play by Konstantin Simonov.

10. *The Big Knife*. Play, 3 acts. Published 1949. Produced National Theatre, Feb. 24, 1949.

11. *The Country Girl*. Play, 3 acts. Published 1951. Produced Lyceum Theatre, Nov. 10, 1950.

12. *The Flowering Peach*. Comedy. Produced Belasco Theatre, Dec. 28, 1954.

13. *The Silent Partner*. Play.

14. *The Law of Flight*. Play.

EDITIONS

Collections
Three Plays, New York, 1935; *Six Plays*, New York, 1939.
Individual Plays
Till the Day I Die. Published in *Famous Plays of 1936*, London, 1936.
Waiting for Lefty. Published in *Modern American Plays*, ed. by F. G. Cassidy, New York, 1949.

CRITICISM

H. Clurman, *The Fervent Years*, New York, 1945; R. B. Shuman, *Clifford Odets*, New York, 1962; Edward Murray, *Clifford Odets: The Thirties and After*, New York, 1968; G. Weales, *Clifford Odets: Playwright*, New York, 1971; H. Cantor, *Clifford Odets*, Metuchen, N.J., 1978.

Oehlenschläger, Adam (1779–1850)

Danish poet and dramatist. Adam Gottlob Oehlenschläger was born on November 14, 1779, in Copenhagen, to a German father and a Danish mother. He was raised at the royal palace in Frederiksberg, where his father held various positions ranging from organist to steward. Having had only a modicum of formal education, the child nevertheless evidenced so precocious a talent for poetry that he was sent to Copenhagen at the age of twelve to study under the poet Edvard Storm. In 1800, after a vain attempt to become an actor, he entered the law school of the University of Copenhagen. His meeting two years later with the Norwegian philosopher Henrich Steffens—who had just returned from Germany, where romanticism was flourishing—marked the beginning of the romantic movement in Denmark. One result was Oehlenschläger's poem *The Golden Horns* (*Guldhornene*, 1802), the first purely romantic work in

Adam Oehlenschläger. [Danish Information Office]

Scandinavian history; another was his first important drama, *A Play of Midsummer Night* (*Sanct Hansaften-Spil*, pub. 1803).

Oehlenschläger rapidly gained recognition as Denmark's leading poet. In 1805, his reputation secure, he left his homeland for five years of travel in Germany, France, and Italy, during which time he was befriended by Goethe, Mme. de Staël, Johann Ludwig Tieck, Johann Schlegal, and the Danish romantic sculptor Bertel Thorvaldsen. In this period he wrote many plays, including *Earl Hakon* (*Hakon Jarl*, 1808), probably his finest work. He returned to Denmark in 1810, famous and much admired, to teach aesthetics at the University of Copenhagen. After 1815 his writing abilities suffered a decline. From 1814 until the late 1820s he was the object of attacks by the poet Jens Baggesen and by Johan Ludvig Heiberg, who favored more modern dramatic modes. Although Oehlenschläger lived to see the growing reaction against the romantic theatre for which he had written, he continued to enjoy the esteem of his countrymen until his death. In 1849 he was decorated by the King at a public festival in his honor. He died in Copenhagen on January 20, 1850.

WORK

Still considered by many to be Denmark's greatest poet, Oehlenschläger was certainly its first and greatest romantic writer. His talent lay primarily in the realm of lyric poetry, and as a result his plays are weak and lacking in dramatic force. Although still widely read in Scandinavia, Oehlenschläger's plays are infrequently performed.

His early work is by far his best, and it is in his first plays that nature predominates. *A Play of Midsummer Night* (pub. 1803) consists of a series of *tableaux vivants* with thinly drawn characters; and *Aladdin* (wr. 1805, prod. 1839) is a heavily symbolic work inspired by nature. Oehlenschläger subsequently came under Schiller's influence, reflected in *Earl Hakon* (1808), the first and best of his many historical tragedies and a play that influenced the young Strindberg. The Middle Ages, a favorite period of the romantic school, served as a backdrop for Oehlenschläger's poetic drama *Axel and Valborg* (*Axel og Valborg*, 1810). So convincingly did it capture the medieval concepts of love, chivalry, and magic that it won the praise even of Oehlenschläger's enemies. *Correggio* (1811), originally written in German and then translated into Danish, is an affirmation of the romantic notion of the sanctity of art.

Confused and disillusioned by the attacks directed at him by his critics, Oehlenschläger wrote works of increasing despondency and decreasing literary value. *Hugo von Rheinberg* (1814) is a pessimistic drama which questions the very truths of art, love, and beauty that the early works had so valiantly affirmed. *The Vaeringers in Constantinople* (*Vaeringerne i Miklagaard*, 1827) marked Oehlenschläger's partial conversion to a certain realism in character and situation. His subsequent plays do not reveal the poetic inspiration found in the works of his youth.

Print of an early production of *Earl Hakon*. [Danish Information Office]

Earl Hakon (*Hakon Jarl*, 1808). Verse dramatization, based on ancient Icelandic sagas, of the struggle for the Crown of Norway in the tenth century. The last stronghold of the primitive gods and barbarism is personified in the doughty warrior Earl Hakon, who rules Norway with a tyrant's hand. Olaf Trygvason, Christian King of Dublin, is persuaded to claim the Crown, to which he is legally entitled. The sensual Hakon's lust for a peasant girl ignites the peasants' smoldering resentment against him. Dogged by bad luck and deception, he is defeated by the pure and noble Olaf and ends his life as a hunted fugitive, dying at his own request at the hands of his faithful slave Karker. Olaf ascends the throne, signaling the dawn of a new religion and a new era.

Oelschlegel, Gerd (1926–)

Post-World War II German dramatist. Oelschlegel served in Hitler's army in the Balkans and was captured by the Allies. Because he engaged in rebellious activities after the war, he was sent to a labor camp by the East German authorities but escaped to West Germany. In Hamburg he gained recognition through his work for radio and television, and his radio play *Romeo and Juliet in Berlin* (*Romeo und Julia in Berlin*, 1954) was later adapted for the stage with simultaneous successful runs in Aachen, Bremen, Hamburg, and Wiesbaden.

One of Oelschlegel's contributions to the stage is a "new realism" that presents the constant questioning of men but never an answer. In this vein he established his reputation as a dramatist with forceful, realistic plays such as *The Deadly Lie* (*Die tödliche Lüge,* 1956), about the plight of people in a divided Germany. Oelschlegel has also written a comedy, *Dust in Heaven* (*Staub auf dem Paradies,* 1957).

[PETER JELAVICH]

Ogunde, Hubert (1916–   )

Nigerian playwright and actor-manager. Born at Ososa near Ijebu-Ose in Western Nigeria, Chief Hubert Ogunde is the "grand old man" of the Nigerian theatre, having founded in 1944 the country's first professional company, the Ogunde Concert Party. He was a teacher and choirmaster at the Church of the Lord in Lagos. His inspiration came from several sources: the church concerts in which Biblical scenes were acted out between musical items; the traditional Yoruba Alarinjo theatre (without its "pagan" masks); the British music hall (which he encountered on a visit sponsored by the British Council in 1947); the American musical (through recordings and the cinema); and the performances of Ghana's Bob Johnson, "father of the concert party," who first toured Nigeria in the 1930s. The term "concert party" is said to derive from the patriotic school concerts held on Empire Day. Ogunde's main debts to the Ghanaian concert party are his use of Western jazz instruments, the chorus line, and transvestite impersonations. C. B. Hutton, Bob Johnson's partner in the act called "The Two Bobs," was a celebrated female impersonator; in Ogunde's theatre, actresses (many of them Ogunde's wives) regularly play male parts.

Ogunde's plays are by no means just escapist entertainments. A brief stint as a policeman brought him into contact with the political realities of Nigeria. His *Strike and Hunger* (1945) and *Bread and Bullets* (1949) were suppressed by the colonial administration, and *Yorubas Must Think* (*Yoruba Ronu*) was banned by the government of the Western Region in 1965. His plays are popular for their topicality as well as for the skill and energy with which they are performed. With the deaths of Kola Ogunmola in 1972 and Duro Ladipo in 1975—both of whom he had influenced greatly—his supremacy in the Nigerian popular theatre world was unchallenged. He made his first feature film in 1979 and was the subject of a BBC television documentary in 1980. *See* LADIPO, DURO; OGUNMOLA, KOLA.

GEOFFREY AXWORTHY

Ogunmola, Kola (1923–1972)

Nigerian playwright and actor-manager. Born in the Ekiti district of Western Nigeria, Ogunmola played a key role in the development of the Yoruba popular theatre. Like Hubert Ogunde, to whose example he owed a great debt, his first dramatic efforts were as a school teacher

The marriage scene of Bisi and the Drinkard (played by Kola Ogunmola, right) in a 1963 production of *The Palmwine Drinkard* at the Arts Theatre of the University of Ibadan, Nigeria. [Photograph courtesy of Geoffrey Axworthy]

and choirmaster. His introduction of "pagan" elements and native musical instruments into the performances did not meet with the approval of the mission school, and Ogunmola left teaching for entertainment. He recuited a little company from his former pupils and walked with them from village to village offering his shows. He based the form of the Yoruba "folk opera" on Ogunde's pattern of alternating songs and dances and traditional ceremonials with dramatic episodes, but he eschewed Ogunde's use of Western elements such as the saxophone, slapstick comedy, and the provacative chorus line. He also avoided the political and controversial themes that got Ogunde into trouble. Ogunmola confined himself to simple moral tales in which virtue was rewarded in the end.

Love of Money (ca. 1954) is typical of Ogunmola's early work. A rich trader risks both his money and his peace of mind when he brings a glamorous but greedy woman into his house as a second wife. Fortunately, his first wife is generous and clever enough to rescue him from his folly.

The Ogunmola "concert party" was adaptable in performance to all kinds of locales, from small courtyard bars to the formal stages of colleges. In 1962, when the University of Ibadan School of Drama was in formation, Ogunmola and his entire company were in residence for a year to revise and record their repertoire. *The Palmwine Drinkard* (1963) based on Amos Tutuola's celebrated story (1952) was the company's graduation exercise.

The protagonist of *The Palmwine Drinkard* is Lanke, whose father, finding him good for nothing except drinking, has indulgently left him a plantation of palm trees, and a tapster to collect the wine from them daily. Thus equipped he would never lack friends, and Lanke's life is one long party until his tapster falls from a tree and dies. Abandoned by his friends, Lanke decides to go to the Land of the Dead and bring the tapster back. This leads him on an Orpheus-like quest and into many adventures. He meets Bisi, the wayward daughter of a Chief, who refuses all the suitors proposed for her and is waiting for her "complete gentleman." Lanke rescues her from the demon she follows into the bush, and from execution at the hands of the Cruel King. Although he claims to be wedded to palmwine, he finally accepts her as his wife, and they have a traditional Yoruba wedding presided over by the Forest Mother. They finally arrive in the Land of the Dead (where everyone walks backward) and find the tapster. He may not return with them or even look at them, but he gives Lanke a magic egg that turns water into wine. So the lifelong drinking party starts again, with the audience joining in.

Brilliantly designed by Demas Nwoko, *The Palmwine Drinkard* was a great step forward for the Yoruba theatre, and it remained in the company's repertoire after the author's untimely death of a heart attack. Wale Ogunyemi, a notable performer and dramatist in English and Yoruba, took over the direction of the company.

GEOFFREY AXWORTHY

CRITICISM

U. Beier, "Yoruba Theatre," in *Introduction to Africa*, Evanston, Ill., 1967, pp. 243–254; E. Sutherland, *The Story of Bob Johnson*, Makers of Ghanaian Theatre Series, no. 1, Accra, 1970; A. Graham-White, *The Drama of Black Africa*, London, New York, 1975; M. Banham and C. Wake, *African Theatre Today*, London, 1976, pp. 1–23; E. Clark, *Hubert Ogunde, the Making of Nigerian* Theatre, 1979.

Ohnet, Georges   (1848–1918)

French novelist and dramatist. In spite of all the critics could do to prevent it, Ohnet's sentimental and psychologically shallow novels and plays were for a time immensely popular. He often treated the same subject in both forms, and his best-known play, *The Ironmaster* (*Le maître de forges*, 1883), is based on a novel published the previous year. A noble lady whose family suffers financial losses is abandoned by her aristocratic lover. She marries instead the proprietor of an ironworks, a man whom she despises as being her social inferior. Eventually, she comes to appreciate her husband's sterling character and even risks her life for him when he fights a duel with her former lover. *Serge Panine* (1882) concerns a middle-class young lady's marriage to a corrupt Polish nobleman. He squanders her dowry and is eventually shot by her mother to save the family honor. Ohnet had a great deal of trouble in obtaining a production of the play, which was not staged until the story had become popular as a novel. Though his plays have little literary worth, like those of Scribe they are carefully constructed mechanisms. They flattered the vanity of middle-class audiences, whose probity and strength they portray with sentimental insistence. Other works of interest are *Last Love* (*Dernier amour*, 1890), *Colonel Roquebrune* (*Le colonel Roquebrune*, 1896), and *The Reds and the Whites* (*Les rouges et les blancs*, 1901).

[JOSEPH E. GARREAU]

Okamoto Kidō   (1872–1939)

Neo-Kabuki dramatist. Okamoto Kidō wrote under the influence of Western realism. His plays often avoid the most characteristic Kabuki techniques, including tableaux, poses, music, and use of the runway (*hanamichi*); instead, they stress poetic allusion, psychological realism, historical accuracy, and restraint. Many of his works are currently performed. The following are the most popular.

The Tale of Shuzenji (*Shuzenji Monogatari*, 1911). Katsura, the daughter of a famous mask-maker, Yashao, becomes the mistress of the shogun after she gives him a mask of himself made by her father. Yashao, dissatisfied with the mask because it lacks life, destroys all his masks. At play's end, however, Katsura returns dying, having been wounded in a battle in which the shogun was killed and in which she, wearing his mask, was mistaken for him. Her father realizes that his skill was so great that he had unknowingly carved death into the shogun's mask. Now he sets to work on a mask of his dying daughter's features.

The Double Suicide at Toribeyama (*Toribeyama Shinjū*, 1915). A young samurai, Hankurō, loves the geisha, Osome. One evening, in a dispute at the geisha house Hankurō tangles with the boorish brother of his best friend, and finally, in a duel, kills him. When he comes to his senses, he realizes that he must now either commit suicide or give himself up to the dead man's brother in order to allow him to exact revenge. Instead, Osome convinces him to allow her to flee with him to Toribe Hill, a cremation ground, and to die with him there.

The Mansion of the Plates (*Banchō Sarayashiki*, 1916). The rare old plates of the Aoyama family are so precious that anyone breaking one is immediately beheaded. The serving maid, Okiku, who is the mistress of the lord, Harima, hears that Harima is to be married. To test his love for her, she purposely breaks a plate. When Harima discovers it, he forgives her, believing it was an accident. When he later discovers, through a spying retainer, that it was broken on purpose, he cannot forgive Okiku for doubting his love. He breaks the remaining plates, kills Okiku and pushes her body into a well, then sets off for a battle which we assume will be suicidal.

LEONARD PRONKO

O'Keefe, John   (1747–1833)

Irish actor-playwright. O'Keefe was born in Dublin. His first play, a farce entitled *The She-gallant* (later renamed *The Positive Man*), was produced in Dublin in 1767. His next success, *Tony Lumpkin in Town*, a kind of sequel to Goldsmith's *She Stoops to Conquer*, was produced at the Haymarket Theater in 1778, a year after O'Keefe and his family had moved to London. A year later his comic opera, *The Son-in-Law*, also put on at the Haymarket, took London by storm. After this success, O'Keefe devoted himself entirely to writing plays and farces. By 1798 he was able to publish a collection of over fifty of his creations, even though he had gone blind in 1781. In 1792 he published *Wild Oats*, considered one of his best plays. The play was produced first by Sheridan at Covent Garden in 1791 and then in New York in 1793. (The play was unearthed again by The Royal Shakespeare Company and had a long and successful run during the 1976–1977 London season).

In 1826 he published *Recollections of the Life of John O'Keefe* in two volumes. During the same year he was given an annual pension of one hundred guineas from the King's private purse. After more than forty years of blindness cheerfully borne, he died in Southampton on February 4, 1833. Today, he is credited with having been the first dramatist of his day to turn eighteenth-century public taste away from dull sentimental comedy toward the sprightly comic humor exhibited in *Wild Oats*.

CAROL GELDERMAN

Olmo, Lauro (1922–)

Spanish novelist and dramatist. His first play, *The Shirt* (*La camisa*, 1962), is a forceful realistic work set in the outskirts of Madrid and has as its central theme the problems of Spanish laborers who wish to emigrate. Involvement in social issues continued to be the prime motivation of Olmo's work in *The Breast of the Sardine* (*La pechuga de la sardina*, 1963), *The Body* (*El cuerpo*, 1966) and *English Spoken* (1968). *The Fourth Estate* (*El cuarto poder*, 1963–1964), *The Decoration* (*La condecoración*, wr. 1964; prod. 1965), *Mare Nostrum* (1966), *Plaza Menor* (1967), and *Leonidas the Great* (*Leónidas el Grande*, 1972) were banned by the government censors. *The News Item* (*La noticia*), which has been translated into English, was written in 1963 as part of *The Fourth Estate*, a group of plays dealing with the state of the Spanish press under the Franco dictatorship. Though basically a writer in the realist tradition, Olmo has occasionally experimented with avant-garde techniques.

ANDRÉS FRANCO

EDITIONS

La camisa, ed. by A. K. and I. F. Ariza, London, 1968; *The News Item*, ed. by M. Benedikt and G. E. Wellwarth, tr. by M. C. Wellwarth, *Modern Spanish Theatre*, New York, 1968; *Teatro* (*La camisa; El cuerpo; El cuarto poder*), ed. by J. Monleón, Madrid, 1970.

CRITICISM

Introductory material in Ariza and Monleón editions; F. Ruiz Ramón, *Historia del teatro español: Siglo XX*, Madrid, 1977 (3rd. ed.), pp. 494–500; M. T. Halsey, "La Generación Realista: A Selected Bibliography," *Estreno*, vol. III, No. 1 (1977), pp. 8–13.

Olsson, Hagar (1893–1978)

Finnish novelist and playwright. A critic and polemicist of considerable stature, and an active champion of "modernism" in Finland-Swedish literature; also a prolific novelist (her *The Woodcarver and Death* [*Träsnidaren och döden*, 1940] appeared in English in 1965) and a dramatist who could be termed a romantic expressionist. She made her debut as a follower of Pär Lagerkvist and Luigi Pirandello, however without sharing the Italian's mordancy (*see* LAGERKVIST, PÄR; PIRANDELLO, LUIGI). In *The Heart's Pantomime* (*Hjärtats pantomim*, 1927), the unnamed hero-

ine (She) refuses to accept the Author's would-be destruction of his play: "The greater drama begins. It cannot be destroyed, it lives within us." Hearing the voice of a beloved (He) from offstage, she follows it, while the Author is left before the curtain, to deliver the final line: "The heart! How banal!", but the stage direction adds that he is only "an impotent shadow of doubt."

S.O.S. (1928) contains numerous echoes of Georg Kaiser's *Gas I–II* and ends with another symbolic triumph of the human spirit (*see* KAISER, GEORG). Maria, struggling against "chemical warfare, humanity's suicide," is arrested; she goes gladly, confident that the "new youth" will conquer the "dead power of machines and gold." Likewise, in *The Blue Wonder* (*Det blå undret*, 1931) a young girl, Louisa, fights the forces of evil, here represented by her beloved brother, Martin, who has become a Fascist. (Olsson alludes to the Finnish "Lapua" movement led by Vihtori Kosola, "Finland's Mussolini.") When Louisa has been condemned to prison (or worse) for participating in a "treasonable demonstration," Martin sees the error of his ways, while Louisa predicts that "developments will set her free."

Another play with a political meaning, *The Snowball War* (*Lumisota*, 1939, Hagar Olsson's only play in Finnish), had its production halted by the Soviet Union's invasion of Finland at the start of the Winter War; here again the extreme right is represented by a young man, the elder son of Finland's foreign minister, and the role of the pure-hearted heroine of the earlier plays is taken by his younger brother, caught, as it were, between two gangs that fight with snowballs. (It is significant that Olsson gives him the name Outi, which is customarily feminine in Finland.) The boys' father is a figure of particular interest, an old-style liberal who argues for compromise and the value of the individual.

In 1944 Hagar Olsson tried the stage once more with *The Robber and the Maiden* (*Rövaren och jungfrun*), a ballad-like play set in the Ostrobothnian countryside during the great famine of 1867. Elk-Matts, a Finnish Robin Hood, is captured after a mystical night of love; miraculously, he escapes after public torture, but nonetheless is broken by his sense of guilt at having taken human life. His beloved, Sanna, defies her grandmother, who has closed the doors of her house to the hungry masses. Sanna feeds them all, and while taking a starving baby to her breast declares: "You shall live . . . you are the one among us who shall live . . . for the new day." The last of Olsson's six dramas, *The Death of Love* (*Kärlekens död*, 1952), is again an accusation hurled at those who scorn the human heart, but once more this altogether valid message is colored by Hagar Olsson's weakness for a vague "collectivism." In this extension of Jean-Paul Sartre's *Huit clos* (*No Exit*), a group of "Western individualists" torment one another in the rooms of a seedy hotel.

The derivative nature of Hagar Olsson's dramatic *oeuvre* is plain enough. As an active journalist, who doggedly kept abreast of continental drama, she could not avoid the influence of what she read and saw. Moreover, as in her novels, there is a monotony of characterization—especially in her affection for the young girl as idealist, martyr, and savior. (In this connection it is regrettable that *The Snowball War*, with its reasonable and humane middle-aged hero, has never been sufficiently known; and the physician in *The Death of Love* is the other example of the type in Olsson's work.) The critic Eric Olssoni, who in the 1920s had saluted Hagar Olsson for the intrepidity with which she brought modern dramatic currents to Finland, subsequently called her a creator of characters who were merely "symbols for her ideas" and of plays which, for all their understanding of the resources of the modern theatre, were "humorless and pretentious." In the future her plays may be of more significance as documents for cultural historians than as living works for the stage.   G. C. SCHOOLFIELD

CRITICISM

O. Enckell, *Den unga Hagar Olsson: Studier i finlandssvensk modernism*, II, Helsinki, 1949; L. Fridell, *Hagar Olsson och den nya teatern: Teatersynen speglad i teaterkritiken 1918–1929 och i Hjärtats pantomim*, Gothenburg, 1973; E. Törnquist, "Hagar Olsson's First Play," *Scandinavica*, 15 (1976): 63–72; C. Zilliacus, "Snöbollskriget som frös bort: Hagar Olsson och dramatiken år 1939," in *Pegas och snöbollskrig: Litteraturvetenskapliga studier tillägnade Sven Linnér*, Turku, 1979, pp. 171–185.

Olyesha, Yury Karlovich (1899–1960)

Soviet Russian novelist and dramatist. He was born on March 3, 1899, in Elisavetgrad, the son of an excise officer, an impoverished member of the gentry. Olyesha grew up in Odessa and soon joined the lively literary life there, counting among his associates Isaac Babel and Valentin Katayev. His novel *Envy* (*Zavist*, 1927) created a sensation, contrasting the old intelligentsia with the new order of hero, without using stereotypes. Dramatized as *A Conspiracy of Feelings* (*Zagovor chuvstv*, 1929), it was staged at the Vakhtangov Theatre and, with the endorsement of the Communist party authorities, had a great success. His most popular work was probably his fairy tale, *Three Fat Men* (*Tri Tolstyaka*), which was made into a play (1930), a ballet (1935), and an opera (1956). Gradually, the authorities began to realize that Olyesha's works were more ambiguous and ambivalent than was permissible, and the organs of public opinion started to attack him. His play *A List of Benefactions* (*Spisok blagodeyaniy*, 1931) was coolly received, and when he affirmed his belief in the importance of the individual at the First All-Union Congress of Writers (1934), he definitely fell from favor. His works went out of print, not to be republished until after Stalin's death, and he himself was relegated to hack work. His only noteworthy theatre piece in later life was an adaptation of Dostoevsky's *The Idiot* (*Idiot*, 1958) for the Vakhtangov Theatre.

WORK

Olyesha's plays are pivoted on an opposition of the romantic, individualistic beliefs of the pre-Revolutionary intelligentsia and the utilitarian, prosaic activists of the new Soviet order. In *A Conspiracy of Feelings*, as in Schiller's *Robbers*, the central contrast is embodied by two brothers: Andrey Babichev, a sausage-maker, stands for vital, rationalist creativity, beneficial to the majority, while half-mad Ivan promotes indulgence of the private passions. Olyesha himself seems torn between the two,

and is represented by the unemployed proletarian Nikolay Kavalyerov, just as in *A List of Benefactions* his mouthpiece is the actress Goncharova. Goncharova, like Olyesha, is alarmed by Soviet crimes against individuality and torn between her personal needs as an artist and her love for her country. These tensions recur in Olyesha's other plays, *The Black Man* (*Chyorniy chelovyek*, 1932) and *A Stern Youth* (*Strogiy molodos*, 1934). The former contrasts art as an instrument of death and as a tool for the reconstruction of the world; the latter, intended as a screenplay and employing a love triangle to depict the struggle between old and new, was greeted with much hostility.

Olyesha's inability to draw black-and-white characters and his posing of strong arguments for both sides distressed the Soviet authorities no less than did the so-called formalist elements in his plays. He dabbled in such expressionist techniques as dream sequences, stark lighting, symbolic props, and grotesque crowd scenes to heighten his realistic pictures of life under communism.

A Conspiracy of Feelings (*Zagovor chuvstv*, 1929). The businessman Andrey Babichev plans a new salami and a new cafeteria to revolutionize the food industry, while his bizarre brother Ivan drifts through Moscow cultivating the pernicious feelings of others, such as jealousy, envy, and covetousness. An unemployed worker, Nikolay Kavalyerov, in love with Ivan's daughter Valya and kept by the repulsive Annichka Prokopovich, falls under Ivan's spell and agrees to assassinate Andrey at a football rally. In Olyesha's original, more ambiguous ending, Nikolay lapses into a stupor and is denounced by Ivan as a worthless museum piece, "the man whose life was stolen away." In the staged ending, Nikolay sees the light in time and murders Ivan, instead of Andrey.

A List of Benefactions (*Spisok blagodeyaniy*, 1931). The actress Yelena Goncharova, who prefers to play *Hamlet* over the Soviet repertory, keeps a diary with two lists, one of the crimes, the other of the benefactions of the Soviet regime. Frustrated by life in Russia, she goes to Paris, where she finds the situation worse. The music hall manager, Margaret, proposes that she play a flute through her rectum on the stage; she is pursued by a febrile emigré; and her diary is stolen and the list of crimes published by the White Russian editor Tatarov. Just when she is most anxious to return home and admit Russian superiority, she is repudiated by her Soviet colleagues. During a march of the unemployed, she steps in front of a bullet meant for the radical leader Henri Santillain, but her last request, to be wrapped in the red banner, goes unheeded.   LAURENCE SENELICK

EDITIONS

Izbrannye sochineniya, Moscow, 1956; *A List of Assets*, tr. by A. MacAndrew, in *Envy and Other Works by Yuri Olesha*, New York, 1960, and in *20th Century Russian Drama*, New York, 1963; *Pyesy, stati o teatri dramaturgiy*, Moscow, 1968; *The Conspiracy of Feelings*, tr. by D. C. Gerould and E. S. Gerould in *Avant Garde Drama*, ed. by B. F. Dukore and D. C. Gerould, New York, 1976.

CRITICISM

P. Novitskiy, *Sovremennye teatral'nye sistemy*, Moscow, 1933; Y. Ostrovskiy, "Problema intelligentsii v tvorchestve Yuriya Oleshi," in *Literaturnyy kritik*, no. 2, Moscow, 1934; A. Gurvich, *Tri dramaturga, Pogodin, Olesha,*

Kirshon, Moscow, 1936; B. Levin, *Yury Olesha: His Times and His "Conspiracy of Feelings,"* Cambridge, Mass., 1962.

O'Neill, Eugene   (1888–1953)

American dramatist. Eugene Gladstone O'Neill was born in New York City on October 18, 1888, the third child of the prominent actor James O'Neill (1847–1920) and Ella Quinlan O'Neill. His older brothers were James Jr. (1878–1923) and Edmund Burke (1883–1885) O'Neill. For the first seven years of his life, Eugene and his mother accompanied his father on tour around the country; summers were spent at the family home in New London, Conn. During these years he acquired an intimate and precocious knowledge of the theatre, along with a tendency to withdraw into a personal fantasy world.

In 1895 O'Neill was enrolled in the St. Aloysius Academy for Boys, a convent boarding school. He disliked it, and as a result his reserve seemed to deepen. In 1900 he was transferred to the DeLaSalle Institute in Manhattan and lived at home with his mother, who had become addicted to morphine. The experience proved to be traumatic for O'Neill; the boy tried in vain to save his mother through prayer and, failing, gave up the last vestiges of his precarious religious faith. In 1902 he entered Betts Academy in Stamford, Conn., where he seemed content. Although not a remarkable student, O'Neill was a voracious reader; the breadth of his knowledge was impressive. Under the influence of his cynical and profligate brother Jamie, he spent weekends away from school in the barrooms and hotels of New York. Incurably romantic, O'Neill was convinced from the first that the prostitutes and other characters he encountered with his brother all had hearts of gold—an impression that was often to be incorporated in his writing.

Eugene O'Neill.

He entered Princeton University in 1906 but spent most of his time dissipating. Remaining in New York after his freshman year, O'Neill fell under the influence of the anarchist Benjamin Tucker and was introduced by him to the works of Friedrich Neitzsche, which were to have a profound influence on O'Neill throughout his life. He roomed with George Bellows, who later achieved fame as a painter of the Ashcan school.

In 1909 O'Neill met Kathleen Jenkins, who soon fell in love with him. James O'Neill, alarmed at his son's involvement, sent him on a mining expedition to Honduras; but on October 3, 1909, before his departure, he married Kathleen. During six fruitless months searching for gold in Honduras, O'Neill became ill with malaria, and he returned to New York in April, 1910. On May 5, Eugene O'Neill, Jr., was born. James had been outraged by the marriage and directed Eugene not to visit his wife and child. Depressed and seemingly indifferent to Kathleen's fate, he obeyed, offering no explanation to her or her family. He left the city with his father, assuming a position as assistant manager in the touring company of *The White Sister.*

Late in the spring of 1910, O'Neill left the company and began a series of sailing indentures which, for the following eighteen months, took him to South America and England. Despite his love of the sea and his long-standing wish to travel, this episode of his life was characterized by a conscious descent into personal degradation. Between voyages he drank until his money ran out and then resorted to panhandling. For six months in Buenos Aires he lived as a derelict, sleeping on park benches and hiding from the police. From the perspective of later years, O'Neill considered these months invaluable to his creative makeup, providing him with material for plays throughout his career, especially his early plays of the sea. However, he never again went to sea.

Back in New York, O'Neill lived for a while in a seamy waterfront hotel called Jimmy-the-Priest's, which later served as the locale for both *Anna Christie* (wr. 1920) and *The Iceman Cometh* (wr. 1939). He continued to ignore his wife and son, and in 1911 Kathleen divorced him. Again under his father's influence, he and his brother toured as actors in a vaudeville version of *The Count of Monte Cristo.* He was drunk most of the time and once attempted suicide.

In the summer of 1912 O'Neill, facing for the first time the possibility of shaping his life, resolved to become a dramatist. His father secured a position for him on the *New London Telegraph.* Although he was a poor journalist, he contributed a quantity of popular but undistinguished poetry to the newspaper and in his spare time began to make notes for future plays. In October he suffered a mild attack of tuberculosis and was sent by his doctor to Gaylord Farm, a private sanatorium near Wallingford, Conn., where his health improved rapidly. He began a number of short plays, completed one—*A Wife for a Life*—and read for the first time the plays of August Strindberg, which were to become another major influence on his own work. *See* STRINDBERG, AUGUST.

In 1914, the year after his release from Gaylord,

O'Neill convalesced in New London and wrote seven plays: *The Web, Fog, Thirst, Recklessness, Warnings, Abortion,* and *Servitude.* Impressed, his father allowed him to enroll in George Pierce Baker's 47 Workshop at Harvard University. Although impatient and offended by some of Baker's criticisms, O'Neill nevertheless was one of the few invited to return for the advanced seminar. Presumably it was his father's parsimony that prevented him from returning and kept him in New York. That winter he met George Cram Cook and Susan Glaspell, who were attempting to organize a new experimental summer theatre in Provincetown. O'Neill's *Bound East for Cardiff* (wr. 1913/14) excited them, and they enthusiastically accepted it to open their Playhouse. Thus O'Neill found himself back in the theatre—staging, directing, and acting in *Thirst. See* BAKER, GEORGE PIERCE.

Before fall the Provincetown group decided to take the theatre to New York under a new name, the Playwrights' Theatre, suggested by O'Neill, who promised to write more plays. By April, 1917, he had completed *'Ile, The Moon of the Caribees, The Long Voyage Home,* and *In the Zone,* his first financial success. Returning to Provincetown, O'Neill worked on *Beyond the Horizon* and on a short story that was to be the basis for *The Hairy Ape* (wr. 1921).

In New York the next winter, O'Neill met Agnes Boulton, a writer of short stories, whom he married in Provincetown on April 12, 1918. There he started revising *Beyond the Horizon* and wrote *Where the Cross Is Made* and *The Rope,* which contains the germ idea for *Desire under the Elms* (1924).

By this time O'Neill's dramatic efforts had begun to gain recognition in New York, but his family, puzzled over his strange genius, was still reluctant to admit it. After the New York success of *In the Zone,* produced in 1917 by the Washington Square Players at the Comedy Theatre, it was booked by a vaudeville circuit, and the Broadway producer John D. Williams took an option on *Beyond the Horizon.* O'Neill also saw three of his one-act plays published in the *Smart Set* by H. L. Mencken and George Jean Nathan.

At the close of the 1918 season, the O'Neills moved into Agnes's house in New Jersey. During the next six months O'Neill completed *The Straw* (wr. 1919), based on his experiences at Gaylord, and began a new play, *Chris Christopherson,* hardly recognizable in its final version, *Anna Cristie.* The next year, O'Neill's second "unplanned" child, Shane, was born and his first Broadway production, *Beyond the Horizon,* was mounted. The play received mixed critical comments but won him a Pulitzer Prize of a much-needed $1,000. Perhaps most gratifying was the long-awaited approval from his father, which came, grudgingly, only a short time before his death in August, 1920.

Between 1920 and 1922, in a burst of activity, O'Neill completed seven full-length plays: *Gold, Anna Cristie, The Emperor Jones, Diff'rent, The First Man, The Hairy Ape,* and *The Fountain.* He began to curtail his activity at the Playwrights' Theatre although his own plays continued to be produced there, and during the rehearsals of

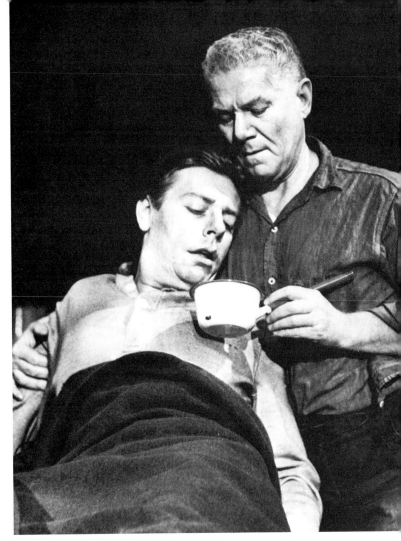

Ken Ruta and Paul Ballantyne in a 1966 production of *Bound East for Cardiff.* [The Guthrie Theater Company]

The Hairy Ape he met Carlotta Monterey, the actress who was to become his third wife.

In 1922 O'Neill's mother died; his brother Jamie died a year later. His marital situation, if reflected by his new drama *Welded* (wr. 1923), was tense. He was beginning to withdraw from the New York social circle, believing that it threatened his privacy and his work. By 1924 he had sequestered himself with his family in a Bermuda retreat to write *Marco Millions* and *The Great God Brown.* His only daughter, Oona, was born there on May 14, 1925, amid tensions created by the rivalry between the two temperamental writer parents.

The next winter, O'Neill worked on *Lazarus Laughed* and *Strange Interlude.* He returned to the United States in 1929 to accept an honorary degree from Yale University. Afterward, in Maine, he once again encountered Carlotta Monterey. Within a year he was divorced from Agnes and was traveling with Carlotta to Europe and the Orient. They were married in Paris on July 22, 1929, and settled in an isolated château in Tours, where O'Neill began his trilogy *Mourning Becomes Electra.* The couple's decision to live abroad began a long period of seclusion which continued until their return to the United States in May, 1931, for the production of *Mourning Becomes Electra.*

They never returned to Europe, as they had planned, but established and abandoned a succession of lavish homes, from Georgia to Seattle and northern California to Marblehead Harbor, Mass., over the following twenty-two years. In 1934 O'Neill began work on *A Tale of Possessors Self-Dispossessed,* a cycle of plays that was to be a definitive history of the American family corrupted by possessiveness and materialism. The cycle was never completed, and of the nine plays he envisioned in 1936, only two are extant: *A Touch of the Poet* (wr. 1935–1942) and *More Stately Mansions* (wr. 1953).

In August, 1936, O'Neill was awarded the Nobel Prize for Literature, but poor health prevented him from attending the ceremonies in Sweden. His remaining productive years, until 1943, were characterized by long periods of illness and physical disability which added to the painfulness of writing his last great plays, *The Iceman Cometh* (wr. 1939), *Long Day's Journey into Night* (wr. 1941), and *A Moon for the Misbegotten* (wr. 1943)—all bleak but candid looks into his past. As a diversion, he also began in 1941 a series of one-act plays to be called *By Way of Obit,* but only *Hughie* (wr. 1942) was completed.

By 1943 O'Neill was physically dependent upon his wife and became increasingly depressed by his inability to write. His health continued to decline, he gradually became paralyzed, and on November 27, 1953, he died in Boston.

Work

Eugene O'Neill, generally considered the foremost American dramatist and certainly the one who has enjoyed the longest sustained reputation in his own country and abroad, is surely in addition the most protean. He essayed almost every dramatic form current in modern drama between 1915 and 1930—naturalism (*Beyond the Horizon,* 1920), symbolism (*The Emperor Jones,* 1920), expressionism (*The Hairy Ape,* 1922). He employed masks in *The Great God Brown* (1926), soliloquies and the stream-of-consciousness technique in *Strange Interlude* (1928), Greek myth in *Mourning Becomes Electra* (1931), and Biblical material in *Lazarus Laughed* (1928). At times, as in *The Great God Brown, Dynamo* (1929), and *Lazarus Laughed,* his use of theatrical effect or heavy symbolism seems to overwhelm his slender ideas. At other times, as in *The Iceman Cometh* (wr. 1939, prod. 1946) and *Long Day's Journey into Night* (wr. 1941, prod. 1956), his style is raw, spare, and utterly devoid of theatrical tricks and machinery. Although he could yield to the windiest sort of idealism and cosmic utterance or write a charming comedy of adolescence, he is remembered as the bleakest and most pessimistic of all American dramatists.

O'Neill's great propensity for experimentation, due in part to the acknowledged influence of August Strindberg, was a mixed blessing. While his eagerness to try new forms enhanced his already considerable gift for theatrical effect, the form frequently became an end in itself or sustained material which would otherwise be exposed as shoddy or puerile. More often, experimentation diverted him from the full exercise of his principal talent,

Lee Richardson (left), John Cromwell, and Tina Sattin in *The Moon of the Caribbees,* Minneapolis, 1966. [The Guthrie Theater Company]

the depiction of character. For this reason the plays that have stood the test of time are most often the realistic ones in which the emphasis is on character delineation.

One weakness which O'Neill was never to overcome but later learned to circumvent, even to use, was his inability to write vital dialogue. At its worst his dialogue sounds borrowed from some dreadful melodrama; at its best it has a commonplace flatness which gives authenticity to the character. It never soars; there is never a *mot juste.* Indeed, scholars have suggested that, in some of his very long plays, O'Neill overwrote in order to overcome this lack of precision.

Throughout his career O'Neill was preoccupied with three principal themes. One was the implacability of natural environment, most often the sea or the bleak areas of New England—the idea that nature tests man and either exposes him or increases his stature. Another theme is materialism and man's greed for the crude forms of wealth. Finally, and the theme to be exploited most successfully, is the problem of identity, the test of discovering the true self beneath the facade.

O'Neill's work may be divided roughly into five periods. The first is that of the "lost" plays, works so poor that their author made no attempt to make them public. Unearthed in the Library of Congress and published in 1958, these plays—*A Wife for Life* (wr. 1913/14), *Servitude* (wr. 1913/14, prod. 1960), *Abortion* (wr. 1913/14), *The Sniper* (1917), and *The Movie Man* (wr. 1916)—add nothing to his reputation. Little better are others of the same period—*Thirst* (1916), *The Web* (wr. 1913/14), *Warnings* (wr. 1913/14), *Fog* (1917), and *Recklessness* (wr. 1913/14)—which he published in 1914 under the title *Thirst and Other Plays*.

O'Neill's second period, during which he first gained recognition, was devoted primarily to short plays of the sea. This compact and somewhat repetitive body of work was considered starkly realistic at the time, but more recently its romantic, even sentimental, quality has been acknowledged. The best of these, generally grouped under the collective title *S.S. Glencairn*, are *Bound East for Cardiff* (1916), a vignette of a dying seaman; *The Long Voyage Home* (1917), in which a sailor's dreams are destroyed when he is robbed and shanghaied; *In the Zone* (1917), in which a sailor's intimate secrets are exposed when he is accused of being a saboteur; and *The Moon of the Caribbees* (1918), a vignette concerning a drunken spreee in a Caribbean port. Similar are *'Ile* (1917), the study of a captain obsessed by the search for whale oil; and *Where the Cross Is Made* (1918), later expanded as *Gold* (1921), in which the greed for gold destroys both father and son.

His third period, and one of his most successful, includes the plays produced between 1920 and 1924. Having served his apprenticeship in the one-act play, O'Neill began writting longer works beginning with the Pulitzer Prize-winning *Beyond the Horizon,* in which a poetic soul is destroyed through his own timidity. After such minor works as *The Straw* (1921), in which love and hope save a woman's life, and the aforementioned *Gold* (1921), he won another Pulitzer Prize with *Anna Christie,* in which the redemption of a prostitute is underlaid by the motif of the power of the sea to both cleanse and destroy. The power of the play is marred by the conventional sentimental treatment of the prostitute. O'Neill's first major departure from realism was the expressionistic and symbolic *The Emperor Jones,* a masterful depiction of an arrogant man's disintegration under the impact of superstition and fear. After two mediocre studies of ''identity,'' *Diff'rent* (1920) and *The First Man* (1922), O'Neill produced a full-fledged expressionistic drama in the style of Georg Kaiser, *The Hairy Ape.* In this play, a brutish stoker is destroyed by the mechanistic civilization of which he is a prime support. *See* KAISER, GEORG.

In rapid succession O'Neill next produced the Strindbergian marriage drama *Welded* (1924); *All God's Chillun Got Wings* (1924), a drama of miscegenation in which the black husband and white wife seek their identity in the other's race; and the sprawling drama about Ponce de León, *The Fountain* (1925). One of the best of the plays of this period is *Desire under the Elms* (1924), which possibly owes something to Leo Tolstoy's *The Power of Darkness.* One of O'Neill's few true tragedies, this story of a son who fathers a child with his own stepmother is a cautionary tale of the eruption of sexuality in a puritan land (New England). *See* TOLSTOY, LEO.

O'Neill's fourth period covers the decade beginning in 1925 and might well be called his ''cosmic'' period. Most of the eight plays written during this time deal with grand issues, often at great length. The conceptions are lofty, often windily idealistic, and there is a heavy dependence upon theatrical effect. In *Marco Millions* (1928), O'Neill uses the full pageantry of fabled Cathay in an episodic satire on materialism that centers on the figure of Marco Polo. *The Great God Brown* (1926) is another experimental drama, in which masks, before employed only for theatrical effect, are central to the play and to the development of the characters who wear them. Lacking in clarity but heavy with significance, it attempts to represent the symbiotic relationship between two people. Brown assumes Dion Anthony's mask but must also at times become Brown. In *Lazarus Laughed* (1928), another pageantlike work, the provocative though ill-dramatized idea that laughter is man's only possible reponse to an imponderable universe is used as a reaffirmation of life.

Strange Interlude (1928), which brought O'Neill his third Pulitzer Prize, is a sentimentalized melodrama which turns into a lengthy psychological study. Its inordinate length and use of long interior monologues, soliloquies patterned on the stream-of-consciousness theory, stirred much critical comment. Similar devices are used in *Dynamo* (1929), in which the machine in a mechanistic society becomes a god to be worshiped. With his return to realism in *Mourning Becomes Electra* (1931), O'Neill produced what is possibly his best work of this period. However, the use of Aeschylus's *Oresteia* as the model for this modern trilogy has, for many critics, falsely in-

Scene from *The Moon of the Caribbees,* **Minneapolis, 1966. [The Guthrie Theater Company]**

flated the play's value, and for the perceptive modern reader the characters may assume a contrived aspect, being so evidently manipulated to conform to the ancient classic theme. *See* AESCHYLUS.

Ah, Wilderness! (1933) is a nostalgic view of the America O'Neill knew as a youth, a comedy with serious overtones which is autobiographical in many respects. The only play of this period with modest pretensions, it is the only one that is completely successful. In *Days Without End* (1934), O'Neill again uses masks in the drama of a man destroyed by his evil alter ego but redeemed through Christ.

By 1935, O'Neill's career seemed at an end. Once acclaimed as America's greatest dramatist, he was all but forgotten; his reputation steadily declined, reaching its nadir in the 1940s and early 1950s. Even the award of the Nobel Prize for Literature (1936) did not stay this decline. Although O'Neill was to write six more plays, only one of these, *The Iceman Cometh,* was produced during his lifetime, and even that was unsuccessful. Not until the play was revived in 1956, a year which also saw the triumphant production of *Long Day's Journey into Night,* was O'Neill's reputation restored. In fact, for many, this fifth and last period was his finest.

In his last plays, O'Neill abandoned theatrical experiments and returned to realism, with the result that for stark power many of these dramas are unmatched in the American theatre. *The Iceman Cometh* is a masterful study of the inmates of a cheap saloon and how their pathetic illusions are nourished and then destroyed by a traveling salesman. The Pulitzer Prize-winning *Long Day's Journey into Night* (1956), generally considered O'Neill's finest play and the greatest American tragedy, is a grim study of a tormented family which O'Neill said was "written in

Two scenes from *Beyond the Horizon.* (Left) Judith Lowry, Aline MacMahon, and Robert Keith. (Below; l. to r.) Thomas Chalmers, Malcolm Williams, Aline MacMahon (holding Elaine Koch), and Robert Keith. New York, Mansfield Theatre, 1926. [Photograph by Vandamm. Theatre Collection, The New York Public Library at Lincoln Center, Astor, Lenox and Tilden Foundations]

blood," based upon his own early life. Similarly biographical is *A Moon for the Misbegotten* (wr. 1943, prod. 1957), in which an alcoholic, despairing young man (based on O'Neill's brother Jamie) meets a robust and exuberant girl who tries unsuccessfully to help him.

Of the massive eleven-play cycle in which O'Neill intended, during his last years, to examine the destructive power of the pursuit of material gain and which was to be entitled *A Tale of Possessors Self-Dispossessed*, only two are extant: *A Touch of the Poet* (wr. 1935–1942, prod. 1958) and *More Stately Mansions* (wr. 1953, prod. 1967). The first two plays of the cycle, *Greed of the Meek* and *Give Me Death*, were burned in manuscript in 1943; the existing two plays of the cycle follow the fortunes of Major Melody and the demise of the poetic spirit (Simon Hartford), corrupted initially by a base, materialistic world.

At the same time O'Neill was at work on a cycle of "light" shorter pieces collectively to be called *By Way of Obit*. Of these, only *Hughie* (wr. 1942, prod. 1958) was completed, and it, too, is a study of pathetic illusion.

Beyond the Horizon (1920). Fatalistic drama of unfulfilled dreams and irresistible forces which work at cross-purposes to the desires of men. Robert Mayo, a poetic young intellectual eager to leave the constraint of the family farm, is about to ship out on a voyage with his uncle. His brother, who is happy on the farm, is looking forward to his marriage to Ruth Atkins, a childhood sweetheart. When Robert tells Ruth he loves her, her response causes him to abandon his chance of escape and to marry Ruth, while Andrew replaces his brother on the sea voyage. Robert proves inept and temperamentally unsuited to farming and brings the farm to slow disintegration and ruin. Too late he realizes that his wife, who has become resentful and morose, has always loved his brother. Andrew returns, successful and wealthy, having grown away from Ruth and life on the farm, to find Robert, surrounded by the ruins he has created, dying of tuberculosis. On his deathbed, Robert still dreams of freedom beyond the horizon and a reconciliation between Ruth and Andrew.

The Straw (1921). Young, pretty Eileen Carmody, stricken with consumption, spends several months in the Hill Farm sanatorium, where she falls in love with Stephen Murray, a small-town journalist. She inspires him to a flurry of creative writing, and he is immediately successful. Believing that Murray does not return her love, Eileen loses all desire for recovery and is expected to die. Informed of her condition, Murray decides he does love her and they become engaged, clinging to the straw of hope that her happiness will work a miracle.

Gold (1921). Psychological drama of obsession and greed set on the California coast. Whaling captain Isaiah Bartlett dreams of and plans for the recovery of a treasure chest he found and buried on a South Sea island years ago when shipwrecked with survivors of his crew. He is tormented by his complicity in the murder of two men on the island, and his mind gradually disintegrates. At the end, a recluse in the ship's cabin built on the roof of his oceanside mansion, he dies, admitting that the treasure was in reality only worthless brass and that his life has been destroyed by a compulsive illusion.

Anna Christie (1920). Drama concerning the redemption of a former prostitute. Chris Christopherson, an old survivor of the days of windjammers in Sweden, is reduced to being skipper of a coal barge running between New York and Boston. He has learned, after suffering and loss, to hate the sea. Not only has it brought death and destruction to the men in his family, but his own wife, unable to endure the life of a sailor's wife, had taken his baby Anna to America to live with relatives in Minnesota. There Anna's mother had died and the child had been raised far from the dangers of the sea. Now, more than fifteen years later, Chris receives a postcard from St. Louis saying that Anna is on her way to New York. Chris, in preparation for Anna's arrival, clears his barge quarters of his longtime companion, a prostitute named Marthy, and receives his daughter at Johnny the Priest's saloon with warmth and affection. Only in his eyes is she the innocent child he had imagined, for it is obvious to everyone else that she has lived the hard life of a prostitute. But Anna softens to her new life, and gradually, by virtue of the cleansing sea, she becomes innocent once again. When the barge picks up the survivors of a shipwreck, Anna is intensely admired by one of them, the gigantic but childlike Mat Burke, and they fall in love. Chris is furious at the prospect of his Anna

A Norwegian production of *Anna Christie*. Oslo, Riksteatret, 1953.
[Royal Norwegian Embassy Information Service]

marrying a seafaring man, and the two men come to blows over her. Now Anna confesses her past, and the men, bewildered by their new knowledge, leave the barge, determined to lose themselves in drink. After two days of drunken revelry, Chris and Mat return. Mat has decided that he still wants to marry Anna and Chris has decided to relent, but both have signed on the same steamer bound for South Africa the next morning. Hopeful but wary of the future on the sea, they prepare to leave, and Anna plans to wait for Mat's return.

The Emperor Jones (1920). Expressionistic drama set in the jungles of a West Indian island. Former pullman porter and murderer Brutus Jones and the Cockney trader Smithers have set up a ruthless monarchy, dominating the ignorant and superstitious natives. Warned by Smithers that the island is in revolt, Jones immediately

Elizabeth Brown (left) and Mary Blair in *Diff'rent*. New York, Princess Theatre, 1921. [Theatre Collection, The New York Public Library at Lincoln Center, Astor, Lenox and Tilden Foundations]

begins his preplanned escape: he will cross the jungle to the coast and safety. As he enters the jungle, however, night falls, and to the incessant accompaniment of pounding drums he confronts the dark forces of his own mind and the history of his race. In a terrifying series of short episodes he is assailed by the phantoms of his victims and his past life, journeying back through auction block and slave ship to his primeval origins in the Congo. Frantic with fear, he has fired all the bullets in his gun at the images which pass before him. At dawn the rebels start their search and find Jones lying prostrate very near the place where he had entered the forest. They fire a silver bullet into his body, believing it the only means to end his life. But, as Smithers concludes from the horrified expression on the dead Jones's face, it was probably fear that caused his death.

Diff'rent (1920). Drama, set in a seaport village in New England, exploring the fatal results of mistaken idealism and unrealistic standards. In the spring of 1890, young captain Caleb Williams returns from his initial voyage as master of his own ship. His betrothed, Emma Crosby, a novel-reading girl who insists that her fiancé be "diff'rent" from other men, prudishly breaks their engagement when she learns of his single indiscretion on a South Sea island. Thirty years later, in 1920, Emma has deteriorated into a prurient spinster, grotesque in her efforts to stay young and pretty and convinced she holds an irresistible attraction for Benny Rogers, the wastrel son of Caleb's sister Harriet. Desperate and bitter, Caleb, who has waited all these years for her to change her mind, hangs himself in the barn. Emma now realizes what she has become and walks out of her home to the same end.

The First Man (1922). Realistic drama set in a small town in contemporary Connecticut. Young and brilliant anthropologist Curtis Jayson, embittered by the deaths of his two beloved children ten years before, has since immersed himself and his devoted wife Martha in his work, which takes him all over the world. About to embark on a lengthy expedition in search of the first man's fossils, Curtis learns to his dismay that Martha is once again pregnant—a pregnancy his snobbish family secretly attributes to his closest friend Ed Bigelow. When Martha dies in agony in childbirth, Curtis, insane with grief, at first refuses to acknowledge the child, but on discovering the rumors about his wife he affirms his fatherhood and accepts the baby, finding in it a continuation of Martha's life and love for him.

The Hairy Ape (1922). Eight-scene drama, considered one of the foremost achievements of expressionism on the American stage, presenting a demonstration of man's alienation within the very environment he has helped to shape. A stoker in the infernolike bowels of a transatlantic liner, the massive, brutish Yank Smith is possessed of a proud dignity that he "belongs" to the age of steam, power, and speed until a simple look of revulsion from a slumming passenger topples his confidence and self-respect. Bewildered and humiliated, Yank sets out to understand and then, by brute force, to destroy the society in which he now feels himself a misfit. First imprisoned

Louis Wolheim in *The Hairy Ape*. New York, Playwrights' Theatre, 1922. [Culver Pictures]

and then peremptorily rejected by a socialist cell, Yank is finally killed in a zoo by the gorilla, a purely instinctive being with whom he can at last feel some affinity.

The Fountain (1925). Sprawling historical drama concentrating on the character of Don Juan Ponce de León and his obsession with the Fountain of Youth. Beginning as a young adventurer whose exploits and ability quickly raise him to the position of governor in the newly formed colony of Porto Rico, Juan's whole life gradually becomes dominated by the legend of the fountain. Spurred on by his love for his young ward Beatriz de Córdova, he sails to the coast of Florida and believes he has reached Cathay. Wounded by Indians just before he realizes that the fountain is a myth, Juan, in delirium, experiences a mystical revelation that age, youth, and death are but manifestations of the rhythm of eternal life. He dies a few months later, reconciled to his life and fate.

Welded (1924). Self-conscious drama of the living hell which the playwright Michael Cape and his actress wife Eleanor endure as a result of their obsessive grip on one another. Cape's insane jealousy of Eleanor precipitates a violent quarrel which drives each to attempt to ruin their marriage, Eleanor with an elderly admirer and Cape with a prostitute. Both are rejected when it becomes obvious that vengeance is their motive. The attempts of each to be free of the other's compulsive hold prove futile, and Cape and Eleanor resume their marriage.

All God's Chillun Got Wings (1924). Powerful drama dealing with the tragic marriage between the sensitive, intelligent Negro Jim Harris and his white wife Ella Downey, each unable to accept his own identity. Growing up in the slums of lower New York, Jim and Ella, in the innocence of childhood, pledge their love. With maturity comes awareness of the disharmony between the races, an awareness which does not, however, prevent them from finding in one another the only sources of understanding and gentleness in their brutal, squalid world. After their marriage Jim's herculean efforts to study law are defeated by his sense of racial inferiority. Ella, driven gradually insane by the rejection of both races and unable to repress a growing revulsion at her own degradation, escapes into a fantasy world of childhood where her relationship with Jim no longer bears the stigma of decadence or the taint of social ostracism.

Desire under the Elms (1924). Stark drama of love and lust, greed and covetousness, set in the rocky countryside of New England in 1850. Seventy-six-year-old Ephraim Cabot, a grim, hard-shelled New England farmer, takes a third wife, the young and sensual Abbie. His stepson Eben is filled with resentment that he will be thus disinherited from the farm which belonged to his deceased mother. He is attracted to Abbie and at first resists her advances, but he eventually succumbs to her seduction and fathers a child which old Cabot believes to be his own. Furious at having been the instrument of his own disinheritance, Eben inadvertently drives Abbie to murder the child, which she feels is an obstacle to their love. Then, horrified at the unnatural crime, he turns her over to the sheriff. Realizing at last the great love which prompted her to the act, Eben gives himself up as her accomplice, determined to share in her punishment and leaving Ephraim sitting alone in "the best farm in the county."

Marco Millions (1928). Satire, often bordering on slapstick, which denounces Western materialism and the absurd contentions of the world's religions. The play focuses on the development of the fabled Marco Polo, who matures from a callow youth into a clumsy and ignorant adult. Tutored by his father and uncle, enterprising Venetian traveling salesmen who take the youthful Marco on a journey to Cathay, with sublime naïveté he impresses the philosophic Kublai, the Great Khan. Under Kublai's amused gaze, Marco rises to high political office by virtue of his blindness to any values other than those of money and of his own egotism coupled with absolute confidence in the superior virtues of Christian-

Scenes from *All God's Chillun Got Wings,* **with Paul Robeson and
Flora Robson. London, Piccadilly Theatre, 1933. [Theatre Collection,
The New York Public Library at Lincoln Center, Astor, Lenox and
Tilden Foundations]**

ity. He is so self-absorbed that he fails to observe that Princess Kukachin, the Khan's granddaughter, loves him with a consuming passion. Marco returns to Venice fabulously rich and with a closed mind, never suspecting that Kukachin will die of unrequited love.

The Great God Brown (1926). Experimental drama which reinforces psychological probing with the use of masks, to represent the public faces people assume as opposed to their inner selves. Dion Anthony, gifted and sensitive, hides his true self behind a mask of Dionysian sensuality and sardonic cynicism. His wife Margaret knows and loves the masked Dion but fears and mistrusts the brooding man who is Dion unmasked. William A. Brown, a successful but stolid, uninspired architect—"the great god Brown"—has always envied and resented his boyhood friend, the masked Dion, and feeds on Dion's talent and gift for life. Understood only by the prostitute Cybel, the "Earth Mother," Dion finally destroys himself through drink and dissipation. Now Brown can assume his friend's identity. Wearing Dion's mask and through it his life, he manages for a time to alternate between the two selves; but, unable to sustain the masquerade, he then assumes the character of Dion for good, is accused of murdering Brown, and dies at the hands of the police.

George C. Scott and Colleen Dewhurst in *Desire under the Elms.* **New York Circle in the Square Theatre, 1963. [Friedman-Abeles]**

Joseph Wiseman (standing), Hal Holbrook, and Zohra Lampert in *Marco Millions.* **New York, Repertory Theatre of Lincoln Center, 1964. [Martha Swope]**

Lazarus Laughed (1928). Pageantlike drama in which all characters wear masks except Lazarus, whom Christ has resurrected and who is considered a deity throughout the Roman Empire. He grows gradually younger as the play progresses and acquires more and more followers; his presence inspires a celebration of life wherever he goes. Traveling to Rome with his wife Miriam, Lazarus encounters the envious Tiberius Caesar and his half-mad nephew Caligula. Miriam is poisoned by the jealous Pompeia, Caesar's mistress, and Lazarus is executed by burning at the bidding of Tiberius. But the laughter of Lazarus rises even from the flames, affirming his teaching that there is no death. Having murdered Tiberius, Caligula witnesses Lazarus's last breath and asks his forgiveness.

Strange Interlude (1928). Psychiatric drama in nine acts, unique for its use of asides and soliloquies which expose the thoughts and motives of its characters to the audience before they are revealed to the players. Covering more than a decade in the lives of its principals, the play is necessarily episodic, concentrating on neurotic Nina Leeds, who seems to exert a strange fascination on the men in her life. Prevented by her possessive father, Professor Harry Leeds, from marrying her first love, Gordon Shaw, who is killed shortly thereafter in World War I, Nina flounders in an aimless, promiscuous life. She is intensely admired by the ineffectual novelist Marsden and the brilliant young physician Dr. Darrell, neither of whom is willing to commit himself to marriage. Thus after Nina's father dies, Darrell, now a sort of father substitute, recommends she wed the dull, inferiority-ridden yet wealthy Sam Evans. Nina acquiesces listlessly. Months later, pregnant with Evans's child, Nina is informed by her mother-in-law of a strain of insanity in the family. She deliberately aborts the child over the protests of Mrs. Evans that fatherhood is just what Sam needs to give him confidence and drive. When Darrell agrees to father another child for her, which the delighted Evans believes to be his own, Nina's circle of power is complete: she reigns over her husband, her lover, her son, and Marsden. Eleven years later, Marsden and Darrell, after backing one of Evans's enterprises, have become wealthy. Nina's son Gordon, though sensing there is no love between his parents, never suspects that Darrell, his "Uncle Ned," is his real father. As the boy grows, Nina's possessiveness almost ruins Gordon's chances for a happy marriage to the rich and beautiful Madeline Arnold. When Evans, whom she has grown to despise, dies of a stroke, Nina turns at last to Marsden, who has been waiting patiently for her all these years.

The Great God Brown, Phoenix Theatre, 1959. [Courtesy of Phoenix Theatre. Photograph by Friedman-Abeles]

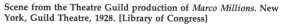

Scene from the Theatre Guild production of *Marco Millions.* New York, Guild Theatre, 1928. [Library of Congress]

Dynamo (1929). Symbolic drama employing the asides and stream-of-consciousness devices of *Strange Interlude* and dealing with the false gods men erect in the wake of their loss of faith in traditional religion. Embittered by the revelation of the true character of his minister father and possessive mother, the young, impressionable Reuben Light undergoes a transformation from a religious, God-fearing youth to a cynical atheist. Mystically attracted to a humming dynamo at the hydroelectric plant where he is employed, Reuben begins to worship this man-made idol as the mother of the universe, offering his sweetheart, the simpleminded Ada, as a blood sacrifice in atonement for his sins of lust and dying himself in a last fatal embrace with the monstrous machine.

Mourning Becomes Electra (1931). Trilogy set in post-Civil War New England, based on the *Oresteia* trilogy of Aeschylus. This modern Freudian adaptation of the Greek legend unfolds a tale of adultery, matricide, and incest leading to the downfall of the Mannon family. It takes 5½ hours to perform.

The Homecoming. Hatred and rivalry fill the Mannon household to which the triumphant soldiers General Ezra Mannon and his son Orin are about to return. Mannon's daughter, Lavinia, adores him and is jealous of his affection for her mother, Christine. During Mannon's absence Christine has had an affair with Captain Adam Brant and is plotting to murder her husband in order to marry her lover, who it seems also has Mannon blood. She quarrels with her husband on the night of his homecoming, and he is stricken with a heart attack. Christine substitutes poison for his medicine, and he dies. Lavinia, at first only suspecting and then confirming the truth, vows to avenge her father's death.

The Hunted. With the arrival of Orin for his father's funeral, Christine and Lavinia begin a battle for his allegiance. His overpowering love for his mother at first reassures her that he will never accept Lavinia's insinuations. Gradually, however, Lavinia's accusations arouse his suspicion. They follow Christine to a meeting with Brant, where they overhear the lovers planning to run away. Orin, insanely jealous, waits until Christine leaves, then murders Brant. Returning to the Mannon house to confront Christine, Lavinia gloats and mocks her with Brant's death until, in a frenzy of grief, her mother shoots herself. Orin then realizes that he has irrevocably lost his mother's love and, consumed by guilt, edges close to madness.

The Haunted. After a long sea voyage, Lavinia has the emotionally twisted Orin under her control. He, in turn, is insanely jealous and possessive of his sister. When Lavinia becomes engaged to Peter Niles, a cousin, Orin threatens to expose their past in order to perpetuate their perverted relationship. Lavinia, however, is no longer able to bear her brother's possessiveness and his obsession with their guilt-ridden past. Subtly she insin-

Glenn Anders (left), Charles Walters, and Lynn Fontanne in *Strange Interlude.* New York, John Golden Theatre, 1928. [Photograph by Vandamm. Theatre Collection, The New York Public Library at Lincoln Center, Astor, Lenox and Tilden Foundations]

uates that suicide would be his only deliverance and Orin dies, shot while cleaning his pistol. Realizing now that she can never be free of the Mannon history or her own guilt, Lavinia breaks her engagement with Peter, orders the windows of the mansion boarded up, and retires into the gloomy house to spend her remaining days with ghosts of the Mannon past.

Ah, Wilderness! (1933). Comedy which focuses on the growing pains of sixteen-year-old Richard Miller, who is in the throes of discovering Swinburne, Omar Khayyam, Ibsen, Shaw, and socialism. Regarded benevolently by his father but with consternation by his doting mother, Richard rebels against the confining life of their small town. On the night of July 4, he tentatively enters the world of barroom frequenters and prostitutes, an experience from which he emerges not a bit older and only slightly wiser, but secure in his resolve to marry one day his innocent childhood sweetheart Muriel. Richard's father, reassured that his son is not on the road to ruin, feels confident that he will successfully weather the storms of adolescence.

Days Without End (1934). Drama which employs the device of a masked individual, the alter ego, who speaks with and sometimes for the protagonist but who remains unseen and unheard by the other characters. The tortured, intellectual John Loving is engaged in a life-and-death conflict with the sneering, cynical element of his psyche which has poisoned his past life, made him prey to false gods and philosophies, and now seeks to destroy him through the final deliverance of suicide. Having been unfaithful to his adored wife Elsa under this evil influence and having caused her to attempt suicide, he seeks a solution from his wise and understanding uncle, Father Matthew Baird. In a cathedral, at the foot of the

The character of Tiberius Caesar in *Lazarus Laughed,* presented by the Pasadena Playhouse in 1928. [Theatre Collection, The New York Public Library at Lincoln Center, Astor, Lenox and Tilden Foundations]

(Above) Stage setting for *Dynamo*. (Left) Glenn Anders and Claudette Colbert in *Dynamo*. New York, Martin Beck Theatre, 1929. [Photograph by Vandamm. Theatre Collection, The New York Public Library at Lincoln Center, Astor, Lenox and Tilden Foundations]

Cross, his masked tormentor perishes as Loving renews his faith in Christ.

The Iceman Cometh (wr. 1939, prod. 1946). Powerful drama describing defeat and illusion and exposing "pipe dreams" which are, paradoxically, both deadly and benevolent to the beaten humans who harbor them, the boarders and barflies of Harry Hope's saloon-hotel located in New York's lower West Side. In the summer of 1912 at Hope's saloon, awaiting the long-overdue arrival of the free-spending, boisterous salesman Hickey on one of his periodic binges is a collection of down-and-outers, each with his own doleful past, their sensibilities and memories numbed with whiskey and never-ending plans for their imminent recovery which is always to take place "tomorrow." When Hickey finally arrives, in time for Harry's birthday, they are shocked to find him greatly changed: he announces that he has finally had the courage to face himself and to lay his pipe dreams to rest, thus finding a kind of peace and contentment. Furthermore he intends to help the others do the same, and he forces his former cronies, one by one, actually to embark on their long-dreamed-of plans in the hope that their failures will at least make them accept what they really are. But the shock of losing their one remaining shred of hope plunges them still further into a despair from which even the whiskey cannot retrieve them. Then, driven by both guilt and exasperation, Hickey reveals the details of his "conversion": his life with the saintly, long-suffering Evelyn who for all the years of their marriage had invariably forgiven his drinking and infidelities; their pipe dream that he truly loved her and would never stray again; and finally his decision, ostensibly to free her from the torment of his presence but actually because he had come to hate her, to put a bullet through her head while she slept, just hours before he had come to Harry's. Having previously telephoned the police, Hickey is arrested and led away while the others, content in the assumption that Hickey was temporarily insane, lapse once more into their comfortable world of whiskey and pipe dreams.

Long Day's Journey into Night (wr. 1941, prod. 1956). Autobiographical drama spanning approximately eighteen torturous hours in the fogbound summer home of the Tyrone family on an August day in 1912, a day during which each member of the family confronts his own failures and guilts and which ends in frustration and futility. Presiding over the tension-filled house is the theatrical James Tyrone, a vain, retired matinee idol whom a childhood of grinding poverty has turned into a miser, penny-wise but dollar-foolish. With him are his delicate and gentle wife Mary, their elder son Jamie—whose alcoholic, wastrel ways are a constant source of irritation to Tyrone—and their younger son Edmund (O'Neill himself), stricken with consumption after years of wandering and dissipation. Addicted to morphine during the birth of Edmund and ravaged by her years of touring with Tyrone and her endless battle against the drug, Mary succumbs once again to the habit, precipitating among the men a flood of accusation, self-recrimina-

Alla Nazimova (standing) and Alice Brady in *Mourning Becomes Electra*. New York, Guild Theatre, 1931. [Library of Congress]

Fern Sloan and Margaret Phillips in *Mourning Becomes Electra*, Minneapolis, 1969. [The Guthrie Theater Company]

(Above) *Days Without End,* with Earl Larimore, Selena Royle, and Stanley Ridges (standing). New York, Henry Miller Theatre, 1934. [Photograph by Vandamm. Theatre Collection, The New York Public Library at Lincoln Center, Astor, Lenox and Tilden Foundations]

Two scenes from *Ah, Wilderness!* (Left) George M. Cohan, Elisha Cook, Jr., and Marjorie Marquis. (Below) John Butler, Ruth Holden, and Elisha Cook, Jr. New York, Guild Theatre, 1933. [Photograph by Vandamm. Theatre Collection, The New York Public Library at Lincoln Center, Astor, Lenox and Tilden Foundations]

The Iceman Cometh, with (l. to r.) Carl Benton Reid, James Barton, Dudley Digges, and Nicholas Joy. New York, Martin Beck Theatre, 1946. [Photograph by Vandamm. Theatre Collection, The New York Public Library at Lincoln Center, Astor, Lenox and Tilden Foundations]

tion, and confession which lays bare their hidden motives and drives and reveals their interdependence. Helpless, unable to fix the guilt of their situation on any one cause, they resign themselves to watching Mary slip deeper and deeper into a world of dream and hallucination.

A Touch of the Poet (wr. 1935–1942, prod. 1958). The third in a projected cycle of nine plays which was to chronicle the history of the Hartfords, a New England family. In 1828, Cornelius Melody, a posturing, alcoholic, Byronic figure, has been reduced to the status of a tavern keeper in a town near Boston. Obsessed by his pretensions to gentlemanly grandeur and the recollections of more dashing days as a dragoon, he has become a constant torment to his long-suffering wife Nora and his spirited daughter Sara. Convalescing in an upstairs bedroom is the Thoreau-like poet Simon, son of the wealthy merchant Henry Hartford. Sara is deeply in love with Simon, and his marriage proposal seems imminent. Though undaunted by a warning visit from Simon's curiously neutral mother Deborah, Sara is fearful that Melody's bungling interference will ruin her chances for happiness. Then, when old Hartford's lawyer appears with an offer to buy the family off, Melody's stiff Irish pride sends him out into the night determined to mend his wounded honor. In the privacy of Simon's bedroom Sara elicits Simon's vow to marry her, after which Melody returns home, having brawled with the police and Hartford's servants. He is a changed man, his illusions tragically shattered—an event for which Nora and Sara had been waiting but which, nonetheless, leaves them saddened.

Hughie (wr. 1942, prod. 1958). Study of character and loneliness, virtually a monologue by the seedy Broadway gambler Erie Smith in the deserted lobby of a fifth-rate hotel on a summer night in 1928. Recovering from a five-day binge brought on by the death of the former night clerk Hughie, Erie regales Hughie's bored and inattentive replacement with the story of his life and with a touching lament for his recently deceased friend. Hughie may have been a dupe, a simple soul, but Erie had found in him a ready believer of his own grandiose pretensions, an uncritical friend whose admiration lent dignity and self-respect to the small-time second-rater. His death was a calamity in Erie's life. His hopes revive, however, when the new night clerk, precisely the same type as Hughie, shows signs of following in his predecessor's footsteps.

Long Day's Journey into Night, with (l. to r.) Bradford Dillman, Jason Robards, Jr., Florence Eldridge, and Fredric March. New York, Helen Hayes Theatre, 1956. [Walter Hampden Memorial Library at The Players, New York]

Scene from a 1957 German production of *Long Day's Journey into Night,* with Elisabeth Bergner as Mary Tyrone. [German Information Center]

A Moon for the Misbegotten (wr. 1943, prod. 1957). Sequel to *Long Day's Journey into Night,* set on the property which the tenant farmer Phil Hogan has leased for twenty years from the now-dead James Tyrone, Sr. The run-down farm has become a haven and retreat for the disconsolate, alcoholic Jim Tyrone while he waits for the settlement of his deceased mother's estate. There the shrewd, garrulous Hogan lives with his daughter Josie, a strong, earthy girl who, though she pretends to be of easy virtue, is in fact pure and very much in love with Jim. Hogan intends to use her as bait for a forced wedding with Jim and tricks her into believing that Jim intends to sell the farm out from under them. Incensed, Josie prepares to seduce him into a marriage proposal. But Jim, in a drunken half-stupor, rejects her advances because he truly loves her, reassuring her that the farm will not be sold. At the same time, he confesses his inconsolable grief over his mother's death and his remorse at his degenerate behavior on the train while bringing the body back from California: he had been drunk, had been with a prostitute during the trip, and, finally, had been too drunk to attend the funeral. Realizing the unutterable sadness of Jim's life, Josie says goodbye and prays that he may soon find deliverance in the death he longs for and that he may rest forever in forgiveness and peace.

Ben Gazzara as Erie Smith in *Hughie*. [Photograph courtesy of Max Eisen]

More Stately Mansions (wr. 1953, prod. 1967). Merciless drama of greed and power continuing the history of Simon Hartford, his wife Sara, and his mother Deborah. The three protagonists are locked in a life-and-death struggle for dominance, each at the mercy of drives and appetites seemingly beyond his control. When Henry Hartford dies, leaving his great business complex near bankruptcy, the once-idealistic Simon, whose four years of managing a modest textile mill have turned him into a shrewd businessman, absorbs the company and moves his family into the Hartford mansion where Deborah has been living in a twilight world somewhere between reality and sensuous dreams. The intimate contact precipitates a desperate battle for the domination of Simon, the roles of wife and mother, husband and son shifting and blending as the sides form and re-form in complex alliances over a period of ten years. Only Sara emerges strong and unbroken. Simon realizes too late that in his ruthless climb to power and wealth he has been advancing toward the destruction of himself and those around him.

[EDWARD MURRAY]

PLAYS

Unless otherwise noted, the plays were first performed in New York.

1. *A Wife for Life*. Play, 1 act. Written 1913/14. Published 1958.

2. *Thirst*. Play, 1 act. Written 1913/14. Published 1914. Produced Provincetown, Mass., Wharf Theatre, summer, 1916.

3. *The Web*. Play, 1 act. Written 1913/14. Published 1914.

4. *Warnings*. Play, 1 act. Written 1913/14. Published 1914.

5. *Fog*. Play, 1 act. Written 1913/14. Published 1914. Produced Playwrights' Theatre, Jan. 5, 1917.

6. *Recklessness*. Play, 1 act. Written 1913/14. Published 1914.

7. *Bound East for Cardiff*. Play, 1 act. Written 1913/14. Published 1919. Produced Playwrights' Theatre, Nov. 3, 1916.

8. *Servitude*. Play, 3 acts. Written 1913/14. Published 1958. Produced Skylark Theatre, New York International Airport, Apr. 23, 1960.

9. *Abortion*. Play, 1 act. Written 1913/14. Published 1958.

10. *The Sniper*. Play, 1 act. Written 1915. Published 1958. Produced Playwrights' Theatre, Feb. 16, 1917.

11. *Before Breakfast*. Play, 1 act. Written 1916. Published 1916. Produced Playwrights' Theatre, Dec. 1, 1916.

12. *The Movie Man*. Comedy, 1 act. Written 1916. Published 1958.

13. *'Ile*. Play, 1 act. Written 1916. Published 1919. Produced Playwrights' Theatre, Nov. 30, 1917.

14. *In the Zone*. Play, 1 act. Written 1916. Published 1919. Produced Comedy Theatre, Oct. 31, 1917.

15. *The Long Voyage Home*. Play, 1 act. Written 1916. Published 1919. Produced Playwrights' Theatre, Nov. 2, 1917.

16. *The Moon of the Caribbees*. Play, 1 act. Written 1916. Published 1919. Produced Dec. 20, 1918.

17. *The Rope*. Play, 1 act. Written 1918. Published 1919. Produced Playwrights' Theatre, Apr. 26, 1918.

18. *The Dreamy Kid*. Play, 1 act. Written 1918. Published 1920. Produced Playwrights' Theatre, Oct. 31, 1919.

19. *Beyond the Horizon*. Play, 3 acts. Written 1918. Published 1921. Produced Morosco Theatre, Feb. 2, 1920.

20. *Where the Cross Is Made*. Play, 1 act. Written 1918. Published 1919. Produced Playwrights' Theatre, Nov. 22, 1918.

21. *The Straw*. Play, 3 acts. Written 1919. Published 1921. Produced Greenwich Village Theatre, Nov. 10, 1921.

22. *Gold*. Play, 4 acts. Written 1920. Published 1920. Produced Frazee Theatre, Jan. 1, 1921.

23. *Anna Christie*. Play, 4 acts. Written 1920. Published 1923. Produced Vanderbilt Theatre, Nov. 10, 1921. Earlier version: *Chris Christopherson*. Written 1919. Produced Atlantic City, N.J., Mar. 8, 1920.

24. *The Emperor Jones*. Play, 8 scenes. Written 1920. Published 1921. Produced Playwrights' Theatre, Nov. 3, 1920.

25. *Diff'rent*. Play, 2 acts. Written 1920. Published 1921. Produced Playwrights' Theatre, Dec. 27, 1920.

26. *The First Man*. Play, 4 acts. Written 1921. Published 1923. Produced Neighborhood Playhouse, Mar. 4, 1922.

27. *The Hairy Ape*. Comedy of ancient and modern life, 8 scenes. Written 1921. Published 1923. Produced Playwrights' Theatre, Mar. 9, 1922.

28. *The Fountain*. Play, 11 scenes. Written 1922. Published 1926. Produced Greenwich Village Theatre, Dec. 10, 1925.

29. *Welded*. Play, 3 acts. Written 1923. Produced Thirty-ninth Street Theatre, Mar. 17, 1924.

30. *All God's Chillun Got Wings*. Play, 2 acts. Written 1923. Published 1924. Produced Provincetown Playhouse, May 15, 1924.

31. *Desire under the Elms*. Play, 3 parts. Written 1924. Published 1925. Produced Greenwich Village Theatre, Nov. 11, 1924.

32. *Marco Millions*. Play, prologue, 3 acts, and epilogue. Written 1925. Published 1927. Produced Guild Theatre, Jan. 9, 1928.

33. *The Great God Brown*. Play, prologue and 4 acts. Written 1925. Published 1926. Produced Greenwich Village Theatre, Jan. 23, 1926.

34. *Lazarus Laughed*. Play, 4 acts. Written 1926. Published 1927. Produced Pasadena, Calif., Playhouse, Apr. 9, 1928.

35. *Strange Interlude*. Play, 2 parts and 9 acts. Written 1927. Published 1928. Produced John Golden Theatre, Jan. 20, 1928.

36. *Dynamo*. Play, 3 acts. Written 1928. Published 1929. Produced Martin Beck Theatre, Feb. 11, 1929.

37. *Mourning Becomes Electra*. Trilogy: *Homecoming*, 4 acts; *The Hunted*, 5 acts; *The Haunted*, 4 acts. Written 1931. Published 1931. Produced Guild Theatre, Oct. 26, 1931.

38. *Ah, Wilderness!* Comedy, 4 acts. Written 1932. Published 1933. Produced Guild Theatre, Oct. 2, 1933.

39. *Days Without End*. Play, 4 acts. Written 1933. Published 1934. Produced Guild Theatre, Jan. 8, 1934.

40. *The Iceman Cometh*. Play, 4 acts. Written 1939. Published 1946. Produced Martin Beck Theatre, Sept. 2, 1946.

41. *Long Day's Journey into Night*. Play, 4 acts. Written 1941. Published 1955. Produced Helen Hayes Theatre, Nov. 7, 1956.

42. *A Touch of the Poet*. Play, 4 acts. Written 1935–1942. Published 1957. Produced Helen Hayes Theatre, Oct. 2, 1958.

43. *Hughie*. Play, 1 act. Written 1942. Published 1959. Produced Stockholm, 1958; New York, Royale Theatre, Dec. 22, 1964.

44. *A Moon for the Misbegotten*. Play, 4 acts. Written 1943. Published 1958. Produced Bijou Theatre, May 2, 1957.

45. *More Stately Mansions*. Play, 2 acts. Written 1953. Published 1964. Produced Broadhurst Theatre, Oct. 31, 1967. Shortened from the rough manuscript by K. R. Gierow and edited by D. Gallup.

EDITIONS

Collections

Thirst and Other One-act Plays, Boston, 1914; *The Moon of the Caribbees and Six Other Plays of the Sea*, New York, 1921; *Complete Works*, 2 vols., New York, 1924; *Nine Plays*, New York, 1932; *The Long Voyage Home: Seven Plays of the Sea*, New York, 1940; *Plays*, 3 vols., New York, 1941, rev. ed., 1955; *Ten ''Lost'' Plays*, New York, 1964; *Later Plays*, ed. by T. Bogard, New York, 1967; *Three Plays*, New York, n.d.; *Six Short Plays*, New York, n.d.

Individual Plays

Ah, Wilderness! Published in *Five Contemporary American Plays*, ed. by W. H. Hildreth and W. R. Dumble, Harper, New York, 1939; *Sixteen Famous American Plays*, ed. by B. A. Cerf and V. H. Cartmell, Garden City, New York, 1941; *Contemporary Drama*, ed. by E. B. Watson and B. Pressey, Scribner, New York, 1959; *Readings for Enjoyment*, ed. by E. R. Davis and W. C. Hummel, Prentice-Hall, Englewood Cliffs, N.J., 1959.

Anna Christie. Published in *Twentieth Century Plays*, ed. by F. W. Chandler and R. A. Cordell, rev. ed., Nelson, New York, 1939; *A New Edition of the Pulitzer Prize Plays*, ed. by K. Cordell and W. H. Cordel, Random House, New York, 1940; *Modern American Plays*, ed. by F. G. Cassidy, Longmans, New York, 1949; *A Treasury of the Theatre*, ed. by J. Gassner, Simon and Schuster, New York, 1951.

Before Breakfast. Published in *A Treasury of Plays for Women*, ed. by F. Shay, Little, Brown, Boston, 1922.

Beyond the Horizon. Published in *The Pulitzer Prize Plays, 1918–1934*, ed. by K. Cordell and W. H. Cordell, Random House, New York, 1935; *Modern Dramas*, ed. by H. H. Hatcher, new ed., Harcourt, Brace, New York, 1948; *Representative American Plays from 1767 to the Present Day*, ed. by A. H. Quinn, 7th ed., rev. and enl., Appleton-Century-Crofts, New York, 1953; *Modern English Readings*, ed. by R. S. Loomis, D. L. Clark, and J. H. Middendorf, 7th ed., Rinehart, New York, 1956.

Bound East for Cardiff. Published in *Contemporary Trends: American Literature since 1900*, ed. by J. H. Nelson and O. Cargill, Macmillan, New York, 1949; *College Reading*, ed. by G. Sanderlin, Heath, Boston, 1953; *The Types of Literature*, ed. by F. X. Connolly, Harcourt, Brace, New York, 1955; *Repertory*, ed. by W. Blair and J. Gerber, Scott, Foresman, Chicago, 1960.

Desire under the Elms. Published in *Twenty-five Best Plays of the Modern American Theatre*, ed. by J. Gassner, Crown, New York, 1949; *Eight Great Tragedies*, ed. by S. Barnet, M. Berman, and W. Burto, New American Library, New York, 1957; *Masters of American Literature*, ed. by G. N. Ray, L. Edel, T. H. Johnson, S. Paul, and C. Simpson, Houghton Mifflin, Boston, 1959; *Modern Drama for Analysis*, ed. by P. M. Cubeta, 3d ed., Holt, New York, 1962.

Diff'rent. Published in *Representative Modern Plays*, ed. by R. A. Cordell, Nelson, New York, 1929.

The Dreamy Kid. Published in *Plays of Negro Life*, ed. by A. L. R. Locke and G. Montgomery, Harper, New York, 1927.

The Emperor Jones. Published in *Chief Contemporary Dramatists*, ed. by T. H. Dickinson, 3d ser., Houghton Mifflin, Boston, 1930; *Modern Drama for Analysis*, ed. by P. M. Cubeta, Sloane, New York, 1950; *The Britannica Library of Great American Writing*, ed. by L. Untermeyer, vol. 2, Lippincott, Philadelphia, 1960; *Masters of Modern Drama*, ed. by H. M. Block and R. G. Shedd, Random House, New York, 1962.

The Great God Brown. Published in *Plays from the Modern Theatre*, ed. by H. R. Steeves, Heath, Boston, 1931; *British and American Plays, 1830–1945*, ed. by W. H. Durham and J. W. Dodds, Oxford, New York, 1947; *Masters of American Literature*, ed. by H. A. Pochman and G. W. Allen, Macmillan, New York, 1949; *Twenty-five Modern Plays*, ed. by S. M. Tucker and A. S. Downer, 3d ed., Harper, New York, 1953.

The Hairy Ape. Published in *Chief Patterns of World Drama*, ed. by W. S. Clark II, Houghton Mifflin, Boston, 1946; *Twenty-five Best Plays of the Modern American Theatre*, ed. by J. Gassner, Crown, New York, 1949; *A Treasury of the Theatre*, ed. by J. Gassner, Simon and Schuster, New York, 1951; *The American Tradition in Literature*, ed. by E. S. Bradley, R. C. Beatty, and E. H. Long, Norton, New York, 1956; *American Drama*, ed. by A. Downer, Thomas Y. Crowell, New York, 1960.

The Iceman Cometh. Published in *Best American Plays*, ed. by J. Gassner, 3d ser., Crown, New York, 1952; *Masters of Modern Drama*, ed. by H. M. Block and R. G. Shedd, Random House, New York, 1962; *Major Writers of America*, ed. by P. Miller, 2 vols., Harcourt, Brace & World, New York, 1962.

'Ile. Published in *Dramas by Present-day Writers*, ed. by R. W. Pence, Scribner, New York, 1927; *Twenty-five Best Plays of the Modern American Theatre*, ed. by J. Gassner, Crown, New York, 1949; *Interpreting Literature*, ed. by K. L. Knickerbocker and H. W. Reninger, rev. ed., Holt, New York, 1960.

In the Zone. Published in *Plays and the Theatre*, ed. by R. B. Thomas, Little, Brown, Boston, 1937; *A Quarto of Modern Literature*, ed. by L. S. Brown and P. G. Perrin, 3d ed., Scribner, New York, 1950; *Our Reading Heritage*, ed. by H. H. Wagenheim, E. V. Brattig, and M. Dolkey, vol. 2,

Holt, New York, 1956; *Introduction to Imaginative Literature*, ed. by B. D. N. Grebanier and S. Reiter, Thomas Y. Crowell, New York, 1960.

Lazarus Laughed. Published in *The Literature of America*, ed. by A. H. Quinn, A. C. Baugh, and W. D. Howe, vol. 2, Scribner, New York, 1929; *Oxford Anthology of American Literature*, ed. by W. R. Benét and N. H. Pearson, Oxford, New York, 1938; *Contemporary Trends: American Literature since 1900*, ed. by J. H. Nelson and O. Cargill, Macmillan, New York, 1949.

Long Day's Journey into Night. New Haven, Conn., 1956.

The Long Voyage Home. Published in *A Book of Dramas*, ed. by B. Carpenter, Prentice-Hall, New York, 1949; *Preface to Drama*, ed. by C. W. Cooper, Ronald, New York, 1955; *Makers of the Modern Theater*, ed. by B. Ulanov, McGraw-Hill, New York, 1961; *Introduction to Literature*, ed. by L. G. Locke, W. M. Gibson, and G. Arms, 4th ed., Holt, New York, 1962.

Marco Millions. Published in *Twentieth Century Plays*, ed. by F. W. Chandler and R. A. Cordell, Nelson, New York, 1934; *American Life in Literature*, ed. by J. B. Hubbell, Harper, New York, 1936; *Nelson's College Caravan*, ed. by A. P. Hudson, L. B. Hurley, and J. D. Clark, 3d ed., Nelson, New York, 1942.

A Moon for the Misbegotten. Published in *Best American Plays*, ed by J. Gassner, 4th ser., Crown, New York, 1958; *Modern Drama: An Anthology of Nine Plays*, ed. by E. J. Lovell and W. R. Pratt, Ginn, Boston, 1963.

The Moon of the Caribbees. Published in *Modern English Readings*, ed. by R. S. Loomis and D. L. Clark, Farrar & Rinehart, New York, 1934; *Plays for the College Theater*, ed. by G. H. Leverton, French, New York, 1934; *Famous American Plays of the 1920's*, ed. by K. Macgowan, Dell, New York, 1959.

Mourning Becomes Electra. Published in *Representative Modern Plays, American*, ed. by R. Warnock, Scott, Foresman, Chicago, 1952.

The Rope. Published in *A College Book of American Literature*, ed. by H. M. Ellis, L. Pound, and G. W. Spohn, American Book, New York, 1939.

Strange Interlude. Published in *The Theatre Guild Anthology*, Random House, New York, 1936; *A New Edition of the Pulitzer Prize Plays*, ed. by K. Cordell and W. H. Cordell, Random House, New York, 1940.

Where the Cross Is Made. Published in *A Book of Modern Plays*, ed. by G. R. Coffman, Scott, Foresman, Chicago, 1925; *Today's Literature*, ed. by D. C. Gordon, V. R. King, and W. W. Lyman, American Book, New York, 1935; *Prose and Poetry of the World*, ed. by J. R. Barnes, Singer, Syracuse, N.Y., 1941; *Adventures in American Literature*, ed. by R. B. Inglis, J. Gehlmann, M. R. Bowman, and W. Schramm, 4th ed., Harcourt, Brace, New York, 1947.

CRITICISM

R. Sanborn and B. H. Clark, *A Bibliography of the Works of Eugene O'Neill*, New York, 1931; V. Geddes, *The Melodramas of Eugene O'Neill: A Critical Study*, Brookfield, Conn., 1934; S. K. Winther, *Eugene O'Neill: A Critical Study*, New York, 1934; R. D. Skinner, *Eugene O'Neill: A Poet's Quest*, New York, 1935; B. H. Clark, *Eugene O'Neill: The Man and His Plays*, New York, 1947; E. A. Engle, *The Haunted Heroes of Eugene O'Neill*, Cambridge, Mass., 1953; J. Y. Miller, *A Critical Bibliography of Eugene O'Neill*, Ann Arbor, Mich., 1957; A. Boulton, *Part of a Long Story*, New York, 1958; D. V. Falk, *Eugene O'Neill and the Tragic Tension*, New Brunswick, N.J., 1958; C. Bowen and S. O'Neill, *The Curse of the Misbegotten: A Tale of the House of O'Neill*, New York, 1959; *O'Neill and His Plays: Four Decades of Criticism*, ed. by O. Cargill, B. N. Fagan, and W. J. Fischer, New York, 1961; D. Alexander, *The Tempering of Eugene O'Neill*, New York, 1962; A. and B. Gelb, *O'Neill*, New York, 1962; J. Y. Miller, *Eugene O'Neill and the American Critic: A Summary and Bibliographical Checklist*, New York, 1962, 2d ed. rev., 1973; C. Leech, *Eugene O'Neill*, New York, 1963; F. I. Carpenter, *Eugene O'Neill*, New York, 1964; *O'Neill: A Collection of Critical Essays*, ed. by J. Gassner, Englewood Cliffs, N.J., 1964; J. Gassner, *Eugene O'Neill*, Minneapolis, 1965; J. Y. Miller, *Playwright's Progress: O'Neill and the Critics*, Glenville, Ill., 1965; D. V. K. Ragharacharyulu, *Eugene O'Neill: A Study*, New York, 1965; J. H. Raleigh, *The Plays of Eugene O'Neill*, Carbondale, Ill., 1965; O. Coolidge, *Eugene O'Neill*, Scribner, New York, 1966; W. D. Frager, *Love as Death in ''The Iceman Cometh,''* Gainesville, Fla., 1967; C. C. Long, *Role of Nemesis in the Structure of Selected Plays by Eugene O'Neill*, New York, 1968; L. Sheaffer, *O'Neill: Son and Playwright*, Boston, 1968; *Twentieth Century Interpretations of ''The Iceman Cometh,''* ed. by J. Raleigh, Englewood Cliffs, N.J., 1968; T. Tivsanen, *O'Neill's Scenic Images*, Princeton, N.J., 1968; *An O'Neill Concordance*, comp. by J. R. Reaver, 3 vols., Detroit, 1971; J. Bryer, *The Merrill Checklist of Eugene O'Neill*, Columbus, O., 1971; H. Frenz, *Eugene O'Neill*, New York, 1971; T. Bogard, *Contour in Time: The Plays of Eugene O'Neill*, New York, 1972; J. M. Salem, ''Eugene O'Neill,'' *A Guide to Critical Reviews—Part I: American Drama 1909–1969*, 2d ed., Metuchen, N.J., 1973, pp. 348–372; L. Sheaffer, *O'Neill: Son and Artist*, Boston, 1973; J. M. Atkinson, *Eugene O'Neill: A Descriptive Bibliography*, Pittsburgh, 1974; L. Chabrowe, *Ritual and Pathos: The Theater of O'Neill*, London, 1976; H. Cronin, *Eugene O'Neill: Irish and American*, New York, 1976; E. Griffin, ed., *Eugene O'Neill*, New York, 1976; J. T. Shipley, *The Art of Eugene O'Neill*, Philadelphia, 1977; V. Geddes, *The Melodramadness of Eugene O'Neill*, Philadelphia, 1978.

Orhan Kemal (1914–1970)

Turkish novelist, film writer, and dramatist; pseudonym of Mehmet Raşit Öğütçü. For political reasons his father, a lawyer and politician, took the family from Adana to Syria, and Orhan Kemal had little formal education. Returning to Turkey in 1932, he worked as a laborer and factory hand. From 1938 to 1943 he was imprisoned, and it was in there that he came to know Nazım Hikmet. After 1951, he settled in Istanbul. He died during a visit to Bulgaria in 1970. *See* NAZIM HIKMET (RAN).

Orhan Kemal is primarily a novelist and short-story writer. His life both in prison and out brought him into contact with Turkey's underprivileged people, and it was from that milieu that he drew his rich material. All his plays are adaptations of his novels and short stories. His *Cell Block No. 72* (*72. Koğuş*, 1967) is a realistic portrayal of prison life. In it he argues that crime prevention can be brought about not by imprisoning people but only by changing the social system that breeds crime. The focus of the play is a ship captain whose goodness, sincerity, love, and tragic death teach the other inmates a lesson in brotherhood. This man is contrasted with the head jailer, who seems determined to increase the sufferings of his prisoners. *The Chaffinches* (*Ispinozlar*, 1964), adapted from his novel *Sweet Bird of Fortune* (*Devlet Kuşu*) depicts the lives of a poor family whose only hope lies in the possibility that the son will marry the enamored daughter of a rich, vulgar neighbor. Though he is in love with a poor girl, he consents to this marriage in order to rescue his family from poverty. This arranged marriage results in unhappiness for all concerned. The play was revised as *The Mayor of Hicksville* (*Yalova Kaymakamı*) in 1968. *Shoemender's Shop* (*Eskici Dükkanı*, 1970) was adapted for the stage from the playwright's novel *The Shoemender and His Sons*. A poor lame cobbler—a patriarchal father and a descendant of a feudal lord—dreams of making rich marriages for his children, but they choose spouses from their own class. In the end the old man is forced to sell

Orhan Kemal.
[Metin And
Collection]

his shop. Destitute, he finds some hope in his neighbors, who unite to help him.

Share and Share Alike (*Kardeş Payı*, 1969), his last play, highlights the tragic situation of workers from rural areas who come to big towns to find work. It realistically depicts their struggle against a cruel labor racketeer who exploits them and threatens to replace them with unemployed workers when they complain. Finally, through the efforts of a brave young woman worker and the man she loves, the workers manage to rebel.

Orhan Kemal's novel *Murtaza* (1968) was adapted by the author, but another stage version was done by the playwright Orhan Asena. A grim comedy, it centers around Murtaza, who works in a cotton mill and acts as a watchdog for his bosses. To avenge themselves against him, the other workers arrange for him to catch his own daughter napping on plant time. Murtaza beats her so cruelly that she dies. *See* ASENA, ORHAN.

METIN AND

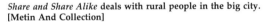

Share and Share Alike deals with rural people in the big city.
[Metin And Collection]

Oriani, Alfredo (1852–1909)

Italian novelist, dramatist, and historian. His works often reflect a taste for realism and romantic anarchism. His philosophical work *The Ideal Revolt* (*La rivolta ideale*, 1908) was hailed by Mussolini as a forerunner of fascist theory in its condemnation of the positivism and materialism of the nineteenth century. *The Unconquerable* (*L'invincibile*, 1902) is a modern adaptation of *Hamlet*. Considered Oriani's best play is *The Last Barbarians* (*Ultimi barbari*, 1903), a reworking of the romantic tragedy of Paolo and Francesca in a peasant milieu.

The Unconquerable (*L'invincibile*, 1902). Modern version of Shakespeare's *Hamlet*. Ruggero, ten years old when his father was murdered, is now a young man greatly disturbed by his hatred of the Count, his mother's second husband. In his attempts to uncover the mystery of his father's death, Ruggero discovers that it

Alfredo Oriani.
[Federico Arborio
Mella, Milan]

came at the hands of the Count's brother. Ruggero confronts the Count with this information and announces that he will not tell the court but only his mother so that she may hate him as he does. The Count takes an overdose of a sleeping potion and dies in his wife's arms. Ruggero then discovers that he alone mourns his father and that he has only succeeded in making his mother forget everything in her deep grief for the loss of the Count.

[PETER BONDANELLA]

EDITIONS

Opera omnia, ed. by B. Mussolini, Bologna, 1923–1933.

CRITICISM

F. Authier, "État présent des études sur Alfred Oriani," *Revue des Études Italiennes* 7 (1960), 250–269.

Örkény, István (1912–1979)

Hungarian playwright and writer. He was born and died in Budapest. At the insistence of his father, a druggist, he was educated as a chemical engineer, but began contributing stories and articles to various literary periodicals in the 1930s. During World War II he served in a forced labor battalion on the Eastern front, and was taken prisoner by the Russians in 1943. His experiences during the war were to become reoccurring themes in both his fiction and drama. Repatriated in 1947, he became the literary assistant of the Theatre of Youth (1949–1951) and then of the Theatre of the Hungarian People's Army (1951–1953). Repeated switches from an initial commitment to Stalinism to support for the uprising of 1956, then back to repenting of this support, resulted in his falling into disfavor in both the literary and theatre worlds. For some time he worked in a chemical plant but in the mid-1960s he was readmitted to literary life and died a celebrated writer and holder of the prestigious Kossuth and Attila József Prizes.

After a promising beginning as a playwright during

and after World War II, he compromised with the Zhdanovist aesthetic expectations of the postwar Stalinist regime of Hungary and wrote no noteworthy plays until *The Tot Family* (*Tóték*, 1967). Though like his close friend Miklós Hubay, Örkény focuses on the absurd aspects of life, his essential approach to drama is that of Brechtian rationalism. The function of irrationalism in his plays is to persuade his audience to side with reason. "You need a hammer to hammer in a nail, and you need the jellylike stuff in your skull to produce thoughts. And mind it: when the train is coming, getting on it and lying under it are two entirely different things!" says his spokesman-hero in *The Key-Seekers* (*Kulcskeresők*, 1976). Örkény tends to represent the alienated and irrational modern world as a machine against which human consciousness rebels. It is the railroad which gives meaning to the life of the protagonists (all called Bokors and related in one way or another) of *Blood Relations* (*Vérrokonok*, 1974), until the computerized, overloaded system breaks down and yields to chaos. In *The Tot Family* a simple village fire chief initially complies with the paranoid caprices of an army officer in order to save the life of his soldier son, but finally rebels and makes mincemeat of the tyrannical major with a bizarre machine the latter has invented. *In Steve in the Bloodshed* (*Pisti a vérzivatarban*, 1969), a young Hungarian Everyman is caught by the merciless machine of modern history which repeatedly makes him either a victimizer or a victim.

Another target of Örkény's criticism is an existence lived as a "winter dream," in submission to fate or in entropy. A revolt against this state is Örkény's answer to absurdity. The most pronounced example of this revolt is in *Catsplay* (*Macskajáték*, 1969). Two elderly sisters, one living amidst modest circumstances in Budapest and the other in sterile comfort in West Germany, look back on their life. At the age of sixty-five Mrs. Erzsi Orbán in Budapest has a male friend and goes through disap-

István Örkény.
[Photograph courtesy
of George Bisztray]

pointments (with his friend, girl friend, and daughter), but heroically fights for life and happiness. Gizi, in Germany, has no need to fight for anything; she lives in luxury, but neither does she know happiness nor does she have any true human connections.

Hungarian critics have emphasized that the exactitude of language in Örkény's plays matches their intellectualism. By the time of his death he had established an international reputation. *The Tot Family* was staged by Washington's Arena Theater in 1977; *Catsplay* had a New York production in 1979 and has been staged in ten European countries.

GEORGE BISZTRAY

PLAYS

1. *Voronyezs (Voronezh, Ukraine).* Drama, 3 acts. Written 1944 or 1948. Produced on television 1969.
2. *Zsugori (The Miser).* Written 1947. Produced Budapest, Madách Színház, 1948. A Molière adaptation.
3. *A borék (The Bor Family).* Comedy. Written 1948.
4. (With Miklós Gyárfás) *A Zichy palota (The Zichy Palace).* Written 1949. Produced Budapest, Ifjúsági Színház, 1949.
5. *Sötét galamb (Dark Dove).* Play, 3 acts. Written 1957. Produced Budapest, Nemzeti Színház, 1970.
6. *Tóték* (The Tot Family).* Tragicomedy, 2 acts. Written 1967. Produced Budapest, Thália Színház, 1967.
7. *Macskajáték* (Catsplay).* Tragicomedy, 2 acts. Written 1969. Produced Szolnok, Szigligeti Színház, 1971.
8. *Pisti a vérzivatarban (Steve in the Bloodshed).* Play, 2 acts. Written 1969. Produced Budapest, Pesti Színház, 1979.
9. (With István Nemeskürty). *A holtak hallgatása (The Silence of the Dead).* Documentary play, 2 acts. Written 1973. Produced Budapest, Pesti Színház, 1973.
10. *Vérrokonok* (Blood Relations).* Written 1974. Produced Budapest, Pesti Színház, 1974.
11. *Kulcskeresők (The Key-Seekers).* Play, 2 acts. Published 1976. Produced Szolnok, Szigligeti Színház, 1975.

EDITIONS

Blood Relations. Published in *New Hungarian Quarterly*, 59, 1975, tr. by M. Kuttna.
Catsplay: A Tragicomedy in Two Acts. Published in *New Hungarian Quarterly*, no. 44, tr. by M. Kuttna, 1971; tr. by C. Györgyey, New York, 1976.
The Tot Family (short excerpts from Act 2). Published in *New Hungarian Quarterly*, no. 28, 1967.

CRITICISM

H. Popkin, "Antic Parable from Hungary," *The New York Times*, Feb. 1, 1976; C. Barnes, Review of *The Tot Family*, Arena Stage Production, *The New York Times*, Feb. 23, 1976; I. Lázár, *Örkény István*, Budapest, 1979.

Orta Oyunu

Genre of Turkish theatre. The similarity between *orta oyunu* and the *karagöz* shadow play as concerns characters, comic elements, and atmosphere is striking in spite of the fact that the former uses live actors and the latter leather puppets. How far was the *orta oyunu* under the influence of *karagöz* or vice versa? Unfortunately, we do not know for sure when *orta oyunu* first constituted itself in Turkey in its final form or even how it arose.

Though Turkish shadow theatre in turn borrowed movements, postures, and costumes from the Ottoman puppet theatre, it was also influenced by human actors such as the jesters and grotesque dancers found in Ottoman miniatures of the sixteenth, seventeenth, and eighteenth centuries. Eventually live actors and puppeteers tried to imitate shadow theatre. As early as 1675 a book on a festival for the circumcision of Mehmet IV's

Seventeenth-century masked clowns of the type that scholars believe found their way into *orta oyunu* performances. [Metin And Collection]

sons in Edirne describes a performance by actors dressed like the puppets in a shadow play. Elsewhere mention is made of a miller's guild entertainment in which the clowns wear hats similar to that worn by Karagöz.

An attempt has been made to trace *orta oyunu* to the ancient Greek mime via Byzantium or the *commedia dell'arte*, there having been a close relationship between the Ottoman Empire and the Italian states. Some scholars, however, are inclined to believe that *orta oyunu* is a

Orta oyunu actors are shown performing on a raft in this eighteenth-century miniature. [Topkapi Palace Museum, Istanbul]

Kavuklu Hamdi (left) and Küçük Ismail were
two great exponents of nineteenth-century *orta oyunu.*
[Metin And Collection]

fairly new type of entertainment, originating after 1790
as an offspring of *karagöz*. Other scholars believe that
orta oyunu did not appear until even later. This point of
view may have been influenced by the fact that the name
orta oyunu is a fairly recent adoption. Previously the form
was known as *kol oyunu* (company play), *meydan oyunu*
(plays in the round), and *tarlit oyunu* (mimicry play). *Orta
oyunu* is first mentioned in a festivity book by the poet
Esat in 1834, and in 1836 a different festivity book by
Lebib reports on two *orta oyunu* companies whose names
were Zuhuri Kolu and Ali Ağa Kolu. The plays performed were *The Raid on a Neighborhood Disorderly House
(Mahalle Baskını)*, *The Play of the Tailor (Terzi Oyunu)*, *The
Play of the Public Scribe (Yazıcı Oyunu)*, *The Play of the
Fountain (Çesme Oyunu)*, *The Play of the Barber (Berber
Oyunu)*, and *The Play of the Fortress (Kale Oyunu)*.

In the early days of *orta oyunu*, plays were preceded
by a diversion in which there were twelve dancers and a
clown called Tiryaki (the opium addict). The latter wore
a pointed hat similar to a dunce's cap and carried a clap-
per consisting of two flat pieces of wood fastened together. (It was used to produce a loud noise when someone was being "beaten.") His job was to make humorous
gestures during the dances, after which the play proper
started.

Turkish ambulatory and processional plays done
during public festivals, on the occasion of court weddings or circumcision ceremonies, and to celebrate the
accession of a new ruler or a military triumph no doubt
also provided models for *orta oyunu*. Usually they were
performed by trade guilds, and elaborately decorated
carts were used as stages. Farces were performed in the
streets, and onlookers took an active part in performances in which a prearranged comic situation was elaborated on by improvisation and spur-of-the-moment
practical jokes. Local officials and shopkeepers were often impersonated, and even the Grand Vizier was not
safe from ridicule. Such skits had the greatest bearing on
the emergence of *orta oyunu*. Sultan Abdülaziz encouraged *orta oyunu* players to ridicule statesmen such as Ali
Pasha, Fuat Pasha, and Yusuf Kamil Pasha—all Grand
Viziers or viziers.

As has been noted, there is some reason for believing that *orta oyunu* is fundamentally a variant of *commedia
dell'arte*, which could have been introduced into the Ottoman Empire either by the Italians themselves or by
Jewish emigrants, who in the fifteenth and sixteenth centuries came to Turkey from Portugal and Spain, where
commedia dell'arte had already been introduced. The latter
explanation is more likely since from that time to the end
of the nineteenth century most of the public entertainers
were Jewish. There is also etymological evidence for accepting this view. For instance, the ground level acting
area in *orta oyunu* is called *palanga*, deriving from the
Spanish *palanque*, which has almost the same meaning.
The word *orta oyunu* itself has several interpretations.
The most common and acceptable of these is that *orta*
literally means "middle" in terms of both place and time.
Thus it may mean a play performed in the middle of an
audience or a play used as an interlude between other
forms of entertainments.

It has also been argued that the word may come
from the fact that the elite Janissary troops were divided
into units known as *orta*. *Orta oyunu* may have been entertainments for these soldiers. In fact, Kavuklu, the
main *orta oyunu* character, mentions in one play that his
costume and the large wadded headgear (which gave
him his name) are a precise copy of the Janissary dress.

As has been noted, the influence of *karagöz* shadow
theatre on *orta oyunu* is considerable. However, another
important element in the development of *orta oyunu* were
the grotesque dancers—the *curcunabaz*, *tulumcu*, and *cin
askeri*. These dancers often had staves at the end of
which were air-filled bladders. Usually they were led by
a man who rode a small donkey. Comically dressed,
their hands and arms concealed in their loose and long
dresses, they would cavort, dance, and somersault, striking out at spectators with their bladders (*tulum*) or in-
dulging in humorous impersonations. Sometimes in their
processions they would display a giant artificial phallus
with which they would salute the spectators.

In the *orta oyunu* eventually presented on the
"stage," mimicry, dance, and comic dialogue evolved
into a play, and the clowns were transformed into actors.
By the seventeenth century public and professional entertainers were very numerous, and Evliya Çelebi, a famous traveler of that period, refers to them in his accounts.

Pişekâr (left) and Kavuklu, whose wadded headgear imitates Janissary dress, square off for a battle of wits. [Metin And Collection]

The *orta oyunu* "stage" consisted of an open space around which the audience sat, the women on a side obscured by a temporary lattice. In rare instances, a low fence marked the playing area. There was no curtain, and the actors dressed and waited for their cues while sitting among the members of the orchestra, remaining visible to the audience during the whole play. The stage scenery was comprised of a screen to represent a house and a smaller, lower one to represent a shop. The rest was left to the imagination of the audience, which displayed great forbearance in regard to the naïve improbabilities of the *mise-en-scène*. A word or gesture was sufficient to transform the playing area.

The main character, Pişekâr, who is also the director and manager of the company, comes onto the stage first. After bowing to the audience on all four sides, he announces the name of the play and from then on remains continuously onstage. He is met by Kavuklu, who usually enters in the company of a dwarf or hunchback dressed like himself. Pişekâr and Kavuklu, the endmen—who much resemble Hacivat and Karagöz in shadow theatre—proceed to a *muhavere* (dialogue), a battle of wits in which Kavuklu tells a farfetched story which he tries to make the audience believe. Eventually it is discovered that Kavuklu is merely relating a dream. To cite two examples:

Kavuklu raises silkworms in Bursa, and when the worms emerge from the cocoons they grow to such a size that half the house is filled with them. He then finds himself in one of the cocoons and begins to perspire and suffocate, but in reality he has only become entangled in the bedclothes.

Kavuklu buys a pumpkin seed, plants it, and the pumpkin grows to an enormous size. It takes four people three days to saw it in half, and then the whole neighborhood eats its insides. Eventually a boat is made from its skin. The boat is so large that it takes sixteen people to row it, but when it gets a little way out to sea, it dis-

Kavuklu (left) and Pişekâr, two of the principal characters in traditional *orta oyunu*. [Metin And Collection]

Early-twentieth-century company of Turkish *orta oyunu* players. [Metin And Collection]

solves and all its occupants fall into the water. Only Kavuklu manages to keep afloat and suddenly someone slaps his face. This turns out to be the cousin who is sharing Kavuklu's bed and who has accidentally hit him while stretching.

After this dialogue comes the main plot, called the *fasıl:* usually Kavuklu asks Pişekâ for a job; some women ask him to help them find a house. Like *karagöz, orta oyunu* lacked a real plot and was merely a series of loosely connected scenes featuring players whose characteristics and limitations the audience easily recognized. Male actors played all feminine roles. As the stage area was surrounded by the audience, the players changed their positions frequently so that all of the spectators could see them. The dialogue was amusing, witty, and utterly unrestrained by technique or decency. On occasion it was sententious and full of puns.

In old times, a full *orta oyunu* company, *kol,* consisted of from twenty-five to thirty players including musicians and dancers. Around 1870 there were eight or ten *orta oyunu* companies in Istanbul. Originally performances were given on ground level, but later raised platforms were used. Eventually roofed theatres, known as *perdeli orta oyunu* ("orta oyunu with curtains"), were used. During the winter *orta oyunu* plays were performed in taverns or inns, and sometimes in the Sultan's Palace or in the homes of the rich. In summer, performances were given at resorts or in public parks.

Orta oyunu plots were ready-made but could easily be adapted for special occasions. The actors specialized in certain roles or well-defined types. To round out his improvisation and give it more substance, each performer always memorized unrelated bits which he could insert as often as was convenient in the improvised dialogues.

The *orta oyunu* actors were deeply aware of the four-sided audience and created a superb sense of intimacy. With minimal sets and props, they summoned up a world in which the spectator's imagination had free rein. When the hero climbed up on a chair, the audience understood that he had reached the second floor of a house, from which vantage point he described the view vividly. With gesture and sound, the actor suggested the opening of a bolt and stepped across the threshold.

An anti-illusionistic and presentational theatre, *orta oyunu* made use of music, dancing, and songs to establish a distance between the action and characters and the audience. This was aided by the fact that female roles were acted by men who spoke in falsetto voices.

In the nineteenth century, intellectuals championing Western culture attacked *orta oyunu* as primitive and vulgar—admittedly, the dialogues emphasized sexual and obscene jokes. As Turkey more and more came under Western influence, *orta oyunu* slowly lost its traditional color and vigor.

Surviving titles and scenarios point up the resemblances and close parallels between *karagöz* and *orta oyunu* plots. Some stock examples follow.

The Sorcerer *(Büyücü Hoca).* Kavuklu insults a *hodja* and is turned to stone. After neighbors ask that Kavuklu be forgiven, the *hodja* brings him back to life. At Kavuklu's request the *hodja* teaches him magic, but he uses his powers to turn the *hodja* and then all his creditors to stone. The *hodja* breaks the spell and decides to punish

Pişekâr cautions Kavuklu, who is accompanied by a dwarf dressed like himself, in this scene from *orta oyunu* comedy. [Metin And Collection]

Kavuklu, but once more he heeds the pleas of the neighbors.

The Chief Eunuch (*Kizlarağasi*). The chief eunuch likes Kavuklu and employs him to act on his behalf in dealing with everybody coming either to seek employment or to press for payment of old bills. Eventually the eunuch is revealed as a swindler. The police arrest him but pardon Kavuklu.

The Prize Wrestling Match (*Ödüllü*). In his will a rich man makes it a condition that his future son-in-law be able to defeat the bride in a wrestling match. The girl is very strong, and though many candidates have come forth, none has been successful. Eventually Kavuklu succeeds, but the girl's mother makes it a further condition that he be able to beat all the other candidates. Kavuklu accepts the challenge and wins the girl.

The Pancake Maker (*Gözlemeci*). With Pişekâr's help some women succeed in finding a house. Kavuklu then becomes an assistant to a man who sells pancakes, and while he is looking after the shop, the women play hide-and-seek and other games with him. Different characters appear as either creditors or customers. Lovers court under Kavuklu's nose without his being aware of it.

METIN AND

Barbra Byrne, Brad Davis, and Gwyllum Evans in the 1981 New York revival of *Entertaining Mr. Sloane*. [Martha Swope]

CRITICISM

T. Menzel, *Meddah, Schattentheater und Orta Ojunu*, Prague, 1941; M. And, "Wie enstand das Türkische Orta Oyunu," *Maske und Kothurn*, XVI-3/4(1970), pp. 201–216; M. And, *A Pictorial History of Turkish Dancing*, 1976; I. Kunos, *Das türkische Volksschauspiel-Orta ojunu*, Leipzig, 1980.

Orton, Joe (1933–1967)

English playwright. He was one of the originators and most gifted exponents of black comedy. In his first staged play, *Entertaining Mr. Sloane* (1964), a frustrated aging spinster and her homosexual brother agree to share the services of young Mr. Sloane rather than expose his murder of their father. *What the Butler Saw* (1969), a play that spans a hectic day in the life of the director of an exclusive psychiatric clinic, is thought to be his best. The source of comedy in both plays lies in the discrepancy between brutal and anarchistic acts and smooth, dispassionate dialogue. Orton also wrote *Loot* (1966), a satire on police corruption; and *The Erpingham Camp* (1967), about the destructiveness of vacationers. His own early and brutal murder could have been taken from one of his plays.

Entertaining Mr. Sloane (1964). Disregarding the opposition of her bad-tempered old father, Kath, a sexually frustrated middle-aged woman with absurd pretensions to refinement, takes in a fair-haired young lodger and seduces him on his first evening in the house. Her homosexual brother, a shady businessman, also has designs on Mr. Sloane, who turns out to be a murderer, and when the old man begins to connect him with an unsolved murder mystery, he is killed. Instead of handing their lodger over to the police, Kath and her brother agree to share him.

Loot (1966). Mrs. McLeavy has been murdered by a nurse who now has designs on her husband. Their son, involved with a close friend in a bank robbery, is expected to conceal the loot in his mother's coffin. A corrupt policeman discovers the facts but exploits them to his own advantage, while McLeavy, the only innocent character, goes to prison.

What the Butler Saw (1969). A philandering doctor persuades the girl he is interviewing for a secretarial job to strip. Complications proliferate with the arrival of his wife, a pageboy who is trying to blackmail her, and a psychiatrist who arrives to investigate the doctor. Confusions of identity and pretexts for making the characters undress soon come to seem rather mechanical.

CRITICISM

J. R. Taylor, *The Second Wave*, London, 1971; J. Lahr, *Prick Up Your Ears*, London, 1978; R. Hayman, *British Theatre since 1955*, London and New York, 1979.

Osborn, Paul (1901–   )

American playwright. He is best known for his adaptations of novels. *On Borrowed Time* (1938), a comedy-fantasy from the novel by Lawrence E. Watkins, concerns an old man whose overpowering love for his orphaned grandson enables him to forestall death for a time. *A Bell for Adano* (1944), from the novel by John Hersey, is a moving portrayal of the confrontation of American military personnel with the simple sentiment of civilians in American-occupied Italy during World War II. Among Osborn's other plays are *Hotbed* (1928); *A Ledge* (1929); *The Vinegar Tree* (1930); *Oliver, Oliver* (1934); *Morning's at Seven* (1939)—a failure at the time but successfully revived on Broadway four decades later; *The Innocent Voyage* (1943), from the novel by Richard Hughes; an adaptation of John P. Marquand's novel *Point of No Return* (1951); and an adaptation of Richard Mason's *The World*

Fredric March in *A Bell for Adano*. New York, Cort Theatre, 1944 [Photograph by Vandamm. Theatre Collection, The New York Public Library at Lincoln Center, Astor, Lenox and Tildon Foundations]

Point of No Return, with (l. to r.) Henry Fonda, Patricia Smith, and Colin Keith-Johnston. New York, Alvin Theatre, 1951. [Walter Hampden Memorial Library at The Players, New York]

of Suzie Wong (1958). He also wrote the screenplays for *Madame Curie* (1943), *East of Eden* (1955), and *South Pacific* (1958).

On Borrowed Time (1938). Fantasy in which Gramps's love for his grandson Pud is so strong, and his fear that Pud might come under the control of Aunt Demetria so great, that when Mr. Brink (death) comes for him, Gramps tricks him into climbing the apple tree. Once in the tree, Mr. Brink discovers that he cannot come down unless Gramps releases him. Gramps intends to keep Mr. Brink in the tree until either Demetria's life-span runs out or Pud grows up. He is forced to change his plans, however, when Pud is hurt and the doctor says he cannot help the boy. Gramps then releases Mr. Brink, and he and Pud set off to spend eternity together. Produced New York, Forty-eighth Street Theatre, February 2, 1938.

[GAUTAM DASGUPTA]

Osborne, John (1929–   )

English actor and dramatist. John James Osborne was born in London on December 12, 1929, the son of a commercial artist. He attended Belmont College, from which he received a certificate of education, but he did not go to a university. For a short time he worked as a journalist on the trade papers *Gas World* and *Miller*. In 1948 he launched his career as an actor in Sheffield in *No Room at the Inn*.

John Osborne. [Courtesy of London International]

It was while working as an actor that Osborne began writing plays. *The Devil inside Him,* written in collaboration with Stella Linden, was presented in Huddersfield in 1950. *Personal Enemy,* written with Anthony Creighton, was performed in Harrogate in 1955; *Epitaph for George Dillon,* written with Creighton in 1954, was not produced until 1958. Meanwhile, Osborne continued working in provincial repertory and together with Creighton managed a small theatrical company at seaside resorts.

For some time he had tried to interest London producers in the play that the English Stage Company finally accepted. It opened in London at the Royal Court Theatre in May, 1956, under the title *Look Back in Anger*. Despite several negative reviews, critics recognized the advent of a new talent, and though the initial run was short, it was almost immediately revived. It was the first momentous success in the English Stage Company's history; not only did it establish Osborne's reputation as a dramatist, but it also gave a name to the host of "angry young men" who followed. In 1957 both critics and public enthusiastically received *The Entertainer*, and in 1958 *Epitaph for George Dillon* was an immediate success. Osborne's subsequent plays include *Luther* (1961), *Inadmissible Evidence* (1964), *Time Present* (1968), *West of Suez* (1971), *A Sense of Detachment* (1972), and *Watch It Come Down* (1976).

Osborne has been married and divorced four times. His first wife was actress Pamela Lane; his second, actress Mary Ure, from whom he was divorced in 1962. In 1963 he married Penelope Gilliatt, and his fourth marriage was to Jill Bennett.

WORK

Osborne's importance to the British theatre was signaled by the opening of *Look Back in Anger* (1956). Osborne was not an innovator of form (*Look Back in Anger* is directly descended from the nineteenth-century well-made play) but he expressed what was thought to epitomize the fury and disillusionment, the frustration and anger, of an entire postwar generation. Although the Labor government had been in power for ten years, nothing substantive had changed and faith in progress had disappeared. The younger generation was helpless to change the "Brave New Nothing-very-much-thank-you" that followed the war. *See* WELL-MADE PLAY in glossary.

Jimmy Porter, the antihero of *Look Back in Anger*, became the spokesman and symbol for the youth of the 1950s, the culture hero of a society that had no good, brave causes left. A neurotic, egotistical, and adolescent young man, he lives in self-inflicted isolation and finds enjoyment in the torment he visits upon his wife in order to revenge himself upon the ruling order, of which she is a member.

Osborne's next play, *The Entertainer* (1957), which was influenced by the epic theatre of Brecht in its form and in its concern with social issues, deals again with disillusionment, despair, and the futility of modern life as reflected in a fading comedian unable and unwilling to communicate with other human beings. *Epitaph for George Dillon*, produced in 1958 but written before *Look Back in Anger*, is a more conventional drama than the other two. George Dillon is a writer-actor who perceives his own deficiencies; in despair, he submits to them and to society by changing his play to make it a financial success and by settling in middle-class suburbia, thereby writing his own epitaph. *Luther* (1961) was a Brechtian play about the first Protestant and the nature of protest.

Of Osborne's other works, *The World of Paul Slickey*

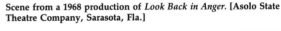

Scene from a 1968 production of *Look Back in Anger*. [Asolo State Theatre Company, Sarasota, Fla.]

(1959), a musical satire about a gossip columnist, was a failure. Equally disastrous was his second attempt at satire, *The Blood of the Bambergs* (1962), a tale of a royal wedding. Killed before the ceremony, the groom is replaced by a look-alike press photographer who is later discovered to be an offspring of the King. The one-act drama *Under Plain Cover* (1962) concerns an apparently normal, happy husband and wife who maintain their stability by secretly acting out their sexual fetishes. Because of the discovery that they are brother and sister, they separate; she remarries but later leaves her husband to return to her brother. *The Blood of the Bambergs* and *Under Plain Cover* were produced together under the title *Plays for England.*

Osborne's next play, *Inadmissible Evidence* (1964), concerns the disintegration of a loquacious middle-aged lawyer whose practice consists of divorce and criminal cases. Self-obsessed, he is unable to concentrate on his clients, who all blend in his mind, a situation presented dramatically by having the same actress play three parts. *A Patriot for Me* (1965), a semihistorical drama loosely based on the life of the spy Redl and his work in the pre-World War I Austro-Hungarian Army, deals with the social problems of the illegality of homosexuality.

Among Osborne's more recent plays are *A Bond Honoured* (1966), an adaptation of Lope de Vega's *The Outrageous Saint* that goes beyond anger to destruction and violence; *Time Present* (1968), another essentially monologue play whose protagonist, a successful actress, accuses her world of superficiality; *A Sense of Detachment* (1971); and *Watch It Come Down* (1976). See VEGA CARPIO, LOPE DE.

Epitaph for George Dillon (wr. 1954, prod. 1958). Dillon, an impecunious aging actor and author, is taken

Wendy Craig and Robert Stephens in *Epitaph for George Dillon.* New York, Golden Theatre, 1958. [Friedman-Abeles]

Laurence Olivier in the title role of *The Entertainer.* [Walter Hampden Memorial Library at The Players, New York]

into the suburban home of Mrs. Elliot. Dillon is a self-centered, cynical bohemian who despairs over his failure, and Mrs. Elliot's sister Ruth alone understands him; in a powerful scene between the two, they reveal themselves to each other with relentless honesty. Dillon makes advances to Ruth, who rejects them, whereupon he seduces Mrs. Elliot's adolescent daughter Josie. One of his plays, which he has cheapened with liberal doses of sex, becomes a hit in the provinces, setting Dillon on the road to commercial success. Trapped into a marriage with Josie, who is pregnant by him, George Dillon the artist is lost, if in fact he ever existed.

Look Back in Anger (1956). Jimmy Porter, the original angry young man, is a state-aided university graduate from the Midlands who chooses to support himself by keeping a sweet stall. His anger at the lack of vitality in life continually erupts in powerfully phrased denunciations of a society that has no worthwhile causes left. His offensiveness to his wife Alison, a gentle, well-bred girl, makes her life intolerable, and she strikes back by refusing to react. Finding herself pregnant, she is persuaded by a visiting friend to leave, and Jimmy thereupon has an affair with the friend. Alison loses her baby, thus achieving the suffering that Jimmy believes necessary, and the two are able to become reconciled in a fantasy world of their own. Cliff, their lodger, is a good, average man who instinctively protects Alison from Jimmy's attacks; and Colonel Redfern, Alison's father, is an Edwardian gentleman, a remnant of a world where hope was possible.

The Entertainer (1957). Play in which England is symbolized by the decayed old music hall known as the Empire. Punctuated by a series of music-hall monologues performed by Archie Rice, the action moves back and forth from the Rices' seedy apartment to the stage of a striptease revue. Rice, lecherous and unprincipled, deliberately arranges an affair between himself and a young girl in order to obtain her parents' financial backing for his new show. His plan fails, and he then persuades his father Billy, a faded Edwardian music-hall star, to try and make a comeback. Finally, with the death of his father and of his son, Archie is forced to admit defeat. The structure, consisting of many short scenes, shows Brecht's influence, as does the frequent topical commentary.

Luther (1961). Twelve scenes combining Brechtian and psychological elements chronicle the history of the Reformation's begetter, Martin Luther. Beginning with his entry into the Augustinian order in 1506 against the judgment of his stern and demanding father, the play presents an angry man struggling with his inability to deal with the father-child relationship, metaphorically expressed by his persistent constipation. The first and last acts portray the personal Luther; the middle act, the public man, a scholarly theologian denying papal authority at the Diet of Worms. But the arch protester himself

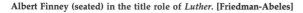

Albert Finney (seated) in the title role of *Luther.* **[Friedman-Abeles]**

Denise Coffey and John Standing in *A Sense of Detachment.* **[Royal Court Theatre. Photograph by John Haynes]**

soon becomes an authority, for Luther refuses to support the German peasants' revolt of 1525. Luther finally achieves a limited peace by marrying a former nun and becoming a father himself.

PLAYS

Unless otherwise noted, the plays were first performed in London.

1. (With Stella Linden). *The Devil inside Him (Cry for Love).* Play. Produced Huddersfield, 1950.

2. (With Anthony Creighton). *Epitaph for George Dillon.* Play, 3 acts. Written 1954. Published 1958. Produced Royal Court Theatre, Feb. 11, 1958.

3. (With Creighton). *Personal Enemy.* Play. Produced Harrogate, 1955.

4. *Look Back in Anger.* Play, 3 acts. Published 1957. Produced Royal Court Theatre, May 8, 1956.

5. *The Entertainer.* Play, 13 scenes. Published 1959. Produced Royal Court Theatre, Apr. 10, 1957. Music: John Addison.

6. *The World of Paul Slickey.* Comedy of manners with music, 2 acts. Published 1959. Produced Bournemouth, Pavilion, Apr. 14, 1959. Music: Christopher Whelen.

7. *A Subject of Scandal and Concern.* Television play, 3 acts. Published 1961. Produced British Broadcasting Corporation, Nov. 6, 1960.

8. *Luther.* Play, 3 acts. Published 1961. Produced Nottingham, The-

atre Royal, June 26, 1961.

The following two plays (Nos. 9 and 10) were produced and published under the collective title *Plays for England*.

9. *The Blood of the Bambergs*. Fairy story, 2 acts. Published 1963. Produced Royal Court Theatre, July 19, 1962.

10. *Under Plain Cover*. Play, 1 act. Published 1963. Produced Royal Court Theatre, July 19, 1962.

11. *Inadmissible Evidence*. Play, 2 acts. Published 1965. Produced Royal Court Theatre, Sept. 9, 1964.

12. *A Patriot for Me*. Play. Published 1965. Produced Royal Court Theatre, June 30, 1965.

13. (Adaptation). *A Bond Honoured*. Play. Produced Old Vic Theatre, June 6, 1966. Based on Lope de Vega's *La fianza satisfecha*.

14. *Time Present*. Play. Produced Royal Court Theatre, May 23, 1968.

15. *The Hotel in Amsterdam*. Play. Produced Royal Court Theatre, July 3, 1968.

16. *West of Suez*. Produced 1971.

17. *A Sense of Detachment*. Produced 1972.

18. *Watch It Come Down*. Produced 1976.

EDITIONS

Look Back in Anger. Published in *Masters of Modern Drama*, ed. by H. M. Block and R. G. Shedd, New York, 1962.

CRITICISM

R. Hayman, *John Osborne*, London, 1968, 3d ed. 1976; M. Banham, *Osborne*, London, 1969; A. Carter, *John Osborne*, London, 1969; S. Trussler, *The Plays of John Osborne: An Assessment*, London, 1969.

Osorio, Luis Enrique (1896–1966)

Colombian playwright. One of the great experimenters in the Colombian theatre, Osorio wrote his first play, *The Happy and Choreographic City* (*La ciudad alegre y coreográfica*, 1919), when he was twenty-three. Although the play contains no specific references, audiences thought they recognized the setting and even identified one of the characters as a well-known socialite; hence the "nerve" of the young dramatist was severely criticized. The following year his *Late-blooming Flower* (*Flor tardía*) brought additional charges—this time of having plagiarized Alberto Insúa's *Amor Tardío*. Discouraged, he took the manuscript of his third play, *Love among the Rubbish* (*Amor de los escombros*, 1920)—subtitled "An American drama adapted to the Colombian scene"—to Mexico, where María Montoya starred in it.

Osorio then moved on to Paris, where his *The Creators* (*Les createurs*, 1926) was the first modern Latin American play ever seen in France. Its success there encouraged him to do a Spanish version for presentation in Madrid, where his *Thirst for Justice* (*Sed de justiciá*, 1921) had already been well received.

Returning to Colombia in 1929, he found so many obstacles put in the way of a career in drama that he settled in Caracas, where theatre was flourishing. Encouraged by Aquiles Certad and other Venezuelan dramatists, he decided to give Bogotá another try. With the cooperation of the mayor he opened a theatre with the promise of a new Colombian play every month. One of his comedies about marriage, *Hard Knot* (*Nudo ciego*, 1943), started off the program. Politicians were the target of *Doctor Manzanillo* (*El Doctor Manzanillo*, 1943). It was so successful that it was followed by a sequel, *Doctor Manzanillo in Power* (*El Doctor Manzanillo en el poder*, 1944), less humorous and more bitter than the first play. Since the seating capacity of his theatre was so small, Osorio began a quarterly, *El teatro*, in which the plays were reprinted.

In 1952, with the excuse that the Municipal Theatre made the presidential palace less imposing—though gossip had it that the attacks in Osorio's plays on political bigwigs had become painful—President Laureano Gómez ordered the Municipal Theatre demolished to give his palace a more attractive frontage. Osorio had by now accumulated enough money and financial backing to build the Teatro de la Comedia, which opened in December 1953 with a prefatory *loa* sent to him from Spain by Jacinto Benavente and with Osorio's own *Yes, Lieutenant* (*Sí, mi teniente*) in his popular national vein (*see* BENAVENTE, JACINTO). After a run of 100 performances, he replaced the latter play with his *Don't Let Your Wife Know* (*Que no lo sepa su esposa*). Then, since the politicians were losing patience with this irritating dramatist, Osorio decided to move to Mexico. His theatre was turned over to the cheaper and more profitable movies and to occasional plays by other Colombian dramatists.

Among his plays satirizing the foibles of his fellow Colombians are *The Man Who Made You Dream* (*El hombre que hacía soñar*, 1945), a satire on Freudianism, and *The Song of My Land* (*El cantar de mi tierra*, 1950).

WILLIS KNAPP JONES and JUDITH A. WEISS

CRITICISM

O. Ricaurte, *Historia Crítica del Teatro en Bogotá*, Bogota, 1927; J. J. Ortega, *Historia de la Literatura en Colombia*, 3d ed., Bogotá, 1935; E. M. Barrera, *Realidad y fantasía en el drama*, Madrid, 1971, 175 pp.

Osten, Suzanne (1944–   )

Swedish theatre director and playwright. She was associated with the ambulatory *Fickteatern* (Pocket Theatre) from 1968 to 1971, and since then with the Klara stage, part of Stockholm's City Theatre. A member of the group theatre movement in Sweden in the 1960s and 1970s, Osten often coauthors her plays with playwrights, performers, and audiences, making great use of movement, mime, and music.

In *A Play about School* (*Ett spel om skolan*, 1968), the Fickteatern group challenged the Swedish school sys-

**Suzanne Osten.
[Swedish Information
Service]**

tem's undemocratic traditions, much to the delight of student audiences but to the chagrin of many teachers and parents. Osten has singled out three particular audiences for her plays: teenagers, children, and women. With Margareta Garpe, Osten wrote *Girl Chat* (*Tjejsnack*, 1971), *Give Me the Address* (*Ge mej adressen*, 1972), and *The Love Performance* (*Kärleksföreställningen*, 1973), all criticizing the widespread exploitation of women in the sexually "permissive" Swedish society.

In *Gee, Girls—Freedom is Near* (*Jösses flickor, befrielsen är nära*, 1974), Osten and Garpe blend realism with caricature in presenting a cavalcade of Swedish women's lib over a period of fifty years. During the royalistic fervor surrounding King Carl XVI Gustaf's marriage to Silvia Sommerlath in 1976, Osten coauthored with Per Lysander *The Princesses at Haga* (*Sessorna på Haga*), a satire on the mythmaking that surrounded the King and his sisters when they were children.

BIRGITTA STEENE

CRITICISM

B. Nolin, "A Successful Realization of Group Theatre in Sweden," *Scandinavian Studies*, Winter, 1971; H. Sjögren, *Stage and Society in Sweden*, Swedish Institute, Stockholm, 1979.

Ostrovsky, Aleksandr Nikolayevich (1823–1886)

Russian dramatist. Ostrovsky was born in Moscow on April 12, 1823 (N.S.). He was the son of a merchant who later became a lawyer and was brought up among the merchant class of *nouveaux riches*, who created a smug and proper *byt* ("way of life") that codified their petty prejudices and concealed their rapacious methods of business. In this "realm of darkness," as the critic Dobrolyubov later called it, isolated from other classes, Ostrovsky had ample opportunity to observe the mores of a class that he was frequently to portray in his plays. Notwithstanding his early passion for the stage, having haunted the Maly Theatre as a schoolboy, Ostrovsky entered the University of Moscow in 1840 to study jurisprudence. In 1843 he left after a dispute with university authorities. He then entered government service as a clerk at a domestic court in Moscow, where he remained until 1845. This apprenticeship, together with his subsequent experiences at the Commercial Court from 1845 to 1851, gave him considerable insight into the seamy side of human relations and the attitudes of Moscow's merchant community.

In 1851 he left the court and from then on devoted himself to literature and the theatre. His first and only nondramatic work, *Notes of a Resident of the Far Side of the Moscow River* (*Zapiski zamoskvoretskogo zhitelya*, 1847), was followed by a continuous flow of dramatic writing. In 1847 he attracted considerable attention with the publication in a Moscow newspaper of two scenes of his comedy *It's a Family Affair—We'll Settle It Ourselves* (*Svoi lyudi—sochtemsya!*; wr. 1849, prod. 1860), whose production was banned by the government of Nicholas I because it showed business frauds going unpunished. As a result, Ostrovsky was placed under police surveillance for a time, but he continued to write. After the produc-

Aleksandr Ostrovsky. [Theatre Collection, The New York Public Library at Lincoln Center, Astor, Lenox and Tilden Foundations]

tion of his play *The Poor Bride* (*Bednaya nevesta*) in 1853, every year saw the appearance of a new play by him for one or another of the imperial theatres. In forty years Ostrovsky produced more than fifty plays as well as translations of Shakespeare, Cervantes, and other European classics. Meanwhile, he became the center of a group of gifted young men eager to produce a literature employing Russian themes in a rich, idiomatic style. He joined the staff of *Moskvityanin* (*The Muscovite*), a Slavophile journal edited by Mikhail Petrovich Pogodin which promoted the ideal of a distinctly national literature and which, until its demise in 1856, was a major influence on Russian literature. During this period Ostrovsky met the poet-critic Apollon Grigoriyev, temporarily the editor of the *Moscovite*. Grigoriyev believed Ostrovsky to be the greatest contemporary writer.

In 1856 Ostrovsky participated in a "literary expedition" through Russia, in particular to the Volga region, whose results are reflected in a number of his plays, notably *The Thunderstorm* (*Groza*, 1859). He enjoyed his greatest popularity in the years that followed this journey. His plays netted theatre managers hundreds of thousands of rubles, although Ostrovsky himself remained poor almost to the end of his life, due to hostility on the part of the Government Administration that ran the Imperial Theatres. Nevertheless, during the 1860s Ostrovsky continued to enjoy a considerable reputation with the public and in literary circles, and he became increasingly concerned with the plight of the artist in Russian society. After his marriage to an actress in 1865 and a brief visit to Western Europe, he founded the Artistic Society of Moscow, which in 1870 was renamed the Society of Russian Playwrights. In 1881, when Alexander III came to the throne, Ostrovsky addressed to him a plea for the establishment of a model national theatre, with low-priced tickets, for the poorer people. "Drama is written not only for the cultured classes, but for all the people!" he declared.

In 1882, through Ostrovsky's efforts, the monopoly of the imperial theatres was abolished and the first private theatre was founded in Moscow by F. A. Korsh, paving the way for the establishment of the Moscow Art

Theatre in 1897. Insofar as his plays demanded a new technique based on realism and his gallery of characters permitted actors much freedom of interpretation, Ostrovsky was responsible for the emergence of a group of fine dramatic actors, including Sadovsky, Martinov, Lensky, Yermolova, Varlamov, and Komissazhevskaya.

Ostrovsky reached the climax of his career in 1885, when, shortly before his death, he was placed in charge of the Moscow Imperial Theatres and appointed head of the Moscow Theatrical School. Now, with the necessary power in his hands, he prepared to democratize the Russian theatre, but he died on June 14, 1886 (N.S.), in Slykovo.

WORK

Ostrovsky occupies a central, perhaps the central, position in the history of Russian drama: his work laid the foundation for a future approach to the theatre based on truth and realism. Although there were a number of Russian dramatic masterpieces before his time, they were largely the efforts of men whose principal concerns lay in other literary fields. Ostrovsky was the first Russian to devote himself exclusively to the drama, and his fifty-four plays form the largest body of Russian drama before the revolution; it singlehandedly comprised a national repertoire. While his reputation in Russia is enormous—in both Czarist and Soviet Russia he has been considered the leading native dramatist—his appeal in other lands has been retarded by the distinctly idiomatic Russian flavor of his work and has been further diminished by poor translations. He was fated to be a dramatist at a time when Russian novelists were in vogue and to die just a decade before Chekhov, Gorky, and Andreyev introduced the Russian dramatic influence into the mainstream of Western drama.

Yet even if his work had been more fortunately timed in terms of Western enthusiasms, his audience, in all likelihood, would not have been much larger, for most of his work is so closely tied to a specific Russian milieu that it is difficult for foreign audiences to penetrate the wealth of local color and typically Russian characterization. With only a few exceptions, Ostrovsky's plays come under the heading of comedy; but his is a particular, peculiarly Russian brand of satirical comedy that bitterly attacks its victims but at the same time retains a measure of compassion for them.

The structure of Ostrovsky's plays is generally loose, resulting in a series of tableaux or conversation pieces or genre scenes, and his dénouements often seem contrived to bring about a happy ending or point a moral. His skill lies in the deft, true-to-life character drawing and his ear for authentic Russian speech, making his dialogue almost untranslatable. Despite attempts to enroll him in the camp of the Slavophiles, he remained politically and artistically independent. His recurrent theme is a universal one: the need for the personal integrity that can develop only when a person is free of social and economic restraints.

Outstanding among the comedies are *Diary of a Scoundrel,* also called *Enough Stupidity for Every Wise Man*

(*Na vsyakogo mudretsa dovolno prostoty,* 1868), perhaps Ostrovsky's best-known play in the West, in which a schemer is unmasked by his diary yet cleverly manages to gain his ends; *It's a Family Affair—We'll Settle It Ourselves* also known as *Bankrupt* (wr. 1849, prod. 1860), in which an unscrupulous merchant is outwitted by his opportunistic clerk; and *A Hangover from Somebody Else's Party* (*V chuzhom piru pokhmelye,* 1856), about a willful domestic tyrant.

Other satires in which Ostrovsky analyzed the growing power of money in Russia, and the greed accompanying it, rely to a large extent on caricature. They include *A Lucrative Post* (*Dokhodnoye mesto;* wr. 1856, prod. 1863), about corrupt civil servants; *Easy Money* (*Beshenye dengi,* 1870), which compares the lavish spending of the aristocracy with the thrift of a new businessman; *Not a Kopek and Suddenly a Ruble* (*Ne bylo ni grosha, da vdrug altyn,* 1872), the study of a miser; *Hard-earned Bread* (*Trudovoy khleb,* 1874), a work that effectively contrasts happy but poor intellectuals with dull, egotistical merchants and scheming speculators; *Wolves and Sheep* (*Volki i ovtsy,* 1875), a powerful work that categorizes all men as predators or victims; and *Poverty Is No Crime* (*Bednost ne porok,* 1854), a comedy that ridicules the rich for their ideas about the poor.

Ostrovsky also used the lives of actors as subject matter, and in *The Forest* (*Les,* 1871), one of his more important plays, he depicted the rich as the real actors in life and actors themselves as the only truly live, fully human, beings. *A Comedian of the Seventeenth Century* (*Komik XVII stoletiya,* 1872), a verse play, and *They Are Guilty though Guiltless* (*Bez viny vinovatye,* 1884) are also comedies built around the theme of the theatre versus life.

The special problem and position of women in mercantile Russian society are portrayed by Ostrovsky in several comedies and in his three tragedies. *The Thunderstorm* (1859), his one successful tragedy and a major work, depicts the desperation of a young wife, suffocated by the banality of merchant-class life, who takes a lover, hoping he will change her existence; his failure to do so leads her to commit suicide. Lesser tragedies are *A Protégée of the Mistress* (*Vospitannitsa;* wr. 1858, prod. 1863), in which a young girl is forced by her protectress to marry a man she detests; and *Sin and Sorrow Are Common to All* (*Grekh da beda na kogo ne zhivyot,* 1863), in which a wife's infidelity causes her shopkeeper husband to stab her. The comedies on the subject of women include *The Rich Brides* (*Bogatye nevesty,* 1875); *A Last Sacrifice* (*Poslednyaya zhertva,* 1877); and *The Bondwomen* (*Nevolnitsy,* 1880), a comedy of two women married to men twice their age. Similar in theme to *A Protégée of the Mistress* is the tragedy *The Girl with No Dowry* (*Bespridannitsa,* 1878).

Two early works are loosely constructed dramas, "scenes" or "sketches": *A Holiday Dream—Before Dinner* (*Prazdnichny son—do obeda,* 1857), the portrait of a petty official who tries unsuccessfully to marry wealth; and *A Cat Has Not Always Carnival* (*Ne vse kotu maslenitsa,* 1871), in which a miser receives his just deserts.

The Snow Maiden (*Snegurochka,* 1873), a fairy tale

evoking Russia's mythic past, is unique among Ostrovsky's works and served as the basis for Rimsky-Korsakov's opera of the same name. Less important than his other plays are his historical dramas, which include *Kozma Zakharich Minin, the One-armed* (*Kozma Zakharich Minin, Sukhoruk;* wr. 1861, rev. 1866), set in seventeenth-century Russia and depicting the heroic victory of Minin over the Polish invaders; *The False Dmitry and Vasily Shuysky* (*Dmitry Samozvanets i Vasily Shuysky,* 1867); *Tushino* (1867); *Vasilisa Melentyeva* (1868), about the reign of Ivan the Terrible; and *The Voivode, or The Dream on the Volga* [*Voevoda (Son na Volge),* 1865], one of several historical verse plays intended as a series under the collective title *Nights on the Volga* (*Nochi na Volge*).

A Domestic Picture (*Semeynaya kartina;* wr. 1847, prod. 1855). Drama that gives a realistic picture of a Moscow merchant's family. Antip Antipych Puzatov is too ignorantly smug and preoccupied to notice that his wife's interests lie outside their home. She and her sister-in-law Marya Antipovna seek adventure with the help of Darya, the maid. Meanwhile, Puzatov and his old mother spend their time drinking with and flattering Paramon Ferapontych Shiryalov, a respected old widower, so that he may be encouraged to marry Marya and thus become Puzatov's brother-in-law.

It's a Family Affair—We'll Settle It Ourselves; also known as **Bankrupt** (*Svoi lyudi—sochtemsya!;* wr. 1849, prod. 1860). Comedy in four acts that chronicles the triumphant career of Lazar Podkhalyuzin, an unscrupulous clerk. A supreme opportunist, Lazar uses the near bankruptcy of his employer as the chance to assume control of the flagging business and even engineers his engagement to his employer's daughter, the dreamy, spoiled Olimpiada. Having achieved his long-desired position of affluence, Lazar shows his true colors in his shoddy treatment of his impecunious father-in-law and others who helped him in his rise to fortune. The play abounds in richly drawn minor characters: the efficient matchmaker Ustinya Naumovna; the alcoholic and penniless lawyer Sysoy Rispolozhensky; the absurdly doting mother Agrafena; and Samson Bolshov, the loud, coarse

merchant who lacks a talent for dishonesty and who is victimized by Lazar.

The Morning of a Young Man (*Utro molodogo cheloveka,* 1853). Scenes from the life of a young wastrel, written in the manner of Gogol but already showing young Ostrovsky's mastery of dramatic technique. Semyon Paramonych Nedopekin, lying in bed at noon, is invited by a servant to visit his mother the next evening. He then receives Sidor Dmitrich Lisavsky, a young fop who reads him his verses, promises to teach him French, and borrows money from him. After the two have left for town, Lisavsky's uncle comes with a message from his mother: unless Lisavsky visits her immediately, she will stop paying his debts.

An Unexpected Occurrence (*Neozhidanny sluchay;* wr. 1850, prod. 1902). Dramatic sketch in which Pavel Gavrilych Druzhnin, a clever young government official, attempts to save his friend Sergey Andreich Rozovy, a naïve landowner, from the clutches of Sofya Antonovna, an experienced widow. Pavel's entreaties and maneuvers prove ineffective against Sofya, her besy ally being Sergey himself, who is hopelessly in love with her.

The Poor Bride (*Bednaya nevesta,* 1853). Satirical comedy rich in characterization, with dramatic overtones describing the urban middle classes of mid-nineteenth-century Russia. Mme. Nezabudkin, the scatterbrained widow of a petty official, is faced with bankruptcy. She hopes to avert it by winning a lawsuit or by marrying her daughter Marya to a rich husband. Meanwhile, Marya, sensitive, idealistic, and surrounded by ineffectual suitors, falls secretly in love with Merich, one of her suitors, who apparently shares her idealism but who is in fact a small-time Don Juan. Mme. Nezabudkin loses her lawsuit and, finding matchmakers no help, arranges for Marya to marry Benevolensky, a boorish official. Marya resists, but eventually capitulates when she discovers that Merich will not marry her. A series of last-act vignettes of the wedding suggest that her future will be unhappy.

Don't Sit in a Sledge You Don't Own (*Ne v svoi sani ne sadis!,* 1853). Comedy in which Viktor Arkadich Vi-

The Thunderstorm, Moscow Art Theatre, 1935. [Theatre Collection, The New York Public Library at Lincoln Center, Astor, Lenox and Tilden Foundations]

khorev, a cavalry officer deeply in debt, hopes to restore his fortunes by marrying Avdotya Maksimovna Rusakova, daughter of a rich merchant. Avdotya falls in love with him, and they elope; but when she tells him that her father is going to leave her penniless, he deserts her. Her father at first refuses to take Avdotya back, but finally a young merchant, Ivan Petrovich Borodkin, promises to marry her; thus the family's honor is restored.

Poverty Is No Crime (*Bednost ne porok*, 1854). Comedy of young love and blundering parents that illustrates the foibles and absurdities of the merchant class. Typical in his upper-class pretensions, the crotchety Gordey Tortsov, a rich merchant, is about to marry his lovely daughter Lyubov to the repulsive Korshunov, another old merchant whose Moscow airs Tortsov admires. Tortsov is finally brought to reason by his ne'er-do-well brother and instead gives his daughter to his penniless but honest clerk, with whom she has been in love from the beginning.

One Must Not Live as One Likes (*Ne tak zhivi, kak khochetsya*, 1854). Moral play, scattered with proverbs and snatches of folk song, based on a popular Russian tale and set in eighteenth-century Moscow during the Shrovetide Fair. Pyotr, the son of Moscow merchant Ilya Ivanovich, is married to Dasha, the daughter of another merchant. After a year their marriage is crumbling, and Pyotr is pursuing Grusha, an innkeeper's daughter who scorns him when she learns that he is married. Dasha wants to return to her parents, but they tell her that her place is with her husband. The frustrated Pyotr gets drunk and sets out to kill Dasha, but the sound of church bells brings him to his senses and he goes quietly home.

A Hangover from Somebody Else's Party (*V chuzhom piru pokhmelye*, 1856). Comedy noted for the first appearance of the *samodur*, a sort of petty and obstinate tyrant not entirely devoid of common sense. Here he is Tit Titych Bruskov, a rich merchant whose son Andrey is in love with Lizaveta Ivanovna, daughter of an impecunious retired teacher, Ivan Ksenofontych Ivanov. Ivanov's shrewd landlady, the widow Agrafena Platonovna, gets Andrey to sign a document promising to marry Lizaveta. Then she sells the document to Bruskov for 1,000 rubles and gives the money to Ivanov. But the honest Ivanov is horrified; he rushes to Bruskov to return the money in exchange for the document. After some hesitation Bruskov gives it to him. He later realizes what a good man Ivanov is and orders Andrey to marry Lizaveta. When Andrey protests that he is ashamed to face Lizaveta, Bruskov states that if Lizaveta is not given to him in marriage, he'd better not come home.

A Lucrative Post (*Dokhodnoye mesto*; wr. 1856, prod. 1863). Ironic comedy centering on Zhadov, an educated and honest young man whose ideals appear naïve in comparison with the views of his uncle and employer Aristarkh Vyshnevsky, a wealthy official and shrewd dealer. Zhadov is in love with Polina Kukushkina, and in order to marry her he requests Vyshnevsky to give him a raise in salary. Vyshnevsky, finding his nephew ignorant of the ways of the world (since he is incorrup-

tible), not only refuses the raise but dismisses him, promoting instead the boorish Belogubov, who marries Polina's sister Yulinka. Months later, Zhadov, now married to Polina and leading a life of toil and privation, discovers that his wife is envious of her sister's money. Giving in to Polina's entreaties he goes to his uncle's house to beg for a more "lucrative post." There, he discovers that Vyshnevsky has just received a blackmailer's letter accusing his wife of infidelity and that he is about to be sued for fraud. Vyshnevsky's ridicule of the "honest generation" reaffirms Zhadov's faith in a tomorrow where honesty will prevail, and he leaves with Polina, who asks his forgiveness.

A Holiday Dream–Before Dinner (*Prazdnichny son–do obeda*, 1857). First of three short playlets dealing with Mikhaylo Balzaminov, a poor government clerk who dreams of marrying money. Balzaminov's mother, Pavla Petrovna, though conscious of her son's limited intelligence, allows herself to be swept along by his dream. She accepts the offer of Akulina Krasavina, a mercenary matchmaker, to visit Kleopatra Nichkina, a wealthy widow whose daughter Kapochka has been platonically courted by Balzaminov and imagines herself in love with him. Out of boredom Kleopatra is inclined to consent to their marriage, but her brother Neuyedenov, uneducated yet shrewd, deftly exposes Balzaminov's real motive, thus leaving him with his dream unfulfilled.

An Incompatibility of Tempers (*Ne soshlis kharakterami!*, 1858). Short play focusing on a marriage for money that takes an unusual turn. Young Pol Prezhnev, son of an impoverished nobleman, has been educated to rich tastes by his romantic mother, who dreams of a "grand passion" for her son. Pol, however, seeing there is little money, listens carefully to the proposal of marriage brought by his former governess: Serafima Karpovna, a wealthy and beautiful young widow, has fallen madly in

The Thunderstorm, **Moscow Art Theatre, 1935. [Theatre Collection, The New York Public Library at Lincoln Center, Astor, Lenox and Tilden Foundations]**

Act III of *The Thunderstorm*, Moscow Art Theatre, 1935. [Theatre Collection, The New York Public Library at Lincoln Center, Astor, Lenox and Tilden Foundations]

love with Pol and wishes to marry him. But Serafima's background, though wealthy, has been coarse and materialistic. She therefore decides with her parents never to allow Pol to touch her capital.

Once married, Pol feels abused by these restrictions and asks Serafima for some money to invest. Minutes later, as Pol is greeting his mother, the butler brings him a letter from Serafima. In it she explains her abrupt departure for her parents' home: she cannot part with her money, she says, despite her love for Pol, for without it she is nothing.

A Protégée of the Mistress (*Vospitannitsa;* wr. 1858, prod. 1862). Drama that alternates between comedy and pathos. Set on a country estate in the mid-nineteenth century, it draws a disturbing picture of the landed gentry and their serfs. Mme. Ulanbekova, old and grotesque owner of 2,000 serfs, has a distorted conception of philanthropy that causes much grief among her subjects. The young and cultivated Nadya is about to be married off by her mistress' inept matchmaking to Negligentov, a boorish drunk. In desperation she holds a clandestine midnight meeting with Mme. Ulanbekova's irresponsible son Leonid, thus enraging her mistress and sealing her engagement to Negligentov. Her soul not her own, Nadya dejectedly acquiesces, intimating that there is always suicide as a last resort.

The Thunderstorm (*Groza,* 1859). Tragedy depicting small-town merchant-class life in the mid-nineteenth century. In Kalinov, a town on the banks of the Volga, Katerina, religious, mystical, and poetic, is married to Tikhon, the son of Mme. Kabanova, a rich, domineering merchant's widow who runs the lives of her children.

Unable to oppose their mother, Tikhon tries to escape through drink, and his sister Varvara through secret flirtations. Katerina becomes infatuated with Boris Grigoryevich, a man she has seen only in church. Nephew of the town's leading merchant Dikoy, who is a tyrant to his workers and his family, Boris is dependent on his uncle's whims for his inheritance.

Discovering Katerina's infatuation, the spirited Varvara arranges a meeting between her and Boris. After a brief encounter they fall deeply in love, but Katerina, distraught with guilt, confesses to her family. As a result, Boris is to be sent away by his uncle and Katerina becomes more than ever the victim of Mme. Kabanova. Realizing that Boris will not take her with him and that Tikhon, though he forgives her, cannot oppose his mother, Katerina drowns herself in the Volga.

An Old Friend Is Better than Two New Ones (*Stary drug luchshe novykh dvukh,* 1860). Drama depicting the social environment of typical Moscow court clerks and satirizing their spurious cultural superiority. Olinka, a young dressmaker of the lower middle class, has hopes that her lover Vasyutin, a court clerk, will marry her, but she learns from her mother's friend, the gossip Pulkheriya, that he is yielding to his mother's wish that he marry an educated girl. Vasyutin, who has neither culture nor character and stoops to taking money from petitioners (a common practice at the time), ruins his chances with his new fiancée by arriving at her house drunk. Pulkheriya reports this contretemps to Olinka's mother Tatyana, and mother and daughter resolve to bring Vasyutin around to asking Olinka to marry him. Skillfully applying female strategy, they succeed, and

Vasyutin even manages to obtain his mother's consent. Only Pulkheriya, commenting on the social incompatibility of the couple, strikes a sour note, but amid general hilarity she is thrown out of the house.

When Your Own Dogs Are Fighting, a Strange Dog Should Not Meddle (*Svoi sobaki gryzutsya, chuzhaya ne pristavay*, 1861). Two-scene sequel to *A Holiday Dream–Before Dinner*. Mikhaylo Balzaminov aspires to marry the wealthy young widow Anfisa Antrygina, who is momentarily willing to pay attention to him because she erroneously believes that her lover Ustrashimov, a colleague of Balzaminov, has been unfaithful to her. The matchmaker Akulina Krasavina appears to discuss the matter with Balzaminov's mother, who, despite some slim doubts, is as ever optimistic about her son's matrimonial chances. Thus Balzaminov, glowing with hope and conceit, visits Anfisa, only to reveal to her inadvertently that Ustrashimov is not, in fact, unfaithful to her. The two lovers are reunited, Akulina receives a generous gratuity from Anfisa, and Balzaminov is the loser.

Whatever You Go After, You Will Find, or Balzaminov's Wedding [*Za chem poydesh, to i naydesh (Zhenitba Balzaminova)*, 1863]. Sequel to *When Your Own Dogs Are Fighting, a Strange Dog Should Not Meddle,* dealing with Balzaminov's third attempt to attract a rich wife. His objective this time is Raisa Pezhenova, locked up at home by her tyrannical brothers while Anfisa, her sister, carries on a romance by correspondence with Lukyan Chebakov, whom Balzaminov admires and trusts. Chebakov persuades Balzaminov that if he delivers a letter to Anfisa, he in turn will help him to elope with Raisa. Confident of success, Balzaminov dismisses Akulina, the matchmaker, who has come to offer him a rich, plump, and phlegmatic bride, Domna Belotelova. Domna lives next door to Raisa, and when Balzaminov has to jump over the Pezhenov garden wall in order to avoid meeting Raisa's brothers, he finds himself face to face with Akulina, who threatens to accuse him of burglary unless he agrees to marry Domna. For a moment Balzaminov romanticizes, imagining himself a Casanova faced with a difficult choice. But Raisa rejects him, Chebakov deceives him, and he has to settle for Domna and her money, which is all that he originally wanted. He realizes that he no longer minds being stupid since he has at long last become rich.

Kozma Zakharich Minin, the One-armed (*Kozma Zakharich Minin, Sukhoruk;* wr. 1861, revised version prod. 1866). Historical play in verse depicting the patriotism and religious loyalty of the people of Nizhny Novgorod, on the Volga River, during the struggle against the Polish invaders of Moscow from 1611 to 1613. The inspired, courageous merchant Minin appeals to the people for volunteers and money for the war. Leading his army in the name of God, he joins the Russian prince Pozharsky at the Moscow River and succeeds in routing the enemy.

Sin and Sorrow Are Common to All (*Grekh da beda na kogo ne zhivyot*, 1863). Melodrama in four acts dealing with the difficulties involved in marriage between titled gentry and the middle class. A marriage of convenience between the beautiful, petulant Tatyana, daughter of a landed family that has fallen on evil times, and the wealthy Lev Krasnov, an honest, hardworking, but clumsy merchant, is doomed from the beginning. His adoration of Tatyana blinds Lev to the shabby way in which she and her unmarried sister have behaved toward him. But when a young nobleman arrives in the neighborhood, Tatyana's blatant flirting and clandestine meetings with the newcomer confirm the accusations that Lev's younger brother Afonya has made against her. Confronted by her irate husband, Tatyana confesses that she never loved him and is about to leave him forever. Outraged by her admission, he murders her and then gives himself up to the law.

Hard Times (*Tyazhelye dni*, 1863). Believing in the superstition that certain days are more unlucky than others, Nastasya Pankratyevna, the ignorant wife of the merchant Bruskov, insists that her husband refrain from doing business on a Monday. He nonetheless chooses that day on which to conduct his affairs in a pub and, half drunk, insults Pertsov, a forger of promissory notes. Pertsov later presents Bruskov with a note for 300,000 rubles and demands payment. Nastasya laments all this as Monday's fault. As a result, Bruskov withdraws his consent to the marriage of his son Andrey to Aleksandra Kruglova, a girl with little money of her own. Then Andrey persuades his friend Dosuzhev, a man of the world, to confront Pertsov when he comes to collect on the note. Using evidence of Pertsov's past forgeries that he has in his possession, Dosuzhev manages to buy the claim against Bruskov for only 100 rubles. He then demands that Bruskov consent to Andrey's marriage to Aleksandra, which he does.

The Jokers (*Shutniki*, 1864). Play depicting the humiliations endured by the retired clerk Obroshenov at the hands of the wealthy, vulgar, and ignorant old Moscow merchant Khryukov. Playing the buffoon in order to obtain loans and maintain a relatively normal standard of living, Obroshenov finds comfort in the love of his daughters: Anna, who at twenty-five has given up hope of marriage; and the younger Verochka, who plans to marry the honest but poor court clerk Goltsov. Obroshenov and Anna, devoted to Verochka, are prepared to help Goltsov raise 300 rubles, which he owes the court, having unintentionally mismanaged public funds. He has vainly tried to obtain the amount from two idle playboys who mislead, intoxicate, and humiliate him. Khryukov seems to be the only hope, and since he has long secretly wished to marry Anna, he seizes the opportunity to put her in his debt. He offers Anna the money on condition that she come to live with him. Obroshenov, enraged by the insult, throws Khryukov out of the house. After enjoying the humiliation of all, Khryukov proposes marriage, and Anna is happy to sacrifice herself for her family.

The Voivode, or The Dream on the Volga [*Voevoda (Son na Volge)*, 1865]. Historical verse play drawing on legends of the mid-seventeenth century and incorporating local folklore about the elderly voivode (military commander) Nechay Grigoryevich Shalygin, who arbitrarily

(Left) Leonid Mironovich Leonidov as Gorudulin and (above) Vara Ninubirg as Manefa in the Moscow Art Theatre production of *Enough Stupidity* (*Enough Stupidity in Every Wise Man*). New York, Jolson's Fifty-ninth Street Theatre, 1923. [Theatre Collection, The New York Public Library at Lincoln Center, Astor, Lenox and Tilden Foundations]

locked away Roman Dubrovin and forcibly took his wife Olena. Shalygin also prepared to marry Praskovya, young daughter of Vlas Dyuzhoy, a wealthy, servile citizen who felt honored by the voivode's choice. Dubrovin, who escaped and wandered for two years in the Volga region pillaging the countryside with an army of peasants, returns–in the prologue–to his hometown in order to see his beloved wife, not knowing her fate. The servants of Semen Bastryukov, an honorable nobleman who disapproves of the voivode's behavior, tell Dubrovin the truth about his wife and hide him in Bastryukov's house without telling their master. Meanwhile, the voivode decides to marry Marya, Praskovya's younger sister, betrothed to Bastryukov's son Stepan. Old Bastryukov secretly goes to Moscow to tell the Czar of the voivode's abuse of power. The servants disclose Dubrovin's presence to the despairing Stepan, who accepts the brave fugitive's plan to abduct Marya and Olena from the voivode's house. Meanwhile, the voivode undertakes a "religious pilgrimage" and, after a nightmarish dream on the Volga in which the ghost of his conscience appears, returns home only to find that Dubrovin has come for his wife, as has Stepan for Marya, and that old Bastryukov has arrived to strip him of his power by order of the Czar, who appoints a new voivode and grants Dubrovin freedom.

At the Jolly Spot (*Na boykom meste*, 1865). Comedy set in the Jolly Spot, an inn run by Bezsudny and Evgeniya, his wife, who flirts with the customers and encourages them to drink so that Bezsudny can more easily steal their money. Anna, Bezsudny's virtuous sister, objects to these shady goings-on, and when she sees her fiancé Milovidov, a landowner attracted by her virtue, kissing Evgeniya, she takes "poison" (in fact a potion used to drug potential victims). When Milovidov finds

her, the truth of Evgeniya's deceit–she had told Milovidov that Anna had a lover–is revealed. Milovidov takes Anna to his home, where they will be married as soon as possible.

The Abyss (*Puchina*, 1866). Tragedy, marred by an unconvincing conclusion, concerning the life of Kiril Kiselnikov (who foreshadows the neurotic protagonists of Chekhov's drama). Against the advice of his friend Pogulyayev, Kiselnikov abandons his university studies to marry into the callous and ignorant merchant family Borovtsov. Robbed of his inheritance by his father-in-law, maltreated by his wife, and openly abused and ridiculed by society for his naïveté, Kiselnikov becomes a lowly court clerk. After the death of his wife and three of his five children for lack of money to pay for a physician, he succumbs to the persuasions of a shrewd stranger and forges a court document for money, thereafter losing his mind. Now gentle and inoffensive, no longer in possession of his faculties, he continues to live in poverty with his devoted mother, Anna Ustinovna, and his only surviving child, Lisa, who works from morning until night to earn a few rubles. Kiselnikov, in his madness, plans to sell her to a wealthy old merchant when Pogulyayev, who has become a well-to-do lawyer, appears. Seeing the abyss into which Kiselnikov has fallen, Pogulyayev asks for Lisa's hand, since he himself feels lonely and useless in this world. For a moment Kiselnikov regains his senses and grants his friend permission to marry Lisa, choosing for himself a life in the gutter.

The False Dmitry and Vasily Shuysky (*Dmitry Samozvanets i Vasily Shuysky*, 1867). Verse play based on history. Vasily Shuysky, a wise old boyar patiently awaiting an outburst of public anger, is pitted against young Dmitry (Demetrius), an imposter sent by the Poles to pose as Czar Ivan's son, long believed dead. Dmitry enters Mos-

Act IV of *Enough Stupidity*, Moscow Art Theatre. New York, Jolson's Fifty-ninth Street Theatre, 1923. [Theatre Collection, The New York Public Library at Lincoln Center, Astor, Lenox and Tilden Foundations]

cow in the winter of 1605–1606 with his Polish and German lackeys and Roman Catholic priests, irritating the patriotic, xenophobic Orthodox Russians and proclaiming himself Czar. Czarina Marfa, Dmitry's mother, does not recognize Dmitry as her son, but she cannot bring herself to deny the youth a mother's tenderness. Although Dmitry is warned of Shuysky's treasonous ideas, he spares his life. Gradually, the boyars recognize the need to curb Dmitry's increasing power. When he decides to marry Marina, a Polish princess, and to crown her Czarina of Russia prior to the wedding, the Russian people can no longer contain their anger, and in an armed uprising Dmitry is killed and Shuysky proclaimed his successor, as Vasily (Basil) IV.

Diary of a Scoundrel, also translated as **Enough Stupidity for Every Wise Man** (*Na vsyakogo mudretsa dovolno prostoty,* 1868). Realistic comedy of manners dealing with a scoundrel of shameless hypocrisy. The shrewd Glumov decides to imitate the bourgeoisie by exploiting the weakness of influential people to gain both a lucrative position and the hand of a young heiress. Flattery of an uncle, bribery, anonymous letters, and carefully planned romances with a benefactor's wife and an eligible widow bring him step by step to his goal. But inadvertently he allows his diary, containing uncomplimentary opinions of those involved, to fall into the hands of a blackmailing journalist, who sends it to Glumov's uncle. Following the reading aloud of the diary, Glumov appears before his victims unruffled and bluntly reminds them that they have all, at one time or another, made similar remarks about each other. They are, in effect, just as hypocritical

as he. Moreover, they need him, for there is no one else to supply them with clever phrases for their speeches and keep their wives happy. Thus Glumov triumphs even after being unmasked.

An Ardent Heart (*Goryachee serdtse,* 1869). Long, loosely constructed play about a purehearted young girl. Parasha is kept under lock and key by her lecherous stepmother Matryona. Matryona is stealing money from her indolent, half-witted husband, the wealthy merchant Kuroslepov, to give to their servant Narkis, who is her lover. After Kuroslepov asks the chief of police to catch the thief, Vasya Shustry, an indecisive, impoverished young man, is found jumping into the garden to meet Parasha, who loves him, and he is promptly jailed as the thief. Suspicion also falls on Gavrilo, a sensitive young man who works for Kuroslepov and who is secretly in love with Parasha. Gavrilo is dismissed, and Parasha, in the hope of getting to see Vasya, runs away with him.

Wishing Parasha's happiness. Gavrilo plots to set Vasya free. His friend Aristarkh induces his wealthy employer Khlynov to bail out Vasya. The immature Vasya, however, fails to use his freedom to marry Parasha. Meanwhile, the extravagant Khlynov and his lackeys embark on an orgy disguised as robbers, meet Narkis in the forest, and ask him to join them. Narkis, in boasting, reveals the truth about the stolen money, and Kuroslepov is informed. He throws out Matryona, apologizes to Parasha, and invites her to choose a husband. Vasya confidently steps forward, but Parasha walks by him and gives her hand to Gavrilo.

Easy Money (*Beshenye dengi*, 1870). Comedy, loosely based on Shakespeare's *The Taming of the Shrew,* in which a spoiled and willful girl submits to the role of humble wife. Having squandered all their money, Lydiya Cheboksarova and her mother decide that Lydiya herself must find a wealthy husband. Believing that Savva Vasilkov, a provincial businessman, owns several gold mines, they contract a marriage with him. But Savva refuses to tolerate Lydiya's spendthrift ways, and she leaves him, only to find that her other "wealthy" suitors are penniless. She pleads with Savva to take her back. He agrees on condition that she prove herself a good wife by serving as his housekeeper at his house in the provinces.

The Forest (*Les,* 1871). Comedy about Raisa Gurmyzhsky, a hypocritically pious old woman who enjoys running other people's lives under the guise of doing good. She has taken in Aksinya, a poor young niece, and wants her to marry Bulanov, a worthless young man to whom she herself has taken a fancy. Aksinya loves Pyotr, but his father, Vosmibratov, demands a dowry of 3,000 rubles. Aksinya's problem is solved by Neschastlivtsev, a wandering actor and nephew of Raisa. He collects 1,000 rubles from his aunt and gives it to Aksinya; Vosmibratov accepts it as her dowry. Raisa decides to marry Bulanov, and Neschastlivtsev leaves, content with having done one good deed in his life.

A Cat Has Not Always Carnival (*Ne vse kotu maslenitsa,* 1871). Comedy based on the Russian saying: "A cat has not always Carnival, she has her Lent also." The "cat" is Yermil Akhov, a rich merchant, and his "Lent" the blow dealt him by his nephew Ippolit, Darya Kruglova, widow of a poor merchant, and her daughter Agniya. Ippolit, while working for his uncle without pay, is courting Agniya. When Akhov also begins to court Agniya, Ippolit finds the courage to assert himself. He tricks Akhov into paying him 15,000 rubles and signing an excellent recommendation for future employment. Then both men ask for Agniya's hand. To Akhov's astonishment he is refused; Ippolit wins Agniya.

Not a Kopek and Suddenly a Ruble (*Ne bylo ni grosha, da vdrug altyn,* 1872). Comedy that through drama and characterization achieves the effect of tragedy. Krutitsky, once a wealthy court clerk, now lives on the outskirts of the city in abject misery with his wife Anna and his young niece Nastya. Although he is seen begging, his family never receives any money. Finally he stoops so low as to send Nastya out to beg money for a trousseau, ordering her to give him every penny she receives. Nastya wishes to invite Baklushin, her former fiancé, to tea in the neighbors' garden so as not to reveal her present poverty, but lacking money to buy the tea, she must get it by begging. Baklushin finally comes to tea, and when the envious neighbors reveal the truth about Nastya's poverty, Baklushin declares that he will nonetheless marry her. But first he must find the money to settle his debt to a ruthless moneylender who has virtually ruined him. Nastya therefore decides to accept the elderly Rasnovezov's offer to set her up in an apartment.

That night Krutitsky becomes involved in a fight with a former court clerk. In the melee his coat is torn and a bundle of notes falls unnoticed out of the lining. Later Yelesya, a neighbor, finds it, Krutitsky claims it, and the police are called in. Krutitsky is finally exposed: not only is this bundle his but he has another 500,000 rubles. In addition, it is revealed that he is the moneylender who had ruined Baklushin and many others. Unmasked, Krutitsky hangs himself, leaving everything to Anna and Nastya, who can now marry Baklushin.

The Snow Maiden (*Snegurochka,* 1873). Poetic fantasy based on traditional Russian folk themes. Snegurochka, the lovely child of Spring and Winter, goes to live with an old peasant couple, Bobyl and Bobylikha, who live in the mythical kingdom of Czar Berendey. A prophecy has it that the sun god Yarilo will destroy Snegurochka should she ever love. However, when Mizgir, betrothed to the maiden Kupava, sees Snegurochka, he falls in love with her, breaking his troth. Kupava's grievance is taken before Czar Berendey, who decrees that Snegurochka must be married by sunrise next morning to appease Yarilo in the yearly fertility rites. Lel, a shepherd, and Mizgir both woo Snegurochka, but in vain. Snegurochka then entreats Spring to make her capable of love. Spring complies, but warns her to stay away from the sun. Snegurochka, now in love with Mizgir, is pressed into participating in the sun ritual and melts away, as prophesied, whereupon Mizgir drowns himself. The sun god appeased, the populace chants praises.

Late Love (*Pozdnyaya lyubov,* 1873). Comedy dealing with the predicaments caused by money. The widow Shablova has two sons, Nikolay, an unsuccessful lawyer, and Dormedont, the good-natured, hardworking, not very bright provider for the family. An old lawyer, Margaritov, once wealthy and successful but now defamed and impoverished as a result of a false charge, lives with his not so young daughter Lyudmila as a tenant in Shab-

Scene from a Moscow production of *The Forest*, 1924. [Theatre Collection, The New York Public Library at Lincoln Center, Astor, Lenox and Tilden Foundations]

lova's house. Dormedont is in love with Lyudmila, but she secretly worships Nikolay and helps him with money, which he spends in gambling houses. Lebedkina, a frivolous young widow whom Nikolay courts, persuades him to extract from Lyudmila a promissory note, now in Margaritov's possession, which she once signed to cover a debt to a client of Margaritov. The client is willing to rehabilitate Margaritov professionally should he collect the money. Lebedkina, who through sheer obstinacy does not wish to pay, promises to settle the debts for which Nikolay is about to go to jail if he brings her the note. Lyudmila, of course, gives Nikolay the document and even tells her father about it. Everything seems lost for the Margaritovs, but Nikolay suddenly comes to his senses, fools Lebedkina with a copy of the note, returns the original to Margaritov, and, moved by Lyudmila's devotion and unselfish love, decides to marry her. His debts are then settled by Margaritov, who has been richly rewarded by his client.

Wolves and Sheep (*Volki i ovtsy*, 1875). Comedy of Meropiya Murzavetskaya, an elderly spinster who owns a large but insolvent estate. She is determined, with the help of Chugunov, a dishonest clerk, to control the money and estate of the widow Evlampiya Kupavina by marrying her to her worthless nephew Apollon. A subplot concerns the attempt of Glafira, a poor relation of Meropiya, to snare the wealthy Lynyayev as her husband. Glafira succeeds in trapping Lynyayev, but Meropiya is foiled by Berkutov, a wealthy neighbor, who not only wins Evlampiya but makes Meropiya help him.

Truth Is Good, but Happiness is Better (*Pravda—khorosho, a schastye luchshe*, 1876). Comedy depicting the discrepancy between theory and practice, truth and destiny, as illustrated in the relationship between a rich girl and a poor young man, a fanatical apostle of truth, who works for the girl's family. The two young people are in love, but all manner of opposition and danger threatens their happiness. Finally, an old, stiff-legged officer, hav-

Truth Is Good, but Happiness Is Better, **Moscow.** [*Moscow Theatres*]

ing once loved the girl's grandmother and promised to keep the intimacy secret, demands that the two young people be allowed to marry. The grandmother must agree lest her past be revealed. The groom, following his own logic, believes this happy outcome to be the result of his devotion to truth, but the grandmother knowingly declares that "truth is good, but happiness is better."

A Last Sacrifice (*Poslednyaya zhertva*, 1877). Comedy in which Vadim Dulchin tells his fiancée Yuliya Tugina to make a last sacrifice: to ask her late husband's friend, the wealthy merchant Flor Pribytkov, for a loan of 5,000 rubles so that Vadim can pay his debts. Unfortunately, Vadim loses the money at cards. Believing that Pribytkov's grandniece Irina will receive a large dowry, Vadim proposes to her and is accepted. But when he discovers she has no money, he breaks off the engagement. He tries to go back to Yuliya, but, having discovered his double-dealing, she has consented to marry Pribytkov. Undaunted, Vadim sets off to woo another wealthy widow.

The Girl with No Dowry (*Bespridannitsa*, 1878). Tragedy, set in a city on the Volga, depicting both the selfishness of the rich and the impotent hopes of a Russian clerk. Young Larisa Dmitriyevna Ogudalova, having lost her father, is dowerless, but not undesirable, and deeply in love with Sergey Paratov, an adventurous nobleman. However, she consents to marry Karandyshev, a clerk of humble means who loves her. In doing so she fails to dampen the dishonorable interest of other suitors who seek her favors. Meanwhile, Paratov returns from a year's absence and appears at the engagement dinner of Karandyshev and Larisa. Without any thought of marriage, for he is engaged to an heiress, Paratov sets out to lure Larisa to follow him on a picnic on the Volga. With

A Russian production of *Wolves and Sheep*. [*Moscow Theatres*]

the naïveté of a girl in love, Larisa leaves with Paratov but soon realizes that she is only an object of amusement to him. Seeking vengeance, Karandyshev runs after them with a gun, but after learning that Paratov has abandoned her, he decides to protect Larisa from all her other suitors. He finds her contemplating suicide and begs her to return to him. When she refuses, mocking him for his lack of pride, he shoots her. Dying, Larisa thanks him for ending her life, while Karandyshev sobs.

The Heart Is Not a Stone (*Serdtse ne kamen*, 1879). Comedy focusing on a young wife and a greedy nephew. Vera Filippovna, the embodiment of womanly virtue, is married to an elderly merchant named Karkunov who has invited his godfather Khalymov to help him draft his will. Konstantin, his young nephew, upset because Vera Filippovna is allotted the lion's share of the estate, bribes Yerast, Karkunov's young employee who lives in the house, to seduce Vera Filippovna and arrange to be caught. Thus, presumably, Karkunov will disinherit her. Meanwhile, Khalymov's wife, an old cynic, informs Vera Filippovna that Konstantin's wife Olga is Yerast's mistress. Vera, however, seems to have some interest in Yerast, and she agrees to visit him in his quarters. Preceding this, Olga, angry and jealous, visits Yerast, and to calm her he explains what is to take place. Vera Filippovna overhears them and leaves. Now Karkunov, looking for his wife, is told by Konstantin that she is in Yerast's bedroom, which in fact is occupied by Olga. Finally Karkunov, gravely ill, makes his wife sole heir to his estate, and she distributes his wealth among the poor, having paid even Konstantin's debts. Nonetheless, Konstantin vainly attempts to rob Vera, who out of magnanimity

Lilia Gritsenko in *The Girl with No Dowry*. [*Moscow Theatres*]

The Heart Is Not a Stone. [*Moscow Theatres*]

grants him an allowance. Yerast then pays tribute to her, confesses his affection, and voices hopes for the future.

The Bondwomen (*Nevolnitsy*, 1880). Comedy of two "bondwomen," Sofya and Yevlaliya. Sofya is bound in marriage to Koblov, a jealous husband twice her age. Yevlaliya's bondage is similar. In her childhood, she was reared in seclusion and "sold" to Styrov, a man twice her age. Sofya points out that Yevlaliya, at least, married a kind, considerate man and advises her to turn to playing cards for amusement. Yevlaliya, however, believes she loves Artemy Mulin, the only other man she has ever known. But Artemy is an opportunist seeking a marriage to further his career. Yevlaliya renounces him when she learns that he is Sofya's lover. Heeding Sofya's advice, Yevlaliya takes up whist and resigns herself to making the best of her life with Styrov.

Talents and Admirers (*Talanty i poklonniki*, 1881). Comedy with overtones of social criticism. Aleksandra Nikolavna Negina, a beautiful and talented actress, lives in near poverty with her mother and her fiancé Pyotr Yegorych Meluzov, a university student who furthers Negina's education but cannot aid her materially. Narokov, an impoverished former entrepreneur, believes in Negina's talent but can do nothing to further her career. Elderly and influential Prince Irakly Stratonych Dulebov and Grigory Antonych Bakin, an important young official, vie for Negina's attentions, but Bakin, aware of Dulebov's wealth, withdraws from the race.

Just before a benefit performance for the troupe, for which the actors are selling tickets, Dulebov visits Negina and is appalled by the misery of her home. To her mother's delight he offers to rent a better apartment for her, but Negina angrily dismisses him. Soon an actress friend arrives with Velikatov, a dignified, wealthy landowner and merchant. Velikatov instantly falls in love with Negina and succeeds, with tact, in presenting her with fabric for her costume. Meanwhile, enraged at his

Scene from Act II of *The Heart Is Not a Stone*. [*Moscow Theatres*]

rejection, Dulebov persuades the theatre manager to cut short Negina's act at the benefit and to dismiss her. Hearing this, Velikatov purchases all the remaining tickets from Negina in order to demonstrate her indispensability.

The benefit a success, Negina declines to celebrate and chooses to spend a last night with Meluzov, whom she loves, for she realizes now there is no other course but to compromise her ideals and accept Velikatov's offer of a brilliant future.

They Are Guilty though Guiltless (*Bezvinny vinovatye*, 1884). Melodrama, set in the world of provincial actors, dealing with the theme of mother love. Lyubov Otradina, a sensitive, educated young orphan, has an illegitimate child by Murov, who abandons her for a wealthy bride. He and old Galchikha, who has been taking care of the child in secret, mislead Lyubov into believing that her little boy has died and then sell him for adoption in a distant province. Lyubov leaves town but returns seventeen years later as Kruchinina, a famous actress, whose only joy is the memory of her child. Among the local actors she meets young Neznamov, a bitter and cynical young man of unknown origin. An almost irrational affinity between the two revives Neznamov's faith in goodness, but envious local actors plot to disillusion him. Meanwhile, Kruchinina learns the truth about her son and, determined to find him, visits Murov, who suggests she forget the boy and marry him. Neznamov, now believing the lies fed to him, becomes drunk at a reception given in her honor and denounces all mothers who abandon their children. In his fury he pulls out a hidden

Scene from Act II of *The Heart Is Not a Stone*. [*Moscow Theatres*]

charm hanging about his neck. Kruchinina recognizes it and faints. Now Neznamov is told the truth, and Murov disappears in the crowd.

[LAURENCE SENELICK]

PLAYS

1. *Semeynaya kartina** (*A Domestic Picture*). Play, 1 act. Written 1847. Published 1847. Produced St. Petersburg, Alexandrinsky Theatre, Oct. 3, 1855.

2. *Svoi lyudi-sochtemsya!** (*It's a Family Affair—We'll Settle It Ourselves; also known as Bankrupt*). Comedy, 4 acts. Written 1849. Published 1850. Produced Voronezh, Cadet Corps Theatre, Apr. 18, 1860; St. Petersburg, Alexandrinsky Theatre, Jan. 16, 1861.

3. *Utro molodogo cheloveka* (*The Morning of a Young Man*). Play, 6 scenes. Written 1850. Produced St. Petersburg, Petersburg Theatre-Circus Theatre, Jan. 16, 1853; Moscow, Maly Theatre, May 11, 1853.

4. *Neozhidanny sluchay* (*An Unexpected Occurrence*). Dramatic study, 2 scenes. Written 1850. Published 1851. Produced St. Petersburg, Alexandrinsky Theatre, May 1, 1902.

5. *Bednaya nevesta** (*The Poor Bride*). Comedy, 5 acts. Written 1851. Published 1852. Produced Moscow, Maly Theatre, Aug. 20, 1853.

6. *Ne v svoi sani ne sadis!* (*Don't Sit in a Sledge You Don't Own*). Comedy, 3 acts. Written 1852. Published 1853. Produced Moscow, Maly Theatre, Jan. 14, 1853; St. Petersburg, Alexandrinsky Theatre, Feb. 19, 1853.

7. *Bednost ne porok** (*Poverty Is No Crime*). Comedy, 3 acts. Written 1853. Published 1854. Produced Moscow, Maly Theatre, Jan. 25, 1854.

8. *Ne tak zhivi, kak khochetsya** (*One Must Not Live as One Likes*). Drama, 3 acts. Written 1854. Published 1855. Produced Moscow, Maly Theatre, Dec. 3, 1854; St. Petersburg, Alexandrinsky Theatre, Jan. 12, 1855.

9. *V chuzhom piru pokhmelye* (*A Hangover from Somebody Else's Party*). Comedy, 2 acts. Written 1855. Published 1856. Produced Moscow, Maly Theatre, Jan. 9, 1856.

10. *Dokhodnoye mesto* (*A Lucrative Post*). Comedy, 5 acts. Written 1856. Published 1857. Produced St. Petersburg, Alexandrinsky Theatre, Sept. 27, 1863.

11. *Prazdnichny son—do obeda* (*A Holiday Dream—Before Dinner*). Play, 3 tableaux. Written 1857. Published 1857. Produced St. Petersburg, Alexandrinsky Theatre, Oct. 28, 1857.

12. *Ne soshlis kharakterami!** (*An Incompatibility of Tempers*). Play, 3 tableaux. Written 1857. Published 1858. Produced St. Petersburg, Alexandrinsky Theatre, Sept. 1, 1858.

13. *Vospitannitsa** (*A Protégée of the Mistress*). Play, 4 tableaux. Written 1858. Published 1859. Produced St. Petersburg, private showing, Jan. 27, 1862; Moscow, Maly Theatre, Oct. 21, 1863.

14. *Groza** (*The Thunderstorm*). Tragedy, 5 acts. Written 1859. Published 1860. Produced Moscow, Maly Theatre, Nov. 16, 1859; St. Petersburg, Alexandrinsky Theatre, Dec. 2, 1859.

15. *Stary drug luchshe novykh dvukh* (*An Old Friend Is Better than Two New Ones*). Play, 3 tableaux. Written 1860. Published 1860. Produced Moscow, Krasnovorotsky Theatre, private showing, Sept. 15, 1860; St. Petersburg, Alexandrinsky Theatre, Oct. 10, 1860.

16. *Svoi sobaki gryzutsya, chuzhaya ne pristavay** (*When Your Own Dogs are Fighting, a Strange Dog Should Not Meddle*). Written 1861. Published 1861. Produced Moscow, Maly Theatre, Oct. 27, 1861.

17. *Za chem poydesh, to i naydesh* (*Zhenitba Balzaminova*) (*Whatever You Go After, You Will Find, or Balzaminov's Wedding*). Play, 3 tableaux. Written 1861. Published 1861. Produced St. Petersburg, Alexandrinsky Theatre, Jan. 1, 1863.

18. *Kozma Zakharich Minin, Sukhoruk* (*Kozma Zakharich Minin, the One-armed*). Drama, 5 acts and epilogue. Written 1861. Published 1862. Revised version: Drama, 5 acts. Written 1866. Published 1904. Produced St. Petersburg, Alexandrinsky Theatre, Dec. 9, 1866.

19. *Grekh da beda na kogo ne zhivyot* (*Sin and Sorrow Are Common to All*). Drama, 4 acts. Written 1862. Published 1863. Produced Moscow, Maly Theatre, Jan. 21, 1863; St. Petersburg, Alexandrinsky Theatre, Jan. 25, 1863.

20. *Tyazhelye dni* (*Hard Times*). Play, 3 acts. Written 1863. Published 1863. Produced Moscow, Maly Theatre, Oct. 2, 1863.

21. *Shutniki** (*The Jokers*). Play, 4 acts. Written 1864. Published 1864. Produced St. Petersburg, Alexandrinsky Theatre, Oct. 9, 1864.

22. *Voevoda* (*Son na Volge*) (*The Voivode, or The Dream on the Volga*). Comedy, 5 acts and prologue. Written 1864. Published 1865. Produced St. Petersburg, Alexandrinsky Theatre, Apr. 23, 1865; Moscow, Bolshoy Theatre, Sept. 9, 1865. Revised version: Written 1885. Published 1890. Produced Moscow, Maly Theatre, Jan. 19, 1886.

23. *Na boykom meste** (*At the Jolly Spot*). Comedy, 3 acts. Written 1865. Published 1865. Produced Moscow, Maly Theatre, Sept. 29, 1865.

24. *Puchina* (*The Abyss*). Play, 4 scenes. Written 1865. Published 1866. Produced Moscow, Maly Theatre, Apr. 8, 1866.

25. *Dmitry Samozvanets i Vasily Shuysky* (*The False Dmitry and Vasily Shuysky*). Drama, 2 parts. Written 1866. Published 1867. Produced Moscow, Maly Theatre, Jan. 30, 1867.

26. *Tushino*. Drama, 8 scenes. Written 1866. Published 1867. Produced Moscow, Maly Theatre, Nov. 23, 1867; St. Petersburg, Alexandrinsky Theatre, Nov. 23, 1867.

27. (With Stepan Alexandrovich Gedeonov). *Vasilisa Melentyeva*. Drama, 5 acts. Written 1867. Published 1868. Produced Moscow, Maly Theatre, Jan. 3, 1868.

28. *Na vsyakogo mudretsa dovolno prostoty** (*Diary of a Scoundrel; also called Enough Stupidity for Every Wise Man*). Comedy, 5 acts. Written 1868. Published 1868. Produced St. Petersburg, Alexandrinsky Theatre, Nov. 1, 1868; Moscow, Maly Theatre, Nov. 6, 1868.

29. *Goryachee serdtse* (*An Ardent Heart*). Comedy, 5 acts. Written 1868. Published 1869. Produced Moscow, Maly Theatre, Jan. 15, 1869.

30. *Beshenye dengi** (*Easy Money*). Comedy, 5 acts. Written 1870. Published 1870. Produced St. Petersburg, Alexandrinsky Theatre, Apr. 16, 1870.

31. *Les** (*The Forest*). Comedy, 5 acts. Written 1870. Published 1871. Produced St. Petersburg, Alexandrinsky Theatre, Nov. 1, 1871.

32. *Ne vse kotu maslenitsa** (*A Cat Has Not Always Carnival*). Four scenes. Written 1871. Published 1871. Produced Moscow, Maly Theatre, Oct. 7, 1871.

33. *Ne bylo ni grosha, da vdrug altyn* (*Not a Kopek and Suddenly a Ruble*). Comedy, 5 acts. Written 1871. Published 1872. Produced St. Petersburg, Alexandrinsky Theatre, Sept. 20, 1872.

34. *Komik XVII stoletiya** (*A Comedian of the Seventeenth Century*). Comedy, 3 acts and epilogue. Written 1872. Published 1873. Produced Moscow, benefit for D. V. Zhivokini Oct. 26, 1872; St. Petersburg, Alexandrinsky Theatre, Aug. 30, 1894.

35. *Snegurochka* (*The Snow Maiden*). Springtide tale, prologue and 4 acts. Written 1873. Published 1873. Produced Moscow, Bolshoy Theatre, May 11, 1873.

36. *Pozdnyaya lyubov* (*Late Love*). Play, 4 acts. Written 1873. Published 1874. Produced Moscow, Maly Theatre, Nov. 22, 1873.

37. *Trudovoy khleb* (*Hard-earned Bread*). Play, 4 acts. Written 1874. Published 1874. Produced Moscow, Maly Theatre, Nov. 28, 1874.

38. *Volki i ovtsy** (*Wolves and Sheep*). Comedy, 5 acts. Written 1875. Published 1875. Produced St. Petersburg, Alexandrinsky Theatre, Dec. 8, 1875.

39. *Bogatye nevesty* (*The Rich Brides*). Comedy, 4 acts. Written 1875. Published 1876. Produced St. Petersburg, Alexandrinsky Theatre, Nov. 28, 1875; Moscow, Maly Theatre, Nov. 30, 1875.

40. *Pravda—khorosho, a schastye luchshe* (*Truth Is Good, but Happiness Is Better*). Comedy, 4 acts. Written 1876. Published 1877. Produced Moscow, Maly Theatre, Nov. 18, 1876.

41. (With Nikolay Yakovlevich Solovyev). *Schastlivy den* (*Lucky Day*). Play, 3 acts. Written 1877. Published 1877. Produced Moscow, Maly Theatre, Oct. 28, 1877.

42. *Poslednyaya zhertva** (*A Last Sacrifice*). Comedy, 5 acts. Written 1877. Published 1878. Produced Moscow, Maly Theatre, Nov. 8, 1877.

43. (With Solovyev). *Zhenitba Belugina* (*Belugin's Wedding*). Comedy, 5 acts. Written 1877. Published 1878. Produced Moscow, Maly Theatre, Dec. 26, 1877.

44. *Bespridannitsa* (*The Girl with No Dowry*). Drama, 4 acts. Written 1878. Published 1879. Produced Moscow, Maly Theatre, Nov. 10, 1878.

45. (With Solovyev). *Dikarka* (*The Wild Woman*). Comedy, 4 acts. Written 1879. Published 1880. Produced Moscow, Maly Theatre, Nov. 2, 1879.

46. *Serdtse ne kamen* (*The Heart Is Not a Stone*). Comedy, 4 acts. Written 1879. Published 1880. Produced St. Petersburg, Alexandrinsky Theatre, Nov. 21, 1879.

47. (With Solovyev). *Svetit, da ne greyet* (*It Lights, but It Does Not Heat*). Drama, 5 acts. Written 1880. Published 1881. Produced Moscow, Maly Theatre, Nov. 6, 1880.

48. *Nevolnitsy** (*The Bondwomen*). Comedy, 4 acts. Written 1880. Published 1881. Produced Moscow, Maly Theatre, Nov. 14, 1880.

49. (With Pyotr Mikhailovich Nevezhin). *Blazh* (*The Whim*). Comedy, 4 acts. Written 1880. Published 1881. Produced Moscow, Maly Theatre, Dec. 26, 1880.

50. (With Nevezhin). *Staroye po-novomu* (*The Old in a New Way*). Comedy, 4 acts. Written 1881. Published 1882. Produced Moscow, Maly Theatre, Nov. 21, 1881.

51. *Talanty i poklonniki** (*Talents and Admirers*). Comedy, 4 acts. Written 1881. Published 1882. Produced Moscow, Maly Theatre, Dec. 20, 1881.

52. *Krasavets-muzhchina* (*A Handsome Man*). Comedy, 4 acts. Written 1882. Published 1883. Produced Moscow, Maly Theatre, Dec. 26, 1882.

53. *Bezvínny vinovatye** (*They Are Guilty though Guiltless*). Comedy, 4 acts. Written 1883. Published 1884. Produced Moscow, Maly Theatre, Jan. 15, 1884.

54. *Ne ot mira sego* (*Not of This World*). Play, 3 acts. Written 1884.

Published 1885. Produced St. Petersburg, Alexandrinsky Theatre, Jan. 9, 1885.

EDITIONS

Collections
Russian *Sochineniya*, 2 vols., St. Petersburg, 1859; *Dramaticheskiye perevody*, 2 vols., St. Petersburg, 1886; *Polnoye sobraniye sochineniy Ostrovskogo*, ed. by M. I. Pisarev, 12 vols., St. Petersburg, 1904–1909; *Teatr Ostrovskogo*, ed. by V. A. Filippov, Moscow, 1937; *Polnoye sobraniye sochineny*, 16 vols., Moscow, 1949; *Polnoye sobraniye sochineny*, 12 vols., Moscow, 1973–1980.
English *Plays*, ed. by G. R. Noyes, New York, 1917; *Easy Money and Two Other Plays*, tr. by D. Magarshack, London, 1944; *Five Plays of Alexander Ostrovsky*, tr. by E. Bristow, New York, 1969; *Plays*, tr. by M. Wettlin, Moscow, 1974.
Individual Plays
Artistes and Admirers. E. Hanson, tr., New York, 1970.
At the Jolly Spot. In *Poet Lore* XXXVI (Spring 1925).
Bondwomen. S. Kurlandzik and G. Noyes, tr., in *Poet Lore* XXXVI (Winter 1925).
A Cat Has Not Always Carnival. J. Campbell and G. Noyes, tr., in *Poet Lore* XL (Autumn 1929).
A Domestic Picture. E. Voynich, tr., in *A Treasury of Classic Russian Literature*, ed. by J. Cournos, New York, 1961.
Enough Stupidity in Every Wise Man. P. Kasherman, tr., in *Moscow Art Theatre Series of Russian Plays*, ed. by O. M. Sayler, 2d ser., New York, 1923; adapted as *The Diary of a Scoundrel*, by Rodney Ackland, London, 1948, and in *The Modern Theatre* Vol. 2, ed. by E. Bentley, New York, 1955.
Fairy Gold. C. Daniels and G. Noyes, tr., in *Poet Lore* XL (Spring 1929).
The Forest. C. Winslow and G. Noyes, tr., New York, 1926.
Incompatibility of Temper. E. Voynich, tr., in *The Humour of Russia*, London, 1895.
The King of Comedy. J. McPetrie, tr., London, 1937.
A Last Sacrifice. E. Korvin-Kroukovsky and G. Noyes, tr., in *Poet Lore* XXXIX (Autumn 1928).
The Poor Bride. J. Seymour and G. Noyes, tr., in *Masterpieces of the Russian Drama*, Vol. I, ed. by G. R. Noyes, New York, 1933.
The Storm. C. Garnett, tr., Chicago, 1911; *The Thunderstorm*, F. Whyte and G. Noyes, tr., New York, 1927, and in *World Drama*, Vol. 2, ed. by B. H. Clark, New York, 1933; *The Storm, and Other Russian plays*, D. Magarshack, tr., New York, 1960; *An Anthology of Russian Plays*, ed. and tr. by F. D. Reeve, vol. 1, New York, 1963; *19th Century Russian Drama*, A. MacAndrew, tr., New York, 1963.
We Won't Brook Interference. J. Seymour and G. Noyes, tr., San Francisco, 1938.
Wolves and Sheep. I. Colby and G. Noyes, tr., in *Poet Lore* XXXVII (Summer 1926).
You Can't Live Just as You Please. P. Winningstad and G. Noyes, tr., in *Poet Lore* XLIX (1943).

CRITICISM

N. Denisov, *Kriticheskaya literatura o proizvedeniyakh Ostrovskogo*, Moscow, 1906–1907; J. Patouillet, *Ostrovsky et son théâtre de moeurs russes*, Paris, 1912; N. Kashin, *Etyudy ob Ostrovskom*, Moscow, 1912–1913; N. Dolgov, *A. N. Ostrovsky*, Moscow, 1923; L. M. Lotman, *A. N. Ostrovsky i russkaya dramaturgiya ego vremeni*, Moscow and Leningrad, 1961; *A. N. Ostrovskiy. Sbornik statey i materialov*, Moscow, 1962; E. M. Kholodov, *Masterstvo Ostrovskogo*, Moscow, 1963; *A. N. Ostrovskiy na sovetskoy stsene*, Moscow, 1974; A. Revyakin, *Iskusstvo dramaturgiy A. N. Ostrovskogo*, Moscow, 1974; M. Hoover, *Alexander Ostrovsky*, New York, 1981.

Otway, Thomas (1651/52–1685)

English poet and dramatist. He was born on March 3, 1651 or 1652, at Trotton, Sussex, the son of a country clergyman. He attended Winchester College and entered Christ Church, Oxford, in 1669. In 1672 he left the university without taking a degree and went to London, where three years later, his first play, the tragedy *Alcibiades*, was presented at Dorset Garden by Thomas Betterton, the leading actor of the day. *Alcibiades* failed, but *Don Carlos, Prince of Spain* (1676), his next tragedy, was a success.

Meanwhile, Otway had fallen in love with the ac-

Engraving of Thomas Otway dated London, 1821, and published in *Effigies Poeticae: Portraits of the British Poets*, 1824. [American Heritage]

tress Elizabeth Barry, Betterton's leading lady. She apparently flirted with Otway (a letter to her exists in which he complains of a broken appointment) but was unwilling to disrupt her permanent liaison with the Earl of Rochester, who briefly became Otway's patron. It is possible that desire to forget Mrs. Barry prompted Otway's enlistment in the army in 1678. He fought in the Netherlands and returned penniless to London in 1679. The same year Betterton presented *The History and Fall of Caius Marius*, and a year later *The Orphan*, an outstanding tragedy in which Mrs. Barry starred. She also appeared in Otway's celebrated tragedy *Venice Preserved* in 1682.

In 1680 Otway wrote *The Poet's Complaint of His Muse*, his one significant poetic work. By 1683, when his last play, a weak comedy entitled *The Atheist*, was produced, he had become a chronic alcoholic, and although his plays were financially successful, he got himself deeply into debt. He hid himself from creditors and friends in a tavern on Tower Hill, where he died, from either starvation or drink, on April 10, 1685.

WORK

Tragedy, which had grown decadent in the late Jacobean and Caroline periods, declined during the Restoration into heroic tragedy of bombast and artificiality. Otway began his theatrical career in this tradition with *Alcibiades* (1675). He moved to a corruption of *Romeo and Juliet* entitled *The History and Fall of Caius Marius* (1679). Soon afterward he created two fine tragedies, *The Orphan, or the Unhappy Marriage* (1680) and *Venice Preserved, or A Plot Discovered* (1682), which set him on a different course from his contemporaries. Otway, although still influenced by heroic drama, took the Elizabethans as his model, substituting ordinary characters for stock, strutting heroic characters and revealing his concern with domestic misfortunes. *See* HEROIC PLAY in glossary.

In *Venice Preserved* the defects of the heroic genre are

less pronounced than in other plays of the time, even though the principal theme is the conventional one of the conflict between love and honor. Jaffeir fluctuates between love for his wife Belvidera and the demands of honor in keeping faith with his friend Pierre in conspiring against the Venetian senate.

The Orphan, a triumph in its day, brought pathos and sentiment to audiences used to banality and heroics. Probing emotions and psychological reactions, the plot centers on the conflict of the brothers Castalio and Polydore over their desire for Monimia, wife of Castalio. *Don Carlos, Prince of Spain* (1676) is a drama of court intrigue and jealousy; *Titus and Berenice* (1676), an adaptation of Racine's tragedy *Bérénice* (1670).

Otway's comedies include *The Soldier's Fortune* (1680), an effective play marked by a sense of disillusionment, in which the soldier Beaugard finds his love for Lady Dunce rekindled although she is now married to a senile old man; *The Cheats of Scapin* (1676), a fairly faithful adaptation of Molière's play (1671); *Friendship in Fashion* (1678); and *The Atheist* (1683), a weak sequel to *The Soldier's Fortune*.

Don Carlos, Prince of Spain (1676). Tragedy in which Ruy Gomez, confidant to Philip II, and his wife, the Duchess of Eboli, plot the downfall of Don Carlos. Gomez makes the King jealously suspicious of his young

Spranger Barry and his wife Ann Barry in *Venice Preserved*. [New York Public Library Picture Collection]

Joyce Henry and Dana Elcar in a Phoenix Theatre production of *Venice Preserved*, 1955. [Courtesy of Phoenix Theatre. Photograph by Leo Friedman]

wife Elizabeth of Valois, who had come to Spain in order to marry his son Carlos. Convinced that his marriage has been dishonored, the King orders the death of his wife and son. Meanwhile, Gomez surprises his wife in the arms of Don John of Austria and stabs her. Before she dies, the duchess reveals to Philip that the Queen and Carlos are innocent. But her confession comes too late to prevent their deaths, and Philip goes mad.

The Orphan, or The Unhappy Marriage (1680). Tragedy in which Monimia, the orphaned ward of Acasto, is loved by Acasto's twin sons Castalio and Polydore. Monimia prefers Castalio. When Acasto is taken ill and thought to be dying, they secretly marry and Castalio makes plans to steal into his wife's chamber that night. But their plan is overheard by Polydore, who, ignorant of the marriage, takes his brother's place while Castalio is kept out by the maid, who thinks he is Polydore. The next day Polydore learns of the marriage and, horrified, provokes his brother to fight with him, and runs against Castalio's dagger. Monimia then takes poison, and Castalio stabs himself.

Venice Preserved, or A Plot Discovered (1682). Tragedy of intrigue, friendship, and love. Jaffeir, a young gentleman of Venice, has married Belvidera, virtuous daughter of Senator Priuli, defying the objections of her father. Now, three years later, virtually penniless, Jaffeir approaches Priuli for help and is again rebuffed. His friend Pierre then has little difficulty in persuading him to join a conspiracy against the Venetian senate. Circumstances force Jaffeir to confide in Belvidera, who urges him to warn the senate and beg pardon for himself and the other conspirators. He agrees, but the gesture misfires and the senate condemns the whole group. Belvidera goes to her father for help, and regretting his former harshness toward her, he obtains a pardon for Jaffeir. But it comes too late. Pierre, a moment before his execution, asks Jaffeir to stab him. He does and then uses the dagger on himself. Tortured by her responsibility for the turn of events, Belvidera goes mad and dies.

PLAYS

All were first performed in London.

1. *Alcibiades.* Tragedy, 5 acts. Published 1675. Produced Dorset Garden Theatre, September, 1675.

2. *Don Carlos, Prince of Spain.* Tragedy, 5 acts. Published 1676. Produced Dorset Garden Theatre, June, 1676.

3. (Adaptation). *Titus and Berenice.* Tragedy, 3 acts. Published 1677. Produced Dorset Garden Theatre, ca. December, 1676. Based on Jean Racine's *Bérénice* (1670).

4. (Adaptation). *The Cheats of Scapin.* Farce, 3 acts. Published 1677. Produced Dorset Garden Theatre, ca. December, 1676. Based on Molière's *Les fourberies de Scapin* (1671).

5. *Friendship in Fashion.* Comedy, 5 acts. Published 1678. Produced Dorset Garden Theatre, April, 1678.

6. *The History and Fall of Caius Marius.* Tragedy, 5 acts. Published 1680. Produced Dorset Garden Theatre, August/September, 1679. Based on William Shakespeare's *Romeo and Juliet* (1591/96).

7. *The Orphan, or The Unhappy Marriage.* Tragedy, 5 acts. Published 1680. Produced Dorset Garden Theatre, February/March, 1680.

8. *The Soldier's Fortune.* Comedy, 5 acts. Published 1681. Produced Dorset Garden Theatre, March, 1680.

9. *Venice Preserved, or A Plot Discovered.* Tragedy, 5 acts. Published 1682. Produced Dorset Garden Theatre, Feb. 9, 1682.

10. *The Atheist, or The Second Part of the Soldier's Fortune.* Comedy, 5 acts. Published 1684. Produced Dorset Garden Theatre, June/November (ca. September), 1683.

A tragedy, *Heroic Friendship* (pub. 1719), has been doubtfully attributed to Otway.

EDITIONS

Complete Works, ed. by M. Summers, 3 vols., New York, 1926; *Venice Preserved.* Published in *Restoration Plays,* New York, 1955.

CRITICISM

E. Schumacher, *Thomas Otway,* New York, 1924; A. M. Taylor, *Next to Shakespeare,* New York, 1950; H. Klingler, *Die Künstleisde Entwicklung in den Trapodien Thomas Otways,* Vienna and Stuttgart, 1971.

Owen, Alun (1926–)

British dramatist. Born in north Wales, he began his theatrical career as an actor and in the 1950s turned to playwriting. His first stage play, *The Rough and Ready Lot* (1959), is a costume drama about two Irish mercenaries, one a Catholic and the other an atheist, and their religious conflict. *Progress to the Park* (1959) is again concerned with religious conflict, this time between a Catholic and a Protestant.

Owen has written numerous plays for television, the best known being a trilogy on Liverpool life: *No Trams to Lime Street*, which returns to the characters first presented in *Two Sons*, a radio play about two sailors and their relationships with their fathers, given on the BBC in 1957; *After the Funeral*, dealing with the relations between members of two generations, grandfather and grandsons; and *Lena, Oh My Lena*, in which a student, alienated from his background by his education, struggles to find himself. In the 1964–1965 London season, collaboration between Owen and Lionel Bart resulted in a musical, *Maggie May*, about a Liverpool tart. The next season, *A Little Winter Love*, a comedy set on a campus in Wales, had a limited run in London, as did *There'll Be Some Changes Made*, about sexual changes, in 1969, and *Shelter*, a drama about an unhappy woman, in 1971. *The Male of the Species*, televised in 1969, was staged in 1974.

Owens, Rochelle (1936–)

American dramatist and poet. She won immediate recognition with her first play, *Futz* (1965). Its shocking subject matter—Cyrus Futz, the protagonist, is in love with his pig, Amanda, and their ensuing sexual relationship calls upon his head the wrath of a puritanical society—and inventive use of language established Owens's reputation as a spokesperson for the budding and radically inclined Off-Off Broadway movement of the sixties. Sexual conflict serves as the basis for *Istanboul* (1965), while in *Homo* (1966) the conflict shifts to a class struggle with racial overtones. Her poetic imagination, coupled with a strongly vivid theatrical bent, resulted in *Belch* (1968), a savage fantasy set in dark Africa with crisscrossing themes of racial, sexual, and cultural domination. Historical subject matter presented as satire is the basis of the musical *The Karl Marx Play* (1973, with music by Galt MacDermot), while mythic and ritual chants pervade the exotic Chinese landscape of *He Wants Shih* (1974). *Emma Instigated Me* (1976) is a subdued feminist tract in a Pirandellian vein as the Author (the playwright herself) mediates between fiction and reality.

GAUTAM DASGUPTA

Oyono-Mbia, Guillaume (n.d.)

Cameroon playwright. Educated in French, Oyono-Mbia is thoroughly acquainted with the classical writers and has found that Molière's satire and comic devices can easily be adapted to certain rather formal African domestic situations. In his *Three Suitors, One Husband (Trois pretendants, un mari)*, which won a BBC Plays in Africa Service Playwriting Award in 1967, the greedy father plays off one suitor against another to get a higher bride price. The daughter takes the money deposited by two of the suitors and gives it to the poor student she loves. The father, who has to refund the payments to the other two, is not unlike Molière's duped fathers, but he has a touch of the cunning Ananse, a spider featured in the dramas of Efua Sutherland (*See* SUTHERLAND, EFUA). *Our Daughter Isn't Going to Marry (Notre fille ne se mariera pas,* 1971) alternates in setting between town and country, satirizing the affectations of townspeople (for example, the Francophile mother who worries because her son dislikes Camembert cheese) and the unsophisticated villagers (one of whom tries to put his goat into a car). The play shows the absurd failures in communication between the two.

GEOFFREY AXWORTHY

Özakman, Turgut (1930–)

Turkish dramatist. He was born in Ankara. After briefly practicing law, he began to attend courses at the Theatre Institute in Cologne. Following a stint as a literary advisor at the Turkish State Theatre, he spent two years (1960–1962) in Bonn as press attaché. He became vice-president (1967) of the Turkish State Radio and TV Corporation. For a number of years he ran his own advertising and film production organization.

Turgut Özakman's chief strength as a dramatist lies in the quality of his dialogue and characterization. His recurrent themes are the causes of criminality, the generational conflict, the process of modernization, and the search for sexual identity. *The Fate of the Pink House (Pembe Evin Kaderi,* 1951), his first play, deals with the confrontation between generations, between tradition

The Cross-stitch Canvas as presented at the State Theatre (Turkey) in 1979. [Metin And Collection]

and change. Three years later, in *Ten People Working on the Sun Newspaper (Güneş'te On Kişi)*, he depicted an idealistic journalist's fight against corruption. *The Flood (Tufan, 1957)*, an antiwar play, retells the story of Noah's Ark, by relating it to a vision of the world after World War III. A psychological and sociological study of the criminal mind is offered in *Beyond the Walls (Duvarların Ötesi, 1958)*, a play about four convicts who take a young girl hostage. This popular work was made into a film in 1964.

The effects of poverty and insecurity are studied in *The Hearth (Ocak, 1962)*, in which a garage mechanic and his wife struggle to keep their family from disintegrating. In 1964 the play was adapted as a film and released as *Migratory Birds (Gurbet Kuşları)*. *The Cross-stitch Canvas (Kanaviçe, 1960)* offers a moving portrait of a young girl's efforts to free herself from the false constraints imposed on her life by three conservative aunts who have brought her up. The title refers to the embroidery work of the older women. The damage done by prudish sexual attitudes is studied in *Ragged and Tattered (Paramparça, 1963)*, a drama about the relationship between a man and his frigid wife.

In 1965 Özakman turned his attention to the aimless lives of urban young people in *Boulevard (Bulvar)*, which featured music by Bülent Arel. The inadequacy of sexual education in Turkey is the focus of *Disciplinary Committee*

of National College (Ulusal Kolej Disiplin Kurulu, 1966), which adopts the adolescent's viewpoint in depicting the search for sexual identity. *Our Neighbors (Komşularımız)* offers a loosely connected series of scenes about family life.

Özakman's later plays are among his best. *Sarıpınar 1914 (1968)* is a successful free adaptation of Reşat Nuri Güntekin's novel *The Windmill*. During the last years of the Ottoman Empire, a false report goes out that Sarıpınar, a provincial town, has suffered an earthquake. The "news" travels from echelon to echelon of the administration, and soon material help is pouring in from all over the world. When the Crown Prince decides to visit the city with a group of foreign journalists, local administrators scheme to simulate an earthquake by demolishing some rickety houses. This turns out to be unnecessary, as the town is already so seedy that the foreigners are convinced that there has been an earthquake. The playwright emphasizes that such a situation could never occur in contemporary Turkey. *See* GÜNTEKIN, REŞAT NURI.

Still unproduced and unpublished, *Fehim Pasha's Mansion (Fehim Paşa Konağı)* won a drama competition in 1979. It is a somewhat lighthearted account of the reign of Sultan Abdülhamid, who employed a villainous pasha to spy for him. In telling this story of the past, Özakman is clearly drawing lessons for the present.   METIN AND

P

Pacheco, Carlos Mauricio (1881–1924)

Uruguayan playwright. When he was four, his family returned to Buenos Aires, from whence it had fled following the death of General Urquiza. Pacheco spent the rest of his life in the Argentine capital, where he attended a French school. A journalist for several important Buenos Aires newspapers, he was attracted to the stage and he got a job as an actor with the company of the famous Jerónimo Podestá. Stage fright ruined his first appearance, and so he spent the rest of his life providing lines for other actors. A string of more than 100 comedies, tragedies, *zarzuelas*, and especially *sainetes* issued from his pen, beginning with *Whites and Reds* (*Blancos y colorados*, 1900), which he later called "a crime of my youth"; its humor was based on the rivalry of the two opposing political parties of Uruguay.

He joined with Pedro E. Pico (1882–1945) in writing *Creole Music* (*Música criolla*, 1906), whose leading role he himself sang, and *Don Costa and Company (Don Costa y compañía)* which exhibited significant dramatic progress. He found his special talent in writing *sainetes*, short plays revolving around a scene, trade, or tradition. He was the greatest *sainetero* of his time, roaming the streets of Buenos Aires at night and taking notes on interesting local color or local scenes.

He first made a name for himself with *The Masqueraders* (*Los disfrazados*, 1906), which takes place during a Buenos Aires carnival and introduces kindly Don Pietro, who never made fun of others but was easily deceived by his friends. Pacheco went on to turn out seventy colorful and lively plays including: *Don Quijote en la Pampa* (1907); *The River Bank* (*La ribera*, 1910); and *The Secret Police* (*La Mazorca*, 1915), a semihistorical play about the secret police of the dictator Rosas. He was not above falsifying details to get a laugh or turning comedy into melodrama. In *The Masqueraders* he introduced a character described as a *cocoliche*, whose barbarous Italianized Spanish became a standard feature of other writers' plays.

Lack of attention to health and bad eating habits as well as long hours at the Café de los Inmortales, gathering place of theatre folk, began to tell on his physical condition. Finally he sought cheaper living quarters in the city's suburbs, where he grew worse and died in 1924. This creator of *sainetes*, so colorful and completely national in spirit and detail, had to be buried at the expense of his friends and the club of which he was an honored, though impoverished, member.

WILLIS KNAPP JONES and JUDITH A. WEISS

CRITICISM

E. M. Barrera, "Aspectos del arte dramático de Pacheco," *LATR* 42, pp. 21–28, Spring 1971.

Pagnol, Marcel (1895–1974)

French novelist, film producer, and dramatist. He is perhaps best known for his charming Marseille trilogy— *Marius* (1929), *Fanny* (1931), and *César* (1936)—the last part of which first appeared as a film and was not reworked into a play until 1946. Against a background of the noisy, sundrenched life of the Old Port, Pagnol relates with direct and unpretentious warmth the romance of Fanny, who urges her lover Marius to follow his heart's desire and sail away on one of the ships that temptingly beckon from the harbor. When Marius returns to reclaim her, he discovers that Fanny, having found herself pregnant with his child, has married the elderly and kindly Panisse. For the sake of their son's future, Marius is persuaded to abandon his claim to Fanny. Twenty years later, after the death of Panisse, Marius and Fanny are reunited by their son.

Pagnol's first successful play was *Merchants of Glory* (*Les marchands de la gloire*, 1925), a satire on civilian profiteers who exploit the heroism of soldiers. It was followed by *Jazz* (1926), and in 1928 Pagnol's international reputation was established with *Topaze*, a witty examination of a naïve schoolteacher dominated by desire for money. Shortly after the introduction of sound films, Pagnol formed his own film company and began producing motion-picture versions of his plays as well as some remarkable films, such as *Harvest* (*Regain*, 1937; literally "aftergrowth") and *The Baker's Wife* (*La femme du boulanger*, 1938), based on the novels of Jean Giono. His later plays include *Judas* (1955), a somewhat uncharacteristic work in which he attempts to explain the betrayal of Christ, and *Fabien* (1956), a cynical account of Parisian mores. In 1946 Pagnol was the first "colloquial" writer

Marcel Pagnol (left) and Jules Romains. [French Cultural Services]

Catherine Rouvel and Jean-Louis Trintignant in *Marius*, Théâtre des Variétés, Paris. [French Cultural Services]

Scenes from *Topaze:* (left) Fernand Gravey in the title role; (right) Gravey and Marie Daëms. Paris, Théâtre du Gymnase, 1957. [French Cultural Services]

Ezio Pinza (left) and Walter Slezak in S. N. Behrman and Joshua Logan's *Fanny,* a musical based on Pagnol trilogy. New York, Majestic Theatre, 1954. [Theatre Collection, The New York Public Library at Lincoln Center, Astor, Lenox and Tilden Foundations]

and film maker to be elected to the Académie Française. *See* GIONO, JEAN.

Jazz (1926). Professor Blaise, who has devoted his life to scholarship, has attributed to Plato the worthless work of a copyist found in an Egyptian convent. Famous and about to be given a chair at the Sorbonne, he is destroyed by another professor of Greek who proves that what Blaise had thought to be *The Phaeton* is but a pastiche written by a first-century grammarian. To make matters worse, Blaise is found to be living with one of his students, the twenty-three-year-old Cécile, who, unable to love, has decided to devote herself to him and care for him. But a young student who loves her takes her away and marries her. Blaise's world falls apart, and he realizes that work of the mind is but nonsense: "Seek the pleasures of life, the one who is telling you failed to do this." Thus speaks Blaise as jazz music seems to invite him to seek pleasures he has ignored for too long. Produced Paris, Théâtre des Arts, December 22, 1926.

Topaze (1928). Naïvely believing in the moral precepts that decorate his classroom, Topaze loses his teaching position when he fails to understand the need to raise the grades of one of his wealthy students. He is tutoring in the home of Suzy Courtois, the mistress and accomplice of Régis Castel-Bénac, a dishonest local politician, when Suzy recruits him to serve as a front man for one of Régis's shady deals. Concocting an elaborate story, she charms Topaze into signing the necessary papers. Though Topaze eventually understands the use being made of him, he is persuaded by Suzy to remain silent. The experience, however, leads him to reconsider his view of life, and he is transformed.

Since the business agency that Suzy and Régis have set up is legally in his name, Topaze informs them that he has decided to run it for his own profit. Régis is furious but helpless. Suzy is charmed into sincere admiration for Topaze, who in a final scene apologetically explains to a former academic colleague that cynicism is the only attitude possible in a world ruled by money. Produced Paris, Théâtre des Variétés, October 11, 1928.

[JOSEPH E. GARREAU]

Pailleron, Édouard   (1834–1899)

French poet and dramatist. He was born in Paris on September 17, 1834, and died there on April 19, 1899. His comedies were extremely popular during the Third Republic but he is best known today for *The Art of Being Bored* (*Le monde où l'on s'ennuie* 1881), a satire on the cultural and social pretensions of Parisian society. Like Molière's *The Learned Ladies*, the play focuses on the literary airs of the female salon. A perennial favorite to this day, the comedy caused a certain amount of scandal in its time as its ludicrous and dishonest Professor Bellac was easily recognized as a thinly veiled portrait of a fashionable Sorbonne philosopher.

As the son-in-law of the director of the journal *La Revue des Deux Mondes*, Pailleron was an influential figure in both literary circles and the theatre. However, he belonged to no literary school, and his comedies were produced at a time when the stage was dominated by the realism of Henry Becque and Dumas *fils*. The success of these comedies was due to the contemporary wit of the dialogue and to Pailleron's talent for comic characterization. Among his more popular plays are *The Triumph of Youth, or The White Mouse* (*La souris*, 1887), in which two women compete for a middle-aged playboy; *Phonies!* (*Cabotins!*, 1894), a satire on bohemians and politicians;

Édouard Pailleron. [Theatre Collection, The New York Public Library at Lincoln Center, Astor, Lenox and Tilden Foundations]

and *The Spark* (*L'étincelle*, 1879), a comedy in which the heart of a young girl is moved by the spark of love.

The Art of Being Bored (*Le monde où l'on s'ennuie*, 1881). Subprefect Raymond and his bride are guests in the home of the pretentious and socially powerful Countess de Céran. Dominating this household is Professor Bellac, whose pedantic, pseudointellectual profundities keep the countess and her bluestocking friends in a constant state of swoon. The only dissenting voice is that of the countess's aunt, the old Duchess of Réville, who mocks this spawning ground of political and literary reputations. Despite the fact that they find their surroundings ridiculous, Raymond and his wife manage to feign sufficient admiration for the countess and her circle to assure the subprefect's promotion. Woven into this main plot is the romance of Roger de Céran, the countess's son, and Suzanne de Villiers, a relative and protégée of the countess. The two young lovers are finally united in spite of the fact that Suzanne has a temporary crush on Professor Bellac and that the countess is determined to marry her son to a lady of her own choosing. Produced Paris, Comédie-Française, April 25, 1881.

[JOSEPH E. GARREAU]

Palaprat, Jean   (1650–1721)

French dramatist. Gifted with a genuine comic flair, he did his best work in collaboration with David-Augustin de Brueys. Together they produced the highly successful comedy of manners *The Grumbler* (*Le grondeur*, 1691) and *The Mute* (*Le muet*, 1691), an ingenious comedy based on Terence's *The Eunuch*. They also wrote a number of one-act plays, including *The Ridiculous Concert* (*Le concert ridicule*, 1689), *The Secret Revealed* (*Le secret revélé*, 1690), and *Difficulties Backstage* (*Les embarras du derrière du théâtre*, wr. 1692/93). Palaprat may have had a hand in an earlier version of Brueys's *The Power of Blood* (*La force du sang*, pub. 1735). The plays he wrote by himself are of less interest, although the one-act satire on opera *The Extravagant Ballet* (*Le ballet extravagant*, 1690) is a lively comedy. His other plays include *Saturnalia, or The Prude of the Time* (*Les saturnales, ou La prude du temps*, 1693) and *Hercules and Omphale* (*Hercule et Omphale*, 1694). *See also* BRUEYS, DAVID-AUGUSTIN DE.

[JOSEPH E. GARREAU]

Panova, Vera Fyodorovna   (1905–1973)

Soviet Russian playwright and novelist. She was born on March 7, 1905, at Rostov-on-Don, and began her career as a journalist in 1922. Her first work in the theatre came in 1933 with *Springtime* (*Vesna*, produced at the Rostov Youth Theatre), which concerned an uprising of rich peasants on the Don. During World War II she acted as a newspaper correspondent attached to a hospital train, and her experiences appeared in such later plays as *Girls* (*Devochki*, 1945), about the plight of evacuees, and *The Captives* (*Plennye*, 1942), later rewritten as *The Snowstorm* (*Metelitsa*, 1956), to display the courage of various classes of Russian society under German occupation. These works were considerably more impassioned and purposeful than her earlier plays, *Ilya Kosogor* (1939) and *In Old Moscow* (*V staroy Moskve*, 1940), naturalistic depictions, in imitation of Gorky and his school, of the petit bourgeoisie traumatized by the Revolution.

Panova often remarked that she felt confined by dramatic form and during the 1950s devoted herself to her prose writing, which was copious, including nine novels. In the 1960s she returned to playwriting, now addressing herself to problems of moral responsibility, modern youth, and the family. Her plays of this period include *Farewell to White Nights* (*Provody belykh nochey*, 1961), *How Goes It, Lad?* (*Kak pozhivaesh, paren?*, 1962), and *It's Been Ages* (*Skolko let, skolko zhit!*, 1966). They are all models of socialist realism, full of carefully observed psychological detail and homiletic intention as well as the poetical echoes of Chekhov, so common to Soviet playwriting. She received three Stalin prizes (1947, 1948, and 1950) and her works were frequently filmed. She died in Leningrad, where she lived with her engineer husband, on March 6, 1973.   LAURENCE SENELICK

EDITIONS

Ilya Kosogor. V staroy Moskve. Metelitsa. Devochki, Leningrad, 1958; *Skolko let, skolko zhit!* in *Novyy Mir* no. 7 (July 1966); *It's Been Ages,* tr. by F. D. Reeve, in *Contemporary Russian Drama,* New York, 1968.

CRITICISM

Z. Boguslavskaya, *Vera Panova,* Moscow, 1963; A. Ninov, "Dramaturgiya Very Panovoy," *Sibirskie ogni,* no. 9, 1963.

Papadat-Bengescu, Hortensia   (1877–1956)

Romanian novelist and dramatist. In her naturalistic plays, such as *The Old Man* (*Batrinul*, 1921), *A Star Has Fallen* (*A cazut o stea*), and *My Sister Anna* (*Sora mea Ana*), Papadat-Bengescu makes no concessions to the sensibilities of middle-class audiences as she analyzes her characters in the urban environment of Bucharest. Choosing her protagonists from the poor, the timid, and the failures in life, she allows them to describe the conditions of physical and moral degradation in which they find themselves. The most viable of her plays is *The Old Man*, which focuses on the psychological reactions of the title character as he discovers the unscrupulous nature of members of his own family.

The dramatist also turns her attention to the position of women in Romanian society of the 1920s and 1930s in *A Star Has Fallen* and *My Sister Anna*. In *A Star Has Fallen* she presents the conflict between an honest woman and an opportunistic man who remains indifferent to the havoc he wreaks. *My Sister Anna* concerns the frustrations of a young woman obliged to sacrifice her youth and love to care for her younger brother and sister.
                                                      RUTH S. LAMB

CRITICISM

E. Lovinescu, *Istoria Literaturii Romane Contemporane,* Bucharest, 1937; H. Papadat-Bengescu, "Despre Teatru," in *Almanahul Teatrului Romanesc,* Bucharest, 1943.

Parabosco, Girolamo   (ca. 1524–1557)

Italian writer, musician, and dramatist. His eight comedies were largely inspired by Boccaccio's *Decameron*, upon which he also modeled his own collection of novellas, *I diporti*. His comedy in verse *The Pilgrim* (*Il pellegrino*, 1552) concerns Gilberto's unrequited love for Clizia and incorporates the usual devices of disguise and mistaken identity. Parabosco wrote only one tragedy, *The Swallow* (*La progne*, 1548), and it is the weakest of his plays. His theatrical talents lay exclusively in the creation of intricate comic situations.

[PETER BONDANELLA]

Parker, Stewart   (1942–   )

Irish-born playwright. Born in Belfast in 1942 as a Protestant, Parker left Ireland at the age of twenty-two to teach composition at Hamilton College in Clinton, N.Y. After two and a half years at Hamilton, Parker moved to nearby Cornell University in Ithaca, N.Y., where he taught creative writing. In 1969 he moved back to Ireland, where he stayed for ten years. He now lives in Edinburgh, Scotland. He has written six radio dramas, three television plays, and three full-length stage plays: *Catchpenny Twist* (1977), *I'm a Dreamer* (1979), and *Spokesong*, his most popular work, which had its premiere at the Dublin Theatre Festival in 1975, was produced in London in 1976, and received its first American production at the Long Wharf Theater in New Haven.

Spokesong (1975). The story of a bicycle-shop owner, Frank, who is passionately convinced that bicycles will be the salvation of the modern city. Frank is a romantic with great nostalgia for the past. His brother Julian, who had been in London, where he became an anarchist, has now returned home determined to destroy what he sees as a hopelessly corrupt society. The conflict between these two brothers lies in Parker's exploration of the roots of the present-day conflict between Protestants and Catholics in Northern Ireland. The story really concerns Frank's painful education into the realities of Belfast life. The play includes a conventional love story and a chorus figure called the Trick Cyclist who sings most of the songs and embodies the spirit of Belfast. Jimmy Kennedy, who wrote "Red Sails in the Sunset," "Isle of Capri," and "South of the Border," did the music for the songs. There are seven songs, ranging from an 1890s music hall song to a 1930s Noel Coward type of song. Not only does the play span eighty years, but it also operates in many styles, from realism to expressionism.

Nightshade (1980). The story of Quinn, a mortician, who performs as an amateur magician, ably assisted by his attractive but morbid tap-dancing daughter, Delia. The disappearance (and death?) of his wife, a strike of coffin-bearers, and the subsequent collapse of the business lead him to a complete breakdown and a kind of living death. Images, allegories, and fairy-tales are all mixed in with bewildering complexity. *Nightshade* is black comedy.

CAROL GELDERMAN

Paso Gil, Alfonso   (1926–1978)

Spanish dramatist. He treated matters of social and emotional content in the framework of comedy, as in *Oh, Mama! Oh, Papa!* (*Cosas de papá y mamá*, 1960), in which widowed older people contract psychosomatic ailments

Alfonso Paso Gil.
[New York
Public Library
Picture Collection]

because they have lost interest in life; *The Poor Little Ones* (*Los pobrecitos*, 1957), a tragicomedy in which starvation is a real and present fear for the poor; and *The Girl's Wedding* (*La boda de la chica*, 1960), in which the difficulties of the lower classes in Madrid are contrasted with the comfort of their wealthy neighbors. Among other works by Paso are *The Sky in the Home* (*El cielo dentro de casa*, 1957); *You Too Can Be an Assassin* (*Usted puede ser asesino*, 1958); *Dinner for Married Couples* (*Cena de matrimonios*, 1958); *Poison for My Husband* (*Veneno para mi marido*, 1953), which portrays the differences between visual and imaginary reality; *Forty-eight Hours of Happiness* (*Cuarenta y ocho horas de felicidad*, 1956); *I'm Sorry, Mr. García* (*Lo siento, señor García*, 1957); *Judgment Against a Scoundrel* (*Juicio contra un sinverguenza*, 1958); *Your Relatives Don't Forget You* (*Tus parientes no te olvidan*, 1959); *There Is No [Special] News, Adela* (*No hay novedades, doña Adela*, 1959); *Catalina Isn't Proper* (*Catalina no es formal*, 1957); *There Is Someone Behind the Door* (*Hay alguien detrás de la puerta*, 1958); *Papa Gets Angry about Everything* (*Papá se enfada por todo*, 1959); *Nice People* (*Las buenas personas*, 1961); *The Necktie* (*La corbata*, 1963); and *The Office* (*La oficina*, 1965).

In terms of sheer output, Paso ranks among the most prolific Spanish playwrights of this century, along with Benavente, Serafín and Joaquín Alvarez Quintero, and Muñoz Seca. In the sixties and early seventies, he virtually monopolized the Madrid stage, as Benavente had once done. The social preoccupations present in some of his earlier plays eventually gave way to more frivolous themes. A dissident in his youth, Paso became increasingly conservative as he got older. His right-wing attitudes did not prevent him, however, from contributing to the wave of pornography that swept the Spanish theatre following the death of Franco in November, 1975. As is frequently the case of playwrights who achieve extraordinary commercial success, Paso's theatre is more interesting as a sociological phenomenon than it is as dramatic art.

ANDRÉS FRANCO

CRITICISM

A. Marquerie, *Alfonso Paso y su teatro*, Madrid, 1960; F. Ruiz Ramón, *Historia del teatro español: Siglo XX*, Madrid, 1977 (3d. ed.), pp. 422–429.

Passeur, Stève   (1899–1966)

French dramatist; pseudonym of Étienne Morin. Passeur was born in Sedan on September 24, 1899, and died in Paris on October 12, 1966. His reputation flourished in the period between the two world wars, when his psychological dramas of the war between the sexes were considered to be in the tradition of Strindberg, though the link with the somewhat explosive theatre of Henry Bernstein now seems more obvious. Passeur's best-known play is *The Buyer* (*L'acheteuse*, 1930), a study of a sadomasochistic marriage. Another of his successes is *I Shall Live a Great Love* (*Je vivrai un grand amour*, 1935), in which one of his typically determined heroines decides that her love for a weak and opportunistic man will be the dominant passion of her life and forthwith engages in a coldly intellectual struggle to win him. By and large Passeur's protagonists are more deeply involved with the idea of love than with love itself. In *The Cheaters* (*Les tricheurs*, 1932), the luckless Jewish hero rigorously denies himself physical possession of the woman he supposedly adores, and she, though indifferent to him, bends all her efforts to make him succumb to her. Other plays by Passeur include *The Chain* (*La chaîne*, 1931), *The House of Cards* (*Le château de cartes*, 1937), and *No Matter What for Her* (*N'importe quoi pour elle*, 1954), a historical play in which physical torture is added to the delights of psychological torture.

The Buyer (*L'acheteuse*, 1930). By paying a debt for which Gilbert would otherwise have gone to prison, Elizabeth, an unattractive spinster, contrives to have him

Scene from a 1947 production of *Je vivrai un grand amour*.
[French Cultural Services]

marry her. When he attempts to desert her for his mistress, Elizabeth's thwarted love turns to hate, but she insists on her claim to what she has "purchased." Though Elizabeth and Gilbert remain together, since they are both denied love, they feed on hate. By the time circumstances remove Gilbert's financial obligation, he has become so well accustomed to the humiliation and suffering he and Elizabeth inflict on one another that he is reluctant to leave her and has to be forced to do so by his father. Elizabeth, denied hate as well as love, prepares to commit suicide as the curtain descends. Produced Paris, Théâtre de l'Oeuvre, April 7, 1930.

[JOSEPH E. GARREAU]

Patrick, John (1907–)

American screenwriter and dramatist. Patrick's experiences as an ambulance driver with the American Field Service during World War II resulted in *The Hasty Heart* (1945), a touching comedy, set in a British Army hospital in Burma, showing the importance of men's interdependence. His Pulitzer Prize-winning *The Teahouse of the August Moon* (1953), a dramatization of Vern Sneider's novel, deals with the hilarious efforts of the military mind to Americanize a remote village in Okinawa. Patrick's other, less successful plays include *Hell Freezes Over* (1935); *The Willow and I* (1942); *The Story of Mary Suratt* (1947); *The Curious Savage* (1950); *Lo and Behold* (1951); *Good as Gold* (1957); *Juniper and the Pagans* (1959); *Everybody Loves Opal* (1961); *Love Is a Time of Day* (1969); and *Lovely Ladies, Kind Gentlemen* (1970). His numerous screenplays include *Three Coins in the Fountain* (1954),

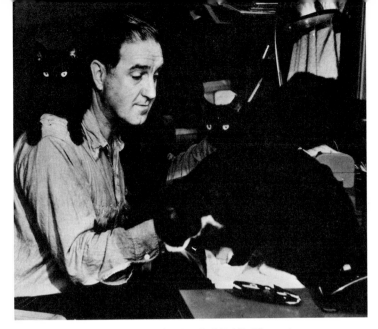

John Patrick. [Theatre Collection, The New York Public Library at Lincoln Center, Astor, Lenox and Tilden Foundations]

Love Is a Many Splendored Thing (1955), *The Teahouse of the August Moon* (1956), and *Les Girls* (1957).

The Hasty Heart (1945). Comedy drama set in the convalescent ward of a British military hospital on the Burma front during World War II. The tranquillity and good-natured banter of the patients are disrupted by the arrival of Sergeant Lachlen McLachlen, a belligerent, dour young Scot, unaware that he has only six weeks to live. The other patients, knowing this, tolerate his "por-

The Hasty Heart, with John Lund (third from right). New York, Hudson Theatre, 1945. [Photograph by Vandamm. Theatre Collection, The New York Public Library at Lincoln Center, Astor, Lenox and Tilden Foundations]

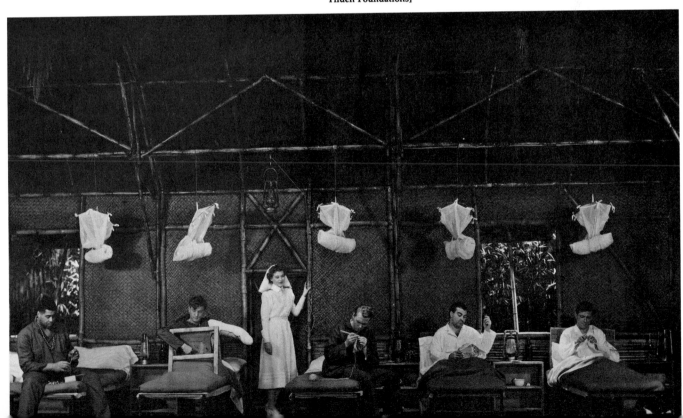

cupine disposition." Finally, through the efforts of a sympathetic American and a compassionate nurse, McLachlen, who is told of his impending death, accepts his fate and begins to realize the value of friendship. Produced New York, Hudson Theatre, January 3, 1945.

The Teahouse of the August Moon (1953). Comedy in which Captain Fisby, sent to Tobiki, Okinawa, to introduce democracy and make the village self-supporting, finds that the only marketable item the villagers produce is potato brandy. Fisby therefore launches them into the brandy business, an enterprise that immediately makes them wealthy. The villagers then vote to use their wealth for a teahouse, rejecting the schoolhouse suggested by the Army; democracy, they have learned, is the will of the majority. At first all goes well. Fisby "goes native," as does the psychiatrist sent to investigate him. Finally, however, Purdy, Fisby's perplexed commanding officer, arrives to survey his officer's accomplishments. Forthwith, he orders the stills and the teahouse destroyed. Although ostensibly razed, the equipment has in reality been hidden. Thus, when a congressional committee, impressed by the villagers' enterprise, comes to visit Tobiki, the teahouse is instantly reassembled. Produced New York, Martin Beck Theatre, October 15, 1953.

[GAUTAM DASGUPTA]

Patrick, Robert (1937–   )

American playwright and actor. His prolific output is characterized by a skillful use of language and the willingness to experiment with diverse modes of dramatic form. *The Haunted Host* (1964) deals humorously (and

Kennedy's Children, with William Devane and Shirley Knight. [Martha Swope]

sympathetically) with the life of a homosexual author who shares a room with the ghost of his dead lover. Through feverish dialogue and fervent stage antics, Patrick creates in most of his plays brief but intense moments of charming theatrical interludes. *Lights, Camera, Action* (1967), a trio of three short skits, offers compelling portraits of human relationships torn asunder by the encroachment of technology and the mechanics of the moving picture—only to point out indirectly the inherent value and power of the immediacy of theatrical encounters. *Still-Love* (1967) is a love story enacted in reverse, and *I Came to New York to Write* (1969) is a series of short plays in chronological succession, each depicting a certain facet of New York life. It is impossible to list Patrick's entire oeuvre, let alone keep up with it. His plays project, at best, a chic, urbane landscape in which the necessity of creating a joyous milieu is highly stressed. *Presenting Arnold Bliss* (1969), another series charting the life of an actor, manages to disarm its audience by gently prodding us about the after-effects of American consumerism and the mass media. *The Golden Circle* (1972) is Patrick's foray into Rosicrucian ritual as characters named after the signs of the Zodiac engage in mythic encounters that have to do with brotherhood, power struggles, and the like. Although to all intents and purposes Patrick has come to symbolize the formidable signal-post of Off-Off Broadway playwriting, his play *Kennedy's Children* (1973) did take him to Broadway after establishing its reputation in London. Basically a series of monologues in a downtown New York bar, the play captures the spirit of a lost generation set adrift in a post-Kennedy-assassination America. Imbued with an aching nostalgia for the Camelot-that-could-have-been, the characters—who range from a Vietnam veteran to a Greenwich Village homosexual to a Marilyn Monroe–type blonde—weave a tender and eloquent tapestry of the social fabric of America in this musically structured play. Other plays by Patrick include *Camera Obscura* (1968), *Fog* (1969), and *T-Shirt* (1981).

GAUTAM DASGUPTA

Peele, George (ca. 1557/58–1596)

English dramatist. He was born in London in 1557 or 1558. His father, James Peele, clerk of Christ's Hospital, was associated with the Ironmongers' pageant of 1566. Peele attended Christ Church, Oxford, and received his B.A. degree in 1577 and his M.A. degree in 1579. He remained at Oxford until 1581 and then spent a year or two in London, where he married. He was called back to Oxford in 1583 to attend to his wife's business affairs, and at this time he staged William Gager's Latin plays *Rivales* and *Dido.*

He is believed to have settled permanently in London, the year of *The Arraignment of Paris,* the earliest of his five extant plays. He wrote for the stage, both public and private, until 1594 and was one of the "university wits." He was a great wit and riotous liver. Several jest books are ascribed to him. Between 1585 and 1595 he wrote several of the Lord Mayor's pageants, four of which are extant.

Peele died in London "by the pox," according to Francis Mere's *Palladis Tamis,* at the age of thirty-eight or thirty-nine. He was buried at St. James's, Clerkenwell, on November 9, 1596.

WORK

George Peele's work, like Lyly's, was important in the transition from the crude plays of public theatres to the literary drama of the later Elizabethans. He experimented widely in various genres fashionable in the decade before he died. His first, and perhaps his best work was a court play, *The Arraignment of Paris* (ca. 1584), which appealed through its poetic fantasy and its pastoral pageantry; Peele used the myth of Paris's judgment between three goddesses to pay an extravagant compliment to Queen Elizabeth. *See* LYLY, JOHN.

The Arraignment of Paris was followed by a rather crude chronicle play, *Edward I* (ca. 1592/93; an adventurous patriotic play, *The Battle of Alcazar* (ca. 1589); a Biblical play in ornate verse, *The Love of King David and Fair Bethsabe* (ca. 1593/94); and a burlesque, *The Old Wives' Tale* (ca. 1591/94), Peele's only surviving comedy. *The Old Wives' Tale* joins romance to a medley of folk incidents, and the action of the whole, though tangled, is delightful. The language is a blend of homely prose and blank verse interrupted by pleasant lyrics.

Although Peele satirized contemporary romantic plays, he himself was as romantic as he was realistic. Throughout his work domestic realism blends with classical myth and legend.

The Arraignment of Paris (ca. 1584). Pastoral comedy recounting the classical story of Paris and designed to flatter Queen Elizabeth. Paris is assigned the task of awarding Ate's Golden Apple to one of three bickering goddesses, Venus, Juno, and Minerva. Dazzled by a vision presented to him by Venus, Paris awards the apple to the goddess of love and thereupon is arraigned before a council of nine deities, including Jupiter and Saturn, to justify his choice. He defends himself so ably that his judges are left in a quandary as to who deserves the apple. Sidestepping the issue, they decide that since the incident occurred in a vale of Ida, Diana's domain, she should adjudicate the matter. After protracted hedging, Diana resolves the problem by awarding the prize to a nymph significantly named Eliza.

The Old Wives' Tale (ca. 1591/94). Comic play-within-a-play that combines elements of fantasy, reality, folklore, romantic adventure, and literary criticism to cast a travesty of chivalric romance within the frame of an old wives' tale. Three knights-errant, Antic, Frolic, and Fantastic, starving and lost in a forest, are rescued by Old Clunch, a smith, who takes them to his cottage. After Madge, his wife, has served her guests supper, she decides to entertain them with a tale, which is no sooner begun than it is interrupted by the arrival of the story's characters, who proceed to act out their parts. The narrative concerns Sacrapant, an evil magician who has imprisoned the fair damsel Delia in a castle; and Venelia, who has been driven mad, and her husband, Erestus, changed into an old man by day and a bear stationed at

a crossroads by night. There follows a tangled series of incidents involving numerous townsfolk and adventurers who, intent on freeing Delia, pass the crossroads. At length, Eumenides, a virtuous knight, assisted by the ghost of Jack the Giant Killer, who is beholden to Eumenides because the latter paid for his burial, kills Sacrapant and frees his victims.

PLAYS

All were first performed in London.
See STATIONERS' REGISTER in glossary.
    1. *The Arraignment of Paris.* Pastoral, 5 acts. Published 1584. Produced Children of the Chapel, ca. 1584.
    2. *The Battle of Alcazar.* Tragedy, 5 acts. Published 1594. Produced Admiral's Men, ca. 1589.
    3. *Edward I.* Chronicle, 5 acts. Published 1593 (Stationers' Register, Oct. 8, 1593). Produced 1592/1593.
    4. *The Love of King David and Fair Bethsabe.* Tragedy, 5 acts; verse. Published 1599 (Stationers' Register, May 14, 1594). Produced ca. 1593/94.
    5. *The Old Wives' Tale.* Comedy, 5 acts. Published 1595 (Stationers' Register, Apr. 16, 1595). Produced Queen's Men, ca. 1591/94.

EDITIONS

Collections
Dramatic and Literary Works, ed. by A. H. Bullen, 2 vols., New York, 1888; *The Dramatic Works of George Peele,* ed. by C. T. Prouty, vol. 2, New Haven, 1961.
Individual Plays
    The Arraignment of Paris. Published *in English Drama, 1580–1642,* ed. by C. F. T. Brooke and N. B. Paradise, Boston, 1933.
    The Love of King David and Fair Bethsabe. Published in *Minor Elizabethan Drama,* vol. 1, London, 1939.
    The Old Wives' Tale. Published in *Five Elizabethan Comedies,* ed. by A. K. McIlwraith, London, 1934.

CRITICISM

D. H. Horne, *The Life and Minor Works of George Peele,* New Haven, Conn., 1952; W. Senn, *Studies in the Dramatic Construction of Robert Greene and George Peele,* Berne, 1973; L. R. H. Ashley, *George Peele,* New York, 1976.

Peking Opera

The most celebrated of the traditional genres of Chinese theatre, Peking opera was born about 1830, though some of its aspects were of much earlier origin. Embracing a variety of other styles of dramatic and musical presentation, it became a fairly homogeneous independent genre in the mid-nineteenth century, maturing into a golden age in about the years 1870–1900. It has remained the major genre of Chinese drama in the twentieth century. *See* CHINESE THEATRE.

The Peking opera plays are usually short—almost two-thirds the length of traditional plays—and consist of one, two, or more acts or episodes from old *zaju* and *chuanqi* dramas of the Yuan, Ming, and Qing dynasties, with the rest deriving from histories, novels, and other writings. This means that background knowledge is often essential to full understanding of a play. There tend to be fewer songs in the texts than in other genres, but the extended manner of singing partly compensates for this. Much depends on the singing in some plays. The respectable young lady roles *(dan)* sing plaintively; the young scholars or young warrior heroes *(sheng)* use falsetto voices; old and lofty male straight roles may sing deeply and more naturally; the forceful *jing* roles (such as warriors and villains) sing raucously and violently; and the comic roles *(chou)* rely mainly on racy, colloquial speech. Apart from the comic roles, a special pronunciation is used, deriving from Anhui, Hubei, and Sichuan provinces and Peking. In Peking opera there are four main role categories (*sheng, dan, jing,* and *chou*) with thirty or more subcategories.

The music is chiefly of two styles, Erhuang-*diao* and Xipi-*diao*—the former for graver or lyrically emotional moments, and the latter for passages of lively cheer or excitement. Orchestras are small. Percussion instruments regulate timing and pace of movements; strings and sometimes the flute accompany or back up the singing. Exits, entrances, and tensions or climaxes are signaled or marked by music, which also provides bridge passages. Early in the nineteenth century the flute is said to have been the leading instrument, but later it was supplanted by the skirling *huqin*-fiddle. In the 1930s the deeper *erhu*-fiddle was introduced.

The guises consist of headgear, a wide variety of costumes, facial makeup, and special footwear. Many of the costumes were inherited from *Kunqu* theatre, but there have been alterations and innovations. Its general qualities are ornateness, symbolism, and type identification, rather than historical accuracy or realism. Rich silks are used for many roles, such as grandee roles, while cottons and simpler attire serve for more humble roles, such as clowns. Colors indicate rank, status, or individual character: an emperor wears yellow robes, important good mandarins wear red, and youth is indicated by pink or turquoise. The costumes are adorned with pictorial motifs and abstract patterns, which have a symbolic significance or designate type—for instance, a tiger's-head motif often appears on a warrior's garb. For young female roles, a major art for the actor to master has been that of walking on false brass-shod wooden "feet," which are bandaged to the ankles to simulate tiny bound feet. Like the showiness of costumes, the colorfulness of much Peking opera makeup may originally have been devised to facilitate audience identification of characters in performances on high stages in vast outdoor spaces. The makeup is generally nonrealistic. The most elaborate face paintings (*lianpu*) are used for *jing* roles. In them, color and pattern symbolize character or signal a type or a particular person. Red, white, black, blue, yellow, green, gold, and purple are used—black, for instance, to convey straightforward integrity. Some famous recurrent characters have their own special makeup. There have been up to five-hundred face patterns in Peking opera, but far fewer are used nowadays.

Until recently no naturalistic scenery was used, but a limited number of objects—principally tables, chairs, cloths, boards, and some small props—assisted the players' words and actions. A brick-patterned cloth or a table can represent a city wall, a wavy-lined board can mean clouds, and chairs can suggest a loom or a well. The spoken or sung word and the actor's gestures also frequently replace props, but swords, spears, tasseled whips, and fly whisks are among the articles wielded on stage. Mime, as when sewing, can be minutely exquisite. Many gestures and movements are symbolic; certain sleeve movements, for instance, sometimes express worry, anger, pleasure, or other feelings. There is likewise a wide range of hand, leg, and other actions which have special meanings. Much of the walking and posturing is done to fixed tempos.

More esoteric than many other genres, traditional Peking opera is attractive even to those who are not connoisseurs, and the more dancelike, acrobatic, and otherwise spectacular items of its repertoire have found much favor with non-Chinese audiences on international tours. There have been modernizations in theme and form, but the largely traditional form of Peking opera still prevails.

The following are some of the best-known plays from the extensive repertoire of Peking opera.

Buying Rouge (*Mai yan-zhi*). Pretty young Wang Yueying is looking after the family cosmetics shop while her mother is out, but her mind is on a young man who has recently visited the shop. Presently the young man, Guo Hua, a scholar neglecting his studies for the imperial examinations, comes into the shop to buy some rouge as a gift for "someone," Wang Yueying herself. As they go behind the counter, their love is forestalled by the appearance of a haberdasher, whose mirror discloses Guo still trying to hide behind the counter. Guo bribes the man to make himself scarce, and snatching a girdle from the haberdasher, he threatens to hang himself with it unless Wang Yueying opens the door, which she has meanwhile barred behind him. As the two young people once more prepare to make love, the pestiferous haberdasher interferes again, and Guo to his abashment plants a kiss on the salesman's mouth instead of Yueying's.

A one-act *zaju* farce, written to be performed with the styles of music and acting known as Bangzi-*qiang* and Chui-*qiang*, it was popular late in the eighteenth century and early in the nineteenth century. It is part of a larger story ultimately deriving from a collection compiled in A.D. 977. The general story was used in earlier plays: an anonymous Yuan *zaju* called *Leaving the Slipper* (*Liu-xie ji*), an early Ming or Yuan *nanxi* of the same title, and a Ming play, a *nanxi* or *chuanqi* entitled *Rouge* (*Yan-zhi ji*).

Capture and Release of Cao Cao (*Zhuo-fang Cao*). Villainous warlord Cao Cao, having just failed in an attempt to assassinate the tyrant Dong Zhuo, comes into the hands of the virtuous magistrate Chen Gong, whom he persuades to join him in his flight and quest to overthrow Dong. As they flee, they stop for a while at the house of kindly Lü Boshe, a sworn brother of Cao Cao's father. While Lü is out, the hypersuspicious Cao hears wild cries, and jumps to the conclusion that he has been betrayed, and kills every member of Lü's household. Chen Gong then discovers that the cries had only been the slaughtering of a pig intended to feast Cao. As they flee once more, Cao and Chen meet Lü returning. Despite Chen's pleading, the bitter, ruthless Cao chops Lü down, too. Shortly after, Chen and Cao take lodging together at an inn. As Cao sleeps, Chen ponders the vileness of his companion and at one point draws his sword to dispatch the villain. Not wishing, however, to let it be thought that he was an adherent of Dong Zhuo's, he instead writes an insulting verse, which he leaves on the table before riding away. When Cao awakes at dawn, he discovers the poem and furiously vows to revenge himself one day on Chen.

This story is based on chapter four of the novel *Saga of the Three Kingdoms (San-guo yan-yi)*, written during the fourteenth century. The chapter is partly based on historical events of A.D. 189.

Cosmos Point (*Yu-zhou Feng*). One of the favorites of the famous actor Mei Lanfang (1894–1961), the play is set under the Second Emperor (r. 209–207 B.C.) of the notorious Qin dynasty. The ruthless prime minister Zhao Gao has married his daughter to Kuang Fu, but later turns on the Kuang family, accusing them of stealing the sword known as Cosmos Point in order to assassinate the Second Emperor. All the Kuang family has been arrested, except Fu himself, whom Zhao's daughter helped escape. Others now assume that Fu is dead. The Second Emperor, visiting Zhao, is much taken with his daughter and wants to have her as a wife. Zhao is only too eager, but the girl refuses, but then realizing that mere refusal will not succeed, she does as her maidservant suggests and pretends to be insane. With great courage and skill she carries through the act of insanity; furthermore, she even uses her madness as a pretext for a face-to-face attack on the Second Emperor's wicked rule. Even his threat of execution does not throw her off guard, and eventually she is dismissed, while Zhao Gao is fined three months' salary. The play rests entirely on the girl's convincing portrayal of her madness, which has to appear real to the Emperor but obviously an act to the audience. More difficult still, while she is acting insane, she has to convey most sanely her inner thoughts to the audience through the medium of songs.

Empty City Ruse (*Kong-cheng ji*). A favorite with both Chinese audiences and foreigners, this spectacular play combines superb tension and plot with a feast of acrobatics. It derives in origin from the fourteenth-century novel *Saga of the Three Kingdoms (San-guo yan-yi)*. Sima Yi, the grand general of Wei, attacks the region of Mount Qi, and Zhuge Liang, the master strategist of the state of Shu, sends his general Ma Su to defend the key point of Jieting. Ma fails, and Sima presses on to menace Xicheng city, where Liang is left with hardly any forces to defend it. Liang sends a few elderly soldiers to sweep the streets at the wide-open city gates, while he himself ascends with his usual feather fan and silk tasselled cap to the open top of the tower above the gates. There, attended only by two pages, he casually sets out table and dulcimer, and airily plays music as if in calm and tranquil seclusion. Sima arrives with his army, and seeing Liang playing so imperturbably assumes—as Liang intends—that it is a trick of his wily enemy, that there must be an ambush lurking within the city. Retreating, he soon learns, however, that he has been fooled, that the city is virtually empty. As he advances once more, the doughty Shu general Zhao Yun rushes to the rescue, in response to an urgent message from Liang, and Sima sagely withdraws.

Kuen Su-shuang in the legend play *The Theft of the Miraculous Herb*. [Peking Opera, 1956]

This play is acted in other genres, such as *jinju* and *huiju*. Sometimes only the episode of the ruse is performed, the *Kong-cheng ji* proper, but what is known as "the whole *Kong-cheng ji*" includes the episodes *Losing Jieting (Shi Jie-ting)* and *Executing Ma Su (Zhan Ma Su)*, the latter being a final scene in which Liang executes Ma for having disobeyed his instructions. This is also known collectively as *Losing, Empty, and Execution (Shi kong zhan)*.

Hegemon King Says Farewell to His Queen (*Ba-wang bie-ji*). Xiang Yu, Hegemon king of Chu, is contending with Liu Bang, king of Han, for mastery of China, but is now isolated and enfeebled. The time has finally come for him to establish himself, or to be broken. The strategic counselor Li Zuoche pretends to change allegience to Xiang's side, and in spite of warnings, Xiang accepts his treacherous advice to go forth against the Han forces. The loyal general Yu Ziqi persuades Xiang's beloved queen, Yu, to try and change the monarch's mind, but Xiang is too headstrong, although he sees the soundness of her counsel. The snapping of a flag and the sudden neighing of his horse, Raven Dapple, are an ill-omened prelude to the battle, and soon it is discovered that Li Zuoche has absconded. Shortly, Liu Bang and Xiang challenge each other, and the fighting begins. Li Zuoche, atop a crag, first urges Xiang to surrender, then lures him into ambush. Xiang Yu is routed and barely man-

Ma Lianliang as Cheng Ying in the Peking opera version of *Zhao-shi gu-er.* [*Beijing jingjutuan fu-Gang yanchutuan,* Hong Kong, 1963]

ages to escape back to his camp.

Yet, despite Queen Yu's advice, Xiang will not rest on the defensive. As he sleeps, she secretly wanders through the camp. Liu Bang's chief general, Han Xin, has his men sing songs of Chu. These are heard by Xiang's men, who assume that Liu Bang has by now conquered Chu, their homeland, and become demoralized. Learning this, the Queen tragically awakens Xiang. He, too, is filled with despair and decides to go forth and fight in one last mighty fling. He has Raven Dapple brought, sadly addresses his noble charger, and then drinks awhile with Queen Yu. He sings a famous song of farewell to his horse and her. She does a sword dance for him and then cuts her throat so that he will not be hampered by longings for her.

After several days of fighting, Xiang is trapped and ambushed in utter defeat by the Yangtse. He sets his horse free and it loyally jumps into the river; Xiang cuts his throat.

This play derives from the long novel *Saga of the*

Western Han (*Xi Han yan-yi*), attributed to Zhong Xing (d. 1625), and other sources. There were earlier plays about Xiang Yu, such as the thirteenth-century *Hegemon King Lifts the Caldrons (Ba-wang ju-ding)* by Gao Wenxiu and *Saying Farewell To Queen Yu (Bie Yu-ji)* by Zhang Shiqi. This Peking opera was a favorite work of the famous actor Mei Lanfang (1894–1961).

Jade Hall Spring (Yu-tang chun). The singing girl and courtesan Su San and the young scholar Wang Jinlong are in love, but once the bawd has deprived the young man of all his money, she drives him away, and later tricks Su San into becoming the number-two wife of a wealthy merchant, Shen Yanlin. Shen's number-one wife, Madam Pi, tries to kill her with poisoned noodles, but Shen eats them instead. The number-one wife accuses Su San of the murder and bribes the magistrate, who cruelly forces a confession. Su San is thrown into jail, to wait for the ratification of her death sentence. Meanwhile, Jinlong has been successful in the imperial examinations, thanks to Su San's financial help, and now holds the lofty post of inspecting commissioner. He presides over a retrial of Su San's case. Finally justice is done and the lovers united in marriage.

This is a much longer and more involved play than the summary above may indicate. There are intricacies concerning their early love and her journey to the retrial in the company of a kindly warder, Chong Gongdao. Above all, the retrial is fraught with emotional and dramatic tensions. Su San long fails to recognize Jinlong, and he is agonizingly unable to disclose the partiality of his feelings toward the prisoner in court. The title of the play is the name of the bower where the lovers initially dally in pleasure. Often only excerpts are performed, most commonly those *Girl under Escort (Nü qi-jie)* and *Trial by Three Judges (San-tang hui-shen),* the latter referring to the fact that the retrial is also jointly conducted by two other mandarins.

Lady Yang Gets Drunk (Gui-fei zui-jiu). This is a snippet from the historical and legendary cycle of the romance between Emperor Minghuang (Xuanzong; r. 712–756) and his favorite wife, Lady Yang Taizhen (Yang Gui-fei). The Emperor has instructed Lady Yang to prepare a party for him in the Hundred Flowers Pavilion, but on arrival she discovers that he has gone instead to give his favors to her rival, Empress Mei. Attended by her eunuch chamberlains Gao and Pei, Lady Yang seeks to drown her sorrows in wine. To avoid a scandal, they scheme to make her return to the palace and stop drinking, at one point even pretending that the Emperor has indeed arrived; but by coaxing, threatening, and slapping them, she obliges them to bring her more and more wine, until after much knockabout and farce, her drunkenness is transformed into more sober sorrow again, and she agrees to be led back.

The success of this play, another of the favorites of the famous actor Mei Lanfang, greatly depends on the minute stress of the right words and gestures, and on maintaining a perfect balance on the tightrope of the psychological portrayal of Lady Yang's mixture of sorrow, wrath, and befuddledness. In particular the slaps she deals have to be executed resoundingly, but in a manner that in no way detracts from her elevated femininity.

Longing for Laity (*Si-fan*). Pretty young girl Zhao Sekong (Zhao "Materiality Void") is an unwilling Buddhist nun who longs for worldly love. Soliloquizing her sorrows, she poohpoohs Buddhism's superstitions and the institution that binds her, and then takes a stroll through the cloisters. Avalokhitesvara, goddess of mercy, and her attendants and holy arhats listen to her as she further declares her yearning for romance and resolves to flee to the lay world. Clearly it is not the plot but, rather, the speech, song, and suggestive miming of this piece that constitute its main attractions. It is identical with act nine of part five of the play *Golden Statutes for Promoting Virtue* (*Quan-shan jin-ke*) by Zhang Zhao (1691–1745), possibly deriving from an earlier play. Later, the appearance of the goddess in the play was often omitted.

Mountain Pavilion (*Shan-ting*). To escape the consequences of crime, Lu Da has turned monk in a monastery on Five Terraces Mountain, changing his name to Lu Zhishen (Lu "Wisdom Deep"). His name changes, but his booming, bullying, bibulous nature does not, and in this play he bursts forth again in no uncertain terms.

Actors performing in the Peking opera *Jiang-xiang he.* [*Beijing jingjutuan fu-Gang yanchutuan,* Hong Kong, 1963]

Qiu Shengrong in the title role of the Peking opera *Yao Qi.* [*Beijing jingjutuan fu-Gang yanchutuan,* Hong Kong, 1963]

Strolling down the mountain, he chances upon and intercepts a wine merchant. The merchant is most reluctant to sell his wares to a monk, supposedly a vegetarian and teetotaler, but Lu scoffingly dismisses all his precepts. When the merchant persists in his refusal, Lu snatches a couple of his wine casks and drains them. Denied payment, the merchant tricks Lu into opening his mouth and then throws in a handful of mud and dust. Returning to the monastery, the drunken Lu practices boxing and in so doing demolishes the mountainside pavilion. Perceiving his state and deeds, the other monks bar the monastery gates to him, then suddenly open them when he threatens to set fire to them. Sent sprawling, he then attacks two guardian statues. The abbot appears on the scene, and expels Lu from the monastery, but gives him ten taels of silver and a recommendation to another monastery. Lu sets off and heads for a village to buy some more wine with the money.

Lu is one of the prominent characters of the sagas of brigand heroes depicted in the fourteenth-century novel *Fenlands/Water Margin* (*Shui-hu zhuan*). This play comes from a section of a mid-seventeenth-century *chuanqi* play, *Tigersack Shot* (*Hu-nang dan*) by Qiu Yuan, which is based on an episode in chapter four of the novel.

Picking Up the Jade Bracelet (*Shi yu-zhuo*). Also a favorite of other genres, this play is a vignette of exquisitely minute actions and gestures. Young Sun Yujiao's mother goes to visit a nearby Buddhist monastery, leaving her daughter to look after the chickens which they sell for their living. Pretty Yujiao sits alone by the door doing some needlework, and she is spied by the young man, Fu Peng. Much taken by her looks, he pretends that he wants to buy a chicken. After chatting, he leaves, but drops a jade bracelet as he goes. Knowing that he has left it as a love token, she is comically bashful and hesitant about picking it up, but finally manages to do so, hides it in her sleeve, and goes indoors. She has, however, been seen in the act by a neighbor, Aunty Liu, a matchmaker. The latter knocks, goes in, and interrogates Yujiao. Yujiao is coyly and cleverly evasive, but Liu reenacts all that she has seen, and the shamefaced young girl is obliged to confess. All is well, for Liu volunteers to act as go-between for the two young people in order to bring them together in marriage. The miming of chicken shooing, sewing, bashfulness, and other sentiments and activities fully compensates for the slightness of the plot.

WILLIAM DOLBY

Pellerin, Jean-Victor (1889–1970)

French poet and dramatist. His expressionist dramas were extremely popular with avant-garde intellectuals during the 1920s. Responding to the theatre of Pirandello and the psychology of Freud, Pellerin created dramas in which the thoughts and preoccupations of his protagonists are externalized onstage. *Intimacy* (*Intimité*, 1922), his first play, features a husband and wife spending a quiet evening at home but surrounded by personifications of their thoughts, including a compliant maid for him and a muscular boxer for her. *Spare Heads* (*Têtes de rechange*, 1926), his most successful play, involves the interplay between a restless modern young man and various externalized aspects of his personality and daydreams. The destructive, impersonal materialism of contemporary society is focused on in *Hearts' Cries* (*Cris des coeurs*, 1928), which consists of three unrelated episodes, the last of which suggests that art is the only remedy for modern man's unhappiness. Other plays of interest include *The Handsomest Man in France* (*Le plus bel homme de France*, 1925) and *Wasteland* (*Terrain vague*, 1931). *See* EXPRESSIONISM in glossary.

Spare Heads (*Têtes de rechange*, 1926). Expressionist drama in which the multiple personalities of Ixe (X) appear onstage and provide most of the action. The restless and disillusioned Ixe is contrasted with his elderly, provincial uncle Opéku (O.P.Q.), who is at home in the world, accepts external reality, and is content to dream only when asleep. Lack of communication between uncle and nephew is total and covers everything from their food preferences to their understanding of the meaning of words. Arriving at a restaurant to have lunch with his uncle, Ixe is accompanied by his various ''spare heads,'' all of which sit down to table. Chance references by Opéku set Ixe to concocting elaborate daydreams, while his uncle continues talking in an exaggerated slow motion that suggests that even time is different for them. Gaston Baty's imaginative staging was an integral part of the play. Produced Paris, Studio des Champs-Élysées, 1926.

[JOSEPH E. GARREAU]

Pellico, Silvio (1789–1854)

Italian author and dramatist. He was born in Saluzzo on June 25, 1789, and died in Turin on January 31, 1854. His major tragedy, *Francesca da Rimini* (1814), transposes Dante's tragic story of Paolo and Francesca into a lightly sentimental bourgeois atmosphere. Lord Byron admired this work and apparently collaborated on the English translation by John C. Hobhouse Broughton. *Eufemio di Messina* (1820) is a romantic tragedy with historical references to the ninth-century Saracen invasion of Sicily. Pellico was a fervent Italian patriot; his active participation in the *Risorgimento* cost him eight years in an Austrian prison in Moravia. His autobiographical account of this confinement, *My Prisons* (*Le mie prigioni*, 1832), became one of the most influential works of the century, rivaling even Manzoni's novel in popularity. Its Christian tone of forgiveness did more damage to the Austrian cause in Italy than the numerous and more violent tracts written by other political firebrands.

Francesca da Rimini (1814). Guido, father of Francesca, arrives in Rimini to learn from his son-in-law Gianciotto that she is extremely melancholy. Both men believe that Francesca hates Paolo, her husband's brother, because he killed her brother in a battle. Therefore, when Paolo returns from the wars to visit Gianciotto, the brothers agree that he must leave home forever. However, Paolo and Francesca meet and confess that they are passionately in love with each other. When their love is discovered by Gianciotto, he attempts to kill his brother, but Francesca intervenes and is slain instead and Paolo asks to die as well. Gianciotto is prevented from committing suicide by Guido, who says enough blood has been spilled, while the dying words of the unfortunate lovers hint at the eternity of their love as recounted by Dante (*Inferno*, V).

Eufemio di Messina (1820). Drama based on Arab and Sicilian chronicles telling of the exploits of a Sicilian warrior, Eufemio, who in revenge for an imagined offense went to North Africa and led the Saracens back to

Silvio Pellico.
[Federico Arborio Mella, Milan]

the walls of his native Messina. The play opens during the siege of Messina and melodramatically presents the despair of King Theodore as he faces the conquering Saracens. Eufemio loves Ludovica, Theodore's daughter, and promises to preserve Theodore's life in return for the girl's hand. Ludovica has become a nun, but the people of Messina send her out of the convent to save the city by emulating the Biblical Judith and killing Eufemio, whom she once loved. Ludovica hesitates to complete her mission but finally kills Eufemio when she sees her father dead on the field of battle. The Saracen commander then sends her back to finish her days in the convent.

[PETER BONDANELLA]

EDITIONS

Rimini, tr. by J. F. Bingham, Cambridge, Mass., 1897; *Opere scelte di Silvio Pellico*, ed. by C. Curto, Turin, 1964.

CRITICISM

J. S. Kennard, *The Italian Theatre from the Close of the Seventeenth Century*, New York, 1964; S. D'Amico, *Storia del teatro drammatico*, Milan, 1968.

Pemán y Pemartín, José María (1897–   )

Spanish journalist, poet, essayist, and dramatist. He is noted for his idealistic drama centering on nationalistic and religious themes. Although Pemán possesses an innate facility as a lyric poet, his most original work has been achieved in the theatre. Many of the motifs of his poetry are also characteristic of his drama: an interest in Andalusian folklore, an attachment to the seventeenth-century tradition, fluid sonority of language, religiosity, and political sentiment. His dramatic effort is generally subordinated to his traditional Catholic and monarchist convictions.

Initially, Pemán wrote historical drama in verse in the style of Eduardo Marquina, with a religious-didactic intention. His first production, *The Anxious Saint* (*El divino impaciente*, 1933), depicts the troubled life of St. Francis Xavier and exalts the Jesuit order. It was followed by other historical dramas in verse, such as *At the Time of the Cádiz Parliament* (*Cuando las cortes de Cádiz*, 1934), of antiliberal inspiration, and *Cisneros* (1934). These plays present a personal vision of history reconstructed according to Pemán's political-religious ideals. Their theatrical effect is weakened by the excessive predominance of the lyric and oratorical values over the dramatic. Pemán's subsequent dramas, written for the most part in prose, were more successful. Among them are *The Saintly Vicereine* (*La santa virreina*, 1939) and *Metternich* (1942). *There Are Seven Sins, Vendimia* (*Hay siete pecados, Vendimia*, 1947), a tragedy set in the Andalusian countryside, is one of Pemán's most powerful dramas.

In recent years, Pemán's theatrical production has been prolific. One of his most popular plays, *Silent as the Dead* (*Callados como muertos*, 1952), protests the evils of society and defends the message of love communicated by saints and poets, who in order to be heard often must die. Among his most recent works are adaptations of classical dramas. In *Oedipus* (*Edipo*, 1954), considered by many to be his masterpiece, Pemán renounced his didac-

José María Pemán y Pemartín. [New York Public Library]

tic aims to create a lyrical and effective dramatic work. Other plays of Pemán are *Lola la Piconera* (1950), a zarzuela with music by Conrado del Campo; the comedy *Heart and Soul* (*Todo el alma*, 1952); the religious-didactic plays *In the Hands of the Son* (*En las manos del hijo*, 1953) and *The Light of Evening* (*La luz de la víspera*, 1954); *Barely Able to Live* (*Vivir apenas*, 1955); *The Wind over the Land* (*El viento sobre la tierra*, 1956); and the farce *The Three Et Ceteras of Don Simón* (*Los tres etcéteras de don Simón*, 1958). See ZARZUELA.

[ANDRÉS FRANCO]

Penzoldt, Ernst (1892–1955)

German sculptor, painter, poet, novelist, and dramatist. He was recipient of the 1948 Literary Prize (Munich) and the 1954 Immermann Prize (Düsseldorf). A lyrical talent influenced by Büchner, he created in his plays, with love and melancholy, pictures of odd and scurrilous types set in an appropriately compelling atmosphere that, for the most part, prevails over the dramatic action and the dramatic tension. His fame came with *The Portuguese Battle* (*Die portugalesische Schlacht*, 1931), a fantastic play subtitled *The Comedy of Immortality* that followed the dramatization of an earlier novel, *Étienne and Luise* (*Étienne und Luise*, 1930). It is "a small tragedy" about a German girl during World War I who, after having sheltered a wounded French soldier, commits suicide when he is shot leaving her house. Penzoldt's next important stage work, *The Youth Karl* (*Der Knabe Karl*, 1931), a dramatization of an earlier "character study" called *Sand*, examines the killer of the dramatist Kotzebue and strips him of the aura of martyrdom for a liberal cause, for at the end Sand discovers that Kotzebue had been eminently inconsequential. *See* KOTZEBUE, AUGUST VON.

With *Thus Was Mr. Brummell* (*So war Herr Brummell*, 1933), Penzoldt turned to comedy marked by charm and grace, portraying George Bryan ("Beau") Brummell, the famous dandy, in late-Georgian England. His other plays include *The Lost Shoes* (*Die verlorenen Schuhe*, 1946), whose central character is the German count Schlabrendorf in the midst of the French Revolution; *The Glass Stork* (*Der gläserne Storch*, 1952), a product of a romantic mood extending into the bizarre; and *Squirrel, or The Gravity of Life* (*Squirrel, oder Der Ernst des Lebens*, 1954), which, significantly, bears Schiller's motto "The creature you worship is you." Penzoldt also wrote the radio play *The Dolphin* (*Der Delphin*, 1952), "a fantastic story told under the influence of wine." [PETER JELAVICH]

Peón y Contreras, José (1843–1907)

Mexican playwright. Trained as a doctor, this facile rhymer and composer, had he been born a generation or even half a generation earlier, would have been writing his poetic plays when romanticism was in flower, rather than in its fading moments. The Spanish playwright García Gutiérrez discovered him in Mérida during a visit to the Yucatán, interested him in writing, and sent him off to Mexico City in 1863 with three plays—*The Punishment of God* (*El castigo de Dios*), *Count Santiesteban*, and *Mad María* (*María la loca*). All had been written during his student days and later produced in Mérida's San Carlos Theatre, later to be rechristened Teatro Peón y Contreras. Theatre managers in the capital returned them unread since audiences wanted neoclassical plays and were not much attracted to theatres even by them. Luckily, President Lerdo eventually decided to launch a drive to encourage Mexican drama, and there was a brief flurry of activity. In response, Peón y Contreras pulled a couple of plays from his files, and one, *As Far As Heaven* (*Hasta el cielo*), a romantic story of the colonial period, was a hit. Soon the dramatist was represented by a score of tragedies involving romantic suitors and lovelorn ladies, all speaking in flowery verse. Once, when *Struggles of Honor and Love* (*Luchas de honra y amor*) was performed in a sort of guessing game, the audience correctly identified it as a work by Peón y Contreras for the beauty of its lines.

Although much of his output has been lost without ever having been produced, several of his earlier works survive to testify to the nature of his drama. In *The King's Daughter* (*La hija del rey*; prod. 1876, pub. 1918), Angelica, illegitimate daughter of Philip II, enters a convent and upon learning that the young man she loved was killed in a duel over her, she goes mad. *By the Jewel on His Hat* (*Por el joyel del sombrero*, 1878) tells of the tragedy that ensues after a gentleman making an illicit visit thoughtlessly leaves his hat in a young lady's room. In the one-act *Gil González de Avila* of the same vintage as the play-

José Peón y Contreras. [Photograph courtesy of INBA]

wright's *King's Daughter*, when the final curtain descends, all the characters except the wronged heroine, Violante, are dead. Peón y Contreras wrote nothing between 1879 and 1885, and then made several attempts at new plays, but Mexican interest in romanticism was dead. WILLIS KNAPP JONES and JUDITH A. WEISS

CRITICISM

E. Abreu Gómez, "Teatro Romántico de Peón y Contreras," in *Clásicas, Románticas, y Modernas*, Mexico City, 1934; A. Magaña Esquivel, *Sueño y Realidad del Teatro*, Mexico City, 1949.

Perelman, S[idney] J[oseph] (1904–1979)

American humorist and playwright. His extraordinary vocabulary, verbal facility, and humor, which rests on exaggeration, made him a popular satirical writer. His satire most often found a target in aspects of contempo-

Mary Martin and Kenny Baker in *One Touch of Venus*, by S. J. Perelman and Ogden Nash. New York, Imperial Theatre, 1943. [Photograph by Vandamm. Theatre Collection, The New York Public Library at Lincoln Center, Astor, Lenox and Tilden Foundations]

rary society, including the advertising and entertainment industries. Following his graduation from Brown University in 1925, Perelman wrote for humor magazines until the publication of his first book, *Dawn Ginsbergh's Revenge,* in 1929 established his reputation and brought offers from Hollywood. There he wrote gags for motion pictures and also turned to the stage, contributing sketches to *The Third Little Show* (1931) and *Walk a Little Faster* (1932), in collaboration with Robert MacGunigle. In 1933 he wrote *All Good Americans* with his wife Laura Perelman. After *Two Weeks with Pay* (1940), he collaborated with his wife on *The Night Before Christmas* (1941). With Ogden Nash he wrote the book for the musical *One Touch of Venus* (1943), and with Al Hirschfeld he wrote the book for *Sweet Bye and Bye* (1946). *The Beauty Part* appeared in 1962. For film, he wrote the script for *One Touch of Venus* (1948) and, with John Farrow and James Poe, *Around the World in 80 Days* (1956).

[GAUTAM DASGUPTA]

Peretz, Isaac Loeb   (1852–1915)

Hebrew- and Yiddish-language novelist, poet, and dramatist. Peretz commands a major place in Yiddish literature. A master of style and mood, he had roots in both the mysticism of the Hasidim and the rationalism of the Haskalah (Jewish Enlightenment). Born in Zamość, Poland, he devoted himself, except for a brief career in the law, to writing, first in Hebrew, but later, to reach the Jewish masses, in Yiddish. Although his preferred genre was the short story, he made a significant contribution to the Jewish theatre, being among the first to introduce symbolism and mysticism to the Jewish stage. In 1911, aspiring to raise the level of Yiddish drama, he organized the Theatre Society. The bulk of his drama consists of one-act plays; of the full-length dramas, *The Golden Chain* (*Die goldene Kaite,* 1907) is the most important.

Peretz's other plays include *After the Funeral* (*Nach di Kvoro;* wr. 1901, pub. 1907), *An Early Morning* (*A frei Morgen;* wr. 1901, pub. 1907), *At the Window* (*Beim Fenster,* 1902), *The Sisters* (*Shvester,* 1903), *The Band* (*Klezmer,* 1907), *Night on the Old Marketplace* (*Beinacht ofen alten Mark,* 1907), *What Lies in the Fiddle* (*Vos in Fidleh shtekt,* 1907), *Chained in the Vestry* (*In Pulish oif der Keit,* 1908), *Champagne* (1908), and *The Hunchback* (*Der Hoiker,* 1914). Peretz's short story, *Bonche the Silent,* was dramatized by Arnold Perl in 1953 as part of *The World of Sholem Aleichem.* Its hero is a meek and silent man who, after a lifetime of poverty, mockery, and abuse, goes to heaven, where he is told he may ask for and receive anything his heart desires; Bonche Shveig replies that he would like a fresh roll with butter for breakfast. *See* YIDDISH DRAMA.

[IRVING SAPOSNIK]

Pérez de Montalván, Juan   (1602?–1638)

Spanish dramatist. Friend, protégé, and biographer of Lope de Vega, this versatile and unjustly neglected author enjoyed enormous popularity in his day. Born in Madrid, Juan Pérez de Montalván (or Montalbán) was

Peretz Cycle, a 1926 Tel Aviv production based on material from Isaac Loeb Peretz. [*Theatre in Israel*]

the son of Lope de Vega's editor, whose bookshop was frequented by prominent men of letters. In 1617, Montalván was granted the Licentiate in philosophy and the humanities by the University of Alcalá de Henares. Shortly thereafter, encouraged perhaps by Lope, he began to write plays. Like many dramatists of the Golden Age, he entered the service of the Church. By 1625 he was an ordained priest, and soon received a doctorate in Theology from the same university where he had earned his previous degree. *See* Siglo de Oro in glossary.

Perhaps in an effort to escape the social stigma of his Jewish ancestry, he obtained a post as an officer of the Inquisition, an institution with which Lope de Vega was also associated. Montalván was often the object of cruel attacks by literary enemies, the most notable of whom was the brilliant satirist Francisco de Quevedo. The latter's hostility seems to have been motivated by a bitter quarrel with the young dramatist's father over pirated editions. Montalván's brief but feverish life was a tragic one. In his thirties he was stricken with a mental disease which reduced him to a state of childishness. The possibility that the personal attacks to which he was subjected may have contributed to his disorder cannot be discarded.

Despite his premature death, he produced an impressive number of plays, several of which have withstood the test of time. Among the hundred-odd plays attributed to him, at least twenty-five *comedias* and three *autos sacramentales* have been definitively identified as having been written by him. In addition, Montalván wrote a few plays in collaboration with other contemporary dramatists—among them Lope de Vega, Calderón, and Mira de Amescua. Many critics and literary historians continue to attribute to him plays which modern research has shown to be spurious. Despite important research and publication in recent years, much remains to be done to ascertain which plays Montalván actually wrote and the pertinent chronological information. To complicate matters further, his plays, except for a few, are not readily available and require modern editing.

Work

While Montalván tried his hand at various branches of literature, including lyric poetry and novelistic prose (he was extremely successful as a writer of short stories, many with erotic themes), he was at his best as a dramatist. Even though his theatre was still being performed in the neoclassical eighteenth century and praised by some critics in the nineteenth, he is now remembered chiefly for *Posthumous Fame* (*Fama póstuma*, 1636), in which he paid tribute to Lope de Vega, and *For Everybody* (*Para todos*, 1632), a miscellany of prose, poetry, and plays in the tradition of Boccaccio's *Decameron*. Intent on providing entertainment above all and a moral lesson to some extent, Montalván, without possessing Lope's genius, attempted to compete with his mentor in fecundity, forcing himself to write with undue rapidity. Despite this weakness, there is considerable substance in his dramatic output. Though in many ways an imitator of Lope de Vega, he at times comes closer to Calderón. A significant figure in the development of the *comedia*, he does not, however, belong in the same category with Lope de Vega, Calderón, Ruiz de Alarcón, or Tirso de Molina. *See* Calderón de la Barca, Pedro; Molina, Tirso de; Ruiz de Alarcón, Juan; Vega Carpio, Lope de.

In one of his finest plays, *The Second Seneca of Spain* (*El segundo Séneca de España*, wr. ca. 1625/28)—for which he also composed a second part—the main feature is character delineation, particularly that of Philip II, the protagonist. The often praised *For a Punishment a Double Revenge* (*De un castigo dos venganzas*, wr. ca. 1630) presents an unusual treatment of the theme of sexual honor, a basic motif in much of the Golden Age drama: the adultress wife and her lover are killed not by her husband but by her lover's discarded mistress. Like other Spanish dramatists before and after him, he was attracted by the famous legend of star-crossed lovers, whose literary roots have been traced back to Boccaccio's tale of Girolamo and Salvestra (*Decameron*, IV, 8). Montalván's *The Lovers of Teruel* (*Los amantes de Teruel*, pub. 1635), like previous versions by other Golden Age dramatists, brings the action forward to the time of Charles V and the conquest of Tunis (1535). (Hartzenbusch, writing at the height of the Romantic era, rejected the sixteenth-century setting in favor of an earlier period in Spanish history, namely the thirteenth century, with the wars of the Reconquest as background.) Montalván's source seems to have been a play by the same title attributed to Tirso de Molina and thought to have been written in 1615. He was especially successful from an artistic point of view in his *capa y espada* ("cloak and sword") plays—comedies of manners based on love-and-honor intrigues. Two of his most delightful efforts of this type are *The Cap Seller of Biscay* (*La toquera vizcaína*, wr. 1628/29) and *The Waiting-Maid* (*La doncella de labor*, pub. 1635), both of which reveal the dramatist's desire to create interesting female characters in the manner of Lope de Vega and Tirso de Molina. Another superb play is *The Divine Portuguese, Saint Anthony of Padua* (*El divino portugués, San Antonio de Padua*, pub. 1638), though its attribution to Montalván is disputed. (Another play of the same title, also attributed to him but not included in any of the three original volumes containing his collected dramatic works, is of inferior quality, and appears not to have been written by Montalván.) As he was a theologian, it is not surprising that he also wrote *autos sacramentales*, short sacramental plays which were performed in the street to celebrate the feast of Corpus Christi. While critical opinions on this aspect of his dramaturgy remain divided, there can be no doubt that his two best-known *autos sacramentales Skander Bey* (*Escanderbech*, wr. ca. 1629), about the Albanian national hero's conversion to Christianity in the fifteenth century, and *Polyphemus* (*El Polifemo*, wr. ca. 1628), were condemned in an excessive and particularly vicious manner by Quevedo, who went so far as to question Montalván's religious orthodoxy, a grave charge in seventeenth-century Spain. *See* Auto Sacramental in glossary.

The Cap Seller of Biscay (*La toquera vizcaína*, wr. 1628/29). Elena, who lives in Valladolid, has two suitors, Don Diego, whom she dislikes, and Don Juan, her favorite. The two rivals fight a duel, and Diego is killed. Juan flees to Madrid, where he takes refuge with Don Lisardo. Before setting out for Madrid to look for Juan, Elena pretends to become a nun (she has her maid's sister enter a Valladolid convent under her name). Once in Madrid she lodges in the home of Magdalena, a Basque headdress seller, and decides to go into the same business herself in order to gain entrance into as many homes as possible in her search for Juan. Eventually she finds him, but he is being pursued by another woman, Flora. After much jealousy, many complications, intrigues, deceptions, and clarifications all ends well: Flora declares her true love for Lisardo, and Elena, revealing her true identity, will marry Juan.

For a Punishment a Double Vengeance (*De un castigo dos venganzas*, wr. ca. 1630). Set in Portugal, the play begins when Don Pedro, having surprised an unknown man at his sister's window in the middle of the night, is slain by him in the ensuing struggle. Leonor was under the impression that the man involved was her lover Don Lope, but it turns out to be Don Juan de Silva, who is immediately imprisoned for his crime. He is released on condition that he marry Leonor at once to restore her honor. The solution is distasteful to all parties, including Violante, a female neighbor, passionately in love with Don Juan. Six months pass: Violante has turned to Don Lope, and the marriage of Don Juan and Leonor is marred by the husband's suspicions that his wife had and continues to have a lover, Don Lope. Violante, who by this time has given herself to Don Lope, is violently jealous of Leonor, who is planning a rendezvous with Lope. Bursting in on the two lovers, she kills both of them with a dagger. Arriving on the scene just at that moment, Don Juan assumes the blame for the double murder and is pardoned as the defender of his family honor. He decides to marry Violante, who has avenged them both.   ANDRÉS FRANCO

EDITIONS

Collections
Dramáticos contemporáneos de Lope de Vega, Biblioteca de Autores Españoles, vol. XLV, ed. by R. de Mesonero Romanos, Madrid, 1858.
Individual Plays
    The Knight of Phoebus (*El caballero del Febo*, wr. ca. 1630). Published as M. G. Profeti's contribution to *Miscellanea di Studi Hispanici*, Pisa, 1966–1967, pp. 218–309.
    Polyphemus (*Polifemo*). Published in *Piezas maestras del teatro teológico español*, 3d ed., ed. by N. González Ruiz, vol. I, Madrid, 1968, pp. 778–798.
    The Second Seneca of Spain (*El segundo Séneca de España*). Published in F. C. Sainz de Robles, *Historia y antología del teatro español*, vol. IV, Madrid, 1943, pp. 509–580.

CRITICISM

G. W. Bacon, ''The Life and Works of Doctor Juan Pérez de Montalván (1602–1638),'' *Revue Hispanique*, XXVI, 1912, pp. 1–474; E. Sylvia, ''A Dramatist of Spain's Golden Age,'' in *More Books*, XIII, 1938, pp. 467–471; V. Dixon, ''Juan Pérez de Montalbán's *Segundo tomo de las comedias*,'' *Hispanic Review*, XXIX, 1961, pp. 91–109; V. Dixon, ''Juan Pérez de Montalbán's *Para todos*,'' *Hispanic Review*, XXXII, 1964, pp. 36–59; M. G. Profeti, *Montalbán: un commediografo dell'età di Lope*, Pisa, 1970; J. H. Parker, *Juan Pérez de Montalván*, Boston, 1975.

Pérez Galdós, Benito   (1843–1920)

Spanish novelist, journalist, and dramatist. He was born in Las Palmas, Canary Islands, on May 10, 1843, the youngest of a large, less-than-prosperous family. His parents having decided that he should follow a legal career, he entered law school at the University of Madrid and remained there until 1868.

In Madrid, Galdós began writing critical articles on art and literature for the newspapers and composed two plays. In 1867 he made his first trip to Paris, where he became acquainted with the works of Balzac, works that inspired him to begin his first full-length novel, *The Fountain of Gold* (*La fontana de oro*, 1871). Having witnessed the overthrow of Isabella II, he became a full-fledged reporter, assigned to cover sessions of the Cortes (Parliament). Meanwhile, he continued his fiction writing, producing a novelette and a second novel.

In 1873 Galdós gave up journalism to devote himself to creative literature. He had begun his famous *National Episodes (Episodios nacionales)*, a series of historical novels, and had written four by the end of 1873. In 1879, after completing twenty *Episodes*, he abandoned historical novels in favor of social novels, and it was through this genre that he achieved his greatest fame. Despite his preoccupation with writing, he traveled a great deal and maintained an active interest in politics: in 1885 he was elected a deputy to the Cortes.

Galdós's interest in the theatre was revived in 1892, when he was persuaded to make a stage version of his novel *Reality (Realidad)*. It was such a popular success that he began adapting his other novels for the stage. In 1897 he became a member of the Royal Spanish Academy. The following year popular demand and financial embarrassment caused him to take up the *National Episodes* again. He worked on them until 1912, by which time he published the forty-sixth and last volume.

When the Spanish dramatist José Echegaray won the Nobel Prize in 1904, Galdós was most often mentioned as more deserving by the outraged Spanish intellectuals, many of whom thought that Galdós was overlooked because of the antagonism of the Catholic Church to his anticlericalism. Soon after he was persuaded by friends

Benito Pérez Galdós.
[Biblioteca Nacional, Madrid]

to enter politics again. In 1906 corruption and dissension were rampant in the government, and Galdós fought vainly for reform. But by 1912 blindness forced him to retire from politics. He devoted his remaining years to his literary work. Dictating to a secretary, he completed one novel and five dramas, leaving one unfinished. He died in Madrid on January 4, 1920.

WORK

Pérez Galdós is an important literary figure by virtue of the advanced ideas he put before the public in his seventy-five novels and his twenty-four plays, which are mainly dramas about the middle class. Although some critics contend that his enlightened progressivism caused him to be overrated as a dramatist, the general consensus is that his lack of dramatic technique and feeling for the resources of the stage prevented him from ranking among the greatest dramatists of Spain. His most frequent theme, which gives a kind of unity to his work, is that the arbitrary barriers between aristocrats and the lower classes must be broken down to allow a free exchange of blood and intellect. It is often his strong women characters who, with a sensible, realistic outlook, defy social conventions and religious strictures to try to secure for themselves a better life. Galdós advocated positive action as the best remedy for misfortune and social ills, and he believed that science and the scientific mode of thought have much to teach a backward nation. He was anticlerical, but he never attacked the spirit of true religion. However, he preferred to see people lead useful, positive lives on earth rather than anticipate rewards in heaven. Personal conduct was Galdós's only measuring stick. He believed that one establishes one's place in the world through one's actions and not through the accident of birth, and he deplored the aristocracy's irrational fear of what would happen if the *status quo* were disturbed. As the titles of many of Galdós's plays indicate, he concentrated mainly on character and achieved a number of notable creations.

The best known of Galdós's plays are *The Madwoman of the House* (*La loca de la casa*, 1893), in which an aristocratic woman marries a wealthy man of no social standing in order to help her father recoup his fortunes; *The Grandfather* (*El abuelo*, 1904), in which an old man drives himself to the brink of madness by trying to determine which of his granddaughters is his legitimate heir; *Electra* (1901), in which a girl weds the man of her choice, a scientist, despite the machinations of her guardians, who want her to become a nun; and *The Duchess of San Quintín* (*La de San Quintín*, 1894), about an impoverished young widow who marries a romantic Socialist without means instead of a rich widower, representative of the declining aristocracy.

Among other well-known plays are *Pedro Minio* (1908), set in a home for the aged, in which Galdós typically aligned himself with the underdog; *Celia in the Slums* (*Celia en los infiernos*, 1913), which underscores the need for the wealthy classes to recognize their obligations toward the poor; *The Miser Solomon* (*El tacaño Sal-*

omón, 1916), a comedy calling for a just distribution of the wealth of the world; *Will Power* (*Voluntad*, 1895), in which an energetic young woman saves her family from financial ruin and changes her status from mistress to wife; and *Mariucha* (1903), in which an aristocratic girl marries the man of her choice, opens a store, and scandalizes her family. Other plays include *Sister Simona* (*Sor Simona*, 1915), about brotherhood and peace; *The Condemned* (*Los condenados*, 1894), about a lusty rascal who pursues a virtuous girl to a convent and there experiences a crisis of conscience that proves disastrous to them both; *Soul and Life* (*Alma y vida*, 1902), a symbolic play asserting the value of the active life; and *Bárbara* (1905), a tragicomedy in which Galdós seems to condemn revolutionary action as a means of achieving justice in the world.

The Madwoman of the House (*La loca de la casa*, 1893). Comedy advocating the dissolution of existing social classes. It has been assumed that Victoria and Gabriela, daughters of the philanthropic Don Juan de Moncada, will marry two brothers, Daniel and Jaime. But Victoria, the impetuous sister of the play's title, decides to enter a convent. When her father suddenly is threatened with bankruptcy, however, she resolves to sacrifice her personal ambition and help him by marrying the wealthy but uncultivated José María Cruz, a "self-made man" whose father once was employed as a cartwright by the Moncadas. After their marriage, Cruz runs the family's business affairs, but his jealousy causes a fight between him and Daniel, inciting Victoria to leave him. Finding that she is about to bear him a child, Cruz begs her to return, and she, realizing that genuine love has developed between them, does so.

The Duchess of San Quintín (*La de San Quintín*, 1894). Comedy in which Rosario de Trastamara, an impoverished duchess, is invited to stay with the wealthy Don José de Buendía and his avaricious son César. There Rosario meets Víctor, an upright young man, César's illegitimate son and a former suitor, who again declares his love for her. When she receives letters proving Víctor is illegitimate, she shows them to him; he vows to accept the truth and its consequences, even though it will cost him a father and an inheritance. When César, after learning Víctor's identity, offers him a bribe to leave, Víctor refuses to take it. Touched by his honesty and aware of his aristocracy of character, Rosario accepts Victor's proposal. Together they set off to start a new life in America.

The Grandfather (*El abuelo*; wr. 1897, as a thesis novel; prod. 1904). Drama depicting old Don Rodrigo's efforts to prove which of his granddaughters Leonora and Dorotea is the illegitimate child of his daughter-in-law Lucrecia. When he confronts Lucrecia with the question in order to determine his legal heir, she refuses to answer. As the old man's efforts drive him to the brink of madness, Lucrecia tries to have him confined to an institution, but Dorotea stands by him. A servant, authorized by Lucrecia, gives Don Rodrigo evidence that Dorotea is the illegitimate child. The old man, however, has come to realize that love and nobility of soul exist beyond the family context. He therefore accepts Dorotea as his heir, for she has proved her humanity and made herself his spiritual if not his actual granddaughter.

Electra (1901). Drama about Electra, daughter of an unwed mother, who falls in love with Don Máximo, a scientist. When pious friends falsely imply that Don Máximo may be her half brother, she is torn by uncertainty and finally flees to the convent where her mother died. At the convent Electra's prayers are answered by her dead mother, who tells her that the insinuations are false, that Máximo is not her brother, and that since God is everywhere, she can find Him by marrying Máximo if she loves him. She must not, says the ghost of her mother, seek sanctuary in the convent, where she cannot be happy. The play is said by some to have allegorical overtones whereby Electra represents Spain, Don Salvador (who suggests the brother-sister relationship between Electra and Máximo in the hope that she will enter the church) the clerical party, and Don Máximo intellectual illumination.   [ANDRÉS FRANCO]

PLAYS

Unless otherwise noted, the plays were first performed in Madrid.

1. *Realidad (Reality).* Drama, 5 acts. Produced Teatro de la Comedia, Mar. 15, 1892.
2. *La loca de la casa (The Madwoman of the House).* Comedy, 4 acts. Produced Teatro de la Comedia, Jan. 16, 1893.
3. *Gerona.* Drama, 4 acts. Produced Feb. 3, 1893.
4. *La de San Quintín (The Duchess of San Quintín).* Comedy, 3 acts. Produced Teatro de la Comedia, Jan. 27, 1894.
5. *Los condenados (The Condemned).* Drama, prologue and 3 acts. Produced Teatro de la Comedia, Dec. 11, 1894.
6. *Voluntad (Will Power).* Comedy, 3 acts. Produced Teatro Español, Dec. 20, 1895.
7. *Doña Perfecta.* Drama, 4 acts. Produced Teatro de la Comedia, Jan. 28, 1896. Based on Pérez Galdós's novel of the same name (1876).
8. *La fiera (The Dragon).* Drama, 3 acts. Produced Teatro de la Comedia, Dec. 23, 1896.
9. *El abuelo (The Grandfather).* Drama, 5 acts. Written 1897, as a thesis novel. Produced Teatro Español, Feb. 14, 1904.
10. *Electra*.* Drama, 5 acts. Produced Teatro Español, Jan. 30, 1901.
11. *Alma y vida (Soul and Life).* Drama, prologue and 4 acts. Produced Teatro Español, Apr. 9, 1902.
12. *Mariucha.* Comedy, 5 acts. Produced Barcelona, Teatro Eldorado, July 16, 1903.
13. *Bárbara.* Tragicomedy, 4 acts. Produced Teatro Español, Mar. 28, 1905.
14. *Amor y ciencia (Love and Science).* Comedy, 4 acts. Produced Teatro de la Comedia, Nov. 17, 1905.
15. *Zaragoza (Saragossa).* Lyric drama, 4 acts; prose. Written 1907. Produced Saragossa, Teatro Principal, June 4, 1908. Music by Arturo Lapuerta.
16. *Pedro Minio.* Comedy, 2 acts. Produced Teatro de Lara, Dec. 15, 1908.
17. *Casandra (Cassandra).* Drama, 4 acts. Produced Teatro Español, Feb. 28, 1910. Based on Pérez Galdós's novel of the same name (1905).
18. *Celia en los infiernos (Celia in the Slums).* Comedy, 4 acts. Produced Teatro Español, Dec. 9, 1913.
19. *Alceste (Alcestis).* Tragicomedy, 3 acts. Produced Teatro de la Princesa, Apr. 21, 1914.
20. *Sor Simona (Sister Simona).* Drama, 3 acts. Produced Teatro de la Infanta Isabel, Dec. 1, 1915.
21. *El tacaño Salomón (The Miser Solomon).* Comedy, 2 acts. Produced Teatro de Lara, Feb. 2, 1916.
22. *Santa Juana de Castilla (St. Juana of Castile).* Tragicomedy, 3 acts. Produced Teatro de la Princesa, May 8, 1918.
23. (With Serafín and Joaquín Álvarez Quintero). *Antón Caballero.* Comedy, 3 acts. Produced Teatro del Centro, Dec. 16, 1921. Completed after Pérez Galdós's death by the Quintero brothers.
24. *Un joven de provecho (A Hardworking Young Man).* Comedy, 4 acts. Published 1935. Written 1867(?).
25. *Quien mal hace, bien no espere (The Doer of Evil Should Expect No Good).* Dramatic experiment in one act. Verse. Written 1861. Published 1974.

EDITIONS

Collections
Obras completas, 6 vols., Madrid, 1941–1942; *Teatro selecto de Pérez Galdós,* Madrid, 1972.
Individual Plays
The Duchess of San Quintín. Published in *Masterpieces of Modern Spanish Drama,* ed. by B. H. Clark and tr. by P. M. Hayden, New York, 1917.
Electra. Published in *Contemporary Spanish Dramatists,* ed. and tr. by C. A. Turrell, Boston, 1919.

CRITICISM

E. Gutiérrez Ganiero, *Galdós y su obra,* vol. III, *El teatro,* Madrid, 1935; J. Casalduero, *Vida y obra de Galdós (1843–1920),* Madrid, 1951; G. Sobejano, "Razón y suceso de la dramática galdosiana," *Anales galdosianos,* V (1970), 39–54; *Estudios escénicos,* Sept. 1970 (issue devoted to Galdós' theatre); M. Alvar, "Novela y teatro en Galdós," *Estudios y ensayos de literatura contemporánea,* Madrid, 1971, pp. 52–110.

Petrescu, Camil (1894–1957)

Romanian dramatist. Petrescu was born in Bucharest on April 9, 1894. During World War I, in August, 1916, he was mobilized and sent to the front, where he was wounded. The first version of *The Play of the Wicked Fairies (Jocul ielolor)* dates from that year. Petrescu rewrote the play in 1917, and in 1918 he was demobilized, having become almost completely deaf. At this time he underwent a period of crisis: "During the whole year 1919, my generation, nearly in its totality, had to wear military jackets with shabby epaulets, drink a coffee with cream a day and live in squalid attics, three of us in a room." The same year he worked as a professor of Romanian, contributed war poems to the review *Zburătorul (The Goblin),* published by Eugen Lovinescu, and wrote the first version of the play *Venetian Act.* In 1924 and 1925 he edited the periodicals *Week of Intellectual and Artistic Work* and *Literary Citadel,* calling upon intellectuals to unite on the ideological front against the social system. In 1925 he brought out the play *Brave Hearts* and finished the drama

Camil Petrescu. [Editura Enciclopedică Română, Bucharest]

Scenes from *Bălcescu*. [Editura Enciclopedică Română, Bucharest]

Danton. In 1925 and 1926 he wrote the play *Mythical Popescu (Mitică Popescu)*. *The Last Night of Love, the First Night of War*, a novel begun about 1919, came out in 1930; *Danton* and the volume of philosophical poems *Transcendentalia*, in 1931; the novel *The Bed of Procrustes*, in 1933. In 1944 the first performance of the play *This Is the Woman I Love* took place, and in 1947 that of *Mitică Popescu*.

Petrescu achieved great success during the interwar period as the author of a drama of ideas. During World War II he directed an experimental seminar of drama. In 1948 he became a member of the Academy of the Romanian People's Republic. The postwar period found him actively working on epic and dramatic reconstructions, notably the play *Bălcescu* (1949). Petrescu was at the height of his journalistic and literary activity when he died suddenly in Bucharest on May 14, 1957, at the age of sixty-three.

In his nondramatic works as well as in his plays Camil Petrescu reflected the problems and the destiny of the Romanian intelligentsia. Proceeding from the classical definition of drama, he believed the theatrical experience to be ideal for the display of passions and intellectual forces. What he strove for was not the breaking down of consciousness but rather revelations in consciousness. He saw the world through his heroes, who, however predictable, are subject to often complex and unforeseeable circumstances. Thus, the world of Petrescu's heroes is a rigorous one, considerably extending the sphere of urban drama, the gallery of Ion Luca Caragiale and of Mihail Sebastian. *See* CARAGIALE, ION LUCA; SEBASTIAN, MIHAIL.

In *The Play of the Wicked Fairies* the starting point is a common, everyday drama, which develops into the tragedy of an honest middle-class intellectual who has detached himself from his class and seeks a solution to his problems and inner contradictions in the workers' movement. The main conflict arises between Gelu Ruscanu, who wants at any cost to publish a damning piece of information regarding the criminal dealings of the Minister of Justice, and the socialist militants, who want to obtain the release of a comrade by holding back its publication. To Gelu such an action means "setting a man's destiny above the cause"; for the activists, it is more important to show the bourgeoisie that the workers' movement, by forcing the release of its fighters, is able to check a wave of terror. Thus the intellectual's passion for absolute justice and the practical development of the class struggle become the conflict; the intellectual is enmeshed in a tangle of ideas, his philosophy being at variance with his social actions.

Although chronologically *The Play of the Wicked Fairies* is followed by *Venetian Act*, *Brave Heart*, and *Sheep* (*Miora*, 1923), the play that continues to explore the range of problems of the first work is *Danton*. The French Revolution of 1789 is here regarded as a progressive event, a necessary stage in the advance of history and a process reaching the limit of intensity with seismic, unforeseen motion. Danton's ascent is actually the ascent of the revolution. The progress of the conflict hinges on

the crucial moments of the revolution: the Prussians' invasion, the dispute with the Girondins, and the clash between Danton and Robespierre. Petrescu here focused on an elaborate profile of a revolutionist and statesman. Danton represents the virtues and capacities that, in Petrescu's view, should characterize a statesman. Yet he is not an ideal hero: his virtues are mixed with vices that seem minor in contrast to the dimensions of the character. Robespierre, on the other hand, is a fanatic immobilized by an irrational fixed idea. Thus he represents a caricatured image of Gelu Ruscanu, his sinister double.

Bălcescu (1949), heralded by the previous works, nevertheless represents a changed point of view. Bălcescu is the first of Petrescu's heroes not to feel alone, disarmed, and useless, harassed by the disagreements of the surrounding world. In this play there is a tragic op-

Venetian Act, presented at the C. I Nottara Theatre, Bucharest. [Editura Enciclopedică Română, Bucharest]

timism not seen before, a firm belief that sacrifice is not in vain. [RUTH S. LAMB]

CRITICISM

C. Petrescu, *Teze si Antiteze (Theses and Antitheses)*, Bucharest, 1936; C. Petrescu, *Modalitatea estetica a teatrului (Aesthetic Principles in the Theatre)*, Bucharest, 1937.

Picard, André (1874–1926)

French dramatist. He wrote *Copper* (*Le cuivre*, 1895; with Paul Adam), a satire on grasping money-makers and corrupt politicians; the light comedy *Kiki* (1918); and the more serious *The Guardian Angel* (*L'ange gardien*, 1910), about a puritanical woman who loves once, only to revert to her original code of morality.

[JOSEPH E. GARREAU]

Piccolo Teatro di Milano

Italy's first national *teatro stabile*, or permanent repertory company, founded on May 14, 1947, by Paolo Grassi (1919–1981) and Giorgio Strehler (1921–   ). Since its inauguration, the Piccolo Teatro di Milano ("Little Theatre of Milan") has developed into one of the finest theatre companies in the world, largely because of the personality and genius of Giorgio Strehler. Strehler's career as a director began with his productions of one-act plays by Luigi Pirandello for student groups during the Fascist period. Forced to flee to Switzerland in 1943–1944, he continued to direct productions of Pirandello in a camp for Italian citizens interned in that country, and then introduced the plays of Thornton Wilder and Albert Ca-

mus in Geneva before returning to Milan.

Under Strehler's direction the Piccolo Teatro has revitalized popular interest in the classics of the Italian stage and introduced new foreign authors and innovative interpretations of more familiar playwrights. In particular, his productions of Goldoni and Pirandello have become mainstays of the company's repertory. More importantly, however, Strehler has emerged as perhaps the most controversial interpreter of Brecht—especially *Galileo* and *The Threepenny Opera*—in contemporary Italy. In addition to productions of works by Eugene O'Neill, T. S. Eliot, Henrik Ibsen, Molière, Georg Büchner, and Peter Weiss, Strehler has worked in the lyric theatre as well, heading productions at Milan's La Scala, Venice's La Fenice, the Florentine Maggio Musicale, and the Salzburg Music Festival.

With Strehler at the helm the Piccolo Teatro has attempted to establish both a national and a popular theatre by bridging the gap between the general public and the most avant-garde intellectual currents in the country. Indeed, it is sometimes difficult to separate his personality from the institution which the Piccolo Teatro now represents. His constant awareness of new trends, his openness to fresh ideas or writers, and his innovative view of staging and acting techniques have made of the Piccolo Teatro a model for any state-subsidized theatrical institution. PETER BONDANELLA

CRITICISM

E. Gaipa, *Giorgio Strehler*, Bologna, 1959; G. Guazzotti, *Teoria e realtà del Piccolo Teatro di Milano*, Turin, 1965; G. Strehler, *Per un teatro umano: pen-*

Piccolo Teatro di Milano's 1967 production of Carlo Goldoni's *Il servitore di due padroni* under the direction of Giorgio Strehler. [Italian Cultural Institute]

sieri scritti, parlati e attuati, ed. by S. Kessler, Milan, 1974; J. Kott, "Prospero or the Director: Giorgio Strehler's *The Tempest* (Piccolo Teatro di Milano)," *Theatre* 10 (1979), 117–122.

Piccolomini, Alessandro (1508–1578)

Italian playwright and professor of philosophy. He eventually held positions of importance in the church in and around the town of Siena, his birthplace. In his youth, he was interested in the theatre and was most likely involved in the composition of an anonymous comic play, *The Deceived* (*Gl'ingannati*, 1537). Critical debate still continues on the authorship of this important work: while some scholars attribute it to Ludovico Castelvetro (1505–1571), the important literary critic and theorist, most recent studies claim that Piccolomini and other members of the Sienese Accademia degli Intronati wrote the work together. As the title suggests, the work owes much to the complicated plot structures of Plautus's *Menaechmi*, but it may also be indebted to Boccaccio's *Decameron* (VII, 7) and to Bernardo Dovizi da Bibbiena's *The Follies of Calandro*. Renaissance audiences were intrigued by its many puzzling disguises, paradoxical relationships, and startling dénouements, and the work has often been suggested as an indirect source for Shakespeare's *Twelfth Night*. In addition to a number of translations from Ovid, Vergil, Aristotle, and Xenophon, Piccolomini completed two lesser comedies: *Constant Love* (*L'amore costante*, 1536) and *Alexander* (*L'Alessandro*, 1544).

[PETER BONDANELLA]

EDITIONS

The Deceived, tr. by T. L. Peacock, in *The Genius of the Italian Theatre*, ed. by E. Bentley, New York, 1964; *Il teatro italiano: la commedia del Cinquecento*, ed. by G. D. Bonino, Turin, 1977.

CRITICISM

F. Cerreta, *Alessandro Piccolomini letterato e filosofo senese del Cinquecento*, Siena, 1960; D. Radcliff-Umstead, *The Birth of Modern Comedy in Renaissance Italy*, Chicago, 1969; M. Celse, "Alessandro Piccolomini, l'homme du ralliement," in *Les écrivains et le pouvoir en Italie à l'epoque de la Renaissance*, ed. by André Rochon, Paris, 1973.

Pichette, Henri (1924–   )

French poet and dramatist. Two theatrical works by Pichette presented in the immediate post-World War II years are interesting avant-garde attempts to return to poetic drama. Though marked by brilliant lyricism and imagination, they are both essentially staged poems stripped of action and conflict. The emphasis is on the musical effects of language and sound, whose emotional impact is heightened by instrumental dissonance and unusual effects achieved with the human voice. *The Epiphanies* (*Les épiphanies*, 1947) is a five-part work about the development and destruction of a poet-lover overcome by the dehumanization of modern society. The basic form of the play is a monologue by the Poet, whose meditations on Genesis, love, war, delirium, and the state are interrupted by the Devil and the Loving Woman.

The somewhat more conventional form and the use of Alexandrines in *Nucléa* (1952) limit the verbal exuberance of Pichette's first play, without, however, achieving

Gérard Philipe and Maria Casarés in
Les épiphanies. Paris, Théâtre Édouard
VII, 1947. [French Cultural Services]

a greater dramatic effect. By dividing the work into two parts in which love and war are treated more or less separately, Pichette sacrificed dramatic confrontation to a static and sometimes shrill lyricism. One of the early presentations of Jean Vilar's Théâtre National Populaire (TNP), *Nucléa* failed to please either the critics or the public.

[JOSEPH E. GARREAU]

Pindemonte, Giovanni (1751–1812)

Italian man of letters and dramatist. His *Cincinnato* (*Cincinnatus*, 1804) is a sociopolitical work involving classical personages and events. *The Bacchanals* (*I baccanali*), an attack on secret societies and rituals, is a formal classical tragedy inspired by a passage from Livy concerning Dionysian rites in ancient Rome. *Adelina and Roberto* (*Adelina e Roberto*, 1827) is a virulent attack on clericalism in which torments are inflicted on husband, wife, and father-in-law by the Spanish inquisitors in Flanders. *Geneva of Scotland* (*Ginevra di Scozia*, 1795) is the adaptation of an episode from Ariosto's *Orlando furioso*. Pindemonte's other plays include *Elena and Gerardo* (*Elena e Gerardo*, 1796), *Mastino I della Scola*, and *The Farmers of Candia* (*I coloni di Candia*, 1807).

[PETER BONDANELLA]

Pindemonte, Ippolito (1753–1828)

Italian man of letters and dramatist. His *Arminius* (*Arminio*, wr. 1797, prod. 1804), a tragedy set in a German forest, represents a struggle between public duties and private affections. *Ulysses* (*Ulisse*, 1788) is a tragedy inspired by Greco-Roman antiquity; and *The Stroke of the Hammer* (*Il colpo di martello*), dedicated to Pindemonte's friend Tetochi Albrizzi (Temira), is a review of the author's life and a preparation for his death. Pindemonte's other plays include *Geta and Caracalla* (*Geta e Caracalla*) and *Ulysses and Palinurus* (*Ulisse e Palinuro*).

Ippolito Pindemonte. [Federico Arborio Mella, Milan]

Arminius (*Arminio;* wr. 1797, prod. 1804). Five-act play possibly inspired by a section of the *Germania* by Tacitus, and also treated by the German poet Klopstock, whom Pindemonte imitated. It observes the Senecan unities but is more closely allied in spirit to Vittorio Alfieri in his *Bruto Secondo*. In the funeral oration pronounced by Telgaste over the body of Baldero, it is reminiscent of Shakespeare's *Julius Caesar*. The general Arminius, urged by his wife Thusnelda, wishes to become King of the Cherusci but is opposed by other warriors who want to remain free. The clash between the two factions takes place in the Teutoburger Wald, and during the battle Arminius's son Baldero is killed. Meanwhile, Telgaste, who has opposed the ambitious Arminius although he is his son-in-law, wins the battle. Arminius himself, seriously wounded, soon dies, his imperial desires having caused nothing but heartbreak and death. *See* SENECAN DRAMA in glossary.

[PETER BONDANELLA]

CRITICISM

N. F. Cimmino, *Ippolito Pindemonte e il suo tempo*, Rome, 1968.

Pinero, Arthur Wing (1855–1934)

English dramatist and actor. Sir Arthur Wing Pinero was born in London on May 24, 1855, the son of a well-to-do solicitor of Portuguese-Jewish origin. When his father's practice began to deteriorate, young Pinero, at the age of ten, was forced to leave school to begin work in the family law office. Nine years later, when his father died, Pinero gave up law to pursue a theatrical career.

He gained experience as an actor in the provinces and on returning to London was invited by Henry Irving to join his company. When his first play, a one-act curtain raiser entitled *£200 a Year*, was performed in 1877 with Pinero in the cast, he had already earned a reputation as a character actor. The play was well received, and he set to work on others. His first full-length play and first real success, *The Money Spinner*, was produced in London in 1881. He abandoned acting to devote himself to writing plays, which he also directed. In 1883 he married the actress Myra Holme.

During the next ten years his output was considerable and varied. His farces *The Magistrate* (1885), *The School Mistress* (1886), and *Dandy Dick* (1887) brought him fame; and their inherent worth has been demonstrated in several recent revivals. From *Sweet Lavender* (1888) to *The Times* (1891) he dealt with more serious topics, and by 1891, he was already at work on *The Second Mrs. Tanqueray*, which did not reach the stage until 1893, partly because managers were doubtful about its theme and partly because it was difficult to find an actress with sufficient daring to take the title role. Finally its production, with Mrs. Pat Campbell as Mrs. Tanqueray, was a triumph. Although Pinero was to write more than twenty plays from this time until 1928, none eclipsed this success, and perhaps only *Trelawny of the "Wells"* (1898)

Arthur Wing Pinero. [Walter Hampden Memorial Library at The Players, New York]

and *Mid-Channel* (1909) are to be regarded as inherently important.

Pinero was knighted in 1909, and he died in London on November 23, 1934.

WORK

Pinero's career in the English theatre lasted some fifty-five years and resulted in plays of all varieties. His work may be divided into three periods: the early years, 1877 to 1893, when he devoted himself with great success to farce; his "serious" period, 1903 to 1919, when he wrote the works that earned him a reputation as a social critic; and the final years, 1919 to 1932, when he tried unsuccessfully to attract an audience for his drama. For a time, *The Second Mrs. Tanqueray* (1893), *Trelawny of the "Wells"* (1898), and *Mid-Channel* (1909) were highly regarded but such contemporary critics as Shaw emphasized that, for all their clever craftsmanship, they did little more than exploit the growing vogue for a more realistic view of society, while remaining essentially conventional. Recently, attention has turned to the early farces, once dismissed as frivolous. In these Pinero's consummate grasp of theatrical technique found its happiest expression. While the "social" plays seem increasingly antiquated, the farces, *The Magistrate* (1885) and *Dandy Dick* (1887) in particular, have been rediscovered and revived. *The School Mistress* (1886) is a study of the catastrophes that

Scene from *Sweet Lavender*. New York, Lyceum Theatre, 1888. [Brander Matthews Dramatic Museum, Columbia University]

Mrs. Patrick Campbell and George Alexander in *The Second Mrs. Tanqueray*. [Theatre Collection, The New York Public Library at Lincoln Center, Astor, Lenox and Tilden Foundations]

Ethel Barrymore starred as the tragic Zoe in the New York production of *Mid-Channel*, a drama of marital infidelity. [Private collection]

befall a man of monumental mediocrity; in *The Amazons* (1893), a woman raises her three daughters as boys; and *The Cabinet Minister* (1890), deals farcically with the higher levels of society. Though influenced by French farce techniques, these plays are English in spirit.

Despite the weaknesses (discerned by some contemporaries and very apparent now) of Pinero's "serious" plays, they were hailed as important. *The Profligate* (1889), his first serious play, deals with the double standard, but the protagonist, rather than being a "fallen woman," is a man who is punished for his actions; *Iris* (1901) is a description of a weak woman's degradation; *The Gay Lord Quex* (1899) shows the reformation of a rake; *The Notorious Mrs. Ebbsmith* (1895) is an improbable drama of an emancipated woman who deserts her ideals; and *The Thunderbolt* (1908) shows the upper classes squabbling over money.

The Magistrate (1885). Court farce concerning the conventional Mrs. Posket. Having been widowed and later married to Mr. Posket, a bumbling police magistrate, she has concealed her true age from her husband. Because of this "sacrifice of five years of girlhood—made only in consideration" for her spouse—her "precocious" son from her former marriage thinks he is fourteen when he is really nineteen. The complexities inherent in this white lie become apparent when Mrs. Posket, in order to silence Colonel Lukyn, her old friend and witness at the baptism of her son, sneaks off to an inn where he is lodging and where, unknown to her, her son and hus-

band are spending the evening. A police raid on the inn brings the characters together in a courtroom; the magistrate, having escaped the clutches of the police, sits in judgment on the "criminals." Informed of his real age, the son leaves for Canada with a bride and the blessings of his stepfather; and the Poskets are happily reunited.

Dandy Dick (1887). Farce about a racehorse which changes the lives of all the characters. For the Reverend Augustin Jedd, Dandy Dick represents a chance to win the £1,000 he needs to finance repairs of his cathedral, but his servant places the bet on the wrong horse with the result that Jedd spends a night in jail. For Jedd's daughters Salome and Sheba, Dandy represents a means of securing their father's consent to marry their Hussar sweethearts. Jedd's widowed sister Georgiana Tidman, who owns a share of Dandy, recoups her lost fortune when Dandy wins, and offers to lend her brother the money he needs. She also accepts a marriage proposal from Dandy's other owner, Tristram Mardon.

The Second Mrs. Tanqueray (1893). Drama in which Aubrey Tanqueray, a middle-aged widower, marries Paula Ray, a woman with a past. They retire to his country house, where they are joined by his daughter Ellean, a convent-reared girl, who refuses to make friends with her stepmother and soon leaves for Paris with a neighbor, causing tension between Aubrey and Paula. Just as they are becoming reconciled, Ellean returns and tells them she has met a young man. Introducing him to Paula, she leaves them alone. The man, Hugh Ardale, is Paula's former lover; she orders him to leave. Ellean, guessing the reason for Hugh's departure, denounces Paula, who kills herself.

Trelawny of the "Wells" (1898). Comedy about the beginnings of realism in the English theatre. Rose Trelawny of the Bagnigge-Wells Theatre leaves on becoming engaged to Arthur Gower, a gentleman. She goes to live with Arthur's grandfather, Sir William, until the wedding but realizing that she cannot adapt herself to her fiancé's society she breaks off the engagement. Back at the "Wells," Rose is told that she can no longer act and is fired. She can no longer declaim the artificial dialogue of the then traditionally "stagy" plays. But her friends Imogen Parrott and Tom Wrench (based on Thomas William Robertson, the first "realistic" dramatist) want to star her in a new, realistic play he has written. Sir William helps Rose by advancing them enough money to finance the production. Meanwhile Arthur, without the knowledge of Rose and Sir William, has become an actor, and Tom hires him to play the male lead. During rehearsal Arthur and Rose are reunited, and Sir William becomes reconciled to their marriage.

Mid-Channel (1909). Drama of Zoe and Theodore Blundell, whose marriage of thirteen years has reached "mid-channel." He treats her with indifference, and she responds with scorn. Their friend Peter Mottram tries to reconcile them, but they separate. Zoe goes to Italy and becomes involved in an affair with Leonard Ferris, while Theodore, in London, takes a mistress. When Zoe returns to London, she quarrels with Leonard and sends him away. Then, with Mottram's help, she attempts a reconciliation with Theodore. She forgives him for his affair, but when he finds she has also strayed, he insists on a divorce so that she can marry Leonard. Zoe goes to Leonard only to discover that he has already become engaged to someone else. In despair, she kills herself.

PLAYS

Unless otherwise noted, the plays were first performed in London.

1. *£200 a Year.* Comedietta, 1 act. Produced Globe Theatre, Oct. 6, 1877.
2. *Two Can Play at That Game.* Play. Produced Lyceum Theatre, Dec. 26, 1877.
3. *La comète, or Two Hearts.* Play. Produced Croydon. Theatre Royal, Apr. 22, 1878.
4. *Daisy's Escape.* Comedietta. Produced Lyceum Theatre, Sept. 20, 1879.
5. *Hester's Mystery.* Comedy, 1 act. Published 1893. Produced Folly Theatre, June 5, 1880.
6. *Bygones.* Play. Produced Lyceum Theatre, Sept. 18, 1880.
7. *The Money Spinner.* Comedy, 2 acts. Published 1900. Produced Manchester, Prince's Theatre, Nov. 5, 1880; London, St. James's Theatre, Jan. 8, 1881.
8. *Imprudence.* Play. Produced Folly Theatre, July 27, 1881.
9. *The Squire.* Play, 3 acts. Published 1881 (private ed.); 1905. Produced St. James's Theatre, Dec. 29, 1881.
10. *Girls and Boys.* Nursery tale. Produced Toole's Theatre, Nov. 1, 1882.
11. *The Rector.* Play. Produced Court Theatre, Mar. 24, 1883.
12. *The Rocket.* Comedy, 3 acts. Published 1905. Produced Liverpool, Prince of Wales Theatre, July 30, 1883; London, Gaiety Theatre, Oct. 10, 1883.
13. *Lords and Commons.* Play. Produced Haymarket Theatre, Nov. 24, 1883.
14. *Low Water.* Play. Published 1905. Produced Globe Theatre, Jan. 12, 1884.
15. (Adaptation). *the Ironmaster.* play. Produced St. James's Theatre, Apr. 17, 1884. Based on Georges Ohnet's *La maître des forges.*
16. *In Chancery.* Fantastic comedy, 3 acts. Published 1905; Produced Edinburgh, Lyceum Theatre, Sept. 19, 1884; London, Gaiety Theatre, Dec. 24, 1884.
17. *The Magistrate.* Farce, 3 acts. Published 1892. Produced Court Theatre, Mar. 21, 1885.
18. (Adaptation). *Mayfair.* Play. Produced St. James's Theatre, Oct. 31, 1885. Based on Victorien Sardou's *Maison Neuve.*
19. *The School Mistress.* Farce, 3 acts. Published 1894. Produced Court Theatre, Mar. 27, 1886.
20. *The Hobby House.* Comedy, 3 acts. Published 1892. Produced St. James's Theatre, Oct. 25, 1886.
21. *Dandy Dick.* Farce, 3 acts. Published 1893. Produced Court Theatre, Jan. 27, 1887.
22. *Sweet Lavender.* Domestic drama, 3 acts. Published 1893. Produced Terry's Theatre, Mar. 21, 1888.
23. *The Weaker Sex.* Comedy, 3 acts. Published 1894. Produced Manchester, Theatre Royal, Sept. 28, 1888; London, Court Theatre, Mar. 16, 1889.
24. *The Profligate.* Play, 4 acts. Published 1892. Produced Garrick Theatre, Apr. 24, 1889.
25. *The Cabinet Minister.* Farce, 4 acts. Produced Court Theatre, Apr. 23, 1890.
26. *Lady Bountiful.* Story of years, 4 acts. Published 1892. Produced Garrick Theatre, Feb. 7, 1891.
27. *The Times.* Comedy, 4 acts. Published 1891. Produced Terry's Theatre, Oct. 24, 1891.
28. *The Amazons.* Farcical romance, 3 acts. Published 1895. Produced Court Theatre, Mar. 7, 1893.
29. *The Second Mrs. Tanqueray.* Drama, 4 acts. Published 1895. Produced St. James's Theatre, May 27, 1893.
30. *The Notorious Mrs. Ebbsmith.* Drama, 4 acts. Published 1895. Produced Garrick Theatre, Mar. 13, 1895.
31. *The Benefit of the Doubt.* Comedy, 3 acts. Published 1896 (private ed.); 1896. Produced Comedy Theatre, Oct. 16, 1895.
32. *The Princess and the Butterfly, or The Fantastics.* Comedy, 5 acts. Published 1896 (private ed.); 1898. Produced St. James's Theatre, Mar. 29, 1897.
33. *Trelawny of the "Wells."* Comedietta, 4 acts. Published 1898. Produced Court Theatre, Jan. 20, 1898.
34. (With J. Comyns Carr). *The Beauty Stone.* Comic opera. Published 1898. Produced Savoy Theatre, May 28, 1898. Music: Sir Arthur Sullivan.
35. *The Gay Lord Quex.* Comedy. Published 1900. Produced Globe Theatre, Apr. 8, 1899.
36. *Iris.* Drama. Published 1902. Produced Garrick Theatre, Sept. 21, 1901.
37. *Letty.* Play. Published 1904. Produced Duke of York's Theatre, Oct. 8, 1903.
38. *A Wife Without a Smile.* Play. Published 1905. Produced Wyndham's Theatre, Oct. 12, 1904.
39. *His House in Order.* Comedy. Published 1906. Produced St. James's Theatre, Feb. 1, 1906.
40. *The Thunderbolt.* Play. Published 1909. Produced St. James's Theatre, May 9, 1908.
41. *Mid-Channel.* Drama. Published 1910. Produced St. James's Theatre, Sept. 2, 1909.
42. *Preserving Mr. Panmure.* Comic play, 4 acts. Published 1912. Produced Comedy Theatre, Jan. 19, 1911.
43. *The "Mind-the-Paint" Girl.* Comedy, 4 acts. Published 1913. Produced Duke of York's Theatre, Feb. 17, 1912.
44. *The Widow of Wasdale Head.* Fantasy, 1 act. Produced Duke of York's Theatre, Oct. 14, 1912.
45. *Playgoers.* Domestic episode, 1 act. Published 1913. Produced St. James's Theatre, Mar. 31, 1913.
46. *The Big Drum.* Comedy, 4 acts. Published 1915. Produced St. James's Theatre, Sept. 1, 1915.
47. *Mr. Livermore's Dream.* Play, 1 act. Produced Coliseum, Jan. 15, 1917.
48. *The Freaks: An Idyll of Suburbia.* Comedy, 3 acts. Published 1922. Produced New Theatre, Feb. 14, 1918.
49. *Monica's Blue Boy.* Wordless play. Produced New Theatre, Apr. 8, 1918. Music: Sir Frederic Cowen.
50. *Quick Work.* Play. Produced Springfield, Mass., Nov. 17, 1919.
51. *A Seat in the Park.* Sketch. Published 1922. Produced Winter Garden, Feb. 21, 1922.
52. *The Enchanted Cottage.* Fable, 3 acts. Published 1922. Produced Duke of York's Theatre, Mar. 1, 1922.
53. *A Private Room.* Play, 2 acts. Published 1928. Produced Little Theatre, May 14, 1928.
54. *Child Man.* Sedate farce, 3 acts. Published 1930.
55. *Dr. Harmer's Holidays.* Contrast, 9 scenes. Published 1930. Produced Washington, Shubert Theatre, Mar. 16, 1931.
56. *A Cold June.* Comedy. Produced Duchess Theatre, May 20, 1932.

EDITIONS

Collections
Social Plays, ed. by C. Hamilton, 4 vols., New York, 1917–1922.
Individual Plays
The Gay Lord Quex. Published in *Representative British Dramas, Victorian and Modern,* ed. by M. H. Moses, new rev. ed., Boston, 1931.
Iris. Published in *Representative Modern Plays,* ed. by R. A. Cordell, New York, 1929.
The Magistrate. Published in *From the Modern Repertoire,* ed. by E. R. Bentley, ser. 3, Bloomington. Ind., 1949–1956.
Mid-Channel. Published in *Edwardian Plays,* ed. by G. Weales, New York, 1962.
The Second Mrs. Tanqueray. Published in *The Victorian Age,* ed. by J. W. Bowyer and J. L. Brooks, 2d ed., New York, 1954.
The Thunderbolt. Published in *Twentieth Century Plays, British,* ed. by F. W. Chandler and R. A. Cordell, rev. and enl. ed., New York, 1941.
Trelawny of the "Wells." Published in *Great Modern British Plays,* ed. by J. W. Marriott, London, 1932.

CRITICISM

H. H. Fyfe, *Sir Arthur Wing Pinero, Playwright,* London, 1902; W. Stöcker, *Pinero's Dramen: Studien über Motive, Charaktere und Technik,* Marburg, 1911; H. H. Fyfe, *Sir Arthur Pinero's Plays and Players,* London, 1930; H. H. Küther, *Arthur Wing Pinero und sein Verhältnis zu Henrik Ibsen,* Bochum—Langendreer, 1937; W. D. Dunkel, *Sir Arthur Pinero,* Chicago, 1941; W. Lazenby, *Arthur Wing Pinero,* New York, 1972.

Pinget, Robert (1919–   )

French novelist and dramatist. Born in Geneva, Switzerland, he is perhaps best known as a leading exponent of the "new novel." His first play, *Dead Letter* (*Lettre morte,* 1960), is actually based on *Sonny* (*Lefiston,* 1959), a novel in the form of a long letter written by a man to his absent son. Pinget has been closely associated with Samuel Beckett, who adapted his radio play *La manivelle* (1960) as *The Old Tune,* conferring a strong Irish flavor on this haunting dialogue between two old men to which a faltering barrel organ provides a sometimes tragic sometimes triumphant counterpoint. *Architruc* (1962) concerns two old men who stave off their feelings of impotence, solitude, and fear of death by a series of elaborate rituals and disguises. *Clope* (*Ici ou ailleurs,* 1962), based on Pinget's novel *Clope's File* (*Clope au dossier,* 1961), contrasts a man's daily life with his spiritual aspirations. *About Mortin* (*Autour de Mortin,* 1965) is not a play in the strict sense of the term but a series of "interviews" meant to bring out the circumstances leading to the suicide of a writer. The figure of Mortin also appears in *The Hypothesis* (*L'hypothèse;* wr. 1961, prod. 1965). He also wrote *Identity* (*Identité,* 1972), *Paralchemy* (*Paralchimie,* 1972), and radio plays, *The Executioner* (*Le bourreau,* 1977), *The Chrysanthemum* (*Le chrysanthème,* 1977), and with Beckett, *Ashes* (*Cendres,* 1978). Though in no way an imitator of Beckett, Pinget closely resembles him in that his work insists on man's inevitable solitude in his hopeless struggle against time and the insufficiency of language. His theatre is stripped to its barest essentials and presents archetypes who nevertheless remain strongly individual. *See* BECKETT, SAMUEL.

Dead Letter (*Lettre morte,* 1960). Old and lonely, M. Levert focuses his hopes on the possibility of a letter from the son who abandoned him years ago. He passes a great deal of his time in a local bar trying to defeat his solitude by establishing some sort of relationship between his own story and the lives of others. A farcical light is thrown on his tragic situation by a group of actors who amuse themselves by rehearsing bits from a comedy about a prodigal son. At the post office, Levert tries to badger the clerk into admitting that the letter may have arrived and been misplaced. The funeral of a young woman passes by, and both Levert and the clerk imaginatively involve themselves in the procession. The clerk is reminded of his sister's funeral and tells Levert about it. After making an attempt to rummage through the post office's dead-letter file, Levert leaves, repeating to himself bits of the clerk's story.   [JOSEPH E. GARREAU]

Pinski, David   (1872–1959)

Yiddish- and Hebrew-language novelist, editor, and dramatist. Pinski became outstanding among Jewish dramatists for the quality and quantity of his work. Born in Russia and originally trained in Talmudic studies, he later attended medical school in Vienna. Eventually he settled in Poland, where, encouraged by his friend I. L. Peretz, he began to write. *See* PERETZ, ISAAC LOEB.

After arriving in New York in 1899, Pinski took courses at Columbia University and then became an editor and a labor-union leader. His first play, *Sorrows* (*Yesurim,* 1899), was followed by *The Mother* (*Die Mutter,* 1900) and *The Zvi Family* (*Die Familie Zvi,* 1903/04). His first great success came with *Isaac Scheftel* (1907), a three-act play exploring the inner turmoil and eventual suicide of a young inventor whose employer steals his invention; translated into German in 1904 by Martin Buber, the play was first performed by the Hirschbein troupe. *Yankel the Smith* (*Yankel die Shmit,* 1906) deals with the

conflict of a man torn between sexual desire for a young girl and love for his sick wife. Pinski first attracted the attention of the non-Jewish world with *The Treasure* (*Der Oitzer,* 1911), a play in which realism joins supernaturalism to comment upon human greed.

Among other outstanding plays by Pinski are *The Eternal Jew* (*Der ebiker Yid,* 1906), a one-act tragedy; *The Dumb Messiah* (*Der shtumer Mashiach,* 1911), a tragedy set in the year 1306; *King David and His Wives* (*Dovid Hamelech und zeine Veiber*), a series of five poetic one-act plays centering on the amours of King David and including *Michal* (1914), *Abigail* (1915), *Bathsheba* (1915), *In the Harem* (1915), and *Abishag* (1916); *To Each His Own* (*Yeder mit zein Got,* 1912); *Gabri and the Women* (*Gabri und die Veiber,* 1916); *Shlomo Molcho* (1930), a tragedy about the sixteenth-century Marrano messianic pretender; *Sabbatai Zevi* (1935), about the seventeenth-century false messiah; and *Not a Fugitive* (*Nisht Antlofer,* 1944), which is set in a concentration camp. When he died, Pinski was in the process of writing plays based on Biblical stories. *See* HEBREW DRAMA; YIDDISH DRAMA.

King David and His Wives (*Dovid Hamelech und zeine Veiber*): *Michal* (1914), *Abigail* (1915), *Bathsheba* (1915), *In the Harem* (1915), *Abishag* (1916). In these five short plays, later brought together under the collective title, David grows older and becomes less a figure of idealism and kingly bearing. In the first episode he is the youthful idealist for whom physical love and Godly love are still inseparable. In *Abigail,* however, physical passion begins to overwhelm him, and while he still remains loyal to his king, he barely disguises his attraction for another man's wife. When Abigail's evil husband finally dies at her feet, she and David are free to marry. His lust for Bathsheba, however, is more immediate and intense. Spying her at her bath, David, now the king, orders her to give herself to him, and when she refuses, he first humiliates her husband, Uriah, and then sends him to his death. By the time of *In the Harem,* David is an aged king, his sons have destroyed each other through lust and jealousy, and his wives, no longer physically attractive, long for his death and squabble about his successor. David, "old and cold," is a remnant of his former self and seeks comfort in the imagined continuity of his physical powers. Yet when Abishag is brought to him in the last of the five plays, he is so taken by her unapproachable beauty and so aware that consummation will provide only temporary satisfaction that he chooses to keep her virginal.

[IRVING SAPOSNIK]

Pinter, Harold   (1930–   )

English actor and dramatist. He was born in the East End of London on October 10, 1930, the only child of a Portuguese-Jewish immigrant family. His successful acting in grammar school plays and an enthusiastic drama teacher led him to an early determination on his career. He enrolled in the Royal Academy of Dramatic Art in 1948. Dissatisfied, he left the following year to join a repertory company. During the next ten years he toured with various companies under the stage name David Baron.

Pinter had begun writing poetry at the age of thirteen. While working as an actor, he began to write short prose pieces, and by 1957 he was writing plays. That year he wrote a one-act play, *The Room*, first produced by the drama department at Bristol University and later by the Bristol Old Vic Drama School; and his first full-length play, *The Birthday Party*, which played only one week at Hammersmith in 1958 after receiving unfavorable criticism in the press. A one-act play, *The Dumb Waiter*, was first produced in Frankfurt am Main in German in 1959. It was not until the 1960 production of *The Caretaker*, in London, that Pinter had his first great success. The same year *The Room* and *The Dumb Waiter* were also well received, and by the end of the season Pinter had been praised as best playwright of the year and had received an award for *The Caretaker* from the *Evening Standard*.

Pinter has written not only for the stage but for all the media adaptable to dramatic writing. Contributing to a couple of revues in 1959, he wrote the sketches *Last to Go, Request Stop, Trouble in the Works,* and *The Black and White;* for radio he wrote *A Slight Ache* (1959) and *A Night Out* (1960); for television, *The Collection* (1961), *The Lover* (1963), *Tea Party* (1965), and *The Basement* (1967); and for the screen, *The Pumpkin Eater* (1964), *Accident* (1965), and *The Quiller Memorandum* (1966). He has adapted several of these works, most notably *A Slight Ache* and *The Collection,* for the stage.

In September, 1956, Pinter married the actress Vivien Merchant, who created many of his female roles until they separated after *Old Times* (1971). They have one son. He later married the writer Lady Antonia Fraser.

WORK

The term "comedy of menace" best describes the early plays of Pinter. Since the source of the menace is often not explicit, the effect is a strong sense of floating anxi-

James LaFerla (left) and Arthur Roberts in a 1969 production of Harold Pinter's *The Birthday Party*. [McCarter Theatre, Princeton, N. J. Photograph by Jim McDonald]

The Birthday Party, with (foreground) Betty Field and Robert Phalen. New York, Repertory Theatre of Lincoln Center, 1971. [Photograph by Martha Swope]

ety. Set in an enclosed area, usually one room, the plays imply that the world outside that room is threatening; the circumstances seem ordinary, but there is a generalized, unspecified horror seething beneath the action. Mystery and terror are frequently created in the form of unanswerable accusations; nothing is verifiable, and there is a chilling sense of the isolation of people. In his later plays, Pinter transfers the menace from the outer, unseen world to the inner world of the mind. Characters in the early plays, although they might communicate on a low level, do not choose to do so. Characters in the later plays tend to be better educated and have the means to communicate, but they still choose not to do so. Pinter's strength in this display of noncommunication lies in his skillful use of language and dialogue, which shows the influence of Samuel Beckett. He uses realistic language to underscore the difference between what people say and what they mean and to emphasize his characters' disinclination to understand one another. Much of the menace as well as the humor of his plays derives from this noncommunication. *See* BECKETT, SAMUEL *See also* THEATRE OF THE ABSURD in glossary.

Menace from without predominates in his first play, *The Room* (1957), in which an elderly couple seems likely to be evicted from the room they have been living in. Likewise, in *The Dumb Waiter* (1959) Pinter employs an unseen menace: two hired murderers, Ben and Gus, wait in a shabby room for orders about their next job, while irrelevant orders for food are transmitted to them by means of a dumbwaiter from above. In *The Birthday Party* (1958), Pinter's first full-length play, Stanley, seemingly safe in a run-down boardinghouse at the seashore, is suddenly confronted with the mysterious and menacing visitors Goldberg and McCann, who work for a mysterious organization. *A Slight Ache* (1959) is the first play in which menace, although apparently coming from without, is abetted by the personalities of the characters themselves. The continual and mysterious presence of a silent old match seller catalyses the disintegration of Edward as a man and husband and his eventual replacement in the eyes of his wife by the old man.

In contrast, *The Caretaker* (1960), Pinter's first commercial success, utilizes the personalities within the inevitable single room to engender menace: characters clash and actively contribute to their own fate. A tramp is manipulated by a jealous brother until he is rejected by the brother who had been his friend. The menace in *The Homecoming* (1965) exists within the brutalizing members of the all-male household into which an older brother, Teddy, brings his wife. In this case, as in *The Caretaker*, the victim comes from outside; here Pinter contrasts the sentimental idea of a homecoming with the vicious forces within the house.

The Dwarfs (1960), based on Pinter's unpublished novel of the same name, is essentially a series of religiously symbolic conversations between three characters who form a nightmarish trinity. *The Collection* (1961) and *The Lover* (1963) both deal with the problem of an individual's reality: in the first, two couples in two separate rooms threaten each other and attempt to work out their real or illusory sexual entanglements; in *The Lover*, a husband and wife indulge in an eerie game in which both pretend infidelity to each other while, in fact, the wife's afternoon lover is her husband dressed in different clothing.

The Birthday Party (1958). Into the relatively peaceful menage of a shabby boardinghouse at the edge of the ocean come two new guests of unknown origin. Before their arrival Stanley, the only boarder, a lethargic and immature man of about thirty, puts up as usual with alternate mothering and flirting from Meg, the owner of the house, while her husband Petey sits behind his newspaper. Stanley's lethargy extends to Lulu, a young girl whose advances he refuses, preferring to lie in bed or sit indoors. When he hears about the imminent arrival of the two visitors, he becomes nervous and irate, and his teasing response to Meg foreshadows the danger to accompany the intrusion of the mysterious newcomers. When they arrive, Goldberg and McCann harry Stanley with inconsequential questions; terror mounts to the point where Stanley lashes out at Goldberg. Meg suc-

Scene from a 1968 production of *The Caretaker,* with (l. to r.) Macon McCalman, Anthony Heald, and David O. Petersen. [Asolo State Theatre Company, Sarasota, Fla.]

The Homecoming, with (l. to r.) Peter Goetz, Fern Sloan, Lee Richardson, and James Lawless, Minneapolis, 1968. [The Guthrie Theater Company]

ceeds in lifting the tension by suggesting a birthday party for Stanley, who maintains that it is not his birthday. Then the party begins. Once again, in a macabre game of blindman's bluff with all the lights extinguished, tension mounts and Stanley again lashes out, apparently to strangle Meg and rape Lulu. McCann and Goldberg overpower him, and the next morning, with a big black car waiting outside, they report that since Stanley has had a nervous breakdown during the night, they will take him away with them and care for him. Stanley appears, now well dressed and clean-shaven, but able to mutter only inarticulate sounds; he goes off meekly with them as they promise to watch over him assiduously. Petey feebly tries to stop them, but he is easily put off by an invitation to accompany them.

The Dumb Waiter (1959). In the basement of an old lodging house two men chat aimlessly about news and sports, and as they nag each other, it becomes evident that they are gunmen waiting for their victim, though still ignorant of his identity. A sense of fear and menace, suggested in the nervous irritability of their chance remarks, is increased when an envelope with a box of matches is slid under the door and when a dumbwaiter goes up and down bearing demands for the sending up of food, demands which the two men frantically, and even farcically, endeavor to fulfill. The tension increases until, at the end, Gus steps out of the room, Ben receives

a final order to shoot the first person to come in, Gus reenters, and Ben levels his revolver at him. All the actions, mingling laughter with a growing terror, are in themselves less important then the general atmosphere of fear enveloping the entire play.

The Caretaker (1960). Davies, an old tramp, has been rescued from a fight by the kind but slow-witted Aston, who takes him back to a junk-filled room in a house that he shares with his brother Mick. Left alone, Davies rummages through the debris that Aston has been collecting with an eye to building a shed. He is surprised by Mick, who tries to establish a bond with the tramp in order to woo him away from his brother. Aston in turn takes Davies into his confidence, and both brothers independently offer him the position of caretaker. Davies, disregarding Aston's trust, now allies himself with Mick, who has subtly goaded him into complaining about Aston. But Mick, having caused a rift in the relationship between his brother and Davies, now rejects Davies's criticisms and tells him he must leave. Too late, Davies turns back to Aston for support; at this point Aston too rejects him. As the curtain falls, Davies leaves the room.

The Homecoming (1965). Teddy, after teaching philosophy at an American university for six years, brings his wife Ruth home to London to meet his family: his father Max, a nagging, aggressive ex-butcher; Max's brother Sam, a weak, ineffectual chauffeur; Teddy's younger brother Lenny, a pimp; and another brother Joey, a prospective boxer. The family has been womanless since the death of Jessie, Teddy's mother, many years before. Teddy and Ruth arrive unexpectedly in the middle of the night and walk about separately. Teddy confronts Lenny but goes to bed without mentioning Ruth, so that when Lenny meets Ruth, they do not know each other and Ruth obliquely offers herself to him. In the morning, Teddy and Ruth see the rest of the family, and Max calls her a tart. After breakfast Teddy, sensing danger, suggests that he and Ruth leave early and return to the States, but she does not respond. Joey and Lenny make love to her while Max and Teddy stand by impassively, and although Teddy makes no sound when his brothers steal his wife, Lenny loudly protests when Teddy eats a cheese roll belonging to him. Teddy leaves alone, and the family sets up Ruth as harlot, cook, mother, and housekeeper.

Old Times (1971). In their converted farmhouse Deeley and Kate are expecting the arrival of a woman apparently known only to Kate; the actress who plays Anna is

George Martin and Amy Van Nostrand in a 1982 New York production of *The Hothouse* by the Trinity Square Repertory Company. The play was written in the 1950s. [Photograph courtesy of Arthur Cantor, Inc.]

already waiting on stage to make her "entrance" into the dialogue. Soon she and Kate are talking as if time had flashed back to when they were flatmates, but Deeley is able to interrupt, and time now seems to flash forward to an after-dinner conversation. Time keeps shifting backward and forward as the balance of power shifts within the triangle, a pair of characters allying to exclude the other.

No Man's Land (1975). A successful man of letters, now apparently a dipsomaniac attended by two male nurses, brings an impecunious writer back to his luxurious Hampstead home. At first it seems that the two men met for the first time earlier in the evening; later the host will reenter after an absence offstage with no apparent memory of ever having seen his guest before; later still the two men will talk as if they have known each other for most of their lives and given each other reasons for sexual jealousy.

Betrayal (1978). The story of a triangular relationship is told backward, ending with the moment at which the best friend makes his first amorous advance to the wife. During the course of the action each of the three betrays both of the others.

PLAYS

1. *The Room.* Play, 1 act. Written 1957. Published 1960. Produced Bristol, Bristol University Drama Department, 1957; London, Hampstead Theatre Club, Jan. 21, 1960; London, Royal Court Theatre, Mar. 8, 1960. Presented as a double bill with *The Dumb Waiter.*

2. *The Birthday Party.* Play, 3 acts. Written 1957. Published 1960. Produced Cambridge, Arts Theatre, Apr. 28, 1958; Hammersmith, Lyric Opera House, May 19, 1958.

3. *The Dumb Waiter.* Play, 1 act. Published 1960. Produced Frankfurt am Main, Frankfurt Municipal Theatre (in German), 1959; London, Hampstead Theatre Club, Jan. 21, 1960; London, Royal Court Theatre, Mar. 8, 1960. Presented as a double bill with *The Room.*

4. *A Slight Ache.* Radio play, 1 act. Published 1961. Produced London, BBC Radio, July 29, 1959; London, Arts Theatre Club, Jan. 18, 1961; London, Criterion Theatre, Feb. 13, 1961. One of three 1-act plays produced under the title *Three.*

5. *Last to Go.* Revue sketch, 1 scene. Published 1961. Produced in the revue *Pieces of Eight,* London, Apollo Theatre, Sept. 23, 1959.

6. *Request Stop.* Revue sketch, 1 scene. Published 1961. Produced in the revue *Pieces of Eight,* London, Apollo Theatre, Sept. 23, 1959.

7. *The Black and White.* Revue sketch, 1 scene. Published 1961. Produced in the revue *One to Another,* Hammersmith, Lyric Opera House, July 15, 1959.

8. *Trouble in the Works.* Revue sketch, 1 scene. Published 1961. Produced in the revue *One to Another,* Hammersmith, Lyric Opera House, July 15, 1959.

9. *A Night Out.* Play, 1 act. Published 1961. Produced London, BBC Radio, Mar. 1, 1960; New York, ABC Armchair Theatre (television), Apr. 24, 1960; Dublin, Gate Theatre (Dublin Theatre Festival), 1961; London, Comedy Theatre, Oct. 2, 1961.

10. *The Caretaker.* Play, 3 acts. Published 1960. Produced London, Arts Theatre Club, Apr. 27, 1960; London, Duchess Theatre, May 30, 1960.

11. *The Dwarfs.* Play, 1 act. Published 1961. Produced London, BBC Radio, Dec. 2, 1960; London, New Arts Theatre, Sept. 18, 1963. Presented with *The Lover.*

12. *Night School.* Play. Produced London, BBC Radio and Television (Associated Rediffusion Ltd.), 1961.

13. *Applicant.* Revue sketch, 1 scene. Published 1961.

14. *The Collection.* Play, short scenes. Published 1963. Produced London, television (Associated Rediffusion Ltd.), May 11, 1961; London, Aldwych Theatre, June 18, 1962.

15. *The Lover.* Play, 1 act; prose. Published 1963. Produced London, BBC Television (Associated Rediffusion Ltd.), Mar. 28, 1963; London, New Arts Theatre, Sept. 18, 1963. Presented with *The Dwarfs.*

16. *Tea Party.* Play. Produced London, BBC Television, March, 1965.

17. *The Homecoming.* Play, 2 acts; prose. Published 1965. Produced London, Aldwych Theatre, June 3, 1965.

18. *The Basement*. Play. Produced London, television, February, 1967.
19. *Landscape* and *Silence*. Two one-act plays. Produced London, Aldwych Theatre, July 2, 1969.
20. *Old Times*. Play, 2 acts. Produced London, Aldwych Theatre, June 1, 1971.
21. *Monologue*. Play. Produced London, BBC Television, Apr. 1973.
22. *No Man's Land*. Play, 2 acts. Published 1975. Produced London National Theatre, Apr. 23, 1975.
23. *Betrayal*. Play, 9 scenes. Published 1978. Produced London National Theatre, Nov. 15, 1978.
24. *Family Voices*. Radio play. Published 1981. Broadcast by the BBC, January, 1981.
25. *The Hothouse*. Black comedy. Written 1958. Published 1980. Produced London, Hampstead Theatre, April, 1980; Providence, February, 1982; New York, Playhouse Theatre, May 6, 1982.

EDITIONS

Collections
Two Plays, New York, 1961; *Three Plays*, New York, 1962; *The Lover; Tea Party; The Basement*, New York, 1967; *Early Plays by Harold Pinter*, New York, 1968.
Individual Plays
The Birthday Party. Published in *Seven Plays of the Modern Theatre*, intro. by H. Clurman, New York, 1962.
The Dumb Waiter. Published in *New English Dramatists*, ed. by E. M. Browne and T. Maschler, vol. 3, Harmondsworth, England, 1962.

CRITICISM

A. P. Hinchcliffe, *Harold Pinter*, New York, 1967; R. Hayman, *Harold Pinter*, London, 1968, 3d ed., 1975; W. Kerr, *Harold Pinter*, New York, 1968; L. G. Gordon, *Stratagem to Uncover Nakedness: The Dramas of Harold Pinter*, Columbia, Mo., 1969; J. R. Hollis, *Harold Pinter: The Poetics of Silence*, Carbondale, Ill., 1970; W. Baker and S. E. Takachnik, *Harold Pinter*, Edinburgh, 1973; R. Hayman, *Theatre and Anti-Theatre*, London and New York, 1979.

Pirandello, Luigi   (1867–1936)

Italian short-story writer, novelist, and dramatist. He was born on June 28, 1867, in Girgenti (now Agrigento), on the south-central coast of Sicily. Both his father and his mother were members of patriotic, pro-Garibaldi families. His maternal grandfather, Giovanni Ricci-Gramitto, had been a member of the provisional Sicilian government of 1848 and had fled to Malta when his property was confiscated after that government was outlawed. His paternal grandfather was a wealthy man, and his father, owner of a rich sulfur mine, played an important role in the industrial and commercial life of Girgenti and Porto Empedocle.

Pirandello had a comfortable childhood and adolescence on his parents' country estate, where the family had taken refuge to avoid drawing public attention to its political beliefs. He studied at first with a private tutor, then went to Girgenti's technical institute, and finally attended its Gymnasium, where he excelled in oratory and literature and where, as a result of his interest in Pellico, the nineteenth-century Italian dramatic poet, he wrote his first tragedy, *Barbaro*, which was subsequently lost. *See* PELLICO, SILVIO.

After completing his early education in Palermo, Pirandello entered his father's business. It was soon apparent that he was unfit for the world of commerce, and in 1887 he enrolled at the University of Rome. He remained there for two years and then, dissatisfied with his professors, went to study at the University of Bonn, where he worked for a degree in letters and philosophy, offering for his doctorate a thesis on the phonetics and morphology of his native dialect. *Painful Joy (Mal giocondo)*,

Luigi Pirandello.
[Italian Cultural
Institute]

the first of several volumes of poetry, was published in 1889. After receiving his degree, he remained in Bonn for a year as a lecturer and returned in 1891 to Rome, where he resided for the rest of his life.

By this time Pirandello had developed literary ambitions. But in 1894 there began a series of melancholy events that were to becloud his entire life. First, his father's business had begun to fail and Pirandello could no longer count on family financial support. Since his literary activity was hardly lucrative, he took, in 1897, a post as a teacher of rhetoric at the Istituto Superiore di Magistero Femminile, a teachers college for women in Rome. He remained there until 1923, first as an instructor and then as a professor.

Also in 1894, Pirandello married Antonietta Portulano, the daughter of a business associate of his father. The wedding had been arranged by the two families, and the couple scarcely knew one another before the ceremony. They were not well matched; his wife's violent, capricious nature contrasted sharply with Pirandello's gentleness. The first five years of marriage, which were relatively untroubled, produced three children, Stefano (now a writer), Rosalie, and Fausto (a painter). Then, in 1904, when her father-in-law went bankrupt, Antonietta suffered a nervous breakdown. She began to show signs of more serious mental imbalance, with frequent hysterical attacks during which she accused her husband of infidelity and deceit. Pirandello did everything possible to soothe his wife and allay her suspicions. He gave up his friends, stayed at home, and even turned over his salary to his wife, keeping only enough money to get him to school. But his efforts were useless, and the situation deteriorated during World War I when their son Stefano, who had enlisted in the Italian Army, was taken prisoner and fell seriously ill. Finally, in 1919, Antonietta was placed in a mental institution.

All through this difficult period Pirandello continued to write. His early volume of poems was followed by two more volumes, and his short stories and novels began to appear in newspapers and magazines. His first novel, *The Outcast (L'esclusa)*, was written in 1893 and serialized

Pirandello in later years. [Italian Cultural Institute]

writings with "bitter compassion for all those who fool themselves."

At forty-two, when he wrote these autobiographical notes, Pirandello had not yet begun his career as a dramatist, but the same personal philosophy of the irony and bitterness of self-deception was to be reflected in each of his more than forty plays. In 1898 he had written *The Epilogue (L'epilogo)*, a one-act play, but it had never been produced. Retitled *The Vise (La morsa)*, it was presented, along with another one-acter, *Sicilian Limes (Lumìe di Sicilia*, wr. 1910), by Nino Martoglio, a Sicilian producer and dramatist who had taken a new theatre in Rome in 1910. From then on Pirandello devoted most of his time to writing plays, and the financial rewards eventually freed him from the tyranny of teaching. He worked intensively and rapidly, in one year writing nine plays, one of which was written, incredibly, in three days and another in six.

His most prolific period occurred between 1916 and 1925. His ambivalent relationship to the Fascist regime became newsworthy as he joined the party in its darkest hour, just after the Matteotti assassination. This gesture won Mussolini's support for his theatrical ventures, although the ideas embodied in his best plays show no evidence of Fascist ideology. In 1925, patronized by Mussolini, he founded his own theatre in Rome and then took his company on a European tour. The enterprise was artistically successful but financially unprofitable, and the dramatist lost a considerable amount of his money. By the last years of his life his fame had spread to North and South America, throughout Europe as far as Turkey, and to Japan. His works were translated into many languages and became the subject of numerous critical studies. He finally received the Nobel Prize for Literature in 1934. The same year his libretto for Gian Francesco Malipiero's opera *The Fable of the Changeling (La favola del figlio cambiato)* met with the disfavor of the Fascist hierarchy, and in 1935 Pirandello felt it necessary to make amends by defending the Ethiopian invasion. He continued to make his home in Rome although he traveled extensively, and he wrote plays until his death in Rome on December 10, 1936. In keeping with his distaste for the deceptions and illusions of life, he requested the simplest possible cremation and funeral.

WORK

Though the roots of Pirandello's unique theatrical works lie within the dramatic traditions of the *commedia dell'arte*, his immediate point of departure was the naturalism represented by such Sicilian writers as Verga, whose major dramatic works include *Cavalleria rusticana* and *The She-Wolf*. Eventually, however, he came to be identified closely with the *teatro del grottesco* ("theatre of the grotesque"), a World War I dramatic school that emphasized the paradoxical and contradictory aspects of life, stressing the conflict between appearance and reality, between the comic mask and the face it hides. The relation between the ideas of Pirandello and dramatists of the grotesque such as Chiarelli (*The Mask and the Face*) and Rosso di San Secondo (*Marionettes, What Passion!*) is

in a Roman newspaper in 1901. This was followed by another novel, *The Turn (Il turno)*, and by volumes of collected short stories. His most famous novel, *The Late Mattia Pascal (Il fu Mattia Pascal)*, appeared in 1904 and established his literary reputation. Between 1904 and 1920 he wrote several novels and produced collections of short stories as well as *Art and Science (Arte e scienza*, 1908), a lengthy book of criticism, and *On Humor (L'umorismo*, 1908), the essay containing his artistic credo, an important definition of modern tragicomedy which is of use in interpreting his best dramatic works. In his essay, Pirandello distinguishes between a comic writer and a humorist (the category to which he belongs) on the basis of self-consciousness and emotion: the comic writer is merely aware of incongruous human situations while the humorist comprehends such situations on both a rational and an emotional level. His emphasis on emotion and sentiment contradicts the views of many recent critics, who see him as a completely cerebral writer.

That he was unhappy can be seen from an autobiographical sketch written in 1909 and finally published in *Le Lettere di Roma* in 1924. In it he describes a colorless existence broken only by daily walks in the company of friends. Teaching became a burden; he fervently wished to retire to the country to write. The important events of his life were all interior, in his work and in his unhappy thoughts. Believing that life was rendered ridiculous by self-deception, by the creation of inner realities sporadically exposed as vain and illusory, Pirandello filled his made clear in Pirandello's own essay *On Humor* (1908). *See* CHIARELLI, LUIGI; ROSSO DI SAN SECONDO, PIER MARIA; VERGA, GIOVANNI. *See also* COMMEDIA DELL' ARTE in glossary.

Pirandello's point of view contains a duality reflecting the Sicilian social structure with its tight-knit family groups in which an austere Catholicism and a rigid code of honor overlay an explosive and violent temperament. Thus, born in a land of contradictions and deceptions, Pirandello became preoccupied with self-deception and peered behind everyday masks to see what lay beneath.

Beyond the land and its tradition of masked violence, Pirandello's personal problems and the intellectual climate of the times—optimism had been shattered by the newly formed Italian kingdom's neglect of faraway Sicily and by a cataclysmic world war—formed the context from which he was to draw his subject matter. Behind him lay, it seemed, the wreckage of religion and science, and ahead lay vast and eternal questions, still unanswered.

Pirandello himself said that these conflicts of his life and his world produced in him an ability to see within every action its opposite, a kind of detachment that placed him outside the event. This detachment can be seen in his protagonists, who suffer in complete awareness of their predicaments. Pirandello considered this point of view the basis of the comic attitude. Yet beyond comedy, his clear vision of life's essential chaos and his conscious avoidance of answers to the questions he posed account for the mystery that is central to his plays—the mystery of life and of human personality. The plays are enigmatic, their characters unpredictable, basically bewildered in the face of life's contradictions and, like life itself, not readily definable.

Because of this vision of the existential predicament of human life, Pirandello became the first of the "absurdists." *Six Characters in Search of an Author* (*Sei personaggi in cerca d'autore,* 1921) had a tremendous impact when it was produced in 1923 in France, where it introduced concepts now taken for granted by Sartre, Camus, Anouilh, Wilder, Beckett, Ionesco, and Genet. It may be said that Pirandello's characters face essentially the same "absurd" abyss; they play life's game by assuming the mask that best permits them to survive, but they are often destroyed in the process. *See* THEATRE OF THE ABSURD in glossary.

Pirandello hated sham and sought to probe the mystery of human personality. Man "creates himself," he felt, choosing whatever personality permits him to live best as a member of society. But society in turn creates itself, inventing forms that make it possible for men to live together. Once codified as religion, law, and morality, these forms then hamper man and become the instruments of his destruction. This theory, carried even further, results in a conflict between form and life and eventually led Pirandello to doubt the reality of art itself. Art becomes the ultimate paradox, a form which simultaneously creates and destroys by giving permanence to material that is in the constant process of change. One finds three dominant themes in Pirandellian drama: man

creates both his personality and his life, ultimately becoming imprisoned by them; reality is relative, changing with the viewer; art is the ultimate reality, superior to life because of its permanence and yet inferior to it because of its immobility. Behind all these themes lie several basic conflicts: those between the primitive life force and life as conceived by man and society, between nature and form, truth and appearance, face and mask.

Although the plays have been termed cerebral, nothing could be further from the truth. For their intensity derives from conflict, the seed of drama. Pirandello's characters live intensely, hate and love, are driven and tossed. At the root is a zest for life often lacking, apparently, in Pirandello's interpreters and critics, who see only the cerebrations, not the motivating actions and emotions. The characters usually act desperately in an absurd and chaotic world; they are fragmented beings with a thirst for ideal truth, beings forced to inhabit a real world that neither suits nor pleases them. Illusion is necessary for survival. Thus, unmasking illusion often causes violence. Sometimes, as with Donata Genzi in *To Find Oneself* (*Trovarsi,* 1932), the illusion is consciously assumed, at times for self-protection and at times for the protection of another. Invariably, however, beneath the mask lies peril.

Thus arises the idea of multiple personalities. If one "creates oneself," then one may change this creation at will. It naturally follows, then, that those who see the creation are themselves creating, and life becomes an endless hall of mirrors within which echoes Pirandello's anguished laughter. So it is that Signora Morli in *Mrs. Morli, One and Two* (*La Signora Morli, una e due,* 1920) buries one personality only to have it emerge when its catalyst reappears; and that Angelo Baldovino in *The Pleasure of Honesty* (*Il piacere dell'onestà,* 1917) assumes a personality created for him by another, gradually submerging his own identity. Perhaps the most extreme expression of these themes is Donata Genzi, an actress in search of her own identity, who learns to her misfortune that life is less real than art, that, in fact, one "creates oneself" in life with far less care than that given to the creations of art.

Although Pirandello experimented with dramatic structure, moving from the appearance onstage of "live" fictional characters in *Six Characters in Search of an Author* through the vagaries of *Tonight We Improvise* (*Questa sera si recita a soggetto,* 1930) and into the poetic symbolism of the unfinished *The Mountain Giants* (*I giganti della montagna,* 1937), he required conventional form in order to exploit his ideas fully. Form suited his purpose of exposing form's rigidity. Thus the play itself becomes a tool. In *Each in His Own Way* (*Ciascuno a suo modo,* 1924) and *Six Characters in Search of an Author,* form is created and then shattered to prove a point. In short, every aspect of reality—even dramatic form itself—can be investigated by opposing illusion and reality and exploring their various levels.

Pirandello, disliking the word "realism," was nevertheless a master of the realistic. Realistic characters, dialogue, and physical detail were his tools but not his material. With these tools he shaped a new dramatic world in which realism becomes the play's mask, just as appearance is life's mask. And beneath this apparent realism whirl the chaos and the contradiction, ready to appear at any moment and prove reality a lie.

His preoccupation with form, with illusion, ultimately led Pirandello to focus on the opposition of life and art. This is seen most simply in his *Diana and Tuda* (*Diana e la Tuda*, 1927), in which the living model is sacrificed to her marble representation, leaving behind a husk of the living woman. But no sooner is a truth captured than its opposite appears. No sooner has a moment taken on artistic life than it becomes falsely immobile. In another sense, however, art is more real than life: the dramatic force of the "six characters," frozen in their fictional moment, is more compelling than life itself; and yet these characters are victims of their moment, unable to move forward or backward without their author. In *Each in His Own Way*, the dramatization of a real event looks absurdly melodramatic. In *Tonight We Improvise*, fiction submerges reality, the characters run away with their actors, and the play takes on a life of its own. In *Henry IV* (*Enrico IV*, 1922), a man is frozen in time; and in *When Someone Is Somebody* (*Quando si è qualcuno*, 1933), an author is trapped in the past by the mass deification of his public personality.

Another variation of the theme of contradictions in life is the relativity of truth. In *Right You Are—If You Think You Are* [*Così è (si vi pare)*, 1917], three people clinging together amid the wreckage of their tragedy create fictions that protect each other and make it impossible to discern the real truth. Truth also can destroy: Ciampa in *Cap and Bells* (*Il berretto a sonagli*, 1917) must destroy truth before it destroys him; in *Naked; To Clothe the Naked* (*Vestire gli ignudi*, 1922), Ersilia Drei must die once she is stripped of her fictions.

Critics have persistently accused Pirandello of nihilism, yet from his world emerges a positive element: the overpowering force of life. Those characters who accept it, with all its inconsistencies, who live life fully—the protagonist of *Liolà* (1916) and the young priest in *Lazarus* (*Lazzaro*, 1929)—are close to God and are "saved." The mother figure in *The New Colony* (*La nuova colonia*, 1928) embodies the life-force emerging from a corrupt world, bearing her child in her arms. In *No One Knows How* (*Non si sa come*, 1934) the women are able to accept chaos while the men are driven to madness and homicide by the disparity between the violence of nature and the demands of their moral codes.

Above the ever-recurring play of illusion and reality stands Pirandello the poet, often forgotten. It is, however, the poetical—the uncapturable moment, the unexplained enigma, the symbolic action, the mythic force, the physical symbol—that often makes his plays unforgettable. It is significant that the basic theme in Pirandello's last play, *The Mountain Giants*, concerns poetry.

Pirandello worked closely with some of the leading Italian actors of his time, and since theatre was not only his form but very often his theme, it seems likely that they influenced his work to some degree. Several of his plays were undoubtedly written with the complex personalities of certain performers, such as Marta Abba and Ruggero Ruggeri, in mind.

The Vise (*La morsa*; wr. 1898, prod. 1910). Drama in which Giulia has abandoned a wealthy family to marry Andrea, who atones for his wife's sacrifice by amassing a fortune. In the process he neglects Giulia, a sentimental girl, who lavishes her affections on Andrea's best friend. Discovering the affair, Andrea tortures his wife by his relentless silence and his refusal to let her see their children. Eventually Giulia is driven to suicide.

If Not So, or Other People's Reasons (*Se non così, o La ragione degli altri*; wr. 1899, prod. 1915). Drama concerning Leonardo Arciani, a writer torn between loyalty to his barren wife and love for his illegitimate infant daughter. The birth of the child has caused him to be fired by his father-in-law from a job on his newspaper. His wife Livia, realizing that things cannot go on with her husband divided between two households, goes to the baby's mother and asks that she make the great sacrifice of giving the child to her so that it may grow up bearing its father's name and in comfortable surroundings. Horrified at first, the mother finally consents and is left brokenhearted and alone.

Scamander (*Scamandro*; pub. 1909; prod. 1928). Drama in which the Scamander River, which flowed near Troy in ancient times, is depicted as a living character, speaking, sighing, and suffering from drought. The play is based on the legend of the Trojan maidens' ritual of betrothal, in which they bathed in the river and uttered the words "Receive, O Scamander, my virginity!" It concerns Callirrhoë, Ascanius's betrothed, who offers the river her virginity in the moonlight and is seen by Eumeus, Ascanius's friend. Hidden in the bushes, Eumeus retorts "And I accept it!" Presenting himself to her as a personification of Scamander, he leads her into the water while Ascanius and her father Caletorus, seeing her disappearance from afar, anxiously search and call for her. After they have given up hope, she emerges from the river and recounts in all innocence her seduction by Eumeus in the guise of Scamander.

Sicilian Limes (*Lumíe di Sicilia*, 1910). Comedy comparing humble Sicilian life with the corruption of the cities. Micuccio Bonavino is a Sicilian musician who has discovered, nurtured, and financially supported the talents of poverty-stricken Teresina. He comes to see her in a bustling city of northern Italy where she now lives in luxury as a successful singer, bringing her a gift of Sicilian limes; but when he discovers how success has corrupted her, he gives the limes, a symbol of the simplicity and beauty of Sicily, to her mother, turns away in anguish, and returns home.

The Doctor's Duty (*Il dovere del medico*, 1913). Naturalistic study revolving around the paradoxical cruelty of an act of humanitarianism. Impetuous Tommaso Corsi, discovered in bed with his friend's wife, has shot the husband in self-defense and then attempted suicide. The family doctor dutifully saves Tommaso but explains that the latter will probably have to spend the rest of his life in prison. Realizing the impossibility of life away from his truly beloved wife and children, Tommaso tears at his bandages and opens his wound. The doctor mercifully refrains from once more doing his "duty."

Chee-Chee (*Cecè*; pub. 1913, prod. 1920). Comedy of the wily Chee-Chee who, in order to retrieve several IOUs for large sums from his mistress Nada, arranges to have Squadriglia, a one-eyed road builder, tell the girl all sorts of lies about him. After listening to his exhortations, Nada assumes that Chee-Chee's notes are valueless and sells them to Squadriglia for almost nothing. Chee-Chee then arrives and accuses Nada of having betrayed him into the hands of an extortionist. To atone for her "betrayal," Nada must redouble her attentions to Chee-Chee.

Think It Over, Giacomino! (*Pensaci, Giacomino!*, 1916). Comedy in which an irrational act—a husband forcing his wife's lover to return to her—becomes right and logical. In revolt against the underpaid drudgery of his government job as a teacher, the elderly Professor Toti decides to marry a young wife so that after his death the government will be compelled to pay his young widow a pension for many years. By marrying a girl whom he discovers just before the wedding to be pregnant, he incurs the scorn of the community. Undeterred, he becomes a father to her, a grandfather to her child, and the protector of her lover Giacomino, who visits the household openly. But Giacomino, urged by his sister and a priest to do something to stop the scandal, becomes engaged to another girl. Indignant, Toti reminds Giacomino that he has a family which he must not abandon, that the woman and child face an uncertain future after Toti's death, and that he must not ruin the lives of three people by marrying another. Giacomino agrees, and the *ménage à trois* is resumed.

At the Gate (*All'uscita*; pub. 1916, prod. 1922). Fantasy in which four ghosts appear in a cemetery, each held to earth by some desire. The Fat Man waits for his unfaithful wife, the Woman, and regrets the lost beauty of nature. The wife, who has been murdered by her jealous lover, still seeks human warmth and motherhood, which she was denied in life. When she sees the Child, whose last, unsatisfied desire had been for a pomegranate, she comforts him. The three disappear beyond the gate where desires cease to matter, leaving behind the Philosopher, who will presumably keep reasoning and wondering until the end of time.

Liolà (1916). "Country comedy," written in Sicilian dialect and later translated into Italian by Pirandello himself. Liolà, a handsome young Sicilian peasant, the Don Juan of the countryside with three illegitimate children, is an earthy symbol of unalloyed joy. Although he once loved the virtuous Mita, she was forced by circumstances to marry Simone, a wealthy old man who now accuses her of barrenness and sends her back home. Mita's cousin Tuzza, jealous of Mita's wealthy marriage and Liolà's attentions, seduces the latter and becomes pregnant. She tells her tale to Simone, hoping to replace Mita by providing him with a child. Liolà, however, realizing that he has been used, persuades the naïve Mita to let him perform the same service for her, thus foiling Tuzza.

Liolà, Turin, 1956–1957 season. [Teatro Stabile di Torino]

Simone, as Liolà predicts, naturally prefers to believe that Mita's child is his own. He rejects Tuzza and her illegitimate child and restores Mita to her honored position.

Right You Are—If You Think You Are [*Cosi è (se vi pare)*, 1917]. Parable describing truth as subjective. Lamberto Laudisi, convinced of truth's inaccessibility, watches amusedly as Councillor Agazzi and his family pry into the life of Signor Ponza, Agazzi's secretary. Ponza's wife has never been seen; his mother-in-law Signora Frola lives alone and is only visited by him late at night; mother and daughter have never been seen together. When Signora Frola appears, she explains that she lives alone because she does not want to interfere with her daughter's life. Then Ponza arrives with the story that Signora Frola is insane, his former wife is dead as a result of an earthquake some years before, and his present wife is humoring Signora Frola by pretending to be her daughter. When he has gone, Signora Frola returns to say that it is Ponza who is mad, that his present wife is her daughter, his first and only wife. The earthquake having destroyed the documents that could have revealed the truth, the bewildered Agazzi finally arranges an "accidental" meeting between the two which results in an emotional scene but reveals nothing. Ponza explains that he pretends to be mad to humor his former mother-in-law. Agazzi then insists that Ponza produce his wife so that she can be questioned. Appearing in heavy veiling, Ponza's wife reveals only that "I am the

Scene from a 1964 Phoenix Theatre production of *Right You Are—If You Think You Are.* [Courtesy of Phoenix Theatre. Photograph by Van Williams]

daughter of Signora Frola, and the second wife of Signor Ponza. As for myself, I am nobody.'' Thus truth can be different to each observer, and Laudisi bursts into bitter laughter at this vain attempt to discover a single truth.

Cap and Bells (*Il berretto a sonagli,* 1917). Comedy in which the irrational triumphs over the rational. In a small Sicilian town, Beatrice Fiorica, aroused by a village gossip, arranges with the police to expose her husband's infidelity with the wife of his elderly clerk Ciampa. Cavalier Fiorica is arrested, but Beatrice becomes the brunt of the town's gossip. As the tide of gossip rises, Ciampa reveals that he had been well aware of his wife's adultery but had, with some difficulty, managed to maintain appearances. Now the mask has been torn away, and Ciampa must find a way to replace it. He persuades the Fiorica ménage that since Beatrice's jealousy caused all the trouble, the only ''honorable'' solution is for Beatrice to be declared mad and to undergo a short confinement in a mental institution. To be declared mad, she need only speak the truth; no one will believe her, society will be satisfied, and all can resume their former lives.

The Jar (*La giara,* 1917). Farce set in Sicily during the olive harvest. Don Lollo Zirata has dought an enormous olive jar because his crop has increased. When he finds it broken, he hires Uncle Zima Licasi to mend it, and in the process old Zima becomes stuck inside. The stubborn Don Lollo, his lawyer, and Zima argue over who will pay what sum to whom, for in order to release Zima the jar must be broken. Zima decides that, rather than pay for the jar, he will stay in it, and he spends his tinker's fee on a celebration. The ensuing noise so infuriates

Lollo that he kicks the jar in anger. It topples over, rolls down the hill, and crashes, releasing the wily Zima.

The Pleasure of Honesty (*Il piacere dell'onestà,* 1917). ''Comedy'' in which Maddelena Renni, wanting her daughter Agata to be happy, tacitly permits her affair with Fabio Colli, a married man separated from his wife. When Agata becomes pregnant, Fabio's cousin Maurizio produces Angelo Baldovino, a bankrupt and dissolute schoolfellow who consents to marry Agata because he wishes to start a new life as an honest member of society. He agrees to carry out the scheme but insists that they all enact their roles scrupulously: Agata must cease her relationship with Fabio. Although Fabio intends to continue relations with Agata, he humors Angelo and the marriage takes place. Angelo then, true to his word, becomes a model husband who refuses to let his wife see her former lover. Fabio soon tires of this situation and attempts to rid himself of Angelo by framing him for embezzlement. Angelo discovers the plot and confronts Fabio. Since he feels himself actually falling in love with Agata (his mask having become his real self) and does not believe that she returns his feelings, he is willing to

Right You Are—If You Think You Are, with (l. to r.) Jennifer Harmon, Sydney Walker, and Helen Hayes. New York, Lyceum Theatre, 1966. [Courtesy of Phoenix Theatre]

Scene from *La giara*. [Italian Cultural Institute]

leave and even pass for a thief, but he insists that the actual stealing be done by Fabio. At this point Agata (her own mask of the dutiful wife now her true self) intervenes and declares that she is, in fact, in love with Angelo.

But It Is Not a Serious Affair (*Ma non è una cosa seria*, 1918). Comedy in which logic is defeated by the vagaries of true sentiment. Memmo Speranza, a rich young Don Juan, marries Gasparina as a joke in order to keep himself from constantly losing his head and proposing to every woman with whom he falls in love. Gasparina agrees in order to escape a life of meanness and insult as a boarding-house drudge. Two months of leisure and life in the country transform her into a desirable woman, and when she visits Memmo in the city and offers to find a way to release him from the marriage, he listens only halfheartedly. Three months later still, his last love affair over, Memmo arrives at the house he has given Gasparina and finds that one of her former boarders, an older man who has long admired her, wishes to marry her. The marriage of Memmo and Gasparina, never consummated, can easily be annulled. This infuriates Memmo, who has fallen in love with his wife and has discovered that his marriage is serious after all.

The Rules of the Game (*Il giuoco delle parti*, 1918). Comedy with tragic undertones in which a man renounces life and becomes an empty shell in order to survive his marriage. Leone Gala has managed to avoid the pain of living with his capricious wife Silia by resigning himself to the role of the betrayed husband and moving

A French production of *The Pleasure of Honesty*. [French Cultural Services]

into a separate apartment where he coldly devotes himself to eating and thinking. He checks daily to see to her needs and discusses her with her lover Guido. When Silia's home is mistakenly invaded one night by a drunken Marquis and his friends, Silia devises a plan to rid herself of Leone. She locks Guido into the bedroom, leads the men on, and then complains to her husband that she has been insulted, knowing that he must challenge the Marquis, an excellent swordsman, to a duel. Leone calmly agrees and insists that it be a duel to the death. Guido is named Leone's second and bears the challenge to the Marquis. The following morning, however, Leone announces that it is really Guido's duel, not his, since Silia belongs to Guido and Guido was present at the time of the outrage. Unable to argue, Guido goes off to his death. A moment later Silia arrives, is told what has happened, and runs out in hysterics while Leone's breakfast is served.

The License (*La patente*, 1919). Comedy in which Rosano Chiarchiaro, suing two people for accusing him of the evil eye, admits to the judge that his life has been made miserable by this superstition. As a result, his only hope lies in having these "powers" sanctioned by law. Loss of this lawsuit, he declares, will be his license, and henceforth people will pay him to stay away. At this point a loose shutter suddenly opens and kills the judge's pet goldfinch. Thinking the accident a result of Chiarchiaro's evil powers, the judge can now license him as a sorcerer.

Grafting (*L'innesto*, 1919). Drama about Laura and Giorgio who, though very much in love and married for seven years, are childless. After a brutal rape by an unknown assailant, Laura conceives and Giorgio wants to have the fetus destroyed. A gardener explains that plants must be in sap to accept a graft, and Laura feels that by analogy only women in love can conceive. She convinces both her husband and herself that the thought of Giorgio's love sustained her at the time of the attack and that he is therefore the "real" father of the child.

Man, Beast, and Virtue (*L'uomo, la bestia e la virtù*, 1919). Comedy written in the tradition of Machiavelli's *The Mandrake Root*, in which the essential target is man's social sham and hypocrisy. Paolino, a schoolmaster, helps his mistress, Signora Perrella, conceal her illegitimate pregnancy from her indifferent husband, Captain Perrella, by helping to entice the latter into her bed on the night of his return from a long voyage. From a druggist friend, Paolino obtains an aphrodisiac which is concealed in a piece of cake destined to be part of the captain's dinner. Then he advises Signora Perrella to dress seductively and to paint her lips and cheeks. However, the captain's response to his "virtuous" wife's primping is an outburst of laughter, and since he is hardly celibate during his voyages, he is difficult to arouse. Eventually he is persuaded to eat the cake, and the next morning Paolino is informed that his mistress's honor is safe.

All for the Best (*Tutto per bene*, 1920). Comedy in which, after a life spent in mourning his dead wife, Martino Lori is brutally informed by his daughter Palma that

L'uomo, la bestia, e la virtù, with Renzo Giovampietro and Adriana Innocenti, Turin, 1960–1961 season. [Teatro Stabile di Torino]

she is not his child. Palma accuses Lori of having known this all along and having behaved toward her with hypocritical unction. Lori, however, previously ignorant of his wife's infidelity, now realizes that his whole life has been an illusion. In his agony he sees no way to continue living except to avenge the insult and the heartbreak by exposing Palma's real father, Senator Manfroni, as a man who has risen to fame on a dead man's discovery. Palma, however, stops Lori by assuring him that she is now capable of giving him the love and respect he has longed for. Since Lori wants to be deluded, he agrees to do what is "all for the best."

As Well as Before, Better than Before (*Come prima, meglio di prima*, 1920). Comedy centering on the tragic figure of a mother who has lost the affection of her child and expressing Pirandello's revulsion at relationships not based on genuine feeling. After thirteen years of going from one lover to another, Fulvia tries to commit suicide and her surgeon husband is summoned to save her. Now she must decide whether to return to her husband or to Mauri, her latest lover, who has given up everything for her. Tired of her gypsylike life and longing for her child, she decides to return to her husband's home. She must do so, however, as his "second" wife, not as the mother of her daughter Livia, who believes her dead. Livia has worshiped her "dead" mother, and she soon grows to despise Fulvia, who she thinks is merely her father's mistress since there has been no marriage ceremony and the old marriage contract cannot be found. A year later, Fulvia has another child. By this time, Livia's attitude has made Fulvia's life unbearable. When she is compelled to reveal her true identity to Livia, Fulvia realizes finally that there is no place for her in this household and decides to rejoin her lover. Referring to the new baby, she cries, "I shall take Livia with me this time, I shall take her alive—and mine!"

Mrs. Morli, One and Two (*La signora Morli, una e due*, 1920). Comedy in which, fourteen years after having abandoned his wife Evelina, the carefree Ferrante Morli returns from America, ostensibly to claim his son Aldo. Evelina has in the interval established a disciplined life for herself as the ''wife'' of a staid lawyer, Lello Carpani, and has borne him a daughter, Titti. She angrily rejects Ferrante's demands, but Aldo elects to go to Rome with his father. Soon after, Evelina receives a telegram informing her that Aldo is dangerously ill, and she rushes to Rome only to discover that Ferrante has tricked her into joining him. She soon finds herself drawn into her earlier carefree life but eventually decides to return to her more straitlaced existence with Titti and Lello. The latter resents her temporary abandonment of him, but Evelina convinces him that she had won her right to return by sacrificing that part of her nature represented by her easygoing life with Ferrante and by electing to go on with her duty-bound life as Lello's illegitimate wife and Titti's mother. Her personality split between the demands of the two egotistical males, Evelina finds psychological unity in her love for and devotion to her children.

Six Characters in Search of an Author (*Sei personaggi in cerca d'autore*, 1921). Comedy in which the creations of art and the reality of life are seen in turn as both illusory and real. Rehearsal preparations of a theatrical company are interrupted by a Father and his family who explain that they are characters from an unfinished dramatic work and ask permission to reenact a crucial moment in their lives, a moment from which the actors can fashion a finished play. The Father explains that, having found that his wife (the Mother) was in love with another man, he had generously made it possible for the two to go off together. He contends that he arranged for his own son to grow up healthily in the country and that he had kept a kindly eye on the welfare of his wife, her lover, and the three illegitimate children born to them—the Stepdaughter, a Young Boy, and a Baby Girl—until they disappeared from the city. His wife challenges this interpretation of events and claims that the Father, tiring of her, had forced her into the arms of another man and cruelly separated her from her legitimate Son. Years later, the Father continues, he failed to recognize the Stepdaughter in a young girl encountered in Mme. Pace's bawdy house; only the last-minute intervention of the Mother saved him from dishonor. The actors who are to play the roles of Father and Stepdaughter now act out this crucial scene in a manner that distorts and vulgarizes the incident. Objecting to the reenactment, the Father explains that finding that the Mother and her illegitimate children were destitute—the lover having died—he took them all to live with him and the Son. However, the Stepdaughter continued to blame the Father for her shame, and the Son not only rejected him as a libertine but refused to acknowledge his Mother or her three illegitimate children. Called upon to play the scene in which he rejects the Mother, the Son refuses and runs into the garden where he finds the Young Boy staring into a fountain at the drowned body of the Baby Girl. Suddenly a shot rings out. The boy has killed himself and is carried into the wings amid the laments of the ''characters'' and the nervous insistence of the actors that the situation is only make-believe. However, the Father vehemently insists that the events they have witnessed are real. Caught in the irreconcilable clash between day-to-day reality and the reality of art, the director of the company bemoans a wasted day.

Six Characters in Search of an Author. New York, Princess Theatre, 1922. [Theatre Collection, The New York Public Library at Lincoln Center, Astor, Lenox and Tilden Foundations]

Scene from a French production of *Six Characters in Search of an Author,* 1968. [French Cultural Services]

Henry IV (*Enrico IV*, 1922). Tragedy centering on a middle-aged nobleman living in a modern Italian villa, who out of madness has played the role of Emperor Henry IV for twenty years. The accident that caused his madness had occurred on a carnival day long ago when, dressed as Henry IV, he had fallen from his horse. Now he dresses his attendants and styles his life to conform to his delusion. Hoping to cure him, four people arrive with a doctor: Matilde Spina, the woman he had loved but who had spurned him; her lover Belcredi; her daughter Frida; and Frida's fiancé, the deluded man's nephew. The doctor hopes to shock him into sanity by presenting him with a simultaneous view of the past and present as represented by Matilde and her daughter. "Henry" rages inwardly at this affront, for his present role has in recent years become a protective device he has consciously used to shield himself from reality, which has passed him by. In a moment of anger he reveals his sanity to his four amazed lackeys, who immediately betray him to Matilde, but she refuses to believe their story. Seeing the image of his former love in Frida recalls old emotions. Henry then reveals that at the time he had regained his sanity, eight years previously, he had decided that he was as well off with one masquerade as with another. He further reveals that on that carnival day his horse had been deliberately pricked by Belcredi. His behavior becomes increasingly wild as his rage is revived, and he stabs Belcredi, who is carried away dying and protesting that his rival is, in fact, sane. The circle is

now closed: to escape the consequences of murder, Henry IV must continue to pretend to be insane.

The Imbecile (*L'imbecille,* 1922). Comedy about Luca Fazio, who overhears Paroni, a provincial editor with political ambitions, call his friend Pulini an imbecile for having committed suicide without first killing Mazzarini, the leader of the rival political party. Ill and about to commit suicide like Pulini, Luca threatens Paroni just as Paroni had wanted Pulini to threaten Mazzarini. Paroni, seeing that Luca carries a pistol, falls on his knees in fear. Then, with great disdain, Luca forces Paroni to write a note saying that Luca had come to kill him but that, seeing his disgusting cowardice on facing death, he had contemptuously spared him. The note will be found on Luca's dead body and will put an end to Paroni's political ambitions.

Naked; To Clothe the Naked (*Vestire gli ignudi,* 1922). Comedy unmasking a lie. The story of an unsuccessful suicide is printed in a Rome newspaper: Ersilia Drei, whose fiancé had abandoned her for another woman, became governess to Consul Grotti's child and tried to poison herself after the tragic fall of the child from a terrace and her subsequent dismissal. Moved by the story, a writer named Ludovico Nota takes Ersilia into his house. Soon afterward, the newspaperman who wrote the story appears with the news that Grotti has demanded a retraction of it and that Franco Laspiga, Ersilia's former fiancé, has been rejected by his betrothed and has appeared to make amends to Ersilia. The girl collapses and is put to bed, but during the night she tries to run away. The following day Franco begs her to marry him, but she refuses. Grotti then arrives and demands to see her. The ensuing scene reveals that a complicated affair between the two is the real cause of the child's death. Later that day, Franco returns, having learned of Ersilia's affair with Grotti, and demands to know if it began before or after his relationship with her. Grotti arrives, denies the affair, and blames Ersilia alone for the child's death. At this point Ersilia enters, having poisoned herself a second time, and explains that she lied "to make herself a pretty dress" to die in and that now she must die naked, stripped of her protective fictions.

The Man With the Flower in His Mouth (*L'uomo dal fiore in bocca*, 1923). Dialogue that takes place in a café at midnight. A commuter who has missed his train regales a stranger with the trivial causes of this catastrophe. In reply, the stranger quietly explains how his zest for life and a great tragedy that weighs him down impel him to use his imagination to participate in the lives of complete strangers. He then reveals that in a short time he will die of cancer of the mouth.

The Life I Gave You (*La vita che ti diedi*, 1923). Tragedy with symbolic overtones. Consumed by his love for the married Lucia Maubel, Donn'Anna Luna's son Fulvio has traveled in her wake for seven years. Shortly after his return home, he dies a broken and changed man. His

Ruggero Ruggeri in the title role of *Enrico IV*. [Italian Cultural Institute]

Enrico IV, Turin, 1963–1964 season. [Teatro Stabile di Torino]

mother knows, however, that his real life was the love she had given him, that he returned a stranger, and that his physical death does not destroy the illusion that her love for him has created. The life she gave him continues. Determined to keep Lucia Maubel's image of him alive as well, she answers the girl's tortured letter to her son, a letter in which she threatens to abandon husband and children for him. Lucia then arrives, but Donn'Anna conceals the truth, saying that her son is away. Lucia then reveals that Fulvio's love has made her feel joy in her role as mother of her husband's children and that she has even more joy in knowing that she is to bear Fulvio's child. Lucia's mother arrives, and Donn'Anna's lie is exposed. Although Lucia wants to stay with Donn'Anna, the resigned woman tells her to go. By giving birth to Fulvio's child Lucia will keep his spirit alive, and she, not Donn'Anna, will then be the guardian of that spirit.

The Other Son (*L'altro figlio*, 1923). Dramatic sketch set in Sicily. Old Maragrazia, who lives in poverty, yearns for her two sons who have gone to Argentina. On a day when other young men of the town are leaving for America, Maragrazia dictates a letter to Ninfarosa, an educated girl, which one of the men will deliver. When the village doctor passes by, Maragrazia asks him to read the letter, and he quickly discovers that nothing had been copied down; Maragrazia had been deceived. Now the doctor discovers from Ninfarosa that Maragrazia has another son, with whom she refuses to live. The other son, Maragrazia then explains, is the result of a bestial attack upon her by one of a gang of bandits who had killed her husband. Can this man, she asks, be called her son? Sympathetic, as Ninfarosa had not been, the doctor writes a real letter to the sons in Argentina.

Scene from a French production of *Henry IV*. [French Cultural Services]

Each in His Own Way (*Ciascuno a suo modo*, 1924). Comedy inspired by a newspaper report of the suicide of a promising sculptor as a result of his fiancée's infidelity. Each of the two acts is followed by an interlude presenting the audience's comments on the play and the reactions of an infuriated couple who rush onstage claiming to recognize their own lives in the play.

A famous painter's suicide owing to the infidelity of his mistress Delia Morello, with his best friend Michele Rocca, causes discussion at a party. Doro Palegari defends Delia, blaming Michele, while Francesco Savio takes the opposing view. The next day Francesco apologizes to Doro, but each has been converted to the other's viewpoint; they argue again and challenge each other to a duel. Delia, visiting Doro to thank him for his defense, is presented with both viewpoints and is herself confused as to what is "true."

During the first interlude the scene represents the theatre lobby where the audience protests the play as a "joke" on them, while the real-life counterparts of Delia and Michele (sitting apart) become furious. In the second act Michele, wanting to defend his honor and fight the duel himself, follows Delia to Francesco's house, where she has gone hoping to stop the duel, and the two lovers confront each other. The violent scene that follows proves to all that neither version of the tragedy is true, that both Delia and Michele were guilty of a violent passion, now turned to hatred because of the suicide.

During the second interlude the real-life counterparts of Delia and Michele go onstage to protest that the situation as presented is preposterous. They attack author and actors, confront each other, and reenact the scene just played, while the audience of the play-within-the-play watches in amazement. The actors go home in a huff, the "audience" is shocked, the management apologizes, and the performance ends.

The Festival of Our Lord of the Ship (*Sagra del Signore della nave*, 1925). Comedy set at a church festival, climaxed by the sacrifice of a pig. The pig's owner debates with his tutor the beast's superiority to man. The guests devour his pig, and a riot starts, interrupted by a procession bearing the statue of Christ in agony. It is this that saves mankind, the tutor maintains, as the rioters fall to their knees.

Diana and Tuda (*Diana e la Tuda*, 1926). Tragedy dealing with attitudes toward art, which is static, and life, which is constantly changing. The aging sculptor Giuncano has destroyed his work, feeling that art kills life, which is ever changing, and that life's animation is the most important thing. He watches in anguish as young Sirio Dossi, who wishes to sculpt one great Diana and die, slowly drains the life from his model Tuda because he denies her the love she wants from him. In an effort to trap him into thinking of her as more than just a model, Tuda maneuvers Sirio into marrying her by threatening to pose for another artist while he is working on his Diana. But the marriage fails to change the relationship, and Sirio even continues his alliance with his mistress Sara Mendel. Finally Tuda, haggard and despondent, is unable to stay with Sirio. After she leaves, however, Sirio finds he cannot finish his sculpture without her. He searches for her, brings her to the studio, and, thinking her move toward the statue menacing, thinking she is about to destroy it, threatens to kill her. Enraged, Giuncano strangles Sirio. Tuda is now nothing, neither model nor wife.

The Wives' Friend (*L'amica delle mogli*, 1927). Tragedy dedicated to Marta Alba, the actress to whom Pirandello entrusted the leading roles in plays written after 1925. Marta Tosolani, in spite of beauty, goodness, and intelligence, has remained unmarried because her reserve frightens men who love her. Although unattainable herself, she nevertheless helps smooth the domestic lives of four married couples, becoming at once a friend of the wives and a secret passion of the husbands. Venzi, one of the men, nurses such painful regrets and jealousies that he destroys her one hope of happiness. Sensing that Marta secretly loves Viani, he plants suspicion of her in the mind of Elena, Viani's ailing wife. In addition, he poisons the minds of Marta and Viani, who, though innocent, realize the possibility of their own marriage should Elena die. Fatally ill, Elena eventually dies in a torment of uncertainty about Marta and Viani. Then, to prevent Viani from marrying Marta after Elena's death, Venzi kills him. Marta is left alone, above the aspirations of ordinary men and the victim of their corruption.

Bellavita (1927). Drama about Bellavita who, cuckolded for ten years, is asked to agree to his rival's offer to send his son away to school. He refuses, asking why his rival hates him so much that he attempts to strip him of everything in spite of the fact that he has always been treated with kindness by Bellavita. Enraged, his rival shows that Bellavita has used kindness as a means of torturing him with remorse. Bellavita jubilantly admits as much and vows to continue to torture his enemy with kindness.

The New Colony (*La nuova colonia*, 1928). Dramatic parable set in a seaside town in southern Italy. Spera, a prostitute reborn through her love of Currao, a smuggler whose child she has borne, urges his outlaw band to begin a new life on a small island. They go, taking with them Dorò, the romantic young son of a prosperous shipowner, Captain Nocio. But one of the colonists, Crocco, jealous of Currao's role as leader, quarrels with him, leaves the island, and, intent on revenge, returns with Nocio and a band of settlers. The old order now gradually reasserts itself. Spera is spurned by all but Dorò; even Currao asks her to give up her child so that he can marry Nocio's daughter and regain his lost power. The jealous Crocco convinces Spera that Currao is going to kill Dorò; enraged, Spera denounces her lover, refuses to give up her child, and flees to the rocky heights of the island warning Currao that should he touch her child, the earth would quake and the sea would rise to destroy them all. Currao, in turn, exposes Crocco's lies. As though in answer to the cries of a mother, an earthquake begins and the island slowly sinks into the sea, taking with it both old and new. Only Spera and her child, clinging to a rocky promontory, are left.

Either of One or of No One (*O di uno o di nessuno*, 1929). Comedy that presents the touching story of a prostitute redeemed by affection and care and purified by motherhood. Tito and Carlino, two young clerks, have brought Melina from their hometown to Rome as their housekeeper-wife-mistress. Everything runs smoothly until she becomes pregnant and Tito and Carlino try, with their lawyer Merletti, to decide which one is the father. Each wants the responsibility of the child if it is truly his own, but neither wishes to support the child of the other. The only solution, they decide, is that it be sent to an institution, even though Melina wishes the child to be her responsibility alone. The friends then quarrel violently, each wishing to consider himself father of the child. Melina, who has been abandoned by her two jealous lovers, dies soon after giving birth but not before she has extracted the promise from Merletti that they will not send the baby to an orphan asylum. The problem is solved when the baby is given to a mother in a nearby villa who has just lost her child. Relieved of their cause for hatred, the two friends weep together over the loss of the mother.

Lazarus (*Lazzaro*, 1929). Drama in which Pirandello attempts to reconcile religious belief with his complex view of reality. Diego Spina, a conventionally religious man, has by his barren insistence on duty driven his wife into a peasant's arms, committed his son to the priesthood at a tender age, and unwittingly caused his daughter to become paralyzed. As the play opens, his son is about to renounce his calling and his wife and her lover are about to leave Diego's farm, which they have tilled and enriched. When Diego meets with an accident and discovers that he has technically died and been restored to life by his doctor, his faith is shaken, for he has tasted death and returned with no knowledge of God. But his son has learned, through a talk with his mother, that life is meant to be lived, and now, mysteriously, he feels his faith confirmed. "Your soul *is* God," he tells his father, to whom he brings a new faith with the force of his newly discovered faith. At this point the real miracle occurs—Diego's crippled daughter begins to walk into her mother's arms.

I'm Dreaming, But Am I? [*Sogno (ma forse no)*, 1931]. One-act drama in which a guilt-ridden girl relives in a dream the dual affair in which she is, in fact, involved. Just as her lover, having exposed her greed and discovered her infidelity in the dream, is strangling her, she awakens. The other man has sent her the gift of a necklace. Quickly, she hides it as her lover arrives, and she feigns innocence while he casually discusses the man's return.

As You Desire Me (*Come tu mi vuoi*, 1930). Tragedy in which being and seeming to be are indistinguishable. Boffi, artist friend of Bruno Pieri, has found in a Berlin cabaret an Unknown Woman who calls herself Elma but who he believes is Cia, Bruno's beautiful and gifted wife who disappeared ten years earlier after the invasion of their villa in northern Italy. He persuades the woman, presently living a dissolute life as the mistress of Salter, a vulgar and sensual German writer, to return with him

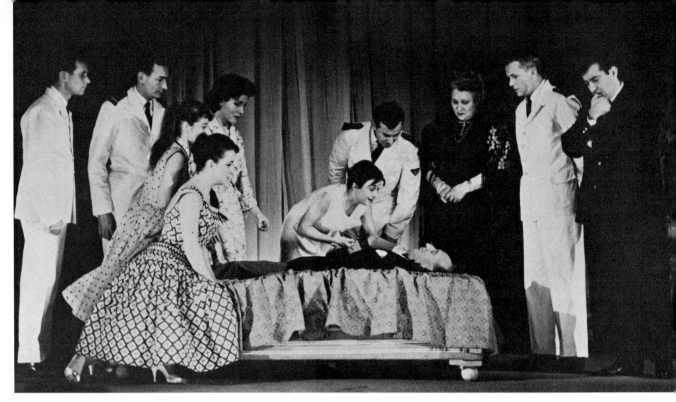

A French production of *Tonight We Improvise* at the Théâtre d'Aujourd'hui, Paris. [French Cultural Services]

and resume her former existence as Cia among people who truly love her. She arrives at the villa and is readily accepted by the aunt and uncle who raised her, as well as by her husband, despite her antisocial behavior while adjusting to her old environment. Gradually she becomes serene, but is disturbed when, to resolve a dispute over some property, Bruno insists that she identify herself by a birthmark. Cia's mark is not on her body, and Bruno is confused, but the woman assures him that she has found her identity: hers is the soul of Cia. Bruno's motives, however, are now in question: is he more interested in Cia's body than in her soul, more concerned about his property than his wife? At this point Salter appears with the Demented One, a shadow of a woman found in a sanitarium, and claims that she is the real Cia. The Unknown Woman, realizing that her identity is once again in question, now hints that the madwoman may well be Cia. Her attempts to start a new life having failed because her husband no longer sustains her as her former self, the Unknown Woman departs with Salter.

Tonight We Improvise (*Questa sera si recita a soggetto*, 1930). Drama that, by means of a play-within-a-play, shows the difficulties of creating a play vis-à-vis the drama of actors who must become the characters they impersonate. As actors mingled in the audience complain impatiently over delays, a pompous stage manager, Dr. Hinkfuss, strides onto the stage, announces an improvised play set in Sicily, and introduces the actors who will play the characters in it. The play then begins. Signor Palmiro, the father of four beautiful and passionate daughters, Mommina, Totina, Dorina, and Nenè, has gone off to a cabaret to hear one of the chorus girls sing, having been touched by her likeness to one of his daugh-

ters. Meanwhile, because of the tutelage of their liberal mother, Signora Ignazia, the girls party with five young aviation officers, one of whom, Verri, true to his constrictive Sicilian background, resents their free and easy attitudes toward love and sex. Eventually, enraged at Mommina's attentions to the other men, he quarrels with his friends, fights with one of them, and then asks her to marry him.

While Hinkfuss interrupts the action to arrange melodramatic tableaux, the action of the play proceeds independent of his efforts. Signor Palmiro is brought home from the café mortally wounded after having taken his singer's part in a scuffle. Now Mommina can do nothing but marry Verri, knowing full well that his jealousy will make her miserable. Hinkfuss interrupts once again with his proposals for stage effects. But the characters, steeped in the emotions of their roles, eject him. Now, in the last act, Mommina has two daughters, but her life with Verri has caused her to age beyond her years. His jealousy compels him to probe even her dreams, lest she derive pleasure from her memories. Weakened by heart disease and tormented by Verri, Mommina is dying, and her memories of the past, her family, and her love of music become reality to her. The familiar figures of her mother and her sisters pass before her as she explains to her enraptured daughters what life could have been like had she not married their father. After singing her favorite aria, she dies. Meanwhile, recriminations between the director, who thinks the playwright artificial, and the actors, who think the director artificial, interrupt the action.

To Find Oneself (*Trovarsi*, 1932). Drama dedicated to Marta Abba, depicting the inner struggle of Donata Genzi, an actress who is bewildered by the feeling that she has lived many fictional lives but never one of her own. Donata, tired and in ill health, visits a schoolmate at her villa on the Riviera. Excusing herself from a dinner party, she slips out for a walk and encounters a late-arriving guest, Elj Nielsen. The antithesis of Donata, whose every action and emotion has at some time been performed on the stage, Elj believes in spontaneity and in living with nature, which epitomizes spontaneity. On a sudden whim Donata suggests they go for a sail in Elj's boat; there is a storm, and he saves her life. While she is recuperating in his studio, he proposes, but Donata is unsure that real life can be as exciting and fulfilling as her life in the theatre, through which she has experienced everything. She returns to the theatre for a test. Elj watches her performance but leaves after the first two acts and returns to nature and the sea. Donata, who has been caught in a profound struggle because of this intruder from life into her artistic world, wins liberation during the third act with realization that "one must create oneself, create! And only then does one find oneself." Since Elj prefers the woman in her to the actress, Donata now realizes that she must forget him.

When Someone Is Somebody (*Quando si è qualcuno*, 1933). Drama about a famous Italian poet, referred to as * * *, who, having secretly fallen in love at fifty with his nephew Pietro's young sister-in-law Veroccia, has written a new and youthful book of poetry. Wanting to strengthen this new literary image before laying public claim to it, he gives the book to his nephew. Pietro publishes it in America, where it receives enthusiastic reviews as the work of Délago. Then * * * writes a second book, also in Délago's style, and leaves for Pietro's villa in Naples to join Veroccia and his wife Natascia. But * * *'s publisher invades his idyll, bringing * * *'s family and a cabinet minister and announcing that he cannot destroy his carefully built image by publishing the new work. After * * * returns with his family, Pietro publishes the book, hoping to free his uncle by revealing Délago's identity. Instead, however, * * * claims the new work to be a joke, for he now knows himself to be forever imprisoned by age and fame. His friends insist on seeing the whole episode as a literary hoax, but for the poet the necessity of resuming his old existence is a sentence to a living death.

The Fable of the Changeling (*La favola del figlio cambiato*, 1934). Verse fantasy with choruses and songs begun as a study for the myth play *The Mountain Giants* and finished as a libretto set to music by Malipiero. It recounts the legend of a baby stolen from its mother and replaced by a dark changeling. The mother's own child has been taken to a king's palace. Some twenty years later, this son, now an ailing prince, returns to his native village and renounces his throne in favor of the changeling, jestingly called Son-of-the-King, for the wearer of the crown is not as important as the crown itself while a mother's love is worth all the power in the world.

No One Knows How (*Non si sa come*, 1934). Drama dealing with the realm of mystery in which events occur "no one knows how." Ginevra Vanzi and Romeo Daddi succumb to a moment's passion although they deeply love their respective mates. To complicate matters further, the two couples are extremely close. Both women,

Scene from a French production of *No One Knows How*. [French Cultural Services]

however, as "bearers of the life-force," are able to accept such an event, and they attempt to keep it from Ginevra's husband Giorgio. Romeo, however, remembering a similar lapse during which he committed a murder that went unpunished, is gradually driven mad by the dichotomy between the self he knows and the violent, inexplicable other self capable of such violence. Finally, in anguished incoherence, he reveals the truth unwittingly and is shot immediately by Giorgio. Thus the original act of passion leads to a final act of violence, and four lives are destroyed.

The Mountain Giants (*I giganti della montagna*, 1937). Unfinished symbolic drama often interpreted as a comment on the perilous situation of the artist under totalitarianism. A poverty-stricken theatrical company, headed by a Count and Countess who have devoted their lives and fortune to producing the masterwork of a dead poet whom the Countess loved, arrives exhausted in the dead of night at a villa on the side of a mountain. A magician, Cotrone, and his troupe of outcasts inhabit the villa. Cotrone informs them that their poetic presentation will be ill received in the area, but he invites them to stay in the villa, where visions come to life and dreams become reality. The following day, accompanied by Cotrone, the group decides, despite Cotrone's warning, to perform at a celebration given by the "Giants of the Mountain." The barbaric audience, unused to poetry and wild with drink, tears two of the actors to pieces and kills the Countess.

[PETER BONDANELLA]

PLAYS

The name of the producing company appears in parentheses after that of the theatre.

1. *La morsa** (*The Vise*). Drama, 1 act. Written 1898. Published as *L'epilogo*, 1898. Produced Rome, Teatro Metastasio (Teatro Minimo), Dec. 9, 1910.

2. *Se non così, o La ragione degli altri* (*If Not So, or Other People's Reasons*). Drama, 3 acts. Written 1899. Published 1916. Produced Milan, Teatro Manzoni (Stabile Milanese), Apr. 19, 1915.

3. *Scamandro* (*Scamander*). Play. Published 1909. Produced Florence, Teatro dell'Accademia dei Fidenti (Gruppo Accademico), Feb. 19, 1928.

4. *Lumìe di Sicilia** (*Sicilian Limes*). Comedy, 1 act. Written 1910. Published 1911. Produced Rome, Teatro Metastasio (Teatro Minimo), Dec. 9, 1910.

5. *Il dovere del medico** (*The Doctor's Duty*). Play, 1 act. Written 1913. Produced Rome, Sala Umberto I (Teatro per Tutti), June 20, 1913.

6. *Cecè** (*Chee-Chee*). Comedy, 1 act. Published 1913. Produced San Pellegrino, Teatro del Casino (Falconi), July 10, 1920.

7. *Pensaci, Giacomino!* (*Think It Over, Giacomino!*). Comedy, 3 acts. Written 1916. Published 1917. Produced Rome, Teatro Nazionale (Musco), in Sicilian dialect, July 10, 1916.

8. *All'uscita** (*At the Gate*). Secular mystery, 1 act. Published 1916. Produced Rome, Teatro Argentina (Picasso), Sept. 29, 1922.

9. *Liolà**. Country comedy, 3 acts. Written 1916. Published 1917. Produced Rome, Teatro Argentina (Musco), in Sicilian dialect, Nov. 4, 1916.

10. *Così è (se vi pare)** (*Right You Are—If You Think You Are*). Parable, 3 acts. Written 1917. Published 1918. Produced Milan, Teatro Olimpia (Talli), June 18, 1917.

11. *Il berretto a sonagli* (*Cap and Bells*). Comedy, 3 acts. Written 1917. Published 1920. Produced Rome, Teatro Nazionale (Musco), in Sicilian dialect, June 27, 1917.

12. *La giara** (*The Jar*). Comedy, 1 act. Written 1917. Published 1925. Produced Rome, Teatro Nazionale (Musco), in Sicilian dialect as *'A Giarra*, July 9, 1917.

13. *Il piacere dell'onestà** (*The Pleasure of Honesty*). Comedy, 3 acts. Written 1917. Published 1918. Produced Turin, Teatro Carignano (Ruggeri), Nov. 27, 1917.

14. *Ma non è una cosa seria* (*But It Is Not a Serious Affair*). Comedy, 3 acts. Published 1919. Produced Leghorn, Teatro Rossini (Gramatica), Nov. 22, 1918.

15. *Il giuoco delle parti** (*The Rules of The Game*). Comedy, 3 acts. Published 1919. Produced Rome, Teatro Quirino (Ruggeri), Dec. 6, 1918.

16. *La patente** (*The License*). Comedy, 1 act. Published 1918. Produced Rome, Teatro Argentina (Teatro Mediterraneo), in Sicilian dialect as *'A Patenti*, Feb. 19, 1919.

17. *L'innesto* (*Grafting*). Comedy, 3 acts. Written 1919. Published 1921. Produced Milan, Teatro Manzoni (Talli), Jan. 29, 1919.

18. *L'uomo, la bestia, e la virtù* (*Man, Beast, and Virtue*). Apologue, 3 acts. Published 1919. Produced Milan, Teatro Olimpia (Gandusie), May 2, 1919.

19. *Tutto per bene* (*All for the Best*). Comedy, 3 acts. Written 1920. Published 1920. Produced Rome, Teatro Quirino (Ruggeri), Mar. 2, 1920.

20. *Come prima, meglio di prima* (*As Well as Before, Better than Before*). Comedy, 3 acts. Written 1920. Published 1921. Produced Venice, Teatro Goldoni (Ferrero-Celli-Paoli), Mar. 24, 1920.

21. *La signora Morli, una e due* (*Mrs. Morli, One and Two*). Comedy, 3 acts. Published 1922. Produced Rome, Teatro Argentina (Gramatica), Nov. 12, 1920.

22. *Sei personaggi in cerca d'autore** (*Six Characters in Search of an Author*). Comedy, 3 acts. Written 1921. Published 1921. Produced Rome, Teatro Valle (Niccodemi), May 10, 1921.

23. *Enrico IV** (*Henry IV*). Tragedy, 3 acts. Written 1922. Published 1922. Produced Milan, Teatro Manzoni (Ruggeri), Feb. 24, 1922.

24. *L'imbecille** (*The Imbecile*). Comedy, 1 act. Published 1926. Produced Rome, Teatro Quirino (Sainati), Oct. 10, 1922.

25. *Vestire gli ignudi** (*Naked; To Clothe the Naked*). Comedy, 3 acts. Published 1923. Produced Rome, Teatro Quirino (Melato), Nov. 14, 1922.

26. *L'uomo dal fiore in bocca** (*The Man with the Flower in His Mouth*). Dialogue, 1 act. Published 1926. Produced Rome, Teatro degli Indipendenti (Indipendenti), Feb. 21, 1923.

27. *La vita che ti diedi** (*The Life I Gave You*). Tragedy, 3 acts. Published 1924. Produced Rome, Teatro Quirino (Borelli), Oct. 12, 1923.

28. *L'altro figlio** (*The Other Son*). Comedy, 1 act. Published 1925. Produced Rome, Teatro Nazionale (Niccòli), Nov. 23, 1923.

29. *Ciascuno a suo modo** (*Each in His Own Way*). Comedy, 2 acts. Published 1924. Produced Milan, Teatro dei Filodrammatici (Niccodemi), May 22, 1924.

30. *Sagra del Signore della nave** (*The Festival of Our Lord of the Ship*). Comedy, 1 act. Published 1924. Produced Rome, Teatro Odesealchi (Teatro d'Arte), Apr. 2, 1925.

31. *Diana e la Tuda** (*Diana and Tuda*). Tragedy, 3 acts. Published 1927. Produced Zurich, Schauspielhaus, Nov. 20, 1926; Milan, Teatro Eden (Pirandello), Jan. 14, 1927.

32. *L'amica delle mogli** (*The Wives' Friend*). Comedy, 3 acts. Written 1927. Published 1927. Produced Rome, Teatro Argentina (Pirandello), Apr. 28, 1927.

33. *Bellavita*. Drama, 1 act. Published 1928. Produced Milan, Teatro Eden (Almirante-Rissone-Tòfano), May 27, 1927.

34. *La nuova colonia** (*The New Colony*). Myth, prologue and 3 acts. Written 1928. Published 1928. Produced Teatro Argentina (Pirandello), Mar. 24, 1928.

35. *O di uno o di nessuno* (*Either of One or of No One*). Comedy, 3 acts. Published 1929. Produced Turin, Teatro di Torino (Almirante-Rissone-Tòfano), Nov. 4, 1929.

36. *Lazzaro** (*Lazarus*). Myth, 3 acts. Written 1929. Published 1929. Produced Huddersfield, England, Theatre Royal, July 9, 1929; Turin, Teatro di Torino (Abba), Dec. 7, 1929.

37. *Sogno (ma forse no)** (*I'm Dreaming, But Am I?*). Play, 1 act. Published 1929. Produced Lisbon, Teatro Nacional, Sept. 22, 1931; Italian Radio, Jan. 11, 1936.

38. *Come tu mi vuoi** (*As You Desire Me*). Comedy, 3 acts. Published 1930. Produced Milan, Teatro dei Filodrammatici (Abba), Feb. 18, 1930.

39. *Questa sera si recita a soggetto** (*Tonight We Improvise*). Drama, 2 acts. Published 1930. Produced Königsberg, Neues Schauspielhaus, Jan. 25, 1930; Turin, Teatro di Torino, Apr. 14, 1930.

40. *Trovarsi** (*To Find Oneself*). Play, 3 acts. Published 1932. Produced Naples, Teatro dei Fiorentini (Abba), Nov. 4, 1932.

41. *Quando si è qualcuno** (*When Someone Is Somebody*). Performance, 3 acts. Produced Buenos Aires, Teatro Odeón, Sept. 20, 1933; San Remo, Teatro del Casino Municipale (Abba), Nov. 7, 1933.

42. *La favola del figlio cambiato* (*The Fable of the Changeling*). Libretto, 3 acts. Published 1934. Produced Brunswick, Landtheater, Jan. 13, 1934; Rome, Teatro Reale dell'Opera, Mar. 24, 1934. Music: Gian Francesco Malipiero.

43. *Non si sa come** (*No One Knows How*). Drama, 3 acts. Published 1935. Produced Prague, National Theatre, Dec. 19, 1934; Rome, Teatro Argentina (Ruggeri), Dec. 13, 1935.

44. *I giganti della montagna** (*The Mountain Giants*). Myth, 3 acts. Pub-

lished 1934. Produced Florence, Giardino di Boboli, June 5, 1937. Incomplete; last act missing.

EDITIONS

Collections

Maschere nude, 1st ed., 4 vols., Milan, 1919–1922; *Three Plays*, New York, 1922; *Each in His Own Way, and Two Other Plays*, tr. by A. Livingston, New York, 1923; *The One-act Plays*, tr. by E. Abbott et al., New York, 1928; *Maschere nude*, 2d ed., 31 vols., Florence, 1920–1929, Milan, 1929–1937; *Maschere nude*, 3d ed., Milan, 1933–1938; *Naked Masks: Five Plays*, ed. by E. Bentley, New York, 1952; *The Mountain Giants and Other Plays*, tr. by M. Abba, New York, 1958; *Opere*, 5 vols., Milan, 1958–1959; *The Rules of the Game; The Life I Gave You; Lazarus*, Harmondsworth, England, 1960; *To Clothe the Naked, and Two Other Plays*, tr. by W. Murray, New York, 1962; *One-act Plays*, tr. by W. Murray, Garden City, N.Y., 1964; *On Humor*, tr. A. Illiano and D. Testa, Chapel Hill, 1974.

Individual Plays

As You Desire Me. S. Putnam, tr., New York, 1931; also published in *Twenty Best European Plays on the American Stage*, ed. by J. Gassner and tr. by M. Abba, New York, 1957.

Each in His Own Way. Published in *Twentieth Century Plays*, ed. by F. W. Chandler and R. A. Cordell and tr. by A. Livingston, rev. ed., New York, 1939.

The Festival of Our Lord of the Ship (Our Lord of the Ships). Published in *The Nobel Prize Treasury*, ed. by M. McClintock, Garden City, N.Y., 1948.

Henry IV. Published in *Makers of the Modern Theater*, ed. by B. Ulanov and tr. by E. Storer, New York, 1961.

The Jar. Published in *Writers of the Western World*, ed. by C. A. Hibbard and H. Frenz and tr. by A. Livingston, 2d ed., Boston, 1954.

Naked. Published in *Chief Contemporary Dramatists*, ed. by T. H. Dickinson and tr. by A. Livingston, 3d ser., Boston, 1930.

Right You Are—If You Think You Are. Published in *Dramas of Modernism and Their Forerunners*, ed. by M. J. Moses and O. J. Campbell and tr. by A. Livingston, rev. ed., Boston, 1941.

Sicilian Limes, Published in *Plays of the Italian Theatre*, ed. by I. Goldberg, Boston, 1921.

Six Characters in Search of An Author. Published in *A Treasury of the Theater*, ed. by J. Gassner and tr. by E. Storer, rev. ed., vol. 2, New York, 1951.

Tonight We Improvise. S. Putnam, tr., New York, 1932.

CRITICISM

Italian

E. Fabbri, *Luigi Pirandello*, Florence, 1921; P. Rost, *Luigi Pirandello*, Milan, 1921; G. A. Borgese, *Tempo di edificare*, Milan, 1923; F. Flora, *Dal romanticismo al futurismo*, new enl. ed., Milan, 1925; M. Alajmo, *Pirandello e il "suo modo,"* Girgenti, 1926; G. Gori, *Il grottesco nell'arte e nella letteratura*, Rome, 1926; F. Pasini, *Luigi Pirandello (come mi pare)*, Trieste, 1927; C. Pellizzi, *Le lettere italiane del nostro secolo*, Milan, 1929; I. Siciliano, *Il teatro di L. Pirandello, ovvero Dei fasti dell'artifico*, Turin, 1929; P. Mignosi, *Il segreto di Pirandello*, Milan, 1935; L. Antonelli, *Maschera nuda di Pirandello*, Rome, 1937; F. Pasini, *Pirandello nell'arte e nella vita*, Padua, 1937; G. Patanè, *Pirandello*, Catania, 1937; M. Bontempelli, *Pirandello, Leopardi, D'Annunzio*, Milan, 1938; U. Cantoro, *L'altro me stesso (il problema della personalità nel dramma pirandelliano)*, Verona, 1939; M. Lo Vecchio Musti, *L'opera di Luigi Pirandello*, Turin, 1939; S. d'Amico, *Il teatro dei fantocci*, Florence, 1940; A. Di Pietro, *Saggio su Pirandello*, Milan, 1941; P. Puliatti and E. Bottino, *Lineamenti sull'arte di Luigi Pirandello*, Catania, 1941; F. V. Nardelli, *L'uomo segreto: Vita e croci di Luigi Pirandello*, 2d ed., Milan, 1944; B. Croce, "Pirandello," in *La letteratura della nuova Italia*, vol. VI, Bari, 1946; L. Baccalo, *Luigi Pirandello*, 2d ed., Milan, 1949; G. Petronio, *Pirandello novelliere e la crisi del realismo*, Lucca, 1950; M. Lo Vecchio Musti, *Bibliografia di Pirandello*, 2d ed., Milan, 1952; L. Ferrante, *Luigi Pirandello*, Florence, 1958; A. Jannu, *Luigi Pirandello*, Florence, 1958; F. Puglisi, *L'arte di Luigi Pirandello*, Messina, 1958; E. Levi, *Il comico di carattere da Teofracto a Pirandello*, Turin, 1959; C. Salinari, "Pirandello," in *Miti e coscienza del decadentismo italiano*, Milan, 1960; G. Giudice, *Luigi Pirandello*, Turin, 1963; G. F. Vené, *Pirandello fascista*, Milan, 1971; A. Illiano, *Introduzione alla critica pirandelliana*, Verona, 1976.

English

J. Palmer, *Studies in the Contemporary Theatre*, London, 1927; D. Vittorini, *The Drama of Luigi Pirandello*, Philadelphia, 1935; L. MacClintock, *The Age of Pirandello*, Bloomington, Ind., 1951; E. R. Bentley, "Pirandello: Joy and Torment," in *In Search of Theater*, New York, 1953; T. Bishop, *Pirandello and the French Theatre*, New York, 1960; F. L. Lucas, *Drama of Chekhov, Synge, Yeats, and Pirandello*, London, 1963; W. F. Starkie, *Luigi Pirandello, 1867–1936*, 3d ed., rev. and enl., Berkeley, Calif., 1965; O. Büdel, *Pirandello*, London, 1966; G. Cambon, ed., *Pirandello: A Collection of Critical Essays*, Englewood Cliffs, N.J., 1967; O. Ragusa, *Luigi Pirandello*, New York, 1968; J. Moestrup, *The Structural Patterns of Pirandello's Work*, Odense, 1972; G. Giudice, *Pirandello*, New York, 1975; R. Oliver, *Dreams of Passion: The Theatre of Luigi Pirandello*, New York, 1980.

Piron, Alexis (1689–1773)

French poet and dramatist. His comedy *The Poetry Craze, or The Poet* (*La métromanie, ou Le poète*, 1738) is considered one of the masterpieces of eighteenth-century comedy. After completing his legal studies, Piron, against his father's wishes, left for Paris to make a name for himself as a poet and playwright. He first drew attention with *Arlequin Deucalion* (1722), a three-act work in the form of a series of monologues that were designed to circumvent a recent interdiction against the performance of dialogue scenes at public fairs. In it, Harlequin, the sole survivor of a flood, amuses himself by re-creating characters according to their social usefulness. In the following four years Piron continued to write for the fair theatres and turned out more than twenty farces, parodies, and comic-opera texts. In 1728, under the influence of the actress Mlle. Quinault, he wrote one of the first middle-class dramas, *The Ungrateful Sons* (*Les fils ingrats*; also

La métromanie. [New York Public Library]

known as *L'école des pères*), in which a father's sacrifices for his children are repaid with ingratitude. Piron also tried his hand at tragedy, but works such as *Gustave Wasa* (1733), a tale of revolution in Sweden, and *Fernand Cortès* (1744) met with little success. Though elected to the Académie Française in 1753, he was never seated in that august body because of the scandal caused by his *Ode to Priapus (Ode à Priape)*, a licentious poem written while he was still a young man. His feud with Voltaire is part of French literary history.

The Poetry Craze, or The Poet (*La métromanie, ou Le poète*, 1738). Damis, a poet who secretly uses the pseudonym M. de l'Empirée, lives in the home of Francaleu, who hopes to marry him to his daughter Lucille. Francaleu secretly writes verse under the name Mlle. de Mériadec de Kersic, and through the agency of the publication *Mercure de France* he and Damis have become involved in a passionate exchange of letters to which they sign their pseudonyms. Damis swears undying fidelity to his unknown Breton muse and writes for Dorante, a young man in love with Lucille, poems that successfully win the girl's heart—for Dorante. Baliveau, Damis's uncle and the epitome of good sense, unsuccessfully attempts to convince his nephew to give up poetry and take up some "gainful" profession. When the various characters come together to perform a play written by Francaleu, the secret of the pseudonymous correspondence is revealed. Even though Damis now knows that his Breton muse is the fifty-year old Francaleu, he insists on remaining faithful to the nonexistent Mlle. de Mériadec de Kersic. Lucille marries Dorante, and Damis is left to devote himself to his real love, poetry.

[JOSEPH E. GARREAU]

Pisemsky, Aleksey Feofilaktovich (1821–1881)

Russian novelist and dramatist. He was born on March 23, 1821 (N.S.), in Rameniye, Kostroma Province, to the impoverished descendants of an ancient family. He earned a degree in mathematics from the University of Moscow in 1844. Soon after his first novel, *Boyarshchina*, written in 1845, was censored because it presented a depressing picture of Russian life, he entered the civil service, there to remain for much of his life. The book finally appeared in 1858. Pisemsky's first published work was "Nina," a short story that appeared in 1848. In 1850, shortly after the publication of another story, "The Simpleton" ("Tyufyak"), Pisemsky joined the writers of the *Moskvityanin*, a periodical with which Ostrovsky and Appolon Grigoriyev were associated. Pisemsky was attracted by the literary originality of the magazine but not by its liberal political ideas, which he as a pessimistic conservative distrusted. *See* OSTROVSKY, ALEKSANDR.

Pisemsky became well known through publication of his novel *One Thousand Souls* (*Tysyacha dush*, 1858), which was followed by the tragic realistic drama *A Bitter Fate* (*Gorkaya sudbina*, wr. 1859). Meanwhile, he had published several humorous tales, including "A Love Match" ("Brak po strasti," 1851) and "Is She to Blame?" ("Vinovata li ona?," 1855), in which he described the baseness of the average man. This view recurs in all his works and is especially apparent in his masterful *Sketches of Peasant Life* (*Ocherki iz krestyanskogo byta*, 1856); Pisemsky's peasants are very different from the idealized peasants of Turgenev, and his realistic interpretation of peasant life alienated the young liberals of St. Petersburg, who were struggling for emancipation of the serfs (1861).

Pisemsky's novel *A Troubled Sea* (*Vzbalomuchennoye more*, 1863), which satirized the younger idealistic generation, completed his estrangement from the liberals. Out of the mainstream of literary style, Pisemsky's novels and plays became less popular in the 1860s and 1870s. The more interesting of his later prose works are *Men of the Forties* (*Lyudi sorokovykh godov*, 1869) and *The Masons* (*Masony*, 1880). Following the suicide of one son and the death of another in the late 1870s, Pisemsky became a hypochondriacal and profoundly bitter man. He died in Moscow on February 2, 1881 (N.S.).

WORK

Pisemsky began in the Gogol tradition: his first play, *The Hypochondriac* (*Ipokhondrik*, 1852), is a loosely knit, wildly inventive comedy centered around Durnopechin, a "humor" character who plays invalid to avoid intrusions on his torpidity. The critical failure of this play led Pisemsky to adopt the well-made play structure for his next comedy, *The Allotment* (*Razdel*, 1852), which featured standard themes of domestic tyranny and social satire. The remainder of his dramatic work sticks to this combination of well-constructed plot and exposure of the abuses of Russian society.

His finest play is *A Bitter Fate* (*Gorkaya sudbina*; wr. 1859, prod. 1863), a powerful drama of peasant life that has often been favorably compared with Tolstoy's *Power of Darkness*; its depiction of the peasants is realistic and unromantic, but the rigorous working out of the action and the protagonist's choice of his destiny bring it close to classical tragedy. When originally produced, the pessimistic ending was changed to one in which the infanticide Yakovlev repents.

Pisemsky's later plays can be divided into two groups, historical melodramas set in the eighteenth century, including *Laws unto Themselves* (*Samoupravtsy*, 1866) and *Lieutenant Gladkov* (*Poruchik Gladkov*, 1864), and dramas satirizing the financial wheeling and dealing of the 1860s and 1870s, such as *Baal* (*Vaal*, 1873), *The Financial Genius* (*Finansoviy geniy*, 1876), and *Predators* (*Khishchniki*, 1872). These plays suffer from an excess of melodrama but in their acrid tone resemble the works of Honoré de Balzac and Henry Becque. *See* BALZAC, HONORÉ DE; BECQUE, HENRY.

The Allotment (*Razdel*; wr. 1852, prod. 1874). Satire in which the prospect of financial gain triggers the display of meanness and hypocrisy among members of a family. Anna Yefremovna Burilenko, a widow, discusses the disposition of her late husband's estate with Ivan and Kiril Manokhin, her brothers; Yemiliya, her niece; and Sergey, her nephew. Pavel, Burilenko's ward, has hidden the dead man's money and appears to control the situation until he is locked in a barn by the others, who then proceed to divide the goods of the estate. Gradually all the heirs become entangled in intrigue, lies, and betrayal. For a time Ivan outwits the others and pauperizes the widow, but presently he loses his mind. A servant announces that Pavel has escaped from the barn and that Sergey and Ivan are at each other's throats; then a shot rings out and the play ends, offering no hint as to the final outcome.

A Bitter Fate (*Gorkaya sudbina*; wr. 1859, prod. 1863). Tragedy about Anany Yakovlev, a peasant tenant who returns to his village, Sokovina, to learn that Lizaveta, his wife by a forced marriage, has become the mistress of a local landowner, Cheglov-Sokovin, and has borne him a child. Proud and principled, Yakovlev refuses to trade his honor for the landowner's money; he proposes instead to move elsewhere and start a new life with Lizaveta and her child. However, Lizaveta and Cheglov-Sokovin love each other. When Cheglov-Sokovin summons Lizaveta to him, Yakovlev, in a rage, kills the infant. Later he gives himself up and begs for punishment. He refuses to explain that Cheglov-Sokovin is the father of Lizaveta's child and is therefore granted no mercy. Witnesses against Cheglov-Sokovin are bribed into silence, and Lizaveta falls at Yakovlev's feet as he goes to his fate.

The Warriors and Those Who Wait (*Boytsy i vyzhidateli*, wr. 1864). Prince Maksata, a meddlesome bureaucrat, intercepts a love note arranging a midnight rendezvous sent by Yevgeniya, the boss's daughter, to Obolonsky, a co-worker. Maksata tells Terkhazin, another co-worker, about the note. Envious, Terkhazin informs Count Poltashev, their superior, that Obolonsky is the writer of an anonymous article exposing certain compromising practices within the count's department. The count, hurt, seeks the consolation of an actress, Mme. Delyabel, who is enamored of Obolonsky. In a servile attempt to ingratiate himself with the actress, Maksata tells her that Yevgeniya and Obolonsky are lovers. She then persuades the count to surprise them at their meeting place, which he does. Charging Obolonsky with treason, the count has him arrested. Yevgeniya, however, manages to incriminate herself in order to share her lover's fate. Over the count's objections the lovers are finally freed, and they leave Russia. At the play's end Mme. Delyabel decides to content herself with the count, who has resigned from his post. Terkhazin moves up to the count's position, and Maksata is appointed to succeed Obolonsky.

[LAURENCE SENELICK]

PLAYS

1. *Ipokhondrik* (*The Hypochondriac*). Comedy, 4 acts. Written 1852. Published 1851 (partial), 1852. Produced St. Petersburg, Sept. 21, 1855.
2. *Razdel* (*The Allotment*). Comedy, 3 acts. Written 1852. Published 1853. Produced St. Petersburg, Alexandrinsky Theatre, Feb. 6, 1874.
3. *Veteran i novobranets* (*The Veteran and the Recruit*). Play, 8 scenes. Written 1854. Published 1854.
4. *Gorkaya sudbina** (*A Bitter Fate*). Drama, 4 acts. Written 1859. Produced St. Petersburg, private performance, July 31, 1863; St. Petersburg, Alexandrinsky Theatre, Oct. 18, 1863.
5. *Poruchik Gladkov* (*Lieutenant Gladkov*). Tragedy, 5 acts. Written 1864. Published 1867.
6. *Byvye sokoly* (*Former Falcons*). Tragedy, 4 acts. Written 1864. Published 1868.
7. *Boytsy i vyzhidateli* (*The Warriors and Those Who Wait*). Drama, 4 acts. Written 1864. Published 1883–1886.
8. *Samoupravtsy* (*Laws unto Themselves*). Tragedy, 5 acts. Wrtten 1865. Published 1867. Produced Moscow, Maly Theatre, Jan. 17, 1866.
9. *Khishchniki* (*The Predators*). Comedy, 5 acts. Written 1872. Published 1873. Produced St. Petersburg, October, 1905.
10. *Vaal** (*Baal*). Drama, 4 acts. Written 1873. Published 1873. Produced St. Petersburg, Alexandrinsky Theatre, Oct. 12, 1873.
11. *Prosveshchyonnoye vremya* (*The Enlightened Time*). Tragedy, 4 acts. Written 1874. Published 1875. Produced Moscow, Maly Theatre, Jan. 30, 1875.
12. *Finansovy geny* (*The Financial Genius*). Comedy, 4 acts. Written 1876. Published 1876.
13. *Ptentsy poslednego sleta* (*The Fledglings of the Last Flight*). Tragedy, 4 acts. Published 1883–1886.
14. *Miloslavskiye i Naryshkiny* (*The Miloslavs and the Naryshkins*). Tragedy, 5 acts. Published 1886.
15. *Materi-sopernitsy* (*The Rival Mothers*). Tragedy, 5 acts. Unfinished.
16. *Semeyny omut* (*The Family Slough*). Drama, 5 acts. Unfinished.

EDITIONS

Komedii, dramy, i tragedii, 2 vols., Moscow, 1874; *Polnoye sobraniye sochineny*, 8 vols., Moscow, 1910–1911; *Pisma*, Moscow, 1936; *Pyesy*, Moscow, 1958.

A Bitter Fate. Published in *Masterpieces of the Russian Drama*, ed. and tr. by G. R. Noyes, New York, 1933; *Baal*, tr. by A. Donskov, in *Russian Literature Triquarterly* IX (1974).

CRITICISM

A. I. Kirpichnikov, *Dostoyevsky i Pisemsky*, Moscow, 1894; I. D. Ivanov, *Pisemsky*, Moscow, 1898; M. P. Yeremin, *Pisemsky*, Moscow, 1956; C. A. Moser, *Pisemsky, a Provincial Realist*, Cambridge, Mass., 1969.

Pixérécourt, René-Charles Guilbert de
(1773–1844)

French dramatist. René-Charles Guilbert de Pixérécourt was born in Nancy on January 22, 1773. He studied law in Nancy and received a degree in 1790, one year after his father had been dispossessed of his land and fortune by a revolutionary decree. To escape the Terror, he was sent in 1791 to Coblenz, where he spent two years. In 1793 he went to Paris, where he shortened his name to Guilbert to diminish its aristocratic associations. There, living in a garret, he adapted Jean de Florian's novel *Selico* into a four-act play that was never staged. He then had to return to Nancy for military service, but trouble with the police forced him to leave. On his return to Paris, he found employment with a friend. In 1795 he married and resumed playwriting, but it was not until 1798 that his first melodrama, *Victor, or The Child of the Forest* (*Victor, ou L'enfant de la forêt*), was produced. In the meantime he earned his living as a fan painter. To secure his future, Pixérécourt became a government inspector of land leases in 1802, holding this position until 1836. He was director of the Opéra Comique in 1827 and privileged director of the Théâtre de la Gaîté from 1825 to 1835. On February 21, 1835, the Gaîté was destroyed by fire, and Pixérécourt had to sell his country house to pay his debts. In June, 1835, plagued by gout and kidney stones, he went to the spa at Contrexéville, where he suffered both sunstroke and severe burns in an overheated bath. Almost complete aphasia followed, and he spent his remaining years in slow agony in Nancy, finally dying there on July 27, 1844.

WORK

The melodrama of Pixérécourt, which epitomized the popular tragedy of the early nineteenth century, was born out of the apparent need of audiences for a change from the classical theatre that predominated at the end of the eighteenth century. Introduced to France from Italy in the eighteenth century, *mélodrame* originally signified "opera," but by the start of the nineteenth century it had come to mean a popular drama with a serious plot, sensational and highly moral in character, interspersed with comic scenes and often accompanied by incidental music. *See* MELODRAMA in glossary.

Pixérécourt became a master of the new genre, which combined the spectacular effects of the original musical melodrama with the serious tone and action of classical tragedy and tragicomedy. His melodrama, however, was only superficially related to classical drama. The complex psychological conflicts essential to a classical form such as the tragicomedy of Corneille were reduced to violent and sensational conflicts that created an emotional effect derived more from circumstances than from character. The dramatic effect of the play was due largely to highly emotional suspense and to surprises resulting from plot contrivances.

Many of the sensational effects of melodrama as exemplified by Pixérécourt came from the use of spectacular scenery intended to appeal to the senses through an exaggerated realism. In *The Belvedere, or The Valley of Etna* (*Le belvéder, ou La vallée de l'Etna*, 1818), Mount Etna erupts; in *Charles the Bold, or The Siege of Nancy* (*Charles le Téméraire, ou Le siège de Nancy*, 1814), there is a flood; and in *The Exile's Daughter, or Eight Months in Two Hours* (*La fille de l'exilé, ou Huit mois en deux heures*, 1819), a river overflows its banks.

Classical elements in plot structure, such as mistaken identities, were introduced by artificial turns in the plot and reduced the classical conception of fate to the mere hazard of circumstance. In *Valentine, or The Seduction* (*Valentine, ou La séduction*, 1821) and in *The Death's Head, or The Ruins of Pompeii* (*La tête de mort, ou Les ruines de Pompéi*, 1827), tragic emotions are aroused through external and arbitrary means rather than proceeding from psychological characterization or a causal development of plot. The classical conception of fate was also replaced by faith in the power of a justice based on bourgeois morality. Thus in *Coelina, or The Child of Mystery* (*Coelina, ou L'enfant du mystère*, 1800) destiny is identified with virtue in the avenging of a crime.

Pathos and sentiment, which arose from the tragic outcome in classical drama, are, in Pixérécourt's melodrama, evoked by stock figures employed specifically to engender pity through stereotyped sentimentality. The characters of Pixérécourt's melodrama are recurrent types: the virtuous heroine who is loved by a brave and equally virtuous young man; the evil villain who threatens their well-being but who has enough good in him to allow for a final conversion; and a comic personage, usually a servant, whose function is to relieve dramatic tension. Around these stock characters Pixérécourt constructed highly moralistic plots. In *Victor, or The Child of the Forest* (1798), Victor pleads with his father to turn away from crime and the father dies regretting his sordid life; in *The Wife of Two Husbands* (*La femme à deux maris*,

1802), a pure, innocent woman is beset by her worthless husband, whom she thought dead; a mother grieves for her children who are torn from her to be offered as hostages to a cruel enemy in *The Moors of Spain, or The Power of Childhood* (*Les maures d'Espagne, ou Le pouvoir de l'enfance*, 1804); and *The Dog of Montargis, or The Forest of Bondy* (*Le chien de Montargis, ou La forêt de Bondy*, 1814) portrays an innocent man condemned for a crime committed by someone else.

In rejecting the clarity and rationality of classical theatre in favor of sentimentality and emotionalism, Pixérécourt reflected the beginning of romanticism. Like the romantics, he found the conventions of classical drama too rigid to permit the free expression of moods and sensations. He created a typically melancholy romantic heroine in *Valentine, or The Seduction*, which is about a young girl who sacrifices herself for love. Similarities between the melodrama of Pixérécourt and romantic drama include a taste for the sublime and the sensational, a fascination with the abstract forces of good and evil, and an almost morbid interest in the emotional suffering and sentimental moods of the hero. However, Pixérécourt was not a romantic and was little concerned with the abstractions of romantic aesthetics, which urged the free expression of the subjective and individualistic nature of the artist. His efforts in the melodrama were directed solely toward obtaining a public and his use of spectacular scenery, violent action, and moralizing sentimentality proved effective on the stage.

Victor, or The Child of the Forest (*Victor, ou L'enfant de la forêt*, 1798). Melodrama based on a novel by François-Guillaume Ducray-Duminil. Victor must choose between killing his real father, a bandit chief named Roger, or showing himself to be a monster of ingratitude by not protecting his adopted father, who has offered him his daughter Clémence in marriage. Victor's dilemma is solved at the last moment when Roger is killed by someone else. As Roger dies, he discloses that he has been a bandit by force of circumstance, not by choice.

Coelina, or The Child of Mystery (*Coelina, ou L'enfant du mystère*, 1800). Melodrama based on a novel by Ducray-Duminil. In the mountain home of Dufour live his niece Coelina and Francisque, a mysterious man who is said to have been struck dumb by bandits. Coelina's odious uncle Truguelin arrives with plans to persuade her to marry his son. Coelina soon discovers that he also plans to murder Francisque. This villainy convinces Dufour that his own son should marry Coelina. Preparations for the wedding begin, but they are stopped abruptly when a letter from Truguelin informs Dufour that Coelina's father was not Dufour's brother but is Francisque. Finally the truth is disclosed: Francisque and Coelina's mother were husband and wife. Truguelin is revealed as the man who mutilated Francisque and is led away to prison. The lovers are united, and everyone lives happily ever after.

Margaret of Anjou (*Marguerite d'Anjou*, 1810). Melodrama based on the Abbé Prévost's life of Margaret (1756), Shakespeare's *Henry VI* and *Richard III*, and *Le comte de Warwick* (1779) by Jean-François de Laharpe.

Margaret, wife of Henry of England, who was killed by Gloucester, sets out with the remnants of an army to oust Gloucester from the throne that he has usurped. Defeated, Margaret falls into the hands of bandits, who become her protectors until Gloucester arrives and seizes her. She is about to be slain when French troops arrive and save her. Gloucester, enraged, sets fire to the forest where he has discovered her and perishes in the flames.

The Belvedere, or The Valley of Etna (*Le belvéder, ou La vallée de l'Etna*, 1818). Melodrama that combines aspects of Charles Nodier's novel *Jean Sbogar* and *The Robbers* by Schiller. Banished from his city, Loredan seeks either glory or death in combat. To achieve his goal, he becomes a barbarian chief known as Spalatro. He falls in love with Emily, daughter of the Duke of Belmont, whose life is threatened by another bandit. Spalatro, known to Emily as Giovanni, disappears and returns as Loredan-Spalatro. He terrifies everyone but saves Emily and the city of Catania. Then he reveals his true identity to his beloved. When he finally saves her father too, his banishment is rescinded. *See* SCHILLER, FRIEDRICH VON.

[JOSEPH E. GARREAU]

PLAYS

All plays are in prose and were first performed in Paris.

1. *Victor, ou L'enfant de la forêt* (*Victor, or The Child of the Forest*). Melodrama, 3 acts. Published 1803. Produced Théâtre de l'Ambigu-Comique, June 10, 1798. Based on the novel of the same name by François-Guillaume Ducray-Duminil.

2. *Les petits auvergnats* (*The Little Auvergnats*). Comedy, 1 act. Published 1799. Produced Théâtre Louvois and Théâtre de l'Ambigu-Comique, 1798.

3. *Le château des Apennins, ou Le fantôme vivant* (*The Château of the Apennines, or The Living Phantom*). Drama, 5 acts. Published 1799. Produced Théâtre de l'Ambigu-Comique, Dec. 9, 1798.

4. *Zozo, ou Le mal-avisé* (*Zozo, or The Imprudent Man*). Comedy, 1 act. Published 1800. Produced Théâtre Montansier-Variétés, Oct. 17, 1799.

5. *Rosa, ou L'hermitage du Torrent* (*Rosa, or the Torrent Hermitage*). Play. Published 1800.

6. *Le petit page, ou La prison d'état* (*The Little Page, or The State Prison*). Comedy, 1 act. Published 1800. Produced Théâtre Feydeau, Feb. 14, 1800. Music: Rodolphe Kreutzer.

7. *Coelina, ou L'enfant du mystère* (*Coelina, or The Child of Mystery*). Melodrama, 3 acts. Published 1803. Produced Théâtre de l'Ambigu-Comique, Sept. 2, 1800. Based on a novel by Ducray-Duminil.

8. *Le chansonnier de la paix* (*The Balladeer of Peace*). Impromptu, 1 act. Published 1802. Produced Théâtre Feydeau, Feb. 19, 1801.

9. (With L. T. Lambert). *Flaminius à Corinthe* (*Flaminius at Corinth*). Opera, 1 act. Published 1801. Produced Théâtre des Arts, Feb. 24, 1801. Music: Kreutzer and Nicolò Isouard.

10. *Le pèlerin blanc.* Drama, 3 acts. Published 1802. Produced Théâtre de l'Ambigu-Comique, Apr. 16, 1801.

11. *L'homme à trois visages, ou Le proscrit** (*The Venetian Outlaw*). Drama, 3 acts. Published 1801. Produced Théâtre de l'Ambigu-Comique, 1801.

12. (With François Léger). *Le vieux major* (*The Old Major*). Vaudeville, 1 act. Published 1801. Produced Théâtre du Montansier, Aug. 24, 1801.

13. (With Lambert). *La peau de l'ours* (*The Bearskin*). Folie, 1 act. Published 1802. Produced Théâtre Montansier-Variétés, Mar. 1, 1802.

14. *Raymond de Toulouse, ou Le retour de la Terre-Sainte* (*Raymond de Toulouse, or The Return from the Holy Land*). Lyric drama, 3 acts. Published 1802. Produced Théâtre de la Rue Bondy, Sept. 16, 1802. Music: Jacques Foignet and François Foignet.

15. *Pizarre, ou La conquête de Pérou* (*Pizarro, or The Conquest of Peru*). Historical melodrama. Published 1802. Produced Théâtre de la Porte-Saint-Martin, Sept. 27, 1802.

16. *La femme à deux maris** (*The Wife of Two Husbands*). Drama, 3 acts. Published 1802. Produced Théâtre de l'Ambigu-Comique, Dec. 27, 1802.

17. *Les deux valets* (*The Two Valets*). Comedy, 1 act. Published 1803. Produced Théâtre de la Porte-Saint-Martin, Apr. 11, 1803.

18. *Les mines de Pologne* (*The Mines of Poland*). Melodrama, 3 acts. Published 1803. Produced Théâtre de l'Ambigu-Comique, May 3, 1803.

19. *Tékéli, ou Le siège de Mongatz* (*Tékéli, or the Siege of Mongatz*). His-torical melodrama, 3 acts. Published 1804. Produced Théâtre de l'Ambigu-Comique, Dec. 29, 1803.

20. *Les maures d'Espagne, ou Le pouvoir de l'enfance* (*The Moors of Spain, or The Power of Childhood*). Melodrama, 3 acts. Published 1804. Produced Théâtre de l'Ambigu-Comique, May 9, 1804.

21. *Avis aux femmes, ou Le mari en colère* (*Advice to Wives, or The Angry Husband*). Comedy, 1 act. Published 1804. Produced Opéra Comique, Oct. 27, 1804. Music: Pierre Gaveaux.

22. (With Joseph-Marie Loaisel de Tréogate). *Le grand chasseur, ou L'île des palmiers* (*The Great Hunter, or The Island of Palms*). Melodrama, 3 acts. Published 1804. Produced Théâtre de l'Ambigu-Comique, Nov. 6, 1804.

23. *La forteresse de Danube* (*The Danube Fortress*). Melodrama, 3 acts. Published 1805. Produced Théâtre de la Porte-Saint-Martin, Jan. 3, 1805.

24. *Robinson Crusoë.* Melodrama, 3 acts. Published 1805. Produced Théâtre de la Porte-Saint-Martin, Oct. 2, 1805. Music: Alexandre Piccini and Gérardin Lacour.

25. *La solitaire de la roche noire* (*The Solitary Lady of the Black Rock*). Melodrama, 3 acts. Published 1806. Produced Théâtre de la Porte-Saint-Martin, May 4, 1806. Music: Piccini.

26. *Les fausses déclarations, ou La veuve* (*False Declarations, or The Widow*). Play, 1 act. Produced Théâtre des Jeunes-Artistes, Aug. 23, 1806.

27. *Koulouf, ou Les chinois* (*Koulouf, or The Chinese*). Comic opera, 3 acts. Published 1807. Produced Opéra Comique, Dec. 18, 1806. Music: Nicolas Dalayrac.

28. *L'ange tutélaire, ou Le démon femelle* (*The Guiding Angel, or The Female Demon*). Melodrama, 3 acts. Published 1808. Produced Théâtre de la Gaîté, June 2, 1808. Music: Piccini.

29. *La citerne* (*The Reservoir*). Melodrama, 4 acts. Published 1809. Produced Théâtre de la Gaîté, Jan. 14, 1809.

30. *La rose blanche et la rose rouge* (*The White Rose and the Red*). Lyric drama, 3 acts. Published 1809. Produced Opéra Comique, Mar. 20, 1809. Music: Gaveaux.

31. *Marguerite d'Anjou* (*Margaret of Anjou*). Melodrama, 3 acts. Published 1810. Produced Théâtre de la Gaîté, Jan. 11, 1810. Music: Lacour.

32. (With Jean-Baptiste Dubois). *Les trois moulins* (*The Three Windmills*). Allegorical divertissement, 1 act. Published 1810. Produced Théâtre de la Gaîté, Mar. 30, 1810.

33. *Les ruines de Babylone, ou Giafar et Zaïda* (*The Ruins of Babylon, or Giafar and Zaïda*). Historical melodrama, 3 acts. Published 1810. Produced Théâtre de la Gaîté, Oct. 30, 1810.

34. *Le précipice, ou Les forges de Norvège* (*The Precipice, or The Norwegian Forges*). Melodrama, 3 acts. Published 1811. Produced Théâtre de la Gaîté, Oct. 30, 1811.

35. *Le fanal de Messine* (*The Banner of Messina*). Melodrama, 3 acts. Published 1812. Produced Théâtre de la Gaîté, June 23, 1812.

36. *Le petit carillonneur, ou La tour ténébreuse* (*The Little Bell Ringer, or The Dark Tower*). Melodrama, 3 acts. Published 1812. Produced Théâtre de la Gaîté, Nov. 24, 1812.

37. *L'ennemi des modes, ou La maison de Choisy* (*The Enemy of Fashion, or The House at Choisy*). Comedy, 3 acts. Published 1814. Produced Théâtre de l'Odéon, Dec. 7, 1813.

38. *Le chien de Montargis, ou La forêt de Bondy** (*The Dog of Montargis, or The Forest of Bondy*). Melodrama, 3 acts. Published 1814. Produced Théâtre de la Gaîté, June 18, 1814.

39. *Charles le Téméraire, ou Le siège de Nancy* (*Charles the Bold, or The Siege of Nancy*). Historical melodrama, 3 acts. Published 1814. Produced Théâtre de la Gaîté, Oct. 26, 1814.

40. *Christophe Colomb, ou La découverte du nouveau monde* (*Christopher Columbus, or The Discovery of the New World*). Historical melodrama, 3 acts. Published 1815. Produced Théâtre de la Gaîté, Sept. 5, 1815.

41. *Le suicide, ou Le vieux sergent* (*The Suicide, or The Old Sergeant*). Melodrama, 2 acts. Published 1816. Produced Théâtre de la Gaîté, Feb. 20, 1816.

42. *Le monastère abandonné, ou La malédiction paternelle* (*The Abandoned Monastery, or The Paternal Malediction*). Melodrama, 3 acts. Published 1816. Produced Théâtre de la Gaîté, Nov. 28, 1816.

43. (With Michel-Nicolas Balisson de Rougemont). *La chapelle des bois, ou Le témoin invisible* (*The Chapel in the Woods, or The Invisible Witness*). Melodrama, 3 acts. Published 1818. Produced Théâtre de la Gaîté, Aug. 12, 1818.

44. *Le belvéder, ou La vallée de l'Etna* (*The Belvedere, or The Valley of Etna*). Melodrama, 3 acts. Published 1818. Produced Théâtre de l'Ambigu-Comique, Dec. 10, 1818.

45. *La fille de l'exilé, ou Huit mois en deux heures* (*The Exile's Daughter, or Eight Months in Two Hours*). Historical melodrama, 3 parts. Published 1819. Produced Théâtre de la Gaîté, Mar. 13, 1819.

46. *Les chefs écossais* (*The Scottish Chiefs*). Heroic melodrama, 3 acts. Published 1819. Produced Théâtre de la Porte-Saint-Martin, Sept. 1, 1819.

47. *Bouton de rose* (*Rosebud*). Fairy-tale melodrama, 3 acts. Published 1819. Produced Théâtre de la Gaîté, Nov. 13, 1819.

48. *Le mont sauvage, ou Le solitaire* (*The Savage Mountain, or The Soli-*

tary). Melodrama, 3 acts. Published 1821. Produced Théâtre de la Porte-Saint-Martin, July 12, 1821.

49. *Valentine, ou La séduction (Valentine, or The Seduction).* Melodrama, 3 acts. Published 1822. Produced Théâtre de la Gaîté, Dec. 15, 1821.

50. *Le pavillon des fleurs, ou Les pêcheurs de Grenade.* Comedy, 1 act. Published 1822. Produced Opéra Comique, May 13, 1822. Music: Dalayrac.

51. *Ali Baba, ou Les quarante voleurs (Ali Baba, or The Forty Thieves).* Melodrama, 3 acts. Published 1822. Produced Théâtre de la Gaîté, Sept. 24, 1822.

52. *Le château de Loch-leven, ou La captivité de Marie Stuart (The Castle of Lochleven, or The Captivity of Mary Stuart).* Historical melodrama, 3 acts. Published 1822. Produced Théâtre de la Gaîté, Dec. 3, 1822.

53. *La place du palais (The Palace Square).* Melodrama, 3 acts. Published 1824. Produced Théâtre de la Gaîté, Mar. 26, 1824.

54. (With Nicolas Brazier and Mélesville). *Le baril d'olives (The Barrel of Olives).* Comedy vaudeville, 1 act. Published 1825. Produced Théâtre des Variétés, Feb. 1, 1825.

55. *Le moulin des étangs (The Mill at the Ponds).* Play. Produced Jan. 28, 1826.

56. *Les Natchez, ou La tribu des serpents (The Natchez, or The Tribe of Serpents).* Play. Produced Théâtre de la Gaîté, June 21, 1827.

57. *La tête de mort, ou Les ruines de Pompéi (The Death's Head, or The Ruins of Pompeii).* Melodrama, 3 acts. Published 1828. Produced Théâtre de la Gaîté, Dec. 8, 1827. Music: Piccini.

58. (With Benjamin Antier). *La muette de la forêt (The Dumb Woman of the Forest).* Melodrama, 1 act. Published 1828. Produced Théâtre de la Gaîté, Jan. 29, 1828.

59. *La peste de Marseille (The Marseille Plague).* Historical melodrama, 3 acts. Published 1828. Produced Théâtre de la Gaîté, Aug. 2, 1828.

60. (With Victor Ducange). *Polder, ou Le bourreau d'Amsterdam (Polder, or The Executioner of Amsterdam).* Drama, 3 acts. Published 1840. Produced Théâtre de la Gaîté, Oct. 15, 1828.

61. (With Antier). *Guillaume Tell (William Tell).* Melodrama, 6 parts. Published 1828. Produced Théâtre de la Gaîté, May 3, 1829. Adapted from Friedrich von Schiller's *Wilhelm Tell.*

62. (With Mélesville). *L'aigle des Pyrénées (The Eagle of the Pyrenees).* Melodrama, 3 acts. Published 1829. Produced Théâtre de la Gaîté, Feb. 19, 1829.

63. *Olivier, ou Les compagnons du chêne (Oliver, or The Companions of the Oak).* Play. Produced June 6, 1829.

64. *Alice, ou Les fossoyeurs écossais (Alice, or The Scots Gravediggers).* Play. Produced Sept. 24, 1829.

65. *Ondine, ou La nymphe des eaux (Ondine, or The Water Nymph).* Fairy play, 4 acts. Published 1830. Produced Théâtre de la Gaîté, Feb. 17, 1830. Music: Piccini.

66. (With Ducange). *Judacin, ou Les filles de la veuve (Judacin, or The Widow's Daughters).* Melodrama, 3 acts. Published 1840, as *Le jésuite.* Produced Théâtre de la Gaîté, Sept. 4, 1830.

67. (With Pigault-Lebrun). *La lettre de cachet (The King's Private Seal).* Play. Produced Feb. 26, 1831.

68. (With H. Martin). *L'abbaye au bois, ou La femme de chambre (The Abbey in the Woods, or The Chambermaid).* Contemporary history, 3 acts. Published 1832. Produced Théâtre de la Gaîté, Feb. 14, 1832.

69. (With Brazier and Pierre-François-Adolphe Carmouche). *Le petit (The Youngster).* Romantic fairy play, 4 acts. Published 1832. Produced Théâtre de la Gaîté, Mar. 19, 1832. Music: Piccini.

70. *Six florins, ou La brodeuse et la dame (Six florins, or The Embroiderer and the Lady).* Play. Produced July 7, 1832.

71. *L'allée des veuves, ou La justice en 1773 (Widows' Way, or Justice in 1773).* Melodrama, 3 acts. Published 1833. Produced Théâtre de la Gaîté, Mar. 16, 1833. Music: Piccini.

72. (With Brazier and Théophile du Mersan). *Les quatre éléments (The Four Elements).* Fantastic fairy comedy, 4 acts. Published 1833. Produced Théâtre de la Gaîté, July 10, 1833.

73. *Valentine, ou Le château et la ferme (Valentine, or The Château and the Farm).* Melodrama, 5 acts. Published 1834. Produced Théâtre de la Gaîté, Mar. 20, 1834.

74. *Latude, ou Trente-cinq ans de captivité (Latude, or Thirty-five Years of Captivity).* Historical melodrama, 3 acts. Published 1834. Produced Théâtre de la Gaîté, Nov. 15, 1834.

75. *Le berceau (The Cradle).* Divertissement, 1 act. Published 1839. Produced Cirque-Olympique, Jan. 31, 1838.

77. (With Brazier and Félix-Auguste Duvert). *Bijou, ou L'enfant de Paris (Jewel, or The Child of Paris).* Fairy play, 4 acts. Published 1839. Produced Cirque-Olympique, Jan. 31, 1838.

EDITIONS

Théâtre, 10 vols., Paris, n.d.; *Théâtre choisi,* 4 vols., Nancy, 1841–1843.

Coelina, ou L'enfant du mystère. Published in *Nineteenth Century French Plays,* ed. by J. L. Borgerhoff, Century, New York, 1931.

CRITICISM

A. Virely, *René Charles Guilbert de Pixérécourt (1773–1844),* Paris, 1909; F. Heel, *Guilbert de Pixérécourt: Sein Leben und seine Werke,* Erlangen, 1912; W. G. Hartog, *Guilbert de Pixérécourt: Sa vie, son mélodrame, sa technique et son influence,* Paris, 1913; A. Lacey, *Pixérécourt and the French Romantic Drama,* Toronto, 1928.

Plautus (ca. 251–ca. 184 B.C.)

Roman dramatist. Mystery surrounds the life of Titus Maccius Plautus; only through references to him by other Latin writers does a skeleton of facts emerge. In *Brutus,* Cicero states that Plautus died in 184 B.C.; in *De senectute,* he states that Plautus was at least sixty when he wrote his *Truculentus* and *Pseudolus,* placing the date of his birth somewhere between 254 and 251 B.C. According to Sextus Pompeius Festus, Roman grammarian of the second century A.D., he was born to humble parents in Sarsina, Umbria. Aulus Gellius, another grammarian of the second century, gives us some insight into Plautus's life. According to Gellius, Plautus went to Rome at an early age and engaged in some sort of theatrical work. Having saved some money, he became involved in an unsuccessful business venture that took him abroad. After this failure, he returned to Rome and took work as a laborer in a mill. During this period he wrote the *Saturio* and the *Addictus* (both lost) and one other play. Gellius may well have simply inferred this scant information from similar incidents in Plautus's comedies, but the association of Plautus with practical theatrical work seems likely.

Plautus. [Giraudon]

Only approximate dates of Plautus's comedies can be determined. The didascaliae, or records of production, however, do indicate the year 200 B.C. for the *Stichus* and 191 B.C. for *Pseudolus.* Mention of current events suggests for *The Braggart Warrior (Miles Gloriosus)* a date soon after 206 B.C. and for *The Casket (Cistellaria)* a date during or soon after the Second Punic War (218–201 B.C.). Since *The Two Bacchides (Bacchides)* contains a reference to the *Epidicus,* it must have been written after the latter. Finally, on stylistic grounds *The Merchant (Mercator)* could be considered early and *The Three Penny Day (Trinummus)* late. The main body of Plautus's work belongs to the latter half of his life.

WORK

Plautus was the most popular writer of *comoediae palliatae*, Latin comedies performed in Greek dress. He based his plays on the work of such Greek writers of New Comedy as Diphilus, Philemon, and Menander, but he recast them in uniquely Roman form. The Greece of his dramatic settings is a comic fantasy land where slaves outwit masters, sons dominate fathers, and romance triumphs over reality. Plautus's diction combines colloquialism and artificiality. His stage action is rapid and broad, his characters often clever versions of stock figures dear to his audience. The resulting plays follow the general outlines of Greek New Comedy but owe much to the peculiarities of the Latin language and to independent Italian traditions of mime and farce. *See* ROMAN DRAMA. *See* NEW COMEDY in glossary.

Plautus's gift for fantasy and his occasional lyricism are reminiscent of Aristophanes, as are his liveliness and vulgarity. The plays are certainly funnier than anything in Terence. The complex plots abound in mistaken identities, recognitions, and farcical scenes. Though Plautus sometimes aimed for continuity of action and clear overall structure, he tolerated contradictions, incongruities, and loose ends when they suited him. He could shorten his Greek original or expand it with new, not always germane comic material. The recent discovery of a hundred lines of Menander's *The Double Deceiver (Dis Exapaton),* the original of *The Two Bacchides,* establishes Plautus's easy omission of scenes, changing of names and meter, and alteration in the very focus of the plot. *Pseudolus,* Plautus's greatest play, includes a scene of abuse patterned on a native Italian custom called *flagitatio,* and much humor depends on the making and breaking of contracts in the typical Roman legal style. These are both clearly original additions, and both are integral to the success of the play. *See* ARISTOPHANES; TERENCE.

Though they vary greatly in theme, structure, and length, many plays present the dilemma of a young, middle-class lover kept from his beloved by a greedy pimp, a stubborn father, or simply lack of cash. A clever slave contrives elaborate intrigues to unite the lovers, and the play follows the ups and downs of the scheme. Plautus lavished much attention on his rogues' gallery of stock types, such as courtesans, pimps, soldiers, and cooks, who are often the blocking characters in these plots. He gives them comic names, self-descriptive monologues, and broad scenes for them to play in character. The inventiveness of these characterizations and the amount of stage time devoted to them make each one unique and memorable. The scheming slaves also receive much attention. They liken themselves to generals or lawyers routing the opposition and proclaim their skill in elaborate monologues. The lovers themselves are usually of less interest to Plautus except when, like Calidorus at the beginning of *Pseudolus,* they play straightman for the stronger comic figure.

Though Plautus's diction was rooted in Roman colloquial speech, it also reflects the stylization characteristic of the developing tradition of the *comoedia palliata.* His puns, alliterations, and verbal twists have many parallels in the comic fragments of his contemporaries. Whereas the early plays are written, like their Greek models, in the meters of dialogue, the later ones show great metrical variety. Exploiting the dramatic effects of varying rhythms, Plautus displayed a metrical agility not equaled again until Horace nearly two hundred years later, and the complexity of his songs is especially remarkable in a language then only beginning to acquire literary polish. Plautus's development of the *canticum,* singing with musical accompaniment, and his use of dance, both of which had almost entirely disappeared from Greek drama, created an early form of musical comedy. His plays also suggest prototypes for other familiar forms, from burlesque and farce to romance, masque, and operetta. *See* CANTICUM in glossary.

In the generations after his death, Plautus was still so popular that mere association of his name with a play was thought a ticket to success. Some 130 plays came to be attributed to him until late in the first century B.C., when the scholar and antiquarian Marcus Terentius Varro trimmed the list to 21 plays he thought authentic. Twenty of these survive, and there are fragments of the twenty-first. Among the best known are *Amphitryon (Amphitruo),* a comedy of character; and *The Twin Menaechmi (Menaechmi),* a deft farce about mistaken identity. A blend of satiric humor and sentimentality characterizes *The Captives (Captivi),* which Lessing called the greatest comedy ever written. *The Rope (Rudens)* features an exotic setting and romantic rescue; the slave and pimp of *Pseudolus* are among the most appealing rogues in Western drama.

Unlike Terence, whose simple elegance made him an ideal school text, Plautus was too difficult an author to be widely read in later antiquity and the Middle Ages. Since 1429, however, when twelve comedies were rediscovered and were added to the eight then known, his influence on Western drama has been considerable. Descendants of his boastful soldiers include the hero of the first English comedy, Nicholas Udall's *Ralph Roister Doister* (who also owes much to Terence's Thraso), Shakespeare's Falstaff, and the swaggering Sergius of Shaw's *Arms and the Man.* Shakespeare built *The Comedy of Errors* upon *The Twin Menaechmi* with a touch of *Amphitryon.* Molière's *The Miser* owes much to *The Pot of Gold,* and Lessing's early plays include adaptations of *Stichus (Weiber sind Weiber)* and *The Three Penny Day (Der Schatz). The Boys from Syracuse,* a Rodgers and Hart musical based upon *The Comedy of Errors,* has many truly Plautine touches, and the slave Pseudolus made a modern appearance in the musical comedy *A Funny Thing Happened on the Way to the Forum* (1962).

The Comedy of Asses (Asinaria). Comedy adapted from a Greek play by Demophilus concerning a father-son rivalry for the affections of a beautiful young woman. Demaenetus, a henpecked old lecher, wants to acquire the funds with which his son Argyrippus may purchase the highly desirable daughter of a procuress. Unable to approach his wife, of whom he is deathly afraid, Demaenetus conspires with his slaves Libanus and Leonida to raise the money. Some asses having recently been sold by the family steward, the trio arrange for Leonida to impersonate the steward and intercept the payment, which is exactly the amount required.

With Demaenetus himself vouching for Leonida's authenticity, the plot succeeds and the young lovers, Argyrippus and Philaenium, are overjoyed at the prospect of their impending union. Argyrippus, however, is understandably distressed when Demaenetus announces his intention of sharing the favors of Philaenium as a reward for his resourcefulness. Diabolus, Argyrippus's rival in love, discovers the plot and exposes Demaenetus to his dreaded wife Artemona, who spies on the old reprobate during a celebration banquet at which he reveals his lust for Philaenium and vents his hatred of his wife. But his flight from bondage is short-lived, for Artemona steps out of her hiding place, and Demaenetus reverts to his henpecked state. Dutifully returning home, he leaves the young lovers to enjoy their passion undisturbed.

The Merchant (*Mercator*). Comedy, based on Philemon's *Emporos*, that exploits a father-son rivalry over a woman. Charinus, an Athenian youth, has just returned from a business trip to Rhodes, where he had been sent to make him forget an Athenian courtesan. He now fears his father's displeasure, for while in Rhodes he fell in love with another girl, purchased her, and has brought her back to Athens with him. Demipho, his lascivious old father, accidentally meets the girl on shipboard and is promptly smitten with her, whereupon Charinus's quick-thinking slave Acanthio claims that his son bought her as a maid for his mother. But Demipho has other plans for her and insists that Charinus sell the girl to him "for a friend." Charinus counters that he too has "a friend" who wants her; father and son proceed to bid against each other. Demipho, of course, outbids his son and rushes off to claim his purchase, plunging Charinus into a depression from which his friend Eutychus cannot lift him. Meanwhile, Demipho has his old neighbor Lysimachus take secret custody of the girl, and the inevitable banquet is planned. The return of Lysimachus's wife interrupts the proceedings. Finding a strange woman in her home, she suspects the worst and threatens divorce. Faithful old Lysimachus, however, will not betray Demipho and is made to suffer the ignominy of being thrown out of his house. Charinus, about to leave town forever, is stopped when he hears from Eutychus that his beloved is in Lysimachus's house. When Eutychus finally informs Demipho that the girl is in reality his son's mistress, the repentant old man yields to his son and is forgiven.

The Braggart Warrior (*Miles Gloriosus*, ca. 205 B.C.). An Ephesian soldier, Pyrgopolynices, believes himself invincible in war and irresistible in love. He has purchased and carried back to Ephesus the Athenian girl Philocomasium against her will and has accidentally come into possession of Palaestrio, the slave of the girl's true lover Pleusicles, who is now secretly living next door. The lovers are able to meet clandestinely through the good offices of Palaestrio, who has dug a passage in the wall between the two houses. Disaster threatens when another of the soldier's slaves spies on the lovers. To convince him that he has not seen Philocomasium but only her twin sister, Palaestrio engineers a complex ruse wherein she poses as her own twin. Tragedy thus averted, Palaestrio sets to work devising Philocomasium's escape. A clever courtesan is hired to pose as the wife of Pleusicles's friend, the old bachelor Periplectomenus. This "wife" is to fall madly in love with the soldier, insist that Philocomasium be thrown out of his house, and then implicate the braggart in a charge of "adultery" by means of an incriminating ring. With Palaestrio and the courtesan's maid acting as go-betweens, the plot works. Philocomasium leaves the soldier's house with "tearful" farewells and is quickly spirited away by her lover in the guise of a ship captain. Periplectomenus has the soldier set upon and beaten for his "adultery," and when the spying slave informs his master that Philocomasium has been taken away by her true lover, he realizes he has been duped. Generously he admits he deserved the lesson.

The Casket (*Cistellaria*, before 201 B.C.). Comedy based on Menander's *The Women at Luncheon* and set in Sicyon, a Greek city where a young gentleman, Alcesimarchus, is involved in an ironic twist of fate. Deeply in love with his mistress Selenium, he is being forced by his father to marry the daughter of Demipho, an old friend. Sadly acquiescing in the arrangement, Selenium leaves the home of her lover and joins her mother, the procuress Malaenis. At this point, the audience learns from the god Succor the story of how an illegitimate child who was given to a slave to dispose of eventually came into the possession of Malaenis; Selenium is in fact only Malaenis's foster daughter. Beseeching Selenium's and Malaenis's forgiveness, Alcesimarchus is plunged to the depths of despair when both women reproach him. A slave enters and informs Demipho's wife Phanostrata that he has finally tracked down the woman who had found the baby she had abandoned. Malaenis, listening from a doorway, realizes that Selenium is Phanostrata's and Demipho's missing daughter, for Demipho had married Phanostrata years after he had wronged her and she had disposed of her baby. A casket of trinkets left with the abandoned child is produced by Malaenis as identification, but it is almost lost when Selenium stops Alcesimarchus's suicide attempt. Phanostrata's slave finds the box and turns it over to his mistress, who immediately recognizes the truth. Demipho is then informed of Selenium's true identity, and the comedy ends joyously for all as Alcesimarchus will surely marry the newly recognized daughter of Demipho.

Stichus (200 B.C.). Comedy, apparently adapted from Menander's first play called *The Brothers*, in which the plot serves as the barest framework for the final scene, a prolonged revelry. Two sisters of Athens are married to two brothers, Epignomus and Pamphilippus, who have been away for three years trying to make their fortunes. The girls' father Antipho, disgusted with the penniless state of his sons-in-law, insists that they divorce their husbands and marry richer men, but his daughters are loyal. Epignomus returns a wealthy man to his overjoyed wife, raising the hopes of the ravenously hungry parasite Gelasimus, who anticipates a banquet and is despondent when he is not offered an invitation. The brother's good fortune placates Antipho, and Epignomus's slave Stichus is given the day off as a holiday. Soon after Pamphilippus also returns a rich man, and the plans for a banquet are confirmed, though the wretched Gelasimus still cannot wangle an invitation. Stichus and his friend the slave Sangarinus, both of whom have designs on the slave girl Stephanium, appear loaded down with food and drink, parodying their masters' meal, and join their sweetheart for an evening of dancing and revelry.

The Pot of Gold (*Aulularia*). Comedy, probably based on a play by Menander, concerning the frantic efforts of a poor and miserly Athenian gentleman to retain a pot of gold. Prompted by the secret pregnancy of Euclio's unwed but pious daughter Phaedria, Euclio's household god has revealed that a pot of gold has long been buried in his house. The god intends that the treasure ensure Phaedria's marriage to her seducer Lyconides, whose uncle Megadorus also has designs on the simple, unspoiled girl. Ignorant of his daughter's condition, Euclio's neurotic worry over the safety of the gold torments his every moment, making him keenly suspicious of his old slave woman Staphyla and even of Megadorus's proposal of marriage. Although finally convinced that Megadorus knows nothing of the treasure, Euclio nonetheless shifts the pot's hiding place to a nearby temple. Meanwhile, Lyconides, hearing rumors of Megadorus's proposal to Phaedria, sends his slave to make inquiries. Learning of the existence of the gold, the slave tries to steal it from the temple. Unsuccessful, he follows Euclio to a field, watches him bury it, and then absconds with the loot. Lyconides, fearful that Phaedria will marry Megadorus, finally confesses his seduction to his mother and asks for her help. She sends him to Euclio to confess the seduction, but when Euclio rants over the disappearance of his gold, Lyconides mistakenly thinks the irate father is ranting over his affair with Phaedria. The mistake is rectified, and Lyconides rightfully claims her hand in marriage just after she delivers the baby. The pot of gold is returned to Euclio, and although the original ending of the play has been lost, it is generally assumed that the gold eventually serves as Phaedria's dowry.

Curculio. Comedy which takes its name from the highly enterprising slave of Phaedromus, a young gentleman of Epidaurus. In love with Planesium, a young virgin belonging to the hypochondriacal procurer Cappadox, Phaedromus is trying to gather enough money to purchase her. Toward this end, he has sent his slave Curculio to Caria, where he meets a captain, Therapontigonus. The captain, having recently purchased Planesium from Cappadox, had deposited the money with an Epidaurian banker with instructions that the girl is to be collected only by a person bearing a letter sealed with his ring. Curculio returns to Epidaurus with the ring; Phaedromus uses it as identification to obtain the captain's deposit from the banker and promptly delivers the money to Cappadox, who emerges from the temple of the god of healing long enough to conclude the bargain and immediately return. Therapontigonus arrives, learns that Planesium has been delivered to Phaedromus, and denounces the hapless Cappadox. Planesium, on seeing the ring, identifies it as one that belonged to her father and produces another identical to it, evidence that she is Therapontigonus's sister, who was separated from her family as a child. Proved to be freeborn, Planesium is free to marry Phaedromus and her brother to reclaim his money from Cappadox, since according to law those born free cannot be bought or sold.

The Haunted House (*Mostellaria*). Comedy derived from Philemon's *The Ghost* and describing riotous goings-on in Athens. Philolaches, once a model Athenian youth, on reaching his twenty-first birthday has turned to debauchery and profligacy, living with Philematum, a simple yet faithful mistress, and squandering the money of his long-absent father Theopropides in revelry with a fellow rake Callidamates. Their latest orgy is interrupted when Philolaches's slave Tranio bursts in with news of the father's return. Philolaches loses his head, but the cunning Tranio promises to save the day; at his order the house is locked and boarded up, and when Theopropides finds his home empty, Tranio regales him with stories of the house's being haunted by a ghost, a victim of the former tenant. The frightened Theopropides is about to investigate the story when Philolaches's irate moneylender appears. Tranio, to create a diversion, informs Theopropides that the vast sums due were borrowed by his son to buy the neighboring house and tricks its owner, Simo, into permitting Theopropides to inspect his home. Impressed, Theopropides believes his son has shown good business sense.

The whole complex of lies collapses when Theopropides intercepts a pair of slaves belonging to Callidamates, come to bear their drunken master home. Gradually the truth is revealed to the furious father. Sobered, Callidamates emerges to inform Theopropides of his son's shame and repentance and of his friends' willingness to repay the money Philolaches has squandered on them. All is finally forgiven as the sowing of wild oats. Even the rascal Tranio is excused.

The Carthaginian (*Poenulus*). Comedy set in Calydon. Agorastocles, born a Carthaginian but kidnaped at an early age and sold to a Calydonian, lives next door to the procurer Lycus, who owns two sisters and their nurse, all likewise Carthaginian-born and kidnapped years ago. The sisters are the daughters of Agorastocles's uncle Hanno, who has been searching for them ever since. Agorastocles, unaware of their relationship, is in love with one of the sisters, Adelphasium, who is growing impatient with his unfulfilled promises to free her. With his slave Milphio, he plans to discredit Lycus by having his overseer Collybiscus pose as a stranger seeking Lycus's services. He is to enter Lycus's house with money in hand and then accuse Lycus as an accessory to the theft of Agorastocles's money. The scheme works. At the same time, Milphio learns that Adelphasium and her sister are freeborn and hurries to inform Agorastocles.

Scene from *Amphitryon*. [Goethe House]

Meanwhile, Hanno arrives. Agorastocles recognizes his uncle. Milphio, knowing Hanno is searching for his long-lost daughters and wanting to help Agorastocles free Adelphasium and her sisters, suggests that Hanno pretend the two girls are his own daughters. But the slave's scheme turns out to be unnecessary when the nurse appears and recognizes Hanno. Adelphasium is promised to Agorastocles; Lycus, learning that the girls are no longer his, is ruined.

Pseudolus (191 B.C.). The cunning slave Pseudolus helps his master Calidorus release his beloved, the courtesan Phoenicium, from the clutches of the tyrannical procurer Ballio. But Phoenicium has already been promised to a Macedonian soldier, who, having made a down payment and left a token of identification, is now sending his slave Harpax with a similar token and the balance of money to collect the girl. Ballio rejects Calidorus's pleas for Phoenicium but grudgingly concedes that if he will produce the full price before Harpax arrives, Calidorus can have Phoenicium. Simo, Calidorus's father, suspects Pseudolus of plotting to steal the money from him, but this Pseudolus denies. Instead he persuades Simo to give him an equivalent sum if he succeeds in tricking Ballio to release the girl. Posing as Ballio's slave, Pseudolus intercepts Harpax and wheedles the token from him. Now Calidorus arrives with a friend, who supplies the necessary balance of money and a rascally slave to impersonate Harpax. The false Harpax presents Ballio with the token and the money, and Phoenicium is freed into the hands of Calidorus. With the arrival of the real Harpax, Ballio realizes he has been tricked, and Simo, unable to restrain his genuine admiration for Pseudolus, willingly pays him the money he has promised.

Epidicus. Comedy of intrigue, about a clever slave who extricates himself from a seemingly impossible situation. Before Stratippocles, a young Athenian, went to war, he commissioned his slave to buy Acropolistis, of whom he was enamored. Epidicus had persuaded his master's father Periphanes to purchase the girl by convincing him that she was his long-lost illegitimate daughter Telestis. Now Stratippocles, returned from the war, is in love with an attractive captive, whom he is to buy with borrowed money. Epidicus must get rid of Acropolistis and raise money to repay the loan. To do so, Epidicus informs Periphanes that his son loves Acropolistis, who is really a slave girl, and has borrowed money to free her; he can avert the undesirable marriage by buying the girl himself and reselling her to a soldier. Periphanes, agreeing to the scheme, gives money to Epidicus, who promptly turns it over to Stratippocles. Epidicus then hires a clever girl to pose as Acropolistis (who is still posing as Telestis) and delivers her to the relieved father. Accidentally learning that neither of the two girls in his house is the person he thought she was, Periphanes realizes he has been thoroughly deceived and imprisons Epidicus. Meanwhile, Epidicus has identified Stratippocles's new love as the real Telestis. He thereupon informs Periphanes of the truth and is freed. Periphanes is reunited with Telestis's mother.

The Two Bacchides (*Bacchides*). Lively comedy set in Athens and based on Menander's *The Double Deceiver*. The young Pistoclerus has been asked by his now-absent friend Mnesilochus to find a Samian courtesan named Bacchis, with whom he is in love. During the search Pistoclerus learns from an Athenian courtesan, also called Bacchis, that the girl he is looking for is her sister, who has recently arrived from Samos. Inevitably, Pistoclerus falls in love with Bacchis of Athens. Meanwhile, Mnesilochus's slave Chrysalus devises a plan to steal from Mnesilochus's father Nicobulus the money needed to free Bacchis of Samos. The plot is thwarted by Mnesilochus himself when, on returning to Athens, he mistakenly assumes that Pistoclerus is in love with his own Bacchis. But Chrysalus concocts a second plan: he tells Nicobulus about Mnesilochus's liaison with Bacchis, claiming that she is a married woman. The "husband," he says, can be bought off and furthermore, states Chrysalus, since his son has repented of his actions, the girl must be bought off with a similar amount. Nicobulus agrees to give the money but soon learns he has been duped. Furious, he is finally softened, together with Pistoclerus's father, by the coaxing of the two charming Bacchides and forgives all.

The Rope (*Rudens*). Comedy derived from a Greek comedy by Diphilus and set in Cyrene, on the shores of North Africa. The Athenian Daemones, having lost his fortune, now lives in rustic simplicity on a farm. His daughter Palaestra was stolen from Athens at an early age and sold to a Cyrenian procurer, Labrax. Her lover Plesidippus has contracted to buy her and made a token payment; but the untrustworthy Labrax has been convinced by an equally dishonest friend to take Palaestra and Ampelisca, another slave, to Sicily, where they will bring higher prices. The party sets sail under cover of night, but a storm wrecks the ship not far from Daemones' farm and the nearby shrine of Venus, where, incidentally, Plesidippus was to have met Labrax with the balance of money.

Plesidippus, come to conclude the bargain, meets Daemones and then hurries to help survivors of the shipwreck, missing by seconds the arrival of Palaestra and Ampelisca, who, having escaped in a small boat, stagger into the shrine for temporary refuge. However, Labrax has also survived the wreck and, learning accidentally from one of Daemones' slaves that Palaestra and Ampelisca are in the temple, rushes to claim them. But when Plesidippus's slave Trachalio sees the violent scene, he fetches Daemones, who rescues the girls. Plesidippus then hauls Labrax into court for fraud. When a trunk bound with rope and containing Palaestra's identification is found, Daemones and Palaestra are joyously reunited. Ampelisca's freedom is purchased with part of the money extorted from Labrax by Daemones for finding the trunk, and the procurer is invited to dinner.

The Captives (Captivi). Comedy set in Aetolia. Hegio, an old man, is trying to effect the return of his son Philopolemus, who is a prisoner of war in Elea. In buying Elean captives to obtain a suitable hostage for exchange, Hegio acquires Philocrates and his slave Tyndarus, who is in reality Hegio's second long-lost son, stolen as a child. Neither Hegio nor Tyndarus is aware of their true relationship. But to enable his master to escape, Tyndarus has changed identities with Philocrates; the ruse works and Hegio, thinking he is only releasing a slave, sends Philocrates back to Elea to arrange the exchange of his son. When the impersonation is accidentally exposed by another Elean captive, Tyndarus is imprisoned. Philocrates returns, however, with Philopolemus and a slave named Stalagmus. At the joyous reunion Hegio learns that Stalagmus was the culprit who had kidnaped his second son and sold him to Philocrates's father. Under questioning, the unsuspecting Philocrates reveals Tyndarus's true identity; released from prison, the long-lost son is restored to his home.

The Three Penny Day (Trinummus). Moral comedy based on Philemon's *The Treasure*, about the amusing confusion caused by a wastrel son. Charmides, having left the country, has entrusted his house, the treasure hidden within, and his affairs to his old friend and neighbor Callicles. Having squandered the family fortune, Lesbonicus, Charmides's spendthrift and dissolute son, tries to sell the house, and Callicles promptly buys it. When reproached, Callicles explains that he purchased the house to safeguard the treasure or to use it as a dowry for Charmides's daughter. In no case must Lesbonicus learn of its existence. Meanwhile, Lysiteles, Lesbonicus's friend, offers to marry Lesbonicus's sister without a dowry, since he knows of the family's penniless state. However, Lesbonicus is offended by this offer and resolves that there shall be a dowry one way or another. Callicles, also wanting to provide a dowry for Charmides's daughter, for three pennies hires a swindler who, posing as an emissary from the absent Charmides, promises to pay the dowry (the money is to come from the treasure).

The scheme has almost succeeded when Charmides himself appears, meets the swindler, and drives him off. He learns the whole story from Callicles and is grateful to his friend for keeping a watch over his interests. He

promises Lysiteles a handsome dowry, for, besides his treasure, he has returned rich. He also forgives his repentant son and announces that Lesbonicus shall marry Callicles's daughter.

Truculentus. Sardonic comedy describing the bondage of three men who vie for the attentions of the scheming courtesan Phronesium. Diniarchus, an Athenian youth, has bankrupted himself for her. The soldier Stratophanes, whom she accuses of fathering her baby, presents her with all his war trophies. Strabax, a spendthrift country youth, showers her with the profits from his farm. Truculentus, plain-spoken slave of Strabax, righteous at first, threatens to inform the boy's father but then himself falls in love with the courtesan's maid Astaphium. Presently Callicles, father of Diniarchus's betrothed, appears and produces proof that the baby, hired by Phronesium from her hairdresser to extort money and promises from Stratophanes, was given to the hairdresser by her maid, who in turn had received it from his daughter; the child is, in fact, Diniarchus's own illegitimate son. Ordered to claim the baby and marry its mother promptly, the startled youth is about to leave when Phronesium persuades him to let her keep the infant a little longer so that she can continue her swindle of the gullible soldier. Strabax's and Stratophanes's arguments over Phronesium are resolved when she agrees to share herself with both. As the two fools enter her house, she happily flirts with the audience.

Amphitryon (Amphitruo). The only extant Roman comedy that employs a theme from Greek mythology. Mercury, speaking the prologue, facetiously coins the word *tragicomoedia* ("tragicomedy") to describe its mixture of seriousness and farce. The original source is believed to be a lost Greek play. Jupiter, in love with the mortal Alcmena, wife of the Theban general Amphi-

A modern (1930s) adaptation of Plautus's *The Twin Menaechmi* was Jean Variot's *La mauvaise conduite,* produced by La Compagnie des Quinze. [*Theatre Arts Monthly.* Photograph by Achay, Paris]

tryon, has come to her disguised as her husband and has delayed the dawn, to prolong the liaison. Meanwhile, his ship having returned to Thebes, Amphitryon sends his slave Sosia to announce his imminent arrival. At the door of Amphitryon's house Sosia meets what appears to be his duplicate. In fact, it is Mercury, disguised as Sosia, standing guard so that Jupiter, his father, may not be disturbed. Astonished and confused, Sosia fetches Amphitryon, who, unable to understand Alcmena's references to their night of love, Jupiter having not long since departed from her, flies into a fury and threatens to leave her because of her infidelity.

Again assuming Amphitryon's form, Jupiter returns and calms Alcmena's despair by claiming that he was only testing her. Inevitably, confusion ensues when the transformed Jupiter and Amphitryon meet; the enraged general is left abandoned before his own home. About to storm his doors, he is stopped by a peal of thunder, and Alcmena's maid Bromia announces that his wife has just given birth to two sons, one fathered by Jupiter and the other by himself. Jupiter claims the child who has strangled two snakes as his own, calling it Hercules, and admonishes Amphitryon not to be harsh with his wife. Amphitryon agrees and rejoins Alcmena.

The Twin Menaechmi *(Menaechmi).* Twin sons were born to a merchant of Syracuse. One, Menaechmus, having wandered away from his father, was found by an Epidamnian merchant who, being childless, adopted him, made him his heir, and married him off to a shrew. The second son, likewise given the name Menaechmus by his grieving family, has engaged, since his father's death, in an endless search for his brother. Menaechmus I of Epidamnus, unhappily married, is having an affair with the courtesan Erotium, for whom he has stolen one of his wife's dresses. Preparing for a banquet at Erotium's house, he leaves minutes before his brother Menaechmus II arrives and is promptly mistaken by Erotium for her lover. Bewildered but delighted, Menaechmus II enjoys the unfathomable situation until the wife of Menaechmus I mistakes him for her husband and begins abusing him for taking the dress. Unable to understand his strange behavior and believing him to be insane, the wife's father summons a doctor to examine his son-in-law. When Menaechmus I returns, he is immediately plunged into confused misunderstandings with Erotium, his wife, his father-in-law, and the doctor. Finally the brothers meet accidentally, and the truth is revealed. Menaechmus I resolves to abandon his wife and property and return to Syracuse with his brother.

The Girl from Persia *(Persa).* Comedy demonstrating that a slave is as vulnerable as his master to a lover's frustrations. Toxilus, an Athenian slave, is deeply in love with a courtesan kept by the procurer Dordalus. In a desperate effort to raise enough money to buy her, he enlists the aid of the parasite Saturio and another slave, Sagaristio. Saturio is to lend Toxilus the use of his daughter so that she may, under the guise of a kidnaped Persian girl, be sold to Dordalus; once the money changes hands, her true identity as a freeborn citizen will be revealed, and by law she will be freed. Toxilus will

then use the money to buy his courtesan. Before the scheme is set in motion, Sagaristio arrives with money given him by his master to purchase oxen. He promptly gives the money to Toxilus, who immediately sets about buying his courtesan legally. Now, to replace the stolen money, the former ploy is enacted, with Sagaristio posing as a Persian and Saturio's reluctant daughter as bait. Dordalus, at first suspicious, cannot resist the girl's obvious charms and hands the money over to the "Persian," who quickly withdraws. Then Saturio emerges, claims the girl as his freeborn daughter, and drags the bewildered Dordalus into court. The celebration banquet, attended by Toxilus, his sweetheart, and Sagaristio, is interrupted by the furious Dordalus, who recognizes the "Persian" as Sagaristio. But subdued by taunts and ridicule, Dordalus acknowledges that for once he has been bested.

Casina. Farce based on the Greek play *The Men Who Draw Lots,* by Diphilus, which deals with a father-son rivalry for the affections of Casina, their sixteen-year-old household slave. The Athenian Lysidamus and his son Euthynicus each plan to have Casina marry his personal slave. Lysidamus favors his overseer Olympio, and Euthynicus his armor-bearer Chalinus. Thus, each thinks he can have Casina for himself. Lysidamus, on learning of his son's passion for Casina, sends him out of town; unrivaled, he can put his plan into operation. But Chalinus exposes the plot to Cleustrata, Lysidamus's wife, who with Pardalisca, her slave woman, hatches a scheme to humiliate Lysidamus once and for all. Chalinus, disguised as Casina, is married to Olympio, and Lysidamus's careful plans for the wedding-night tryst are thwarted. Olympio is beaten by his "bride," and Lysidamus is driven half naked into the street, where he begs his wife's forgiveness. The epilogue announces Casina to be the long-lost daughter of a neighbor, making her an Athenian citizen, a suitable bride for Euthynicus.

[SANDER M. GOLDBERG]

PLAYS

The plays are listed in an order inferred from internal evidence; the only definite dates are those for Nos. 5 and 10.

1. *Asinaria** *(The Comedy of Asses).*
2. *Mercator** *(The Merchant).*
3. *Miles Gloriosus** *(The Braggart Warrior).* ca. 205 B.C.
4. *Cistellaria** *(The Casket).* before 201 B.C.
5. *Stichus*.* November, 200 B.C.
6. *Aulularia** *(The Pot of Gold).*
7. *Curculio*.*
8. *Mostellaria** *(The Haunted House).*
9. *Poenulus** *(The Carthaginian).*
10. *Pseudolus** 191 B.C.
11. *Epidicus*.*
12. *Bacchides** *(The Two Bacchides).*
13. *Rudens** *(The Rope).*
14. *Captivi** *(The Captives).*
15. *Trinummus** *(The Three Penny Day).*
16. *Truculentus*.*
17. *Amphitruo** *(Amphitryon).*
18. *Menaechmi** *(The Twin Menaechmi).*
19. *Persa** *(The Girl from Persia).*
20. *Casina*.* 185 or 184 B.C.

EDITIONS

Latin Texts and Commentaries
Comoediae, ed. by W. M. Lindsay, 2 vol., Oxford Classical Texts, Oxford, 1903; *The Captives,* ed. by W. M. Lindsay, New York, 1921; *Works,* ed. P.

Nixon, 5 vol., Loeb Classical Library, Cambridge, Mass., 1928–1938; *Mercator*, ed. by P. J. Enk, 2 vol., Leiden, 1932; *Epidicus*, ed. by G. Duckworth, Princeton, 1940; *Truculentus*, ed. by P. J. Enk, 2 vol., Leiden, 1953; *Menaechmi*, ed. by M. Hammond et al., Cambridge, Mass., 1961; *Miles Gloriosus*, ed. by M. Hammond et al., Cambridge, Mass., 1963; *Amphitruo*, ed. by T. Cutt, Detroit, 1970; *Casina*, ed. by W. T. MacCary and M. M. Willcock, Cambridge, 1976; *Curculio*, ed. by J. Wright, Chico, Ca., 1980.

English

G. Duckworth, *The Complete Roman Drama*, New York, 1942; P. W. Harsh, *An Anthology of Roman Drama*, New York, 1960; L. Casson, *Six Plays of Plautus*, Garden City, N.Y., 1963; E. F. Watling, *The Rope and Other Plays*, Penguin Classics, Baltimore, 1964; ibid., *The Pot of Gold and Other Plays*, Penguin Classics, Baltimore, 1965; F. O. Copley and M. Hadas, *Roman Drama*, Indianapolis, 1965.

CRITICISM

F. Leo, *Plautinische Forschungen*, 2d ed., Berlin, 1912; G. Duckworth, *The Nature of Roman Comedy*, Princeton, 1952; E. Fraenkel, *Elementi Plautini in Plauto*, Florence, 1960; E. W. Handley, *Menander and Plautus: A Study in Comparison*, London, 1968; J. Wright, *Dancing in Chains, the Stylistic Unity of the comoedia palliata*, Rome, 1974; E. Segal, "Scholarship on Plautus 1965–1976," *Classical World* 74 (1981), pp. 353–433.

The Play of Adam

Oldest French drama with dialogue entirely in French, although the stage directions are in Latin. Although both author and place of performance are unknown, *The Play of Adam* (*Le jeu d'Adam*) was probably written in Normandy or in a Norman community in the south of England about 1175 (it was found and published in 1854). The complicated scenery, requiring vast space, suggests production in a cloister. The dramatic form and vivacious dialogue are remarkable and form a prelude to the fifteenth-century mystery plays. The drama actually consists of three separate plays related to one another by the common theme of man's redemption. To separate the first, *The Fall of Adam and Eve* (*La chute d'Adam et d'Ève*), from the second, *The Murder of Abel* (*Le meurtre d'Abel*), the poet departs from the Biblical sequence by presenting Adam's death before that of Abel. The third drama, *The Procession of Prophets from Abraham to Nebuchadnezzar* (*Le défilé des prophètes d'Abraham à Nabuchodonosor*), is an annunciation of the coming of the Messiah. In all likelihood the work was written to be played at Christmas but was probably performed on other religious occasions too. *See* MYSTERY PLAY in glossary.

[JOSEPH E. GARREAU]

Pogodin, Nikolay Fyodorovich (1900–1962)

Soviet journalist and dramatist; pseudonym of Nikolay Fyodorovich Stukalov. He was born in the Cossack village of Gundorovsky on November 16, 1900 (N.S.), into a peasant family. Having worked as a farmhand and later in blacksmith shops and book binderies, Pogodin embarked on a career in journalism in 1920. His newspaper sketches and stories were almost exclusively documentary, drawn from his own experiences. In 1922 he became a correspondent for the daily newspaper *Pravda*, retaining his position until 1930, when, partly on the strength of the encouragement he received from Maxim Gorky, he decided to devote himself exclusively to the theatre. *See* GORKY, MAXIM.

In the early years of the First Five-Year Plan (1928–1933) to promote economic growth in the

Nikoly Fyodorovich Pogodin. [Theatre Collection, The New York Public Library at Lincoln Center, Astor, Lenox and Tilden Foundations]

U.S.S.R., Pogodin's newspaper assignments took him to many new construction sites in Siberia, the Urals, and Transcaucasia, and he accumulated an abundance of facts that he later wove into his journalistic plays. When this period ended and the Communist party under Stalin began curbing writers through the All-Union Writers' Organization (VAPP) and the Russian Organization of Proletarian Writers (RAPP), Pogodin joined RAPP, wholeheartedly supporting its appropriation of the theatre for party propaganda purposes and becoming a staunch advocate of socialist realism.

Concentrating at first on topical issues, Pogodin soon introduced into the Soviet theatre plays dealing with Lenin and Stalin. Other party-oriented dramatists quickly followed suit, and a series of plays appeared in which Lenin is saintly and omnipotent and Stalin is faithful, the rightful heir to the throne. After this theatrical exploration of communism's leaders, Pogodin, by World War II a successful and celebrated dramatist, once more entered the mainstream of party literature, the discussion of current problems, and often admittedly wrote to formula to avoid censorship. Decorated several times (Stalin Prize, 1941; R.S.F.S.R. Arts Award, 1949; Lenin Prize, 1958), he remained one of the most successful official dramatists in the U.S.S.R. until his death in Moscow on September 19, 1962.

WORK

Pogodin's nearly thirty plays almost without exception focus on contemporary Soviet issues. An admitted propagandist and a reverent portraitist of famous Communist leaders, he considered his plots unimportant; suspense rests not on personal conflicts but on the efforts of the working masses to meet production quotas and set records for new construction. His plays established a traditional pattern of preliminary difficulties to be overcome, the worker's increasing zeal, and the final victory. A doc-

Maria Babanova in *Poem about an Ax*. [*Moscow Theatres*]

umentary naturalism prevails, and in some plays Pogodin employed an episodic technique derived from the cinema. His characters are stock types: heroes are generally loyal, doctrinaire Communists or else Stakhanovite workers, who outproduce average workers and have a "positive" effect on their colleagues; and villains are the "class enemies," those who try to sabotage the hard work and enthusiasm of the faithful.

His best-known plays are *Tempo* (*Temp*, 1930); *The Aristocrats* (*Aristokraty*, 1934); *Snow* (*Sneg*, 1932); and *The Chimes of the Kremlin* (*Kremlyovskiye kuranty*, 1942), Part II of the much-praised Lenin cycle, which is Pogodin's major dramatic achievement. The other two plays of the cycle are *The Man with a Gun* (*Chelovek s ruzhyom*, 1937), showing the symbolic encounter of a simple soldier with Lenin and Stalin in 1917; and *The Third, Pathétique* (*Tretya, pateticheskaya*, 1959), which depicts Lenin's death. The two earlier works of this cycle had to be reworked in 1955 with regard to Stalin's role in Soviet history.

Among Pogodin's earlier plays are *Poem about an Ax* (*Poema o topore*, 1931), describing the discovery of stain-

less steel and advocating close cooperation between labor and science; *After the Ball* (*Posle bala*, 1934), which, with puppetlike characters, combines kolkhoz heroics, farcical humor, and melodramatic young love; *The Moth* (*Mol*, 1939), in which a bourgeois wife attempts to undermine her husband's Communist beliefs; and *The Missouri Waltz* (*Missurysky vals*, 1950), an anti-American satire on President Truman. *A Petrarchan Sonnet* (*Sonet Petrarki*, 1957), depicting the vulgarization of an aged Communist's love for a young girl by malicious "virtuous" citizens and party officials, was considered adventurous for a man who had always adhered to party formula. Thus Pogodin, in his last period of drama, chose to break with strict socialist realism and treat his subject and characters in a more sober and realistic manner.

Tempo (*Temp*, 1930). Journalistic depiction of the construction of a tractor plant in Stalingrad with superficially delineated characters, including enthusiastic Communists, anti-Communist saboteurs, and an American engineer, who is initially shocked by the primitiveness of Soviet methods but later discovers that the results outshine the best American records. Carter, the American, is sympathetic with the efforts of the Soviets, and watching the transformation of inefficient peasants into responsible industrial workers, he is inspired to help meet the deadline. The climax comes when the construction is completed in record time.

The Aristocrats (*Aristokraty*, 1934). Drama set in a prison camp where various criminals have been brought together to help build the Baltic-White Sea Canal. They have been tempted to join construction crews by promises of better food and reductions in their sentences. Some see at once the advantages of working; others are reluctant. One who rebels against the pressure to work is Sonya; another is her buoyant and clever friend, the Captain. Gradually, however, Sonya complies, but the Captain is taken to a detention camp for further persuasion. After trying unsuccessfully to knife himself, he dubiously agrees to take charge of a rock-blasting expedition. Soon he finds himself enjoying his new role. The

The Man with a Gun. [*Moscow Theatres*]

Scene from a Moscow production of *The Aristocrats*. [Theatre Collection, The New York Public Library at Lincoln Center, Astor, Lenox and Tilden Foundations]

prisoners are awarded new privileges, and the canal is completed. When, however, a girl calls the Captain a thief, he suddenly reverts to his old self and tries to escape but changes his mind and returns to camp. He is not punished, and the workers celebrate the opening of the canal.

The Chimes of the Kremlin (*Kremlyovskiye kuranty*; first version, 1942; second version, 1956). Middle play in the Lenin trilogy. In 1920, while famine rages, Lenin, as-

sisted by Stalin and Dzerzhinski, plans the electrification of Russia. Presented as the driving force behind the people, Lenin performs miracles with his fervor, faith, and humanity as well as his humor and enjoyment of life. He approaches a Jewish workingman with simplicity and friendliness and converses with such wit and natural goodness that the worker is inspired to repair the chimes in the Kremlin tower so that the "Internationale" can be played.

The Chimes of the Kremlin. [*Moscow Theatres*]

A Petrarchan Sonnet. produced in Moscow in 1957. [*Moscow Theatres*]

A Petrarchan Sonnet (*Sonet Petrarki*, 1957). Drama in three acts. Sukhodolov, a middle-aged Communist construction engineer who is unhappily married to Kseniya, a philistine termagant, conceives an idealistic love for Maiya, a young researcher in a library. Feeling truly

The Third Pathétique. [*Moscow Theatres*]

happy for the first time in his life, Sukhodolov confides his feelings to his friend Armando, a concert violinist. When Clara, Maiya's roommate, finds the letters written to Maiya by Sukhodolov, she turns them over to Pavel, his superior, as evidence that Sukhodolov is morally corrupt and a corrosive influence upon the party. At the same time, Armando informs Kseniya, whose jealousy leads her to publicize the innocent romance, making it appear to be a sordid affair.

The furor thus caused culminates in Sukhodolov's official reproval for holding an incorrect party line. Now Armando, Clara, and even Kseniya regret their roles as informants. Maiya confesses to Sukhodolov that his idealized love has aroused her passion and that his detachment is a disappointment to her. As he bids her farewell, she runs away, but the play ends with a suggestion that he may follow her to realize his romantic dream.

[LAURENCE SENELICK]

PLAYS

1. *Temp* (Tempo)*. Comedy, 4 acts and 9 scenes. Written 1929. Published 1931. Produced Moscow, Vakhtangov Theatre, Nov. 11, 1930; Leningrad, Red Army Theatre, 1930.

2. *Derzost (Impertinence)*. Play, 3 acts. Written 1930. Published 1960. Produced Moscow, Gorky Academic Art Theatre, Oct. 12, 1930.

3. *Poema o topore (Poem about an Ax)*. Drama; prologue and epilogue, 3 acts. Written 1928/30. Published 1932. Produced Moscow, Theatre of the Revolution, Feb. 6, 1931.

4. *Sneg (Snow)*. Comedy, prologue and 4 acts. Written 1932. Published 1932. Produced Moscow, MOSPS Theatre, Nov. 7, 1932.

5. *Moy drug (My Friend)*. Play, 3 acts and epilogue. Written 1932. Published 1932. Produced Moscow, Theatre of the Revolution, Nov. 11, 1932.

6. *Posle bala (After the Ball)*. Comedy, 3 acts and 12 scenes. Written 1933. Published 1934. Produced Moscow, Theatre of the Revolution, Apr. 12, 1934.

7. *Aristokraty* (The Aristocrats)*. Comedy, 4 acts and 24 episodes. Written 1933/34. Published 1935. Produced Moscow, Realistic Theatre, Dec. 30, 1934; Vakhtangov Theatre, May 6, 1935.

8. *Chelovek s ruzhyom* (The Man with a Gun)*. Drama, 3 acts, 13 scenes, and finale. Written 1937. Published 1937. Produced Moscow, Vakhtangov Theatre, Nov. 13, 1937.

9. *Pad serebryanaya (The Silvery Canyon)*. Drama, 3 acts and 9 scenes. Written 1937/38. Published 1939. Produced Moscow, Central Army Theatre, Jan. 16, 1939.

10. *Mol (The Moth)*. Satiric comedy, 4 acts and 12 scenes. Written 1938. Published 1960. Produced Moscow, Lenin Komsomol Theatre, December, 1939.

11. *Dzhiokonda (La Gioconda)*. Comedy, 3 acts. Published 1939. Produced Moscow, Theatre of Satire, January, 1939.

12. *Kremlyovskiye kuranty* (The Chimes of the Kremlin)*. Drama, 4 acts and 11 scenes. First version: Written 1939/41. Produced Saratov, Moscow Academic Art Theatre, Jan. 22, 1942. Second version: Written 1955. Produced Moscow Academic Art Theatre, February, 1956.

13. *Lodochnitsa (The Boatwoman)*. Drama, 4 acts and 6 scenes. Written 1943. Produced Stalingrad, Gorky Theatre, February, 1943.

14. *Sotvoreniye mira (The Creation of the World)*. Drama, 4 acts and 6 scenes. Written 1945. Published 1946. Produced Moscow, Maly Theatre, Jan. 5, 1946.

15. *Minuvshiye gody (The Bygone Years)*. Drama, 3 acts. Written 1947. Published 1948. Produced Tyumen, 1947; Moscow, Maly Theatre, Mar. 17, 1948.

16. *Barkhatny sezon (The Velvety Season)*. Comedy, 4 acts and 7 scenes. Published 1961. Produced Moscow, Yermolova Theatre, 1949.

17. *Missurysky vals (The Missouri Waltz)*. Drama, 4 acts and 8 scenes. Published 1950. Produced Moscow, Vakhtangov and Yermolova Theatres, 1950.

18. *Kogda lomayutsya kopya (When the Lances Are Broken)*. Comedy, 4 acts and 11 scenes. Written 1952. Published 1953. Produced Moscow, Maly Theatre, Mar. 22, 1953.

19. *Zagovor Lokkarta (The Lockhart Plot)* or *Vikhri vrazhdebnye (Hostile Hurricanes)*. Dramatic chronicle, 4 acts and 17 episodes. Written 1953. Published 1954. Produced Moscow, Central Transport Theatre, Nov. 7, 1953.

20. *Bagrovye oblaka (The Purple Clouds)*. Drama, 3 acts and 7 scenes.

Written 1955. Published 1956. Produced Moscow, Central Transport Theatre, Nov. 4, 1955.

21. *Rytsari mylnykh puzyrey (The Knights of Soap Bubbles).* Grotesque comedy, 3 acts and 6 scenes. Published 1961. Produced Moscow, Theatre of Satire, 1955.

22. *My vtroem poyekhali na tselinu (We Three Went to the Virgin Lands).* Play, 4 acts and 9 scenes. Written 1955. Published 1955. Produced Moscow, Central Children's Theatre, 1955.

23. *Sonet Petrarki* (A Petrarchan Sonnet).* Drama, 3 acts and 10 scenes. Published 1956. Produced Moscow, Mayakovsky Theatre, 1957; Leningrad, Pushkin Dramatic Theatre, 1957.

24. *Tretya, pateticheskaya (The Third, Pathétique).* Drama, 4 acts and 13 scenes. Written 1958. Published 1958. Produced Moscow Academic Art Theatre, Jan. 3, 1959.

25. *Ne pomerknet nikogda (It Will Never Get Dark).* Drama; prologue, 3 acts, and 7 scenes. Published 1958. Produced Ivanovo Regional Theatre, 1959; Moscow, Central Army Theatre, October, 1960.

26. *Malenkaya studentka (The Little Student).* Drama, 12 scenes. Published 1959. Produced Moscow, Mayakovsky Theatre, 1959; Leningrad, Lenin Komsomol Theatre, 1959.

27. *Tsvety zhivye (The Living Flowers).* Drama, 3 acts and 9 scenes. Published 1960. Produced Moscow, Lenin Komsomol Theatre, 1960; Moscow Academic Art Theatre, 1961.

28. *Vernost (Loyalty).* Drama of contemporary life, 3 acts. Published 1961.

EDITIONS

Collections
Teatr i zhizn Pogodina, Moscow, 1953; *Sobraniye dramaticheskikh proizvedeny,* 5 vols., Moscow, 1960–1961.
Individual Plays
The Aristocrats. Published in *Four Soviet Plays,* tr. by A. Wixley and R. Carr, New York, 1937.
The Chimes of the Kremlin. Published in *Soviet Scene,* ed. and tr. by A. Bakshy, New Haven, Conn., 1946.
The Man with a Gun. Published in *International Literature,* vol. 7, pp. 3–40, 1938.
A Petrarchan Sonnet. Published in *Contemporary Russian Drama,* ed. by F. D. Reeve, New York, 1968.
Tempo. Published in *Six Soviet Plays,* ed. by E. Lyons, Boston, 1934.

CRITICISM

N. N. F. Zaytsev, *Pogodin,* Moscow, 1953.

Poliakoff, Stephen (1953–   )

English playwright. After leaving Oxford without completing his course, Poliakoff launched himself into a series of violent plays which question accepted values and criticize not only the old hierarchical institutions such as army and university but organizations such as commercial radio which profit from the mindlessness of pop culture.

Poliakoff was only twenty-one when he wrote *Clever Soldiers* (1974), an uncompromising indictment of privileged education. Set just before and just after the outbreak of the First World War, it shows how a popular, good-looking public school boy, habituated to idolization, becomes an undergraduate and later a subaltern who comes to question why other people should do what he tells them to. His sense of superiority snaps back into self-destructiveness.

Heroes (1975) is set ambiguously in a large city which might be either German or British, at a time which might be either the 1920s or the 1980s. The object of the ambiguity is to validate the assumption that we are currently in danger of a fascist resurgence. Poliakoff succeeds well in evoking the atmosphere of the city, conveying strong impressions of desperation and militancy among the victims of unemployment and inflation. The two "heroes," Julius and Rainer, are representatives of the upper and

Scene from *A Shout across the River,* with Lynn Farleigh and Gwyneth Strong, as presented at the Warehouse Theatre in 1978. [Royal Shakespeare Company. Photograph by Chris Davies]

lower classes, and, as in *Clever Soldiers,* the self-destructiveness of the aristocrat is the subject of some highly effective sequences, as when Julius peps himself up with painful electric shocks. But the plot depends too heavily on development in the two men's relationship, which is sketched out only perfunctorily.

The central relationship in *Hitting Town* (1975) is more convincing: we believe in the possibility that the brother and sister will commit incest, though the development of their behavior, once they have, is less plausible; the sister, alternating between defiant complicity and numbed reticence, is less well characterized than her aggressive, reckless brother.

The companion piece, *City Sugar* (1976), centers on a provincial radio disc jockey who was once a schoolteacher. Though he despises himself for seasoning rubbishy music with bad jokes, he cannot resist the attraction of a better-paid job in London. Toward the audience he feels more contempt than compassion or guilt, and when he contrives a meeting with a girl whose voice he has heard over the telephone, a girl typical of his audience, his ambivalence emerges in the confrontation.

Poliakoff's more recent plays, *Strawberry Fields* (1977), *A Shout across the River* (1978), *American Days* (1979), and *Favourite Nights* (1981), have not been quite so successful.   RONALD HAYMAN

CRITICISM

R. Hayman, *British Theatre since 1955,* London and New York, 1979.

Polish Drama

Poland has a continuous tradition in drama going back to the Middle Ages, and its dramatic literature is one of the most original in all of Europe, although its very Polishness has often made it inaccessible to outsiders; only in the second half of the twentieth century have Polish plays started to become part of the world repertory. Closely tied to the vicissitudes of history, drama in Poland occupies a very special position in the cultural life of the country. During the partitions of Poland and its domination by foreign powers, drama became a prime force for maintaining national identity and arousing the conscience of a people. To this day, Polish drama has preserved its function as a public forum and major expression of issues that affect the life of the nation. For this reason, the theatre in Poland has evolved as a poetic and metaphoric art that deals with political, social and philosophical concerns, rather than with the purely private and psychological.

MIDDLE AGES AND RENAISSANCE

The earliest period of Polish drama, which saw the gradual development of vernacular plays on religious themes from liturgical texts in Latin, corresponds to that of many other European countries. As the place of performance moved from the altar to the church steps and then to the marketplace, and craftsmen replaced clergy as the performers, the drama grew more secular in content and adopted Polish as its language.

The oldest surviving Polish mystery and morality plays are of a relatively late date, coming, for the most part, from the fifteenth and sixteenth centuries. *The Life of Joseph (Zywot Józefa)* in 1545 is the work of the Calvinist poet Mikołaj Rej, the first major Polish writer to use the vernacular. Derived from the Biblical story of Joseph and Potiphar's wife and based on a Latin source, *The Life of Joseph* takes the form of a medieval mystery but contains many farcical episodes and reflects contemporary manners and dress. It was successfully staged by Kazimierz Dejmek in 1958. (Rej also wrote poetry in dialogue form as well as other verse plays.) *See* MORALITY PLAY; MYSTERY PLAY in glossary.

The most famous Polish folk mystery, *The Story of the Most Glorious Resurrection of Our Lord (Historia o chwalebnym zmartwychwstaniu Pańskim)*, was first set down by Mikołaj of Wilkowiecko, a Pauline monk from Częstochowa, in 1570, although it draws upon texts from at least a century earlier. Similar to the fifteenth-century French *Mystère de la Passion, The Story of the Most Glorious Resurrection of Our Lord* contains episodes showing Christ's visit to the three Maries, his descent to hell, and his appearance to his disciples, presented in a naive and vivid colloquial style. Equipped with detailed stage directions and offering rich possibilities for combining pageantry and music to drama, the play has been adapted for the twentieth-century theatre, first by Leon Schiller in 1925, then by Kazimierz Dejmek in 1961.

Classical plays by Seneca, Plautus, and Terence were given in Latin at the court and by students at the University of Cracow; vernacular adaptations of these works appeared soon afterward. Jesuit school theatres flourished for over two hundred years, from the sixteenth to the eighteenth century, often using both Polish and Latin and serving as political propaganda in the battle against Protestantism. *See* PLAUTUS; SENECA; TERENCE.

Toward the end of the sixteenth century there appeared a brilliant example of a new type of drama, humanist tragedy based on classical models. The play was *The Dismissal of the Greek Envoys (Odprawa posłów greckich)* by the greatest Polish Renaissance poet Jan Kochanowski (1530–1584), who composed the work for a wedding at the royal court in 1578. In accord with Renaissance poetics, *The Dismissal of the Greek Envoys* is divided into five acts (although it is only slightly over six hundred lines), has a messenger and a chorus of Trojan maidens, and is written in blank verse. A dramatization of portions of Book III of *The Iliad*, Kochanowski's tragedy deals with the arrival in Troy of the Greek messengers bringing offers of peace on condition that Helen be returned to her husband. In form only a historical drama, *The Dismissal of the Greek Envoys*

Mikolaj of Wilkowiecko's *Story of the Most Glorious Resurrection of Our Lord,* **a sixteenth-century Easter play, was staged in Łodz in 1961.** [*Theatre in Modern Poland*]

is actually concerned with contemporary issues and addressed to the audience of the times, stressing the need to strengthen the power of the king in order to avoid disaster. A political rather than a personal drama, *The Dismissal of the Greek Envoys,* in its use of myth to explore problems of statehood, political power, and national destiny, forecasts one of the basic traits of much subsequent Polish theatre. Kochanowski's metaphoric treatment of the fable to make a topical point becomes a characteristic method of Polish playwrights.

By the early seventeenth century, popular drama also took root in Poland. Wandering bands of minstrels gave performances in marketplaces and at fairs, and foreign troupes toured throughout Poland. As early as 1611 a company of English comedians led by John Greene came to Poland with Shakespeare's plays. Noteworthy among native forms of popular drama is the *komedia rybałtowska,* a crude species of realistic comedy featuring lower-class characters such as beggars and braggart soldiers. Piotr Baryka's satirical verse comedy, *Peasant Turned King (Z chłopa Król,* 1637), is the best known of these works. About a drunken peasant tricked into believing that he is king, Baryka's play is probably derived from the Introduction to *The Taming of the Shrew,* which had been performed by Greene's company some years earlier.

At the court and palaces of the nobility Italian opera and *commedia dell'arte* enjoyed a vogue, and foreign plays, particularly French works, were translated, adapted, and performed. Corneille's *Le Cid,* in a Polish version by Andrzej Morsztyn, was first presented at Zamość in 1660 and then at the royal court in 1662 for King Jan Kazimierz, who was both a lover of French culture and an enthusiast of the theatre. But by the middle of the seventeenth century social and political upheavals within the country and the invasion by Sweden interrupted the natural development of Polish drama. *See* Commedia dell'Arte in glossary.

Eighteenth Century

A permanent theatre had yet to be established in Poland. Italian, French, and German companies played at the Polish court throughout most of the eighteenth century, and following the lead of the monarch, the most powerful nobles set up their own private theatres, in which they, their guests, and serfs (who became the earliest professional actors in Poland) took part. It was not until 1765 that the first theatre with a professional company acting in Polish was opened to the general public. Founded by Stanisław August Poniatowski, the last king of Poland, who had developed a strong interest in the drama while visiting Paris, London, and St. Petersburg, the National Theatre in Warsaw staged as its first play *The Intruders (Natręci)* by Józef Bielawski, which was adapted from Molière's *Les fâcheux* and commissioned by the king.

It was not, however, until the actor, director, and playwright Wojciech Bogusławski (1757–1829) assumed direction of the National Theatre that it achieved a high level of artistic excellence and began producing a reper-

tory of original Polish plays. Bogusławski was responsible for changing the status of the Polish actor and making the profession respectable, and he staged the first Polish *Hamlet* in 1797 in Lwów, in his own adaptation made from the German, and produced a number of Molière's works transposed to Polish settings, with Polish characters and national costumes. His own plays include *The Supposed Miracle, or The Cracovians and the Mountaineers (Cud mniemany czyli Krakowiacy i Górale,* 1794), a colorful vaudeville with songs or comic opera, which because of its sympathetic portrayal of the people took on revolutionary significance during the insurrection against the Russians led by Kościuszko; and *Henry VI at the Hunt (Henryk VI na łowach,* 1792), the first Polish historical comedy, in prose with songs, and imbued with political sentiments of a democratic nature. *The Cracovians and the Mountaineers* has been successfully revived many times in the modern Polish theatre, starting with Leon Schiller's 1946 production in Łódź.

At the end of the eighteenth century, the archeologist, traveler, and adventurer Jan Potocki (1761–1815), who wrote in French a number of learned works on Slavic prehistory and the picaresque and fantastic novel *The Saragossa Manuscript* (1805), also composed a group of six short one-act comedies, *Collection of Parades (Recueil des Parades)* which in 1792 were performed in French in the private theatre belonging to Izabela Lubomirska at her palace in Łańcut. Using the traditional characters (Giles, Leander, Cassander, and Zerzabelle) and ludicrous plots of the *parade,* a fairground derivative of the Italian *commedia* that became popular in the mid-eighteenth century with aristocratic French audiences, Potocki created a series of lighthearted sketches abounding in absurd humor, non sequiturs, and plays on words. Performed by the hosts and guests at the palace, including a number of French exiles fleeing the terror reigning in Paris, Potocki's *parades* even deal mockingly with class antagonisms and the repercussions of the French Revolution.

The Partitions of Poland and the Romantic Period

In 1772 Poland underwent the first of three partitions (the others came in 1793 and 1795) at the hands of her more powerful neighbors, Russia, Austria, and Prussia, and as a result lost her independence until 1918. Ill-fated uprisings—against Russia in 1831, against Austria and Prussia in 1846, and against Russia again in 1863—were cruelly suppressed and followed by ever harsher reprisals and restrictions. The consequences for cultural life, and especially the theatre, were disastrous, yet somehow theatrical life continued even under conditions of material and political hardship. Censorship was severe, particularly in the territory occupied by the Russians, which constituted over half the area of the country, including the capital and theatrical center, Warsaw.

The tsarist administration and police attempted to suppress all manifestations of Polishness and to russify the theatre. In those restricted theatres where Polish plays could be performed and the Polish language used,

Adam Mickiewicz. [*Galerie des Contemporains Illustres*]

all national allusions and references were forbidden as dangerous and liable to incite insurrection. Even so, the theatre became the natural bulwark for the country's language and culture, since Polish had been outlawed in schools, offices, and all other public places. After Poland lost its independence, literature and above all the drama acquired a national mission, and poets and playwrights took on the role of inspired political leaders and messiahs.

This sense of high calling, which has given the drama such a preeminent position in Polish cultural life, is nowhere more evident than in the case of the three great Polish poets of the first half of the nineteenth century, Adam Mickiewicz (1798–1855), Juliusz Słowacki (1809–1849), and Zygmunt Krasiński (1812–1859), who had left their partitioned homeland and lived abroad as members of the great emigration occasioned by the failure of the 1831 rebellion against the tsarist oppression. Writing in exile, these dramatists created a unique form of romantic drama written for a theatre that existed only in the imagination of its authors and designed to transcend the bounds of reality and the prosaic stage imitating it. Intensely patriotic in spirit and obsessed with Poland and Polishness, the plays devised by these visionary artists are vast dramatic poems, inspired by the example of Goethe's *Faust* and Byron's *Manfred* and soaring far beyond the limits of the traditional theatre in both boldness of expression and freedom of form.

The masterworks of these authors—Mickiewicz's *Forefathers' Eve (Dziady*, 1823), Słowacki's *Kordian* (1834), and Krasiński's *The Undivine Comedy* (*Nie-Boska Komedia*, 1833)–anticipate the techniques of expressionism in their use of short, fragmentary scenes, loose episodic structure, the blending of real and unreal worlds, alternation of mundane and fantastic scenes, and free flow of associations as in a dream. Only the Italian opera and the Parisian Olympic Circus were grandiose enough to provide the Polish romantic poets with ideas for the actual theatrical realization of their works. At the time of their composition, the resources of the conventional playhouse were simply inadequate to a concept of total theatre that would unite the various arts. The immense possibilities for imaginative staging inherent in these dramatic poems could be brought to the stage only in the twentieth century, first at the *fin de siècle* by Stanisław Wyspiański, then in the interwar years by Leon Schiller, and finally in the 1960s and '70s by the major contemporary directors, using all the modern techniques and theories of avant-garde theatre. Polish romantic drama has proved prophetic in its artistic daring as well as in its philosophical and moral perceptions. *See* KRASIŃSKI, ZYGMUNT; MICKIEWICZ, ADAM; SŁOWACKI, JULIUSZ.

Even though forbidden by the censor and considered unstageable, the plays of Mickiewicz, Słowacki, and Krasiński lived in the imagination of their compatriots and helped mold the national consciousness. These authors were not considered simply playwrights, like their Western European contemporaries, but bards or seers who practiced an art of the drama that would overcome the separation of the poet and his audience, draw the spectator into the performance, and directly influence his life. The aim of the romantics was nothing less than the transformation of passive onlookers into active participants in a morality play, whose hero, Poland, must be saved. Although seemingly defeated and alone, the human protagonists of these visionary works embody a suprapersonal ideal and identify themselves with the entire nation, for whose deliverance they become willing sacrifices.

Created without regard for the material conditions necessary for performance and existing in a cosmic dimension beyond ordinary categories of time and space, Mickiewicz's *Forefathers' Eve* has become Poland's national sacred drama and the very basis of the Polish theatrical tradition. This modern passion play celebrating the martyrdom of Poland depicts the entire universe of heaven, hell, and earth, with man at its center, surrounded by supernatural powers and struggling for redemption. Drawing upon pre-Slavic folklore and primitive religion, Mickiewicz returns to the ancient roots of sacral theatre. In a prolonged scene of magical intensity, the poet shows a group of peasants chanting incantations; they have gathered together to enact the primeval rites of calling upon the dead and offering them food. Later, during a night of startling visions and hallucinations, Gustaw, the protagonist, is transformed from an individual preoccupied with personal problems to a hero dedicated to the cause of his nation and of humanity.

Through his vivid descriptions of the cruel oppression experienced by his fellow countrymen under the tyranny of the tsar, Mickiewicz poses the problem of human suffering, portraying Poland as the Christ of nations

Scene from a 1963 Polish production of Mickiewicz's *Forefather's Eve*. [Agencja Autorska, Warsaw]

and its agony as comparable to Christ's crucifixion. Now renamed Konrad as a sign of his spiritual metamorphosis, the hero of *Forefathers' Eve* challenges God, in a famous scene known as the "great improvisation," accusing the Creator of injustice for allowing an entire people to suffer such a destiny. Despite this blasphemy, Konrad is ultimately saved by his good angels, and the drama contains messianic prophecies telling of a great man who will lead Poland and all humanity to a glorious future.

In the sixteenth lecture of his course on Slavic literature given in French at the Collège de France in 1843, Mickiewicz gave the theoretical basis for his view of a new, visionary drama. Declaring that the actual theatre of his day could not stage romantic plays such as *Forefathers' Eve* and Krasiński's *The Undivine Comedy*, which he greatly admired, the poet predicted that the Slavic theatre of the future would be the true heir to Greek tragedy and the medieval religious theatre, thereby revitalizing the concept of the mystery. As for staging, Mickiewicz argued that the theatre should fuse architecture, painting, and music with drama—a credo that has been adopted by most twentieth-century Polish directors. In fact, Mickiewicz's notions of romantic drama anticipated by more than a century two of the principal goals of modern theatre: first, a return to myth and ritual, and second, the creation of a total spectacle.

Mickiewicz's contemporary and rival, Juliusz Słowacki, was the most prolific of the Polish romantic

Zygmunt Krasiński's *Iridion,* as produced in Warsaw. [Agencja Autorska, Warsaw]

Zygmunt Krasiński's *The Undivine Comedy* as produced in
Poland in 1937; design by Jarnutowski. [*Theatre in Action*]

A contemporary production of Krasiński's *The Undivine
Comedy* shows freer staging than the above version. [Agencja
Autorska, Warsaw]

dramatists, writing more than twenty plays on a wide variety of subjects, ranging through European history (*Beatrix Cenci* and *Maria Stuart*), Polish history and legend [*Kordian, Horsztyński,* and *The Silver Dream of Salomei, (Sen srebrny Salomei)*], and folklore and fairytale (*Lilla Weneda* and *Balladyna*), even to a comic satire on romantic poses (*Fantazy*). Słowacki evolved a complex dramatic technique, capable of shifting tones and styles, of mixing the lofty and mystical with the horrible and cruel, and of including both the dreamlike and the grotesque. *Kordian,* with its weak, Hamlet-like hero who proves incapable of effecting a true revolution against the tsar, was intended by Słowacki as a counterstatement to *Forefathers' Eve* and introduced what would become a characteristic procedure in the Polish dramatic tradition: commentary on an earlier work as a springboard to new creativity.

In *The Undivine Comedy* Krasiński at the age of twenty-one produced one of the first great European dramas on the theme of modern revolution. Unlike other Polish romantic drama, it is written in prose, has an unspecified European setting, and is not directly based on Polish history. For these reasons, Krasiński's masterpiece has proved accessible in translation to non-Polish readers. Its powerful theatricalization of the dynamics of violent class revolution (conceived in almost Hegelian terms) is unmatched in world literature and quite universal in appeal.

A unique phenomenon in the history of European theatre and the very antithesis of the well-made plays of Scribe that began to dominate Western theatre in the 1840s, Polish Romantic drama shaped the entire course and evolution of modern theatre in Poland. It is scarcely possible to understand the accomplishments of twentieth-century Polish drama without tracing its roots back to this unusual tradition, where politics and poetry, history and dream, the real and the fantastic are freely intermingled.

OTHER NINETEENTH-CENTURY CURRENTS

The romantic tradition of poets in exile was not the only significant manifestation of Polish drama in the nineteenth century. The author of more than thirty comedies, Aleksander Fredro was unquestionably the most important playwright active in Poland during the early part of

Scene from Słowacki's *Balladyna* as produced at the Teatr Polski Szczecin in 1965. [Agencja Autorska, Warsaw]

the century. With Fredro, Polish verse comedy, developed by writers such as Franciszek Zabłocki (1754–1821), now reached its point of perfection. Written in supple octosyllabic rhymed couplets that are both clever and poetic, Fredro's plays have quick tempos, lively intrigue plots, and colorful eccentric characters, derived, for the most part, from eighteenth-century Polish neoclassical comedy and, behind that, from Molière and his French successors. *See* FREDRO, ALEKSANDER.

Often set in prepartition Poland, Fredro's comedies give a vivid picture of the life and manners of the Polish gentry in a happier and more stable era, already part of a bygone age when they were written. *Maidens' Vows* (*Śluby panieńskie,* 1833), *Ladies and Hussars* (*Damy i huzary,* 1825), and *Vengeance* (*Zemsta,* 1834) are among his best-known works. These plays, along with a number of Fredro's other early comedies (he had written twenty of his finest works by 1835), have become a central part of the Polish repertory and, ever since the author's own day, have offered actors and actresses choice roles and provided theatres with splendid material for imaginative productions that can appeal to audiences of all complexions. Many of the remarks in his plays have passed into the spoken language as proverbial sayings, and Fredro now is a genuine national classic.

A far more esoteric playwright was the poet, prose writer, sculptor, and painter, Cyprian Norwid (1821–1883), who spent much of his life abroad, first in Italy, Germany, and the United States, and then ultimately in Paris, where he knew Mickiewicz and other members of the romantic emigration. Younger by a generation, Norwid rejected the romantics' yearning for suffering and martyrdom and with it their political rhetoric of revenge and uprisings. Almost totally unknown in his

Stefan Jaracz as Don Fernando in *The Constant Prince*, a Juliusz Słowacki work based on Calderón. [*Theatre in Modern Poland*]

Stefan Jaracz in the title role of Aleksander Fredro's *Pan Geldhab*, with Ewa Bonacka as Flora. [*Theatre in Modern Poland*]

lifetime, Norwid died in extreme poverty in a Paris garret, but he has become recognized in the twentieth century as a major poet and an original, if obscure, playwright.

Norwid left behind ten plays and seven dramatic fragments; most of these have reached the stage only in recent times. In his avoidance of passion and violence, which he felt led to vulgar melodrama, and in his preference for irony, understatement, silence, and sculptural gesture, Norwid diverges from the romantic school and anticipates the turn-of-the-century symbolists and modernists who, in fact, first discovered his poetry some twenty years after his death.

Norwid's work for the theatre includes mystery plays using legendary characters from Polish prehistory (*Wanda* and *Krakus*, both 1851); play-within-a-play dramas dealing with the theme of life and art, reality and illusion, such as *The Actor* (*Aktor*, 1867) and *Behind the Scenes* (*Za kulisami*, 1869); dramatic miniatures on the battle of the sexes, such as *The One Thousand and Second Night* (*Noc tysiączna druga*, 1850) and *Pure Love in a Spa by the Sea* (*Miłość czysta u kąpieli morskich*, 1880); a high comedy about the artist and his isolation in society, *The Ring of a Grand Lady* (*Pierścień wielkiej damy*, 1872); and historical drama, *Cleopatra and Caesar* (*Kleopatra i Cezar*, 1872). Written either in elegant prose or subtle verse, these rarefied and abstruse dramas have often survived only in highly defective texts lacking many lines or even scenes. Nonetheless, Norwid has been widely performed in the contemporary Polish theatre, perhaps because he

provides the sort of challenge to stage the seemingly unstageable that proves irresistible to modern Polish directors.

At the end of the nineteenth century, two innovative new trends in Western European drama, naturalism and symbolism, reached Poland from France and quickly became assimilated into the modernist movement, known as Młoda Polska (Young Poland), that dominated Polish literature and art in the early 1900s. Although symbolism proved to be more influential and took root within the native Polish dramatic tradition, naturalism produced at least one outstanding playwright in the person of Gabriela Zapolska. An actress and novelist as well as a dramatist, Zapolska was the prototype of the new woman in revolt who enjoyed shocking contemporaries and outraging critics. Her novels dealt with forbidden subjects, such as prostitution, venereal disease, and alcoholism. Although her career as an actress proved less than brilliant, two years with the Théâtre Libre in Paris, from 1892 to 1894, gave her firsthand knowledge of both the theory and practice of naturalism in the theatre. Upon her return to Poland, she began writing plays that draw upon the ideas of Émile Zola, ideas which she had absorbed while working with André Antoine (1858–1943), founder of the Théâtre Libre and leading spokesman for naturalism in the theatre. *See* ZAPOLSKA, GABRIELA.

In her dramas, which blend sharp satire and brutal melodrama, Zapolska exposes the hypocritical morality of the bourgeoisie and defends the helpless victims of the smug and wealthy. Her most celebrated play, *The Morality of Mrs. Dulska* (*Moralność pani Dulskiej*, 1906), is a tragicomic unmasking of the fraudulent standards of a respectable wife and mother from a provincial bourgeois milieu. Zapolska's devastating portrait is masterfully drawn, as witness the fact that Mrs. Dulska's name has become synonymous in Poland for a narrow-minded, self-righteous hypocrite. Other plays by Zapolska deal with the plight of a young actress victimized by predatory males and the prejudices of society, *Miss Maliczewska* (*Panna Maliczewska*, 1910), and with Jewish life in Poland, *Małka Szwarcenkopf*, (1897).

Because her works are said to be crude and sensational, Zapolska does not enjoy as high a position in Pol-

A contemporary Warsaw revival of Fredro's *Vengeance*. [Agencja Autorska, Warsaw]

Scene from a 1962 Warsaw production of Gabriela Zapolska's *The Morality of Mrs. Dulska*. [Agencja Autorska, Warsaw]

ish literature as she deserves. Her best dramas and comedies are tightly constructed, the characters are drawn with great satirical verve, and the dialogue is lively and biting; on stage, her plays are immensely effective and constant favorites with both actors and audiences. In fact, Zapolska was one of the finest naturalist playwrights in all of Europe and one of the two most important women dramatists of the period (only Lady Gregory in Ireland is of equal stature).

Several other talented writers, belonging to the same general movement, excelled in disabused dramas that probe the sores of family life. *In the Net* (*W sieci*, 1899) by Jan August Kisielewski (1876–1918) shows the attempted rebellion of a young girl against her parents and their repressive ideas. Włodzimierz Perzyński (1877–1933) created subtle psychological studies of middle-class manners, as in his Chekhovian *Frank's Luck* (*Szczęście Frania*, 1909). Tadeusz Rittner, who lived in Vienna and frequented the Schnitzler and Hermann Bahr circles, wrote in both Polish and German. His ironic dramas about the foibles of bourgeois life include *Silly Jacob* (*Głupi Jakub*, 1910) and *In a Little House* (*W małym domku*, 1904). Karol Hubert Rostworowski, the author of many historical verse plays, also wrote one powerful naturalistic tragedy, *The Surprise* (*Niespodzianka*, 1929), about a peasant woman who robs and kills her own son, failing to recognize him when he returns home unannounced from America. Here Rostworowski, while drawing on a true event, returned to an ancient tragic plot, first known in a lost play by Euripides and also used in George Lillo's *The Fatal Curiosity* (1736), Zacharias Werner's *Der vierundzwanzigste Februar* (1810), and Albert Camus's *Le Malentendu* (1944). *See* RITTNER, TADEUSZ.

Despite these real accomplishments, naturalism was but a minor phase in the development of the Polish dramatic tradition. In its primary concern with the material values of middle-class culture, the naturalist movement lay outside the broader poetic mainstream of theatre in Poland.

FIN DE SIÈCLE AND THE EARLY TWENTIETH CENTURY

Although directly influenced by the ideas and examples of both Wagner and Maeterlinck, Polish symbolism in drama and theatre was less a foreign importation than a natural continuation of the poetic, metaphoric tradition begun by the romantic poets and given a theoretical basis by Mickiewicz in his remarks about the Slavic theatre of the future. The heir to this tradition was Stanisław Wyspiański, the most important Polish dramatist at the turn of the century and one of the greatest European symbolists. An immensely talented and versatile artist, Wyspiański was painter, book illustrator, and maker of stained-glass windows as well as stage designer, director, and complete man of the theatre. He made his own costumes, properties, and sets and often worked on staging his own and others' plays, including the first production of Mickiewicz's *Forefathers' Eve* in a condensed version presented in Cracow in 1901. His two large cycles of dramas, one on classical Greek mythological subjects and the other on national issues, reexamined the problems already taken up by the romantics and pursued the dialogue they had already started on the destiny of Poland. *See* WYSPIAŃSKI, STANISŁAW.

Wyspiański's plays are scenarios for the theatre rather than self-sufficient literary tests. Using both ancient Greek theatre and Wagner's music-drama as his models and drawing upon folk arts, village customs, popular ceremonies, processions, and the Polish *szopka* (Christmas puppet shows featuring Herod, Death, and the Devil), Wyspiański created a total theatre that succeeds in uniting many different arts and comes alive through its images of shape, sound, and color.

One of Wyspiański's unusual accomplishments was

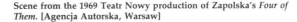

Scene from the 1969 Teatr Nowy production of Zapolska's *Four of Them*. [Agencja Autorska, Warsaw]

to embody myth and ritual within the concrete reality of Polish life and history. In *The Wedding* (*Wesele*, 1901), the rural wedding of a poet and a peasant girl, uniting two different classes and offering hope of a new national purpose, becomes the occasion for the appearance of various legendary and phantasmagoric figures from Poland's glorious past who mingle with the real guests at the festivities, which are presided over by an eerie strawman, or Mulch (the protective covering for the rosebush in the garden). The drama ends with an arresting scenic effect, characteristic of Polish drama at its best. At dawn, the assembled guests weary of waiting for the great revelation that never comes, begin a slow somnambulistic dance to creaking music played on a broken fiddle by the Mulch. As the curtain falls, the entire puppet show, as though in a deep sleep, goes through its trancelike motions. Wyspiański's enchanted Mulch dance—a powerful theatrical image of stagnation and hopelessness—is taken up again and again by later Polish playwrights, novelists, and filmmakers (for example, Tadeusz Konwicki's film *Salto* (1965) and Andrzej Wajda's cinema version of Jerzy Andrzejewski's novel *Ashes and Diamonds*, 1958).

Dispensing with normal plot, Wyspiański has his dramas played out on two different planes, the real and the supernatural, which collide and interact. In *November Night* (*Noc listopadowa*, 1904), Wyspiański's drama about the first great Polish uprising against the tsar, Greek mythology comes to life in Polish history. The action of the play takes place on the night of November 29, 1830, while at the same time the actual events of the insurrection are presented within the eternal context of the ancient myth of Demeter and Persephone. Through striking theatrical use of juxtaposition and synchronism, the nineteenth-century Polish soldiers become Greek warriors, playthings in the hands of the Homeric gods, and the 1830 rebellion is transformed into an Eleusinian seasonal mystery of death and rebirth.

Stanisław Wyspiński's *The Return of Odysseus*. [Agencja Autorska, Warsaw]

During his years of study in Paris as a young painter in the early 1890s, Wyspiański had been initiated into the occult sciences and came under the influence of Edouard Schuré's ideas about the "theatre of the soul," in which the mythopoetic higher consciousness fuses past and present time. In a second drama of death and resurrection, *Acropolis* (*Akropolis*), written in 1903 but not performed in its original version until 1926, Wyspiański fashions a syncretism of Judaic, Greek, and Christian religious mythology through a series of correspondences between Old Testament, Homer, and Polish history. Set on Easter eve in the royal castle of Wawel overlooking the city of Cracow and the river Vistula (analogues for the Acropolis, Athens, and the Scamander), Wyspiański's drama has no human characters, only figures from tapestries, wall hangings, and sculptures, who come to life and enact scenes from the Bible and the *Iliad*.

In *The Deliverance* (*Wyzwolenie*, 1903), Wyspiański, almost two decades before Pirandello's *Six Characters in Search of an Author*, uses the device of the play-within-a-play to explode conventional canons of stagecraft and, at the same time, to carry on Polish drama's running dialogue with its own past, a practice which, to an outsider, may sometimes seem almost incestuous. The action of *The Deliverance* takes place on the bare stage of a contemporary Cracow theatre, where Konrad, the hero of Mickiewicz's *Forefathers' Eve*, has come to lead the nation to salvation. Konrad first addresses the theatre workmen, then the stage manager and actors who are putting on their costumes, but he declares that there will be no play today, only a *commedia* improvisation through which the hero hopes to awaken the nation from paralyzing dreams of the past. Determined to destroy the false illusions of the old theatre, Konrad hopes to build a new one out of its ruins that will represent the nation. *The Deliverance* is a reckoning with the masks and voices of the past and a settlement of accounts with romantic drama; these devices of theatrical appropriation and allusion become characteristic procedures of modern Polish drama.

Although Wyspiański opened the way for the later triumphs of twentieth-century Polish theatrical production, his farsighted ideas about a new stagecraft were too advanced for his own day and became widely accepted only in the 1920s, when several of his later plays, such as *Achilles* (*Achilleis*, 1903) were presented for the first time. Now Wyspiański's dramas, along with the romantic classics, are the mainstay of the Polish repertory.

Far more obscure but equally innovative are the plays of the poet and novelist Tadeusz Miciński, who shared Wyspiański's notions of the sacred function of theatre and called for drama to return to its origins in the religious mysteries of ancient Greece, India, Persia, and medieval Christendom. A mystical sage, pan-Slavist, and student of the occult—known to his admirers as the Magus—Miciński believed that the theatre should be a temple, not a place of entertainment, and wrote more than a dozen plays which, he hoped, would unite East and West, reconcile Christianity and the Orthodox faith, and bring Poland and Russia together on the basis of gnosticism and esoteric philosophy. *See* MICIŃSKI, TADEUSZ.

Scene from Stanisław Przybyszewski's *Snow*, Teatr Dramatyczny, Warsaw. [Agencja Autorska, Warsaw]

Miciński's *The Revolt of the Potemkin* (*Kniaź Patiomkin*, 1906), which deals with the 1905 revolt of Russian sailors on the Black Sea battleship and covers many of the same events as does Sergei Eisenstein's famous film, is both rigorously documentary and wildly visionary. The playwright invests with mystical significance a wealth of realistic details taken from a wide range of sources, including newspaper articles, memoirs, eyewitness accounts, and songs of the period. The antithetical yet complementary pair of Christ and Lucifer, who dominate all Miciński's work and give it a metaphysical dimension, appear in *The Revolt of the Potemkin*, not as symbolic figures but as two actual Russian officers in a daring fusion of the topical and the mythical. In the Walpurgis Night of Act III, during which the port of Odessa is looted and burned, Miciński, inspired by the orgy scenes in Krasiński's *The Undivine Comedy*, presents the grotesque underside of the revolutionary saga in the form of the Putrescent Man in the Garbage Can (half a century before Beckett's *Endgame*), the Syphilitic Madonna, and the Unknown Figure proclaiming his vision of a world ruled over by microbes. The final apocalyptic act of the drama takes place on a reef in the middle of the sea, where the *Potemkin*'s crew, both dead and alive, see visions of the Golden City of Lhasa in Tibet amidst the Himalayas and make contact with the ghost of the infant Dalai Lama. *The Revolt of the Potemkin* was first staged in 1925 by Leon Schiller and was revived in 1979.

In the Shades of the Golden Palace, or Basilissa Teophano (*W mrokach złotego pałacu, czyli Bazilissa Teofanu*, 1909), Miciński's historical drama about the decline of the Byzantine Empire, has the weird structure of a dream, intermingling the most disparate elements of the everyday, the erudite, and the fantastic. Long thought to be unperformable, *Basilissa* reached the stage only in 1967, and in the 1970s a revival of interest in Miciński's work brought about several other productions as well as a new edition of his dramas.

A dabbler in satanism and the black arts, Stanisław Przybyszewski (1868–1927) was a quintessential *fin-de-siècle* figure who wrote a number of novels, essays, and plays depicting an anguished demonic universe. Trained as a physician in Berlin, Przybyszewski was an influential member of the German artistic circles frequented by his friends August Strindberg and Edvard Munch; at the beginning of his literary career, he wrote for the most part in German, switching to Polish around 1900. *See* Przybyszewski, Stanisław.

In his own day one of the most celebrated modernists in all of Europe, whose plays were performed throughout the world, particularly in Russia where Vsevolod Meyerhold was his champion, Przybyszewski combined a brutal psychological naturalism in his portrayal of the battle of the sexes with a highly subjective and impressionistic style. A flamboyantly exhibitionistic art resulted, in which the author's personality emerged as more fascinating than his creations. Plays such as *For the Sake of Happiness* (*Dla szczęścia*, 1900), *The Golden Fleece* (*Złote runo*, 1901), and *Snow* (*Śnieg*, 1903), which seemed so daring to Przybyszewski's contemporaries, now strike audiences as dated and even comical in their overinsistence on hysterical passions leading to murder and suicide, as though in illustration of the author's well-known dictum, "In the beginning there was lust." *See* Meyerhold, Vsevolod.

Yet certain of Przybyszewski's dramatic works retain a nervous power and originality of form. In *Visitors* (*Goście*, 1901), a dramatic epilogue in one act published with *The Golden Fleece*, the protagonist, Adam, is pursued by a divided self that takes the form of his shadow and double. Here Przybyszewski shows man in the clutches of unseen diabolic forces that first awaken him to a consciousness of evil and then drive him to suicide as the only way out. The torments of a "naked soul" (Przybyszewski's preferred field of exploration)—outside time, independent of environment, beyond experience and reality—are dramatized through the striking theatrical image of a mansion being invaded by unknown visitors, a device later adopted by the Russian dramatist Leonid Andreyev in his *Black Maskers* (1908). *See* Andreyev, Leonid.

BETWEEN THE TWO WORLD WARS

In 1918, as a result of the Treaty of Versailles, Poland regained its independence, but the interwar years proved to be only a brief and unstable interlude before a new disaster struck; in 1939 first Nazi Germany and then the Soviet Union invaded their neighbor and divided it

A self-portrait by Stanisław Ignacy Witkiewicz (Witkacy). [Agencja Autorska, Warsaw]

stage effects, Witkacy's theatre springs first of all from feelings of fear and loneliness in the face of an inexplicable universe, and next from the impingement of society on the individual as the concrete embodiment of the dilemma of the self confronted by all that is outside it. Thus Witkacian drama is both metaphysical and social. In plays such as *The New Deliverance* (*Nowe wyzwolenie*, 1920) with its ironic allusion to Wyspiański's *Deliverance*, *The Water Hen* (*Kurka wodna*, 1921), parodying the bird titles of Ibsen's *Wild Duck* and Chekhov's *Seagull*, and *The Anonymous Work* (*Bezimienne dzieło*, 1921), Witkacy shows the collapse of an *ancien régime* composed of obsolete individualists—decadent artists, demonic women, Nietzschean supermen—which is overrun by the gray masses representing the new anthill civilization.

Although his plays show certain affinities to both expressionism and surrealism in themes and techniques, Witkacy's "comedies with corpses" and "non-Euclidian dramas"—to use the playwright's own terms—remain unique in their urgently personal and constantly ironic vision of an insane world heading for disaster. In *They* (*Oni*, 1920), a prophetic play dealing in thought control, confession to uncommitted crimes, the destruction of modern art, and government by informers and secret organizations, Witkacy explores the real, as opposed to the apparent, sources of power. In *The Shoemakers* (*Szewcy*, 1927–1934), his last surviving work for the theatre, after a pair of old-fashioned revolutions from the right and from the left, the insidious technocrats come to power and institute their passionless tyranny over all aspects of public and private life.

Unlike the Czech Karel Čapek in *R.U.R.* and the German Georg Kaiser in the *Gas* trilogy, the Polish painter-playwright was little concerned with the enslavement of man to the machine or the dangers inherent in

among themselves. During these twenty years of precarious freedom, a number of new playwrights appeared and attempted to create an avant-garde Polish drama that would be attuned to the postwar realities of urban life, mechanization, and mass culture. Once the national issue appeared to be settled, writers abandoned the grandiose neoromantic style bequeathed by the nineteenth century and sought dynamic new forms that could keep pace with the automobile and cinema. Although some interesting theatrical experiments resulted, these innovative dramatists did not find a receptive audience for their work in a society that was fragmented into mutually antagonistic classes and parties and was little concerned with artistic ground-breaking. Many of the best Polish plays of the 1920s and '30s had to wait until after 1956 to be accepted in the theatre.

Undoubtedly the most extraordinary Polish artist in the interwar years was the painter, playwright, novelist, aesthetician, philosopher, and drug expert Stanisław Ignacy Witkiewicz, or Witkacy, as he called himself. After an idyllic childhood and stormy adolescence in the picturesque mountain resort of Zakopane, where he was educated entirely at home according to his father's elite system, Witkacy went with his friend Bronisław Malinowski on an anthropological expedition to Australia and then served four years as a tsarist officer in Russia, witnessing the last days of St. Petersburg and living through the February, 1917, Revolution. Both experiences—with primitive tribal life and modern communism—decisively shaped the writer's view of the collectivist threat to the individual, which would be the central theme of his work. *See* WITKIEWICZ, STANISŁAW IGNACY.

Upon his return to Poland in 1918, the thirty-three-year-old painter began his career as a playwright, creating in the next eight years some forty works for the stage; many of these dramas remained unpublished and unperformed in his lifetime and more than a dozen are lost or preserved only in fragments. Characterized by grotesque humor, dreamlike illogicality, vivid color (showing a strong pictorial inspiration), and spectacular

Witkiewicz wrote *They* in 1920. This prophetic drama about mind control was revived by Warsaw's Teatr Polski in 1966. [Photograph by Fr. Myszkowski]

The title of Witkiewicz's *The Water Hen*, shown here in a 1964 production, parodies the bird titles used by Ibsen and Chekhov. [Photograph by Fr. Myszkowski]

advanced industrialization. For Witkacy, modern science and modern art are allies in the struggle against the ant-hill; both are subversive to stability and uniformity and must be rigidly controlled by the new dictators. Well versed in the theories of Einstein, Whitehead, Cantor, and Heisenberg, Witkacy recognized that the conventions of realistic drama are based on mechanistic Newtonian physics. In his own plays he attempted to create a new dramatic model, which he called Pure Form, derived as much from the discoveries of the new mathematics and physics as from Picasso's breakthrough in nonrepresentational painting.

Ridiculed or ignored in his own lifetime, Witkacy left a rich legacy to the future Polish avant-garde. Rejecting the prevalent national mode, which he found inflated and insular, he created an international dramatic idiom capable of reflecting the problems of the modern world rather than of the Polish past. In the face of the absurdities and contradictions of contemporary life, he adopted an irreverent, mocking tone full of self-irony that contrasted sharply with the pompous solemnity of the earlier Polish tradition. Finally, by his efforts to liberate drama from old-fashioned storytelling, conventional psychology, and Stanislavsky's tenets of realistic acting, Witkacy strove to give Polish theatre all the formal possibilities of modern art and music. At the outbreak of World War II in September, 1939, Witkacy committed suicide, unrecognized and forgotten. It was only after 1956 that his ideas and accomplishments could bear fruit in the theatre.

Other tragic casualties of the interwar years include the communist playwrights Witold Wandurski and Bruno Jasieński, who unsuccessfully attempted to establish workers' theatre in Poland and later emigrated to the Soviet Union hoping to find a warmer welcome there;

instead, they were both liquidated during the purges under Stalin. Wandurski's *Death in a Pear Tree* (*Śmierć na gruszy*, 1925), which called forth boos and showers of rotten eggs when it was first presented in Cracow at the Słowacki Theatre, is an antiwar folk fable about how Death was imprisoned by a crafty peasant; it was revived in 1964 by Józef Szajna (cocreator with Jerzy Grotowski of *Acropolis*, famous for his many stagings of the Holocaust). The futurist Jasieński wrote *The Ball of the Mannequins* (*Bal manekinów*, 1931), in which a group of fashion dummies stage a revolt, after he had settled in Moscow and assumed the editorship of the international publication *The Literature of the World Revolution*, where the play was published. It was first presented on the Polish stage in 1957 and has received several notable revivals since then.

The socialist poet and editor Tadeusz Peiper (1891–1969) fared no better with his experimental plays, *Six o'clock! Six o'clock!* (*Szósta! Szósta!*, 1925), which contrasts stage time with real time by inversions of chronological order, and *If There Isn't Any Him* (*Skoro go nie ma*, 1933), a drama of revolution and the loss of self. These unusual works had to wait until the mid-1970s before reaching the stage and are further evidence of the wealth of exciting Polish drama neglected and ignored in its own era. An outstanding dramatist of the interwar years, who suffered a similar fate, was Stanisława Przybyszewska, the illegitimate daughter of Stanisław Przybyszewski, who wrote a brilliant trilogy about Danton and the French Revolution. Only the first of these plays, *The Danton Affair* (*Sprawa Dantona*, 1931), was performed

Scene from Witkiewicz's *The Mother*, an "unsavory play" written in 1924 but not produced until forty years later. [Agencja Autorska, Warsaw]

during the author's lifetime, but since 1967 Przyby-szewska's historical dramas have been highly acclaimed in the theatre and have eclipsed in importance her father's work for the stage. *See* PRZYBYSZEWSKA, STANISLAWA.

More successful in the 1920s were plays by the celebrated social novelist Stefan Zeromski (1864–1925), who had begun his career as a playwright before the war with *Rose* (*Róża*, 1908–1909), a study of the failure of the revolution of 1905, brilliantly staged by Leon Schiller in 1926. Żeromski produced several other plays in the last years of his life, including *My Little Quail Has Flown Away* (*Uciekła mi przepióreczka*, 1924), about a utopian scheme that miscarries. Jerzy Szaniawski (1886–1970) wrote a number of subtle and poetic comedies throughout the interwar years, but only his later *The Two Theatres* (*Dwa teatry*, 1946), reflecting the experiences of the war and, through the device of the play-within-a-play, contrasting two views of art (as petty realism or as fantasy), left a lasting mark.

A major figure in twentieth-century Polish literature, the novelist Witold Gombrowicz began his work as a playwright in the 1930s but did not achieve any recognition in the theatre until many years later. His first play, *Ivona, Princess of Burgundia* (*Iwona, księżniczka Burgunda*), was written and published in Poland in 1935 but only reached the stage in 1957, after the Thaw. His second, *The Marriage* (*Ślub*), was written in 1946 in Argentina (Gombrowicz was on a summer cruise when the war broke out in 1939, and he remained in South America for twenty-five years), published in Paris in 1953, and first produced there ten years later. His final work for the theatre, *Operetta* (*Operetka*), was written and published in France in 1966 and performed throughout Europe shortly thereafter. Because Gombrowicz chose never to return to Poland and wrote as an exile critical of the regime, his last two plays could not be performed professionally in the Polish theatre until after his death. Now his three dramas are an important part of the Polish rep-

Leon Schiller (left), probably Poland's greatest twentieth-century stage producer, is shown with his friend and mentor, Gordon Craig. [*Theatre in Modern Poland*]

ertory, especially attractive to contemporary directors because of their self-consciously theatrical use of parody, political parable, and the grotesque. *See* GOMBROWICZ, WITOLD.

Gombrowicz's plays, which take place in absurd fairytale kingdoms, pit the conflicting images of reality held by the characters one against the other in a battle between restrictive forms that are socially imposed and creative immaturity. In *Ivona, Princess of Burgundia*, the ugly, repellent, and morosely silent heroine—chosen by the young Prince as his betrothed simply as a joke—makes the members of the royal court realize how ridiculous they themselves are. To regain their sense of self-importance and dignity, the courtiers decide to murder Ivona and watch with satisfaction as she slowly chokes on a fishbone. Written in both prose and verse and utilizing stylized literary devices, *The Marriage* is a vast and complex dream play, rich in allusions to Shakespeare, the romantics, and Wyspiański's *The Wedding*, and full of the dazzling and ambiguous transformations of time, place, and identity characteristic of the Polish tradition in drama. Gombrowicz's masterpiece for the stage, *The Marriage* is an exploration of the self, its endless possibilities for creation through words and images, and its intricate poses and diversions. According to the author, everything is created by and among people as they artificially form one another by means of imagination, pretense, and lies. In *Operetta* the playwright tellingly uses the absurd conventions and style of operetta to deal with the equally preposterous events of modern history. In a total spectacle of great theatrical power, Gombrowicz charts the course of the decline and fall of Europe from the turn of the century to the present—including two world wars and two revolutions—by means of the ludicrously colorful characters and situations of a Viennese operetta.

WORLD WAR II AND THE POSTWAR PERIOD

The outbreak of World War II in September, 1939, once again threatened to obliterate Poland as a nation, and even more drastically than the nineteenth-century parti-

Witold Gombrowicz. [Grove Press. Photograph by Bogdan Paczowski]

tions disrupted Polish cultural life and brought to a temporary halt the development of the drama. During six years of an inhuman Nazi occupation, no open theatre—except for some collaborationist light entertainment—was possible in Poland; clandestine performances had to be given in private homes and apartments. Still more disastrous for Polish culture, many of the most talented young writers and artists were put in concentration camps or killed. Andrzej Trzebiński (1922–1943), an underground poet and soldier, wrote one remarkable play, *To Pick Up the Rose (Aby podnieść różę)* about revolution, political power, and Ping-Pong, at the age of twenty, a year before he was shot by the Nazis in a random street execution.

Despite the great losses and immense physical destruction (no theatres were left standing in Warsaw after the 1945 Uprising had been crushed), reconstruction began as soon as the war ended, and within a matter of months theatrical life was reestablished throughout the country. Prewar playwrights like Szaniawski picked up their careers again, and a number of new talents appeared. *Święto Winkelrida (Winkelried's Day)*, a topical political fable written by the novelist Jerzy Andrzejewski and the poet Jerzy Zagórski during the occupation, was published in 1946 but could not be staged until ten years later. The celebrated poet Konstanty Ildefons Gałczyński (1905–1953) created a miniature nonsense theatre in the pages of a popular Cracow weekly. Called *The Little Theatre of ''The Green Goose,''* Gałczyński's irreverent parodies mock the solemnities of Polish cultural and political life and render absurd the hallowed traditions and conventions of the theatre.

Before the new Polish drama had time to find its di-

Scene from a postwar production of Andrzej Trzebiński's *To Pick Up the Rose.* [Photograph by Zofia Myszkowska]

Barbara Krafftowna in Gombrowicz's *Ivona, Princess of Burgundia* in a 1957 production by Halina Mikołajska. [*Theatre in Modern Poland*]

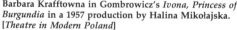

rection, a new misfortune struck. In January, 1949, socialist realism was proclaimed as the reigning style for all the arts, and later that year a Festival of Soviet Drama was instituted to show Polish playwrights how drama should be written. Soon all theatres were put under totally centralized bureaucratic control, the Polish romantic classics were forbidden, and Stalinism dominated the arts for the next five years. Deeply alien and inimical to the Polish tradition of a metaphoric theatre, enforced socialist realism produced ludicrous results, spawning lifeless productivity plays set in factories and construction sites or cold war dramas attacking America and the West, such as *Julius and Ethel (Juliusz i Ethel,* 1954), a polemic about the Rosenbergs by Leon Kruczkowski (1900–1962). But even such an officially sanctioned communist author as Kruczkowski could not fit comfortably into the straitjacket of socialist realism, and his most universal play, *The Death of the Governor (Śmierć Gubernatora)* a penetrating study of political power based on Leonid Andreyev's story ''The Governor,'' could appear only in 1961.

After the death of Stalin in 1953, the entire mechanism of repression and lies started to crumble. Polish student theatres, such as STS, Bim-Bom, and Kalambur, played a pioneering role in liberating drama from official constraints as early as 1954, but it was only with the bloodless October revolution of 1956, following the Poznań workers' riots in June of the same year, that the Thaw set in and Poland acquired an autonomous policy in the arts. The effects on the theatre were quite extraordinary.

Recently cut off from all contact with the West, Polish drama immediately became responsive to foreign influences and attuned to modern sensibility. Starting with the Polish production of *Waiting for Godot* in 1957, all the plays of Beckett and Ionesco were translated and performed as soon as they appeared in France. Ghelderode, Adamov, Genet, Dürrenmatt, Frisch, Pinter, and Brecht became popular theatrical fare. The entire Western avant-garde was quickly understood, accepted, and assimilated by Polish actors, audiences, and writers.

As had been the case before in Poland, the theatre proved to be the only public place where certain national obsessions and grievances could be aired, at least in an oblique form. Liberalized state support and control had both positive and negative consequences but unquestionably played an important role in the flowering of Polish drama after 1956 as a significant voice in the world of modern artistic expression. Lavish subsidization made possible the creation throughout the country of a highly sophisticated theatrical enterprise capable of enlisting the best talent. At the same time the constant pressure of censorship, while ruling out truthful presentation of everyday reality and its problems, naturally inclined playwrights to parable and metaphor, devices central to the Polish dramatic tradition.

A sudden explosion of playwriting occurred in the late 1950s in Poland as a result of the changes in cultural policy produced by the Thaw. Not only professional

The *Greedy Eve* sequence from Ildefons Gałczyński's *The Little Theatre of "The Green Goose"* as presented at the Walden Theatre, New York, under the direction of William Korff. [Photograph by Warren C. Levy]

dramatists, but nearly everyone in the literary world—outstanding poets like Zbigniew Herbert, Stanisław Grochowiak, Tymoteusz Karpowicz, and Tadeusz Różewicz as well as Marxist philosophers like Leszek Kołakowski—turned to the theatre as the most effective platform from which to be heard. Conditioned by the grim experiences of the war, occupation, concentration camps, and Stalinist repression, the new Polish drama took an ironic view of ideals and ideologies, including romantic heroics, and subjected to penetrating scrutiny the operations of the machinery of governing, as in Jerzy Broszkiewicz's philosophical allegory, *The Names of Power* (*Imiona władzy*, 1956), in which the arbitrary nature of political power is shown in three scenes set in different historical epochs.

As part of the wholesale rejection of socialist realism, the poet Miron Białoszewski set up his private Theatre Apart (1953–1961) in his own apartment, where the author and his friends gave performances of his radical linguistic experiments. In 1956 the playwright and critic Adam Tarn established the influential magazine *Dialog*, in which almost all important new Polish plays are published prior to performance. Witkacy was rediscovered and became a potent force for shaping the new drama. At the same time a whole group of gifted young directors, such as Kazimierz Dejmek, Jerzy Grotowski (best known for his influential theories on actor training and for his innovative productions, such as *Apocalypsis cum figuris*, 1968), Zygmunt Hübner, Tadeusz Kantor, Konrad Świnarski, Jerzy Jarocki, and Józef Szajna, contributed to the ferment and excitement. By the mid-1960s modern Polish drama and theatre had gained recognition as the best in Europe.

The two playwrights who have dominated the Polish stage for the two decades since 1960 and become the best known abroad are Sławomir Mrożek and Tadeusz Różewicz. Utilizing vaudeville, music hall, and cabaret techniques, Mrożek, who is also a cartoonist and author of humorous sketches, turns highly intellectualized concepts into dynamic theatrical spectacles. His plays, which have affinities with the Theatre of the Absurd, are characterized by absence of psychology, generic types, rapidly accelerating tempos, and sudden reversals producing striking *coups de théâtre*. In his early one-act parables of power, such as *Out at Sea* (*Na pełnym morzu*, 1960), *Striptease* (1961), and *Charlie* (*Karol*, 1961), the playwright thrusts helpless victims into unforeseen situations from which there is no escape and then develops the absurd premises to logical, if drastic, conclusions. Ironically juxtaposing extremes of civilization and barbarism, Mrożek explores the precarious position of man in society and in the universe, which, in the playwright's sardonic view, is responsible for the blind human determination to survive, even at the cost of cannibalizing one's fellow man. *See* MROŻEK, SŁAWOMIR; RÓŻEWICZ, TADEUSZ.

With characteristic fusion of precise analytical thought and malicious slapstick fun, Mrożek's dramas reveal the complex bonds between the hunter and the hunted in a world of illusory freedom where both victim and victimizer use reason to accommodate to unreason. In *Tango* (1964), Mrożek's most important play of the

1960s, the playwright treats family drama as parable in order to trace the history of European civilization from nineteenth-century liberalism to modern totalitarianism. Through a system of citations from and allusions to Wyspiański's *The Wedding*, Gombrowicz's *The Marriage*, and Shakespeare's *Hamlet* (with its opposition of the strongman Fortinbras and the intellectual Prince, a source for much modern Polish literature), Mrożek makes the farcical collapse of a single family composed of three generations of would-be artists and thinkers tell the story of how the failure of culture leads to the reign of brute strength.

Ten years later, with *Emigrés* (*Emigranci*, 1974), Mrożek produced a second masterpiece that has played in theatres throughout the world. A two-character play about an intellectual and a peasant from Eastern Europe who share a grimy basement in a Western European city where they have gone in consequence of contrasting attitudes to their homeland, *Emigrés* is a profound and disturbing comic study of human illusion and of man's freedom, and its limitations. Himself an emigré to the West since the early 1960s, Mrożek continues to write for the Polish stage, and his more than twenty-five plays are a central part of the modern Polish repertory.

A major poet as well as an essayist, novelist, and playwright, Mrożek's older contemporary Różewicz also writes about problems of survival in a world of instant apocalypse, but he totally abandons the accepted canons of stagecraft and dramatic structure for what he calls open dramaturgy, in which the director and actors are invited to create the performance with the author. Rejecting traditional notions of artistic beauty and form, Różewicz creates both poetry and drama out of the refuse of modern civilization. His highly experimental plays include *The Card Index* (*Kartoteka*, 1960), whose anonymous hero of indefinite age, profession, and outlook experiences life—past, present, and future—while in bed at a crossroads of existence, *Interrupted Act* (*Akt przerywany*, 1964), an antiplay challenging theatrical convention by means of long polemical stage directions, and *The Old Woman Broods* (*Stara kobieta wysiaduje*, 1968), depicting civilization as a rubbish heap that continues to function even after the great cataclysm. The worldwide success of *White Marriage* (*Białe małżeństwo*, 1974), an ironic, touching, and ultimately ambiguous treatment of sexual awakening in two adolescent girls at the turn of the century, reaffirms Różewicz's position as a leading practitioner of a higher, poetic realism.

Różewicz and Mrożek are only two highly personal voices among many talented modern Polish dramatists. Others worthy of note include Ernest Bryll, whose *November Story* (*Rzecz listopadowa*, 1968) deals with national history in a neoromantic style and whose *Over Hills, Over Clouds. . .* (*Po górach, po chmurach . . .*, 1968) imitates a folk nativity play. Ireneusz Iredyński has written a number of neonaturalistic plays dealing with sex and violence: *A Modern Nativity Play* (*Jasełka-moderne*, 1966) concerns a group of prisoners in a concentration camp who are forced to rehearse a mystery play and who become the characters whom they portray; *The Third Breast*

Tadeusz Różewicz's *White Marriage* as presented in Wrocław in 1975. [Agencja Autorska, Warsaw]

(*Trzecia pierś*, 1973) is a shocking thriller about the totalitarian mentality; and *Quadraphonia* (*Kwadrofonia*, 1977) is a radio play for four voices. The poet and director Helmut Kajzar has written a number of plays that break new ground, among them *Paternoster* (1970), which reconstructs a dream in scenic images.　　　DANIEL GEROULD

CRITICISM

E. Csató, *The Polish Theater*, Warsaw, 1963; K. Puzyna, "Prologue," *Theatre in Modern Poland*, Warsaw, 1963; S. Marczak-Oborski, *Życie teatralne w latach, 1944–1964*, Warsaw, 1968; C. Miłosz, *The History of Polish Literature*, New York, 1969; B. Taborski, "Poland," *Crowell's Handbook of Contemporary Drama*, New York, 1971; T. Kudliński, *Rodowód Polskiego Teatru*, Warsaw, 1972; R. Szydłowski, *The Theatre in Poland*, Warsaw, 1972; H. B. Segel, "Introduction," *Polish Romantic Drama*, Ithaca, N.Y., 1977; W. Filler, *Contemporary Polish Theatre*, Warsaw, 1977; D. Gerould, "Introduction," *Twentieth-Century Polish Avant-Garde Drama*, Ithaca, N.Y., 1977; L. Eustachiewicz, *Dramaturgia polska w latach 1945–77*, Warsaw, 1979; S. Gąssowski, *Współcześni dramatopisarze Polscy*, Warsaw, 1979.

Poliziano, Angelo (1454–1494)

Italian poet, humanist, and dramatist; pseudonym of Angelo Ambrogini. His *Orpheus* (*La fabula d'Orfeo*, 1480?) is a landmark of Renaissance theatre. The earliest extant secular play in Italian, deriving from the linguistic tradition of medieval religious drama, *Orpheus* is the prototype of the pastoral genre, while the author's attempt to individuate the psychology of his characters is important in the evolution of tragicomedy as well. *See* PASTORAL DRAMA; TRAGICOMEDY in glossary.

Orpheus (*La fabula d'Orfeo*, 1480?). Verse tragedy composed in Italian, based on Virgil's *Georgics*. It was written in only two days in Mantua when Poliziano was requested to provide entertainment for the visit of Duke Galeazzo Mariá Sforza. Following a prologue in which Mercury outlines the plot of the drama, the shepherd Aristaeus first confesses to Mopsus his love for Eurydice in a melancholy song and then pursues Tirsi. The poet Orpheus, husband of Eurydice, appears, and in a Sapphic ode chants the honor of Poliziano's patrons, the Gonzagas. Then, having learned from a shepherd that Eurydice has died after being bitten by a snake, Orpheus descends at once into Hades, where he begs Pluto, Minos, and Persephone for the return of his wife. His wish is granted on condition that he precede Eurydice out of Hades without looking back at her until they are again aboveground. Shortly thereafter, however, Eurydice expresses her fear of being drawn back into the underworld, and when Orpheus turns to her too soon, she disappears. The embittered husband then sings of his hatred for women. An orgiast invokes Orpheus's death and in conclusion describes the macabre wounds inflicted on his body.   [PETER BONDANELLA]

EDITIONS

H. M. Ayres, "A Translation of Poliziano's *Orfeo*," *Romanic Review* 20 (1929), 13–24; *Il teatro italiano dalle origini al Quattrocento*, ed. Emilio Faccioli, Turin, 1975.

CRITICISM

B. Croce, *Poesia popolare e poesia d'arte*, Bari, 1933; G. De Robertis, *Saggi*, Florence, 1939; B. Maier, "Angelo Poliziano," in *Letteratura italiana: I maggiori*, Milan, 1956.

Popescu, Dumitru Radu (1935–   )

Romanian dramatist. The editor of *A Tribuna*, a weekly literary magazine, Popescu is also deeply involved in the writing of his plays. Enthusiastic about all foreign theatre, he believes that he and others of his generation have been influenced by contemporary French and American dramatists—especially Tennessee Williams, Eugene O'Neill, Arthur Miller—as well as Chekhov and Tolstoy among the Russians.

Several of Popescu's plays have been published under the collective title *These Sad Angels* (*Acesti ingeri tristi*, 1970). Of these, one of the best is *Caesar, the Pirates' Play* (*Cezar, mascariciul piratilor*, 1968), in which the captain of a ship on which Caesar is held captive presents a drama that foretells the future of the Roman leader and how he will be assassinated. *Cat on New Year's Eve* (*Pisica in noaptea anului*, 1971), a psychological study that avoids conflict with prescribed Communist guidelines, was produced in Cluj in 1971, and later filmed for television, as was his naturalistic *Dwarf in the Summer Garden* (*Un suris in plina vara*).

Popescu admits censorship of plays is a problem. Noting that writing plays and having them produced are two different things, he points out that he does not focus on politically sensitive matters.   RUTH S. LAMB

CRITICISM

R. S. Lamb, *The World of Romanian Theatre*, Ocelot, Calif., 1976.

Popović, Jovan Sterija (1806–1856)

Serbian dramatist, poet, and novelist. Born in Vršac on January 1, 1806, of a Greek merchant father and a Serbian mother, he became a high-school teacher and then a lawyer in his hometown. In 1840 he went to Serbia, where he was a college professor, a school administrator, and a theatre organizer. He was instrumental in founding the Serbian Academy of Sciences, the Science Museum, and the National Library. In addition to writing dramas, he also organized, staged, and directed plays. His own plays constituted the repertory of the young Serbian theatre. In 1848 he returned to Vršac disillusioned with politics and in poor health, which forced him to withdraw from public life in a strongly pessimistic mood, in which he remained until his death.

Popović attained his greatest success with satires and comedies. His *Liar and Superliar* (*Laža i paralaža*, 1830), *The Miser* (*Tvrdica ili Kir Janja*, 1837), *An Evil Woman* (*Zla žena*, 1838), *An Upstart* (*Pokondirena tikva*, 1838), *The Wedding* (*Ženidba i udadba*, 1841), *Belgrade Then and Now* (*Beograd nekad i sad*, 1853), and *Patriots* (*Rodoljupci*, 1903) are among the best Serbian dramas and have remained very popular. With genuine humor Popović depicts the life of the middle class, championing the little man but also lampooning his foibles and idiosyncrasies, such as greed, falsehood, and pseudopatriotism. Some of his themes and types are admittedly borrowed from other writers (Shakespeare, Molière, Kotzebue), but they have local color and application.

Liar and Superliar (*Laža i paralaža*, 1830). Two destitute friends, Aleksa and Mita, decide to improve their lot by using lies and trickery. They visit the richest merchant in town and so overwhelm his daughter that betrothal soon follows; however, Aleksa's earlier girlfriend spoils their plans, and his intended bride marries her original fiancé.

The Miser (*Tvrdica ili Kir Janja*, 1837). In this comedy, patterned after Molière's *The Miser*, the playwright depicts a smalltown merchant of Greek origin whose passion is money and property and whose main character trait is miserliness. He calculates every penny and tries to save even on food, only to end up losing rather than saving money. He even tries to marry his daughter to a man of his age only because the man does not demand a dowry. In the end he loses both his property and his daughter to a young notary public who outwits him. What makes this play more than a mere imitation is Popović's creation of original characters based on local circumstances and on genuinely comic situations.

An Upstart (*Pokondirena tikva*, 1838). In another comedy of morals, Popović presents Fema, widow of a shoemaker, who after inheriting some money decides to abandon her past and start a new life on a much higher social level. To achieve that goal she pretends that she is of a higher class, imitates the speech mannerisms and social behavior of aristocracy in large foreign cities, and wreaks havoc among her relatives, friends, and neighbors. The only results of her efforts are a ruined family and a reputation as a ludicrous and pathetic upstart.

Patriots (*Rodoljupci*, 1903). During the revolution of 1848 a number of Voyvodina Serbs proclaim their patriotism by villifying the Hungarians in favor of the Austrians, hoping in that way to bring greater autonomy for the Serbs. In the course of the play, however, it becomes clear that all of them have been subservient to the Hungarians all along, and when it becomes evident that nothing will come of their struggle, they put their Hungarian insignias back on, hiding the Serbian ones. Popović lashes out at false patriotism among his compatriots and in the process creates several prototypes of chameleons who sell their allegiance for a few ducats. Because of its touchy subject matter, the play was not performed until long after the author's death.

VASA D. MIHAILOVICH

Porter, Cole   (1893–1964)

American composer and lyricist. Porter is known for his sparkling melodies and sophisticated and witty lyrics. Perhaps his two greatest stage successes were *Anything Goes* (1934) and *Kiss Me, Kate* (1948), the latter based on Shakespeare's *The Taming of the Shrew*. His other musicals include *Fifty Million Frenchmen* (1929), *Gay Divorce* (1932),

Danny Kaye as Jerry Walker in *Let's Face It*. New York, Imperial Theatre, 1941. [Photograph by Vandamm. Theatre Collection, The New York Public Library at Lincoln Center, Astor, Lenox and Tilden Foundations]

Jimmy Durante in *Red, Hot, and Blue*. New York, Alvin Theatre, 1936. [Theatre Collection, The New York Public Library at Lincoln Center, Astor, Lenox and Tilden Foundations]

Helen Broderick in *Fifty Million Frenchmen*. New York, Lyric Theatre, 1929. [Photograph by Vandamm. Theatre Collection, The New York Public Library at Lincoln Center, Astor, Lenox and Tilden Foundations]

Red, Hot and Blue (1936), *Du Barry Was a Lady* (1939), *Let's Face It* (1941), *Can-Can* (1953), and *Silk Stockings* (1955). Porter also composed original scores for a number of musical films including *Born to Dance* (1936) and *Rosalie* (1937). *See* MUSICAL COMEDY.   [GAUTAM DASGUPTA]

Porter, Henry   (fl. 1599)

English dramatist. Little is known of Porter except that he may have studied at Oxford, that he worked for Philip Henslowe, owner of several theatres in London, and that he was famous for his comedies, which may have influenced Ben Jonson. Porter collaborated with Jonson on the now-lost *Hot Anger Soon Cold* (1598). Henslowe's diary records other plays in which Porter had a hand, all of which are lost except *The Two Angry Women of Abington* (before 1598), a comedy of country life, which was one of the few plays of the late 1500s to stray from the prevailing romanticism and move toward realism. In a bourgeois milieu, two families oppose the union of their respective offspring but finally blunder through to a happy resolution. *See* JONSON, BEN.

Porto-Riche, Georges de   (1849–1930)

French dramatist. Born in Bordeaux on May 20, 1849, he is generally considered the founder of the modern *théâtre d'amour* ("theatre of love"), a descriptive title under which his collected works were eventually published. Porto-Riche focused on the physical tyranny of passion, and at the height of his career his works were somewhat overenthusiastically compared to the plays of Racine. He emphasized the basically polygamous nature of men and its conflict with the possessive monogamy of women. Porto-Riche's first plays, however, were historical verse dramas in the tradition of Victor Hugo, and it was not until *The Luck of Françoise* (*La chance de Françoise*, 1888), produced by André Antoine at his Théâtre Libre, that he hit upon the themes and the realistic manner that were to establish his reputation. In that play, an intelligent and indulgent woman saves her husband from the consequences of his philandering.

A *Loving Wife* (*Amoureuse*, 1891), Porto-Riche's most celebrated play, is a penetrating analysis of the different conceptions of love held by men and women. Porto-Riche's protagonists are generally the slaves of their passions, but in *The Past* (*Le passé*, 1897) a young widow seduced and betrayed by a professional Don Juan manages to break his spell over her when she recognizes his emotional dependence on his promiscuity. In *The Malefilâtres* (*Les Malefilâtre*, 1904), a man breaks with his re-

Jean Chevrier and Annie Ducaux in *Amoureuse*. Paris, Comédie-Française, 1949. [French Cultural Services]

spectable and puritanical family rather than give up his wife, who he knows has been unfaithful to him. *The Old Man* (*Le vieil homme*, 1911), which some critics consider his best play, concentrates on the tragic romantic rivalry of an aging roué and his neurotic son, ending with the suicide of the latter. Porto-Riche's influence is most strongly seen in the plays of Paul Géraldy, but it is also apparent in the theatre of Henri Bataille, Tristan Bernard, Édouard Bourdet, and Sacha Guitry as well as in contemporary boulevard theatre generally. Other plays of interest by Porto-Riche include *The Print Merchant* (*Le marchand d'estampes*, 1917) and *The True Gods* (*Les vrais dieux*, 1920). He died in Paris on September 4, 1930. *See* BOULEVARD COMEDY in glossary.

A Loving Wife (*Amoureuse*, 1891). Though in love with his wife Germaine, Étienne Fériaud, a distinguished physician, is wearied by her demanding and all-consuming passion. He had hoped to find in marriage the domestic tranquillity that would allow him to pursue his career in peace, but now he finds that her possessiveness interferes with the outside interests that are as important to him as physical passion. Irritated when she forces him to forgo an important scientific congress, he announces his intention of turning their marriage into a strictly formal arrangement, thus forcing his wife into the arms of a family friend who has long been in love with her. Étienne is initially pleased to be able to purchase peace and tranquillity at this price. Eventually, however, he and Germaine both realize that the bond between them, though satisfactory to neither, is too strong to be broken. Porto-Riche originally intended to call the play *The Enemy* (*L'ennemie*). Produced Paris, Théâtre de l'Odéon, April 25, 1891.

[JOSEPH E. GARREAU]

Portuguese Drama

Portuguese drama as a written literature began in 1502, when Gil Vicente presented his *Play of the Visitation* (*Auto da visitação*) at the royal palace at Lisbon on the occasion of the birth of Prince John. Vicente was the only speaking character, a cowherd who expressed amazement at the decorations of the palace, congratulated the King and Queen upon the birth of their son, and then introduced a group of some thirty companions, each bearing a gift for the infant. The Queen Mother Leonor, widow of John II, became the playwright's protector. Her husband, in spite of his high position, had been an actor in the court mummeries (*momos*). *See* VICENTE, GIL.

FIFTEENTH AND SIXTEENTH CENTURIES

In fifteenth- and sixteenth-century Portugal the *momo* was not just a pastime; it was a mirror of the age. In these fanciful creations of a society which had reached the height of its trajectory, the medieval allegories mixed an exoticism which evoked worlds of long ago. The themes, inspired in ballads or other poems, gained actuality when inserted in the landscapes of adventure and conquest in which the Portuguese were involved in Africa, India, and Brazil. Dragons, men, giants, and devils simultaneously signified the fight of medieval man

Gil Vicente. [Portuguese National Tourist Office]

against evil and the triumph of modern man against the elements.

It was with *momos* that Prince Henry celebrated the Epiphany of 1414 in Viseu. In 1451 King Alfonso V organized *momos* in Lisbon on the occasion of the marriage of his sister, Princess Leonor, to Frederick III. In one *momo* King Manuel was seen gliding down the Tejo River aboard a frigate decorated with damask and Oriental silks, according to his chronicler Damião de Góis. The seas and the empire had accustomed the Portuguese to magnificent masques. A spark of genius would transform this material into theatre.

Gil Vicente was the court playwright from 1502 to 1536, the year in which he wrote his last play. Vicente's appearance as a dramatist coincided with Portugal's emergence as a great power by virtue of its exploration and colonization. From simple eclogues and pastoral and morality plays, he progressed to comedies, tragicomedies, farces, and pageants, most of which received elaborate productions at court. He wrote some of his plays in Spanish, some in Portuguese, and others in a combination of both languages. They were always written in accord with classical license, which permitted Vicente to attack the dissolute habits of the clergy and to refer critically to important personages of the time. Despite his criticism of the human element in the church, Vicente was deeply religious. He was a medieval writer, as he did not observe the Renaissance rules of dramatic structure, although they were well known in the Portugal of his time. Sá de Miranda introduced the new Renaissance techniques when he returned to Portugal in 1526.

The customs, characters, social relationships, and the folklore of the medieval world were portrayed in Vicente's plays. He was unequaled in his lyricism and comic sense. The morality play and the romantic comedy

Luis de Camões. [Portuguese National Tourist Office]

were theatrically the most promising forms evolved by Vicente, but in the last twelve years of his life he turned principally to secular allegorical fantasies, and away from the main paths that European drama was to follow in the sixteenth and seventeenth centuries.

The splendor and complexity of the stage designs used in these works, such as *Festival Play* (*Auto da feira*, 1528) and *Forge of Love* (*Fragoa de amor*, 1524), are a direct outcome of the fifteenth-century court mummeries. Vicente's plays moved away from the kind of drama that would develop outside the court, and when the court lost interest soon after Vicente's death, the way of his successors was difficult.

Post-Vicente dramatists can be divided into main groups: those who tried to follow the techniques used by Vicente, and those who turned to classical and Renaissance models. One of the earliest figures of importance in the first group was Afonso Álvares, a mulatto, who in the sixteenth century probably originated hagiographic drama in Portugal. Vicente had written a short play in Spanish on St. Martin, but had never developed the form. Álvares, commissioned by the Church, combined stories from the *Golden Legends of Saints* (*Aurea Legenda Sanctorum*) with comic elements taken from Gil Vicente. His *Play of San António* (*Auto do Santo António*) was performed in 1531; three more of his plays survive. The blind Baltasar Dias, born in the Madeira Islands in the

sixteenth century, also wrote plays about saints as well as other types of plays. Despite the poor literary quality of his works, they retained their popularity by circulation in chapbooks.

Antonio Ribeiro Chiado (d. 1591) was a Franciscan monk of Évora who left the priesthood and went to Lisbon to become author, actor, and libertine. He became a very popular figure of the time, whose plays, unlike Vicente's, were written for the general public rather than the court. He wrote short plays about Lisbon life, and for these he had a good eye for character types and a good ear for dialogues as would be heard in the public squares. There are four extant plays by Chiado, among them, *Play of the Fishwives* (*Auto das regateiras*, sixteenth century) and *Customs of Eight Characters* (*Prática de octo figuras*, 1543).

The plays of Antonio Prestes (d. 1587?) were published in the *First Part of the Plays and Comedies of Antonio Prestes and of Luis de Camões and Other Portuguese Authors, Whose Names Appear at the Beginning of Their Works* (*Primeira parte dos autos e comedias portuguesas, feitas por Antonio Prestes e por Luis de Camões, e outros autores portugueses cujos nomes vao no principio de suas obras*), an edition organized by Afonso Lopes in 1587. Highly regarded by his contemporaries, Prestes has been condemned by most modern critics for the structural weakness of the plays and for the obscurity of his language. Prestes was a judicial functionary in Santarem, and most of his plays are about judicial affairs, as, for example, *Play of the Attorney* (*Auto do procurador*, 1587) and *Play of the Judge of the Appeals Court* (*Auto do dezembargador*, 1587). Seven of his plays are extant: six domestic comedies and an ambitious morality, *Play of Ave Maria* (*Auto da Ave Maria*).

Another author noteworthy of the period is Francisco da Costa (1553–1591), who died in captivity in Morocco. During his long imprisonment he wrote many poems and seven plays on Biblical subjects, some of which were performed by the Christian captives. They survived in manuscripts, which have recently been published. In the closing years of the sixteenth century Simão Machado (b. mid-sixteenth century; d. first half of seventeenth century), composed two original plays, successful modifications of the Vicentine tradition: a historical drama, *The Wall of God* (*O cerco de Deus*, 1601), and a pastoral comedy, *Comedy of the Shepherdess Alfea* (*Comedia da pastora Alfea*, 1601).

The Portuguese tradition was founded by Francisco Sá de Miranda (1481–1558). Sá de Miranda returned from Italy in 1526, having been influenced by the works of Terence and Plautus, and by the drama of Renaissance Italy. In the preface to his first play, *Strangers* (*Estrangeiros*, 1526?), he states his aims as a writer. Both this play and the later *Os vilhalpandos* (1538?) are in prose and divided into acts and scenes; the plots are complex and the influence of both classical and Renaissance comedy is seen. Where as Vicente's strength was in performance, Sá de Miranda's was in literary correctness.

Greater success was achieved by Antonio Ferreira (1525–1580). Ferreira, a judge of the Civil Court in Lisbon, wrote two prose comedies which take their names from their protagonists: *O Cioso* and *Bristo* (1554). Though moralistic in tone, they are essentially meant as lighthearted entertainments. His greatest achievement was his work, *Tragedy of Lady Inês de Castro* (*Tragédia de Dona Inês de Castro*, pub. 1598). His subject was the tragic story of Inês de Castro, mistress of the heir to the throne, Crown Prince Pedro; her murder wrecked the lives of her lover and the king. In writing the play Antonio Ferreira combined elements from Sophocles's *Electra*, from a fragmentary tragedy of *Cleopatra* by Sá de Miranda, and from Latin plays written and performed in the College of Coimbra and at the Jesuit College in Évora. The first four acts show the uneasiness of Inês and her sons, the vacillations of King Alfonso IV, and the fiery temperament of the crown prince. The comments of the chorus increase the tension, which reaches its height at the end of the fourth act, when the interests of state prevail over humane sentiments and the King orders the death of Inês. The final act—which does not observe the classical unities as the place of the action changes—presages the terrible vengeance Pedro will wreak on Inês's killers.

Luis de Camões, best known for his epic poem *The Lusiads* (*Os Lusiadas*, 1572), was also the author of three plays: *Hosts* (*Anfitriões*, 1587), *King Seleucus* (*El Rei Seleuco*, pub. 1645), and *Philodemus* (*Filodemo*; prod. in India ca. 1555, pub. 1587 with *Anfitriões*). Camões resembles Vicente in his comic techniques as well as in his use of anachronism, but he is essentially a transitional author, coming between Portugal's first playwright and the Renaissance "theatre to be read." *See* CAMÕES, LUIS DE.

Many plays were heavily censored by the Inquisition and the church. Some of Vicente's plays and others, including chapbook plays, were undoubtedly lost owing to this censorship. The Inquisition and the church also extended their prohibitions to theatrical performances. Another factor was the court's loss of interest before the drama had established itself elsewhere.

SEVENTEENTH CENTURY

Theatrical productions flourished in seventeenth-century Portugal, but at the same time native drama was almost nonexistent. The only important Portuguese play was *The Apprentice Hidalgo* (*O fidalgo aprendiz*, ca. 1646) by Francisco Manuel de Melo (1608–1666). This farce in three acts is very interesting for its dramatic composition, for the suitability of the dialogue, and for the characterization of the personages. Many other dramatists tried to write plays in Portuguese or Spanish for the ambulatory theatres of the provinces, but none of their works have survived. Among these no longer extant works are the religious dramas of the mulatto cleric Antão Pires Gonge; the twenty-four *entremeses* published in Coimbra by Manuel Coelho Rebelo in 1658 under the title *Musa entretenida de varios entremezes*; and *Play of Birth of Christ* (*Auto del nascimento de Cristo*) by Francisco Rodrigues Lobo. Francisco Manuel de Melo's play was popular, but it failed to revive vernacular drama in Portugal.

In the Jesuit colleges elaborate dramatic productions were used for teaching purposes. At the University of Évora as well as at the colleges maintained by the society in Lisbon, Coimbra, and Braga, the Jesuits produced theatrical works in Latin based on Biblical passages and classical in form. For more than two hundred years the theatre of the Jesuits flooded the Portuguese-speaking countries. Classical themes and constructions were used in many tragicomedies, comedies, ecologues, and musical dramas.

EIGHTEENTH CENTURY

In contrast to the lack of interest in drama which characterized Portugal in the seventeenth century, the succeeding period showed an extraordinary development of theatrical activity. The Cord Theatre (Teatro de Cordel) was so called because the plays were printed in pamphlet form and suspended on cords in the newstands for sale to the public. Hundreds of comedies, farces, and interludes, including adaptations and translations, were published and performed. In 1756, the Arcádia Lusitana Society was founded. One of its principal objectives was to return theatre to an active state rather than limit it to mere literature.

Slowly the influence of the Spanish theatre disappeared and was replaced by Italian opera, by melodrama, and by the French classical theatre. Whereas in 1606 writers were translating Lope de Vega's *New Art of Making Plays* and Boileau's *L'art poétique*, in 1697 they were translating the plays of Goldoni, Maffei, Chiari or Molière, Corneille, Racine, and, later, Voltaire. The Portuguese writers adapted these to Portuguese taste and substituted them for Calderón, Lope, and Tirso on the stages of Lisbon.

Francisco Manuel de Melo's *The Apprentice Hidalgo* **as staged in 1966 by A. M. Couto Viana. [Portuguese National Tourist Office]**

During the eighteenth century the professional standing of the actor evolved until it was officially established in 1771 by the Marquis of Pombal. Queen Maria I forbade the participation of women in public performances, but this was revoked in 1800 at the request of the actor Antonio José de Paula, then impresario of the theatre in the Rua dos Condes.

Antonio José da Silva, a Jew, was the most important dramatist between Gil Vicente and João Baptista de Almeida Garrett (1799–1854). Born in Rio de Janeiro in 1705, he was burned at the stake by the Inquisition in 1739 "because of Jewish errors." His first play, *Life of the Great Don Quixote and of the Fat Sancho Panza (Vida do Grande Don Quixote e do Gordo Sancho Panza),* was presented with puppets "made of painted cork moved by wires" in 1733. He used episodes from Cervantes, probably others from an *entremez* by Nuno Nisceno Sutil, and some of his own ideas to produce a more narrative than dramatic play. He also wrote *The Life of Aesop (A vida de Esopo,* 1734), *The Enchantment of Medea (Os encantos de Medeia,* 1735), *Jupiter and Alcmena (Jupiter e Alcmena,* 1736), *The Varieties of Proteus (Variedades de Proteu), Wars of Alecrim and of Manjerona (As guerras do Alecrim e da Manjerona,* 1737), and *Fall of Phaeton (Precipio de Faetonte,* 1738). With the exception of *The Life of Aesop* and *Wars of Alecrim and of Manjerona,* all of his dramas were on mythological themes. *See* SILVA, ANTONIO JOSÉ DA.

NINETEENTH CENTURY

There was not a great difference between the historical dramas of Garrett and the romantic melodramas which dominated the Lisbon stages for the next fifty years of the nineteenth century. Garrett inspired playwrights to use historical material with certain modern psychological interpretations. His imitators limited themselves to developing certain exterior and marginal aspects of Garrett's work to create subgenres vitiated by an intense patriotic nationalism and conditioned by a formula which they attributed to Victor Hugo and Alexandre Dumas *père*. Moreover, from a limited interpretation of the aesthetics of Victor Hugo the Portuguese romantics acquired a vision of the universe in which good and evil were systematically separated. The writers offered the theatre inflexible characters, models of truculence, and boring wordiness. *See* GARRETT, JOÃO BAPTISTA DE ALMEIDA.

The first romantic drama written by José da Silva Mendes Leal (1818–1886) was *The Two Renegades (Os dois renegados,* 1839). In his prologue he wrote: "The dramatic poet must elevate himself, as the cedar of Lebanon, among the trees of our forests. God placed Virtue in his right hand and Vice in his left; he must fling both at the multitude; Vice in all its turpitude; Virtue in all the splendor of its beauty. . . ." His recipe was simple, and animated by the success of *The Two Renegades*. Mendes Leal continued to write one melodrama after another: *The Man in the Black Mask (O homem da máscara negra,* 1840), *The Page of Aljubarrota (O pajem de Aljubarrota,* 1846), *The First Loves of Bocage (Os primeiros amores de Bocage,* 1865), and others.

Then times changed. Costa Cabral left the dictatorship, and the country was evolving toward a liberal, democratic regime, in which climate the ultraromantic dramas were out of style. Mendes Leal realized this. He had one hand in politics, where he was a Cabralista, and another in literature. He knew how to play his cards right and created around his person an aura of interest and sympathy which assured the success of each new play. When the historical formula seemed exhausted, Mendes Leal felt the moment had arrived to play the social card. He began to write thesis dramas, such as *Pedro* (1849), *Men of Marble (Homens de marmore,* 1854), and *Shameful Poverty (Pobreza envergonhada,* 1857). He also wrote comedies of manners, the so-called comedy-dramas, in which the great passions of the romantic drama were replaced by more tender feelings, and the characters no longer came from a heroic and mysterious past, but from the present and the bourgeoisie.

There were many dramatists in this period who followed the artistic and patriotic appeal of Garrett: Antonio da Silva Abranches (1810–1868), who wrote *Captive of the Fez (Cativo de Fez,* 1841) inspired by the story of Friar Luis de Sousa; Joao de Andrade Corvo (1824–1890), author of *Maria Teles;* José Freire de Serpa Pimentel (1814–1870), writer of cataclysmic dramas, such as *Almansor Aben-Afan, The Last King of Algarve (O Almansor Aben-Afan, último rei do Algarve,* 1840); Pedro Sousa de Macedo (1821–1901), who started writing plays at the age of twenty with *The Two Champions or The Court of D. João I (Os dois campeões ou a corte de D. João I,* 1841).

By the middle of the nineteenth century every writer in Portugal seemed interested in writing romantic histo-

Lisbon's Maria Vitoria National Theatre has for many years been a major center for Portuguese drama. [Portuguese National Tourist Office]

The São Carlos Opera House in Lisbon is a rare
example of eighteenth-century theatrical architecture.
[Portuguese National Tourist Office]

rical dramas, including the novelists Alexandre Herculano (1810–1877), Júlio Dinis (1839–1871), Rodrigo Pagan-
ino (1835–1863), João de Lemos (1819–1890), and finally
Camilo Castelo Branco (1825–1890), the most imaginative
and in a certain sense, the most authentic of the Portuguese novelists. These writers almost always wrote historical dramas, such as *The Frontier of Africa (O Fronteiro
de África)* by Herculano, and *Agostinho de Ceuta,* by Castelo Branco.

The theatre between 1850 and 1860 was saturated
with historical plays, and the public tried to find relief in
comic opera and operetta. As one critic, Andrade Ferreira, wrote, "The historical drama has become the night-
mare of our theatres." It was necessary to do something
and there were two choices: parody or the new social
realism. The first reaction was in a certain way easier,
but it did not produce lasting works. Parody and thesis
drama were essayed by Francisco Gomes de Amorim
(1827–1891), who wrote *Courage of the Tiger (Fígados de
tigre,* 1857), a parody of melodrama.

The public responded well and parodies inundated
the Portuguese theatres. Even the writers of ultraromantic dramas turned to parody. For example, Francisco
Palha (1862–1890), founder and impresario of the Teatro
da Trinidade, put together a volume of parodies called
Parodias (1859). Besides parodies, many highly polemic
pieces appeared. In 1860 one of the greatest successes
was Castelo Branco's *The Heir of Fafe in Lisbon (O morgado
de Fafe em Lisboa),* a satire about a hidalgo from the province who finds himself in Lisbon.

The social note already touched on by Mendes Leal
became the background of many plays during the second
half of the nineteenth century. The literary winds from
Europe came to Portugal with the "generation of the
1870"—writers who were proponents of "good sense
and good taste in literature." In the Casino de Lisboa
they declared war on the old mentors of national culture.
Among them were Eça de Queirós, Ramalho Ortigão,
Olveira Martins, Antero de Quental, and Teófilo Braga,
but none were dramatists; hence the breath of European
change which benefited Portuguese fiction had little effect on the national theatre repertory. Thus, neglected by
the reformers, the theatre continued as before. While the
literary men of the 1870 generation were anticlerical re-
publicans and socialists, and the literary revolution they
espoused was effected in the name of realism and naturalism, the dramatists continued to be anchored to romantic and social plays.

By the end of the nineteenth century the new aesthetic movements in Europe had reacted violently to positivism. Positivism reached Portugal by the 1890s, and
when it became inadequate, Parnassianism and symbolism were blended with it to form new models. It is not
easy to determine the extent of the influences, since the
new European movements arrived in Portugal fifty years
late and were mixed with cultural elements of previous

waves. The French symbolist poets Charles Baudelaire (1821–1867) and Paul Verlaine (1844–1896) influenced in turn the same authors and schools. The program of "art for art's sake" present in decadentism would turn later to new relationships and emblematic values in symbolism. Maurice Maeterlinck was the writer most revered by the Portuguese symbolists. Representative of the first symbolist theatre in Portugal were the dramatists Eugénio de Castro (1869–1944), Fernando Pessoa (1888–1935), António Patrício (1878–1930), and Raul Brandão (1867–1930). *See* Maeterlinck, Maurice. *See also* Symbolism in glossary.

Twentieth Century

The dramatic texts of Eugénio de Castro are works of sensational symbolism in which the sound is always much more important than the story narrated. His four symbolist plays, written in the 1890s and the first decade of the new century, are *The Eyes of Illusion* (*Os olhos da ilusão*, 1896); *Sagramor* (1895), dealing with Faustian ambitions and preoccupations; *King Galaor* (*O Rei Galaor*, 1897), the story of a morbid king; and *Belkiss* (1894), an evocation of the Oriental world of the Queen of Saba, Axum, and Himiar. After that, the symbolism seems to have vanished from the work of Eugénio de Castro, although the magic and affected language remained.

In a certain sense the theatre of Fernando Pessoa fits within the symbolist experience. The modern Portuguese poet conceived and structured all his literary work as an immense drama. In spite of that, his contribution to the theatre was small: a one-act symbolist play, *The Sailor* (*O marinheiro*), written in 1913 and published in 1915 in the first issue of the modernist magazine *Orpheu*; a fragmentary *First Faust* (*Primeiro Fausto*, 1908); and outlines of several other pieces in prose. *The Sailor* was the war cry of Portuguese modernism. Pessoa called it a "static drama" and believed that it surpassed the real symbolist theatre on which he modeled it. He said: "I call static theatre the one whose dramatic plot does not constitute action—that is, where the figures not only don't move, but don't even have feelings capable of producing an action. . . . There must be revelation of souls without action, and creation of situations of inertia, moments for the soul without windows or doors to reality." The influence of Maeterlinck in *The Sailor* is evident. The action, purely verbal, is born and develops through the dialogue of three characters—young women who watch over the body of a dead woman in a room of an ancient castle. Seated facing the window and immobile for the entire duration of the spectacle, the women evoke "a past which hadn't happened." From the dream emerges the fiction of a sailor lost on a distant island.

The best example of the return to classicism was Eugénio de Castro's dramatic poem *Constance* (*Constança*, 1900), in which the author utilized the theme of King Pedro and his beloved Inês. His *The Ring of Policrates* (*O anel de Polícrates*, 1896) is also classical in form but is poetically of lesser quality. *The Prodigal Son* (*O filho prodigo*, 1910) follows the example of *Sagramor* in exploring the morality of the 1500s.

Like Castro, António Patrício (1878–1950) began his career under the sign of symbolism. His itinerant existence as a diplomat enriched his work with cosmopolitan experiences, a pantheistic mysticism, and the literature of the decadents. He was an over-refined narrator who left few dramatic pieces: *The End* (*O fim*, 1909); the dramatic poem *Pedro, o Cru* (1918), once more about King Pedro and Inês; a "story of spring" entitled *Dinis and Isabel* (*Dinis e Isabel*, 1919); and the tragic fable *Don Juan and the Mask* (*D. João e a máscara*, 1924), about that eternal seducer. Don João oscillates between love and death, and the Portuguese interpretation of death. In Patrício's version of the tale, Don Juan's desire for death becomes almost a religion. Patrício's words, like Castro's, are extremely plastic, sonorous, and allusive; and his verses have great musicality in their play of internal rhymes and assonances.

Some dramatists were associated with the literary group known as Orpheu, which published a magazine by that name. In 1915 this group initiated Portuguese modernism. Among the playwrights in the group were Teixeira de Pascoais, Fernando Pessoa, Jaime Cortesão, and José de Almada Negreiros.

Before their experience with modernism, some of the members of Orpheu had already passed through a period of *saudosismo*, a feeling of national nostalgia or mystical patriotism, which was to mark Portuguese literature profoundly in the first thirty years of the twentieth century; however, it had more influence on lyric poetry than on the novel or the theatre. Teixeira de Pascoais (1877–1952), chief exponent of the movement, had only casual and sporadic contacts with the theatre. Raul Brandão had him as a collaborator on *Jesus Christ in Lisbon* (*Jesus Cristo em Lisboa*, 1924), a Dostoievskian fantasy. Pascoais wote only one other piece for the theatre—the dramatic poem *D. Carlos* (1925).

Jaime Cortesão (1884–1960), another *saudosista*, had greater interest in the theatre. His first dramatic pieces assumed the form of neoromantic historical dramas, as in *The Prince of Sagres* (*Infante de Sagres*, 1916). After World War I he became profoundly interested in social problems, and turned to writing satire, such as *Adam and Eve* (*Adão e Eva*, 1921).

José de Almada Negreiros (1893–   ) was an artist before turning to poetry and drama. His theatre was dissociated from any type of intellectualism, and he maintained an ingenuous and elementary expression by "reinventing" each word. Almada Negreiros considered the theatre a figurative art, and he created amusing spectacles, such as the plays *Before Beginning* (*Antes de começar*, 1919), the dialogue *Pierrot and Arlequim* (1924), and the musical comedies *Make Yourself Desirable, Woman* (*Deseja-se mulher*, 1928) and *S.O.S. Theatre in Three Acts* (*S.O.S. teatro em tres actos*, 1929).

Between the two world wars the theatre gradually turned toward realism and became involved in social and cultural ferment. Historical drama had given playwrights the sense of social criticism, and the realistic themes became tinged with psychological aspects. Examples of this theatre are the works of Vasco de Mendonça Alves, Car-

Tá-Mar by Alfredo Cortês, as produced in 1936. [Portuguese National Tourist Office]

los Selvagem, and Amilcar Ramada Curto.

Vasco de Mendonça Alves (1883–1963) became known for his historical pieces, such as *The Conspirator* (*A Conspiradora*, 1913), but after World War I he began to write comedies of manners and moralistic middle-class dramas. He was particularly successful with *My Love is Treacherous* (*Meu amor e traiçoeiro*, 1935), a picture of Lisbon life painted with a vague populism and illuminated by lively dialogue; *The Street Door* (*A porta da rua*, 1943); and *Lost in the World* (*Perdida no mundo*, 1946).

In 1917 Carlos Selvagem (1890–   ) produced his *Midst the Broom* (*Entre giestas*), a rural drama. He was also interested in psychological investigation, as was revealed in his later plays, such as *Child of Eagles* (*Ninho de aguias*, 1920), and in African dramas, such as *Telmo, or the Adventurer* (*Telmo, o aventureiro*, 1937). In 1944 Selvagem turned to farce, inserting certain Portuguese ingredients into the Spanish myth of Don Quixote. His *Dulcinea or the Last Adventure of D. Quixote* (*A Dulcineia ou a ultima aventura de D. Quixote*) transports the Knight of the Sad Figure to the island of Tristiania, a "cidade esquemática" governed by tyranny. There the idealistic efforts of Don Quixote fail as he is not able to install a reign of love and justice. But quixoticism does not die since the idea gains followers among his own enemies, thus saving dreams and hopes from defeat. Notable

among Selvagem's later plays is the comedy *Farce of Love* (*Farsa do amor*, 1951), written in collaboration with Henrique Galvão (1895–   ), author in his own right of African dramas and comedies of customs, such as *Comedy of Death and Life* (*Comedia da morte e da vida*, 1950).

Amilcar Ramada Curto (1886–1961), had a good knowledge of theatrical technique. His theatre oscillates between the grotesque of Raul Brandão and satire. To those who accused Ramada Curto of conforming to middle-class values, he replied that his theatre did not have moralistic implications, but only served to photograph life. Nevertheless, under the photographic realism of Ramada Curto is hidden a whole series of preconcepts which suggest sympathy with certain characters, even though they may be irregular elements of society. Such is the case with *The Man Who Compromised Himself* (*O homem que se arranjou*, 1928), the story of a government official whom all respect because they believe him corrupt, and who on the contrary is such an honest person that he cannot arrange for a place in a sanatorium for his sick daughter. The theatrical work of Ramada Curto maintained itself on a decorous commercial level from 1905 to 1956. His thirty-six plays are imposing for the variety of their dramatic motives.

The successors to the Orpheu generation were the members of another literary group which took its name from the magazine *Presenca*, published in Coimbra from 1927 to 1940. The principal collaborators of *Presenca* were Branquinho da Fonseca, João Gaspar Simões, José Régio, Antonio Botto, and Miguel Torga. Their theatrical endeavors were more or less consequential, although once again the interests of the group were principally lyric or narrative, not dramatic. The *Presenca* group proposed the critical diffusion and the "deprovincialization" of Portuguese culture, and the writers tried to get away from the influence of the *saudosistas*.

José Régio was the most authentic dramatic writer of the *Presenca* group. He published his mystery *Jacob and the Angel (Jacob e o anjo)* in 1937. Several years later his first volume of plays, *Three Masks (Tres máscaras)* appeared. Many of his plays have not been staged because of censorship, although they have been published, as have his criticism and articles on dramatic theory. *See* RÉGIO, JOSÉ.

In 1929 the National Theatre company led by the actors Amélia Rey-Colaço and Robles Monteiro began a very discreet work of renovation, although they continued to put on light, so-called "boulevard" dramas. In the 1930s the performance of *Gladiators (Gladiadores*, 1934) by Alfrêdo Cortês and the staging of some classical works, like those of Ferreira Castro, and of Gil Vicente's *Amadis of Gaul (Amadis de Gaula)* stood out. In the early 1940s the performance of Eugene O'Neill's *Mourning Becomes Electra*, Hauptmann's *Assumption of Joan*, and Carlos Selvagem's *Dulcinea, or Don Quíxote's Last Adventure*, with staging by Almada Negreiros and music by Ernesto Halffter, showed that the development of the National Theatre was beginning to gather momentum. A further contribution was made in 1944 by the formation of the company called Comediantes de Lisboa. Under Francisco Ribeiro the company introduced foreign playwrights such as Giraudoux, Shaw, and Tolstoy to the Portuguese public. They also performed Alfredo Cortês's *Lipstick (Baton)*. *See* CORTÊS, ALFREDO.

Portuguese drama was updated by the immediate post-World War II generation. Theatre had been paralyzed by outdated structures and other hindrances,

which had prevented it from being a "public mirror," as Molière had referred to it. The first sign of change came in 1946 with the creation of an experimental theatre, the Teatro-Estudio Salitre. Its purpose was expressed in the "manifesto" distributed at its first performance. This was "to recover the rhythm, the style, the poetry of acting in the words of the text, in the actors' gestures, in the groups, in the colors, in the whole atmosphere of stage performance, which had been distorted through long years of submission to a naturalistic aesthetic which, once released from its initial revolutionary impact, was no longer capable of satisfying the interests of a new public."

The Teatro-Estudio Salitre, installed in the rooms of the Italian Cultural Institute, gave its first performance in April 1946. The desire for a different kind of interpretation and performance of drama was already evident. The Salitre company soon inspired other groups, such as the Casa da Comédias, the Modern Drama Group of the Faculty of Letters of Lisbon, the Companheiros do Patio das Comédias, and the companies directed by Manuela Porto and Pedro Bom.

The Teatro-Estudio Salitre brought a practical, active awareness of the need for change. Among those whose work and example opened the way for this movement were the playwrights Raul Brandão and Alfredo Cortês—the first for the existential anguish underlying all of his plays and the second for the rigor of his social criticism, which ventures into hitherto unexplored regions of expressionism. Some writers, such as Almada Negreiros, Branquinho da Fonseca, João Pedro de Andrade, and José Régio, who had previously published their plays in books and magazines, finally saw them reach the stages of the Teatro-Estudio Salitre and the National Theatre. *See* BRANDÃO, RAUL.

A basic role in the experimental revolution was played by the painter Antonio Pedro, who in 1948 joined the group called Companheiros do Patio das Comédias, and in 1953 began to lead the Oporto Experimental Theatre. Few directors find themselves able to do without scenographers. Julio Resende, Arthur Bual, Relogio, João Abel Mante, João Vieira, Sá Nogueira, Espiga Pinto, Augusto Gomes, Fernando Azevedo, Noronha de Costa, Lagoa Henriques, Antonio Alfredo, Paulo Guilherme, and José Rodrigues Vespeira, to mention a few, have created decors to which performances owe much of their dramatic effectiveness.

Modern Portuguese theatre is characterized by experimentalism. Small theatres such as the Teatro-Estudio Salitre, the Patio das Comédias, and the Teatro Experimental de Pedro Bom opened between 1946 and 1953. All of these groups have given contemporary Portuguese theatre a special character: however, what the Portuguese theatre needed and continued to need, according to Stegagno Picchio, was "pure air, different voices, new themes and spirit."

The university groups of Coimbra and Oporto, guardians of an academic tradition dating from the sixteenth century, reworked and modernized the classics of the national repertory and presented foreign plays as

João Agonia's Sin by Bernardo Santareno as staged by Rogério Paulo for the Teatro Capitólio in 1969.
[Portuguese National Tourist Office]

Prista Monteiro's *The Fiddle* as staged in
1961 by Luís de Lima for Coimbra's CITAC.
[Portuguese National Tourist Office]

well. The little theatres in Lisbon and Oporto spoke the new language of a Thornton Wilder, an Arthur Miller, or a Samuel Beckett. The little theatres served as pulpit and public meeting places. It did not matter that their programs were often in confusion, their repertories heterogeneous or contradictory, and almost all of them ephemeral and limited to small audiences. Their ultimate function was to restore literary and artistic dignity to the theatre, to educate a small but more conscious public, and to stimulate dramatic vocations. Those objectives were attained. Almost all of the new generation of Portuguese dramatists came from the experimental groups: Alves Redol (1911–   ), Rodrigo de Melo, Pedro Bom (1914–   ), Luíz Francisco Rebello (1924–   ), Carlos Montanha, and David Mourão-Ferreira from the Salitre Teatro Estudio, directed by the Italian Gino Saviotti; Costa Ferreira (1918–   ) and Jorge de Sena (1919–   ) from the Patio das Comédias; and Bernardo Santareno (1924–   ) from the Teatro Experimental of Oporto. To these one must add the names, proposals, ambitions, and, many times, the real merit of those who only published texts written for the theatre. Many economic and political reasons made this phenomenon more important in Portugal than in other countries. *See* REBELLO, LUÍZ F.

One can distinguish schools, tendencies, and styles among the new generation of Portuguese dramatists. The postwar generation assimilated Pirandello, O'Neill, García Lorca, and even the lessons of the Brechtian epic theatre. From these sources comes Portuguese neorealism, brought to the Portuguese theatre in about 1950 by Pedro Serodio (1887–1966) and Alves Redol (1911–   ), a vigorous and intellectual narrator concerned with social issues. Another neorealist, Romeu Correia (1917–   ), has introduced into his pieces, and with good results—above all in *The Vagabond with the Hands of Gold (Vagabundo dos maos de ouro*, 1960)—an eclectic experimentalism, with a mixture of expressionism and the somewhat abstract color populism that characterizes a great part of modern Portuguese literature.

Pedro Bom (1914–   ), who came from the Teatro Estudio of Salitre, does not conceive of experimentalism as a tournament of ideas or as a stage for ideologies but, rather, as a means of perfecting the theatre. His goal is a theatre made to please the public, not to correct its defects. It has been said that plays such as *The Girl and the Apple (A menina e a maça*, 1948) and *The Devil Comes Any Time (A qualquer hora o diabo vem*, 1951) are commercial, but this qualification is unjust, since the work of this experimentalist implies that it is part of a legitimate artistic search.

Owing to the postwar activity in the theatre the Portuguese writers felt more and more attracted to writing for the stage. Plays and publications began to appear in greater numbers, the public and the critics became more demanding, and the names and plays of some dramatists created hope and certainty of a renaissance in writing for the theatre. This renaissance started in the 1960s with the appearance of plays by younger dramatists, such as Bernardo Santareno, Augusto Abelaira, José Cardoso Pires, and Luís de Sttau Monteiro.

RUTH S. LAMB

CRITICISM

T. Braga, *Historia do Theatro Português*, 4 vols, Oporto, 1870–1871; J. M. Esteves Pereira, *Monumentos da Litteratura Dramatica Portuguesa*, vol. 2, Lisbon, 1918; A. Forjas de Sampaio, *Subsidios para a História do Teatro Po-*

tuguês: Teatro de Cordel, Lisbon, 1922; J. T. da Silva Bastos, *Historia da Censura Intelectual em Portugal: Ensaio Sobre a Compreensão do Pensamento Português*, Coimbra, 1926; R. B. Williams, "Staging of Early Spanish Plays in Spanish Peninsula Prior to 1555," in *Iowa University Studies*, N. S. no. 289, Dec. 15, 1934, pp. 7–140; A. J. da Costa Pimpão, *O Frei Luis de Sousa de Almeida Garrett*, in *Biblos*, 16, Coimbra, 1940; A. Crabbe Rocha, *O Teatro de Garrett*, Coimbra, 1944; J. de Carvalho, *Estudos sobre a Cultura Portuguesa do Século XVI*, vol. 1, Coimbra, 1947; *A Evolução e o Espírito do Teatro em Portugal*, 2 vols., Lisbon, 1947–1948; L. F. Rebello, *Imagens do Teatro Contemporâneo*, Lisbon, 1957, 1961; L. F. Rebello, *Teatro Moderno: Caminhos e Figuras*, Lisbon, 1957; 2d ed., 1966; W. H. Roberts, "Portuguese Theatre de Fauteuil 1945–1955," *Hispania*, 40 (1957), pp. 297–302; J. Gaspar Simões, *Perspectiva da Literatura Portuguesa do Século XIX*, 2 vols., Lisbon, 1959; *Dicionario das Literaturas Portuguesa, Galega e Brasileira*, ed. by J. Prado Coelho, Oporto, 1960; L. F. Rebello, *Teatro Português, do Romanticismo aos Nossos Dias*, Lisbon, 1960; A. J. Saraiva, "A Evolução do teatro de Garrett: Os temas e as formas," in *Para a Historia da Cultura em Portugal*, vol. 2, Lisbon, 1961, pp. 15–62; M. Vilaca, *Panorama do Teatro Português Contemporaneo*, vol. 23, Lisbon, 1963; L. Stegagno Picchio, *Historia do Teatro Português*, Lisbon: Original title: *Storia del Teatro Portoghese*, Rome, 1964; L. F. Rebello, *História do Teatro Português*, 2d ed., Lisbon, 1972; I. Cruz Duarte, *Introdução ao Teatro Português do Século XX (Seguido de una Antología)*, Lisbon, n.d.; L. F. Rebello, *50 anos de Teoria e Pratica do Teatro em Portugal*, Lisbon, n.d.

Potekhin, Aleksey Antipovich   (1829–1908)

Russian playwright and theatre administrator. Potekhin was born on July 1, 1829 (N.S.) and graduated from the Demidov Lyceum in Yaroslavl in 1849. His first play, *The People's Verdict Isn't God's* (*Sud lyudskoy—Ne Bozhiy*, 1853), is a keen if technically naïve condemnation of serfdom; it would certainly have been censored if not for the intercession of the Grand Duke Konstantin Nikolaevich. The play's great success in Moscow in 1854 made Potekhin's reputation, and throughout the 1860s he was known as a leading exponent of liberal causes, and his plays became standard repertory pieces. In the early 1880s he managed the Repertory Division of the Alexandrinsky Theatre in St. Petersburg, became manager of the acting troupes of the Imperial Theatres, and in 1900 was elected a member of the Academy of Sciences.

Potekhin's plays, like those of Ostrovsky, attempt to portray the life of the lower classes and can be divided into two types, dramas of peasant life and comedies of officialdom and provincial society. His peasants tend to be idealized and impossibly noble, as in *A Sheepskin Coat, but a Human Heart* (*Shuba ovechya, dusha chelovechya*, 1854), in which a valiant muzhik defends his sister's honor against all comers. But in the character Mishenka, in *Another's Goods Do Me No Good* (*Chuzhoe dobro vprok ne idyot*, 1855), he invented a weak-willed, expansive, more psychologically complex peasant, a character which became a model for later dramas. Potekhin's comedies expose bribery in the civil service and the follies of middle-class society. *The Latest Oracle* (*Noveyshiy orakul*, 1858), a sardonic satire on fortune tellers and spiritualists, may have inspired Ostrovsky's *Enough Stupidity for Every Sage* (*The Diary of a Scoundrel*). *See* OSTROVSKY, ALEKSANDR NIKOLAYEVICH.

Potekhin never learned to manage a plot, and his characters are often overdrawn; but his plays provided juicy roles for actors and were often enlivened by colorful language and courageous thrusts at current abuses. He was one of the most popular dramatists of his time.

LAURENCE SENELICK

EDITIONS

Sochineniya Alekseya Potekhina, St. Petersburg, 1873–1874; *Sochineniya A. A. Potekhina*, 12 vols., St. Petersburg, n.d.

CRITICISM

L. A. Lotman, *A. N. Ostrovskiy i russkaya dramaturgiya ego vremeni*, Moscow-Leningrad, 1961; S. Ketchian, *The Plays of Aleksej Potexin* (Ph. D. diss. Harvard University, 1974).

Pradon, Jacques   (1644–1698)

French tragic dramatist. His popularity, in his day, rivaled that of Racine. His first tragedy, *Pyramus and Thisbe* (*Pyrame et Thisbé*, 1673), attracted favorable attention. It seems probable that the aristocratic and literary enemies of Racine considered this fresh new talent an admirable tool to use against the celebrated dramatist. Thus, Pradon's *Phaedra and Hippolytus* (*Phèdre et Hippolyte*) was performed on January 3, 1677, just two days after the premiere of Racine's *Phaedra*. Pradon's play, obviously a partial plagiarism, had been hastily and crudely assembled in three months. Despite its inferiority, *Phaedra and Hippolytus* was initially far more successful than the rival masterpiece—a fact that may have contributed to Racine's sudden retirement from the stage. In the controversy over the two plays, Pradon became involved in an exchange of verses and critiques with the great critic Boileau, who vigorously defended Racine. *See* RACINE, JEAN.

Phaedra and Hippolytus is, in fact, Pradon's weakest play. His others, although far from distinguished, are generally well constructed and eminently playable. Of his seven extant tragedies, *Régulus* (1688), which deals with Roman heroism during the Punic Wars, is the best. Among the others are *Tamburlaine* (*Tamerlan*, 1675), *The Trojan Woman* (*La Troade*, 1679), *Statira* (1679), and *Scipio Africanus* (*Scipion l'Africain*, 1697).

[JOSEPH E. GARREAU]

Praga, Marco   (1862–1929)

Italian writer, critic, and dramatist. He was born in Milan on June 20, 1862. The son of the poet and dramatist Emilio Praga, Marco inherited neither his father's romantic temperament nor his inclination to the irregular bohemian life of the Milanese Scapigliatura (an anticlassical avant-garde literary group). After having completed studies in bookkeeping and accounting, he began to take an interest in writing plays and revealed his natural talent for the theatre in *The Encounter* (*L'incontro*, wr. 1883). *The Friend* (*L'amico*, 1886) made him successful, and he went on to become a theatre administrator and a critic. He was director, then president, and finally councillor of the Italian Society of Authors and Publishers, which he revived financially by obtaining the privilege of taxing public performances as a source of revenue for the organization.

From 1912 to 1915 he headed the important experimental Teatro Manzoni in Milan, forming and directing the group in an only partially realized attempt to renew traditional repertory and scenery for the production of artistically serious plays. He thus became one of the first in Italy to stage the plays of Pirandello. Praga was also, for a short period, general artistic director of Silentium Films of Milan (founded in 1916). From 1919 to 1929 he was drama critic for *L'Illustrazione Italiana*, writing a series of articles that were later published in ten volumes. Praga also wrote sketches, novels, short stories, and libretti in collaboration with Leoncavallo, Oliva, and Luigi Illica and worked with Giacosa and others on the libretto of Puccini's *Manon Lescaut* (1893). He died in Varese on January 31, 1929. *See* GIACOSA, GIUSEPPE.

WORK

Among the Italian realists of the late nineteenth century, Praga stood out principally as a follower of the French mode because of his preoccupation with moral conflict. Despite his reaction against the didacticism of Giacosa and his followers, Praga revealed in his dramas an essentially conventional cast of mind. Although he criticized contemporary society for keeping up appearances to conceal social ills beneath the surface, he was basically conservative: frequently depicting women driven to immorality by the forces of society, he nevertheless disapproved of "fallen women." He was attracted by the social pretensions of the bourgeois world and repeatedly focused in his plays upon the institution of marriage with its often hypocritical role-playing and subterfuges. *See* REALISM in glossary.

His most notable play, which reveals a strong Ibsenite influence, is *The Virgins* (*Le vergini,* 1889). The heroines, ironically called virgins, barter their favors for material rewards. When true love comes to Paolina, she is pressed by an excess of conscience to reveal her former life and in this honest act loses her lover. Having firmly established Praga's reputation, this drama is considered most representative of his notion that true love has a purifying power, that society often confuses immorality and morality, and that morality of the soul cleanses away vice. *See* IBSEN, HENRIK.

Later, Praga struck a satirical note in *The Ideal Wife* (*La moglie ideale,* 1890), in which he depicted a wife who carries on an affair but, out of true fondness for her husband, remains an "ideal wife" by being particularly careful to conceal it. The painful consequence of an affair is the theme of *The Closed Door* (*La porta chiusa,* 1913), in which an illegitimate son breaks away from his overaffectionate mother. Another immoral relationship, treated conventionally, is the basis of *The Moral of the Fable* (*La morale della favola*; wr. 1893, prod. 1899), in which a woman, having yielded to her lover, is psychologically incapable of returning to her husband and children until told by her priest to do so and to atone by living in constant awareness of her sin. Other interesting plays are *Alleluia* (1892), in which a husband punishes his unfaithful wife, finding her responsible for their daughter's immoral ways; and *The Crisis* (*La crisi,* 1904), which portrays Pietro, a weak-willed husband, Nicoletta, his overbearing, faithless wife, and the morally stern brother-in-law Raimondo, who challenges the lover to a duel, thus revealing his brother's weakness.

Marco Praga.
[Italian Cultural
Institute]

The Virgins (*Le vergini,* 1889). Drama of a middle-class family in which three sisters, Nini, Selene, and Paolina, move in an elegant but dissolute circle, seeking only pleasure and enrichment, while their mother tries to maintain the mask of respectability. Only Paolina objects to the loose morals of her sisters and their friends. When she finds true love with Dario and he asks her to marry him, her honesty compels her to tell him of the single incident that long ago marred her purity. As a result, the unfeeling Dario turns against her and suggests that they continue their liaison although he no longer wants her for a wife. Paolina rejects his proposal and thereby loses her chances for happiness. The sisters continue in their dissolute ways, untouched by the scruples of Paolina.

The Closed Door (*La porta chiusa,* 1913). Drama that deals with marriage and the consequences of infidelity. Giulio, before he breaks free from his mother's constricting affection, must admit to her that he knows that he is the son of her former lover. Bianca has long since broken off her relationship with Giulio's real father and has, for the sake of her son, endured her dandy husband, who has treated her with indulgence but not love. Giulio takes his leave, forgiving Bianca but bound to be free of her, promising to return for her when he has made a success for himself in the colonies of East Africa. Bianca sees the justice of her lot and rejects the suggestion that she start life anew with her lover. Alone, she will wait for Giulio to return.

[PETER BONDANELLA]

PLAYS

1. *L'incontro* (The Encounter). Play. Written 1883.
2. (With V. Colombo). *Le due case* (The Two Houses). Play. Produced Milan, Teatro Manzoni, Jan. 11, 1884.
3. *L'amico* (The Friend). Play, 1 act. Written 1886. Published 1893. Produced Milan, Teatro Manzoni, Oct. 25, 1886.
4. *Le vergini* (The Virgins). Play, 4 acts. Written 1889. Published 1890. Produced Milan, Teatro Manzoni, Dec. 16, 1889.

5. *La moglie ideale (The Ideal Wife)*. Play. Written 1890. Published 1891. Produced Turin, Teatro Gerbino, Nov. 11, 1890.

6. *L'innamorata (The Sweetheart)*. Play. Written 1891. Published 1893. Produced Turin, Teatro Carignano, Oct. 5, 1891.

7. *Alleluia*. Play, 1 act. Written 1892. Published 1893. Produced Rome, Teatro Valle, Feb. 19, 1892.

8. *L'incanto (Enchantment)*. Play. Produced Milan, Teatro Filodrammatici, Dec. 9, 1892.

9. *L'erede (The Heir)*. Play. Written 1893. Published 1894. Produced Turin, Teatro Gerbino, December, 1893.

10. *La morale della favola (The Moral of the Fable)*. Play, 1 act. Written 1893. Published 1908. Produced Turin, 1899.

11. *Il bell'Apollo (The Beautiful Apollo)*. Play, 4 acts. Written 1894. Published 1920. Produced Venice, Teatro Goldoni, Dec. 3, 1894.

12. *La mamma (The Mother)*. Play. Produced Turin, Teatro Alfieri, Nov. 19, 1895.

13. *Il dubbio (The Doubt)*. Play, 1 act. Published 1921. Produced Milan, Teatro Manzoni, May 13, 1899.

14. *L'ondina (Undine)*. Play, 4 acts. Written 1903. Published 1920. Produced Turin, Teatro Alfieri, Apr. 24, 1903.

15. *La crisi (The Crisis)*. Play. Written 1904. Published 1905. Produced Turin, Teatro Alfieri, Oct. 24, 1904.

16. *La porta chiusa* (The Closed Door)*. Play. Written 1913. Published 1914. Produced Milan, Teatro Manzoni, Jan. 23, 1913.

17. *Il divorzio (The Divorce)*. Play, 2 acts. Published 1921. Produced Milan, Teatro Manzoni, Apr. 7, 1925.

EDITIONS

The Closed Door. Published in *The Eleonora Duse Series of Plays*, ed. by O. M. Sayler and tr. by A. MacDonald, New York, 1923.

CRITICISM

L. MacClintock, *The Age of Pirandello*, Bloomington, 1951; G. Pullini, *Marco Praga*, Bologna, 1960.

Preston, Thomas   (before 1569–after 1589)

English dramatist. Little is known except that he was the author of *Cambyses, King of Persia* (before 1570), a tragedy that mixes passionate rhetoric with broad comedy.

Cambyses, King of Persia (before 1570). Bombastic verse play, half allegory and half chronicle, that relates the sordid history of the vices, murders, and treachery of Cambyses, King of Persia, in the sixth century B.C., and introducing the popular stock figure of the "Vice," here called Ambidexter. While commenting on the action, Ambidexter also instigates it by corrupting Sisamnes, Lord Deputy of Persia, during Cambyses' absence from the country. On the monarch's return, Sisamnes, condemned for his corruption, is flayed before his son's eyes. When Cambyses' just councillor Praxaspes urges his king to renounce vice and intemperance, the cruel tyrant proves his sobriety by shooting an arrow into the heart of Praxaspes' son. Crimes and vices mount until Cambyses, smitten with incestuous love for a kinswoman and infuriated by her rejection, orders her execution. He is accidentally killed by his own sword.

Priestley, J[ohn] B[oynton]   (1894–   )

English dramatist, novelist, and essayist. John Boynton Priestley was born in Bradford on September 13, 1894, the son of a schoolmaster. In World War I he enlisted in the infantry, working his way up from the ranks to become a commissioned officer, and was wounded in action three times. After the war he attended Cambridge University, where he took honors in English literature, modern history, and political science. Since the age of sixteen he had been writing steadily, contributing articles to London and provincial newspapers, and the money

J. B. Priestley. [Raymond Mander and Joe Mitchenson Theatre Collection]

he earned helped put him through the university. In 1918 he published a volume of verse entitled *The Chapman of Rhymes* and, in 1922, *Brief Diversions*, both written while he was still at Cambridge.

In 1922 Priestley arrived in London and established himself as a reviewer and critic. His first real success came in 1929 with the novel *The Good Companions*; in all, he has written more than twenty novels. Having established himself as a novelist, he began a new career as a dramatist, in 1931 when he collaborated with Edward Knoblock in adapting *The Good Companions*, and in 1932 when he wrote *Dangerous Corner*. Since then some thirty of his plays have been produced, and he has managed his own company and directed two of London's theatres. He is also a prolific writer of essays and miscellaneous prose.

During World War II, Priestley became popular as a radio broadcaster with his series "Postscripts." He has represented his country as chairman of two international theatre conferences, in Paris and Prague, has been chairman of the British Theatre Conference, and has served as director of the weekly *New Statesman and Nation*.

Priestley's first wife, Patricia Tempest, died in 1925, leaving two daughters. Later on he married Mrs. Mary Wyndham Lewis, with whom he had three daughters and a son. In 1953 he married the author Jacquetta Hawkes.

WORK

Although most British dramatists of the 1930s were content to write realistic drawing-room drama, Priestley, while dabbling with established formulas, was ready to experiment outside realism. His plays, in fact, range from the country farce and horseplay of *When We Are Married* (1938) to the nonrealistic allegory of *Johnson over Jordan* (1939).

His first real success was *Dangerous Corner* (1932), a psychological melodrama that returns in the end to the point at which it began. This so-called time-continuum technique, in which the present seems to merge with the past held Priestley's interest. *Time and the Conways* (1937), *I Have Been Here Before* (1937), and *An Inspector Calls*

(1946) are all explorations into the nature of time. Priestley was influenced by the time-theories of J. W. Dunne and P. D. Ouspensky; characters from another time scale descend upon the scene with unpleasant truths, and the unconscious is explored.

Laburnum Grove (1933) is a conventional comedy drama of lower-middle-class English suburbia. *Eden End* (1934) attempts to reproduce the atmosphere of the theatre at the turn of the century but is not effective. *Duet in Floodlight* and *Cornelius,* both written and produced in 1935, are pedestrian pieces, but the latter holds some technical interest. *Bees on the Boat Deck* (1936) explores capital and labor in a combination of fantasy and comedy.

Other plays include *Music at Night* (1938), in which Priestley tried to show the effects of music on people's minds and emotions; *The Long Mirror* (1940), which depicts an extrasensory relation between a girl and a man; and *Goodnight Children* (1942), a satire on the BBC. *They Came to a City* (1943) and *Desert Highway* (1944) deal with the impact of World War II; in the former Priestley proclaimed concern for the formation of a better world, and in the latter he depicted the reactions of a group of British soldiers. His last produced play, *A Severed Head* (1963), written in collaboration with Iris Murdoch, was an adaptation of her novel. J. B. Priestley's reputation as a dramatist rests largely on the fact that he trod where others had not ventured before.

Dangerous Corner (1932). Prompted by an offhand remark concerning a cigarette box, a gathering of friends in the country home of Robert Chatfield begin a chain of disclosures and confessions, each linked to the next and

Scene from *Time and the Conways.* London, Duchess Theatre, 1937. [Raymond Mander and Joe Mitchenson Theatre Collection]

Thomas Mitchell and Rene Ray in *An Inspector Calls.* New York, Booth Theatre, 1947. [Photograph by Vandamm. Theatre Collection, The New York Public Library at Lincoln Center, Astor, Lenox and Tilden Foundations]

leading to a shattering revelation of the causes behind the supposed suicide of Robert's eccentric brother months before. Theft, infidelity, homosexuality, and narcotics are gradually revealed as inextricably woven into the fabric of events. Switching back to the moment before the cigarette-box remark, the play concludes with the undisturbed tranquillity and hypocrisy that prevail when the error is not made and the chain never begun.

Laburnum Grove (1923). The quintessence of solid, dull London suburbia is the setting for this "immoral comedy in three acts." Respectable, boring George Radfern suddenly informs his restless daughter and her spineless suitor, together with his sponging sister-in-law and her husband, that, unbeknown to them and his wife, he has for some time been a member of an international counterfeiting ring. Understandably disturbed, the others are relieved when Mrs. Radfern tells them that it couldn't possibly be true and that George was making a joke. Though allowing them all to believe he invented the story, George was actually telling the truth, and after a close call with a Scotland Yard inspector, he suspends operations and happily departs with his wife and daughter on a lengthy world trip.

Time and the Conways (1937). The play begins on an autumn night in 1919, the twenty-first birthday of Kay, second-eldest daughter of the Conways. The other six members of the family and some close friends celebrate the occasion in joyous, youthful high spirits. Kay, an aspiring novelist, watches her little world acting and reacting in a game of charades and then lapses into a private reverie. Act II shifts to the same room twenty years later, dramatizing Kay's vision in a chilling atmosphere of unfulfilled dreams and vicious quarreling, the same characters all having failed in life and love. Kay is consoled by her gentle brother Alan, who points out, with William Blake, that "Man was made for joy and woe." Act III reverts to the birthday party, with Mrs. Conway prophesying a warm and cosy future for her children and all save Kay unaware of coming disasters.

I Have Been Here Before, with (l. to r.) Lydia Sherwood, Ernst Deutsch, and Eric Portman. New York, Guild Theatre, 1938. [Photograph by Vandamm. Theatre Collection, The New York Public Library at Lincoln Center, Astor, Lenox and Tilden Foundations]

An Inspector Calls (1946). Intricate metaphysical drama that investigates the responsibility each person bears for all others in the far-reaching causal chain of events. Living in England under the growing threat of World War I, the members of the wealthy and complacent Birling family spend a harrowing evening when the daughter's engagement party is interrupted by the sudden arrival of Inspector Goole, an enigmatic, moralistic figure who informs them that a pregnant girl has just committed suicide. With relentless, probing questioning, he reveals that each of them was acquainted with her and each helped drive her to her death, and must all therefore share the guilt. On his departure they discover that there is no Inspector Goole on the police force and are momentarily elated, but a telephone call informs them that a girl has just committed suicide and that an inspector is coming to ask questions.

PLAYS

Unless otherwise noted, the plays were first performed in London.

1. (With Edward Knoblock). *The Good Companions.* Play, 2 acts. Published 1935. Produced His Majesty's Theatre, May 14, 1931.
2. *Dangerous Corner.* Play, 3 acts. Published 1932. Produced London, Lyric Theatre, May 17, 1932; New York, Empire Theatre, Oct. 27, 1932.
3. *The Roundabout.* Comedy, 3 acts. Published 1933. Produced Liverpool, Playhouse, Dec. 14, 1932.
4. *Laburnum Grove.* Immoral comedy, 3 acts. Published 1934. Produced Duchess Theatre, Nov. 28. 1933.
5. *Eden End.* Play, 3 acts. Published 1934. Produced Duchess Theatre, Sept. 13, 1934.
6. *Duet in Floodlight.* Comedy. Published 1935. Produced Liverpool, Playhouse, Feb. 13, 1935; London, Apollo Theatre, June 4, 1935.
7. *Cornelius.* Business affair in 3 transactions. Published 1935. Produced Birmingham, Theatre Royal, Mar. 11, 1935; London, Duchess Theatre, Mar. 20, 1935.
8. *Bees on the Boat Deck.* Farcical tragedy, 2 acts. Published 1936. Produced Lyric Theatre, May 5, 1936.
9. (With George Billam). *Spring Tide.* Comedy, 3 acts. Published 1936. Produced Duchess Theatre, July 15, 1936.
10. *Time and the Conways.* Play, 3 acts. Published 1937. Produced Duchess Theatre, Aug. 26, 1937.
11. *Bad Samaritan.* Play. Produced 1937.
12. *I'm a Stranger Here.* Play. Produced 1937.
13. *I Have Been Here Before.* Play, 3 acts. Published 1937. Produced Royalty Theatre, Sept. 22, 1937.
14. *People at Sea.* Play, 3 acts. Published 1937. Produced Apollo Theatre, Nov. 24, 1937.
15. *Mystery at Greenfingers.* Comedy of detection, 3 acts. Published 1938. Produced Fortune Theatre, Jan. 18, 1938.
16. *Music at Night.* Play, 3 acts. Published 1947. Produced Malvern, Festival Theatre, April, 1938; London, Westminster Theatre, Oct. 10, 1939.
17. *When We Are Married.* Yorkshire farcical comedy. 3 acts. Published 1938. Produced St. Martin's Theatre, Oct. 11, 1938.
18. *Johnson over Jordan.* Play, 3 acts. Published 1939. Produced New Theatre, Feb. 22, 1939.
19. *The Long Mirror.* Play, 3 acts. Published 1940. Produced Oxford, Playhouse, March, 1940; London, Gateway Theatre, Nov. 6, 1945.
20. *Goodnight Children.* Comedy on broadcasting, 3 acts. Published 1942. Produced New Theatre, Feb. 5, 1942.
21. *They Came to a City.* Play, 2 acts. Published 1944. Produced Globe Theatre, Apr. 21, 1943.
22. *Desert Highway.* Play, 3 acts. Published 1944. Produced Playhouse, Feb. 10, 1944.
23. *How Are They at Home?* Topical comedy, 2 acts. Published 1944. Produced Apollo Theatre, May 4, 1944.
24. *The Golden Fleece.* Comedy, 3 acts. Published 1948. Produced Bradford, Civic Theatre, 1944.
25. *Jenny Villiers.* Play. Produced Bristol, Theatre Royal, March, 1946.
26. *Ever since Paradise.* Discursive entertainment, chiefly referring to love and marriage, 3 acts. Published 1950. Produced Sheffield, Lyceum Theatre, Aug. 19, 1946; London, New Theatre, Jan. 4, 1947.
27. *An Inspector Calls.* Play. Published 1947. Produced Manchester,

Opera House, Sept. 9, 1946; London, New Theatre, Oct. 1, 1946.

28. *The Rose and Crown*. Play. Published 1947.

29. *The Linden Tree*. Play, 2 acts. Published 1948. Produced Sheffield, Lyceum Theatre, June 23, 1947; London, Duchess Theatre, Aug. 15, 1947.

30. *The High Toby*. Play for the toy theatre, 3 acts. Published 1948.

31. *Home Is Tomorrow*. Play. Published 1949. Produced Cambridge Theatre, Nov. 4, 1948.

32. *The Olympians*. Play. Published 1949.

33. *Summer Day's Dream*. Play, 2 acts. Published 1950. Produced St. Martin's Theatre, Sept. 8, 1949.

34. *Bright Shadow*. Play of detection, 3 acts. Published 1950. Produced Oldham, Coliseum, Apr. 3, 1950; London, Q Theatre, Apr. 25, 1950.

35. *Treasure on Pelican*. Play. Published 1953. Produced King's Theatre, Hammersmith, Feb. 18, 1952.

36. (With Jacquetta Hawkes). *Dragon's Mouth*. Dramatic quartet, 2 parts. Published 1952. Produced Winter Garden Theatre, May 13, 1952.

37. *Try It Again*. Play. Published 1953.

38. *Private Rooms*. Comedy in the Viennese style, 1 act. Published 1953.

39. *Mother's Day*. Play. Published 1953.

40. (With Miss Hawkes). *The White Countess*. Play, produced Saville Theatre, March 24, 1954.

41. *A Glass of Bitter*. Play, 1 act. Published 1954.

42. *The Golden Entry*. Play. Produced 1955.

43. *The Scandalous Affair of Mr. Kettle and Mrs. Moon*. Comedy, 3 acts. Published 1955. Produced Duchess Theatre, Sept. 1, 1955.

44. *Take the Fool Away*. Play. Produced Vienna, Burgtheater, February, 1956; Nottingham, Playhouse, Sept. 28, 1959.

45. *These Our Actors*. Play. Produced Glasgow, Citizens' Theatre, Oct. 1, 1956.

46. *The Glass Cage*. Play, 2 acts. Published 1958. Produced Toronto, Crest Theatre, 1957; London, Piccadilly Theatre, Apr. 26, 1957.

47. *The Thirty-first of June*. Play. Produced Toronto, Crest Theatre, 1957.

48. (With Iris Murdoch). *A Severed Head*. Play. Produced Bristol Old Vic, 1963.

49. *The Pavilion of Masks*. Play. Produced 1963.

EDITIONS

Collections
Plays, 3 vols., London, 1948–1950.
Individual Plays
Cornelius. Published in *Six Plays of Today*, London, 1939.
Dangerous Corner. Published in *Sixteen Famous British Plays*, ed. by B. A. Cerf and V. H. Cartmell, Garden City, N.Y., 1942.
Dragon's Mouth. Published in *The Off-Broadway Theatre*, ed. by R. A. Cordell and L. Matson, New York, 1959.
An Inspector Calls. Published in *Angles of Vision*, ed. by E. Huberman and R. R. Raymo, Boston, 1962.
Laburnum Grove. Published in *Seven Plays*, London, 1935.

CRITICISM

R. Pogson, *J. B. Priestley and the Theatre*, Clevedon, Somerset, 1947; D. Hughes, *J. B. Priestley: An Informal Study of His Work*, London, 1958; G. L. Evans, *J. B. Priestley: The Dramatist*, London, 1964.

Przybyszewska, Stanisława (1901–1935)

Polish dramatist. The illegitimate daughter of the celebrated turn-of-the-century Polish writer Stanisław Przybyszewski, Przybyszewska, who was educated in France and Germany, wrote in the years between 1925 and 1929 a trilogy of plays about the French revolution: *Ninety-three* (*Dziewięćdziesiąty trzeci*, 1969), *The Danton Affair* (*Sprawa Dantona*, 1931), and *Thermidor* (wr. in German, prod. in Polish translation, 1971). Although only *The Danton Affair* was staged in the author's lifetime, since 1967 Przybyszewska's plays have received a number of impressive productions and are now recognized as one of the most significant treatments of the French revolution since Büchner's *Danton's Death* and Romain Rolland's *Theatre of the Revolution*. Remarkable for its vivid psychological portraits, Przybyszewska's trilogy was published for the first time in 1975.   DANIEL GEROULD

Przybyszewski, Stanisław (1868–1927)

Polish dramatist. He was born in Łojewo on May 7, 1868, in what was then Prussian Poland. After attending secondary schools in Thorn (Toruń) and Wągrowiec, he studied architecture in Charlottenburg (Berlin) in 1889. The following year he started to study medicine at the University of Berlin but was forced to abandon his studies in 1893 for having taken part in the workers' movement: he had collaborated on the *Workers' Gazette (Gazeta Robotnicza)*, a Polish-language paper for workers in Germany. Also in 1893, he married a Norwegian girl, Dagny Juel, who was to be murdered in 1901. Przybyszewski spent four years in Norway with his parents-in-law and was influential in making Scandinavian writers like Ibsen and Strindberg popular in Germany—the first stepping-stone to their world fame. His own writings were strongly naturalistic but not without romantic undertones.

Stanisław Przybyszewski; portrait by Władysław Jarocki. [Agencja Autorska, Warsaw]

In 1898 he lived in Cracow as the editor of the magazine *Życie (Life)*. There followed several years in Russia during which he met his second wife, Jadwiga Kasprowiczowa. In 1906 he settled in Munich, where he was a leading member of the expressionist movement. In the years 1917–1918 he edited the expressionist magazine *Zdrój (The Torrent)*. *See* EXPRESSIONISM in glossary.

Snow, **as performed at the Teatr Dramatyczny,**
Warsaw. [Agencja Autorska, Warsaw]

After 1919 he returned to newly independent Poland and became a civil servant, first in the post office, then the state railroads, and finally the Office of the Presidency. He died in Jaronty on November 23, 1927.

WORK

A member of the Young Poland movement, Przybyszewski was nevertheless proud of his individualism. His main concern in literary terms was to express the dilemma of souls brought face to face with the infinite. He rejected reason and praised intuition and "absolute art." He separated the psyche and the soul from the external world. The most characteristic of his postulates was the idea that the function of art is to present the human soul in all its "holy" manifestations; hence in his fiction and drama the inner lives of his heroes are of prime importance while the external world is reduced to a minimum. The realistic interpretation of human behavior is replaced by metaphysical motivation. Przybyszewski thus influenced Polish literature by his unorthodox treatment of plot and his lofty neoromanticism. A forerunner of expressionism, he shocked his generation by his demoniacal works in which satanic passion predominates; his popularity lasted only a short time.

In *For Happiness* (*Das grosse Glück; Dla szczęścia,* 1897), a man named Micki wants to terminate his liaison with his mistress Helena to marry Olga, but a friend surreptitiously poisons the minds of all three characters, and Helena finally drowns herself. For this psychological

drama Przybyszewski created a new type of dramatic expression, the declaration of something undeclared and seemingly undeclarable. In addition, he created a new breed of heroes, contemporary people beset by inner struggles and communicating in broken dialogue ranging from railing hysteria to utter silence.

Another psychological drama, *Snow* (*Śnieg; Der Schnee,* 1903), is also obsessed with sex in the *fin de siècle* fashion. Once again death comes as a result of inner doubts and insecurity.

Snow (*Śnieg,* 1903). Drama in which Bronka, the young, happily married wife of Tadeusz, discovers that her visiting friend Eva is Tadeusz's former lover. Although Tadeusz attempts to reassure her that he no longer loves Eva, Bronka is obsessed with the idea that she is losing her husband. Tadeusz's brother Kazimierz, seeing Bronka's anxiety, reveals his own love for her and offers his help. Bronka asks him to murder Tadeusz, but he cannot bring himself to do so. Bronka, powerless against her demonic qualities, refuses to believe her husband's reassurances of his love for her. Certain that all hope of happiness is lost, she orders a servant to clear the pond of snow and chip out two fishing holes, whereupon she and Kazimierz go to the pond and drown themselves.   [DANIEL GEROULD]

PLAYS

Both the German and the Polish versions of the plays are by Przybyszewski.

1. *Das grosse Glück* (For Happiness).* Drama 5 acts. Written 1897.

Published 1897. Produced Prague, 1898. Polish version: *Dla szczęścia (For Happiness)*. Published 1900. Produced Cracow Feb. 18, 1899.

The following two plays (Nos. 2 and 3) from the sequence *Taniec śmierci i miłości (Dance of Death and Love)*. Published Cracow, 1901. German version: *Totentanz der Liebe*. Published Berlin, 1902.

2. *Złote runo (The Golden Fleece)*. Drama, 3 acts. Produced Lvov, Mar. 27, 1901. German version: *Das goldene Vlies*. Produced Vienna, 1906.

3. *Goście* (Visitors)*. Dramatic epilogue, 1 act. Produced Cracow, Mar. 27, 1901. German version: *Die Gäste*. Produced Berlin, 1903.

4. *Matka (Mother)*. Drama, 4 acts. Published 1903. Produced Cracow, Sept. 27, 1902. German version: *Die Mutter (The Mother)*. Produced Vienna. 1905.

5. *Srebrne gody (Silver Jubilee)*. Scene from a drama. Fragment published 1903.

6. *Śnieg* (Snow)*. Drama, 4 acts. Published 1903. Produced Łódź Nov. 17, 1903. German version: *Der Schnee (Snow)*. Produced Vienna, 1906.

7. *Odwieczna baśń (The Eternal Tale)*. Dramatic poem in 3 acts. Published 1906. Produced Lvov, May 2, 1906.

8. *Śluby (The Vows)*. Dramatic poem, 3 acts. Published 1906. Produced Cracow, Feb. 17, 1906. German version: *Gelübde*. Produced Munich, 1906.

9. *Gody życia (The Feast of Life)*. Contemporary drama, 4 acts. Published 1910. Produced Poznań, Nov. 27, 1909.

10. *Topiel (Dangerous Shallows)*. Drama, 3 acts. Published 1912. Produced Lvov, Mar. 8, 1912. German version: *Untiefen*. Produced Munich. 1913.

11. *Miasto (The City)*. Legend, 4 acts. Published 1914. Produced Lvov, before 1920; Poznań, Feb. 6, 1920.

12. *U wrót Twoich (At Your Gate)*. Drama, 3 acts. Written 1925. Fragment published 1932.

13. *Ostatnia miłość Don Juana (Don Juan's Last Love)*. Drama, 1 act. Fragment published 1927.

14. *Mściciel (The Avenger)*. Drama, 3 acts. Published 1927. Produced Warsaw, Mar. 11, 1924.

EDITIONS

For Happiness. L. Baron, tr., *Poet Lore*. vol. XXIII, 1912.

Snow. O.F. Theis, tr., New York, 1920.

Visitors. D. Gerould and J. Kosicka, trs., New York Literary Forum, 1980.

CRITICISM

J. Krzyżanowski, "Stanisław Przybyszewski: A Critical Appraisal," *Slavonic Review*, vol. 6, 1927; M. Viumewieg. "A Polish Satanist: Stanisław Przybyszewski," *Polish Review*, vol. XIV, no. 2, 1964; Stanisław Helsztyński, *Stanisław Przybyszewski*, Cracow, 1966.

Psathas, Dimitris (1907–1980)

Greek playwright. Born in Trapezounda in Asia Minor, he came to Athens in 1923 to finish his studies and there began his career as a journalist with a strong interest in the theatre. Throughout his long career he wrote numerous humorous books and travel collections about his visits to other countries, such as France, England, the United States, Turkey, and Egypt.

Psathas has become even more acclaimed for his social comedies, many of which are among the longest-running shows in Greek theatrical history. Using a style called "satiric reportage," Psathas has managed to create, with seeming ease, characters and situations that are both topical and universal, stereotypic and individualistic. As the critic Y. Fteris has put it, the playwright's characters project a "depth of human nature itself" that goes beyond the world of farce, situation comedy, and satire. Finally, with his clever plots and sharp ear for common Greek speech, Psathas has captured a truly "popular laughter" that suggests how closely he understood both human nature and Greek society in particular.

His plays include *The Crossbeam (To stravoxilo*, 1940), *Little Me (O eaftoulis mou*, 1941), *The Lightheaded Ones (E elafromiale*, 1942), the extremely popular *Madam Sousou* (1942), *Scenes of the Times (Skitsa tis epohis*, 1944), *Von Dimitrakis* (1947), *Life Is Wonderful (E zoi einai oraio*, 1952), *The Very Stupid One (Enas vlakas kai misos*, 1956), *Marie Will Tell All (E Mairi ta leei ola*, 1960), *The Woman Cardshark (Hartopaichtra)*, and *The Gossip (O koutsopolis)*.

Psathas's concern for Greek culture and history is clear not only in his plays but also in his long historical study of the Greeks who migrated to Greece from Asia Minor between the two world wars: *The Land of Pontos (Ye tou Pontu*, 1966).

Typical of his comedies is *Von Dimitrakis* (1947). Combining satire, social drama, and comedy, Psathas unfolds the story of one Greek family and how it responds to the German Occupation. Dimitris is the central protagonist. Forty-five years old, he is the father of his middle-class family and eager to cooperate with the Germans in order to further his career. His self-serving interests lead him finally to become Minister of Public Security, punishing his own people with twice the severity of the Germans in order to impress the latter with his devotion.

In contrast to Dimitris—who comes to be known as "Von" Dimitrakis—are his brother, Leonidas, a philosophy professor turned revolutionary who quietly runs guns for the Resistance through his grocery store, and his daughter, Anna, who appears to be a "proper" middle-class girl but is in fact an active member of the Resistance. Another response to the Germans is shown in the character Zarlas, a polite and seemingly civilized "gentleman" who is a double agent for the Greeks and Germans. Dimitrakis is motivated by bourgeois values, and Leonidas and Anna by democratic ideals, but Zarlas represents the amoral man who sells himself, his friends, and his country to the powers in control at the time.

Psathas manages to evoke a surprising amount of humor out of a situation fraught with tragedy. In fact, the first act, set in Dimitris's living room, is very much in the tradition of conventional bourgeois comedy of manners, as we listen to the pretentious banter of Maria, Dimitris's lightheaded wife, and hear of his concerns for his own career.

But while Psathas uses such traditional comedy as a framework, he quickly moves on to a more serious and more experimental level as he shifts the action in act two to Leonidas's "underground" grocery store and in the final act to Dimitris's office of national security. The movement of the play is thus from the private world of a family to the public drama of all Greek society. The play is likewise a reflection on one family's involvement in the Occupation and, at the same time, emblematic of Greek society in general.

Classical allusions are made throughout the play, especially by Leonidas, the professor-revolutionary. Psathas's drama therefore identifies itself with the whole tradition of Greek drama as well as with the continuity of the Greek urge for democracy and respect for the individual. For instance, one of the most important characters, Dimitris's son Alekos, never appears on stage but looms heavy in the background. He is an *andartis*, a member of the Greek guerrilla forces in the mountains, whom Leonidas compares to the fighting heroes of the *Iliad*. Leonidas (whose own name is properly symbolic) sees the average Greek, however, as needing to be more like Odysseus in the *Odyssey*, surviving and fighting with cleverness while living under the noses of the oppressors. With humor, wit, sympathy and courage, Leonidas succeeds at his task until he is arrested by his brother, Von Dimitrakis, who tries to claim that he "no longer has a brother."

Psathas demonstrates his ability to create strong characters throughout the play in a series of important clashes of personalities and philosophies. Anna, who seems so quiet at the beginning of the play, becomes a modern Antigone. In order to secure his position, Dimitrakis is willing to marry off his daughter to the traitor Zarlas. At this point bourgeois comedy blends with Greek tragedy as Anna defies her father, preferring to be handed over to the Germans rather than marry a traitor.

A "happy" ending occurs as Alekos, who has been offstage appears like Orestes to claim revenge; he murders Zarlas, and as the play ends, there is the fear that he may also murder his father, Von Dimitrakis.

Von Dimitrakis is labeled a comedy. But Psathas goes far beyond the usual scope of domestic comedy to evoke the Greek past, the present reality, and the dangers of a future in which people like Von Dimitrakis exist.

ANDREW HORTON

Puerto Rican Drama

Drama seems to have been the last literary genre to appear in the cultural panorama of Puerto Rico. Although there is evidence that during the first half of the seventeenth century theatrical presentations were held to celebrate royal weddings in Spain and church feasts, it was not until the early part of the nineteenth century that narrative drama was produced in the country.

NINETEENTH CENTURY

The first play written in Puerto Rico, dating from 1811, is a comedy in verse of which only pages 17–34 have survived. The beginning and the end have been lost along with the name of the author. From the remaining pages it can be inferred that the action of the comedy occurs in Puerto Rico at the end of the eighteenth century and in the first decade of the nineteenth, when Spain was at war with Great Britain. The plot seems to hinge around the themes of adultery and bigamy.

By 1823 three provisional theatres were built on the island, and that same year saw the publication of the tragedy *Mucén or The Triumph of Patriotism* (*Mucén O El triunfo del patriotismo*), as well as other pieces which reflected the patriotic and liberal feelings of the island's population. By the end of 1824, with the absolutist regime of the Bourbons back in power, the government press printed *The Triumph of the Throne and Puerto Rican Loyalty* (*El triunfo del trono y lealtad puertorriqueña*), a prose comedy in three acts by Pedro Tomas de Córdova

(1785–1869), who held the position of secretary of the insular government. The absolutist and colonialist position of the government after the fall of the liberal constitutional regime of 1820–1823 and the return to power of Ferdinand VII is clearly reflected in the comedy. The purpose of the comedy was to inspire Puerto Ricans with obedience and loyalty to the Madrid government and its island representatives. In 1832 the Municipal Theatre of San Juan was built, but because of heavy censorship no plays of Puerto Rican origin were submitted for presentation and the theatre was used mostly by theatrical companies from Europe and Cuba.

Romanticism had its first manifestation in Puerto Rican literature after 1839, mainly among poets and prose writers. Like the other literary genres, the drama written in the island after 1839 followed peninsular trends. Main themes in nineteenth-century Puerto Rican drama were honor, unrequited love, adventure, and historical themes. Church and state censorship made it impossible to deal with insular history, and so foreign history and historical persons provided the plots and themes of the dramas. Many were written in verse, as were their classical and neoclassical models, but combinations of verse and prose, as well as prose exclusively, were common. Though dramatists made some effort to introduce peasant characters and to reproduce the spoken language of the peasantry, most of the plays stuck to the themes and forms of the romantic Spanish theatre. In quality and quantity, romantic drama in Puerto Rico during the nineteenth and the early years of the twentieth century fell behind poetry, which was to be the preferred vehicle of the island writers.

Carmen Hernández de Araújo (1832–1877) and María Bibiana Benítez (1783–1875) were unusual and

Stage design by Carlos Marichal for a contemporary revival of *La Cuarterona*, a nineteenth-century drama by Alejandro Tapia y Rivera. [Instituto de Cultura Puertorriqueña]

early examples of women playwrights in a society which did not grant their sex access to the educational or artistic opportunities allowed to men. Hernández focused on common subjects in romantic literature: history, as in *The Kindred Rivals (Los deudos Rivales)*; unrequited love, as in *Ideal Love (Amor ideal)*; and didacticism, as in *Returning Good for Evil, the Best Punishment (Hacer bien al enemigo, el mayor castigo)*. Benítez, Puerto Rico's first woman poet, is best known for her historical drama, *The Morro Cross (La cruz del Morro)*, about the Dutch attack on San Juan in 1625. It is perhaps the best example of the influences of romanticism and of Calderón on Puerto Rican drama of the second half of the nineteenth century. *See* CALDERÓN DE LA BARCA, PEDRO.

Ramon F. Caballero (b. 1820) wrote, as far as we know, only one drama, *The Cock Fight or The Black Muzzle (La juega de gallos o El negro bozal*, 1852), but he was the first Puerto Rican dramatist to portray the peasant and the black slave. In the play the author cuts through the social strata of his times, thus giving us an idea of what life in Puerto Rico was like in the middle of the nineteenth century. The drama presents the triple circumstances of the peasant, the slave, and the white landowner. Interestingly enough, the two female characters, one the daugher of landed gentry and the other a black slave, reject marriage and opt for freedom.

Though Alejandro Tapia y Rivera (1826–1882) was also a poet, novelist, and historian, he became best known as a dramatist. A key figure in ninteenth-century Puerto Rican literature, Tapia was in constant difficulties with the official censors. He therefore often chose as his subjects periods and places far from home. Given his romantic temperament and the literary influences upon him, this allowed him to develop his favorite themes: honor and unrequited love. In Tapia's work primary importance is given to themes, locale, and historical veracity, while character development and motivations are of secondary importance. His plays are essentially dramatized biographies with metaphysical overtones.

His first dramatic work was *Roberto D'Evreux*. Written in 1848, it was based on the love affair between Queen Elizabeth I and the Earl of Essex. He noted in his memoirs that the censors would not allow it to be presented because "in America it should not be allowed to publish or present dramas in which kings are represented as human, or having human feelings." After some modifications, *Roberto D'Evreux* was staged in 1856. It has generally been considered the first dramatic presentation of any importance on the island.

Tapia's other historical plays include: *Guarionex* (1854), a libretto for an opera based on the pre-Columbian Taino indians of Puerto Rico; *Bernardo de Palissy* (1857), a didactic drama focusing on the life of the sixteenth-century Huguenot potter and savant; *Camoens* (1868), inspired by the love of Portugal's epic poet for Catalina de Ataíde; and *Vasco Núñez de Balboa* (1873), recounting the life and loves of the Spanish explorer credited with discovering the Pacific Ocean.

In Tapia's best-known play, *The Quadroon (La Cuarterona*, 1867), the action occurs in the second half of the

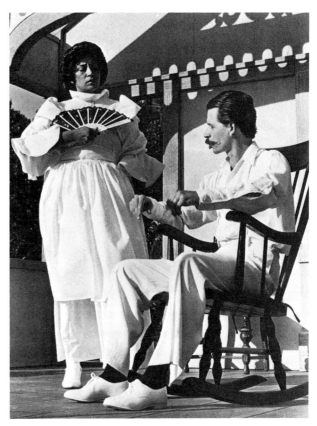

Marta de la Cruz and Freddy Valle in the Puerto Rican Traveling Theatre's revival of Ramón Méndez Quiñones's *Los jíbaros progresistas*. [Photograph by Ken Howard]

nineteenth century in colonial Havana, a locale chosen by the playwright to avoid conflict with Spanish censors in Puerto Rico. Julia, the mulatto daughter of a slave, works as a maid in the house of a somewhat impoverished Countess, whose son Carlos is in love with her. However, the Countess wants to marry Carlos to Emilia, daughter of a wealthy and vulgar merchant, who favors the marriage because it would improve his social status. Carlos rather meekly opposes the marriage and wants to leave the island with Julia, and settle somewhere free of racial prejudice. Nevertheless the Countess finally has her way; Carlos and Emilia are married, and Julia poisons herself.

To some extent, poet, novelist, essayist, and historian Salvador Brau (1842–1912) continues the tradition begun by Tapia. His verse plays closely adhere to the spirit of Spanish romanticism. His first play, *Hero and Martyr (Héroe y mártir*, 1871) is based on the *communard* rebellions in Castille. While it contains the necessary love subplot, it is obvious that social and political problems are the playwright's chief concern. *The Return Home (La vuelta al hogar*, 1877) presents the struggle of honor, courage, and sacrifice against greed and intrigue, all within the exotic world of pirates. *The Horror of Triumph (Los horrores del triunfo*, 1887) is inspired by the Sicilian Vespers, the thirteenth-century struggle on that Mediter-

Manuel Méndez Ballester [Instituto de Cultura Puertorriqueña]

ranean island to throw off French domination. The parallels with the situation in nineteenth-century Puerto Rico make this an obvious political statement by Brau, who also focuses on the theme of freedom and social justice, as does his poetry.

Though Ramón Méndez Quiñones (1847–1889) chose as the subject of his theatre the rural peasantry in Puerto Rico during the last decades of the nineteenth century, he was not so interested in social conditions as in peasant humor and local color. His dramas are essentially short sketches in which the everyday language of the peasant finds form in octosyllabic verse. Beneath the surface charm of Méndez's theatre, there is a strong moralistic and didactic vein. In both *A Countryman* (*Un jíbaro*, 1881), Méndez's first play, and *A Countrywoman* (*Una jíbara*, 1881), the author opposes the honest peasant to the corrupt city dwellers. In later dramas the author continues this series of "portraits." *The Progressive Peasants* (*Los jíbaros progresistas*, 1882) is a comic sketch concerning the argument between a man and wife; *A Local Police Commissioner* (*Un comisario de barrio*, n.d.) lets us listen in while four men playing cards express their dissatisfaction with the conservative Spanish regime; *Poor Sinda!* (*¡Pobre Sinda!* n.d.) is a serious analysis of a day in the life of a slave. The topic of slavery had been touched on earlier by Caballero, but it was more extensively developed by Méndez.

TWENTIETH CENTURY

Like all aspects of Puerto Rican life, the theatre underwent a significant change following the Spanish-American War (1898) and the 1902 Treaty of Paris, under which the island ceased being a Spanish colony and became an American colony. Puerto Rican drama of the first three decades of the new century was characterized by a strong realism which had its source in the class struggle caused by (1) organized union labor, (2) the overall political situation, (3) the evolution toward modernization of

the traditional social institutions, and (4) changes in the educational system, which under the United States had become an instrument of Americanization and forced assimilation. The organization of workers into labor unions was to become a main theme for island writers, of whom José Limón de Arce (1877–1940), also a poet and journalist, is perhaps the best known. His drama *Redemption* (*Redención*, 1904) presents labor unions as the only instrument capable of redeeming the working class.

More overt political theatre dealing with the problems of man and his relationships within social groups and society appeared during the 1920s and early 1930s. José Perez Losada (1879–1937) and Rafael Martínez Alvarez (1882–1959) are the key figures of these years. Both were to write under the influence of the Spanish dramatists of the early twentieth century, closely following the urban realism and "costumbrismo" of Benavente (*see* BENAVENTE, JACINTO). The works of these dramatists are distinguished by irony, a critical attitude toward the new bourgeoisie, a stage language closely approximating that of the man on the street, and a dash of sentimentalism. Pérez Losada and Martinez Alvarez's concern with social analysis approaches the theatre of Ibsen but lacks its universal appeal. The influence of the Norwegian master can also be seen in the theatre of Antonio Coll Vidal (1898–   ), especially in his *A Man of Forty* (*Un hombre de cuarenta*, 1928), which owes a debt to Ibsen's *A Doll House* and *Hedda Gabler*. Similarly, Nemesio Canales (1878–1923) in his *The Galloping Hero* (*El héroe galopante*, 1923) shows an awareness of George Bernard Shaw's comic *Arms and the Man*.

In 1938 playwright Emilio Belaval (1903–1972) in his manifesto *What Puerto Rican Theatre Could Be* (*Lo que podría ser un teatro puertorriqueño*) called for the creation of a truly Puerto Rican theatre, in which themes, actors, sets, ideas, and esthetics would be of authentic national origin. Some months later a group of Puerto Rican artists created the dramatic society Areyto, which in seven months presented four dramas. Areyto served as an example for the formation of other dramatic groups. The island, politically and economically, was now an American colony, but culturally it was still linked to Spain—"la Madre Patria" as it was called. Belaval had matured as a writer during those politically volatile years: the Nationalist Party with its call to and affirmation of the Puerto Rican nationality appealed to young intellectuals, who saw the traditional parties as trying to suppress the people's cry for social reforms. Independent of political parties was the growth of a nationalistic consciousness that led to increased interest in halting cultural assimilation by North Americans and in searching for the island's historical and cultural roots.

Of the four plays produced by Areyto during it's brief existence, *The Dead Season* (*Tiempo muerto*, 1940) by Manuel Méndez Ballester (1909–   ) is most representative of its time and has become a recognized classic. Méndez Ballester's theatre has been termed "bitter drama of the land." *The Dead Season* followed *The Clamor of the Furrows* (*El clamor de los surcos*), which was produced in 1939 but written much earlier, and shows a firmer grasp of dramatic technique. The title refers to that time of the year when there is no sugar cane to cut and unemployment is widespread. Simon, a former cutter now too old to work in the fields, must beg to survive. Throughout the drama he functions as a choruslike commentator and a living example of the eventual fate of nonunionized workers. The aged and tubercular Ignacio is also no longer able to support his family. His son Samuel decides to leave the cane fields, which he equates with a prison, to work as a hired hand on a cargo boat. His sickly daughter Rosa is sent off to work as a maid in the overseer's house. Samuel returns to find that Rosa has been raped by the overseer, and that his father, fearful of starvation, is willing to allow her to become the overseer's mistress. To restore the family's honor, Samuel sets out to kill the overseer with a knife, but is himself killed. Ignacio avenges his son and turns himself in. Her hopes obliterated, Juana, the matriarch of the family, takes her life.

The short-lived Areyto (1940–1941) and the various drama groups which followed had a profound effect on the island's theatre. Playwrights, directors, designers, and actors now had a foundation on which to build a theatre which would contribute to the search for national identity. Important concerns of this theatre were the political, economic, and cultural ties with United States and the search for the Puerto Rican ethos.

Some of the post-Areyto groups which were to play a fundamental role in the development and promotion of all aspects of theatre were: Tinglado Puertorriqueño (1944), which began as a high school group and evolved into a "traveling theatre"; Teatro Nuestro (1950), an independent group formed by René Marqués (1919–1978); and Teatro Experimental del Ateneo (1952), a sort of repertory and experimental group. Of lasting importance were to be the creation in 1941 of the Department of Drama at the University of Puerto Rico, and the foundation in 1955 of the Instituto de Cultura Puertorriqueña (I.C.P.), a government agency responsible for "contributing to preserve, promote, and develop the cultural values of Puerto Rico." In 1958 the I.C.P. produced its first Festival of Puerto Rican Theatre, now an annual event, and later it established the Festival of International Theatre.

In 1944 the Department of Drama at the University of Puerto Rico presented The Offended Woman (La resentida), by Enrigue Laguerre (1906–   ), a moving drama about an aristocratic family caught in the problems of class and race in 1898, the year of the United States invasion of the island. After that production the staging of any work by a Puerto Rican playwright was forbidden by the department for political reasons. The department then turned to the international repertoire and set out to train young people as actors, designers, and directors.

Francisco Arriví (1915–   ), founder of Tinglado Puertorriqueño, is representative of the post-Areyto dramatists. His experience as director, translator, and author of radio dramas won him a Rockefeller Foundation grant in 1949 for studies in direction and play writing at Columbia University. Later Arriví became director

of the Office of Theatre Programs at the I.C.P. From his office the annual Festival of Puerto Rican Theatre took form. The first festival (1958) presented four plays focusing on four distinct facets of Puerto Rican life: Crossroads (Encrucijada) by Manuel Méndez Ballester, dealing with the problems of adaptation encountered by the Puerto Rican emigrants to New York, a theme that would also interest Pedro Juan Soto (1928–   ), author of Spiks (1956) and Ardent Ground, Cool Season (Ardiente suelo, fria estación, 1961); The Hacienda of the Four Winds (La hacienda de los cuatro vientos) by Emilio Belaval (1903–1972), depicting the rural Puerto Rico of the nineteenth century and the generational and social conflict between a "criollo" son who repudiates the support of his father; Fanlights (Los soles truncos) by René Marqués (1919–1978), a symbolic representation of the conflict between three aged sisters who represent the past versus the aggressive forces of the present; and Masks (Vejigantes, 1957) by Arriví, which with Bolero y Plena (1956) and Siren (Sirena, 1959) makes up the trilogy Máscara Puertorriqueña. Arriví has described his trilogy as "a nucleus of racial shame, not about racial prejudice . . . [but] about a people formed largely by a visible mixture of the white man, which is predominant, and the black man, plus a few diluted teaspoons of the Indian." The trilogy brings to fruition some of Arriví's early experiments in The Case of the Living Dead Man (Caso del muerto en vida, 1951) with the utilization of the technical possibilities of stage lighting and nonrealistic sets; mastering the technique of flashback, he was able to do away with the exigencies of chronological action and unity of place.

Set in 1910, Masks begins with the feast of St. James the Apostle, during which Benedicto, a local Spaniard

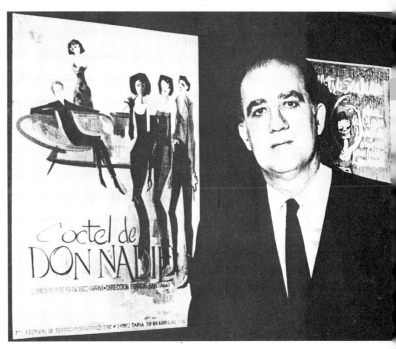

Francisco Arriví. [Instituto de Cultura Puertorriqueña]

Sketch for a costume used in a 1966 production of
Arriví's *Vejigantes*. [Instituto de Cultura
Puertorriqueña]

tually, Clarita convinces her mother to accept her blackness and Toña is allowed to come out of the back room and be seen by all. The black music at the beginning of the play is heard once more, this time on a recording which Marta plays loud enough for her neighbors to hear.

René Marqués (1919–1978) is perhaps the Puerto Rican dramatist best known abroad. Though trained as an agronomist, he never practiced that profession. In 1939 he founded the Areyto chapter in his hometown, and in 1948 he was awarded a Rockefeller Foundation grant to study playwriting at Columbia University and Erwin Piscator's Dramatic Workshop in New York. The theme most frequently recurring in Marqués's writing was political independence for Puerto Rico. He was the first playwright of the island to write about the revolutionary activities of the Nationalist Party and its leader Pedro Albizu Campos (1891–1965), who advocated armed struggle as a means of achieving independence.

After three early experimental plays, *The Man and His Dreams* (*El hombre y sus sueños*, 1946), *The Sun and the MacDonalds* (*El sol y los MacDonald*, 1946), and *Palm Sunday* (1949), written in English, whose main interest lies in certain technical innovations rather than their literary value, Marqués turned to a naturalistic style closer to that of Méndez Ballester's *The Dead Season*.

The Ox Cart (*La carreta*, 1952), while not representative of the dramatist at his most creative, is Marqués's best known and most accessible play. It begins in the mountains, where Luis, adopted son of the matriarch

merchant, dons the mask and costume of a vejigante (symbol of diabolical forces) and seduces the mulatto girl Toña. Pride and prejudice will not allow him to marry her, and Toña agrees to become his domestic. Throughout the action the black music of Bomba reinforces a crucial African presence and a sense of foreboding. Fortyeight years later Marta, Toña's daughter and the widow of a Spaniard, greets with pleasure the possibility that Clarita, her quadroon daughter, is on the verge of marrying an American, Bill Hawkins. Ashamed of her black blood, Marta hides her hair under a turban, covers her face with white powder, and always wears long sleeves and high-collared dresses. When visitors come, she insists that Mama Toña remain hidden in a back room. When Bill, unaware of Clarita's black ancestry, gives vent to his racist feeling, the young people quarrel. To patch things up, Marta lies about her racial heritage, but Clarita insists on telling the truth and Bill leaves. Even-

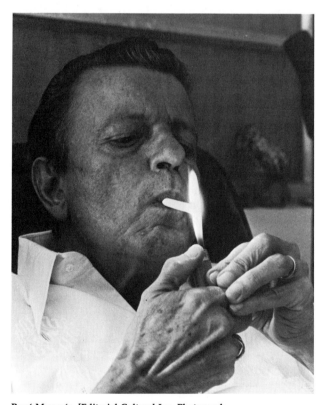

René Marqués. [Editorial Cultural Inc. Photograph by Francisco M. Vazquez]

Poster for Joe Lacomba's 1966 production of
Marqués's *Los soles truncos*. [Instituto de Cultura
Puertorriqueña]

Marqués's most outstanding play, *Fanlights* (1958), is based on his short story "Purificación en la calle del Cristo." It relates the tragedy of three elderly sisters, members of a once wealthy family now living as recluses in their mortgaged home on Cristo Street. The guilt and envy, which are the principal bond between the protagonists, are expiated in the final scene by the funeral pyre which the sisters erect for themselves and for their house. A novelist and poet as well as a playwright, Marqués turned late in his life to various themes for inspiration. Puerto Rican history was the basis for *Mariana, or The Dawn* (*Mariana o El Alba*, 1965), which recounts an unsuccessful nineteenth-century revolt against Spain but suggests present-day Puerto Rican desires for independence from the United States. Contemporary events on the island provided the subject matter of *Death Shall Not Enter the Palace* (*La muerte no entrará en palacio*, 1956), and Biblical themes inform *Mount Moriah Sacrifice* (*Sacrificio en el Monte Moriah*, 1969) and *David and Jonathan* (*David y Jonatán*, 1970).

In the cast of the 1958 premiere of Arriví's *Masks* there was a young actor, at the time a student in the Department of Drama at the University of Puerto Rico, who was to develop into one of the island's most promising and talented writers; Luis Rafael Sánchez (1935–   ). That same year he won a prize for his two-

Doña Gabriela, unable to maintain the small family farm, has arranged for the whole family to move to San Juan, where he hopes to find factory work. But Luis is unable to find a job and has to work as a gardener. Meanwhile life in the city slums takes its toll. After one son is jailed for a petty theft and Juanita attempts suicide following a rape, Luis decides to move the family to New York. There he is able to find work with the machines he considers a symbol of technological advancement and civilization. Though he is able to provide Doña Gabriela with material comforts, he cannot prevent further disintegration of the family. Juanita becomes a prostitute and Luis himself is killed by one of the machines which so fascinate him. Doña Gabriela returns to Puerto Rico with what is left of her family. Much of the controversy surrounding *The Ox Cart* stems from the earthy naturalistic quality of the language and the fact that Marqués used a phonetic imitation of popular Puerto Rican speech, causing some difficulty for readers more familiar with standard Spanish.

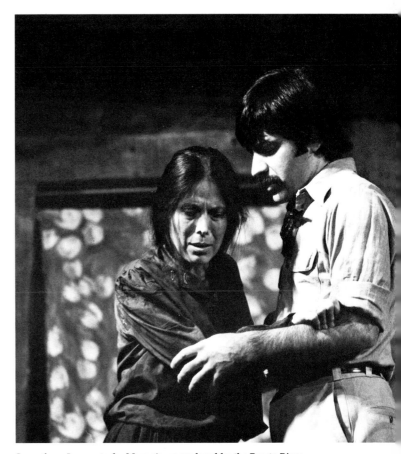

Scene from *La carreta*, by Marqués, as produced by the Puerto Rican Traveling Theatre. [Photograph courtesy of Miriam Colon]

The 1977 production of Marqués's *La carreta* by the Puerto Rican Traveling Theatre. [Photograph courtesy of Miriam Colon]

act play, *The Wait (La espera)*, which in 1960 was adapted as a scenario for a ballet by Ballet de San Juan.

But it was *Sol 13, Interior* (1961), a suite of two plays, which inaugurated Sánchez's meteoric career as a writer of major importance. *Sol 13, interior*, is the address of a tenement in old San Juan. In the title play Píramo and Tisbe, a childless septuagenarian couple, try to escape their misery by playing the lottery. Saints, deceased friends, and spirits are invoked to reveal the lucky number. Furniture is pawned for the price of a lottery ticket.

Luis Rafael Sánchez. [Instituto de Cultura Puertorriqueña]

All is to no avail, and the old couple is about to be evicted for nonpayment of rent. Píramo decides to kill himself with rat poison so that his ghost may discover and reveal the winning number to Tisbe.

The second play in Sánchez's suite, *The Angels Are Weary (Los angeles se han fatigado)*, is a two-act monologue in which Angela, a thirty-five year old prostitute, addresses herself to the unseen Petra, the manager of the bordello in which Angela works. She relates the events which turned her into a whore who in an act of rebellion and liberation murdered the pimp who originally seduced her and then put her on the streets. The action of the play takes place as Angela is waiting to be taken to a mental institution.

Sánchez's use of the monologue form in which the character mixes past and present, illusion and reality, was to be a major contribution to Puerto Rican drama, though Cesáreo Rosa-Nieves (1901–1975) had used it earlier in a minor one-act verse, play, *The Other One (La otra, 1949)*. In terms of themes Sánchez also differs somewhat from his predecessors. *Almost the Soul (O casi el alma, 1964)*, an "auto-da-fe in three acts," is the story of Maggie, a prostitute, who is visited by a man who claims to be the Son of God. He convinces her that she has had a vision and is reformed. The people and the church accept her as a saint—the church because she draws worshippers and financial benefits. The whole drama draws upon religious imagery and liturgy and is heavily seasoned with irony and criticism armed at the commercialization of the church as an institution.

Sánchez's best play to date is *The Passion According to*

Antígona Pérez (*La pasión según Antígona Pérez*, 1968), which the author describes as a "cronica americana" occuring in the imaginary Latin American republic of Molina. Though he closely follows Sophocles's *Antigone* in terms of characters and plot, he has set the personal and ideological conflict between his Antígona and Creon within the perspective of contemporary Latin America. The result is a dialectical drama about the eternal conflict between individual rights and the laws of a dictatorship.

The play opens with an address to the audience in which Antígona summarizes the action it is about to see. This technique, in which Antígona assumes the function of the chorus in Greek tragedy, is used throughout the "cronica." A group of reporters representing the "yellow press" inform the audience of Creon's version of the story, all within the context of international events of the 1960s.

Arrested by the Generalissimo Creon Molina, her uncle, Antígona refuses to confess the whereabouts of the bodies of two comrades she has buried. Throughout the two acts the protagonist is confronted by her mother, by Creon, by the First Lady, a Monsignor, and an old friend, all of whom vainly try to make her change her stand. These characters stand for both themselves and the social institutions in contemporary Latin America. In the end, Antígona is shot, a fact reported by the newspapers and the radio, sandwiched between news of Jackie Kennedy's vacation in the Swiss Alps and Pierre Cardin's new line of fashions.

Both Sánchez's *The Passion According to Antígona Pérez* and Marqués's *The Ox Cart* have enjoyed many productions and much critical success in Europe, the United States, and Latin America.

Other significant contemporary Puerto Rican playwrights are Gerard Paul Marin (1922–   ), Jaime Carrero (1931–   ), and Pedro Santaliz (1938–   ). Marin has written historical plays, such as *At the End of the Street* (*Al final de la calle*, 1959); farcical sketches, such as *The Puppet Theatre and Guignol of Juan Canelo* (*El retablo y guiñol de Juan Canelo*, 1967); and psychological dramas, such as *In the Beginning the Night Was Calm* (*En el principio la noche era serena*, 1960). Carrero has brought to the contemporary stage the language, situations, and characters of the New York Puerto Rican in his *Pipo Subway Don't Know How to Laugh* (*Pipo subway no sabe reir*, 1971), *The FM Safe* (1973), and *Noo jork* (1972). The participation of Puerto Rican draftees in the Vietnam War is dealt with in *Flag Inside* (1966). Santaliz, after living many years in New York, where he directed a small group of young actors, has returned to the island, where he has settled in a slum area and continued his work using members of the community as actors, designers, and workers. The influence of Poland's Jerzy Grotowski is obvious in his work with the Nuevo Teatro Pobre de America. Santaliz has been crucial to the spread of the "street theatre" concept throughout the island.

Mention should be made of the most professional drama group in Puerto Rico, the collective Teatro del Sesenta. More than any other group since Areyto, it has developed a consistent flow of excellent productions

In Sánchez's *O casi el alma*, Maggie, a prostitute, reforms and becomes a saint. [Instituto de Cultura Puertorriqueña]

and, even more important, has developed a steadily increasing audience. The Puerto Rican community in New York, which grew steadily after the collapse of the Puerto Rican agricultural economy and the imposition of U.S. citizenship in 1916, did not develop any continuing theatre activity until the 1960s. Prior to that the most significant event had been the premiere of Marqués's *The Ox Cart* in 1953 at the Hunts Point Palace, a production paid for completely by the actors. Miriam Colon's Puerto Rican Traveling Theatre debuted in 1965 with a bilingual production of *The Ox Cart*. Since then the P.R.T.T. has remained active, presenting Latin American plays in Spanish and English, and in 1981 it acquired a permanent home—a renovated firehouse and presented a season of play by Marqués, Carrero and other island playwrights. To do this Miss Colon raised $1 million from sources including the Kresge Foundation, the Rockefeller

Scene from Sánchez's *La pasión según Antígona Pérez*. [Instituto de Cultura Puertorriqueña]

Foundation, the National Endowment for the Arts, and the U.S. Department of Housing and Urban Development. Other recent groups are: Nuevo Teatro Pobre de America, Teatro de Orilla, Puerto Rican Ensemble, and The Family, a group of ex-convicts including Miguel Piñero (1946–   ), author of an English-language play entitled *Short Eyes* (1974). The common goal of the above groups, except The Family, has been creation of a new form of Puerto Rican theatre: low-budgeted, brief works that are either adaptations of short stories or based on real life incidents linked by a central theme and sometimes music.

Today, a new crop of young Puerto Rican playwright-poets has emerged in New York City: Pedro Pietri (1944–   ), with *Lewlu* (1980); Jesus Papoleto Melendez (1951–   ), with *The Junkies Stole the Clock* (1971); Miguel Algarín (1941–   ), also director of the Puerto Rican Playwrights/Actors Workshop, with *The Murder of Pito* (1976); and Tato Laviera (1951–   ), with *Piñones* (the name of a beach). The new generation writes in English or in a mixture of English and Spanish which is meant to reflect not just the reality of the ghetto but also the cultural ambivalence of a people still in search of its identity.

RAFAEL RODRIGUEZ

CRITICISM

W. Green, "Puerto Rican Portrait," *Theatre Arts*, vol. 40, pp. 79–80, 93–95, March 1956; W. Green, "Puerto Rico—Theatrical History," *Enciclopedia dello Spettacolo*, VIII (1961), cols. 377–378; F. Dauster, "Drama and Theater in Puerto Rico," *Modern Drama*, vol. 6, p. 183, September 1963; M. T. Babin, "Veinte años de teatro puertorriqueño (1945–1964)," *Asomante*, vol. 20, pp. 7–20, 1964; W. Braschi, *Apuntes sobre el teatro puertorriqueño*, San Juan, 1970; E. J. Pasarell, *Origenes y desarollo de la afición teatral en Puerto Rico*, San Juan, 1970; J. B. Phillips, *Contemporary Puerto Rican Drama*, New York, 1972; A. Sáez, *El teatro en Puerto Rico: notas para su historia*, Rio Piedras, P.R., 1972; M. Casas, "Theatrical Production in Puerto Rico from 1700–1824," Ph.D., New York University, 1974; N. González, *Bibliografía de teatro puertorriqueño (Siglos XIX y XX)*, Rio Piedras, P.R., 1979; A. Morfi, *Historia crítica de un siglo de teatro puertorriqueño*, I.C.P., San Juan, 1980; V. Fragoso, *Notas sobre la expresión teatral puertorriqueña en Nueva York, 1965–1975*, Centro de Estudios Puertorriqueños, New York (CUNY), n.d.

Puget, Claude-André   (1905–1975)

French journalist, poet, and dramatist. He is best known for the triumphal success of his comedy *Les jours heureux* (1938), in which an aviator, the embodiment of the

Denise Noël and Jean Davy in *La peine capitale*. Paris, Comédie-Française, 1952. [French Cultural Services]

dreams of several adolescents, forced down near their campsite, temporarily causes heartbreak in the girls and jealousy in their boyfriends. Puget's first full-length play was the popular *La ligne de coeur* (1931), followed in 1932 by another success, *Valentin le désossé*, and a failure, *Tourterelle* (1934). *Échec à Don Juan* (1941) broke away from the romantic comedies that had preceded it, as did many subsequent works. The maturation of the artist as well as the tragic events of the time gave an increasingly somber quality to Puget's later plays. *Le grand poucet* (1943) is a fairy tale that introduces a modern moral; *La peine capitale* (1948), a historical drama set in Renaissance Italy; and *Un nommé Judas* (1954), which Puget wrote with Pierre Bost, an investigation of the nature of solitude and individual responsibility. In addition to his original plays, Puget has provided the French stage with translations of Shakespeare, Shaw, and Noël Coward.

[JOSEPH E. GARREAU]

Pushkin, Aleksandr Sergeyevich   (1799–1837)

Russia's greatest poet, who also made a significant contribution to the growth of Russian drama. Pushkin was born in Moscow on June 6, 1799, and died in St. Petersburg on February 10, 1837 (N.S.). In his only full-length drama, *Boris Godunov* (wr. 1825, prod. 1870), he intended to release Russian theatre from the prevalent mold of French classicism and reconstruct it along lines more congenial to the national temperament. In giving minor attention to romantic intrigue, dispensing with the unities, mingling verse with prose, using colloquial Russian to produce natural dialogue, and developing the action on two planes, historical and psychological, *Boris Godunov* was remarkably innovative, and it forced a drastic change in the Russian theatre. *See* UNITIES in glossary.

Pushkin knew Shakespeare's work primarily through the translations and criticisms of A. W. Schlegel and François Guizot; what he admired in the English playwright was his mixture of comedy and tragedy, his wide-ranging and episodic scene structure, his accuracy in finding appropriate speech for each level of character, and his exploitation of national history as source material. *Boris Godunov* was planned on a Shakespearean model and introduced a supple blank verse into Russian drama. Despite the title, Boris, a kind of Slavic Macbeth who sees visions of murdered children, is not the true protagonist; that role Pushkin assigned to the Russian people, who are mute sufferers and survivors of the events. This transference of focus from the individual to the collective is a striking trait of Russian drama.

Disappointed by the censor's ban on *Boris*, which prevented its stage production, Pushkin began experiments with his "Little Tragedies" (1830). Using traditional European literary types (the miser, the Don Juan figure, the artistic genius), he created a series of masterly sketches of passion, and characters destroyed by monomania. In *The Covetous Knight* (*Skupoy rytsar*), the protagonist is subject to the gold he loves; Don Juan in *The Stone Guest* (*Kamyennyy gost*) is torn between an ideal and a corporeal love; and in *Mozart and Salieri* (*Motsart i Salyeri*) the mediocrity poisons the genius to enable his be-

Aleksandr Sergeyevich Pushkin; portrait by O. Kipienski. [American Heritage]

er, Boris. Traveling to Lithuania and Poland, Grigory gathers support among political opportunists who have been seeking a plausible pretext to invade Russia.

Meanwhile, Boris has proved to be a repressive tyrant, alienating both the famished masses and the boyars, whose power he has sedulously eroded. The stage thus set for insurrection, he nevertheless staves off his foes with the assistance of Prince Shuysky and Basmanov, the boyar in charge of defense. Undermined by a guilty conscience, however, Boris succumbs to a fatal stroke, whereupon his power falls to Fyodor, his feckless son. Basmanov then defects, convinced by Grigory's emissary that the people will forsake Fyodor for the charismatic Dmitry, and hands over his entire command to the opposition. When the boyars storm the palace to seize Fyodor and his mother, they discover that the two have taken poison. Emerging to announce the new order to the crowd outside, the boyars expect cheers; but, stunned by the mounting carnage, the people stand in numb silence.

[LAURENCE SENELICK]

PLAYS

Original Plays

1. *Vadim.* Unfinished tragedy. Written 1821.
2. [*Skazhi, kakoy sudboy . . .*] (*Say, what fate . . .*). Unfinished comedy. Written 1821.
3. *Boris Godunov**. Historical tragedy, 21 scenes, with 2 supplemental scenes. Written 1824–1825. Published 1831. Produced (with cuts) St. Petersburg, Mariinsky Theatre, Sept. 17, 1870.
4. *Stsena iz Fausta* (*Scene from Faust*). Fragment. Written 1827. Published 1828.
5. *Skupoy rytsar** (*The Covetous Knight*)."Little tragedy," 3 scenes. Written 1830. Published 1836. Produced St. Petersburg, Alexandrinsky Theatre, Sept. 23, 1852; Moscow, Maly Theatre, Jan. 9, 1853.
6. *Motsart i Salyeri** (*Mozart and Salieri*). "Little tragedy," 2 scenes. Written 1830. Published 1832. Produced St. Petersburg, Bolshoy Dramatic Theatre, Jan. 27, 1832.
7. *Kamyennyy Gost** (*The Stone Guest*). "Little tragedy," 4 scenes. Written 1830. Published 1839. Produced St. Petersburg, Alexandrinsky Theatre, Nov. 18, 1847.
8. *Pir vo vryemya chumy** (*The Feast in Plague Time*). "Little tragedy," 1 scene. Written 1830. Published 1832. Produced St. Petersburg, Alexandrinsky Theatre, 1899; Moscow, Moscow Art Theatre, 1915. Based on *The City of the Plague* by John Wilson (pseud. of Christopher North).
9. *Rusalka** (*The Nixie*). Lyrical tragedy, 6 scenes. Written 1829–1832. Published 1837. Produced St. Petersburg, Alexandrinsky Theatre, Apr. 25, 1838.
10. *Stseny iz rytsarskikh vryemen* (*Scenes from the Age of Chivalry*). Unfinished drama. Written 1835. Produced Leningrad, Bolshoy Dramatic Theatre named after Gorky, 1937.
11. *Papessa Ioanna* (*The She-Pope Joan*). Outline of a drama. Written 1834–1835.

Operas Based on Pushkin's Plays

1. *Rusalka* (*The Nixie*). Composed by A. S. Dargomyzhsky, 1855. Produced St. Petersburg, Mariinsky Theatre, May 16, 1856.
2. *Boris Godunov.* Composed by Modest Mussorgsky, 1868–1869. Produced St. Petersburg, Mariinsky Theatre, Jan. 27, 1874.
3. *Kamyennyy Gost* (*The Stone Guest*). Composed by A. S. Dargomyzhsky, 1869. Produced Mariinsky Theatre, Feb. 28, 1872.
4. *Motsart i Salyeri* (*Mozart and Salieri*). Composed by Nikolay Rimsky-Korsakov, 1898. Produced Moscow, Moscow Private Russian Opera, Dec. 7, 1898.
5. *Pir vo vryemya chumy* (*The Feast in Plague Time*). Composed by Cesar Cui, 1900. Produced Moscow, Novyy Theatre, 1901.
6. *Skupoy Rytsar* (*The Covetous Knight*). Composed by S. V. Rachmaninov, 1905. Produced Moscow, Bolshoy Theatre, 1906.

EDITIONS

Collections

The Poems, Prose and Plays of Aleksandr Pushkin, ed. by A. Yarmolinsky, New York, 1936; *Polnoe sobranie sochineniy*, 16 vols., Moscow, 1948; *Pushkin i teatr*, ed. by N. Litvinenko, Moscow, 1953; *Little Tragedies*, tr. by E.

loved art to survive. With their concise strokes and resonant language, these plays resemble chamber music. Terse psychological studies, they contain monologues impressive for their emotional complexity and dialogue deft in its mingling of the colloquial and the lyrical.

Pushkin's later, rather fragmentary plays include *The Nixie* (*Rusalka*, 1831), a revenge tragedy of a miller's daughter who turns into a water sprite after her seduction and abandonment by a prince; and *Scenes from the Age of Chivalry* (*Stseny iz rytsarskikh vremen*, 1835), an unfinished historical drama.

Boris Godunov (wr. 1825, prod. 1870). Chronicle play in verse and prose, showing a strong Shakespearean influence and set in Russia and Poland during the tumultuous reign of Boris Godunov (1598–1605), the regent who became Tsar after the death of Ivan the Terrible. Determined to quash suspicions following his assassination of Dmitry, Ivan's heir apparent, and his own ascent to the throne, Boris provides for "spontaneous" public demonstrations in his favor, thus making his usurpation of the throne appear a reluctant deference to a popular mandate. Grigory, a restless young monk, plots his own coup: by claiming that he is Dmitry, miraculously saved, he will lead a rebellion against the usurp-

M. Kayden, Yellow Springs, 1965; *Polnoe sobranie sochineniy*, Moscow, 1973–

Individual Plays

The Avaricious Knight. E. Simmons, tr., in *Harvard Studies and Notes in Philology and Literature* XV (1933).

Boris Godunov. A. Hayes, tr., New York, 1918; P. Barbour, tr., New York, 1953, Westport, Conn., 1975; F. D. Reeve, tr., in *Anthology of Russian Plays*, vol. 1, New York, 1961.

Don Juan (The Stone Guest) A. Werth, tr., in *Slavonic Review* V, 15 (1926–1927); A. MacAndrew, tr., in *19th Century Russian Drama*, New York, 1963.

A Feast in the City of the Plague, A. Werth, tr., in *Slavonic Review* VI, 6 (1927–1928).

Mozart and Salieri. F. P. Marchant, tr., in *Anglo-Russian Literary Society Proceedings* 89 (1920); N. Lubimov, tr., in *Poet Lore* XXXI, 4 (1920); A. Werth, tr., in *Glasgow Book of Prose and Verse*, ed. by J. B. Weir and M. Peock, Glasgow, 1923–1924; A. Clark, tr., in *University of Toronto Quarterly* 4 (1933); V. Nabokov, tr., in *New Republic* CIV (1941).

The Rusalka, R. Newmarch, tr., in *Poetry and Progress in Russia*, London, 1907.

Criticism

Russian

D. Darskiy, *Malenkie tragediy Pushkina*, Moscow, 1915; L. P. Grossman, *Pushkin v teatralnykh kreslakh*, Leningrad, 1928; N. N. Ardens, *Dramaturgiya i teatr A. S. Pushkina*, Moscow, 1939; M. Zagorskiy, *Pushkin i teatr*, Moscow-Leningrad, 1940; S. Durylin, *Pushkin na stsene*, Moscow, 1951; N. Litvinenko, *Pushkin i teatr*, Moscow, 1974.

English

D. S. Mirsky, *Pushkin*, London, 1926; E. Simmons, *Pushkin*, Cambridge, Mass., 1937; *Pushkin the Man and the Artist*, New York, 1937; T. A. Woolf, "Shakespeare's influence on Pushkin's dramatic work," *Shakespeare Survey* 5 (1952); Henri Troyat, *Pushkin, a Biography*, Garden City, 1970; *Pushkin on Literature*, ed. and tr. by T. A. Woolf, London, 1971; J. Bayley, *Pushkin, a Comparative Commentary*, Cambridge, 1971.

Q

Qi Rushan (1876–1962)

Chinese playwright. Qi Rushan from Gaoyang in Hebei province was born of an illustrious literary family. He received a traditional Confucian education and later studied French and German. On visits to France in 1908, 1911, and 1913, he attended the theatre frequently and was stirred to try and improve the Chinese theatre. A 1913 lecture of his in China was attended by the famous actor Mei Lanfang (1894–1961), and led to a twenty-year association between them. In 1915 he devised for Mei a modern-style play, *Moon Fairy Flees to the Moon* (*Chang E ben-yue*), employing an ancient theme, old dance forms, and modern costumes. Thereafter he wrote or adapted over twenty plays for Mei, who relied greatly on him. He did much to further Mei's career at home and abroad, being the chief organizer of Mei's tour of the United States in 1930. Though he did not accompany Mei to Russia in 1935, he was responsible for organizing the program. During the 1930s he edited and published a great deal of his research, wrote about Mei, and set up both the Guoju Xuehui (Study Society of Traditional Chinese Drama) and the Guoju Chuanxisuo (Transmission and Training Institute for Traditional Chinese Drama). The latter set up a museum to which he devoted himself after the Japanese entered Peking in 1937. In 1948 he went to Taiwan, where he was active in theatre affairs as well as writing and publishing copiously on Chinese theatre and social customs. He became director of a drama training school established in 1956.

In partnership with Mei Lanfang, as well as in his own right, Qi Rushan was an important figure in the movement to maintain and restore the power and respect of traditional Chinese drama in the twentieth century, as well as to spread its reputation internationally. *See* CHINESE THEATRE.

WILLIAM DOLBY

Quinault, Philippe (1635–1688)

French dramatist. His tragedies were popular with the *précieuses* of the court of Louis XIV and with the King himself. Of somewhat lower social origins than most of his rival dramatists—Corneille, Mairet, Du Ryer—Quinault, the son of a baker, became a valet to the dramatist Tristan L'Hermite, who encouraged his social and literary ambitions. At eighteen he wrote his first play, *The Rivals (Les rivales*, 1653), which, through the influence of Tristan, was produced at the Hôtel de Bourgogne. A series of comedies quickly established Quinault's popular reputation, and in 1655 his *The Comedy Without Comedy (La comédie sans comédie)* was a considerable success. *See* TRISTAN L'HERMITE, FRANÇOIS.

Quinault next wrote several popular tragicomedies more or less modeled on the genre established by Thomas Corneille's *Timocrates*. Magdeleine de Scudéry's popular novel *Le grand Cyrus* was the source for his *The Death of Cyrus (La mort de Cyrus*, 1659), and the same interminable novel provided the inspiration for Quinault's best-known tragedy, *Astrates (Astrate*, 1665). The latter play was ridiculed by Boileau for its extreme sentimentality and defended by Edme Boursault in his biting *La satire des satires*. In 1660 Quinault had married a rich widow who objected to his writing for the popular stage, and he began to turn his attention to the composition of opera libretti, which many critics feel show his slight poetic talent to best advantage. He was elected to the Académie Française in 1670, and the following year he collaborated with Molière on the opera-ballet *Psyche*. Other Quinault works of interest include *The Indiscreet Lover, or The Giddy Master* (*L'amant indiscret, ou Le maistre étourdi*, 1654) and *The Flirtatious Mother, or The Confused Lovers* (*La mère coquette, ou Les amants brouillés*, 1665), both of which are comedies.

The Comedy Without Comedy (*La comédie sans comédie*, 1655). La Roque and Hauteroche, two actors, are in love with Sitvanire and Aminte, daughters of a wealthy merchant named La Fleur. They convince La Fleur of the value of their profession by enacting four playlets that comprise the four acts of the comedy: a pastoral, a burlesque, a tragedy, and a tragicomedy. Finally, La Fleur allows his daughters to wed their talented admirers. The material for the individual playlets is drawn from works by Rabelais, Cervantes, and Tasso.

Astrates (*Astrate*, 1665). To strengthen her rule, Elissa, usurper Queen of Tyre, has had the long-imprisoned former King and two of his three sons murdered. However, a third son, spirited to safety while still an infant, is now said to have returned to Tyre to raise the people against her. Elissa reveals to the strangely reluctant Sichaeus, her adviser, that to consolidate her illegal grip on the throne she plans to marry his warrior son Astrates, whom she genuinely loves and knows to be in love with her. To prevent this union, Sichaeus informs Astrates that he is really the son of the murdered King and therefore the rightful ruler of Tyre. Astrates, however, places his love for Elissa above his duty to avenge his father. He takes arms against Sichaeus and his followers, who want to depose Elissa and make him King. After learning Astrates's true identity, Elissa, moved by this demonstration of his love, sacrifices herself for him by taking poison.

[JOSEPH E. GARREAU]

Quiñones de Benavente, Luis (1589?–1651)

Spanish dramatist. Little about his life is known. He was ordained a priest and probably began to write by 1609, but the *entremés* (interlude) *Good Manners* (*Las civilidades*), dated 1612, is his first known work. The first allusion to his fame as a writer is found in an *entremés* entitled *Miser Palomo*, dated 1618, by Antonio Hurtado de Mendoza. See ENTREMÉS in glossary.

A fecund writer, Quiñones had composed some 300 works by 1620: *loas*, *jácaras*, *entremeses*, and *bailes*, of which 140 survive. Within the next ten years, he composed another 300 works, and at the time of his death he had written a total of 900.

Quiñones was recognized by his contemporaries as the master of the *entremés*, the short interlude that was performed between the acts (*jornadas*) of the Spanish *comedia*. Unlike the one-act play, which was a later dramatic development, the *entremés* was not meant to stand alone. It depended on the witty development of a single situation but could not give much scope to plot or character development. One or two final lines would resolve the conflict, and the interlude could then conclude with a verse, song, or dance. See COMEDIA in glossary.

Quiñones's talents were perfectly attuned to the requirements of the *entremés* form. His gift for verse enabled him to make use of the comic possibilities of rhyme. He expanded his verse beyond the limits of literary Spanish, interspersing it with slang, Portuguese, and bits and scraps of other languages and dialects. He also exploited the full range of slapstick and low comedy and even combined them with literary conceits. For example, in *The Drunkard* (*El borracho*) a soldier delights a barber with a tale of five men trying to rescue a captive maiden while the five fingers of his hand are occupied in lifting the barber's purse. In this play Quiñones played on the metaphor of "stealing the barber's treasure," carrying the meaning of both his purse and his beautiful daughter.

In *The Moneybag* (*El talego-niño*), the miser Taracea, while in the process of moving his residence, entrusts his moneybag to his servant Carrote. Disguising himself as a woman, Carrote wraps the bag in blankets and carries it like a baby. On the road he meets Doña Salpullida and Doña Revesa, who convince him they knew each other in the Indies and trick him into giving them the "baby." Poor Carrote is beaten by his master for his stupidity.

Little of Quiñones's work was published in his lifetime. A volume of his works, *Jocoseria, burlas veras o reprehensión moral y festiva de los desórdenes públicos* (1645), denotes by its title the gentle combination of mockery and moralizing that composed his successful formula. Toward the end of his life, Quiñones belonged as did the majority of the literary men of his time, to the Third Order of San Francisco and to the Slaves of the Holy Sacrament.

[ANDRÉS FRANCO]

EDITIONS

Entremeses de Luis Quiñones de Benavente, ed. by C. Rosell, Madrid, 1872, 2 vols. (*Libros de Antaño*); *Colección de entremeses, bailes, jácaras y mojigangas*, ed. by E. Cotarelo y Mori, NBAE, vol. 18, Madrid, 1911; *Entremeses*, ed. by J. Hurtado and A. González Palencia, Madrid, 1925.

CRITICISM

Introductions, editions cited; E. Asensio, *Itinerario del entremés. Desde Lope de Rueda a Quiñones de Benavente*, Madrid, 1965; H. E. Bergman, *Luis Quiñones de Benavente y sus entremeses*, Madrid, 1965; id., *Luis Quiñones de Benavente*, New York, 1972.

R

Rabe, David [William] (1940–   )

American dramatist. Drafted in 1965 after he dropped out of Villanova University, where he was working for a master's degree in theatre, he was sent to Vietnam one year later and remained there as part of a hospital support group for two years. The experience inspired a series of powerful dramas—*The Basic Training of Pavlo Hummel* (1968), *Sticks and Bones* (1969), and *Streamers* (1975)—which cover the draftee's experience from basic training and combat to homecoming. In *Basic Training* Pavlo Hummel is indoctrinated into warped concepts of masculinity that are considered best to prepare him for combat. Attempting to pattern himself after Ardell, a black super-soldier ideal, he perfects the robot reflexes that lead him to smother a live grenade. In *Sticks and Bones* a soldier is returned from the madness of combat to his uncomprehending family for whom the war is a mixture of national debate and television show. *Streamers*, which derives its title from the nylon plume formed when a parachute malfunctions, and from the soldier who plummets past the others in terror, focuses on three soldiers whose different social conditioning leads to an explosion of hatred and murder.

Also of note is *In the Boom Boom Room* (1972), in which a hapless Philadephia go-go dancer is defeated by the thoughtless behavior of the men in her life. Rabe also wrote the screenplay for the 1982 film *I'm Dancing As Fast As I Can*.

Sticks and Bones (1969). Comedy in which David, an embittered, blinded veteran, returns to his perfect American home. His parents, Ozzie and Harriet, offer David cake and coffee while Rick, David's younger brother, happily takes photos with his Instamatic. David complains of feeling lost and anguished. Harriet lovingly understands, suggesting warm milk, prayer, and two Ezy Sleep pills. But David is haunted by the horrors he still sees and by the Vietnamese woman he loved. He lashes out at his family, but they feel he is being unnecessarily moody. They invite Father Donald by, but David assaults him, first verbally, then with his cane. The level of tension rises, and the family seems about to disintegrate, when a solution is found. The family talks David into suicide, and as the blood drips from his slit wrists Ozzie

Dolph Sweet (left) and Kenneth McMillan in the 1976 production of *Streamers*. [Martha Swope]

and Harriet happily return to normalcy. Produced New York, Public Theatre, November 7, 1971; John Golden Theatre, March 1, 1972.

TERRY MILLER

Racine, Jean (1639–1699)

French dramatist. He was born in December, 1639, in La Ferté-Milon, a small town near Soissons, northeast of Paris. His family belonged to the upper bourgeoisie and had been technically ennobled some generations earlier. Racine's mother died when he was only thirteen months old, and his father, a *procureur* (attorney), died two years later. The boy was raised by his paternal grandparents, who were ardent Jansenists, members of a Counter Reformation Catholic sect that denied free will and stressed the necessity of grace for salvation.

At the age of nine Racine was sent to the grammar school at Beauvais, an institution influenced by the Jansenists. In 1655 he was transferred to an affiliated school at Port-Royal, where his special masters were Pierre Nicole, the famous Jansenist moralist and theologian, and Antoine Le Maître, a celebrated advocate whose family (the Arnaulds) had long been connected with the disputes between the Jansenists and the Jesuits. Deprived of companions his own age, Racine spent three years there, secretly gorging himself on books often forbidden by his strict mentors. The documents of both schools indicate that Racine was a diligent student who often wrote poems in both Latin and French. While still a student, Racine composed his *Port-Royal Odes (Promenades de Port-Royal)*, describing the abbey and the surrounding landscape.

In 1658 Racine went to study at the Collège de Harcourt in Paris, where he boarded with his cousin, who was the steward of the Duc de Luynes, an ardent Port-Royalist. Thus Racine continued to live in Jansenist surroundings, although his correspondence suggests that he was not inclined to austerity. His letters of this time also indicate that he had committed himself to a literary ca-

Jean Racine; portrait by his son, Jean-Baptiste Racine. [French Cultural Services]

reer. His friends included the playwright Molière, the fabulist La Fontaine, and the poet-critic Boileau. *See* MOLIÈRE.

During this period he composed a sonnet celebrating the marriage of Louis XIV to Marie-Thérèse of Spain and submitted his first play, *Amasie* (1660), to the actors of the Théâtre du Marais. The play was rejected and has been lost. Racine began another play, *The Loves of Ovid (Les amours d'Ovide)*, for the celebrated Hôtel de Bourgogne company, but as far as is known, he never finished it. In November, 1661, he went to live with his uncle in Uzès, and a vain attempt was made to get him an ecclesiastical sinecure; less than two years later Racine was back in Paris. By 1663 he had written two more sonnets to the King, *Ode on the King's Convalescence (Ode sur la convalescence du roi)* and *The Goddess Fame Speaks to the Muses (La Renommée aux Muses)*, and had finished his first extant tragedy, *The Thebans, or The Enemy Brothers (La Thébaïde, ou Les frères ennemis)*. He submitted this to Molière's company, which performed it on June 20, 1664, at the Palais-Royal. Eighteen months later, on December 4, 1665, the Palais-Royal produced Racine's second tragedy, *Alexander the Great (Alexandre le Grand)*, but on December 18 of the same year the play was also performed with Racine's approval by the rival company at the Hôtel de Bourgogne. This brought about his alienation from Molière, and henceforth his plays were written for the Hôtel de Bourgogne.

In 1666 an incident occurred that Racine was later to regret. The chief writer of the Port-Royalist group, Nicole, published a letter criticizing an unnamed author as an *empoisonneur publique* ("public poisoner"). Racine mistakenly assumed that the reference was to himself, and he refuted the charge by publishing a letter filled with disparaging anecdotes and caricatures of the people he knew in the Jansenist movement.

Racine's break with the Jansenists also signified the end of the first phase of his life. The next decade saw the full blossoming of his professional career. In 1667 *Andromache (Andromaque)* was produced, and Racine was hailed as Corneille's equal. During the production he met the actress Thérèse du Parc, who played the title role; she was his mistress until her death a year later. Racine's next play, his only comedy, *The Litigants (Les plaideurs, 1668)*, was a failure. In 1669 Racine invaded Corneille's domain with a political tragedy, *Brittanicus*. The versification was declared excellent, but the play itself was thought inferior at the time, although its popularity increased in revivals. Racine felt that his play had been the victim of a cabal headed by Corneille and in his introduction to *Britannicus* he attacked the elder poet, although not by name. His conviction that he was Corneille's superior was soon to be tested, as both dramatists were at work on a tragedy about Titus and Berenice. Racine's *Berenice (Bérénice)* was produced on November 21, 1670, and Corneille's *Titus and Berenice* a week later. Racine's work was quickly recognized as the better of the two. *See* CORNEILLE, PIERRE.

During the production of *Berenice*, Racine formed a liaison with the actress La Champmeslé, who played the title role, and for the next seven years she was his mistress and leading lady. There then followed *Bajazet* (1672) and *Mithridates* (*Mithridate*, 1673). The day before *Mithridates* opened, Racine, only thirty-three, was elected to the Académie Française, as its youngest member. In October, 1674, the King appointed him government treasurer of Moulins, a town in central France which he never visited but from which he received an annual income of 2,400 livres. The same year *Iphigenia* (*Iphigénie*) was given a lavish outdoor production at court and was a tremendous success.

Racine's next play, *Phaedra* (*Phèdre*), his last for the professional theatre, was to cause him unhappiness even before it opened in January, 1677. During his career, Racine had made many enemies, among them the powerful Duchess de Bouillon, a niece of Mazarin, the French Cardinal and statesman, and sister of the Duc de Nevers. When she discovered the subject of Racine's new play, the Duchesse and Jacques Pradon, a minor dramatist and member of her coterie, composed their own play about Phaedra and Hippolytus. It opened two days after Racine's and for a time enjoyed greater success. There then followed the so-called War of the Sonnets. A sonnet was published by the Bouillon coterie ridiculing Racine's *Phaedra*. A countersonnet from the Racine faction slandered the Mazarin family, infuriating the Duc de Nevers and requiring the intervention of a friend of Racine to smooth things over. The reputation of Racine's *Phaedra* survived the cabal, and its superiority over the Pradon play was eventually established. But the episode impressed upon Racine the vulnerability of his position. His professional reputation had been challenged by a coterie, and his personal safety had been threatened by the Duc de Nevers. The effect on Racine was profound and considerably altered his life. *See* PRADON, JACQUES.

His affair with La Champmeslé had just ended, and on June 1, 1677, Racine married Catherine de Romanet. He was now in his mid-thirties and at the height of his career. When the King offered Racine and his friend Boileau the joint post of Royal Historiographer, Racine accepted the condition that he give up the theatre. He became reconciled with the Jansenists at Port-Royal, severed connections with the professional theatre, and devoted himself to his family. He and his wife had seven children, two boys and five girls. Racine was also an active courtier. As Royal Historiographer, he held a recognized position, official as well as literary, and enjoyed access to influential circles and the financial security of an annual salary of 6,000 livres. It was his duty to accompany the King on his military campaigns and record his exploits. In so doing, Racine became a creditable war correspondent: he said once that writing the truth was easy; finding it was the difficulty.

Thus Racine's life passed for the next ten years. Then Mme. de Maintenon, the King's morganatic wife, asked him to compose a play. A pious woman who exercised a profound influence over Louis, she had founded a school at Saint-Cyr for the daughters of impoverished nobility. The school's activities included the performance of a play and Mme. de Maintenon appealed to Racine. The result was *Esther*, a complete departure from anything he had written before. Based on the Old Testament story of Esther, it was written as a dramatic poem in three acts, interspersed with choruses, both recited and sung; the music was written by Jean-Baptiste Moreau, the court composer and organist of Saint-Cyr. *Esther* was given a lavish production at Saint-Cyr on January 26, 1689, before the King and an invited audience. The King was so greatly impressed that he ordered another performance three days later. The play was also repeated four times in February. Delighted by this rediscovery of his genius, Racine immediately set to work on *Athaliah* (*Athalie*), which he probably finished before the end of 1690. In December of that year the King had conferred on him still another honor, the post of *Gentilhomme ordinaire du roi*.

Athaliah was presented at Saint-Cyr in 1691, but because Mme. de Maintenon feared that the lavish production of *Esther* had had an unsettling effect on the students, the new play was privately given without costumes or scenery. Because of this it failed to make an impression, though many critics consider it the finest religious play since the classical Greek tragedies. Racine wrote no more except for four *Spiritual Hymns* (*Cantiques spirituelles*) and *A Shortened History of Port-Royal* (*Abrégé de l'histoire de Port-Royal*). Eight years later, on April 21, 1699, he died after a long illness and was buried at Port-Royal.

WORK

Racine, unlike his closest rival, Pierre Corneille, found the simplicity of the neoclassical tragic form well suited to his themes and style. The classical unities provided an ideal framework for the concise action of his tragedies, often motivated by a single dominant passion. Corneille, more inventive and concerned with acts of will rather than passion, found his style in constant conflict with the limitations and dicta imposed by the neoclassical tradition. Only Racine seemed at ease in the midst of these restrictions, which in other hands made the form seem almost an academic curiosity, far removed from the powerful simplicity of the Greek models it imitated. *See* NEOCLASSICISM; UNITIES in glossary.

The measure of Racine's genius cannot be taken without realizing that although neoclassicism was the most recurring of dramatic traditions, it had failed to produce a masterpiece. Since the Italian Renaissance, when neoclassicism developed from an imperfect understanding of Greek tragedy, it had been considered the epitome of dramatic excellence. The form was established by the Italians, and its rejection by English and Spanish dramatists was not without some defensiveness in the highest intellectual circles. Corneille was the only French dramatist capable of establishing the successful alternative of tragicomedy, as in *The Cid*, but after being humiliated by the criticism of Richelieu's newly founded Académie Française, he wrote only within the strict classical framework. Thus, this neoclassical idiom, which had been the ideal for more than 200 years, though its results were for the most part mediocre, became the absolute standard for perfection in tragedy. Racine took the form, which had become so rigidly conventional that it seemed doomed to obsolescence, and imbued it with such vitality that it survived for another 150 years. *See* TRAGICOMEDY in glossary.

Racine was educated at a Jansenist school at Port-Royal by some of the most brilliant scholars of his time. The Jansenist teaching, with its emphasis on original sin and predestined salvation, was to mark him for life, and its influence may be seen in his tragic characters, who are totally motivated by ungovernable passions and unable to bring their will to bear on events.

Racine used the same basic plot structure for most of his tragedies: an omnipotent king or queen, as in *Bajazet* (1672), *Phaedra* (1677), and *Athaliah* (1691), makes certain demands on a princess or a prince. Usually the demand is for love. This being denied, the monarch tries to force compliance. Racine's characters, unlike those of Corneille, are unable to subordinate the demands of passion to their duty to the state. Only in *Berenice* (1670) did he alter this structure, and here it is not Titus's passion for Berenice, but his lack of passion, that forms the tragedy. Having been proclaimed Emperor of Rome, he would lose support and power by marrying Berenice; so he sacrifices her love. In *Iphigenia* (1674), Agamemnon must sacrifice his daughter Iphigenia to the goddess Artemis, but unlike Racine's other victims of sovereign will, Iphigenia is ready to obey his command. The opposition is provided by her mother Clytemnestra, her betrothed

Elizabeth White Hartley as Andromache. [Theatre Collection, The New York Public Library at Lincoln Center, Astor, Lenox and Tilden Foundations]

Achilles, and finally by Agamemnon himself, who defies the gods in an attempt to save her. The perspective of the conflict is changed again in *Esther* (1689), in which Racine refrained from using sexual motivations. The focus here is on Esther's struggle to save her people, the Jews, from the destruction planned for them by Haman, the trusted minister of Ahasuerus, King of Persia.

Racine's only comedy, *The Litigants* (1668), does not conform to this structure. It is a satire on litigation, allegedly based on Racine's own experience, and shows the caustic wit that earned him so many enemies during his lifetime.

Though Racine's first two tragedies, *The Thebans, or The Enemy Brothers* (1664) and *Alexander the Great* (1665), were strongly influenced by the sentimentality and eloquence of Corneillian tragedy, they contain elements that were to be considered strictly Racinian. It is interesting that the motivation in his first tragedy, the struggle of the brothers Polynices and Eteocles for power, is to some extent paralleled in his last play by the conflict between Athaliah and Jehoiada. In the intervening tragedies, with only a few exceptions the protagonists are motivated largely by sexual passion and to a lesser extent by a wish for power. Although Racine's monarchs have physical power over their victims, they demand emotional and spiritual sovereignty as well. In failing to submit, the loved one must perish by murder or suicide.

Racine's protagonists are usually mature men and women at the height of their worldly greatness. The one exception, Nero, is depicted in *Britannicus* (1669) as a young ruler at the beginning of his reign. Driven by invincible passions, these characters are brought into violent moral conflict. Although Racinian man is aware of the distinction between right and wrong, the force of his desire overcomes his sense of honor and leads to his destruction.

Racine's princes and princesses are shadowy figures controlled by the sovereign; yet they precipitate events. Another type of subordinate character often essential to the action of the play is the confidant, usually a person of lower station than the principal characters. The protagonist confides his inner thoughts and feelings to this minor figure, who in turn has the power to influence the action by giving advice or information. Thus, in *Britannicus*, Narcissus's counsel encourages Nero to crime. In *Phaedra*, Oenone precipitates the tragedy by telling Theseus that Hippolytus lusts for Phaedra. In *Esther*, Haman persuades Ahasuerus to destroy the Jews. In *Athaliah*, Mattan urges Athaliah to pursue her vengeance. The confidant shows a shrewdness and cunning his master lacks, and his dispassionate simplicity contrasts sharply with the emotional complexity of the protagonist. *See* CONFIDANT in glossary.

An understanding of Racine demands an appreciation of his linguistic style, which is so stripped of conventional eloquence that it often borders on prose. Unlike that of Corneille, it never gives way to inflated rhetoric but pinpoints an idea or emotion, expressing it in precise images that heighten the impact of the facts

Scene from *Britannicus*. [French Cultural Services]

they convey. In addition, Racine's lines are justly famous for their rhythmic and harmonious flow.

Though Racine's plays were designed to reflect the interests and preoccupations of the royal court, they surpass all class barriers because of their stress on the passions, the common denominator of all men.

The Thebans, or The Enemy Brothers (*La Thébaïde, ou Les frères ennemis*, 1664). Tragedy based on the story of Oedipus's sons Polynices and Eteocles, who are in conflict for the throne of Thebes. Their fratricidal strife is encouraged by Creon, who wants the throne for himself. Their mother Jocasta, their sister Antigone, and their cousin Haemon endeavor in vain to reconcile them. Eventually, Haemon is killed as he tries to separate the brothers, who slaughter each other in combat. Jocasta and Antigone both commit suicide, the latter to avoid being forced into marriage with Creon, who kills himself in remorse.

Alexander the Great (*Alexandre le Grand*, 1665). Tragedy in which Alexander, the great Macedonian conqueror, having subdued the Persians, approaches the camp of the Indian king Taxila, whose sister Cleophila he loves. Taxila, encouraged by Cleophila, surrenders to Alexander, betraying his royal comrade Porus, who continues to oppose the Macedonian. Porus is believed to have been killed in the ensuing battle, and Alexander rewards Taxila with Porus's beloved Axiana, but she rejects him as a traitor. When it is learned that Porus and a few followers have arrived and are continuing their resistance to Alexander, Taxila, in despair, seeks out his rival for Axiana and is killed by him. However, Porus is eventually defeated by Alexander, who is so much impressed by his bravery that he restores to him both his kingdom and Axiana.

Andromache (*Andromaque*, 1667). Tragedy that takes place at the end of the Trojan War. Hector's widow Andromache and her son Astyanax have been given as slaves to the son of Achilles, Pyrrhus, who is the King of Epirus. Though he is betrothed to Menelaus's daughter Hermione, Pyrrhus has fallen in love with Andromache and wants to make her his Queen, but she is resolved to remain faithful to the memory of Hector. The tragedy is precipitated when Orestes, who has long been in love with Hermione, is sent by the Greeks to Epirus to demand the death of Astyanax, the last of the Trojan royal line. By threatening to surrender her son to the Greeks, Pyrrhus forces Andromache to marry him. Enraged, Hermione promises to marry Orestes if he will slay Pyrrhus. Orestes does so, but as soon as he and Hermione are married, she denounces him, hastens to the temple, and stabs herself over Pyrrhus's body. Thus, Andromache has preserved the purity of her love for Hector; Pyrrhus and Hermione, victims of obsessive love, are destroyed; and Orestes, having compromised the purity of his love by becoming involved in Hermione's passion, is driven mad with grief and shame.

The Litigants (*Les plaideurs*, 1668). Comedy satirizing the legal profession and based on Aristophanes's *The Wasps*. Dandin ("ninny") is a mad judge with a mania for his profession. His compulsion to judge everything and everyone has caused his son Leander to keep him locked in his house. Chicanneau ("quibble"), a bourgeois litigant who brings suit against everyone, and the Countess de Pimbesche, also an ardent litigant, become involved in an argument. When the countess brings suit against Chicanneau, they present their case to Dandin, who, shut in his house, listens to them first from a garret window and then from his cellar.

Meanwhile, the suit gives Leander, who is in love with Chicanneau's daughter Isabelle, the opportunity to disguise himself as a magistrate and trick Chicanneau into signing a marriage contract. Leander then obtains his own father's consent by presenting him with a hypothetical marriage suit for judgment: the lover is eager, the girl is willing, and her father consents. Having "judged" that the marriage should take place immediately, Dandin is unable to retract his decision. *See* ARISTOPHANES.

Britannicus (1669). Tragedy based on events in Roman history. Agrippina, widow of the emperor Claudius, has had Nero, her son by an earlier marriage, named Emperor in place of Claudius's son Britannicus. However, to maintain her hold over Nero, Agrippina has favored the marriage of Britannicus to Junia, a descendant of Emperor Augustus. Fearing that such a marriage will strengthen his rival's claim to the throne, Nero abducts Junia. He himself then falls in love with her; when she rejects him, he has Britannicus arrested. Agrippina appeals to Nero on behalf of Britannicus, and the young ruler yields to a similar plea by his tutor Burrhus (Burrus). But at the instigation of Britannicus's treacherous tutor Narcissus, Nero finally poisons his half brother during a celebration of their supposed reconciliation. Junia flees to the temple to become a vestal virgin. Nero dares not interfere with the mob that aids her flight. Narcissus, striving to please his Emperor, tries to stop her, but the angry crowd beats him to death. Nero is driven insane by the sight and is able only to mutter Junia's name.

Berenice (*Bérénice*, 1670). Tragedy based on the classic love story of Titus and Berenice. Berenice, Queen of Palestine, and Titus, heir to the Roman throne, have been in love for five years but are unable to marry because of political opposition to their union. Now that Vespasian is dead and Titus has become Emperor, it is assumed that he will be strong enough to do as he pleases. At this time Antiochus, King of Commagene, comes to take his leave of Berenice because he too loves her. But Titus reveals to his confidant Paulinus that his duty as Emperor will not permit him to marry Berenice; such a marriage, being contrary to Roman law, would threaten the stability of his rule. He asks Antiochus to tell Berenice this and to take her away with him. Refusing to believe Antiochus, Berenice hastens to Titus, who convinces her that his duty must take precedence over their love. Berenice agrees to leave, but she insists that Antiochus renounce his love for her, just as she has renounced her love for Titus.

Bajazet (1672). Tragedy supposedly based on actual events in Constantinople in 1638. The grand vizier Acomat is caught in a losing power struggle with the sultan Amurath (Murad), who has left his favorite, Roxane, in charge of the seraglio while he leads his army on a campaign. To save himself, Acomat plans to dethrone Amurath and place in power the latter's younger brother Bajazet, who is a prisoner in the palace awaiting execution on a command from the Sultan. He therefore contrives to have Roxane fall in love with Bajazet. Thinking that the Sultan's brother returns her love, Roxane promises that she and Acomat will seize the throne for him if he will marry her. When Bajazet refuses, Roxane discovers that he is in love with Atalide, the girl she has used as an intermediary.

Orcan, a slave devoted to Amurath, arrives with orders to have Bajazet put to death. Roxane, however, offers to save him if he will marry her and also agree to have Atalide put to death before his eyes. When he refuses, Roxane, in a frenzy of jealousy, carries out Amurath's order and has him put to death. However, she in

Scene from Roger Planchon and Jacques Rosner's production of *Bérénice*. The set and costumes were by René Allio. [French Cultural Services]

turn is executed by Orcan, acting on orders from Amurath, who has learned of his favorite's faithlessness. Atalide commits suicide when she hears of Bajazet's death, and Acomat escapes on a ship he has kept in readiness.

Mithridates (*Mithridate*, 1673). Tragedy in which the half brothers Pharnaces and Xiphares, hearing that their father Mithridates, King of Pontus, has been defeated and killed by the Romans, both come to Nymphaeum to claim Monime, who was to have married their father. As the elder brother, Pharnaces demands that Monime marry him, but the girl tells Xiphares that she loathes his brutal brother and would rather kill herself than marry him. Realizing that Monime returns his own love, Xiphares has agreed to protect her when the supposedly dead Mithridates arrives at Nymphaeum. From Monime's coolness to him, he concludes that she is in love with someone else. Suspecting that Pharnaces desires Monime, Mithridates commands him to make a political marriage with a Parthian princess in order to gain the support of Parthia for his invasion of Italy. Pharnaces refuses the match and reveals Xiphares's love to his father. Mithridates then tricks Monime into admitting that she returns the love of Xiphares.

Pharnaces, in the meantime, has treacherously joined forces with the Romans in an attack on the palace. Before going off to fight, Mithridates gives orders for Monime to take poison. She is about to do so when she learns that the King, fearing capture by the Romans, has stabbed himself. Before dying, he was bravely defended by Xiphares and with his last breath had revoked Monime's death sentence and united her to her lover.

Iphigenia (*Iphigénie*, 1674). Tragedy based on Euripides's *Iphigenia in Aulis*. The Greek ships lie becalmed at Aulis and the high priest Calchas states that they cannot set sail for Troy until Agamemnon sacrifices his daughter Iphigenia to the goddess Artemis. Iphigenia is sent for and made to believe that she has come to wed her betrothed Achilles before he leaves for the Trojan War. When the lovers discover the true reason for Iphigenia's presence in Aulis, Achilles swears to defend her. But Iphigenia protests that as it is her father's duty to sacrifice her, she must obey. Agamemnon, finally realizing that he cannot sacrifice his own daughter, tries to help her flee the Greek camp with her mother Clytemnestra. But her escape is disclosed to the high priest by Eriphyla, a young prisoner from Lesbos who loves Achilles, and Iphigenia is captured. As Iphigenia is led to the altar to be sacrificed, Calchas reinterprets the oracle, discovering that is it Eriphyla's death the gods demand, as she is the daughter of Helen and Theseus and was also named Iphigenia at birth. Eriphyla stabs herself, and the gods are placated. The lovers are reunited, and the Greeks are free to sail for Troy. *See* EURIPIDES.

Phaedra (*Phèdre*, 1677). Tragedy based on Euripides's *Hippolytus*. Phaedra, wife of Theseus, confesses to her nurse Oenone that the cause of her mysterious illness is her criminal love for her stepson Hippolytus. When word comes that the long-absent Theseus is dead, at Oenone's urging Phaedra sends for Hippolytus and

Phèdre, with Marie Bell (left) in the title role, Théâtre du Gymnase, Paris. [French Cultural Services]

reveals her love, but he spurns her in horror. Theseus unexpectedly returns, and Oenone, fearing that Hippolytus will denounce her mistress, secures permission from the frenzied Queen to act first and accuse Hippolytus of incestuous love for Phaedra. Confronted by Theseus, Hippolytus denies the charge and reveals that he loves Aricia, an Athenian princess, but his father angrily refuses to listen. After banishing Hippolytus, Theseus calls on Neptune to punish his son. Phaedra would like to clear Hippolytus's name, but the news that she has a rival in Aricia revives her jealous frenzy, and she lapses into silence. After the death of Hippolytus through the intervention of Neptune, Phaedra poisons herself, but before dying she confesses her guilt. The grief-stricken Theseus honors his son's memory by adopting Aricia.

Esther (1689). "Choral" tragedy based on the Old Testament Book of Esther. Esther, having been chosen from all the maidens of Persia to be the wife of King Ahasuerus, has become his Queen without revealing that she is a Jewess. Later, Haman, one of the King's favorites, convinces Ahasuerus that the Jews are disloyal and obtains an order for their massacre. Esther's uncle Mordecai persuades her to intercede for her people, even at the risk of her own life. She invites her husband to dine with her and so pleases him that he offers to grant any request she may make. She asks that the Jews be spared and reveals that she too is Jewish. When Ahasuerus realizes that Haman's plot against the Jews came from his hatred of Mordecai, he revokes the order for their extermination and has Haman put to death. A chorus of young Israelites comments throughout the play on the vicissitudes of the plot and ends the action with a song of thanks to God, protector of innocence.

Phaedra as produced at the National Theatre in Warsaw in 1957 with a set by Jan Kosiński. [*Theatre in Modern Poland*]

Athaliah (*Athalie*, 1691). "Choral" tragedy based on the Old Testament. A pagan worshiper of Baal, Athaliah, Queen of Judah, has slain her grandchildren so that the royal line of King David shall not ascend the throne. Thus she has avenged the death of her mother at the hands of the Jews. Unknown to her, however, her grandson Joash has been saved by Johosheba, wife of Jehoiada, the Jews' high priest. The latter has brought Joash up in the Temple but has concealed his identity and plans to claim the kingship for him later. Athaliah, troubled by dreams in which a youth slays her, finds no help in her god Baal, who plays upon her fears, tells her that Jehoiada is plotting against her, and urges her to demand Joash, who so resembles the slayer in her dream, as a hostage. However, Jehoiada refuses to give Joash up, and while Athaliah masses her troops to destroy the Temple, he calls the Levites together and crowns Joash king. Jehoiada then tricks Athaliah into entering the Temple alone and there presents Joash, revealing the secret of his birth. Joash is then presented to the people, who rally to him. Athaliah's troops flee, and she is led away to execution after acknowledging the power of the God of the Jews. The action of the play is commented on by a chorus of young Israelite maidens.

[JOSEPH E. GARREAU]

PLAYS

All plays are in verse. Unless otherwise noted, they were first performed in Paris.

1. *La Thébaïde, ou Les frères ennemis** (*The Thebans, or The Enemy Brothers*). Tragedy, 5 acts. Published 1664. Produced Palais-Royal, June 20, 1664.
2. *Alexandre le Grand** (*Alexander the Great*). Tragedy, 5 acts. Published 1666. Produced Palais-Royal, Dec. 4, 1665; Hôtel de Bourgogne, Dec. 18, 1665.
3. *Andromaque** (*Andromache*). Tragedy, 5 acts. Published 1668. Produced Hôtel de Bourgogne, Nov. 7, 1667.
4. *Les plaideurs** (*The Litigants*). Comedy, 5 acts. Published 1669. Produced Hôtel de Bourgogne, late 1668. Based on Aristophanes's *The Wasps*.
5. *Britannicus**. Tragedy, 5 acts. Published 1670. Produced Hôtel de Bourgogne, Dec. 13, 1669.
6. *Bérénice** (*Berenice*). Tragedy, 5 acts. Published 1671. Produced Hôtel de Bourgogne, Nov. 21, 1670.
7. *Bajazet**. Tragedy, 5 acts. Published 1672. Produced Hôtel de Bourgogne, Jan. 1, 1672.
8. *Mithridate** (*Mithridates*). Tragedy, 5 acts. Published 1673. Produced Hôtel de Bourgogne, January, 1673.
9. *Iphigénie** (*Iphigenia*). Tragedy, 5 acts. Published 1675. Produced Versailles, Aug. 18, 1674; Paris, Hôtel de Bourgogne, late 1674.
10. *Phèdre** (*Phaedra*). Tragedy, 5 acts. Written 1676. Published 1677. Produced Hôtel de Bourgogne, Jan. 1, 1677.
11. *Esther**. Tragedy, 3 acts. Written 1688. Published 1689. Produced Saint-Cyr, Mme. de Maintenon's school for young ladies, Jan. 26, 1689; Paris, Comédie-Française, May 8, 1721.
12. *Athalie** (*Athaliah*). Tragedy, 5 acts. Written 1690/91. Published 1691. Produced Versailles, by students from Mme. de Maintenon's school for young ladies, February, 1691; Paris, Comédie-Française, Mar. 3, 1716.

EDITIONS

Collections

Oeuvres, 2 vols., Paris, 1679; *Oeuvres*, 3 vols., Paris, 1767; *Oeuvres*, 7 vols., ed. by P. Luneau de Boisjermain, Paris, 1768; *Oeuvres complètes*, 4 vols., Paris, 1796; *Oeuvres*, 5 vols., Paris, 1801; *Oeuvres*, 5 vols., Paris, 1805; *Oeuvres*, 5 vols., ed. by C. Petitot, Paris, 1810; *Oeuvres*, 4 vols., Paris, 1813; *Théâtre complet*, 5 vols., ed by J.-F. de Laharpe, Paris, 1817; *Oeuvres complètes*, 6 vols., ed. by L.-A. Martin, Paris, 1820–1822; *Oeuvres complètes*, ed. by P.-R. Auguis, Paris, 1826; *Oeuvres*, ed. by L. Racine, Paris, 1854; *Théâtre complet*, ed. by L.-S. Auger, Paris, 1856; *Théâtre complet*, ed. by C. Louardre, Paris, 1855, 1870; *Oeuvres poétiques*, ed. by L.-A. Martin, 3 vols., Paris, 1886; *Oeuvres*, 8 vols., ed. by P. Mesnard, Paris, 1865–1873, 1885–1890; *Oeuvres complètes*, 3 vols., Paris, 1892–1897; *The Dramatic Works*, tr. by R. B. Boswell, 2 vols., London, 1890–1908; *Théâtre*, 3 vols., ed. by D. Mornet, Paris, 1912; *Six Plays of Corneille and Racine*, ed. by P. Landis, New York, 1931; *The Best Plays of Racine*, tr. by L. Lockert, Princeton, N.J., 1936; *Théâtre*, 4 vols., Geneva, 1944; *Oeuvres complètes*, 2 vols., Paris, 1940–1952; *Théâtre*, 5 vols., ed. by P. Mélèse, Paris, 1951–1952; *Mid-career Tragedies*, tr. by L. Lockert, Princeton, N.J., 1958; *Five Plays*, tr. by K. Muir, New York, 1960; *Théâtre complet*, ed. by M. Rat, Paris, 1960; *Three Plays*, tr. by G. Dillon, Chicago, 1961; *Oeuvres complètes*, ed. by P. Clarac, Paris, 1962; *Phaedra and Other Plays*, tr. by J. Cairncross, Harmondsworth, England, and Baltimore, 1963; *Andromache and Other Plays*, tr. by J. Cairncross, Harmondsworth, England, and Baltimore, 1967; *Complete Plays*, 2 vols., tr. by S. Solomon, New York, 1967.

Individual Plays

Andromache. Published in *The Genius of the French Theatre*, ed. by A. Bermel and tr. by L. Abel, New York, 1961.

Athaliah. Published in *An Anthology of World Literature*, ed. by P. M. Buck, Jr., and H. S. Alberson and tr. by R. B. Boswell, 3d ed., New York, 1951.

Berenice. Published in *World Drama*, ed. by B. H. Clark and tr. by R. B. Boswell, vol. 2, New York, 1933.

Esther. Published in *Nine Classic French Plays*, ed. by J. Seronde and H. Peyre, Boston, 1936.

The Litigants. Published in *The Drama: Its History, Literature and Influence on Civilization*, ed. by A. Bates and tr. by I. Browne, vol. 7, London, 1903–1904.

Phaedra. Published in *Classical French Drama*, ed. and tr. by W. Fowlie, New York, 1962.

CRITICISM

French

L. Racine, *Mémoire sur la vie de Jean Racine*, 2 vols., Lausanne and Geneva, 1747; M.-H. Beyle, *Racine et Shakespeare*, 2d ed., Paris, 1854; F. Deltour, *Les ennemis de Racine au XVIIe siècle*, Paris, 1859; J.-J.-E. Roy, *Histoire de Jean Racine*, Tours, 1863; P. Mesnard, *Notice bibliographique de Racine*, Paris, 1865–1873; P. Robert, *La poétique de Racine*, Paris, 1890; É. Deschanel, *Racine*, 2 vols., Paris, 1891; P. Monceaux, *Racine*, Paris, 1892; G. Larroumet, *Racine*, Paris, 1898; J. Lemaître, *Jean Racine*, 18th ed., Paris, 1908; G. Truc, *Le cas Racine*, Paris, 1921; L. Dubech, *Jean Racine, politique*, Paris, 1926; E. Renan, *Sur Corneille, Racine et Bossuet*, Paris, 1926; G. Truc, *Jean Racine: L'artiste, l'homme et le temps*, Paris, 1926; F. Mauriac, *La vie de Jean Racine*, Paris, 1928; H. Bremond, *Racine et Valéry*, Paris, 1930; J. Giraudoux, *Racine*, Paris, 1930; J. Lichtenstein, *Racine, poète biblique*, Paris, 1934; J. Talagrand, *Racine*, Paris, 1935; M.-M.-L. Saint-René Taillandier, *Racine*, enl. ed., Paris, 1940; J.-L.-P. Segond, *Psychologie de Jean Racine*, Paris, 1940; E. E. Williams, *Racine depuis 1885: Bibliographie raisonnée*, Baltimore, 1940; P. Brisson, *Les deux visages de Racine*, Paris, 1944; O. Mornet, *Jean Racine*, Paris, 1944; P. Moreau, *Racine: L'homme et l'oeuvre*, Paris, 1945; A. Bailly, *Racine*, Paris, 1946; P. Guéguen, *Poésie de Racine*, Paris, 1946; P. de Lacretelle, *La vie privée de Racine*, Paris, 1946; F. Lion, *Les rêves de Racine*, Paris, 1948; G. C. May, *Tragédie cornélienne, tragédie racinienne*, Urbana, Ill., 1948; M. Cambier, *Racine et Madame de Maintenon*, Brussels, 1949; G. C. May, *D'Ovide à Racine*, Paris, 1949; R. C. Knight, *Racine et la Grèce*, Paris, 1951; E. Vinaver, *Racine et la poésie tragique*, Paris, 1951; J.-J.-M. Pommier, *Aspects de Racine*, Paris, 1954; L. Goldmann, *Le Dieu caché: Étude sur la vision tragique dans les Pensées de Pascal et dans le théâtre de Racine*, Paris, 1956; id., *Jean Racine, dramaturge*, Paris, 1956; J.-D. Hubert, *Essai d'exégèse racinienne*, Paris, 1956; R. Picard, *La carrière de Jean Racine*, Paris, 1956; M. Descotes, *Les grands rôles du théâtre de Jean Racine*, Paris, 1957; C. Mauron, *L'inconscient dans l'oeuvre et la vie de Racine*, Gap, France, 1957; R. Jasinski, *Vers le vrai Racine*, 2 vols., Paris, 1958; P. Butler, *Classicisme et baroque dans l'oeuvre de Racine*, Paris, 1959; L. Vaurois, *L'enfance et la jeunesse de Racine*, Paris, 1964; M. Blom, *Le thème symbolique dans le théâtre de Racine*, 2 vols., Paris, 1962–1965; J. Mercanton, *Racine*, Paris, 1966; O. de Mourgues, *Autonomie de Racine*, Paris, 1967; R. Picard, *Racine polémiste*, Paris, 1967; B. C. Freeman, ed., *Concordance de théâtre et des poésies de Jean Racine*, 2 vols., Ithaca, N.Y., 1968; J. J. Roubine, *Lectures de Racine*, Paris, 1971; G. Borgal, *Racine*, Paris, 1974; R. C. Night, *Racine et la Grèce*, Paris, 1974; A. Niderst, *Les tragédies de Racine. Diversité et unité*, Paris, 1975; E. Batache-Watt, *Profils des heroïnes raciniennes*, Paris, 1976; *Racine: Mythes et réalités*, W. Ontario, 1976.

English

M. B. de Bury, *Racine and the French Classical Drama*, London, 1845; F. Hawkins, *Annals of the French Stage from Its Origin to the Death of Racine*, London, 1884; D. F. C. Fisher, *Corneille and Racine in England: A Study of the English Translations of the Two Corneilles and Racine*, New York, 1904; M. Cowley, *Racine*, Paris, 1923; M. Duclaux, *The Life of Racine*, London, 1925, New York, 1926; J. Giraudoux, *Racine*, tr. by P. M. Jones, Cambridge, England, 1938; A. F. B. Clark, *Jean Racine*, Cambridge, Mass., 1939; M. Turnell, *The Classical Moment: Studies of Corneille, Molière and Racine*, London, 1946; V. Orgel, *A New View of the Plays of Racine*, London, 1948; G. Brereton, *Jean Racine*, London, 1951; K. Wheatley, *Racine and English Classicism*, Austin, Tex., 1956; E. Vinaver, *Racine and Poetic Tragedy*, tr. by P. M. Jones, Manchester, England, 1955; New York, 1959; K. Muir, *Last Periods of Shakespeare, Racine, Ibsen*, Detroit, 1961; M.-H. Beyle, *Racine and Shakespeare*, tr. by G. Daniels, New York, 1962; B. Weinberg, *The Art of Jean Racine*, Chicago, 1963; R. Barthes, *On Racine*, tr. by R. Howard, New York, 1964; L. Goldmann, *The Hidden God: A Study of Tragic Vision in the Penseés of Pascal and the Tragedies of Racine*, tr. by P. Thody, London and New York, 1964; J. C. Lapp, *Aspects of Racinian Tragedy*, Toronto, 1964; J. A. Stone, *Sophocles and Racine*, Geneva, 1964; P. France, *Racine's Rhetoric*, Oxford, 1965; R. J. Nelson, *Corneille and Racine: Parallels and Contrasts*, Englewood Cliffs, N.J., 1966; O. de Mourgues, *Racine, or The Triumph of Relevance*, London, 1967; A. A. Tilley, *Three French Dramatists: Racine, Marivaux, Musset*, reprint, New York, 1967; B. L. Knapp, *Jean Racine: Mythos and Renewal in Modern Theater*, Alabama, 1971; G. Brereton, *Jean Racine: A Critical Biography*, London and New York, 1973.

Raimund, Ferdinand (1790–1836)

Austrian dramatist; pseudonym of Jakob Raimann. Ferdinand Raimund was born into an artisan's family on June 1, 1790, in Mariahilf, a district of Vienna. Having lost his parents at an early age, he worked as a baker's apprentice and made his first acquaintance with the theatre while selling pastries during intermissions. He dreamed of becoming a tragic actor, but at the beginning of his stage career in the provinces in the years 1808–1814 he became typed as a comedian. Back in Vienna in 1814, he met the theatre director J. A. Gleich (1772–1841), who employed him at the Theater in der Josefstadt. In 1817 he transferred to the Theater in der Leopoldstadt, of which he was director from 1828 to 1830.

Raimund's apparent naturalness, charm, and wit soon made him one of the most popular actors in Vienna. In fact, he was the opposite of his stage image, given to melancholy and choleric outbursts. Contributing to his bitterness was his marriage to the actress Luise Gleich, an unhappy union into which her father had forced him in 1821. The couple separated one year later, and from then on Raimund lived with Toni Wagner, his former love.

Ferdinand Raimund.
[Goethe House]

The success of Raimund's first play, *The Barometer Maker on the Enchanted Isle* (*Der Barometermacher auf der Zauberinsel,* 1823) encouraged him to continue as a dramatist. Extremely gifted in comedy, he began to write in the tradition of the Viennese *Zauberposse* ("fairy-tale farce"), which he raised to an artistic level, and soon became the foremost dramatist of the Viennese *Volkstheater* ("people's theatre"). However, he was never able fully to enjoy his success. The rising popularity of Johann Nestroy seemed to eclipse his fame, and, more important, Raimund turned to high tragedy, for which he had no talent. This failure to accept his limitations aggravated his depression and hypochondria. Fearing that he might have contracted rabies from a dogbite, he shot himself. Several days later, on September 5, 1836, he died in Pottenstein.

Work

While inheriting the traditions of the Viennese baroque theatre and the Italian *commedia dell'arte,* Raimund saw in the long-established form of fairy-tale farce the medium in which to present his idealistic longings for a more nearly perfect world. At best, he fused realism and illusion, injecting elements of social satire into his fairy-tale comedies while looking nostalgically back on a romantic past. Flashes of inner doubt and pain permeate his humor, lending a bittersweet quality to much of his work. Raimund thus transcended the usual superficialities of the fairy-tale genre, giving it reality and depth. *See* Commedia dell'Arte in glossary.

Raimund's most important plays are *The Girl from Fairyland or The Farmer as Millionaire* (*Das Mädchen aus der Feenwelt oder Der Bauer als Millionär,* 1826), in which he first found his distinctive voice, suffusing routine situations with romantic melancholy, with Farmer Wurzel's scenes becoming philosophical comments on life's transitoriness; *The King of the Alps and the Enemy of Man* (*Der Alpenkönig und der Menschenfeind,* 1828), considered his

Die gefesselte Phantasie. **Berlin, Theater am Kurfürstendamm. 1955. [Goethe House]**

Scene from *Das Mädchen aus der Feenwelt.* [Theater-Museum, Munich]

finest play, an outstanding example of poetic realism; and *The Spendthrift* (*Der Verschwender,* 1834), his most popular play, a serious work containing some of his most beautiful songs.

His first two plays, *The Barometer Maker on the Enchanted Isle* (1823) and *The Diamond of the King of Spirits* (*Der Diamant des Geisterkönigs,* 1824), both written in the traditional vein, are accomplished but shallow. Two attempts to combine tragedy and fairy-tale melodrama were unsuccessful: *The Magic Curse of Moisasur* (*Moisasurs Zauberfluch,* 1827), set in a Hindu milieu, with the gods declaiming in verse and the peasants conversing in dialect, and depicting the tribulations of an Indian queen who builds a temple of virtue but offends the demons; and *Fettered Fancy* (*Die gefesselte Phantasie,* 1828), in which the problems of a frustrated poet are presented in the framework of a conventional love story. *The Fatal Crown* (*Die unheilbringende Krone,* 1829), an inferior fairy-tale play, depicts the quest of a village tailor to find a king without a kingdom, a hero without courage, and a

A 1965 Austrian television production of *Der Alpenkönig und der Menschenfeind.* [Austrian Federal Press Service]

beauty without youth.

Even though Raimund never gained great popularity outside Austria, he played a vital role in the continuation of the Austrian folk tradition and the revival of the fairy-tale farce, which he endowed with deeper meaning and great artistic qualities. Many songs of his plays have become folk songs, and his dramas are often staged in the standard repertory of Viennese theatres. A theatre, a prize, and a society bearing his name have been founded to continue his endeavors to give the fairy-tale comedy a place alongside the great Austrian classic dramas.

The Girl from Fairyland or The Farmer as Millionaire (*Das Mädchen aus der Feenwelt oder Der Bauer als Millionär*, 1826). Fairy-tale drama in which the powerful fairy Lacrimosa, having once loved an earthling, has borne his daughter Lottchen. For her transgression she has been stripped of her powers and will regain them only if Lottchen marries a poor young man before she reaches her eighteenth birthday. With this end in mind, Lacrimosa entrusts Lottchen's upbringing to a farmer, Fortunatus Wurzel. Envy, whose advances Lacrimosa once rejected, now revenges himself on her by making Fortunatus a millionaire and causing him to forbid Lottchen to marry Karl Schilf, a poor fisherman. As Lottchen's birthday draws near, Lacrimosa appeals to her friends for help. Youth and Old Age appear to Fortunatus to say farewell; disturbed by these apparitions, he comes to realize the vanity of riches and renounces them. Hate, in a last desperate effort on behalf of Envy, showers Karl with wealth and magic ornaments, but Contentment redeems him. Karl casts the treasures aside and marries Lottchen. Lacrimosa regains her powers, and Wurzel once again becomes an honest farmer.

The King of the Alps and the Enemy of Man (*Der Alpenkönig und der Menschenfeind*, 1828). Fairy-tale comedy in which Rappelkopf, a rich landowner, is also a petty tyrant and a misanthrope. Distrusting his family, he forbids his daughter Malchen to marry the painter August Dorn. Finally, he leaves home and settles as a hermit in a mountain hut. His wife sends for her brother Silberkern to help her. Meanwhile, Astragalus, King of the Alps, swears to bring Rappelkopf to his senses and unleashes a storm so fierce that Rappelkopf is frightened into promising that he will reform. Not satisfied, Astragalus transforms Rappelkopf into his brother-in-law Silberkern and sends him to face his family. The sight of their love for him melts his heart. Astragalus himself then appears disguised as Rappelkopf and mistreats the family and servants in the misanthrope's former manner. The true Rappelkopf, feeling compelled to defend his family, barely escapes fighting a duel with his own image. Transformed by the experience, Rappelkopf becomes a friend to all humanity, and Malchen and August are reunited.

The Spendthrift (*Der Verschwender*, 1834). Romantic fairy drama, also considered an allegory depicting man's greatness and weakness. Julius von Flottwell, richly endowed from childhood by the fairy Cheristane, who loves him, spends his money generously but unwisely. Cheristane sends the spirit Azure disguised as a beggar, as a warning of what the future will bring. The beggar visits Flottwell four times; each time Flottwell lavishes money on him, and each time the beggar demands more, until finally in a rage Flottwell attempts to kill him. Twenty years later Cheristane's prediction comes true: Flottwell is an impoverished beggar. His castle is owned by his former secretary Wolf, who has made his fortune by robbing Flottwell. When Flottwell is turned away, Valentin, his former servant, takes him in; but he is then turned out by Valentin's wife Rose. At this point Flottwell is again visited by Cheristane and Azure, who restore his fortune. Valentin meanwhile has persuaded Rose to change her mind and seeks out Flottwell to offer him a home with them once again. Flottwell repays this loyalty by inviting Valentin and Rose to live with him and share his newly gained wealth. [VIOLET B. KETELS]

PLAYS

All were first performed in Vienna.

1. *Der Barometermacher auf der Zauberinsel* (The Barometer Maker on the Enchanted Isle). Fairy-tale farce, 3 acts. Written 1823. Published 1837. Produced Theater in der Leopoldstadt, Dec. 18, 1823.

2. *Der Diamant des Geisterkönigs* (The Diamond of the King of Spirits). Fairy-tale farce, 3 acts. Written 1824. Published 1837. Produced Theater in der Leopoldstadt, Dec. 17, 1824.

3. *Das Mädchen aus der Feenwelt oder Der Bauer als Millionär* (The Girl from Fairyland or The Farmer as Millionaire). Fairy-tale drama, 3 acts. Written 1826. Published 1837. Produced Theater in der Leopoldstadt, Nov. 10, 1826.

4. *Moisasurs Zauberfluch* (The Magic Curse of Moisasur). Fairy-tale drama, 3 acts. Written 1827. Published 1837. Produced Theater an der Wien, Sept. 25, 1827.

5. *Die gefesselte Phantasie* (Fettered Fancy). Fairytale drama, 2 acts. Written 1828. Published 1837. Produced Theater in der Leopoldstadt, Jan. 8, 1828.

6. *Der Alpenkönig und der Menschenfeind* (The King of the Alps and the Enemy of Man). Drama, 3 acts. Written 1828. Published 1837. Produced Theater in der Leopoldstadt, Oct. 17, 1828.

7. *Die unheilbringende Krone oder König ohne Reich, Held ohne Mut, Schönheit ohne Jugend* (The Fatal Crown or King Without a Kingdom, Hero Without Courage, Beauty Without Youth). Fairy-tale drama, 2 acts. Written 1829. Published 1837. Produced Theater in der Leopoldstadt, Dec. 4, 1829.

8. *Der Verschwender** (The Spendthrift). Fairy-tale drama, 3 acts. Written 1833. Published 1837. Produced Theater in der Josefstadt, Feb. 20, 1834.

EDITIONS

Dramatische Werke, ed. by G. Pichler, 1960; *Sämtliche Werke*, ed. by F. Brukner and E. Castle, Munich, 1960; *Gesammelte Werke*, ed. by O. Rommel, Gütersloh, 1962.

CRITICISM

R. Smekal, *Ferdinand Raimund*, Vienna, 1920; id., *Grillparzer und Raimund*, Vienna, 1920; O. Rauscher, *Ferdinand Raimund*, Leipzig, 1936; H. Kindermann, *Ferdinand Raimund*, Vienna, 1943; O. Rommel, *Ferdinand Raimund und die Vollendung des Alt-Wiener Zauberstückes*, Vienna, 1947; J. Hein, *Ferdinand Raimund*, Stuttgart, 1970; D. Prohaska, *Raimund and Vienna: A Critical Study of Raimund's Plays in their Viennese Setting*, Cambridge, 1970; F. Schaumann, *Gestalt und Funktion des Mythos in F. Raimunds Bühnenwerk*, Vienna, 1970; G. Wiltschko, *Raimunds Dramaturgie*, Munich, 1973; L. Harding, *The Dramatic Art of Ferdinand Raimund and Johann Nestroy: A Critical Study*, The Hague, 1974; J. Hein, *Das Wiener Volkstheater: Raimund und Nestroy*, Darmstadt, 1978.

Ramos, José Antonio   (1885–1946)

Cuban playwright. Born in Havana, the son of a professor of botany, Ramos proclaimed himself to be a free thinker, influenced by Voltaire, while still in secondary school. He remained an eclectic reader, devouring Rousseau, Mirabeau, Nietzsche, Rénan, and the anarchists Proudhon and Bakunin. At least four intellectual reviews flourished during Ramos's lifetime as a forum for ideas in Cuba, and Ramos was, above all, a man of ideas. He wrote novels, essays, and plays, concerned with what he called "the conflict between Reality and the Ideal."

Early in his career, Ramos advocated a program of political reform in Cuba to eliminate corruption and disorder and to create a national consciousness through education: the country's hope lay in its youth and its children. His view of history and society is based on a materialistic, economic analysis, but it is not Marxist.

Ramos traveled to Paris and Madrid and returned to cofound the Sociedad de Fomento del Teatro, in 1909. He served as Cuban consul in Spain and Mexico before being posted to Philadelphia. He resided in the United States for over ten years; consequently, his view of the United States combined an admiration for its success as a nation and concern with its expansionist policies. He often criticized Latin America for not dealing with its own internal weaknesses, which made it susceptible to foreign exploitation.

Ramos was a defender of trade unionism, feminism, and civil rights. He opposed the dictatorship of Gerardo Machado and was exiled after being stripped of his diplomatic post. His early reformism grew into a closer identification with the working classes. This is sometimes attributed to the favorable response he found among them, after failing to gain a large following among wealthier audiences with his social drama.

As assistant director of the National Library, he promoted a policy of building up Cuba's lending libraries, and he reorganized the library, often at his own personal expense. He willed his personal library to the Cuban Workers' Federation, and it is now housed in the Workers' Palace.

Ramos's writings are sometimes excessively verbose, and his social concerns overwhelm technical refinement. Influenced by Ibsen and Pirandello, the "solitary star of Cuban theatre" did, however, have an excellent dramatic sense and won several awards. He is considered one of the best exponents of naturalist theatre in Latin America.

Quaking Earth (*Tembladera*, 1917), which was awarded first prize by the National Academy of Cuba, is regarded as his most successful play. The title refers to the name of the sugar estate of the Gonsalvez de la Rosa family; the action is itself like a hurricane that sweeps the characters along in quick succession. Don Fernando Gonsalvez de la Rosa, an honest, hard-working Spanish immigrant, made his fortune and raised a family in Cuba. He and his wife, Maela (a caring but nonassertive person), failed to instill the same values in their children that made "Tembladera" a successful venture.

Mario, the eldest son, educated in Spain, feels like a stranger in Cuba, and is totally ineffectual. Gustavo is a corrupt young rake. Luciano, the widower of a daughter of Fernando and Maela, is a sincere but defeated man. Only Isolina, the daughter, and Joaquín Artigas, Fernando's foster son, have a dream of saving the family estate from foreign takeover. Isolina has a natural son, Teófilo, an alienated adolescent, and Joaquín has a daughter, Isabel, a loving young woman, who is seduced by Gustavo.

Financial setbacks are forcing Don Fernando to sell "Tembladera." Gustavo is arrested for murder and is bailed out by a Mr. Carpetbagger, who wants "Tembladera" transferred to the United States sugar company that is buying up all the land in the area. Joaquín believes he can administer the estate and persuades Don Fernando not to sell, and he also insists that Gustavo be brought to trial for his crime.

Isabel confronts Gustavo before he can escape for Mexico, and Joaquín and the others discover that he has tricked Isabel. Don Fernando disowns Gustavo (who later commits suicide offstage) and allows Joaquín and Isolina to take over "Tembladera," which they are determined to turn into a productive enterprise once more.

Ramos's other plays include *A Stray Bullet* (*Una bala perdida*, 1907), *The Hydra* (*La hidra*, 1908), *Nanda* (1908), and *When Love Dies* (*Cuando el amor muere . . .*, 1911).

JUDITH A. WEISS

Raphaelson, Samson   (1899–   )

American director, script and short-story writer, and dramatist. He is best known for *The Jazz Singer* (1925), a highly successful comedy drama starring George Jessel,

Nicholas Hannen and Constance Cummings in *Accent on Youth*. New York, Plymouth Theatre, 1934. [Theatre Collection, The New York Public Library at Lincoln Center]

about a Jewish youth belonging to a family of famous cantors and the conflict caused by his becoming a jazz singer. In 1927 *The Jazz Singer* was made into a now-famous motion picture, with Al Jolson in Jessel's role. Raphaelson also wrote *Young Love* (1928), *The Wooden Slipper* (1934), *Accent on Youth* (1934), *White Man* (1936), *Skylark* (1939), *The Perfect Marriage* (1944), and *Hilda Crane* (1950).

[GAUTAM DASGUPTA]

Terence Rattigan.
[Courtesy of
International
Copyright Agency.
Photograph by
Angus McBean]

Rattigan, Terence (1911–1977)

English dramatist. Rattigan was born in London, on June 10, 1911, the son of a diplomat. He went to Oxford with a history scholarship to prepare himself for the diplomatic service, but his early interest in the theatre soon reengaged him completely. He joined the Oxford University Dramatic Society and played a small part in a production of *Romeo and Juliet* staged by John Gielgud. His first play, *First Episode*, written in collaboration with Philip Heimann, was performed in London in 1933. It failed, but Rattigan left Oxford determined to become a dramatist.

Within the next two years he wrote five plays, none of which was produced. Then, in 1936, his farcical comedy *French Without Tears* was staged. It enjoyed an immediate success and one of the longest runs in British theatrical history. His next three plays failed, however.

During World War II, Rattigan served as an air gunner in the Royal Air Force, from 1940 to 1945. His roman-

tic drama *Flare Path* was successfully produced in 1942. This was followed by the comedy *While the Sun Shines*, in 1943, and the popular hit *Love in Idleness (O Mistress Mine)* in 1944. But not until 1946, with *The Winslow Boy*, did Rattigan convince the critics that he merited serious attention. A popular success, the play won the Ellen Terry Award in London; and when it was produced in New York the following year, the New York Drama Crit-

The Winslow Boy, with (l. to r.) Alan Webb, Frank Allenby, Michael Kingsley, Valerie White, and Michael Newell. New York, Empire Theatre, 1947.

(Top) Alfred Lunt and Lynn Fontanne in *O Mistress Mine.* New York, Empire Theatre, 1946; (bottom) *French Without Tears,* with Penelope Dudley Ward. New York, Henry Miller's Theatre, 1937.

ics Circle acclaimed it the best foreign play of the year. Rattigan again received the Ellen Terry Award in 1948, for *The Browning Version*. *The Deep Blue Sea* (1952) had an unenthusiastic reception from the public and critics but *Separate Tables* was the biggest hit of the London season in 1954–1955 and was successfully produced in New York in 1956.

Rattigan has also written several original film scenarios as well as the screen versions of *The Winslow Boy*, *The Browning Version*, and *The Prince and the Showgirl* (from his own play *The Sleeping Prince*).

WORK

Rattigan has had one of the most successful careers in the modern English theatre. *French Without Tears* (1936), which describes romantic entanglements among the students in a French cram course conducted on the Riviera, ran for more than 1,000 performances and was followed by several other equally popular and frivolous comedies. Rattigan's reputation as a dramatist rests, however, on such solid plays as *The Winslow Boy* (1946), *The Browning Version* (1948), *Separate Tables* (1954), and *Ross* (1960), all of which demonstrate his theatrical dexterity. *The Winslow Boy*, based on the Archer-Shee case that agitated England during the first decade of this century, is propelled by the elder Winslow's determination to secure justice, even if this means financial ruin for himself and his family, and by the determination of the lawyer, Sir

Eric Portman and Margaret Leighton in *Separate Tables*. New York, Music Box Theatre, 1956. [Photograph by Vandamm. Theatre Collection, The New York Public Library at Lincoln Center, Astor, Lenox and Tilden Foundations]

Margaret Sullavan and James Hanley in *The Deep Blue Sea*. New York, Morosco Theatre, 1952. [Photograph by Vandamm. Theatre Collection, The New York Public Library at Lincoln Center, Astor, Lenox and Tilden Foundations]

Robert Morton. In *The Browning Version,* Rattigan portrays a failure who, while suffering yet another humiliation, suddenly musters the power to rise up to life. *Separate Tables* examines the lonely lives of four contrasted characters. One of the best examples of Rattigan's craftsmanship is *Ross,* a biographical drama about T. E. Lawrence. While the dialogue is held taut, the action ranges between England and Arabia, as the romantic personality of Lawrence unfolds through dramatic episodes.

The Winslow Boy (1946). Drama concerning Ronnie Winslow, who at the age of fourteen is falsely accused of having stolen a 5-shilling postal order and is consequently dismissed from the Royal Naval College at Osborne. His proud father insists that his son's name be cleared, and gradually the case becomes a *cause célèbre.* The cold, logical, but idealistic Sir Robert Morton, engaged to defend Ronnie, fights the case through to the House of Lords, where he wins an acquittal under the battle cry "Let right be done."

The Browning Version (1948). One-act play that takes place in the living room of Andrew Crocker-Harris, a formal, reserved classics schoolmaster, "the Himmler of the lower fifth." Feared by his pupils, despised by his unfaithful wife, his dreams of a headmastership dissolved after eighteen years of unrequited drudgery and domestic turmoil, he is deeply moved when one of his students presents him with a copy of Browning's translation of *Agamemnon.* The impact of this incident rejuvenates Harris's soul, and he begins for the first time in years to assert his individuality and his rights.

Separate Tables (1954). Two short plays, both set in a drab residential hotel where the clearheaded manageress, Miss Cooper, involves herself in the private lives of her clientele. *Table by the Window* concerns the stormy reconciliation, after eight years of divorce, of an eccentric leftwing writer and his cold, lonely ex-wife, a model now dreading the ravages of time. *Table Number Seven* focuses on the pathetic figures of a self-styled "Major," recently charged with indecency, and the mousy daughter of a snobbish old woman. The fake military man and the shy girl draw sustenance from each other and thus begin to assert their emotional rights as human beings.

Ross (1960). The title refers to the pseudonym under which T. E. Lawrence (Lawrence of Arabia) enlisted in the Royal Air Force in 1922. In sixteen dreamlike scenes in episodic form, the play portrays the puzzling soldier-mystic. In a malarial fever Ross relives his exploits in unifying the Arabs against their Turkish oppressors during World War I: he dwells on his ambition, his hankering after fame and adulation, and his descent into callous inhumanity after being obscenely violated by his enemies. Despite his subsequent search for anonymity and peace of mind, his identity is discovered and he is discharged from the RAF, whereupon he resolves to change his name once again and reenlist.

PLAYS

Unless otherwise noted, the plays were first performed in London.

1. (With Philip Heimann) *First Episode.* Play. Produced London, Q Theatre, Sept. 11, 1933.

2. *French Without Tears.* Comedy, 3 acts. Published 1937. Produced Criterion Theatre, Nov. 6, 1936.

3. *After the Dance.* Play. Produced St. James's Theatre, June 21, 1939.

4. (With Anthony Maurice). *Follow My Leader.* Play. Produced Apollo Theatre, Jan. 16, 1940.

5. (With Hector Bolitho). *Grey Farm.* Play. Produced New York, Hudson Theatre, May 3, 1940.

6. *Flare Path.* Play, 3 acts. Published 1942. Produced Apollo Theatre, Aug. 12, 1942.

7. *While the Sun Shines.* Comedy, 3 acts. Produced Globe Theatre, Dec. 24, 1943.

8. *Love in Idleness (O Mistress Mine).* Play, 3 acts. Published 1945. Produced Lyric Theatre, Dec. 20, 1944.

9. *The Winslow Boy.* Drama, 4 acts. Published 1946. Produced Lyric Theatre, May 23, 1946.

The following two plays (Nos. 10 and 11) were produced and published under the collective title *Playbill.*

10. *The Browning Version.* Play, 1 act. Published 1949. Produced Phoenix Theatre, Sept. 8, 1948.

11. *Harlequinade.* Play, 1 act. Produced Phoenix Theatre, Sept. 8, 1948.

12. *Adventure Story.* Play; prologue, 2 acts, and epilogue. Published 1950. Produced St. James's Theatre, Mar. 17, 1949.

13. *Who Is Sylvia?* Light comedy, 3 acts. Published 1951. Produced Criterion Theatre, Oct. 24, 1950.

14. *The Deep Blue Sea.* Drama, 3 acts. Published 1952. Produced Duchess Theatre, Mar. 5, 1952.

15. *The Sleeping Prince.* Occasional fairy tale, 2 acts. Published 1954. Produced Phoenix Theatre, Nov. 5, 1953.

The following two plays (Nos. 16 and 17) were produced and published under the collective title *Separate Tables.*

16. *Table by the Window.* Play, 3 scenes. Published 1955. Produced St. James's Theatre, Sept. 22, 1954.

17. *Table Number Seven.* Play, 2 scenes. Published 1955. Produced St. James's Theatre, Sept. 22, 1954.

18. *Variation on a Theme.* Play, 2 acts. Published 1958. Produced Globe Theatre, May 8, 1958.

19. *Ross.* Dramatic portrait. Published 1960. Produced Haymarket Theatre, May 12, 1960.

20. *Joie de Vivre.* Musical. Produced Queen's Theatre, July 14, 1960. Music: Robert Stolz. Lyrics: Paul Dehn. Based on Rattigan's play *French Without Tears.*

21. *Man and Boy.* Play. Produced Queen's Theatre, Sept. 4, 1963.

22. *A Bequest to the Nation.* Play, 2 acts. Produced Haymarket Theatre, Sept. 23, 1970.

23. *All on Her Own.* Published 1970. Televized 1968. Produced 1974.

24. *High Summer.* Published 1973. Televized 1972.

25. *In Praise of Love: Before Dawn and After Lydia.* Published 1973. Produced as *IPOL,* 1974.

EDITIONS

After the Dance. Published in *Six Plays of 1939,* London, 1939.
The Deep Blue Sea. Published in *Famous Plays of Today.* London, 1953.
French Without Tears. Published in *Theatre Omnibus,* London, 1938.
The Winslow Boy. Published in *Drama II,* ed. by C. E. Redmond, New York, 1962.

CRITICISM

M. Darlow and G. Hodson, *Terence Rattigan: The Man and His Work,* London, 1979.

Raynal, Paul (1885–1971)

French dramatist. His reputation flourished in the period between the two world wars. Turning his back on the dominant naturalism, Raynal wrote psychological dramas that were cast in the mold of French classical tragedy. His highly symbolic plays employ elevated language and feature protagonists who are seldom identified by more than name and sometimes only by their social role: "the father," "the soldier," and so on. *The Master of His Heart (Le maître de son coeur;* wr. 1913, prod. 1920) focuses on the complex relationship between two men and a woman. Resenting the friendship between the men, the woman tries to introduce dissent. The younger of the men dies convinced that he has been betrayed by both the woman and his friend. Raynal's best-known play is *The Tomb Beneath the Arch of Triumph*

Jean Yonnel as Christ in *A souffert sous Ponce Pilate.* **Paris, Comédie-Française, 1946. [French Cultural Services]**

(*Le tombeau sous l'Arc de Triomphe,* 1924), also known as *The Unknown Warrior,* which highlights misunderstanding between the soldiers at the front and civilians safely ensconced at home. The play respects the three classical unities and employs a stylized prose that approximates the rhythm of Alexandrine verse. *Has Suffered under Pontius Pilate* (*A souffert sous Ponce Pilate,* 1939) attempts to explain the betrayal of Judas by showing him as a simpleminded man who was merely trying to protect Christ from what he considered a greater danger. *Human Material* (*Le matériel humain;* wr. 1935, prod. 1948), considered by some critics to be his best play, is based on an incident that occurred during the French Army mutinies of 1917. It contrasts national necessity and personal freedom and shows the impossibility of interrupting military disciplinary machinery once it has been set in action. Raynal's other plays include *Under the Sun of Instinct* (*Au soleil de l'instinct,* 1932) and *La Francerie* (1933). *See* UNITIES in glossary.

The Tomb Beneath the Arch of Triumph; The Unknown Warrior (*Le tombeau sous l'Arc de Triomphe,* 1924). A disillusioned young soldier returns home on an overnight leave to see his father and his fiancée. He finds them both apathetic and unable to understand the concerns of the men in the trenches. Given his long absence, his fiancée Aude, the only one of the three symbolic characters to be given a name, is no longer sure that she is in love with him. He manages, however, to rekindle her affection, and they spend the night together. Having reawakened courage and hope in Aude and in his father,

he returns to the front the next morning to carry out a dangerous mission that is almost sure to mean his death. Produced Paris, Comédie-Française, February 1, 1924.

[JOSEPH E. GARREAU]

Razzi, Girolamo or Silvano   (fl. 1550–1600)

Italian dramatist. He wrote three comedies in prose and a tragedy in verse before taking up a monastic life. *The Magpie* (*La cecca,* 1556) is a lively Renaissance comedy of student life at the University of Pisa. Razzi's other two comedies, *The Nurse* (*La balia,* 1560) and *La Gostanza* (1564), were created in the belief that comedies should instruct as well as delight; they are therefore in a more serious vein. Razzi's tragedy *Gismunda* (1569) is directly inspired by the novella about the same subject in Boccaccio's *Decameron* (IV, 1).

[PETER BONDANELLA]

Reaney, James   (1926–   )

Canadian playwright. His work is a unique amalgam of verse, children's play and games, fairy tale and myth, docudrama, and conventions borrowed from Oriental theatrical forms. An academic who has taught at the University of Manitoba and the University of Western Ontario, he completed his doctoral dissertation under the supervision of Northrop Frye, whose theories of mythic pattern and literary archetype have had a profound influence on Reaney's creative work. Reaney initially gained recognition as a poet; his first book of verse, *The Red Heart,* won the Governor-General's Award in 1949. His first dramatic work was a libretto for a chamber opera, *Night-Blooming Cereus,* written in 1952 but not performed until 1960. The way in which the sharply observed reality of southwestern Ontario is linked to universal myth through a magical act of transformation is typical of the writer's work. *One-Man Masque* (1960), a poetic tour of objects encountered in the cycle of life to death to life again, was written to accompany the opera in its first production. *The Killdeer* (1960), *The Easter Egg* (1962), and *The Sun and the Moon* (1964), all set in rural Ontario, are pastoral comedies with the sinister and macabre (murder, suicide, abortion) lurking in the green shade; in each, the forces of death are ultimately defeated by the liberating power of the imagination, by the power of words and metaphor, a recurrent theme in Reaney's work.

The earlier plays lose some power through the form's contradicting the content; the structural conventions are usually those of the realistic play, portraying a homely and familiar reality, but the fantastic turns of event, fairy-tale transformations and revelations, and nonrealistic use of image seemed out of place to many audiences. However, in *Listen to the Wind* (1966) the child's activity of make-believe is made part of the theatrical method as well as the poetic content. A sickly boy attempts to reunite his separated parents, to give structure to his world, by enlisting other children to stage a melodrama in which good and evil are clearly delineated. Through the charming and deliberately makeshift performance, in which anything can represent anything else, the myth is shown to be part of the homely reality. The playwright employed similar techniques in *Colours in the Dark*, which had its first production at the Stratford Festival's Avon Theatre in 1967. The play, which Reaney describes as a "play box" packed with "memory objects," comprises forty-two short scenes viewed through the imagination of a child confined, blindfolded, to bed with measles, and again, through the memory of an adult recalling the incident. The vignettes, songs, skits, chants, and games are linked by projected images, large mythic and metaphorical patterns, and a theatrical framework to constitute a model of a developing imagination, individual and national.

After a brief excursion into academic comedy, *Three Desks* (1967), Reaney used the highly theatrical presentational style again in *The Donnelly Trilogy: Sticks and Stones* (1973), *St. Nicholas Hotel* (1974), and *Handcuffs* (1975). The plays are based on a nineteenth-century religious feud which resulted in the massacre, in Biddulph, of an entire family; legend has made the victims, the "black Donnellys," the villains of the piece, and Reaney's trilogy is, in effect, a vindication; but, more importantly, it is also an exploration of the nature of legend and of "truth." An account of the NDWT Company's crosscountry tour with the trilogy is contained in Reaney's book, *Fourteen Barrels from Sea to Sea. Baldoon*, written with G. H. Gervais and first produced in 1976, is based on another rural Ontario legend, this one of ghosts and witchcraft, while *The Dismissal* (1977) is about a student strike at the University of Toronto in 1894; one of those involved was William Lyon Mackenzie King, later prime minister of Canada. *Wacousta*, based on the novel of the same name by John Richardson, was published in 1979.

Throughout his career, Reaney has written and produced children's plays and puppet plays; a number of these were collected and published as *Apple Butter and Other Plays for Children* in 1973.

CHRIS JOHNSON

Rebello, Luiz F. (1924–   )

Portuguese playwright and critic. Rebello was one of the founders and directors of Teatro-Estudio Salitre, which presented his expressionistic play *The World Began at 5:47* (*O mundo começou as 5 e 47*, 1947). Most of his theatre is in a neorealistic vein and deals with the middle classes. An authority on the dramatic literatures of other countries, Rebello published many valuable articles in *Imagens do Teatro Contemporâneo* (1961). His texts and essays have appeared under the titles *Teatro moderno; Teatro Português do romantismo aos nossos dias; Teatro português das origins ao romantismo*; and *D. João da Cámara e os caminhos do teatro português* (in *Perspectiva da literatura portuguesa no Século XIX*, 1949; 2d ed., 1962).

RUTH S. LAMB

Reed, Mark (1890–1969)

American architect and dramatist. He was best known for his comedy *Yes, My Darling Daughter* (1937), in which the phases of feminine freedom are presented through an erstwhile suffragist, a middle-aged aunt, product of

the 1920s, and the daughter, a maturing, freethinking college girl. Of Reed's other plays, only *Petticoat Fever* (1933) enjoyed a moderate success.

[GAUTAM DASGUPTA]

Régio, José (1901–   )

Portuguese playwright, novelist, and poet. Influenced by Pirandello, the German expressionist theatre, and the French surrealists, Régio writes dramas in which the protagonists were often considered mad in spite of—or perhaps because of—the superhuman lucidity and perception they display. In *Jacob and the Angel* (*Jacob e o anjo*, 1937) the protagonist finds understanding and the capacity to love only as a result of bodily pain and mortification of his soul. The playwright suggests that spirit cleanses by consuming all and that the love of God as it settles upon men is fearful. The protagonist of *Benilde or the Virgin Mother* (*Benilde ou a Virgem Mãe*, 1947) is a young woman who is convinced that her imminent motherhood is a divine miracle. *King Sebastian* (*El Rei Sebastião*, reworks Portuguese history as expressionist drama. Misunderstood by noblemen who oppose his African adventure, Dom Sebastian lives his mad dream of glory and self-destruction in an attempt to redeem himself.

Intellectual and often highly abstract—for example, as in his *The Salvation of the World* (*A salvação do mundo*, 1954)—Régio's theatre is not of a nature that appeals to the general theatregoing public. Other plays by him are *Three Masks* (*Tres máscaras*, 1934), *My Situation* (*O meu caso*, 1957), and *Mario or Myself or Another* (*Mario ou eu proprio o outro*, 1957).

RUTH S. LAMB

Regnard, Jean-François (1655–1709)

French dramatist. The exact date of his birth is unknown, but he was baptized in Paris on February 8, 1655. His father, a wealthy fish merchant, died when the boy was three, and by the time Regnard reached twenty he was in control of a large fortune. As a result of his mother's assiduous attention to his upbringing as a gentleman, he became a man of letters and manners, widely traveled and accomplished in sports. At the age of seventeen he went to Italy, remaining there two years. On October 3, 1678, he was captured by Algerian pirates, who took him to Constantinople, where he had to wait seven months before being ransomed. He gave an account of this adventure in *The Provençale* (*La Provençale*, 1731), a posthumously published romance. In 1681 he set off again, visiting Scandinavia, Poland, Hungary, and Germany. In 1683, having returned to France, he purchased the office of Trésorier de France au Bureau des Finances de Paris, which contributed to his knowledge of finance without unduly restricting his time. Shortly thereafter he wrote his only tragedy, *Sapor*, which was never produced. Turning to comedy, he began contributing to the Comédie-Italienne in 1688, sometimes in collaboration with Charles Dufresny. *See* DUFRESNY, CHARLES RIVIÈRE.

By 1694 Regnard had begun to write for the Comédie-Française. That year he wrote his *Satire Against*

Husbands (Satire contre les maris) in reply to Nicolas Boileau's *Satire Against Wives*, arousing the enmity of the powerful critic. With the production of *The Gambler (Le joueur)* in 1696, Regnard achieved a success that was to remain undiminished until his death. In 1699 he purchased the handsome Château de Grillon, near Dourdan, not far from Paris, where he lived for a decade. His sudden death on September 4, 1709, has been attributed to poisoning, but this seems unlikely.

Work

With the exception of Molière, Regnard was undoubtedly the finest French comic dramatist in the second half of the seventeenth century. He was a "laughing" dramatist who presented the foibles of his time realistically and amusingly, without the fierceness of the satirist. Although he wrote in the manner of Molière, he lacked his predecessor's insight and his ability to reveal the very core of a character. Yet in wit, cleverness, flexibility, and craftsmanship, Regnard was not far behind, and some critics have considered his verse as good as or better than Molière's. His masterpiece, *The Gambler* (1696), a study of a gambler who sacrifices love to his incurable habit, and *The Sole Heir (Le légataire universel,* 1708), the story of a successful deception, are expertly written and are still being performed. Only slightly inferior are *The Amorous Follies (Les folies amoureuses,* 1704), a charming play about a clever orphan who, outwitting the man who keeps her cloistered, succeeds in eloping with her lover; *The Absentminded Man (Le distrait,* 1697), an interesting portrait of a scatterbrained hero; *Democritus in Love (Démocrite amoureux,* 1700), a romantic comedy enlivened by the antics of the servants; *The Menaechmi, or The Twins (Les Ménechmes, ou Les jumeaux,* 1705), a successful adaptation of Plautus's comedy *The Twin Menaechmi;* and *Wait for Me under the Elm (Attendez-moi sous l'orme,* 1694), an excellent one-act play in which a group of peasants outwit an officer. *See* MOLIÈRE; PLAUTUS.

Plays for the Comédie-Italienne include *Harlequin the Lady Killer (Arlequin homme à bonnes fortunes,* 1690); *The Coquette, or the Ladies' Academy (La coquette, ou L'académie des dames,* 1691); and two others written in collaboration with Dufresny, *The Chinese (Les chinois,* 1692) and the highly successful *The Saint-Germain Fair (La foire Saint-Germain,* 1696).

The Gambler (*Le joueur,* 1696). Comedy dealing with the adventures of Valère, a handsome and agreeable young man who has but one fault: he is hopelessly addicted to gambling. His refusal to mend his ways costs him the love of Angélique, who agrees instead to marry his uncle Dorante. The repentant Valère again wins her confidence, and Géronte, his father, agrees to pay the young man's debts. However, when Angélique gives Valère a jeweled portrait of herself, the temptation becomes too great. He pawns it, gambles, and wins but postpones redeeming the portrait. Word of the transaction reaches Angélique, and the portrait falls into the hands of Dorante. Meanwhile, Valère has gambled again and has lost. Angélique confronts him with the portrait, ignores his lies and pleas, and agrees to marry Dorante.

Jean-François Regnard. [Culver Pictures]

Disinherited by his father, Valère is left penniless and friendless, but he still hopes to make his fortune by gambling.

The Sole Heir (*Le légataire universel,* 1708). Comedy centering on Éraste, who is in love with Isabelle. Mme. Argante, Isabelle's mother, promises Éraste her daughter's hand if he inherits the major portion of his uncle Géronte's fortune. Although an invalid, the old man takes a fancy to Isabelle and plans to marry her himself, but he is dissuaded. He finally decides to make Éraste his heir but also plans to make bequests to a rural nephew and niece. Masquerading as each of these two characters, Éraste's rascally valet Crispin makes them appear so disagreeable that Géronte changes his mind about their bequests. Soon afterward he falls into a coma and, to the horror of his heir presumptive, seems about to die intestate. Crispin disguises himself as the elderly invalid, calls the notaries, and makes a will, also providing generous annuities for himself and Géronte's servant Lisette, whom he loves. When Géronte recovers from his coma, the worried conspirators finally manage to convince him that he himself dictated the will. He is persuaded to let it stand. Thus Éraste marries Isabelle, and Crispin marries Lisette.

[JOSEPH E. GARREAU]

Plays

All were first performed in Paris.

1. *Sapor.* Tragedy, 5 acts; verse. Written ca. 1682/86? Published 1731.

2. *Le divorce (The Divorce).* Comedy, 1 act. Published 1694. Produced Comédie-Italienne, Mar. 17, 1688.

3. *Arlequin homme à bonnes fortunes (Harlequin the Lady Killer).* Comedy, 3 acts. Published 1694. Produced Comédie-Italienne, Jan. 10, 1690.

4. *Critique de "L'homme à bonnes fortunes" (Critique of "The Lady Killer").* Comedy, 1 act. Published 1700. Produced Comédie-Italienne, Mar. 1, 1690.

5. *Les filles errantes, ou Les intrigues des hôtelleries (The Wandering Girls, or The Hotel Intrigues).* Comedy, 3 acts. Published 1700. Produced Comédie-Italienne, Aug. 24, 1690.

6. *La coquette, ou L'académie des dames (The Coquette, or The Ladies' Academy).* Comedy. Published 1700. Produced Comédie-Italienne, Jan. 17, 1691.

7. (With Charles Rivière Dufresny). *Les chinois (The Chinese).* Comedy, 4 acts, Published 1700. Produced Comédie-Italienne, Dec. 13, 1692.

8. (With Dufresny). *La baguette, ou L'augmentation de Vulcain (The Rod, or The Rise of Vulcan)*. Comedy, 1 act. Published 1694. Produced Jan. 10, 1693.

9. *La naissance d'Amadis (The Birth of Amadis)*. Comedy. Published 1697. Produced Comédie-Italienne, Feb. 10, 1694.

10. *Attendez-moi sous l'orme (Wait for Me under the Elm)*. Comedy, 1 act. Published 1694. Produced Comédie-Française, May 19, 1694.

11. *La sérénade (The Serenade)*. Comedy, 1 act. Published 1694. Produced Comédie-Française, July 3, 1694.

12. (With Dufresny). *La suite de la foire Saint-Germain, ou Les momies d'Égypte (The Sequel to the Saint-Germain Fair, or The Mummies of Egypt)*. Comedy, 1 act. Published 1700. Produced Comédie-Italienne, Mar. 19, 1696.

13. *Le bourgeois de Falaise, ou Le bal (The Bourgeois of Falaise, or The Ball)*. Comedy, 1 act; verse. Published 1696. Produced Comédie-Française, June 14, 1696.

14. (With Dufresny). *La foire Saint-Germain (The Saint Germain Fair)*. Comedy, 3 acts. Published 1696. Produced Comédie-Italienne, Dec. 19, 1696.

15. *Le joueur (The Gambler)*. Comedy, 5 acts; verse. Published 1697. Produced Comédie-Française, Dec. 19, 1696.

16. *Le distrait (The Absentminded Man)*. Comedy, 5 acts; verse. Published 1698. Produced Comédie-Française, Dec. 2, 1697.

17. *Le carnaval de Venise (The Carnival of Venice)*. Comedy ballet, 3 acts; verse. Published 1699.

18. *Démocrite amoureux (Democritus in Love)*. Comedy, 5 acts; verse. Published 1700. Produced Comédie-Française, Jan. 12, 1700.

19. *Le retour imprévu* (The Unforeseen Return)*. Comedy, 1 act. Published 1700. Produced Comédie-Française, Feb. 11, 1700.

20. *Les folies amoureuses (The Amorous Follies)*. Comedy, 3 acts; verse. Published 1704. Produced Comédie-Française, Jan. 15, 1704.

21. (Adaptation). *Les Ménechmes, ou Les jumeaux (The Menaechmi, or The Twins)*. Comedy, 5 acts; verse. Published 1706. Produced Comédie-Française. Dec. 4, 1705. Adapted from Plautus's comedy *The Twin Menaechmi*.

22. *Le légataire universel (The Sole Heir)*. Comedy, 5 acts; verse. Published 1708. Produced Comédie-Française, Jan. 9, 1708.

23. *Critique du "Légataire universel" (Critique of "The Sole Heir")*. Comedy, 1 act. Published 1708. Produced Comédie-Française, Feb. 9, 1708.

24. *Les souhaits (The Wishes)*. Comedy, 1 act; verse. Published 1731.

25. *Les vendanges, ou Le bailli d'Anières (The Profits, or The Bailiff of Anières)*. Comedy, 1 act; verse. Published 1731.

EDITIONS

Oeuvres complètes, ed. by É. Fournier, new ed., Paris, 1875.

The Sole Heir (The Residuary Legatee). Published in *French Comedies of the XVIIIth Century*, ed. and tr. by R. Aldington, London, 1923; *Eighteenth Century French Plays*, ed. by C. D. Brenner and N.A. Goodyear, New York, 1927.

CRITICISM

J. Guyot, *Le poète Jean François Regnard en son château de Grillon*, Paris, 1907; A. Hallays, *Regnard*, Paris, 1929.

Rehfisch, Hans José   (1891–1960)

German dramatist. Originally a judge, Rehfisch achieved worldwide popularity with the tragicomedy *Who Weeps for Juckenack (Wer weint um Juckenack*, 1924). One of the most famous playwrights in Germany before World War II, Rehfisch, after his return from exile, launched on the postwar German stage new versions of his early comedies *Nickel and the Thirty-six Just Men (Nickel und die sechsunddreissig Gerechten*, 1925) and *Duel on the Beach (Duell am Lido*, 1926) as well as many new plays, and he reestablished himself as a leading and prolific dramatist. Technically skillful, realistic in a style often reminiscent of journalism, and dealing with a wide range of vital problems, including the pet concerns of expressionism, his thirty-one plays paint lucid pictures in black and white that are sometimes indebted to Sternheim and Wedekind, sometimes to Kaiser and Shaw. Of his early plays, *The Gynecologist (Der Frauenarzt*, 1927); *The Dreyfus Affair (Die Affaire Dreyfus*, 1929), written in collaboration

with Wilhelm Herzog; and *Brest-Litovsk* (1931) won great praise. In the postwar drama *Beyond Fear (Jenseits der Angst*, 1958), Rehfisch touched on the hazards of nuclear research and asked whether scientists should divulge the results of their work to irresponsible politicians. *Boomerang (Bumerang*, 1960) satirized the 1872 Leipzig trial and indictment of August Bebel and Wilhelm Liebknecht as dangerous Socialists because they had refused to vote in favor of war credits in the North German Bundestag.

[PETER JELAVICH]

Renard, Jules   (1864–1910)

French novelist and playwright. His reputation in the theatre is based on three brilliant one-act plays; however, he also employed the dialogue form in much of his fiction. Renard's theatre is classical in terms of its precision, purity of language, and penetrating psychology. In his first play, *The Pleasure in Parting (Le plaisir de rompre*, 1897), a middle-class young man on the eve of a "respectable" marriage comes to pay a final visit to his mistress. With a sharp eye for detail, Renard shows them examining their liaison and deciding with bittersweet calm that it was perfect, since they always behaved toward one another with admirable civilization and restraint. When the man "sentimentally" suggests that they spend this final night together, his former mistress wisely decides that when something is over, it is over.

Poil de Carotte (1900), Renard's most popular play, is based on his celebrated autobiographical novel. In the dramatic adaptation, the unhappy adolescent hero is

Scene from *Le plaisir de rompre*. Paris, Comédie-Française, 1949. [French Cultural Services]

John Gray and Patricia Mertens in *The Pleasure of Parting,* as staged in 1978 by the Festival Theatre Foundation. [Photograph courtesy of Robert O'Rourke]

somewhat older and the action centers on his attempt at suicide. *Household Bread* (*Le pain de ménage,* 1902) concerns a bored middle-class husband momentarily attracted by the idea of infidelity. Recognizing him as an essentially fainthearted and overimaginative type, the woman to whom he proposes a liaison paints his psychological portrait in the following terms: "You have the wingspan of an eagle, but the appetite of a swallow. You need only shift a piece of furniture to convince yourself that you are moving your household, or open a window to believe that you are free." Under the circumstances, she suggests that if he merely kisses her hand, he will feel that he has betrayed his wife. Some of Renard's

Jean-Paul Roussillon in a Comédie-Française production of *Poil de Carotte.* [French Cultural Services]

other plays include *Monsieur Vernet* (1903), based on his novel *The Sponger* (*L'écornifleur,* 1902); and *The Bigot* (*La bigote,* 1909), which takes up some of the characters who originally appeared in *Poil de Carotte.*

Poil de Carotte (1900). Somewhat sentimentalized version of Renard's brilliant and acerbic novel of the same name (1894). The action takes place on the Lépic farm, where young François–whose red hair has earned him the somewhat nasty nickname "Poil de Carotte" (carrottop)–is spending an uneasy vacation from school under the vigilant and malevolent eye of his mother. Relations between the Lépics are strained: for unspecified reasons M. Lépic has not spoken to his wife in years, and she, an unloved and unlovable woman, finds release in tyrannizing over Poil de Carotte, who is convinced that his father is indifferent to him. A variety of small incidents pinpoint the boy's unhappy situation, and the action hinges on his attempted suicide when Mme. Lépic secretly forces him to refuse to accompany his father on a fishing trip. Saved by the intervention of his father, Poil de Carotte blurts out his unhappiness and his inability to love his mother. His father's response makes Poil de Carotte realize that his own misery is matched by the solitude and wretchedness of his father. A bond is thus formed between father and son, victims of the terrible Mme. Lépic.

[JOSEPH E. GARREAU]

Rendra, W. S. (1935–   )

Indonesian poet, playwright, translator, and critic. Although born into a Roman Catholic family on November 7, 1935, in Solo, central Java, Willibordus Surendra Rendra was also nurtured on the deeply rooted Javanese court traditions. His father was a devotee of old Javanese literature, and his mother had been a *srimpi* dancer in Jogjakarta. (*Srimpi* is a highly ritualistic court dance of central Java.) After completing his secondary education in a Catholic school, Rendra studied Western literature at Gajah Mada University in Jogjakarta. By 1957, before he made any appreciable impact as a dramatist, Rendra had established himself as an innovative poet of the first rank. *A Ballad for Lovers* (*Ballada Orang Tjinta*), his first volume of poetry, won the literature prize of the National Cultural Consultative Council in 1957. A Harvard University seminar on literature took him to the United States in 1964, but it was only three years later that he returned home. In those years he traveled, and after winning a scholarship, he studied at the American Academy of Dramatic Arts in New York City.

Soon after his return to Jogjakarta he formed the Little Workshop (Bengkel Kecil), which incorporated some of the avant-garde ideas of a theatre collective found on Off and particularly Off-Off Broadway in the 1960s. Within a year of the formation of his group, Rendra presented the notorious "mini-theatre" performance events. The titles of the improvisational pieces, such as *Piiiiip* and *Sssssstt,* may not have made any sense, but their implicit message that theatre should be autonomous of literature, rather than its adjunct, was abundantly clear. In subsequent years, Rendra transformed a host of Western and especially classical Greek plays into Indonesian cultural events. For instance, Oedipus of *Oedipus Rex,* performed in 1970, was presented as a Balinese ruler wearing a mask from the Balinese *Topeng,* or masked dance drama. On the other hand, the missionizing Oedipus of *Oedipus at Colonus,* staged in 1974, appeared, as befitted his new status, as a Javanese monk.

In spite of the fact that Rendra was weaned on the Javanese court tradition, he also turned for inspiration to the popular and profane theatre of Java. Thus Vladimir and Estragon in his translation of Samuel Beckett's *Waiting for Godot (Menantikan Godot),* performed in 1969, were without much difficulty accepted as *ludruk* clowns. Many of these innovations appear in retrospect to be preparations for the building of a scaffolding of traditional performing genres for use in his own plays. He turned to satire in his play *Mastadon and Eagle (Mastadon dan Burung Kondor),* which he produced in 1973. Set in a South American republic, the play broadly and farcically draws frequent analogies between the adversities of the Latin American poor and the downtrodden of Indonesia. Two years later Rendra's *The Struggle of the Naga Tribe (Kisah Perjuangan Suku Naga)* crystallized his lessons on the political economy of the Third World. This play, more than any other, is almost entirely built upon a traditional framework—the coherent form of Javanese *wayang kulit,* or shadow theatre. While audiences seemed to have enjoyed the play, many local critics bred on the ironic ambiguities of the modern stage did not entirely embrace Rendra's attempts to transplant the mythic vision of good against evil forces to the contemporary world.

Following a protest poetry reading by Rendra, the Indonesian authorities arrested him on May 1, 1978. After his release on August 12 of the same year, he was placed under "town arrest" until October 15, when he was unconditionally freed. Since then Rendra has encountered difficulties in getting sponsors for his performances. Even if Rendra does not write or stage another play, his pioneering contribution in forging an alliance between traditional and modern theatre will continue to be a sustaining force in contemporary Indonesian Theatre. *See* SOUTHEAST ASIAN THEATRE.

KRISHEN JIT

Requena, María Asunción (1918–)

Chilean playwright. A member of the Generation of 1950, María Asunción Requena, a dentist, wrote plays as a relaxation from her profession. Her first play, *Mister Jones Arrives at Six o'Clock (Míster Jones llega a las seis),* set in the pampas of southern Chile, won the Teatro Nacional competition in 1952.

Within the next six years this dramatist from southern Chile wrote eleven plays. *Fort Bulnes (Fuerte Bulnes,* 1953), was sent to the Teatro Experimental Universidad de Chile. It was a portrait of frontier life in colonial Chile. *A Winter's Tale (Cuento de invierno),* more appropriately retitled *Magellan Fox Farm (El criadero de zorros de Magallanes,* 1957), had as its protagonist a woman administrator of a large Tierra del Fuego estate who must choose

María Asunción Requena. [Republic of Chile]

between her devotion to the desolate southern land and its inhabitants and her love for the man who is courting her.

Further glimpses of the desolate Chilean southland appear in *Hot Bread (Pan caliente,* 1958), which won a prize in the play contest of the Experimental Theatre. *A Longer Road (Un camino más largo,* 1959) dramatized the lengthy struggle of Ernestina Pérez, Chile's first woman physician, to earn her degree. Abandoning Chilean history, Requena tried her hand at farce with *Tiger Skin (Piel de tigre,* 1961), but the play was not well received.

WILLIS KNAPP JONES and JUDITH A. WEISS

CRITICISM

F. Alegría, "Chile's Experimental Theatre," *InterAmerican Review,* vol. 4, no. 10, p. 1945, Oct. 1945; R. A. Latcham, "Curtain Time in Chile," *Americas,* vol. 4, no. 9, pp. 16–19, Sept. 1952; W. K. Jones, "New Life in Chile's Theatre," *Modern Drama,* May 1959; W. K. Jones, "Chile's Dramatic Renaissance," *Hispania,* vol. 45, pp. 89–94, Mar. 1961.

Riaza, Luis (1925–)

Spanish avant-garde dramatist. Riaza has won recognition as a writer of exceptional imagination and originality. Born in Madrid, he was forced to leave school at the age of fourteen to help support his family. Though he soon started writing plays, it was not until he became associated with the Independent Theatre (Teatro Independiente)—a loosely formed alliance of amateur and semiprofessional groups which sprang up in the late 1960s—that his career took a serious turn. It was almost exclusively to these groups that he owed his earliest productions: *The Puppets (Los muñecos,* 1968); *The Cages (Las jaulas,* 1970); *Ferdinand (El Fernando,* 1971), a collective work in which eight authors collaborated; *The Circles (Los círculos,* 1972); *The Palace of the Monkeys (El palacio de los monos,* 1977); and *The Garret of the Males and the Cellar of the Females (El desván de los machos y el sótano de las hembras,* 1974).

Riaza's only commercial production so far, *Portrait of*

a Lady with a Dog (Retrato de dama con perrito), was premiered in Madrid's Bellas Artes Theatre in 1979 under the auspices of the National Dramatic Center (Centro Dramático Nacional). It established his reputation as an outstanding vanguard dramatist but failed at the box office. (Riaza's plays are full of literary allusions and demand of the public a rather high level of sophistication.)

The theatre of Luis Riaza attempts to renovate contemporary Spanish dramaturgy and offers a radical assessment of present-day political, social, and cultural structures. Its ambiguous allegories suggest various levels of meaning (a practice which proved useful during the years when censorship was in operation). He not only attacks social, religious, and sexual myths but strikes out against aesthetic myths, particularly those related to the theatre. Employing the technique of parody, he questions the authenticity and value of new dramatic styles that became fashionable before they were properly assimilated.

Like his fellow avant-garde dramatists Miguel Romero Esteo and Francisco Nieva, with whom he is frequently compared, Riaza is extremely concerned with language and literary rhetoric. His theatre is richly baroque, but the spell of fascination which it casts over the audience is often abruptly broken by the unexpected injection of coarse expressions. He achieves a surrealistic effect not only by means of the ritualistic nature of the movements and dialogue but by the effective use of life-size puppets and characters who assume multiple roles, often sexually interchangeable ones. Among the current crop of vanguard Spanish dramatists, none exploits the theatrical possibilities of the tranvestite (usually a male actor interpreting a female character) as frequently or as skillfully as Riaza. Like the majority of serious contemporary Spanish playwrights, he has been highly influenced by Ramón del Valle Inclán, the creator of the *esperpento*, a grotesque type of farce which he developed during the 1920s.

Performance of Don Juan Tenorio by the Company of Traveling Prostitutes (Representación de Don Juan Tenorio por el carro de las meretrices ambulantes)—published in 1973 but never performed—satirizes attempts by the conservative cultural establishment during the Franco era to revitalize and modernize José Zorrilla's famous romantic play which is traditionally staged every year on All Souls' Day. *Portrait of a Lady with a Dog* demonstrates that literary language often serves not so much to beautify life but to conceal it. *The Garret of the Males and the Cellar of the Females* is a parabolic meditation on the dynamics of power in a patriarchal society. *The Palace of the Monkeys*, classified by the author as an "epic opera," is written entirely in free verse. Inspired by recent events in Spain following Franco's death, it is a bitter denunciation of the struggle among those most closely associated with the deceased dictator to lay claim to his legacy. *Drama of the Lady Who Washes amidst the White Flames (Drama de la dama que lava entre las blancas llamas, 1974)* and *Medea Is a Good Fellow (Medea es un buen chico, 1981)* have appeared in theatre journals, but have not yet been performed.

ANDRÉS FRANCO

CRITICISM

F. Nieva, Introduction, *Portrait of a Lady with a Dog*, Madrid, 1976, pp. 7–13; F Ruiz Ramón, *Historia del teatro español: Siglo XX*, 3d ed., Madrid, 1977, pp. 553–555; A. Castilla, Introduction to Cátedra edition of *The Garret of the Males and the Cellar of the Females* and *The Palace of the Monkeys*, Madrid, 1978, pp. 11–34; L. T. Valdivieso, *España: Bibliografía de un teatro "silenciado,"* Society of Spanish and Spanish-American Studies, 1979, pp. 73–76; H. Cazorla, "La invención de la libertad o el triunfo de la imaginación en el teatro de Luis Riaza," *Pipirijaina-Textos,* no. 18 (1981), pp. 11–24; ibid., "The Duality of Power in the Theatre of Luis Riaza," *Modern Drama* (scheduled to appear in 1981).

Rice, Elmer (1892–1967)

American dramatist. He was born Elmer Leopold Reizenstein on September 28, 1892, in New York, the son of Jacob Reizenstein, a bookkeeper, and his wife, the former Fanny Lion. A solitary child in a bookless house, Rice soon became a habitué of the public library. At twelve he entered the High School of Commerce, but the family's financial problems forced him to leave school when he was fourteen. He took a job as an office boy in a law firm, continuing to study on his own. Within a year he was able to pass the New York State examinations that certified him as a high school graduate. He entered New York Law School in 1910, graduated *cum laude* in 1912, and was admitted to the New York bar the following year. During this period Rice became an avid theatregoer, and it was not long before he decided to write plays instead of practicing law. In 1914, for the first time using the name Elmer Rice, he wrote *On Trial*, a murder melodrama that met with extraordinary success. In 1915 he married Hazel Levy, with whom he had two children, Robert in 1916 and Margaret in 1919. In the years after *On Trial* was produced, he became associated with amateur dramatic groups around Columbia Univer-

The Adding Machine, set design by Lee Simonson. New York, Garrick Theatre, 1923. [Theatre Collection, The New York Public Library at Lincoln Center, Astor, Lenox and Tilden Foundations]

Scene from the London production of *Street Scene*, with Erin O'Brien-Moore (center). [Theatre Collection, The New York Public Library at Lincoln Center, Astor, Lenox and Tilden Foundations]

sity, where he also took courses and worked in settlement houses.

In 1923 the Theatre Guild produced his *The Adding Machine,* one of the early successful American dramas of expressionism. It was followed by another highly praised play, *Street Scene* (1929), which portrayed life in the slums of New York. Increasingly dissatisfied with the artistic and financial values of the Broadway theatre, Rice assumed control over the production of his own plays, but this move yielded little financial success except in the case of *Judgment Day,* which succeeded in London in 1937 after failing in New York three years earlier. At this time he was recruited to organize the Federal Theatre Project. Although the project lasted only a short time, Rice was able to realize some of his plan to popularize theatre across the country, to renovate many theatres with federal funds, and to secure lasting benefits for people employed in the arts. When the government began to impose censorship on the project, Rice was outraged and resigned. His advocacy of the prime importance of the dramatist in theatrical production led to the formation in 1939 of the Playwrights' Company, of which he was a founding member. *See* EXPRESSIONISM in glossary.

After his divorce in 1942, Rice married the actress Betty Field, who had starred in *Two on an Island* and *Flight to the West* in 1940. The marriage lasted through three children, John, Judy, and Paul, and terminated in divorce in 1955.

Although *Dream Girl,* the play written in 1945 for his new wife, was a financial success, Rice made little impact on the American theatre after World War II. During the last two decades of his life his name became associated with liberal causes such as the American Civil Liberties Union. In 1967, en route to England, he was stricken with a heart attack, and he died in Southampton on May 8.

WORK

Rice's plays consistently champion spiritual freedom, the existence of which he believed to be contingent upon man's liberation from social, political, economic, and religious enslavement. Although thematically devoted to this single idea, Rice's work shows no such constancy in dramatic form. His dramaturgy is marked by restless experimentation and innovation. He wrote comedies, tragedies, melodramas, parables, panoramas, mysteries, and ideological and psychoanalytical plays, demonstrating in all an impressive versatility and range. *On Trial* (1914) is a play in which a murder trial furnishes the framework for flashback scenes, a technique invented by Rice and later imitated by innumerable playwrights and scriptwriters. *The Iron Cross* (1917) and *Judgment Day* (1934) are both antiwar plays. *American Landscape* (1938) is a drama using historical contexts and fantasy to condemn racism and economic inequity. *Flight to the West* (1940) is a melodrama containing bitter denunciation of Nazism. *The House in Blind Alley* (wr. 1916) is a comedy that speaks out against child labor. *For the Defense* (1919) and *It Is the Law* (1922) are both mystery plays. *Wake Up, Jonathan!* (1921) is a romantic comedy written with Hatcher Hughes in which a woman must choose between a businessman and a poet. It starred the famous American actress Minnie Maddern Fiske.

In addition, Rice produced the one-act comedies *The Passing of Chow-Chow* (1915), about newlyweds who quar-

Betty Field and Wendell Corey in *Dream Girl.* New York, Coronet Theatre, 1945. [Photograph by Vandamm. Theatre Collection, The New York Public Library at Lincoln Center, Astor, Lenox and Tilden Foundations]

rel over the wife's dog; *The Home of the Free* (1917), a spoof on liberalism; and *A Diadem of Snow* (1918), concerning a czar who becomes a happy worker after the Russian Revolution. His full-length comedies include *Close Harmony, or The Lady Next Door* (1924), a criticism of suburban monotony written with Dorothy Parker; and *Cock Robin* (1928), an amusing mystery written with Philip Barry.

Tragedy predominates in *The Adding Machine* (1923), a satire on modern man's social regimentation, and in *The Subway* (wr. 1924, prod. 1929), an expressionistic play portraying the destruction of human compassion and innocence by mechanization. Unlike *The Adding Machine* and *The Subway*, the tragedy of *Street Scene* (1929), a portrayal of squalid urban life, is realistic; in 1947 it was turned into a musical play for which Kurt Weill wrote the music and Langston Hughes the lyrics.

In *We, the People* (1933) and *Two on an Island* (1940), panoramic episodes replace traditional dramatic construction. Rice's best-known melodrama is *Counsellor-at-Law* (1931), in which the hero is a man of goodwill who becomes a slave to careerism. Other melodramas are *The Grand Tour* (1951), a sentimental romance about a schoolteacher's European vacation; *The Winner* (1954), about the relation between morals and money; and *Love among the Ruins* (wr. 1950, prod. 1963), about selfless love in the contemporary world. Drama becomes a forum for discussions about political systems in *Between Two Worlds* (1934), about the expatriate artist in *The Left Bank* (1931), and about the nature of success in *Black Sheep* (wr. 1921, prod. 1932).

Rice's late plays indicate his preoccupation with psychoanalysis: *Dream Girl* (1945) is a comedy about an excessively imaginative young woman who discovers that real life can be romantic, and *Cue for Passion* (1958) is the story of Hamlet retold in modern psychiatric terms.

The Adding Machine (1923). Expressionistic drama about Mr. Zero, the eternal "little man," shallow yet possessing some dignity, who murders his boss when he learns that, after twenty-five years of being a bookkeeper, he is to be replaced by an adding machine. Condemned to death despite his piteous stream-of-consciousness appeal to the jury, he is executed and appears next in the Elysian Fields, where he meets and enjoys a brief idyll with Daisy, his deceased co-worker, whose love he had secretly desired. But conventional Mr. Zero cannot abide the freedom of paradise for long, and he leaves. Confused by encounters with such people as Shrdlu, who cannot understand why after killing his mother he has been sent to heaven, Zero finds happiness while operating a heavenly adding machine. Presently, however, he is sent back to earth by a celestial overseer to be reborn, endure again his insignificant life, and die, a perpetual victim of a depersonalizing world.

Street Scene (1929). Tragic naturalistic drama set in the seamy milieu of a tenement house in New York where the emotions of the inhabitants are inflamed by the heat of summer. The brutal Joneses, the good-natured Fiorentinos, and the old intellectual Mr. Kaplan are neighbors of the unhappy Maurrants. Mrs. Maurrant,

Paul Muni in *Counsellor-at-Law*. [Theatre Collection, The New York Public Library at Lincoln Center, Astor, Lenox and Tilden Foundations]

the talk of the neighborhood, has been carrying on with Sankey, the local milk-bill collector. Her daughter Rose fears Maurrant's discovery of the affair and urges her mother to be more discreet. But Mrs. Maurrant meets once too often with her lover, and Maurrant shoots them to death. Returning from her mother's deathbed at the hospital, Rose says good-bye to her young admirer Sam Kaplan, whose bigoted sister has thwarted the innocent love between them. Rose accepts this frustration just as she has accepted the tragic fate of her parents. She leaves Sam and the tenement house, avowing her new faith that love will come out of self-knowledge. Life goes on in the tenement as new people move into the vacated apartment.

Counsellor-at-Law (1931). Drama set in the office of George Simon, an eminent New York lawyer, who by dint of hard work and shrewd intelligence has risen to prominence from an impoverished lower East Side background. Clients, friends, and favor seekers troop through his office. Among them is a politician who reveals that disbarment proceedings have been started against George for once having furnished a client with a false alibi. The motivating force behind the bar's action is its anti-Semitic prosecuting lawyer. Needing time to quash the proceedings, Simon cancels a European trip he has planned with his snobbish society wife Cora. By discovering a shameful fact in the personal life of the opposing attorney, George is able to trade his silence for the other's forbearance. George is elated and asks Cora to postpone their trip for a week while he puts his affairs in order. She, however, is annoyed and makes plans to sail to Europe with Roy Darwin, a socially prominent admirer, on the original date. When George discovers the liaison, he considers suicide, but the devotion of his secretary and the challenge of a new and major lawsuit persuade him to make a fresh start.

Dream Girl (1945). Comedy about Georgina Allerton, a young woman who entertains romantic daydreams about Jim Lucas, her ineffectual brother-in-law. One morning, while she tends her failing bookstore, she is wooed by a brusque young journalist, Clarke Redfield, whom she decides she despises. Later she is offered an illicit romance by a debonair businessman, George Hand, who seems more appealing. But when Lucas, who has been rejected by his wife, proposes that Georgina fly with him to Reno, she nearly accepts him. Redfield, however, energetically pursues Georgina, taking her to dinner, the theatre, and a nightclub. At 3 A.M., Georgina's parents are awakened by a call from their daughter telling them that she and Redfield have eloped.

[GAUTAM DASGUPTA]

PLAYS

Unless otherwise noted, the plays were first performed in New York.

1. *The Passing of Chow-Chow*. Comedy, 1 act. Written 1913. Published 1925. Produced (amateur), 1915.

2. *On Trial*. Drama, 4 acts. Published 1919. Produced Candler Theatre, Aug. 19, 1914.

3. *The Iron Cross*. Play, 4 acts. Written 1915. Produced Comedy Theatre, Feb. 13, 1917.

4. *The House in Blind Alley*. Comedy, 3 acts. Written 1916. Published 1932.

5. *The Home of the Free*. Comedy, 1 act. Written 1917. Published 1917. Produced Comedy Theatre, Apr. 22, 1917.

6. *A Diadem of Snow*. Comedy, 1 act. Written 1917. Published 1929. Produced (amateur), 1918.

7. *For the Defense*. Play. Written 1918. Produced Playhouse, Dec. 19, 1919.

8. (With Hatcher Hughes). *Wake Up, Jonathan!* Comedy, prologue and 3 acts. Written 1919. Published 1928. Produced Henry Miller's Theatre, Jan. 17, 1921.

9. *Black Sheep*. Comedy, 4 acts. Written 1921. Published 1938. Produced Morosco Theatre, Oct. 13, 1932.

10. (Adaptation). *It Is the Law*. Play. Written 1922. Produced Ritz Theatre, Nov. 19, 1922. Based on the novel of the same name by Hayden Talbot.

11. *The Adding Machine*. Expressionistic drama, 7 scenes. Written 1922. Published 1923. Produced Garrick Theatre, Mar. 19, 1923.

12. (With Dorothy Parker). *Close Harmony, or The Lady Next Door*. Comedy, 3 acts. Written 1924. Published 1929. Produced Gaiety Theatre, Dec. 1, 1924.

13. (Adaptation). *The Mongrel*. Play. Produced New York, Longacre Theatre, Dec. 15, 1924. Based on a play by Hermann Bahr.

14. *The Subway*. Play, 9 scenes. Written 1924. Published 1929. Produced Cherry Lane Theatre, Jan. 25, 1929.

15. *Landscape with Figures*. Interlude with words, 1 act. Written 1925. Published 1934.

16. *Run in Urbe*. Pastoral without words, 1 act. Written 1925. Published 1934.

17. *Exterior*. Pageant without words, 1 act. Written 1925. Published 1934.

18. *The Gay White Way*. Romantic comedy without words, 1 act. Written 1925. Published 1934. Produced (amateur), 1934.

19. *Life Is Real*. Written 1926. Published in Germany, as *Wir in Amer-*

ika, 1928. Produced Munich, January, 1929; San Francisco, June 4, 1937.

20. (Adaptation). *The Blue Hawaii*. Play. Produced Boston, September, 1927. Based on a play by Rudolph Lothar.

21. (With Phi.ip Barry). *Cock Robin*. Comedy drama, 3 acts. Written 1927. Published 1929. Produced Forty-eighth Street Theatre, Jan. 12, 1928.

22. *Street Scene*. Naturalistic drama, 3 acts. Written 1928. Published 1929. Produced Playhouse, Jan. 10, 1929.

23. *See Naples and Die*. Comedy, 3 acts. Written 1928. Published 1929. Produced Vanderbilt Theatre, Sept. 24, 1929.

24. *The Left Bank*. Play, 3 acts. Written 1930. Published 1931. Produced Little Theatre, Oct. 5, 1931.

25. *Counsellor-at-Law*. Drama, 3 acts. Written 1931. Published 1931. Produced Plymouth Theatre, Nov. 6, 1931.

26. *We, the People*. Play, 21 scenes. Written 1932. Published 1933. Produced Empire Theatre, Jan. 21, 1933.

27. *Judgment Day*. Melodrama, 3 acts. Written 1934. Published 1934. Produced Belasco Theatre, Sept. 12, 1934.

28. *Between Two Worlds*. Play, 9 scenes. Written 1934. Published 1935. Produced Belasco Theatre, Oct. 25, 1934.

29. *Not for Children*. Comedy, 3 acts. Written 1934. Published 1935, revised 1950. Produced London, Fortune Theatre, Nov. 25, 1935; Calif., Pasadena Playhouse, Feb. 25, 1936; New York, Coronet Theatre, Feb. 13, 1951.

30. *American Landscape*. Drama, 3 acts. Written 1938. Published 1939. Produced Cort Theatre, Dec. 3, 1938.

31. *Two on an Island*. Comedy, 11 scenes. Written 1939. Published 1940. Produced Broadhurst Theatre, Jan. 22, 1940.

32. *Flight to the West*. Melodrama, 3 acts. Written 1940. Published 1941. Produced Guild Theatre, Dec. 30, 1940.

33. *A New Life*. Drama, 9 scenes. Written 1943. Published 1944. Produced Royale Theatre, Sept. 9, 1943.

34. *Dream Girl*. Comedy, 2 acts. Written 1945. Published 1946. Produced Coronet Theatre, Dec. 14, 1945.

35. (Adaptation). *Street Scene*. Musical. Written 1946. Published 1948. Produced Adelphi Theatre, Jan. 9, 1947. Music: Kurt Weill. Lyrics: Langston Hughes. Based on Rice's play.

36. *Love among the Ruins*. Play, 2 acts. Written 1950. Published 1963. Produced University of Rochester (N.Y.), May 3, 1963.

37. *The Grand Tour*. Play, 2 acts. Written 1951. Published 1952. Produced Martin Beck Theatre, Dec. 10, 1951.

38. *The Winner*. Play, 4 scenes. Written 1953. Published 1954. Produced Plymouth Theatre, Feb. 17, 1954.

39. *Cue for Passion*. Play, 5 scenes. Written 1958. Published 1959. Produced Henry Miller's Theatre, Nov. 25, 1958.

EDITIONS

Collections

Plays, London, 1933; *Three Plays Without Words*, French, New York, 1934; *Two Plays*, Coward-McCann, New York, 1935; *Seven Plays*, Viking, New York, 1950; *Three Plays*, Hill and Wang, New York, 1965.

Individual Plays

The Adding Machine. Doubleday, New York, 1923; also published in *Contemporary Plays*, ed. by T. H. Dickinson and J. R. Crawford, Houghton Mifflin, Boston, 1925; *A College Treasury*, ed. by P. A. Jorgenson and F. B. Shroyer, Scribner, New York, 1956; *The Range of Literature*, ed. by E. W. Schneider, A. L. Walker, and H. E. Childs, American Book, New York, 1960; *Best American Plays*, ed. by J. Gassner, Crown, New York, 1961.

American Landscape. Coward-McCann, New York, 1939.

Black Sheep. Dramatists' Play Service, New York; 1938.

Close Harmony. French, New York, 1929.

Counsellor-at-Law. French, New York, 1931; also published in *Famous Plays of 1932–33*, Gollancz, London, 1933.

Cue for Passion. Dramatists' Play Service, New York, 1959.

A Diadem of Snow. Published in *One-act Plays for Stage and Study*, 5th ser., French, New York, 1929.

Dream Girl. Coward-McCann, New York, 1946; also published in *Best Plays of the Modern American Theatre*, ed. by J. Gassner, 2d ser., Crown, New York, 1947.

Flight to the West. Coward-McCann, New York, 1941.

The Gay White Way. Published in *One-act Plays for Stage and Study*, 8th ser., French, New York, 1934.

The Grand Tour. Dramatists' Play Service, New York, 1952.

The House in Blind Alley. French, New York, 1932.

Judgment Day. Coward-McCann, New York, 1934; also published in *Famous Plays of 1937*, Gollancz, London, 1937.

The Left Bank. French, New York, 1931.

Love among the Ruins. Dramatists' Play Service, New York, 1963.

A New Life. Coward-McCann, New York, 1944.

On Trial. French, New York, 1919; also published in *Famous Plays of*

Crime and Detection, ed. by V. H. Cartmell and B. A. Cerf, Blakiston, Philadelphia, 1946.

The Passing of Chow-Chow. Published in *One-act Plays for Stage and Study*, 2d ser., French, New York, 1925.

See Naples and Die. French, New York, 1930; also published in *Famous Plays of 1932*, Gollancz, London, 1932.

Street Scene. French, New York, 1929; also published in *Twentieth Century Plays*, ed. by R. A. Cordell, 3d ed., Ronald, New York, 1947; *Living Theatre*, ed. by A. S. Griffin, Twayne, New York, 1953; *Famous American Plays of the 1920's*, ed. by K. Macgowan, Dell, New York, 1959; *Three Dramas of American Realism*, ed. by J. E. Mersand, Washington Square, New York, 1961.

The Subway. French, New York, 1929.

Two on an Island. Coward-McCann, New York, 1940.

Wake Up, Jonathan! French, New York, 1928.

We, the People. Coward-McCann, New York, 1933.

The Winner. Dramatists' Play Service, New York, 1954.

CRITICISM

E. Rice, *Minority Report: An Autobiography*, New York, 1963; R. Hogan, *The Independence of Elmer Rice*, Carbondale, Ill., 1965; F. Durham, *Elmer Rice*, New York, 1970; A. Palmieri, *Elmer Rice: A Playwright's Vision of America*, Madison, N.J., 1980.

Richardson, Howard   (1917–   )

American actor, educator, and dramatist. He is best known for his folk drama *Dark of the Moon* (1945), written with William Berney. His other plays, few of which have appeared in New York, include *Top Hats and Tenements* (1936); *Catch on the Wing* (1948), with William Goforth; *Sodom, Tennessee* (1949), *Design for a Stained Glass Window* (1950), and *Mountain Fire* (1954), all with Berney; and *Protective Custody* (1956).

Dark of the Moon (1945). Tragedy based on a folktale of the Great Smoky Mountains. John, a witch boy, becomes human for love of Barbara Allen. The change is wrought by the Conjur Woman on condition that Barbara remain true to him for one year. After John and Barbara are married, John grows restless under the yoke of human responsibility and begins to walk the mountainside by night. Some months later, Barbara has a child born with witchlike deformities. Because of this, the baby is destroyed by the midwife. Now rumors that John is a witch race through the town. In despair, Barbara's mother drags her to church, where, swayed by the hypnotic mass confessional, she submits to a man, thus breaking her marriage vow. Repentant, she later seeks John on the mountaintop. But at the moon's rise he tells her that she has been doomed by a witch's pact, and she dies in his arms. Once again a witch, John looks without recognition at the body of the girl he once loved. Produced New York, Forty-sixth Street Theatre, March 14, 1945.

[GAUTAM DASGUPTA]

Richardson, Jack [Carter]   (1935–   )

American novelist and playwright. Relatively unknown outside experimental circles, Richardson has been influenced by Shaw and shows affinities to Dürrenmatt, Giraudoux, and Anouilh. His first play, *The Prodigal* (1960), for which he received the *Village Voice* Off Broadway Award, is an existentialist adaptation of the Oresteia legend. In it the tragic element resides in the conventions of society; Orestes accepts his role as avenger not out of conviction but out of weakness and the failure to define

another role for himself. *Gallows Humor*, which appeared a year later, comprises two sardonic one-act plays preceded by a prologue in which Death introduces the theme of the plays: "The grave's dimensions suddenly have grown to include those who have not yet achieved the once necessary technicality of ceasing to breathe." *Lorenzo* (1963) is a play about reality and the force of illusion as seen in a traveling theatrical company in Renaissance Italy; and *Xmas in Las Vegas* (1965), perhaps Richardson's weakest play, deals with a gambler and his family. Other plays by Richardson include *As Happy as Kings* (1968) and *Juan Feldman* (pub. 1968).

[GAUTAM DASGUPTA]

Richepin, [Auguste] Jean   (1849–1926)

French poet and dramatist. His work, like Rostand's represents the late flowering of romantic verse drama. His poetry is in the vein of François Villon (1431–1463?), celebrating the life of the tramps and beggars of his time, and his free use of slang shocked and titillated many readers. Richepin tried his hand at just about every theatrical genre—adaptations of Shakespeare, Cervantes, and Sem Benelli; musical comedies; fairy tales; melodramas—but he is best remembered for his engagingly sentimental comedies, the most celebrated of which is *The Tramp* (*Le chemineau*, 1897), a bittersweet tale of a carefree vagabond who temporarily returns after a twenty-year absence to help a woman he once seduced and abandoned. Other plays of interest include *Nana-Sahib* (1883), written for Sarah Bernhardt; *Monsieur Scapin* (1886), about the later days of Molière's rascally creation; *The Sleeping Beauty* (*La belle au bois dormant*, 1907), in which he collaborated with Henri Cain on a dramatization of Charles Perrault's immortal fairy tales; and *The Vagrants* (*Les truands*, 1899), a play set in the medieval Paris of François Villon.

The Tramp (*Le chemineau*, 1897). A carefree young vagabond seduces and abandons Toinette, a village girl, and returns twenty years later to discover that she bore him a son, Antoine, whose putative father is her present husband, François. Antoine is in love with a girl whose father refuses to let her marry him, and François is bedridden and dying. Setting to work, the tramp manages to win Antoine's bride for him by curing her father's ailing cattle. At a Christmas celebration the tramp recounts his vagabond life, and everyone urges him to remain. In a burst of insight, just before dying, François tries to slip his wedding ring onto the tramp's finger as a sign that he wants him to marry Toinette. Though tempted by his love for Toinette, his pride in Antoine, and the security of domestic life, the tramp eventually decides to return to his vagabond life. Produced Paris, Théâtre de l'Odéon, February 6, 1897.

[JOSEPH E. GARREAU]

Rifat, Oktay (Horozcu)   (1914–   )

Turkish poet, novelist, and dramatist. He was born in Trabzon, northern Turkey. His father was the poet Samih Rifat. After graduating from the law faculty of An-

Oktay Rifat (Horozcu).
[Metin And Collection]

kara University, he went to Paris to study political science. He was later appointed to the Press and Information Bureau in Ankara, and until 1973 he was a lawyer of the state railways.

During World War II he and two friends, Orhan Veli Kanık and Melih Cevdet Anday, launched a school of poetry that has remained influential. *The Jealous Ones* (*Kıskançlar*, 1950), one of his earliest plays, was written with Melih Cevdet Anday. A light comedy, it deals with the jealousy and misunderstanding of two husbands. In a similar vein is his earlier *Play within a Play* (*Oyun İçinde Oyun*, 1949), in which two amateur actors of the Turkish traditional improvisatory theatre are deceived by their wives. The structure of the play allows us to witness their lives both on and off stage and to contrast Eastern and Western values. *Among the Women* (*Kadınlar Arasında*, 1948) focuses on four women from the third generation of an aristocratic family now faced with poverty. In *A Group of People* (*Bir Takım İnsanlar*, 1960) a number of passengers gathered by chance at a small boat-landing stage on the Bosporus reconstruct their lives and dream their dreams with the help of a dockhand who serves as narrator and chorus.

A Speckled Cock deals with the plight of rural migrants to the big city. [Metin And Collection]

Knights and Bishops (*Atlar ve Filler*) was first produced in 1962, but the title was changed to *Health and Wealth* (*Dirlik Düzenlik*) when the play was revived in 1977. It depicts a family in which the rhythm of life is determined not by the dictates of the heart but by money and food. The family members are presented as having dual personalities, and they behave very much like pieces in a chess game. *A Speckled Cock* (*Çil Horoz*, 1964) is set in a big-city shantytown inhabited by people who have emigrated from rural areas in search of work. No longer peasants and not yet city folk, they are in the process of creating their own values and culture. The lives of three sisters give insight into the economic and sexual problems of these people. The title refers to a young cab driver who puts on airs because women are attracted to him. A domineering mother is the focus of *Officer Fatma's Little Lamb* (*Zabit Fatma'nın Kuzusu*, 1965), in which a middle-aged man, married for the third time, becomes impotent when he recognizes in his new wife certain characteristics of his mother.

Among Oktay Rifat's more important plays is *Depression before Rain* (*Yağmur Sıkıntısı*, 1970), a verbal duel between a man and woman whose marriage is devoid of love and mutual affection. Giving insight into a domestic hell, it also provides the playwright with an opportunity for indirect comment on the social and economic system which has forged the characters.

METIN AND

Riggs, Lynn   (1899–1954)

American poet and dramatist. His folk play *Green Grow the Lilacs* (1931), a cowboy love story, reflects his sensitive grasp of the lyrical atmosphere of his native state of

Green Grow the Lilacs, as presented by the Theatre Guild. New York, Guild Theatre, 1931. [Walter Hampden Memorial Library at The Players, New York]

Oklahoma and its people. The play was later adapted by Rodgers and Hammerstein into the celebrated musical comedy *Oklahoma!* (1943). Among Riggs's other plays are *Big Lake* (1927), *Knives from Syria* (1928), *Roadside* (1930), *Cherokee Night* (1932), *Russet Mantle* (1936), *The Cream in the Well* (1941), and *The Year of Pilar* (1952).

[GAUTAM DASGUPTA]

Rittner, Tadeusz (1873–1921)

Polish playwright. Although Rittner was raised in Vienna, his birthplace in eastern Poland always remained a moving force in his life. The irony and skepticism of an expatriate longing for but never going home suffused his plays. The tragedies and comedies he described are not heroic or larger than life; rather they are events that could happen to ordinary people. *The Little Home* (*W małym domku*, 1904) illuminates the tragedy of a provincial doctor who kills his wife after learning that she has succumbed to another man. Tried and acquitted yet unable to bear his loss, the doctor finally takes his own life. *On the Way* (*Unterwegs*, 1909) describes a Don Juan-like baron who is killed by one of the husbands he has cuckolded. *Foolish Jacob* (*Głupi Jakub*, 1910) deals with a theme not unlike that of Somerset Maugham's *Of Human Bondage*. *Summer* (*Lato*, 1912) is a light comedy about visitors to a bourgeois seaside resort. *Wolves in the Night* (*Wilki w nocy*, 1916) is another light comedy about a pedant, and *The Garden of Youth* (*Ogród młodości*, 1917) one that verges on fairy tale.

[DANIEL GEROULD]

Wolves in the Night, Gdańsk, 1970. [Agencja Autorska, Warsaw]

Scene from *The Little Home*, as presented in Lublin. [Agencja Autorska, Warsaw]

Rivarola Matto, José María (1917–   )

Paraguayan playwright. One of the leading literary figures of his nation, this Asunción lawyer has written little, but his plays are important examples of local color.

His first effort, *The Fate of Cipriano Gonzalez* (*El fin de Chipí Gonzalez*, 1954), while a fantasy, is yet a realistic picture of lower-class life in a rural Paraguayan family. Among the characters are a football player who lives only for sports, several girls attracted to him, a farmer worried about the price of his crops, and a crooked politician who does unto others as has been done unto him. The fact that the cast includes a good and a bad angel does not turn it into a fairy tale, for they do not unduly exert their magic power. The language of the play is neither Castilian Spanish nor the Guaraní spoken in Paraguay, but a sort of Guaraní-ized Spanish that adds to the local color.

Rivarola Matto's one-act *A Coffin for a Usurer* (*Un ataúd para un usurero*) was begun as a humorous sketch but ended up as a metaphysical play that proved unpopular with audiences, as did *The Sectarian* (*El sectario*), in which the conflict grows out of political sectarianism. His *Holy Spirit Crossroads* (*Encrucijada del Espíritu Santo*, 1973), is a historical play dealing with the founding and closing of the Jesuit *reducciones* in Paraguay. After its appearance, the Paraguay critic Rodriguez Alcalá called its author "the best Paraguayan dramatist of his generation."

WILLIS KNAPP JONES and JUDITH A. WEISS

CRITICISM

W. K. Jones, "Paraguay's Theatre," *Books Abroad*, vol. 15, pp. 40–42, 1941; W. Rela, "Fundamentos para una historia del teatro Paraguayo," *Jornadas de Cultura Paraguaya*, Montevideo, 1953, pp. 23–42.

Rivemale, Alexandre (1918–   )

French poet, novelist, and dramatist. In his first play, *Azouk*, presented at the Théâtre Fontaine in 1953, a rather eccentric grandfather, bored by village life, enjoys

Scene from *Némo*. Paris, Théâtre Marigny, 1956. [French Cultural Services]

scribbling adventure stories, a jug of red wine by his side, when the rest of the family are out of the house. One afternoon, fumbling through his manuscripts, he accidentally breaks an Indian vase, out of which materializes a white elephant, named Azouk, who speaks excellent French, but with a typical Provençal accent, and regales the befuddled and astonished grandfather with an amazing repertory of tales in addition to sagely settling most of the family's problems. The play was followed by *Némo* (1956) and *Le mobile* (1960).

JOSEPH E. GARREAU

Robertson, Thomas William (1829–1871)

English dramatist and actor. Robertson was born in Newark, Nottinghamshire, on January 9, 1829. Born into a theatrical family, he made his first appearance onstage

T. W. Robertson. [Walter Hampden Memorial Library at The Players, New York]

in 1834. In 1836 he was sent away to school, first to Spalding and then to Whittlesea. He left school in 1843 to join the Lincoln Circuit company, which his father managed. His jobs as scene painter and prompter were interspersed with occasional acting until the company broke up in 1848, when he went to London. There he took odd jobs teaching, acting, and writing for newspapers, and there, in 1851, his *A Night's Adventure* was produced. Three years later *Castles in the Air* was produced, but neither play was successful.

In 1856 he married the actress Elizabeth Burton, and they traveled to Dublin, where they worked in the theatre. A son was born in 1857, and a daughter in 1858.

After her death in 1860 he temporarily abandoned the theatre. For a time in London he found work on a mining journal, wrote articles for magazines, and translated plays from the French for Walter Lacy. In 1861 his farce *The Cantab* was produced, but his first real success came with *David Garrick* in 1864. The following year his reputation as a playwright was established when *Society* was produced at the Prince of Wales's Theatre in London. A series of his plays, all produced by actor-manager Sir Squire Bancroft at the Prince of Wales, proved him to be an innovator with a new form of realism later called "cup and saucer." *See* REALISM in glossary.

His wife died in 1865 and he married again in 1867, the year his masterpiece, *Caste*, was produced. His young German wife Rosetta Feist bore a daughter, but the marriage lasted only three years. Robertson died in London on February 3, 1871.

WORK

T. W. Robertson pioneered simple realistic comedies portraying contemporary middle-class domestic life. These comedies, roundly approved by audiences, played an important part in the movement toward realism. Robertson brought real life and characters to the stage, offering a refreshing alternative to the sentimentality and romanticism of the mid-Victorian theatre. Characters were given credible speeches; dialogue was made natural. Realistic stagecraft was introduced: a drawing room was a drawing room in every detail, and people's behavior in it was accurately reproduced.

Before Robertson's success with *Society* (1865), the first of the "cup-and-saucer comedies," he wrote a series of melodramas, farces, and comedies in the prevalent style. Among them were *The Battle of Life* (licensed 1847), *The Haunted Man* (1843/49), *The Star of the North* (1855), *The Muleteer of Toledo* (1856), and *The Half Caste, or The Poisoned Pearl* (1856). In the mid-1850s he made innumerable adaptations including *The Ladies' Battle* (1851), based on *Bataille des dames*, by Eugène Scribe and Gabriel-Jean-Baptiste Legouvé. The one play that met with success was *David Garrick* (1864), a free adaptation of a French play, *Sullivan*, by Mélesville (Anne-Honoré-Joseph Duveyrier), in which a famous actor succeeds in disillusioning a young admirer by behaving badly offstage. Though sentimental, it was more truthful than most plays of the time and attracted audiences by its freshness and charm.

The technique that succeeded in *Society* was developed in *Ours* (1866), a play about three romances during the Crimean War. Improving the technique still further, Robertson had his greatest success with *Caste* (1867), his most famous play, about a young actress who marries into an aristocratic family and is troubled by the social pretensions of her husband's mother. After deviating from the successful formula with a few old-style melodramas, he returned to the style of *Caste* in *Play* (1868), a more melodramatic comedy set in a German gambling resort; *School* (1869), an exquisitely delicate romance about two teachers in a girls' school and their impact on the surrounding community; and *The M.P.* (1870), about romances cutting across social boundaries.

Society (1865). Comedy about John Chodd, Sr., and his son John Chodd, Jr., who are anxious to be accepted in society. They approach Sidney Daryl, an impoverished gentleman, and offer payment for introductions to his friends. When Sidney refuses, young Chodd swears to avenge the rebuff. He begins by courting Maude Hetherington, the girl Sidney loves. He is encouraged by her aunt, Lady Ptarmigant, who is more interested in his money than his character. He then runs for Parliament in a constituency that has always been represented by a member of the Daryl family. This time Sidney fights back and wins both the election and the support of Lady Ptarmigant, who has learned that Sidney has been enriched and ennobled by his older brother's death. She now accepts him as Maude's fiancé.

Caste (1867). Comedy about the caste system. A member of the aristocracy, the Honorable George D'Alroy, falls in love with a lower-class girl, Esther Eccles, whose father is a vulgar wastrel and a drunkard. Disregarding the advice of his closest friend, George insists on marrying immediately. When he is ordered to join his regiment in India, his mother, the Marquise de St. Maur, arrives to say good-bye and she is horrified to discover the marriage, which George has kept secret; she will have nothing to do with her daughter-in-law. A year later, Esther, believing her husband has been killed, is living in desperate privation with her baby son. Her father has squandered the money left her by D'Alroy, and the Marquise is trying to take away her baby. Her situation seems hopeless but suddenly D'Alroy reappears, having been saved from death by a native. He and Esther are reunited, and the marquise, affected by Esther's goodness of nature, gives her blessing to their marriage.

PLAYS

Unless otherwise noted, the plays were first performed in London.

1. (Adaptation). *The Chevalier de St. George*. Drama, 3 acts. Published 1879. Produced Princess's Theatre, May 20, 1845. Based on a play by Mélesville (Anne-Honoré-Joseph Duveyrier) and Roger de Beauvoir (Édouard-Roger de Bully).

2. (Adaptation). *Ernestine*. Drama, 2 acts. Published 1856, as *Noémie*. Produced Princess's Theatre, Apr. 14, 1846. Based on a play by Adolphe Dennery and René Clément.

3. *The Battle of Life*. Drama. Licensed Jan. 23, 1847.

4. (Adaptation). *The Haunted Man*. Farce. Produced Boston, 1843/49; London, Queen's Theatre, Jan. 1, 1849. Based on Charles Dickens's tale of the same name (1848).

5. (Adaptation). *A Night's Adventure, or Highways & Byways*. Comic Drama. Produced Olympic Theatre, Aug. 25, 1851. Based on Edward Bulwer-Lytton's novel *Paul Clifford* (1830).

6. (Adaptation). *The Ladies' Battle*. Drama. Published 1856? Produced Haymarket Theatre, Nov. 18, 1851. Based on *Bataille des dames*, by Eugéne Scribe and Gabriel-Jean-Baptiste Legouvé.

7. *Faust and Marguerite*. Drama. Published 1854. Produced Princess's Theatre, Apr. 19, 1854. Sometimes attributed to Dion Boucicault.

8. *Castles in the Air*. Drama. Produced City of London Theatre, Apr. 29, 1854.

9. (Adaptation). *A Wife's Journal*. Comedietta, 1 act. Published 1855, as *My Wife's Diary*. Produced Olympic Theatre, Dec. 18, 1854. Based on *Les Mémoires des deux jeunes mariées*, by Dennery and Louis-François Clairville.

10. *A Row in the House*. Farce, 1 act. Written ca. 1854. Published 1888. Produced Toole's Theatre, Aug. 30, 1883.

11. (Adaptation). *The Star of the North*. Drama. Published 1872, as *The Northern Star*. Produced Sadler's Wells Theatre, Mar. 5, 1855. Based on a play by Scribe.

12. (Adaptation). *The Clockmaker's Hat*. Farce. Produced Adelphi Theatre, Mar. 7, 1955, as *Betty Martin*. Based on Delphine de Girardin's *Le chapeau d'un horloger*.

13. *Peace at Any Price*. Farce, 1 act. Published 1872. Produced Strand Theatre, Feb. 13, 1856.

14. (Adaptation). *Two Gay Deceivers, or Black, White and Grey*. Farce. Published 1856. Produced Strand Theatre, 1858? Based on Eugène Labiche's play *Deux profonds scélérats*.

15. *The Muleteer of Toledo*. Comedietta. Licensed May 6, 1856.

16. *The Half Caste, or The Poisoned Pearl*. Drama. Published 1872. Produced Surrey Theatre, Sept. 8, 1856.

17. *Our Private Theatricals*. Comedy, 2 acts. Published 1860. Licensed 1894.

18. *Jocrisse, the Juggler*. Drama, 3 acts. Produced Paris, Théâtre de la Gaîté, Oct. 12, 1860; London, Adelphi Theatre, Apr. 1, 1861. Based on *L'escamoteur*, by Dennery and Jules Brésil.

19. *The Cantab*. Farce, 1 act. Published 1861. Produced Strand Theatre, Feb. 14, 1861.

20. (Adaptation). *David Garrick*. Comic drama, 3 acts. Published 1870? Produced Birmingham, Prince of Wales's Theatre, April, 1864; London, Haymarket Theatre, Apr. 30, 1864. Based on Mélesville's *Sullivan*.

21. *Constance*. Operetta. Produced Covent Garden, Jan. 23, 1865. Music: Frederick Clay.

22. *Society*. Comedy, 3 acts. Published 1866. Produced Liverpool, Prince of Wales's Theatre, May 8, 1865; London, Prince of Wales's Theatre, Nov. 11, 1865.

23. *Ours*. Comedy, 3 acts. Published 1890. Produced Liverpool, Prince of Wales's Theatre, Aug. 23, 1866; London, Prince of Wales's Theatre, Sept. 15, 1866.

24. *Shadow-Tree Shaft*. Drama. Produced Princess's Theatre, Feb. 6, 1867.

25. (Adaptation). *A Rapid Thaw*. Comedietta. Produced St. James's Theatre, Mar. 2, 1867. Based on Victorien Sardou's *Le dégel*.

26. *A Dream in Venice*. Operetta. Produced Royal Gallery of Illustration, Mar. 18, 1867.

27. *Caste*. Comedy, 3 acts. Published 1878. Produced Prince of Wales's Theatre, Apr. 6, 1867.

28. *For Love*. Drama. Produced Holborn Theatre, Oct. 5, 1867.

29. *The Sea of Ice, or The Prayer of the Wrecked*. Play. Produced Glasgow, Nov. 28, 1867.

30. *Play*. Comedy, 4 acts. Published 1890. Produced Prince of Wales's Theatre, Feb. 15, 1868.

31. *Passion Flowers*. Drama. Produced Haymarket Theatre, Jan. 14, 1869.

32. (Adaptation). *Home*. Comedy, 3 acts. Published 1879. Produced Haymarket Theatre, Jan. 14, 1869. Based on Émile Augier's *L'aventurière*.

33. *School*. Comedy, 4 acts. Published 1879. Produced Prince of Wales's Theatre, Jan. 16, 1869.

34. *My Lady Clare*. Drama. Published 1875(?), as *Dreams*. Produced Liverpool, Alexandra Theatre, Feb. 22, 1869; London, Gaiety Theatre, Mar. 27, 1869 (as *Dreams*).

35. *A Breach of Promise*. Farce, 2 acts. Published 1888. Produced Globe Theatre, Apr. 10, 1869.

36. *Dublin Bay*. Comedietta. Produced Manchester, Theatre Royal, May 18, 1869; London, Folly Theatre, Dec. 18, 1875.

37. (Adaptation). *Progress*. Comedy. Published 1891. Produced Globe Theatre, Sept. 18, 1869. Based on Sardou's *Les ganaches*.

38. *The Nightingale*. Drama, 5 acts. Published 1890. Produced Adelphi Theatre, Jan. 15, 1870.

39. *The M.P.* Comedy, 3 acts. Published 1890. Produced Prince of Wales's Theatre, Apr. 23, 1870.

40. *Birth*. Comedy, 3 acts. Published 1891. Produced Bristol, New Theatre Royal, Oct. 5, 1870.

41. *War*. Comic drama. Published 1891. Produced St. James's Theatre, Jan. 16, 1871.

42. *Policy*. Comedy. Produced Glasgow, Feb. 13, 1871.

43. *Not at All Jealous*. Farce, 1 act. Published 1872. Produced Court Theatre, May 29, 1871.

44. *Birds of Prey, or A Duel in the Dark*. Drama. Published 1872.

45. *Which Is It?* Comedietta. Licensed July 27, 1881.

46. *Other Days*. Play. Produced Hull, Theatre Royal, Apr. 12, 1883.

47. *A Row in the House*. Play. Produced Toole's Theatre, Aug. 30, 1883.

48. *Cinderella*. Play. Produced Newcastle, Aug. 15, 1892; London, Grand Theatre, Oct. 3, 1892.

49. *Over the Way*. Play. Produced Court Theatre, Jan. 20, 1893.

50. (Translation). *Down in Our Village*. Play. Based on Édouard Plouvier's *Le sang mêlé*.

EDITIONS

Collections
Principal Dramatic Works, 2 vols., London, 1889.
Individual Plays
Caste. Published in *Nineteenth Century Plays*, ed. by G. Rowell, London, 1953.
Society. Published in *Great English Plays*, ed. by H. F. Rubinstein, New York, 1928.

CRITICISM

T. E. Pemberton, *Life and Writings of T. W. Robertson*, London, 1893; M. Savin, *Thomas William Robertson*, Providence, 1950.

Robinson, Lennox (1886–1958)

Irish novelist, director, and dramatist. Esme Stuart Lennox Robinson was born in Douglas, County Cork, on October 4, 1886, the son of a Protestant clergyman. A frail and ailing child, he was forced by poor health to suspend his formal education at Bandon Grammar School in his teens and to live a quiet life until he was twenty. During this period he familiarized himself with music and literature and observed the rural and small-town Irish life he was later to use as material in many of his plays.

After a brief attempt at teaching and writing, Robinson, impressed by a performance at the Abbey Theatre of Yeats's *Cathleen ni Houlihan* (1902), became a convert

Lennox Robinson.
[Irish Tourist Board]

the United States during a teaching engagement. In 1951, after fire consumed the Abbey Theatre, Robinson published its history, entitled *Ireland's Abbey Theatre: A History 1899–1951,* and helped the Abbey board continue its work at the Queen's Theatre in Dublin. He also wrote *Curtain Up, An Autobiography* (1942) and *Pictures in a Theatre* (1951). His essay "The Man and the Dramatist" was published in Stephen Gwynne's *Scattering Branches* (1940). Despite failing health, his last decade was filled with writing and lecturing in the United States. Robinson, still a director of the Abbey, died of a heart attack in Dublin on October 14, 1958.

WORK

Although Lennox Robinson never achieved major stature as a dramatist, his contribution to the Abbey Theatre as a producer and director was substantial. His plays, while frequently commonplace and facile, are invariably entertaining. Many of them deal with serious subjects concerning Irish rural life and politics, but his strength as a dramatist is to be found in his comedies.

His first play, *The Clancy Name* (1908), is a tragedy concerning an old woman whose mainstay in life is the pride she feels for her family. Thus, when her son kills a man, threatening their name with dishonor, she urges him not to confess. Her pride is secured when the son is killed while saving the life of a child. The first of Robinson's political dramas was *Patriots* (1912), about an old revolutionary, James Nugent, who is released from prison after serving a fifteen-year sentence. He expects to be greeted as a hero, but ironically his sacrifice is treated with indifference as he has long since been forgotten. *The Dreamers* (1915) is a historical drama about Robert Emmet's ill-fated uprising of 1803. *The Lost Leader* (1918), another political drama, concerns an old recluse thought to be Charles Parnell (at the time the play was written, there was a widespread notion in Ireland that Parnell was still living), who is inadvertently killed be-

to Irish nationalism and to a career in the Irish theatre. Soon after, his first one-act play, *The Clancy Name,* was produced at the Abbey Theatre on October 8, 1908, when he was in his early twenties. Between that October day and the other October day on which he died fifty years later, his association with the Abbey Theatre was almost unbroken. In 1909 Robinson was hired by Yeats and Lady Gregory as director and manager of the Abbey and sent to England to study production methods there. He became its manager, one of its best directors, a member of its board, and one of its most prolific writers. The number of his plays and the frequency of their revivals probably put him on a par with George Shiels in his influence on the style of the modern Abbey Theatre drama. *See* SHIELS, GEORGE.

In 1909, soon after his return to Dublin, he presented his own play, *Harvest* (1910). In 1913 Robinson managed the Abbey's second tour in America with Lady Gregory, but her criticism of his work led to his break with the Abbey in 1914. During his absence he established the Drama League for the fostering of international theatre in Ireland. After various nontheatrical activities, the publication of a novel, *A Young Man from the South* (1917), and the production of three more of his plays at the Abbey, Robinson returned in 1919 to his old post there, and by 1923 he was a permanent member of the board of directors. *See* GREGORY, LADY AUGUSTA; IRISH DRAMA.

Never satisfied with a single job, Robinson wrote a drama column for the London *Observer* (1924–1925) and at the same time established the Peacock Theatre, an experimental addition to the Abbey, where in the next three years he helped organize a school of acting and ballet. The decade ended with the production of his *The Far-off Hills* (1928) and *Give a Dog———* (1929).

Following his marriage to Dorothy Travers Smith in 1931, Robinson divided his time between productions at the Abbey and lecturing and teaching in the United States. In 1938 he established the Abbey Theatre Festival. Ten years later his play *The Lucky Finger* was produced in

An Abbey Theatre production of *The Big House,* with F. J. McCormick and Shelagh Richards. [Irish Tourist Board]

fore his identity can be verified by Parnell's old associates.

His most popular play, a comedy, was the early *The Whiteheaded Boy* (1916), which was followed by other notable comedies like *The Far-off Hills* (1928), *Is Life Worth Living* (1933), and *The Lucky Finger* (1948). His best-known serious dramas are *The Big House* (1926), *Killycreggs in Twilight* (1937), and *Bird's Nest* (1938). Less conventional plays—many of which the Abbey Theatre refused to stage, but which were accepted by the more tolerant Dublin Gate Theatre—were *The White Blackbird* (1925), *Give A Dog———* (1929), *All's Over Then?* (1932), *Church Street* (1934), *When Lovely Woman* (1936), *Roly Poly* (1940), and *The Demon Lover* (1954). Excursions into satire like *Ever the Twain* (1929) were not popular. Although he experimented, Robinson's most successful plays are his more conventional realistic ones.

The White-headed Boy (1916). Comedy about Denis Geoghegan, the youngest of six children, who has always been his mother's white-headed (favorite) boy. She has decided he will be a doctor, but when he fails his examinations for the third time, brother George refuses to continue supporting him. Denis, he says, must break his engagement with Delia Duffy and go to Canada, where he must learn to support himself. The girl's father threatens to sue for breach of promise, and to avoid a court suit, Denis's family secretly pays him off. Nevertheless, Denis and Delia marry, and Denis finds work as a day laborer. Appalled, Mr. Duffy gives Denis all the money he has collected, and the family offers to make him manager of a store, which Delia assures them she will run for him.

The Far-off Hills (1928). Comedy in which Marian, the oldest daughter of Patrick Clancy, has temporarily forsaken her ambition to enter a convent so that she may take care of her blind father and two sisters. A domineering moralist, she assumes command of the household, objects to her father's friends, and controls her sisters' lives. The family is relieved when Patrick decides to marry Susie Tynan, thinking that now Marian will retire to the convent. But Marian feels duty-bound to watch over her sisters until they finish school. By now Marian realizes that she enjoys her role as ruler of the house and that she could not be happy in a convent. Finally, she agrees to marry the ambitious Pierce Hegarty, an enterprising businessman who wins her by claiming that she will help him "run the town."

[CAROL GELDERMAN]

PLAYS

Unless otherwise noted, the plays were first performed in Dublin.

1. *The Clancy Name*. Tragedy, 1 act. Published 1909. Produced Abbey Theatre, Oct. 8, 1908.
2. *The Cross Roads*. Play, prologue and 2 acts. Published 1909. Produced Abbey Theatre, Apr. 1, 1909.
3. *The Lesson of His Life*. Farce, 1 act. Produced Cork, Dunn Theatre, Dec. 2, 1909.
4. *Harvest*. Play, 3 acts. Published 1911. Produced Abbey Theatre, May 19, 1910.
5. *Patriots*. Play, 3 acts. Published 1912. Produced Abbey Theatre, Apr. 11, 1912.
6. *The Dreamers*. Play, 3 acts. Published 1915. Produced Abbey Theatre, Feb. 10, 1915.
7. *The White-headed Boy*. Comedy, 3 acts. Published 1921. Produced Abbey Theatre, Dec. 13, 1916.

8. *The Lost Leader*. Play, 3 acts. Published 1918. Produced Abbey Theatre, Feb. 19, 1918.
9. *The Round Table*. Comic tragedy, 3 acts. Published 1924. Produced Abbey Theatre, Jan. 31, 1922. Revised version: Published 1928. Produced Liverpool, Playhouse Theatre, Mar. 16, 1927.
10. *Crabbed Youth and Age*. Comedy, 1 act. Published 1924. Produced Abbey Theatre, Nov. 14, 1922.
11. *Never the Time and the Place*. Comedy, 1 act. Published 1924. Produced Abbey Theatre, Feb. 19, 1924.
12. *Portrait*. Play, 2 sittings. Published 1926. Produced Abbey Theatre, Mar. 31, 1925.
13. *The White Blackbird*. Play, 3 acts. Published 1926. Produced Abbey Theatre, Oct. 12, 1925.
14. *The Big House*. Play, 4 scenes. Published 1928. Produced Abbey Theatre, Sept. 6, 1926.
15. *The Far-off Hills*. Comedy, 3 acts. Published 1931. Produced Abbey Theatre, Oct. 22, 1928.
16. *Give a Dog———*. Play, 3 acts. Published 1928. Produced London, Strand Theatre, Jan. 20, 1929.
17. *Ever the Twain*. Comedy, 3 acts. Published 1930. Produced Abbey Theatre, Oct. 8, 1929.
18. *All's Over Then?* Play, 3 acts. Published 1935. Produced Abbey Theatre, July 25, 1932.
19. *Is Life Worth Living? Drama at Inish*. An exaggeration, 3 acts. Published 1933. Produced Abbey Theatre, Feb. 6, 1933.
20. *Church Street*. Play, 1 act. Published 1935. Produced Abbey Theatre, May 21, 1934.
21. *When Lovely Woman*. Comedy, 3 acts. Produced Gate Theatre, Aug. 18, 1936.
22. *Killycreggs in Twilight*. Play, 3 acts. Published 1939. Produced Abbey Theatre, Apr. 19, 1937.
23. *Bird's Nest*. Play, 3 acts. Published 1939. Produced Abbey Theatre, Sept. 12, 1938.
24. *Roly Poly*. Play, 12 scenes. Based on Guy de Maupassant's story "Boule de suif." Produced Gate Theatre, Nov. 19, 1940.
25. *Let Well Alone*. Radio comedy. Published 1941. Produced 1941. Produced Radio Eireann, Dec. 25, 1940.
26. *Forget Me Not*. Play, 3 acts. Produced Abbey Theatre, Dec. 26, 1941.
27. *The Lucky Finger*. Comedy, 3 acts. Published 1949. Produced Bowling Green, Ohio, University Theatre, Jan. 19, 1948; Dublin, Abbey Theatre, Aug. 23, 1948.
28. *Speed the Plough*. Absurdity, 3 acts. Written 1953.
29. *The Demon Lover*. Play, 3 acts. Produced London, Gaiety Theatre, June 21, 1954.

EDITIONS

Collections
Plays, London, 1928.
Individual Plays
The Big House. Published in *Plays of the Irish Renaissance, 1880–1930*, ed. by C. Canfield, New York, 1929.
Church Street. Published in *Plays of Changing Ireland*, ed. by C. Canfield, New York, 1936.
The Far-off Hills. Published in *Twentieth Century Plays, British*, ed. by F. W. Chandler and R. A. Cordell, rev. and enl. ed., New York, 1941.
The White-headed Boy. Published in *My Best Play*, London, 1934.

CRITICISM

M. J. O'Neill, *Lennox Robinson*, New York, 1934.

Rocca, Gino (1891–1941)

Italian journalist, novelist, dramatist, and critic. His works were popular between the two world wars. *The Jungle Vines* (*Le liane*, 1920) is an exotic play, taking place in the Congo, in which the relationship between black men and their white overlords is explored. Other plays include *The Blue Baskets* (*I canestri azzurri*, 1921), satirizing feminism; *The Impossible Lovers* (*Gli amanti impossibili*, 1925), a love story; *The Lambs* (*Le pecorelle*, 1925), another ironic tale concerning the gullibility of women; *The Dying Gladiator* (*Il gladiatore morente*, 1928), again about the plight of the black man in a white society; *The Third Lover* (*Il terzo amante*, 1929), in which an actress must choose between love and her theatrical vocation; *The World Without Crayfish* (*Il mondo senza gamberi*, 1932), concerning the scientist's responsibility to control those of his inventions that are capable of destroying mankind; and *The Poor King* (*Il re povero*, 1939), in which the corrupting powers of industry are explored. It is evident that Rocca's interests were varied and vital. He also wrote extensively for the Venetian-dialect stage.

[PETER BONDANELLA]

Rodgers, Richard   (1902–1979)

American composer and producer. He wrote for the musical stage for more than fifty years, mostly in collaboration with two lyricists, Lorenz Hart, in the period 1925–1943, and Oscar Hammerstein II, in the period 1943–1959. Rodgers's successes include *Garrick Gaieties* (1925); *A Connecticut Yankee* (1927); *Jumbo* (1935); *On Your Toes* (1936), for which he also collaborated on the book; *The Boys from Syracuse* (1938), based on Shakespeare's *The Comedy of Errors; Too Many Girls* (1939); *Pal Joey* (1940); *Oklahoma!* (1943); *Carousel* (1945); *South Pacific* (1949); *The King and I* (1951); and *The Sound of Music* (1959). One of his finest scores was written for the film musical *Love Me Tonight* (1932); he composed original scores for several other films including *State Fair* (1945). He also wrote the lyrics for the 1962 musical *No Strings. See* HAMMERSTEIN, OSCAR, II; HART, LORENZ; MUSICAL COMEDY.

[GAUTAM DASGUPTA]

Rodrigues, Nelson   (1912–   )

Brazilian dramatist. He was born in Recife, Pernambuco, on August 23, 1912, to journalist Mário Rodrigues and Maria Ester Falcão Rodrigues. Nelson moved to Rio de Janeiro in 1916, and at the age of thirteen wrote crime columns for his father's newspaper, *A Manhã.* In later years he worked as a journalist for *Crítica, O Globo, Diários Associados,* and *Última Hora* and for the magazines *O Cruzeiro* and *Manchete.* In recent years he has been closely associated with *O Jornal da Tarde.* Rodrigues made his debut as a dramatist in 1939 with his play *Woman Without Sin (A mulher sem pecado)* and attracted wide critical attention with *The Wedding Dress (Vestido de noiva),* produced by Os Comediantes in Rio's Teatro Municipal in 1943. He has also written a novel, *The Wedding (O casamento,* 1966), and a collection of short stories, *Life As We Know It (A vida como ela é,* 1961).

WORK

The name of Nelson Rodrigues is irrevocably linked with a radical change of direction in contemporary Brazilian drama. His first play, *Woman Without Sin,* set the pattern for all his subsequent plays. The "happenings" on which his dramas are based are almost like extracts from the sensational press, but these are admirably transformed

Too Many Girls by Rodgers and Lorenz Hart, with (l. to r.) Eddie Bracken, Desi Arnaz, Hal LeRoy, and Marcy Westcott. New York, Imperial Theatre, 1939. [Photograph by Vandamm. Theatre Collection, The New York Public Library at Lincoln Center, Astor, Lenox and Tilden Foundations]

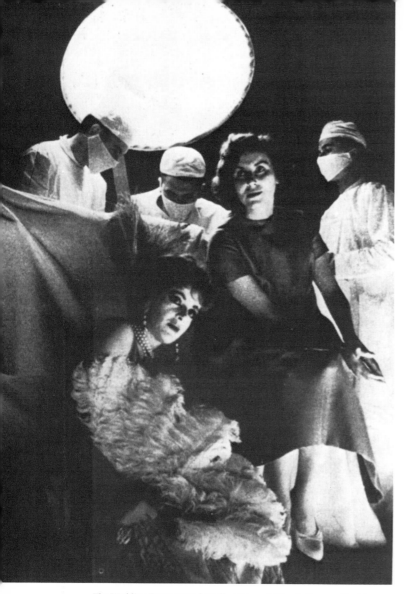

The Wedding Dress starred Nydia Licia and Wanda Kosmo. [Archives IDART-PMSP]

by the sheer concentration and power of Rodrigues's writing. In his first play a woman is tortured by her husband's uncontrolled jealousy and absurd suspicions. She finally abandons him just as he decides to reform. The sheer intensity of the dialogue sustains this slender plot of conflict. Pace and economy are the two salient features of Rodrigues's art. Every word and phrase has its own particular resonance.

His avant-garde approach to drama is best seen in his second play, *The Wedding Dress.* Theatre managements, company directors, actors, audiences, and even certain prominent critics were unprepared for the expressionism in this major work, which explores the subconscious of a dying woman. And for some time both censorship by state authorities and incomprehension by audiences made life difficult for this intransigent innovator.

But Rodrigues persevered with his controversial plays, which challenge conventional morality and traditional codes of conduct. *The Deceased Woman* (*A falecida*, 1953) deals with the private frustrations of a suburban housewife. The gulf between her dreams and the harsh

realities of her existence is beyond endurance and even her secret desire of having a splendid funeral after death fails to materialize.

Obsessive in his themes and techniques, some of Rodrigues's plays degenerate into melodrama. Such plays as *Forgive Me for Betraying Myself* (*Perdoa-me por me traíres*, 1957) and *The Seven Kittens* (*Os sete gatinhos*, 1958) fall into this category.

But he regains his form with *The Man with Gold Teeth* (*Bôca de ouro*, 1959), in which his most striking technique, namely the interplay between objective and subjective planes, is admirably sustained. Tragedy, comedy, and lyricism are skillfully combined in this work as the main protagonist Dona Guigui projects her inner world with its inherent contradictions. Each of the three acts presents a different version of the same story. Meaningful comparisons have been drawn between Rodrigues's play and the Japanese film *Rashomon* by Kurosawa. The influence of Pirandello is also strong, and the techniques of *The Man with Gold Teeth* have been studied alongside those of the Italian dramatist's first major play *Così è se vi pare* (1916.) Rodrigues engages in the same perusal of man's multiple personality, and the human soul becomes a mirror of endless reflections.

In another important work *The Kiss on the Pavement* (*O beijo no asfalto*, 1960), Rodrigues once more draws inspiration from an incident reminiscent of a police file and builds up unsuspected complexities with an intricate pattern of motivations and consequences. The father-in-law Aprígio reveals the pederast in his nature as the uneasy relationships between father, daughter, and son-in-law gradually unfold.

Intent upon probing man's inner contradictions, Ro-

Sérgio Cardoso and Sonia Oiticica in *The Deceased Woman.* [Archives IDART-PMSP]

Set for *The Deceased Woman*. [Archives IDART-PMSP]

drigues depicts a world tainted by sin and evil. His characters hover between moments of puritanical autoflagellation and a rebellious desire to show their contempt for all social propriety.

Other plays of note are *All Nudity Will Be Punished* (*Toda nudez será castigada*) and *The Snake* (*A serpente*), produced in 1979. Nelson Rodrigues firmly believes that every writer is sustained by his obsessions, but in the case of Rodrigues these obsessions appear to have drawn him into a vicious circle.

The Wedding Dress (*Vestido de noiva*, 1943). In its time this play was considered a "cerebral enigma." A woman is run over in the street by a car. She undergoes an emergency operation, and there seems little hope of saving her life. In her delirium her mind works incessantly, confusing fact and fiction, things imagined and actually experienced, past and present. From this mental jigsaw there emerges a coherent pattern in which two facts dominate: Alaide, the protagonist, had married her sister's boy friend; and as a girl Alaide lived in a house where a fashionable prostitute Mme. Clessy had once operated until she was brutally murdered by a seventeen-year-old youth. Alaide's rambling thoughts construe crosscurrents of intrigue and motivation in her subconscious. These betray her uneasy relationship with her husband Pedro and her sister Lucia. They also reveal mysterious parallels between intention and accident, between premeditated crime and circumstantial death. Images range from the sordid to the sublime, and the intricate multiplicity of the human personality is insistently explored. The disordered, feverish inner world of the individual and the dark side of his psyche are cruelly unmasked. The peril of the human state is expressed in a suggestive juxtaposition of guilt and remorse, hatred and compassion, love and lust, and life and death.

GIOVANNI PONTIERO

EDITIONS

Teatro, 2 vols., Rio de Janeiro, 1959; *Teatro Quase Completo*, 4 vols., Rio de Janeiro, 1966.

CRITICISM

A. Fonseca Pimentel, *O teatro de Nelson Rodrigues*, Rio de Janeiro, 1951; S. Magaldi, *Panorama do teatro brasileiro*, São Paulo, 1962, pp. 202–211.

Rodríguez Méndez, José María (1925–   )

Spanish critic, essayist, and dramatist. Rodríguez Méndez was born in Madrid but has spent most of his life in Barcelona. In 1954 he emigrated to Argentina, but the following year returned to Spain and served a tour of duty in the army. Though he holds a law degree from the University of Zaragoza, he supports himself by working as a civil servant and a parttime journalist. Deeply committed to the concept of a popular theatre, he has collaborated with various theatrical groups that perform before working-class audiences and on a number of occasions has acted in their productions.

He is a member of the "Realist Generation," a group of dissident playwrights who emerged in Franco Spain in the 1950s and whose plays address themselves to social issues. His first plays were produced by amateur groups in Barcelona, and until very recently only two of his twenty-odd works were staged in Madrid: *The Innocents of the Moncloa* (*Los inocentes de la Moncloa*, 1964) and *Story of a Few* (*Historia de unos cuantos*, 1975). In 1978 the government-funded National Dramatic Center (Centro Dramático Nacional) successfully produced *The Once Famous Wedding of Pingajo and Fandanga* (*Bodas que fueron famosas del Pingajo y la Fandanga*) in Madrid's Bellas Artes Theatre.

Like most dramatists of the Realist Generation, he began writing in the naturalist manner of Antonio Buero Vallejo's *Story of a Staircase* (*Historia de una escalera*, 1949) and has remained fundamentally faithful to this conception of the drama. He has sought artistic inspiration in the Hispanic dramatic tradition, particularly in those authors and genres most closely related to popular culture: the *sainetes* (picturesque sketches, usually short, of lower-class life) of Carlos Arniches; the *género chico* (a light, popular form of theatrical entertainment that flourished in the late nineteenth century and includes the *sainete*); the grotesque farces, or *esperpentos*, of Ramón del Valle Inclán; and the *entremeses* (short comic interludes which are the forerunners of the modern *sainete*) of Cervantes. His theatre is characterized by what might be termed a tragic sense of humor, which had immediate antecedents in Arniches and Valle Inclán.

The characters in his plays almost invariably belong to or identify with the lower strata of Spanish society: the socially alienated and exploited. In his most recent dramas, those written after 1965, Rodríguez Méndez focuses on socially disfranchised types which bourgeois Spanish theatre has normally excluded from the stage: impoverished peasants, prostitutes, delinquents, drifters, and homosexuals. His dramatic method is direct, his language harsh and free of ambiguities.

Among his most important plays are *The Innocents of the Moncloa* (*Los inocentes de la Moncloa*; originally performed 1961); *The Chalk Circle of Cartagena* (*El círculo de tiza de Cartagena*, 1963); *The Once Famous Wedding of Pingajo and Fandanga* (*Bodas que fueron famosas del Pingajo y la*

Fandanga; wr. 1965, but not performed until 1978); and *Autumn Flower (Flor de Otoño),* written in 1972 but still unperformed on the stage, although it has been made into a film.

The Innocents of the Moncloa deals with a familiar aspect of Spanish life, the system of *oposiciones,* or competitive examinations, for those who aspire to civil service positions. Set in a contemporary Madrid boardinghouse, the play revolves around a group of students who are preparing themselves for their *oposiciones,* a system which the author denounces as alienating, cruel, and absurd. The presence of Valle Inclán and his *esperpento* style appear for the first time in *The Chalk Circle of Cartagena,* a historical drama about a nineteenth-century popular uprising. The play additionally shows the influence both of Bertolt Brecht (who had a powerful impact on many Spanish playwrights of the 1960s and 1970s) and of the *entremeses* of Cervantes. *The Once Famous Wedding of Pingajo and Fandanga* marks a turning point in Rodríguez Méndez's theatre and his maturity as a dramatist. The influence of Valle Inclán remains, but it is now possible to detect another source of artistic inspiration, the *género chico.* The action takes place in Madrid just after the defeat of Spain by the United States in 1898 and consists of a series of individual *cuadros* (he labels them *estampas*), or tableaux, that employ music and song. *Autumn Flower,* written seven years later, also focuses on a segment of the Spanish past: 1930, the last months of the dictatorship of Primo de Rivera, who had ruled since 1923 and whose downfall ushered in the Second Spanish Republic, against which the forces of the right were to rebel in July, 1936. The action takes place against a background of social unrest and terrorist bombings. The protagonist, a female impersonator, is a member of a prominent upper-class family but rebelliously seeks the company of those underworld types who inhabit the cabarets and dance halls of Barcelona's red-light district. A major portion of the dialogue is realistically written in the idiomatic Catalan speech of Barcelona, phonetically transcribed. Needless to say, Rodríguez Méndez's historical plays, like those written by Buero Vallejo and the younger dramatists who came after him, utilize the past as a means of reflecting on the present. *See* CATALAN DRAMA.

ANDRÉS FRANCO

CRITICISM

J. Monleón, ed., *Teatro* (miscellaneous material), Madrid (Col. Primer Acto, no. 8), 1968; J. Monleón, *Cuatro autores críticos,* Granada, 1976; M. Halsey, "La Generación Realista: A Select Bibliography," *Estreno,* vol. III, no. 1 (1977), pp. 8–13; F. Ruiz Ramón, *Historia del teatro español: Siglo XX,* 3d ed., Madrid, 1977, pp. 509–516; C. Oliva, *Cuatro dramaturgos realistas: sus contribuciones estéticas,* Murcia, 1978; ibid, *Disidentes de la generación realista,* Murcia, 1979.

Roepke, Gabriela   (1920–   )

Chilean playwright. One of the founders of the Teatro de Ensayo, after studying drama in the United States, she began writing psychological dramas. On her return to Santiago, she initiated drama programs in several local schools and continued her own writing. *Invitation (Invitación)* won both the Santiago and the Caupolicán prizes

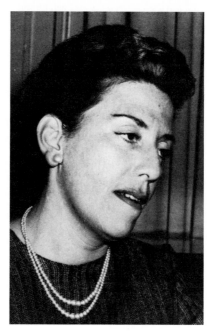

Gabriela Roepke.
[Republic of Chile]

for that year in 1954. *White Butterfly (Mariposa blanca)* appeared in 1957, but it was actually written while she was in the United States. *Cobweb (Telaraña,* 1958) contributed an excellent example of mystery drama to the Chilean stage. In 1959 her *Blessed Women (Las santas mujeres)* was given a production by the Teatro de Ensayo. Her *Conferencia dialogada,* published in 1968, was the outcome of a discussion with another local playwright and covers aspects of theatre history in Chile.

WILLIS KNAPP JONES and JUDITH A. WEISS

Roger-Ferdinand   (1898–1967)

French film writer and dramatist; pseudonym of Roger Ferdinand. He is best known for his comedy *The J-3s, or The New School (Les J-3, ou La nouvelle école,* 1943). (J-3 was a wartime administrative designation for adolescents from sixteen to twenty.) The comedy deals with the influence of a determined young teacher on a group of young boys disoriented by the pressures of a wartime society.

Roger-Ferdinand was originally an English instructor and made his debut as a dramatist with *The Memory Machine (La machine à souvenirs,* 1924). After the success of Aurélien Lugné-Poë's production of *A Man of Gold (Un homme en or,* 1927), he quit teaching to devote himself to the theatre. He soon became one of France's most prolific and popular playwrights. Among some of his better-known comedies are *Irma* (1926); *Chotard and Company (Chotard et Cie,* 1928); *Batoche* (1932), which starred Raimu; *Three Boys and a Girl (Trois garçons, une fille,* 1947); *The Folks Are Fine (Les croulants se portent bien,* 1959); and *The Kikota Sign (Le signe de Kikota,* 1960). He is also known for his adaptations of foreign plays, including Robert Anderson's *Tea and Sympathy* (1956).

[JOSEPH E. GARREAU]

Rojas, Fernando de   (2d half 15th cent.–1541)

Spanish dramatist. Fernando de Rojas, celebrated for his play *La Celestina*, was born in La Puebla de Montalbán, Toledo Province, into a family of *conversos*, Spanish Jews recently converted to Catholicism. Rojas studied law at the University of Salamanca, from which he was graduated shortly before or during the last decade of the century. Thereafter he moved with his family to Talavera de la Reina, where he practiced law and served as chief administrative and judicial officer for some years. No longer young, he married the converted Jewess Leonor Álvarez, whose father, Álvaro de Montalbán, was subsequently tried by the Inquisition. Rojas died in early April, 1541.

WORK

Rojas's fame rests upon a single work, the prose drama *Comedia de Calisto y Melibea*, more commonly known as *La Celestina*, the name of its central character. The first extant edition, containing sixteen acts, was published anonymously in Burgos in or about 1499. *La Celestina* is generally considered the most important work of Spanish literature before Cervantes' *Don Quixote*, both because of its intrinsic merits and because of its influence on the European novel and theatre. Rojas's sources are to be found in the writings of the ancients as well as in the medieval and early Renaissance literature of Spain and Italy. In essence, the author is caught up in an insoluble conflict between the medieval and the Renaissance conceptions of romantic love and resolves it through the classical expediency of death, meted out to all the protagonists.

The play concerns the consummation of the love, both sensual and spiritual, of Calisto for Melibea, brought about under the aegis of the amoral procuress Celestina, which ends in the tragic death of all three. The characters are portrayed with a knowledge of the complexity of human emotions and an understanding of hu-

Maureen Mileski (right) in the title role of *La Celestina* bewitches Melibea, played by Moana Diamond in this 1979 production by San Francisco's Stagegroup. [Photograph by Charles Farruggia]

Woodcut of a scene from *La Celestina*, 1538. [Goethe House]

man fallibility that are astounding at such an early date. The behavior of the secondary characters serves as a foil for the greater intricacies of the relationships existing between the protagonists. The style of the work is rich and varied, and the language as realistic as the characters who speak it.

In the beginning of *Don Quixote*, Cervantes wrote of Rojas's *Celestina* that it would have been a "divine book" if it had allowed human passion to remain in somewhat greater obscurity.

The second known edition, published in Toledo in 1500, contains a preface in which the author, in the form of a letter addressed to a friend, writes that while on vacation he has discovered an anonymous transcription of the first act and has completed the work in a fortnight. Rojas's authorship is revealed in acrostic verses that state that "the baccalaureate Fernando de Rojas finished the

Comedy of Calisto and Melibea, who was born in La Puebla de Montalbán." A version of the play with five additional acts and other changes, entitled *Tragicomedy of Calisto and Melibea (Tragicomedia de Calisto y Melibea),* was published in Salamanca no later than 1502, although the earliest extant editions of this revision are the Italian translation published in Rome in 1506 and the Saragossa edition of 1507. In the 1514 and 1526 editions, a twenty-second act was added. However, it is generally believed that Rojas was the author of Acts II through XXI.

The play was reprinted in Spanish at least sixty times in the sixteenth century alone, and it was translated into Italian, French, German, English, Flemish, Hebrew, and Latin. Its inordinate length prevented its actual performance, however, until the twentieth century, when it was cut and adapted for the stage on several occasions.

La Celestina had an important influence on the Spanish literature of the Siglo de Oro (Spanish Golden Age), perhaps most notably on *La Dorotea* of Lope de Vega. Some critics believe that Shakespeare knew the work, probably in an Italian version, and used it for certain elements of *Romeo and Juliet,* although this latter play is quite different in tone from *La Celestina. See* SHAKESPEARE, WILLIAM. *See also* SIGLO DE ORO in glossary.

La Celestina (first version, pub. 1499; second version, pub. 1502). Prose drama depicting the tragic consequences of the unrestrainable passion of two young lovers, the consummation of which is fostered by an amoral procuress. Calisto, a selfish young nobleman, falls in love with the beautiful Melibea, only daughter of Pleberio and Alisa, when he sees her one day in her garden. After she rebuffs his first declarations of love, he asks his servants Sempronio and Parmeno for help in winning her love. Against the advice of Parmeno, Sempronio enlists the services of Celestina, a wily procuress, in exchange for monetary reward. Celestina arranges a meeting between Calisto and Melibea through the practice of sorcery. That night, while Calisto seduces Melibea, Celestina, having refused to share her monetary gain with Sempronio and Parmeno as she had promised, is killed by the two servants, who are later arrested and put to death in the public square. Celestina's women accuse Calisto of causing her death and employ the braggart soldier Centurion to kill him and Melibea. Hearing this, Calisto leaves Melibea's garden in great haste and is accidentally killed as he falls from the top of the wall. When Melibea learns of her lover's death, in order to follow him to the grave, she throws herself from the top of a tower in the presence of her father, to whom she had declared her love for Calisto. On the point of death, she asks to be buried beside her lover.

[ANDRÉS FRANCO]

PLAYS

The following is a partial list of twentieth-century adaptations of *La Celestina* for the stage.
1. Adaptation in 5 acts by Felipe Pediell. Published 1903.
2. Adaptation in 5 acts by Francisco Fernández Villegas. Produced Madrid, Teatro Español, October, 1909.
3. Adaptation by Felipe Lluch. Produced Madrid, Nov. 13, 1940; Parma, April, 1955; Cáceres, 1955.
4. Adaptation of translation by C. Alvaro. Published 1940. Produced Rome, Teatro delle Arti, 1941; Teatro dell'Ateneo, 1950.
5. Adaptation by P. Achard. Published 1942. Produced Paris, Théâtre Montparnasse–Gaston-Baty, Feb. 20, 1942.
6. Adaptation by Huberto Pérez de la Ossa. Produced Madrid, Teatro Eslava, May 10, 1957.
7. Adaptation of translation by James Mabbe (1631). Produced Stratford, England, Theatre Royal, Feb. 21, 1958.
8. Adaptation by Georges Brousse. Produced Montauban, July, 1960.
9. Adaptation by C. J. Cela. Produced Madrid, 1979.

EDITIONS

The following is a list of editions of *La Celestina* in various languages.
Spanish
M. Menéndez Pelayo, ed., 2 vols., Vigo, 1899–1900 (reprint of 1514 edition); R. Foulché-Delbosc, ed., *Bibliotheca hispánica,* vols. I and XII, Barcelona, 1900, 1902 (reprints of 1499 and 1500 editions); Hispanic Society, New York, 1909 (facsimile of 1499 edition); J. Cejador, ed., *Clásicos castellanos,* vols. XX and XXIII, Madrid, 1913; M. Criado de Val and G. D. Trotter, eds., *Clásicos hispánicos,* ser. II, vol. III, Madrid, 1958; Valencia, 1958 (facsimile of 1502 edition).
English
L. B. Simpson, tr., *The Celestina: A Novel in Dialogue,* Berkeley, Calif., 1955; M. H. Singleton, tr., Madison, Wis., 1958; P. Hartnoll, tr., London and New York, 1959; J. M. Cohen, tr., New York, 1964.
French
P. Achard, ed., Paris, 1942.
Italian
C. Alvaro, ed., 2 vols., Milan, 1943.

CRITICISM

M. Menéndez Pelayo, *Orígenes de la novela,* vol. III, pp. 219–458, Madrid, 1943; S. Gilman, *The Art of the Celestina,* Madison, Wis., 1956; M. Bataillon, *La Célestine selon Fernando de Rojas,* Paris, 1961; M. R. Lida de Malkiel, *La originalidad artística de La Celestina,* Buenos Aires, 1962; J. A. Maravall, *El mundo social de "La Celestina,"* Madrid, 1964; A. Castro, *"La Celestina" como contienda literaria,* Madrid, 1965; S. Gilman, *The Spain of Fernando de Rojas. The Intellectual and Social Landscape of "La Celestina,"* Princeton, 1972; P. N. Dunn, *Fernando de Rojas,* New York, 1975.

Rojas Zorrilla, Francisco de (1607–1648)

Spanish dramatist. Rojas Zorrilla was born in Toledo on October 4, 1607, but was brought up in Madrid, where his father moved the family after resigning as an ensign in the Royal Navy. He is believed to have studied at a university, probably Salamanca, but it is not known whether or not he finished his studies there. By 1631 Rojas had returned to Madrid and was asked to contribute a sonnet to a collection in which eighty-nine poets celebrated the shooting of a bull by Philip IV. Early in his career Rojas was accepted as the collaborator of such prominent dramatists as Calderón, Coello, Pérez de Montalbán, and Vélez de Guevara. The early 1630s, however, brought him recognition in his own name. In 1635 he wrote a sonnet on the occasion of the death of Lope de Vega. *See* CALDERÓN DE LA BARCA, PEDRO; COELLO Y OCHOA, ANTONIO; VEGA CARPIO, LOPE DE; VÉLEZ DE GUEVARA, LUIS.

The year 1636 was perhaps the most important in Rojas Zorrilla's life, as it saw the production of six of his plays, including *To Marry for Vengeance (Casarse por vengarse).* On January 29, 1637, his play *No Jealousy Without Cause, or The Servant Master (Donde hay agravios no hay celos, o El amo criado)* was produced as part of the festivities honoring the arrival in Spain of Doña María de Borbón, Princess of Carignan. In 1638 an unsuccessful attempt was made on his life, presumably by someone who was the butt of a literary lampoon written by Rojas as a contribution to festivities organized to amuse Philip

Francisco de Rojas Zorrilla. [New York Public Library Picture Collection]

IV. When, on February 4, 1640, a new theatre was opened in the Palace of Buen Retiro in Madrid, Rojas's play *The Two Households of Verona (Los bandos de Verona)* was chosen as the inaugural piece.

On November 21, 1640, Rojas married Doña Catalina Yáñez Trillo de Mendoza, and a few days later a collection of his plays, *The First Part (Primera parte)*, was published; *The Second Part (Segunda parte)*, was to follow in 1645. Although it is not certain that after 1640 he wrote any more *comedias* (the last recorded one is *The Two Households of Verona*), his succeeding plays invariably took the form of more profitable *autos sacramentales. See* AUTO SACRAMENTAL; COMEDIA in glossary.

Philip IV honored Rojas in 1643 by awarding him a knighthood in the Order of Santiago. During the subsequent investigation into the purity of his bloodlines, Rojas was accused of bribing witnesses to hide the fact that he had Moorish and Jewish ancestors. Before he could receive the habit, a special papal dispensation was necessary because Rojas's father had accepted gainful employment as a notary in his later years. Between 1646 and 1649 the king banned all theatrical productions because of the death of his son. Nevertheless, in 1647 Rojas was called on to contribute the *auto sacramental The Great Courtyard of the Palace (El gran patio de palacio)* to the Corpus Christi Festival in Madrid. By the time the ban was lifted, Rojas had died under suspicious circumstances in Madrid on January 23, 1648. He was survived by a son and an illegitimate daughter, Francisca Bezón, who became the famous actress La Bezona.

WORK

Among the Spanish dramatists of the seventeenth century, Rojas Zorrilla, the author of tragedies, *comedias, autos sacramentales,* and *entremeses (see* ENTREMÉS in glossary) and the collaborator of such dramatists as Calderón and Vélez de Guevara, was the innovator and rebel. He challenged the concept of royal omnipotence, the prevailing adulation of the King, and the aristocratic code of

honor. In his *comedias de pundonor* (plays based on a serious treatment of the Spanish code of honor) it is often the women who extract vengeance for a "point of honor" flouted; Rojas championed the rights of women against the double standard of the day, treating questions of matrimony, incompatibility, unfaithfulness, and love outside marriage with a frankness that sometimes infuriated his audiences. By exposing moral issues to a new, skeptical scrutiny and by showing the fallibility of institutions until then regarded as sacrosanct, Rojas brought freshness and vigor into Spanish theatre. For Calderón's opulent decoration and elaborate ceremonial, he substituted a sense of reality and throbbing life and created a gallery of vigorous, sometimes hyperbolic burlesque types: he invented the *çomedia de figurón,* which extended the *comedia de carácter* into the realm of caricature, thus breaking new ground in the comedy genre.

Rojas incorporated into his plays details of everyday life that previously had not been used. He generally avoided obscurity and exaggeration, employing a simple style and a clear idiom cast in sonorous, fluid verse, less poetic than that of Lope, and a lively dialogue with a sprinkling of satire. His plots are intricate but less so than those of his contemporaries; a looser structure allowed him to interweave frequent comic passages, at which he excelled. He also broke the convention that confined humor to the *gracioso* ("clown"). Rojas Zorrilla had an important influence outside Spain, on Thomas Corneille, Scarron, Marivaux, and Lesage. *See* CORNEILLE, THOMAS; LESAGE, ALAIN-RENÉ; MARIVAUX, PIERRE CARLET DE; SCARRON, PAUL.

The most famous among his approximately 100 stage works (excluding works of doubtful authorship) are *None But the King (Del rey abajo, ninguno,* pub. 1650) a *comedia de pundonor* developed into authentic tragedy, in which a young peasant is dishonored by a courtier he mistakes for the King; *The Sport of Fools (Entre bobos anda el juego,* wr. 1638), a *comedia de figurón* in which a repulsive old man sends a young cousin to escort his reluctant bride-to-be; and *No Jealousy Without Cause* (1637) a *comedia de capa y espada* in which a suitor changes places with his servant in order to observe his intended wife, who has never seen him. Three *comedias de enredo,* in which all elements are subordinated to a complex plot, are also outstanding examples of Rojas Zorrilla's art: *Keep Your Eyes Open (Abre el ojo,* 1640) describes the way gentlemen take revenge on the courtesans who have been using them; *What Women Are (Lo que son las mujeres,* pub. 1645) deals with the complicated courtship of two women, one beautiful and the other ugly, by four suitors; and *Treachery Seeks Punishment (La traición busca el castigo,* wr. 1637?) portrays a villain who dupes his rival in love into killing an innocent man.

Other *comedias* of note are *Don Diego by Night (Don Diego de noche,* pub. 1654), about two girls in love with the same man; *To Each His Own (Cada cual lo que le toca),* a violent play, in which a nobleman discovers that his bride is not a virgin, that defends a woman's right to choose her own husband; *A King, Not a Father (No hay ser padre siendo rey,* wr. ca. 1635?), depicting the conflicting duties of a man who is both father and King; and *The Most Improper Executioner for the Most Just Vengeance* (*El más impropio verdugo para la más justa venganza*, 1637), in which a father disguises himself and kills his degenerate son in order to restore his own honor.

No Jealousy Without Cause, or The Servant Master (*Donde hay agravios no hay celos, o El amo criado*, 1637). *Comedia de capa y espada* in which Juan, seeing another young man near the house of Inés, his bride-to-be, suspects that she has been unfaithful to him. He persuades his servant Sancho to change places with him so that he, as a servant, will see Inés's reaction to her intended husband, whom she has never seen. Inés has another suitor, Lope, who while attempting to seduce Juan's sister had killed her other brother as he tried to defend her. Sancho, comical and cowardly, finds himself threatened by Lope and informs Juan, who quickly avenges himself both as brother and as suitor against Lope.

Scarron imitated this *comedia* in his *Jodelet, or The Master-Valet*.

The Sport of Fools, or Don Lucas del Cigarral (*Entre bobos anda el juego, o Don Lucas del Cigarral*, wr. 1638). *Comedia de figurón* in which Lucas del Cigarral, rich, old, and uncouth, decides to marry and sends his young cousin Pedro to escort Isabel, his reluctant bride, from Madrid to Toledo. On the way, Pedro rescues Isabel from a bull, and the two fall in love. When they are joined by Lucas, Isabel's evasiveness compels Lucas to ask Pedro to intercede for him. At first Pedro is shy, and Lucas urges him to be more forceful; when he becomes bolder, Lucas tries to restrain him. During the journey Lucas becomes increasingly suspicious of Pedro, whom he sees entering Isabel's room at night.

A newcomer, Luis, now appears, ready to declare his love for Isabel, but by mistake he enters the room of Alfonsa, Lucas's sister, and courts her instead. After Lucas learns that both Luis and Pedro love Isabel, he abandons his plans to marry, reluctant to wed someone whose romantic life is so active. Isabel marries Pedro, and Lucas comforts himself with the thought of their future poverty.

Lucas is one of the most original and lively caricatures of Golden Age drama, and the play furnished the plot for Thomas Corneille's *Don Bertrand de Cigarral*.

None But the King, or The Most Honored Peasant, or García del Castañar (*Del rey abajo, ninguno, o El labrador más honrado, o García del Castañar*, pub. 1650). *Comedia de pundonor* set in the fourteenth century. King Alfonso XI of Castile receives from a peasant vassal a lavish gift of food and wine to feed his army. He learns that the donor is García del Castañar, a man of incomparable valor. Although García is actually the son of the exiled Regent who held the throne until Alfonso came of age, he has chosen to live in rustic serenity away from the dangers of court factions. His wife Blanca is also of noble blood, though she is unaware of it. When the King and his courtier Don Mendo set out in disguise to knight García, Mendo attempts to seduce Blanca. Believing Mendo to be the King because he wears a royal sash, García is unable to avenge the dishonor.

In deep sorrow he vows to kill his beloved wife even though he believes her to be innocent. But he wavers, and she escapes to the court of the Queen. García follows and finds Mendo once more trying to force her submission. Finally realizing that Mendo is not the King, he fatally stabs him. García's noble ancestry is admitted, and he is pardoned. He then agrees to lead Alfonso's troops in battle.

[ANDRÉS FRANCO]

PLAYS

Rojas Zorrilla's plays are separated into appropriate categories and listed alphabetically.

Comedias

1. *Abre el ojo* (*Keep Your Eyes Open*). Play. Published 1645. Produced Toledo, Aug. 3, 1640.
2. *Los áspides de Cleopatra* (*Cleopatra's Asps*). Play. Published 1645.
3. *Los bandos de Verona* (*The Two Households of Verona*). Play. Published 1645. Produced Madrid, Coliseo del Buen Retiro, Feb. 4, 1640.
4. *Cada cual lo que le toca* (*To Each His Own*). Tragedy.
5. *El Caín de Cataluña* (*The Cain of Catalonia*). Play. Published 1663.
6. *Casarse por vengarse* (*To Marry for Vengeance*). Play. Published 1636. Produced Valencia, 1636; Madrid, 1640.
7. *Los celos de Rodamonte* (*Rodamonte's Jealousy*). Play. Published 1638.
8. *La confusión de la fortuna* (*The Confusion of Fortune*). Play. Written 1638/39.
9. *Del rey abajo, ninguno, o El labrador más honrado, o García del Castañar** (*None But the King, or The Most Honored Peasant, or García del Castañar*). Play. Published 1650.
10. *El desafío de Carlos V* (*The Challenge of Charles V*). Play. Published 1861. Produced May 28, 1635.
11. *La difunta pleiteada* (*The Disputed Corpse*). Play. Published 1663.
12. *Donde hay agravios no hay celos, o El amo criado* (*No Jealousy Without Cause, or The Servant Master*). Play. Written 1635/36. Published 1640. Produced Madrid, El Prado, Jan. 29, 1637.
13. *Don Diego de noche* (*Don Diego by Night*). Play. Published 1654.
14. *Los encantos de Medea* (*Medea's Spells*). Play. Published 1645.
15. *Entre bobos anda el juego, o Don Lucas del Cigarral* (*The Sport of Fools, or Don Lucas del Cigarral*). Play. Written 1638. Published 1645.
16. *Esto es hecho, o No hay contra la muerte industria?* (*This Is Done, or Is There No Remedy Against Death?*). Play.
17. *La hermosura y la desdicha* (*Beauty and Misfortune*). Play. Published 1671.
18. *Hierusalem castigada* (*Jerusalem Punished*). Play.
19. *Lo que quería ver el Marqués de Villena* (*What the Marquis of Villena Wished to See*). Play. Published 1645.
20. *Lo que son las mujeres* (*What Women Are*). Play. Published 1645.
21. *El más impropio verdugo para la más justa venganza* (*The Most Improper Executioner for the Most Just Vengeance*). Play. Published 1645. Produced Madrid, Coliseo del Buen Retiro, Feb. 2, 1637.
22. *El médico de su amor* (*The Surgeon of His Love*). Play.
23. *El mejor amigo, el muerto, o El capuchino escocés* (*The Best Friend Is the Dead One, or The Scottish Capuchin*). Play.
24. *Morir pensando matar* (*To Die Intending to Kill*). Play. Published 1642.
25. *No hay amigo para amigo, o Las cañas se vuelven lanzas* (*True Friends Do Not Exist, or Reeds Become Lances*). Play. Published 1640. Produced Madrid, Coliseo del Buen Retiro, July 1, 1636.
26. *No hay duelo entre dos amigos* (*No Duel Between Two Friends*). Play.
27. *No hay ser padre siendo rey* (*A King, Not a Father*). Play. Written ca. 1635? Published 1640. Based on Guillén de Castro's *La justicia en la piedad*. Play.
28. *No intenta el que no es dichoso* (*One Who Is Unhappy Does Not Try*). Play.
29. *Nuestra Señora de Atocha* (*Our Lady of Atocha*). Play. Published 1645. Produced Madrid, Feb. 11, 1639.
30. *Numancia cercada* (*Numantia Encircled*). Play.
31. *Numancia destruída* (*Numantia Destroyed*). Play.
32. *Obligados y ofendidos, o El gorrón de Salamanca* (*Obliged though Offended*). Play. Published 1640. Produced Madrid, June 6, 1635.
33. *Peligrar en los remedios* (*A Risk amid Remedies*). Play. Published 1640. Produced December, 1634.
34. *Persiles y Segismunda* (*Persiles and Segismunda*). Play. Published 1636. Produced Madrid, Feb. 7, 1633. Based on a novel by Miguel de Cervantes (1617).
35. *El primer Marqués de Astonga, o Fronterizo español* (*The First Marquis of Astonga, or Spanish Frontier*). Play. Produced ca. 1634.
36. *Primero es la honra que el gusto* (*Honor before Pleasure*). Play. Published 1861.
37. *El profeta falso Mahoma* (*Mohammed, the False Prophet*). Play. Pub-

lished 1640. Produced June 8, 1635.

38. *Progne y Filomena* (*Progne and Philomena*). Play. Published 1640. Produced Madrid, Jan. 10, 1636.

39. *La prudencia en el castigo* (*Prudence in Punishment*). Play. Published 1678.

40. *Saber de una vez* (*To Know Once*). Play.

41. *Santa Isabel, reina de Portugal* (*St. Isabel, Queen of Portugal*). Play. Published 1638. Produced Madrid, Sept. 18, 1635.

42. *Santa Tais* (*St. Thais*). Play.

43. *La segunda Magdalena, o La sirena de Nápoles* (*The Second Magdalen, or The Siren of Naples*). Play.

44. *Selva de amor y celos* (*Forest of Love and Jealousy*). Play. Published 1669.

45. *Sin honor no hay amistad* (*Without Honor There Is No Friendship*). Play. Published 1645.

46. *Los trabajos de Tobías* (*The Labors of Tobias*). Play. Published 1642.

47. *La traición busca el castigo* (*Treachery Seeks Punishment*).Play. Written 1637? Published 1640.

48. *La vida en el ataúd* (*Life in the Coffin*). Play. Published 1669.

Plays Written in Collaboration

1. (With Antonio Coello y Ochoa and Luis Vélez de Guevara). *La Baltasara* (*Baltasara*). Play, 3 acts. Published 1652. Act I, Vélez de Guevara; Act II, Coello y Ochoa; Act III, Rojas Zorrilla.

2. (With Jerónimo de Cáncer y Velasco and Pedro Rosete Niño). *El bandolero Solposto* (*Solposto the Bandit*). Play, 3 acts. Published 1669. Act I, Cáncer; Act II, Rosete Niño; Act III, Rojas Zorrilla.

3. (With Coello y Ochoa and Vélez de Guevara). *El catalán Serrallonga, o Los bandos de Barcelona*. Play, 3 acts. Published 1636. Produced Toledo, Palacio, Jan. 10, 1635. Act I, Coello y Ochoa; Act II, Rojas Zorrilla; Act III, Vélez de Guevara.

4. (With Coello y Ochoa and Pedro Calderón de la Barca). *El jardín de Falerina* (*The Garden of Falerina*). Play, 3 acts. Act I, Rojas Zorrilla; Act II, Coello y Ochoa; Act III, Calderón.

5. (With Juan de Zabaleta and Calderón). *La más hidalga hermosura* (*Beauty Most Noble*). Play, 3 acts. Published 1650. Produced 1645. Act I, Zabaleta; Act II, Rojas Zorrilla; Act III, Calderón.

6. (With Luis Belmonte y Bermúdez and Calderón). *El mejor amigo el muerto* (*The Best Friend Is the Dead One*). Play, 3 acts. Written ca. 1635. Published 1657. Act I, Belmonte; Act II, Rojas Zorrilla; Act III, Calderón.

7. (With Calderón and Juan Pérez de Montalbán). *El monstruo de la fortuna, o La lavandera de Nápoles* (*The Monster of Fortune, or The Washerwoman of Naples*). Play, 3 acts. Published 1666. Act I, Calderón; Act II, Pérez de Montalbán; Act III, Rojas Zorrilla.

8. (With Vélez de Guevara and Antonio Mira de Amescua). *Pleito que tuvo el diablo con el cura de Madrilejos* (*The Devil's Dispute with the Priest of Madrilejos*). Play, 3 acts. Written 1639/40. Published 1652. Act I, Vélez de Guevara; Act II, Rojas Zorrilla; Act III, Mira de Amescua.

9. *El robo de las sabinas* (*The Rape of the Sabine Women*). Play. Published 1659. Produced Madrid, Coliseo del Buen Retiro, June 24, 1637.

10. (With Vélez de Guevara and Coello y Ochoa). *También la afrenta es veneno* (*The Affront Is Also Poison*). Play, 3 acts. Published 1697. Act I, Vélez de Guevara; Act II, Coella y Ochoa; Act III, Rojas Zorrilla.

11. (With Vélez de Guevara and Juan Claudio Hoz y Mota?). *También tiene el sol menguante, o No hay privanza sin envidia* (*The Sun Also Wanes, or There Is No Favor Without Envy*). Play, 3 acts. Published 1666. Produced Madrid, Nov. 17, 1655.

12. (With Coello y Ochoa). *Los tres blasones de España*. Play, 3 acts. Published 1645. Act I, Coello y Ochoa; Act II, Rojas Zorrilla; Act III, Rojas Zorrilla.

13. (With Jerónimo de Villanueva and Gabriel de Ros). *El villano gran señor, o El gran Tamerlán de Persia* (*The Lowborn Lord, or The Great Tamerlane of Persia*). Play, 3 acts. Written 1635. Act I, Rojas Zorrilla; Act II, Villanueva; Act III, Ros.

Autos Sacramentales

1. *Los acreedores del hombre* (*Man's Creditors*). Play.

2. *Los árboles* (*The Trees*). Play. Published 1675.

3. *Galán, valiente y discreto* (*Gallant, Brave, and Discreet*). Play. Published 1655.

4. *El gran patio de palacio* (*The Great Courtyard of the Palace*). Play. Published 1656. Produced 1647.

5. *Hércules* (*Hercules*). Play. ced Madrid, 1639.

6. *El más bueno y el más malo* (*The Best and the Worst*). Play.

7. *Los obreros del Señor* (*The Lord's Workers*). Play. Published 1655.

8. *El rico avariento* (*The Miserly Rich Man*). Play.

9. *El robo de Elena* (*The Abduction of Helen*). Play.

10. *La viña de Nabot* (*Naboth's Vineyard*). Play. Produced Granada, 1648.

Entremeses

1. *El alcalde ardite* (*The Penny Mayor*). Play.

2. *El doctor* (*The Doctor*). Play.

Doubtful Plays

1. *Donde hay valor hay honor* (*Where There Is Bravery, There Is Honor*).

Play. Published 1640. Produced Madrid, before Sept. 9, 1637. Attributed to Rojas Zorrilla, Diego de Rosas, and Diego de Rojas.

2. *Don Gil de la Mancha* (*Don Gil of La Mancha*). Play.

3. *El pleito del demonio con la Virgen* (*The Devil's Dispute with the Virgin*). Play. Published 1654.

4. *El sordo y el montañés* (*The Deaf Man and the Man from the Mountains*). Play. Published 1678.

5. *La trompeta del juicio* (*The Trump of Doom*). Play. Published 1669.

EDITIONS

Comedias de Don Francisco de Rojas Zorrilla, 2 parts, Madrid, 1640–1645; *Comedias escogidas*, ed. by R. de Mesonero Romanos, *Biblioteca de autores españoles*, vol. LIV, Madrid, 1861.

None But the King. Published in *Three Classic Spanish Plays*, as *None Beneath the King*, ed. by H. Alpern and tr. by I. Goldberg, Washington Square, New York, 1963; *The Genius of the Spanish Theater*, ed. by R. O'Brien and tr. by R. Benson, Mentor Books, New American Library, New York, 1964.

CRITICISM

E. Cotarelo y Mori, *Don Francisco de Rojas Zorrilla*, Madrid, 1911; J. A. Barrett, *Some Aspects of the Dramatic Technique of Francisco de Rojas Zorrilla* (thesis), University of North Carolina, Chapel Hill, N.C., 1938; F. C. Sainz de Robles, *Dramaturgos de la escuela de Calderón: Rojas Zorrilla*, Madrid, 1947; R. R. MacCurdy, *Francisco de Rojas Zorrilla and the Tragedy*, Albuquerque, 1958; R. R. MacCurdy, *Francisco de Rojas Zorrilla*, New York, 1973.

Rolland, Romain (1866–1944)

French novelist, musicologist, and dramatist. He is best known for *Jean Christophe*, a *roman-fleuve* whose idealist hero strongly resembles Beethoven. An internationalist and a pacifist under the philosophical influence of Tolstoy and the immediate personal influence of Mme. Malwida von Meysenbug's highly idealistic circle, Rolland developed a view of the social utility of art. He therefore exposed a concept of ''popular'' theatre that had emerged during the French Revolution and was in his own time advanced by Maurice Pottecher's Théâtre du Peuple in Bussang and the Théâtre Civique established in Paris in 1897 by Octave Mirbeau and others. Rolland's views were expounded in a collection of essays called *The Theatre of the People* (*Le théâtre du peuple*, 1903) that had originally been published in Charles Péguy's famous *Les Cahiers de la Quinzaine*. The concrete results of these theories were two cycles of chronicle plays based on inci-

Romain Rolland.
[Italian Cultural
Institute]

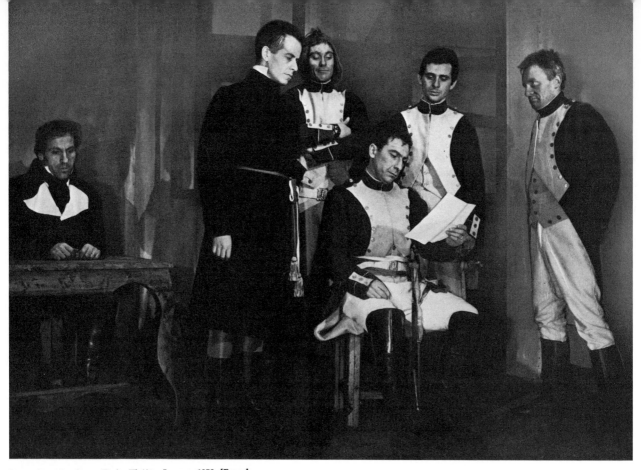

Scene from *Les loups*. Paris, Théâtre Lancry, 1953. [French Cultural Services]

dents in French history. *The Tragedies of Faith (Les tragédies de la foi,* published collectively in 1913) includes *Saint Louis* (wr. 1895), *Aërt* (1898), and *The Triumph of Reason (Le triomphe de la raison,* 1899). Intended as a cycle of ten plays on the French Revolution, the never-completed *Theatre of the Revolution (Théâtre de la Révolution)* included, when first published in 1909, *The Fourteenth of July (Le quatorze juillet,* 1902), *Danton* (1900), and *The Wolves (Les loups,*1898), but *The Triumph of Reason* was later transferred to the collection, and the following were added: *The Game of Love and Death (Le jeu de l'amour et de la mort,* 1924), *Flowering Easter (Pâques fleuries,* 1925), *The Leonids (Les Léonides,* 1927), and *Robespierre* (wr. 1938). Declamatory, didactic, and lacking in dramatic focus, Rolland's plays were more successful in post-World War I Germany, where they no doubt influenced Brecht's concept of epic theatre, than in his native France. Though the plays are historical in incident, Rolland stressed the contemporary relevance of the "experience" gained. *The Wolves,* for example, was presented at the time of the Dreyfus case, and the inference contained in the story of an attempt to railroad an honest if unsympathetic man on the basis of forged evidence was not lost on its intended audience. Nor could the relevance of *Danton,* in which the spirit of the French Revolution is shown being sacrificed to revolutionary discipline, be lost in an era when the Moscow purge trials were making headlines. *See* EPIC THEATRE in glossary.

In 1915 Rolland's international stature was recog-
nized when he was awarded the Nobel Prize for Literature. The following year, he alienated many of his countrymen by publishing *Above the Conflict (Au-dessus de la mêlée),* in which he advocated a pacifist stand. (He abandoned his pacificism at the beginning of World War II.)

In addition to the two dramatic cycles mentioned above, other plays of interest by Rolland include *The Time Will Come (Le temps viendra,* 1903; *Liluli* (wr. 1918, prod. 1923), "a lyric farce"; and *Savonarola (Savonarole,* 1896), an unfinished work.

[JOSEPH E. GARREAU]

Romains, Jules (1885–1972)

French poet, novelist, journalist, and dramatist; pseudonym of Louis Farigoule. Jules Romains became his legal name on July 9, 1953. He was born in Saint-Julien-Chapteuil on August 26, 1885. He grew up in Paris, where he attended the Lycée Condorcet and the École Normale Supérieure. After his graduation, he taught philosophy in the *lycées* of Laon, Paris, and Nice, finally giving up teaching in 1918. He began to write in 1908, publishing a book of poems, *Unanimous Life (La vie unanime),* propounding the philosophy of unanimism, a belief that modern man's character is no longer created by his own individualism, but by his life within various interacting social groups, or *unanimes.* Some aspect of this doctrine, which reflects the theories expounded in Émile Durkheim's enormously influential *The Rules of Sociological Method* (1894), is evident in all Romains's work. Although not a literary movement, unanimism has had influence in countries other than France; its most notable exponent is James Joyce.

Romains's first successful play was *Monsieur Le Trouhadec Seized by Debauchery* (*Monsieur Le Trouhadec saisi par la débauche*, 1923). It was followed by what is generally considered his best play, *Doctor Knock, or The Triumph of Medicine* (*Knock, ou Le triomphe de la médecine*, 1923). In 1928 he translated Stefan Zweig's adaptation of Ben Jonson's *Volpone*. Almost all the plays that have introduced him to a wide public were written before 1932. In that year he published a scientific paper based on research in extraretinal vision, and he began the twenty-seven-volume novel *Men of Good Will* (*Les hommes de bonne volonté*), a huge fresco of French society between the years 1908 and 1933. The final volume was completed in 1946, the year in which Romains was elected to the Académie Française. In 1956 he wrote a radio play entitled *Barbazout*.

Romains, in his later years, devoted himself to writing essays for various newspapers and magazines, to political studies, and to the supervision of film versions of his plays. He died in Paris on August 14, 1972.

WORK

Rejecting the commercial theatre of his youth, Romains called for a return to the classical sources of inspiration and for dramas of literary worth that focus on the fundamental and universal in human experience. His plays, like his novels and poems, were to provide a platform for demonstrations in dramatic form of the psychological and sociological ideas that contributed to the doctrine of unanimism, a view in which the adjustment and interrelation of man and his environment create a group psychology that transcends the individual and ultimately determines his behavior.

For example, Romains's first play, *The Army in the Town* (*L'armée dans la ville*, 1911), is a blank-verse drama depicting the conflict between two *unanimes*, or social groups, the troops of an occupying power and the inhabitants of a small city. Each group forms a united front against the other, but when the mayor's wife inspires her fellow townspeople to attempt the massacre of the enemy troops, it is the occupiers who emerge victorious because of the superior discipline and internal cohesion of the group they form. Romains's second play, *Cromedeyre-le-Vieil* (1920), the last of his verse dramas, pits the inhabitants of a strongly led and psychologically unified mountain town against those of a fragmented and impersonal society in the valley. Because only males are born in Cromedeyre, the men abduct the women of a neighboring valley town. At first rebellious, these modern Sabines come to prefer their lives in a male-dominated society based on ancient traditions and given psychological orientation by strong leadership.

A more jaundiced view of the possibilities of unanimism is given in Romains's best-known comedy, *Doctor Knock, or The Triumph of Medicine* (1923). Here the unifying principle does not spring from the group but is imposed on it by a charlatan doctor who brings an irritatingly healthy town to heel by converting the inhabitants to the "religion" of medicine.

In *The Dictator* (*Le dictateur*, 1926) interest is focused on the psychological transformation of a Socialist leader

Comédie-Française production of *Monsieur Le Trouhadec saisi par la débauche*, with (l. to r.) Hélène Perdrière, Jean Meyer, and Jean Debucourt. [French Cultural Services]

who becomes head of state when the constitutional monarchy is overthrown. Inexorably transformed into a tyrant by the exigencies of power, he eventually orders the death of his friend, who has become the leader of the opposition. *Jean le Maufranc* (1926) is a satirical attack on the tendency of the modern state to encroach on individual liberty. The hero first finds escape in hypocrisy, but he soon realizes that he has thus exposed himself to an even greater danger than the loss of freedom, the loss of his soul. The play was revised in 1930 as *Jean Musse, or The School for Hypocrites (Jean Musse, ou L'école de l'hypocrisie)*, and in the new version even the refuge of hypocrisy is sealed off when science finds a way to detect lies.

The comedies *Donogoo-Tonka* (1930), *Monsieur Le Trouhadec Seized by Debauchery* (1923), and *Monsieur Le Trouhadec's Marriage (Le mariage de Monsieur Le Trouhadec,* 1925) form a trilogy with a common hero, an aging and easily corruptible geographer of dubious scholarly ability. In this trio of satires Le Trouhadec turns a map error into a reality when the people who believe in the fictitious existence of an Argentinian Eldorado actually create it; is led on by a unanimist scoundrel to win the favors of an actress at the Monte Carlo gambling tables; and finally gives up his glamorous mistress to make a respectable marriage and so become leader of the Party of Honest Men, a political group whose chief activity consists of nonstop talk. Le Trouhadec first appeared in Romans's novel *Donogoo-Tonka, or The Miracles of Science (Donogoo-Tonka, ou Les miracles de la science,* 1919), which provided the plot for the first part of the trilogy (actually written and produced last).

In *Boën, or The Possession of Goods (Boën, ou La possession des biens,* 1930) a millionaire philanthropist finds that his wealth cuts him off from the possibility of true friendship and of honestly sharing in the concerns of the community. *Spare the Earth Again (Grâce encore pour la terre;* wr. 1939, prod. 1947) reflects the anguish and hope of all men of goodwill just before World War II. *The Year 1000 (L'an mil,* 1947) deals with an outbreak of mass terror that accompanied the approach of the first millennium, a time in which many believed the world would end.

Romains's one-act plays seem to be mere sketches for unanimist themes he planned to develop later. In *The "Peach" (La scintillante,* 1924), for example, the owner of a bicycle shop finds that it is not her feminine charms but her social role as the proprietor of a prosperous business that attracts the love of a nobleman, and in *The Moroccan Lunch (Le déjeuner marocain,* 1929) a unanimist convinces a French family to sell its daughter to a Moroccan chieftain.

Cromedeyre-le-Vieil (1920). Verse drama in which the people of Cromedeyre, governed by tradition and established custom, live peacefully together enjoying a rich communal life. The town lacks enough women, however, to provide wives for all the unmarried men. When one of the young men falls in love with a girl from a more modern village, his wifeless fellow townsmen join him in abducting her and other women of her village.

The women initially rebel against their captors, but they soon discover the beauty and strength of the collective existence in Cromedeyre and forget the shallow individualistic world they had known.

Monsieur Le Trouhadec Seized by Debauchery (*Monsieur Le Trouhadec saisi par la débauche,* 1923). The famous geographer Professor Le Trouhadec, vacationing at Monte Carlo under an assumed name, falls in love with Rolande, an actress. He confides his passion to Bénin, who sees to it that the two meet. Counseled by M. Trestaillon, a guest at the same hotel, the professor undertakes the conquest of Rolande, who develops a sudden interest in Le Trouhadec after he wins a fortune at the casino. Unfortunately, Rolande's tastes are expensive, and the professor soon has to return to the gaming tables to win enough money to take her to dinner. This time his luck is bad, and he emerges from the casino a ruined and debt-ridden man. He meets Trestaillon, who has just completed a successful jewel robbery, and the latter gives the naïve professor part of the proceeds. Happily for the professor's reputation the clever Bénin is able to return the jewels to the police. He also manages to rebuild Le Trouhadec's depleted fortune by putting him in touch with M. Josselin, who is writing a guide for gamblers. Impressed by Le Trouhadec's well-advertised former success at the casino, Josselin pays the professor handsomely for lending his name to the proposed book. Le Trouhadec is therefore able to continue his liaison with Rolande.

Doctor Knock, or The Triumph of Medicine (*Knock, ou Le triomphe de la médecine,* 1923). Unanimist comedy involving the medical profession. Having contracted for his first practice sight unseen, Dr. Knock arrives to claim it and discovers from his predecessor, Dr. Parpalaid, that the inhabitants of this French mountain village are disgustingly healthy. Knock, who practiced for years without a license and has just received his medical degree at forty, shrewdly sets about changing things. He persuades the town crier to announce a free weekly consultation, induces the schoolmaster to lecture on hygiene, and reaches a lucrative "agreement" with the druggist. Then, insisting that there is no such thing as a healthy man, Knock begins to discover the undiagnosed ailments of the citizenry. When Parpalaid returns three months later, he finds a thriving practice and a delighted community. The townspeople, united by their belief in medicine, blame Parpalaid for having allowed them to go on ignorantly believing in their good health. Knock, meanwhile, blissfully dreams of an entire countryside filled with patients. Before Parpalaid can escape, he himself is put under "observation."

[JOSEPH E. GARREAU]

PLAYS

Unless otherwise noted, the plays were first performed in Paris.

1. *L'armée dans la ville (The Army in the Town).* Drama, 5 acts; verse. Published 1911. Produced Théâtre de l'Odéon, Mar. 4, 1911.

2. *Cromedeyre-le-Vieil.* Tragedy, 5 acts; verse. Published 1920. Produced Théâtre du Vieux-Colombier, May 27, 1920.

3. *Monsieur Le Trouhadec saisi par la débauche (Monsieur Le Trouhadec Seized by Debauchery).* Comedy, 4 acts. Produced Comédie des Champs-Élysées, Mar. 13, 1923.

4. *Knock, ou Le triomphe de la médecine* (Doctor Knock, or The Triumph*

of Medicine). Comedy, 3 acts. Produced Comédie des Champs-Élysées, Dec. 15, 1923.

5. *Amédée et les messieurs en rang (Amédée and the Gentlemen in Line).* Mystery, 1 act. Produced Comédie des Champs-Élysées, Dec. 15, 1923.

6. *La scintillante* (The ''Peach'').* Comedy, 1 act. Produced Comédie des Champs-Élysées, Oct. 7, 1924.

7. *Le mariage de Monsieur Le Trouhadec (Monsieur Le Trouhadec's Marriage).* Comedy, 4 acts. Produced Comédie des Champs-Élysées, Jan. 31, 1925. Music: Georges Auric.

8. *Démétrios.* Comedy, 1 act. Produced Comédie des Champs-Élysées, Oct. 9, 1925.

9. *Le dictateur (The Dictator).* Comedy. Produced Comédie des Champs-Élysées, Oct. 5, 1926.

10. *Jean le Maufranc.* Mystery, 5 acts. Produced Théâtre des Arts, Dec. 1, 1926. Early version of *Jean Musse, ou L'école de l'hypocrisie.*

11. (Adaptation). *Volpone.* Comedy, 5 acts. Produced Théâtre de l'Atelier, Nov. 23, 1928. Music: Auric. Based on Stefan Zweig's version of Ben Jonson's play.

12. *Le déjeuner marocain (The Moroccan Lunch).* Play, 1 act. Produced Théâtre Saint-Georges, Feb. 9, 1929.

13. *Donogoo-Tonka.* Play; prologue and epilogue, 3 acts. Produced Théâtre Pigalle, Oct. 25, 1930. Music: Jacques Ibert.

14. *Jean Musse, ou L'école de l'hypocrisie (Jean Musse, or The School for Hypocrites).* Play. Produced Théâtre de l'Atelier, Nov. 21, 1930. Revision of *Jean le Maufranc.*

15. *Boën, ou La possession des biens (Boën, or The Possession of Goods).* Comedy, 3 acts. Produced Théâtre de l'Odéon, Dec. 4, 1930.

16. *Le roi masqué (The Masked King).* Comedy, 3 acts. Published 1932. Produced Théâtre Pigalle, Dec. 19, 1931.

17. *Grâce encore pour la terre (Spare the Earth Again).* Play, 3 acts. Written 1939. Published 1941. Produced Rio de Janeiro, June 24, 1947.

18. *L'an mil (The Year 1000).* Play, 3 acts. Published 1947. Produced Théâtre Sarah-Bernhardt, Mar. 13, 1947.

19. *Barbazout.* Radio play. Produced Paris, January, 1956.

EDITIONS

Cromedeyre-le-Vieil. Published in *The Contemporary French Theatre,* ed. by S. A. Rhodes, New York, 1942.

Doctor Knock. Published in *From the Modern Repertoire,* ed. by E. R. Bentley and tr. by H. Granville-Barker, ser. 3, Bloomington, Ind., 1949–1956.

CRITICISM

M. Israël, *Jules Romains: Sa vie, son oeuvre,* Paris, 1931; M. Berry, *Jules Romains: Sa vie, son oeuvre,* Paris, 1953; A. Cuisenier, *Jules Romains et l'unanimisme,* 3 vols., Paris, 1935–1954; P. J. Norrish, *Drama of the Group: A Study of Unanimism in the Plays of Jules Romains,* London, 1958; D. Boak, *Jules Romains,* New York, 1974.

Roman Drama

Formal Latin literature is said to have begun when a Greek from Tarentum named Livius Andronicus produced Latin versions of a Greek tragedy and comedy at the Roman games (ludi Romani) of 240 B.C. Though Cicero later remarked that the plays of Livius were not worth a second reading (*Brutus* 18.71), they nevertheless initiated a rich and varied dramatic tradition. More plays and more playwrights followed, and dramatic performances became a fixture of Roman festivals. By the late third century B.C. a Roman dramatist had more opportunities to present plays than the dramatists of fifth-century Athens had known. The kind of theatre that developed in Rome was shaped not only by efforts to reproduce Greek dramatic forms but also by indigenous traditions. Native Italian precursors of drama include the so-called Fescennine verses of Etruria, the Atellan farce of Campania, and the mime.

ROMAN COMEDY

Fescennine verses, which probably take their name from the Etruscan town of Fescennium, were joking, abusive, and often obscene improvisations performed in response

Stage setting for *La mauvaise conduite,* Jean Variot's modern adaptation of the *Twin Menaechmi* by Plautus as given by La Compagnie des Quinze in the 1930s. [Photograph by Achay, Paris]

sion and traditionally associated with weddings and harvest festivals. Many different types of abusive verse eventually came to be called Fescennine. Atellan farce (*fabula Atellana,* from the Oscan town of Atella between Naples and Capua) consisted of short improvised sketches, usually with rural settings. Like the *commedia dell'arte* they employed stock masked characters: Maccus the clown, Bucco the glutton, Pappus the old man, and Dossenus the scoundrel. The humor of these sketches was undoubtedly broad, and the action was set to music. The third native dramatic form, mime, was for centuries the favorite form of popular entertainment in the ancient world. Mimes were performed in the Italian countryside by bands of traveling players who did their short improvisations on makeshift stages. More elaborate performances took place in cities, and their scenarios could have literary pretentions. Character drawing was broad, and the performances featured dramatic situations, generally farcical and indecent, rather than real plots. Adultery was a favorite subject, and the pace was lively. Such forms of humor were deeply rooted in the Italian taste and had a profound effect on the literary drama that developed from Livius's experiments.

The best-known form of Roman drama is the *comoedia palliata*—comedy performed in Greek dress (*pallium* is the Latin word for the characteristic Greek cloak). These plays were based upon Greek originals of the New Comedy, but the Roman dramatists were not simply translators. Plautus (ca. 251–ca. 184 B.C.) was the foremost writer of such plays, and comparisons with the surviving Greek dramas of Menander reveal quite different concepts of comedy. Menander's plays are quiet and elegant, deriving their dramatic effects from subtle character portrayals and poignant humor. Plautus deliberately cultivates the broad and familiar. Roman audiences, rather like modern opera audiences, were conservative and demanding. They enjoyed seeing favorite characters and familiar situations. They liked song and dance, farce, and spectacle. The stock characters of Atellan farce, the musical vulgarity of the Fescennine verses, and the broad action of mime all find counterparts in the superficially Greek adaptations of Plautus and his contemporaries. *See* MENANDER. *See also* NEW COMEDY in glossary.

Stock figures abound in these plays. The clever slaves, boastful soldiers, cruel and greedy whores and pimps, lovesick young men, and angry fathers indicate less a poverty of imagination among the writers of *palliatae* than a readiness to capitalize on the tastes and expectations of Roman audiences, surprising and delighting the spectators with the new tricks that the dramatists could teach these old dogs. In Cicero's day the great comic actor Roscius was famous for the role of Ballio, the pimp in Plautus's *Pseudolus,* not because Ballio was a unique pimp, but because he was the archetypal one. The tradition was a bond between dramatists and audience that neither wanted to sever.

The language of *palliata* comedies suggests a lively colloquialism but is actually quite deliberately artificial. In the generation between Livius and Plautus, dramatists perfected a comic diction that was uniquely Latin and preeminently theatrical: full of alliteration, assonance, word play, and complex rhythmic patterns. All Roman drama is in verse. Lines might be spoken, performed as recitative, or actually sung. Songs are particularly common in the later plays of Plautus, whose characters sing elaborate arias when they make their entrances; so strong a musical element is unique to Roman drama. Song and dance were limited to nondramatic entr'actes in Greek New Comedy, and recitative was rare. The Roman dramatists must have thoroughly rewritten large sections of their models and created quite new dramatic

Ninth-century manuscript showing masks from Terence's comedy *Phormio.* [*Codex Vaticanus Latinus,* 3868]

effects. The origins of this practice are obscure, perhaps due in part to nondramatic Greek models and in part to other native Italian forms of entertainment.

Whereas Greek New Comedy offered a wide range of dramatic effects, from the psychological subtleties of Menander to the spectacles of Diphilus, Roman dramatists limited themselves to a comparatively small range of plots. Romantic intrigues, mistaken identities, and sudden recognitions seized their attention because they provided the kind of broad action best suited to Roman taste. Plautus, for example, seeks complex and rapid action. He cheerfully sacrifices consistency of plot and character to comic effects, while his characters speak their artificial but engaging approximation of colloquial Latin. They are obviously Romans who have found themselves in Greek costumes and settings, and Plautus plays brilliantly on the contrast between Greek and Roman elements in his material. The result is a vivacious, fantastic kind of comedy that is much closer to the Old Comedy of Aristophanes than to Menander or, for that matter, to the well-made domestic comedies of the past century. *See* ARISTOPHANES; PLAUTUS. *See also* OLD COMEDY in glossary.

Terence (ca. 195–159 B.C.) apparently sought to write comedies that were closer to the subtleties of Menander. He avoids the artificialities and coarse colloquialisms of Plautine diction and puts greater emphasis on the consistency of character and action. He is very sparing in his use of song. He constantly experimented with Roman equivalents for the Greek techniques of his originals, but he had difficulty keeping his audience. His prologues suggest a dramatist at odds with his time. Though he achieved considerable success with *The Eunuch* and *Phormio,* he fought constantly with his fellow dramatists and never displayed the easy mastery of his craft demon-

Father confronts drunken son in this marble relief of a scene typical of the New Comedy. [Naples National Museum]

strated by Plautus. *See* TERENCE.

Though Plautus and Terence are the only writers of *palliatae* whose works survive, they are nevertheless only two dramatists among many working in this tradition at Rome in the third and second centuries B.C. The verse epigram of a grammarian named Volcacius Sedigitus rates ten comic writers. Plautus was only second in this list. A poet named Caecilius was first. Terence was sixth, after Naevius, a pioneer in many forms of Latin literature, and two unknowns named Licinius and Atilius. Ancient opinion was nearly unanimous in calling Caecilius the master of the *comoedia palliata*. Only fragments of his work survive, but they have proven crucial for identifying both the extent and the nature of the traditional comic style that characterized Plautus and that Terence sometimes tried so hard to escape. *See* CAECILIUS.

As early as 207 B.C. the Roman state recognized a guild of poets and actors in Rome called the *Collegium poetarum,* an organization that probably helped preserve the continuity of the dramatic tradition. It may well have been members of this guild that Terence attacked in his prologues. Establishment of such a guild gave the Roman theatre a certain status, but it could not guarantee its continued creativity. Toward the end of the second century B.C. the *comoedia palliata* went into decline. An increasing and sometimes pedantic fidelity to Greek originals sapped its vitality, and it ceased to be a living dramatic form. The last writer of *palliatae* for the stage was Turpilius, who died in 103 B.C.; however, dramatic performance in Rome did not die with him. Old plays were frequently revived. The extant prologue of Plautus's *Casina* is the product of one such revival and laments the worthlessness of contemporary theatre. In the first century B.C. comedies by Plautus, Terence, and Turpilius played to enthusiastic audiences; the famous Roman ac-

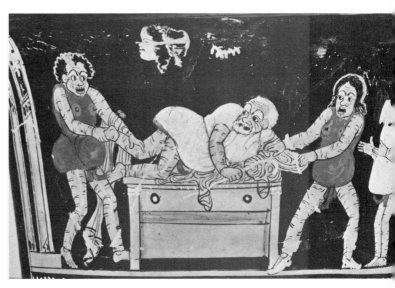

A fourth-century B.C. Roman vase painting shows a miser and thieves scene probably suggested by *The Pot of Gold* by Plautus. [Staatliche Museen, Berlin]

tors Aesopus and Roscius made their reputations in roles that were by that time classics. As classics, however, they soon suffered the fate of classics. *Palliata* comedies came to be more read than performed. Cicero quotes from them frequently, but there is something bookish about his allusions.

A second form of Latin comedy was the *fabula togata,* comedy performed in Roman dress. We know some sixty titles of *togatae* and the names of three dramatists—Titinius, Afranius, and Atta—but only fragments of their work survive. Titinius, the traditional founder of

Plautus is reading to friends in this painting by Miola Camillo in Florence's Nazionale. [Italian Cultural Institute]

the genre, may have been a contemporary of Terence. Atta died in 77 B.C. The sources of the genre were mixed. In the prologue to a play called *The Crossroads Caper (Compitalia)*, Afranius acknowledges debts to several predecessors—Menander is first among them. Cicero and Horace also link Afranius and Menander. *Togata* plays had original plots and Italian settings, but they must have featured Italian equivalents of the Greek domestic situations of New Comedy. The surviving fragments certainly have strong stylistic affinities with the *comoedia palliata*. There were, however, some interesting differences between the two forms of Roman comedy. Because women enjoyed greater freedom in Roman society than they had known in Athens, they played a larger part in the action of *togata* comedies. There are frequent references in the fragments to romances between children of respectable families. There are also references to pederasty, a rare theme in New Comedy and the *palliata*. An interesting difference is mentioned by the grammarian Donatus, who reports that "in the *palliata* comic poets were permitted to represent slaves who were smarter than their masters, a thing that could not be done in the *togata*." The Romans may not have cared to glorify deceit among their own slaves. Nevertheless, a fragment of Afranius's play *The Conflagration (Incendium)* reads as follows:

> I have a slave named Nicasio,
> a meddlesome rascal. He has been weaving
> some plot or other with my son to get money.

The old man of this speech sounds like several old men in Plautus and Terence. Donatus's remark therefore probably means not that *togatae* did not have clever slaves but only that their masters were cleverer still. The material for humor in the two forms of comedy was probably the same. *Palliata* and *togata* coexisted as active dramatic forms for a considerable time, and the oppor-

tunities for sharing material and techniques were frequent. They certainly shared the same death, though perhaps the *togata* grew a little colder a little faster. Revivals of these comedies were few, and the scanty remains indicate that they were not much read by later generations.

ROMAN TRAGEDY

Even if continuous texts of Plautus and Terence had not survived, the rich and varied life of comedy in republican Rome would be apparent. The situation for tragedy was a little different. After the initial attempts to adapt Greek tragedies by Livius Andronicus, the poet Naevius (ca. 270–201 B.C.) experimented with tragedies on Roman subjects: the *fabula praetexta*. Naevius was a successful writer of *palliatae* and composed a famous epic on the Punic War, but neither he nor Livius had much success with tragedy. Rome produced only three tragedians of stature during the republic, and they followed Naevius at the rate of one a generation. Ennius (239–169 B.C.), the first indisputably great Latin poet, wrote successful tragedies in addition to a famous epic on Roman history, *The Annals*, and some mediocre comedies. Twenty titles and about four hundred lines of his tragic writing survive. The plays are based, perhaps rather loosely, on Greek originals, and some interesting comparisons are possible. The musical element so essential to Plautine comedy is also present in Ennius, who freely changed the simple spoken meters of his originals to complex lyrics. There are also curious examples of Greek rhetorical tricks yielding to native Italian logic. Euripides, for example, had begun his *Medea* with a famous inversion as Medea's nurse laments first the coming of the ship Argo to Colchis and then the felling of the timber that built it. Ennius's nurse first laments the felling of the trees, and only then the coming of the ship.

Pacuvius (220–ca. 130 B.C.), said to be a nephew of Ennius, was the first Roman dramatist to specialize in tragedy, though he was also a painter of some note. Thirteen titles and about four hundred lines have come down to us. Twelve of his tragedies used Greek material; the thirteenth is a *praetexta* about Aemilius Paulus, who defeated the Macedonians at Pydna in 168 B.C. The fragments reveal a rhetorical style and considerable violence in the dramatic action. Cicero thought highly of Pacuvius, and his plays were undoubtedly effective on the stage. Accius (170–ca. 90 B.C.) knew Pacuvius, and Cicero implies that as a young man he himself had discussed literary questions with Accius. We know of forty-six tragedies, for Accius was quite famous and often quoted by later writers. He was also a grammarian and a historian of the theatre. His dramatic writing had a tendency toward bombast and continued the trend toward violence already evident in Pacuvius. "Powerful" was an adjective often applied to Accius in antiquity.

The fragmentary evidence makes a true picture of republican Roman tragedy difficult to draw, but a few things are clear. Many of the stylistic devices familiar from the *comoedia palliata* also appear in the tragic fragments, especially metrical complexity, alliteration, and

Initial from the fourteenth-century *Codex Urbin* shows scenes from Seneca's *Mad Hercules.* [Vatican Library]

A 1971 production of Seneca's *Medea* at the Teatro Español, Madrid. [Photograph courtesy of Spanish Embassy]

word play. Isolated examples of Latin tragic style can make us wince. "Salmacida spolia sine sudore et sanguine" ("Spoils of Salamis won without sweat or blood") ran a line of Ennius's *Ajax*, but such devices could be very effective. Ennius's *Alexander* (that is, Paris, the son of King Priam of Troy) featured a mad scene in which the alliterations and sudden metrical shifts of Cassandra's prophecy about Paris have a haunting power. Throughout the writings of Cicero there are allusions to tragic scenes whose theatricality is unmistakable: a contest in self-sacrifice between Orestes and Pylades in Pacuvius's *Orestes in Thrall (Dulorestes)*, and the ghost of a dead child begging his mother for burial in Pacuvius's *Iliona*. The Romans certainly liked these plays, and even later generations knew them well. Horace alludes to the unlucky actor Fufius, who, playing the title role of Iliona, actually fell asleep onstage and missed his cue when the ghost of Polydorus called to him, "Mother, I beseech you," and the whole audience joined in to awaken him (*Satires* II 3.60). Suetonius records in his life of Julius Caesar that at the funeral games for Caesar some lines from Pacuvius's *Judgment of Arms (Armorum Iudicium)* were sung to incite the crowd against the conspirators. "Did I save these men so that they might destroy me?" said Pacuvius's Ajax, an allusion that gained point for those able to recognize its source.

By the first century B.C. tragedy, like comedy, had gone into decline. The last documented performance of a new tragedy at Rome was a play by Varius, a distinguished poet of the early empire and coeditor of the *Aeneid* after Vergil's death. His *Thyestes* was performed in 29 B.C. at the games held in celebration of Octavian's victory at Actium. Ovid (43 B.C.–A.D. 17) wrote a *Medea* that was praised by Quintilian (X 1.98), but it was almost certainly not intended for performance. Only two verses survive. The plays of Seneca (4 B.C.–A.D. 65) are a perennial subject of debate. There are ten tragedies, a *praetexta* called *Octavia* not actually written by Seneca himself, and nine plays on Greek mythological subjects. When Seneca wrote these plays and what his intention was remain uncertain. Public performance is unlikely because by Seneca's time the public theatre had become less than respectable. The dominant forms of entertainment were mime and pantomime, in which actors performed a dumb show while a chorus sang. Writing plays had become a literary pastime for the upper class. Seneca may have envisioned private performances or simply dramatic readings by one or more speakers. The actability of his plays is frequently debated. The Elizabethans certainly appreciated his theatrical skill, and we can see how time and again Seneca chose more stagy versions of his material than his Greek predecessors had used. His Medea murders her children on stage; his Phaedra confronts Hippolytus. Even Theseus' macabre reassembly of Hippolytus's body is by no means unstageable, and there is an increasing feeling among modern critics that Seneca may well have had stage performance in mind. Whether these plays were actually ever produced is a separate historical question that cannot now be answered. *See* SENECA.

One cannot escape the feeling, however, that even during Rome's republican heyday the Romans were a little uncomfortable with tragedy. The *comoedia palliata* certainly had a popular following, but love of tragedy was

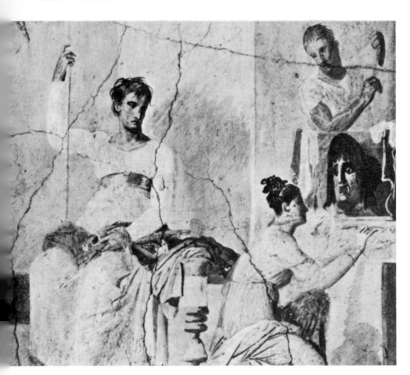

Herculaneum wall painting of a victorious tragedian after the agon. The woman kneels to write a dedicatory inscription. [Naples National Museum]

not so deeply rooted: its effects and its appeal were superficial. Whereas Greek tragedy was profoundly appealing to fifth-century Athenians, and comic dramatists learned from it even as they satirized its mannerisms, tragedy and comedy went their separate ways in Rome. The occasional parodies of tragedy in Plautus and Terence do not cut very deep, partly because the Roman idea of tragedy was influenced less by the subtle poetry of fifth-century Athens than by the more florid tragedy of the Hellenistic period. Beginning in the fourth century B.C. tragic poets in Greece yielded their status and their control of the theatre to producers and actors organized in professional troupes. Set speeches and theatrical effects established the tone, and choral poetry of the old Athenian type became a lost art. The bombast and spectacle in Ennius, Pacuvius, and Accius was an established part of the tragic style they knew from the contemporary Greek world.

But this is only part of the story. Roman tragedians might have breathed new life into the style had they so desired, just as the comic poets had revitalized Greek New Comedy, but they did not do so because the Roman character was at odds with tragedy. For one thing, tragedy requires extremes, and the Romans went to great lengths to avoid extremes. It also centers on noble losers, and the Romans liked noble winners. Roman heroes like Regulus might die, but they die gloriously for their country. The decision to die is simple, and there is nothing tragic about a simple course of action. Moreover, Roman culture subordinates the individual to the state, whereas the Greek myths focus on individuals rather than states,

and the power of tragedy lies in the single heroic figure. This too runs counter to traditional Roman values. The Coriolanus of Livy's history, for example, is simply a threat to Rome overcome by a courageous and patriotic woman (Livy 2.40). The conflict of loyalties that Shakespeare saw in this story and turned into tragedy is quite alien to the Roman point of view. The resulting lack of sympathy for the tragic spirit led not just to the failure of the *fabula praetexta* to develop depth, but also impeded the creative reworking of mythology that was the key to tragedy's vitality among the Greeks. The problems of fate and will that the Greeks explored through tragedy were simply not such important issues for the Romans, or were at least not issues that the Romans thought suitable for drama. The focus on human emotions in Senecan tragedy owes more to other literary forms, especially Hellenistic and Roman epic, and more to Stoic philosophy than to earlier Greek or Roman tragedy. Seneca's tragic vision looks ahead to new traditions, not back to old ones.

DRAMATIC PERFORMANCE

The conditions of dramatic performance in republican Rome were quite different from those of classical Athens. Although Roman drama was also presented at festivals, it was always a professional business rather than an amateur civic function. Plays were performed at six annual religious festivals and also at the dedicatory and funeral games that were held at irregular intervals. In 200 B.C. the regular dramatic festivals (*ludi scaenici*) alone provided eleven days for dramatic performances. By 194 B.C. that number had increased to seventeen, and by the early empire it was forty-three. In addition, various religious irregularities could necessitate the restagings of the festivals called *instaurationes*, which easily increased the number of days for dramatic presentations by five to seven each year. By comparison, the dramatists of fifth-century Athens had hardly more than six performance days a year, though as many as five plays were performed each day.

Roman actors were organized in troupes, and the dramatists probably sold their plays to the managers of them. These managers would then have to win the right to perform from the magistrates responsible for the festival. The size of the acting companies is unknown, but the surviving comedies could probably all have been staged by no more than five speaking actors and a few mutes. The actors' skill no doubt grew with time. The increasing metrical complexity of Plautus's later plays is plausibly attributed at least in part to the increasing ability of actors to handle these demanding roles. The acting style was probably always broad, with elaborate, stylized gestures and "out front" delivery. In Cicero's day actors wore masks. They may well have done so from the beginning, but the evidence is confused and unreliable.

Although the establishment of the theatrical guild (*Collegium poetarum*) in 207 B.C. gave actors and playwrights themselves a certain social standing, the conditions under which they worked were remarkably crude.

Inherent Roman conservatism—and perhaps deep-seated distrust of what was after all a Greek art form—delayed the construction of a permanent theatre in Rome for generations. Instead, a temporary wooden structure was built for each festival. In 195 B.C. the first few rows of seats were reserved for senators, which at least implies that seats were provided. Proposals for a more permanent arrangement came to nothing in 179 and again in 174. In 154 B.C. construction was actually begun on a stone theatre, but was soon halted by a decree of the senate condemning drama as harmful to public morals. Pompey built the first permanent theatre in Rome in 55 B.C., though provincial towns had had them much earlier. The dimensions of the stage known by Plautus and Terence are thus uncertain, but Greek precedent suggests a long and narrow platform, perhaps over sixty feet in length and raised as much as five feet off the ground. Since there was no integral chorus, the circular Greek orchestra was reduced to a semicircle used for seating. The backdrop represented two or three houses, with the stage platform as the street. Entrances could be made from the house doors or from the wings—one wing traditionally representing the direction of the forum and the other the direction of the harbor. The length of the stage certainly facilitated the large processions and running messenger scenes of comedy. It also made more plausible such common devices as eavesdropping and the inability of one character to see another character who was plainly visible to the audience.

This audience was a curious assortment of people from all social classes and of both sexes. Plautus's long, witty, and repetitious prologues suggest some difficulty in getting the audience to settle down and hear the actors' words. There was no curtain and, unlike Greek New Comedy, no act breaks. The play might also have to compete with other simultaneous entertainments. The prologues to Terence's *Mother-in-Law (Hecyra)* claim that on two occasions audiences abandoned the play, once to watch a tightrope walker and once to see gladiators. The modern inference that Roman audiences were obtuse and inattentive, however, is not really tenable. The repetitions and broad actions of Roman drama can be ascribed at least in part to the exigencies of outdoor performance, while the richness of the language implies a knowledgeable and attentive audience. The pressure throughout the republican period to increase the number of opportunities for dramatic performances suggests an appreciative and demanding population. Even after the great creative period was over, the theatre continued to increase in popularity. Roscius never lacked audiences and grew rich playing the old classics.

Although the Romans never produced plays to rival the artistry of the Greeks, theirs became the tradition that shaped the course of later Western drama. They recast the very idea of theatre to suit their needs, and our own idea was derived from theirs. By the time Greek drama was again read with understanding in the West, the Roman concept of theatre had already taken root. There have since been many changes and many experiments with form and subject, but our comedy is far more

Fourth-century ivory relief shows a Roman pantomime actor holding a three-faced mask. [Staatliche Museen, Berlin]

the comedy of Plautus and Terence than of Aristophanes and Menander, and our tragedy is Senecan, not Sophoclean. Our concept of secular, professional theatre is wholly Roman. A modern traveler in time might well be awed by the theatrical experience of the Athenian Dionysia, but it would be the shows of the *ludi Romani* that he would really understand.

SANDER M. GOLDBERG

CRITICISM

G. Duckworth, *The Nature of Roman Comedy*, Princeton, N.J., 1952; P. W. Harsh, *A Handbook of Classical Drama*, Stanford, Calif., 1960; W. Beare, *The Roman Stage*, 3d ed., London, 1964; *Roman Drama*, ed. by T. A. Dorey and D. R. Dudley, London, 1965; L. A. McKay, "The Roman Tragic Spirit," *California Studies in Classical Antiquity*, no. 8, 1975, pp. 145–162; E. Fantham, "Adaptation and Survival: A Genre Study of Roman Comedy in Relation to its Greek Sources," *Versions of Medieval Comedy*, Norman, Okla., 1977, pp. 297–327.

Romanian Drama

Romania lies at the crossroads of the Slavic world, the world of ancient Byzantium, and the Western world. This region, inhabited since ancient times, has been successively conquered and reconquered. In the lands now comprising Romania certain types of theatre existed in pre-Christian times.

Greek settlers from Asia Minor settled the rich lands

on the Black Sea coast in the seventh century B.C., founding the cities of Histria, Tomi, and Callatia. They followed the cult of Dionysus and Aphrodite. The Romans came in the first century B.C., conquered the Greek cities, and resettled them. They developed a rich slave-owning civilization in Provincia Dacia. To defend this distant part of their empire, the Romans built walled cities, a network of roads, and huge defense walls against the migratory peoples who had repeatedly devastated the region. Archaeological finds in the Roman cities of Dacia reveal a remarkable level of development there. Ruins of the public buildings, baths, and amphitheatres still exist.

The amphitheatres were built close to the cities, and certain officials called *aediles* were charged with organizing festive events. Undoubtedly classical and popular Roman plays were performed in these amphitheatres. Andrei Otetea in his *History of the Romanian People* writes: "A taste for immortalizing thoughts, deeds, and persons in inscriptions and through artistic representations was widespread here as in all the provinces."

THE BYZANTINE EMPIRE

With the fall of the Roman Empire (A.D. 476) the greater part of its dramatic achievement was lost in the East, although some activity continued in Constantinople, which became the capital of the Byzantine Empire. From the writings of the early fathers of the Church and from reports of ceremonies and festivities by historians it is known that certain kinds of drama existed.

Although Byzantium did not create a genuine theatre or any truly dramatic poetry, there were dramatic elements in its festivals, games, mummeries, and masquerades. There are records of four early theatres in Constantinople, and of at least one theatre each in other cities of the Byzantine Empire. Herman Reich, a German scholar, indicates in his book, *Der Mimus*, that pure mime continued in the East throughout the Dark Ages. In Constantinople and other centers many of the primitive forms of the Roman mime were preserved unchanged, continuing as an independent branch of theatre into modern times.

According to Ionnes Lydus, a sixth-century Byzantine historian, the main forms of Roman comedy continued to be performed in Byzantium. Although no written texts survive, it is evident that the *mimus, pantomimus,* and *tragoedia* competed for attention with jugglers, acrobats, and horse racing. In spite of the Edict of the Trullan Council and the active opposition of the church, the *mimus* remained popular until the capture of Constantinople by the Turks in 1453. Its subject matter varied from simple buffoonery to social satire, especially protests against corrupt state officials. It sometimes took its themes from mythology and history, and even ridiculed Christian rites and beliefs. In the *pantomimus* a solo dancer, sometimes impersonating several characters, mimed the entire plot to offstage singing. In the *tragoedia* the actor himself sang while miming the story, but he did not dance. There is no evidence that classical tragedy and comedy were staged.

Liturgical drama in Byzantium, which appears to have been closely linked with the sermons, consisted of fully dramatized episodes from the life of Christ accompanied or followed by oratorical passages. The homily drama, or mystery play, developed from these sermons. The dramatic elements formed a complete play, to which the fundamental idea gave unity of purpose and meaning. The homily drama first appeared as part of the Panegyris, reserved for the great liturgical feasts. However, it can also be traced to three other sources: the Apocrypha, the *mimus*, and the Syriac *sogitha*, or homily canticle, in which the hymn writers dramatized sacred history. There were apparently two cycles, each involving a trilogy: the Annunciation, Nativity, and Flight into Egypt; the Baptism of Jesus, the Passion, and the Harrowing of Hell.

Little is known of the inhabitants of Dacia from the end of the third until the beginning of the eleventh century. They probably continued with the *mimus, pantomimus, tragoedia,* and *karagöz* in their festivities and with the dramatic elements related to the liturgical feasts. In Dacia the homily drama came to be known as *Vicleim,* from the name Bethleem or Bethlehem, or as *Irods,* after King Herod.

THIRTEENTH TO SIXTEENTH CENTURIES

Late in the thirteenth and early in the fourteenth centuries the Romanian principalities of Wallachia and Moldavia were established. The ruling princes in this feudal society were surrounded by household officials, landed nobles *(boyars)*, and a military gentry, all rivals for control of the power of the state. Masquerades, mummeries, and games were part of the festivals in the courts of the princes. Later, under Turkish influence, particularly in Wallachia, one finds the appearance of the Turkish *karagoz,* or shadow theatre, which burlesqued characters in village life. The great temporal power of the church made for a more elaborate liturgical drama.

Prior to the acceptance of Turkish suzerainty in the fifteenth and early sixteenth centuries, the political situation in the principalities was chaotic. The ruling prince was busy defending his rights from infringements by the leading secular and religious magnates. Surrounded by hostile countries, the prince was forced to make concessions which lessened his authority as the price of noble and church support. Turkish control over Moldavia and Wallachia was to a large extent exerted and maintained with the cooperation of the boyars.

For the three hundred years from 1415 to the establishment of the Phanariot regime in 1711, the Romanian principalities of Wallachia and Moldavia were ruled by the native princes *de jure* but by the Turks and boyars *de facto*. The boyars intrigued with the Porte to ensure succession to the Wallachian and Moldavian thrones by members of their families; however, when an outstanding military or political leader arose, such as Michael the Brave of Wallachia (1593–1601) or Peter (Petru) Rares of Moldavia (1527–1546), selfish interests would be temporarily put aside and support against the Turks was secured by the ruler with little difficulty.

SEVENTEENTH AND EIGHTEENTH CENTURIES

As a result of unstable political and economic conditions, the first two centuries of Turkish vassalage are regarded as one of the darkest periods in Romanian history. The social structure of the country was virtually reduced to two groups: nobles (lay and clerical) and peasants (serfs). There was an almost complete lack of cultural activity except at the courts of the princes of Moldavia and Wallachia. In the seventeenth century the courts at Jassy (Iaşi), capital of Moldavia, and Bucharest, capital of Wallachia, were often visited by strolling troupes of actors on their way to Poland or Russia. There are records of such visits to the court of Vasile Lupu, Prince of Moldavia from 1634 to 1654, and by the eighteenth century they were quite common.

In the early years of the eighteenth century, when the reliability of rulers and boyars could no longer be counted on, and when their funds became insufficient to ensure purchase of the thrones against the higher bids and more adroit intrigues of the Phanariots (Greek merchants of Constantinople), the latter replaced the former.

Meanwhile, in the seventeenth and eighteenth centuries Western influence predominated in Transylvania. The Hapsburg rulers carried on an extensive campaign stressing the Roman and Latin elements in the Romanian population for religious and political reasons. At the same time the Roman Catholic Church was actively introducing the French and Italian cultures. Consequently, Transylvania, although politically separated from the rest of Romania in the nineteenth and early twentieth centuries, served as a cultural bridge between the Romanians and Western Europe. European drama was introduced into Romania by traveling companies of actors who came first to Transylvania and then to Moldavia and Wallachia. By 1787 there were two resident drama companies at the court of Bucharest—one French and the other German.

The Phanariot rulers and their entourage of Romanian boyars and Greek merchants and politicians ushered in a period of chaos (1711–1821) at the highest level of the state, accompanied by ruthless exploitation of the peasants. The population, in addition to paying the expenses incurred by their Greek rulers to secure the throne, also had to pay the increasingly greater tribute imposed upon the principalities by the destitute Porte. The Romanian nobility and the Greek entourage of the princes freely participated in this abuse of the country's wealth and did not hesitate to betray or even murder competitors.

From this Machiavellian atmosphere many young nobles went to travel and study abroad, primarily in France. Not only Romanians but the Phanariots themselves developed interest in French political ideas and those of the Greek nationalist thinker Rhiger, who advocated the overthrow of Turkish control of the Greek nation. The first Greek revolutionary organization, the Hetairia, also contributed to the growth of the seeds of nationalism, which brought about the next important period in Romanian history—the struggle for and achieve-

In 1966 Horia Lovinescu's *Petru Rares,* a Shakespearean drama focusing on a sixteenth-century political leader, was staged in Bucharest at the Theatre "C. I. Nottara." [Editura Enciclopedică Română, Bucharest]

Vasile Alecsandri's *Madame Chirita* as presented in a modern adaptation by Tudor Musatescu. [Embassy of the Socialist Republic of Romania]

ment of national independence.

The Hetairists started a drama movement in their school in Bucharest in 1780. The students acted in plays by Greek and French writers under the direction of Costache Aristia (1799–1840), a Greek. The plays were usually nationalistic and antidespotic. A similar repertoire was organized at the Greek school in Jassy and in the French schools directed by émigrés. The Hetairists were suppressed in 1821, but not before their schools had introduced acting and stagecraft to Romania. The first formal theatrical performances took place in the schools of Transylvania, Wallachia, and Moldavia. The first performance in Romanian, given in Transylvania in 1782, was that of *Achilles in Sciro (Achille in Sciro)*, with Metastasio's libretto translated by Iordache Slatineau.

Historical circumstances prevented the flowering of a truly national literature until the first quarter of the nineteenth century. Some of the Phanariot princes appointed by Constantinople in the eighteenth century attempted to create a happier cultural climate in Wallachia and Moldavia. But the literature supported by the courts and therefore by the nobility and the clergy was Greek. There was no encouragement for Romanian writers apart from the theatre, which became a rallying point for the rebels against the Ottoman and Greek authorities. It was not until after the Revolution of 1821 and the establishment of schools which taught Romanian that there

emerged a public that could read its own literature.

NINETEENTH CENTURY

An Italian company acted in Jassy about 1800, a Russian company performed in 1809 to 1812, and an Italian *commedia dell'arte* troupe came to Bucharest in 1813. These foreign companies created a strong interest in drama among the nobility. Princess Ralu, daughter of Prince Ioan Caragea of Wallachia, ordered the rebuilding of a ballroom in Bucharest to provide a permanent theatre. In 1815 a Romanian theatre was opened in Oravita, Transylvania. The following year Gheorghe Asachi (1788–1869) recruited an amateur company at Jassy, and in 1836 he founded the Philharmonic-Dramatic Society, which taught singing, acting, and declamation. Also in Jassy the first National Theatre opened in 1840.

This early theatrical activity at Jassy was paralleled in Bucharest, where Iancu Vacaresu (1791–1863) and Ion Eliade Radulescu (1802–1872) presented Euripides's *Hecuba* and Molière's *L'avare* in Romanian in 1819. Much of the extraordinarily rapid growth of Romanian literature and theatre in the second quarter of the nineteenth century can be attributed to Radulescu. A teacher, poet, journalist, printer, philologist, and historian, Radulescu played an important role in the Revolution of 1848 in Wallachia. He helped found the Bucharest Conservatory and the Philharmonic Society, devoted to the promotion of music and the growth of a national drama. The society's emphasis on social and revolutionary drama caused its suppression in 1837; however, thanks to its work a theatre which opened in Bucharest on December 31, 1852, became the National Theatre two years later. In 1866 Radulescu became the first president of the Romanian Academy.

By 1840 the Romanian intelligentsia could satisfy its desire to study the culture of the West. There were many translations available, and many young writers who had studied in France, Prussia, or Switzerland returned to Romania imbued with the philosophy of romanticism. A school of Romanian dramatists appeared in the 1830s and 1840s: the Francophiles Costache Balacescu (1800–1880), Cezar Boliac (1813–1881), and Costache Faca (1800–1845), author of *The Frenchified Ones (Frantuzitele)*, a play which preserves in its dialogue the curious half-French, half-Romanian argot spoken by the Francophiles of the period.

The Romanians, like romantics elsewhere, turned to their homeland for inspiration. Their task, they said, was not the imitation of foreign literature but, rather, the creation of a literature original in form with its sources in the historical past of the nation and in all that was most characteristic of Romanian life. The leading voice of this school was Mihail Kogălniceanu (1817–1891), who played an important part in the political and literary achievements of the century. Publisher of *Dacia Literară (Literary Dacia,* 1840), the magazine of the romantic school, and of the more political *Steaua Dunarit (Star of the Danube),* he was also responsible for the first publication of Romanian documents, *Arhiva Romaneasca* (1840, 1845), and the chronicles of Moldavia.

In *Dacia Literară* and later literary magazines, such as *Propăsirea (Progress,* 1844) and *Romania Literară (Literary Romania,* 1855), Kogălniceanu, Vasile Alecsandri, and others promoted the national and popular current which was part of European romanticism. Romantic drama was popular in Romania throughout the nineteenth century, and Romanian dramatists placed emphasis on the use of national history as a source of inspiration, as well as on a comparison of the past with the present and on an evaluation of folk arts, local color, and popular types.

One of the most universally recognized dramatists was Vasile Alecsandri, poet, man of letters, and diplomat, who reigned over Romanian letters for almost forty years. He was well known for his participation in literary magazines of the day, for his abundant literary output, for the gaiety and optimism of his poetry, and for his glamorous diplomatic career. He served as Prince Cuza's personal envoy to Napoleon III in 1859 and later as minister plenipotentiary in Paris. Always faithful to the historical tradition, Alecsandri sang the glory of Romania's heroes in an impressive number of plays, among them *Horatio (Horatiu), Ovid (Ovidiu),* and *Despot Vodă (Voivode,* 1881), and in more than fifty patriotic poems. *See* ALECSANDRI, VASILE.

The period that followed the union of the principalities in 1859 was also romantic, but quieter, more balanced, and marked by greater national achievement. The writers were of an encyclopedic cast. For example, Bogdan Petriceicu Hasdeu opened a new era in the study of Romanian history, archeology, and linguistics, as well as in paleography and folklore. Moreover, he published poetry, prose, and a historical drama, *Razvan and Vidra, (Razvan si Vidra),* which has continued to be staged in the twentieth century.

While Alecsandri and his contemporaries continued the historical school of romanticism, a new literary movement, the Junimea (Young People's) Society, appeared in Romanian letters in the late 1870s. It was dedicated to artistic purity, to art for art's sake. Junimea's central figure was Ion Maiorescu (1840–1917), writer, lawyer, professor of philosophy, leader of the Conservative Party, and later prime minister during the Balkan War of 1913. For many years he reigned as the great critic and mentor of Romanian letters, insisting in the pages of Junimea's magazine, *Convorbiri Literare (Literary Conversations,* 1876), on perfect control of language and harmony between form and substance.

Maiorescu's rigorous spirit, and the high standards of the Junimea Society, had a strong and beneficial influence on all Romanian literature, but perhaps its great achievement was the encouragement it gave to such writers as Eminescu, Creanga, Caragiale, and Delavrancea. Eminescu became the great national poet. Ion Creanga (1837–1889), the poet's friend, brought to Romanian letters the rich vocabulary of the Moldavian peasant and an original gaiety and gusto comparable to that of Rabelais. He drew from folklore the inspiration for his stories and fairy tales, which have been dramatized for children's theatre. The children's theatre in Bucharest is named for him. Ion Luca Caragiale (1852–1912)

Ion Luca Caragiale's *The Lost Letter* as presented by Bucharest's Bulandra Theatre. [Embassy of the Socialist Republic of Romania]

watched with amusement the effects of foreign mannerisms on Romanian society. In his comedies and short stories he displayed a precise wit and a cutting satire which made his works popular successes in his lifetime and classics to all Romanians. He depicted contemporary society and its evils in such plays as *A Stormy Night, or Number 9* (*O noapte furtunoasă sau numărul 9*, 1879), *The Lost Letter* (*O scrisoarce pierdută*, 1884), and *Mr. Leonida and the Reactionaries* (*Conul Leonida faţă cu reacţiunea*, pub. 1880), but at the same time he created characters of universal value. *See* CARAGIALE, ION LUCA.

It was also under the auspices of the Junimea Society that Barbu Ştefănescu (1858–1918), who wrote under the name of Delavrancea, entered the world of literature as a playwright and prose writer. He wrote historical dramas, of which the best known are the trilogy *Sunset* (*Apus de soare*, 1909), *The Blizzard* (*Viforul*, 1909), and *The Morning Star* (*Luceafarul*, 1910). They are historical evocations of fifteenth-century Prince Stephen the Great of Moldavia and two of his descendants, Ştefăniţă and Petru Rares. The plays present three aspects of power in distinct historical moments. *See* DELAVRANCEA, BARBU.

The National Theatre and National Opera were united into the Romanian Society of Drama and Acting in 1877. This encouraged the native dramatists and gave them the opportunity to acquaint themselves with foreign plays, such as those of Corneille, Racine, Scribe, Sardou, Ibsen, Pirandello, and Maeterlinck. The new theatre flourished under several directors, among them

Prince Ion Chica. It was an age of brilliant stars and elaborate stage machinery. Shakespeare was constantly performed. Among the actors, Mihail Pascaly and Grigore Manolescu were successful Hamlets, and Aristiza Romanescu was famous as Ophelia.

Meanwhile the leaders of the Junimea Society did not remain unchallenged. The last three decades of the nineteenth century witnessed the appearance of varied schools of thought and many new talents. Each new circle, each new magazine, announced a program in which one could, however dimly, distinguish one of two trends: The first, inspired by Junimea, banned anything but intrinsic merit in literary work, while the second stressed "national characteristics" as a criteria for Romanian literature.

The literary orientation of *Convorbiri Literare* was criticized by the writers of the nationalist magazines *Columna lui Traian* (*Trajan's Column*, 1870), *Revista Noua* (*New Review*, 1887), *Noua Revista Romana* (*New Romanian Review*), *Semanatorul* (*The Sower*, 1901), *Luceafarul* (*The Morning Star*, founded in Budapest in 1902), *Vatra* (*The Fireside*), and *Viata Romaneasca* (*Romanian Life*, 1906). "We think," wrote Slavici in *Vatra*, "that we Romanians have not yet reached that point of cultural development where our writers can aspire to write for all times and all nations. Let us then be satisfied to write for our Romanian contemporaries."

The proponents of art for art's sake were just as active as the nationalists. Poets, prose writers, and drama-

Scene from *Alizuna* by Victor Eftimiu as produced by the National Theatre "Ion Luca Caragiale." [Editura Enciclopedică Română, Bucharest]

tists used the pages of their literary magazines *Transactiuni Literari si Scientifice* (*Literary and Scientific Transactions*, 1872), *Revista Contemporana* (*Contemporary Review*), *Pagini Literare* (*Literary Pages*, 1899), *Revista Idealista* (*Idealist Review*, 1903), *Linea Dreapta* (*Straight Line*), *Convorbiri Critice* (*Critical Conversations*, 1907), and *Flacara* (*The Flame*) to carry on, with considerable variations, the tradition of Junimea. Opposed to both these movements were the socialists, whose magazines were *Contemporanul* (*The Contemporary*, 1881), and *Curentul Nou* (*New Trend*, 1905). Although virtually nonexistent as a political force in Romania at this time, socialism attracted considerable literary attention.

As men of letters the dramatists were attracted to one or another of these literary groups and wrote their plays accordingly. For example, following the nationalist trend two Transylvanian poets and dramatists, Octavian Goga (1881–1938) and St. O. Iosif (1875–1913), found their themes in village life. Goga wrote *Mr. Notary* (*Domnul notar*, 1913) and a folklore piece, *Master Manole* (*Mesterul manole*, 1927). Iosif wrote *Gossamer Legend* (*Legenda funigeilor*, 1922) and *The Comet* (*Cometa*), with Dimitrie Anghel.

TWENTIETH CENTURY

The turn of the century saw the debut of the French-inspired symbolists, whose works were published in *Viata Noua* (*New Life*, 1906) and *Simbolul* (*The Symbol*), which appeared in 1912 under the direction of Ion Vinea and S. Samyro, better known as Tristan Tzara. Symbolism entered Romanian drama with the plays of Ion Minulescu, Victor Eftimiu, Adrian Maniu, N. Davidescu, G. V. Bacovia, and Dimitrie Anghel. These writers took a more subjective view of reality, attempting to capture in their plays man's subconscious reality in dramatic images. They turned away from the idea of the dramatist as the objective recorder of the details of everyday life and created a more abstract drama (*see* SYMBOLISM in glossary). Ion Minulescu (1881–1944), influenced by Pirandello, wrote ironic plays in *The Man Who Needs His Mill* (*Omul care trebuie sa moara*, 1924), *Sentimental Puppet* (*Machinul sentimental*, 1926), *Allegro, Ma Non Troppo* (1927), and *Anonymous Sweetheart* (*Amantul anonim*, 1928). Victor Eftimiu (1888–   ?), wrote contemporary comedies and tragedies, historical plays, and reinterpretations of Greek tragedies. His comedies, such as *The Man Who Has Seen Death*, analyze the Romanian middle class of the 1920s. Adrian Maniu (1891–   ?) combined the styles of Maeterlinck and Ibsen with the traditions of Romanian folklore in *Yellow Wolves* (*Lupii de arama*, 1929) and *The Master Builder* (*Mesterul*, 1922).

Beginning in the years before World War I, Romania witnessed an increasingly voluminous literary production in all schools and genres, including works for the theatre. Garabet Ibraileanu was the mentor of the writers grouped around *Viata Romaneasca*; Eugen Lovinescu was at the center of those identified with the magazine *Zburatorul*; and Nichifor Crainic was the director of *Gandirea*, located in Cluj. In this period the new drama of Ibsen and Sudermann, and the stagecraft of Antoine and Stan-

Cuckolded lovers prepare to slug it out in Caragiale's *Carnival Scenes*, as staged at the Bulandra Theatre by Liviu Ciulei and Giulio Tinou. [Embassy of the Socialist Republic of Romania]

islavsky, came to the National Theatre under the directorships of Alexandru Davila and Pompiliu Eliade. During the years 1909–1911 Davila also promoted the new ideas as director of the Modern Theatre, the first private theatre in Romania.

In the interwar period there was a veritable renaissance in the writing of plays by new authors. Dramatic art was influenced by contradictory tendencies in the artistic and literary revolutions of expressionism, symbolism, biomechanics, constructivism, surrealism, and dadaism. Realism and naturalism continued to be popular. Within the different styles much emphasis was placed on social satire, social drama, modern psychological analysis, themes from mythology and folklore, and historical drama. Historical plays were especially popular in the late 1920s, when historical settings were used to present contemporary political problems.

In the same period the greatest success was scored by the plays of Mihail Sorbul, Victor Eftimiu, George Ciprian, Caton Theodorian, Tudor Musatescu, Camil Petrescu, Adrian Maniu, and Victor Ion Popa. Many popular novelists of the day also wrote plays, including Hortensia Papadat-Bengescu, Gib Mihaescu, and A. O. Teodoreanu. *See* CIPRIAN, GEORGE; EFTIMIU, VICTOR; PAPADAT-BENGESCU, HORTENSIA; PETRESCU, CAMIL.

After a brilliant career as an actor with the National Theatre in Bucharest, George Ciprian made his debut as a dramatist in 1927 with his play *The Man with the Nag* (*Omul eu mirtoago*). This delightful social satire analyzes in a humorous way those who want to create the impossible dream. The play was very successful in Romania and abroad, where it played in Berlin, Prague, Berne, and Paris. His most important play, *The Duck's Head* (*Capul de ratoi*), was premiered much later—in January 1940. In this play one finds a definite link between Ciprian, Caragiale, and Urmuz. Caragiale satirized certain segments of society; Urmuz in his *Bizarre Pages* emphasized the unusual and the grotesque in society; and Ciprian used the comic, the farcical, and the surrealistic approaches to reality in his criticism of society.

Liviu Rebreanu, Tudor Musatescu, Bogdan Amaru, Alexandru Kiritescu, Ion Luca, Andrei Corteanu, and Ion Sava were among those who wrote comedies in the same vein as George Ciprian and Victor Eftimiu. Playwrights who continued to use the conventions of logic and order that had dominated the realistic and naturalistic theatre of the nineteenth century included Victor Ion Popa, Mihail Sorbul, Mircea Stefanescu, Hortensia Papadat-Bengescu, Mihail Sebastian, and George Mihail Zamfirescu. These writers adhered to the naturalistic thesis and presented a "slice of life" in all its harsh reality. They were pessimistic and shared with the expressionists their enmity toward family, bourgeois society, war, materialism, and corruption. They objected to the conventions and authority which hampered the individual and kept him from realizing his full potential. For example, Victor Ion Popa (1895–1946), considered an "experimental psychologist" in his plays, applied his theories in *Take, Ianke and Cadir (Take, Ianke si Cadir)*, a psychological study of the love of two young people of different religious faiths and the opposition of their families to their marriage. Popa wrote other plays, *The Great Crossroads (Raspintia cea mare, 1922)*, based on experiences in World War I, *The Deer (Ciuta, 1922)*, and *Revenge of the Soul (Razbunarea sufleorului)*, with accents of social criticism. *See* SEBASTIAN, MIHAIL; ZAMFIRESCU, GEORGE MIHAIL.

The expressionists considered themselves visionaries who would bring about man's regeneration by giving dramatic form to his inner struggle against the evil forces of the world. Expressionist echoes are seen in the plays

Sanda Toma, Mircea Şeptilici, and Ştefan Tapalaga in Mihail Sebastian's *The Island,* as staged by Bucharest's Theatre of Comedy. [Editura Enciclopedică Română, Bucharest]

Constantin Brezeanu and Eugenia Bădulescu in Camil Petrescu's *Venetian Act* as staged at the Theatre "C. I. Nottara" in Bucharest. [Editura Enciclopedică Română, Bucharest]

of Ion Marin Sadoveanu and Lucian Blaga. Sadoveanu (1893–1964) was greatly influenced by the work and thought of Paul Claudel and followed the mystical nature of Catholic themes. His plays may be seen, too, as stages in a search for the nature of God and for Christian salvation. In *Anno Domini* (1927) he expresses his obsession with death, a theme generally absent in Romanian dramaturgy. His first play, *Metamorphosis (Metamorfoze)*, which appeared in the magazine *Viata Romaneasca* in 1926, is in a lighter vein, about the search for escape in the world of spirits and fairies. In *Epidemic (Molima, 1939)*, he returns to the theme of emotional adjustment in a changing world.

Lucian Blaga (1895–1961), poet and dramatist, displays certain expressionist tones, nuances of Paul Claudel and Henrik Ibsen. Blaga admitted that the expressionists had rejected the psychological realism of the nineteenth century "as an inadequate, old-fashioned tool" which stopped at appearances, incapable of getting to the essence of things. His social dramas *Daria* (1925) and *The Feat (Fapta, 1925)*, written in the style of Ibsen, set forth his doctrine of human values and his view of the individual in conflict with society. His *Avram Iancu* (1934) is a historical play, an interpretation of the hero of the Transylvanian revolt against Hungary in 1848. It was first staged in the National Theatre in Cluj in January 1935, and as a character piece it has been popular ever since. *Zamolxe* (1921), called a "pagan mystery," distorts external reality in order to express the subjective, inner reality of the old prophet who stands alone in his opposition to the ancient pagan rituals.

When Romania became a Communist country after the defeat of the Germans on August 23, 1944, the theatres, like all other aspects of national life, were collectivized. The theatres were nationalized in 1948, and became an instrument for the building of socialism. The party gives strict and detailed instructions on handling this tool, which is directly under the Ministry of Culture and the Association of Theatre Workers.

The drama companies are state subsidized through central or regional councils. Theatre workers, producers, actors, and directors are elected as deputies to the regional districts, to the people's councils, and to the National Assembly, and thus they participate in public affairs.

Each permanent theatre company has a director who is responsible for the general management as well as for the artistic side of the productions. An assistant director looks after the finances of the company. He places the advertising and sells the tickets. The literary secretary has the task of selecting plays for consideration by the troupe, and he writes the advertising. A chief producer, also called director at times, oversees the actual production of each play. Every theatre company has its own council, which consists of the aforementioned, as well as the stage designer, stage manager, lighting technician, chief engineer, and representatives of the actors. The council discusses plans for the repertory and the allocation of work to producers, actors, and crew; however, the final decision rests with the director, although regular conferences are held with the council during the preparation of each new production. After the premiere a meeting of the company is held in the theatre to discuss the play with the official censors.

Today this country of some twenty million people

Scene from a Bucharest production of George Ciprian's *The Duck's Head*. [Photograph courtesy of Ruth S. Lamb]

Barbu Delavrancea's *Sunset* is the first play in a trilogy focusing on events in fifteenth-century Romania. [Embassy of the Socialist Republic of Romania]

The communist state in Romania quickly asserted its interest in dramatic literature. To ensure control over individual playwrights, the writing profession was institutionalized. By 1949 a writer had to belong to a union before he could get his ration card; his plays could not be presented unless the Ministry of Culture approved them. Only those plays favorable to the regime and to the Soviet Union could appear. If the dramatist successfully followed the party line, his work would be carefully scrutinized by the censors for "deviationism," "abstractism," or "schematism." Communist "realism," often called "socialist realism," demands heroic figures, larger than life, who nonetheless behave naturally. The dramatist must project himself into what will be the best of all possible worlds and describe the noble individuals he sees there in terms that will inspire his audience to imitation.

The main task of the Romanian dramatists has been to present the "fight for socialism in dynamic terms." The writers who did not take their places in the literary battle line were soon faced with the loss of livelihood and liberty or subject to exile. The literary magazine *Flacara (The Flame)* affirmed that the "writers must follow the example of their comrades in the mines and at the lathes." The Ministry of Culture became the sole patron of the theatre, and commissioned plays on set themes.

The Romanian playwright must not only build socialism, but he must also build friendship for the Soviet Union. Russian plays are held up as models to the Romanian dramatist, and translations of Russian plays are given high priority. Festivals of Russian plays are held

An adaption by Zoe Anghel Stanca of Ion Creanga's *White Moor.* [Embassy of the Socialist Republic of Romania]

has more than forty dramatic and repertory theatres as well as thirty-six state theatres in the provinces. This does not include some thirty professional puppet theatres, numerous opera and ballet groups, social and music hall companies. Apart from the professional theatres there are many amateur groups attached to farm cooperatives, factories, and recreation centers, known as houses of culture. They are provided with stages and receive help and encouragement from the professional actors and producers. Romania, which constitutionally guarantees the linguistic and cultural rights of minority nationalities, supports theatre companies in Hungarian, German, and Yiddish.

Bucharest is the center of theatrical activity and has the largest number of playhouses, including the National Theatre, the Bulandra, Comedie, Nottara, Giulesti, Mic (Pocket Theatre), Ion Creanga Children's Theatre, the Constantin Tanase Variety Theatre, the Jewish State Theatre, State Operetta Theatre, the Opera and Ballet Theatre. The new National Theatre building opened its doors to the public in December 1973, with the presentation of two patriotic plays, Barbu Delavrancea's *Sunset (Apus de soare)* and Aurel Baranga's *Pathetic Symphony (Simfonie patetic)*. For the theatregoing Romanians this new theatre ushered in a new age. The old theatre had been destroyed in the Nazi bombing of the city in 1944. As the manager of the new theatre, Radu Beligan, said: "The history of our National Theatre is an integral part of Romanian history. This theatre is traditionally the first stage of the country, but it will have to live up to its title by acts of artistic pride as well. And these can only be expected from steadily promoting our national drama and cultivating the best values of world theatre in performances of a higher artistic quality."

Serafima Birman in a Russian production of Horia Lovinescu's *The Crumbling Citadel*. [New York Public Library]

once a year in the different provinces of Romania; the programs include works by Chekhov, Dostoievsky, Gogol, and Gorky. Literary specialists have been sent from Moscow to evaluate the progress of the Romanian people toward socialism, and to authorize or censor the performance of certain plays.

To exploit the literary heritage of the past, the Romanian Communists have selected certain nineteenth-century dramatists—Caragiale, Creanga, and Delavrancea—as the best subjects for this "working over and development." This is not because of their "progressive elements," for they were apolitical, but because of their stature. The party has liberated these writers from the "falsehoods made up by the literary lackeys of the exploiting class." Creanga's stories, now widely dramatized in Romania, supposedly show the misery of the peasants, and Caragiale is presented as an unconscious socialist. Caragiale's comedies of manners, so popular with his contemporaries, are presented as illustrative of pre-Communist social decay. Delavrancea's historical plays are presented in oversized heroic proportions to fit the needs of "socialist realism."

The Communist regime has developed a school of new dramatists, unknown before 1944: Horia Lovinescu, Aurel Baranga, Lucia Demetrius, Paul Everac, Alexandru Mirodan, Ecaterina Oproiu, Sidonia Dragusanu, Alexandru Voitin, Alecou Popovici, Dumitru Radu Popescu, and others. They are talented writers, but they are obliged to write within the guidelines of state policy. According to the resolutions of the central committee of the party every play must further communism. If the changing party line invalidates one of the basic themes, the plays which it inspired are taken out of circulation. For instance, *The Wolves (Lupii)*, a play by Radu Boureanu which "exposed" Titoist espionage in Romania, was

withdrawn when the Soviet Union began to make overtures to Yugoslavia in 1953. Liviu Ciulei's production of Gogol's *Inspector General* suffered a similar fate in 1972 because of Russian criticism of the interpretation.

Horia Lovinescu is one of the representative figures of the new Romanian dramaturgy under the Communist system. Director of the Nottara Theatre in Bucharest, he made his debut as a playwright in 1953 with *Light at Ulmi* (*Lumina de la Ulmi*, 1953), whose theme supports the new political philosophy in Romania. *The Crumbling Citadel* (*Citadela sfarimata*, 1954) brought him recognition and the state prize. It concerns the destruction of bourgeois individualism. He has written many other plays, including the patriotic *Town of Victory* for the opening of the new National Theatre in Bucharest in 1973. When Lovinescu was asked, "What is the rapport between art and politics in Romania?" he replied, "The writer can be a political man, independent of his career as a writer. I hold that the social role of the writer is to make an authentic image of reality stand out for the political man and public opinion." *See* LOVINESCU, HORIA.

Aurel Baranga, popular dramatist and prose writer, concerns himself with the individual living in a socialist society. He has written many comedies dealing with present-day social and political concerns such as *Public Opinion* (*Opinia publica*, pub. 1967), *Adam and Eve* (*Adam si Eva*, pub. 1963), *Recipe for Happiness* (*Reteta fericirii*, pub. 1967), and *Be Obedient, Christopher* (*Fii cuminte, Cristofor*, pub. 1967). His patriotic drama *Arch of Triumph* (*Arcul de Triumf*, 1954) has been played many times in theatres throughout the country. *Travesty* (*Travesti*, ca. 1973) treats the theme of the dissolution of the family because of the changing role of the wife and mother in the new society. His *Pathetic Symphony (Symfonie patetic)* was chosen in 1973 as one of the patriotic plays to open the new National Theatre in Bucharest. *See* BARANGA, AUREL.

Stage, screen, and television writer Paul Everac in his play *Moth on the Lamp* (*Un fluture pe lampa*, 1973) debates the concept of individual freedom in a Communist society as opposed to a capitalist society. He uses Paris as the location and Romanian exiles there as the protagonists. His answer is that the socialist way of life offers more to the individual. His plays *Chimera* (*Himera*, 1964), *White Eyes* (*Ochiul albastru*, 1961), and *Open Windows (Fenestre deschise)* express the same line of thought. *See* EVERAC, PAUL.

Alexandru Mirodan (1927–   ) has written many short plays, but a longer comedy, *The Moon's Mayor and His Sweetheart* (*Primarul lunii si tubita sa*, 1969), gives an interesting twist to the story of cosmonauts who find an organized socialist society on the moon. Alecou Popovici writes children's plays for special programs in the schools and for children's theatre. He recreates the child's world with humor, using old themes and inventing new ones that are in line with Communist philosophy. Examples are *A Discovered Letter, Unfinished Story*, and *The Boy in the Second Row* (*Baiatul din banca a doua*, 1961). Dumitru Radu Popescu, dramatist from Cluj and editor of the literary magazine *A Tribuna*, has written contemporary social plays, such as *Those Sad Angels* (*Acesti ingeri tristi*, 1970) and *Cat on New Year's Eve* (*Pisica in noaptea anului*, 1971), as well as historical plays like *Caesar, the Pirates' Play* (*Cezar, mascariciul piratilor*, 1968), about a captive Caesar. *See* POPESCU, DUMITRU RADU.

Foremost among the imaginative women dramatists are Sidonia Dragusanu, who analyzes the contemporary soul and mind; Lucia Demetrius, author of many plays such as *Men from Now On* (*Oameni de azi*, 1952) and *Three Generations* (*Trei generatii*, 1956), who is concerned with moral behavior in modern family life; and Ecaterina Oproiu, a sophisticated film critic, who studies the individual's basis for happiness within the socialist society in her modern allegory *I Am Not the Eiffel Tower* (*Nu sint turnel Eiffel*, 1964).

The post-World War II period witnessed the rise in popularity of the short play owing to the demands of radio, television, and amateur and laboratory theatres. The one-act play provided a more unitary development, fewer characters, and a more rapid crescendo of the plot. The short play had first appeared during World War I, when there developed the custom of presenting a curtain raiser before the beginning of the main play. Curtain raisers became very popular, and the Society of Dramatic Authors set up an annual competition for them with prizes. As the number of amateur theatrical groups grew, some of the well-known dramatists were asked to write short comedies for them. One of the most popular to provide this type of light drama was the writer and stage director Victor Ion Popa.

The true flowering of the short play occurred after World War II, when "the existence of almost ten thousand groups of amateur actors created a genuine thirst for short plays." Old plays were used, longer plays were shortened, and a great demand arose for dramatists to write more short plays, since even the professional theatre groups had begun to use them. During the 1940s, 1950s, and 1960s established writers such as Alexandru Kiritescu, Tudor Musatescu, Mircea Stefanescu, Mihail Davidoglu, Aurel Baranga, Lucia Demetrius, Horia Lovinescu, Alexandru Mirodan, and Paul Everac published numerous short plays. They took their themes from contemporary life and current problems, including those based on changes in the structure of Romanian society.

The most recent generation of short-play writers has tried to produce a more daring, original, and parabolic dramaturgy by penetrating into the territories of the absurd, surrealism, neosymbolism, and epic theatre. But probably their most important characteristic is the tendency to embrace allegorically the universe of modern man. They are interested in man the builder and prophet, man the explorer of the microcosm and navigator among the galaxies, and man who is menaced by catastrophes but generally triumphs in the struggle against nature and himself.

Among the younger pleiad are Teodor Mazilu, Marin Sorescu, Dumitru Radu Popescu, Ion Baiescu, Leonida Teodorescu, Iosef Naghiu, Dumitru Solomon, Paul Cornel Chitic, Nelu Ionescu, Ilie Paunescu, Cezar Ivanescu, Romulus Vulpescu, Gheorghe Astalos, Valeriu Sirbu, Mihai Georgescu, A. T. Popescu, Mihail Neagu Bassarab, Radu Dumitru, and Sorana Coroama. All are concerned with "man's dramatic condition" in its many aspects. Some use themes based on war, social inadaptability, civic pride, and bureaucracy; others portray more personal relationships, such as interference in the individual's private life, or the dialogue between man and his conscience.

The Romanian critic Valentin Silvestru disapproves of the generalizations and abstract conclusions reached

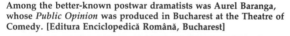

Among the better-known postwar dramatists was Aurel Baranga, whose *Public Opinion* was produced in Bucharest at the Theatre of Comedy. [Editura Enciclopedică Română, Bucharest]

Liviu Ciulei's staging of Georg Büchner's *Leonce and Lena* at the Bulandra Theatre in 1970. [Embassy of the Socialist Republic of Romania]

These Sad Angels by Dumitru Radu Popescu, as staged in Bucharest at the Giuleşti Theatre. [Editura Enciclopedică Română, Bucharest]

in some of these plays. He also criticizes the use of certain themes, such as eroticism, death, and incommunicability, which he believes endanger their genuine originality. However, he concludes that "beyond these incertitudes, a new and splendid dramaturgy is arising, and we firmly believe that some of the works of this new Romanian drama are most original contributions to modern world culture."

According to Liviu Ciulei and Radu Beligan, both well-known directors, 1962 was a year of crisis in the Romanian theatre. Modernization was needed in directing, repertoire, and acting. New directors were sought to bring a more genuinely creative approach to the theatre. Radu Beligan, himself an actor, was allowed to experiment in the Sala Comedie with a small number of good actors, a new repertoire, and modern staging. Liviu Ciulei, then a young director and now an international figure, began to make changes at the Bulandra Theatre. Horia Lovinescu, dramatist and director, took over the managership of the Nottara Theatre in 1965.

Other prominent director-producers today are Radu Penciulescu, Dinu Cernescu, Lucian Pintilie, Lucian Giurchescu, Mihai Berechet, and Horea Popescu. They work in various theatres with well-trained companies of actors and direct plays for the stage, cinema, and television. In recent years the National Theatre Institute has trained other younger directors, such as David Esrig, Alexa Visarion, Catalina Buzoianu, Ivan Helmer, Nada Budeianu, Andre Serlan, Aurel Manea, Magda Bordeianu, Soran Coroama, and Sanda Manu, all of whom are making a name for themselves.

Stage designing should be mentioned for its current variety and vitality, covering all styles from the conventional to the abstract. Before 1948 stage design fell into two categories: the symbolic and impressionistic, and the naturalism of the Stanislavsky school. The reaction in the following period led to constructivism. The Romanians followed in the footsteps of Meyerhold; wings, borders, and painted drops were replaced by revolving wheels, ladders, lifts, stairs, and stands. The theatre became a factory with actors as workers and the performance as a process of production. This was an excellent symbolic gesture to socialism, but audiences crowding the Romanian theatres wanted color and evocative settings. Thus constructivism went out of fashion, and scenographers—Dan Nemteanu, Liviu Ciulei, Jules Perahim, Ervin Kutler, Cataline Buzoianu, Sanda Musatescu, and others—turned to different styles, including the most contemporary designs. The creative ability of the scenographers, directors, and actors is of high quality, and their staging and performances have brought international fame to Romanian theatre.

Ruth S. Lamb

CRITICISM

R. W. Seton-Watson, *A History of the Roumanians*, Cambridge, 1934; B. Munteano, *Modern Rumanian Literature*, Bucharest, 1939; S. Fischer-Galati, *Romania*, New York, 1957; G. Oprescu, *Teatrul in Romania dupa 23 August 1944. (Theatre in Romania After 23 August, 1944)*, Bucharest, 1959; *Istoria Teatrului in Romania (History of Theatre in Romania)*, ed. by G. Oprescu, Bucharest, 1965; R. A. Petrescu, *100 Years of Drama Tuition*, Bucharest, 1965; P. Hartnoll, *The Oxford Companion to the Theatre*, London, 1967; V. Rapeanu, *Dramaturgie Romana Contemporana (Contemporary Romanian Dramaturgy)*, 2 vols., Bucharest, 1967; J. Gassner and E. Quinn, *The Reader's Encyclopedia of World Drama*, New York, 1969; *The History of the Romanian People*, ed. by A. Otetea, New York, 1970; *Aspects du Theatre Roumain Contemporain*, Bucharest, L'Association des Artistes des Institutions Theatrales et Musicales de la Republique Socialiste de Roumanie, 1971; M. Matlaw, *Modern World Drama, an Encyclopedia*, New York, 1972; M. Vasiliu, *Istoria Teatrului Romanesc (A History of Romanian Theatre)*, Jassy (Iaşi), Romania, 1972; *Istoria Teatrului in Romania (A History of the Theatre in Romania)*, ed. by S. Alterescu, Bucharest, 1973; L. Pride, *International Theatre Directory: A World Directory of the Theatre and Performing Arts*, New York, 1973; D. Cocea, "The Theatre, a Messenger of National Culture," *Romania Today*, no. 5, 1974; R. S. Lamb, *The World of Romanian Theatre*, California: Ocelot, 1976.

Romero Esteo, Miguel (1930–)

Spanish dramatist, poet, and essayist. Romero Esteo was born in Montoro (Córdoba). At the end of the Spanish Civil War (1936–1939), his family was forced by circumstances to immigrate to Málaga. He was able to continue his studies thanks to a scholarship from a religious institution. Trained for the priesthood, he left the seminary before being ordained. In his mid-twenties he moved to Madrid, where he obtained degrees in journalism and political science. A literary critic for a national newspaper for several years, he now teaches courses in theatre at the University of Málaga and directs a drama workshop there.

Romero Esteo wrote his first play, *The Hilarious Pizzicato and Grand Pavane of the Owls (Pizzicato irrisorio y gran pavana de los lechuzos)* in 1963, but it was not until four years later that his name began to attract attention in avant-garde theatre circles. In 1967 he completed *Pontifical* and submitted it for performance at the first annual Sitges (Barcelona) International Theatre Festival. The play was rejected on political grounds, despite the objections of several members of the selection committee. The following year the same situation repeated itself, giving rise to another "affaire." In 1971 mimeographed copies of the two volumes of *Pontifical* began to circulate clandestinely among the groups and writers associated with the "New Spanish Theatre," the underground movement which sprang up in the 1960s and is still struggling to assert itself. Even before any of his plays had been performed or published, Romero Esteo's originality was an established fact.

With the exception of *The Paper Boat (El barco de papel*, 1975), all his plays were banned during Franco's dictatorship. The original ban was later lifted in only two cases, *Paraphernalia of the Potpourri, Mercy and Much Consolation (Paraphernalia de la olla podrida, la misericordia y la mucha consolación*, 1971) and *Pasodoble* (1973), but performances were restricted to experimental (that is, noncommercial) productions, a method devised by the Spanish censorship to limit the number of spectators without outright prohibition of the play. *Paraphernalia* was first performed by Ditirambo, one of the better "Independent Theatre" groups, at the Sitges Festival in October 1972 and later in Paris and Madrid. *Pasodoble* was first staged in Madrid, at the Teatro Alfil, on October 26, 1974, as part of the First International Independent Theatre Festival. Ditirambo, which was also responsible for this production, later took it on a national tour. (In 1976 it was selected for performance at the Venice Biennial and in

1978 Ditirambo embarked on a tour of American colleges and universities with *Pasodoble* and a work by another vanguard Spanish dramatist, Luis Riaza.) There have yet to be professional productions in Madrid of *The Vaudeville of the Pale, Pale, Pale, Pale Rose* (*El vodevil de la pálida, pálida, pálida, pálida rosa*, 1974) and *The Merry Feasts of Wine and Eats* (*Fiestas gordas del vino y del tocino*, 1973).

Hailed as a major dramatist by some of the leading critics in the Hispanic world, Romero Esteo tends to write long, complex texts which cannot be performed in their entirety: *Pontifical*, the longest of his plays, runs 442 pages in typescript, while *Pasodoble*, one of his shortest, is about one fourth as long but still approximately twice the length of the average play staged in Spain. His theatre defies classification. Unlike his fellow avant-garde dramatists, he writes neither allegories nor parables; and while he makes copious use of symbols, he cannot be regarded as an essentially symbolic writer. His plays reveal an extremely intricate structure with many overlapping layers of text and are full of multifaceted allusions. Like Valle Inclán, Romero Esteo writes grotesqueries, but he actually goes beyond the *esperpento*, the term the former bestowed on his experiments in the grotesque manner (*see* VALLE INCLÁN, RAMÓN MARÍA DE). (Romero Esteo has very shrewdly observed that the *esperpento* is basically naturalist theatre subjected to a process of deformation.) The complexity of Romero Esteo's theatre also extends to the linguistic level. In fact, linguistic distortions, achieved by combining the ceremonial forms of Catholicism and high-flown literary language with slang, colloquialisms, and obscenities of a sexual and scatological nature, are his trademark. The clever juxtaposition of noble concepts and debased words results in a systematic degradation of those concepts. By degrading the language of his characters he not only exposes their hypocrisy as individuals, but also the moral bankruptcy of the class ideology which that language embodies.

Romero Esteo, who characterizes his plays as Theatre of Derision, also employs a number of other stylistic devices, among them: the obsessive repetition of sentences or parts of sentences, which imparts a nightmarish, psychotic quality to the dialogue; the frequent use of puns, usually involving a word's formal meaning and its vulgar significance; and the deliberate overuse of rhyme and other rhetorical devices based on the repetition of sounds. Drawing on his liturgical and musical background (he became an accomplished organist during his years as a seminarian), Romero Esteo has created a unique form of ceremonial theatre. Behind his torturous system of linguistic allusions and complex symbols lies a deep historical reflection on the structure of power and its repercussions for the individual. Romero Esteo's ferociously satirical vision of life is tempered by a boundless Rabelesian ribaldry, deeply rooted, as he himself has declared on a number of occasions, in the sensibility of the Spanish populace. *See* SPANISH DRAMA.

ANDRÉS FRANCO

EDITIONS

The Hilarious Pizzicato and Grand Pavane of the Owls (*Pizzicato irrisorio y gran pavana de los lechuzos*, 1963). Published with an introduction by the author and bibliographical material, Madrid, 1978.

The Merry Feasts of Wine and Eats (*Fiestas gordas del vino y del tocino*, 1973). Published Madrid, 1975.

Pasodoble (1973). Published in *Primer Acto*, no. 162, pp. 15–49, 1973.

Paraphernalia of the Potpourri, Mercy and Great Consolation (*Paraphernalia de la olla podrida, la misericordia y la mucha consolación*, 1971). Published in *Estreno*, no. 2, T1–T32, 1975 (condensed version staged by Ditirambo).

The Vaudeville of the Pale, Pale, Pale, Pale Rose (*El vodevil de la pálida, pálida, pálida, pálida rosa*, 1974). Published Madrid, 1979.

CRITICISM

G. E. Wellwarth, *Spanish Underground Drama*, University Park, Pa., and London, 1972, pp. 81–90; M. Pérez Coterillo, "Un sueño inigualable de destrucción," *Primer Acto*, no. 162, pp. 12–15, 1973; C. Isasi Angulo, "Entrevista con Miguel Romero Esteo," in *Diálogos del teatro español de la postguerra*, Madrid, 1974, pp. 389–413; F. Ruiz Ramón, *Historia del teatro español*, 3d. ed., vol. 2, Madrid, 1977, pp. 564–569; L. T. Valdivieso, *España: Bibliografía de un teatro "silenciado*," Society of Spanish and Spanish-American Studies, 1979, pp. 77–82.

Rosenow, Emil (1871–1904)

German novelist, journalist, and dramatist. He began his career as editor of the socialist newspapers *Chemnitzer Beobachter* and *Rheinisch-westfälische Arbeiterzeitung*, in Dortmund, but his principal importance lies in his dramatic work. The force and originality of his talent were heralded by the one-act play *At Home* (*Daheim*), a compelling milieu piece with a haunting quality that grew out of personal experience and suffering. This was followed by *The Playful Grouse* (*Der balzende Auerhahn*), a rather conventional play patterned after Ibsen's *A Doll's House*. Rosenow's fame came with the naturalistic comedy *Lampe, the Cat* (*Kater Lampe*, 1902), his best and most mature work, comparable to Gerhart Hauptmann's *The Beaver Coat*, in which light and shadow are combined in perfect equilibrium and the authentic presentation of environment, people, and dialect provides a climate of understanding and gaiety.

Of Rosenow's other plays, *Prince Frederick* (*Prinz Friedrich*) and *The Hope of the Wandering Scholar* (*Die Hoffnung des Vaganten*) remained mere fragments, while the miners' tragedy, *Those Who Live in the Dark* (*Die im Schatten leben*, 1912), survives as a document of the times, an outcry against the dormant conscience of society, an accusation of the heart, whose profound sincerity overshadows any political bias.

[PETER JELAVICH]

Rosso di San Secondo, Pier Maria (1887–1956)

Italian journalist, short-story writer, and dramatist. He was born on November 30, 1887, in Caltanissetta, Sicily, the first of five sons of a titled family. After secondary school he studied law at the University of Rome and began writing short stories and plays. Before receiving his degree, he had completed his first play, *The Siren Sings Again* (*La sirena ricanta*, 1908), the text of which is now lost, and a group of short stories entitled *The Shut Eye* (*L'occhio chiuso*, 1911). During his sojourn in Rome, Rosso knew Pirandello, who read his short stories and theatrical works and encouraged him to continue his literary activity. *See* PIRANDELLO, LUIGI.

For a while, at the age of twenty, Rosso traveled on the Continent, settling finally in the Netherlands, where he remained for two years. His experiences abroad led

Pier Maria Rosso
di San Secondo.
[Italian Cultural
Institute]

him to write a notable group of stories, *Elegies to Marike* (*Elegie a Marike*, 1914), which were published in *Lirica*, the Roman periodical. After World War I, during which Rosso served in the army, he joined the editorial staff of *L'Idea Nazionale* and later was editor in chief of *Il Messaggero della Domenica*, a literary weekly under the direction of Pirandello, with whom by now Rosso had formed a close friendship.

During these early postwar years Rosso wrote many short stories and several plays, becoming a celebrated playwright almost overnight with *Marionettes, What Passion!* (*Marionette che passione!*, 1918), a work derived from one of his earlier short stories. He traveled frequently thereafter, as a journalist, to France and Germany, returning to those countries for lengthy stays between 1926 and 1932 as correspondent for the Turin *La Stampa*. In 1934 he was awarded the prize of the Italian Academy, which enabled him to build a house at Lido di Camaiore, where he lived with his German-born wife, the former Inge Redlich, until the outbreak of World War II.

Rosso returned to Rome after the war as theatre critic for the *Giornale d'Italia*. In 1954 he was awarded the Melpomene Prize for his last play, *The Rape of Persephone* (*Il ratto di Proserpina*). He died in Lido di Camaiore on November 22, 1956.

WORK

One of the most imaginative and gifted Italian dramatists of the early twentieth century, a writer usually placed in the "grotesque" school, whose work falls somewhere between Pirandello's abstractions and the far-ranging symbolism of outright grotesquerie, Rosso di San Secondo brought to the theatre a vision distinctly his own. In his more than thirty plays, his style developed from the poignant yet deeply tragic unfolding of character and motive in the puppetlike figures of his first and perhaps best drama, *Marionettes, What Passion!* (1918), to the epic scale of his last drama, *The Rape of Persephone* (1954), in which poetic fantasy, rhetoric, sheer theatricality, and profound

thought are intermingled in a brilliant if bizarre display of dramatic skill. Favorable criticism contends that Rosso's "inward" vision is as fascinating and compelling as that of Strindberg in the "dream plays," while negative opinion maintains that the symbolic characters and events, that "inwardness" of vision which is Rosso's true distinction, are incomprehensible. *See* TEATRO DEL GROTTESCO in glossary.

There is an intoxicating atmosphere arising from romantic illusion and an intuitive psychological perceptiveness in *The Sleeping Beauty* (*La bella addormentata,* 1919), in which the central character, a prostitute, represents beauty betrayed by man but rescued by a modern mediating hero. In *Stone and Monuments* (*La roccia e i monumenti,* 1923), the surface narrative depicts the meeting of Brunetto, a World War I hero, and Isabella, who once had loved him but now is married and deeply devoted to a blind man; on a deeper level, however, the play depicts the symbolic clash of instinctual man, ignorant of moral ties (Brunetto, the unworked stone), with moral character refined through the acceptance of civilized values (monuments).

Also of great interest is *The Terrestrial Adventure* (*L'avventura terrestre,* 1924), in which Rosso created a powerful character called Alessandra, a Russian woman who follows Ruggiero to his native Sicily and there, in the atmosphere of southern primitivism, finds relative peace for her troubled northern soul. A more pathetic female figure is portrayed in *The Staircase* (*La scala,* 1925), the story of a tormented woman whose only hope is the illusion that her dead child is still alive. The mingling of the symbolic and real are also to be found in Rosso's remaining plays, which include *Dog Days* (*Canicola,* 1925), *Fever* (*Febbre,* 1926), and *Among Clothes that Dance* (*Tra vestiti che ballano,* 1926).

Marionettes, What Passion! (*Marionette che passione!,* 1918). Grotesque drama about the futility of human attempts at meaningful contact and communication. Three characters meet by chance in a telegraph office. Each is attempting to compose an important telegram. The Man in Grey is suffering from an inner torment; the Lady in Blue Fox has left her husband, who insulted and mistreated her; the Man in Mourning has worn black since his wife ran away with her lover.

The Lady in Blue Fox and the Man in Mourning are drawn to each other and hope to begin a new life together that will dispel past misfortunes. The Man in Grey attempts to dissuade them from trying to create an illusion of happiness; yet he himself momentarily gives in to the same desire when he makes a declaration of love to a singer, the friend of the Lady in Blue Fox. In a restaurant that evening, the members of the group feign gaiety and drink a toast to themselves and to their absent spouses. Suddenly, the husband of the Lady in Blue Fox appears and leads his wife away; the Man in Grey, who feels that his love is dead and sees his position as forever hopeless, poisons himself. The Man in Mourning is left, clinging to the singer and begging her to help him live.

The Sleeping Beauty (*La bella addormentata,* 1919). Poetic fantasy in which the central character, the Beauty, an enigmatic personification of loveliness betrayed, is a pregnant prostitute who, in a somnambulistic fashion, goes from one place of public entertainment to another, from carnival to fair, selling herself to all who come to pay homage to her beauty. The only man to succeed in awakening her passion is the Black of the Sulfur Mine, who becomes her sole interest and effectively rids her of all other admirers. Now the Black takes the Beauty to the Notary, who first seduced and then abandoned her. At the insistence of his aunt, the Notary marries the Beauty, while the Black is carried away under arrest. In the original version, the play ends with the dream of the Beauty holding her newborn infant to her breast. As the music of a Jew's harp is heard, signifying the return of the Black, the Notary hangs himself. In the second edition of the play, it is the Beauty who dies in the end, after forgiving the Notary.

The Staircase (*La scala*, 1925). Tragedy in which Clotilde is forced by her husband to live like a kept woman because she has been unfaithful. Her only reason for wanting to live is to see her daughter once again. She does not know that the child has died; in a spirit of vindictiveness, her husband maintains her illusion.

[PETER BONDANELLA]

PLAYS

1. *Madre* (*Mother*). Play. Produced Milan, Teatro Verdi, 1908.
2. *La tunisina* (*The Tunisian*). Play. Produced Genoa, Teatro Paganini, February, 1918.
3. *Marionette che passione!** (*Marionettes, What Passion!*). Play. Published 1919. Produced Milan, Teatro Manzoni, Mar. 4, 1918.
4. *Per fare l'alba* (*Daybreak*). Play. Produced Rome, Teatro Argentina, Feb. 14, 1919.
5. *La bella addormentata* (*The Sleeping Beauty*). Play. Produced Milan, Teatro Olimpia, July, 1919.
6. *Primavera* (*Spring*). Play. Produced Milan, Teatro Olimpia, July, 1920.
7. *L'ospite desiderato* (*The Desired Guest*). Play. Published 1921. Produced Milan, Teatro Olimpia, April, 1921.
8. *La roccia e i monumenti* (*Stone and Monuments*). Play. Published 1923. Produced Milan, Teatro Olimpia, March, 1923.
9. *Amara* (*Bitter*). Play. Produced Modena, Teatro Storchi, May 29, 1923.
10. *I peccati di gioventù* (*The Sins of Youth*). Play. Published 1930. Produced Milan, Teatro Manzoni, June, 1923.
11. *La danza su di un piede* (*Dance on One Foot*). Play. Published 1924. Produced Milan, Teatro Manzoni, Nov. 23, 1923.
12. *L'avventura terrestre* (*The Terrestrial Adventure*). Play. Produced Milan, Teatro Manzoni, Apr. 11, 1924.
13. *Una cosa di carne* (*A Thing of Flesh*). Play. Published 1925. Produced Buenos Aires, Teatro Cervantes, Oct. 18, 1924.
14. *Canicola* (*Dog Days*). Play. Published 1925. Produced Rome, Teatro di Villa Ferrari, Mar. 20, 1925.
15. *L'illusione dei giorni e delle notti* (*The Illusion of Days and Nights*). Play. Published 1936. Produced Milan, Teatro del Convegno, Apr. 7, 1925.
16. *Il fiore necessario* (*The Necessary Flower*). Play. Published 1958. Produced Rome, Teatro degli Indipendenti, 1925.
17. *Il delirio dell'oste Bassà* (*The Delirium of the Innkeeper Bassà*). Play. Produced Rome, Teatro Argentina, Nov. 10, 1925.
18. *La scala** (*The Staircase*). Play. Published 1936. Produced Milan, Teatro Olimpia, November, 1925.
19. *Le esperienze di Giovanni Arce filosofo* (*The Experiences of the Philosopher Giovanni Arce*). Play. Published 1930. Produced Milan, Teatro Olimpia, 1926.
20. *Febbre* (*Fever*). Play. Produced Venice, Teatro Goldoni, May, 1926.
21. *Tra vestiti che ballano* (*Among Clothes that Dance*). Play, 3 acts. Published 1927. Produced Milan, Teatro Olimpia, Dec. 3, 1926.
22. *La madonnina del Belvento* (*The Little Madonna of Belvento*). Play. Published 1936. Produced Milan, Teatro Filodrammatici, Feb. 10, 1928.
23. *La Signora Falkestein* (*Mrs. Falkestein*). Play. Published 1931. Produced Milan, Teatro Olimpia, 1929.

24. *La fidanzata dell'albero verde* (*The Sweetheart of the Green Tree*). Play, 1 act. Published 1936.
25. *Per l'arte bisogna soffrire* (*One Must Suffer for Art*). Play. Produced Milan, Teatro Odeon, Dec. 16, 1936.
26. *I fiori del cielo* (*The Flowers of Heaven*). Play. Produced Florence, Teatro Verdi, Oct. 20, 1939.
27. *L'ammiraglio degli oceani e delle anime* (*The Admiral of the Oceans and of the Spirits*). Play, 1 act. Produced Rome, Teatro delle Arti, February, 1940.
28. *Storiella di Montagna* (*The Little Story of the Mountain*). Play. Produced Rome, Teatro delle Arti, Feb. 17, 1940.
29. *L'uomo che ha avuto il successo* (*The Man Who Was Successful*). Play. Produced Rome, Teatro delle Arti, Feb. 17, 1940.
30. *Lo spirito della morte* (*The Spirit of Death*). Play. Produced Rome, Teatro delle Arti, Dec. 12, 1941.
31. *Finestre* (*Windows*). Play. Produced Palermo, Piccolo Teatro, Jan. 28, 1954.
32. *Il ratto di Proserpina* (*The Rape of Persephone*). Play. Published 1954. Produced 1954.

EDITIONS

The Staircase (*The Stairs*). Published in *Eight European Plays*, comp. and tr. by W. Katzin, New York, 1927; *Teatro (1911–1925)*, ed. by L. Ferrante, Bologna, 1962; *Teatro*, Rome, 1976.

CRITICISM

A. Tilgher, *Studi sul teatro contemporaneo*, Rome, 1923; L. MacClintock, *The Age of Pirandello*, Bloomington, 1951; L. Ferrante, *Rosso di San Secondo*, Bologna, 1959.

Rostand, Edmond (1868–1918)

French poet and dramatist. Edmond-Eugène Rostand was born in Marseille on April 1, 1868. His father was an economist and poet, a member of the Marseille Academy and the Institute de France. After attending schools in Marseille, Rostand was sent to Paris, where he studied literature, history, and philosophy at the Collège Stanislas. At this time he began writing for the marionette theatre, and his poems and essays appeared in the literary review *Mireille* as early as 1884. His first play, *The Red Glove* (*Le gant rouge*), written when he was twenty, was produced in 1888 at the Théâtre Cluny with little success. Two years later a volume of poetry, *The Idlers* (*Les musardises*), was published, and he married Rosemonde Gérard, the poet.

Rostand's first significant play was *The Romantics* (*Les romanesques*), sometimes called *The Fantasticks*, which

Edmond Rostand. [Walter Hampden Memorial Library at The Players, New York]

Jean Piat in a Comédie-Française production of *Cyrano de Bergerac.*[French Cultural Services]

symbolism of Maeterlinck and Claudel and the psychological plays of Georges de Porto-Riche. Along with Henri de Bornier and François Coppée, Rostand remained a neoromanticist.

The appeal of Rostand's plays is due to his dramatic sense, combined with his facility with verse forms. His use of traditional themes and forms familiar to French audiences of his day was welcomed as a reaction to the naturalistic currents being introduced. He first gained recognition with *The Romantics* (1894). This is a comedy of romantic intrigue centered on young lovers who seek adventure and romance. His next play, *The Faraway Princess (La princesse lointaine),* was presented the following year at the Théâtre de la Renaissance with Sarah Bernhardt. It is based on the story of the love of the troubadour Joffroy Rudel, Prince of Blaye, for the Countess of Tripoli, recounting his travels, the hardships endured in the Crusades in the year 1147, and his death just as he has reached his love. Rostand's treatment of this legend is suited to the romantic theme of courtly love. The rich imagery and fine cadence of the verses were much praised. *The Woman of Samaria (La samaritaine)* was presented in the spring of 1897 with Sarah Bernhardt. A drama in three parts, it retells the Biblical story of Jesus and the woman at the well and mingles the themes of sacred and profane love.

It is on *Cyrano de Bergerac,* written for Coquelin Aîné and presented in December, 1897, that Rostand's fame rests. This heroic comedy, inspired by the personality of the seventeenth-century author of *Comic History of the Stages of the Moon and the Sun,* seemed to contain all the elements that the public craved: heroic action, heroic characters, humor, wit, and exalted language. It reintro-

was produced at the Comédie-Française in 1894. Three years later *Cyrano de Bergerac* was hailed by both the public and the critics, who saw in it a revival of verse drama. This success was repeated by *L'Aiglon* (1900), a tragedy based on the life of Napoleon's son. Rostand's reputation and popularity were such that in 1901, when he was only thirty-three, he was elected to the Académie Française.

In poor health, Rostand then retired to the Basque country, where he wrote *Chantecler* (1910), an allegorical drama in which the characters are barnyard animals. His first play in ten years, it was poorly received and was more or less the swan song of postromantic verse drama. Rostand spent the years of World War I writing poetry and working on a drama, *The Last Night of Don Juan (La dernière nuit de Don Juan),* which was published posthumously in 1921. He died in Paris on December 2, 1918.

WORK

Rostand's work stands apart from the literary movements seeking to revitalize the French theatre at the turn of the twentieth century. He avoided the most vigorous of these movements, naturalism, as reflected in the work of Henry Becque and in the plays of foreign authors, notably Ibsen, who was introduced to the French public through the Théâtre Libre. He also stood clear of the

Walter Hampden in the title role of *Cyrano de Bergerac.* [Private collection]

Scene from *L'Aiglon*, presented at the Paris Opéra, with music by Arthur Honegger and Jacques Ibert. [French Cultural Services]

Sarah Bernhardt in 1900 as the ill-fated Duke of Reichstadt in *L'Aiglon.* [Private collection]

duced the Alexandrine verse to the stage at a time when its success was guaranteed by public nostalgia for the dead romantic era. The hero, whose nose is so ludicrous that he feels he cannot openly aspire to court Roxane, writes her letters and love poems in Christian's name and is content to share vicariously in the love these letters inspire.

L'Aiglon (1900) is the story of the ill-fated Duke of Reichstadt, son of Napoleon I. The unhappy young duke, in his agonized self-searching, has often been compared to Hamlet. The part was played by Sarah Bernhardt and became one of her most famous roles. Ten years later, Rostand presented *Chantecler* (1910). This allegorical verse comedy moved closer to the symbolist movement and was a departure from Rostand's earlier dramas. It was not a success on the stage, but it is appreciated by many who believe it is more suitable for reading. Rostand's last play, *The Last Night of Don Juan,* was produced posthumously in 1922.

The Romantics (*Les romanesques,* 1894). Romantic comedy in which Bergamin, father of Percinet, and his neighbor Pasquinot, father of Sylvette, pretend to be enemies because they know that romance thrives on obstacles and therefore hope their children will fall in love. Their plan succeeds and is capped when a hired abductor, Straforel, pretends to be routed by Percinet's sword. The fathers are overjoyed but soon fall to quarreling in earnest. Finally, in a moment of pique, they tell Sylvette the truth; she tells Percinet. Both pretend not to care. But when Straforel returns for his pay and deftly diverts Percinet's attack, the boy angrily goes off to seek real adventure. Hoping to obtain his money, which the fathers now refuse to pay, Straforel poses as a marquis, steals into Sylvette's garden, and terrifies her with feverish plans for a real abduction. Disillusioned by his adventure seeking, Percinet returns soon after, and the lovers are reunited, for their feelings are genuine despite the plot that brought them together.

Cyrano de Bergerac (1897). Romantic verse drama in which Cyrano, a daring soldier and poet, hides his deep love for his beautiful cousin Roxane, because he believes his grotesquely large nose renders him ludicrous as a suitor. Discovering Roxane's attraction to Christian, his handsome comrade in the Gascon Guards, Cyrano gallantly fosters their romance by writing love letters in Christian's name. One night, hidden beneath Roxane's balcony and pretending to be Christian, he woos and wins Roxane for the latter. When the Guards' commanding officer De Guiche discovers that Roxane, with whom he is infatuated, is married to Christian, he orders the unit off to fight against the Spaniards. During the subsequent siege of Arras, Cyrano crosses Spanish lines each night to send letters to Roxane in Christian's name. When she makes an impromptu visit to the battlefield, Christian, hearing her speak of the letters, realizes that it is not his own good looks but Cyrano's letters that have won Roxane. He loyally urges his friend to speak, but before Cyrano can confess authorship of the letters, Christian is killed.

To preserve Roxane's romantic memories, Cyrano decides to conceal the truth. Grieving, Roxane retires to a convent, and Cyrano returns to Paris to fight with his pen his "ancient enemies—Falsehood . . . . Prejudice . . . Compromise . . . Cowardice. . . ." His outspoken idealism wins him numerous enemies, but he is sustained by the love of his old friends and the affection of Roxane, whom he visits weekly. Wounded in a treacherous attack, Cyrano pays a last visit to Roxane. He asks if he may read Christian's last letter. As he reads it aloud in the growing darkness, Roxane realizes that the voice under her balcony that night many years ago was Cyrano's as was the soul behind "Christian's" letters. As Cyrano dies, she tells him of her love.

L'Aiglon (1900). Romantic tragedy in verse in which Rostand advanced the factors of heredity and environment as explanations for the unsuccessful life of the Duke of Reichstadt, Napoleon's son. Confined at the Austrian court by Metternich, the young duke grows to manhood dreaming of his father's accomplishments and the day when he will regain his lost throne. Sympathizers effect his escape, and on the way to France, L'Aiglon spends a night on the battlefield of Wagram, where Napoleon had fought. As the ghosts of the dead rise and the voices of past wars echo, the young man realizes that his life must be a sacrifice, or a "ransom to the past." He is recaptured and forced to return to Vienna. Eventually he dies at the Hapsburg court calling out his father's name—"a harp's sweet note heard after martial music."

Chantecler (1910). Allegorical verse comedy. Chantecler, a barnyard cock, lives joyously in his little valley, ruling his domain. He secretly believes that his crowing makes the sun rise, and he is both humbled and elevated by his role. He keeps his secret until a golden hen Pheasant enters his life; falling in love with her, he reveals that he is "the Voice of Earth." But the Night Birds, envying him, bring to the Guinea Pig's Monday at home a variety of exotic cocks, including a fighting cock, in the hope of humbling Chantecler. Disillusioned by his friend's attempts to discredit him, he flees with his Pheasant to the forest. There, distracted by the Nightingale's song, he watches as the sun rises without his call. Nonetheless, Chantecler decides to return to the barnyard and resume his daily crowing, for "all worthy life is effort and a dream."

[JOSEPH E. GARREAU]

PLAYS

Unless otherwise noted, the plays were first performed in Paris.
1. *Le gant rouge* (The Red Glove). Farce, 1 act. Published 1888. Produced Théâtre Cluny, Aug. 24, 1888.
2. *Les deux pierrots, ou Le souper blanc** (The Two Pierrots, or The White Supper). Play. Published 1891.
3. *Les romanesques** (The Romantics; The Fantasticks). Comedy, 3 acts; verse. Produced Comédie-Française, May 21, 1894.
4. *La princesse lointaine** (The Faraway Princess). Comedy, 4 acts; verse. Produced Théâtre de la Renaissance, Apr. 5, 1895.
5. *La samaritaine** (The Woman of Samaria). Gospel, 3 parts; verse. Published 1898. Produced Théâtre de la Renaissance, Apr. 14, 1897.
6. *Cyrano de Bergerac**. Heroic comedy, 5 acts; verse. Published 1898. Produced Théâtre de la Porte-Saint-Martin, Dec. 28, 1897.
7. *L'Aiglon**. Drama, 6 acts; verse. Published 1900. Produced Théâtre Sarah-Bernhardt, Mar. 15, 1900.
8. *Chantecler**. Play, 4 acts; verse. Published 1910. Produced Théâtre de la Porte-Saint-Martin, Feb. 7, 1910.
9. *La dernière nuit de Don Juan** (The Last Night of Don Juan). Dramatic poem, prologue and 2 parts; verse. Published 1921. Produced 1922.

EDITIONS

Collections
Oeuvres complètes, 7 vols., Paris, 1910–1911; *Plays,* tr. by H. D. Norman, 2 vols., New York, 1921.
Individual Plays
Cyrano de Bergerac. Published in *The Play: A Critical Anthology*, ed. by E. R. Bentley and tr. by H. Wolfe, New York, 1951.
The Last Night of Don Juan. Published in *Poetic Drama*, ed. by A. Kreymborg and tr. by T. Riggs, New York, 1941.
The Romantics. Published in *The Genius of the French Theater*, ed. by A. Bermel and tr. by B. Clark, New York, 1961.

CRITICISM

G. Haraszti, *Edmond Rostand*, Paris, 1913; J. Suberville, *Le théâtre d'Edmond Rostand: Étude critique*, Paris, 1919; *id.*, *Edmond Rostand*, Paris, 1921; A. Lautier and F. Keller, *Edmond Rostand: Son oeuvre*, Paris, 1924; P. Faure, *Vingt ans d'intimité avec Edmond Rostand*, Paris, 1928; J. W. Grieve, *L'oeuvre dramatique d'Edmond Rostand*, Paris, 1931; E. Katz, *L'esprit français dans le théâtre d'Edmond Rostand*, Toulouse, 1934; R. Rostand, *Edmond Rostand*, Paris, 1935.

Rotimi, Ola (1938–)

Nigerian playwright. Born of Yoruba and Ljaw parents, Emmanuel Gladstone Olawole Rotimi was educated at the Methodist Boys High School in Lagos. He received a bachelor degree in theatre arts from Boston University in

1963 and a master of fine arts degree from Yale in 1965. His early play *To Stir the God of Iron* was produced at Boston University in 1963, and a more mature work *Our Husband Has Gone Mad Again* was chosen as the major Yale play of the year in 1965.

Rotimi returned to Nigeria in 1966 to a research fellowship at the University of Ife. His *The Gods Are Not to Blame* (1969), based on *Oedipus Rex*, was first presented at the Ori-Olokun Centre in Ife and has had many subsequent productions, including one (in 1978) sponsored by the Drum Arts Centre, London, directed by the author. Since 1977 he has been head of the Creative Arts Centre and arts director at the University of Port Harcourt. *Kurunmi* (1969) is an epic of the nineteenth-century Ijaiye war. *Ovonramwen Nogbaisi* (1971) is also a historical play, dealing with the conflict leading to the destruction of Benin. Of his latest play, *If*, Rotimi says, "It lets ordinary Nigerians in a multi-tenancy building run through the giddy gauntlet of survival imposed by the socio-political truths of present-day Nigeria."

Rotimi acknowledges a number of influences on his work: including family involvement in amateur productions of plays ranging from Shakespeare to O'Neill; the indigenous cultural elements in the theatre of John Pepper Clark and Wole Soyinka; and the linguistic forms of the Yoruba traveling theatre companies. He admits to a certain disassociation from his Nigerian background and lack of fluency in the vernacular.

Rotimi's style is characteristically bold, theatrical, and emotional. Some critics accuse him of melodramatic triteness and superficiality on political and cultural matters. But no one challenges his ability to hold and move an audience or denies the great contribution he has made to the Nigerian theatre through his robust productions and extensive touring. He alone of the Nigerian dramatists writing in English has achieved the kind of rapport with Nigerian audiences enjoyed by the vernacular touring companies.

GEOFFREY AXWORTHY

Rotrou, Jean de (1609–1650)

French dramatist. He was born on August 19 or 20, 1609, in Dreux, Normandy, into an influential local family. While still in his teens, he went to Paris to study and soon began to write plays. By 1628 two of his plays had been staged by the company at the Théâtre de l'Hôtel de Bourgogne, the most important theatre in Paris, where he is thought to have succeeded Alexandre Hardy as official dramatist. His success was so great that in 1634 he was selected as one of the Richelieu group, a committee of five dramatists—including Pierre Corneille, François de Boisrobert, Guillaume Colletet, and Claude de L'Estoile—organized by Cardinal Richelieu to collaborate on new plays. *See* CORNEILLE, PIERRE.

Although he enjoyed the patronage of several noblemen, Rotrou lived by his pen. By the age of twenty-five he had written thirty plays. In 1639 he bought the post of *lieutenant particulier au baillage* in Dreux; the following year he was married. Having gained financial security, Rotrou spent the last few years of his life with his wife

and six children in his native town, where he continued to write while holding office in the town government. Refusing to leave Dreux during an outbreak of the plague in 1650, he died there on June 28, 1650.

WORK

Next to Corneille, Rotrou is undoubtedly the finest French dramatist of the first half of the seventeenth century. Most of his early work, based on Spanish, classical, or Italian material, shows signs of haste despite flashes of dramatic effectiveness and some fine poetry. After 1639 he devoted more care to his work, eventually producing his three best-known plays: *The True St. Genesius* (*Le véritable Saint Genest*, 1646/47), his most popular work, containing his finest poetry; *Wenceslaus* (*Venceslas*, 1647?), a vigorous "dark" tragicomedy of sibling rivalry; and *Chosroes* (*Cosroès*, 1647), a powerful tragedy of blood. Only slightly inferior to these are the comedies *The Doubles* (*Les sosies*, 1636/37), based on the Amphitryon legend, and *The Sister* (*La soeur*, 1645?); and the tragicomedies *Laura Persecuted* (*Laure persécutée*, 1637?) and *Don Bernardo of Cabrera* (*Dom Bernardo de Cabrère*, ca. 1646). His other plays include *Lost Opportunities* (*Les occasions perdues*, 1633); *The Dying Hercules* (*Hercule mourant*, 1634); *Antigone* (1636/37); and *The Ring of Forgetfulness* (*La bague de l'oubli*, 1629?), the first French play to be based on a Spanish source, a precedent soon to be followed in Corneille's *The Cid* and *The Liar* and in several of Molière's comedies. *See* MOLIÈRE. *See also* TRAGEDY OF BLOOD; TRAGICOMEDY in glossary.

The True St. Genesius (*Le véritable Saint Genest*, 1646/47). Tragedy in which the emperor Diocletian, in celebration of his daughter's marriage, orders the actor Genesius to prepare a play on the martyrdom of a Christian. Genesius agrees, and in the process of writing and rehearsing the play becomes converted to Christianity. At the performance Genesius sees flames in the sky and is miraculously baptized. Returning to the stage, he proclaims his conversion. Diocletian offers to spare him from punishment if he recants, but Genesius clings to his faith and becomes a martyr.

Wenceslaus (*Venceslas*, 1647?). Tragicomedy about the two sons of King Wenceslaus of Poland—Ladislas, the unruly elder son, and Alexander, a man of excellent qualities—who both love the duchess Cassandra. She loves Alexander, but they conceal their love with the help of the King's minister Frederick, who, although in love with Theodora, the King's daughter, pretends to be Cassandra's lover. In a fit of jealousy, Ladislas secretly enters Cassandra's palace and kills her lover, whom he discovers to be Alexander, his brother. Condemned to death by his father, Ladislas is about to be executed when Theodora and Cassandra plead for his life. Since Ladislas can be saved only if he is placed above the law, King Wenceslaus abdicates in his favor. Theodora marries Frederick, and Ladislas proposes to Cassandra.

Chosroes (*Cosroès*, 1647). Tragedy of Chosroes (Khosrau) II, King of Persia, who is burdened with guilt for the murder of his father. Strong-willed Queen Sira persuades him to abdicate in favor of their son Mardesanes, over the vigorous protests of the legitimate heir, Siroes (Kavadh), Chosroes's son by a previous marriage. Mardesanes is named King and orders the arrest of Siroes, who manages to escape. He soon returns to Persia, however, with a large force and succeeds in capturing Sira but not Chosroes and Mardesanes, who flee. Believing Sira to be the mother of Narsea, the girl he loves, Siroes decides to spare her life. Later, learning that Sira is not Narsea's mother, he orders Sira poisoned. Mardesanes and Chosroes commit suicide.

[JOSEPH E. GARREAU]

PLAYS

1. *L'hypocondriaque (The Hypochondriac)*. Tragicomedy. Written 1628. Published 1635. Produced ca. 1628.

2. (Adaptation). *La bague de l'oubli (The Ring of Forgetfulness)*. Comedy. Written 1629. Published 1635. Produced 1629? Based on Lope de Vega's *La sortija del olvido*.

3. (Adaptation). *Les Ménechmes (The Menaechmi)*. Comedy. Written 1630/31. Published 1636. Produced 1630/31. Based on Plautus's *Menaechmi*.

4. *Céliane*. Tragicomedy. Written 1631/32. Published 1637. Produced ca. 1631/32.

5. (Adaptation). *Diane*. Comedy. Written 1632/33. Published 1635. Produced 1633. Based on Lope de Vega's *La villana de Getafe*.

6. (Adaptation). *La pèlerine amoureuse (The Amorous Pilgrim)*. Play. Written 1632/33. Published 1637. Produced 1633? Based on Girolamo Bargagli's *La pellegrina*.

7. *La filandre (The Thread)*. Comedy. Written 1633. Published 1637. Produced 1633.

8. (Adaptation). *Les occasions perdues (Lost Opportunities)*. Tragicomedy. Written 1633. Published 1635. Produced 1633. Based on Lope de Vega's *La ocasión perdida*.

9. *Célimène*. Comedy. Written 1633. Published 1636. Produced 1633.

10. (Adaptation). *L'heureuse constance (Happy Constancy)*. Tragicomedy. Written 1633. Published 1636. Produced ca. 1633. Based on Lope de Vega's *El poder vencido* and *Mirad a quien alabáis*.

11. *Amélie*. Tragicomedy. Written ca. 1633. Published 1637. Produced ca. 1633.

12. (Adaptation). *Cléagénor et Doristée*. Tragicomedy. Written 1634. Published 1634. Produced 1634. Based on Charles Sorel's novel *Histoire amoureuse de Cléagénor et de Doristée*.

13. (Adaptation). *Hercule mourant (The Dying Hercules)*. Tragicomedy. Written 1634. Published 1636. Produced 1634. Based on Seneca's *Hercules oetaeus*.

14. *L'heureux naufrage (The Happy Shipwreck)*. Play. Written 1634. Published 1637. Produced 1634?

15. *L'innocente infidélité (Innocent Infidelity)*. Tragicomedy. Written 1634/35. Produced 1634/35.

16. *Crisante*. Tragedy. Written 1635. Published 1640. Produced 1635?

17. *Florimonde*. Comedy. Written 1635. Published 1654. Produced ca. 1635/36.

18. *Clorinde*. Comedy. Written 1635. Published 1637. Produced 1635.

19. *La belle Alphrède*. Comedy. Written 1636. Published 1639. Produced 1636?

20. (Adaptation). *Agésilan de Colchos*. Tragicomedy. Written 1636. Published 1637. Produced 1636. Based on the romance *Amadís de Gaula*.

21. (Adaptation). *Les deux pucelles (The Two Maidens)*. Comedy. Written 1636. Published 1639. Produced 1636? Based on Cervantes' *Las dos doncellas*.

22. (Adaptation). *Les Sosies (The Doubles)*. Play. Written 1636. Published 1638. Produced 1636/37. Based on Plautus's *Amphitryon*.

23. *Antigone*. Tragedy. Written ca. 1636/37. Published 1639. Produced 1636/37.

24. (Adaptation). *Laure persécutée (Laura Persecuted)*. Play. Written 1637? Published 1639. Produced 1637? Based on Lope de Vega's *Laura perseguida*.

25. (Adaptation). *Les captifs (The Captives)*. Comedy. Written 1638. Published 1639. Produced 1638? Based on Plautus's *Captivi*.

26. (Adaptation). *Iphigénie (Iphigenia)*. Tragedy. Written 1639/40. Published 1641. Produced 1640? Based on Euripides's *Iphigenia ē en Auludi*.

27. (Adaptation). *Clarice*. Play. Written 1641. Published 1644. Produced 1641. Based on Sforza Oddi's *L'erofilomachia*.

28. (Adaptation). *Bélisaire (Belisarius)*. Play. Written ca. 1642/43. Published 1644. Produced ca. 1642/43. Based on Antonio Mira de Amescua's *El ejemplo mayor de la desdicha* (ca. 1625).

29. *Célie*. Tragicomedy. Written ca. 1644. Published 1646. Produced ca. 1644/45. Based on Giambattista Della Porta's *I due fratelli rivali*.

30. (Adaptation). *La soeur (The Sister)*. Comedy. Written ca. 1645. Published 1647. Produced 1645? Based on Della Porta's *La sorella*.

31. (Adaptation). *Le véritable Saint Genest* (The True St. Genesius)*. Tragedy. Written ca. 1646. Published 1647. Produced 1646/47. Based on Lope de Vega's *Lo fingido verdadero*.

32. *Dom Bernard de Cabrère (Don Bernardo de Cabrera)*. Tragicomedy. Written ca. 1646. Published 1647. Produced ca. 1646. Based on the anonymous *Prospera fortuna de Don Bernardo de Cabrera*.

33. (Adaptation). *Venceslas* (Wenceslaus)*. Tragicomedy. Written ca. 1647. Published 1648. Produced 1647? Based on Francisco de Rojas Zorrilla's *No hay ser padre siendo rey*.

34. (Adaptation). *Cosroès* (Chosroes)*. Tragedy. Written 1647. Published 1648. Produced 1647. Based on Fr. Cellot's Latin school drama *Chosroës*.

35. (Adaptation). *Dom Lope de Cardone (Don Lope de Cardona)*. Tragicomedy. Written 1650. Published 1652. Produced 1651. Based on Lope de Vega's play of the same name.

EDITIONS

Collections
Oeuvres complètes, ed. by E.-E. Viollet-le-Duc, 5 vols., Paris, 1820; *Théâtre choisi*, ed. by F. Hémon, new ed., Paris, 1928.
Individual Plays
Chosroes. Published in *The Chief Rivals of Corneille and Racine*, ed. and tr. by L. Lockert, Nashville, 1956.
Wenceslaus. Published in *The Chief Rivals of Corneille and Racine*, ed. and tr. by L. Lockert, Nashville, 1956.

CRITICISM

J. Jarry, *Essai sur les oeuvres dramatiques de Jean Rotrou*, Paris, 1868; L. Person, *Histoire du véritable Saint-Genest de Rotrou*, Paris, 1882; H. Chardon, *La vie de Rotrou mieux connue*, Paris, 1884.

Roussin, André (1911–)

French actor and playwright. He is one of the most successful writers of popular melodramatic plays in the erotic boulevard tradition. Although his themes are typically conventional, his virtuosity of stagecraft and brilliant dialogue camouflage this flaw.

After having studied law, Roussin first turned to journalism and then became a comic actor in the troupe Rideau Gris of Louis Ducreux. He became known as a dramatist with *Am-Stram-Gram* (1941), which was followed by *Just a Big Girl* (*Une grande fille toute simple*, 1942); *Jean-Baptiste le mal aimé* (1944), inspired by Pierre

André Roussin.
[French Cultural Services]

Fernand Gravey and Suzanne Flon in *La petite hutte*. [French Cultural Services]

Brisson's *Molière* (1943); and *The Holy Family* (*La sainte famille*, 1946). His first great success came with *The Little Hut* (*La petite hutte*, 1947), a three-act comedy about a shipwrecked couple and lover on a tropical island. The sharing of the wife results in a growing jealousy on the part of the lover while the husband becomes ever more carefree.

Among Roussin's other plays are *Nina* (1949), about a husband who comes to shoot his wife's lover but catches a cold and stays on as a patient, developing a friendship with the lover and joining forces with him against the common enemy, the wife-mistress; *Ostrich Eggs* (*Les oeufs de l'autruche*, 1949); *Bobosse* (1950); *The Hand of Caesar* (*La main de César*, 1951); *When the Child Appears* (*Lorsque l'enfant paraît*, 1952), a situation comedy in which every female member of a bourgeois household, including the maid, finds herself embarrassingly pregnant; *Helene, or The Joy of Living* (*Hélène, ou La joie de vivre*, 1952), written in collaboration with Madeleine Gray, an adaptation of John Erskine's novel *The Private Life of Helen of Troy* (1925) and a completely altered version of the famous legend presented through the eyes of the palace doorkeeper; *The Husband, the Wife, and Death* (*Le mari, la femme et la mort*, 1954); *Mad Love, or The First Surprise* (*L'amour fou, ou La première surprise*, 1955); *Mamma* (*La Mamma*, 1957), an adaptation of Vitaliano Brancati's *Handsome Antonio* (*Il bell'Antonio*; 1949, tr. 1978), a comedy of male impotence; *The Glorious Women* (*Les glorieuses*, 1960), written in Alexandrine verse, about a woman exploiting her husband's glory; *The Fibber* (*La coquine*), adapted from the play *The Liar* (*La bugiarda*, 1956), by Diego Fabbri; *The Seer* (*La voyante*, 1963); *Love Without End* (*Un amour qui ne finit pas*, 1963), about a faithless husband who in search of undying love enters into a platonic relationship with a reluctant girl; *The Lo-*

comotive (*La locomotive*, 1967), about a sentimental Russian refugee who continues to live in the past; *One Never Knows . . .* (*On ne sait jamais . . .*, 1969); *The Slap* (*La claque*, 1972); *April Night* (*Nuit d'avril*, 1972); and *The Kidnapped Pope* (*Le pape kidnappé*, 1975), adapted from Béthencourt. His reflections on his comedies are expressed in *A Reasonable Satisfaction* (*Un contentement raisonnable*, 1965), his childhood memories are published in *The Box of Crayons* (*La boîte à couleurs*, 1974), and *The Red Curtain* (*Le rideau rouge*, 1982) tells of his contacts with certain famous actors. In 1973 he was elected to the Académie Française. *See* Brancati, Vitaliano; Fabbri, Diego.

After an absence from the theatre of several years, Roussin was again represented on the Paris stage in 1981 when he offered *Life Is Too Short* (*La vie est trop courte*), a comedy about a still attractive middle-aged woman who finds herself suffering from the "empty nest syndrome" when her children grow up and leave home.

The Little Hut (*La petite hutte*, 1947). Philippe, his wife Suzanne, and Henri, his best friend, are shipwrecked on a tropical island. Exiled to a small hut, the sexually deprived bachelor confesses to Philippe that he has been Suzanne's lover and argues that "morality" requires that she live with each of them in alternate weeks. Philippe accepts this proposal and finds that competition for Suzanne's affections rejuvenates his enthusiasm. Jealous, Henri now suggests that both men live celibate lives and that Suzanne inhabit the small hut. A black appears, binds up the men, and makes Suzanne his mistress. Willing enough as long as she believes the black to be a native king, Suzanne becomes indignant when she discovers that he is really a shipwrecked crew member. The men overwhelm the black, who agrees to be their cook and servant if they will free him. When a ship appears, Henri and Suzanne prepare for their return to Paris by convincing Philippe that they were never really lovers.

La coquine. [French Cultural Services]

The black accepts a position as cook in Philippe's Paris house. Produced Paris, Théâtre des Nouveautés, December 19, 1947; reviewed several times and produced in a new version, Théâtre des Nouveautés, 1979.

[JOSEPH E. GARREAU]

Rovetta, Gerolamo (1851–1910)

Italian novelist and playwright. He was notable for his extraordinary skill in characterizing the hypocrites and corrupt surroundings of his social milieu. He was extremely pessimistic in his view of life, even in his comedies. A major influence upon his work was Balzac, whose example encouraged Rovetta to depict an entire human comedy in his works and to reveal the often sordid economic factors in human affairs which determine social conduct. *In the City of Rome* (*Alla città di Roma*, 1888) concerns a husband's tacit acceptance of his wife's adultery in order to avoid provoking her into opening a competing millinery shop across the street from his. *Dorina's Trilogy* (*La trilogia di Dorina*, 1889) is the ironic story of a poor girl's rise to fame as an entertainer and the concomitant vagaries of her relations with her would-be suitors. In *The Barbarò Family* (*I Barbarò*, 1890), Rovetta challenged the moral hypocrisy of a society that considered money an indication of virtue. *The Dishonest Ones* (*I disonesti*, 1892) is the drama of a man victimized by the financial situation caused by his wife's adultery. In the tragedy *Reality* (*La realtà*, 1895), the protagonist is forced to kill himself to avoid the repercussions of his wife's perfidy. *Romanticism* (*Romanticismo*, 1901) portrays the Italian people's aspirations to unification and freedom in the mid-nineteenth century. *An Excellent Father* (*Papà eccellènza*, 1907) depicts an honest government official whose daughter has involved him in a scandal from which he cannot emerge without the censure of society. Rovetta committed suicide, remaining faithful to his pessimistic view of life to the end.

The Dishonest Ones (*I disonesti*, 1892). Drama concerning the corrupt values of a bourgeois society in which Carlo Moretti, a modest bank clerk, does not notice that his wife Elisa keeps their home furnished in a manner surpassing his means. Following the death of Sigismund, president of the bank, his wife receives a sudden deluge of bills. It seems that during a recent lengthy illness of Moretti, his wife had been drawn into an illicit affair by Sigismund. By the time she wished to break with Sigismund, she had received too much of his largesse. Moretti is now afraid that a sudden drop in their living standard will cause him and Elisa to lose face. When De Fornaris, a bank employee, stands accused of embezzlement and his wife gives Moretti an amount to cover the theft, he misappropriates that sum for his own use, manipulating the books so that, with his testimony, De Fornaris is judged guilty. Terrified at the moral abyss into which he has sunk, Moretti flees, leaving wife and family in the hope that somehow, established in another city, he may make amends.

An Excellent Father (*Papà eccellènza*, 1907). Drama of Pietro Mattei, an honest government minister who is forced to resign when he is accused of having been the beneficiary of some privileged information and of having used this to invest profitably in the stock market. Actually, it is Mattei's daughter who has connived with her lover to profit from the information that she has accidentally acquired. Nevertheless, Mattei is inexorably condemned by society. The daughter, originally ignorant of her wrongdoing, suffers pangs of remorse when she realizes she has erred, but she does not have the moral strength to reveal the truth when she is asked why her father has resigned. For this Mattei does not forgive her, and although she dismisses her lover, it is too late; her father dies of a broken heart.

[PETER BONDANELLA]

EDITIONS

Romanticismo, Milan, 1903.

CRITICISM

G. Pullini, *Teatro italiano fra due secoli*, Florence, 1958; C. Reimold, " 'A Passing Smile': On Some Plays of Rovetta," *Italica* 51 (1974), 215–235.

Rowe, Nicholas (1674–1718)

English poet, editor, and dramatist. Rowe was born in Little Barford, Bedfordshire, in 1674. The oldest son of a successful London barrister, he was educated at Westminster School, became a King's scholar at the age of fifteen, and in 1691 entered the Middle Temple to study law. He completed his studies there and was called to the bar, but never practiced. Instead, he became a dramatist, living on the independent fortune willed him by his father.

His first work, *The Ambitious Step-Mother* (1700), enjoyed a small success. It was followed by *Tamerlane* (1701) and the highly successful *The Fair Penitent* (1703). Rowe's one attempt at farce, *The Biter* (1704), failed. He wrote only four more plays, the most notable of which is *The Tragedy of Jane Shore* (1714). Among Rowe's important literary accomplishments was the publication of a six-volume edition of Shakespeare (he is known as the first modern editor of Shakespeare), including a biography, in 1709, followed by the first English translation of Lucan's *Pharsalia*, published posthumously. *See* SHAKESPEARE, WILLIAM.

Nicholas Rowe. [National Portrait Gallery, London]

An ardent supporter of the Whigs, Rowe was appointed to lucrative posts. From 1709 to 1711 he was Undersecretary of State for Scotland, and in 1715 George I named him Poet Laureate.

In 1698 he married Antonia Parsons, who died in 1706 after bearing a son. His second wife, Anne Devenish, whom he married in 1717, had one daughter. Rowe died on December 6, 1718, and was buried in Westminster Abbey.

WORK

Rowe was the chief exponent of the tragic style that had emerged in the works of Thomas Otway. In Rowe's plays tragedy depends on pathos rather than awe and terror. Central interest is shifted from a male character to a female; indeed, his dramas are often characterized as "she-tragedies." He was, in effect, the last tragedian in whom the Elizabethan spirit was still alive. Though his blank verse lacks the power of his greater predecessors, there are occasional resplendent Shakespearean echoes and touches of heroic grandeur. *See* OTWAY, THOMAS.

Rowe began his career in the "heroic" tradition: the Otway-inspired drama *The Ambitious Step-Mother* (1700) concerns a wicked stepmother, Artemisa, who attempts to gain the throne of Persia for her son instead of accepting its inheritance by Artaxerxes, the rightful heir. His second play, *Tamerlane* (1701), draws a thinly concealed political parallel: the ennobled Scythian warlord represents William III, and Tamerlane's enemy Bajazet is thought to symbolize Louis XIV. *See* HEROIC PLAY in glossary.

It was not long before Rowe developed the "domestic" style for which he is principally remembered. The moral drama *The Fair Penitent* (1703) is notable on several counts: it reduced tragedy from the austerity of the royal court to "a melancholy tale of private woes," eliciting tearful responses rather than deep tragic emotions; it spoke out for women's rights; and it presented the character of a heartless yet lovable libertine, the lighthearted yet despicable Lothario.

Still later, Rowe turned to history. *The Tragedy of Jane Shore* (1714) is set against the background of Richard III's reign; and *The Tragedy of Lady Jane Gray* (1715), his most ably constructed play, concentrates on the pitiful situation of the heroine in a period of dynastic struggles.

The Fair Penitent (1703). Blank-verse tragedy about Calista, a Genoese maiden who, although in love with Lothario, has been given in marriage to young Lord Altamont by her father. On their wedding night, Altamont discovers the lovers together and kills Lothario in a duel. Then he dispatches Calista, who had been condemned by her father and who mourns the fate of young girls subject to their fathers' discipline and of older women subject to their husbands' whims. Brought to justice for his actions, Altamont is acquitted, only to be killed by one of Lothario's friends.

The Tragedy of Jane Shore (1714). Blank-verse tragedy with strong echoes of Shakespeare's *Richard III*. During her pathetic final days, Jane Shore, former mistress of the recently deceased Edward IV, is denounced to the Duke of Gloucester (soon to be Richard III) by Lady Alicia, who is jealous of the attentions that her lover Lord Hastings has showered on Jane. Having rebuffed Hastings, Jane now refuses to use her influence to persuade him to support Gloucester in his attempt to gain the throne, and the two are punished. Hastings is ordered killed, and Jane is condemned to do public penance; should anyone offer her food or shelter, he too shall be killed. Finally her husband, who had been in her service disguised as Dumont, comes to her aid. He is arrested, but not before he has forgiven his wife as she dies, repentant, in his arms.

PLAYS

All were first performed in London.

1. *The Ambitious Step-Mother*. Tragedy, 5 acts; verse. Published 1701. Produced Lincoln's Inn Fields Theatre, ca. December, 1700.
2. *Tamerlane*. Tragedy, 5 acts; verse. Published 1701. Produced Lincoln's Inn Fields Theatre, ca. December, 1701.
3. *The Fair Penitent*. Tragedy, 5 acts; verse. Published 1703. Produced Lincoln's Inn Fields Theatre, ca. May, 1703.
4. *The Biter*. Farce, 3 acts; prose. Published 1705. Produced Lincoln's Inn Fields, ca. December 1704.
5. *Ulysses*. Tragedy, 5 acts; verse. Published 1706. Produced Haymarket Theatre, Nov. 23, 1705.
6. *The Royal Convert*. Tragedy, 5 acts; verse. Published 1708. Produced Haymarket Theatre, Nov. 25, 1707.
7. *The Tragedy of Jane Shore*. Tragedy, 5 acts; verse. Published 1714. Produced Drury Lane Theatre, Feb. 2, 1714.
8. *The Tragedy of the Lady Jane Gray*. Tragedy, 5 acts; verse. Published 1715. Produced Drury Lane Theatre, Apr. 20, 1715.

EDITIONS

Collections
Works, 2 vols., London, 1766; *Three Plays*, ed. by J. R. Sutherland, London, 1929.
Individual Plays
The Fair Penitent. Published in *Plays of the Restoration and Eighteenth Century*, ed. by D. MacMillan and H. M. Jones, New York, 1938.
The Tragedy of Jane Shore. Published in *Eighteenth-century Plays*, intro. by R. Quintana, New York, 1952.

CRITICISM

O. Intze, *Nicholas Rowe*, Leipzig, 1910.

Rowley, William   (?–before 1625)

English actor and dramatist. Very little is known about Rowley. Most of his work was done in collaboration with such famous dramatists as Middleton, Ford, Heywood, and Massinger. The extant plays attributed to Rowley alone are of little interest: *A Shoemaker a Gentleman* (ca. 1608), *A New Wonder, a Woman Never Vexed* (pub. 1632), *A Match at Midnight* (pub. 1633), and *The Birth of Merlin* (pub. 1662). *See* FORD, THOMAS; HEYWOOD, THOMAS; MASSINGER, PHILIP; MIDDLETON, THOMAS.

Royle, Edwin Milton   (1862–1942)

American actor, producer, and dramatist. His realistic Western-style play *The Squaw Man* (1905) became the first motion picture to be made in Hollywood. In the play, an Englishman goes to the American West and marries the Indian girl who saves his life. Royle's first play, the melodrama *Friends* (1892), depicts show people in their struggle for recognition and success. Among his other plays are *My Wife's Husbands* (1903), a farce revised into the musical comedy *Marrying Mary* (1906); *The Struggle Everlasting* (1907), a contemporary morality play; the melodrama *The Unwritten Law* (1913); and *Lancelot and Elaine* (1921).

[Gautam Dasgupta]

Różewicz, Tadeusz (1921–   )

Polish poet, short-story writer, essayist, and dramatist. He was born on October 9, 1921, in Radomsk, where his father was a court clerk. As an adolescent, Różewicz published his first literary works in high school magazines. During the German occupation he worked as a manual laborer and messenger boy, attended secret military classes, and became a soldier in the London-directed underground (or Home Army). After the war Różewicz completed his secondary education and attended the Jagiellonian University in Cracow, where he studied art history. His first volume of poetry, *Anxiety (Niepokój)*, appeared in 1947, and new collections of verse followed almost every year. In 1955 Różewicz received several state prizes for his long poem *The Plain (Równina)*, written the previous year, and brought out a volume of stories—*Leaves Fell from the Trees (Opadły liście z drzew)*—and more verse. By 1960 he was already the author of twelve collections of poetry as well as several volumes of prose and recognized as one of the outstanding postwar writers. In the same year his first play *The Card Index (Kartoteka)* was presented at the Teatr Dramatyczny in Warsaw, directed by Wanda Laskowska with sets by Jan Kosiński, and Różewicz immediately became an important new voice in contemporary Polish drama. The volume *Nothing in Prospero's Cloak (Nic w płaszczu Prospera)*, which appeared in 1962, contained poetry and two new plays: *The Witnesses, or Things Are Almost Back to Normal (Świadkowie, czyli nasza mała stabilizacja)* and *The Group of Laocoön (Grupa Laokoona)*. In 1966 Różewicz received another state prize, and collections of his plays and stories were published. Since 1968 Różewicz has lived in Wrocław. His works are translated into many languages, and two of his later plays, *The Old Woman Broods (Stara kobieta wysiaduje, 1970)* and *White Marriage (Białe małżeństwo, 1974)*, have been widely performed abroad as well as in Poland.

Work

A member of the war generation marked by the grim experiences of the occupation, Różewicz brings to the drama an omnivorous poetic sensibility for the concrete and a radical skepticism as regards ideologies. His first literary works, published after the war, were poems exposing literature as a lie and attacking all artistic convention. In fiction and poetry, as well as in drama, Różewicz has sought to obliterate the distinctions and limitations of genre and form. Deliberately striving for maximum impurity, he creates "junk art" out of scraps of quotations, clippings, lists, and documents. His playwriting resembles a poetic collage made up of disparate pieces of trash.

Różewicz's plays are without normal dramatic action, have no beginning, middle, or end, and mix the lyric, epic, and dramatic. Rather than repeat the formulas of the avant-garde, Różewicz challenges the very nature of drama, often substituting stage directions for dialogue or admitting the impossibility of making reality submit to the conventions of the theatre. Any device, technique, or tradition can be adopted or discarded so long as it serves the purposes of what Różewicz calls poetic realism. In his first play, *The Card Index*, Różewicz celebrates the anonymous man through a montage of shreds and fragments, misplaced emotions, stray characters, and quotations, all lost in a world of fluid time and space. The nameless hero of the drama mistrusts big words and seeks truth in the bare biological facts of the human organism and the world of things that surround it. Throughout all of Różewicz's works there runs a deep suspicion of abstract principles, particularly those forcibly imposed on human beings in the name of humanity; for the poet a crucial difference exists between individual

A 1975 production of *White Marriage*. [Agencja Autorska, Warsaw]

The Card Index as produced by Wanda Laskowska in a setting by
Jan Kosiński. [*Theatre in Modern Poland*]

humanness and humanity in general.

As Różewicz continued his attempts to write plays
in the face of what he felt to be the impossibility of such
an enterprise, commentary increasingly replaced dramatic text. Instead of finished plays, the poet produced
arguments with the theatre and scenarios in which
dramatist and performers must be co-creators. In *The Interrupted Act* (*Akt przerywany,* 1964) Różewicz makes a
play out of his dissatisfaction with all existing dramatic
forms. The conflict in the drama is between the idea of
the play and the impossibility of its execution. Remarks
by the author, personal intrusions, theoretical delibera-
tions, and polemics interrupt the play and produce a
new kind of narrative script. In *The Old Woman Broods*
(1968) the poet creates an open score for the theatre. The
stage directions, which constitute over a third of the
printed play, offer the director suggestions that he is free
to carry out as he wishes. Brilliantly realized by Jerzy
Jarocki at the Współczesny Theatre in Wrocław in 1969,
The Old Woman Broods is a series of variations on the
theme of rubbish, portraying the contemporary world as
a giant trash heap and graveyard, or cosmic garbage can,
for all culture and civilization. Różewicz calls *Birth Rate*
(*Przyrost naturalny,* 1968) "the biography of a play." As
in conceptual art the author's inability to write the play
becomes the drama. About biological proliferation and
the population explosion, *Birth Rate* cannot fit into normal theatrical molds, and the playwright must leave his
piece unwritten, asking some future director and theatre
to compose it for him. *Birth Rate* was first staged in 1979

by Kazimierz Braun, who incorporated some of Różewicz's poetry in the production. *White Marriage* (1974),
Różewicz's most successful work for the stage, is also a
biological drama, but of a more private nature, dealing
with the sexual coming of age of two adolescent girls at
the turn of the century and subtly probing contemporary problems of male and female identity. For twenty
years Różewicz has maintained his position as one of the
most inventive and original playwrights in all of Europe.

The Card Index (*Kartoteka,* 1960). During the entire
drama the nameless hero—a man of indefinite age,
profession, and outlook—lies in bed in his room,
through which a street appears to run, and passers-by
wander in and question him about his life and commitments. These figures make up the cast of characters of
his life: friends, relatives, and acquaintances out of his
past, present, and future. Interrogated by these ghosts
and voices, the hero tries desperately to resist all pressures by remaining totally passive and irresponsible.
Lying in bed, looking at his own hand, and opening and
closing his fingers, this modern Everyman clutches at his
own concrete humanness like a baby and hides from
those forces outside himself that seek to fit him into restrictive categories. "I like the little toe on my left foot
better than I do all of humanity," the inert protagonist
asserts, rejecting all noble sentiments and big emotions.
When a journalist, pen and notebook in hand, interviews
the hero and asks him a series of questions about his
goals in life, his political beliefs, his love of mankind,
and his desire for world peace, the anonymous man is

unwilling and unable to answer anything. He does not know and simply keeps quiet.

The Old Woman Broods (*Stara kobieta wysiaduje*; pub. 1968, prod. 1969). Amid refuse, in a café-necropolis, a grotesque old woman wearing multiple layers of discarded clothing imagines that she is giving birth to new life. She celebrates the abdomen: digestion and gestation. She is hatching something in all the pollution and filth. While the old woman talks about childbirth, larches, and the most beautiful river in all Europe, refuse and old papers pour through the window. The sound of dustbins clanking and the roar of the garbage truck can be heard outside. The characters' conversation is also junk, old scraps from the newspaper and radio about the weather, the new world crisis, the possibility of war. Human beings are fighting a losing battle with rubbish and ugliness; they are garbage themselves. The old woman realizes that she has no time to lose; she must give birth. In this refuse culture, people copulate, buy things, and get rich. Trenches are dug, and war is waged; young girls sunbathe and gossip; a gentleman gets his hair cut, and the old woman has a pedicure at the beauty parlor; hands come up out of the rubble; and the young waiter appears covered with bandages from the "third war." The old woman announces that she has given birth to one boy and three girls and is sitting on the boy. The street sweepers keep dumping and shoveling human artifacts and bodies (some real, some dummies). Paper continues to pile up.

White Marriage (*Białe małżeństwo*; wr. 1973, pub. 1974, prod. 1975). In a well-to-do family at the turn of the century two pubescent girls discover sex and sensuality, while at the same time the members of the older generation are tormented by their own failures to come to terms with love and lust in human life. Brought up more as a boy than a girl, Bianca, engaged to the pure and inexperienced Benjamin, is disturbed by the physical side of love; her companion Pauline, with whom she has been raised, has an earthy humor and is able to accept the bodily functions as an integral part of daily existence. Bianca's mother, repelled by the incessant sexual demands of a husband she does not love, somehow imagines that her daughter will find happiness in marriage and proudly catalogues the various items that make up the bride's trousseau. Bianca's father, driven by desire, never stops his pursuit of the buxom cook and other female servants, turning into a lustful Bull-Father and terrifying his daughter. Even Grandfather cannot confront approaching death with dignity, but is more obsessed with sex than ever, bribing the girls with sweets so that he may pet them or treasure their stockings. At a gathering where Benjamin reads romantic poetry, Bianca grows hysterical when she imagines she sees a huge phallus between her fiance's legs. The onset of menstruation is another shock for Bianca, whose erotic longings are transmuted into strange poetic dreams and fantasies. The Aunt, who is more sensual by nature than her sister, realizes that she should have married Bianca's father. During a picnic in a fairy-tale forest the girls gather mushrooms, which are grotesquely phallic in

shape, and are haunted by visions of male animality. Frightened of her marriage, which is drawing near, Bianca tears and cuts up her bridal linen. At the wedding, the guests become transformed into wild beasts, and the bed is like a coffin in which Bianca lies stiffly. Having made Benjamin promise that theirs will be a *marriage blanc* until she feels ready for physical love, Bianca has her new husband put his clothes back on. In the final scene, which takes place in the bedroom in broad daylight, Bianca looks intently at her image in the mirror, removes her clothes slowly, and throws them in the fire. Then, after closely cropping her hair, she turns to Benjamin, covers her breasts with her hands, and says, "I am your brother."

DANIEL GEROULD

PLAYS

1. *Będą się bili, dramat o Marianie Buczku* (They'll Come To Blows, a Drama About Marian Buczek). Published 1949–1950.

2. *Kartoteka** (The Card Index). Published 1960. Produced Warsaw, Teatr Dramatyczny, Sala Prób, Mar. 25, 1960.

3. *Grupa Laokoona* (The Group of Laocoön). Published 1961. Produced Warsaw, Teatr Dramatyczny, Sala Prób, Apr. 4, 1962.

4. *Świadkowie albo Nasza mała stabilizacja** (The Witnesses, or Things Are Almost Back to Normal). Published 1962. Produced West Berlin, Schiller Theatre, June 1963; Warsaw, Teatr Ludowy, Jan. 13, 1964.

5. *Akt przerywany, Komedia niesceniczna** (The Interrupted Act, a Non-Theatrical Comedy). One Act. Published 1964. Produced Ulm, West Germany, Dec. 12, 1965; Lublin, Teatr im. Osterwy, Feb. 28, 1970.

6. *Śmieszny Staruszek** (The Funny Old Man). Comedy. Two Scenes. Published 1964. Produced Warsaw, Teatr Ateneum, Dec. 21, 1965.

7. *Wyszedł z domu** (Gone Out). A so-called comedy. Published 1964. Produced Cracow, Teatr Stary, Apr. 25, 1965.

8. *Spaghetti i miecz* (Spaghetti and the Sword). Published 1964. Produced Warsaw, Teatr Dramatyczny, Sala Prób, July 16, 1967.

9. *Przyrost naturalny: Biografia sztuki teatralnej** (Birth Rate: Biography of a Play for the Theatre). Published 1968. Produced Wrocław, Teatr Współczesny im. Edmunda Wiercińskiego, Dec. 30, 1979.

10. *Stara kobieta wysiaduje** (The Old Woman Broods). Published 1968. Produced Wrocław, Teatr Współczesny im. Edmunda Wiercińskiego, June 28, 1969.

11. *Rajski Ogródek* (The Garden of Eden). Published 1970. Produced Kalisz, Teatr im. Wojciecha Bogusławskiego, Feb. 20, 1971.

12. *Pogrzeb po polsku* (Polish-style Funeral). Tragifarce. Published 1972. Produced Wrocław, Teatr Polski (Scena Kameralna), Oct. 14, 1971.

13. *Na czworakach* (On All Fours). Published 1971. Produced Warsaw, Teatr Dramatyczny, Mar. 25, 1972.

14. *Białe małżeństwo* (White Marriage). Published 1974. Produced Warsaw, Teatr Mały, Jan. 24, 1975.

15. *Odejście Głodomora* (The Starveling's Departure). Published 1976. Produced Wrocław, Teatr Współczesny im. Edmunda Wiercińskiego, Feb. 9, 1977.

16. *Do piachu* (Dead and Buried). Written 1955–1972. Published 1979. Produced Warsaw, Teatr na Woli, Mar. 30, 1979.

17. *Teatr niekonsekwencji* (Theatre of Inconsistencies). Short plays. Written and published during 1970s. Produced Warsaw, Teatr Popularny, Apr. 7, 1979.

EDITIONS

Collections

Utwory dramatyczne, Cracow, 1966; *The Card Index and Other Plays* (The Interrupted Act, Gone Out), tr. by A. Czerniawski, New York, 1970; *The Witnesses and Other Plays* (The Funny Old Man, The Old Woman Broods), tr. by A. Czerniawski, London, 1970; *Teatr niekonsekwencji*, Warsaw, 1970; *Sztuki teatralne*, Wrocław, 1972; *Białe Małżeństwo i inne utwory sceniczne*, Cracow, 1975; *Teatr niekonsekwencji*, Wrocław, 1979.

CRITICISM

S. Gębała, *Teatr Różewicza*, Wrocław, 1977.

Rozov, Viktor Sergeyevich (1913–)

Soviet Russian dramatist. Rozov was born in Yaroslavl and began taking part in amateur theatricals while working at a factory. He was a student at the Theatre of the

The Reunion, a drama which examines the conflict between personal and professional goals, as directed by Yefremov in 1967.

Revolution in Moscow (1934–1938) and remained an actor and director with that company, playing for the troops after the outbreak of war, until he was wounded. In 1949 he began his playwriting career and entered the Gorky Literary Institute in Moscow. Rozov's earliest plays, among them *Her Friends* (*Yeyo druzya*, 1949), *A Page of Life* (*Stranitsa zhizni*, also known as *Your Path* [*Tvoy put'*], 1953), and *In a Lucky Hour* (*V dobryy chas*, 1954), dealt with the personality and labor problems of Soviet youth in a low-keyed and intimate manner; these plays regularly had their premieres at the Central Children's Theatre in Moscow and are still revived there.

The climax of this period of Rozov's writing came in *Alive Forever* (*Vechno zhivyo*, 1956), a reworking of *The Serebrisky Family* (*Semya Serebriskikh*), a play written in 1943, which opened at the Sovremennik Theatre, Moscow, in 1957. Telling of an adolescent soldier and his friends during wartime, it eschews the heroic stances of the Stalinist period for a warmer, more honest look at human reactions. The play became his best-known work when filmed as *The Cranes Are Flying* (*Letyat zhuravli*; co-author M. K. Kalatozov), the first of many screenplays Rozov has created.

In the 1960s he turned towards the problems of adults, although youth continues to appear as an element of hope and revitalization in his dramas. The first of these plays, *Before Supper* (*Pered uzhinom*, 1962), struck the note that runs through them all: the contrast between those who preserve their personal integrity and those who compromise. *Wedding Day* (*V den svadby*, 1964) features a bride who abandons her groom on their wedding day because he still loves another; it is almost a reversal of Aleksandr Ostrovsky's classic play *The Poor Bride*. Other dramas of this period include *The Reunion* (*Traditsiony sbor*, 1967), which pivots on the theme of professional success versus personal fulfillment, and *From Night to Noon* (*S vechera do poludnya*, 1969), which, like

Rozov's earlier plays, confines the action to a single household.

Although the psychology of everyday life is well observed by Rozov, his plays are somewhat formulaic; the characters are either those who function well in society by becoming callous or those failures who still retain their sensitivity. If he avoids clumsy happy endings, he nevertheless provides a rosy atmosphere at the fall of the curtain.

Rozov remains active, providing stage adaptations of novels by Dostoevsky and Goncharov; his play *Four Drops* (*Chetyre kapli*, 1975) was produced by the Lenin Komsomol Theatre in Leningrad, and he himself was honored on his sixtieth birthday by the Supreme Soviet.

LAURENCE SENELICK

EDITIONS

Pyesy, Moscow, 1959; *In Search of Happiness*, tr. by N. Froud, London, 1961; *Alive Forever*, tr. by F. D. Reeve, in *Contemporary Russian Drama*, New York, 1968; *Moi shestidesyatye*, Moscow, 1969; *From Night till Noon*, tr. by R. Daglish, in *Nine Modern Soviet Plays*, Moscow, 1977; *The Young Graduates* in *Russian Plays for Young Audiences*, ed. and tr. by M. Morton, Rowayton, Conn., 1979.

CRITICISM

Y. Vishnevskaya, "Viktor Rozov i ego geroi," *Teatr*, vol. VI, 1963; A. Anastasyev, *Viktor Rozov, ocherk tvorchestva*, Moscow, 1966.

Rucellai, Giovanni (1475–1525)

Italian man of letters and dramatist. His tragedy *Rosmunda* (wr. 1515, prod. 1525) was inspired by the literary theories of his friendly rival Trissino. Rucellai combined medieval and classical sources for his subject matter and loosely imitated Latin dramatic modes. Rucellai's tragedy *Orestes* (*Oreste*; wr. 1515–1520, prod. 1723) adheres more rigidly to formal classical prototypes (it is an adaptation of Euripides' *Iphigenia in Tauris*) but lacks their dramatic impact and declines into melodrama. *See* TRISSINO, GIANGIORGIO.

[PETER BONDANELLA]

Rudkin, David (1936–   )

British dramatist. He began writing stories as a child, later studied music (which he now teaches), and eventually turned to playwriting. His first play, *Afore Night Come* (1962), was produced by the Royal Shakespeare Company. Set in an orchard, it seems at first to be a slice-of-life drama about fruit pickers, but it quickly takes on sinister overtones as the play moves inexorably toward the climax, the ritual sacrifice of an inoffensive Irish tramp. He has also written for television and the ballet. His most successful play is *Ashes* (1974).

Ashes (1974). The play probes uninhibitedly into the privacy of a couple eager to have a child, and persuaded by the medical profession to submit to indignities such as sperm counts, postcoital smears, and lovemaking in a prescribed position. Finally a miscarriage is followed by a hysterectomy, but even in their efforts to adopt a child they are fated to frustration. The play becomes less compelling when it changes course. Under the pretext of linking the private barrenness to public barrenness, the playwright requires the audience to refocus its attention on the situation in Northern Ireland.

CRITICISM

R. Hayman, *British Theatre since 1955*, London, and New York, 1979.

Rueda, Lope de   (1510?–1565)

Spanish actor-manager, poet, and dramatist. He was born in Seville, probably in 1510. A goldbeater by trade, he made the theatre his profession and is considered by many scholars to be the true founder of the Spanish theatre, being the first Spanish dramatist to write directly for the popular stage rather than for production at court or in the homes of the nobility. In addition, Rueda formed and managed his own company, for which he wrote plays and also acted, and toured the provinces, playing in marketplaces, inns, and, occasionally, great houses. The company performed both original plays and adaptations.

About 1552 Rueda married a young singer and dancer named Marianita who had joined his troupe. Two years later he was engaged by the Count of Benavente to present a play in honor of Philip II's arrival in Benavente. Afterward he took his company through Segovia (1558), Seville (1559), and Valladolid; by 1561 he was in Madrid. Now a widower, he married Rafaela Angela Trillas, of Valencia, where he settled in 1562, remaining for the next two or three years while collecting his works for publication. Their one child, Juana, who was baptized in Seville in 1564, died in Córdoba in 1565. Rueda died the same year and is said by Cervantes to have been buried in the Cathedral of Córdoba, but no grave bearing his name is to be found there.

Lope de Rueda. [Biblioteca Nacional, Madrid]

WORK

As the manager of a small traveling theatrical company, Lope de Rueda composed plays and playlets that appealed to a wide audience which, seldom having seen truly sophisticated theatre, was eager for the experience. Like the *commedia dell'arte* troupes of Italy, Rueda's company performed in the open air, and his fame attests to the extraordinary popularity of his farces. But despite this encouraging popular acceptance, few of his contemporaries followed his lead in the use of prose for dramatic writing. *See* COMMEDIA DELL'ARTE in glossary.

Rueda composed five full-length dramas in imitation of Plautus and the Italian theatre, the best of which, *Eufemia* (wr. 1544?), incorporating a plot drawn from Boccaccio's *Decameron*, is mediocre. His real genius is revealed in his *pasos*. These compositions are very brief, farcical one-act skits, with negligible plots, depicting everyday scenes in a realistic and comical fashion. Their sole purpose was to entertain. Rueda made no effort to communicate an ideological message. Episodic in nature, the *pasos* were perhaps originally intended to be used as prologues to longer plays or to be presented between the acts for comic relief, but it appears that they were actually staged several at a time as part of an afternoon's entertainment in some public place.

Rueda based these compositions on real life by focusing on some amusing incident and observing with a keen sense of realism the customs and manners of the time. His farcical theatre evinces little variety, but the comic force is always strong, reinforced by the use of a vivid, spicy popular diction and frequent allusions to the proverbs, phrases, and superstitions of the people. Since the short pieces precluded character analysis, Rueda created stereotyped figures, such as the Negress, the gypsy, the matchmaking Jew, the Biscayan, and the *bobo* ("fool"). Drawn almost exclusively from the lower classes, they are portrayed faithfully and naturally.

The most famous of the *pasos* is *The Olives* (*Las aceitunas*, wr. 1548?), in which a husband and wife, after planting a tiny olive tree that will not bear fruit for years, quarrel over the price they will charge for the olives. *Cuckolds Go to Heaven* (*Cornudo y contento*, wr. 1546?) describes the efforts of a man to cure his wife of a feigned illness while she cuckolds him with a student. In *The Guest* (*El convidado*, wr. 1546?) a student tries to avoid paying for his guest's dinner by pretending to be ill.

Similar to *Eufemia* are Rueda's other prose comedies. *Medora* (wr. 1550?), based upon Giancarli's *La zingana* (pub. 1545), deals with the confusion caused by identical twins; *The Deceived* (*Los engañados*, wr. 1556?) is a sharply etched version of the anonymous Italian comedy *The Cheats* (*Gl'ingannati*); and *Armelina* (wr. 1545?) employs the traditional Italian elements of mistaken identities and long-lost children being restored to their parents. *See* GIANCARLI, GIGIO ARTEMIO.

Eufemia (wr. 1544?). Drama, derived from Boccaccio's *Decameron*, interesting largely because of the comic dialogue and spirited embroilments of the servants. Leonardo, a gentleman, embarks on a journey, leaving behind his sister Eufemia. He becomes a secretary in the household of Valiano, a baron to whom he extols Eufemia's virtues, hoping to promote a marriage between the two. An old servant, Pedro, arrives to tell Valiano that Eufemia is a woman of loose morals whose bed he has shared and produces as evidence a bit of hair allegedly taken from a mole on her shoulder. Believing himself betrayed, Valiano sentences Leonardo to death. Pedro's treachery is revealed by Eufemia's maid Christina, who confesses to having given a token of her mistress's person to a persistent stranger (Pedro), in whose scheme to supplant Leonardo in the baron's favor she (the maid) was not an accomplice. In the baron's presence Eufemia and Christina trick Pedro into disclosing his perfidy, which results in Leonardo's freedom and a proposed marriage between Valiano and Eufemia.

PLAYS

The dramatic works of Rueda are best listed by category since the dates provided by Moratín (and given below) have been widely questioned.

Pasos (Prose)

1. *Los criados* (*The Servants*). Play, 1 act. Written 1544? Published 1567.
2. *La carátula* (*The Mask*). Play, 1 act. Written 1545? Published 1567.
3. *Cornudo y contento** (*Cuckolds Go to Heaven*). Play, 1 act. Written 1546? Published 1567.
4. *El convidado* (*The Guest*). Play, 1 act. Written 1546? Published 1567.
5. *La tierra de Jauja* (*The Land of Jauja*). Play, 1 act. Written 1547? Published 1567.
6. *Pagar y no pagar* (*To Pay and Not to Pay*). Play, 1 act. Written 1547? Published 1567.
7. *Las aceitunas** (*The Olives*). Play, 1 act. Written 1548? Published 1567.
8. *El rufián cobarde* (*The Cowardly Ruffian*). Play, 1 act. Written 1556? Published 1570.
9. *Los lacayos ladrones* (*The Thieving Servants*). Play, 1 act. Written 1556? Published 1570.
10. *La generosa paliza* (*The Generous Beating*). Play, 1 act. Written 1588? Published 1570.

Comedias in Prose

1. *Eufemia*. Play, 8 scenes. Written 1544? Published 1567. Based on a tale from Giovanni Boccaccio's *Decameron* (1353).
2. *Armelina*. Play, 6 scenes. Written 1545? Published 1567.
3. *Medora*. Play, 6 scenes. Written 1550? Published 1567. Based on Gigio Artemio Giancarli's *La zingana*.
4. *Los engañados* (*The Deceived*). Play. Written 1556? Published 1567.

Comedia in Verse

Discordia y cuestión de amor (*Discord and Question of Love*). Play. Published 1617.

Colloquies in Prose

1. *Camila*. Play, 1 long act. Written 1551? Published 1567.
2. *Tymbria*. Play, 1 long act. Written 1552? Published 1567.

Colloquy in Verse

Prendas de amor (*Pledges of Love*). Play, 1 act. Written 1556? Published 1570.

Dialogue in Verse

El diálogo sobre la invención de las calzas (*Dialogue on the Invention of Breeches*). Play, 1 act. Published 1567.

Play Doubtfully Attributed to Rueda

Farsa del sordo (*Farce of the Deaf Man*). Play, 1 act; verse. Written 1549? Published 1568?

EDITIONS

Obras, ed. by the Marquis of Fuensanta del Valle, 2 vols., Madrid, 1895–1896; *Obras*, ed. by E. Cotarelo y Mori, 2 vols., Madrid, 1908.

The Olives. Published in *Spanish Drama*, ed. and tr. by A. Flores, New York, 1962.

CRITICISM

E. Cotarelo y Mori, *Lope de Rueda y el teatro español de su tiempo*, Madrid, 1901; N. Alonso Cortés, *Un pleito de Lope de Rueda*, Madrid and Valladolid, 1903; S. Salazar, *Lope de Rueda y su teatro*, Havana, 1911; R. E. Chandler and K. Schwartz, *A New History of Spanish Literature*, Baton Rouge, 1961; V. Tusón, *Lope de Rueda: Bibliografía crítica*, Madrid, 1965; J.

P. Wickersham Crawford, "Lope de Rueda, Italianate Comedy and the Farce," in *Spanish Drama before Lope de Vega*, Philadelphia, 1922, 3d ed., with *Bibliographical Supplement* by W. T. McCready, 1967.

Ruederer, Josef (1861–1915)

Pre-World War I German novelist and dramatist. His fame in the theatre rests almost exclusively on his rural comedy *Presentation of Colors* (*Fahnenweihe*, 1895). "A finely carved piece," according to Alfred Kerr, the most influential critic of the day, it is "made up of contours rather than shades, an outlandish land-symphony, an orchestrated scherzo on the theme 'Human, all too human.' " Ruederer's was a starkly satirical talent; he presented people naked and unadorned, shamefully incongruous with the ethics then commonly preached and supposedly upheld.

His second play, *The Dawn* (*Die Morgenröte*, 1905), proved less successful than his first. It centers on the hypocritical, philistine motives of the Munich students in their expulsion of the dancer Lola Montez, mistress of King Louis I of Bavaria, in 1848. The characters in this play are named and portrayed in detail but appear unconvincing. *The Smith from Kochel* (*Der Schmied von Kochel*, 1911), Ruederer's attempt to make a heroic episode from the history of Bavaria the subject of a tragedy, was ill fated. It showed only that the author's forte did not extend beyond the realm of polemical satire.

[PETER JELAVICH]

Ruibal, José (1925–)

Spanish playwright. Ruibal was born in the Galician city of Pontevedra and educated in Santiago de Compostela. At twenty he began publishing poems in a local newspaper. Economic difficulties created by his father's dismissal from the civil service following Franco's victory in the Spanish Civil War prevented him from continuing his studies. After living in Madrid from 1948 to 1951 he emigrated to South America. He resided primarily in Montevideo and Buenos Aires, devoting himself to journalism. Although he traveled extensively in Europe in 1955, he did not return to Spain until 1960. For a number of years he continued to work as a journalist, but in 1967 he was fired from an important Madrid newspaper for political reasons. Encouraged by friends and by a contract from a Swiss publisher, he decided to concentrate exclusively on the theatre.

One of the pioneers of contemporary avante-garde Spanish drama, he had been writing plays since 1956, but his work had received scant attention. He had come close to winning the important Valle Inclán Prize in 1963 with *The Jackass* (*El asno*, 1962), but the selection committee could not reach a final decision and the award was not given that year. Winning the competition would have meant production of the play. It was a moment in Spain when what might be termed the "opposition" or dissident theatre (as compared to the "official" or conformist theatre) was oriented toward social realism. Ruibal's play, an allegorical satire about the economic colonization of underdeveloped countries by more powerful ones (Spanish society was beginning to undergo vast

Norman Briski (left) and Lázaro Pérez in the Puerto Rican
Traveling Theatre's production of *The Man and the Fly*.
[Photograph by Peter Krupenye]

changes as a result of recent foreign investment, particularly from North American sources), is in an avant-garde style which has not yet been fully accepted in Spain, where the realist-naturalist conception of drama continues to predominate. Ruibal, like Fernando Arrabal before him (it was the negative reaction to vanguard dramaturgy which prompted Arrabal to leave Spain definitively in 1958 and settle in Paris), found himself confronted not only with the problem of censorship but also with a lack of support for avant-garde experimentation (*see* ARRABAL, FERNANDO). From 1963 to 1967 he wrote only one play, *His Majesty the Jack* (*Su majestad la sota*, 1966), an allegorical depiction of the principal methods used by totalitarian rulers to maintain themselves in power.

In the late 1960s and early 1970s a number of foreign critics and scholars—among them G. E. Wellwarth, who was chiefly responsible for the discovery of an ''underground'' theatre in Franco's Spain—began to take an interest in him. A translation of *The Jackass* was published in 1968 in *Modern International Drama*, which also chose it as the recipient of its annual award for the best foreign play published by the review that year. That same year, 1968, Ruibal wrote *The Man and the Fly* (*El hombre y la mosca*), a play which has undergone several revisions. It

is considered by most critics his masterpiece and one of the best pieces of dramatic literature to come out of post-Civil War Spain. Banned by Spanish censors, this brilliant satire on political power (the two principal characters are an aging dictator and a double whom he has been secretly training to succeed him) had its world premiere in 1971 at the State University of New York in Binghamton, with Ruibal in attendance. Although some of his plays have been performed abroad, especially in the United States, and he has been translated into several languages, Ruibal continues to be ignored by the theatrical establishment in Spain.

During a period of intense creativity, 1968–1970, Ruibal wrote, in addition to *The Man and the Fly*, six skits for cabaret theatre, *The Pious Monkey* (*El mono piadoso*, 1969), *The Begging Machine* (*La máquina de pedir*, 1969), and *Curriculum Vitae* (1970). He also adapted the text of *The Jackass* into an opera libretto under the title *The Electronic Jackass* (*El asno electrónico*, 1969). After a respite of several years, during which he sought new directions for his dramaturgy, he produced *Controls* (*Controles*, 1976), a work which combines ceremonial techniques with animal symbolism (the characters are ostriches) to present the grim reality of a world bent on destroying itself. An ardent admirer of the Spanish drama of the Golden Age,

Ruibal has done an adaptation of Fernando de Rujas's *La Celestina* and is preparing several adaptations of Calderón's works.

A master of abstract symbolism, Ruibal focuses on themes most pertinent to our times: the abuse of power, the exploitive and repressive nature of a society ruled by greed, and the dehumanization of life as a result of a technological revolution used to further oppress humankind. Employing symbols which spring from the fantasy of his imagination, he creates a world in which animals and electronic creatures abound. His linguistic skills enable him to impart an extraordinary plastic dimension to all aspects of his theatre. Even though there are allusions in some of his works to Hispanic society, the scope of his plays tends to be universal, as is characteristic of the "New Spanish Theatre," the movement with which Ruibal is closely associated.

ANDRÉS FRANCO

EDITIONS

Spanish

The Beggars (*Los mendigos*, 1957). Published in *Teatro sobre teatro*, Madrid, 1975, pp. 129–160. This play was originally published in a volume titled *Los mendigos y seis piezas de café teatro*, Colección Teatro, no. 632, Madrid, 1969. Before the edition could be put on sale, it was banned by the censors and thereupon reissued as *El mono piadoso y seis piezas de café teatro* (see below).

The Begging Machine (*La máquina de pedir*, 1969). Published in *La máquina de pedir. El asno. La ciencia de birlibirloque*, Madrid, 1970, pp. 9–85; also in *Teatro sobre teatro*, Madrid, 1975, pp. 53–127.

The Codfish (*El bacalao*, 1960). Published in *A Reader in Spanish Literature*, ed. by A. Zahareas and B. Mújica, New York, 1975, pp. 325–351. Fragments of this play appear in a collection of plays by various authors, *Teatro difícil*, Colección Teatro, no. 690, Madrid, pp. 187–196.

Curriculum Vitae (1970). Published in *El Urogallo*, no. 2, 1970; also in *Teatro difícil*, Madrid, 1971, pp. 177–185; and in *Nuevas Lecturas*, ed. by B. Mújica, New York, 1974, pp. 185–195.

The Man and the Fly (*El hombre y la mosca*, 1968). Published in *España en el siglo XX*, ed. by A. Regalado, G. D. Keller, and S. Kerr, New York, 1974, pp. 360–408; a revised edition of the play, with a preface by the author and various critical essays, Madrid, 1977.

The Manager-in-Chief (*El supergerente*, 1968). Published in *El mono piadoso y seis piezas de café teatro*, Madrid, 1969, pp. 73–82; also in *Teatro sobre teatro*, Madrid, 1975, pp. 201–210.

The Mutants (*Los mutantes*, 1968). Published in *Primer Acto*, no. 112, pp. 61–52, 1969; also in *El mono piadoso y seis piezas de café teatro*, Madrid, 1969, pp. 43–48; and in *Teatro sobre teatro*, Madrid, 1975, pp. 169–174.

The Pious Monkey (*El mono piadoso*, 1969). Published in *El mono piadoso y seis piezas de café teatro*, Madrid, 1975, pp. 14–31.

The Science of Blarney (*El arte de birlibirloque*, 1956). Published in *La máquina de pedir. El asno. La ciencia de birlibirloque*, Madrid, 1970, pp. 179–195.

The Secretary (*La secretaria*, 1968). Published in *El mono piadoso y seis piezas de café teatro*, Madrid, 1969, pp. 35–41; also in *Teatro sobre teatro*, Madrid, 1975, pp. 161–167; and in *Contemporary Spanish Theatre: Seven One-Act Plays*, ed. by P. W. O'Connor and A. M. Pasquariello, New York, 1980, pp. 129–139.

Tails (*El rabo*, 1968). Published in *Revista de Occidente*, June 1969; also in *El mono piadoso y seis piezas de café teatro*, Madrid, 1969, pp. 49–56; and in *Teatro sobre teatro*, Madrid, 1975, pp. 175–184.

English

The Beggars (*Los mendigos*, 1957). Published in *Drama and Theatre*, tr. by J. Pearson, Winter 1968–1969, pp. 56–63.

The Codfish (*El bacalao*, 1960). Published in *Modern International Drama*, vol. 5, tr. by J. Pearson, pp. 5–18, 1972.

The Jackass (*El asno*, 1962). Published in *Modern International Drama*, vol. 2, tr. by T. Seward, pp. 31–56, 1968; also in *The New Wave Spanish Drama*, ed. by G. E. Wellwarth, New York, 1970, pp. 55–101.

Tails (*El rabo*, 1968). Published in *Drama Review*, vol. 13, tr. by M. C. Wellwarth, pp. 157–159, 1969.

The Man and the Fly (*El hombre y la mosca*, 1968). Published in *The New Wave Spanish Drama*, ed. by G. E. Wellwarth and tr. by J. Zelonis, New York, 1970, pp. 1–53; also in *Themes of Drama: An Anthology*, ed. by G. E. Wellwarth, New York, 1973, pp. 481–507. A new translation of this play by G. Rabassa has not yet been published.

The Begging Machine (*La máquina de pedir*, 1969). Published in *Modern International Drama*, vol. 9, tr. by J. Bernstein, pp. 5–63, 1976.

CRITICISM

G. E. Wellwarth, *Spanish Underground Drama*, University Park, Pa., and London, 1972, pp. 21–37; Articles by G. Gillespie, M. Romero, F. Lázaro Carreter, A. Berenguer, M. Castellví de Morr, and B. Mújica in the Fundamentos edition of *The Man and the Fly*, Madrid, 1977; F. Ruiz Ramón, *Historia del teatro español*, 3d ed., vol. 2, Madrid, 1977, pp. 531–535; L. T. Valdivieso, *España: Bibliografía de un teatro "silenciado,"* Society of Spanish and Spanish-American Studies, 1979, pp. 83–91.

Ruiz de Alarcón, Juan (1580/81–1639)

Spanish poet and dramatist. Juan Ruiz de Alarcón y Mendoza was born at the end of 1580 or the beginning of 1581 in Mexico City to Pedro Ruiz de Alarcón, a superintendent of mines in Tasco, and Leonor de Mendoza. The child, one of five, was an unattractive hunchback, but instead of becoming bitter and resentful, he developed a spirit of magnanimity and a sense of morality, which are clearly evident in his plays. In 1592 he enrolled at the Liberal Arts School of the Universidad Real y Pontífica of Mexico; four years later he entered the Law Preparatory School of the university, from which he was graduated in 1598. After attending the Civil Law Division of the Law Institute for two years, he decided to continue his education at the University of Salamanca, and in 1600 he left the New World for Spain.

For a time he was financially dependent on a relative, but in 1606, though he still lacked his law license, he embarked on a successful law practice in Seville, where no license was required. During this period he also became acquainted with the literati of the city. In 1608 Alarcón returned to Mexico, and in 1609 he finally received his law degree. He soon became legal counsel to the mayor of Mexico City, frequently pleading in the Royal High Court. In 1613 he returned to Spain, where he began revising previously written plays and working on new ones. Their successful production, and perhaps Alarcón's tendency to see himself as something of a Don Juan, aroused the antagonism of his literary colleagues (Lope de Vega, Quevedo, Góngora, Pérez de Montalbán,

Juan Ruiz de Alarcón. [New York Public Library Picture Collection]

among others), who did not hesitate to lampoon him cruelly for his physical defects.

In 1626 Alarcón obtained a post in the Council of the Indies and thereafter ceased writing. He was by now highly regarded in professional and governmental circles, but the bitter attacks of his literary rivals are said to have made him despondent. During his lifetime his *comedias* were published in two volumes, *Parte primera* (1628) and *Parte segunda* (1634). After his death in Madrid on August 4, 1639, his will disclosed that he had a daughter, whom he named his sole heiress and whose mother was Angela Cervantes.

WORK

Although born in the New World, Alarcón proved to be an outstanding dramatist of Spain's Siglo de Oro (Golden Age) and its most modern though least prolific representative. (Of the twenty-four plays attributed to him, only twenty are definitely known to be from his pen.) He followed the tradition established by Lope de Vega, yet he strayed from it perhaps more than any other writer of his time. Despite a sprinkling of Latin-American allusions in his early works, his plays have a distinct Spanish flavor but lack the baroque ornamentation and conscious melodrama with which his contemporaries held their audiences. Instead, Alarcón, writing vivid and authentic *comedias de carácter*, in which specific character traits are examined, sought to instruct his audiences even as he entertained them. The result was a number of "serious" comedies that rank among Spain's greatest dramatic works, notable for their humanism, balance, subtlety, and discrimination—eighteenth-century qualities that place Alarcón ahead of his time and were to be influential in the theatre of Corneille, Molière, and Goldoni. His characterizations are realistic and psychologically true although Siglo de Oro concepts of chivalry, honor, and patriotism are described as virtues worthy of praise and cultivation. His idiom is dry and devoid of imagery, but his verse has a quiet, sober dignity that mirrors the personality of the author and his careful craftsmanship. *See* VEGA CARPIO, LOPE DE. *See also* COMEDIA; SIGLO DE ORO in glossary.

Alarcón's general theatrical technique was based on the presentation of a character who would demonstrate the results of some specific personal or social vice in action. Thus, his best-known play, *The Truth Suspected* (*La verdad sospechosa*, ca. 1619/21), presents a chronic liar who is finally the major victim of his own failing. This play was to serve as the basis for Corneille's only comedy, *The Liar*, and was also indirectly to provide the model for Goldoni's *The Liar*. *See* CORNEILLE, PIERRE; GOLDONI, CARLO.

A handsome slanderer loses a beautiful lady to an unattractive but virtuous suitor in *The Walls Have Ears* (*Las paredes oyen*, 1617), a play in which Alarcón ventured to paint his own psychological portrait. Fickleness is the theme of *A Change for the Better* (*Mudarse por mejorarse*, pub. 1628), in which a young nobleman unsuccessfully courts the niece of the lady to whom he is betrothed and finds that others too can make "a change for the bet-

ter." In *The Test for Husbands* (*El examen de maridos*, pub. 1634) two suitors debate their views on marriage before the lady of their choice. Ingratitude is the undoing of the protagonist of *The Proof of the Promises* (*La prueba de las promesas*, pub. 1634), who forgets that he owes his success and charm to the spells of a powerful magician.

The Weaver of Segovia, Parts I and II (*El tejedor de Segovia, primera y segunda partes*, pub. 1634), both *comedias históricas*, trace the downfall and eventual restoration to honor of the noble Ramírez family, falsely accused of treachery. Only the second of the two parts is known definitely to be the work of Alarcón. Another genre employed by Alarcón was the *comedia de capa y espada*, one of the lightest of the *comedia* forms, which focuses on the intrigue of the upper classes, portraying them with wit, masquerade, and numerous turns of plot. Probably the best example of this type is *Privileged Bosoms* (*Los pechos privilegiados*, wr. 1625), a drama about a king's jealous persecution of a supposed rival in love. *The Cave of Salamanca* (*La cueva de Salamanca*, pub. 1628), which combines magic with plots involving students, is a *comedia de enredo*, a genre in which most elements are subordinated to the machinations of a fantastically complicated plot.

Among other plays of note are *Feigned Misfortune* (*El desdichado en fingir*, pub. 1628), which explores various aspects of love; *His Own Double* (*El semejante a sí mismo*, pub. 1628), about the testing of a woman's fidelity, based on an episode in Cervantes' *Don Quixote* (1605, 1615); *Wits and Luck* (*La industria y la suerte*, pub. 1628), in which a lucky hidalgo outwits a rich merchant; *The Favors of the World* (*Los favores del mundo*, pub. 1628), depicting a conflict between prince and vassal and the difficulties of life at court; *All Is Due to Fortune* (*Todo es ventura*, pub. 1628), which demonstrates the role of luck in social success; *An Error's Obligations* (*Los empeños de un engaño*, pub. 1634), about a woman in pursuit of a man; *Melilla's Trick* (*La manganilla de Melilla*, 1617), Alarcón's only *comedia* with a Moorish background; *The Antichrist* (*El Anticristo*, 1623), about the rise and fall of a tyrant, Alarcón's only religious play; *Cruelty for Honor* (*La crueldad por el honor*, wr. ca. 1625), in which themes of vengeance and loyalty are presented against a historical background; *The Master of the Stars* (*El dueño de las estrellas*, pub. 1634), about a vassal who chooses suicide as a means of redeeming his honor; and *Friendship Punished* (*La amistad castigada*, pub. 1634), about the conflict between friendship and duty to the King.

The Walls Have Ears (*Las paredes oyen*, 1617). Doña Ana is courted by two gentlemen, Don Mendo, who is handsome and rich, and Don Juan, who is ugly and poor. Although she is attracted to Don Mendo because of his looks, his insincerity and tendency toward scandalmongering soon become apparent. Doña Ana overhears a conversation in which Don Mendo, in an attempt to ward off another potential suitor, maligns her character. When Don Mendo proposes to Doña Ana, he is rejected and the only explanation given is that "the walls have ears." Frustrated in his bid for her hand, Don Mendo tries to abduct Doña Ana, but she is rescued by Don Juan, who, in doing so, wounds his rival. Gradually

Doña Ana is won over by the true worth of Don Juan and marries him. Don Mendo's discomfort is complete when he is rejected by another lady to whom he has been paying court.

The Truth Suspected (*La verdad sospechosa*, ca. 1619/21). Don García, a young law student with a passion for lying, encounters two beautiful women, Lucrecia and Jacinta, on his return to Madrid from Salamanca. Though he is immediately attracted to Jacinta, she is wrongly identified to him as Lucrecia. Then, when he meets Don Juan, Don García falsely boasts of having entertained a lady named Jacinta. Don Juan, who has courted Jacinta unsuccessfully because he lacks a military commission, is outraged and jealous.

Meanwhile, Don Beltrán, Don García's father, has arranged a marriage between his son and Jacinta. To avoid the marriage, Don García, who still believes his love's name is Lucrecia, tells his father that he had been forced to marry a noblewoman in Salamanca. Eventually Don Beltrán learns that the story of a previous marriage is a lie. When he confronts his son, the latter confesses to loving ''Lucrecia,'' for such he believes is Jacinta's name. Thinking he has finally learned the truth from his son, Don Beltrán arranges a marriage between Don García and Lucrecia. Don Juan, who has now received his commission, is free to ask for Jacinta's hand. When all four young people are brought together and the true identities of the two women are disclosed, both men claim Jacinta. The latter, however, disgusted by Don García's lies, accepts Don Juan. Don García is forced to apologize to Lucrecia and ask for her hand.

Privileged Bosoms (*Los pechos privilegiados*, wr. 1625). *Comedia de capa y espada* mingling documented fact with fiction. Rodrigo de Villagómez, a nobleman who is in love with Leonor, daughter of Melendo González, Count of Galicia and previous tutor of King Alfonso, needs the King's consent to marry her, but he incurs Alfonso's wrath when he indignantly refuses to act as the King's mediator with Elvira, the Count's other daughter. Ramiro, another nobleman in love with Leonor and jealous of Rodrigo, persuades the King that Rodrigo is his rival for Elvira's heart, and in an encounter in the countryside of Valmadrigal, Alfonso tries in vain to kill Rodrigo. Meanwhile, the King of Navarre falls in love with Elvira and asks for her hand. Finally, realizing that he alone possesses Elvira's love, Alfonso decides to restore honor to Rodrigo and grant him the right to marry Leonor. Throughout the play Rodrigo is aided by his faithful nurse Simena, and because of her constancy the King announces that she and all future nurses in the Villagómez family are to be known as ''privileged bosoms.''

A Change for the Better (*Mudarse por mejorarse*, pub. 1628). Don García transfers his affections from the widowed Doña Clara to her niece Leonor, who has come to Madrid to find a husband. Reproached with his fickleness, he replies that he has made ''a change for the better.'' When Don García has his friend Don Félix accompany him to Doña Clara's house and pretend to court the aunt while he secretly woos the niece, Don Félix discovers that Doña Clara is the unidentified woman he has long secretly loved. Although Leonor temporarily responds to Don García's passion, she ridicules his fickleness.

At this point, the Marquis, Doña Clara's relative, meets Leonor, decides to seduce her, and therefore becomes a frequent visitor to Doña Clara's house. Don García, desperate for an excuse to break with Doña Clara, accuses her of unfaithfulness with the Marquis. Meanwhile, the wily Leonor, although not indifferent to Don García, uses him to arouse the Marquis's jealousy and induce the libertine aristocrat to propose. Doña Clara consents to her niece's marriage, pleased by this proof that the Marquis's visits to her house had been occasioned by his interest in her niece. When the outraged Don García demands that Leonor explain this change in her affections, she repays the fickle lover in his own coin by replying that it is ''a change for the better.'' Doña Clara and Don García are reunited, and only Don Félix is left unhappy and unmarried.

The Proof of the Promises (*La prueba de las promesas*, pub. 1634). Don Illán de Toledo, a famous magician, disapproves of his daughter Blanca's desire to marry Juan de Robera. Juan offers Illán money and power in exchange for lessons in magic, and the magician casts a spell that enables Juan to climb the social and political ladder until he is a leading figure at court. But when Illán asks favors for his son Mauricio, Juan turns a deaf ear to his benefactor. Now wishing to make a match with a more important family, he is no longer interested in marrying Blanca and threatens Illán with persecution as a wizard. Illán retaliates by breaking his spell, and all the characters find themselves as they were at the beginning of the play.

The Test for Husbands (*El examen de maridos*, pub. 1634). The beautiful and wealthy Doña Inés subjects her suitors to rigorous tests of conduct and reputation. She loves Marquis Fadrique, who, along with Count Carlos, Don Alberto, Don Guillén, and Don Juan de Guzmán, aspires to marry her. Doña Blanca, trying to win back the now-rich Marquis, whom she had rejected because of his poverty, appears before Inés disguised as a servant and maliciously convinces her that Don Carlos is the man she ought to marry. Meanwhile, Ochado, Fadrique's servant, learns that Blanca's slander has thus far prevented his master from being chosen by Inés and promptly tells the Marquis. Carlos and Fadrique debate their views on marriage before Inés, and Carlos, who has championed the cause of love as stronger than reason, wins; but he must concede his award to Don Fadrique so that his thesis may be translated into practice.

The Weaver of Segovia, Part I (*El tejedor de Segovia, primera parte*, pub. 1634). *Comedia histórica* in which Beltrán Ramírez finds letters incriminating two nobles, Suero Peláez and his son Don Juan, of plotting with the Moors against King Alfonso VI. however, the two guilty noblemen succeed in convincing the King that Beltrán Ramírez is the traitor, and the latter is executed. Fernando, Ramírez's son, returns victorious from battles with the Moors and barely escapes his father's fate. He is helped by Doña María, but the two lovers must take refuge by disguising themselves as a weaver (Pedro Alonso) and his wife (Teodora). Fernando had given poison to his sister Ana, who was imprisoned by Don Juan, to prevent her from being dishonored; she, however, survives the poison and is forced to become Don Juan's mistress. The two treacherous nobles rise in royal favor, and Fernando, swearing vengeance, sees them enter Segovia as honored friends of the King.

The Weaver of Segovia, Part II (*El tejedor de Segovia, segunda parte*, pub. 1634). Sequel to *The Weaver of Segovia, Part I*. Don Fernando and Doña María, who are secretly married, have found refuge in Segovia disguised as Pedro Alonso and Teodora, a weaver and his wife. Teodora has attracted the attention of Don Juan, who proceeds to court her. But when he learns about Teodora's relations with Pedro Alonso, he attacks the weaver, who fights bravely and kills two of Don Juan's servants. Escaping from prison with Teodora to the mountain country, he finds his sister Ana, whom he has believed dead. When his whereabouts are discovered, he flees, but later, in the house of his rival Don Juan, he reveals his identity and forces Juan to marry his sister. Then Juan, wounded in a duel with Fernando, confesses that he and his father committed the felony attributed to Fernando's father. Fernando and his friends repulse the attacking Moors, and the King rehabilitates the name Ramírez.

[ANDRÉS FRANCO]

PLAYS

There is no adequate chronology of the plays of Ruiz de Alarcón; they are therefore listed in alphabetical order.

1. *La amistad castigada* (*Friendship Punished*). Play. Published 1634.
2. *El Anticristo* (*The Antichrist*). Comedia de magia o milagros. Published 1634. Produced Madrid, Dec. 14, 1623.
3. *La crueldad por el honor* (*Cruelty for Honor*). Teatro heróico nacional. Written ca. 1625. Published 1634.
4. *La cueva de Salamanca* (*The Cave of Salamanca*). Comedia de enredo. Published 1628.
5. *La culpa busca la pena y el agravio la venganza* (*Crime Seeks Punishment and Grievance Revenge*). Play. Published ca. 1642–1650.
6. *El desdichado en fingir* (*Feigned Misfortune*). Comedia de enredo. Published 1628.
7. *El dueño de las estrellas* (*The Master of the Stars*). Play. Published 1634.
8. *Los empeños de un engaño* (*An Error's Obligations*). Comedia de capa y espada. Published 1634.
9. *El examen de maridos* (*The Test for Husbands*). Play. Published 1634.
10. *Los favores del mundo* (*The Favors of the World*). Play. Published 1628.
11. *Ganar amigos* (*Gaining Friends*). Comedia de capa y espada. Written 1621. Published 1634. Produced 1621.
12. *La industria y la suerte* (*Wits and Luck*). Comedia de enredo. Published 1628.
13. *La manganilla de Melilla* (*Melilla's Trick*). Play. Written 1617. Published 1634. Produced 1617.
14. *Mudarse por mejorarse* (*A Change for the Better*). Play. Published 1628.
15. *No hay mal que por bien no venga, o Don Domingo de Don Blas* (*Look for the Silver Lining, or Don Domingo de Don Blas*). Play. Published 1653.
16. *Las paredes oyen* (*The Walls Have Ears*). Play. Written 1617. Published 1628. Produced 1617.
17. *Los pechos privilegiados* (*Privileged Bosoms*). Comedia de capa y espada. Written 1625. Published 1634.
18. *La prueba de las promesas* (*The Proof of the Promises*). Play. Published 1634.
19. *Quien mal anda en mal acaba* (*Evil Works Make an Evil End*). Play. Published 1652?
20. *El semejante a sí mismo* (*His Own Double*). Comedia de enredo. Published 1628. Based on an episode in Miguel de Cervantes' *Don Quixote* (1605, 1615).

21. *El tejedor de Segovia, primera parte* (*The Weaver of Segovia, Part I*). Comedia histórica. Published 1634.
22. *El tejedor de Segovia, segunda parte* (*The Weaver of Segovia, Part II*). Comedia histórica. Published 1634.
23. *Todo es ventura* (*All Is Due to Fortune*). Play. Published 1628.
24. *La verdad sospechosa** (*The Truth Suspected*). Play. Written ca. 1619/21. Published 1634. Produced ca. 1619/21.

EDITIONS

Collections
Parte primera, Madrid, 1628; *Parte segunda*, Barcelona, 1634; *Comedias*, in *Biblioteca de autores españoles*, vol. XX; *Teatro completo*, ed. by E. Abreu Gómez, Mexico City, 1951; *Obras completas*, ed. by A. Millares Carlo, Mexico City, 3 vols., 1957–1959.
Individual Plays
Look for the Silver Lining. Published in *Cuarto comedias*, ed. by J. M. Hill and M. M. Harlan, New York, 1941.
The Truth Suspected. Published in *Spanish Drama*, ed. by A. Flores and tr. by R. C. Ryan, New York, 1962.
The Walls Have Ears. Published in *Representative Spanish Authors*, ed. by W. T. Pattison, New York, 1942.

CRITICISM

L. Fernández-Guerra y Orbe, *Don Juan Ruiz de Alarcón y Mendoza*, Madrid, 1871; P. Henríquez Ureña, *Don Juan Ruiz de Alarcón*, Mexico City, 1914; E. Abreu Gómez, *Ruiz de Alarcón: Bibliografía crítica*, Mexico City, 1939; J. Jiménez Rueda, *Juan Ruiz de Alarcón y su tiempo*, Mexico City, 1939; A. Castro Leal, *Juan Ruiz: Su vida y su obra*, Mexico City, 1943; R. E. Chandler and K. Schwartz, *A New History of Spanish Literature*, Baton Rouge, La., 1961; W. Poesse, *Ensayo de una bibliografía de Juan Ruiz de Alarcón y Mendoza*, Valencia, 1964; W. Poesse, *Juan Ruiz de Alarcón*, New York, 1973.

Ruiz Iriarte, Víctor (1912–)

Spanish journalist, film scenarist, and dramatist. His play *The Six-horse Landau* (*El landó de seis caballos*, 1950) is an absurd farce that, like many of his successful plays, possesses an undercurrent of human tragedy. Themes of man's eternal striving for love, happiness, and affection or of his anguished loneliness are skillfully placed within the context of comedy or farce in such plays as the famous *Play-Game* (*Juego de niños*, 1952), *The Poor Little Hypocrite* (*El pobrecito embustero*, 1953), *The Café of the Flowers* (*El café de las flores*, 1953), *The Rebellious Spinster* (*La soltera rebelde*, 1952), and *The Apprentice Lover* (*El aprendiz de amante*, 1949). While it is true that the majority of Ruiz Iriarte's works are farces, a number of his more exceptional dramatic plays are written in a serious, transcendental vein: *The Blind Birds* (*Los pájaros ciegos*,

Víctor Ruiz Iriarte.
[New York
Public Library]

Scene from *El carrusell*. Madrid, Teatro de Lara, 1964. [New York Public Library Picture Collection]

1948), *Juanita Goes to Rio de Janeiro* (*Juanita va a Río de Janeiro*, 1948), *Esta noche es la víspera* (1958), the transcendental satire *One Day of Glory* (*Un día de gloria*, 1943), and *The Grand Minuet* (*El gran minué*, 1950. Three of his best plays were written during the sixties: *The Carousel* (*El carrusel*, 1964), *A Letter Comes*, 1967, and *Story of a Deceit* (*Historia de un adulterio*, 1968).

Ruiz Iriarte won the Premio Piquor of the Royal Spanish Academy for his comedy *The Academy of Love* (*Academia de amor*, 1946) and has served as president of the Sociedad de Autores de España.   [ANDRÉS FRANCO]

CRITICISM

P. Zatlin Boring, *Víctor Ruiz Iriarte*, New York, 1980.

Russell, George William (1867–1935)

Irish writer and activist; known as AE. Russell was born in Lurgan, Ireland, on April 10, 1867, and died in Bournemouth, England, on July 17, 1935. He was a second-rate writer, painter, and politician, but a first-rate influence on politics and literature. He continually challenged, instructed, and disturbed his lifelong friend and occasional amicable opponent, William Butler Yeats. He became a familiar figure in Dublin as the host of a weekly gathering of writers that included Yeats, George Moore, Padraic Colum, and James Stephens. Moore described Russell in his autobiography, *Hail and Farewell* (1911–1914). *See* COLUM, PADRAIC; YEATS, WILLIAM BUTLER.

The Irish Literary Theatre founded by Yeats, Lady Gregory, and Edward Martyn was replaced by the Irish National Dramatic Company which became known as the Irish National Theatre Society. Yeats was made president, and AE vice-president. The first series of the society's plays took place at St. Theresa's Hall on Clarendon Street, Dublin, in April 1902. One of the plays, George Russell's *Deirdre*, his single contribution to the repertoire, was destined to become a cornerstone in the building of a national theatre because of its great popularity. It is a well-constructed play based on the Deirdre legend from *Cuchulain of Muirthemne*, a legend used dramatically by Yeats and Synge as well. Although Russell did not, as Yeats expected, write other plays, he often gave plots or incidents that suggested plots to other dramatists. Lady Gregory attributes to him the story of *The Image* and acknowledges hints from AE used in her *Aristotle's Bellows* (1923) and *The Jester* (1923). *See* GREGORY, LADY AUGUSTA.

AE and most of the actors drawn from the various nationalist groups in Dublin looked upon membership in the theatre as part of their political activities. Yeats, Lady Gregory, Synge, and the Fays tried to keep the theatre out of politics. When Synge's *In the Shadow of the Glen* (1903) was accepted, the first open split occurred. Actresses Maud Gonne and Maire Quinn and actor Dudley Digges resigned at the "insult to Irish womanhood." Yeats was relieved and in a letter to Frank Fay indicated that this defection of the strongest national element would make it easier "to keep a pure artistic ideal." But differences erupted again during the 1903–1904 season, ending in AE's resignation. In the struggle between nation and art Yeats had won, at least temporarily. *See* IRISH DRAMA; SYNGE, JOHN MILLINGTON.

Deirdre (1902). Tragedy of Deirdre, who, because of the prophecy that she would cause the downfall of the house of the reigning monarch, is hidden away in a valley by King Concobar. One day Naisi and his brothers enter the valley; he comes upon Deirdre, and they fall in love. Concobar, who is also in love with Deirdre, swears vengeance. For two years the lovers live blissfully in Scotland, but Naisi longs to return home. Thus, when an envoy from Concobar arrives offering amnesty they leave for Erin despite Deirdre's pleadings and warnings. When Concobar sees Deirdre, now more beautiful than ever, his jealousy returns. Naisi and his brothers are murdered, and Deirdre dies over Naisi's body.

CAROL GELDERMAN

Russian Drama

Russian drama began, like so much drama, in rituals of rural life: magical ceremonies to ensure fertility and abundance; the oral tradition of charms and songs; the choric round dances, or *khorovody*, that accompanied peasant weddings; and the *potekhi*, the "sport" of village buffoons. These gradually became incorporated into folk drama. The antiphonal responses of participants in fertility rites, divided into two groups like their ancient Greek counterparts, acted as a rudimentary kind of play. The first professional players, the *skomorokhi*, or "minstrels" (the word derives from the Greek *skommarkhos*, or master of mirth), wandered over Russia as musicians, storytellers, dancers, bear-leaders, and clowns, and by the eleventh and twelveth centuries had developed a specialized repertory of puppet plays, bear shows, and improvisational comedy. Details of everyday life were staples: a standby of the puppet plays was the horse-trading scene in which Petrushka, the Russian Punch, out-haggles a gypsy. But wish fulfillment played a part too. *The Farce of the Boyar*, which survived well into the nineteenth century, was a typical *skomorokh* gibe at the ruling classes, in which a boyar magistrate is bribed by wicker baskets full of rubbish and eventually thrashed by his suppliants.

Christianity fostered the mystery plays performed within the precincts of a church, although the ecclesiastical authorities often frowned on these activities. Primarily *peshchnye dramy* ("dramas of martyrdom"), they rapidly took on a comic element in the dialogues between two "Chaldeans" who act as tormentors and whose antics resembled those of the *skomorokhi*. The highly popular *vertep*, or nativity play, made a physical division between secular and religious content by staging Christ's birth on an upper platform and the comic interludes on a lower. *See* MYSTERY PLAY in glossary.

By the seventeenth century folk drama had evolved certain standard plays capable of extensive variation and often commenting on social and political situations. The most famous of these is the *Tsar Maximilian and His Disobedient Son Adolph* (*Komediya o tsare Maksimilyane i nepokornom syne ego Adolfe*), in which a heathen king executes his Christian (or in some versions, robber chieftain) son. Its episodes are common to all European folk drama: heroic combats between paladins, a fight with Death, comic resurrections, and punning gravediggers; but there are also literary vestiges, for the play may have been founded on an unknown scholastic drama, with allusions to Peter the Great's quarrel with his son Alexis and, in some late variants, to doctors out of Molière and to the English mummers' play. In the widely popular *The Boat* (*Lodka*), otherwise known as *The Sloop* (*Shlyupka*) or *The Robber Band* (*Shayka razboiynikov*), bandits are glorified for drowning a local landowner. Other folk plays like *Mavrukh* and *Pakhomukha* parodied church services. In short, they served as escape valves for social discontent.

SEVENTEENTH CENTURY

Russian drama entered literature in the 1670s and 1680s with the school dramas, translated from Latin and Polish Jesuit plays into a stilted Old Church Slavonic jargon. Some, like the *Play of Martyrdom* (*Peschoe deystvo*), were merely embroidered church rituals or, like the *Comedy of Christ's Birth* (*Komodiya na rozhdestvo Khristovo*), formal nativity dramas; others, like the *Play of Alexis Man of God* (*Deystvo ob Aleksee bozhyem cheloveke*), were hagiographic dialogues of saints' lives. Morality plays such as Georgý Konissky's *The Resurrection of the Dead* (*Voskresenie myortvykh*) would mingle allegorical figures like Vice, Pride, and Truth with Biblical or historical personages. As in the church plays, the declamatory passages were enlivened by comic interludes and even musical and dance

An illustrated page from a late-seventeenth-century publication of Simeon of Polotsk's *Comedy-Parable of the Prodigal Son*.

numbers. The first playwright of note was the monk and poet Simeon of Polotsk, whose tragedy *King Nebuchadnezzar, the Golden Calf, and The Three Children Unburnt in the Furnace* (*O Navkhodonosore tsare, o tele zlate i trekh otrotsekh v peshchi ne sozhzhyonnykh*) and *Comedy-Parable of the Prodigal Son* (*Komediya-prichta o bludnom syne*), written in rhymed syllabic verse, added a modicum of character conflict and realistic elements to the old Biblical stories. *See* MORALITY PLAY in glossary.

Tsar Alexis Mikhailovich founded a court theatre in 1672 and ordered the Lutheran pastor Johann Gregori to recruit an acting company from the children of scribes to perform religious and historical dramas. The plays of this court theatre were adapted from the repertory of the so-called English Comedians, originally Elizabethan actors who had toured and settled in Germany. Although pompous and didactic, such plays as *The Comedy of Esther, or The Play of Artaxerxes* (*Komediya ob Esfiri, ili Artakserksovo deystvo*, 1672), *Judith* (*Ob Iudifi*, 1674), and *Bajazet and Tamerlane* (*Bazhazet i Tamerlan, ili Temir-aksakovo deystvo,* 1675) contributed action and pathos to the rhetoric of the school dramas. Prologues, epilogues, lengthy asides, and coarse clowning kept the spectators' interest and alerted them to the emblematic meaning of the events. For instance, Tamerlane's victory over the Persian king Bajazet was related to the Russo-Turkish hostilities.

In 1694 the folk theatre received a blow when Tsar Alexis, following the "Copper Revolt," ordered all *skomorokhi* to "desist from ungodly practices" and exiled them to border towns, prohibiting improvisational entertainments. His son, Peter I, however, encouraged public gatherings at performances, but the performers were imported from abroad to propagandize for Peter's reforms. Drama in the Petrine era tended to be spectacular apotheoses of the Tsar's military victories—not so much plays as elaborate divertissements with music, fireworks, allegories, and grandiose speeches. *The Triumph of the Orthodox Peace* (*Torzhestvo mira pravoslavnogo,* 1703), depicting a Russian Mars overcoming the Lion of Sweden, or *God Brings Low the Prideful* (*Bozhie unichizhitely gordykh unichizhenie,* 1710), about the Battle of Poltava, can be likened to the pageants and masques of European courts. Comic interludes were translated from German and used as weapons of satire against conservative enemies of Peter's policies.

EIGHTEENTH CENTURY

Although the school drama no longer entertained the court and returned to the seminary, it reached its highest level with St. Dimitry Tuptalo of Rostov, who staged his own plays with the students of the Kiev Religious Academy. His baroque blend of the solemn and comic in his version of the nativity drama was particularly interesting. Another innovator was Feofan Prokopovich, whose tragicomedy *Prince Vladimir* (*Vladimir Slavenorossiyskikh stran knyaz i povelitel, ot neveriya tmy v svet evangelskoy privedennoy dukhom svyatym,* 1702) was structured according to Renaissance Italian models and neo-Aristotelian rules, and equated the idolatrous priests who opposed Vladi-

Illustration for Simeon of Polotsk's *King Nebuchadnezzar, the Golden Calf, and The Three Children Unburnt in the Furnace.*

Aleksey Petrovich Sumarokov. [Academy of Art Archives]

mir's Christianizing of Russia to those retrograde reactionaries who fought against Peter's Westernization. Feofan was the first theorist of Russian drama, calling on poets to portray "general virtues and vices" and draw on national history for subject matter.

The first established company of actors in Russia, headed by Fyodor Volkov of Yaroslavl, played before the Empress Elizabeth in 1752. Three years earlier she had attended a performance of the tragedy *Khorev,* by Aleksey Sumarokov, performed by the amateurs of the Cadet School. Up to that time the major foreign influences on secular drama had been the bombastic German *Haupt- und Staatsaktionen,* as a model for tragedy, and the stereotyped action of the Italian *commedia dell'arte* as a model for comedy. When, in 1756, Sumarokov was appointed director of the first permanent professional Russian theatre with Volkov as his star, he introduced the French neoclassical influence. Under the spell of Boileau's *Art poétique,* Sumarokov's own nine tragedies and twelve comedies, the foundation of the basic Russian repertoire of the 1750s and 1760s, closely copied Racine and Molière. In Alexandrine verse and observing the unities, such tragedies as *Khorev* (1747), *Sinavius and Truvor* (*Sinav i Truvor,* 1750), and *Dimitry the Pretender* (*Dimitry Samozvanets,* 1771) drew on a quasi-legendary Russian past to teach lessons of civic duty and the submission of personal ambitions to a higher duty. *See* SUMAROKOV, ALEKSEY PETROVICH. *See also* COMMEDIA DELL' ARTE; NEOCLASSICISM; UNITIES in glossary.

Sumarokov's drama is at best intense with virtue but too often vitiated by flabby plotting, frigid diction, and rationally abstract characters. Nevertheless, his example was followed for decades and tragedy became a forum for liberal ideas. The scientist and man of letters M. V. Lomonosov used his *Tamira and Selim* (*Tamira i Selim,* 1751) to defend the rights of man; but as Catherine the Great abandoned the Enlightenment principles of her early reign, she repressed outspoken tragedies. Ya. B. Knyazhnin's *Vadim of Novgorod* (*Vadim Novgorodsky,* 1789) was ordered seized and burnt by the common hangman because of its insurgent hero and antityranni-

Contemporary drawing of a scene from M. V. Lomonosov's *Tamira and Selim*, a classical defense of human rights.

cal sentiments. Catherine's own historical plays *From the Life of Rurik* (*Iz zhizni Ryurika*, 1786) and *The Early Reign of Oleg* (*Nachalnoe upravlenie Olega*, 1786) were apologies for her dynasty, and by the end of the century tragedies like Mikhail Kheraskov's *Moscow Liberated* (*Osvobozhdyonnaya Moskva*, 1798) were loud in their praise of the monarchy.

In comedy, although Sumarokov drew his plots and situations from Molière, he added the spice of Russian manners and allusions, making such plays as *The Monstrosity* (*Chudovishcha*), *An Empty Quarrel* (*Pustaya ssora*), and *The Inveigled Dowry* (*Pridanoe obmanom*, 1750–1772) the foundation for national dramatic satire. For the most part, and in the tradition of European "new comedy," the targets of mockery were personal affectation, eccentricity, and abnormality and could become extremely didactic, like Kheraskov's *The Atheist* (*Bezbozhnik*, 1761), an attack on freethinking. But comedy was the only form of drama that portrayed the common man: peasants became standard personnel in comic opera, sometimes absurdly idealized as in V. I. Maykov's *The Village Holiday, or The Benefactor Crowned* (*Derevensky prazdnik, ili Uvenchannaya dobrodetel*, 1777), sometimes reasonably close to the truth in their oppressed state, as in Knyazhnin's *Mis-*

fortune from a Carriage (*Neschastie ot karetu*, 1779). However, the most popular comic opera of the period, frequently revived, was Aleksandr Ablesimov's rollicking *Miller-Magician, Mountebank, and Matchmaker* (*Melnik-koldun, obmanshchik i svat*, 1779). *See* NEW COMEDY in glossary.

Sentimentality and the modes of "lachrymose comedy" made their appearance in the sentention *The Rake, Corrected by Love* (*Mot, lyuboviyu ispravlennyy*, 1765) of V. I. Lukin, an effective propagandist for feeling over reason in drama. Lukin recommended that classical rules and standard plots be retained in comedy but that the characters and their foibles come from Russian life; these tenets were upheld by M. A. Matinsky in his satire on government clerks, *The Central Market of St. Petersberg* (*Sanktpeterburgsky gostinny dvor*, 1782), and by Knyazhnin in his comic opera *The Mead Vendor* (*Sbitenshchik*, 1784), which introduced wholly Russian types into conventional intrigues. The leading exponent of Russian subject matter for both comedy and tragedy was P. A. Plavilshchikov, who argued that audiences could not relate to Greek or Tatar heroes and that it was better for citizens to learn their own history. His own comedies foreshadow Ostrovsky and Potekhin in depicting the mores of peasants in *The Landless Farmer* (*Bobyl*, 1790) and of merchants in *The Shopkeeper* (*Sidelets*, 1793). But the aristocratic audiences who formed the taste of the time were not interested, and Plavilshchikov's example remained unimitated for many years.

The dramatist who most clearly set the stage for an indigenous Russian comic drama was Denis Fonvizin, who drew his characters and their language from everyday Russian life in addition to attacking mindless Francophilia and the abuse of serfs by landowners. His *The Brigadier* (*Brigadir*, 1766) was welcomed as a mirror image of the gentry (the statesman Count Panin said, "You put our own aunties and grannies in it"), and his best play, *The Minor* (*Nedorosl*, 1782), although prolix and stodgy in its sententious passages, introduced characters who became synonyms for stupidity and loutishness. Several features which consistently recur in Russian drama made an early appearance in Fonvizin's plays: the harsh mistress who wilfully tries to wreck the love life of her innocent *protégée*; the government as *deus ex machina* to set all things right at the end; and the prosy *raisonneur* to point the moral. *See* FONVIZIN, DENIS IVANOVICH.

NINETEENTH CENTURY

An even more outspoken satirist of corruption was Vasily Kapnist, whose comedy in verse *Chicanery* (*Yabeda*, 1798) is a garish castigation of bribery and peculation in the law courts, a precursor to the works of Gogol and Sukhovo-Kobylin as well as to Ostrovsky's *A Lucrative Post* (*Dohbodnoe mesto*, 1856). But Fonvizin's chief successor was the fabulist Ivan Krylov, who ridiculed classicism in *Triumphus, or The Princess Podshchipa* (*Triumf, ili Podshchipa*, 1800), and in *The Notion Shop* (*Modnaya Lavka*, 1806) and *School for Daughters* (*Urok dochkam*, 1807) contrasted the native wit of the average Russian with affected French airs and graces.

A great wave of sentimentality washed over Russian drama, leaving it sodden with tears, in the wake of the German dramatist August von Kotzebue, who headed the German theatre in St. Petersburg in the last years of the reign of Emperor Paul I, whose vanity he had flattered in a play. Not only were his own melodramas immensely popular, but his cult of natural feelings and virtuous self-sacrifice and his contrived plots and overheated emotionalism infected Russian playwrights. The first great hit of this school was V. M. Fyodorov's dramatization of Nikolay Karamzin's tearful novella, *Poor Liza* (*Bednaya Liza*), as *Liza, or The Consequences of Pride and Seduction* (*Liza ili Sledstvie gordosti i obolshcheniya*, 1803), and his lead was followed by N. I. Ilyin. Sentimentality also suffused tragedy. V. A. Ozerov took the old neoclassic formulas and revitalized them with the new sensibility; whether his subjects were drawn from Greek mythology, as in *Oedipus in Athens* (*Edip v Afinakh*, 1804) and *Polixena* (*Poliksena*, 1809), or from the pseudo-Gaelic poems of Ossian as in *Fingal* (1805), or from medieval Russian history, as in his patriotic effusion *Dimitry of the Don* (*Dimitry Donskoy*, 1807), the treatment was equally generalized and elevated, and the emotions impossibly noble and pathetic. Yet the favor of actors and audiences alike allowed his tragedies to dominate the boards for years.

The idiosyncratic development of Russian drama was retarded by two principal factors, the government and the audience. All the theatres of Moscow and Petersburg, which set the style for the provinces, were governmental agencies, staffed by career bureaucrats answerable to the Tsar's chief-of-staff; no play could be staged until it had passed the censor. State censorship, which grew particularly strict during the reign of Nicholas I, eliminated serious discussion of social issues or an accurate depiction of whole sectors of Russian life. It also limited dramatic genres to those already established. Audiences were composed either of a fashionable aristocracy which preferred French culture and regarded native art as crude and irrelevant or of a more or less illiterate and untutored mass, eager to be entertained. In the first half of the nineteenth century, the stage was overrun with imported French vaudevilles and romantic melodrama tailored to suit Russian political decorum. Emasculated versions of Hugo and Dumas were the inspiration for the fatuous patriotic melodramas and spectacles of Nestor Kukolnik, whose *The Hand of the Almighty the Fatherland Hath Saved* (*Ruka vsevyshnego otechestvo spasla*, 1833) was the Tsar's favorite play, and of Nikolay Polevoy, who blared out such heart-stirring fanfares as *Grandfather of the Russian Fleet* (*Dedushka Russkogo flota*, 1837). Polevoy, however, is also responsible for the popularization of Shakespeare. His translation of *Hamlet*, played by the tragedian Pavel Mochalov in 1837, was the closest to the original the Russians had yet seen.

The vaudeville, a one-act farce sprinkled with witty verses set to popular tunes, had been welcomed with open arms by Prince A. A. Shakhovskoy, who used it to attack the romantics in *School for Coquettes, or The Lipets Spa* (*Urok koketkam, ili Lipetskie vody*, 1815), and it soon became naturalized. Such deft vaudeville writers as A. I. Pisarev, M. N. Zagoskin, and N. I. Khmelnitsky used the form as a weapon in literary quarrels and to poke fun at current fads. Another vaudeville author, Aleksandr Griboyedov, produced one genuine masterpiece, *Woe from Wit* (*Gore ot uma*, 1824), a high comedy in verse, which, as a culmination of earlier attempts at social satire and an embodiment of a new, more intellectual approach, is worthy of comparison with Molière's *The Misanthrope*. Griboyedov subordinated the love plot and quirks of character to the conflict of ideas; while drawing a vivid picture of Moscow high life at a specific moment in history, he also created universal types. Preserving the unities, he invented dialogue so pithy and aphoristic that much of it became proverbial, even while the play was still circulating in manuscript. *See* GRIBOYEDOV, ALEKSANDR SERGEYEVICH.

As *Woe from Wit* pointed out a new direction in comedy, so *Boris Godunov* (1825) blazed a trail in tragedy. The poet Aleksandr Pushkin hoped to found a school of national tragedy by following Shakespearean models, using a looser scene arrangement, more realistic dialogue, and a subtler presentation of human psychology in the exploration of national history. "Our theatre," he insisted, "is suited to the popular laws of Shakespeare's drama and not to the courtly usages of Racine's tragedy." *Boris Godunov*, based on historical data provided by Karamzin, was written in blank verse and set in some thirty locales. Following his dictum that "human fate is national fate," Pushkin made the title character less important than "the People," whose passive reactions to events produce the residual impression. When Nicholas I forbade a performance of the play, suggesting that Pushkin turn it into a novel of the Walter Scott variety, the poet retreated to his more intimate *Little Tragedies* (*Malenkie tragediy*, 1830),

Aleksandr Griboyedov's *Woe from Wit,* as produced in Moscow with Shchepkin (center) as Famusov. [*Moscow Theatres*]

I. Tolchanov as Arbenin in Mikhail Lermontov's *Masquerade*, Vakhtangov Theatre, Moscow. [Theatre Collection, The New York Public Library at Lincoln Center, Astor, Lenox and Tilden Foundations]

four short plays based on European literary types like the miser and Don Juan, using terse verse dialogue, soliloquies, and archetypical characters to explore human passions and contradictions. *See* PUSHKIN, ALEKSANDR SERGEYEVICH.

Another contemporary innovator in tragedy was Mikhail Lermontov, whose earliest plays, *The Spaniards* (*Ispantsy*, 1830), *Men and Passions* (*Menschen und Leidenschaften*, 1830), and *The Strange Man* (*Stranny chelovek*, 1831), run the romantic gamut from full-blown outbursts to mysterious gloom. His finest play, *Masquerade* (*Maskarad*, 1835–1836), is a typical moral rebellion. It combines a sardonic indictment of society's duplicity with a portrait of a latter-day Othello, isolated, incapable of compromise, ruthless in pursuit of a private truth, and destroyed by the mendacity around him and his own implacability. Awkward and hysterical as it is at times, the play is far more powerful and emotionally authentic than any other tragedy of its age. *See* LERMONTOV, MIKHAIL YURYEVICH.

But Griboyedov, Pushkin, and Lermontov failed to have a direct effect on Russian playwriting because their works were forbidden on the stage for decades or, when produced, were heavily cut. The greatest dramatist to influence the contemporary stage was Nikolay Gogol, and this was due largely to the support of the liberal critic Vissarion Belinsky and sympathetic actors like Mikhail Shchepkin and Ivan Sosnitsky. Always fascinated by the theatre, Gogol had begun by writing a historical play about Alfred the Great, but he soon found his best material in the world of the bureaucracy. *The Inspector General* (*Revizor*, 1836), a hilariously funny exposure of small-town corruption, passed the censorship, it was rumored, because the Tsar wanted to see it performed; but Gogol was dismayed that it was played as a farce and annoyed the audience with its truth-telling. To the charge that there were no "positive characters," Gogol cited Laughter as the noble protagonist and insisted that high comedy has a duty not only to reflect life but to judge it. In fact, *Revizor* is only superficially realistic; like many of Gogol's works, it is a fanciful verbal construct whose events exist in the characters' imaginations, and its grotesque caricature and hyperbole were vastly influential on later Russian comedy. *See* GOGOL, NIKOLAY VASILYEVICH.

Gogol's other plays, *Marriage* (*Zhenitba*, 1842) and *Gamblers* (*Igroki*, 1842), are closer to traditional situation comedies, although the dialogue and characterizations are saturated with Gogolian absurdity. He himself condemned vaudevilles as inexpressive of Russian life, but by the time of his death the vaudeville had become a fully assimilated genre, depicting aspects of ordinary existence seldom seen on the stage. Its masters were Dmitry Lensky, F. A. Koni, Pavel Karatygin, and even the poet Nikolay Nekrasov (under the pseudonym Perepelsky); its subjects are usually backstage intrigues, Petersburg apartment dwellers, and trends in literary or millinery fashion; and its language is racy and colloquial, interspersed with ditties of considerable verve. *See* LENSKY, DMITRY TIMOFEYEVICH.

The themes of "the little man" and "the humiliated and offended" that occur in Gogol's late stories and Dostoevsky's early novels appear in dramatic form in the plays of Ivan Turgenev. The work of a novelist and short-story writer, Tugenev's plays make up in character-drawing and emotional nuance what they lack in action or stagecraft. His farce *Luncheon with the Marshal* (*Zavtrak u predvoditelya*, 1839) is Gogolian in its accumulation of misunderstandings, while *The Charity Case* (*Nakhlebnik*, 1848) and *The Bachelor* (*Kholostyak*, 1849), written for the actor Shchepkin, are infused with a Dostoevskyan pity for society's outcasts. Other plays, such as *Thin Ice* (*Gde tonko, tam i rvetsya*, 1848) and *Evening in Sorrento* (*Vecher v Sorrente*, 1852), approximate the *comédies-proverbes* of Alfred de Musset. But his best play, *A Month in the Country* (*Mesyats v derevne*, 1850), is the first drama to portray refined, indolent landowners whiling away their time in idle love affairs; the play's milieu, the low-keyed modulations of the characters' feelings, the psychological acuity, and the poetic atmosphere are direct forerunners of

"Chekhovian mood." But even when these plays were staged in Turgenev's lifetime, audiences failed to recognize their originality. *See* TURGENEV, IVAN SERGEYEVICH.

The most important plays of the nineteenth century thus seem to exist in a vacuum, outside the mainstream of theatrical activity. This holds true of the grotesque satiric trilogy of Aleksandr Sukhovo-Kobylin—*Krechinsky's Wedding* (*Svadba Krechinskogo*, 1855), *The Lawsuit* (*Delo*, 1861), and *Tarelkin's Death* (*Smert Tarelkina*, 1869)—wherein Gogolian hyperbole, vaudeville devices, and the author's personal bitterness intermingle to present a nightmarish view of the world. A kindred savage indignation leers from Mikhail Saltykov-Shchedrin's comedy *Pazukhin's Death* (*Smert Pazukhina*, 1857), which boasts not one virtuous character. A skewed, almost absurdist universe is reflected in Aleksey Pisemsky's first play, the bizarre character comedy *The Hypochondriac* (*Ipokhondrik*, 1852), and in the parodies of "Kozma Prutkov," a civil servant with literary tastes, invented by Aleksey K. Tolstoy and his cousins to mock the excesses of the vaudeville, the folk opera, and the metaphysical tragedy. All these plays either went unperformed until the turn of the century or were misunderstood and condemned when they did manage to reach the stage in their own time. Later they would provide considerable inspiration for early Soviet comedy. *See* PISEMSKY, ALEKSEY FEOFILAKTOVICH; SALTYKOV-SHCHEDRIN, MIKHAIL YEVGRAFOVICH; SUKHOVO-KOBYLIN, ALEKSANDR VASILYEVICH.

The writer responsible for creating almost single-handedly a Russian repertory is Aleksandr Ostrovsky, who may be seen as another descendant of Plavilshchikov, Fonvizin, and Gogol, but whose voice is quite dis-

The Lawsuit, the second play in a trilogy by Aleksandr Sukhovo-Kobylin, as produced in 1927 with Podgorny as the Prince. [Theatre Collection, The New York Public Library at Lincoln Center, Astor, Lenox and Tilden Foundations]

Vsevolod Meyerhold's production of Nikolay Gogol's *The Inspector General.* [*Moscow Theatres*]

Enough Stupidity in Every Wise Man by Aleksandr Ostrovsky, as staged in New York in 1923 by the Moscow Art Theatre. [Theatre Collection, The New York Public Library at Lincoln Center, Astor, Lenox and Tilden Foundations]

tinct and independent. Without attempting or achieving "naturalism," Ostrovsky created a *bytovaya drama* ("way-of-life drama") that presented the manners and speech patterns of merchants, shopkeepers, and petty bureaucrats of the cities, and peasants and smallholders of the country. His plays are imbued with local color and his characters defined by their environment, professions, and domestic arrangements. He was immediately claimed by both opposing camps of Russian ideology. The radical Westernizers hailed him as the scourge of conservative domestic tyranny and homegrown corruption, for excoriating what the critic Dobrolyubov called "the kingdom of darkness." The Slavophils, on the other hand, lauded him for preserving and enhancing folk customs and bygone lore in his plays. Ostrovsky himself tried to remain aloof from categorization, and his plays are of all sorts: comedies of Moscow merchant life like *It's a Family Affair—We'll Settle It Ourselves* (*Svoy lyudi—sochtyomsya*, 1850) and *Poverty Is No Crime* (*Bednost ne porok*, 1854); satires of high society like *Enough Stupidity in Every Wise Man* (*Na vsyakogo mudretsa dovolno prostoty*, 1868); tragedies of provincial intolerance like *The Thunderstorm* (*Groza*, 1859), often called the first true Russian tragedy; folk drama like *The Snow Maiden* (*Snegoruchka*, 1873); genre pictures of actors' lives like *Talents and Admirers* (*Talanty i poklonniki*, 1881); and studies of economic oppression like *The Last Sacrifice* (*Poslednyaya zhertva*, 1877). Allied to both the melodrama and the social satire traditions, his plays are rather leisurely in tempo, the plots uninvolved, as the emphasis is put on the workings of character within a sharply drawn ambience. *See* OSTROVSKY, ALEKSANDR NIKOLAYEVICH.

Ostrovsky also wrote historical drama, such as *Kozma Minin the One-armed* (*Kozma Zakharich Minin, Sukhoruk*, 1866) and *The Voivod, or The Dream on the Volga* (*Voevoda, ili Son na Volge*, 1865), participating in a movement inspired by Slavophil antiquarianism and governmentally nurtured chauvinism. Most of these plays about Ivan the Terrible and the Time of Troubles such as L. A. Mey's *The Tsar's Bride* (*Tsarskaya nevesta*, 1840) and *Maid of Pskov* (*Pskovityanka*, 1859) survive as opera librettos or, like D. V. Averkiev's *Olden Kashira* (*Kashirskaya starina*, 1871), as silent film scenarios. The idealization of patriarchal times and feudal Rus reached its apogee in the trilogy of blank-verse tragedies by Aleksey K. Tolstoy: *Death of Ivan the Terrible* (*Smert Ioanna Groznogo*, 1867), *Tsar Fyodor Ioannovich* (1868), and *Tsar Boris* (1870), not devoid of fustian but memorable for their vivid characterizations and resonant rhetoric. *See* TOLSTOY, ALEKSEY KONSTANTINOVICH.

If Slavophil tendencies appeared in historical drama, liberal attempts at reform crop up in dramas of peasant life and in problem plays. There is an eighteenth-century flavor to Aleksey Potekhin's *Human Judgment Isn't God's* (*Sud lyudskoy—ne bozhiy*, 1854) and *A Sheepskin Coat but a Human Heart* (*Shuba ovechya—dusha chelovechya*, 1855) which, despite the sedulously rendered peasant idioms, possess impossibly virtuous heroes and sentimental plots. The best of this lot is Aleksey Pisemsky's *A Bitter Fate* (*Gorkaya sudbina*, 1859), which raises the injustices of the peasant-master relationship to the level of classical tragedy and which both preceded and surpassed Leo Tolstoy's better-known *The Power of Darkness* (*Vlast tmy*, 1886). *See* POTEKHIN, ALEKSEY ANTIPOVICH; TOLSTOY, LEO.

The problem drama, ostensibly addressed to burning issues of the day, was, for the most part, a sensational melodrama featuring a *raisonneur* commenting superficially on a social question. The plays of Aleksey Potekhin's brother Nikolay, V. A. Dyachenko, I. V. Shpazhinsky, and Modest Chaikovsky, the composer's brother, are paragons of a mediocre genre, but one can single out Nikolay Leskov's *The Profligate* (*Rastochitel*, 1867), with its investigation of industrial profit sharing, as the best of a bad lot. The reactionary political temper of the 1880s put an end to even this token social commentary in drama. When the monopoly of the State theatres was ended in 1882, the private theatres, instead of rushing to put on experimental drama or socially conscious works, turned to translations of European boulevard farces and love intrigues, adventure extravaganzas, and historical spectacle. However, F. A. Korsh's theatre in Moscow gave special Friday matinees as a showcase for the better class of literary drama, thus creating an audience for the later Moscow Art Theatre, and Suvorin's theatre in St. Petersburg performed a similar service for serious contemporary playwrights. *See* MOSCOW ART THEATRE.

The various, often contradictory influences of Ibsen, Sudermann, Hauptmann, and Sardou can be perceived in the work of Aleksandr Sumbatov-Yuzhin, whose melodramatic effects and juicy roles for actors camouflage his feeble treatment of domestic problems—*Gentlemen* (*Dzhentlemen*, 1897); *Ties That Bind* (*Tsepi*, 1888)—and of Vladimir Nemirovich-Danchenko, in his intelligent, ultrarealistic, but turgid treatments of the dilemmas of the intellectual class—*Gold* (*Zoloto*, 1895); *The Price of Life* (*Tsena zhizni*, 1896).

Respected as a short-story writer, Anton Chekhov was regarded, at the start of his dramatic activity, as simply another of this group. His early farces—*The Bear*

The original production of Anton Chekhov's *Three Sisters*, with (l. to r.) Olga Knipper, M. G. Savickaya, and N. N. Litovceva as Masha, Olga, and Irina. [Moscow Art Theatre]

(*Medved*, 1888), *The Marriage Proposal* (*Predlozhenie*, 1888), *The Wedding* (*Svadba*, 1889), *The Jubilee* (*Yubiley*, 1891)—were efficient, mirth-raising equivalents of his humorous anecdotes. But his full-length plays *Ivanov* (1887) and *The Wood Demon* (*Leshy*, 1889) were, as investigations of the failed intelligentsia, similar to the dramas of his colleagues and, indeed, so clumsy in contrast to the usual professional hackwork that the most prolific play-doctor of the period, Viktor Krylov, offered himself to Chekhov as a collaborator. Chekhov found his distinctive voice in *The Seagull* (*Chayka*, 1896), a "comedy" about art and the

Leo Tolstoy's *The Power of Darkness*, with Y. Shatrova as Matryona, B. Gorbatov as Pyotr, I. Ilyinsky as Akim, and O. Chuvayeva as Anisya. [*Moscow Theatres*]

V. I. Kachalov in the title role of Chekhov's *Ivanov* in a Moscow Art Theatre production. New York, Jolson's Fifty-ninth Street Theatre, 1923. [Theatre Collection, The New York Public Library at Lincoln Center, Astor, Lenox and Tilden Foundations]

uses of talent; although still bound to old-fashioned devices like soliloquies and offstage gunshots, the play held the Chekhovian ethos. Each element, from locale and weather to a character's slightest remark, is intricately woven into the atmospheric pattern. The seeming inaction and inconsequentiality of the dialogue are a still surface beneath which bubbles the true inner life of the characters and the meaning of their behavior. *See* CHEKHOV, ANTON PAVLOVICH.

Chekhov owed his success and ability to develop this technique further to Nemirovich-Danchenko, who insisted on staging him at the Moscow Art Theatre, which he had founded in 1898 along with the amateur actor Konstantin Stanislavsky. The Art Theatre, which stressed ensemble playing, the expression of *perezhivanie* (inner feelings, subtext), and sensitivity to nuance, was an ideal advocate in the popularization of Chekhov's drama, although he himself often felt that it went overboard in the way of naturalistic effects and plangent emotionalism. After the Art Theatre's successful revival of *The Seagull*, Chekhov reworked *The Wood Demon* into *Uncle Vanya* (*Dyadya Vanya*, 1899), with new comic overtones and a dense, allusive dialogue composed of images of suffocation. On a broader canvas, in *Three Sisters* (*Tri sestry*, 1901) he achieved a fugal or symphonic structure, the themes of hopeless aspiration and overwhelming

vulgarity struck and restruck in different keys. By his final play, *The Cherry Orchard* (*Vishnyovy sad*, 1904), the straightforward tale of the sale of a mortgaged estate had taken on a symbolic cast, the characters comically realistic on one level, puppets of fate on another. What provides the special quality of Chekhov's plays are his ironic distance and his bemused objectivity. These qualities are lacking in his imitators, such as Boris Zaytsev, who reproduced his atmosphere of genteel futility but little else. Chekhov remains unique. *See* STANISLAVSKY, KONSTANTIN.

TWENTIETH CENTURY

The millenarianism that accompanied the dawn of the twentieth century was expressed in Russian drama in two diametrically opposite fashions. Political protest became louder, especially in the first plays of Maxim Gorky, romantic polemics with a naturalistic coating. Generally two groups of persons are pitted against one another, with a superman overcoming the reactionaries. *The Petty Bourgeois* (*Meshchane*, 1902), with its conflict between the older and younger generations, features Nil the engine driver, athirst for a social upheaval, a prototype of the positive hero in Soviet drama. *The Lower Depths* (*Na dne*, 1902), a slice of life more ambiguous in its praise of human potential and its contempt for "lifelies," has retained its popularity because it allows its audience to slum safely. Gorky adopted a more Chekhovian approach in his plays about the intelligentsia, *The Vacationists* (*Dachniki*, 1904) and *Children of the Sun* (*Deti solntsa*, 1905); his confrontation of intellectuals with factory workers, *Enemies* (*Vragi*, 1906), was banned. *See* GORKY, MAXIM.

Gorky's publishing house, Znaniye (Knowledge) fostered a number of writers who copied his style in drama, among them S. A. Naidyonov, whose plays of domestic oppression in a mercantile surrounding—*Vanyushin's Children* (*Deti Vanyushina*, 1901) and *Avdotya's Life* (*Avdotyina zhizn*, 1904)—conjure up a more outspoken, cruder Ostrovsky. E. N. Chirikov's plays—*Jews* (*Yevrey*, 1904) and *Peasants* (*Muzhiki*, 1907)—and the dramas of Semyon Yushkevich—*In Town* (*Vgorode*, 1906) and *Hunger* (*Golod*, 1907)—are impassioned, revolutionary outcries, relevant to their times but of no lasting value.

The other trend of dramatic innovation was antirealistic, a turn toward decadence and symbolism, inspired partly by Maurice Maeterlinck's poetic plays and partly by Friedrich Nietzsche's theories of the Dionysian origins of tragedy. The first Russian symbolist dramatist was also its first Jewish playwright, Nikolay Minsky (real name, Vilenkin), with *The Sun* (*Solntse*, 1881), a "neo-mystery," and *Alma* (1900), a garrulous case study of a neurasthenic personality, with vague, other-worldly connections. But the movement was spearheaded by the classical scholar Vyacheslav Ivanov, who demanded a return to the *sobornost* or communion of Dionysiac celebrations, the poet entering the theatre as an hierophant into the temple in order to bring his audience or congregation in touch with the higher realities. Ivanov's own plays, paraphrases of the tragedies of Aeschylus, were not very convincing, but his ideas recur in Andrey Bely (real name, Boris Bugayev), whose *He That Hath Come* (*Prishedshy*, 1903) and *The Jaws of Night* (*Past nochi*, 1907) are modern mystery plays of more than ordinary portentousness; Valery Bryusov, whose *Earth* (*Zemlya*, 1904) is an allegorical vision of an underground race striving to reach the sun and dying in the attempt; and Innokenty Annensky, who in *Thamyras the Cithäerist* (*Famira Kifared*, 1906) and other tragedies turned to Greek mythology for his content and, to some degree, form. Each of these works is couched in carefully wrought, self-conscious poetic diction, and none was staged at the time of writing. One that was, Konstantin Balmont's *Three Blooms* (*Tri rasveta*, 1906), was almost hissed off the stage. *See* ANNENSKY, INNOKENTY FYODOROVICH.

Fyodor Sologub (real name, Teternikov) promulgated his pessimistic, antihumanist views of man in a hostile universe in verse drama set in Capetian France—*The Triumph of Death* (*Pobeda smerti*, 1906)—and legendary Greece—*The Gift of the Wise Bees* (*Dar mudrykh pchel*, 1906)—although the lyric mood softened the harshness of his message. But despite his cynical tone, Sologub's other plays were lighter, the best being the double-plotted *Vanka the Butler and Jean the Page* (*O Vanka klyuchnik i pazh Zhean*, 1909), a scabrous comedy contrasting seduction in medieval France and Russia. The sprightly eroticism of Sologub's "blackouts" was in keeping with the flourishing of cabarets and miniature theatres at the time, which poked fun at the latest innovations in avant-garde art or revived folk themes. The Flitter-Mouse in Moscow staged brightly colored sketches and songs; the Stray Dog was primarily a literary cabaret; and the Crooked Mirror in St. Petersburg mounted elaborate parodies of opera and directorial excesses. *See* SOLOGUB, FYODOR.

The leading light of the Crooked Mirror, Nikolay Yevreinov, subscribed to a theory of "theatricality," make-believe as a human instinct and need, and many of his plays, such as *A Gay Death* (*Vesyolaya smert*, 1908), a bittersweet harlequinade, and *The Chief Thing* (*Samoe glavnoye*, 1919), embody this concept. Theatre for theatre's sake became popular, especially among those writers who disdained naturalism but were unattracted by the earnestness of Ivanov's mystery cult. Aleksey Remizov turned to Russian folk theatre for his elaborate pastiches, *The Devil's Play* (*Besovskoe deystvo*, 1907), *The Tragedy of Judas, Prince of Iscariot* (*Tragediya ob Iude, printse*

Michael Redgrave (behind table) in the title role of Chekhov's *Uncle Vanya*. The cast also included Robert Lang, Rosemary Harris, Joan Plowright, Max Adrian, Sybil Thorndike, Laurence Olivier, and Lewis Casson. [Photograph courtesy of Arthur Cantor, Inc.]

Vera Pashennaya (left) in the title role of Maxim Gorky's *Vassa Zheleznova*. [*Moscow Theatres*]

Iskariotskom, 1909), and a new version of *Tsar Maksimilian* (1919). Another poet, Mikhail Kuzmin, spun airy confections of rococo pastorals and mildly sensuous imitations of miracle plays, such as *Eudoxia of Heliopolis, or The Repentant Courtesan* (*O Yevdoky iz Geliopolya, ili obrashchonnaya kurtizanka*, 1908). *See* KUZMIN, MIKHAIL ALIEKSEY EVICH, YEVREINOV, NIKOLAY NIKOLAYEVICH.

The tension between the despair brought about by the failed Revolution of 1905 and the prankishness of the cabaret theatre is clearly manifested in the "lyrical dramas" of Aleksandr Blok: *The Little Showbooth* (*Balaganchik*), *The Unknown Woman* (*Neznakomka*), and *The King in the Town Square* (*Korol na ploshchadi*)—all 1906—highly personal statements of the inability of the sublime to survive in the mundane sphere. Blok was one of the more successfully performed of the antirealistic playwrights, thanks to the experiments of Vsevolod Meyerhold, who espoused the cause of many new dramatists in order to expand the possibilities of the stage. *The Rose and the Cross* (*Roza i krest*, 1913), Blok's full-length drama of troubadour France, phrased in a poignant if not always stageworthy idiom, added a human dimension to his symbols. *See* BLOK, ALEKSANDROVICH; MEYERHOLD, VSEVOLOD EMILYEVICH.

However, the most fashionable of these writers was also the least durable: Leonid Andreyev, whose works exhibit the contradictions and ambivalences of literature on the eve of Revolution. A member of Gorky's Znaniye group, Andreyev produced more or less realistic plays such as *To the Stars* (*Kzvezdam*, 1906) and *Tsar Hunger* (*Tsar golod*, 1908), condemning the status quo and envisaging an uprising of the world's people. But he also expounded a pessimistic belief in man's impotence and isolation in the face of a malevolent fate in overwrought symbolist drama like *The Life of a Man* (*Zhizn cheloveka*, 1907) and *Anathema* (*Anatema*, 1909) before returning to a rephrasing of the same creed in a more "psychologized," Dostoevskyan vein. *See* ANDREYEV, LEONID NIKOLAYEVICH.

Moscow Art Theatre production of Gorky's *The Lower Depths*, in which Konstantin Stanislavsky (on table) played the role of Satin. [*Moscow Art Theatre Plays*]

Vsevolod Ivanov's *Armored Train 14-69,* as produced by the Moscow Art Theatre in 1934. [Theatre Collection, The New York Public Library at Lincoln Center, Astor, Lenox and Tilden Foundations]

The October Revolution of 1918 opened the floodgates for new theatrical forms. A vast, untapped proletarian audience, ripe for instruction in socialist ideals, required fresh means of communication, and such experimental modes as the mass spectacle, the "eccentric" multimedia show utilizing circus, variety, and cinema techniques, and the "living newspaper" were much in evidence, and brilliant directors like Meyerhold, Tairov, and Sergey Eisenstein attempted all manner of exciting innovations in the first years of uncensored artistic freedom. Unfortunately, there were few dramas to supply the needs of a Bolshevik theatre. The Commissar of Public Enlightenment A. V. Lunacharsky could provide only half-baked historical parallels in his *Oliver Cromwell* (1920) and *Thomas Campanella (Foma Kampanella,* 1921). The so-called first Soviet play was Vladimir Mayakovsky's *Mystery-bouffe (Misteriya-buff,* 1918), which, as its name implied, yoked together the ritual communion of the religious drama with the cartoon humor of the propaganda poster. In an effort to reeducate the public by means of theatre, popular novels were dramatized, and the literacy campaigns among the peasants and workers were portrayed in such plays as A. S. Serafimovich's *Maryana* (1920) and A. S. Neverov's *Peasant Women (Baby,* 1920).

Arguing for a "factographic" approach, Sergey Tre-

taykov created strident melodramas calling for world revolution and attacking foreign interference in the Communist advance, as in *Listening, Moscow?! (Slushayte, Moskva?!,* 1923) and *Roar, China! (Rychi, Kitay!,* 1926), immediate dramatization of current events that were to influence Bertolt Brecht. His lead was followed by V. N. Bill-Belotserkovsky, whose *Gale Winds (Shtorm,* 1924) showed a whole village in upheaval during the civil war. Revolutionary exploits and the conversion of various social classes to communism became the common themes of drama, as seen in Mikhail Bulgakov's *Days of the Turbins (Dni Turbinykh,* 1926), depicting the divided loyalties in the family of a White Guard officer; Leonid Leonov's *The Badgers (Barsuki,* 1927), in which the Red and White sides are personified by two brothers; Konstantin Trenyov's *Lyubov Yarovaya* (1926), in which a schoolmistress must choose between her White Guard husband and her revolutionary sympathies; Vsevolod Ivanov's *Armored Train 14-69 (Bronepoezd 14-69,* 1927), in which revolutionary peasants capture a White train; and V. A. Lavrenyov's *The Breakup (Razlom,* 1927), about the mutiny on the cruiser *Aurora* during the October Revolution. These plays, comprising a wide panorama of scenes and large casts of variegated characters, became the classics of the Soviet repertory, and their heroes the first psychologically elaborated communist characters in a new id-

Conflict between the White and the Red Guards as seen in Mikhail Bulgakov's *The Days of the Turbins*. [Moscow Art Theatre]

iom. *See* IVANOV, VSEVOLOD VYACHESLAVOVICH; LEONOV, LEONID MAKSIMOVICH; TRENYOV, KONSTANTIN ANDREEVICH; TRETYAKOV, SERGEY MIKHAILOVICH.

The period of the New Economic Policy (NEP), which permitted a certain amount of private enterprise to flourish, engendered a resurgence of grotesque comedy, for the most part outrageous and farcical, howling with laughter at bourgeois throwbacks, pretentious poseurs, and misfits in the brave new world of socialism. Boris Romashov's *Meringue* (*Vozdushny pirog*, 1924) and

The Mattress (*Matrats*, 1926) were uproarious assaults on NEP-men and their policies, while Nikolay Erdman's *Credentials* (*Mandat*, 1925) and *The Suicide* (*Samoubiytsa*, 1928) turned an almost Gogolian searchlight on self-seeking climbers and Tsarist flotsam. Similar preoccupations appear in Bulgakov's *Up in Zoya's Flat* (*Zoykina kvartira*, 1926), in which a NEP fashion salon is used as a brothel, and in Ilf and Petrov's *The Power of Love* (*Silnoe chuvstvo*, 1933), an updating of Chekhov's *The Wedding*. The real culmination of this trend was reached in Mayakovsky's *The Bedbug* (*Klop*, 1929) and *The Bathhouse* (*Banya*, 1930) which directed the satire at the bureaucracy and seemed dubious about the direction Soviet society was taking. It is not surprising that as governmental repression increased and the NEP policies rescinded, these free-wheeling hijinks were halted. *See* BULGAKOV, MIKHAIL AFANASYEVICH; ERDMAN, NIKOLAY; MAYAKOVSKY, VLADIMIR VLADIMIROVICH.

Gorky's romantic realism remained the model for most Soviet playwrights, and his last plays, *Yegor Bulychev and Others* (*Yegor Bulychev i drugie*, 1932) and *Dostigayev and Others* (*Dostigayev i drugie*, 1933), were among his best, wry depictions of the old age succumbing to the new. Under his aegis, melodrama throve, as in A. M. Faykov's *The Man with a Briefcase* (*Chelovek s portfelem*, 1928). But meanwhile a debate proceeded concerning the proper format for Soviet drama. Nikolay Pogodin and Vsevolod Vishnevsky supported the concept of an epic play, unfolding the exploits of a large number of persons. Pogodin, in works like *Tempo* (*Temp*, 1930) and *Poem About an Ax* (*Poema o topore*, 1931), made the masses his protagonist, discarded the old act and scene structure for a staccato arrangement of short episodes, bursting out like news bulletins, and built his conflicts

Vladimir Mayakovsky's *The Bathhouse* was seen as a major political and artistic statement when staged in Poland in 1954 under the direction of Kazimierz Dejmek. [*Theatre in Modern Poland*]

The Optimistic Tragedy, by Vsevolod Vishnevsky. Moscow, Kamerny Theatre, 1934. [Theatre Collection, The New York Public Library at Lincoln Center, Astor, Lenox and Tilden Foundations]

around the sacrifice of personal feelings to collective needs. Vishnevsky's style in *The First Cavalry* (*Pervaya Konnaya*, 1930), *The Ultimate Decisive* (*Posledny reshitelny*, 1931), and his best work, *An Optimistic Tragedy* (*Optimisticheskaya tragediya*, 1933), blazoned forth a heroic appeal to future generations. An opposite view, that psychological chamber drama was the best means of reflecting the contemporary scene, was held by Vladimir Kirshon and Aleksandr Afinogenov. Afinogenov's finest play, *Fear* (*Strakh*, 1931), managed to portray the winning of the old intelligentisia to socialism without simplifying the viewpoints of either side, although it is marred by the Pollyanna ending that had come to be *de rigueur* in Soviet drama. *See* AFINOGENOV, ALEKSANDR NIKOLAYEVICH; POGODIN, NIKOLAY FYODOROVICH; VISHNEVSKY, VSEVOLOD VITALYEVICH.

The plays of the early 1930s are concerned with industrialization, as in Kirshon's *The Rails Are Humming* (*Relsy gudyat*, 1928) about the fulfillment of the five-year-plan, and *Bread* (*Khleb*, 1930), depicting the class struggle in a farming village; Kirshon contrived to make his plays' rhythms reflect the new industrial tempo. The new protagonists were doctors, as in A. E. Korneychuk's *Platon Krechet* (1934), and rehabilitated criminals working on the Baltic Sea Canal, as in Pogodin's entertaining *Aristocrats* (*Aristokraty*, 1935).

But by 1936 a monolithic standardization was being applied to Russian literature; party congresses set strict rules for dramatic composition, and deviation might have fatal consequences. Attacks on "Formalism" and the "internal émigré" annihilated experimentation: content was to inform and uplift the people and support the leadership of Stalin and the Communist party; style was to adhere to socialist realism, a larger-than-life, re-

touched photograph of the Soviet world picture. On the twentieth anniversary of the Revolution, Lenin became a perennial dramatic figure, as in Pogodin's trilogy, beginning with *The Man with a Gun* (*Chelovek s ruzhyom*, 1937), Aleksandr Korneychuk's *Truth* (*Pravada*, 1937), and Konstantin Trenyov's *On the Banks of the Neva* (*Na beregu Nevy*, 1937). These plays are icons, which distort history and echo the party line.

To achieve some measure of free expression, many gifted dramatists wrote for children's theatres, among them A. Ya. Brushtein, Sergey Mikhalkov, Samuil Marshak, and, most important, Yevgeny Shvarts. In his

Howard Renensland and Sally Parish in Nikolay Erdman's *The Suicide* as produced Off Broadway in 1978. [Festival Theatre Foundation, Inc.]

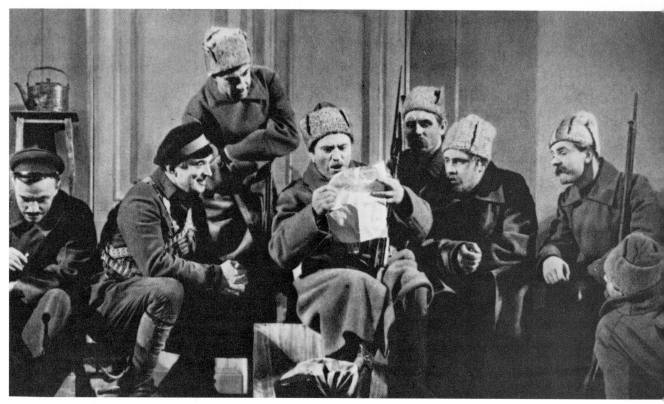

Scene from Nikolay Pogodin's *The Man with a Gun*. [*Moscow Theatres*]

fairytales for adults—*The Naked King* (*Goly korol*, 1934), *The Shadow* (*Ten*, 1940), and *The Dragon* (*Drakon*, 1943)—Shvarts created complex metaphors applicable on several levels, animadverting on the compromise of integrity and appealing for the preservation of humane ideals. His medley of folkloric humor and shrewd sophistication constitutes a dramatic poetry of great originality. *See* SHVARTS, YEVGENY LVOVICH.

But for the most part, Russian playwriting of the 1940s and 1950s is a dreary roster of time-serving platitudes. The war effort required propaganda pieces, displaying the heroism of the Russian people and exhorting the populace to resistance against the invader: the most successful (or least banal) of these are Konstantin Simonov's *The Russian People* (*Russkye lyudi*, 1942), Korneychuk's *Front* (1942), and Leonov's *Invasion* (*Nashestvie*, 1942). Concurrently, the Stalinist cult of personality inspired a school of historical drama that equated the Leader with great men of the past. V. A. Solovyov's *Feldmarshal Kutuzov* (1940), and A. N. Tolstoy's chronicles of Peter the Great— *Pyotr I* (1930–1938)—and Ivan the Terrible— *The Eagle and Its Mate* (*Oryol i orlitsa*, 1945) and *The Difficult Years* (*Trudny gody*, 1946)—were typical. Even more egregious was Vishnevsky's sycophantic *Unforgotten 1919* (*Nezabyvaemy 1919-y*, 1949), which attributes to Stalin a part in putting down the Cronstadt Rebellion he never actually played. The period of the cold war was perhaps the nadir. In addition to blatant attacks on the United States in such works as Simonov's *The Russian Question* (*Russky vopros*, 1947) and Lavrenyov's

The Voice of America (*Golos Ameriki*, 1950), the doctrine of "conflictlessness" prevailed, holding that no authentic conflicts existed in Soviet life and therefore no such conflicts could be presented in drama. *See* SIMONOV, KONSTANTIN MIKHAILOVICH; TOLSTOY, ALEKSEY NIKOLAYEVICH.

With the thaw that followed Stalin's death, playwrights stepped off the pedestals and soapboxes and returned to more intimate pictures of family life and romantic entanglements. The most prolific and popular of this group, Alexey Arbuzov, had come to the fore in the prewar years with *Tanya* (1939); he now created a host of lyrical dramas of youth such as *The Irkutsk Story* (*Irkutskaya istoriya*, 1959) and *The Promise* (*Moy bedny Marat*, 1964). Similar works were produced by Viktor Rozov—*Alive Forever* (*Vechno zhivyo*, 1956)—and Vera Panova—*It's Been Ages!* (*Skolko let, skolko zhit!*, 1966). Mayakovsky's works were revived for the first time since their original productions, and many of Shvarts's plays were rediscovered and staged, although neither of these authors had much influence on postwar playwriting. The general mode remained realism, but a realism tempered by a pseudo-Chekhovian lyricism. The general aim remained social betterment, but this too was mitigated by a recognition of human frailty and a mild disillusionment. *See* ARBUZOV, ALEXEY NIKOLAYEVICH; PANOVA, VERA FYODOROVNA; ROZOV, VIKTOR SERGEYEVICH.

Isolated so long from developments in the Western theatre, Russian drama failed to register the effects of Brecht or the "absurdists" until, in the late 1960s,

Brecht's plays became widely produced in the Soviet Union and translations of Ionesco and Pinter, though unpublished, passed from hand to hand. The resultant breakthroughs came, however, in theatrical production, such as Yury Lyubimov's treatment of literary material by Bulgakov—*The Master and Margarita (Magister i Margarita)*—Voznesensky, and John Reed at the Taganka Theatre, Moscow, and Georgy Tovstonogov's reinterpretation of Russian classics in Leningrad. A surrealistic drama of sorts had occurred in the 1920s with the Oberyuty group: Daniil Kharms's *Elizaveta Bam* (1928), and Aleksandr Vvedensky's *Christmas at the Ivanovs'* (*Yolka v Ivanoyykh*, ca. 1929), oddly similar to Karl Valentin's German cabaret sketch *The Christmas Tree*. But the only evidence of suprarealistic styles in postwar playwriting appears in the rather feeble plays of the dissident Andrey Amalrik and in Vasily Aksyonov's two comedies *Always on Sale* (*Vsegda v prodazhe*, 1965) and *Your Murderer* (*Vasha ubiytsa*, 1975), which hark back to the farcical expressionism of the NEP period and especially to Yury Olyesha's *The Conspiracy of Feelings* (*Zagovor chuvstv*, 1929). *See* OLYESHA, YURY KARLOVICH.

At the present time, Soviet playwriting follows certain distinct paths. There is a nostalgia for the Great Patriotic War, when sympathies were clearly defined and possibilities of individual heroism existed; one of the most effective plays of this type is Mikhail Roshchin's *Troop Train* (*Eshelon*, 1975), with its emotional depiction of a rather cliché assortment of women in wartime. Roshchin is also the author of *Valentin and Valentina* (*Valentin i Valentina*, 1971), a highly successful transference of the youth theme of the postwar years to the 1970s. Another trend is the play devoted to problems of industry, conservation, and consumerism, which may evoke

David Dukes and Dana Larson in an American production of Alexey Arbuzov's *The Promise*. [Courtesy of American Conservatory Theatre, San Francisco, Calif. Photograph by Hank Kranzler]

Banned in the Soviet Union, Yevgeny Shvarts's *The Dragon*, an allegory about the struggle against dictatorship, was given its world premiere in Poland in 1961. [*Theatre in Modern Poland*]

Stalinist drama about collectivization but is far more open-ended and subtle than its predecessors; the leading practitioner of this genre is Aleksandr Gelman, with his *The Party Committee Meeting* (*Zasedanie Partkoma*, 1975) and *Feedback Circuit* (*Obratnaya svyaz*, 1977), who is socially concerned but not dogmatic. One of the most interesting trends is the revival of the vaudeville and farce of the past, combining theatrical playfulness with shrewd characterizations; in his latest dramas Arbuzov has exhibited this trait, and in his brief career Aleksandr Vampilov successfully revived the Chekhovian "joke." Still somewhat constrained by didacticism and conformity to socialist ideals, modern Russian drama is as informed of human nature and as technically proficient as ever, and as it gains freedom to develop beyond the realist model, it will show that the heirs of Gogol and Chekhov are worthy of their ancestors. *See* VAMPILOV, ALEKSANDR.

LAURENCE SENELICK

EDITIONS

Russian

Rossiiskiy teatre, 43 vols., St. Petersburg, 1786–1794; *Staryy russkiy vodvil, 1819–1849*, ed. by M. Paushkin, Moscow, 1937; *Sovetskaya dramaturgiya 1917–1947*, 6 vols., Moscow-Leningrad, 1948; *Russkaya narodnaya drama XVII–XX vekov*, ed. by P. N. Berkov, Moscow, 1953; *Pyesy sovetskikh pisateley*, 12 vols., Moscow, 1953–1956; *Pervye sovetskye pyesy*, ed. by V. F. Pimenov, Moscow, 1958; *Russkaya dramaturgiya XVIII v.*, 2 vols., Moscow-Leningrad, 1959; *Dramaturgiya Znaniya*, ed. by V. Chuvakov, Moscow, 1964; *Stikhotvorenaya komediya kontsa XVIII–nachala XIX v.*, ed. by M. O. Yankovsky, Moscow-Leningrad, 1964; *Sovetskaya odnoaktnaya dramaturgiya*, 2 vols., Moscow, 1967; *Russkiy vodvil*, ed. by T. Shantarenkov, Moscow, 1970; *Odnoaktnye pyesy*, Moscow, 1971; *Rannaya russkaya dramaturgiya XVII–pervoy poloviny XVIII v.*, ed. by O. Z. Derzhavina, K. N. Lomunov, and A. N. Robinson, 5 vols., Moscow, 1972–1976; *Russkaya teatralnaya parodiya XIX–nachala XX veka*, Moscow, 1976.

English

A. Bates, *The Drama: Its History, Literature, and Influence on Civilization*, Vol. 18: *Russian Drama*, London, 1903; C. E. B. Roberts, *Five Russian Plays with One from Ukrainian*, London, 1916; *The Moscow Art Theatre Series of Russian Plays*, 2 vols, New York, 1923; G. R. Noyes, *Masterpieces of the Russian Drama*, 2 vols., New York, 1933; B. Blake, *Four Soviet Plays*, London, 1937; H. Marshall, *Soviet One-Act Plays*, London, 1944; A. Bakshy, *Soviet Scene. Six Plays of Russian Life*, New Haven, 1946; *Seven Soviet Plays*, with intro. by H. W. L. Dana, New York, 1946; D. Magarshack, *The Storm and Other Russian Plays*, New York, 1960; N. Houghton, *Great Russian Plays*, New York, 1960; J. Gassner, *Nineteenth Century Russian Drama*, tr. by A. McAndrew, New York, 1963; J. Gassner, *Twentieth Century Russian Drama*, tr. by A. McAndrew, New York, 1963; F. D. Reeve, *Anthology of Russian Plays*, 2 vols., New York, 1963; F. D. Reeve, *Contemporary Russian Drama*, New York, 1968; M. Glenny, *Three Soviet Plays*, Harmondsworth, 1969, 1975; V. Komissarzhevsky, *Nine Modern Soviet Plays*, Moscow, 1977.

CRITICISM

Russian

A. R. Kugel, *Russkie dramaturgi*, Moscow, 1923; V. Vsevolodskiy-Gerngross, *Istoriya russkogo teatra*, 2 vols., Leningrad, 1929; B. V. Varneke, *Istoriya russkogo teatra XVII–XIX vv.*, Moscow-Leningrad, 1939; Y. Osnos, *Sovetskaya istoricheskaya drama*, Moscow, 1947; S. S. Danilov, *Ocherki po istoriy russkogo dramaticheskogo teatra*, Moscow-Leningrad, 1948; V. Vsevolodskiy-Gerngross, *Russkiy teatr ot istokov do serediny XVIII v.* Moscow, 1957; B. N. Aseyev, *Russkiy dramaticheskiy teatr XVIII–XVIII vekov*, Moscow, 1958; *Russkie dramaturgi XVIII–XIX vv. Monograficheskie ocherki*, 3 vols., Moscow, 1959–1962; V. Vsevolodskiy-Gerngross, *Russkiy teatr votory poloviny XVIII v.*, Moscow, 1960; L. Tamashin, *Sovetskaya dramaturgiya v gody grazhdanskoy voyny*, Moscow, 1961; A. A. Anikst, *Teoriya dramy v Rossii ot Pushkina do Chekhova*, Moscow, 1972; S. S. Danilov and M. G. Portugalova, *Russkiy dramaticheskiy teatr XIX veka*, 2 vols., Leningrad, 1974; *Istoriya russkogo dramaticheskogo teatra*, 7 vols., Moscow, 1977–in progress.

Other Languages

J. Patouillet, *Le Théâtre de moeurs russes*, Paris, 1912; H. W. L. Dana, *Handbook on Soviet Drama*, New York, 1938; N. Evreinov, *Histoire du théâtre russe*, Paris, 1947; B. V. Varneke, *History of the Russian Theatre*, New York, 1951; E. Lo Gatto, *Storia dello teatro russo*, 2 vols., Florence, 1952; P. Yershov, *Comedy in the Soviet Theatre*, New York, 1956; M. Slonim, *Russian Theatre from the Empire to the Soviets*, New York, 1962; D. J. Welsh, *Russian Comedy 1765–1823*, The Hague-Paris, 1966; L. Warner, *Russian Folk Drama*, The Hague, 1978; R. Zguta, *Russian Minstrels, a History of the Skomorokhi*, Pittsburgh, 1978; H. B. Segel, *Twentieth Century Russian Drama from Gorky to the Present*, New York, 1979; L. P. Senelick, *Russian Dramatic Theory from Pushkin to the Symbolists*, Austin, Tex., 1981.

Rutebeuf   (1248?–?1285)

French poet and dramatist. Little is known of his life, but he appeared in Paris as a jongleur during the reign of Louis IX. Some fifty surviving poems attributed to Rutebeuf speak of an elderly wife, the loss of his right eye, and extreme poverty, which he was constantly appealing to persons in power to relieve. His importance in French dramatic history is due to *The Miracle of Theophilus* (*Le miracle de Théophile*, ca. 1261), the first-known theatrical text in which the Holy Virgin appears as a figure of special importance and power. Based on a legend recounted in medieval Latin texts and in French by Gautier de Coincy (1177/78–1236) in his collection *Miracles de Notre-Dame*, the drama is often seen as a forerunner of *Faust*, since it concerns a pious man's pact with the Devil. Rutebeuf is also known to be the author of a dramatic monologue entitled *Le dit de l'herberie*, a satire on a charlatan who claims to have collected powerful herbs that can restore health and youth.

The Miracle of Theophilus (*Le miracle de Théophile*, ca. 1261). Theophilus, a high dignitary of the church of Adana, is deprived of his position and wealth by the new bishop. Reduced to begging, he seeks the aid of Salatin, an evil man said to have dealings with the Devil. Salatin arranges for Theophilus to meet the Devil, and the latter agrees to restore Theophilus to his former wealth and power if he will renounce God. After some hesitation, Theophilus agrees and signs a pact with the Devil. Though Theophilus is restored to his previous functions in the church, he is consumed by guilt. Eventually he appeals to the Holy Virgin, who in response to his fervent prayers makes it possible for him to regain possession of his pact with the Devil.

[JOSEPH E. GARREAU]

Ruzzante, Il   (ca. 1502–1542)

Italian actor and dramatist. Il Ruzzante (Il Ruzante) was the stage name for Angelo Beolco, born in Padua about 1502, the illegitimate son of a physician who died in 1524, leaving him a modest inheritance. He was not permitted a share in the rest of his father's estate, which was divided among the physician's legitimate children. It seems that Beolco was never financially well-off, but from the context of his plays, in which humanist and literary references abound, it appears certain that he was brought up in a refined and cultured atmosphere. He was always welcome in the intellectual and aristocratic society of Padua, his closest friend being the humanist scholar Alvise Cornaro, one of the most cultured and temperate men of his time. Beolco stayed frequently at

Cornaro's homes in the country, one of which had a private theatre. For this stage Beolco organized performances and wrote and acted in comedies.

Beolco made his acting debut in 1520 at the Palazzo Foscari in Venice. For the rest of his life he wrote and acted for princes, cardinals, and dukes in northern Italian cities such as Milan, Ferrara, and Padua, producing his own plays as well as those of other dramatists at banquets, fetes, and balls in palaces and piazzas. He was arranging a performance for the Accademici Infiammati of Padua when he died suddenly on March 17, 1542, as the result, according to some of his biographers, of having led an intemperate life.

WORK

Beolco wrote at a time when Italian farce was flourishing in Venice. As a Paduan with an almost fanatic love for his city, he scorned its citizens for imitating the refined Florentines. Paduans, he felt, should not adopt the clothes, food, language, or customs of their more aristocratic neighbors. His peasant characters, with their exuberance and enjoyment of life, act naturally and spontaneously. For Beolco, the natural and the spontaneous contained the essence of great art. Because of this belief (as well as his Paduan patriotism and hatred for Tuscan pedantry), Beolco wrote most of his greatest works in the dialect of the region.

The popular comedy form created by Beolco did not influence the dramatists who came after him, and only slight traces are found in the later *commedia dell'arte*. See COMMEDIA DELL'ARTE in glossary.

Beolco's twelve plays date from about 1520 to 1533. Three of his farces feature the popular peasant Ruzzante from whom Beolco took his stage name: *Ruzzante Returns from the Wars* (*Primo dialogo in lingua rustica, o Parlamento de Ruzzante che iera vegnù de campo, o Il reduce*, wr. before 1528), in which Ruzzante returns from the tribulations of war to find that his wife has been unfaithful; *The Flirt* (*Moschetta*, 1528), a farce of domestic entanglements; and *Fiorina* (wr. ca. 1529/30), a comedy culminating in agreeable love matches. The second and third of these plays center on arguments between a still-rustic peasant husband and his urbanized wife. Beolco also wrote comedies, including *The Girl of Ancona* (*Anconitana*, 1522), written in both the Tuscan and the Paduan dialects; *Bìlora, or the Second Rustic Play* (*Secondo dialogo in lingua rustica, o Bìlora*, wr. before 1528), about a peasant who goes to the city to retrieve his unfaithful wife; *The Cowshed* (*Vaccaria*, 1533), taken from *The Comedy of Asses* of Plautus; and *The Rainstorm* (*Piovana*, wr. 1532/33), an adaptation of Plautus's *The Rope*. See PLAUTUS.

Beolco replaced the verse of the early *Comedy Without a Title, or Betìa* (*Commedia senza titolo, o Betìa*, wr. late 1521 or ca. 1524) with prose closer to the Paduan speech of everyday life. The use of dialect offended his refined audience, and he was obliged to explain in the plays that a story about Paduans must be told in the native idiom in order to preserve its authenticity. His best plays, however, transcend their locales; they are comedies and

Il Ruzzante.
[Goethe House]

farces of man's life everywhere.

Ruzzante Returns from the Wars (*Primo dialogo in lingua rustica, o Parlamento de Ruzzante che iera vegnù de campo, o Il reduce*, wr. before 1528). Comedy in which Ruzzante, having deserted from the army out of cowardice, returns to his native village to find that his wife Gnua has left him for a bullying ruffian. She is interested in Ruzzante's vaunted heroism only out of vanity and would rather he had been wounded and maimed in order to prove his love for her than have him back. Ruzzante's attempts to deceive himself and his friend Menato are evident as he brags about his exaggerated exploits and tries to turn cowardly motives into heroic ones. He tries to convince Menato that the beating he has received from Gnua's new man was inflicted by 100 men and that he could not possibly have defended himself. His rationalizations do not convince either Menato or the audience, and the play ends with Ruzzante protesting that he does not care about his timidity.

Bìlora, or the Second Rustic Play (*Secondo dialogo in lingua rustica, o Bìlora*, wr. before 1528). Comedy in which a peasant tries to win back his unfaithful wife. Bìlora, exhausted after days of travel across the fields to Venice, seeks his young wife Dina, who lives with Andronico, an old usurer known for his short temper. In the city Bìlora meets Pittora, another peasant who is a friend of Andronico. At Pittora's suggestion, Bìlora asks his wife, who is alone in Andronico's house, whether she wants to return to him. Dina tells Bìlora that she is tired of Andronico and will go back to her husband whether the usurer agrees or not. She gives Bìlora money for dinner and advises him to return when Andronico is home so that the matter can be settled. Bìlora persuades Pittora to speak for him with the moneylender, but when Pittora pleads Bìlora's case, Andronico swears he will never let Dina go. When Pittora proposes that Dina be allowed to choose what she wants, she declares that the idea of returning to Bìlora is preposterous; he beats her daily and looks like a wolf. Though Pittora accepts her reply, Bìlora is furious. He plans to bully Andronico into returning Dina. Then he will sell his opponent's coat, buy a horse, and go into the army. When

Andronico comes out of his house, Bìlora, possessed by fury, kills him, feeling that he has given Andronico sufficient warning.

The Flirt (*Moschetta*, 1528). Comedy in which the peasant Menato is in love with Bettia, coquettish wife of Ruzzante, but the handsome soldier Tonin pleases her much more. Menato decides to upset Ruzzante's household and suggests that Ruzzante test his wife's fidelity by disguising himself as a stranger. The adventure ends badly, for it is Tonin who profits from Bettia's favors. Ruzzante, completely baffled, ends by asking his wife's pardon.

Fiorina (wr. ca. 1529/30). Comedy in Paduan dialect that opens with a lecture on dress and manners addressed to the ladies of the court. Ruzzante, in love with Flora (Fiorina), has as a rival Marchioro, whom she prefers and incites to fight Ruzzante. Ruzzante is soundly beaten and in revenge carries off Flora, bound and gagged, and seduces her. Marchioro swears revenge, but on his way to do battle he meets the fathers of Ruzzante and Flora, who urge him to marry Ruzzante's sister, who will have a large dowry. Marchioro agrees without too much reluctance, and the comedy ends with the formation of two happy couples. [PETER BONDANELLA]

PLAYS

1. *Pastoral*. Pastoral, 5 acts; prose. Written ca. 1520. Published 1951.
2. *Prima orazione* (*First Oration*). Play. Written 1521. Published 1551. Produced September, 1521.
3. *Anconitana* (*The Girl of Ancona*). Comedy, 5 acts; prose. Written 1522. Published 1551. Produced 1522.
4. *Commedia senza titolo, o Betìa* (*Comedy Without a Title, or Betìa*). Comedy, 5 acts; Paduan dialect; verse. Written late 1521 or ca. 1524. Published 1894.
5. *Primo dialogo in lingua rustica, o Parlamento de Ruzzante che iera vegnù de campo, o Il reduce** (*Ruzzante Returns from the Wars*). Farce. Written before 1528. Published 1551.
6. *Secondo dialogo in lingua rustica, o Bìlora** (*Bìlora, or The Second Rustic Play*). Farce. Written before 1528. Published 1551.
7. *Dialogo facetissimo et ridiculosissimo, o Ménego* (*Most Ridiculous and Most Facetious Dialogue, or Menego*). Play. Written 1528. Published 1554. Produced 1528.
8. *Seconda orazione* (*Second Oration*). Play. Written 1528. Published 1551. Produced 1528.
9. *Moschetta* (*The Flirt*). Comedy, 5 acts; Paduan and Bergamask dialect; prose. Written 1528. Published 1551. Produced 1528.
10. *Fiorina*. Comedy, 5 acts; Paduan dialect; prose. Written ca. 1529/30. Published 1551.
11. *Piovana* (*The Rainstorm*). Comedy; prose. Written 1532/33. Published 1548.
12. *Vaccaria* (*The Cowshed*). Comedy; prose. Written 1533. Published 1551. Produced Feb. 25, 1533.

EDITIONS

Collections
Oeuvres complètes, tr. by A. Mortier, Paris, 1926; *Dialoghi*, Turin, 1953; *Opere*, vols. 4, 6, and 8, Padua, 1951–1954; *Teatro*, ed. by L. Zorzi, Turin, 1967.
Individual Plays
Bilora, or the Second Rustic Play. Published in *World Drama*, ed. by B. H. Clark and tr. by B. and G. Hughes, vol. 2, New York, 1933.
Ruzzante Returns from the Wars. Published in *The Classic Theatre*, ed. by E. R. Bentley and tr. by A. Ingold and T. Hoffman, Garden City, N.Y., 1958–1961.

CRITICISM

G. Boldrin, *Angelo Beolco detto il Ruzzante*, Padua, 1924; A. Mortier, *Un dramaturge populaire de la renaissance italienne: Ruzzante (1502–1542)*, Paris, 1925; A. Cataldo, *Il Ruzzante*, Milan, 1933; C. Grabher, *Ruzzante*, Milan, 1953; E. Lovarini, *Studi sul Ruzzante e la letteratura pavana*, Padua, 1965; D. Radcliff-Umstead, *The Birth of Modern Comedy in Renaissance Italy*, Chicago, 1969.

Ryga, George (1932–   )

Canadian playwright. He is noted for his social protest, use of western Canadian speech and folksong in his work, and dramaturgical experiment. His boyhood in northern Alberta, where his Ukrainian immigrant parents worked a marginal farm, and the years of his early manhood, during which he frequently worked as a manual laborer, have had a lasting influence on the attitudes reflected in his work, particularly his sympathy for the underdog. After leaving school early, Ryga received scholarships to study creative writing for two sessions at the Banff School of Arts in the early 1950s. He then worked as a copywriter and producer for a commercial radio station in Edmonton. After readings of some of his short stories were broadcast by the Canadian Broadcasting Corporation, he turned his hand to radio plays, the beginning of a long involvement with media drama: most of his over seventy produced plays were written for radio or television. The technique of his stage plays is influenced by the electronic media: one critic describes the writer's disruption of time, his use of cinematic cuts and repeated motifs, and abrupt shifts in convention as "Ryga's liquid dramaturgy." Ryga's style is also influenced by his activities as a composer, songwriter, and folklorist; another critic describes Ryga's plays as "folk ballads."

Ryga's first published play, *Indian* (1965), was written originally for television; it cleverly enlists the audience's sympathy for the protagonist, a nameless native Indian transient laborer, by encouraging racist attitudes initially, then reversing those attitudes during the Indian's confrontation with an Indian Agent to give the audience a taste of the cultural isolation and deprivation that constitute the protagonist's life. *The Ecstasy of Rita Joe* (1967) is the play for which Ryga is best known. It is also concerned with the plight of the Indian lost in contemporary Western society, and it too is designed to encourage a middle-class audience to exchange its point of view and accompanying self-satisfaction for the position of people who do not share that point of view and who suffer because of it. A young Indian woman stands trial on a number of charges, several court appearances being merged into one. The audience's assumptions are challenged through reversal of chronological order, through flashback sequences offering glimpses of the heroine's earlier life, through song, mime, and direct confrontation between stage and auditorium, until the audience discovers with Rita Joe that the crime for which she stands charged is, essentially, that of being an Indian. The play has been extensively produced across Canada, including Quebec in a translation by Gratien Gélinas, and has also been performed in Washington, D.C., and London. *See* GÉLINAS, GRATIEN.

Grass and Wild Strawberries (1968) is not sympathetic to the flower children's withdrawal from society but examines some of the reasons for their dropping out. A civil servant and his proletarian kidnapper are compelled to delineate their positions in *Captives of the Faceless Drummer* (1971); the situation parallels the political kidnapping at the center of the 1970 October Crisis in Quebec, resulting in a stormy production history for the play and one of Ryga's many confrontations with the Canadian cultural establishment. *Paracelsus* (1971) is a historical epic based on the life of the Swiss-German physician and alchemist, and *Sunrise on Sarah* (1972), commissioned and first produced by the Banff School, explores the mind of a woman confused by the changes in women's social roles. *Seven Hours to Sundown* (1976) presents the conflict between commercial and cultural forces in a representative Canadian small town. A similar clash, between an obsessed gold miner and an equally obsessed but reformist newspaper editor, is at the centre of *Ploughmen of the Glacier* (1976). While Ryga's recent work is not often performed in the large Canadian theatres, he has been more successful than most playwrights in his attempts to take theatre to small communities and to audiences who seldom attend more formal theatrical performances.

CHRIS JOHNSON

S

Saavedra, Ángel de   (1791–1865)

Spanish politician, poet, and dramatist. Ángel de Saavedra Ramírez de Baquedano, Duke of Rivas, was born in Córdoba on March 19, 1791. He was well educated and took an early interest in both literature and politics. In 1814 he published his first volume of poetry; this was followed by other volumes and by numerous tragedies. By 1820 he was not only a prominent literary figure but a respected member of the Liberal party, which protested the corrupt despotism of King Ferdinand VII. A leading member of the Cortes (Parliament) and an active participant in the abortive revolution that overthrew and imprisoned the King, Saavedra fled into exile under penalty of death when Ferdinand was rescued by French forces in 1823.

Exiled for eleven years in England, Malta, France, and Italy, Saavedra came into close contact with theatrical trends in other parts of Europe. After a general amnesty was decreed in 1834, he returned to Spain and the following year produced his masterpiece, *Don Álvaro, or The Force of Destiny (Don Álvaro, o La fuerza del sino)*. Having succeeded his brother as Duke of Rivas, Saavedra was again drawn into politics. He served briefly as Minister of the Interior, fled the caprices of the King, but returned once again in 1837 to reenter politics. Thereafter he served sporadically in the occasional "moderate" governments during the Carlist Wars, as Ambassador to Naples and Paris and as President of the Council of State. His health failed in 1858, and he retired to Córdoba. He died in Madrid on June 22, 1865.

Ángel de Saavedra. [Biblioteca Nacional, Madrid]

WORK

By virtue of his romantic themes and tone, presented in sonorous, emotional verse, Saavedra is most frequently considered a thoroughgoing Spanish romantic. Certainly his most famous drama, *Don Álvaro* (1835), which Verdi translated into the opera *La forza del destino* (1862), does much to support this view. Nevertheless, in his use of local color, realistic details, and scenes of comic relief, Saavedra continued the traditions of the pre-Golden Age (Siglo de Oro) and Golden Age drama. Even when his plots and characters were highly romantic, he showed a neoclassical preoccupation with form and structure. The specificity of his instructions for sets and scenery indicate his unusual consciousness of stagecraft. *See* NEOCLASSICISM; SIGLO DE ORO in glossary.

A lesser-known but perhaps no less fine a play than *Don Álvaro* is *Dissillusion in a Dream* (*El desengaño en un sueño;* wr. 1842, prod. 1875), in which Saavedra made effective use of the dream-versus-reality theme employed by Calderón in *Life Is a Dream.* Other romantic dramas are *The Solace of a Prisoner* (*Solaces de un prisonero,* 1841), set in Madrid, about King Francis I of France; *The Moorish Woman of Alajuar* (*La morisca de Alajuar,* 1841), which portrays the expulsion of the Moriscos from Valencia in 1609; and *The Crucible of Loyalty* (*El crisol de la lealtad,* 1842), based on Ruiz de Alarcón's *Cruelty for Honor* (pub. 1634). *See* CALDERÓN DE LA BARCA, PEDRO; RUIZ DE ALARCÓN, JUAN.

Among his other works are *Ataúlfo* (wr. 1814), originally banned by the censor but later produced; *Aliatar* (1816), set in Moorish times; *Doña Blanca de Castilla* (prod. 1917), after the style of Moratín; *The Duke of Aquitaine* (*El duque de Aquitania,* 1817), a tragicomedy imitating Alfieri's *Orestes; Malek-Adhel* (1818); *Lanuza* (1822); *The Inn of Bailén* (*El parador de Bailén,* 1843); *Arias Gonzalo* (wr. 1826), a medieval tragedy considered by some the best of Saavedra's neoclassical works and by others his first mildly romantic drama; and *You Are Worth as Much as You Own* (*Tanto vales cuanto tienes;* wr. 1828, prod. 1834), a comedy inspired by Moratín. *See* ALFIERI, VITTORIO; MORATÍN Y CABAÑA, AGUSTÍN.

Don Álvaro, or The Force of Destiny (*Don Álvaro, o La fuerza del sino,* 1835). Tragedy about Don Álvaro, who loves Leonor, daughter of the Marquis of Calatrava, but whose suit the marquis rejects because Don Álvaro's mother was not of noble birth. As the couple prepare to elope, the marquis apprehends them, but he is mortally wounded when Don Álvaro's pistol accidentally discharges. Dying, the marquis curses Leonor. Years pass, and now Leonor is a hermit living in a cave in the vicinity of a Franciscan monastery, while Don Álvaro and Don Carlos, Leonor's brother, who has sworn vengeance on the lovers, are soldiers in Italy. Neither man knows the true name of the other, and, each having saved the other's life, they become fast friends until their identities are revealed. Now the two are forced to duel, and Don Álvaro kills Don Carlos.

Years later, Don Álvaro withdraws to the same monastery, where he becomes a paragon of humility. Don Alfonso, Leonor's remaining brother, seeks him out and compels him to duel. Alfonso, fatally wounded, begs Álvaro to fetch him a priest. Álvaro goes to the hermit's cave and, mistaking Leonor for a monk, forces her to follow him. Alfonso recognizes her immediately, and as she stoops over him, he stabs her in revenge. When he realizes the tragedy, Don Álvaro hurls himself over a precipice.

Disillusion in a Dream (*El desengaño en un sueño;* wr. 1842, prod. 1875). Dramatic fantasy about Marcolán, an old magician living in seclusion with his restless son Lisardo, who wishes to go out into the world. While Lisardo is asleep, Marcolán causes him to dream of adventures in the outside world. First, Lisardo marries his beloved Zora, but soon, coveting wealth and fame, he deserts her. With the Queen's assistance, he murders the King and reigns in his place. But this does not bring him happiness. He discovers that the Queen is plotting against him, that the people too have turned against him, and that Zora is dead. He tries to escape but is captured. While awaiting execution, he is awakened by Marcolán, to whom he confesses that he is, after all, content to remain where he is.

[ANDRÉS FRANCO]

PLAYS

1. *Ataúlfo.* Tragedy, 5 acts. Written 1814.
2. *Aliatar.* Tragedy, 5 acts. Written 1814. Published 1816. Produced Seville, July 8, 1816.
3. *El duque de Aquitania (The Duke of Aquitaine).* Tragedy, 5 acts. Written 1817. Published 1820. Produced Seville, 1817.
4. *Malek-Adhel.* Tragedy, 5 acts. Written 1818. Published 1820. Produced Barcelona, ca. 1818. Based on Marie Cottin's novel *Mathilde* (1805).
5. *Lanuza.* Tragedy, 5 acts. Written 1822. Published 1823. Produced Madrid. Teatro de la Cruz, Dec. 17, 1822.
6. *Arias Gonzalo.* Tragedy, 5 acts; verse. Written 1826. Published 1894.
7. *Tanto vales cuanto tienes (You Are Worth as Much as You Own).* Comedy, 3 acts; verse. Written 1828. Published 1840. Produced Madrid, Teatro del Príncipe, July 2, 1834.
8. *Don Álvaro, o La fuerza del sino (Don Álvaro, or The Force of Destiny).* Drama, 5 acts; prose and verse. Written 1835. Published 1835. Produced Madrid, Teatro del Príncipe, Mar. 22, 1835.
9. *Solaces de un prisionero, o Tres noches de Madrid (The Solace of a Prisoner, or Three Nights in Madrid).* Comedy, 3 acts; verse. Written 1840. Published 1841. Produced Madrid, 1841.
10. *La morisca de Alajuar (The Moorish Woman of Alajuar).* Comedy, 3 acts; verse. Written 1841. Published 1841. Produced November, 1841.
11. *El crisol de la lealtad (The Crucible of Loyalty).* Comedy, 3 acts; verse. Written 1842. Published 1842. Produced Seville, 1842.
12. *El desengaño en un sueño (Disillusion in a Dream).* Fantastic drama, 4 acts. Written 1842. Published 1844. Produced Madrid, Teatro de Apolo, Dec. 11, 1875.
13. *El parador de Bailén (The Inn of Bailén).* Comedy, 3 acts. Written 1843. Published 1844. Produced Seville, 1843.
14. *Doña Blanca de Castilla.* Play. Produced Seville, Nov. 28, 1917.

EDITIONS

Obras completas, 5 vols., Madrid, 1854–1855; *Obras completas,* 2 vols., Barcelona, 1884–1885; *Obras completas,* 7 vols., Madrid, 1894–1904; *Obras completas,* ed. by J. Campos, *Biblioteca de autores españoles,* vols. C, CI, and CII, Madrid, 1957.

Don Álvaro, or The Force of Destiny. Published in *Spanish Plays of the Nineteenth Century,* ed. by R. O'Brien and tr. by R. Lima, Las Américas, New York, 1964.

CRITICISM

E. A. Peers, "Ángel de Saavedra, Duque de Rivas: A Critical Study," *Revue Hispanique,* vol. LVIII, 1923; G. Boussogol, *Angel de Saavedra, duc de Rivas: Sa vie, son oeuvre poétique,* Toulouse and Paris, 1926; E. M. Rosell, "Valores clásicos y románticos en el teatro del Duque de Rivas," *Boletín de la Biblioteca Menéndez Pelayo,* vol. X, 1928; N. González Ruiz, *El*

Duque de Rivas, Madrid, 1944; G. H. Lovett, *The Duke of Rivas*, Boston, 1977.

Sachs, Hans (1494–1576)

German *Meistersinger* and dramatist and the earliest important figure in German drama. He was born in Nürnberg on November 5, 1494. The son of a tailor, he received an excellent education for one of his class and time. By 1509 he had mastered Latin and had acquired some knowledge of Greek. About this time he was apprenticed to a shoemaker and, in 1510, began a five-year tour of the German cities known for their excellence in this craft. During these crucial years he not only became proficient as a shoemaker but gained a wide knowledge of German life and was introduced to the *Meistergesang*, the art of the *Meistersinger*, who were artisans and members of the musical and literary guilds that flourished in the larger towns in the fifteenth and sixteenth centuries.

In 1518 Sachs settled in Nürnberg, where he became a master of the shoemakers' guild and a prominent member of the community. He married in 1519 and then again in 1561 after the death of his first wife. Besides practicing his craft, Sachs found ample time for the composition of prodigious numbers of poems, tales, and plays of all sorts. According to an inventory that he made in 1567, at the age of seventy-three, he had written 4,275 *Meisterlieder* ("master songs"); 1,700 tales, fables, and anecdotes; and more than 200 plays, including comedies, tragedies, and *Fastnachtsspiele* ("Shrovetide plays"). In the 1520s he wrote a number of works supporting Luther in the Protestant Reformation.

By the time Sachs died, on January 19, 1576, in Nürnberg, the bulk of his work had been published, indicating that he was considered a person of some importance during his lifetime. However, he was all but forgotten during the seventeenth and eighteenth centuries, until Goethe, in a poem published in *Deutscher Merkur* (April, 1776), brought him to the attention of the German public. Since then interest in Sachs has grown, assisted by Richard Wagner's partially fictional account of his life in *Die Meistersinger von Nürnberg* (1868).

WORK

During a lifetime of prolific literary productivity, Hans Sachs wrote sixty-three tragedies, sixty-four comedies, and eighty-five *Fastnachtsspiele*, in addition to some 1,700 *Schwänke* ("farces"), more than 4,000 *Meisterlieder*, and a considerable number of didactic poems, many in defense of Protestantism. For his subject matter he drew on the Bible, Greek and Roman classics, romances, history, and anecdotes, often substituting Nürnberg for foreign locales. The tragedies and comedies deal with realistic contemporary subjects: the grievances of priests, artisans, and peasants and the contentiousness of lovers, gamblers, and drinkers. The tragedies culminate in the hero's death, while the comedies, though not necessarily humorous, end happily. These plays are rather rambling and verbose, with arbitrary act divisions and no sense of historical perspective or tragic depth. The plays that are comic in the modern sense, Sachs labeled farces. A few titles serve to indicate their folk roots and peasant milieu: *The Doctor with the Big Nose* (*Der Doktor mit der langen Nase*, pub. 1559), *St. Peter and the Goat* (*Sankt Peter mit der gais*, pub. 1555), and *The Breeding of Calves* (*Das Kälberbrüten*, pub. 1551).

Sachs's fame and greatest popularity are due chiefly to his Shrovetide plays, which display a fresh, childlike humor. He embarked on an especially fruitful period of dramatic composition in 1544, when he began turning out Shrovetide plays rapidly, producing as many as thirteen in one year. Since he often reworked material from his short, humorous narrative poems, many of the early Shrovetide plays are essentially stories told in rhymed dialogue. Sach's treatment of situation in these plays is straightforward, even crude, but never indecent. He seeks to satirize the follies of the world in the person of the bickering housewife, the boorish simpleton, or the unfaithful spouse, and he always concludes with a moral observation involving a rhyme on his name. Although real dramatic structure is lacking, the plays are still amusing reading today. Among the notable examples of this type are *The Wandering Scholar in Paradise* (*Der fahrende Schüler im Paradies*, pub. 1550), in which a wanderer leads a peasant woman to believe that he is on his way to paradise; *The Hot Iron* (*Das heisse Eisen*, pub. 1551), in which a husband accused of infidelity by his wife effectively turns the tables on her; *The Pregnant Peasant* (*Der schwangere Bauer*, pub. 1544), about the efforts of a group of peasants, aided by a physician, to convince a notorious miser that he is pregnant; *Eve's Dissimilar Children* (*Die ungleichen Kinder Evas*, pub. 1553), which relates a visit by God to Adam and Eve; and *The Stolen Shrovetide Hen* (*Die gestohlene Fastnacht's Henne*, pub. 1550), in

Hans Sachs. [German Information Center]

which a missing hen becomes a bone of contention between two village couples.

The Pregnant Peasant (*Der schwangere Bauer*, pub. 1544). *Fastnachtsspiel* about the conspiracy of a group of peasants who, with the aid of a physician, convince a notorious miser that he is pregnant and extract from him a sizable doctor's fee by means of which they provide themselves with food and drink at Shrovetide. The pathetic patient begins not only to feel the fetus in his body but also to worry about acquiring a godfather and nursing the infant. As in almost all his Shrovetide comedies, Sachs employs grotesque gestures rather than language to create comic effects.

The Stolen Shrovetide Hen (*Die gestohlene Fastnacht's Henne*, pub. 1550). Comedy in which a village couple accuse another village couple of stealing a hen. A heated argument ensues. The men are satisfied with crossing verbal swords, but the women resort to violence. While the women are at each other's throats, the men decide to settle their differences over a glass of wine.

The Wandering Scholar in Paradise (*Der fahrende Schüler im Paradies*, pub. 1550). Short comedy on the simplemindedness and gullibility of a peasant woman who, in an encounter with a wandering scholar, mistakes his destination, which is Paris, for paradise. She entrusts him with money and clothing for her deceased first husband, who "walks around in heaven in his shroud." On hearing of his wife's folly, the woman's second husband rides after the departed stranger. Having caught up with him, he fails to recognize him and falls prey himself to the roguishly sly wanderer, who advises the husband to leave his horse with him and continue the chase on foot. Having lost his horse, the peasant returns home too proud to admit his own naïveté and informs his wife that he has entrusted his horse to the wandering scholar to be given to the deceased in heaven. She tells the neighbors of the incident, and husband and wife become the laughingstock of the village.

The Hot Iron (*Das heisse Eisen*, pub. 1551). Expertly contrived comedy in which a husband suspected of infidelity must expiate his guilt by holding a hot iron. He passes the test without burning himself by adroitly slipping a wooden peg under the iron. He then demands the same "trial" of his wife, who as the iron comes closer and closer, admits her own unfaithfulness and divulges in a comical progression of panic all her sinful escapades. Finally she burns herself despite her confessions. Funny in itself, the buffoonery is greatly enhanced by psychological insight when the wife attributes her estrangement from her husband to his infidelity whereas the reverse is true: her need for other men has alienated them from each other.

Eve's Dissimilar Children (*Die ungleichen Kinder Evas*, pub. 1553). Comedy based on a Latin version of Melanchthon's legend. Sachs brings God himself to the stage, portraying Him as a typical German country priest. Through an angel the Lord announces His forthcoming visit to Adam and Eve, who are also depicted with all the idiosyncrasies of rural Germans. The couple resolve to present only their good and obedient children, keeping the mischievous ones hidden. Impressed, God awards them rank and riches. Encouraged by his graciousness, Eve brings out the naughty children too. God is amused by their dirty faces, but He blesses them with equanimity and appoints them to menial callings in various trades. The parents are obviously disillusioned. However, God reproaches them for failing to understand that all work is equal in His eyes.

[PETER JELAVICH]

PLAYS

Tragedies

Sachs's tragedies are listed in the order of their appearance in his *Register der Tragödie*. Proper names are not capitalized in the original.

1. *Lukretia, die Römerin mit Sextus* (Lucretia, the Roman Woman, and Sextus); also called *Tragödie der Lukretia aus der Beschreibung des Livius* (Tragedy of Lucretia from Livy's Account). 1 act. Published Jan. 1, 1527.

2. *Virginia, die keusche Römerin* (Virginia, the Chaste Roman Woman). Published Dec. 12, 1530.

3. *Caron mit den abgestorben Seelen*; also called *Caron mit den Seelen der Verstorbenen* (Charon with the Souls of the Dead). Also registered as a comedy. Published Jan. 28, 1531.

4. *Gismunda mit Guiscardus*; also called *Eine klägliche Tragödie des Fürsten Concret* (i.e. Tancred) (A Lamentable Tragedy of Prince Concret, i.e., Tancred). 5 acts. Published Nov. 17, 1545.

5. *Lisbeth mit Lorenz* (Elizabeth and Lawrence). 5 acts. Also registered as a comedy. Published Dec. 31, 1545.

6. *Die sechs Kämpfer* (The Six Warriors). 4 acts. Published July 1, 1549.

7. *Die Enthauptung Johannes* (The Decapitation of John the Baptist). Published Jan. 15, 1550.

8. *Jocasta, die unglückliche Königin* (Jocasta, the Unfortunate Queen). Published Apr. 19, 1550.

9. *Der reiche Mann stirbt* (The Rich Man Dies); also called *Hecastus* or *Von dem sterbenden Reichen, Hecastus genannt* (The Dying Rich Man Called Hecastus). 5 acts. Also registered as a comedy. Published Sept. 6, 1549.

10. *Judith mit Holophernes* (Judith and Holofernes). Also registered as a comedy. Published Mar. 17, 1551.

11. *Jeremias, der Prophet* (The Prophet Jeremiah). 5 acts. Published Aug. 3(?), 1551.

12. *Absalom, der Aufrührer, mit seinem Vater, König David* (Absalom, the Rebel, with His Father, King David). 5 acts. Published Oct. 26, 1551.

13. *König Rehabeam mit seinem jungen Rat(?)* (King Rehoboam and His Young Council); also called *Der junge, stolze König Rehabeam mit Jeroboam* (The Arrogant Young King Rehoboam and Jeroboam), Published Nov. 12, 1551.

14. *Lazarus wird auferweckt* (Lazarus Is Resuscitated); also called *Die Auferweckung des Lazarus* (The Resuscitation of Lazarus). 3 acts. Published Nov. 19, 1551.

15. *Die falsche Kaiserin mit dem (unschuldigen) Grafen* [The False Empress and the (Innocent) Count]. 5 acts. Published Nov. 27, 1551.

16. *Der Ritter von Burgund* (The Knight of Burgundy); also called *Die zwei Ritter von Burgund* (The Two Knights of Burgundy). 5 acts. Published Jan. 16, 1552.

17. *König Ysboset wird umgebracht* (King Ysboset Is Killed); also called *Der König mit seinen untreuen Hauptleuten* (King Ysboset and His Unfaithful Captains). 5 acts. Published Feb. 4, 1552.

18. *König David lässt sein Volk zählen liess* (King David Has His People Counted); also called *Wie König David seine Mannen zählen liess* (How King David Had His Following Counted). 3 acts. Published Dec. 5, 1552.

19. *Die Belagerung von Samaria* (The Siege of Samaria). 5 acts. Published July 6, 1552.

20. *Die Belagerung von Jerusalem von dem assyrischen König Sanherib* (The Siege of Jerusalem by the Assyrian King Sennacherib). 5 acts. Published July 9, 1552.

21. *Herodes mit seinen Söhnen* (Herod and His Sons); also called *Wie der Wüterich, König Herodes, seine drei Söhne und seine Gemahlin umbrachte* (The Raging King Herod: How He Killed His Three Sons and His Wife). 5 acts. Published Nov. 2, 1552.

22. *Die Kindheit von Moses* (The Childhood of Moses). 5 acts. Published Jan. 26, 1553.

23. *Tristan mit Isolde* (Tristan and Iseult); also called *Von der strengen Liebe des Herrn Tristan zu der schönen Königin Isolde* (The Strong Love of Lord Tristan for the Beautiful Queen Iseult). 7 acts. Published Feb. 7, 1553.

24. *Fortunatus mit dem Wunschhut*; also called *Fortunatus Wünschhütlein (Glücksäckel)* [Fortunatus and His Magic Hat (Magic Sack)]. 7 acts. Published Mar. 4, 1553.

25. *Priester Eli mit seinen ungeratenen Söhnen* (Eli the Priest and His Un-

dutiful Sons). 5 acts. Published Aug. 27, 1553.

26. *Die Opferung des Isaak (The Sacrifice of Isaac).* Published Nov. 4, 1553.

27. *Clitemnestra, die möderische Königin (Clytemnestra, the Murderous Queen);* also called *Klytämnestra, die blutdürstige Königin (Clytemnestra, the Bloodthirsty Queen).* 5 acts. Published Jan. 2, 1554.

28. *Achilles mit Polyxena: Die Zerstörung von Troya (Achilles and Polyxena: The Destruction of Troy);* also called *Die Zerstörung der Stadt Troya von den Griechen . . . Der Held Achilles mit Polyxena, der Königstochter von Troya (The Destruction of the City of Troy by the Greeks . . . The Hero Achilles and Polyxena, Daughter of the King of Troy).* 6 acts. Published Apr. 28, 1554.

29. *Rosamunda, die falsche Königin (Rosamund, the False Queen);* also called *Die Königin Rosamunda (Queen Rosamund)* or *Die untreue Königin Rosamunda (The Unfaithful Queen Rosamund).* 5 acts. Published Aug. 10, 1555.

30. *Alcestis, die getreue Fürstin (Alcestis, the Faithful Princess);* also called *Die getreue Frau Alcestis mit ihrem getreuen Mann Admetus (The Faithful Princess Alcestis and Her Faithful Husband Admetus).* 3 acts. Published Aug. 30, 1555.

31. *Agatocles mit Clinia (Agathocles and Clinia);* also called *Von Clinia und Agatocles, den zweien Griechen (Clinia and Agathocles, the Two Greeks).* 3 acts. Published Sept. 12, 1555.

32. *Das Kebsweib (des Leviten) (The Concubine of the Levite);* also called *Des Leviten Kebsweib (The Levite's Concubine).* 5 acts. Published Nov. 5, 1555.

33. *Die Zerstörung Jerusalems (The Destruction of Jerusalem).* 6 acts. Published Oct. 21, 1555. Produced Nürnberg, guild of *Briefmaler* (writers or painters of official documents), February, 1556.

34. *Herzog Wilhelm mit Agaley (Duke William and Aglaia);* also called *Herzog Wilhelm mit seiner Agaley, der Königstochter von Griechenland (Duke William of Austria and His Aglaia, the King's Daughter from Greece).* 7 acts. Published Dec. 3, 1555.

35. *Jephta (Jephthah);* also called *Jephta mit seiner Tochter (Jephthah and His Daughter).* Published Dec. 11, 1555.

36. *Simson (Samson);* also called *Der Richter Simson (Samson the Judge).* 5 acts. Published Jan. 31, 1556.

37. *Melusine (Melusina).* 7 acts. Published Feb. 15, 1556.

38. *Thamar (Tamar);* also called *Thamar, die Tochter des Königs David mit ihren Brüdern, Amnon und Absalom (Tamar, Daughter of King David and Her Brothers Amnon and Absalom).* 3 acts. Published May 12, 1556.

39. *Die Makkabäer;* Original title, *Die Machabeer (The Maccabees).* 7 acts. Published Oct. 30, 1556.

40. *Die vier Liebhabenden (The Four Lovers);* also called *Die vier liebhabenden Personen* or *Die vier verliebten Personen (Four Persons in Love).* 7 acts. Published Nov. 12, 1556.

41. *Hagwart mit seiner Signe (Hagwart and His Signe);* also called *Von zwei Liebhabenden, Hagwart mit Signe, der Königstochter aus Dänemark (The Two Lovers: Hagwart and Signe, Daughter of the King of Denmark).* 5 acts. Published Nov. 30, 1556.

42. *Antaphila mit den Tyrannen (Antaphila and the Tyrants);* also called *Das kühne Weib Antaphila mit den zwei Tyrannen (The Brave Woman Antaphila and the Two Tyrants).* 5 acts. Also registered as a comedy. Published Dec. 8, 1556.

43. *Die Kindheit Christi (The Childhood of Christ);* also called *Die Empfängnis und Geburt Christi und des Johannes (The Conception and Birth of Christ and John the Baptist).* 9 acts. Also registered as a *geistige Komödie oder Tragödie* ("spiritual comedy or tragedy") and as a comedy. Published June 16, 1557. Production permitted by Nürnberg City Council, Jan. 11, 1558.

44. *König Saul mit David (King Saul and David);* also called *Tragödie des König Sauls mit Verfolgung des Königs David (The Tragedy of King Saul and the Persecution of King David).* Two versions; 5 acts each. Published Aug. 28, 1557. Production permitted by Nürnberg City Council, Jan. 14, 1558.

45. *Geburt, Leben und Ende von König Cyrus (The Birth, Life, and Death of King Cyrus);* also called *Des König Cyrus Geburt, Leben und Ende (King Cyrus's Birth, Life, and Death).* 7 acts. Published June 30, 1557. Production permitted by Nürnberg City Council, Jan. 14, 1558.

46. *Die Tyranei des Königs Saul und sein Ende (The Tyranny of King Saul and His Death);* also called *Die Verfolgung von Saul des Königs David (The Persecution of King David by Saul).* 5 acts. Published Sept. 6, 1557. Production permitted by Nürnberg City Council, Jan. 14, 1558.

47. *Der gehörnte Siegfried (The Armored Siegfried);* also called *Der gehörnte Siegfried, Sohn des Königs Sigismund aus den Niederlanden (The Armored Siegfried, Son of King Sigismund of the Netherlands).* 7 acts. Published Sept. 14, 1557.

48. *Nabot und König Achab (Naboth and King Ahab);* also called *Der gottlose König Achab mit dem frommen Nabot (The Godless King Ahab and the Pious Naboth).* 5 acts. Published Oct. 4, 1557.

49. *Phöbus und Daphne (Phoebus and Daphne);* also called *Daphne, eine Königstochter (Daphne, a King's Daughter).* 5 acts. Published Mar. 22, 1558.

50. *Die Passion Christi (The Passion of Christ);* also called *Die ganze Passion nach dem Text der vier Evangelisten, vor einer christlichen Versammlung*

zu spielen (The Entire Passion after the Text of the Four Gospels to Be Played before a Christian Gathering). 10 acts. Published Apr. 12, 1558.

51. *Das jüngste Gericht (The Day of Judgment);* also called *Der Tag des jüngsten Gerichtes aus der (heiligen) Schrift zusammengestellt (The Day of Judgment, Gathered from the Entire Holy Writ).* 7 acts. Published May 25, 1558.

52. *Abraham und Lot (Abraham and Lot);* also called *Abraham, Lot samt der Opferung Isaaks (Abraham, Lot, and the Sacrifice of Isaac).* 7 acts. Published Sept. 13, 1558.

53. *Alexandrus Magnus (Alexander the Great);* also called *Von Alexandrus Magnus, dem König von Makedonien, seiner Geburt, seinem Leben und Ende (Alexander the Great, King of Macedonia: His Birth, Life, and Death).* 7 acts. Published Sept. 27, 1558.

54. *Der Gott Bel mit den Pfaffen (The God Baal and the Priests).* 3 acts. Published Jan. 14, 1559.

55. *Die Frau Beritola (The Lady Beritola);* also called *Die edle Frau Beritola mit ihrem mannigfaltigen Unglück (The Noble Lady Beritola and Her Many Misfortunes).* 7 acts. Also registered as comedy. Published Aug. 16, 1559.

56. *Puera, die Märtyrerin (Puera the Martyr);* also called *Die Jungfrau Puera und der Ritter Gottfried (The Virgin Puera and the Knight Gottfried).* 3 acts. Published Nov. 11, 1559.

57. *Ptolemäus, der Tyrann (Ptolemy the Tyrant);* also called *Die fromme Königin Arsinoes mit ihrem tyrannischen Bruder, König Ptolemäus Ceraunus (The Pious Queen Arsinoë and Her Tyrannical Brother, King Ptolemy Keraunos).* 6 acts. Published Dec. 19, 1559.

58. *Kleopatra, die Königin von Ägypten;* original title, *Cleopatra, die Königen von Ägypten (Cleopatra, Queen of Egypt);* also called *Die Königin Kleopatra von Ägypten mit Antonius, dem Römer (Queen Cleopatra of Egypt and Antony the Roman).* 7 acts. Published Sept. 10, 1560.

59. *Romulus und Remus, die Brüder (The Brothers Romulus and Remus);* also called *Romulus und Remus, die Erbauer der Stadt Rom (Romulus and Remus, Builders of the City of Rome).* 7 acts. Published Sept. 20, 1560.

60. *Des Königs Artaxerxes Unglück (King Artaxerxes the Unfortunate);* also called *Artaxerxes, der König Persiens, mit den mancherlei Unfällen der Seinen (Artaxerxes, King of Persia, and the Many Misfortunes of His People).* 7 acts. Published Oct. 12, 1560.

61. *König Andreas von Ungarn (King Andrew of Hungary);* also called *Andreas, der ungarische König, mit Bancbano, seinem getreuen Stadthalter (Andrew, King of Hungary, and Viceroy Bánk, His Faithful Regent).* Published Dec. 7, 1561.

62. *Theseus mit dem Minotaurus (im Irrgarten) (Theseus and the Minotaur in the Labyrinth).* 7 acts. Published February, 1564 (not printed).

63. *Euricles mit Lukretia (Euricles and Lucretia).* 5 acts. Published Jan. (?) 1, 1565 (not printed).

Comedies

Sachs's comedies are listed in the order of their appearance in *Das Register der Komödie.*

1. *Die Göttin Pallas, mit Venus, worin die Göttin Pallas die Tugend und die Göttin Venus die Wollust verficht (The Goddess Pallas Athena and Venus, in Which the Goddess Pallas Represents Virtue and the Goddess Venus Lust);* also called *Die Göttin Venus wider Pallas (The Goddess Venus versus Pallas).* 3 acts. Published Feb. 3, 1530.

2. *Henno.* Published Jan. 9, 1531. Adaptation of the Latin play (1497) by Johann Reuchlin, which was taken from the medieval French play *Maître Pierre Pathelin.*

3. *Judicium Paridi (The Judgment of Paris).* 5 acts. Published Jan. 9, 1532.

4. *Disputation über Messias (Disputation on the Messiah);* also called *Komödie, dass Christus der wahre Messias ist (Comedy that Christ is the True Messiah).* Published Dec. 8, 1530.

5. *Plutos, der Gott des Reichtums (Plutus, the God of Wealth);* also called *Plutos, ein Gott aller Reichtümer (Plutus, a God of All Wealth).* 5 acts. Published Jan. 13, 1531.

6. *Tobias;* original title, *Thobias;* also called *Die ganze Historie von Tobias (The Whole Story of Tobias).* 5 acts. Published Jan. 7, 1530.

7. *Die Stupidität und ihr Hofgesinde;* original title, *Die Stultitia und ihr Hofgesinde (The Goddess Stupidity and Her Court).* Published Feb. 1, 1532.

8. *Esther mit dem König Ahasverus;* original title, *Hester mit dem König Ahasverus (Esther and King Ahasuerus);* also called *Die ganze Historie von Esther (The Whole Story of Esther).* 3 acts. Published Oct. 8, 1536.

9. *Der Gott Jupiter mit der Göttin Juno (Jupiter the God and Juno the Goddess);* also called *Komödie oder Kampfgespräch zwischen Jupiter und Juno, ob Weiber oder Männer zum Regiment fähiger sind (Comedy or Dispute Between Jupiter and Juno on Whether Men or Women Are Better Fitted to Rule).* Published Apr. 30, 1534.

10. *Kampfgespräch: Das Alter gegen die Jugend (Dispute: Youth versus Age).* Published Jan. 12, 1534.

11. *Violanta, Tochter eines Ritters (Violanta, a Knight's Daughter).* 5 acts. Published Nov. 27, 1545.

12. *Griseldis, die Geduldige (Griselda, the Patient Woman);* also called *Die geduldige und gehorsame Marquise Griseldis (The Patient and Obedient Marchioness Griselda).* 5 acts. Published Apr. 15, 1546.

13. *Titus und Gisippus, zwei getreue Freunde (Titus and Gisippus, Two Faithful Friends)*; also called *Die zwei getreuen Freunde, Titus und Gisippus (The Two Faithful Friends Titus and Gisippus)*. 5 acts. Published May 25, 1546.

14. *Hiob, der Geduldige (Job the Patient)*. 5 acts. Published Nov. 9, 1547.

15. *Die Gebrüder Lucius*; original title, *Die zwei Brüder Lucius (The Two Brothers Lucius)*; also called *Eine Komödie von Plautus . . . genannt Menechmus (A Comedy of Plautus Called Menaechmus)*. 5 acts. Published Jan. 17, 1548.

16. *Genura, die Unschuldige (Genura the Innocent)*; also called *Die unschuldige Frau Genura (The Innocent Woman Genura)*. 5 acts. Published Mar. 6, 1548.

17. *Schöpfung und Fall von Adam*; original title, *Geschopff und Fall von Adam (The Creation and Fall of Adam)*; also called *Tragödie von Schöpfung, Fall und Austreibung Adams aus dem Paradies (The Tragedy of the Creation, Fall, and Expulsion from Paradise of Adam)* or *Eine Komödie von der Schöpfung und dem Fall des Menschen (A Comedy of the Creation and Fall of Man)*. 3 acts. Published Oct. 17, 1548.

18. *Die Königin aus Frankreich (mit dem falschen Marschall) (The Queen of France and the False Marshal)*. Two versions: 5 acts and 8 acts. Published Dec. 12, 1549.

19. *Jakob mit (seinem Bruder) Esau [Jacob and (His Brother) Esau]*. 5 acts. Published Jan. 31, 1550.

20. *Circe mit Odysseus (Circe and Ulysses)*; also called *Die Göttin Circe (The Goddess Circe)*. 5 acts. Published Feb. 22, 1550.

21. *Salomonisches Urteil*; original title, *Das Gericht Salomonis*; also called *Judicium Salomonis (The Judgment of Solomon)*. Published Mar. 6, 1550.

22. *Der König von Frankreich mit dem Kind (The King of France and the Child)*; also called *Der König Dagobert von Frankreich mit Kind des Försters (King Dagobert of France and the Forester's Child)*. Published Jan. 31, 1551.

23. *Bianceffora mit dem Pfaffen (Blanchefleur with the Priest)*; also called *Florian, der Königssohn aus Spanien mit der schönen Bianceffora (Floris, Son of the King of Spain, and the Beautiful Blanchefleur)*. Published Apr. 17, 1551.

24. *Die Kaiserin mit den Aussätzigen (dem Aussätzigen) [The Empress and the Leper (Lepers)]*; also called *Die unschuldige Kaiserin von Rom (The Innocent Empress of Rome)*. 5 acts. Published Aug. 31, 1551. Production permitted by Nürnberg City Council, Feb. 5, 1552.

25. *Jonas, der Prophet (The Prophet Jonah)*; also called *Der ganze Prophet Jonas (The Entire Prophet Jonah)*. 4 or 5 acts.

26. *Waldbruder mit dem Engel (The Forest Hermit and the Angel)*; also called *Waldbruder vom heimlichen Gericht Gottes (The Forest Hermit from the Secret Court of God)*. 3 acts. Published Nov. 23, 1551.

27. *Der Alte Bürger mit 3 Söhnen (The Old Burgher and His Three Sons)*; also called *Der alte reiche Bürger, der seinen Söhnen sein Gut übergab (The Rich Old Burgher Who Gave His Property to His Sons)*. 5 acts. Produced July 22, 1552.

28. *Ritter Galmi mit der Herzogin (aus Britannien) [The Knight Galmi and the Duchess (of Britain)]*. 7 acts. Published Dec. 24, 1552.

29. *David mit Abigail (David and Abigail)*; also called *Abigail*. 5 acts. Published Jan. 4, 1553.

30. *David's Ehebruch mit Bathseba (David's Adultery with Bathsheba)*; also called *David begeht Ehebruch mit Bathseba*; original title, *David mit Bathseba in Ehebruch (David Commits Adultery with Bathsheba)*. 5 acts. Published Oct. 4(?), 1553.

31. *Mucius Scävola, der Römer (Mucius Scaevola the Roman)*; also called *Mucius Scävola, der getreue, kühne und edle römische Bürger (Mucius Scaevola, the Loyal, Brave, and Noble Citizen of Rome)*. Two versions: 4 acts and 5 acts. Published Oct. 5, 1553.

32. *Die ungleichen Kinder Evas (wie sie Gott, der Herrn anspricht) (Eve's Dissimilar Children)*. Written 1552. Published Nov. 6, 1553.

33. *Der falsche Schulmeister (The False Schoolmaster)*; also called *Von dem ehrenfesten Hauptmann Camillus mit dem untreuen Schulmeister in der Stadt Valisco (The Honorable Captain Camillus and the Unfaithful Schoolmaster in the City of Valisco)*. Published Dec. 8, 1553. Production permitted by Nürnberg City Council on date of completion, Dec. 8, 1553?

34. *Persones, die Königin, mit Aristoteles (Queen Persones and Aristotle)*; also called *Die Königin Persones reitet auf dem Philosophen Aristoteles (Queen Persones Rides the Philosopher Aristotle)*. 5 acts. Published (?) January 1554?

35. *Die Irrfahrt des Odysseus (mit den Freiern und seiner Gemahlin Penelope) (The Wanderings of Ulysses and the Suitors of His Wife Penelope)*. 7 acts. Published Feb. 20, 1555.

36. *Die vertriebene fromme Kaiserin (The Pious Empress Exiled)*; also called *Die vertriebene Kaiserin mit den zwei verlorenen Söhnen (The Expelled Empress and the Two Lost Sons)*. 6 acts. Published Nov. 13, 1555.

37. *Die schöne Magelone (The Beautiful Magelona)*. 7 acts. Published Nov. 19, 1555. Produced Frankfurt am Main, by Nürnberg citizens, Easter fair, 1585.

38. *Gideon*. 5 acts. Published Jan. 25, 1556.

39. *Der verlorene Sohn [The Lost (Prodigal) Son]*. 5 acts. Published Apr. 18, 1556.

40. *Hugo Schapler (Hugh Capet)*; also called *Von Hugo Schapler, dem streitbaren Helden in Frankreich (Hugh Capet, the Battling Hero of France)*. 7 acts. Published June 11, 1556.

41. *Sohn des Marschalls (The Marshal's Son)*; also called *Von dem Marschall mit seinem Sohn (The Marshal and His Son)*. Published July 4, 1556.

42. *Frau Marina mit dem Doktor (The Woman Marina and the Doctor)*; also called *Die schöne Marina mit dem Doktor Dagmanus (The Beautiful Marina and Doctor Dagman)*. 3 acts. Published Sept. 1, 1556.

43. *König Darius mit dem Kammerherrn (King Darius and the Chamberlain)*; also called *König Darius mit drei Kammerherren (King Darius and Three Chamberlains)*. 3 acts. Published Sept. 23, 1556.

44. *Kaiser Julian im Bad (The Emperor Julian in the Bath)*; also called *Julian, der Kaiser, im Bad (Julian the Emperor in the Bath)*. 5 acts. Published Sept. 23, 1556.

45. *Josua mit den 5 Königen (Joshua and the Five Kings)*; also called *Der Josua mit seinen Streitigkeiten*; original title, *Der Josua mit seinem Streiten (Joshua and His Struggles)*. 7 acts. Published Oct. 19, 1556.

46. *(Der Prophet) Elias mit dem Ölkrug (The Prophet Elijah and the Jar of Oil)*; also called *Das Fräulein mit dem Ölkrug (The Girl and the Jar of Oil)*. 3 acts. Published Dec. 18, 1556.

47. *Oliver mit Artus (Oliver and Artus)*; also called *Die getreuen Gesellen und Brüder, zwei Königssöhne Oliver und Artus (The Two Faithful Friends and Brothers Oliver and Artus)*. 7 acts. Published Dec. 3, 1556.

48. *Der Jüngling im Kasten (The Young Man in the Box)*. 3 acts. Published Jan. 13, 1557.

49. *Der weltliche verlorene Sohn (The Worldly Prodigal Son)*; also called *Der verlorene Sohn, den man richten wollte (The Prodigal Son Whom People Wanted Judged)*. 3 acts. Published Mar. 11, 1557.

50. *(Die) Jael mit Sisera (Jael and Sisera)*. 4 acts. Published July 8, 1557.

51. *Marina, die Königstochter aus Frankreich (Marina, Daughter of the King of France)*. 5 acts. Published July 20, 1557.

52. *(Der) Daniel (mit seinen Gesellen) [Daniel (and His Companions)]*; also called *Die Komödie Daniels (The Comedy of Daniel)*. 7 acts. Published Aug. 10, 1558.

53. *(Der) Mephiboset, König Sauls Sohn (Mephibosheth, Son of King Saul)*. Published Oct. 5, 1557.

54. *Pontus mit seiner Sidonia (Pontus and His Sidonia)*; also called *Pontus, ein Königssohn aus Galizien, mit seiner schönen Sidonia, eine Königstochter aus Britannien (Pontus, Son of the King of Wales, and His Beautiful Sidonia, Daughter of the King of Britain)*. 7 acts. Published Jan. 17, 1558.

55. *Andromeda mit Perseus (Andromeda and Perseus)*; also called *Perseus mit Andromeda (Perseus and Andromeda)*. 5 acts. Published Mar. 22, 1558.

56. *Die zwölf erlauchten (getreuen) Frauen [The Twelve Illustrious (Faithful) Ladies]*. Published Mar. 30, 1559.

57. *Esthers ganze Historie*: original title, *Hester's ganze Historie (The Whole History of Esther)*; also called *Die Komödie der Königin Esther (The Comedy of Queen Esther)*. 7 acts. Published Aug. 8, 1559.

58. *Herzog Wilhelm von Orleans (Duke William of Orléans)*; also called *Der Fürst Wilhelm von Orleans mit seiner Amalie, der Königstochter aus England (Prince William of Orléans and His Amalie, Daughter of the King of England)*. 7 acts. Published Oct. 18, 1559.

59. *König Sedras mit Helebat (King Sedras and Helebat)*; also called *König Sedras mit der Königin Helebat und dem Fürsten, Pillerus (King Sedras, Queen Helebat, and Prince Pillerus)*. 7 acts. Published June 13, 1560.

60. *König Artaxerxes' Unglück (The Misfortunes of King Artaxerxes)*; also called *Artaxerxes, der König Persien, mit seinen mannigfaltigen Unfällen der Seinen [Artaxerxes, King of Persia, and the Many Mishaps of His Family (People)]*. 7 acts. Also registered as a tragedy. Published Oct. 12, 1560.

61. *König Andreas von Ungarn (King Andrew of Hungary)*; also called *Andreas, der ungarische König mit Bancbano, seinem getreuen Stadthalter (The Hungarian King Andrew and Viceroy Bánk, His Faithful Regent)*. Also registered as a tragedy. Published Dec. 17, 1561.

62. *Terenz mit Thrassus und Thaisa (Terence, Thraso, and Thais)*; also called *Eine Komödie von Terenz: Der Ritter Thrassus mit seinen Buhlen (A Comedy of Terence: The Knight Thraso and His Courtesans)* or *Eine schöne Komödie von dem Poeten, Terenz, vor 1700 Jahren von der Buhlin Thais und ihren zwer Buhlen, dem Ritter Thrassus und Phödria beschrieben (A Beautiful Comedy Written by the Poet Terence 1,700 Years Ago about the Courtesan Thais and Her Two Lovers, the Knight Thraso and Phaedria)*. 5 acts. Published Nov. 4, 1564.

63. *Judicium Paridis, für kleine Knaben (oder Kinder) gekürzt [The Judgment of Paris, Adapted for Little Boys (or Children)]*. 3 acts Published (?) January, 1565 (not printed).

64. *Geschichte von Jakob und Joseph (History of Jacob and Joseph)*. Comedy started by Sachs and left unfinished, according to Puschmann.

Shrovetide Plays

Sachs's Shrovetide plays are listed as registered in his *Register der Fastnachtsspiele*. All have only one act.

1. *Von dem Liebesstreit (A Love Quarrel)*; also called *Von der Eigenschaft der Liebe (The Quality of Love)*. Published Jan. 8, 1518.

2. *Der Frau Venus Hofgesinde*; also called *Das Hofgesinde der Venus*

[*The Court of (Lady) Venus*]. Published Feb. 21, 1517.

3. *Reichtum wider Armut* (*Wealth versus Poverty*). Also registered as a comedy. Published (?) 1531.

4. *Das böse Weib mit ?* (*The Bad Woman and ?*). Published Oct. 8, 1530.

5. *Buhler, Spieler und Trinker* (*Lovers, Gamblers, and Drinkers*); also called *Ein Richter, ein Buhler, ein Spieler und ein Trinker* (*A Judge, a Lover, A Gambler, and a Drinker*). Published Feb. 9, 1535.

6. *Der ungeratene Sohn* (*The Undutiful Son*). Also registered as a comedy. Published Feb. 9, 1535.

7. *Die Milde und der Geiz* (*Charity and Greed*); original title, *Der Milde und Karge*; also called *Von einem Vater mit zwei Söhnen* (*A Father and Two Sons*). Published Feb. 17(?), 1538.

8. *Der Fürwitzige mit dem Eckhardt* (*The Meddler and Eckhardt*). Published July 12, 1538.

9. *Die sechs (armen) Klagenden* [*The Six (Poor) Plaintiffs (Complainers)*]. Published Dec. 21, 1536.

10. *Die Spinnstube*; original title, *Der Rockenstube* (*The Spinning Room*). Published Dec. 28, 1536.

11. *Das Narrenschneiden* (*The Cutting Up of Fools*). Published Oct. 3, 1536. Produced Torgau Court, February 1680; Weimar Theatre, by Goethe; Nürnberg marketplace, June 24, 1874; Nürnberg, garden of the German National Museum, 1874. Based on an episode in Sebastian Brant's *Ship of Fools* (1494).

12. *. . . . holen im deutschen Hof* (*Fetching in the German Court*). Published Nov. 21, 1539.

13. *Die fünf elenden (oder armen) Wanderer* [*The Five Miserable (or Poor) Wanderers*]. Published Dec. 15, 1539.

14. *Der Heuchler und der wahre Freund* (*The Hypocrite and the True Friend*); also called *Unterschied zwischen einem wahren Freund und einem Heuchler* (*The Difference Between a True and a False Friend*). Published Dec. 30, 1540.

15. *Der tölpelhafte Fritz holt Krapfen* (*Silly Fritz Sent to Fetch Doughnuts*); also called *Ein Bürger, ein Bauer und ein Edelmann; die holen Krapfen* (*A Burgher, a Peasant, and a Nobleman Go to Fetch Doughnuts*). Published Dec. 31, 1540.

16. *Der schwangere Bauer* (*The Pregnant Peasant*). Published Nov. 25, 1544.

17. *Die Arznei gegen Lasten*; original title, *Die Lasten Arznei* (*The Remedy for Vices*). Published Dec. 10, 1544.

18. *Der Teufel mit den alten Weibern* (*The Devil and the Old Women*). Published Nov. 19, 1545.

19. *Der Kaufmann mit dem Teufel* (*The Merchant and the Devil*); also called *Der Teufel mit dem Kaufmann und den alten Weibern* (*The Devil, the Merchant, and the Old Women*). Published Nov. 27, 1549.

20. *Der Nasentanz*; also called *Nasentanz* (*The Nose Dance*). Published Feb. 4, 1550.

21. *Die gestohlene Fastnacht's Henne* (*The Stolen Shrovetide Hen*). Published Oct. 4, 1550.

22. *Der fahrende Schüler im Paradies** (*The Wandering Scholar in Paradise*). Published Oct. 8, 1550.

23. *Nikola, der junge Kaufmann* (*The Young Merchant Nicola*). Published Oct. 10, 1550.

24. *Frau Wahrheit mit dem Bauern* (*The Lady Truth and the Peasant*); also called *Frau Wahrheit will niemanden beherbergen* (*The Lady Truth Will Shelter No One*). Published Nov. 10, 1550.

25. *Der Kuhdieb mit dem Bauern* (*The Cow Thief and the Peasant*). Published Nov. 25, 1550.

26. *Die zwei Bürger mit Salomon* (*The Two Burghers and Solomon*). Published Nov. 29, 1550.

27. *Der Abt im Wildbad* (*The Abbot at the Hot Springs*). Published Dec. 17, 1550. Production not permitted.

28. *Der böse Rauch* (*The Evil Smoke*). Published Jan. 13, 1551.

29. *Die drei Studenten* (*The Three Students*). Published (?) February, 1551.

30. *Gott Apollo mit Fabius* (*The God Apollo and Fabius*); also called *Fastnachtsspiel zwischen dem Gott Apollo und dem Römer Fabius* (*Shrovetide Play about the God Apollo and the Roman Fabius*). Published Sept. 2, 1551.

31. *Der Halbfreund (und Heuchler)* (*The Half-Friend and Hypocrite*). Published Aug. 28, 1551.

32. *Der Geizhunger* (*Greedy Hunger*); also called *Der unersättliche Geizhunger* (*The Insatiable Greedy Hunger*). Published Sept. 5, 1551.

33. *Der bodenlose Pfaffensack* (*The Priest's Bottomless Sack*). Published Oct. 7, 1551.

34. *Das Ausbrüten von Kälbern*; original title, *Das Kälberbrüten* (*The Breeding of Calves*). Published Oct. 7, 1551.

35. *Die fettige Buhlerei*; original title, *Die speckige Buhlerei* (*Fat Lechery*). Published Oct. 20, 1551.

36. *Der Bauerknecht will zwei Weiber* (*The Farm Laborer Wants Two Wives*); also called *Der Bauerknecht will zwei Frauen haben* (*The Farm Laborer Wants to Have Two Wives*). Published Oct. 21, 1551.

37. *Der fahrende Schüler mit dem Teufel** (*Raising the Devil; The Wander-ing Scholar and the Devil*); also called *Teufelsaustreibung*; original title, *Teufelsbannen* (*The Devil's Expulsion*). Published Nov. 5, 1551.

38. *Das heisse Eisen** (*The Hot Iron*). Published Nov. 16, 1551.

39. *Die verschwätzte Buhlschaft* (*Love Chattered Away*); also called *Von der unglücklichen verschwätzten Buhlschaft* (*The Unfortunate Love that Was Chattered Away*). Published Aug. 9, 1552.

40. Untitled play. Published Dec. 2, 1552.

41. *Der gestohlene Pack* (*The Stolen Package*). Published Dec. 6, 1552.

42. *Der Bauer im Fegefeuer* (*The Peasant in Purgatory*). Published Dec. 9, 1552.

43. *Die listige Buhlerin* (*The Clever Courtesan*). Published Dec. 17, 1552.

44. *König Alexander mit Diogenes* (*King Alexander and Diogenes*); also called *Das Gespräch von Alexandrus Magnus mit dem Philosophen, Diogenes* (*The Conversation Between Alexander the Great and the Philosopher Diogenes*). Published Dec. 30, 1552.

45. *Der Eiferer hört sein Weib beichten* (*The Jealous Man Hears His Wife Confess*). Published Jan. 14, 1553.

46. *Das Weib im Brunnen* (*The Woman in the Well*). Published Jan. 15, 1553.

47. *Der Tyrann Dionysius (mit Damon)* (*The Tyrant Dionysius and Damon*). Published Jan. 28, 1553.

48. *Reichstag von Deutschland* (*The Parliament of Germany*). Published (?) March, 1553.

49. *Das böse Weib mit Wort, Gewürz und Stein* (*The Wicked Woman: Words, Spices, and Stones*); also called *Das böse Weib mit den Worten, Gewürzen und Steinen gut zu machen* (*Improving a Wicked Woman with Words, Spices, and Stones*). Published Sept. 4, 1553.

50. *Der verdorbene Edelmann im Bett* (*The Depraved Nobleman in Bed*); also called *Der verdorbene Edelmann mit dem weichen Bett, das Kaiser Augustus kaufen wollte* (*The Depraved Nobleman and His Soft Bed, which Emperor Augustus Wanted to Buy*). Published Sept. 9, 1553.

51. *Eulenspiegel mit dem Blinden* (*Eulenspiegel and the Blind Man*). Published Sept. 14, 1553. Produced Berlin, summer festival of the Academy of Arts, July 2, 1887.

52. *Die ungleichen Kinder Evas* (*Eve's Dissimilar Children*); also called *Wie Gott, der Herr, die Kinder von Adam und Eva segnet* (*How the Lord God Blesses Adam and Eve's Children*). Published Sept. 23, 1553.

53. *Kellermeister mit seinem Suppenkessel* [*The Cellarman (Butler) and His Soup Kettle*]; also called *Kellermeister mit seinem Kessel voll Suppe* [*The Cellarman (Butler) and His Full Kettle of Soup*] or *Kellermeister mit dem Suppenkessel* [*The Cellarman (Butler) and the Soup Kettle*]. Published Oct. 2, 1553.

54. *Der Bauer mit dem . . .* (*The Peasant and . . .*). Published Oct. 12, 1553.

55. *Der schalkhafte Bauernkneckt* (*The Sly Farmhand*). Published Oct. 1 (?), 1553.

56. *Bürgerin mit dem Pfaffen* (*The Townswoman and the Priest*); also called *Die Bürgerin mit dem Domherrn* (*The Townswoman and the Canon*). Published Oct. 24, 1553.

57. *Die alte (verschlagene) Kupplerin mit dem Domherrn* [*The (Wily) Old Procuress and the Canon*]. Published Oct. 27, 1553.

58. *Eulenspiegel mit der Kellnerin* (*Eulenspiegel and the Housekeeper*); also called *Eulenspiegel, the Priest's Housekeeper, and the Horse*). Published Dec. 16, 1553.

59. *Der Rossdieb von Fünzing (mit dem tollen diebischen Bauern)** (*The Horse Thief*). Published Dec. 16, 1553.

60. *Der tote Mann (wurde lebendig)* (*The Dead Man Returns to Life*). Published Jan. 11, 1554.

61. *Das weinende Hündlein* (*The Crying Little Dog*). Published Jan. 25, 1554.

62. *Der wohl zerzauste alte Buhle* (*The Well-ruffled Old Lover*); also called *Der alte Buhle mit der Zauberei* (*The Old Lover and Magic*). Published Feb. 1, 1554.

63. *Wie man wunderliche Männer zähmt*; original title, *Wunderlichen Mann geschlacht zu machen* (*How to Make Rough Men Smooth*); also called *Wie man wunderliche Männer und unhäusliche Weiber zähmt und häuslich macht* (*How to Make Rough Men Smooth and to Smooth and Domesticate Shrews*). Published Apr. 24, 1554.

64. *Das geifernde Weib* (*The Gossipy Woman*); original title, *Das munkelnd Weib*; also called *Der faule Mann mit dem geifernde Weib* (*The Lazy Man and the Gossipy Woman*). Published May 24, 1554.

65. *Pfarrer mit dem ehebrecherischen Bauern* (*The Vicar and the Adulterous Peasant*). Published May 30, 1554.

66. *Des Krämers Korb*; also called *Der Krämerskorb* (*The Grocer's Basket*).

67. *Sankt Peter mit seinen Freunden* (*St. Peter and His Friends*); also called *Sankt Peter feiert (originally, letzt sich) Abschied mit seinen Freunden* (*St. Peter Celebrates Farewell with His Friends*). Published Aug. 28, 1554.

68. *Der Kampf zwischen Armut und Glück* [*The Struggle Between Poverty and Luck (Happiness; Success)*]; also called *Der Kampf von Frau Armut gegen Frau Glück* (*The Struggle Between Lady Poverty and Lady Luck*). Also registered as a comedy. Published Sept. 5, 1554.

69. *Der blinde Totengräber (originally, Mesner) mit de Pfaffen [und der Totengräberin (originally, Mesmerin)]* (*The Blind Gravedigger, the Priest, and*

the Gravedigger's Wife). Published Oct. 25, 1555.

70. *Der Tod im Schraubstock (Death in the Vice).* Published Aug. 8, 1555.

71. *Die Disputation zwischen Thales und Solon (The Debate Between Thales and Solon);* also called *Die Disputation zweier Philosophen über den Ehestand, ob es besser sei, ledig zu bleiben oder einen weisen Mann zu heiraten (The Debate Between Two Philosophers on Whether It Is Better to Stay Single or to Marry a Wise Man).* Published Sept. 27, 1556.

72. *Das Pelzwaschen (The Fur Washing);* also called *Eulenspiegel mit der Pelzwäsche in Nügstetten (Eulenspiegel and the Fur Washing in Nügstetten).* Published Feb. 5, 1556.

73. *Lucius Papirius mit dem Weibern (Lucius Papirius and the Women);* also called *Der Knabe Lucius Papirius Cursor (The Boy Lucius Papirius Cursor).* Published Feb. 8, 1556.

74. *Die fromme Schwiegermutter kuppelt ihre Tochter (The Pious Mother-in-law Panders for Her Daughter);* also called *Die kupplerische Schwiegermutter mit dem alten Kaufmann (The Matchmaking Mother-in-law and the Old Merchant).* Published Mar. 17, 1556.

75. *Der Neidhart mit dem Pfeil (The Envier with the Arrow).* Published Mar. 17, 1556.

76. *Der Teufel nahm ein altes Weib (zur Frau) (The Devil Married an Old Woman).* Published Sept. 24, 1557.

77. *Eulenspiegel mit dem Tuch (Eulenspiegel and the Cloth);* also called *Eulenspiegel mit dem blauen Hosentuch und dem Bauern (Eulenspiegel, the Blue Pants Cloth, and the Peasant).* Published Sept. 30, 1557.

78. *Der Gott mit dem Wucherer (God and the Profiteer);* also called *Eine Klage über den Wucher und Verkauf (A Complaint about Usury and Trade)* or *Fastnachtsspiel, den Wucher und andere Beschwerden betreffend (A Shrovetide Play on Usury and Other Burdens).* Published Dec. 23, 1557.

79. *Hermann mit dem Safran (Herman and the Saffron);* also called *Der Bauer mit dem Safran (The Peasant and the Saffron).* Published Nov. 10, 1558.

80. *Der schwangere Bauer mit dem Füllen (The Pregnant Peasant and the Colt).* Published Feb. 26, 1559.

81. *Der Schellentanz (der verspielte Reiter);* original title *Klas Schellentanz [The Dance of the Bells (The Lost Rider)].* Published Nov. 16, 1559. Produced Rothenburg an der Tauber, June 6, 1892.

82. *Die zwei sich raufenden Gevattern (The Two Quarreling Godfathers);* also called *Die zwei Gevattern voller Zorn (The Two Godfathers Full of Anger).* Published Nov. 23, 1559.

83. *Der Doktor mit der (langen) Nase (The Doctor with the Big Nose).* Published Dec. 13, 1559.

84. *Franziska wehrt zwei Buhlen ab [Francisca Evades (Wards Off) Two Lovers];* also called *Die junge Witwe Franziska (The Young Widow Francisca).* Also registered as a comedy. Published Oct. 31, 1560.

85. *Aesop mit Xanthus (Aesop and Xanthus).* Also registered as a comedy. Published Nov. 23, 1560.

EDITIONS

Collections
Sämtliche Fastnachtsspiele, ed. by E. Götze, 7 vols., Halle, 1880–1886; *Werke,* ed. by A. von Keller and E. Götze, 26 vols., Tübingen, 1870–1908; *Werke,* ed. by K. M. Schiller, 2 vols., 1960.
Individual Plays
The Horse Thief. Published in *Adventures in World Literature,* ed. by R. B. Inglis and W. K. Stewart and tr. by W. Leighton, New York, 1936.
Raising the Devil. Published in *The Drama: Its History, Literature and Influence on Civilization,* ed. by A. Bates and tr. by W. Chambers, vol. 10, London, 1903–1904.
The Wandering Scholar in Paradise. Published in *Poetic Drama,* ed. by A. Kreymborg and tr. by S. Eliot, New York, 1941.

CRITICISM

E. Götze, *H. Sachs,* Bamberg, 1890; R. Genée, *Hans Sachs,* Leipzig, 1902; M. Herrmann, *Die Bühne des Hans Sachs,* Berlin, 1923; P. Landau, *Hans Sachs,* Berlin, 1924; L. Wohlrab, *Die Bedeutung Boccaccios für die Werke des Hans Sachs,* Leipzig, 1924; E. Geiger, *Das Meistergesang des Hans Sachs,* Bern, 1956; B. Koenneker, *Hans Sachs,* Stuttgart, 1971.

Sackler, Howard   (1929–   )

American poet, film and television writer, and dramatist. His Broadway debut in 1968 with *The Great White Hope,* a play about the world of boxing and racial conflict, won him his greatest success. Among his other plays are *Uriel Acosta* (1954), *Mr. Welk and Jersey Jim* (1960), *The Pastime of Monsieur Robert* (1960), and *The Yellow Loves* (1960). He also wrote the screenplays for *Fear and Desire* (1953) and *The Great White Hope* (1970).   [GAUTAM DASGUPTA]

The Great White Hope, with James Earl Jones (center) and Jane Alexander (right). Washington, Arena Stage, 1967. [Arena Stage, Washington]

Sackville, Thomas   (1536–1608)

English poet, statesman, and dramatist. Sackville, the 1st Earl of Dorset, is known in theatrical circles for his collaboration with Thomas Norton on the tragedy *Gorboduc or Ferrex and Porrex* (1562). He was also the author of a distinguished long poem entitled *Induction,* which served as an introduction to the volume of poetry entitled *A Mirror for Magistrates.* The book exerted a powerful influence on the chronicle play. *See* CHRONICLE PLAY in glossary.

Sagan, Françoise   (1935–   )

French novelist and playwright; pseudonym of Françoise Quoirez. Her first novel, *Bonjour tristesse* (Prix des critiques, 1954), written when she was nineteen, brought her instant fame, as much for her clear and classical style

Françoise Sagan. [Agence de Presse Bernand]

as for her mature understanding of human nature and bourgeois society. She subsequently wrote numerous novels with uneven success; her last one to date is *The Unmade Bed* (*Le lit défait*, 1977).

Her first plays, *Castle in Sweden* (*Château en Suède*, 1960) and *Violins Sometimes* (*Les violons parfois*, 1961), were only moderately successful. Like her novels they depict the loose morals and sentimental problems of a blasé bourgeois society. *The Purple Dress of Valentine* (*La robe mauve de Valentine*, 1963) was better received. In 1964 she wrote *Happiness, Odd and Pass* (*Bonheur, impair et passe*), in which a young army officer who has decided to die declares being in love with his game partner's wife, thus hoping to be killed, but finally becomes the lover of the beautiful young woman.

In 1966 two works were produced: *The Splinter* (*L'écharde*) and *The Vanishing Horse* (*Le cheval évanoui*). In the latter play, Hubert Darsay, in search of a dowry, wants to wed the rich heiress Priscilla and make his girl friend Coralie marry his fiancée's brother, but Coralie prefers Priscilla's father. Here, Sagan develops one of her favorite themes: the amorous conflict between two generations. Sagan's *A Piano on the Lawn* (*Un piano dans l'herbe*) was produced in 1970. Sagan has hardly any rivals in the bourgeois comedy of manners, as most young and talented authors seem to prefer the medium of the film to that of the boulevard.

JOSPEH E. GARREAU

Salacrou, Armand (1899–   )

French dramatist. He was born on August 8, 1899, in Rouen. In 1902 his family moved to Le Havre where he attended school and as a young man was active in the

Armand Salacrou. [French Cultural Services]

organization of the local branch of the Jeunesses Socialistes. After initial studies in medicine, Salacrou turned to philosophy and was eventually granted a licentiate's degree after submitting a thesis on the work of Benedetto Croce, whom he had met on a visit to Florence. In Paris he studied law for a time and worked as a journalist for *L'Humanité* and the *Internationale*. Salacrou was a Communist until 1923, when he quit the party and drew closer to the surrealists. His friends at the time included Antonin Artaud, Robert Desnos, and Charles Dullin, the actor-director who was to help launch his career. *See* AR-TAUD, ANTONIN.

Salacrou's early plays were poorly received by the public and critics, who were accustomed to theatre in a naturalistic vein, but he retained the enthusiastic support of Dullin, Louis Jouvet, Aurélien-François Lugné-Poë, and other important figures in the theatrical world. His first popular success was *Atlas-Hôtel* (1931). For almost a decade he divided his time between writing and operating an advertising agency that he had founded to supplement his income. The latter enterprise became so successful and time-consuming that in 1939, with his theatrical career also firmly established, he gave it up to devote all his time to writing.

Christian Wolff and Ann Smyrner in the 1962 Berlin production of *Castle in Sweden*. [German Information Center]

Salacrou enlisted in the army at the outbreak of World War II, was captured by the Germans, and escaped. After France demobilized in 1940, he moved to Lyon, where he edited the clandestine newspaper *Front National.* Salacrou's experiences in the Resistance are reflected in his play *Nights of Anger* (*Les nuits de la colère,* 1946), which shows his deep commitment to the cause of French liberation. In 1946 he and Jean-Louis Barrault jointly directed the Théâtre de l'Odéon, but he refused the post of administrator of the theatre when it was offered him the following year. Salacrou was a member of UNESCO's First Congress of the International Theatre Institute in 1948, and in 1949 he became a member of the Goncourt Academy. His autobiographical writings and ideas on theatre are contained in various prefaces and appendixes to his *Théâtre* and in two published volumes of memoirs entitled *Nocturnal Ideas* (*Les idées de la nuit,* 1960) and *In the Waiting Hall Loves* (*Dans la salle des pas perdus les amours,* 1976).

WORK

Salacrou's early plays are in a vein closely associated with the Dadaist and surrealist experiments, and even in his later, more conventional plays he was never to abandon the artistic and poetic devices developed by these movements. These techniques find their purest expression in an unproduced one-act play entitled *The Plate*

Histoire de rire, with (l. to r.) Yves Robert, Danièle Delorme, and Pierre Dux, Théâtre Saint-Georges, Paris. [French Cultural Services]

Scene from *Une femme libre.* Paris, Théâtre Saint-Georges, 1946. [French Cultural Services]

Breaker (*Le casseur d'assiettes,* pub. 1925), which also announced what was to be a dominant intellectual theme of Salacrou's theatre: the impossibility of reconciling the fact of evil with the existence of a just God. In this surrealist sketch God is compared to a plate juggler who purposely breaks his plates, and the existence of a mechanistic universe is found to be less "absurd" than the postulation of a God who judges and condemns his own imperfectly made creations.

Salacrou soon turned his attention to Pirandellian demonstrations of the discontinuity of human personality and to investigations of the influence of the past on the present. Exemplifying this trend is *The Bridge of Europe* (*Le pont de l'Europe,* 1925), in which a group of actors is invited by a king to represent key events in his life. As time went on, Salacrou made less consciously literary use of poetic techniques and philosophically probed everyday characters and situations. His adamantly deterministic view of life gave his plays a tone that oscillated between anguish and cynical burlesque.

After the success of *Atlas-Hôtel* (1931), a more or less typical boulevard drama in which a romantic who dreams of creating a tourist empire at the foot of the Atlas Mountains struggles to retain the love of his wife, Salacrou returned to themes closer to his heart with *A Free Woman* (*Une femme libre,* 1934). In it a young woman rejects the confining limits of bourgeois marriage in favor of personal freedom. Salacrou was one of the first modern playwrights to experiment with dramatic flashback, and in *The Frenzied Ones* (*Les frénétiques,* 1934), he made extensive use of this technique in dealing with the life of a domineering film mogul. Time is also a central preoccupation in *The Unknown Woman of Arras* (*L'inconnue d'Arras*, 1935), the action of which takes place between the moment a man shoots himself and the instant of his death. Reviewing the events of his life, he finds its justification in acts of charity as symbolized by kindness to an unknown woman on the Arras battlefield; but the bullet has been discharged, and all perspectives are closed by death.

Aspects of adultery and the problem of imposing a moral code in a world from which God is seemingly absent are central concerns of both *A Man Like the Others* (*Un homme comme les autres*, 1936) and *When the Music Stops* (*Histoire de rire*, 1939).

The World Is Round (*La terre est ronde*, 1938), one of Salacrou's major philosophical plays, emphasizes the cyclical return of totalitarianism as an accident in man's eternal struggle for freedom. Events in Savonarola's Florence in 1492, when Columbus's voyage challenged basic Christian beliefs, provided a striking parallel with contemporary Hitler-dominated Europe. After the liberation Salacrou presented a drama on the Resistance, *Nights of Anger* (1946), which probes modern morality by taking its characters back in time to show how decent men may be led to act dishonorably.

Among other plays of interest by Salacrou are *No Entry, or The Ages of Life* (*Sens interdit, ou Les âges de la vie*, 1953), in which the characters are born old and then progress to innocent youth and eventual unconsciousness; and *Boulevard Durand* (pub. 1960, prod. 1971, Liège), a realistic presentation of the events that led to the judicial "error" that resulted in the imprisonment of a union leader in Le Havre, where Salacrou was raised.

The Unknown Woman of Arras (*L'inconnue d'Arras*, 1935). Episodic drama depicting past events in the life of a man about to die. Ulysse, a middle-aged salesman, shoots himself when he discovers that his wife Yolande and his best friend Maxime are having an affair. As the shot rings out, time stops and Ulysse's past unfolds before him; he recalls words he spoke, things he heard, and people he knew, particularly the women who af-

Scene from *Boulevard Durand*. [Courtesy of Centre Dramatique National Nord]

Sens interdit. Paris, Théâtre du Quartier Latin, 1953. [French Cultural Services]

fected him most: his old nurse; a girl who left him for another; a woman who loved him so deeply that she attempted suicide when he left her; and finally, "the unknown woman," briefly met in wartime, who represents the poignant mystery in Ulysse's life. He then probes the relationship between Yolande and Maxime. In his final moment of life, Yolande reveals her deep shame. Ulysse then reverses his decision: he wants to live, but it is too late. The shot has been fired, and his life is over.

The World Is Round (*La terre est ronde*, 1938). Drama about extreme religious zeal, set in Florence in 1492 but generally accepted as an allegory of Nazi fanaticism. Savonarola, prior of St. Mark's, denounces man's depravity and exhorts his flock to repudiate pleasure and consecrate itself to God. These appeals to the spirit are, however, accompanied by cruel and tyrannical coercion. The worried papacy has tried in vain to control Savonarola by offering him a cardinalate. It now dares him to ascend a burning pyre with another monk, assuming that God will save the one He considers His own. Savonarola refuses to undergo the ordeal, thereby losing credit among his puerile and fanatical followers. Arrested and tortured, he goes to his death proclaiming that "nothing exists but the light of God." The story emphasizes the interaction of Savonarola's world with the voluptuous world of Renaissance Italy, and it shows the effect of the situation on two lovers, Silvio and Lucciana.

Nights of Anger (*Les nuits de colère*, 1946). Drama depicting the moral problem of a group of French citizens in German-controlled Chartres in April, 1944. Dead, dying, and live characters all participate in a discussion. Bernard Bazire, a storekeeper who values his comfort and peace of mind above all and who always obeys the ruling authority, shelters his old friend Jean Cordeau when he comes to Bazire's home with an injury he says he received in an accident. In fact, his wound was sustained while he was sabotaging a train as a member of the Maquis. Sensing that his friend is in trouble and not wanting to become involved, Bazire betrays him to a neighbor who is a collaborator. Finally, they are both killed, Jean by the Gestapo and Bernard by members of the Resistance, and as corpses they continue to argue about morality and guilt.

[JOSEPH E. GARREAU]

PLAYS

Unless otherwise noted, the plays were first performed in Paris.

1. *La boule de verre (The Glass Bull).* Play, 1 act. Published 1924.
2. *Le casseur d'assiettes (The Plate Breaker).* Play, 1 act. Published 1925.
3. *Tour à terre (Shore Leave).* Play, 3 acts. Published 1929. Produced Théâtre de l'Oeuvre, Dec. 24, 1925.
4. *Le pont de l'Europe (The Bridge of Europe).* Play, 3 acts. Published 1929. Produced Théâtre de l'Oeuvre, Dec. 24, 1925.
5. *Patchouli.* Play, 3 acts. Published 1930. Produced Théâtre de l'Atelier, Jan. 22, 1930.
6. *Atlas-Hôtel.* Play, 3 acts. Published 1931. Produced Théâtre de l'Atelier, Apr. 15, 1931.
7. *La vie en rose (A Rosy Life).* Impromptu, 1 act. Published 1936. Produced Théâtre du Vieux-Colombier, Dec. 3, 1931.
8. *Une femme libre (A Free Woman).* Play, 3 acts. Published 1934. Produced Théâtre de l'Oeuvre, Oct. 4, 1934.
9. *Les frénétiques (The Frenzied Ones).* Play, 5 tableaux. Published 1935. Produced Théâtre Daunou, Dec. 5, 1934.
10. *L'inconnue d'Arras* (The Unknown Woman of Arras).* Play, 3 acts. Published 1936. Produced Comédie des Champs-Élysées, Nov. 22, 1935.
11. *Un homme comme les autres (A Man Like the Others).* Play, 3 acts. Published 1937. Produced Théâtre de l'Oeuvre, Nov. 23, 1936.
12. *La terre est ronde* (The World Is Round).* Play, 3 acts. Published 1938. Produced Théâtre de l'Atelier, Nov. 7, 1938.
13. *Histoire de rire* (When the Music Stops).* Dramatic farce, 3 acts. Published 1940. Produced Théâtre de la Madeleine, Dec. 22, 1939.
14. *La Marguerite* (Marguerite).* Play, 1 act. Published 1941. Produced Théâtre Pigalle, Oct. 28, 1944.
15. *Les fiancés du Havre (The Fiancés of Le Havre).* Play, 3 acts. Published 1944. Produced Comédie-Française, Dec. 10, 1944.
16. *Le soldat et la sorcière (The Soldier and the Witch).* Historical divertissement, 2 parts. Published 1946. Produced Théâtre Sarah-Bernhardt, Dec. 5, 1945.
17. *Les nuits de la colère (Nights of Anger).* Play. Produced Théâtre Marigny, Dec. 12, 1946.
18. *L'Archipel Lenoir, ou Il ne faut pas toucher aux choses immobiles (The Lenoir Archipelago, or One Must Not Touch Immobile Things).* Comedy, 2 parts. Published 1946. Produced Théâtre Montparnasse, Nov. 8, 1947.
19. *Pourquoi pas moi? (Why Not Me?).* Play, 1 act. Produced Brussels, Théâtre du Rideau, Sept. 4, 1948; Paris, Théâtre Édouard VII, Oct. 26, 1950.
20. *Poof*.* Comedy ballet, 1 long act. Produced Théâtre Édouard VII, Oct. 26, 1950.
21. *Dieu le savait, ou la vie n'est pas sérieuse (God Knew It, or Life Isn't Serious).* Play, 3 acts. Published 1951. Produced Théâtre Saint-Georges, Dec. 2, 1950.
22. *Sens interdit, ou Les âges de la vie* (No Entry, or The Ages of Life).* Psychodrama, 1 act. Published 1952. Produced Théâtre du Quartier-Latin, Jan. 6, 1953.
23. *Les invités du bon Dieu (God's Guests).* Vaudeville, 3 acts. Published 1953. Produced Théâtre Saint-Georges, Sept. 23, 1953.
24. *Le miroir* (The Mirror).* Play, 4 acts. Published 1956. Produced Théâtre des Ambassadeurs, Sept. 21, 1956.
25. *Une femme trop honnête (Too Honest a Woman).* Play, 3 acts. Published 1956. Produced Théâtre Édouard VII, December, 1956.
26. *Boulevard Durand.* Drama, 2 parts. Published 1960. Produced Liège, 1971.
27. *Comme des chardons (Like Thistles).* Play. Produced Comédie-Française, Oct. 18, 1964.
28. *Histoire de cirque (Circus Story).* Play. Def. ed. 1977.
29. *La rue noire (The Black Street).* Play. Produced 1967.
30. *Poof.* Comedy-ballet for television, 1973.

EDITIONS

Théâtre, 8 vols., Paris, 1942–1966; *Three Plays,* tr. by N. Stokle, Minneapolis, 1967.

CRITICISM

J. Van den Esch, *Armand Salacrou, dramaturge de l'angoisse,* Paris, 1947; S. Radine, *Anouilh, Lenormand, Salacrou: Trois dramaturges à la recherche de leur vérité,* Geneva, 1951; F. di Franco, *Le théâtre de Salacrou,* Paris, 1970; A. Ubersfeld, *Armand Salacrou,* Paris, 1970; B. Bébon, *Salacrou,* Paris, 1971.

Saltykov-Shchedrin, Mikhail Yevgrafovich (1826–1889)

Russian satirist, journalist, novelist, and critic; pseudonym of Mikhail Yevgrafovich Saltykov. He was born to a noble family of landowners in the province of Tula. From his earliest stories ("An Intricate Business," 1848), he attacked abuse of privilege and social inequity, and found himself out of favor with the authorities. Using the pen name N. Shchedrin for his satirical *Provincial Sketches* (1856–1857), he became under his own name deputy governor of Ryazan and Tver and editor of *The Contemporary (Sovremennik)* and *Notes of the Fatherland (Otechestvennye zapiski),* two leading organs of liberal opinion. His most important prose works are *The Golovlyov Family (Gospoda Golovlyovy,* 1880), the picture of a rapacious, degenerating clan of landowners; *The History of a Town (Istoriya goroda,* 1870), in which a chronicle of Russian tyranny is camouflaged as the history of one small town; and *Fairy Tales (Skazki,* 1869–1886), fables whose Aesopian language enabled him to expose all sorts of political abuses and follies.

Many of Saltykov's writings are in dialogue form and were staged during his lifetime. His importance as a dramatist rests, however, on two plays, *Pazukhin's Death (Smert Pazukhina;* wr. 1857, prod. 1889) and *Shadows (Teni;* wr. 1862–1865, pub. 1914, prod. 1914). The former is a savagely caustic comedy of provincial life, a kind of Russian *Volpone* in which the machinations of the characters to procure an inheritance reveal no redeeming virtues. *Shadows* is a more traditional satire of the civil service and high society. *Pazukhin's Death* received its strongest production from the Moscow Art Theatre in 1914, when its caricatural qualities were emphasized.

Pazukhin's Death (*Smert Pazukhina,* 1857). The deathbed of old Pazukhin, once a peasant, now a millionaire, is surrounded by relatives and hangers-on anxious to secure the inheritance. His son Prokofy, who angered his father by retaining the habits and religion of the merchant class, fears that, if a will is made, his rights will be violated. He tries scheming with his brother-in-law, the hypocritical councilor Furnachyov, and the impoverished General Lobastov, who wants to marry his spinster daughter to Porfiry's son, but they disclaim him. He even shaves off his beard, but old Pazukhin is unimpressed and dies after an angry scene among the family. Furnachyov is surprised in the act of robbing the corpse by the rightful heir, Prokofy, and is publicly humiliated. The last line is, "Virtue—oops, I mean, Vice—

Vice is punished, and Virtue—where is Virtue, any-way?''

LAURENCE SENELICK

EDITIONS

Polnoe sobranie sochineniy, Moscow-Leningrad, 20 vols. 1933–1941; *Sobranie sochineniy*, 20 vols., Moscow, 1965–   ; *Pazukhin's Death*, tr. by L. Senelick, in *Russian Literature Triquarterly* 14 (Winter 1976).

CRITICISM

E. Zenkevich, *M. E. Saltykov-Shchedrin—teatralnyy kritik*, Moscow, 1953; D. Zolotnitskiy, *Shchedrin-dramaturg*, Leningrad-Moscow, 1961.

Salviati, Lionardo   (1539–1589)

Italian dramatist. Lionardo Salviati, an influential Florentine literary critic and academician, was one of a number of Italian humanists responsible for transferring the cultural aims of humanism from the classics to the Italian language and literary classics. Elected consul of the important Accademia Fiorentina, Salviati turned to the theatre in order to produce vernacular works based upon Roman practice. His two comedies—*The Crab* (*Il granchio*, 1566) and *The Thorn* (*La spina*, 1592)—are most important from a linguistic perspective, for in them Salviati attempts to reproduce on the stage the comic language of Giovanni Boccaccio's *Decameron*. Later, Salviati would become famous for his revision of *The Decameron* (1582), which aimed to make Boccaccio's masterpiece conform to post-Tridentine morality by editing, expurgating, and moralizing. More influential as a scholar than as a playwright, Salviati always championed the Florentine literary classics as a linguistic model for all of Italy.

PETER BONDANELLA

EDITIONS

Opere complete del cavaliere Lionardo Salviati, Milan, 1810.

CRITICISM

P. M. Brown, *Lionardo Salviati: A Critical Biography*, Oxford, 1974.

Sánchez, Florencio   (1875–1910)

Uruguayan journalist and dramatist. He was born in Montevideo on January 17, 1875. After having spent his childhood and youth in Uruguay, Sánchez went to Argentina, where he produced most of his journalistic and dramatic work. His literary talents developed early, and he began writing for a newspaper while still in his teens. His life thereafter was generally unsettled and impoverished, as he eked out a living as a journalist for a variety of newspapers in Montevideo, Rosario, and Buenos Aires, where he eventually established residence.

After 1897 Sánchez became interested in the theatre. His first play, *Decent Folk* (*La gente honesta*), was to have opened in Rosario in June, 1902, but was banned because of its satire of several prominent persons. *The Newspaper Boy* (*Canillita*), however, was performed in Rosario that fall and enjoyed an immediate success. In 1903 Sánchez presented his play *My Son the Lawyer* (*M'hijo el dotor*) in Buenos Aires and achieved both critical and popular acclaim.

During the next five years Sánchez completed the rest of his major works. He wrote feverishly, composing in this time some eighteen plays while continuing his journalistic career. *The Immigrant Girl* (*La gringa*, 1904) and *The Dead* (*Los muertos*, 1905) were said to have been written in single nights. In 1909 a subsidy from the Republic of Uruguay enabled Sánchez to travel through France and Italy, and in the spring of 1910 he settled in Milan, where he died.

Generally considered the most important South American theatrical literature of the early twentieth century, the plays of Sánchez are based on contemporary sociological themes. Technically, his theatre detached itself from the prevalent romantic melodramatic drama in its use of natural idiomatic language, realistic settings, and situations of everyday life. Rooted in the reality of the people of the Rio de la Plata region, Sánchez's drama exhibits the influence of Uruguayan folklore and Argentinian gaucho theatre. Of his prolific production (twenty-three works in six years), twenty integral texts and some fragments remain. Sánchez's dramas may be divided into three groups: the early works, including *Inner Doors* (*Puertas adentro*, 1897) and *Decent Folk*, works set in the country; and those set in an urban environment. Two of his rural dramas, *My Son the Lawyer* and *The Immigrant Girl*, are based on the conflict between older gaucho traditions and more modern social values. Perhaps his best rural play is *Down the Gully* (*Barranca abajo*, 1905), a fatalistic drama that follows the decline of the family of an old rancher, Zoilo. Most of Sánchez's urban plays deal with the lower classes. Among them is *The Newspaper Boy*, the story of a newsboy from Rio de la Plata who labors to help his impoverished family. Most notable of his plays set in the city and dealing with the bourgeoisie are *The Family Circle* (*En familia*, 1905); *Our Children* (*Nuestros hijos*, 1907); and *The Rights of Health* (*Los derechos de la salud*, 1907), which centers on the destructive ramifications of illness in the lives of both the sick and the well. Sánchez's zarzuela (musical comedy) *Chief Pichuleo* (*El cacique Pichuleo*) was written in 1906 in collaboration with the musician Francisco Payá. He died on November 7, 1910. *See* ZARZUELA in glossary.

My Son the Lawyer (*M'hijo el dotor*, 1903). Drama dominated by Julio, a law student in revolt against the country society in which he grew up. In his struggle for independence from social conventions, he alienates Olegario, his Old World father, begets a child by his father's ward Jesusa, and loses the love of his city sweetheart. Through the unselfishness of Jesusa, Julio comes to realize that he has unconsciously achieved his ideal of love, and he marries her.

The Immigrant Girl (*La gringa*, 1904). The title refers to Victoria, the daughter of Don Nicola, an Italian rancher, who is in love with Próspero, an Argentine. The play deals mainly with the downfall of Cantalicio, Próspero's Creole father. Having lost his ranch, his herd, and his son to the successful, hardworking ''gringos,'' Cantalicio refuses any further dealings with them and leaves his home, bitter and heartbroken. A reconciliation between Cantalicio and the landowner is achieved when Don Nicola allows Próspero to marry Victoria, and the play concludes with the hope that a new and stronger kind of people will issue from their union.

Down the Gully (*Barranca abajo*, 1905). Tragic drama about Zoilo Carbajal, a gentleman whose refusal to compromise his self-respect renders him and his family helpless before economic and moral ruin. Throughout his misfortunes, he retains the love of his consumptive daughter Prudencia, who becomes his only reason for living. There is momentary hope for a new life when an old friend offers to marry Prudencia, but the girl dies, leaving Ziolo with no escape from his misery but suicide.

Our Children (*Nuestros hijos*, 1907). Domestic drama in which Eduardo Díaz, a man of liberal views, has retired from social life, ostensibly to make a study of social taboos. His wife and children continue to circulate in society until Mercedes, the eldest daughter, reveals that she is pregnant by her former sweetheart Enrique, whom she no longer loves. A conflict erupts between Díaz, who wants to keep Mercedes at home, and his wife and other children, who want her either to marry Enrique or to enter a convent. Threats from his self-righteous son force Díaz to divulge that he has actually retired because of his wife's unfaithfulness, and he leaves with Mercedes to start a new life.

WILLIS KNAPP JONES and JUDITH A. WEISS

CRITICISM

R. T. House, "Florencio Sánchez, a Great Uruguayan Dramatist," *Poet Lore*, Summer 1923; W. K. Jones, "The Gringo Theme in River Plate Drama," in *Hispania*, no. 25, pp. 326–332, 1942; also in *Boletín de Estudios de Teatro*, Buenos Aires, Oct. 1943, and in *Revista Nacional del Uruguay*, no. 7, pp. 75 ff; May, 1944.

Sánchez de Badajoz, Diego (1479?–ca. 1550?)

Spanish theologian, poet, and dramatist. He was one of the most prolific authors of *farsas* in sixteenth-century Spain and an important figure in the development of religious theatre. Little is known about his life: the only source of biographical data is the posthumous edition of his collected works, *Recopilación en metro*, published by his nephew, Juan de Figueroa, in 1554. He earned a bachelor's degree, most likely in theology, and was a priest in Talavera la Real, near Badajoz, from 1533 to 1549. Primarily he was a theologian and a moralist, and he wrote many sermons and plays in verse, but his *autos*, one-act allegorical dramas with religious themes, which he wrote in Spanish rather than the customary Latin, were the cause of his renown. These *autos* were also known as *farsas*, *farsa* being the general sixteenth-century Spanish term for a play written in the vernacular.

From the license to publish the *Recopilación* given to Juan de Figueroa on April 23, 1552, and from the dedication of the book to the Count of Feria, we know that Sánchez died before this date.

WORK

The primary importance of the work of Diego Sánchez de Badajoz is its contribution to the evolution of Spanish religious theatre. All twenty-eight of his known plays have religious or moralistic orientation. His drama has its roots in the medieval liturgical theatre, analogous to the morality and mystery plays of other parts of Europe. Sánchez made use of secular elements without discarding the religious symbolism and theological discussions of the liturgical plays. In so doing he added touches of everyday life to allegory and often presented his plays, written in Spanish, in the streets and plazas. In the *Dance of the Sins* (*Danza de los pecados*), a shepherd precedes the actors and makes room for them by pushing the crowd back with his staff. Allegorical figures are realistically represented as contemporary Spaniards, not abstract symbols, in *The Marriage of Reason* (*La farsa racional*). *See* ALLEGORY; MORALITY PLAY; MYSTERY PLAY in glossary.

Sánchez was one of the first Spanish playwrights to use pagan elements in sacred drama. A sybil in *The Reed-Spear Tournament* (*Farsa del juego de cañas*), a Nativity drama, describes a competition between the virtues and the vices. In this play, Sánchez followed the tradition of sybil plays in representations of the Nativity, using a sybil or prophetess as a narrator and leader of other prophets as they foretell the birth of Christ. As is true of many of his other plays, *The Reed-Spear Tournament* embodies much symbolism, particularly in its representation of the struggle between vice and virtue and the allusion to the prophets of the Old Testament through the narration of the sybil.

Sánchez's plays are also notable for their elaborate props and scenery and varied stage effects. In *Play of the Most Holy Sacrament* (*Farsa del Santísimo Sacramento*), music, carts, banners, and masks are employed, and the festivities include dances and tournaments. The actors appear on a cart decorated as a garden of flowers in the *Play of St. Susanna* (*Farsa de Santa Susaña*). Perhaps Sánchez's greatest achievement in the theatre was his ability to relate theological subjects to average people in a meaningful and entertaining manner.

The Marriage of Reason (*Farsa racional*). Allegory of the ideal but arduously achieved marriage of Reason and Free Will. The Body, personified as an insistent and forceful father, is anxious to marry his daughter Sensuality to Free Will, represented as an ingenuous and timid young man. Free Will is reluctantly engaging in a conversation with the Body when Sensuality arrives, passionately declaring her love for the young man. Although Free Will finds the girl's love enticing, he refuses her request for an embrace. Indecisive, he feels the need to ask the advice of his brother Understanding. Her pride wounded, Sensuality mocks Free Will's timidity and simplicity. Understanding, dressed as a doctor, counsels Free Will to forget the frivolous Sensuality and to consider an engagement with a more serious girl, Reason. However, Free Will decides that there is no harm in enjoying the beauty and passion of Sensuality for the time being, even if he should change his mind later. He returns to Sensuality to find her less attractive and disdainful. When he discovers that she has faithlessly formed a liaison with his brother Indolence, Free Will realizes his error and decides to marry the serious and loving Reason.

Dance of the Sins (*Danza de los pecados*). Allegorical drama, written for the Feast of Corpus Christi, in which the capital sins struggle against humanity, personified in Adam. The play is introduced by a Shepherd, who delivers a prologue about the ruin of sin. He continues to comment upon the action as the play evolves. Seven beautiful maidens, representing the sins, entice the ingenuous Adam into a dance. They maliciously cause him to fall repeatedly. After his seventh fall, he realizes his error. The Shepherd intervenes to exhort Adam to penitence. Agreeing to repent, Adam rejoices in the mercy of God.

[ANDRÉS FRANCO]

PLAYS

The only extant plays of Diego Sánchez de Badajoz are the following twenty-eight *farsas*, first published posthumously in *Recopilación en metro* (Seville, 1554) and most recently under the same title in Buenos Aires, 1968, ed. by F. Kurlat.

1. *Farsa teologal (Theological Play).*
2. *Farsa de la Natividad (Nativity Play).*
3. *Farsa de Santa Bárbara (Play of St. Barbara).*
4. *Farsa de Salomón (Play of Solomon).*
5. *Farsa moral (Morality Play).*
6. *Farsa del colmenero (Play of the Beekeeper).*
7. *Farsa de Tamar (Play of Tamar).*
8. *Farsa militar (Military Play).*
9. *Farsa racional (The Marriage of Reason).*
10. *Farsa del matrimonio (Play of Matrimony).*
11. *Farsa del Santísimo Sacramento (Play of the Most Holy Sacrament).*
12. *Farsa de los doctores (Play of the Learned Men).*
13. *Farsa de la fortuna ó hado (Play of Fortune or Fate).*
14. *Farsa de Isaac (Play of Isaac).*
15. *Farsa de molinero (Play of the Miller).*
16. *Farsa del Moysén (Play of Moses).*
17. *Farsa de Santa Susaña (Play of St. Susanna).*
18. *Farsa del rey David (Play of King David).*
19. *Farsa de Abrahán (Play of Abraham).*
20. *Farsa de la Iglesia (Play of the Church).*
21. *Farsa del herrero (Play of the Blacksmith).*
22. *Farsa de la Salutación (Play of the Angel's Greeting to Mary).*
23. *Farsa de San Pedro (Play of St. Peter).*
24. *Farsa de la hechicera (Play of the Witch).*
25. *Farsa de la ventura (Play of Fortune).*
26. *Farsa de la muerte (Play of Death).*
27. *Farsa del juego de cañas (The Reed-Spear Tournament).*
28. *Danza de los pecados (Dance of the Sins).*

CRITICISM

J. López Prudencio, *Diego Sánchez de Badajoz: estudio crítico, biográfico bibliográfico,* Madrid, 1915; B. W. Wardropper, *Introducción al teatro religioso del Siglo de Oro,* Salamanca, 1953.

Sandeau, Jules   (1811–1883)

French dramatist and novelist. He collaborated with George Sand on the short story "Prima Donna" (1831) and the novel *Rose et Blanche* (1831). He is best remembered for the novel *Mlle. de la Seiglière* (1848). His collaboration with Émile Augier resulted in a number of plays, including *La pierre de touche* (1853) and *Le gendre de M. Poirier* (1854). A dramatization of his novel *Jean de Thommeraye* enjoyed much success in 1874 because of its treatment of contemporary political problems. *See* AUGIER, ÉMILE.

[JOSEPH E. GARREAU]

Sandor, Malena   (1913–1968)

Argentine playwright; pseudonym of María Janes de Terza. Her first play, *I'm Getting a Divorce, Papa (Yo me divorcio, papá,* 1937), was followed the next year by *A Free Woman (Una mujer libre,* 1938), which won the National Culture Prize. In it, a divorced woman who opts

for a career as a sculptor finds that she is a focus of attention for too many men. Underlying the action is the protagonist's concern for going through life alone.

After a tour of duty as Italian correspondent of a Buenos Aires newspaper, she wrote *I Am the Strongest (Yo soy la más fuerte,* 1943), in which the protagonist tries to prevent the marriage of her stepson; *Your Life and Mine (Tu vida y la mía,* 1945), in which the protagonist forces her sister into an unwilling marriage; and—after another stay in Rome—*And the Reply Was Given (La respuesta fue dada,* 1956), which showed an Italian aristocrat questioning the values for which he had sacrificed himself during World War II. *An Almost Unbelievable Story (Una historia casi inverosímil,* 1966) was honored by Argentores, the national organization of dramatists. Malena Sandor was also the author of the musical comedy *Penelope No Longer Weaves (Penélope ya no teje,* 1946).

WILLIS KNAPP JONES and JUDITH A. WEISS

Sardou, Victorien   (1831–1908)

French dramatist. He was born in Paris on September 5, 1831. He was initially a medical student but soon abandoned medicine for history. Upon the completion of his studies he began to write, earning a meager living between 1850 and 1860 by working in a succession of badly paid jobs and by turning out newspaper articles on a wide variety of topics. His first play to be produced, *The Student Tavern (La taverne des étudiants),* appeared at the Odéon in 1854. It failed, however, and Sardou then began to write semiscientific stories in the manner of Edgar Allan Poe. In 1858, poor and in ill health, he was nursed by a young neighbor, Mlle. de Brécourt, whom he married soon after his illness. His wife introduced him to a friend, the well-known actress Pauline Déjazet, who encouraged his dramatic writing and, when she opened her own theatre in 1859, hired him to write plays. After his first success, *A Scrap of Paper (Les pattes de mouche,* 1860), a comedy, Sardou began to turn out comedies, historical dramas, melodramas, and opera libretti in such rapid succession that critics called him a "dealer in literature." He wrote twenty plays between 1860 and 1864 but thereafter decreased his output to about one play a year.

The Franco-Prussian War of 1870–1871 was finan-

Victorien Sardou. [Walter Hampden Memorial Library at The Players, New York]

cially disastrous for Sardou because the theatres were closed. He retreated to his château in Marly-le-Roi, became mayor of the town, and was active in aiding the wives and families of soldiers who lived there. In 1872, six years after the death of his first wife, he married Anne Soulié, with whom he had three children. In 1878 he was elected to the Académie Française. After Mlle. Déjazet's death in 1875, Sardou began to write plays for Sarah Bernhardt, notably *Fédora* (1882), *Théodora* (1884), and *La Tosca* (1887). During the 1880s and 1890s he achieved great popular success. He was burdened, however, by a lawsuit he instituted against the librettists of Puccini's opera *Tosca*, Luigi Illica and Giuseppe Giacosa, for plagiarism. The suit was finally settled in his favor in 1908. Soon after that, Sardou was stricken with pneumonia, and he died in Marly on November 8, 1908.

WORK

Sardou succeeded Eugène Scribe as the foremost French writer of the well-made play and managed to put his own stamp on the genre. He was concerned primarily with theatricality and, exercising prodigious powers of assimilation, made use of anything that was likely to increase the impact of a play. Thus he was a synthesizer, mixing melodrama, farce, and the elements of the well-made play. *See* WELL-MADE PLAY in glossary.

Happily embracing the increasingly complex scenic effects that new stage machinery was able to provide, he gave his historical plays spectacular settings, based on thorough research so as to be accurate in every detail. He was as accomplished a director as he was a play constructor, and he swept crowds about the stage with ease, achieving almost cinematic effects. But he could also cre-

Diplomacy, the English adaptation of *Dora*, with (l. to r.) Leslie Faber, William Gillette, and Giorgio Majeroni. New York, Empire Theatre, 1914. [Theatre Collection, The New York Public Library at Lincoln Center, Astor, Lenox and Tilden Foundations]

William Kendal and his wife, Dame Madge Kendal, in *A Scrap of Paper*. [Brander Matthews Dramatic Museum, Columbia University]

ate suspense with such simple stage props as a letter or a shawl. Audiences held their breath and came back for more. This was especially true when Sarah Bernhardt was acting one or another of the roles he created for her. Their first collaboration was the melodrama *Fédora* (1882), with a Russian setting and a characteristically involved plot; it was a triumph and established the "two S's" as an unbeatable team. They followed it with *Théodora* (1884), a Byzantine extravaganza; *La Tosca* (1887); and *Cleopatra* (*Cléopâtre*, 1890), which gave Bernhardt a death scene complete with live garter snakes.

Less spectacular but no less accomplished are Sardou's comic farces or vaudevilles. In *Let's Get a Divorce* (*Divorçons*, 1880) he envisioned the comic situations resulting from a proposed liberalization of the divorce law; and in *Madame Sans-Gêne* (1893) he plucked a minor figure from history, Napoleon's devil-may-care washerwoman, and built a comedy around her. The famous French actress Réjane scored a triumph in the title role.

Sardou's last play to be produced, *The Poison Scandal* (*L'affaire des poisons*, 1907), was a historical thriller based on a plot to poison Louis XIV.

Among other notable plays by Sardou are *A Scrap of Paper* (1860), his first theatrical success, inspired by a reading of Poe's *The Purloined Letter*; *The Benoîton Family*

(*La famille Benoîton*, 1865), a melodrama-farce; *Rabagas* (1872), a portrayal of political corruption; *Native Land!* (*Patrie!*, 1886), a melodrama-spectacle dealing with the French Revolution; *Spiritualism* (*Spiritisme*, 1897), in which a husband's interest in the occult creates marital difficulties; and *The Sorceress* (*La sorcière*, 1903), the last play Sardou wrote for Bernhardt, in which she played a Spanish gypsy at odds with the Inquisition.

Though Sardou had great theatrical gifts, his characters never rise above the level of cleverly manipulated puppets. Even in his own day critics attacked him for pandering to the tastes of his audiences. George Bernard Shaw best summed up critical distaste for the popular French dramatist with his coined word "Sardoodledom." Sardou's plays are rarely performed now, but in 1957 Jean-Louis Barrault successfully revived *Madame Sans-Gêne*.

A Scrap of Paper (*Les pattes de mouche*, 1860). Prosper and Clarisse, former lovers, have been forced by circumstances to part. Clarisse marries Vanhove, and three years later Prosper returns to court Clarisse's sister Marthe, who loves Paul, a young student. Prosper learns that Clarisse's last letter to him has remained for three years under the statue that the lovers had used as a mailbox. To Clarisse's horror, Prosper obtains the letter. Accompanied by her friend Suzanne, she goes to see Prosper in an attempt to get it back. Vanhove unexpectedly arrives, and though initially suspicious, he decides that it is Suzanne who has come to see Prosper. At Suzanne's

Katarina Hübscher and Ljerka Šram in an 1894 Zagreb production of *Madame Sans-Gêne*. [Private collection]

Sarah Bernhardt in an 1889 production of *Cléopâtre*. [Private collection]

urging, Prosper burns the letter, but a scrap blows into the street just as Vanhove is passing by with M. Thirion, Paul's tutor, who uses it to wrap an insect specimen. Later, Paul unknowingly uses the scrap of paper to scribble a hurried note to Marthe, a note that is mistakenly given to Mme. Thirion while everyone is dining at the Vanhove home. After some confusion, Prosper, who has meanwhile transferred his affections to Suzanne, manages to convince Vanhove that Suzanne had always been the object of his passion. This leaves the way open for the marriage of Marthe and Paul.

Let's Get a Divorce (*Divorçons*, 1880). Farce in which Cyprienne Des Prunelles, excited by discussion in government circles of a new divorce law, has begun a flirtation with Adhémar, her husband's cousin, with a view to marrying him after a divorce. Adhémar sends a telegram falsely stating that the proposed law has been passed, whereupon Des Prunelles suggests an amicable divorce with a ten-month truce until the decree can be secured. Adhémar is accepted as Cyprienne's fiancé, but when Des Prunelles tries to resume his bachelor habits, his wife becomes jealous. She accepts an invitation to dine with her husband in a private restaurant room and falls in love with him again. Thus, husband and lover change roles, and to Adhémar's complete discomfiture there is a happy reunion between Des Prunelles and Cyprienne.

Fédora (1882). Drama of the Russian princess Fédora, who resolves to avenge what she believes to

Two scenes from a Comédie-Française production of *Madame Sans-Gêne*: (top) with Béatrice Bretty (holding basket) in the title role; (bottom) with Jean Davy and P. E. Deiber. [French Cultural Services]

have been the political murder of her fiancé, son of the head of the Russian police. She denounces Loris, the suspected murderer, and follows him to Paris, where they fall in love. Loris confesses to the crime and discloses that it was actually a crime of honor; his wife and Fédora's fiancé had been lovers. To her horror, Fédora learns that Loris's mother and brother have been brutally killed as his accomplices in the murder. In despair she takes poison and dies, having discovered that the desire for personal revenge brings nothing but agony.

La Tosca (1887). Melodrama of the love affair between the singer Tosca and Mario, a liberal republican. During the Napoleonic conquest of Italy, Rome is governed by the cruel and lascivious Baron Scarpia, a reactionary opposed to Napoleon, who makes use of Tosca to trap Mario. He tortures her lover, then promises the horrified woman to let him go if she will become his mistress. Pretending to agree, Tosca obtains a safe-conduct for Mario and herself before stabbing Scarpia to death. She then hastens to the Castel Sant'Angelo, where a simulated execution of Mario is scheduled to take place. But Scarpia has given orders for Mario's actual execution, and when she realizes that her lover is dead, Tosca commits suicide by leaping from the parapet of the prison.

The play was the basis for the famous opera by Puccini (1900).   [JOSEPH E. GARREAU]

PLAYS

Unless otherwise noted, the plays were first performed in Paris.
1. *La taverne des étudiants (The Student Tavern).* Play. Produced Théâtre de l'Odéon, Apr. 1, 1854.
2. *Les premières armes de Figaro (Figaro's First Campaign).* Play. Produced Théâtre Déjazet, Sept. 27, 1859.
3. *Les gens nerveux (The Excitable People).* Play. Produced Théâtre du Palais-Royal, Nov. 4, 1859.
4. *Les pattes de mouche* (A Scrap of Paper).* Play. Produced Théâtre du Gymnase, May 15, 1860.
5. *Monsieur Garat.* Play. Produced Théâtre Déjazet, May 31, 1860.
6. *Les femmes fortes (The Strong Women).* Play. Produced Théâtre du Vaudeville, Dec. 31, 1860.

7. *L'écureuil (The Squirrel).* Play. Produced Théâtre du Vaudeville, Feb. 9, 1861.

8. *Piccolino.* Comedy. Produced Théâtre du Gymnase, July 18, 1861.

9. *Nos intimes (Our Friends).* Play. Produced Théâtre du Vaudeville, Nov. 16, 1861.

10. *La papillonne (The Butterfly).* Play. Produced Théâtre-Français, Apr. 11, 1862.

11. *La perle noire (The Black Pearl).* Play. Produced Théâtre du Gymnase, Apr. 12, 1862.

12. *Les prés Saint-Gervais (The Saint-Gervais Meadows).* Comedy. Produced Théâtre Déjazet, Apr. 26, 1862.

13. *Les ganaches (The Blockheads).* Play. Produced Théâtre du Gymnase, Oct. 29, 1862.

14. *Bataille d'amour (Battle of Love).* Libretto. Produced Opéra Comique, Apr. 13, 1863.

15. *Les diables noirs (The Black Devils).* Play. Produced Nov. 28, 1863.

16. *Le dégel (The Thaw).* Play. Produced Théâtre Déjazet, Apr. 12, 1864.

17. *Don Quichotte (Don Quixote).* Play. Produced Théâtre du Gymnase, June 25, 1864.

18. *Les pommes du voisin (The Neighbor's Apples).* Play. Produced Théâtre du Palais-Royal, Oct. 15, 1864.

19. *Le capitaine Henriot (Captain Henriot).* Libretto. Produced Opéra Comique, Dec. 29, 1864.

20. *Les vieux garçons (The Old Bachelors).* Play. Produced Théâtre du Gymnase, Jan. 21, 1865.

21. *La famille Benoîton (The Benoîton Family).* Play. Produced Théâtre du Vaudeville, Nov. 4, 1865.

22. *Nos bons villageois (Our Good Yokels).* Play. Produced Théâtre du Gymnase, Oct. 3, 1866.

23. *Maison neuve (The New House).* Play. Produced Théâtre du Vaudeville, Dec. 4, 1866.

24. *Séraphine.* Play. Produced Théâtre du Gymnase, Dec. 29, 1868.

25. *Patrie!* (Native Land!).* Drama. Produced Théâtre de la Porte-Saint-Martin, Mar. 18, 1869.

26. *Fernande.* Play. Produced Théâtre du Gymnase, Mar. 8, 1870.

27. *Le roi carotte (The King Swindles).* Libretto. Produced Théâtre de la Gaîté, Jan. 15, 1872.

28. *Rabagas.* Play. Produced Théâtre du Vaudeville, Feb. 1, 1872.

29. *Andréa.* Play. Produced Théâtre du Gymnase, Mar. 17, 1873.

30. *L'oncle Sam (Uncle Sam).* Play. Produced Théâtre du Vaudeville, Nov. 6, 1873.

31. *Les merveilleuses (The Exquisites).* Play. Produced Théâtre des Variétés, Dec. 16, 1873.

32. *Le magot.* Play. Produced Théâtre du Palais-Royal, Jan. 14, 1874.

33. *Les prés Saint-Gervais (The Saint-Gervais Meadows).* Libretto. Produced Théâtre des Variétés, Nov. 14, 1874.

34. *La haine (Hatred).* Play. Produced Théâtre de la Gaîté, Dec. 3, 1874.

35. *Ferréol.* Play. Produced Théâtre du Gymnase, Nov. 17, 1875.

36. *Piccolino.* Libretto. Produced Théâtre des Variétés, Apr. 11, 1876.

37. *L'hôtel Godelot (Hotel Godelot).* Play. Produced Théâtre du Gymnase, May 13, 1876.

38. *Dora.* Play. Produced Théâtre du Vaudeville, Jan. 22, 1877. Early version of *L'espionne*. Adapted for the English stage as *Diplomacy*.

39. *Les exilés (The Exiles).* Play. Produced New York, Boston Theatre, Dec. 10, 1877.

40. *Les bourgeois de Pont-Arcy (The Bourgeoisie of Pont-Arcy).* Play. Produced Théâtre du Vaudeville, Mar. 1, 1878.

41. *Les noces de Fernande (Fernande's Wedding).* Libretto. Produced 1878.

42. *André Fortier.* Play. Produced New York, Boston Theatre, Mar. 11, 1879.

43. *Daniel Rochat.* Play. Produced Théâtre-Français, Feb. 16, 1880.

44. *Divorçons* (Let's Get a Divorce).* Comedy. Produced Théâtre du Palais-Royal, Dec. 6, 1880.

45. *Odette.* Play. Produced Théâtre du Vaudeville, Nov. 17, 1881.

46. *Fédora.* Play. Produced Théâtre du Vaudeville, Dec. 11, 1882.

47. *Théodora.* Play. Produced Théâtre de la Porte-Saint-Martin, Dec. 26, 1884.

48. *Georgette.* Play. Produced Théâtre du Vaudeville, Dec. 9, 1885.

49. *Patrie! (Native Land!).* Libretto. Produced Théâtre de l'Opéra, Dec. 17, 1886.

50. *Le crocodile (The Crocodile).* Play. Produced Théâtre de la Porte-Saint-Martin, Dec. 21, 1886.

51. *La Tosca.* Play, 3 acts. Produced Théâtre de la Porte-Saint-Martin, Nov. 24, 1887.

52. *Marquise.* Play. Produced Théâtre du Vaudeville, Feb. 12, 1889.

53. *Belle-maman (Mama-in-law).* Play. Produced Théâtre du Gymnase, Mar. 15, 1889.

54. *Cléopâtre (Cleopatra).* Play. Produced Théâtre de la Porte-Saint-Martin, Oct. 23, 1890.

55. *Thermidor.* Play. Produced Théâtre-Français, Jan. 24, 1891.

56. *Les américaines à l'étranger* (American Women Abroad).* Play. Produced New York, Lyceum Theatre (in English), 1892.

57. *A Woman's Silence.* Play. Produced New York, Lyceum Theatre (in English), 1892.

58. *Madame Sans-Gêne.* Play. Produced Théâtre du Vaudeville, Oct. 27, 1893.

59. *Gismonda.* Play. Produced Théâtre de la Renaissance, Oct. 31, 1894.

60. *Marcelle.* Play. Produced Théâtre du Gymnase, Dec. 21, 1895.

61. *Spiritisme (Spiritualism).* Play. Produced Théâtre de la Renaissance, Feb. 8, 1897.

62. *Paméla, marchande de frivolité (Pamela, Lace Merchant).* Play. Produced Théâtre du Vaudeville, Feb. 11, 1898.

63. *Robespierre.* Play. Produced London, Lyceum Theatre, Apr. 15, 1899.

64. *La fille de Tabarin (Tabarin's Daughter).* Libretto. Produced Opéra Comique, Feb. 20, 1901.

65. *Les barbares (The Barbarians).* Libretto. Produced Théâtre de l'Opéra, Oct. 23, 1901.

66. *Dante.* Play. Produced London, Drury Lane Theatre, Apr. 30, 1903.

67. *La sorcière* (The Sorceress).* Play. Produced Théâtre Sarah-Bernhardt, Dec. 15, 1903.

68. *Fiorella.* Play. Produced London, Waldorf Theatre, June 7, 1905.

69. *La piste.* Play. Produced Théâtre des Variétés, Feb. 15, 1906.

70. *L'affaire des poisons (The Poison Scandal).* Play. Produced Théâtre de la Porte-Saint-Martin, Dec. 7, 1907.

71. *Les amis imaginaires (Imaginary Friends).* Play.

72. *La reine Ulfra (Queen Ulfra).* Play.

73. *Bernard Palissy.* Play.

74. *Fleur de liane.* Play.

75. *Le bossu (The Hunchback).* Play.

76. *Candide.* Play.

77. *Paris à l'envers (Paris in a Whirl).* Play.

78. *L'espionne (The Spy).* Play. Revised and revived version of *Dora*.

EDITIONS

Collections
Théâtre complet, 15 vols., Paris, 1934–1961.
Individual Plays
Native Land! (Patrie!). Published in *Plays for the College Theater,* ed. by G. H. Leverton and tr. by B. Clark, French, New York, 1934.

A Scrap of Paper (Les pattes de mouche). Published in *Dramatic Masterpieces,* ed. by A. E. Bergh and tr. by L. Gilmour, rev. ed., Collier, New York, 1900; *Camille and Other Plays,* ed. by S. S. Stanton and tr. by L. Gilmour, Hill and Wang, New York, 1957.

CRITICISM

French
L. Lacour, *Trois théâtres: Émile Augier, Alexandre Dumas fils, Victorien Sardou,* Paris, 1880; H. Rebell, *Victorien Sardou: Le théâtre et l'époque,* Paris, 1903; G. Mouly, *Vie prodigieuse de Victorien Sardou,* Paris, 1931.
English
B. R. Maccheta, *Victorien Sardou: Poet, Author, and Member of the Academy of France,* London, 1892; J. A. Hart, *Sardou and the Sardou Plays,* Philadelphia, 1913.
German
J. V. Sarrazin, *Das moderne Drama der Franzosen in seinen Hauptvertretern, mit zahlreichen Textproben aus hervorragenden Werken von Augier, Dumas, Sardou und Pailleron,* Stuttgart, 1888.

Sarkadi, Imre (1921–1961)

Hungarian playwright and writer. After his university studies, Imre Sarkadi became a journalist during World War II. In the postwar period he was actively involved in the socialist transformation of Hungary's traditional economic structure and values. At that time he was a newspaper editor and also worked for the nationalized broadcasting system and film industry. In 1955, he received the prestigious Kossuth Prize. His brief visit to France and the uprising of 1956 drove Sarkadi into a chronic crisis from which he never recovered. He became a factory worker and committed suicide a year later.

Reflections of the individual development of their au-

**Imre Sarkadi.
[Photograph courtesy
of George Bisztray]**

thor, Sarkadi's plays are uneven and full of paradoxes. One of his critics characterized him as a writer with two souls: one belonging to a social revolutionary and the other to a decadent, impressionist artist. Of his fourteen dramas, only six were completed. Artistically they vary in value, from *The Way from the Farmlands* (*Út a tanyákról*, 1951), an exercise in Stalinist propaganda, to *Simeon on the Pillar* (*Oszlopos Simeon*, 1960), a drama about lost illusions, alienation, and inhumanity, which many consider one of the best modern Hungarian plays.

Sarkadi's dramas present heroes whose ideals are in the process of sudden or slow disintegration, and show how they cope with disillusionment. In addition, his heroes are or were "leaders" who are pampered by those around them in expectation of the great things they may—but never do—accomplish. The protagonist of *The Prophet* (*A próféta*, 1943) proves to be a false prophet; and *Simeon on the Pillar* features an antihero who has awaited a miracle for so long that eventually he can believe in nothing at all. In Sarkadi's dramas even the great heroes and heroines of history (Hannibal) and mythology (Electra) are represented as losers or as hopeless idealists doomed to disillusion.

Disillusionment is an important element in the lives of Sarkadi and his generation who enthusiastically accepted the social reformist slogans of Hungary's postwar regime and found themselves serving an inhuman system. But Sarkadi also shows the bankruptcy that can result from the extreme cynicism that corrupts and degrades all human values. In his last plays there is always at least one character (usually a woman) who refuses to condone such behavior and takes action. In *Simeon on the Pillar* the morally corrupt artist who sells out his mistress is killed by her. *The House near the Town* (*Ház a város mellett*, 1958) and *Paradise Lost* (*Elveszett paradicsom*, 1961) are unique, highly charged dramatic representations of human derailment in a society which has done away with the old values but has been unable to develop new

ones. *Paradise Lost*, especially, has been praised as a drama of supreme humanism. One of the central figures is a cynical young doctor who causes a woman's death while performing an abortion. His developing love for a girl makes him accept the consequences in hope of a new start.

Sarkadi resembles Strindberg and Miller in his approach to drama and his insistence on clinging to humanist values in an inhuman world.

GEORGE BISZTRAY

PLAYS

1. *A próféta* (*The Prophet*). Play, 3 acts. Written 1943. Produced Budapest, Madách Színház Kamaraszínháza, 1968.
2. *Hannibal "a portás"* (*Hannibal The Porter*). Unfinished drama. Written 1943.
3. *Hannibal*. Unfinished drafts of a drama. Written 1943–1957.
4. *Kőműves Kelemen* (*Clement Mason*). Unfinished drafts of a drama. Written ca. 1947–1953. A compilation produced Veszprém, Petőfi Színház, 1974.
5. *Lucretia*. Unfinished drafts of a drama. Written 1948–1949.
6. *Elektra*. Unfinished drafts of a drama. Written ca. 1948–1949.
7. *Január* (*January*). Drama outline and fragments. Written ca. 1949–1953.
8. *Út a tanyákról* (*The Way from the Farmlands*). Drama, 3 acts. Written 1951. Produced Budapest, Madách Színház, 1952.
9. *Párbaj* (*Duel*). Unfinished drafts of a drama. Written 1953–1954.
10. *Szeptember* (*September*). Drama, 3 acts. Written 1955. Produced Budapest, Madách Színház, 1955.
11. *Balassi Menyhárt árultatása* (*Melchior Balassi's Treacheries*). Play originally written for broadcasting ca. 1956.
12. *Ház a város mellett* (*The House near the Town*). Play, 3 acts. Written 1958. Produced Veszprém, Petőfi Színház, 1967.
13. *Oszlopos Simeon* (*Simeon on the Pillar*). Drama, 3 acts. Written 1960. Produced Budapest, Madách Színház Stúdió Színpada, 1967.
14. *Elveszett paradicsom* (*Paradise Lost*). Drama, 2 acts. Written 1961. Produced Budapest, Madách Színház Kamaraszínháza, 1961.

CRITICISM

L. B. Nagy, "Sarkadi Imre," in *Élő irodalom*, ed. by D. Tóth, Budapest, 1969; J. Kónya, *Sarkadi Imre*, Budapest, 1971; R. Hajdu, *Sarkadi Imre*, Budapest, 1973.

Sarment, Jean (1897–1976)

French actor, poet, novelist, and dramatist; pseudonym of Jean Bellemère. He was born in Nantes on January 13, 1897, and died on March 29, 1976. His plays, in a vague contemporary echo of Musset, feature romantic and disenchanted young men unable to reconcile their illusions with reality. He first attracted attention when Aurélien Lugné-Poë produced *The Cardboard Crown* (*La couronne de carton*, 1920), in which a romantic and sincere young prince is able to win the women he loves only by pretending to be a cynic. Sarment's best-known play, *Rude Awakening* (*Le pêcheur d'ombres*, 1921) set the tone for much of what was to follow. In it a delicate and sensitive youth, restored to sanity by the love of a girl who had previously rejected him, commits suicide when he becomes convinced that the girl is not in fact the one he had loved. Hamlet and Ophelia get a second chance at happiness in *Hamlet's Marriage* (*Le mariage d'Hamlet*, 1922), but the ineluctably melancholy Dane once again forces his tragic destiny. *The Most Beautiful Eyes in the World* (*Les plus beaux yeux du monde*, 1925) concerns a romantic young man who for one brief night is able to create the illusions that win him the girl he loves. *The Trip to Biarritz* (*Le voyage à Biarritz*, 1936) focuses on the disappointment of a man who, after years of planning a fabulous family vacation, finds that the circumstances that gave birth to his dream have altered and rendered the trip pointless.

Sarment's early plays show a talent for sensitive comedy with a tragic or bittersweet undercurrent; but he increasingly accommodated himself to public taste, and his comic effects became obvious and unconvincing. His better-known plays include *Leopold the Well Beloved* (*Léopold le Bien-Aimé*, 1927), *Aboard My Fine Ship* (*Sur mon beau navire*, 1928), *Bobard* (1930), *Terra Firma* (*Le plancher des vaches*, 1931), *Madame Quinze* (1935), *The Paris Impromptu* (*L'impromptu de Paris*, 1935), *Two Pigeons* (*Deux pigeons*, 1937), *On the Steps of the Palace* (*Sur les marches du palais*, 1938), *Parisian Idyll* (*Idylle parisienne*, 1939), *Madame Souris* (1939), *River* (*Rivière*, 1941), *Mamouret* (1941), *Voice over the Water* (*Voix sur l'eau*, 1949), *There Were Three of Us* (*Nous étions trois . . .*, 1951), *The Municipal Billposter* (*L'afficheur municipal*, 1951), *The Jade Necklace* (*Le collier de jade*, 1953), and *The Pavilion of Children* (*Le pavillon des enfants*, 1955). In addition, he has translated into French Shakespeare's *Much Ado about Nothing* (1936), *Othello* (1938), and *Romeo and Juliet* (1952).

Rude Awakening (*Le pêcheur d'ombres*, 1921). Gentle and mad, Jean fishes for shadows (or the fish called in French *ombre chevalier*) to pass his time. In an effort to cure Jean's melancholia, his mother invites Nelly, the girl he once loved, to stay with the family. Nelly comes to love Jean, and he seems to be recovering; however, his elder brother, jealous of Nelly's love, tells Jean that she is not the same girl he had once loved. In spite of protests, Jean insists that "the real Nelly did not love me," and he again retreats into madness. Finding an antique pistol, he begins to shoot at the shadowy fish. Eventually, he turns the pistol on himself, convinced that all

Madame Quinze, Théâtre du Luxembourg, Paris. [French Cultural Services]

things in life, including all forms of love, are mere shadows. Produced Paris, Théâtre de l'Oeuvre, Apr. 15, 1921.

The Most Beautiful Eyes in the World (*Les plus beaux yeux du monde*, 1925). Napoleon insists upon living up to his ideals, but he cannot meet life's demands; his friend Arthur is a grasping egotist who likes to think of himself as a soulful poet. Loved by both men, Lucie chooses the worldly and successful Arthur, and Napoleon leaves to seek his fortune. Returning poverty-stricken some years later, he finds Lucie unhappy and deserted. Since Lucie is blind, Napoleon is for one night able to hide his poverty; for a short time he becomes the happy man of his youth. Arthur's return, however, destroys the fantasy. Arthur still loves Lucie, and he jealously discloses Napoleon's true condition. Brokenhearted, Napoleon departs once again. Produced Paris, Salle du Journal, October 24, 1925.

[JOSEPH E. GARREAU]

Saroyan, William   (1908–1981)

American author and dramatist. He is remarkable in the history of the American drama for his consistent optimism, unaffected by historical change or public taste. Without denying the miseries of modern society and the material world, Saroyan affirms an innate and universal benevolence in mankind in the face of evil and corruption. Most frequently, the characters in his dramas are simple people who, having been rejected by society, intuitively find happiness in sharing the mysteries and beauties of life. The plays are loosely constructed, with highly emotional dialogue, and reflect the spontaneity of life as envisioned by the author. The approach to reality is poetic, deriving from an emotional perception of truth and a need for an innocent enjoyment of life.

In the late 1930s, when the American public seemed to share the playwright's need for optimism, Saroyan's long one-act play *My Heart's in the Highlands* (1939) appeared, establishing his popular reputation. Because of the dramatist's rambling dialogue and insufficiently disciplined thematic structure, the play was adversely received by a number of critics, but Saroyan defied them. The same characteristics were a target for critics even in his later plays. *The Time of Your Life* (1939), a better-integrated play, was successful with both critics and public. It was awarded the New York Drama Critics Circle award and the Pulitzer Prize; Saroyan rejected the latter.

The advent of World War II brought a sharp decline in Saroyan's popularity; his optimism seemed no longer relevant. Nonetheless, he refused to conform to public taste. In 1941 *The Beautiful People*, although a well-structured play, was unconvincing in its presentation of humble people who overcome poverty through love and fantasy. After 1945, in the face of demands made by the political and philosophical climate, Saroyan seemed more and more out of date. By 1949, when both *Don't Go Away Mad*, set in a hospital for the hopelessly ill, and *Sam Ego's House*, which draws an analogy to the United States, were published, Saroyan was attempting to grapple with the new postwar morality, as he did in *The Slaughter of the Innocents* (1952), in which man is identified as the author of his own ills.

Julie Haydon and Eddie Dowling in *The
Time of Your Life.* New York, Booth Theatre, 1939.
[Photograph by Vandamm. Theatre Collection, The
New York Public Library at Lincoln Center, Astor,
Lenox and Tilden Foundations]

Saroyan never regained the success he had enjoyed before the war. The failures of *Love's Old Sweet Song* (1940), in which a migratory worker from Oklahoma gives birth while camping on a California lawn, *Jim Dandy* (1947), set in a transparent eggshell, and *The Cave Dwellers* (1957), about a group of outcasts, brought together in an abandoned theatre, who find contentment in self-acceptance and sharing, were all due to Saroyan's inability to come to terms with the materialism and urbanity of the second half of the twentieth century.

Saroyan spent a great deal of time in Europe and many of his later plays were premiered there: *The Paris Comedy; or The Secret of Lily* (1960), *The London Comedy; or Sam, the Highest Jumper of Them All* (1960), and *Settled Out of Court* (1960), an adaptation of a novel by Henry Cecil. His reputation also partly rests on such powerful one-act plays as *Hello Out There* (1942).

My Heart's in the Highlands (1939). Lyrical comedy about nine-year-old Johnny Alexander, his Armenian grandmother, and his poet father, who live in cheerful poverty while they await the arrival of a check from the *Atlantic Monthly* for the poetry Johnny's father has submitted. Macgregor, an aging actor, suddenly appears, lilting "My Heart's in the Highlands" on his golden bugle. The neighbors offer him food in payment for his music until he is returned to the old folks' home from which he has strayed. Soon a letter of rejection arrives from the *Atlantic Monthly*, as well as a notice of the Alexanders' impending eviction. Shocked out of his dream world, Johnny's father bravely marches his family out into the rain. Produced New York, Guild Theatre, April 13, 1939.

The Time of Your Life (1939). Comedy of derelicts and their dreams that unfolds in Nick's waterfront saloon in San Francisco. Joe, the pivotal character, gently observes the lives swirling about him. Young Dudley waits for Elsie, his true love, to say yes to his marriage proposal; Willie tries obsessively to beat the pinball machine; Harry, a lugubrious comic and dancer in need of a job, softshoes his way into Nick's heart and employment; and Wesley, a down-and-out Negro pianist, is also hired. When Kitty Duval, a prostitute who dreams of home, arrives, the giant Tom, Joe's simpleminded factotum, falls in love with her. Suddenly the peaceful scene is menaced by the appearance of Blick, a sadistic vice-squad detective. He threatens Nick with police pressure for allowing prostitutes on his premises and then conducts a raid, during which he forces Kitty to undress and has several of the habitués beaten. Finally, Blick is killed by Kit Carson, an eccentric ex-trapper and raconteur whom Blick had once thrashed. Harmony returns to Nick's, and dreams triumph as Elsie and Dudley unite, Willie beats the machine at last, and Kitty and Tom go off together. Produced New York, Booth Theatre, October 25, 1939.

The Beautiful People (1941). Play set in an old house in San Francisco, where Jonah Webster, who subsists on pension checks still being sent to a former tenant, now deceased, encourages his children to indulge in fantasies. Owen, fifteen, writes books consisting of one word ("tree") and caters to Agnes, his seventeen-year-old sis-

A 1976 Polish production of *The Time of Your Life*, starring Wiesław Komasa, Leszrek Dąbrowski, and Halina Łabonarska under the direction of Wanda Laskowska. [*Le Théâtre en Pologne*]

ter, by rescuing her pet mice. Owen and Agnes imagine they can hear their brother Harold playing the cornet, although Harold is 3,000 miles away in New York. When Mr. Prim, vice-president of the firm dispensing the pension checks, arrives to announce that the money will be discontinued, the Webster family so enchants him that he promises to increase the payments instead. The sound of the cornet grows louder, Harold appears, and the family is happily united. Produced New York, Lyceum Theatre, April 21, 1941.

[Gautam Dasgupta]

Sartre, Jean-Paul (1905–1980)

French novelist, philosopher, critic, and dramatist. He was born in Paris on June 21, 1905, and died there on April 15, 1980. Orphaned by the death of his father, a naval officer, before his second birthday, the boy was taken by his mother, a niece of Dr. Albert Schweitzer, to live with her parents. The consequent influence of his grandfather Charles Schweitzer, a teacher of German, was marked. Sartre first studied at the Lycée Henry IV, then at the select École Normale Supérieure. He proved to be a brilliant student and graduated in 1928 with a degree in philosophy. He received his *agrégation* in 1929, after which military service placed him in the Meteorological Corps. He was then appointed professor of philosophy at the Lycée of Le Havre, where he taught until 1933. He spent the next year at the Institut Français in Berlin and returned to France to teach in Le Havre, in Laon, and from 1937 to 1939, at the Lycée Pasteur in

Jean-Paul Sartre.
[French Cultural
Services]

Paris. During these years he met Simone de Beauvoir, with whom he formed an enduring alliance, although they never married.

Between 1936 and 1939 Sartre published three philosophical works as well as his first important works of fiction, the novel *Nausea* (*La nausée*, 1938) and *The Wall and Other Stories* (*Le mur*, 1939). Although these were successful, his great fame did not come until the end of World War II.

In 1939 Sartre joined the army, and from June, 1940, until 1941 he was held as a prisoner of war. After escaping, he became, as a member of the Resistance, an influential literary force during the years of the German occupation. He published an underground newspaper in association with Camus as well as his monumental work on phenomenology, *Being and Nothingness* (*L'être et le néant*, 1943), and his first play, the anti-Vichy *The Flies* (*Les mouches*, 1943), written virtually under the eyes of the Germans. His second play, *No Exit* (*Huis clos*), became the literary event of 1944. *See* Camus, Albert.

When the war ended, Sartre's fame quickly spread in his own country and throughout Europe and the United States. Interest grew in his philosophy of atheistic existentialism. The experiences of the war, as well as the events leading up to it, the humiliation of the Occupation, and, above all, his participation in the Resistance, a movement embracing both human isolation and human solidarity, had greatly influenced the development of Sartre's thinking. Existential concepts such as commitment (*engagement*), dreadful freedom, and responsible choice became associated with his name, and thus he gave existentialism a wider audience.

In 1944, after having taught philosophy at the Lycée Condorcet since 1941, Sartre gave up teaching to devote himself to writing. His productivity during the succeeding ten years was impressive. Among other works, he wrote six plays; his novelistic trilogy *The Roads to Freedom* (*Les chemins de la liberté*, 1945–1949); and his studies of Baudelaire, *Baudelaire* (1947), and Jean Genet, *Saint Genet:*

Actor and Martyr (*Saint Genet: Comédien et martyr*, 1952), which combine philosophy and psychoanalysis with literary biography. In 1946 he published one of his most brilliant essays, *The Portrait of an Anti-Semite* (*Réflexions sur la question juive*), which was later expanded into a book. That same year, he founded the literary monthly *Les Temps Modernes*, which in 1952 featured a notable debate on history and ethics between himself and Camus.

These productive years, the postwar period, were marked by a growing involvement with communism. Always a controversial figure, aggressively antibourgeois, outspoken on political and social issues, and practicing the doctrine that man is nothing unless he exercises his freedom of choice, Sartre, although he never became a Communist, allied himself with the party, and he defended the Soviet Union during the first years of the cold war. In 1956, however, his affiliation with the Communists came to an end when he condemned the Soviet Union's intervention in the Hungarian revolt. After that, although his sympathies committed him to supporting the Communist cause and thus the Eastern bloc, he argued for peaceful coexistence but chose to remain a ''witness'' of both East and West.

During the latter 1950s his great popularity declined, notwithstanding a residual ability to stir controversy and obtain newspaper coverage. His play *The Condemned of Altona* (*Les séquestrés d'Altona*), presented in 1959, aroused much discussion, as did his stand in favor of Algerian independence; and the autobiography of his formative years, *The Words* (*Les mots*, 1964), received wide acclaim. When, in 1964, he was awarded the Nobel Prize for Literature, he again aroused controversy by rejecting it on the personal ground that accepting official awards transforms a writer into an institution and on the objective ground that, in the context of the East-West conflict, past Nobel literary awards had gone only to Westerners or to ''rebels of the East.''

Throughout his career, Sartre traveled extensively. He also wrote numerous literary and political essays and articles; prefaces to the works of other writers; and film scenarios, the most notable being *The Chips Are Down* (*Les jeux sont faits*, 1946) and *The Crucible*, based on Arthur Miller's drama. *See* Miller, Arthur.

WORK

Despite the fact that Sartre's dramatic output was small, his commanding position as a man of letters and as one of the most popular writers in post-World War II France makes his plays of particular significance in the history of recent European drama. Whether his plays have the same major significance as literature that they have as history is still a disputed point. That they are important as creative products of their time is, however, indisputable.

Sartre's plays have been aptly described as philosophical melodramas, or melodramas of ideas, a description applicable to all but *Kean, or Disorder and Genius* (*Kean, ou Désordre et génie*, 1953) and the comedy *Nekrassov* (1955). Except for *Nekrassov*, his plays are intellectually oriented and heavily thematic. Though dramatically forceful, they lack both tragic grandeur and fully realized tragic protagonists. Nevertheless, they are eminently theatrical and suspenseful, emphasizing external action and often employing violence and evil, albeit for moralizing ends.

Although Sartre's plays range from myth to historical allegory and even farce, all of them remain within the bounds of realism. He did not originate any genres, nor did he experiment with special language for the theatre, even though a certain pithiness in the dialogue came to be identified as Sartrean. Because of the existentialist emphasis on the importance of an individual's acts, Sartre's plays go beyond the confines of psychological realism and its concern with *why* something is done. Rather, they are concerned with *what* is done. The private and public significance of an action is often explored, as in *Dirty Hands* (*Les mains sales*, 1948) and *The Condemned of Altona* (1959).

Prior knowledge of existential philosophy is not necessary for an understanding of the plays. One finds the atheistic existentialist tenets easily enough: the sharp split and consequent "alienation" between the internal and the external world or, as existentialists put it, between each individual's subjective consciousness and "everything else," including other human beings; the futility of inventing absolutes such as God or truth to justify one's existence; and the compelling semantics of choice—that one must reconcile oneself to a life of responsible choosing because whether or not one wishes to choose, one does "choose," or "will," every act or decision, not to act being a choice. That one may never be happy in being responsible, but that one can be honest and, depending on the greatness of one's concerns, can achieve heroic status, is revealed. In fact, Sartre's honest men must be concerned with great issues precisely because of their honesty.

The problem of identity—the fallacy of finding meaning through other people—is touched upon in *Kean* and *No Exit* (1944). Man's responsibility for his actions is treated in *The Flies* (1943), *The Victors* (*Morts sans sépulture*, 1946; also translated as *Men Without Shadows*), *No Exit*, and *The Condemned of Altona*. *The Respectful Prostitute* (*La putain respectueuse*, 1946) shows people trapped by social myths: the Negro cannot free himself from his belief in white superiority, and the prostitute from her belief in the "good family." The destructively fallacious search for absolutes is depicted in *Dirty Hands* and *The Devil and the Good Lord* (*Le Diable et le Bon Dieu*, 1951). In the three last-named plays as well as in *The Condemned of Altona*, political situations are used to make philosophical points, a peculiarly Sartrean technique. The typical Sartrean "hero" is like the protagonist of these last four plays. He is a highly intelligent and articulate outsider in the community of the play. His world being an exceptional one, it demands from him exceptional, if not heroic, action. The real world of local, national, or international crises, continually testing his commitments and his wits, precipitates an internal crisis. His stages of growth are marked by what he sees in himself and how he han-

dles what he sees: the protagonists of *The Flies* and *The Devil and the Good Lord* come to a proper understanding and exercise of their free will.

The Flies (*Les mouches*, 1943). Philosophical retelling of the *Oresteia*. Orestes, a still-uncommitted young intellectual, returns to Argos, the city of his birth, to seek the meaning of life. He finds a cowering, servile city, doing penance for having been the silent accomplice years before to the murder of Orestes' father, King Agamemnon, by Queen Clytemnestra and her lover, the tyrant Aegisthus—a city punished by the gods with a plague of flies. Orestes meets his sister Electra and later discloses his identity to her. She rejoices, having awaited his return to avenge Agamemnon's honor. Orestes prefers to leave rather than to kill, but Electra's resoluteness persuades him to change his mind. To free Argos and to find his self-realization in public service, Orestes decides to slay Aegisthus and Clytemnestra.

After he has murdered them, the flies, or Furies, goddesses of remorse, swarm down on Orestes and Electra, who flee to Apollo's shrine. There, Zeus visits them, first coaxing and then attempting to coerce them into remorse and subjugation. Electra succumbs, but Orestes defies Zeus; asserting his freedom, he deliberately takes upon himself the collective Argive guilt. Urging the people to recognize their freedom, he leaves Argos pursued by the Furies.

In its original presentation, guilt-ridden Argos was associated with occupied France under the Vichy government of Pétain (Aegisthus), crawling before the German Zeus and plagued by Nazis (flies).

No Exit (*Huis clos*, 1944). One-act philosophical melodrama. Three recently dead strangers arrive in hell, which is represented as a Second Empire drawing room. Estelle is a nymphomaniac who drove her lover to suicide when she killed their illegitimate child; Inez is a lesbian who corrupted her cousin's wife and drove her to suicide; and Garcin is a militant pacifist who betrayed his own cause and was shot while attempting to escape. They discover that in the economy of hell each is de-

Les mouches, Théâtre du Vieux-Colombier, Paris.
[French Cultural Services]

signed to serve as the torturer of the others. Estelle's sexual needs draw her to Garcin, but the latter, obsessed by his desire for assurance that he did not die a coward's death, is drawn to the intellectually lucid Inez, who is herself anguished by Estelle's preference for Garcin. Realizing that ''hell is other people,'' they determine to ignore one another. But cut off from the future and dependent on the others for self-definition, they are again and again drawn into contact. Unable to make Inez admit that he really died for heroic principles, Garcin attempts to make love to Estelle, but her vapid reassurances fail to drown out Inez's taunts of ''coward.'' At one point the door to their room opens, but they are afraid to venture beyond it. Aware of their hopeless situation, they break into hysterical laughter, growing silent as the curtain falls.

The Victors; Men Without Shadows (*Morts sans sépulture*, 1946). Drama set in France in 1944. A small band of captured *maquisards*, French Resistance fighters, await interrogation and torture by Vichy officers. Actually, they have nothing to confess and do not even know the whereabouts of their leader Jean. Among the prisoners are Jean's mistress Luci and her teen-age brother François. Suddenly Jean is thrown among them,

Huis clos, with Michel Vitold, Gaby Sylvia, and Tania Balachova, Comédie Caumartin, Paris. [French Cultural Services]

An Israeli production of *No Exit,* with Stella Avni, Pnina Gary, and Shumel Atzmon, Tel Aviv, 1964. [*Theatre in Israel*]

his identity not being known to his captors. They agree that Jean can and must be freed to warn others of a suspected trap. While some of the other *maquisards* undergo torture, François breaks down and declares that he will denounce Jean. The others strangle François. Before Jean is freed, he devises a plan to save the group: they can pretend to inform on him by sending their captors to a place where they will find a corpse that they will mistakenly believe to be Jean's.

Although the *maquisards* prefer to maintain silence, they come to realize that dying unnecessarily is pride, not heroism. They ''confess,'' but a sadistic officer has them shot anyway.

The Respectful Prostitute (*La putain respectueuse,* 1946). One-act drama set in the United States. Lizzie, a prostitute newly arrived in the South, has witnessed the murder of a Negro by a white man. Fred, her first customer, who is a cousin of the murderer and the son of Senator Clarke, then the police, and finally Senator Clarke himself try to bribe, threaten, and coax Lizzie into giving false testimony. Senator Clarke induces her by flattery to accuse the murdered Negro and his companion of raping her and to state that the white man, in defending her, shot one Negro but that another escaped.

The town immediately forms a lynch hunt for the escaped Negro, who hours later seeks refuge at Lizzie's house. When Fred returns, he discovers the hidden Negro, who escapes once more. Fred insists on making the bewildered and intimidated Lizzie his mistress, and she wearily submits.

Dirty Hands (*Les mains sales,* 1948). Political melodrama set in German-occupied Illyria before the Russian

John Dall (extreme left) and Charles Boyer (at center of table) in the New York production of *Red Gloves (Dirty Hands)*. [Photograph by Vandamm. Theatre Collection, The New York Public Library at Lincoln Center]

La putain respectueuse. Paris, Théâtre du Gymnase, 1961. [French Cultural Services]

liberation. As the play opens, Hugo, a young idealist just released from prison after a two-year sentence for killing the Communist party boss Hoederer, flees to the home of Olga, a party comrade. He is followed there by Louis, the Communist leader who has been commissioned to kill him. Olga pleads with Louis to be allowed to hear Hugo's story before his fate is decided.

An explanatory flashback follows. Two years earlier, a split in Communist policy resulted in Hoederer's desire to compromise with other political parties, but Louis and the party majority had refused to do so. Admiring Louis's principles, Hugo became Hoederer's secretary in order to assassinate him. However, Hugo and his wife came to admire Hoederer, although Hugo maintained his rigid adherence to the party line. At the moment when he was about to waver because of Hoederer's friendship, Hugo discovered his wife in Hoederer's arms. Not knowing she had thrown herself there, he impulsively shot Hoederer.

In the next act, the party line has changed to support Hoederer's position, making Hugo *persona non grata.* Olga, wishing to reinstate Hugo, attempts to persuade him to say that he killed Hoederer not out of duty but out of passion. Finding his political idealism compromised, Hugo declines the suggestion and chooses what he believes to be an honorable death both for himself and for Hoederer.

The Devil and the Good Lord (*Le Diable et le Bon Dieu*, 1951). Massive historical drama set in sixteenth-century Germany during the Peasants' War and the beginning of the Reformation. Germany's greatest captain, Goetz, a wanton evildoer, is dissuaded from sacking Worms by Heinrich, a renegade priest. Goetz is demoniacally proud, seeing himself as God's unique concern. Heinrich challenges this belief with the notion that God has willed that man can only do evil and that good on earth is impossible. Goetz then decides to challenge God by doing only good but discovers that it is harder to do absolute good than to do absolute evil. All Goetz's attempts at goodness fail; they reach a climax in his attempt to found a utopian City of the Sun, which is destroyed because of its pacificism and Goetz's refusal to lead troops. After a period of self-abasement, he concludes that there is no God, that his challenge to God was pure egoism, and that there are only other men, compromise, and struggle. He decides that if he wants his share of good, he must accept his share of evil. Influenced by Nasti, the Lutheran prophet and leader of the Peasants' War, Goetz becomes the general of the rebelling peasants and sets about ruthlessly and cruelly enforcing the discipline in which lies their only hope.

Kean, or Disorder and Genius (*Kean, ou Désordre et génie*, 1953). Romantic comedy set in the 1830s and based on the play by Alexandre Dumas *père*. England's idol, actor Edmund Kean, has an assignation with one of his many admirers, Countess Elena de Koefeld, but is prevented from keeping it by the Prince of Wales. Meanwhile, another admirer, Anna Danby, determined to become both an actress and Kean's wife, pursues Kean and

Scene from *Kean*, Théâtre Sarah-Bernhardt, Paris. [French Cultural Services]

Nekrassov, Théâtre Antoine, Paris. [French Cultural Services]

badgers him into letting her perform. Jealous of Anna, Elena flirts with the Prince of Wales during Kean's performance, thus provoking Kean to step out of his role and insult the Prince and the audience. Subsequently, Kean's popularity declines, and his romance with Elena dies because it is the actor she loves and not the man. The forgiving Prince of Wales saves Kean from debtors' prison with a writ granting him exile rather than imprisonment. Kean chooses to go to New York and marry Anna. *See* DUMAS, ALEXANDRE, PÈRE.

Nekrassov (1955). Political satire set in Paris in 1955. Georges de Valera, the swindler of the century, escapes the police by pretending to be Nekrassov, the Soviet Minister of the Interior, who has supposedly defected. The right-wing government newspaper *Soir à Paris*, in need of new and sensational anti-Communist propaganda, believes he is Nekrassov and adopts him. He is full of horror tales, including one of a plan for occupying France and using a list of 100,000 Frenchmen who will be shot.

De Valera discovers, however, that his masquerade can have serious consequences. French government agents, learning his true identity, try to blackmail him into testifying against two innocent left-wing journalists whom the government wants jailed. They suggest that there will be others to inform on in the future. De Valera escapes from the government agents and plans to give an exclusive exposé of the hoax to a Communist newspaper. *Soir à Paris* counters with news that the real Nekrassov was abducted by Soviet agents and that De Valera sold out to the Communists.

The Condemned of Altona (*Les séquestrés d'Altona*, 1959). Drama set in Germany in 1959. Von Gerlach, a powerful industrialist and a former Nazi collaborator, is dying and calls his family together to settle affairs. He forces his unwilling younger son Werner to pledge himself to take over the family empire, because his elder son Frantz has hidden himself for the last thirteen years in an upstairs room from which he excludes everyone but his sister Leni. Werner's wife Johanna, wishing to prevent his being sacrificed by being forced into a life he rejects, persuades Von Gerlach to promise to release Werner if she convinces Frantz to come downstairs.

Frantz, obsessed by Germany's crimes, lives under the illusion of being both mankind's "witness" and the defender of a still-desolate 1945 Germany. Johanna, interrupting Frantz's solitude, gradually learns his secret: he, too, was steeped in Nazi crime. No longer able to hide after this confrontation, he descends and sees his father. Painfully acknowledging their responsibility for Nazi outrages, both Frantz and his father decide on suicide.

[JOSEPH E. GARREAU]

PLAYS

All were first performed in Paris.

1. *Les mouches* (The Flies)*. Drama, 3 acts. Published 1943. Produced Théâtre de la Cité (Sarah-Bernhardt), June 3, 1943.
2. *Huis clos* (No Exit)*. Play, 1 act. Published 1945. Produced Théâtre du Vieux-Colombier, May 27, 1944.
3. *Morts sans sépulture* (The Victors; Men Without Shadows)*. Play, 2 acts. Published 1946. Produced Théâtre Antoine, Nov. 8, 1946.
4. *La putain respectueuse* (The Respectful Prostitute)*. Play, 1 act. Published 1946. Produced Théâtre Antoine, Nov. 8, 1946.
5. *Les mains sales* (Dirty Hands)*. Play, 7 scenes. Published 1948. Produced Théâtre Antoine, Apr. 2, 1948.
6. *Le Diable et le Bon Dieu* (The Devil and the Good Lord)*. Play, 3 acts. Published 1952. Produced Théâtre Antoine, June 7, 1951.
7. *Kean, or Disorder and Genius* (Kean, ou Désordre et génie)*. Play, 5 acts. Published 1952. Produced Théâtre Sarah-Bernhardt, Nov. 17, 1953.
8. *Nekrassov**. Play, 8 scenes. Published 1956. Produced Théâtre Antoine, June 8, 1955.
9. *Les séquestrés d'Altona* (The Condemned of Altona)*. Play, 5 acts. Published 1960. Produced Théâtre de la Renaissance, Sept. 23, 1959.
10. *L'engrenage (Clockwork)*. Play. Produced Paris, Théâtre de la Ville, Feb. 25, 1969. Based on a film scenario written by Sartre in 1946.

EDITIONS

Collections
No Exit and Three Other Plays, tr. by S. Gilbert and L. Abel, New York, 1956; *The Devil and the Good Lord and Two Other Plays*, tr. by K. Black, G. Leeson, and S. Leeson, New York, 1960.
Individual Plays
Dirty Hands. Published in *The French Theater since 1930*, ed. by O. F. Pucciani, Boston, 1954.
The Flies. Published in *A Treasury of the Theatre*, ed. by J. Gassner and tr. by S. Gilbert, rev. ed., vol. 2, New York, 1951.

CRITICISM

M. Beigbeder, *L'homme Sartre*, Paris, 1947; F. Jeanson, *Le problème moral et la pensée de Sartre*, Paris, 1947; R.-M. Albérès, *Jean-Paul Sartre*, Paris, 1953; *Sartre par lui-même*, ed. by F. Jeanson, Paris, 1955; R. R. Champigny, *Stages on Sartre's Way, 1938–1952*, Bloomington, Ind., 1959; I. Murdoch, *Sartre: Romantic Rationalist*, New Haven, Conn., 1959; W. D. Desan, *Tragic Finale*, New York, 1960; P. Thody, *Jean-Paul Sartre: A Literary and Political Study*, New York, 1960; S. U. Zuidema, *Sartre*, Philadelphia, 1960; F. Jameson, *Sartre: The Origins of a Style*, New Haven, Conn., 1961; *Sartre: A Collection of Critical Essays*, ed. by E. Kern, Englewood Cliffs, N.J., 1963; W. D. Desan, *The Marxism of Jean-Paul Sartre*, Garden City, N.Y., 1965; J. P. Fell III, *Emotion in the Thought of Sartre*, New York, 1965; M. W. Cranston, *Jean-Paul Sartre*, 2d ed., New York, 1966; E. H. Falk, *Types of Thematic Structure*, Chicago, 1967; M. Adereth, *Commitment in Modern French Literature: Politics and Society in Péguy, Aragon, and Sartre*, New York, 1968; H. Peyre, *Jean-Paul Sartre*, New York, 1968; L. Richter, *Jean-Paul Sartre*, tr. by F. D. Wieck, New York, 1968; J. McMahon, *Human Being: The World of Jean-Paul Sartre*, Chicago, 1971; R. Royle, *Sartre, l'enfer et la liberté, Étude de Huis clos et des Mouches*, Québec, 1973; J. M. King, *Sartre and the Sacred*, Chicago, 1974; R. Lorris, *Sartre dramaturge*, Paris, 1975; R. Wilcocks, *J.-P. Sartre, A Bibliography of International Criticism*, Edmonton, 1975; *La révolte dans le théâtre de Sartre*, Paris, 1976; F. Lapointe, ed., *J.-P. Sarte and His Critics: An International Bibliography, 1938 to 1980*, rev. 2d ed., New York, 1981.

Sastre, Alfonso (1926–)

Spanish dramatic theorist and dramatist. He was born on February 20, 1926, in Madrid. He received his bachelor's degree from the Instituto Cardenal Cisneros in Madrid and then entered the University of Madrid. There he studied literature and philosophy and also showed a deep concern for social issues, especially as reflected in the theatre. Desiring an active role in the shaping of the artistic and dramatic trends of the time, Sastre, while still a student, established with a number of contemporary authors the Arte Nuevo (New Art) society (1945), a theatrical group that declared itself opposed to the *status quo* in the Spanish theatre. The society presented experimental plays until 1948, when it disbanded. Then as later, Sastre and his associates were controversial on more than an artistic level: much of their experimentation involved social commentary highly unpalatable to the Franco regime, and as a result Sastre can to some extent be considered an underground writer.

During these three years Sastre wrote his first plays and continued his studies at the University of Murcia; he obtained a licentiate in philosophy. His next venture into active theatre was the establishment, with the critic José María de Quinto, of the Teatro de Agitación Social (Theatre of Social Agitation; T.A.S.) in 1950; Sastre also issued his *Manifiesto del T.A.S.* at this time. Since then he has influenced the Spanish stage not only as a dramatist but also as a theorist and an essayist. His ideas of theatre as a reflection of social reality and as an instrument in its reform are set forth in such articles as "Subsidies" ("Subvenciones," 1950) and "The Social Aspects of Drama" ("Sobre las formas sociales del drama," 1952) and in his books *Drama and Society (Drama y sociedad*, 1956), *Anatomy of Realism (Anatomía del realismo*, 1965), and *Revolution and Criticism of Culture (La revolución y la crítica de la*

Alfonso Sastre.
[New York Public Library]

cultura, 1970). In 1956, while continuing his promotion of new forms of theatre, experimental attempts to communicate a heightened awareness of reality, Sastre founded the Grupo de Teatro Realista (Realist Theatre Company; G.T.R.), which staged works by Pirandello, Carlos Muñiz, Sastre himself, and others.

During the Franco regime, Sastre was in the paradoxical position of being an acknowledged influence on contemporary Spanish drama while relatively few of his major works were produced or even published in Spain owing to their controversial themes. He was imprisoned in 1974 for alleged subversive activities, and released after eight and a half months. Because of threats on his life from right-wing extremists, Sastre was forced to seek exile in France. He has subsequently returned to Spain.

Work

Despite Sastre's avowed preoccupation with social issues and his belief that the mission of art is to point the way toward improvements that are badly needed in an imperfect world, his plays have nothing propagandistic about them and contain no explicit indictment of society. Instead, he has created dramas rich in suggestion and implication, employing symbols that most critics have found open to interpretation as social commentary. Usually he places an individual in opposition to an inexorable fate, a situation destined to end in tragedy. Murder, suicide, and violent death are frequent elements in Sastre's drama, but they are played out on the personal level; the audience must draw its own conclusions concerning the broader social significance. The influence of Sartre, Camus, and Pirandello is evident, as well as that of American playwrights such as O'Neill and Arthur Miller, but the voice that is heard is essentially Sastre's own, the voice of a "revolutionary" who necessarily presents his ideas with indirection and subtlety, this perhaps being the only path for a socially conscious dramatist writing in a nation ruled by a dictator. *See* Camus, Albert; Miller, Arthur; O'Neill, Eugene; Pirandello, Luigi; Sartre, Jean-Paul.

Sastre's most notable plays are *Pathetic Prologue* (*Prólogo patético,* wr. 1949), a drama concerning Spanish revolutionaries; *The Condemned Squad* (*Escuadra hacia la muerte,* 1953), banned by the government after the initial performances, which portrays the emotions and actions of five soldiers and their leader as they face death on a military frontier; *The Raven* (*El cuervo,* 1957), a one-act drama focusing on the complexities of time and memory; and *Death Thrust* (*La cornada,* 1960), the story of the last hours of a bullfighter who is inhumanly exploited by his ambitious manager.

Among other outstanding plays are *The Gag* (*La mordaza,* 1954), an existential drama based on an internationally famous murder case; *Everyman's Bread* (*El pan de todos,* 1957), which depicts a puritanical Communist in a Communist country who commits suicide after denouncing his mother; *Death in the Neighborhood* (*Muerte en el barrio,* wr. 1959), about an alcoholic physician whose negligence leads to the death of an injured youth and who is

subsequently lynched by a group of students and neighbors, led by the victim's father; and *In the Web* (*En la red,* 1961), an intense drama set in Algeria, which depicts the condition of the alienated man in a callous and hypocritical world. The last-named play was originally banned by the Spanish censors. Generally speaking, although Sastre's work is known and admired in his native country, it is seldom produced there.

Pathetic Prologue (*Prólogo patético,* wr. 1949). Drama about a band of terrorists working for the Spanish Revolution. Their leader, Pablo, allows no dissension over policy; when Antón questions the killing of innocent people, Pablo silences him with a blow.

Oscar is ordered to set off an explosion. After completing his assignment, he is arrested by the police and told that he has killed his own brother. With the help of a revolutionary, he escapes from prison. Believing Pablo responsible for the death of his brother, Oscar kills him. He then discovers that his brother is alive and that the explosion actually killed the Minister of War. When the police come for him, Oscar refuses to flee, seeing his impending arrest and execution as an atonement for the murder of Pablo. He wishes his suffering to be a moral contribution to the cause of the revolution and a "pathetic prologue" to happier days for the Spanish people.

The Condemned Squad (*Escuadra hacia la muerte,* 1953). Drama in two parts about outcast soldiers during a third world war. Goban is the heartless leader of five soldiers who form a patrol in the woods on a military front. Each man has been assigned to the squad because of previous misconduct. Goban, who has killed three men from his own side, tells the squad that a soldier must know how to die and that under his guidance they will learn how. The pressure of their danger, alone in the woods, puts the men on edge. Against Goban's wishes they get drunk; this leads to a scuffle and Goban's death. Thereupon, Adolfo and Andrés run off to brave the unknown, and Javier, an ex-professor, kills himself. Pedro, unwilling to shirk his part in the collective responsibility for Goban's death, remains to comfort Luis, the youngest and most innocent of the soldiers. He tells Luis, who feels guilty for having outlived his companions, that he must live on for all the men of the squad who have lost or will lose their lives.

The Raven (*El cuervo,* 1957). Drama concerning the relativity of time and reality. On a snowy New Year's Eve, exactly one year after John's wife, Laura, was murdered in their chalet garden by a madman while John, Peter, Inez, and Al were celebrating in the living room, John and his housekeeper are obsessed by the notion that they are reliving the events of that tragic evening. John becomes convinced of this by the unexpected arrival of Peter, Inez, and Al, who claim they were invited. While remaining conscious of the present, John and his guests relive minor events of the previous New Year's Eve. Finally, Laura appears; living totally in the past she believes she has only been absent from the room for a few moments. Terrified by their inability to distinguish the dream from the reality or the past from the present, the guests decide to leave in order to avoid the circumstances that led to Laura's death. The snow prevents their departure, however, and when Laura disappears into the garden, they are once more too drunk to come to her aid. Al tries to convince John that they have dreamed it all. Quoting from Poe's *The Raven*, he claims that Laura is truly dead and will nevermore return. Nevertheless, John continues to believe in the dual reality of their experience that evening.

Death Thrust (*La cornada*, 1960). In a prologue, a doctor and his assistant play chess in the bullring infirmary where bullfighter José Alba is brought, already dead from a wound that, it is discovered, he had received before the fight. The scene flashes back to the events preceding José's death. In a hotel room José and his manager Marcos discuss Marcos's plans for bringing José "to the top" in spite of José's attacks of panic; Marcos's insane ambition is revealed. Gabriela, José's estranged wife, is deterred from meeting with her husband by Marcos, but finally she encounters him, and their love for each other is rekindled. Marcos, who sees in this reconciliation a threat to the total domination of José's life by the bullring, cruelly abandons his support of José. In panic José stabs himself, but is forced by Marcos to go on with the fight. In an epilogue Marcos tries to inflame the bullring ambitions of Pastor, José's former auxiliary; but Pastor, who sees the lies and exploitation in Marcos's formula for success, refuses to be manipulated.

[ANDRÉS FRANCO]

PLAYS

1. (With M. Fraile). *Ha sonado la muerte (Death Has Sounded)*. Play. Written 1946. Published 1948. Produced Madrid, Teatro Beatriz, Jan. 31, 1946.
2. *Uranio 235 (Uranium 235)*. Play, 1 act. Written 1946. Published 1948. Produced Madrid, Teatro Beatriz, April 11, 1946.
3. *Cargamento de sueños (Cargo of Dreams)*. Play, 1 act. Written 1946. Published 1948. Produced Madrid, Teatro Ramiro de Maeztu, Jan. 9, 1948.
4. (With Fraile). *Comedia sonámbula (Sleepwalking Comedy)*. Play. Published 1948.
5. *Prólogo patético* (Pathetic Prologue)*. Play, 6 scenes. Written 1949.
6. *El cubo de la basura (The Trash Can)*. Play. wr. 1951.
7. *Escuadra hacia la muerte* (The Condemned Squad)*. Drama, 2 parts. Produced Madrid, Teatro María Guerrero, Mar. 18, 1953.
8. *La mordaza (The Gag)*. Drama, 6 scenes and epilogue. Published 1956. Produced Madrid, Teatro Reina Victoria, Sept. 17, 1954.
9. *Ana Kleiber* (Anna Kleiber)*. Drama, 3 acts. Written 1955. Published 1960. Produced Gijón, Teatro Ateneo, Mar. 25, 1958.
10. *La sangre de Dios (The Blood of God)*. Drama, 2 acts. Produced Valencia, Teatro Serrano, Apr. 22, 1955.
11. *El pan de todos (Everyman's Bread)*. Drama; prologue and epilogue, 4 acts. Written 1955. Produced Barcelona, Teatro Windsor, Jan. 11, 1957.
12. *El cuervo* (The Raven)*. Drama, 1 long act. Published 1960. Produced Madrid, Teatro María Guerrero, Oct. 31, 1957.
13. *Medea*. Play. Produced Montjuich, Teatro Griego, July 3, 1958.
14. *Muerte en el barrio (Death in the Neighborhood)*. Play; prologue and epilogue, 5 scenes. Written 1959. Published 1960.
15. *Asalto nocturno (Nocturnal Assault)*. Play. Written 1959.
16. *Guillermo Tell tiene los ojos tristes* (Sad Are the Eyes of William Tell)*. Drama, 7 scenes. Published 1960.
17. *Tierra roja (Red Earth)*. Drama, 4 scenes and epilogue. Published 1960.
18. *La cornada* (Death Thrust)*. Drama; prologue and epilogue, 2 acts. Published 1960. Produced Madrid, Teatro Lara, Jan. 14, 1960.
19. *En la red* (In the Web)*. Drama, 3 acts. Produced Madrid, Teatro Recoletos, Mar. 8, 1961.
20. (Adaptation). *Los acreedores (Creditors)*. Drama, 3 acts. Produced Madrid, Teatro Valle Inclán, Dec. 19, 1962. Based on August Strindberg's *Fordringsägare* (1889).

21. *Oficio de tinieblas (Tenebrae Service)*. Written 1962. Produced Madrid, Teatro de la Comedia, Feb. 8, 1967.
22. *Historia de una muñeca abandonada (Tale of an Abandoned Doll)*. Play for children. wr. 1964.
23. *Mulato*. Play. Produced Madrid, Teatro de la Comedia, Apr. 4, 1963.
24. *El circulito de tiza (The Little Chalk Ring)*. Play for children. wr. 1962.
25. *La sangre y la ceniza (Blood and Ash)*. Play. Written 1965. Produced Madrid, Sala Cadarso, 1977.
26. *El banquete (The Banquet)*. Play. Written 1965.
27. *La taberna fantástica (Fantastic Tavern)*. Play. Written 1966.
28. *Crónicas romanas (Roman Chronicles)*. Play. Written 1968. Published 1970.
29. *Ejercicios de terror (Exercises in Terror)*. Play. Written 1970. Published 1973.
30. *Askatasuna*. Play. Written 1971.
31. *Las cintas magnéticas (The Recording Tapes)*. Radio play. Written 1971. Published 1973.
32. *El camarada oscura (Dark Comrade)*. Play. Written 1972.

EDITIONS

Collections
Teatro, Buenos Aires, 1960; *Teatro*, ed. by J. Monleón, Madrid, 1964; *Teatro selecto*, Madrid, 1966; *Obras completas*, I, Madrid, 1967.
Individual Plays
Anna Kleiber. Published in *The New Theatre of Europe*, ed. by R. W. Corrigan and tr. by L. C. Pronko, New York, 1962.
Death Thrust. Published in *Masterpieces of the Modern Spanish Theatre*, ed. by R. W. Corrigan and L. C. Pronko, New York, 1967.
The Condemned Squad. Published in *The Modern Spanish Stage: Four Plays*, ed. by M. Holt and tr. by L. C. Pronko, New York, 1970.
Sad Are the Eyes of William Tell. Published in *The New Wave Spanish Drama*, ed. by G. E. Wellwarth and tr. by L. C. Pronko, New York, 1970.

CRITICISM

F. Anderson, *Alfonso Sastre*, New York, 1971; A. C. Van der Naald, *Alfonso Sastre. Dramaturgo de la revolución*, New York, 1973; F. Ruiz Ramón, *Historia del teatro español: Siglo XX*, 3d ed., Madrid, 1977.

Saunders, James (1925–)

English dramatist. A chemistry teacher by profession, Saunders made his mark as a dramatist in the provinces. Having begun playwriting as a hobby, he has attempted various styles, ranging from the Ionesco-influenced *Alas, Poor Fred* to the traditional idea play *The Ark* (1959). *Alas, Poor Fred* is a dialogue between a husband and a wife about Fred, who was cut in half some time ago: Fred symbolizes their love and life together. In *The Ark* Saunders is concerned with human responsibility and divine justice. The play is a reinterpretation of the story of Noah, with a new central character, Noah's son Shem. Noah is represented as self-righteous and inhuman, and his other two sons, Japhet and Ham, are portrayed respectively as sensualist and simpleton. Shem, concerned with the fate awaiting mankind, tries to cast his lot in with those who will be left behind but is finally forced to board the ark.

In 1960 three of Saunders's one-act plays—*Barnstable, Committal* and *Return to a City*—were produced under the title *Ends and Echoes*. His reputation depends on two plays written in the 1960s. In the first, the existential *Next Time I'll Sing to You* (1963), a group of actors gathered together to rehearse a play probe for the essential meaning of their respective roles. By seeking the truth of the role of the Hermit, they are shown the meaning of life and the essence of individuality. The second play, *A Scent of Flowers* (1964), depicts the events leading up to the suicide of a sensitive young girl. His subsequent plays include *The Borage Pigeon Affair* (1969), *The Island* (1975), and *Bodies* (1978).

Savoir, Alfred (1883–1934)

French dramatist of Polish-Jewish origin; pseudonym of Alfred Posznanski. His plays to some extent provided a link between the avant-garde theatre and the traditional boulevard theatre. Savoir's early dramas, such as *The Third Place Setting* (*Le troisième couvert*, 1906), in which an illegitimate child is driven to suicide, were so pessimistic that producers preferred to have him collaborate with other authors. With Fernand Nozière he wrote *The Baptism* (*Le baptême*, 1907), a satire on Parisian Jewish families who cynically convert to Catholicism; and *The Kreutzer Sonata* (1910), an adaptation of Tolstoy's novel. His first individual success was *Bluebeard's Eighth Wife* (*La huitième femme de Barbe-Bleu*, 1921), a clever comedy on husband taming. *The Grand Duchess and the Bellboy* (*La grande-duchesse et le garçon d'étage*, 1924) concerns the romance between an exiled Russian duchess and a millionaire's son whom she mistakes for a bellboy. *See* NOZIÈRE, FERNAND.

Savoir's most ambitious works were published in 1930 under the title *The Flight Forward: Three Avant-garde Comedies* (*Le fuite en avant: Trois comédies d'avant-garde*). They include *The Lion Tamer* (*Le dompteur, ou L'anglais tel qu'on le mange*, 1925), the story of an English lord who replaces a brutal lion tamer he had hoped to see eaten and is himself eaten by the lion when he loses confidence in his humane, whipless approach to taming; *The Supernumerary at the Gaîté* (*Le figurant de la Gaîté*, 1926), a Pirandellian comedy opposing man and his mask; and *He* (*Lui*, 1929), which focuses on the strange events in a snowbound Swiss hotel that convince members of a congress of freethinkers that an escaped lunatic's claim to be

Claude Rains and Violet Kemble Cooper in *He*. New York, Guild Theatre, 1931. [Photograph by Vandamm. Theatre Collection, The New York Public Library at Lincoln Center, Astor, Lenox and Tilden Foundations]

God may have some validity. Other plays of interest include *Banco!* (1922); *Little Catherine* (*La petite Catherine*, 1930), which concerns Catherine the Great as a child; and *The Margravine* (*La margrave*, 1932).

The Supernumerary at the Gaîté (*Le figurant de la Gaîté*, 1926). In love with the beautiful Princess, Albert Landier is forced by a reversal of fortune to work as a Gaîté supernumerary. After playing a rajah one night,

(Left) Gérard Philipe in *Le figurant de la Gaîté*, Théâtre Montparnasse, Paris; (right) scene from *La huitiéme femme de Barbe-Bleu*. [French Cultural Services]

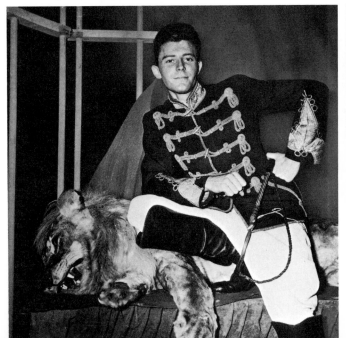

La petite Catherine, **Théâtre des Bouffes-Parisiens, Paris. [French Cultural Services]**

Albert wears his costume to a restaurant, where everybody takes him for the Maharajah of Kashmir. The Princess' imagination is stirred and she agrees to meet Albert again the following night. But Albert is in a new play, and this time he shows up dressed as an archbishop and immediately sets about preaching virtue to the Princess. She is nevertheless taken with this false prince of the church, "since where there is no mask, there is no love." Albert, however, wants to be loved for himself. The Princess agrees to meet him at the zoo, and this time Albert shows up dressed as a lion tamer and enters the cage of a dead lion. When the Princess announces her readiness to follow him even into the jaws of death, he risks her love by exposing his fraud. The Princess admits that her imagination falsifies life and agrees to love Albert for himself. Nevertheless, she asks that he show up at their next meeting in the "poor bohemian costume" he will be wearing in the next Gaîté play.

[JOSEPH E. GARREAU]

Scarron, Paul (1610–1660)

French novelist, poet, and playwright. Scarron was originally destined to be a priest but soon abandoned this career in favor of a riotous life in Paris. About 1637 his legs were paralyzed as the result of a severe attack of rheumatism, and he became financially dependent on a small clerical benefice and whatever income he could derive from his pen. His early works are romances and burlesques of classical literary forms, such as the unfinished *Virgil Parodied* (*Virgile travesti*, wr. 1648–1652), a comic form of the *Aeneid*. Scarron's masterpiece is *The Comic Novel* (*Le roman comique*, wr. 1651–1657), a picaresque novel focusing on the lives of a troupe of itinerant actors.

His first play was the enormously successful comedy *Jodelet, or the Master-Valet* (*Jodelet, ou Le maître valet*, 1643), which, like most of his dramatic works, was inspired by a Spanish source, in this case Rojas Zorilla's *No Jealousy Without Cause, or The Servant Master*. His next work, *The Three Dorothies, or Jodelet Slapped* (*Les trois Dorothées, ou Le Jodelet souffleté*, 1645), features the same *gracioso* ("clown") as a foolish and cowardly servant, but in *Don Japhet of Armenia* (*Don Japhet d'Arménie*, 1647), the figure of Jodelet is replaced by that of the buffoon of Charles V. *The Ridiculous Heir* (*L'héritier ridicule*, 1650), in which an enterprising servant disguises himself as a gentleman and courts a lady of quality, is often considered to have inspired Molière's *The Affected Ladies* (1659), which presents a vaguely similar situation. In his later works Scarron favored the romantic rather than the comic elements, and *The Salamancan Schoolboy, or The Gracious Enemies* (*L'écolier de Salamanque, ou Les ennemis généreux*, 1654) bears the identification "tragicomedy" on the title page of the published version. His posthumously published *The Corsair Prince* (*Le prince corsaire*, 1663), another tragicomedy, is the only one of Scarron's plays not based on a Spanish source. *See* TRAGICOMEDY in glossary.

Jodelet, or the Master-Valet (*Jodelet, ou Le maître valet*, 1643). Juan de Alvarado's scatterbrained valet Jodelet mistakenly sends his master's betrothed, Don Fernando's daughter Isabel, his own portrait instead of Juan's. Taking advantage of this error and the fact that he and Isabel have never met, Juan decides to switch places with Jodelet so that he may study the character and conduct of the woman destined to be his wife. A complicated series of misunderstandings ensue as Jodelet responds overenthusiastically to his role as "Juan." Isabel is so greatly repelled by "Juan" that she secretly asks her cousin Luis to help her out of her dilemma. Juan is smitten with jealousy when he sees Luis leaving Isabel's room, but he soon becomes furious when he recognizes Luis as the man who betrayed his sister Lucresse. Dropping his disguise, he intends to revenge himself on Luis but is prevented from doing so by the sudden appearance of Lucresse, who, after being abandoned by Luis, sought refuge in Don Fernando's house. Luis explains his conduct and is pardoned. The play ends with the marriage of Juan to Isabel, Luis to Lucresse, and Jodelet to Isabel's maid.

The Salamancan Schoolboy, or The Generous Enemies (*L'écolier de Salamanque, ou Les ennemis généreux*, 1654). Two young friends are caught in the toils of an exacting code of honor. When Félix, father of Leonor, discovers the Count in her bedroom, he sends for his son Pedro, a student at Salamanca, to avenge his family's honor. Unfortunately Pedro, a friend of the Count and in love with his sister Cassandra, killed her younger brother when the latter attacked him in an effort to defend Cassandra's honor. Arrested for murder, Pedro is released by the Count, and Pedro in turn frees the Count when the latter is arrested by Félix. Pedro and the Count begin to duel to avenge the honor of their families, but eventually their mutual affection leads them to mutual forgiveness. The count's offer to marry Leonor is accepted by Pedro and his father, and the Count gives Cassandra to Pedro.

[JOSEPH E. GARREAU]

Schéhadé, Georges (1910–   )

Lebanese dramatist and poet. Born in Alexandria, Egypt, he writes in French and now lives in Paris. Schéhadé first wrote poems in a surrealist vein. His plays are distinguished by an atmosphere of poetry and fantasy and by an emphasis on the theme that the fate of purity in a world gone mad is either death or corruption. *Monsieur Bob'le* (1951), his first play, recounts the life and death of a poet-prophet who is the soul of the small village of Paolo Scala and who chooses a path that ends in his death in a far-off hospital. It was greeted by the surrealist André Breton as a major dramatic event.

The Evening of Proverbs (*La soirée des proverbes,* 1954) relates the preparations for a mysterious celebration in a forest inn. Recognizing a young intruder as the reincarnation of his dead and innocent youth, the tormented hunter Alexis kills him to prevent his eventual corruption. *The Story of Vasco* (*Histoire de Vasco,* 1956) shows how a purehearted and terrified young barber is drawn into the machinations of the military and transformed into a hero and martyr. Considered his best work, it abounds in such poetic contrivances as prophetic dreams, soldiers disguised as beautiful girls and as trees, and mysterious forest encounters.

In *The Violets* (*Les violettes,* 1960) Schéhadé turned his poetic imagination to a world threatened with destruction by modern weaponry. *The Voyage* (*Le voyage,*

Scene from a Swedish production of *The Violets.*
[Swedish Information Service]

Le voyage, with Jean-Louis Barrault (left). Paris, Théâtre de France, 1961. [French Cultural Services]

1956) shows its protagonists undergoing a series of imaginary journeys. It was followed by *The Brisbane Emigrant* (*L'émigré de Brisbane,* 1965) and *The Clothes Make the Prince* (*L'habit fait le prince,* pub. 1973), a "pantomine inspired (if one wants) from Gottfried Keller's *novella: Kleider machen Leute.*"

The Story of Vasco (*L'histoire de Vasco,* 1956). In an unspecified nineteenth-century nation, a general, convinced that frightened people "have a feeling for nuances," selects an innocent and terrified barber, Vasco, for a dangerous wartime mission to the enemy. Lieutenant Septembre is dispatched to win Vasco's consent and fails, but Vasco is tricked into agreement by the mayor, who promises him the opportunity to dress "the most beautiful head in Europe." Remorseful, Septembre objects, but he is assured by the General that Vasco's stupidity will protect him. Convinced that he is merely delivering a message to a trout fisherman, Vasco sets out, and his progress is watched by enemy soldiers disguised as trees and girls. At Post 1 he meets Marguerite, who, having dreamed of Vasco's scissors, believes him to be her destined lover; however, Vasco fails to recognize himself in the girl's description of the hero for whom she is searching. Eventually learning of his fame as a spy, Vasco, though terrified, is piqued into living up to the myth. As the crows patiently wait overhead, he delivers the general's false information to the enemy, who fall into a trap. But Vasco is executed, and Septembre and Marguerite come upon his bullet-riddled body.

[JOSEPH E. GARREAU]

Schildt, Runar (1888–1925)

Finnish novelist and playwright. Schildt had been interested in the theatre long before he began his brief career as dramatist. Educated at the University of Helsinki, in 1913 he was appointed a director at the newly instituted domestic section of the capital's Swedish Theatre. Schildt remained for only two seasons; a man of withdrawn and self-critical disposition, he disliked the holding of authority. Furthermore, he had been offered a post in a cousin's recently established publishing house, which would afford him more time, he thought, for literary work. (He had made his debut in 1913 as a writer of novellas with the collection *Eros Triumphant* (*Den segrande Eros*), in which the long title story deals with a traveling theatrical troupe in early-nineteenth-century Finland.) After the seventh and last collection of tales appeared in 1920, he turned to writing plays. Despite his growing fame at home and in Sweden, he once again fell into a depression and committed suicide in September 1925.

WORK

The Gallows Man (*Galgmannen,* 1922) has only two characters, Colonel Toll and his young housekeeper Maria. The Colonel is the owner of a talisman—a mandrake root—which bestows on him the power to control other human beings. The mandrake root cannot be given away; it can only be sold at a price lower than the one paid by the owner. If the owner dies without having gotten rid of the root,"he will lose his eternal bliss." Suddenly realizing that she loves the Colonel, Maria takes the talisman for "nothing at all," and it turns to dust in her hands. The Colonel dies, asking her forgiveness for his attempt to seduce her—to make her the last in his long catalogue of conquests. The effectiveness of the play depends to an extent on its atmosphere (the scene is a snowbound manor house in eastern Finland, in the 1840s), and still more on the presentation of Toll's mixture of brutal arrogance, sensitivity, and fear. The part did not immediately find a competent interpretation; later, after Schildt's death, it became a vehicle of the Danish star Poul Reumert (1883–1968).

Conversely, *The Great Role* (*Den stora rollen,* 1923) instantly won public favor, both because of a brilliant performance by the Finland-Swedish character actor Axel Slangus (1880–1965), and because the play seemed to infer that the Reds, the losers in Finland's recent Civil War, had attracted self-seekers and cowards to their ranks. Schildt's intention had been to portray a specific personality, the middle-aged failure who makes a last try at gaining importance whatever the cost to others. Armas Fager, a bit player at the Swedish Theatre, had first appeared in a fragmentary novel by Schildt published in 1920. There Fager had been seen in happier prewar times flirting with chorus girls at summer performances in a city park, whereas in *The Great Role* it is the winter of 1918 and the capital is held by the Reds. Dreams of playing Cyrano de Bergerac are replaced by dreams of cutting a fine figure in the Red Guard. Deaf to the arguments of his wife, Wendla (a descendant of Gina in Ibsen's *The Wild Duck,* just as her husband has something of Hjalmar Ekdal about him), Fager enlists, dragging his crony Hagert with him (*see* IBSEN, HENRIK). The butt of his new comrades' jokes, Fager plans to save himself from service at the front by capturing his daughter's student lover, as the two young people have been smuggling guns to the Whites. Realizing that Fager, in his selfishness, is willing to risk his daughter's life, Hagert allows Fager to be shot in the ambush set for the student.

Schildt's tragicomedy bears considerable resemblance in characters, milieu, and even in some aspects of the plot to Sean O'Casey's *Juno and the Paycock* (1925); while Schildt's Wendla does not have the depth of O'Casey's Juno, Armas, with his dangerous bluster, is as complex a dramatic creation as "Captain" Jack Boyle. *See* O'CASEY, SEAN.

Not unreasonably, critics have seen Schildt's last play, *The Fortune-Hunter* (*Lyckoriddaren,* 1923), as a kind of self-criticism and personal prophecy. Dr. Stephen Irben, an ambitious and gifted man, fears that his existence will peter out in "giving tutorials . . . or writing accounts of visits to tourist spots for the newspapers." Threatened with the revelation of a past episode which will destroy his diplomatic career, Irben kills himself, having refused to understand the arguments of a woman, Gerda Bruun, who deeply loves him and who has tried to persuade him that he is in a way the victim of his own vanity. Indeed, all three of Schildt's heroes—Toll, Fager, and Irben—suffer from a species of vainglory.

G. C. SCHOOLFIELD

EDITIONS

The Gallows Man, tr. by Henry Alexander, in *Scandinavian Plays of the Twentieth Century: First Series,* Princeton, N. J. 1944.

CRITICISM

George C. Schoolfield, "Runar Schildt and Swedish Finland," *Scandinavian Studies,* 1960, pp. 7–17.

Schiller, Friedrich von (1759–1805)

German historian, poet, and dramatist. Johann Christoph Friedrich von Schiller was born of Lutheran parents on November 10, 1759, in Marbach, Württemberg. His father, Johannes Kaspar Schiller, a captain and surgeon in the army of Duke Charles Eugene of Württemberg, was a stern and staunch bourgeois; his mother, Elisabeth Dorothea, who exercised a very strong formative influence, was a pious, serious-minded woman for whom Friedrich retained a deep affection all his life. The idyllic childhood Friedrich shared with his five sisters was short-lived, for his obvious intellectual gifts, uncovered in the demanding Latin School at Ludwigsburg, where he was enrolled at seven, soon marked him for the clergy, in those days the natural profession for middle-class men of talent and intelligence.

This career, however, never materialized. In 1773, at the age of fourteen, Schiller was uprooted from his family and placed in the elite Karlsschule in Stuttgart, a military academy that was the pet project of Duke Charles Eugene, whose prerogatives allowed him to draft the most promising young intellectuals among his subjects' sons. There Schiller entered the newly created medical department and, always a brilliant student, distinguished himself in his studies.

It was in Stuttgart that Schiller became interested in

Friedrich von Schiller. [Walter Hampden Memorial Library at The Players, New York]

poetry, especially in the lyric and epic works of Friedrich Gottlieb Klopstock. He had fed his interest in secret because, in his words, "an inclination for poetry infringed the laws of the academy and ran counter to the plan of its founder." With the extraordinary capacity for intense concentration that characterized him all his life, Schiller managed, in addition to his medical studies, to ground himself in the literary activity of his day, moving from Klopstock through Shakespeare to settle finally and firmly in the *Sturm und Drang* movement. The lanky red-headed student resolved to write a book "that would positively have to be burnt by the public hangman." He was almost to be granted his wish, for in 1780, when at the age of twenty-one he left the Karlsschule, he carried with him the complete manuscript of *The Robbers (Die Räuber)*. See KLOPSTOCK, FRIEDRICH GOTTLIEB. *See also* STURM UND DRANG in glossary.

Assigned to Stuttgart as regimental surgeon, Schiller had *The Robbers* published at his own expense (1781), thus incurring the first of many debts that plagued all but the last years of his life. The book caused an instantaneous sensation, one enthusiastic reviewer making the resounding declaration, "If ever we may have hopes of a German Shakespeare, this is he!" In Mannheim the bookseller Schwan brought the play to the attention of Wolfgang Heribert von Dalberg, the director of the Nationaltheater there, and in January, 1782, *The Robbers* received its premiere in an atmosphere of frenzied enthusiasm. A contemporary report describes the occasion: "Rolling eyes, clenched fists, strangers falling sobbing into one another's arms. . . . Everything dissolved as in the chaos from whose mists a new world breaks forth."

Schiller was soon to learn the price of fame, for Duke Charles Eugene, informed of the revolutionary fervor and ecstatic poetry of the play, forbade his radical officer any further literary activity. On September 22, 1782, Schiller fled the restrictions of Stuttgart. He settled finally in Mannheim, where he entered a financially difficult period because of the vacillation of Dalberg, who, having offered him a theatre contract, withdrew the offer and then cautiously signed him on in 1783 as resident dramatist for one year. Schiller was thus rescued from his half-fugitive, half-celebrity existence. His second drama, *Fiesco, or The Conspiracy of Genoa (Die Verschwörung des Fiesko zu Genua)*, completed in 1783, received a lukewarm reception when performed in Mannheim in 1784, in a version revised by Dalberg. *Love and Intrigue (Kabale und Liebe)*, first performed in Frankfurt on April 13 of the same year, was a resounding success, and it appeared that Schiller had become, at twenty-four, one of the masters of German drama.

Intrigues and petty jealousies within the acting company, however, made his life difficult, and in April, 1785, he broke with Dalberg and the Mannheim theatre and moved to Leipzig at the invitation of a circle of admirers headed by Christian Gottfried Körner. There he edited the theatrical magazine *The Rhenish Thalia (Die Rheinische Thalia)*, published poetry, began but never finished a novel, and completed *Don Carlos, Infante of Spain (Don Carlos, Infant von Spanien,* 1787). This marked the end of his first period of theatrical activity; almost ten years elapsed before he turned seriously to playwriting again.

In July, 1787, Schiller visited Weimar, where Goethe lived. Although Goethe was in Italy at the time, the city's intellectual atmosphere was permeated by his influence, and Schiller chose to stay. Not least of the attractions in Weimar was the presence of Charlotte von Kalb, the wife of an army officer and the woman who had inspired Schiller to lyrical works of great beauty while he was still in Mannheim. Soon, however, he met the Lengefeld family, whose daughter he was later to marry. *See* GOETHE, JOHANN WOLFGANG VON.

In September, 1788, Schiller and Goethe made their first contact, which several years later deepened into a lasting friendship. Until Schiller's death they exercised a great influence on each other, exchanging ideas and offering mutual encouragement. Their ballads were published together in Schiller's *Muses' Almanac* (*Musenalmanach*, 1797).

The following December, Schiller, through the intervention of Goethe, was appointed professor of history at the University of Jena. Schiller occupied the chair with enormous success, for he had become a hero to the idol-worshiping youth of his day. Although the meager salary contributed little to his economic security, apparently it was encouraging enough, for in December, 1789, he became engaged to Charlotte von Lengefeld, whom he married the following February.

The years between 1788 and 1798 were devoted to study and research. Schiller's output, as historian, poet, and philosopher, was prodigious; in fact, he worked in almost every field of literary activity except the drama. These years saw the publication of the *History of the Thirty Years' War* (*Geschichte des dreissigjährigen Krieges*, 1793), out of which was to evolve the *Wallenstein* trilogy; and his major aesthetic treatises based upon the philosophy of Kant, *On Grace and Dignity* (*Über Anmut und Würde*, 1793), *Letters on the Aesthetic Education of Man* (*Briefe über die ästhetische Erziehung des Menschen*, 1795), and *On Naïve and Sentimental Poetry* (*Über naive und sentimentalische Dichtung*, 1795).

In January, 1791, Schiller was stricken with what is now thought to have been pneumonia and pleurisy, complicated by an intestinal infection, which was painful and debilitating. He never fully recovered his health.

In 1793 the plan for the monumental *Wallenstein* trilogy had begun to form in Schiller's mind, but it was not until three years later that he seriously set to work on this great historical drama. The autumn of 1798 saw the first production of *Wallenstein's Camp* (*Wallensteins Lager*) in Weimar; the following winter and spring, *The Piccolominis (Die Piccolomini)* and *Wallenstein's Death* (*Wallensteins Tod*). This was the beginning of Schiller's second great period of dramatic composition, in which he turned from the *Sturm und Drang* to a more classically oriented drama.

With remarkable industry, as though knowing he had not long to live, Schiller produced *Mary Stuart (Maria Stuart)* in 1800, which was followed the next year by *The*

Maid of Orleans (Die Jungfrau von Orleans), his greatest popular success. In March, 1803, came the premiere of *The Bride of Messina (Die Braut von Messina);* one year later, almost to the day, *William Tell (Wilhelm Tell)* was performed for the first time.

Schiller immediately began work on another drama, *Demetrius*, a project he never completed, for his illness attacked him with renewed force, suddenly and, this time, fatally. For ten days he lay in a delirium, attended by his loving wife Lotte, who never left his side; on May 9, 1805, he died quietly and peacefully in Weimar.

Goethe, who was himself ill at the time, was not told of his friend's death until later, and he could not bring himself to visit the bereaved family for weeks thereafter. His own sense of loss was expressed in his poem *Epilogue to Schiller's Bell* (*Epilog zu Schillers Glocke*, 1806).

WORK

Schiller and his great contemporary Goethe played major roles in the movement (to which Lessing made many early contributions) that elevated Germany to a position of equity, even temporary dominance, in Western drama. Although Schiller wrote only eleven full-length original plays, all are important in the history of German drama and several remain in the German repertoire. His language, which tends toward bombast and rhetoric, thus limiting his appeal to modern audiences and presenting unusual difficulties to translators, is not entirely inappropriate to the revolutionary passions that suffuse his plays. He shows great skill in dramaturgy, for the structure of his plays almost always provides a sound dramatic framework for his ideas.

Ideas are central to Schiller's drama as they are not to the plays of Shakespeare or Goethe. Whereas Goethe was the eternal skeptic and endless investigator, unwilling to accept any code or dogma at the expense of the alternatives it might foreclose, Schiller's work reveals the intensity of his commitment and the strength of his loyalties. As he matured as a dramatist, he tended to move toward the kind of objectivity that was instinctive to Goethe. In so doing, however, he replaced old commitments with a new one, a passionate adherence to aesthetic principles of his own formulation. Schiller's position was based on adherence to intellectual concepts of a revived classicism: universal balance and eventual harmony. The very intensity of Schiller's ideological commitment limited his concern for well-rounded characterization. The vitality his characters possess is due largely to the force of his language and the degree to which he is successful in shaping them as vehicles for his ideas.

Schiller's work, like that of Goethe, can be divided into three periods. The three earliest plays belong to the period of the *Sturm und Drang*, the earliest dramatic manifestation of the romantic movement that was to sweep Europe. The first of these plays, *The Robbers* (1782), established Schiller's reputation. While it is similar to Goethe's *Götz von Berlichingen* (1774) in the sweep and intensity of its action, its clear defense of the idea of justice marks it as Schiller's creation. In his second play, *Fiesco, or The Conspiracy of Genoa* (1783), in many ways the least interesting of his major plays, Schiller deals with a revolution gone sour, in which the revolutionary becomes far more vicious than the system he attempts to destroy. The third of these plays, *Love and Intrigue* (1784), is a bourgeois tragedy that forms a link in the development of the form from the plays of Lessing to Hebbel's *Maria Magdalena* (1846). In all three of these plays Schiller is at some pains to make clear that reaction against injustice or tyranny can itself assume tyrannical aspects. *See* HEBBEL, FRIEDRICH; LESSING, GOTTHOLD.

Schiller's second period was one of transition, during which he wrote only one play, *Don Carlos, Infante of Spain* (1787), which provides a sort of coda to his earlier dramatic efforts. The first of his verse plays (all later original plays are in verse), it recalls his earlier efforts in its stout plea for political freedom. After *Don Carlos*, Schiller turned to historical writing and the study of philosophy. For the better part of a decade he produced no plays. During this period he was greatly influenced by the philosophical writings of Kant.

Kant's influence is apparent in a series of essays in which Schiller set forth his belief that drama, and especially tragedy, should be an instrument for the moral perfection of mankind. *Letters on the Aesthetic Education of Man* (1795) and *On Naïve and Sentimental Poetry* (1795) reveal his belief in a universal order modified by the understanding that all social systems are necessarily flawed. This principle is the basis for his growing concern with harmony. The harmonious soul incorporates both beauty and morality, desire and responsibility. If conflicts appear, the soul achieves new harmony by triumphing over desire. Thus, rejecting the flawed, self-

Scene from Act III of *Die Räuber*. [German Information Center]

destructive heroes of the earlier plays, Schiller anticipates the reappearance of the tragic hero who achieves moral regeneration through the acceptance of guilt, suffering, and ultimate atonement. In *On Naïve and Sentimental Poetry*, Schiller distinguishes between the "naïve" (instinctive) writer such as Shakespeare or Goethe, who more or less realistically depicts his environment as it is, and the "sentimental" (reflective) writer such as himself, who as an idealist or visionary shows the world as it could or should be. Although he praises the naïve writers, he justifies his own position and his growing tendency toward classicism.

Schiller's final period, during which he gave dramatic form to his theories, opens with the so-called *Wallenstein* trilogy—*Wallenstein's Camp* (1798), *The Piccolomini* (1799), and *The Death of Wallenstein* (1799)—considered by many to be his masterpiece. *Wallenstein* might be more aptly termed a ten-act tragedy with a two-part prologue. It illustrates the tentative embodiment of Schiller's new theories, but the hero is not yet "sublime" because his death is not a self-induced liberating act. Yet in Wallenstein Schiller has created a hero equivalent, in modern terms, to those of the Greeks.

His next two plays are the most precise embodiments of his theories. In *Mary Stuart* (1800), the regenerative process is most clear. For the Scottish Queen is required to admit to Darnley's murder in order that a moral redemption may be achieved and her death at Elizabeth's hands be justified. In fulfillment of Schiller's desire for harmony, Mary must also atone for the additional crimes of pride and love of luxury so that the play may present a morally instructive whole. *The Maid of Orleans* (1801) poses similar problems for its heroine, for in one of his frequent distortions of historical fact Schiller has Joan of Arc assume full guilt for her actions before she is allowed a glorious death on the battlefield.

A 1926 Berlin production of *Die Räuber* directed by Erwin Piscator. [Theater-Museum, Munich]

In his last two plays Schiller seemed less concerned with giving his theories dramatic form than with moving beyond them in both form and content. *The Bride of Messina* (1803) is the most classical of all his plays and, in its original form, followed Greek models by ignoring act divisions. In this, his bloodiest work, he treads a fine line between the predestined fatalism that his material seems to demand and his own insistence upon free will. *William Tell* (1804) represents yet another departure. A loosely constructed work, it provides a certain synthesis of all his plays to date. The vigor of the action recalls the early plays, as does the familiar plea for religious freedom. Yet Tell is obviously a hero of tragic proportions, although he both triumphs over his adversaries and escapes death.

Of *Demetrius* (wr. 1804/05), the fragment of a tragedy left unfinished at Schiller's death, little can be said, except that, if completed, it would probably have been a major work.

The Robbers (*Die Räuber*, 1782). Drama set in the sixteenth century and dealing with the hostility of two brothers who, each in his own way, have rejected the conventions and authority of their father's court. Karl Moor has fled to the forests of Bohemia, where he has

Die Verschwörung des Fiesko zu Genua, with Rolf Henniger (left) and Walter Franck, Berlin, 1958. [Goethe House]

Scene from *Kabale und Liebe*, illustrated by Daniel Nikolaus Chodowiecki. [Theater-Museum, Munich]

become the captain of a band of outlaws and has lived like a German Robin Hood. Franz Moor has succeeded in poisoning his father's mind against his favorite son Karl by telling the old man of Karl's misdeeds. Meanwhile, Karl, now disillusioned by greed and baseness manifest in the robber band, wishes his father's forgiveness. He despairs of a reconciliation when a messenger brings him a letter from Franz falsely claiming that his father has disowned him. Impatient for his inheritance, Franz tries to hasten his father's death by telling him that Karl is dead. At the same time he attempts, first by deceit and then by force, to win the favor of Karl's beloved Amalia.

Karl returns in disguise to his father's castle to find that Franz has become a tyrannical lord over the estates and that Amalia has remained faithful to him. He believes himself guilty of his father's death until he discovers, by accident, the old servant Hermann bringing food to a prisoner in a nearby tower. The emaciated prisoner turns out to be the father, who has been imprisoned and left to starve to death by Franz. Led by Karl, the robber band sets fire to the castle and goes to seize Franz, who kills himself in a paroxysm of fear. Karl's father dies when he realizes that Karl is indeed the captain of a band of outlaws, and Amalia, who does not want to live without Karl and sees that he is bound by his oath never to leave the robbers, asks Karl to kill her. Karl kills his beloved and then abandons the band and goes to surrender himself to justice.

Fiesco, or The Conspiracy of Genoa (*Die Verschwörung des Fiesko zu Genua*, 1783). Drama dealing with a struggle for power in the republic of Genoa,

Werner Hinz as Philip II in *Don Carlos, Infant von Spanien.* [Städtische Bühnen, Frankfurt am Main]

which is ruled by the honorable and doughty Andreas Doria. An ambitious nobleman, Fiesco, heads an underground movement that threatens to wrest control from Doria. When Doria's arrogant young nephew Gianettino assaults the daughter of the nobleman Verrina, Fiesco seizes the opportunity for open rebellion. He initiates a successful coup, the Dorias are forced to flee, and Fiesco is acclaimed Duke of Genoa. Realizing that Fiesco's unbridled ambition threatens the freedom of the Genoese people, Verrina first pleads with him to renounce his newly acquired power and then, when his entreaties fail, kills him by throwing him into the sea from the gangplank of a galley.

Love and Intrigue (*Kabale und Liebe,* 1784). Bourgeois tragedy of lovers destroyed in their attempt to overcome the social barriers that keep them apart. The play is set in a German principality whose Chancellor, President von Walter, wishes his son to marry the Prince's former mistress so that he himself may acquire more power. When Von Walter's son Ferdinand falls in love with Luise, daughter of the town musician, the proposed match is denounced by both their fathers. In an attempt to destroy their romance, Von Walter threatens violence against Luise's father, but he is dissuaded from such a

desperate measure by his son, who threatens to expose the dishonest means by which Von Walter has gained his position. Thus thwarted, Von Walter allows his secretary, Wurm, to foment a plot in which Luise, in order to save her father from Walter's threats, is forced to compromise herself with Chamberlain Von Kalb by means of an incriminating letter. The intrigue succeeds, and the jealous Ferdinand refuses to believe Luise's innocence even though Von Kalb confesses his own role. Ferdinand poisons both Luise and himself, realizing the truth too late.

Don Carlos, Infante of Spain (*Don Carlos, Infant von Spanien,* 1787). Blank-verse tragedy of court intrigue in sixteenth-century Spain. Don Carlos, heir to the neurotically suspicious Philip II, is excluded by his father from participation in affairs of state. His efforts to assume responsibility and power are complicated by his love for his stepmother, Elizabeth of Valois, to whom he was once engaged. Don Carlos pledges himself to help his friend the Marquis of Posa, newly returned from Spanish-occupied Flanders, to alleviate Philip's repressive policies there, in return for Posa's confidence and eventual help with regard to the Queen. The two become entangled in a web of intercepted letters, disguises, and rendezvous. When Posa approaches Philip concerning the situation in Flanders, Don Carlos misunderstands his intentions and commits the blunder of confiding in Princess Eboli, who is ill-disposed toward him because of his love for Elizabeth. Posa makes himself a willing scapegoat for Philip's suspicions that Don Carlos has intrigued against him in Flanders and is killed by an agent of Philip.

Carlos makes the King aware of his mistake, and Philip, who had come to consider Posa his only friend, turns in anger against his son. Carlos decides to flee the country and to carry on the struggle in Flanders in the spirit of his friend Posa. He risks a last visit to Elizabeth, however, and is discovered by the King, arrested, and handed over to the Grand Inquisitor.

Wallenstein. Trilogy in blank verse depicting a small but highly dramatic segment of the Thirty Years' War. The three plays constituting the trilogy are *Wallenstein's Camp, The Piccolomini,* and *The Death of Wallenstein.* Schiller condensed the events of the winter of 1633–1634, at the end of which General Albrecht von Wallenstein, commander of the Catholic forces opposing the Protestant armies of Bohemia, was accused of complicity with the enemy and was assassinated. Wallenstein is still an enigma to historians, who have painted him both as shabbily treated by Emperor Ferdinand II and as disillusioned and about to defect to the other side for personal gain.

Wallenstein's Camp (*Wallensteins Lager,* 1798). First part of trilogy. A kind of prologue, the short play *Wallenstein's Camp* introduces none of the main characters but sets the tone and temper of the times. Rumors fly thick and fast in the winter quarters of the Catholic forces, bivouacked outside the town of Plzeň in Bohemia. The cavalrymen, bombardiers, and other soldiers are trying to make themselves comfortable during a lull in the

(Top left) *Wallensteins Tod,* as produced at Weimar. (Top right) Scene from *Die Piccolomini.* (Bottom) *Wallensteins Lager,* Weimar, 1805. [Theater-Museum, Munich]

fighting. Although of various backgrounds and different nationalities, they are unanimous in their admiration of and affection for their commander, General von Wallenstein.

The Piccolominis (*Die Piccolomini*, 1799). Second part of trilogy. The wheels of fate begin to turn when Wallenstein's trusted friend and lieutenant, General Octavio Piccolomini, receives word that Wallenstein is planning to defect to the Protestant forces of King Gustavus Adolphus of Sweden. Wallenstein is motivated partly by the treatment he has received from the Emperor and partly by his own plans for his beloved daughter Thekla, for in return for his allegiance to Sweden he is to be made King of Hungary. Piccolomini is ordered to assume command of the army and arrest Wallenstein, but the devotion of the troops and officers to Wallenstein prevents Piccolomini from taking direct action. Even Piccolomini's son Max, who is in love with Thekla, cannot believe the accusations against his commander. Wallenstein's suspicions that he has been found out are aroused, however, and he manages to implicate some of his officers by persuading them while they are carousing at a banquet to sign a document pledging their loyalty to him rather than to the Emperor. Then Wallenstein's messenger to the Swedes is captured, but even this fails to convince Max of his beloved general's duplicity, and he resolves to determine the facts for himself.

The Death of Wallenstein (*Wallensteins Tod*, 1799). Third part of trilogy. Receiving orders to divide his army

Scene from *Turandot, Prinzessin von China,* Theater der Stadt, Bonn. [German Information Center]

and learning that a Spanish force is about to arrive under a different commander, Wallenstein feels certain that his days are numbered unless he acts quickly. General Piccolomini finally convinces the officers of Wallenstein's treacherous intentions, and the regiments under Wallenstein's command begin to desert. Determined to carry out his plan to defect, Wallenstein is preparing to leave to meet the Swedish forces at Eger when Max Piccolomini appears with Thekla and asks his permission to marry her. Wallenstein's refusal is final proof to Max of the general's treacherous intentions; he is imprisoned by Wallenstein but rescued by his own troops. Wallenstein then sets out for Eger. In the remnants of his army is an Irish adventurer, Colonel Buttler, who harbors a deep hatred of Wallenstein for having interfered with his becoming a count. After news arrives that Max has been killed in an attack on the Swedish lines and Thekla leaves her father to go to his grave, the vengeful Buttler breaks into Wallenstein's apartments and assassinates him. General Piccolomini arrives at Eger to find Wallenstein dead, and a messenger arrives with the news that the Emperor has bestowed the rank of prince on Piccolomini.

Mary Stuart (*Maria Stuart*, 1800). Blank-verse historical drama about Mary Queen of Scots in her last days, when she was held captive in the Castle of Fotheringhay, unjustly convicted of complicity in an attempted assassi-

Illustration of Act III of *Maria Stuart.* [Theater-Museum, Munich]

nation of Queen Elizabeth. There Mary awaits the stroke of Elizabeth's pen to send her to the headsman's block. The warm, womanly Mary is the antithesis of the brittle, authoritative Elizabeth, surrounded by intrigues and harried by the demands of government. Two attempts are made to save Mary, but both fail. The plot of the zealous young Mortimer to storm the castle ends in his suicide when the plan is exposed; and an "accidental" confrontation of Mary and Elizabeth, the central scene of the play, is arranged but results not in conciliation but in a moral victory for Mary that seals her fate. Deliberately issuing ambiguous orders so as to cloud her own responsibility, Elizabeth precipitates Mary's execution.

The Maid of Orleans (*Die Jungfrau von Orleans*, 1801). Verse drama giving a highly unorthodox portrait of Joan. Writing before her canonization, at a time when her reputation was at low ebb, Schiller turns Joan into a veritable Valkyrie, whose sacred mission can be accomplished only as long as she remains free of any taint of earthly appetites. After turning the tide of defeat and returning the vengeful Duke of Burgundy to the French cause, she is smitten with love for the English general Lionel, a passion that fills her with remorse and guilt. She allows herself to be denounced as a sorceress and captured by the King's mother Isabeau, who had, like Burgundy, allied herself with the English. The imminent defeat of her beloved French troops rekindles her former ardor, and after miraculously bursting her bonds, she leads them to victory once more, dying gloriously on the field, reinstated

Turandot, as produced in Bonn during the 1956–57 season. [German Information Center]

Die Braut von Messina, produced at Weimar about 1810. [Theater-Museum, Munich]

in the love and esteem of her fellow warriors, who recognize in her an angel of God.

The Bride of Messina (*Die Braut von Messina*, 1803). Tragedy with chorus, consciously constructed along the lines of Greek tragedy and set in a fictionalized Sicily, concerning two brothers unwittingly in love with their sister. The King, their father, long ago had dreamed that a daughter, yet unborn, would bring about the destruction of his two sons and the kingdom. Thus when his wife gave birth to Beatrice, he ordered his daughter put to death. However, her mother, Donna Isabella, secretly took her to a convent, where she grew up knowing nothing of her family. The play, which spans a day and a night, opens as Donna Isabella publicly reconciles her sons, Manuel and Caesar, who have been in open conflict since their father's death. She also reveals to them the existence of their sister, not knowing that each of the boys, without the other's knowledge, has met and fallen in love with Beatrice. This entanglement results in Caesar's unknowingly causing Manuel's death. When he discovers that they have all been the pawns of a cruel fate, Caesar kills himself to atone for his crime.

William Tell (*Wilhelm Tell*, 1804). Loosely constructed drama in which Schiller paid tribute to the freedom and the dignity of men living close to nature, unspoiled by the corruption of civilization. The drama consists of two separate, parallel stories, alike only in

their central theme of resistance to the tyrannical Gessler, Viceroy of the Emperor of Austria in Switzerland: the individual defiance of the heroic forester William Tell and the first rumblings of insurrection among the freedom-loving Swiss. The familiar legend of William Tell and the apple is interwoven with the first efforts of the Swiss mountaineers to band together under the leadership of the stalwart Walter Furst and with the wavering of the nobleman Ulrich von Rudenz between the Swiss cause and the attraction of the Austrian court. William Tell is ordered by Gessler to shoot an apple from his own son's head but holds a second arrow ready for the Viceroy's heart if the first would miss its mark. After Tell has been arrested by Gessler for his act of defiance, a storm provides the opportunity for his escape, and with his famous crossbow he puts an end to Switzerland's oppressor, thereby signaling the start of the revolution. Ulrich proves himself a true Swiss by his courage in leading the aroused cantons. With the assassination of the Emperor by his own nephew and the Count of Luxemburg's assumption of the throne, peace is restored and William Tell is hailed as a savior in the cantons.

[PETER JELAVICH]

PLAYS

1. *Die Räuber** (*The Robbers*). Tragedy, 5 acts; prose. Written 1780. Published 1781. Produced Mannheim, Nationaltheater, Jan. 13, 1782.

2. *Die Verschwörung des Fiesko zu Genua** (*Fiesco, or The Conspiracy of Genoa*). Republican tragedy, 5 acts; prose. Written 1783. Published 1783. Produced Bonn, July 20, 1783; Mannheim, Nationaltheater, Jan. 11, 1784.

3. *Kabale und Liebe** (*Love and Intrigue; Cabal and Love*). Bourgeois tragedy, 5 acts; prose. Written 1783. Published 1784. Produced Frankfurt am Main, Apr. 13, 1784; Mannheim, Nationaltheater, Apr. 15, 1784.

4. *Don Carlos, Infant von Spanien** (*Don Carlos, Infante of Spain*). Tragedy, 5 acts; verse. Written 1787. Published 1787. Produced Hamburg, Nationaltheater, Aug. 29, 1787; Mannheim, Nationaltheater, Mar. 8, 1788.

5. (Translation). *Der Parasit, oder Die Kunst sein Glück zu machen** (*The Parasite, or The Art to Make One's Fortune*). Comedy, 5 acts; prose. Written 1797. Published 1797. Produced Weimar, Hoftheater, Oct. 12, 1803. Based on Louis-Benoît Picard's *Médiocre et rampant* (1797).

The following three plays (Nos. 6, 7, and 8) form the *Wallenstein* trilogy.

6. *Wallensteins Lager** (*Wallenstein's Camp*). Play, prologue and 1 act; verse. Written 1798. Published 1800. Produced Weimar, Hoftheater, Oct. 12, 1798.

7. *Die Piccolomini** (*The Piccolominis*). Play, 5 acts; verse. Written 1799. Published 1800. Produced Weimar, Hoftheater, Jan. 30, 1799.

8. *Wallensteins Tod** (*The Death of Wallenstein*). Tragedy, 5 acts; verse. Written 1799. Published 1800. Produced Weimar, Hoftheater, Apr. 20, 1799.

9. (Adaptation). *Macbeth*. Tragedy, 5 acts; verse. Written 1800. Published 1801. Produced Weimar, Hoftheater, May 14, 1800. Based on William Shakespeare's *Macbeth* (ca. 1606).

10. *Maria Stuart** (*Mary Stuart*). Tragedy, 5 acts, verse. Written 1800. Published 1801. Produced Weimar, Hoftheater, June 14, 1800.

11. *Die Jungfrau von Orleans** (*The Maid of Orleans*). Romantic tragedy, 5 acts; verse. Written 1801. Published 1802. Produced Leipzig, Sept. 11, 1801.

12. (Adaptation). *Turandot, Prinzessin von China* (*Turandot, Princess of China*). Tragicomedy, 5 acts; verse. Written 1801. Published 1802. Produced Weimar, Hoftheater, Jan. 30, 1802. Based on Carlo Gozzi's play *Turandot* (1762).

13. *Die Braut von Messina, oder Die feindlichen Brüder** (*The Bride of Messina*). Tragedy with chorus, 5 acts; verse. Written 1802/03. Published 1803. Produced Weimar, Hoftheater, Mar. 19, 1803.

14. (Translation). *Der Neffe als Onkel* (*The Nephew as Uncle*). Comedy, 3 acts; prose. Written 1803. Published 1808. Produced Weimar, Hoftheater, May 18, 1803. Based on Louis-Benoît Picard's *Encore de Ménechmes* (1791).

15. *Wilhelm Tell** (*William Tell*). Drama, 5 acts; verse. Written 1804. Published 1804. Produced Weimar, Hoftheater, Mar. 17, 1804.

16. *Die Huldigung der Künste** (*Homage of the Arts*). Festival play, 1 act; verse. Written 1804. Published 1805. Produced Weimar, Hoftheater, Nov. 12, 1804.

Attila Hörbiger (left) and Ernst Deutsch in *Wilhelm Tell,* Düsseldorf, 1959. [German Information Center]

17. (Translation). *Phädra (Phaedra)*. Tragedy, 5 acts; verse. Written 1805. Published 1805. Produced Weimar, Hoftheater, Jan. 30, 1805. Based on Jean Racine's play *Phèdre* (1677).

18. *Demetrius**. Fragment. Tragedy, first two acts only; verse. Written 1804/05. Published 1815.

EDITIONS

Collections

Historical Dramas, London, 1847; *Early Dramas and Romances*, London, 1849; *Dramatic Works*, London, 1851; *Sämtliche Werke*, ed. by O. Güntter and G. Witkowski, 10 vols., Leipzig, 1910–1911; *Sämtliche Werke*, ed. by G. Fricke, H. G. Göpfert, and H. Stubenrauch, 5 vols., Munich, 1958–1959; *Schillers Werke*, 43 vols., Weimar, 1943—(14 vols. published thus far).

Individual Plays

The Death of Wallenstein. Published in *Poetic Drama*, ed. by A. Kreymborg and tr. by S. Coleridge, New York, 1941.

Don Carlos, Infante of Spain. Published in *The Classic Theatre*, ed. by E. R Bentley and tr. by J. Kirkup, vol. 2, Garden City, N.Y., 1958–1961.

Mary Stuart. Published in *The Classic Theatre*, ed. by E. R. Bentley and tr. by J. Mellish, vol. 2, Garden City, N.Y., 1958–1961; *Classical German Drama*, tr. by T. H. Lustig, New York, 1963.

Wallenstein's Camp. Published in *The Drama: Its History, Literature and Influence on Civilization*, ed. by A. Bates and tr. by J. Churchill, vol. 10, London, 1903–1904.

William Tell. Published in *World Drama*, ed. by B. H. Clark and tr. by T. Martin, New York, 1933.

CRITICISM

German

G. Schwab, *Urkunden über Schiller und seine Familie*, Stuttgart, 1840; K. Hoffmeister, *Schillers Leben, Geistesentwicklung und Werke im Zusammenhang*, 5 vols., Stuttgart, 1838–1842; K. von Wolzogen, *Schillers Leben*, Stuttgart, 1845; E. Palleske, *Schillers Leben und Werke*, 2 vols., Berlin, 1858; K. Tomaschek, *Schiller in seinem Verhältnisse zur Wissenschaft*, Vienna, 1862; W. Feilitz, *Studien zu Schillers Dramen*, Leipzig, 1876; K. Fulda, *Leben Charlottens von Schiller, geborene von Lengefeld*, Berlin, 1878; O. Brosin, *Schillers Vater: Ein Lebensbild*, Leipzig, 1879; H. Düntzer, *Schillers Leben*, Leipzig, 1881; A. Buttmann, *Die Schicksalsidee in Schillers Braut von Messina*, Berlin, 1882; F. Überweg, *Schiller als Historiker und Philosoph*, Leipzig, 1884; V. Golde, *Schillers Abhandlung über naive und sentimentalische Dichtung*, Berlin, 1889; E. Kühnemann, *Die Komposition des Wallenstein im Zusammenhang mit den Kantischen Studien Schillers*, Marburg, 1889; J. Minor, *Schiller: Sein Leben und seine Werke*, 2 vols., Berlin, 1890; L. Bellermann, *Schiller: Dramen*, Berlin, 1891; K. Fischer, *Schiller als Philosoph*, Heidelberg, 1892; K. Gneisse, *Schillers Lehre von der ästhetischen Wahrnehmung*, Berlin, 1893; K. Berger, *Die Entwicklung von Schillers Ästhetik*, Weimar, 1894; E. Müller, *Schillers Mutter: Ein Lebensbild*, Leipzig, 1894; E. Kühnemann, *Kants und Schillers Begründung der Ästhetik*, Munich, 1895; R. Weltrich, *Friedrich Schiller*, Stuttgart, 1885–1899; E. Müller, *Regesten zu Friedrich Schillers Leben und Werken*, Leipzig, 1900; J. Hartmann, *Schillers Jugendfreude*, Stuttgart, 1904; J. Petersen, *Schiller und die Bühne*, New York, 1904; O. Harnack, *Schiller*, Berlin, 1905; R. Petsch, *Freiheit und Notwendigkeit in Schillers Dramen*, Munich, 1905; G. Kettner, *Studien zu Schillers Dramen*, Berlin, 1909; A. Ludwig, *Schiller und die deutsche Nachwelt*, Berlin, 1909; K. Wolff, *Schillers Theodizee bis zum Beginn der Kantischen Studien*, Leipzig, 1909; L. Bellermann, *Schiller*, Leipzig, 1911; K. Berger, *Schiller: Sein Leben und seine Werke*, Munich, 1914; K. Vorländer, *Kant, Schiller, Goethe*, Leipzig, 1923; P. Böckmann, *Schillers Geisteshaltung als Bedingung seines dramatischen Schaffens*, Dortmund, 1925; W. Goether, *Schiller*, Leipzig, 1925; W. Iffert, *Der junge Schiller und das geistige Ringen seiner Zeit*, Halle, 1926; F. Koch, *Schillers philosophische Schriften und Plotin*, Leipzig, 1926; W. Böhm, *Schillers Briefe über die ästhetische Erziehung des Menscher*, Halle, 1927; G. Fricke, *Der religiöse Sinn der Klassik Schillers*, Munich, 1927; F. A. Hohenstein, *Schiller: Die Metaphysik seiner Tragödie*, Weimar, 1927; H. Jensen, *Schiller zwischen Goethe und Kant*, Oslo, 1927; E. Kühnemann, *Schiller*, Munich, 1927; F. Strich, *Schiller: Sein Leben und sein Werk*, Leipzig, 1927; H. H. Borcherdt, *Schiller: Seine geistige und künstlerische Entwicklung*, Leipzig, 1929; K. Cunningham, *Schiller und die französische Klassik*, Bonn, 1930; E. Deye, *Shakespeare und Schiller*, Munich, 1931; W. Spengler, *Das Drama Schillers: Seine Genesis*, Leipzig, 1932; H. Schneider, *Vom Wallenstein zum Demetrius*, Stuttgart, 1933; A. Tenenbaum, *Kants Ästhetik und ihr Einfluss auf Schiller*, Berlin, 1933; H. Cysarz, *Schiller*, Halle, 1934; H. Örtel, *Schillers Theorie des Tragischen*, Dresden, 1934; W. Deubel, *Schillers Kampf um die Tragödie*, Berlin, 1935; M. Hecker, *Schillers Tod und Bestattung*, Leipzig, 1935; H. Pongs, *Schillers Urbilder*, Stuttgart, 1935; G. Baumecker, *Schillers Schönheitslehre*, Heidelberg, 1937; F. Meinecke, *Schiller und der Individualitätsgedanke*, Leipzig, 1937; G. Storz, *Das Drama Friedrich Schillers*, Frankfurt am Main, 1938; B. von Wiese, *Die Dramen Schillers: Politik und Tragödie*, Leipzig, 1938; E. Spranger, *Schillers Geistesart*, Berlin, 1941; G. M. Bruckner, *Schiller in Bauerbach*, new ed., Bielefeld, 1947; H. H. Borcherdt, *Schiller und die Romantiker*,

Stuttgart, 1948; K. May, *Schiller: Idee und Wirklichkeit im Drama*, Göttingen, 1948; F. W. Wentzlaff-Eggebert, *Schillers Weg zu Goethe*, Tübingen and Stuttgart, 1949; M. Gerhard, *Schiller*, Bern, 1950; R. Buchwald, *Schiller*, new ed., Leipzig, 1953; F. Prader, *Schiller und Sophokles*, Zurich, 1954; A. Abusch, *Schiller*, Berlin, 1955; T. Piana, *Friedrich Schiller: Bild-Urkunden zu seinem Leben und Schaffen*, Weimar, 1957; B. von Heiseler, *Schiller*, Gütersloh, 1959; W. Muschg, *Schiller: Die Tragödie der Freiheit*, Bern, 1959; W. Vulpius, *Schiller: Bibliographie; 1893–1958*, Weimar, 1959; B. von Wiese, *Friedrich Schiller*, Stuttgart, 1963; E. Müller, *Der Herzog und das Genie: Friedrich Schillers Jugendjahre*, Stuttgart, 1965; *ibid.*, *Schillers Dramaturgie*, Stuttgart, 1965; H. G. Nerjes, *Ein unbekannter Schiller: Kritiker des Weimarer Musenhofes*, Berlin, Bielefeld, and Munich, 1965; N. Öllers, *Schiller: Geschichte seiner Wirkung bis zu Goethes Tod (1805–1832)*, Bonn, 1966; H. Koopmann, *Friedrich Schiller*, 2 vols., Stuttgart, 1966; E. Staiger, *Friedrich Schiller*, Zurich, 1967; F. Burschell, *Schiller*, Reinbek, 1968; H. Rischbieter, *Friedrich Schiller*, 2 vols., Velber, 1969; N. Oellers, ed., *Schiller: Zeitgenosse aller Epochen: Dokumente zur Wirkungsgeschichte in Deutschland*, 2 vols., Frankfurt am Main, 1970, 1976; G. Sautermeister, *Idyllik und Dramatik im Werk Friedrich Schillers: Zum geschichtlichen Ort seiner klassischen Dramen*, Stuttgart, 1971; G. Ueding, *Schillers Rhetorik*, Tübingen, 1971; K. Berghahn and R. Grimm, *Schiller: Zur Theorie und Praxis der Dramen*, Darmstadt, 1972; D. Borchmeyer, *Tragödie und Öffentlichkeit. Schillers Dramaturgie im Zusammenhang seiner ästhetisch-politischen Theorie und die rhetorische Tradition*, Munich, 1973; K. Berghahn, *Friedrich Schiller: Zur Geschichtlichkeit seines Werkes*, Kronberg, 1975.

English

T. Carlyle, *The Life of Friedrich Schiller*, London, 1825; E. Ellet, *The Characters of Schiller*, Boston, 1839; F. Werner, *The Characteristics of Schiller's Dramas*, London, 1859; H. H. Boyesen, *Goethe and Schiller: Their Lives and Works*, New York, 1879; J. Sime, *Schiller*, London, 1882; H. Duntzer, *The Life of Schiller*, tr. by P. E. Pinkerton, London, 1883; H. W. Nevinson, *The Life of Schiller*, New York, 1889; L. Rudolph, *Schiller: Lexicon*, 2d ed., 2 vols., New York, 1890; C. Thomas, *The Life and Works of Schiller*, New York, 1901; P. Carus, *Friedrich Schiller*, La Salle, Ill., 1905; E. C. Parry, *Friedrich Schiller in America*, Philadelphia, 1905; J. G. Robertson, *Schiller after a Century*, Edinburgh, 1905; T. Rea, *Schiller's Dramas and Poems in England*, London, 1906; F. Ewen, *The Prestige of Schiller in England*, New York, 1932; F. W. Kaufman, *Schiller: Poet of Philosophical Idealism*, Oberlin, Ohio, 1942; W. Witte, *Schiller*, Oxford, 1949; H. B. Garland, *Schiller*, New York, 1950; E. L. Stahl, *Friedrich Schiller's Drama: Theory and Practice*, Oxford, 1954; W. F. Mainland, *Schiller and the Changing Past*, London, 1957; J. R. Frey, ed., *Schiller, 1759–1959: Commemorative American Studies*, Urbana, Ill., 1959; F. Norman, ed., *Schiller: Bicentenary Lectures*, rev. ed., New York, 1960; S. S. Kerry, *Schiller's Writings on Aesthetics*, New York, 1961; A. L. Willson, ed., *A Schiller Symposium*, Austin, Tex., 1961; B. von Heiseler, *Schiller*, tr. by J. Bednall, London, 1962; R. D. Miller, *The Drama of Schiller*, Harrogate, England, 1963; E. K. Kostka, *Schiller in Russian Literature*, Philadelphia, 1964; H. J. Sandberg, *Thomas Mann's Schiller Studies*, Boston, 1965; R. M. Longyear, *Schiller and Music*, Chapel Hill, N.C., 1966; H. B. Garland, *Schiller, the Dramatic Writer*, New York and London, 1969; T. Calvin, *The Life and Works of Friedrich Schiller*, New York, 1970; J. E. Prudhoe, *The Theatre of Goethe and Schiller*, Oxford, 1973; I. Graham, *Schiller's Dramas: Talent and Integrity*, London, 1974; *ibid.*, *Schiller: A Master of the Tragic Form: His Theory and Practice*, Pittsburgh, 1975; C. E. Passage, *Friedrich Schiller*, New York, 1975.

Schisgal, Murray (1926–)

American dramatist. He began his theatre career as a writer for the Off Broadway stage. Three one-act plays, *The Typists*, *The Postman*, and *A Simple Kind of Love Story*, opened first in London in 1960. *The Typists*, about the aspirations and fears of two aging office workers, was presented in New York in 1963 along with *The Tiger*, a comedy about an abduction for the purpose of conversation. Meanwhile, *Ducks and Lovers* (1961) had appeared. After *Knit One, Purl Two* (1963), which never saw Broadway, Schisgal's zany three-character love-triangle comedy *Luv* (1964) amused New York audiences during a long run. Among his other plays are *Windows* (1965), *Reverberations* (1967), *A Way of Life* (1969), *The Chinese and Dr. Fish* (1970), and *Twice Around the Park* (1982), two one-act, two-character plays. In the United States, his theater is closely identified with the performances by Eli Wallach and Anne Jackson.

Schlegel, Johann Elias (1719–1749)

German dramatist. Schlegel was initially an exponent of Johann Christoph Gottsched's concept of tragedy, and later became an early admirer of Shakespeare and is thus considered a forerunner of Lessing. He wrote such classical dramas as *The Trojan Women* (*Die Trojanerinnen*; wr. 1735, pub. 1747), *Siblings of Tauris* (*Die Geschwister in Taurien*, 1739), revised under the title *Orestes and Pylades* (1742), and *Dido* (1739); historical dramas including *Hermann* (1741) and *Canute* (*Canut*, 1746); and several successful comedies, such as *Busy Idlers* (*Geschäfftigen Müssiggänger*, 1743), *The Secretive Man* (*Der Geheimnisvolle*; wr. 1743, pub. 1747), *The King of the Gardeners* (*Gärtnerkönig*, 1746), and *The Triumph of Good Women* (*Der Triumph der guten Frauen*, 1748), which were rated second only to Lessing's works. *Canute*, his most popularly successful and influential drama, pits the evil barbarian Ulfo against Canute, the virtuous, kind King of Denmark. Although virtue is victorious, Ulfo is by far the more interesting figure—an evil hero, a revolutionary innovation in a narrowly rationalistic age.

[PETER JELAVICH]

Schnitzler, Arthur (1862–1931)

Austrian novelist and dramatist. Arthur Schnitzler was born on May 15, 1862, in Vienna, the son of Professor Johann Schnitzler, a prominent Jewish physician. He was exposed early to the influence of literature and drama and at the age of twelve wrote verse tragedies, of which his father disapproved. Nevertheless, Schnitzler held his father in high esteem; the title character of *Professor Bernhardi* (1912) is supposedly modeled after him.

Arthur Schnitzler. [Bildarchiv der Österreichischen Nationalbibliothek]

In accordance with his father's wishes, Schnitzler studied medicine at the University of Vienna, where he proved to be a brilliant student even while pursuing his ambition to write. He developed a keen interest in psychiatry, and his close acquaintance with Sigmund Freud, who was six years his senior, later led him to write a thesis on the hypnotic treatment of neuroses. On his part, Freud hailed the poetic intuition of Schnitzler, which, he contended, had anticipated or paralleled some of his own findings.

After obtaining his degree in medicine in 1885, Schnitzler became a practicing physician and edited and wrote for a medical journal. At the same time, he was producing literary pieces under the pen name Anatol. His artistic inclinations drew him to the Café Griensteidl, a favorite meeting place of many Viennese writers. One of them, Hugo von Hofmannsthal, later prefaced Schnitzler's first short-play cycle, *Anatol* (wr. 1889–1892), with verses signed Loris (*see* HOFMANNSTHAL, HUGO VON). At about the same time Schnitzler met Theodor Herzl, a talented journalist and the founder of political Zionism; he paid tribute to him in the character of Leo Gowolsky in his autobiographical novel *The Road to the Open* (*Der Weg ins Freie*, 1908). Though Schnitzler characterized himself as a "German writer of Jewish origin," he never embraced the political credo of Zionism. Nevertheless, he was a frequent target of anti-Semitism, particularly after his play *Fair Game* (*Freiwild*, 1896) exposed bigotry in the Austro-Hungarian army.

Schnitzler never entirely abandoned his medical practice, but he gave increasing priority to his literary activities after 1895, the year his *Light o' Love* (*Liebelei*) changed the Burgtheater's policy of barring naturalistic plays and established him as the leading dramatist of his day. In 1901 controversy over his short novel *Leutnant Gustl* brought about his resignation from the army medical reserve.

Most of Schnitzler's later years, spent in a luxurious villa overlooking Vienna, were devoted almost entirely to writing, although he took time to travel all over Europe and the Orient. In 1912 his close associate Otto Brahm, the Berlin theatre director, died. Subsequently Schnitzler devoted much of his time to writing short stories and novelettes. This shift from playwriting to fiction was also due to World War I, which shattered the world that had provided him with most of the characters for his plays, the Hapsburg monarchy and the Viennese *fin de siècle* culture.

Schnitzler's narrative work consists of numerous short stories and the later, more ambitious and melancholy novelettes: *Fräulein Else* (1924), *Rhapsody* (1925), *Frau Berta Garlan, Doktor Gräsler* (1917), *Spa Doctor* (*Badearzt*, 1917), and *Flight into Darkness* (*Flucht in die Finsternis*, 1926). He wrote only two full-length novels, *The Road to the Open* (1908) and *Therese* (1928).

Schnitzler died on October 21, 1931, in Vienna, one year after suffering the severe shock of his married daughter's suicide. About a year after his death his works were banned by the Nazi party in Germany and, shortly after that, also in Austria.

Anatol as staged in Munich in 1925.
[Theater-Museum, Munich]

WORK

Held in very high esteem during his lifetime, Schnitzler's work faded after the 1914 cataclysm swept away the foundations of his culture. His plays, while reflecting the rise of realism, convey the subtle flavor of a *fin de siècle* Viennese culture that was soon to become a charming and sophisticated obsolescence in modern Europe. His dramas explore the tenor of this society, particularly its amoral leisure classes, revealing wistfulness and melancholy beneath the frivolity. He continually illustrated the elements of playacting and game in his worldlings, whose glossy surface activity masks vacuity and futility. Schnitzler possessed a melancholic awareness of the limitations of human experience that led him to reject all dogmatism and religious faith. Fatalistically, he attributed man's frailty, treachery, and promiscuity to his multiple nature, to the "thousand souls within him."

Schnitzler dealt with the theme of illusion and reality in many variations: dream and death, play and necessity, appearance and being, mask and essence. This preoccupation connected him with other Viennese writers of the period who sometimes dealt with similar motifs from slightly different points of view. Thus the portrayal of the theme of transitoriness, for example, in *The Sisters, or Casanova in Spa* (*Die Schwestern, oder Casanova in Spa*, 1919) is reminiscent of Hofmannsthal's *Yesterday*.

Schnitzler was a master of conversation through which characters inadvertently expose themselves by what they fail to say. In his plays allusions are more important than objects, gestures more significant than words, the manner of speech more expressive than the text. The unsaid is ever present.

Sexuality figures prominently in Schnitzler's characters. They seek sensual pleasures despite their fastidious attention to social protocol. Thus, *Hands Around, or La Ronde* (*Reigen*; wr. 1897, prod. 1920), is a series of "dialogues" between diverse men and women, each of which culminates in sexual union. In Schnitzler's plays, women are important as catalysts in the dynamics of the erotic process.

Combining psychological acumen with his art, Schnitzler dissected jealousy, exhibiting it as nothing more than erotic possessiveness. This theme found elaborate expression in his first full-length play, *The Fairy Tale* (*Märchen*, 1893), and in *The Green Cockatoo* (*Der grüne Kakadu*, 1899), in which jealousy motivates murder. Unhappiness between a man and a woman is portrayed in *Light o' Love* (1895), in which sincerity and naïveté in love are contrasted with the intellectuals' decadence and cynicism. Love, for Schnitzler, was short-lived and inconstant, made tragic by disparity between the sexes and inevitable loneliness. He elegantly but forcefully excoriated conventional morality, for dooming a woman in *The Legacy* (*Das Vermächtnis*, 1898) and for sponsoring senseless duels in *Fair Game* (1896). *The Wide Country*, or *The Vast Domain* (*Das weite Land*, 1911), shows how the idle affairs of Viennese aristocrats cost two young lives; *The Countess Mizzi, or The Family Reunion* (*Komtesse Mizzi, oder Der Familientag*, 1909) deals again with the follies of the privileged classes. *Paracelsus* (1899) is an examination of the suppressed instincts that reside in the unconscious. In *Beatrice's Veil* (*Der Schleier der Beatrice*, 1900), Schnitzler wrestled with the enigma of a female soul capable of destroying two men and itself. In *The Mate* (*Die Gefährtin*, 1899), a husband discovers after his wife's death that she had been a virtual stranger to him; *Intermezzo* (*Zwischenspiel*, 1905) repeats the notion of marriage as failure.

Schnitzler's facility for evoking mood through dialogue led him to compose several series of short plays such as *Living Hours* (*Lebendige Stunden*, 1902), four one-act plays; *The Puppets* (*Die Marionetten*, 1903–1906), three one-act plays; and *Comedy of Words* (*Komödie der Worte*, 1915), three one-act plays. None of these has the thread of unity that Anatol and his friend Max maintain throughout the episodes of *Anatol* (wr. 1889–1892, prod. 1910). That Schnitzler preferred the short form is evident from the fact that he wrote twice as many one-act plays as he wrote full-length dramas. In addition, *The Sisters, or Casanova in Spa*, a comedy in verse, is denoted as three acts in one.

Other plays by Schnitzler are *The Lonely Way* (*Der einsame Weg*, 1904), showing how youth suffers from parental indiscretions; *The Call of Life* (*Der Ruf des Lebens*, 1906); and *The Young Medardus* (*Der junge Medardus*, 1910). *Professor Bernhardi* (1912) explores anti-Semitism and the rift between religion and science. World War I and the passing of the Hapsburg monarchy affected Schnitzler deeply; his few subsequent writings are dominated by pessimism and despondency.

Anatol (wr. 1889–1892, prod. 1910). Sequence of sophisticated one-act comedies about the perpetual, sometimes overlapping affairs of Anatol, a Viennese *flâneur* ("idler"). In seven short dialogues, Anatol is observed by Max, his philosophical friend and adviser, as he drifts through one adventure after another in his bewildering game of love. As soon as he has learned one lesson, the rules seem to change, leaving him always with more to learn. In the final scene, in which he is setting off for his wedding, he seems slightly sadder but all the wiser.

Light o' Love (*Liebelei*, 1895). Drama set in Vienna. Fritz, a wealthy bachelor, is involved in an affair with a married woman. Theodor and Mizzi, Fritz's friends, try to break up the relationship by introducing Fritz to Christine, the young daughter of an opera-house violinist. While the four gather in the lighthearted atmosphere of Fritz's flat, Fate, disguised as an elegant gentleman, intrudes and predicts death. Christine falls deeply in love with Fritz, but he secretly continues his amour until the other woman's husband discovers them and challenges Fritz to a duel. Recalling the premonition, Fritz bids Christine farewell, pretending to go on a trip. When he fails to return, Christine learns from his friends that Fritz has been killed over another woman. The thought that she had been only a diversion to Fritz is unbearable, and Christine commits suicide.

Hands Around; La Ronde (*Reigen;* wr. 1897, prod. 1920). Short play cycle in ten dialogues, all of which conclude with sexual consummation. Beginning with the seduction of a soldier by a whore, each subsequent dialogue is related to its predecessor by the reappearance of one of the characters who has first been seen in the passive role and who now appears as the aggressor in the sexual relay. Following his seduction by a whore, the soldier makes love to a chambermaid, who in turn has an amour with her employer's son. The son's mistress is an elegant lady married to the seducer of a charming young girl who, in turn, makes love with a poet. The poet becomes involved with an actress, she seduces a count, and the count goes on to the whore with whom the drama began. Thus the cycle is complete, and a round of the game is ended.

The Green Cockatoo (*Der grüne Kakadu*, 1899). One-act play-within-a-play, set in France on the eve of the French Revolution. Various noblemen visit a sordid cellar tavern and observe a group of actors who are disporting themselves in wild mimicry. The merriment takes a tragic turn when Henri, the star of the company, who had been impersonating a jealous husband, learns that his wife is involved with one of the noblemen in the party. Henri mortally stabs the aristocrat, shattering the

A Munich production of *Reigen.* [Theater-Museum, Munich]

tavern's bacchanalian atmosphere. Now those inside the tavern realize that outside on the street a mob is storming the Bastille and the revolution has begun.

The Lonely Way (*Der einsame Weg*, 1904). Psychological drama about people in the autumn of their lives. Professor Wegrat discovers that his son is, in fact, the offspring of his wife and her former lover, the painter Fichtner. Now an aging bachelor belatedly seeking a purpose in life, Fichtner claims the young man as his illegitimate son, but the boy rejects him. At the same time, Wegrat's daughter falls in love with the fading Von Sala, Fichtner's friend. Von Sala, trying to recapture his youth, proposes to the girl even though he foresees the end of the relationship. Terrified by her sense of emptiness and her own impending loneliness, the girl drowns herself in the river.

The Wide Country; The Vast Domain (*Das weite Land*, 1911). Drama in which both virtue and promiscuity lead to tragedy. Although Friedrich Hofreiter, a forty-year-old Viennese industrialist, has a wife, Genia, and a son, he indulges in affairs with other women. When a young pianist commits suicide because of his love for Genia, Hofreiter is shocked that his wife's virtue has cost the young man's life. To distract himself he goes to the mountains with his friend Dr. Mauer and begins an affair with Erna Wahl, a woman who has loved him since her childhood and whom Dr. Mauer now loves. When Hofreiter returns, he discovers that in his absence his wife has also taken a young lover. He challenges the young man to a duel and kills him.

Professor Bernhardi (1912). Drama dealing with anti-Semitism and the theme of science versus religion. Bernhardi, a prominent liberal Jewish physician and the head

Liebelei. Vienna, Akademietheater, 1954. [Goethe House]

Scenes from *Anatol*: (above, l. to r.) Joseph
Schildkraut as Anatol, Dennie Moore, and Walter
Connolly as Max; (right) Connolly and
Schildkraut. New York, Lyceum Theatre,
1931. [Photographs by Vandamm. Theater
Collection, The New York Public Library at Lincoln
Center, Astor, Lenox and Tilden Foundations]

of a large Vienna hospital, refuses to permit a Catholic
priest to visit a dying girl. He does this so that her last
hours may be unmarred by the knowledge of her impending end. Bernhardi's gesture proves both futile and
unfortunate, since the patient learns from a nurse about
her state of health and dies without the last rites. A political scandal explodes in which Bernhardi finds himself
the focus of a *cause célèbre*. Both Jews and Christians
caught in the situation are satirized, and anti-Semitic attitudes are bitterly criticized. As recriminations multiply,
Bernhardi is accused of behavior inimical to religion and
sentenced to two months in prison. After his release, because he regards himself as an apolitical scientist, Bernhardi adamantly opposes his friends' efforts to call a
mass meeting and arouse public support for him as a
persecuted Jew.

The Comedy of Seduction (*Komödie der Verführung*, 1924). Drama set in Europe shortly before World War I. Aurelie must choose one from among three suitors: Prince Ardulin von Perosa, the poet Ambros Dohl, and Ulrich von Falkenir, all of whom are expecting her at a ball given by the prince. She appears at midnight and chooses Falkenir, but he refuses to marry her, believing that her beauty and versatility must not be chained to one man. Falkenir thus opens for Aurelie the possibilities of lust and promiscuity. As she proceeds to drift freely from one affair to another, she suffers such disorientation that she begins to experience herself as disembodied, a mere shadow. When war erupts, she meets Falkenir again, in a small Danish seashore resort. Aurelie tells him that though she has had countless lovers, she has never loved another. Falkenir is profoundly moved and wants to begin their relationship anew. Aurelie, now entirely without illusions, says "yes" to him but then takes a boat and sails into the open sea. Realizing that union in death is all they can hope for, Falkenir follows. Calmly, they let the sea engulf them.

[VIOLET B. KETELS]

PLAYS

The "play" Anatol is a sequence of one-act plays written between 1889 and 1892 and arranged in the following order: Nos. 2, 7, 3, 6, 9, 10, and 4 below. Except for Nos. 3 and 6, the sequence was first produced in Prague in 1893 in the Czech language; the first German productions were in the Berlin Lessingtheater and the Vienna Deutsches Volkstheater, on Dec. 3, 1910. The entire sequence has not yet been produced.

1. *Das Abenteuer seines Lebens* (*The Adventure of His Life*). Comedy, 1 act. Published 1888. Produced Vienna, Volkstheater in Rudolfsheim, Apr. 11, 1891.

2. *Die Frage an das Schicksal** (*Ask No Questions and You'll Hear No Stories*). Play, 1 act. Written 1889. Published 1890. Produced Leipzig, Carola-Theater, Jan. 26, 1896.

3. *Episode** (*An Episode*). Play, 1 act. Published 1889. Produced Leipzig, Ibsen-Theater, June 26, 1898.

4. *Anatols Hochzeitsmorgen** (*The Wedding Morning*). Play, 1 act. Published 1890. Produced Berlin, Langenbeck-Haus, Oct. 13, 1901.

5. *Alkandis Lied* (*The Song of Alkandis*). Play. Published 1890.

6. *Denksteine** (*Keepsakes*). Play, 1 act. Published 1891. Produced Vienna, Urania Theatre, Jan. 10, 1916.

7. *Weihnachtseinkäufe** (*A Christmas Present*). Play, 1 act. Published 1891. Produced Vienna, Sofien-Säle, Jan. 13, 1898.

8. *Das Märchen* (*The Fairy Tale*). Play, 3 acts. Written 1891. Published 1891. Produced Vienna, Deutsches Volkstheater, Dec. 1, 1893.

9. *Abschiedssouper** (*A Farewell Dinner*). Play, 1 act. Published 1893. Produced Bad Ischl, July 14, 1893.

10. *Agonie** (*Dying Pangs*). Play, 1 act. Published 1893. Produced 1893.

11. *Liebelei** (*Light o' Love*). Play, 3 acts. Written 1894. Published 1896. Produced Vienna, Burgtheater, Oct. 9, 1895.

12. *Die überspannte Person* (*The Eccentric One*). Play, 1 act. Written 1894. Published 1896. Produced Vienna, Deutsches Volkstheater, Mar. 29, 1932.

13. *Halbzwei* (*One-thirty*). Play, 1 act. Written 1894. Published 1897. Produced Vienna, Deutsches Volkstheater, Mar. 29, 1932.

14. *Freiwild* (*Fair Game*). Play, 3 acts. Published 1898. Produced Berlin, Deutsches Theater, Nov. 1, 1896.

15. *Paracelsus** . Verse play, 1 act. Written 1897. Published 1898. Produced Vienna, Burgtheater, Mar. 1, 1899.

16. *Reigen** (*Hands Around; La Ronde*). Play, 10 scenes. Written 1897. Published 1900. Produced Berlin, Kleines Schauspielhaus, Dec. 23, 1920.

17. *Das Vermächtnis** (*The Legacy*). Play, 3 acts. Published 1899. Produced Berlin, Deutsches Theater, Oct. 8, 1898.

18. *Der grüne Kakadu** (*The Green Cockatoo*). Grotesque, 1 act. Written 1898. Published 1899. Produced Vienna, Burgtheater, Mar. 1, 1899.

19. *Die Gefährtin** (*The Mate*). Play, 1 act. Written 1898. Published 1899. Produced Vienna, Burgtheater, Mar. 1, 1899.

20. *Der Schleier der Beatrice* (*Beatrice's Veil*). Play, 5 acts. Published 1901. Produced Breslau, Lobe-Theater, Dec. 1, 1900.

21. *Sylvesternacht* (*New Year's Night*). Dialogue, 1 act. Written 1900. Published 1901. Produced Vienna, Theater in der Josefstadt, Dec. 31, 1926.

The following four plays (Nos. 22–25) form a cycle under the title *Lebendige Stunden* (*Living Hours*).

22. *Lebendige Stunden** (*Living Hours*). Play, 1 act. Written 1901. Published 1901. Produced Berlin, Deutsches Theater, Jan. 4, 1902.

23. *Die Frau mit dem Dolche** (*The Lady with the Dagger*). Play, 1 act. Written 1901. Published 1902. Produced Berlin, Deutsches Theater, Jan. 4, 1902.

24. *Die letzten Masken** (*Last Masks*). Play, 1 act. Written 1901. Published 1902. Produced Berlin, Deutsches Theater, Jan. 4, 1902.

25. *Literatur** (*Literature*). Comedy, 1 act. Written 1901. Published 1902. Produced Berlin, Deutsches Theater, Jan. 4, 1902.

The following three plays (Nos. 26–28) form a cycle under the title *Die Marionetten* (*The Puppets*).

26. *Der Puppenspieler* (*The Puppet Player*). Study, 1 act. Written 1902. Published 1903. Produced Berlin, Deutsches Theater, Sept. 12, 1903.

27. *Der tapfere Kassian** (*The Gallant Kassian*). Comic opera, 1 act. Written 1904. Published 1909. Produced Berlin, Kleines Theater, Nov. 22, 1904. Musical version: Produced Leipzig, Neues Stadtheater, Oct. 30, 1909. Music: Oscar Straus.

28. *Zum grossen Wurstel* (*The Great Show*). Burlesque, 1 act. Written 1904. Published 1905. Produced Vienna, Lustspieltheater, Mar. 16, 1906.

29. *Der einsame Weg** (*The Lonely Way*). Play, 5 acts. Published 1904. Produced Berlin, Deutsches Theater, Feb. 13, 1904.

30. *Zwischenspiel** (*Intermezzo*). Comedy, 3 acts. Published 1906. Produced Vienna, Burgtheater, Oct. 12, 1905.

31. *Der Ruf des Lebens* (*The Call of Life*). Play, 3 acts. Published 1906. Produced Berlin, Lessingtheater, Feb. 24, 1906.

32. *Die Verwandlungen des Pierrot* (*The Transformations of Pierrot*). Pantomime, 6 scenes. Published 1908.

33. *Komtesse Mizzi, oder Der Familientag** (*The Countess Mizzi, or The Family Reunion*). Comedy, 1 act. Written 1907. Published 1908. Produced Vienna, Deutsches Volkstheater, Jan. 5, 1909.

34. *Der junge Medardus* (*The Young Medardus*). Historical drama, prologue and 5 acts. Published 1910. Produced Vienna, Burgtheater, Nov. 24, 1910.

35. *Der Schleier der Pierrette* (*Pierrette's Veil*). Pantomime, 3 scenes. Published 1910. Produced Dresden, Königliches Opernhaus, Jan. 22, 1910. Music: Ernst von Dohnányi.

36. *Das weite Land* (*The Wide Country; The Vast Domain*). Tragicomedy, 5 acts. Published 1911. Produced Berlin, Lessingtheater; Breslau, Lobe-Theater; Munich, Residenztheater; Hamburg, Deutsches Schauspielhaus; Prague, Deutsches Landestheater; Leipzig, Altes Stadttheater; Hannover, Schauburg; Bochum, Stadttheater; Vienna, Burgtheater, Oct. 14, 1911.

37. *Professor Bernhardi** . Drama, 5 acts. Published 1912. Produced Berlin, Kleines Theater, Nov. 28, 1912.

The following three plays (Nos. 38–40) form the cycle *Komödie der Worte* (*Comedy of Words*).

38. *Stunde des Erkennens** (*Hour of Recognition*). Drama, 1 act. Published 1915. Produced Vienna, Burgtheater, Oct. 12, 1915.

39. *Grosse Szene** (*The Great Scene*). Play, 1 act. Published 1915. Produced Vienna, Burgtheater, Oct. 12, 1915.

40. *Das Bacchusfest** (*The Festival of Bacchus*). Play, 1 act. Published 1915. Produced Vienna, Burgtheater, Oct. 12, 1915.

41. *Fink und Fliederbusch*. Comedy, 3 acts. Published 1917. Produced Vienna, Volkstheater, Nov. 14, 1917.

42. *Die Schwestern, oder Casanova in Spa* (*The Sisters, or Casanova in Spa*). Comedy, 3 acts in 1; verse. Published 1919. Produced Vienna, Burgtheater, Mar. 26, 1920.

43. *Komödie der Verführung* (*The Comedy of Seduction*). Drama, 3 acts. Published 1924. Produced Vienna, Burgtheater, Oct. 11, 1924.

44. *Der Gang zum Weiher* (*The Walk to the Pond*). Drama, 5 acts. Written 1921. Published 1926. Produced Vienna, Burgtheater, Feb. 14, 1931.

45. *Das Wort* (*The Word*). Fragment. Tragicomedy, 5 acts. Written 1927. Published 1966.

46. *Im Spiel der Sommerlüfte* (*In the Play of Summer Breezes*). Play, 3 acts. Published 1930. Produced Vienna, Deutsches Volkstheater, Dec. 21, 1929.

47. *Anatols Grössenwahn* (*Anatol's Megalomania*). Play, 1 act. Published 1932. Produced Vienna, Deutsches Volkstheater, Mar. 29, 1932.

48. *Die Mörderin* (*The Murderess*). Tragic sketch, 1 act. Published 1932. Produced Vienna, Deutsches Volkstheater, Mar. 29, 1932.

49. *Die Gleitenden* (*The Gliders*). Play, 1 act. Published 1932. Produced Vienna, Deutsches Volkstheater, Mar. 29, 1932.

EDITIONS

Collections

The Green Cockatoo and Other Plays, tr. by H. B. Samuel, London and Edinburgh, 1913; *Gesammelte Werke*, 7 vols., Berlin, 1918; *The Lonely Way, Intermezzo, Countess Mizzie*, tr. by E. Björkman, Boston, 1922; *Reigen, The*

Affairs of Anatol and Other Plays, tr. by M. Mannes and G. I. Colbron, New York, 1933; *Die dramatischen Werke*, 2 vols., Frankfurt am Main, 1962; *Entworfenes und Verworfenes: Aus dem Nachlass*, ed. by R. Urbach, 6 vols., Frankfurt, 1977.

Individual Plays

Anatol. Published in *From the Modern Repertoire*, ed. by E. R. Bentley and tr. by H. Granville-Barker, vol. 3, Bloomington, Ind., 1949–1956.

Ask No Questions and You'll Hear No Stories (Questioning the Irrevocable). Published in *The Drama: Its History, Literature and Influence on Civilization*, ed. by A. Bates and tr. by W. Chambers, vol. 12, London, 1903–1904.

A Farewell Dinner (A Farewell Supper). Published in *Reading Drama*, ed. by F. B. Millett and tr. by H. Granville-Barker, New York, 1950.

The Game of Love (Liebelei). Published in *Masterpieces of the Modern Central European Theater*, tr. by C. Mueller and ed. by R. Corrigan, New York, 1967.

The Green Cockatoo. Published in *Plays for the College Theater*, ed. by G. H. Leverton and tr. by E. Van der Meer, New York, 1934.

Hands Around (La Ronde). Published in *The Modern Theatre*, ed. and tr. by E. R. Bentley, vol. 2, Garden City, N.Y., 1955–1960.

Intermezzo. Published in *Plays from the Modern Theatre*, ed. by H. R. Steeves and tr. by E. Björkman, Boston, 1931.

La Ronde (Reigen). Published in *Masterpieces of the Modern Central European Theatre*, tr. by C. Mueller and ed. by R. Corrigan, New York, 1967.

Light o' Love. Published in *Twenty-five Modern Plays*, ed. by S. M. Tucker and A. J. Downer and tr. by B. Morgan, 3d ed., New York, 1953.

Literature. Published in *German Classics of the Nineteenth and Twentieth Centuries*, ed. by K. Francke and tr. by A. Coleman, vol. 20, New York, 1913–1914.

Living Hours. Published in *Chief Contemporary Dramatists*, ed. by T. H. Dickinson and tr. by G. I. Colbron, 2d ser., Boston, 1921.

The Lonely Way. Published in *Representative Modern Dramas*, ed. by C. H. Whitman and tr. by J. Leigh, New York, 1936.

Professor Bernhardi. Published in *Famous Plays of 1936*, tr. by L. Borell and R. Adam, London, 1936.

Round Dance (Reigen). Published in *Themes of Drama*, tr. by E. Bentley and ed. by G. Wellwarth, New York, 1973.

CRITICISM

German

J. Kapp, *Arthur Schnitzler*, Leipzig, 1912; T. Reik, *Arthur Schnitzler als Psycholog*, Minden, 1913; J. Körner, *Arthur Schnitzlers Gestalten und Probleme*, Vienna, 1921; R. Specht, *Arthur Schnitzler: Der Dichter und sein Werk*, Berlin, 1922; G. Baumann, *Arthur Schnitzler: Die Welt von Gestern eines Dichters von Morgen*, Frankfurt am Main, 1965; R. H. Allen, *An Annotated Arthur Schnitzler Bibliography*, Chapel Hill, N.C., 1966; C. Melchinger, *Illusion und Wirklichkeit in dramatischen Werk Arthur Schnitzlers*, Heidelberg, 1968; R. Urbach, *Arthur Schnitzler*, Velber bei Hannover, 1968, 1972; H. U. Lindken, *Interpetation en zu Arthur Schnitzler*, Munich, 1970; K. Killian, *Die Komödien Arthur Schnitzlers: Sozialer Rollenzwang und kritische Ethic*, Dusseldorf, 1972; E. Offermanns, *Arthur Schnitzler: Das Komödienwerk als Kritik des Impressionismus*, Munich, 1973; H. Rieder, *Arthur Schnitzler: Das dramatische Werk*, Vienna, 1973; A. Fritsche, *Dekadenz im Werk Arthur Schnitzlers*, Bern, 1974; G. Selling, *Die Einakterzyklen Arthur Schnitzlers*, Amsterdam, 1976; J. B. Berlin, *An Annotated Arthur Schnitzler Bibliography 1965–77*, Berlin, 1977; B. Gutt, *Emanzipation bei Arthur Schnitzler*, Berlin, 1977; R. P. Janz and K. Laermann, *Arthur Schnitzler: Diagnose des Wiener Bürgertums im Fin de Siecle*, Stuttgart, 1977; H. Schieble, *Arthur Schnitzler und die Aufklärung*, Munich, 1977.

English

S. Liptzin, *Arthur Schnitzler*, New York, 1932; *Studies in Arthur Schnitzler*, ed. by H. W. Reichert and H. Salinger, Chapel Hill, N.C., 1963; P. Bauland, *The Hooded Eagle: Modern German Drama on the New York Stage*, New York, 1968; E. Bentley, "Reigen Comes Full Circle", in *What is Theater?* New York, 1968; M. P. Alter, *The Concept of Physicians in the Writings of Hans Carossa, Arthur Schnitzler*, Bern, 1971; M. Swales, *Arthur Schnitzler: A Critical Study*, London, 1971; E. Urbach, *Arthur Schnitzler*, tr. by G. Daviau, New York, 1973; C. E. Williams, *The Broken Eagle: The Politics of Austrian Literature from Empire to Anschluss*, New York, 1974.

Scholz, Wilhelm von   (1874–1969)

German poet, novelist, essayist, translator, publisher, theatre director, and dramatist. He is best known for his stage works. Considered by Hermann Hesse to be "one of the most serious writers of our time," Scholz never employed superficial reality, believing imagination to be the essence and source of all art. In the age of naturalism he began as a neoclassicist, following in the wake of Paul Ernst yet using Kleist and Hebbel as models and showing a distinct inclination toward the mystical, the occult, and the enigmatic. His early lyric-symbolic dramas, such as the one-act *My Prince* (*Mein Fürst*, 1898), the mystical *The Vanquished* (*Der Besiegte*, 1899), and the verse play *The Guest* (*Der Gast*, 1900), were followed by his first successful play, the medieval tragedy *The Jew of Konstanz* (*Der Jude von Konstanz*, 1905); and *Meroë* (1906), a forceful tragedy depicting the conflict between royalty and priesthood, father and son, which is resolved by Queen Meroë through murder and suicide. Thereafter Scholz turned away from moralistic neoclassicism toward the metaphysical and wrote the comedy *Exchanged Souls* (*Vertauschte Seelen*, 1910), a new version of the tale of the king and the pauper; *Dangerous Love* (*Gefährliche Liebe*, 1913); *Empedocles* (*Empedokles*, 1916), an adaptation of Hölderlin's *Empedocles's Death*; *The Enemies* (*Die Feinde*, 1917), set in the Napoleonic era and published anonymously; *Homage* (*Die Huldigung*, 1917), written for the twenty-fifth anniversary celebration of Baron Pistlitz; *Junk from the Fairs* (*Der Plunder von Jahrmarktsweilern*, 1917), a "slapdash comedy"; *The Two-headed One* (*Doppelkopf*, 1918), a grotesque puppet play; *Wonder of the Heart* (*Das Herzwunder*, 1918); and *Troilus and Cressida* (1919), an adaptation of Shakespeare's work.

Scholz's first worldwide success came with the drama *Race with a Shadow* (*Der Wettlauf mit dem Schatten*, 1920), whose subject, the rivalry between a writer and one of his creations, fully reflects the author's bent toward the twilight of the soul and the mysteries of fate. *Glass Woman* (*Die gläserne Frau*, 1924), typically mystical and profound, is really dramatized psychoanalysis. Scholz's other dramatic works include *Frankfurt Christmas* (*Die Frankfurter Weihnacht*, 1938), *Claudia Colonna* (1940), *The Cry* (*Der Schrei*, 1941), *Ayatari* (1944), *Eternal Youth* (*Ewige Jugend*, 1948), *Trumpet Playing in Säckingen* (*Das Säckinger Trompetenspiel*, 1953), and *Spanish World Theatre* (*Spanisches Welttheater*, 1961). He also wrote adaptations of four Calderón plays: *Love, the Greatest Enchantment* (*Über allen Zauber Liebe*, 1931), *Life Is a Dream* (*Das Leben ein Traum*, 1933), *The Judge of Zalamea* (*Der Richter von Zalamea*, 1937), and *The Great German Theatre of the World* (*Das deutsche grosse Welttheater*, 1941). See CALDERÓN DE LA BARCA, PEDRO.

Scholz wrote a number of radio plays based on his own novels as well as several theatrical essays on drama including *New Thoughts on Drama* (*Gedanken zum Drama: Neue Folge*, 1915).   [PETER JELAVICH]

Schönherr, Karl   (1867–1943)

Austrian dramatist. Karl Schönherr was born on February 24, 1867, in Axams, in the Austrian Tyrol, the son of a teacher. As a child he came under the spell of the Tyrolese popular theatre. Although the early death of his father exposed the family to many hardships, Schönherr began studying medicine in Innsbruck. In 1891 he moved to Vienna and in 1896 received his medical degree at the University of Vienna. Choosing to stay there, he made his literary debut in 1898 with a volume of short stories. Fame followed with the production of his play *The Woodcarver* (*Der Bildschnitzer*) in 1900.

Karl Schönherr.
[Bildarchiv der
Österreichischen
Nationalbibliothek]

Literary success enabled Schönherr to give up his medical practice in 1905 and devote himself to writing. His career was enlivened by critical controversies and feuds with the leadership of Vienna's Burgtheater. In 1910 he established a close working relationship with the Exl-Bühne, the outstanding Tyrolese folk theatre group, and its founder Ferdinand Exl. Inflation after World War I deprived Schönherr of most of his property. In 1922 he married Malvine Chiavacci. He became gravely ill in 1938 and produced no more plays. Schönherr died in Vienna on March 15, 1943. His many literary awards include three Grillparzer Prizes.

WORK

The earthiness and violence of Schönherr's drama—an extension of the naturalistic folk plays of Ludwig Anzengruber—contrast sharply with the fashionable aestheticism and symbolism of his contemporaries. Schönherr, closely connected with the mountain people of his province, focused on the portrayal of Austrian peasant life in a terse and vigorous style. His "peasant" plays revolve around the central symbols of earth and motherhood. *See* ANZENGRUBER, LUDWIG.

He is best known for *The Earth* (*Erde*, 1908), about a mountain peasant who refuses to die, and *Faith and Fireside* (*Glaube und Heimat*, 1910), which deals with the conflict between religion and patriotism. Other plays of note include *Solstice Day* (*Der Sonnwendtag*, 1902), an anticlerical work depicting a clash between vestigial paganism and Catholicism; *The Wood-carver* (1900), about an ailing wood-carver who voluntarily chooses death because his friend is better suited to take care of his family; *A People in Distress* (*Volk in Not*, 1916), about the uprising against Napoleon led by Andreas Hofer; *The Flag Waves* (*Die Fahne weht*, 1937), also about the Tyrolese fight for freedom; *The She-Devil* (*Der Weibsteufel*, 1915), depicting a love triangle in which a desperate woman goads a customs man into murdering her husband; *It* (*Es*, 1922), a two-character drama about motherhood; and *The King-*

dom (*Das Königreich*, 1909), a symbolist play with overtones of Ferdinand Raimund that is unique among Schönherr's dramas. The plays dealing with the postwar misery of the middle class— *The Struggle* (*Der Kampf*, wr. 1922), *Life's Mad Pranks* (*Narrenspiel des Lebens*, 1919), and *The Doctor of the Poor* (*Der Armendoktor*, 1926)—are weak, although prompted by sincere compassion. *See* RAIMUND, FERDINAND.

Schönherr's work is characterized, probably more strongly than that of any other Austrian playwright, by its close connection to a specific geographical area. With very few exceptions, such as *It* and *The Doctor of the Poor*, all his plays remain within the peasant world of his Tyrolean home and illustrate its folklore, traditions, and problems.

The Earth (*Erde*, 1908). Comedy of rustic life. Obstinate old Grutz refuses to turn over his farm to his twenty-six-year-old son Hannes. "I won't die!" he insists. The housekeeper Mena and the maid Trina compete for Hannes's affections in the hope of sharing in his future inheritance, and Mena finally wins. Afraid of losing Mena to another farmer who has proposed to her, Hannes asks his father to retire, but the old man still refuses. Then suddenly it appears that Hannes will get the farm after all, for Grutz is kicked by a wild horse and suffers a severe injury. Grutz becomes weaker but refuses a doctor, ordering his grave dug and his coffin made. Three weeks later, however, he recovers, leaves his bed, and exclaims: "The earth bears me again!" Discouraged, Mena leaves the farm to marry elsewhere despite the pleas of Hannes. Old Grutz then hacks his coffin to pieces for firewood.

Faith and Fireside (*Glaube und Heimat*, 1910). Tragedy concerning the movement against the Reformation that takes place among Tyrolese Protestants who are faced with the choice of either renouncing their faith or being driven from their land. Father Rott, a Catholic, refuses to shelter Protestants, but his son Christopher is converted to Protestantism after witnessing the death of an old woman, stabbed by some soldiers for refusing to yield her Lutheran Bible. Christopher's family faces exile, but old Rott refuses to join them; he wants to spend his last years at home. Christopher is told that his son "Spatz" must stay behind because the law forbids migration of minors. Learning that he cannot go with his father, the boy tries to run away, and he is accidentally killed by a mill wheel. Enraged, Christopher attacks a Catholic soldier but, remembering Christ's commandment, spares his life. The soldier watches Christopher and his wife depart with their dead son, then breaks his sword in two.

[VIOLET B. KETELS]

PLAYS

1. *Der Judas von Tirol* (*The Judas of Tyrol*). Folk play. Published 1897. Produced Vienna, Theater an der Wien, Oct. 10, 1897. New version: Produced 1927.

2. *Der Bildschnitzer* (*The Wood-carver*). Tragedy, 1 act. Written 1899. Published 1900. Produced Vienna, Deutsches Volkstheater, Sept. 13, 1900.

3. (With Rudolf Greinz). *Die Altweibermühle* (*The Fountain of Youth*). German carnival play. Produced Vienna, Kaiser-Jubiläumstheater, Jan. 22, 1902.

4. *Der Sonnwendtag (Solstice Day)*. Play, 3 acts. Written 1902. Published 1902. Produced Vienna, Burgtheater, Apr. 19, 1902. Early version of *Die Trenkwalder*.

5. *Karrnerleut' (The Carters)*. Play. Written 1904. Published 1905. Produced Vienna, Theater in der Josefstadt.

6. *Familie (The Family)*. Play, 3 acts. Written 1905. Published 1906. Produced Vienna, Burgtheater, Nov. 30, 1905.

7. *Erde (The Earth)*. Comedy of life, 3 acts. Written 1907. Published 1908. Produced Vienna, Burgtheater, Feb. 22, 1908. Preceded by premiere at Agram (Zagreb), Stadttheater, in the Croatian language.

8. *Das Königreich (The Kingdom)*. Fairy-tale play, 3 acts. Written 1908. Published 1908. Produced Vienna, Deutsches Volkstheater, Feb. 13, 1909. Rewritten 1917.

9. *Über die Brücke (Over the Bridge)*. Comedy, 5 acts. Produced Vienna, Burgtheater, Nov. 27, 1909. Early version of *Der Komödiant*.

10. *Lorbeer (Laurels)*. Comedy, 3 acts. Title used for revision of *Über die Brücke* in *Gesammelte Werke*.

11. *Glaube und Heimat* (Faith and Fireside)*. Tragedy, 3 acts. Written 1910. Published 1910. Produced Vienna, Deutsches Volkstheater, Dec. 17, 1910.

12. *Die Trenkwalder (The Trenkwalders)*. Comedy. Written 1913. Published 1914. Revision of *Der Sonnwendtag*.

13. *Der Weibsteufel (The She-Devil)*. Play, 5 acts. Written 1914. Published 1914. Produced Vienna, Burgtheater, Apr. 8, 1915. Burgtheater production preceded by a charity performance at Johann-Strauss Theater.

14. *Volk in Not (A People in Distress)*. Heroic drama, 3 acts. Written 1915. Published 1916. Produced Vienna, Volkstheater, July 2, 1916.

15. *Frau Suitner (Mrs. Suitner)*. Play, 5 acts. Written 1916. Published 1916. Produced Vienna, Burgtheater, Nov. 18, 1917.

16. *Narrenspiel des Lebens (Life's Mad Pranks)*. Play, 5 acts. Written 1918. Published 1918. Produced Berlin, Das Deutsche Theater, Feb. 4, 1919.

17. *Kindertragödie (Children's Tragedy)*. Tragedy, 3 acts. Written 1918. Published 1919. Produced Vienna, Deutsches Volkstheater, Nov. 28, 1919.

18. *Vivat Academia (Long Live the University)*. Play, 5 acts. Written 1922. Published 1922. Produced Vienna, Deutsches Volkstheater, Apr. 1, 1922.

Plays Nos. 19, 20, and 21 are revisions of *Vivat Academia*.

19. *Der Spurius*. Comedy, 3 acts. Published 1926.

20. *Der Kampf (The Struggle)*. Play, 3 acts. Written 1922.

21. *Herr Doktor, haben Sie zu essen (What About a Bite, Doctor)*. Play. Published 1930. Produced Vienna, Burgtheater, Mar. 29, 1930.

22. *Es (It)*. Tragedy, 5 acts. Written 1922. Produced Vienna, Deutsches Volkstheater, Dec. 23, 1922.

23. *Maitanz (May Dance)*. Tragedy, 3 acts. Published 1922. Produced Vienna, Burgtheater, Jan. 13, 1923.

24. *Der Komödiant (The Comedian)*. Comedy, 5 acts. Published 1924. Produced Vienna, Burgtheater, Nov. 14, 1924. Revision of *Über die Brücke*.

25. *Hungerblockade 1919 (Hunger Blockade of 1919)*. Play, 3 acts. Published 1925.

The following two plays (Nos. 26 and 27) are revisions of *Hungerblockade 1919*.

26. *Der Armendoktor (The Doctor of the Poor)*. Play, 3 acts. Written 1925. Published 1927. Produced Vienna, Deutsches Volkstheater, Jan. 26, 1926.

27. *Der Nothelfer (Helper in Need)*. Play. Produced Innsbruck, Exl-Bühne, Aug. 13, 1926.

28. *Passionspiel (Passion Play)*. Religious play. Written 1930. Published 1933. Produced Troppau, Oct. 23, 1933.

29. *Das Lied der Liebe (The Song of Love)*. Comedy, 3 acts. Produced Vienna, Burgtheater, Mar. 24, 1936.

30. *Die Fahne weht (The Flag Waves)*. Play, 3 acts. Published 1937. Produced Graz, Stadttheater, Apr. 7, 1937.

EDITIONS

Gesammelte Werke, ed. by V. Chiavacci, 2 vols., Vienna, 1948; *Gesamtausgabe*, ed. by V. K. Chiavacci, 3 vols., Vienna, 1976.

Faith and Fireside. Published in *The German Classics of the Nineteenth and Twentieth Centuries*, ed. by K. Francke and tr. by E. Mach, vol. 16, New York, 1913–1914.

CRITICISM

R. Sedlmaier, *Karl Schönherr und das österreichische Volksstück*, Würzburg, 1920; H. Kienzl, *Karl Schönherr und seine wichtigsten Bühnenwerke*, Berlin, 1922; M. Lederer, *Karl Schönherr als Dramatiker*, Vienna, 1925; A. Bettelheim, *Karl Schönherr*, Leipzig, 1928; K. Paulin, *Karl Schönherr und seine Dichtungen*, Innsbruck, 1950; T. Schuh, "Kunstlerischen Wert der Mundart in Schonherrs Dramen," in *Germanische Studien*, ed. by J. Erben and E. Thurnher, Innsbruck, 1969.

Schreyvogl, Friedrich   (1899–   )

Austrian essayist, novelist, poet, and dramatist. In his numerous well-constructed plays the central theme is the Christianization of all life. Typical of his religious dramas are *The Mariazell Mother-of-God Play* (*Mariazeller Muttergottesspiel*, 1924), a mystery in the tradition of Max Mell; and *God in the Kremlin* (*Der Gott im Kreml*, 1937), a tragedy about Demetrius, the pretender to the Russian throne in 1605. Austrian history finds dramatic expression in *The Legend of the Hapsburgs* (*Habsburgerlegende*, 1933; originally entitled *Johan Orth*, 1928). Several plays reveal Schreyvogl's long heritage of Austrian *Konversationsstück* ("conversation comedy"): *The Wise Viennese Woman* (*Die kluge Wienerin*, 1941), a popular success set in the Rome of Marcus Aurelius; *Titania* (1943), reviving a Raimundian fairy kingdom; and *The Temptation of Tasso* (*Die Versuchung des Tasso*, 1956), based on an episode in Goethe's life. Schreyvogl is also active as a critic and acts as the chief *Dramaturg* (artistic director) of the Burgtheater of Vienna.

[VIOLET B. KETELS]

Scribe, Eugène   (1791–1861)

French dramatist. Augustin-Eugène Scribe was born in Paris on December 24, 1791. His father, a silk merchant, died in 1798, but the boy continued at school on a scholarship. Scribe studied law until his mother's death in 1811; then, in collaboration with two friends, he began writing theatrical vaudevilles. With *Another Night in the National Guard* (*Encore une nuit de la Garde Nationale*, 1815), his first success, Scribe demonstrated his competence as a businessman by instituting a system for royalties considerably more protective for dramatists than any method hitherto employed in France.

In 1820 he agreed to write plays for Charles-Gaspard Delestre-Poirson, director of the Théâtre du Gymnase, under an arrangement that lasted until 1830. He wrote a large number of plays, alone or in collaboration, and trained and directed actors; these activities earned him

Eugène Scribe. [Walter Hampden Memorial Library at The Players, New York]

the reputation of running a "play factory." Scribe's wide range comprised vaudevilles, comedies of manners, and romantic and historical dramas. He originated a type of light opera in which story is as important as music, and he worked for Boieldieu, Cherubini, and Rossini. His tragic dramas became the books for such famous operas as *Les Huguenots* (1836), by Meyerbeer; *La Juive* (1835), by Halévy; and *Les vêpres siciliennes* (1855), by Verdi. Scribe also devised the ballet-opera, a form previously unknown. By 1860, alone or in collaboration, he had produced more than 300 dramatic works.

He was elected to the Académie Française in 1834 and in 1839 married Mme. Biollay, the widow of a friend. From then until his death he lived lavishly, befriended young dramatists, enjoyed huge success, and won praise for his contributions to French musical drama; but he never received critical acclaim.

Napoleon III appointed Scribe a member of the Paris Municipal Council in 1860. As he approved of the re-

Scene from *Adrienne Lecouvreur,* as performed at the Comédie-Française in 1849. [Bibliothèque de l'Arsenal]

Sarah Bernhardt as Adrienne Lecouvreur. [Theatre Collection, The New York Public Library at Lincoln Center, Astor, Lenox and Tilden Foundations]

gime, he accepted the post and fulfilled its duties faithfully until his death in Paris, from apoplexy, on February 20, 1861.

WORK

From 1811 through 1860, Eugène Scribe, working alone or with such collaborators as Henri Dupin, Gabriel-Jean-Baptiste Legouvé, Germain Delavigne, Xavier Saintine, and Mélesville (Anne-Honoré-Joseph Duveyrier), supplied the Paris stage with hundreds of plays. He is recognized as the architect of the well-made play (*pièce bien faite*), a genre characterized by intricate plotting, methodical development, and tight construction. Through his inventive and prolific output of one-act vaudevilles, full-length vaudeville-comedies, dramas, and libretti for grand and comic operas, Scribe left his mark on French drama by exerting a strong influence upon his contemporaries and successors: Augier, Sardou, Dumas *fils*, Labiche, and Feydeau. No matter what subject he treated—politics, money, marriage, history, or military and social life—Scribe sought always to entertain. A light manner, slight characterization, witty dialogue, and action that unfolds along lines carefully indicated in the opening scenes typify his constructions. Scribe's attitude was frequently satirical, but he never became didactic, preferring to let the action reveal his satire. *See* WELL-MADE PLAY in glossary.

Outstanding among Scribe's vaudevilles are *The Truthful Liar* (*Le menteur véridique*, 1823), in which a mistress uses her maid's assistance to arrange her marriage; *Another Night in the National Guard* (1815), a satirical treatment of the military; and *The Bear and the Pasha* (*L'ours et le pacha*, 1820), a farce poking fun at royal whimsies and the Parisian interest in performing animals.

Marriage for Money (*Le mariage d'argent*, 1827), a five-act comedy of manners, concerns three couples whose love interests revolve around money; *The Clique* (*La camaraderie*, 1837) is a social satire of political intrigue; and

Bertrand and Raton (*Bertrand et Raton*, 1833), a semihistorical play, shows the ironical course of a palace revolution. In *The Glass of Water* (*Le verre d'eau*, 1840) Scribe shows how a trivial incident sets off a chain of significant historical events. Scribe's only tragedy is *Adrienne Lecouvreur* (1849), based on the life of the French actress whose mysterious death in 1730 became a *cause célèbre*.

Among other noteworthy plays are *The Queen's Gambit* (*Bataille de dames*, 1851) and *The Savoy Frontier* (*La frontière de Savoie*, 1834), comedies in which women use unwanted admirers to protect the men they love; *The Marriage of Convenience* (*Le mariage de raison*, 1826); *Slander* (*La calomnie*, 1840), a comedy showing how scandal mongering affects a young engaged couple; *A Chain* (*Une chaîne*, 1841), a comedy in which a young musician drops his mistress, an older woman who had helped his career, to marry a young cousin; and *Puffery* (*Le puff*, 1848), a satire about a bluestocking and a would-be author who gain their goals through fraud.

In spite of his immense popularity, Scribe's reputation began to decline even during his lifetime, and afterward there was a tendency to hold him responsible for the shortcomings of the dramatists who followed him. Though he was an excellent craftsman with an unerring ability to meet the demands of his audience, the middle classes who dominated the postrevolution period, his plays are almost completely lacking in psychological depth or character development, and their language is undistinguished. They are seldom seen on the stage now, and aside from the various opera libretti, they have survived in textbooks merely as interesting examples of skillful dramatic construction.

The Bear and the Pasha (*L'ours et le pacha*, 1820). Farcical vaudeville, written in collaboration with Saintine, which takes place in a mythical Eastern kingdom. Fearing the wrath of the Pasha, the court conceals the news that his favorite white bear has died. La Gingeole and Tristapatte, two animal trainers whose animals have died, arrive, and Tristapatte, attired in a black bear suit, entertains the Pasha by dancing and playing the harp. Delighted, the Pasha asks La Gingeole to give similar training to his beloved white bear. At this point it seems that the truth must be told, until Gingeole thinks of disguising the Grand Vizier in the fur of the deceased white bear. When black impostor meets white impostor, however, both are terrified, each believing the other to be an authentic bear. They both flee, their bears' heads come off, and they realize the situation and confer. Interrupted by the Pasha, each hastily grabs a head, the wrong one, and puts it on. Astonished by the resulting color combinations and suspicious of all the goings-on, the Pasha orders that both bears' heads be cut off. The imposters then reveal themselves, and the Pasha, less cruel than his reputation, pardons them.

The Truthful Liar (*Le menteur véridique*, 1823). Comedy-vaudeville in one act and seventeen scenes. A maid, Rose, is to receive a dowry on the day that her mistress, Lucie marries Édouard. Édouard, however, is an invet-

Scene from a Russian production of *Adrienne Lecouvreur*. Moscow, Kamerny Theatre, 1919. [Theatre Collection, The New York Public Library at Lincoln Center, Astor, Lenox and Tilden Foundations]

erate liar, and Lucie's father opposes her marriage to such a man. With the help of her fiancé, a valet named Lolive, Rose assists in making all Édouard's lies appear to be true. After a series of incidents that completely baffle Édouard, both couples are happily united.

Marriage for Money (*Le mariage d'argent*, 1827). Exploration from six points of view, three feminine and three masculine, of the idea that a marriage for money gives one everything but happiness. The banker Dorbeval believes he owns his wife because she was poor when they married. She, in turn, hates him and is miserable, for the novelty of possessing money has worn off. Poligini thinks that money is the most important thing in life; so he agrees to marry Hermance, a rich woman so empty-headed that she can never know what love is. He thus loses the love of a woman he really cares for, and she finds happiness with Olivier, an artist who can love for love's sake alone.

Bertrand and Raton, or The Art of Conspiracy (*Bertrand et Raton, ou L'art de conspirer*, 1833). Political comedy loosely based on the Danish palace conspiracy of 1772 against Count Johann von Struensee, a German adventurer and physician, who as Chief Minister to the mentally incompetent King Christian VII virtually controlled the government. Count Bertrand de Rantzeau, a diplomat who plots the revolt, creates a hero for the common people in order to ally them to his cause. He instigates Raton de Burkenstaff, a pretentious silk merchant, who is furious at having been turned away from the palace without an audience after he had been summoned to show his wares, to make disparaging remarks about Queen Caroline Matilda. When Raton's comments reach higher quarters, soldiers are sent to arrest him, but Jean, his clerk, so incites the populace that the soldiers are forced to back down. An involved series of events complicates the plot, but Bertrand finally succeeds in toppling Struensee. The love of Eric, Raton's son, for Christine, daughter of the Minister of War, provides a romantic subplot.

The Clique, or the Helping Hand (*La camaraderie, ou La courte échelle*, 1837). Satire on political maneuvering and the influence of coteries in promoting candidates for parliamentary election. Césarine de Miremont, the redoubtable wife of a doddering senator, is the leader of a mutual advancement society composed of mediocre persons who manufacture reciprocal success by vaunting each other's nonexistent abilities. A worthy young lawyer, Edmond de Varennes, seeks election as deputy to the National Assembly but is opposed by Césarine and her cohorts because he once failed to requite her affections. Edmond is in love with Césarine's stepdaughter Agathe, who decides to help him by enlisting the aid of her friend Zoé de Montlucar, whose husband belongs to the clique. Zoé cozens Césarine into believing that Edmond loves her, causing the clique to align itself behind him and secure his election. By the time Césarine discovers the truth, it is too late. The manipulators have been manipulated.

The Glass of Water, or Causes and Effects (*Le verre d'eau, ou Les effets et les causes*, 1840). Comedy of intrigue based on the controversy between Viscount Bolingbroke and the Duke of Marlborough over England's policy in the War of the Spanish Succession. To help her husband, the Duchess of Marlborough prevents the bearer of a private treaty from Louis XIV from reaching Queen Anne. Bolingbroke, knowing that both the Duchess and the Queen are secretly enamored of Cadet Masham (who himself is in love with Abigail, the Queen's attendant), plays on the mutual jealousy of the two women. Informed that the Queen's signal for a rendezvous with Masham will be her request for a glass of water, the Duchess becomes so agitated that she upsets the glass over the Queen's dress. This seemingly trivial incident causes the Duchess to request her own dismissal and leaves the way open for Bolingbroke's maneuvering to get the treaty signed and bring peace to Europe. Masham is sent to the Queen's boudoir with the treaty, and he obtains her signature. When he is discovered there by the Duchess, scandal is avoided by Abigail's false declaration that he had come there to meet her. In gratitude the Queen "commands" Masham to marry Abigail.

Adrienne Lecouvreur (1849). Drama in which Scribe and Legouvé fictionalized the circumstances surrounding the death of Adrienne Lecouvreur, a famous actress who in 1730 apparently committed suicide because her lover, Maurice de Saxe, had deserted her for the Princess de Bouillon. The play begins with the Princess discovering that Maurice has a new mistress and determining to learn her identity. In order to be free to pursue Maurice, she decides to encourage her husband, the Prince, in his affair with La Duclos, another actress and Adrienne's rival. Through La Duclos the Princess arranges a rendezvous with Maurice, but the Prince, Adrienne, and others arrive and surprise them. Adrienne helps Maurice's unidentified companion escape, although she realizes that the woman is Maurice's mistress. However, neither woman yet knows the other's identity.

At a reception the Princess overhears Maurice talking to Adrienne, and she realizes that the actress is her rival. The Princess insults Adrienne, who takes revenge by reciting lines from *Phèdre* that affront the Princess. Shortly thereafter a bouquet that Adrienne had given to Maurice falls into the Princess' hands. She treats it with a poisonous powder and returns it to the actress. Assuming that Maurice has rejected the flowers, Adrienne inhales them deeply and then throws them into the fire. The poison takes immediate effect, and Maurice, arriving to propose marriage, is too late.

[JOSEPH E. GARREAU]

PLAYS

Unless otherwise noted, the plays were first performed in Paris.
Comedy-Vaudevilles

1. (With Germain Delavigne). *Les dervis* (*The Dervishes*). Vaudeville, 1 act. Produced Théâtre du Vaudeville, Sept. 2, 1811.

2. (With Delavigne). *L'auberge, ou Les brigands sans le savoir* (*The Tavern, or The Unwitting Robbers*). Vaudeville, 1 act. Produced Théâtre du Vaudeville, May 19, 1812.

3. (With Delavigne). *Thibaut, Comte de Champagne* (*Thibaut, Count of Champagne*). Vaudeville, 1 act. Produced Théâtre du Vaudeville, Sept. 27, 1812.

4. (With Henri Dupin and Delavigne). *Le bachelier de Salamanque* (*The Squire of Salamanca*). Comedy, 1 act. Produced Théâtre des Variétés, Jan. 18, 1815.

5. (With Charles-Gaspard Delestre-Poirson). *La mort et le bûcheron (Death and the Woodcutter)*. Vaudeville, 1 act. Produced Théâtre du Vaudeville, Nov. 4, 1815.

6. (With Delestre-Poirson). *Encore une nuit de la Garde Nationale, ou Le poste de la barrière (Another Night in the National Guard, or The Guard Post at the City Gate)*. Vaudeville, 1 act. Produced Théâtre de la Porte-Saint-Martin, Dec. 15, 1815.

7. (With Delestre-Poirson). *Flore et Zéphyre (Flora and Zephyr)*. Vaudeville, 1 act. Produced Théâtre du Vaudeville, Feb. 8, 1816.

8. (With Dupin). *Farinelli, ou La pièce de circonstance (Farinelli, or The Improvised Play)*. Vaudeville, 1 act. Produced Théâtre du Vaudeville, July 25, 1816.

9. (With Dupin). *Gusman d'Alfarach*. Comedy-vaudeville, 2 acts. Produced Théâtre du Vaudeville, Oct. 22, 1816.

10. (With Delestre-Poirson and Dupin). *Les montagnes russes, ou Le temple à la mode (The Roller Coaster, or The Fashionable Temple)*. Vaudeville, 1 act. Produced Théâtre du Vaudeville, Oct. 31, 1816.

11. (With Dupin). *La jarretière de la mariée (The Bride's Garter)*. Comedy-vaudeville, 1 act. Produced Théâtre des Variétés, Nov. 12, 1816.

12. (With Delestre-Poirson). *Le Comte Ory, anecdote du XIe siècle (Count Ory: An Eleventh-century Anecdote)*. Vaudeville, 1 act. Produced Théâtre du Vaudeville, Dec. 16, 1816.

13. (With Delestre-Poirson). *Le nouveau Pourceaugnac (The New Pourceaugnac)*. Comedy-vaudeville, 1 act. Produced Théâtre du Vaudeville, Feb. 18, 1817.

14. (With Jean-Gilbert Ymbert and Antoine-François Varner). *Le solliciteur, ou L'art d'obtenir des places (The Applicant, or The Art of Obtaining Employment)*. Comedy, 1 act. Produced Théâtre des Variétés, Apr. 17, 1817.

15. (With Dupin and Delestre-Poirson). *Wallace, ou La barrière Montparnasse (Wallace, or The Montparnasse Gate)*. Vaudeville, 1 act. Produced Théâtre du Vaudeville, May 8, 1817.

16. (With Charles Moreau). *Les deux précepteurs, ou L'asinus asinum (The Two Tutors, or Asinus Asinum)*. Play. Produced Théâtre des Variétés, June 19, 1817.

17. (With Dupin). *Le combat des montagnes, ou La folie-Beaujon (The Mountain Fight, or the Beaujon Madness)*. Folie-vaudeville, 1 act. Produced Théâtre des Variétés, July 12, 1817.

18. (With Dupin). *Le Café des Variétés (The Variety Café)*. Play. Produced Théâtre des Variétés, Aug. 5, 1817.

19. (With Marc-Antoine Désaugiers and Delestre-Poirson). *Tous les vaudevilles, ou Chacun chez soi (Every Trick in the Bag, or Each Man for Himself)*. Vaudeville, 1 act. Produced Théâtre du Vaudeville, Sept. 18, 1817.

20. (With Delestre-Poirson and Mélesville). *Le petit dragon (The Little Dragon)*. Comedy-vaudeville, 2 acts. Produced Théâtre du Vaudeville, Sept. 18, 1817.

21. (With Varner). *Les comices d'Athènes, ou Les femmes agricoles (The Athenian Comitia, or The Farm Women)*. Comedy-vaudeville, 1 act. Produced Théâtre du Vaudeville, Nov. 7, 1817.

22. (With Dupin). *Les nouvelles Danaïdes (The New Danaides)*. Vaudeville, 1 act. Produced Théâtre des Variétés, Dec. 3, 1817.

23. (With Dupin). *La fête du mari, ou Dissimulons (The Husband's Party, or Let's Pretend)*. Comedy-vaudeville, 1 act. Produced Théâtre de la Gaîté, Dec. 24, 1817.

24. (With Dupin). *Chactas et Atala (Chactas and Atala)*. Drama, 4 acts. Produced Théâtre des Variétés, Mar. 9, 1818.

25. (With Delestre-Poirson and Mélesville). *Les dehors trompeurs, ou Boissy chez lui (Deceitful Appearances, or Boissy at Home)*. Comedy-vaudeville, 1 act. Produced Théâtre des Variétés, Apr. 6, 1818.

26. (With Delestre-Poirson). *Une visite à Bedlam (A Visit to Bedlam)*. Comedy-vaudeville, 1 act. Produced Théâtre du Vaudeville, Apr. 23, 1818.

27. (With Dupin and Varner). *Les vélocipèdes, ou La poste aux chevaux (The Velocipedes, or The Relay Station)*. Vaudeville, 1 act. Produced Théâtre des Variétés, May 2, 1818.

28. (With Delestre-Poirson and Mélesville). *La volière de Frère Philippe (Brother Philip's Birdcage)*. Comedy-vaudeville, 1 act. Produced Théâtre du Vaudeville, June 15, 1818.

29. (With Dupin). *Le nouveau Nicaise (The New Nicasius)*. Comedy-vaudeville, 1 act. Produced Théâtre des Variétés, Oct. 15, 1818.

30. (With Dupin and Nicolas Brazier). *L'Hôtel des Quatre-Nations (The Four Nations Hotel)*. Vaudeville, 1 act. Produced Théâtre des Variétés, Nov. 7, 1818.

31. *Le fou de Péronne (The Madman of Péronne)*. Comedy, 1 act. Produced Théâtre du Vaudeville, Jan. 18, 1819.

32. (With Varner). *Les deux maris (The Two Husbands)*. Comedy-vaudeville, 1 act. Produced Théâtre des Variétés, Feb. 3, 1819.

33. (With Delestre-Poirson and Alphonse-Théodore Cerfbeer). *Le mystificateur (The Mystifier)*. Comedy-vaudeville, 1 act. Produced Théâtre du Vaudeville, Feb. 22, 1819.

34. (With Constant Ménissier). *Caroline*. Comedy-vaudeville; 1 act. Produced Théâtre du Vaudeville, Mar. 15, 1819.

35. (With Dupin and Varner). *Les bains à la papa (The Baths Papa's Way)*. Vaudeville, 1 act. Produced Théâtre du Vaudeville, Oct. 9, 1819.

36. (With Mélesville). *Les vêpres siciliennes (The Sicilian Vespers)*. Vaudeville, 1 act. Produced Théâtre du Vaudeville, Nov. 17, 1819.

37. *La somnambule (The Sleepwalker)*. Comedy-vaudeville, 2 acts. Produced Théâtre du Vaudeville, Dec. 6, 1819.

38. (With Dupin and Mélesville). *L'ennui, ou Le Comte Derfort (Boredom, or Count Derfort)*. Comedy-vaudeville, 2 acts. Produced Théâtre des Variétés, Feb. 2, 1820.

39. (With Xavier Saintine). *L'ours et le pacha (The Bear and the Pasha)*. Vaudeville, 1 act. Produced Théâtre des Variétés, Feb. 10, 1820.

40. (With Delestre-Poirson). *Le spleen (Spleen)*. Comedy, 1 act. Produced Théâtre des Variétés, Mar. 20, 1820.

41. (With Dupin and Pierre Carmouche). *Marie Jobard*. Burlesque, 6 acts. Produced Théâtre des Variétés, Apr. 11, 1820.

42. (With Mélesville and Delestre-Poirson). *Le chat botté (Puss in Boots)*. Fantasy-vaudeville, 2 acts. Produced Théâtre du Vaudeville, Apr. 19, 1820.

43. (With Varner and Ymbert). *L'homme automate (The Automated Man)*. Folie-parade. Produced Théâtre des Variétés, May 10, 1820.

44. *Le vampire (The Vampire)*. Comedy-vaudeville, 1 act. Produced Théâtre du Vaudeville, June 15, 1820.

45. (With Dupin). *L'éclipse totale (The Total Eclipse)*. Tableau-vaudeville, 1 act. Produced Théâtre des Variétés, Sept. 6, 1820.

46. (With Mélesville and Saintine). *Le témoin (The Witness)*. Comedy-vaudeville, 1 act. Produced Théâtre des Variétés, Sept. 28, 1820.

47. (With Mélesville and Saintine). *Le déluge, ou Les petits acteurs (The Flood, or The Little Actors)*. Vaudeville, 1 act. Produced Théâtre des Variétés, Oct. 12, 1820.

48. (With Dupin). *L'homme noir (The Black Man)*. Vaudeville, 1 act. Produced Théâtre du Vaudeville, Nov. 18, 1820.

49. (With Dupin). *L'hôtel des bains (The Beach Hotel)*. Tableau-vaudeville, 1 act. Produced Théâtre des Variétés, Nov. 22, 1820.

50. (With Saintine and Frédéric de Courcy). *Le beau Narcisse (Handsome Narcissus)*. Vaudeville, 1 act. Produced Théâtre de la Porte-Saint-Martin, Dec. 9, 1820.

51. (With Moreau and Mélesville). *Le Boulevard Bonne-Nouvelle*. Vaudeville, 1 act. Produced Théâtre du Gymnase, Dec. 28, 1820.

52. (With Mélesville). *L'amour platonique (Platonic Love)*. Comedy-vaudeville. Produced Théâtre du Gymnase, Jan. 18, 1821.

53. (With Mélesville). *Le secrétaire et le cuisinier (The Secretary and the Cook)*. Comedy-vaudeville, 1 act. Produced Théâtre du Gymnase, Jan. 18, 1821.

54. (With Mélesville). *Frontin mari-garçon (Frontin Bachelor-Husband)*. Comedy-vaudeville, 1 act. Produced Théâtre du Vaudeville, Jan. 18, 1821.

55. (With Delavigne). *Le colonel (The Colonel)*. Comedy-vaudeville, 1 act. Produced Théâtre du Gymnase, Jan. 29, 1821.

56. (With Dupin). *L'intérieur de l'étude, ou Le procureur et l'avoué (Inside the Office, or The Procurator and the Solicitor)*. Comedy-vaudeville, 1 act. Produced Théâtre des Variétés, Feb. 1, 1821.

57. (With Brulay). *Le gastronome sans argent (The Gourmet Without Money)*. Vaudeville, 1 act. Produced Théâtre du Gymnase, Mar. 10, 1821.

58. (With Dupin). *Le ménage de garçon (The Bachelor's Household)*. Comedy-vaudeville, 1 act. Produced Théâtre du Gymnase, Apr. 27, 1821.

59. (With Dupin and Mélesville). *La campagne (The Country)*. Comedy-vaudeville, 1 act. Produced Théâtre des Variétés, May 7, 1821.

60. (With Mélesville). *La petite soeur (The Little Sister)*. Comedy-vaudeville, 1 act. Produced Théâtre du Gymnase, June 6, 1821.

61. (With Delavigne). *Le mariage enfantin (The Childhood Marriage)*. Comedy-vaudeville, 1 act. Produced Théâtre du Gymnase, Aug. 16, 1821.

62. (With Mélesville and Vaudière). *L'amant bossu (The Hunchbacked Lover)*. Comedy-vaudeville, 1 act. Produced Théâtre du Gymnase, Oct. 22, 1821.

63. (With Adrien Perlet). *L'artiste (The Artist)*. Comedy-vaudeville, 1 act. Produced Théâtre du Gymnase, Nov. 23, 1821.

64. (With Mélesville). *Les petites misères de la vie humaine (The Little Miseries of Human Life)*. Comedy-vaudeville, 1 act. Produced Théâtre du Gymnase, Dec. 3, 1821.

65. (With Dupin). *Michel et Christine (Michael and Christine)*. Comedy-vaudeville, 1 act. Produced Théâtre du Gymnase, Dec. 3, 1821.

66. (With Moreau). *Philibert marié (Philibert Married)*. Comedy-vaudeville, 1 act. Produced Théâtre du Gymnase, Dec. 26, 1821.

67. (With Mélesville). *Le plaisant de société (Society's Clown)*. Folie-vaudeville, 1 act. Produced Théâtre des Variétés, Feb. 18, 1822.

68. (With Dupin and De Courcy). *La demoiselle et la dame, ou Avant et après (The Young Girl and the Lady, or Before and After)*. Comedy-vaudeville, 1 act. Produced Théâtre du Gymnase, Mar. 11, 1822.

69. (With Mélesville). *La petite folle (The Little Madwoman)*. Drama, 1 act. Produced Théâtre du Gymnase, May 6, 1822.

70. (With Delavigne). *Le vieux garçon et la petite fille (The Old Bachelor and the Little Girl)*. Comedy-vaudeville, 1 act. Produced Théâtre du Gymnase, May 24, 1822.

71. (With Delavigne). *Les nouveaux jeux de l'amour et du hasard (The New Games of Love and Chance)*. Comedy-vaudeville, 1 act. Produced Théâtre du Gymnase, June 21, 1822.

72. (With De Courcy and Saintine). *Les eaux du Mont-Dore (The Waters of Mont-Dore)*. Vaudeville, 1 act. Produced Théâtre du Gymnase, July 25, 1822.

73. (With Mélesville). *La veuve du Malabar (The Widow of Malabar)*. Vaudeville, 1 act. Produced Théâtre du Gymnase, Aug. 19, 1822.

74. (With Dupin). *La nouvelle Clary, ou Louise et Georgette (The New Clary, or Louise and Georgette)*. Comedy-vaudeville, 1 act. Produced Théâtre du Gymnase, Nov. 11, 1822.

75. (With Mélesville and Georges-Henri Saint-Georges). *L'écarté, ou Un coin du salon (Écarté, or A Corner of the Drawing Room)*. Tableau-vaudeville, 1 act. Produced Théâtre du Gymnase, Nov. 14, 1822.

76. (With Mélesville). *Le bon papa, ou La proposition de mariage (The Good Papa, or The Marriage Proposal)*. Comedy-vaudeville, 1 act. Produced Théâtre du Gymnase, Dec. 2, 1822.

77. (With Édouard-Joseph Mazères). *La loge du portier (The Doorkeeper's Apartment)*. Tableau-vaudeville, 1 act. Produced Théâtre du Gymnase, Jan. 14, 1823.

78. (With Ymbert and Varner). *L'intérieur d'un bureau, ou La chanson (Inside an Office, or The Song)*. Comedy-vaudeville, 1 act. Produced Théâtre du Gymnase, Feb. 25, 1823.

79. (With Carmouche). *Trilby, ou Le lutin d'Argail (Trilby, or The Goblin of Argail)*. Vaudeville, 1 act. Produced Théâtre du Gymnase, Mar. 13, 1823.

80. (With Dupin and Mélesville). *Le plan de campagne (The Campaign Plan)*. Comedy-vaudeville, 1 act. Produced Théâtre du Gymnase, Apr. 14, 1823.

81. (With Mélesville). *Le menteur véridique (The Truthful Liar)*. Comedy-vaudeville, 1 act. Produced Théâtre du Gymnase, Apr. 24, 1823.

82. (With Dupin and Théophile Dumersan). *La pension bourgeoise (The Middle-class Boardinghouse)*. Comedy-vaudeville, 1 act. Produced Théâtre du Gymnase, May 27, 1823.

83. *La maîtresse au logis (The Mistress of the House)*. Comedy-vaudeville, 1 act. Produced Théâtre du Gymnase, June 9, 1823.

84. (With Francis-Cornu and Brazier). *Partie et revanche (Game and Return Match)*. Comedy-vaudeville, 1 act. Produced Théâtre du Gymnase, June 16, 1823.

85. (With Delavigne). *L'avare en goguettes (Miser on a Spree)*. Comedy-vaudeville, 1 act. Produced Théâtre du Gymnase, July 12, 1823.

86. (With Dupin). *Les grisettes (The Lively Working Girls)*. Vaudeville, 1 act. Produced Théâtre du Gymnase, July 12, 1823.

87. (With Mazères). *La vérité dans le vin (The Truth in the Wine)*. Comedy-vaudeville, 1 act. Produced Théâtre du Gymnase, Oct. 10, 1823.

88. (With Dupin). *Le retour, ou La suite de Michel et Christine (Return, or The Sequel to Michael and Christine)*. Comedy-vaudeville, 1 act. Produced Théâtre du Gymnase, Oct. 17, 1823.

89. (With Louis-Emmanuel Dupaty). *Un dernier jour de fortune (One Last Day of Fortune)*. Comedy-vaudeville, 1 act. Produced Théâtre du Gymnase, Nov. 11, 1823.

90. (With Mazères). *Rossini à Paris, ou Le grand dîner (Rossini in Paris, or The Banquet)*. Vaudeville, 1 act. Produced Théâtre du Gymnase, Nov. 29, 1823.

91. (With Delavigne). *L'héritière (The Heiress)*. Comedy-vaudeville, 1 act. Produced Théâtre du Gymnase, Dec. 20, 1823.

92. (With Mazères). *Le coiffeur et le perruquier (The Hairdresser and the Wigmaker)*. Vaudeville, 1 act. Produced Théâtre du Gymnase, Jan. 15, 1824.

93. (With Carmouche). *Le fondé de pouvoirs (The Agent)*. Vaudeville, 1 act. Produced Théâtre du Gymnase, Feb. 18, 1824.

94. (With Dupin and Varner). *La mansarde des artistes (The Artists' Garret)*. Comedy-vaudeville, 1 act. Produced Théâtre du Gymnase, Apr. 2, 1824.

95. *Les trois genres (The Three Types)*. Prologue, 1 act. Produced Théâtre de l'Odéon, Apr. 27, 1824.

96. (With Saintine and Carmouche). *Le Leicester du Faubourg, ou L'amour et l'ambition (Suburban Leicester, or Love and Ambition)*. Vaudeville, 1 act. Produced Théâtre du Gymnase, May 1, 1824.

97. (With Justin Gensoul and De Courcy). *Le baiser au porteur (The Kiss for the Porter)*. Comedy-vaudeville, 1 act. Produced Théâtre du Gymnase, June 9, 1824.

98. (With Mélesville). *Le dîner sur l'herbe (The Picnic Dinner)*. Tableau-vaudeville, 1 act. Produced Théâtre du Gymnase, July 2, 1824.

99. (With Mélesville). *Les adieux au comptoir (Good-bye to the Cashier's Desk)*. Comedy-vaudeville, 1 act. Produced Théâtre du Gymnase, Aug. 9, 1824.

100. (With Dupin and Varner). *Le château de la poularde (The Castle of the Fatted Fowl)*. Comedy-vaudeville, 1 act. Produced Théâtre de Madame, Oct. 4, 1824.

101. (With Dupin). *Le bal champêtre, ou Les grisettes à la campagne (The Rustic Ball, or The Young Working Girls in the Country)*. Tableau-vaudeville, 1 act. Produced Théâtre de Madame, Oct. 21, 1824.

102. (With Mélesville). *Coraly, ou La soeur et le frère (Coralee, or The Sister and the Brother)*. Comedy-vaudeville, 1 act. Produced Théâtre de Madame, Nov. 19, 1824.

103. (With Mélesville). *Monsieur Tardif (Mister Backward)*. Comedy-vaudeville, 1 act. Produced Théâtre de Madame, Dec. 1, 1824.

104. *La haine d'une femme, ou Le jeune homme à marier (A Woman's Hatred, or The Eligible Young Man)*. Comedy-vaudeville, 1 act. Produced Théâtre de Madame, Dec. 14, 1824.

105. (With Mazères). *Vatel, ou Le petit-fils d'un grand homme (Vatel, or The Grandson of a Great Man)*. Comedy-vaudeville, 1 act. Produced Théâtre de Madame, Jan. 18, 1825.

106. (With Mazères). *La quarantaine (The Forty)*. Comedy-vaudeville, 1 act. Produced Théâtre de Madame, Feb. 3, 1824.

107. (With Varner). *Le plus beau jour de la vie (The Most Beautiful Day in Life)*. Comedy-vaudeville, 2 acts. Produced Théâtre de Madame, Feb. 22, 1825.

108. (With Varner). *La charge à payer, ou La mère intrigante (The Debt to Pay, or The Intriguing Mother)*. Comedy-vaudeville, 1 act. Produced Théâtre de Madame, Apr. 13, 1825.

109. (With Dupin). *Les inséparables (The Inseparables)*. Comedy-vaudeville, 1 act. Produced Théâtre de Madame, May 2, 1825.

110. (With Mazères). *Le charlatanisme (Quackery)*. Comedy-vaudeville, 1 act. Produced May 10, 1825.

111. (With Alexandre). *Les empiriques d'autrefois (Bygone Empirics)*. Comedy-vaudeville, 1 act. Produced Théâtre de Madame, June 11, 1825.

112. *Les premières amours, ou Les souvenirs d'enfance (First Loves, or Childhood Memories)*. Comedy-vaudeville, 1 act. Produced Théâtre de Madame, Nov. 12, 1825.

113. (With Mélesville). *Le médecin des dames (The Ladies' Doctor)*. Comedy-vaudeville, 1 act. Produced Théâtre de Madame, Dec. 17, 1825.

114. (With Mélesville). *Le confident (The Confidant)*. Comedy-vaudeville, 1 act. Produced Théâtre de Madame, Jan. 5, 1826.

115. (With Mélesville). *La demoiselle à marier, ou La première entrevue (The Eligible Young Lady, or The First Interview)*. Comedy-vaudeville, 1 act. Produced Jan. 18, 1826.

116. (With Moreau and A. M. Lafortelle). *Le testament de Polichinelle (Punchinello's Will)*. Comedy-vaudeville, 1 act. Produced Théâtre de Madame, Feb. 17, 1826.

117. (With Varner and Dupin). *Les manteaux (The Overcoats)*. Comedy-vaudeville, 2 acts. Produced Théâtre de Madame, Feb. 20, 1826.

118. (With Jean-François-Alfred Bayard). *La belle-mère (The Mother-in-law)*. Comedy-vaudeville, 1 act. Produced Théâtre de Madame, Mar. 14, 1826.

119. (With Mazères). *L'oncle d'Amérique (The Uncle from America)*. Comedy-vaudeville, 1 act. Produced Théâtre de Madame, Mar. 14, 1826.

120. (With Mélesville and Carmouche). *La lune de miel (The Honeymoon)*. Comedy-vaudeville, 2 acts. Produced Théâtre de Madame, Mar. 31, 1826.

121. (With De Courcy). *Simple histoire (The Unvarnished Story)*. Comedy-vaudeville, 1 act. Produced Théâtre de Madame, May 26, 1826.

122. (With Mélesville). *L'ambassadeur (The Ambassador)*. Comedy-vaudeville, 1 act. Produced Théâtre de Madame, Oct. 10, 1826.

123. (With Varner). *Le mariage de raison (The Marriage of Convenience)*. Comedy-vaudeville, 2 acts. Produced Théâtre de Madame, Oct. 10, 1826.

124. (With Mélesville). *La chatte métamorphosée en femme (The Cat Changed into a Woman)*. Folie-vaudeville, 1 act. Produced Théâtre de Madame, Mar. 3, 1827.

125. (With Saintine). *Les élèves du conservatoire (The Conservatory Students)*. Tableau-vaudeville, 1 act. Produced Théâtre de Madame, Mar. 28, 1827.

126. (With Delavigne). *Le diplomate (The Diplomat)*. Comedy-vaudeville, 2 acts. Produced Théâtre de Madame, Oct. 23, 1827.

127. (With Joseph-Philippe Lockroy and Jules Chabot de Bouin). *La marraine (The Godmother)*. Comedy-vaudeville, 1 act. Produced Théâtre de Madame, Nov. 27, 1827.

128. (With Mélesville). *Le mal du pays, ou La batelière de Brienz (Homesickness, or The Boatwoman of Brienz)*. Tableau-vaudeville, 1 act. Produced Théâtre de Madame, Dec. 28, 1827.

129. (With Delestre-Poirson and Dupin). *Le Prince Charmant, ou Les contes de fée (Prince Charming, or The Fairy Tales)*. Folie-vaudeville, 1 act. Produced Théâtre de Madame, Feb. 14, 1828.

130. (With Paul Duport). *Le voyage dans l'appartement, ou L'influence des localités (The Journey in the Apartment, or The Influence of Localities)*. Comedy-vaudeville, 5 tableaux. Produced Théâtre des Variétés, Jan. 18, 1833.

131. *Les malheurs d'un amant heureux (The Misfortunes of a Happy Lover)*. Comedy-vaudeville, 2 acts. Produced Théâtre du Gymnase, Jan. 29, 1833.

132. (With Bayard). *Le gardien (The Guardian)*. Produced Théâtre du Gymnase, Mar. 11, 1833. Based on George Sand's novel *Indiana* (1832).

133. (With Mélesville). *Le moulin de Javelle (The Mill of Javelle)*. Com-

edy-vaudeville, 2 acts. Produced Théâtre du Gymnase, July 8, 1833.

134. (With Mélesville and Carmouche). *Jean de Vert (Jean of the Green)*. Fairy play, 5 tableaux. Produced Théâtre du Vaudeville, Aug. 19, 1833.

135. (With Duport). *Un trait de Paul I, ou Le czar et la vivandière (An Anecdote about Paul I, or The Czar and the Canteen Woman)*. Comedy-vaudeville, 1 act. Produced Théâtre du Gymnase, Sept. 12, 1833.

136. (With Duport). *La Dugazon, ou Le choix d'une maîtresse (La Dugazon, or The Choice of a Mistress)*. Comedy-vaudeville, 1 act. Produced Théâtre du Gymnase, Oct. 30, 1833.

137. *Le lorgnon (The Lorgnette)*. Comedy-vaudeville, 1 act. Produced Théâtre du Gymnase, Dec. 21, 1833.

138. (With Francis-Cornu). *La chanoinesse (The Canoness)*. Comedy-vaudeville, 1 act. Produced Théâtre du Gymnase, Dec. 21, 1833.

139. (With De touremont and Alexis Decomberousse). *Salvoisy, ou L'amoureux de la reine (Salvoisy, or The Queen's Lover)*. Comedy-vaudeville, 2 acts. Produced Théâtre du Gymnase, Apr. 18, 1834.

140. (With Bayard). *La frontière de Savoie (The Savoy Frontier)*. Comedy-vaudeville, 1 act. Produced Théâtre du Gymnase, Aug. 20, 1834.

141. *Estelle, ou Le père et la fille (Estelle, or Father and Daughter)*. Comedy-vaudeville, 1 act. Produced Théâtre du Gymnase, Nov. 7, 1834.

142. *Être aîmé, ou Mourir (To Be Loved, or To Die)*. Comedy-vaudeville, 1 act. Produced Théâtre du Gymnase, Mar. 10, 1835.

143. *Une Chaumière et son coeur (Love in a Cottage)*. Comedy-vaudeville, 2 acts. Produced Théâtre du Gymnase, May 12, 1835.

144. (With Varner). *La pensionnaire mariée (The Married Boarder)*. Comedy-vaudeville, 1 act. Produced Théâtre du Gymnase, Nov. 3, 1835.

145. (With Mélesville). *Valentine*. Drama, 2 acts. Produced Théâtre du Gymnase, Jan. 4, 1836.

146. *Chut! (Shhh!)*. Comedy-vaudeville, 2 acts. Produced Théâtre du Gymnase, Mar. 26, 1836.

147. (With Bayard). *Sir Hugues de Guilfort*. Comedy-vaudeville, 2 acts. Produced Théâtre du Gymnase, Oct. 3, 1836.

148. (With Decomberousse). *Avis aux coquettes, ou L'amant singulier (Advice to Coquettes, or The Peculiar Lover)*. Comedy-vaudeville, 2 acts. Produced Théâtre du Gymnase, Oct. 29, 1836.

149. (With Dupin). *Le fils d'un agent de change (The Son of a Stockbroker)*. Comedy-vaudeville, 1 act. Produced Théâtre des Variétés, Nov. 30, 1836.

150. (With Alexis-Félix Arvers). *Les dames patronesses, ou À quelquechose malheur est bon (The Patronesses, or Misfortune Is Good for Something)*. Proverb, 1 act. Produced Théâtre du Gymnase, Feb. 14, 1837.

151. (With Varner). *César, ou Le chien du château (Caesar, or The Castle Dog)*. Comedy-vaudeville, 2 acts. Produced Théâtre du Gymnase, Mar. 4, 1837.

152. (With Mélesville). *L'étudiant et la grande dame (The Student and the Great Lady)*. Comedy-vaudeville, 2 acts. Produced Théâtre des Variétés, Mar. 30, 1837.

153. (With Varner). *Le bout de l'an, ou Les deux cérémonies (The Year's-end Mass, or The Two Ceremonies)*. Comedy-vaudeville, 1 act. Produced Théâtre du Palais-Royal, June 2, 1837.

154. (With Louis-Émile Vanderburch). *Clermont, ou Une femme d'artiste (Clermont, or An Artist's Wife)*. Comedy-vaudeville, 2 acts. Produced Théâtre du Gymnase, Mar. 30, 1838.

155. *Cicily, ou Le lion amoureux (Cicily, or The Lion in Love)*. Comedy-vaudeville, 2 acts. Produced Théâtre du Gymnase, Dec. 8, 1840.

156. (With Dupin). *Le veau d'or (The Golden Calf)*. Comedy, 1 act. Produced Théâtre du Gymnase, Feb. 26, 1841.

157. (With Jean-François Roger). *Les surprises (The Surprises)*. Comedy-vaudeville, 1 act. Produced Théâtre du Gymnase, July 31, 1844.

158. (With Saintine). *Babiole et Joblot (Babiole and Joblot)*. Comedy-vaudeville, 2 acts. Produced Théâtre du Gymnase, Oct. 1, 1844.

159. *Rebecca*. Comedy-vaudeville, 2 acts. Produced Théâtre du Gymnase, Dec. 2, 1844.

160. (With Thomas Sauvage). *L'image (The Image)*. Comedy-vaudeville, 1 act. Produced Théâtre du Gymnase, Apr. 17, 1845.

161. (With Varner). *Jeanne et Jeanneton (Jeanne and Jeanette)*. Comedy-vaudeville, 2 acts. Produced Théâtre du Gymnase, Apr. 20, 1845.

162. *La loi salique (The Salic Law)*. Comedy-vaudeville, 2 acts. Produced Théâtre du Gymnase, Dec. 30, 1845.

163. *Geneviève, ou La jalousie paternelle (Genevieve, or Paternal Jealousy)*. Comedy-vaudeville, 1 act. Produced Théâtre du Gymnase, Mar. 30, 1846.

164. *La protégée sans le savoir (The Protégée Who Didn't Know It)*. Comedy-vaudeville, 1 act. Produced Théâtre du Gymnase, Dec. 5, 1846.

165. (With Dupin). *Maître Jean, ou La comédie à la cour (Master Jean, or The Comedy at Court)*. Comedy-vaudeville, 2 acts. Produced Théâtre du Gymnase, Jan. 14, 1847.

166. (With Lockroy). *Irène, ou Le magnétisme (Irene, or Magnetism)*. Comedy-vaudeville, 2 acts. Produced Théâtre du Gymnase, Feb. 2, 1847.

167. *D'Aranda, ou Les grandes passions (D'Aranda, or The Great Passions)*. Comedy-vaudeville, 2 acts. Produced Théâtre du Gymnase, Apr. 6, 1847.

168. (With Gustave Lemoine). *Une femme qui se jette par la fenêtre (A Woman Who Throws Herself Out of a Window)*. Comedy-vaudeville, 1 act. Produced Théâtre du Gymnase, Apr. 19, 1847.

169. (With Saintine). *La déesse (The Goddess)*. Comedy-vaudeville, 3 acts. Produced Théâtre du Gymnase, Oct. 30, 1847.

170. (With Varner). *O amitié! ou Les trois époques (O Friendship! or The Three Periods)*. Comedy-vaudeville, 3 acts. Produced Théâtre du Gymnase, Nov. 14, 1848.

171. (With Michel Masson). *Les filles du docteur, ou Le dévouement (The Doctor's Daughters, or Devotion)*. Comedy-vaudeville, 2 acts. Produced Théâtre du Gymnase, Feb. 10, 1849.

172. (With Masson). *Héloïse et Abélard, ou À quelquechose malheur est bon (Héloïse and Abelard, or Misfortune Is Good for Something)*. Comedy-vaudeville, 2 acts. Produced Théâtre du Gymnase, Apr. 22, 1850.

173. (With Varner). *Madame Schlick*. Comedy-vaudeville, 1 act. Produced Théâtre du Gymnase, Feb. 9, 1852.

174. (With Mélesville). *Mémoires d'un colonel de hussards (Memoirs of a Colonel of the Hussars)*. Comedy, 1 act.

Comedy-Dramas

1. (With Delavigne). *Le valet de son rival (His Rival's Valet)*. Comedy, 1 act. Produced Théâtre de l'Odéon, Mar. 19, 1816.

2. (With Mélesville and Delestre-Poirson). *Les frères invisibles (Invisible Brothers)*. Melodrama, 3 acts. Produced Théâtre de la Porte-Saint-Martin, June 10, 1819.

3. (With Mélesville). *La bohémienne, ou L'Amérique en 1775 (The Bohemian Lady, or America in 1775)*. Historical drama, 5 acts. Produced Théâtre du Gymnase, June 1, 1820.

4. (With Delestre-Poirson and Mélesville). *Le parrain (The Godfather)*. Comedy, 1 act. Produced Théâtre du Gymnase, Apr. 23, 1821.

5. (With Mélesville). *Valérie*. Comedy, 3 acts. Produced Théâtre Français, Dec. 21, 1822.

6. (With Mélesville). *Rodolphe, ou Frère et soeur (Rudolph, or Brother and Sister)*. Drama, 1 act. Produced Théâtre du Gymnase, Nov. 20, 1823.

7. (With Camille). *Le mauvais sujet (The Worthless Fellow)*. Drama, 1 act. Produced Théâtre du Gymnase, July 16, 1825.

8. *Le mariage d'argent (Marriage for Money)*. Comedy, 5 acts. Produced Théâtre Français, Dec. 3, 1827.

9. *Les inconsolables (The Inconsolable Ones)*. Comedy, 1 act. Produced Théâtre Français, Dec. 8, 1829.

10. (With Thomas Terrier). *Dix ans de la vie d'une femme, ou Les mauvais conseils (Ten Years from the Life of a Woman, or Bad Advice)*. Drama, 5 acts. Produced Théâtre de la Porte-Saint-Martin, Mar. 17, 1832.

11. *Bertrand et Raton, ou L'art de conspirer (Bertrand and Raton, or The Art of Conspiracy)*. Comedy, 5 acts. Produced Théâtre Français, Nov. 14, 1833.

12. *La passion secrète (The Secret Passion)*. Comedy, 3 acts. Produced Théâtre Français, Mar. 13, 1834.

13. *L'ambitieux (The Ambitious One)*. Comedy, 5 acts. Produced Théâtre Français, Nov. 27, 1834.

14. *La camaraderie, ou La courte échelle (The Clique, or The Helping Hand)*. Comedy, 5 acts. Produced Théâtre Français, June 19, 1837.

15. *Les indépendants (The Independent Ones)*. Comedy, 3 acts. Produced Théâtre Français, Nov. 20, 1837.

16. *La calomnie (Slander)*. Comedy, 5 acts. Produced Théâtre Français, Feb. 20, 1840.

17. *La grand'mère, ou Les trois amours (The Grandmother, or Three Loves)*. Comedy, 3 acts. Produced Théâtre du Gymnase, Mar. 14, 1840.

18. (With Vanderburch). *Japhet, ou La recherche d'un père (Japhet, or The Search for a Father)*. Comedy, 2 acts. Produced Théâtre Français, July 20, 1840.

19. *Le verre d'eau, ou Les effets et les causes* (The Glass of Water, or Causes and Effects)*. Comedy, 5 acts. Produced Théâtre Français, Nov. 17, 1840.

20. *Une chaîne (A Chain)*. Comedy, 5 acts. Produced Théâtre Français, Nov. 29, 1841.

21. (With Mélesville). *Oscar, ou Le mari qui trompe sa femme (Oscar, or The Husband Who Deceives His Wife)*. Comedy, 3 acts. Produced Théâtre Français, Apr. 14, 1842.

22. *Le fils de Cromwell, ou Une restauration (The Son of Cromwell, or a Restoration)*. Comedy, 5 acts. Produced Théâtre Français, Nov. 20, 1842.

23. (With Duport). *La tutrice, ou L'emploi des richesses (The Guardian, or The Use of Riches)*. Comedy, 3 acts. Produced Théâtre Français, Nov. 29, 1843.

24. *Le puff, ou Mensonge et vérité (Puffery, or Lie and Truth)*. Comedy, 5 acts. Produced Théâtre Français, Jan. 22, 1848.

25. (With Gabriel-Jean-Baptiste Legouvé). *Adrienne Lecouvreur*. Comedy-drama, 5 acts. Produced Théâtre Français, Apr. 14, 1849.

26. (With Legouvé). *Les contes de la reine de Navarre, ou La revanche de Pavie (Tales of the Queen of Navarre, or Pavia's Revenge)*. Comedy, 5 acts. Produced Théâtre Français, Oct. 15, 1850.

27. (With Legouvé). *Bataille de dames, ou Un duel en amour* (The Queen's Gambit, or A Duel of Love)*. Comedy, 3 acts. Produced Théâtre Français, Mar. 17, 1851.

28. *Mon étoile (My Star)*. Comedy, 1 act. Produced Théâtre Français, Feb. 6, 1854.

29. *La czarine (The Czarina)*. Drama, 5 acts. Produced Théâtre Français, Jan. 15, 1855.

30. (With Charles Potron). *Feu Lionel, ou Qui vivra verra (The Late Lionel, or Live and Learn)*. Comedy, 3 acts. Produced Théâtre Français, Jan. 23, 1858.

31. (With Legouvé). *Les doigts de fée (Fairy Fingers)*. Comedy, 5 acts. Produced Théâtre Français, Mar. 29, 1858.

32. (With Henry Boisseaux). *Les trois Maupins, ou La veille de la Régence (The Three Maupins, or The Eve of the Regency)*. Comedy, 5 acts. Produced Théâtre du Gymnase, Oct. 23, 1858.

33. (With Charles-Henry Desnoyers de Biéville). *Rêves d'amour (Dreams of Love)*. Comedy, 3 acts. Produced Théâtre Français, Mar. 1, 1859.

34. (With Émile de Najac). *La fille de trente ans (The Thirty-year-old Woman)*. Comedy, 4 acts. Produced Théâtre du Vaudeville, Dec. 15, 1859.

35. *La frileuse (The Chilly One)*. Comedy, 3 acts. Produced Théâtre du Vaudeville, Sept. 6, 1861.

Operas and Ballets

1. (With Pierre Aumer). *La somnambule, ou L'arrivée d'un nouveau seigneur (The Sleepwalker, or The Arrival of a New Master)*. Ballet-pantomime, 3 acts. Produced Théâtre de l'Opéra, Sept. 19, 1827. Music: Ferdinand Hérold.

2. (With Delavigne). *La muette de Portici (The Mute Woman of Portici)*. Opera, 5 acts. Produced Théâtre de l'Opéra, Feb. 29, 1828. Music: Daniel Auber.

3. (With Delestre-Poirson). *Le Comte Ory (Count Ory)*. Opera, 2 acts. Produced Théâtre de l'Opéra, Aug. 20, 1828. Music: Gioacchino Rossini.

4. (With Aumer). *La belle au bois dormant (Sleeping Beauty)*. Ballet-pantomime, 3 acts. Produced Théâtre de l'Opéra, Apr. 27, 1829. Music: Hérold.

5. (With Haussens). *Alcibiade (Alcibiades)*. Opera, 2 acts. Produced Brussels, Grand-Théâtre, Oct. 30, 1829.

6. (With Aumer). *Manon Lescaut*. Ballet-pantomime, 3 acts. Produced Théâtre de l'Opéra, May 3, 1830. Based on the novel by the Abbé Prévost (1721). Music: Jacques Halévy.

7. *Le dieu et la bayadère, ou La courtisane amoureuse (The God and the Indian Dancing Girl, or The Amorous Courtesan)*. Opera-ballet, 2 acts. Produced Théâtre de l'Opéra, Oct. 13, 1830. Music: Auber.

8. *L'enfant prodigue (The Prodigal Son)*. Opera, 5 acts. Produced Théâtre de l'Opéra, Dec. 6, 1830. Music: Auber.

9. *Le philtre (The Philter)*. Opera, 2 acts. Produced Théâtre de l'Opéra, June 20, 1831. Music: Auber.

10. (With Jean Corallé). *L'orgie (The Orgy)*. Ballet-pantomime, 3 acts. Produced Théâtre de l'Opéra, July 18, 1831. Music: Michele Enrico Carafa.

11. (With Delavigne). *Robert le Diable (Robert the Devil)*. Opera, 5 acts. Produced Théâtre de l'Opéra, Nov. 21, 1831. Music: Giacomo Meyerbeer.

12. (With Mazères). *Le serment, ou Les faux-monnayeurs (The Oath, or The Counterfeiters)*. Opera, 3 acts. Produced Théâtre de l'Opéra, Oct. 11, 1832. Music: Auber.

13. *Gustave III, ou Le bal masqué (Gustavus III, or The Masked Ball)*. Historical opera, 5 acts. Produced Théâtre de l'Opéra, Feb. 27, 1883. Music: Auber.

14. (With Mélesville). *Ali-Baba, ou Les quarante voleurs (Ali Baba, or The Forty Thieves)*. Opera, prologue and 4 acts. Produced Théâtre de l'Opéra, July 22, 1833. Music: Luigi Cherubini.

15. *La Juive (The Jewess)*. Opera, 5 acts. Produced Théâtre de l'Opéra, Feb. 23, 1835. Music: Halévy.

16. *Les Huguenots (The Huguenots)*. Opera, 5 acts. Produced Théâtre de l'Opéra, Feb. 29, 1836. Music: Meyerbeer.

17. *Guido et Ginevra, ou La peste de Florence (Guido and Ginevra, or The Plague of Florence)*. Opera, 5 acts. Produced Théâtre de l'Opéra, Mar. 5, 1838. Music: Halévy.

18. (With Thérèse Essler and Gide). *La volière, ou Les oiseaux du bocage (The Aviary, or The Birds of the Grove)*. Ballet-pantomime, 1 act. Produced Théâtre de l'Opéra, May 5, 1838.

19. (With Corallé and Gide). *La tarentule (The Tarantula)*. Ballet-pantomime, 2 acts. Produced Théâtre de l'Opéra, Jan. 24, 1839.

20. (With Mélesville). *Le lac des fées (The Lake of the Fairies)*. Opera, 5 acts. Produced Théâtre de l'Opéra, Apr. 1, 1839. Music: Auber.

21. (With Marliani). *La Xacarilla*. Opera, 1 act. Produced Théâtre de l'Opéra, Oct. 28, 1839.

22. *Le drapier (The Draper)*. Opera, 3 acts. Produced Théâtre de l'Opéra, Jan. 6, 1840. Music: Halévy.

23. *Les martyres (The Martyrs)*. Opera, 4 acts. Produced Théâtre de l'Opéra, Apr. 10, 1840. Music: Gaetano Donizetti.

24. (With Alphonse Royer and Gustave Vaëz). *La favorite (The Favorite)*. Opera, 4 acts. Produced Théâtre de l'Opéra, Dec. 2, 1840. Music: Donizetti.

25. *Carmagnola*. Opera, 2 acts. Produced Théâtre de l'Opéra, Apr. 19, 1841. Music: Ambroise Thomas.

26. *Dom Sébastien, roi de Portugal (Don Sebastian, King of Portugal)*. Opera, 5 acts. Produced Théâtre de l'Opéra, Nov. 13, 1843. Music: Donizetti.

27. *Jeanne la Folle (Juana la Loca)*. Opera, 5 acts. Produced Théâtre de l'Opéra, Nov. 6, 1848. Music: Antonin-Louis Clapisson.

28. *Le prophète (The Prophet)*. Opera, 5 acts. Produced Théâtre de l'Opéra, Apr. 16, 1849. Music: Meyerbeer.

29. *La tempête (The Tempest)*. Opera, prologue and 3 acts. Produced London, Queen's Theatre, June 8, 1850; Paris, Théâtre Italien, Feb. 25, 1851. Music: Halévy.

30. *Zerline, ou La corbeille d'oranges (Zerline, or The Basket of Oranges)*. Opera, 3 acts. Produced Théâtre de l'Opéra, May 16, 1851. Music: Auber.

31. *Florinde, ou Les maures en Espagne (Florinda, or The Moors in Spain)*. Opera, 4 acts. Produced London, Queen's Theatre, July 3, 1851. Music: Jean-Jacques Debillemont.

32. (With Saint-Georges). *Le juif errant (The Wandering Jew)*. Opera. Produced Théâtre de l'Opéra, Apr. 23, 1852. Music: Halévy.

33. (With Delavigne). *La nonne sanglante (The Blood-stained Nun)*. Opera, 5 acts. Produced Théâtre de l'Opéra, Oct. 18, 1854. Music: Charles Gounod.

34. (With Mélesville). *Les vêpres siciliennes (The Sicilian Vespers)*. Opera, 5 acts. Produced Théâtre de l'Opéra, June 13, 1855. Music: Giuseppe Verdi.

35. (With Joseph Mazillier). *Marco Spada, ou La fille du bandit (Marco Spada, or The Bandit's Daughter)*. Ballet-pantomime, 3 acts. Produced Théâtre de l'Opéra, Apr. 1, 1857. Music: Auber.

36. *Le cheval de bronze (The Bronze Horse)*. Opera-ballet, 4 acts. Produced Théâtre l'Opéra, Sept. 21, 1857. Music: Auber.

37. *L'africaine (The African)*. Opera. Produced Théâtre de l'Opéra, Apr. 28, 1865. Music: Meyerbeer.

Comic Operas

1. (With Adolphe Guénée). *La chambre à coucher, ou Une demi-heure de Richelieu (The Bedroom, or A Half Hour of Richelieu)*. Comic opera; 1 act. Produced Théâtre de l'Opéra-Comique, Apr. 29, 1813.

2. (With Mélesville). *La meunière (The Miller's Wife)*. Comic opera, 1 act. Produced Théâtre du Gymnase, May 16, 1821. Music: Manuel García.

3. (With Mélesville). *Le paradis de Mahomet, ou La pluralité des femmes (Mohammed's Paradise, or The Plurality of Wives)*. Comic opera, 3 acts. Produced Théâtre de l'Opéra-Comique, Mar. 23, 1822. Music: Rodolfe Kreutzer and Charles-Frédéric Kreubé.

4. (With Mélesville). *La petite lampe merveilleuse (The Little Magic Lamp)*. Comic opera, 3 acts. Produced Théâtre du Gymnase, July 29, 1822. Music: Niccolò Piccini.

5. (With Mélesville). *Leicester, ou Le château de Kenilworth (Leicester, or The Castle of Kenilworth)*. Opera. Produced Théâtre de l'Opéra-Comique, Jan. 25, 1823. Music: Auber.

6. (With Mélesville). *Le valet de chambre (The Valet)*. Comic opera, 1 act. Produced Théâtre de l'Opéra-Comique, Sept. 16, 1823. Music: Carafa.

7. (With Delavigne). *La neige, ou Le nouvel Eginhard (Snow, or The New Eginhard)*. Comic opera, 4 acts. Produced Théâtre de l'Opéra-Comique, Oct. 8, 1823. Music: Auber.

8. (With Mélesville). *Concert à la cour, ou La débutante (Concert at Court, or The Debutante)*. Comic opera, 1 act. Produced Théâtre de l'Opéra-Comique, June 3, 1824. Music: Auber.

9. (With Mélesville). *Léocadie (Leocadia)*. Lyric drama, 3 acts. Produced Théâtre de l'Opéra-Comique, Nov. 4, 1824. Music: Auber.

10. (With Delavigne). *Le maçon (The Mason)*. Comic opera, 3 acts. Produced Théâtre de l'Opéra-Comique, May 3, 1825. Music: Auber.

11. *La dame blanche (The White Lady)*. Comic opera, 3 acts. Produced Théâtre de l'Opéra-Comique, Dec. 10, 1825. Music: François Boieldieu.

12. (With Delavigne). *La vieille (The Old Lady)*. Comic opera, 1 act. Produced Théâtre de l'Opéra-Comique, Mar. 14, 1826. Music: François-Joseph Fétis.

13. (With Saintine). *Le timide, ou Le nouveau séducteur (The Timid One, or The New Seducer)*. Comic opera, 1 act. Produced Théâtre de l'Opéra-Comique, May 30, 1826. Music: Auber.

14. *Fiorella*. Comic opera, 3 acts. Produced Théâtre de l'Opéra-Comique, Nov. 28, 1826. Music: Auber.

15. (With Mazères). *Le loup-garou (The Werewolf)*. Comic opera, 1 act. Produced Théâtre de l'Opéra-Comique, Mar. 10, 1827. Music: Louise-Angélique Bertin.

16. *La fiancée (The Betrothed)*. Comic opera, 3 acts. Produced Théâtre de l'Opéra-Comique, June 10, 1829. Music: Auber.

17. (With Jean-Nicolas Bouilly). *Les deux nuits (Two Nights)*. Comic opera, 3 acts. Produced Théâtre de l'Opéra-Comique, May 20, 1829. Music: Boieldieu.

18. *Fra Diavolo, ou L'hôtellerie de Terracine (Fra Diavolo, or The Guesthouse of Terracine)*. Comic opera, 3 acts. Produced Théâtre de l'Opéra-Co-

mique, Jan. 28, 1830. Music: Auber.

19. (With Castil-Blaze). *La Marquise de Brinvilliers (The Marquise de Brinvilliers).* Lyric drama, 3 acts. Produced Théâtre de l'Opéra-Comique, Oct. 31, 1831. Music: Auber, Désiré Batton, Henri Montan Berton, Giuseppe Blangini, Boieldieu, Carafa, Cherubini, Hérold, and Ferdinando Paër.

20. (With Bayard). *La médecine sans médecin (Medicine Without a Doctor).* Comic opera, 1 act. Produced Théâtre de l'Opéra-Comique, Oct. 17, 1832. Music: Hérold.

21. (With François de Planard). *La prison d'Edinbourg (The Prison of Edinburgh).* Comic opera, 3 acts. Produced Théâtre de l'Opéra-Comique, July 20, 1833. Music: Carafa.

22. *L'Estocq, ou L'intrigue et l'amour (L'Estocq, or Intrigue and Love).* Comic opera, 4 acts. Produced Théâtre de l'Opéra-Comique, May 24, 1834. Music: Auber.

23. (With De Feltre). *Le fils du prince (The Son of the Prince).* Opera. Produced Théâtre de l'Opéra-Comique, Aug. 28, 1834.

24. (With Mélesville). *Le châlet (The Chalet).* Comic opera, 1 act. Produced Théâtre de l'Opéra-Comique, Sept. 25, 1834. Music: Adolphe Adam.

25. *Le cheval de bronze (The Bronze Horse).* Fairy opera, 3 acts. Produced Théâtre de l'Opéra-Comique, Mar. 23, 1835. Music: Auber.

26. (With José Melchior Gomis). *Le portefaix (The Porter).* Comic opera, 3 acts. Produced Théâtre de l'Opéra-Comique, June 16, 1835.

27. *Actéon (Actaeon).* Comic opera, 1 act. Produced Théâtre de l'Opéra-Comique, Jan. 23, 1836. Music: Auber.

28. *Les chaperons blancs (The White Hoods).* Comic opera, 3 acts. Produced Théâtre de l'Opéra-Comique, Apr. 9, 1836. Music: Auber.

29. (With Lemoine). *Le mauvais oeil (The Evil Eye).* Comic opera, 1 act. Produced Théâtre de L'Opéra-Comique, Oct. 1, 1836. Music: Loïsa Puget.

30. (With Saint-Georges). *L'ambassadrice (The Ambassadress).* Comic opera, 3 acts. Produced Théâtre de l'Opéra-Comique, Dec. 21, 1836. Music: Auber.

31. *Le domino noir (The Black Domino).* Comic opera, 3 acts. Produced Théâtre de l'Opéra-Comique, Dec. 2, 1837. Music: Auber.

32. (With Saint-Georges). *Le fidèle berger (The Faithful Shepherd).* Comic opera, 3 acts. Produced Théâtre de l'Opéra-Comique, Jan. 11, 1838. Music: Adam.

33. (With De Planard). *Marguerite.* Comic opera, 3 acts. Produced Théâtre de l'Opéra-Comique, June 18, 1838. Music: Boieldieu.

34. (With Dupin). *La figurante, ou L'amour et la dame (The Supernumerary, or Love and the Lady).* Comic opera, 3 acts. Produced Théâtre de l'Opéra-Comique, Aug. 24, 1838. Music: Clapisson.

35. *Régine, ou deux nuits (Regina, or Two Nights).* Comic opera, 2 acts. Produced Théâtre de l'Opéra-Comique, Jan. 17, 1839. Music: Adam.

36. (With Duport). *Les treize (The Thirteen).* Comic opera, 3 acts. Produced Théâtre de l'Opéra-Comique, Apr. 15, 1839. Music: Halévy.

37. (With Mélesville and Alexandre Montfort). *Polichinelle (Punch).* Comic opera, 1 act. Produced Théâtre de l'Opéra-Comique, June 14, 1839.

38. *Le shérif (The Sheriff).* Comic opera, 3 acts. Produced Théâtre de l'Opéra-Comique, Sept. 2, 1839. Music: Halévy.

39. (With Saint-Georges). *La reine d'un jour (Queen for a Day).* Comic opera, 3 acts. Produced Théâtre de l'Opéra-Comique, Sept. 19, 1839. Music: Adam.

40. (With Saint-Georges). *Zanetta, ou Jouer avec le feu (Zanetta, or Playing with Fire).* Comic opera, 3 acts. Produced Théâtre de l'Opéra-Comique, May 18, 1840. Music: Auber.

41. (With Saint-Georges). *L'opéra à la cour (Opera at Court).* Comic opera, 4 parts. Produced Théâtre de l'Opéra-Comique, July 16, 1840. Music: Albert Grisar and Boieldieu.

42. *Le Guitarrero.* Comic opera, 3 acts. Produced Théâtre de l'Opéra-Comique, Jan. 21, 1841. Music: Halévy.

43. (With Saint-Georges). *Les diamants de la couronne (The Crown Jewels).* Comic opera, 3 acts. Produced Théâtre de l'Opéra-Comique, Mar. 6, 1841. Music: Auber.

44. (With Adolphe de Leuven). *La main de fer, ou Un mariage secret (The Hand of Iron, or A Secret Marriage).* Comic opera, 3 acts. Produced Théâtre de l'Opéra-Comique, Oct. 26, 1841. Music: Adam.

45. (With Ernest-Henri-Alexandre Boulanger). *Le diable à l'école (The Devil in School).* Legend, 1 act. Produced Théâtre de l'Opéra-Comique, Jan. 17, 1842.

46. (With Saintine). *Le Duc d'Olonne (The Duke of Olonne).* Comic opera, 3 acts. Produced Théâtre de l'Opéra-Comique, Feb. 4, 1842. Music: Auber.

47. *Le codex noir (The Black Codex).* Comic opera, 3 acts. Produced Théâtre de l'Opéra-Comique, June 9, 1842. Music: Clapisson.

48. (With Duport and Jacques Mazas). *Le kiosque (The Kiosk).* Comic opera, 1 act. Produced Théâtre de l'Opéra-Comique, Nov. 2, 1842.

49. (With De Leuven). *Le puits d'amour (The Well of Love).* Comic opera, 3 acts. Produced Théâtre de l'Opéra-Comique, Apr. 20, 1843. Music: Michael William Balfe.

50. *La part du diable (The Devil's Share).* Comic opera, 3 acts. Produced Théâtre de l'Opéra-Comique, June 16, 1843. Music: Auber.

51. (With Mélesville). *Lambert Simnel.* Comic opera. Produced Théâtre de l'Opéra-Comique, Sept. 14, 1843. Music: Hippolyte Monpou.

52. (With Saint-Georges). *Cagliostro.* Comic opera, 3 acts. Produced Théâtre de l'Opéra-Comique, Feb. 10, 1844. Music: Adam.

53. (With Dupin). *Oreste et Pylade (Orestes and Pylades).* Comic opera, 1 act. Produced Théâtre de l'Opéra-Comique, Feb. 28, 1844. Music: Thys.

54. *La sirène (The Siren).* Comic opera, 3 acts. Produced Théâtre de l'Opéra-Comique, Mar. 26, 1844. Music: Auber.

55. *La barcarolle, ou L'amour et la musique (The Barcarolle, or Love and Music).* Comic opera, 3 acts. Produced Théâtre de l'Opéra-Comique, Apr. 22, 1845. Music: Auber.

56. (With Théodore Labarre). *Le ménétrier (The Fiddler).* Comic opera, 3 acts. Produced Théâtre de l'Opéra-Comique, Aug. 9, 1845.

57. (With Mélesville and Montfort). *La charbonnière.* Comic opera, 3 acts. Produced Théâtre de l'Opéra-Comique, Oct. 13, 1845.

58. (With Vaëz and Dominique-François-Xavier Boisselot). *Ne touchez pas à la reine (Don't Meddle with the Queen).* Comic opera, 3 acts. Produced Théâtre de l'Opéra-Comique, Jan. 16, 1847.

59. (With Dupin and Luigi Bordese). *Le sultan Saladin (Sultan Saladin).* Comic opera, 1 act. Produced Théâtre de l'Opéra-Comique, Feb. 8, 1847.

60. *Haÿdée, ou Le secret (Haidée, or The Secret).* Comic opera, 3 acts. Produced Théâtre de l'Opéra-Comique, Dec. 28, 1847. Music: Auber.

61. *La nuit de Noël, ou L'anniversaire (Christmas Night, or The Anniversary).* Comic opera, 3 acts. Produced Théâtre de l'Opéra-Comique, Feb. 9, 1848. Music: Napoléon-Henri Reber.

62. (With Saint-Georges). *La fée aux roses (The Rose Fairy).* Comic opera, 3 acts. Produced Théâtre de l'Opéra-Comique, Oct. 1, 1849. Music: Halévy.

63. *Giralda, ou La nouvelle Psyché (Giralda, or The New Psyche).* Comic opera, 3 acts. Produced Théâtre de l'Opéra-Comique, July 20, 1850. Music: Auber.

64. (With De Leuven and Victor). *La chanteuse voilée (The Veiled Singer).* Comic opera, 1 act. Produced Théâtre de l'Opéra-Comique, Nov. 26, 1850.

65. *La dame de pique (The Queen of Spades).* Comic opera, 3 acts. Produced Théâtre de l'Opéra-Comique, Dec. 28, 1850. Music: Halévy.

66. (With Vaëz and Boisselot). *Mosquita la sorcière (Mosquita the Sorceress).* Comic opera, 3 acts. Produced Théâtre de l'Opéra-National, Sept. 27, 1851.

67. (With Delavigne). *Les mystères d'Udolphe (The Mysteries of Udolpho).* Comic opera, 3 acts. Produced Théâtre de l'Opéra-Comique, Nov. 4, 1852.

68. *Marco Spada.* Comic opera, 3 acts. Produced Théâtre de l'Opéra-Comique, Dec. 21, 1852. Music: Auber.

69. (With De Courcy). *La lettre au bon Dieu (Letter to the Good Lord).* Comic opera, 2 acts. Produced Théâtre de l'Opéra-Comique, Apr. 28, 1853. Music: Louis Duprez.

70. (With Hippolyte Romand). *Le nabab (The Nabob).* Comic opera, 3 acts. Produced Théâtre de l'Opéra-Comique, Sept. 1, 1853. Music: Victor Massé.

71. *L'étoile du nord (The North Star).* Comic opera, 3 acts. Produced Théâtre de l'Opéra-Comique, Feb. 16, 1854. Music: Meyerbeer.

72. (With Romand). *La fiancée du diable (The Devil's Betrothed).* Comic opera, 3 acts. Produced Théâtre de l'Opéra-Comique, June 5, 1854. Music: Massé.

73. *Jenny Bell.* Comic opera, 3 acts. Produced Théâtre de l'Opéra-Comique, June 2, 1855. Music: Auber.

74. *Manon Lescaut.* Comic opera, 3 acts. Produced Théâtre de l'Opéra-Comique, Feb. 23, 1856. Music: Auber.

75. (With Mélesville). *La chatte métamorphosée en femme (The Cat Changed into a Woman).* Comic opera, 1 act. Produced Théâtre des Bouffes-Parisiens, Apr. 19, 1858. Music: Jacques Offenbach.

76. (With Boisseaux). *Broskovano.* Comic opera, 2 acts. Produced Théâtre Lyrique, Sept. 29, 1858. Music: Pierre-Louis Deffès.

77. (With Lopez and De Leuven). *Les trois Nicolas (The Three Nicholases).* Comic opera, 3 acts. Produced Théâtre de l'Opéra-Comique, Dec. 16, 1858. Music: Clapisson.

78. (With Boisseaux). *Les petits violons du roi (The Little Violins of the King).* Comic opera, 3 acts. Produced Théâtre Lyrique, Sept. 30, 1859. Music: Deffès.

79. *Yvonne.* Comic opera, 3 acts. Produced Théâtre de l'Opéra-Comique, Nov. 29, 1859. Music: Armand Limnander de Nieuwenhove.

80. (With Delestre-Poirson and Hignard). *Le nouveau Pourceaugnac (The New Pourceaugnac).* Comic opera, 1 act. Produced Théâtre des Bouffes-Parisiens, Jan. 14, 1860.

81. (With Boisseaux). *Barkoaf.* Opera buffa, 3 acts. Produced Théâtre de l'Opéra-Comique, Dec. 24, 1860. Music: Offenbach.

82. *La circassienne (The Circassian Woman).* Comic opera, 3 acts. Produced Théâtre de l'Opéra-Comique, Feb. 2, 1861. Music: Auber.

83. (With Boisseaux). *Madame Grégoire.* Comic opera, 3 acts. Produced Théâtre Lyrique, Feb. 8, 1861. Music: Clapisson.

84. (With De Najac and Giulio Alary). *La beauté du diable (The Freshness of Youth).* Comic opera, 1 act. Produced Théâtre de l'Opéra-Comique, May 28, 1861.

85. (With Saint-Georges). *La fiancée du roi de Garbe (The Betrothed of the King of Garbe).* Comic opera, 3 acts and 6 tableaux. Produced Théâtre de l'Opéra-Comique, Jan. 11, 1864. Music: Auber.

86. (With Saintine). *L'ours et le pacha (The Bear and the Pasha).* Opera buffa, 1 act. Produced Théâtre de l'Opéra-Comique, Feb. 21, 1870. Music: François-Emmanuel-Joseph Bazin.

Editions

Collections
Oeuvres complètes, 76 vols., Paris, 1874–1885.
Individual Plays
Fairy Fingers. (With Gabriel-Jean-Baptiste Legouvé). Published in *Easy French Plays,* ed. by C. W. Benton, Chicago, 1901.
The Glass of Water. Published in *Nineteenth Century French Plays,* ed. by J. L. Borgerhoff, New York, 1931; *Camille and Other Plays,* ed. by S. S. Stanton and tr. by D. Bodee, New York, 1957.
The Savoy Frontier (A Peculiar Position). (With Jean-François-Alfred Bayard). Published in *Camille and Other Plays,* ed. by S. S. Stanton and tr. by J. Planche, New York, 1957.

Criticism

E. de Mirécourt, *Scribe,* Paris, 1854; E. Legouvé, *Eugène Scribe,* Paris, 1874; J. Rolland, *Les comédies politiques de Eugène Scribe,* Paris, 1912; N. C. Arvin, *Eugène Scribe and the French Theatre,* Cambridge, Mass., 1924, New York, 1967.

Sebastian, Mihail   (1907–1945)

Romanian playwright. Sebastian was born in Brăila on October 8, 1907. After passing his examination for a doctoral degree in economics and political law in Paris, he made his debut as a newspaperman in 1927 with a literary critique in the daily *Cuvîntul (The Word).* At the same time he contributed essays and literary criticism to several other publications. His first book, *Fragments from a Found-out Notebook,* appeared in 1932. It was followed by several novels. However, it was not until the appearance of the plays *Playing at Holiday* (1938), *The Nameless Star* (1944), and *Stop News* (1946) that Sebastian achieved real recognition. In 1944 and 1945 he worked on his drama *The Island,* which remained unfinished at his death in an

Gina Patrichi and George Oancea in
Playing at Holiday, Lucia Sturdza Bulandra
Theatre, Bucharest. [Editura Enciclopedică
Română, Bucharest]

automobile accident in Bucharest on May 29, 1945.

The simple, linear development of his plays notwithstanding, Sebastian, with an uncommon power of suggestion, created unusual nuances of meaning. His language is both precise and full of implications; it creates an atmosphere and numberless echoes: ". . . a supple, well-ordered, linear book in which life should develop minutely enough so as to be known, yet secretly enough so as to preserve its mystery."

Playing at Holiday (Jocul de-a vacanta, 1938) takes place in a boardinghouse in the mountains. The arrival of a riotous holidaymaker disrupts the calm. He intends to relax at any cost by "playing at holiday." The play pro-

Mihail Sebastian.
[Editura
Enciclopedică
Română,
Bucharest]

Scene from *The Nameless Star,* I. L. Caragiale National Theatre, Bucharest. [Editura Enciclopedică Română, Bucharest]

Playing at Holiday, Lucia Sturza Bulandra Theatre, Bucharest.
[Editura Enciclopedică Română, Bucharest]

gresses, scene by scene, zigzagging from what *is* to what *seems*, demonstrating in the end that there is no complete happiness, that a poignant sadness results from a brave new experiment in living.

In *The Nameless Star* (*Steava fava nume,* 1944) Sebastian stressed the illusions of life that come into conflict with its realities. The small town of the play, a symbol of torpid, flat provincial life, is a perfect universe, with its own scale of values. In this setting events tend to acquire gigantic proportions; people come to be ruled by more or less inoffensive passions. Professor Udrea, for example, has worked all his life at composing a symphony, for the performance of which, however, he lacks an English horn; and Miron is absorbed in the study of the heavens and sidereal maps. With this technique, Sebastian approached the threshold of caricature. Thus, the merchant Pascu is a "kind of general store," for he sells anything whatever; the conductor is a "fast train," and therefore constantly hurried; the stationmaster can pretend that he and the "railway station" are one and the same; and Miss Cucu, the schoolmistress, is the embodiment of nonsensical school regulations. At the other pole of this dramatic universe is a brilliant, meteoric appearance. It is the unknown, the remote, the beautiful, the dreams of the schoolgirls and their teacher as they watch the hasty passing through town of the Sinaia express train. When a messenger of this miraculous universe, Mona, the fair stranger, disrupts the harmony of the town, the two worlds suffer reciprocal defeat. Mirage and reality annihilate each other.

Stop News (*Ultima ora,* 1946) admits us farther into the exotic universe of *The Nameless Star.* The rhythm of life in a city actuates the conflict in the play. If at the end of *The Nameless Star* we have seen Miron lost in his astronomy treatises, in *Stop News* Professor Andronic, the protagonist, and his enthusiastic pupil Magda Minu achieve their highest dream, a research journey in the footsteps of Alexander the Great. Magda in this play is the first of Sebastian's heroines to rise above feminine passivity. The play suggests that happiness implies struggle.

[RUTH S. LAMB]

EDITIONS

Stop News (*Ultima edición*). Buenos Aires, 1959.
The Nameless Star (*Der Stern ohne Namen*). Vienna, 1963.

CRITICISM

Istoria Teatrului in Romania (*A History of the Theatre in Romania*), ed. by S. Alterescu, Bucharest, 1973.

Secchi, Niccolò (ca. 1500–1560)

Italian man of letters and dramatist. He wrote four prose comedies. *The Deceptions* (*Gl'inganni;* prod. 1549?, pub. 1562) has a classic plot based on disguises, mistaken identities, and intricate romantic intrigue. *Self-interest* (*Interesse,* 1581) concerns a young girl, disguised in male costume at her father's command, who falls in love with a young man and becomes pregnant by him. *The Chambermaid* (*La cameriera,* 1583) and *The Servant Beffa* (*Il Beffa,* pub. 1584) also document the unlikely situations created by ostensibly ill-starred lovers seeking to legitimize their relationships.

[PETER BONDANELLA]

Sedaine, Michel-Jean (1719–1797)

French poet and dramatist. He is best known for *A Philosopher Without Knowing It* (*Le philosophe sans le savoir,* 1765), which is generally considered the finest example of the *drama bourgeois* ("bourgeois drama"). As formulated by Diderot, this eighteenth-century prose genre stressed the social conditions that had created its protagonists. Turning its back on the classical verse theatre and its focus on the abstract moral problems created by the heroic clash of passions, the *drama* concentrated on the domestic life and secret tragedies of the middle class. Sedaine's play presents a moving picture of virtuous middle-class family life and of a loved and respected father meeting his anguishing responsibilities. The play had originally been entitled *Le duel,* but title and text were altered as a result of police objections to the father's originally calm acceptance of his son's decision to fight a duel. It remained so popular in France that in 1851 George Sand wrote a sequel, *Victorine's Marriage* (*Le mariage de Victorine*), in which the family is involved in events leading to another marriage. *See* BOURGEOIS DRAMA in glossary.

Sedaine's initial ventures in the theatre were in the field of vaudeville and comic opera, the best-known examples of which are *Rose and Colas* (*Rose et Colas,* 1764), *The King and the Farmer* (*Le roi et le fermier,* 1762; adapted from Robert Dodsley's *The King and the Miller of Mansfield*), and *Richard the Lion-Hearted* (*Richard Coeur de Lion,*

1784). His only other dramatic play of note is a one-act comedy called *The Unforeseen Gamble* (*La gageure imprévue*, 1768). Sedaine was made a member of the Académie Française in 1786, but he was dropped from that body when it was reconstituted in 1796. He died in poverty the following year. Though considered a writer of secondary importance, he provided in his masterpiece an interesting if somewhat sentimentalized vision of middle-class virtues, habits, and concerns. His work is often considered a link to the later realism of Augier and Dumas *fils*.

A Philosopher Without Knowing It (*Le philosophe sans le savoir*, 1765). On the morning of his daughter's wedding, Vanderk, a wealthy businessman, surprises his son stealing away from the house with his dueling pistols. Upon questioning him, Vanderk learns that the son is going to settle a quarrel that occurred the day before. A man of honor and professional integrity, Vanderk does not stop his son, although he bemoans the cruelty of social pressures and of fate. When the hour for the wedding arrives and the young man has not returned, Antoine, the household's old and faithful servant, who has secretly watched the duel, announces the son's death. A few minutes later, however, the son appears, explains the error that caused Antoine to believe him dead, and joins the wedding party as the curtain falls on general rejoicing. Produced Paris, Comédie-Parisienne, December 2, 1765.

[JOSEPH E. GARREAU]

Sée, Edmond (1875–1959)

French writer, critic, and dramatist. His career in the theatre began with short pieces in 1894. Two years later his reputation was established with *The Ewe Lamb* (*La brebis*). The short but substantial comedies of morals that followed are modeled on the comedy of the eighteenth century. Irony coupled with sharp psychological analysis, especially of love, characterize these cleverly constructed plays, which include *Crumbs* (*Les miettes*, 1899), *The Disorderly* (*L'irrégulière*, 1913), *The Season of Love* (*Saison d'amour*, 1918), *The Trustee* (*La dépositaire*, 1924), *Lover by Profession* (*Le métier d'amant*, 1928), *Flexible* (*L'élastique*, 1930), *Behind the Door* (*Derrière la porte*, 1931), and *Charity* (*Charité*, 1932). Sée also published a number of critical volumes about the theatre, among them *Le théâtre des autres* (2 vols., 1912–1913); *Ce soir: Notes et impressions dramatiques* (4 vols., 1921; *Entr'actes* (1924); and *Théâtre français contemporain* (1928), which deals with the development of contempory French drama.

[JOSEPH E. GARREAU]

Seneca (4 B.C.–A.D. 65)

Roman Stoic moralist and dramatist. Lucius Annaeus Seneca was born in Corduba (modern Córdoba), capital of Baetica, the most civilized Roman province in Spain, in 4 B.C. Notable members of Seneca's distinguished and wealthy family were his father Marcus Annaeus Seneca (ca. 55 B.C.–A.D. 37/41), a writer on rhetoric; his brother Junius Annaeus Gallio, the proconsul of Achaia who contemptuously dismissed St. Paul's quarrel with the

Seneca. [Goethe House]

Jews of Corinth (Acts 18:12–17); and the epic poet Lucan (A.D. 39–65), Seneca's nephew.

As a child, Seneca was brought to Rome, where he studied rhetoric and philosophy, especially Stoicism under the Stoic Attalus. In A.D. 32 he became a quaestor, or financial administrator, a position that was traditionally a first step in the political career of a promising young Roman nobleman. By the beginning of Caligula's principate in A.D. 37, Seneca was famous for his oratory and writings. The mad Emperor, jealous of his cleverness, almost put him to death but decided he would soon perish from frail health; Caligula contented himself with calling Seneca's orations "sand without lime."

In A.D. 41, following a charge of adultery with Julia, niece of Caligula's successor Claudius, Seneca was banished to Corsica despite the fact that the charge was without foundation. After many unstoical pleas he was recalled to Rome in 49 by Agrippina, Claudius's second wife, to become tutor to her son Nero. When Nero was made Emperor in 54, Seneca and Sextus Afranius Burrus became his chief ministers, and for five years they provided Rome with an able and just administration. In 59, unable to restrain Nero, they reluctantly acquiesced in his murder of his mother. Three years later, after the death of Burrus, Seneca resigned. He offered to restore his great wealth to the Emperor, but Nero denied his request. In A.D. 65 Seneca was accused of complicity in the conspiracy of Gaius Calpurnius Piso against the Emperor's life. Commanded to take his own life, he did so with a calmness that did honor to his Stoicism. His wife Paulina would have died willingly with him but for Nero's orders that she be saved. Since his infant son by his first marriage had died, Seneca left no children.

A paradox of Seneca's life is the terrific tension between the Stoicism which he professed to believe and of which he was an ardent advocate and the behavior forced on him by his wealth and position at court, which involved much compromise. For all his idealism Seneca can be severely criticized for his personal life, but the very ambiguities that make him imperfect as a moral philosopher are the source of his violent, epigrammatic brilliance as a playwright.

WORK

The ten plays ascribed to Seneca are the only extant examples of Roman tragedy. Of these, *The Phoenician Women* is unfinished, the authorship of *Hercules on Oeta* is debated, and *Octavia,* the only surviving tragedy with a Roman subject (Nero's divorce and subsequent execution of his first wife), is now generally thought to have been written by someone else. Classical Greek prototypes are known for the mythological tragedies, but Seneca probably based his work not directly on plays by Aeschylus, Sophocles, and Euripides but on works of the later, Hellenistic period. His five-act structure, inorganic chorus, and various details of structure and stage business are foreign to fifth-century drama but typify later Greek tragedy, which subordinated high poetry and thought to theatricality and rhetoric. Whether Seneca's plays were ever staged in antiquity is uncertain, but he may well have at least envisioned stage production when writing them. *See* ROMAN DRAMA.

The virtues that won Seneca's philosophic work great praise in the Middle Ages and Renaissance also characterize his tragic poetry: a terse and epigrammatic style, an honest acceptance of terror and pain, and imposing meditations on divinity and destiny. The concern with irrationality and terror underlying some of the prose is given free reign in the tragedies. In his hands the gruesome murders of Greek mythology are not the distant savagery of legend but mirror the gladiatorial arena of Seneca's Rome and the dark uncertainties of court life under the Caesars. The palace of Seneca's Atreus and Thyestes might be the Roman imperial palace, and Atreus himself sounds more like the Caligula or Nero described by Tacitus than like figures of the Greek stage. Some scenes, such as Thyestes' recognition of his sons' heads brought to him on a platter and Theseus' attempt to reassemble the dismembered body of Hippolytus, may now seem almost like Grand Guignol or even the Theatre of the Absurd. *See* GRAND GUIGNOL; THEATRE OF THE ABSURD in glossary.

This preoccupation with violence and morbid psychology has limited Seneca's appeal in certain ages and nurtured it at other times. His influence on the theatre was most profound in the Renaissance, when secular drama was just beginning to revive and Greek drama was not widely known. The bloody revenge plays of Elizabethan times have Senecan roots, as does Shakespearean tragedy, and T. S. Eliot has suggested that Elizabethan blank verse was designed in imitation of Seneca's spoken meters. Seneca's concept of dramatic action and many details of his imagery certainly influenced a wide variety of Renaissance writers, and through them the development of Western tragedy. Victorian scholars tended to dismiss the violent world of Senecan drama as unreal and silly, a judgment still echoed in some histories of literature, but appreciation of Seneca has grown again in our own time. There is much new scholarly work and a renewed influence on contempo-

rary theatre both through revivals of Senecan plays and through influence on such writers as Antonin Artaud.

Seneca's tragedies are divided into five acts, with a prologue and choral interludes in which the chorus comments on the action and provides a kind of meditative background for it. Some of the interludes, such as the chorus on death in *The Trojan Women* and the chorus on true and false kingship in *Thyestes,* are masterpieces of Latin lyric poetry. Dialogue is often simply an exchange of biting epigrams; speeches are ornate and sometimes a little long-winded. Characterization tends to be two-dimensional, largely because Seneca is more interested in depicting the passions themselves than the toll those passions take on individuals. His imagery reflects the Stoic tradition of drawing parallels between order and disorder in the mind and in the cosmos. Thus when Phaedra reveals her passion, Hippolytus has an elaborate vision of the heavens torn with disorder and the stars speeding out of their courses.

Phaedra, in which this scene occurs, is one of Seneca's most effective plays, with deft portrayals of a selfish, passionate queen and a virtuous, troubled boy. *Medea* presents a sorceress even more terrifying than Euripides' Medea. Much of Seneca's meaning is compressed into its concluding lines. "Go," Jason cries to Medea in her winged chariot, "fly through the air and testify wherever you go that there are no gods!" *Thyestes,* with its straightforward plot, its brilliant portrayal of the corruption and insanity of absolute power, and its haunted visions of obscenity and horror, is both great and repulsive. *Oedipus* pictures a very different kind of hero from the Oedipus of Sophocles. Seneca's king is a querulous, suspicious tyrant obsessed with premonitions of guilt. The harrowing scenes of necromancy and magic, a theme that fascinated Seneca and other Roman poets, are aimed at producing terror different from the slow revelation of guilt in Sophocles's play. An almost hysterical note of horror and dread is maintained throughout the play, and the finale, in which Jocasta stabs herself in her womb with her husband's sword, has a phallic symbolism that could hardly be more explicit. *The Trojan Women,* an interesting but wordy play, reveals an anti-war attitude much like that of Euripides and includes some fine meditations on human suffering.

Agamemnon. In Agamemnon's absence during the Trojan War, his wife Clytemnestra, who has betrayed him with Aegisthus, now half-reluctantly plans his murder. Resenting his sacrifice of their daughter Iphigenia, his infidelities, and his present pursuit of the prophetess Cassandra, Clytemnestra prepares a murderous celebration for his return. Though Cassandra warns him of impending disaster, Agamemnon remains oblivious to Clytemnestra's plan for Aegisthus to murder him. Weak-willed, Aegisthus cannot do the job, and Clytemnestra herself murders Agamemnon with an ax. Her young son Orestes is the sole avenger of his father's death, but he must flee "the impious butchers' hands" with his sister Electra. Soon Orestes is rescued by Strophius, King of Phocis, but Electra is captured by Clytemnestra and Aegisthus. Rather than reveal Orestes' whereabouts, Electra prefers death, foretelling the revenge that he will wreak on her captors. Aegisthus, however, decides life in exile and chains is a far greater punishment than death, and Electra is led away.

Mad Hercules (*Hercules furens*). Tragedy also found in Euripides' *Heracles*, describes the tribulations visited on Hercules by the queen of the gods, Jupiter's wife Juno. Jealous of Hercules, her husband's bastard son, Juno (as she tells us in the prologue) has inflicted on him the Twelve Labors. While he is in Hades seeking to accomplish the last of his labors, the capture of the three-headed dog Cerberus, Hercules has left his wife Megara, his mortal father Amphitryon, and his children in the care of Creon, his father-in-law and King of Thebes. But a chorus of Thebans exhorts them to bear the miseries of human life with resignation; for Creon has been assassinated by the brutal Lycus, who, having usurped the throne, now lusts after Megara. She resists his advances, and to avenge himself, Lycus plans to murder the entire family. They are preparing for death when Hercules returns with Cerberus and his friend Theseus, King of Athens, whom he has rescued from Hades. Hercules promptly disposes of Lycus and offers prayers and sacrifice. But Juno, who cannot bear to see Hercules at peace, now sends Madness to torment him. Crazed, he believes his children to have been fathered by Lycus and kills both them and Megara. When his sanity returns and he realizes what he had done, Hercules decides to commit suicide, but Theseus persuades him to bear his fate stoically and offers him asylum in Athens, which he accepts.

Hercules on Oeta (*Hercules oetaeus*). Tragedy paralleled by Sophocles's *The Women of Trachis*, describing the death of Hercules. After conquering Euboea, Hercules takes Iole, daughter of King Eurytus of Oechalia, as a mistress and sends word of his victory to Trachis, where his wife Deianira awaits him. Consumed with jealousy, and in the hope of regaining his love, Deianira sends Hercules a robe smeared with the blood of the centaur Nessus, whom Hercules had killed to protect her honor. Nessus, as he died, prophesied that the robe would one day be used as a charm to regain Hercules's love. Too late Deianira learns that the robe is impregnated with poison and that Hercules is dying. Smitten with remorse, she commits suicide. Hercules, despite his pain, orders his son Hyllus to marry Iole and his friend Philoctetes, to whom he bequeaths his bow and arrows, to prepare a funeral pyre for him on Mount Oeta. After his death, Alcmena, his mother, enters with Hercules's ashes and recounts his exploits on behalf of mankind, while from above the voice of Hercules proclaims that he has ascended to heaven and the chorus sings praises of the brave.

Medea. Medea, daughter of the King of Colchis, had fallen in love with Jason when he came to her land in quest of the Golden Fleece. To win Jason's love, Medea had tricked her father and slain her brother to help Jason secure the Golden Fleece. Then, setting sail for Iolcos, Medea had tricked the daughters of Pelias, who had usurped Jason's father's throne, into slaying their father.

Medea and Jason had then escaped to Corinth, where she had borne two children and had lived happily until Jason was offered and decided to accept the hand of Creusa, daughter of Creon.

Now Medea, consumed by hatred and shattered pride, makes elaborate preparations for her inhuman revenge. Creon, fearful that Medea will use her powers of sorcery against Creusa and Jason, orders her to leave Corinth forever, leaving her sons with Jason. Gaining permission to remain in Corinth for one more day in order to plan her exile, Medea, after quarreling with Jason, pretends to recant and accept his marriage; instead, she has prepared a poisoned robe and chaplet to be sent as a gift to Creusa. After both Creon and his daughter have been killed by the poison, Medea, to complete her revenge on Jason, murders one of her sons. Outraged, the Corinthians attack, but Medea, waiting until Jason can witness the deed, brutally kills their second son, hurls both corpses down before him, and escapes in a dragon-drawn chariot.

Oedipus. According to the Delphic oracle, which Creon, brother-in-law of Oedipus, has consulted, the plague that torments Thebes can be ended only if the unknown murderer of former King Laius is banished from the city. King Oedipus asks the blind seer Tiresias to discover the identity of the killer and, with the help of his daughter Manto, performs an elaborate sacrifice and discovers omens that give dark hints about the future of the house of Thebes. Tiresias announces that only the ghost of Laius can name the murderer. His ghost, together with several others, is summoned, names the son of Laius as the killer, and recounts the grisly history of the family.

Despite fears and suspicions, Oedipus, who is married to Jocasta, former wife of Laius, believes himself to be the son of Polybus of Corinth and thus not the man whom the oracle has decreed to be the murderer of Laius. He accuses Tiresias and Creon of collusion and imprisons Creon. However, as the various witnesses are brought forth, the truth that Oedipus is indeed Laius's son and, therefore, Jocasta's son is revealed. Oedipus rushes into the palace and as a punishment for his sins blinds himself. When he returns, Jocasta rushes out in horror, takes Oedipus's sword, and kills herself, stabbing her own womb. The blind Oedipus leaves Thebes.

Phaedra. Phaedra convinces herself that Theseus, her long-absent husband, is dead, thus vindicating the overpowering lust she feels for her stepson Hippolytus. Phaedra tells Hippolytus of her love and, unable to control her passion, attempts to seduce him, an action that horrifies the youth. Smarting under humiliating rejection, Phaedra skillfully convinces Theseus, who has now returned, that during his absence Hippolytus had violated her. Theseus rashly uses one of three wishes granted him by Neptune to invoke the death of his son, and Hippolytus, riding along the shore, is dashed against the rocks by his own chariot when the horses are frightened by tidal waves. When Phaedra sees the grisly remains, she accuses Theseus of causing the tragedy, confesses her guilt, and commits suicide, leaving The-

Medea, **produced by the Teatro Español, Madrid.**
[Courtesy of Spanish Embassy]

seus to curse her and his fate as he tries to reassemble his son's body.

The Phoenician Women (Phoenissae). Tragedy paralleled by Euripides' play of the same name. The guilt-tortured Oedipus, accompanied by his daughter, the faithful Antigone, is wandering through the countryside near Thebes, bewailing his fate. He recounts his story of patricide and incest, ignoring Antigone's stoic admonitions to accept life as it is, and laments over the impending war between his sons Eteocles and Polynices for the throne of Thebes. In Thebes, Jocasta, mother of the two brothers, explains how after the self-imposed exile of Oedipus a pact had been made whereby the brothers would reign alternately. After the first year, however, Eteocles had refused to relinquish the throne and had banished his brother. Polynices took refuge in Argos, where he married the daughter of the Argive king Adrastus. There also, aided by Adrastus, Polynices joined with six other Greek heroes, the famed Seven Against Thebes, in raising an army to win the throne from Eteocles. Now, persuaded by the pleading Antigone, Jocasta hastens to prevent the impending battle; she beseeches Polynices to refrain from attacking his native city, however just his cause may be. The unfinished text ends with Eteocles's resolve to retain his power.

Thyestes. Tragedy that follows traditional accounts of the conflict between Atreus and Thyestes, although a specific model is unknown. The play begins with an elaborate ghost scene, a recitation of the crimes of the house of Pelops and the curses upon Tantalus, father of Atreus, and Pelops. Years before, Atreus had exiled his brother Thyestes for having seduced his third wife, Pelopia, and stolen the golden-fleeced ram, the owner of which could rightfully rule Mycenae. Feigning gestures of reconciliation, Atreus now invites Thyestes to come home and share his kingdom. Thyestes, who has become used to freedom and poverty, resists but is urged by his ambitious sons to accept the offer. Atreus "honors" him at a banquet. There, Thyestes, dulled with drink, unknowingly dines upon the flesh of his own sons, whom the vengeful Atreus has killed. Later Atreus reveals his treachery and presents Thyestes with a platter bearing the heads of his slaughtered sons. Unnatural darkness falls over Mycenae, and the sun vanishes as Thyestes calls down a curse upon Atreus and his descendants.

The Trojan Women (Troades). Tragedy, paralleled by Euripides' *Hecuba* and *The Trojan Women,* which takes place before the ruined walls of Troy, where Hecuba, Andromache, and the chorus of Trojan women await their fates. After Hecuba recounts the disasters and tragedies of the ten years' war, the women are informed that the ghost of Achilles has demanded the sacrifice of Hecuba's daughter Polyxena, a barbarism which the enlightened Agamemnon denounces but which Achilles' son, the arrogant Pyrrhus, demands. The prophet Calchas rules in favor of the sacrifice and insists that Andromache's son Astyanax be sacrificed as well to assure the safe return home of the Greeks. The chorus in one of Seneca's greatest odes voices the Stoic belief that death is annihilation and that resignation in the face of life's sorrows is best for mortals. Andromache's pitiful efforts to hide her son from the cunning Ulysses fail. Meanwhile, Helen, unfaithful wife of the Spartan Menelaus, having instigated the war, now deludes Polyxena into believing she is to be wed to Pyrrhus. In a sudden burst of honesty, however, Helen confesses that Polyxena will become a human sacrifice. Polyxena accepts her fate calmly. Then, with the reports of Astyanax's and Polyxena's deaths, Hecuba calls down curses upon the Greeks and prophesies their tormented future as the remaining captives are led away to their separate fates.

[SANDOR M. GOLDBERG]

PLAYS

No dates are known, and the plays are therefore listed in alphabetical order.
1. *Agamemnon.**
2. *Hercules furens** (*Mad Hercules*).
3. *Hercules oetaeus** (*Hercules on Oeta*).
4. *Medea**.
5. *Oedipus**.
6. *Phaedra**.
7. *Phoenissae* or *Thebais** (*The Phoenician Women*). Unfinished.
8. *Thyestes**.
9. *Troades** (*The Trojan Women*).

A *fabula praetexta* (historical drama), *Octavia*, formerly included with Seneca's work, is probably later (ca. A.D. 70).

EDITIONS

Latin Texts and Commentaries
Tragedies, ed. by F. J. Miller, 2 vols., Loeb Classical Library, New York, 1917; *Tragoediae*, ed. by G. C. Giardina, 2 vols., Bologna, 1966; *Three Tragedies of Seneca (Hercules Furens, Troades, Medea)*, ed. by H. M. Kingery, Norman, Okla., 1966; *Medea*, ed. by C. D. N. Costa, Oxford, 1973; *Agamemnon*, ed. by R. J. Tarrant, Cambridge, 1976.
Translations
The Complete Roman Drama, ed. by G. Duckworth, 2 vols., New York, 1942; *Seneca, His Tenne Tragedies*, tr. by T. Newton, with intro. by T. S. Eliot, Bloomington, Ind., 1966 (reprint of 1581 edition); *Seneca: Four Tragedies and Octavia*, tr. by E. F. Watling, Penguin Classics, Baltimore, 1966.

CRITICISM

C. J. Herington, "Senecan Tragedy," *Arion* 5 (1966):422–471; A. L. Motto, *Seneca*, Twayne World Author Series, New York, 1973; C. D. N. Costa, ed., *Seneca*, London and Boston, 1974; R. J. Tarrant, "Senecan Drama and its Antecedents," *Harvard Studies in Classical Philology* 82 (1978): 213–263.

Shadwell, Thomas   (1641/42–1692)

English dramatist and Poet Laureate. Shadwell was born in either Broomhill or Santon Hill, Norfolk, in 1641 or 1642, the son of a Royalist lawyer. He studied law at the

Thomas Shadwell. [Theatre Collection, The New York Public Library at Lincoln Center, Astor, Lenox and Tilden Foundations]

Middle Temple in London and married an actress, Ann Gibbs, probably between 1663 and 1667. His first comedy, *The Sullen Lovers*, adapted from Molière's *The Bores* (*Les fâcheux*, 1661), was successfully presented in 1668; it was followed by seventeen other plays, among the most notable of which are *The Squire of Alsatia* (1688) and *Bury Fair* (1689). *See* MOLIÈRE.

Early in Shadwell's career, he and Dryden became friendly adversaries, but in the 1680s their differences grew to enmity over politics: Shadwell was a Whig, Dryden a Tory. Though Dryden always triumphed over Shadwell in literary matters, Shadwell finally triumphed politically: upon the accession of William and Mary in 1689, Dryden lost the post of Poet Laureate to Shadwell. *See* DRYDEN, JOHN.

In his later years Shadwell suffered from gout and took opium to relieve the pain. He is thought to have succumbed to an overdose of the drug when he died in Chelsea on November 19 or 20, 1692.

WORK

The Restoration produced not only the brilliant comedies of manners for which the period is famous but also comedies of intrigue and of humors, which were equally popular. As the principal exponent of the Jonsonian comedy of humors, Thomas Shadwell figured prominently during the last third of the seventeenth century. But his plays have suffered an eclipse in the repertory of the modern theatre. Though not so scintillating in wit and not so melodic as the works of William Congreve, his comedies are distinctive, especially as pictures of the ordinary life of the period. *See* JONSON, BEN. *See also* COMEDY OF HUMORS in glossary.

In the first of his eighteen plays, *The Sullen Lovers, or The Impertinents* (1668), the pompous Sir Positive and the poet Ninny are probably reflections of the contemporary dramatist Sir Robert Howard and his versifying brother Edward. The play brims with realism: Emilia's letter writing; Ninny's talk of his barber; the coxcomb Woodcock boasting of his new house. Another major work, *The Humorists* (1670), concerns the love affairs of Crazy, who has the pox. Desiring Theodosia, he induces the maid to help him gain entrance to her bedchamber, but after the wrong window has been pointed out to him, he makes advances to Lady Loveyouth, Theodosia's guardian. The intricate plot of *Epsom Wells* (1672) concerns the tangled affections of two lively young girls and the two gallants they hope to catch. *Bury Fair* (1689) centers on Oldwit's outwitting of his affected wife and stepdaughter. *The Squire of Alsatia* (1688), freely adapted from Terence's *The Brothers* (160 B.C.), contrasts the upbringing of two sons. *The Virtuoso* (1676), one of the clearest expositions of eccentric humors, in which the characters reveal themselves through various spoken asides, deals with the pursuit of Sir Nicholas Gimcrack's wards by Bruce and Longvil. *See* TERENCE.

The Squire of Alsatia (1688). Comedy in which Tim Belfond, brought up in seclusion in the country, journeys to London and immediately falls in with a group of knaves who try to strip him of his inheritance. When Sir

William, Tim's father, arrives in London and hears of Squire Belfond's wild exploits he assumes this squire to be his younger son Ned, who has been brought up in London by an uncle. Most of the action turns on this confusion. Ned, who finally resolves the situation, saves his brother Tim from a disastrous marriage and wins for himself the girls he loves.

Bury Fair (1689). Comedy in which Mr. Wildish, in love with Oldwit's daughter Gertrude, journeys to Bury St. Edmunds to ask her to marry him. There he meets his friend Lord Bellamy, who has also come to court Gertrude. With Bellamy is his page Charles, in reality Gertrude's sister, who is in love with Bellamy and is posing as a boy in order to be with him. Gertrude rejects both her suitors, declaring that she values her freedom more than a husband. When the page's true identity is discovered, Bellamy proposes and is accepted. Thereupon, Gertrude is persuaded to accept Wildish as her husband.

PLAYS

All were first performed in London.

1. *The Sullen Lovers, or The Impertinents.* Comedy, 5 acts. Published 1668. Produced Lincoln's Inn Fields Theatre, May 2, 1668. Based on Molière's *Les fâcheux* (1661).
2. *The Royal Shepherdess.* Tragicomedy, 5 acts. Published 1669. Produced Lincoln's Inn Fields Theatre, Feb. 25, 1669.
3. *The Humorists.* Comedy, 5 acts. Published 1671. Produced Lincoln's Inn Fields Theatre, ca. December, 1670.
4. *The Miser.* Comedy, 5 acts. Published 1672. Produced Theatre Royal, ca. January, 1672.
5. *Epsom Wells.* Comedy, 5 acts. Published 1673. Produced Dorset Garden Theatre, December, 1672.
6. *The Tempest, or The Enchanted Island.* Dramatic opera, 5 acts; verse. Published 1674. Produced Dorset Garden Theatre, Apr. 30, 1674.
7. *Psyche.* Tragedy, 5 acts; verse. Published 1675. Produced Dorset Garden Theatre, Feb. 27, 1675.
8. *The Libertine: A Tragedy.* Comedy, 5 acts. Published 1676. Produced Dorset Garden Theatre, June 15, 1675.
9. *The Virtuoso.* Comedy, 5 acts. Published 1676. Produced Dorset Garden Theatre, May 25, 1676.
10. *The History of Timon of Athens, the Man-Hater.* Tragedy, 5 acts; verse. Published 1678. Produced Dorset Garden Theatre, ca. January, 1678.
11. *A True Widow.* Comedy, 5 acts. Published 1679. Produced Dorset Garden Theatre, ca. December, 1678.
12. *The Woman-Captain.* Comedy, 5 acts. Published 1680. Produced Dorset Garden Theatre, ca. September, 1679.
13. *The Lancashire Witches and Tegue o Divelly, the Irish Priest.* Comedy, 5 acts. Published 1682. Produced Dorset Garden Theatre, ca. September, 1681.
14. *The Squire of Alsatia.* Comedy, 5 acts. Published 1688. Produced Drury Lane Theatre, May, 1688. Adapted from Terence's *Adelphi* (160 B.C.).
15. *The Amorous Bigot with the Second Part of Tegue o Divelly.* Comedy, 5 acts. Published 1690. Produced Drury Lane Theatre, ca. March, 1689.
16. *Bury Fair.* Comedy, 5 acts. Published 1689. Produced Drury Lane Theatre, ca. April, 1689.
17. *The Scowrers.* Comedy, 5 acts. Published 1691. Produced Drury Lane Theatre, ca. December, 1690.
18. *The Volunteers, or The Stock-Jobbers.* Comedy, 5 acts. Published 1693. Produced Drury Lane Theatre, November, 1692.

EDITIONS

Collections
Dramatic Works, 4 vols., London, 1720; *Thomas Shadwell,* ed. by G. Saintsbury, London, 1903; *Dramatic Works,* 5 vols., ed. by M. Summers, London, 1927, New York, 1968.

Individual Plays
Bury Fair. Published in *English Plays, 1660–1820,* ed. by A. E. Morgan, New York, 1935.
The Lancashire Witches and Tegue o Divelly, the Irish Priest. Published in *The Drama: Its History, Literature and Influence on Civilization,* ed. by A. Bates, vol. 22, London, 1903–1904.
The Squire of Alsatia, Published in *Plays of the Restoration and Eighteenth Century,* ed. by D. MacMillan and H. M. Jones, New York, 1938.

CRITICISM

A. S. Borgman, *Thomas Shadwell: His Life and Comedies,* New York, 1928; M. W. Alssid, *Thomas Shadwell,* New York, 1967.

Shaffer, Peter   (1926–   )

British dramatist. His work is notable for its strict and traditional construction, coherent plots, and realistic characters and dialogue. Unlike many of his contemporaries, he remains impersonal, a hidden hand that manipulates plot and characters. His first works as a dramatist were written for television: *The Salt Land* is a classical tragedy set in modern Israel; and *Balance of Terror,* an espionage thriller. Neither showed promise of the great success of his first stage play, *Five Finger Exercise* (1958), a cleverly written drama in which the characters reveal themselves by their reactions to a mysterious and impersonal tutor, the catalyst of the action. In 1962 a double bill of Shaffer's one-act plays was produced: *The Private Ear,* concerning a shy clerk whose illusions about the girl he met at a concert are destroyed by his friend; and *The Public Eye,* a high comedy in which a private detective, hired to spy on a young wife, ends by reuniting wife and husband. Shaffer's epic drama *The Royal Hunt of the Sun* (1964) depicts the conquest of the Inca Empire by the Spaniards and focuses particularly on the developing friendship between Pizarro and the Inca ruler Atahuallpa. Soon after, he produced *Black Comedy* (1965), a farce that draws its inspiration from the Chinese classical theatre, presenting scenes in clear view of the au-

The Public Eye, with (l. to r.) Moray Watson, Geraldine McEwan, and Barry Foster. New York, Morosco Theatre, 1963. [Walter Hampden Memorial Library at The Players, New York]

Five Finger Exercise, with (l. to r.) Michael Bryant, Juliet Mills, and Brian Bedford. New York, Music Box Theatre, 1959. [Friedman-Abeles]

dience that, for the characters onstage, are occurring in the dark. In 1968 it appeared in a double bill with a new play entitled *The White Liars*, set in a fortune-teller's booth at a seaside resort. *The Battle of Shrivings*, produced in 1970, centers on two characters, a philosopher and a poet, who although they have jointly won a prize in humanist studies, are poles apart in their beliefs about man. His subsequent plays include *Equus* (1973) and *Amadeus* (1979).

Five Finger Exercise (1958). Drama depicting what happens to a prosperous upper-middle-class family when the presence of a young German tutor upsets the equilibrium of their lives. A subtle and complex pattern of relationships develops between five characters: Stanley Harrington, the staunchly middle-class father; Louise, his frivolous wife; Clive, their sensitive nineteen-year-old son; Pamela, their teen-age tomboy daughter, and Walter Langer, the tutor. Each member of the family reacts to the presence of Walter according to his or her own needs: Louise dreams of him as a lover, Stanley is able to communicate with him as he is unable to do with his own son, Clive finds in him the companion for whom he has longed, and Pamela finds him disturbing. Finally, in the fury resulting from Walter's declaration that his feelings for her are uncompromisingly filial, Louise insinuates that Walter has encouraged a homosexual relationship to develop between himself and Clive. The misunderstandings, lack of communication, infatuations,

and suppressed resentments result in the tutor's attempted suicide. The basic idea derives from Turgenev's *A Month in the Country*. Produced London, Comedy Theatre, July 17, 1958.

The Royal Hunt of the Sun (1964). Series of scenes that chronicle the conquest and rape of sixteenth-century Peru by the Spanish adventurer Francisco Pizarro and his tiny army of 167 men. Narrated by an aged Martin Ruiz, who as a boy was Pizarro's page on the venture, the play, employing music, dance, and mime, delves into the motivation of Pizarro, a virtual nihilist devoid of country, God, and material ambition. His eventual friendship with the Incan king-god, the youthful Son of the Sun, Atahuallpa, causes his conversion to sun worship, and he tries to prevent the Inca's death. But he is overruled by his bloodthirsty band. Atahuallpa is killed, and Pizarro, in search of solace, awaits proof of the existence of a power greater than death. When Atahuallpa does not rise from death, Pizarro is brokenhearted. Produced Chichester, Festival Theatre, July 7, 1964.

Equus (1973). A young boy employed as a groom in a stable blinds six horses, the witnesses of his first sexual experience with a girl. Dysart, the analyst called in to treat the boy, discovers the religious origins of his obsession with horses, but, caught himself in a loveless marriage with a dentist, questions his right to cauterize the boy's capacity for passion.

Amadeus (1979). A serio-comic investigation of the rumor that Mozart was poisoned by a rival composer, Salieri. The play suggests that Salieri was innocent of the murder but guilty of harboring murderous intentions.

Shakespeare, William   (1564–1616)

English dramatist and poet. He was born in Stratford-on-Avon and baptized on April 26, 1564. His birthday is traditionally celebrated on April 23. The eldest son and first surviving child of John Shakespeare and his wife, Mary Arden, he had three brothers and two sisters. His father, a tenant farmer's son, was a glovemaker who through hard work became a landowner, a justice of the peace, high bailiff (the town's highest political officer), and a gentleman with a coat of arms. His mother was a member of the gentry from Wilmcote. About 1578 John Shakespeare's fortunes began to decline; he ran into debt and was forced to sell some property. Nevertheless, William passed his youth as the son of one of the leading families of a prosperous market town.

It seems likely that he attended a "petty" school from the age of five and, at seven, entered the Stratford Grammar School, which seems to have provided an education as good as any in England. The curriculum was heavily classical, concentrating on Latin and possibly including some Greek. Ben Jonson's statement that Shakespeare had "small Latin and less Greek" was not an attempt to belittle his achievement, for in the same breath he compared him to Aeschylus, Euripides, and Sophocles. *See* JONSON, BEN.

In 1582, at the age of eighteen, William Shakespeare married the twenty-eight-year-old Anne Hathaway, who came from a modest landowning family of Shottery.

Their daughter Susanna was baptized on May 26, 1583, six months after the marriage. Shakespeare's two other children, the twins Hamnet and Judith, were christened on February 2, 1585.

The seven years between 1585 and 1592 have been called "the lost years," for there are no records of Shakespeare's activities after the twins' christening until Robert Greene's contemptuous reference to him in *A Groatsworth of Wit* (1592). By then Shakespeare had obviously enjoyed some success as an actor and dramatist, for otherwise he would have been beneath Greene's contempt. A suggestion that he was a soldier during the lost years seems to be based on confusion about a man with a similar name; a man called William Shakeshafte was a provincial actor; and a late contemporary, William Beeston, states that Shakespeare was a schoolmaster. Recent investigation into the dates of his plays suggests that Shakespeare left Stratford for London between 1584 and 1586 and that, by chance or by evidence of his genius, he quickly established himself there as an actor-dramatist. Some four to nine of Shakespeare's extant plays seem to have been written by 1592. These include the three parts of *Henry VI, Richard III,* and possibly *Titus Andronicus, The Comedy of Errors, The Two Gentlemen of Verona,* and *The Taming of the Shrew. King John* may also date from this early period. *See* GREENE, ROBERT.

Just as little is known of Shakespeare's private life during these lost years. It is almost certain that his wife and children remained in Stratford, and it has been suggested that since his wife's father and brother received Puritan funerals, she too was a Puritan and disapproved of her husband's theatrical activities. Between 1592 and 1594, when the plague closed London's theatres, he probably composed his narrative poems *Venus and Adonis* (1593) and *The Rape of Lucrece* (1594), both authorized for publication by Shakespeare and dedicated to Henry Wriothesley, 3d Earl of Southampton, a young, brilliant, and wealthy member of the court. Both poems were extremely popular; their success and the probable patronage of Southampton suggest that Shakespeare need not have returned to the less distinguished task of writing for the theatre unless he chose to.

He appears to have been dedicated to the theatre, for, unlike most of his fellow dramatists, he wrote almost exclusively for the stage from then on, though popular drama was not considered seriously as literature. Like so many of his contemporaries, he composed sonnets, but they were published without his authority. Shakespeare seems to have been uninterested in preserving his works for posterity, for from then on he published nothing. Only the short poem "The Phoenix and the Turtle," appearing in the volume *Loves Martyr* (1601) in honor of Sir John Salisbury, is "subscribed" by Shakespeare. His plays became the property of his theatre company to dispose of as it chose.

In 1594 he joined the Lord Chamberlain's company as an actor and writer, and he remained for at least sixteen years in what appears to have been a harmonious and profitable artistic and business venture. The Chamberlain's Men, under the patronage of Queen Elizabeth's Lord Chamberlain, was headed by the actor Richard Burbage and his brother Cuthbert, the sons of the actor James Burbage, who had built the Theatre, London's first playhouse, in 1576. It was a joint stock company with ten shares, five owned by the Burbages and the rest divided among Shakespeare and four other actors. With Richard Burbage as leading actor and Shakespeare as principal dramatist, the company prospered, presenting more plays before Queen Elizabeth than any other London company. When it lost the lease of the land on which the Theatre stood, some of the members, including Shakespeare, formed in 1599 a syndicate to finance and build a new theatre, the Globe. In 1603, when James I became King, the Chamberlain's Men received royal patronage and became the King's Men, or King's Servants, London's leading theatrical company. In 1608 the syndicate owning the Globe took over a second theatre, the Blackfriars.

Shakespeare's name appears on the cast lists as one of the "principal comedians" of Jonson's *Every Man in His Humour* and as one of the "principal tragedians" in Jonson's *Sejanus His Fall.* He is reputed by an early biographer to have played Adam in *As You Like It* and the ghost in *Hamlet.*

From 1594 until his retirement in 1611 or 1612, he seems to have been the most popular dramatist of his time. Even his closest rival, Ben Jonson, acknowledged Shakespeare's genius in verses that were extravagant in their praise: "He was not of an age, but for all time!" Shakespeare did not become involved in controversies as

William Shakespeare; engraving on the title page of the First Folio, 1623; from a proof state of the engraving in the Folger Shakespeare Library.

Jonson did, for example, in the so-called war of the theatres; he seems to have been well liked by his contemporaries, for all references to him, except Greene's in *A Groats-worth of Wit*, emphasize his mildness, gentleness, and goodwill.

Much research has been done on the sonnets and toward identifying "Mr. W. H.," to whom they are dedicated. While there is no evidence that Shakespeare authorized or was in any way involved in publishing the 1609 edition of the *Sonnets*, attempts have been made to identify the "fair youth" and the "dark lady" to whom he so frequently alluded. Various critical studies suggest that the "dark lady" was Queen Elizabeth; a courtesan called Lady Negro; the wife of an Oxford innkeeper; or Mary Fitton, the mistress of the Earl of Pembroke. It has also been suggested that the sonnets were private hymns to Shakespeare's homosexual lover. But the feelings of Shakespeare continue to remain an enigma.

The evidence indicates that Shakespeare was careful in money matters, investing his savings (actors in Shakespeare's day were well paid) wisely and cautiously so that in his later days he was a man of some substance. In 1597 he paid £60 for New Place, the second largest house in Stratford, to which he later retired. He received his coat of arms and title "gentleman" after his father's death in 1601. (It is probable that John Shakespeare's coat of arms, granted in 1596, had been financed by his increasingly prominent son.) Purchases of land for £320 in 1602 and for a smaller amount in 1611 made him one of the largest landowners in the district. In 1605 he bought a lease for tithes that brought him an income of about £60 a year. In 1613 he paid £140 for a house in London, in the Blackfriars district.

When Shakespeare retired to his native town in 1611 or 1612, he did not sever his ties with London. In 1612 he was summoned there as a witness in a lawsuit between members of a family in whose house he had lodged years before. In 1613 he took part in the tournament held on the anniversary of the King's accession, helping Richard Burbage design the emblem of the Earl of Rutland's shield. What became of his relationship with his acting company and how and when he disposed of his shares in it are not known. Perhaps his connection with the theatre ended when the Globe burned down in June, 1613, during a performance of his *Henry VIII.*

It appears that Shakespeare enjoyed the life of a country gentleman in Stratford and took some part in local affairs. Little is known about his relationship with his wife; she is mentioned only casually in his will, where she is left his "second-best bed." Their son Hamnet died in 1596, and by 1613 Shakespeare's mother, brothers, and one sister were all dead. Shakespeare's first daughter, Susanna, had married a prominent Puritan physician, John Hall, in 1607; their daughter Elizabeth was born in 1608. Judith, his other daughter, married in 1616. Shakespeare died soon after, on April 23, 1616, and was buried in Stratford. His purchase of tithes entitled him to be buried inside the chancel rail of the parish church.

WORK

Supreme among English dramatists, Shakespeare is probably the greatest dramatist of all time, his only possible competitors being Aeschylus, Sophocles, and Euripides. His work represents the culmination of English Renaissance drama. But it was not until after 1750, 150 years after his death, that Shakespeare's work began to be a major influence upon world drama. Since then his reputation has soared: internationally, his plays have been produced more often than those of any other dramatist, and in many countries more often than plays of native dramatists, a fact all the more remarkable in view of the difficulty of translating his rich, idiomatic Elizabethan language.

Shakespeare's capacity to break through linguistic barriers derives from his perceptive compassion for people, his ability to dramatize abstractions, his appreciation of the dramatic impact of ambiguity, and his magical language. He was influenced by Lyly's prose; Greene's female characterizations; Kyd's revenge tragedy; and Marlowe's heroic characters, style, and verse. Marlowe endowed his characters with majestic and lyrical speech and introduced blank verse into dialogue. Shakespeare transformed this blank verse and varied its rhythms. More self-aware than Marlowe's, Shakespeare's characters become complex and credible human beings, acting from realistic motives lacking in *Tamburlaine the Great* and *Dr. Faustus.* Kyd's *The Spanish Tragedy* helped Shakespeare to acquire the technical mastery he displayed in *Hamlet*, the plot of which is similar to that of *The Spanish Tragedy*, and also in the earlier *Titus Andronicus. See* KYD, THOMAS; LYLY, JOHN; MARLOWE, CHRISTOPHER.

For the chronicle plays, Shakespeare had no important model except Marlowe's *Edward II*; and, in his grasp of complex historical material, his innate sense of drama, and his empathy, no peer. Lyly's euphuistic language and Greene's treatment of romance influenced Shakespeare's romantic drama. Adopting Greene's use of historical framework, adventure, magic, and fantasy, Shakespeare set his romances in remote countries, based their plots on simple tales, and he made fantasy come to life and the impossible seem real by using realistic characters, including comic, ordinary people. *See* CHRONICLE PLAY in glossary.

Historical Plays

Nearly all Shakespeare's historical plays were written early in his career; only *Henry VIII* was written after 1600. But five of the ten histories—*Richard II, Richard III, Henry IV: Part I, Henry IV: Part II,* and *Henry V*—continue to enjoy popular and critical acclaim.

Shakespeare was the first major dramatist to create a cycle of plays based on chronological events significant to the history of his country. He focused on such political crises as rebellion, usurpation, conspiracy, and war, generally showing disorder resolved to order. The only comparable series of plays by another writer is Strindberg's Swedish historical plays, which were based on Shakespeare's pattern. *See* STRINDBERG, AUGUST.

John Barrymore as Richard III. New York, Plymouth Theatre, 1920. [Photograph by Vandamm. Theatre Collection, The New York Public Library at Lincoln Center, Astor, Lenox and Tilden Foundations]

royalty and the nobility but the populace. Falstaff is one of the very few major fictitious characters in any of the histories.

With *Henry V* Shakespeare completed his historical cycle. The next two years yielded *Julius Caesar* and *Hamlet*, and from then on he devoted himself to tragedies and comedies. His final history, *Henry VIII* (if, indeed, it is his, in whole or in part), is merely a sequel to the cycle, a coda on the triumph of the Tudors.

Comedies

Shakespeare's comedies are widely divergent, including rowdy farces, serious romances, and problem satires.

Approximately between 1584 and 1594 he wrote his early comedies: *The Comedy of Errors, The Taming of the Shrew, The Two Gentlemen of Verona,* and *Love's Labour's Lost.* While showing the distinct influence of classical comedy such as that of Plautus in the relationship between servants and masters and the device of mistaken identity, *The Comedy of Errors* is suffused with romantic love and held together by a sympathetic plot. *The Taming of the Shrew,* realistic and boisterous, similarly employs classical techniques, most obviously the courtship plot. Classical literature gave the Elizabethans the stock comic types of the miser and the wealthy girl courted by a rake, a fop, and a *miles gloriosus* ("boastful soldier"); the troublemaking slave derives from both the classical parasite and the native medieval Vice. *See* PLAUTUS *See also* COMEDY; COMMEDIA DELL'ARTE in glossary.

Shakespeare probably had no intention of chronicling English monarchical history when he wrote the three parts of *Henry VI.* In characterization and construction they are relatively simple. In his next play, *Richard III* (1587), Shakespeare's style, rough with Marlovian vitality, provides an effective consonance with the harsh character of Richard III, "hell's black intelligencer."

King John, a mediocre play by Shakespearean standards, is difficult to place in the chronology of his work. It seems to be an adaptation of an earlier effort, possibly a hasty attempt to meet the demands of the company in which Shakespeare had a financial interest. *Richard II* is equally difficult to place chronologically, but it is constructed to combine purity of line with splendor of thematic imagery, a combination as appropriate to the personality of Richard II as is the robust construction of *Richard III* to its hero.

The trilogy consisting of *Henry IV: Part I, Henry IV: Part II,* and *Henry V* is generally considered to be Shakespeare's finest historical achievement. It not only fills the chronological gap between *Richard II* and *Henry VI* but extends the possibilities of the historical play. In earlier historical plays, Shakespeare had progressed from mere chronicles of events to a drama focusing on the character of the particular King; here he was concerned with the nature of monarchy itself. Through his description of the transformation of Prince Hal into Henry V, Shakespeare characterized the qualities essential in a king without lapsing into humorless didacticism. Equally important is his extension of the "historical" form to include not only

Laurence Olivier in the role of Hotspur in an Old Vic Company production of *Henry IV: Part I.* London, New Theatre, 1945. [Culver Pictures]

The Two Gentlemen of Verona and Love's Labour's Lost are true harbingers of Shakespeare's comedic maturity. Despite the incredibility of both the situations and the characters in The Two Gentlemen of Verona, in which two friends court the same woman, the dramatic devices and philosophical attitudes presage the great comedies. Love's Labour's Lost, in which a king and three courtiers renounce a secluded life of study in order to court a princess and three ladies, is heady with verbal wit and innovation.

The mature romantic comedies belong to the period 1594–1600: A Midsummer Night's Dream, The Merchant of Venice, Much Ado about Nothing, As You Like It, and Twelfth Night, or What You Will. They introduce unrealistic situations, fantasy, disguises, clowns, and ultimately happy love. Their style is charming and subtle, and their poetry superb. Incarnations of Shakespeare's humor and rationality, they reflect his observations on human strengths and limitations, and his consciousness of man's constant vulnerability to his own capriciousness. Their range extends from the fantasy and farce of A Midsummer Night's Dream to the threshold of tragedy in The Merchant of Venice, whose central figure is the villain Shylock. Between these two is As You Like It, a delicate pastoral romance in which cynicism shadows but never seriously menaces the idyll. Much Ado about Nothing deals with appearance and reality, and the main interest in the play lies in the subplot's brilliant dialogue and witty repartee, which ultimately leads to love. In

Joseph Shepherd Munden as Autolycus in The Winter's Tale; engraved for the Theatrical Inquisitor, 1813. [Theatre Collection, The New York Public Library at Lincoln Center, Astor, Lenox and Tilden Foundations]

Frances Ternan as the Countess of Rousillon and Lewis Ball as her clown in All's Well That Ends Well. [Theatre Collection, The New York Public Library at Lincoln Center, Astor, Lenox and Tilden Foundations]

Twelfth Night happiness is threatened, but only temporarily, by presumptuousness and indulgence. In The Merry Wives of Windsor, Shakespeare turns to middle-class comedy, reviving the Falstaff of Henry IV, not as the master of impertinence but as a fatuous victim, the dupe of two women.

Between 1602 and 1604 Shakespeare produced the problem, or dark, comedies: Measure for Measure and All's Well That Ends Well. Full of ambiguities, concerned with crucial human and social problems, they are more serious than comic. In All's Well That Ends Well, triumph comes by way of fraud. In Measure for Measure hypocrisy and social corruption are denounced. In both, ethical concepts are questioned.

From 1608 to 1611 Shakespeare wrote the bittersweet comedies: Pericles, Prince of Tyre; The Winter's Tale; Cymbeline; and The Tempest. In all four, sadness results in joy and pain in pleasure. Pericles, dignified in suffering, stands fast against the ugly Dionyza and receives his reward in the loveliness and virtue of Marina. Even at his most vicious, Leontes in The Winter's Tale shows glimmers of repentance. Cymbeline combines the fairy-tale quality of *Pericles* and the pathos of *The Winter's Tale*. Imogen's pure and delightful nature makes her one of Shakespeare's best-loved heroines. In the enchanted world of *The Tempest* despair is transformed to wonder, and reality is inseparable from fantasy.

Tragedies

Eight monumental tragedies were written between 1599 and 1608, the years that also yielded *Twelfth Night* and the problem comedies. *Titus Andronicus* and *Romeo and Juliet* were both written earlier.

Titus Andronicus, while abounding in Senecan horror and sensationalism, reflects the same moral and political concerns as the histories and it juxtaposes order and disorder, duty and disloyalty. By the time of *Romeo and Juliet*, Shakespeare had found his form, and the ensuing tragedies display his mature powers as dramatist and poet. Like Shakespeare's later tragedies, *Romeo and Juliet* assigned a prominent role to fatal coincidence. Splendid characterization, beautiful if not always dramatic poetry, and the magnetic story account for its perennial popularity and frequent revival all over the world.

The four major tragedies are *Hamlet, Othello, King Lear,* and *Macbeth.* With tremendous sweep and cosmic resonances, all four explore the mysteries and fascinations of evil. The unity of tone in each play is unique; language, with its special rhythms and images, evokes thematic content, each play having its own cadences; philosophical significance emanates from the action. Hamlet questions man and society after he learns of his

Act III, scene i, of *Measure for Measure;* from a painting by William Hamilton. [New York Public Library]

Ben De Bar as Falstaff in *The Merry Wives of Windsor.* [Theatre Collection, The New York Public Library at Lincoln Center, Astor, Lenox and Tilden Foundations]

father's murder, and Lear utters a bitter social critique only when he himself is an outcast.

Two plays grouped with the tragedies in the folio but uncharacteristic of Shakespearean tragedy are *Troilus and Cressida* and *Timon of Athens,* both based on Greek history. The former presents the Greeks of the Trojan War in such cynically realistic terms that scholars have variously classified the play as "comedy," "satirical tragedy," and "problem play." *Timon of Athens* is equally pessimistic in its account of human brutishness.

The distinction of Shakespearean tragedy lies in its intensely dramatic power, its grandeur and universality of theme, and its magnificence of poetry and thematically integrated imagery. Shakespeare's most outstanding achievements, the great plays of human motivation, reflect not only his genius as a writer but his depth as a human being.

HISTORICAL PLAYS

The following synopses of historical plays are arranged in chronological order corresponding to the reigns of the various kings.

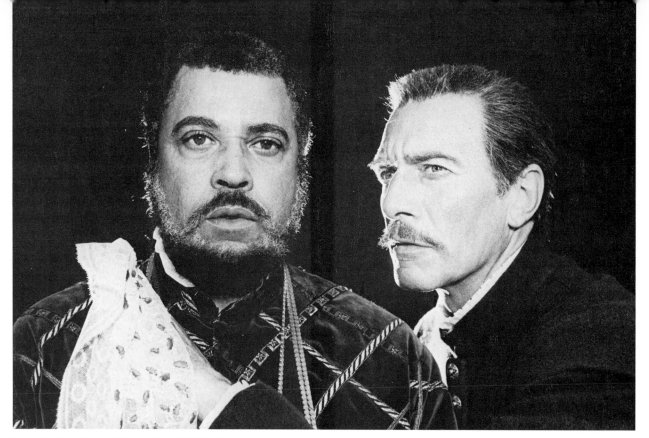

James Earl Jones in the title role of the 1981 Broadway production of *Othello*. Christopher Plummer was Iago. [Martha Swope]

Maude Adams as Juliet. [Brander Matthews Dramatic Museum, Columbia University]

King John (ca. 1596/97). The only historical play not belonging to the continuous chronicle of the conflict between the houses of York and Lancaster that culminated in the Wars of the Roses and the subsequent rise of the Tudors; the events it treats antedate those of the other plays by almost 200 years. The play makes no reference to the Magna Carta (1215), which the historical John's nobles forced him to sign, since for Elizabethans the Magna Carta had little significance. For Shakespeare's contemporaries King John was above all a man bold enough to stand up to the Pope.

John (r. 1199–1216), after the death of his brother King Richard I Coeur de Lion, seizes the throne, which was inherited by Richard's nephew, the "little prince" Arthur of Brittany. Seeking her son's right to the throne, Constance, Arthur's mother, enlists the aid of France and Austria. King Philip II of France upholds Arthur's claims and demands that John relinquish throne and territories to the rightful heir. Instead, John invades France.

Under the leadership of Philip Faulconbridge, illegitimate son of Richard, the English engage the French and Austrian armies at Angiers (Angers), but the battle proves indecisive. The citizens of Angiers, however, propose that the matter be settled by a marriage of conciliation between Lewis (Louis), Dauphin of France, and John's neice, Lady Blanch of Spain. The marriage secures a precarious peace, but John encounters new difficulties when he rejects as Archbishop of Canterbury the papal legate, Cardinal Pandulph (Pandulf). In the furor that ensues, John denies all papal authority and is excom-

Russian actor Nikolay Mordvinov as Othello.

of Lancaster, and Thomas of Woodstock, Duke of Gloucester. In 1397 Gloucester was killed, and Henry Bolingbroke, John of Gaunt's son, accused Thomas Mowbray, Duke of Norfolk, of complicity in the murder, an accusation which precipitated a conflict that was to result in Richard's destruction.

Shakespeare characterizes Richard as "that sweet lovely rose," an elegant, luxurious, sensitive monarch who is "too favorable" to his enemies and who permits or encourages the exploitation of the people by his favorites. When Bolingbroke accuses Mowbray of murder and treason, the vacillating Richard first demands trial by combat, then at the last moment banishes Mowbray for life and Bolingbroke for six years. Soon afterward John of Gaunt dies of old age, after reproaching Richard for his lax and degenerate ways and the consequent decline of England. Disregarding the remonstration, the King seizes John of Gaunt's properties to help finance his Irish wars. Leaving the honest Duke of York to govern England in his absence, Richard departs for Ireland amid growing resentment that culminates in open rebellion when Bolingbroke returns from exile determined to reclaim the title and estates of Lancaster. He immediately becomes the nucleus of a faction that attracts both commoners and nobles, among them the Earl of Northum-

municated by the Cardinal, who threatens King Philip of France with similar treatment unless he breaks the alliance made at Angiers and wages a holy war against the heretic. The renewed hostilities prove disastrous to the French. Arthur is captured and taken to England, where John orders his chamberlain, Hubert de Burgh, to put out his eyes. De Burgh spares the Prince, imprisoning him instead, but the boy is later killed by falling from a tower while trying to escape. Meanwhile, Peter of Pomfret, a prophet, foretells the loss of John's crown on Ascension Day and is jailed immediately.

The death of Arthur provokes a group of disgusted noblemen to defect to the French, who have rallied their forces and, under the Dauphin, invaded Britain. Sensing defeat, John makes his peace with Rome and in a symbolic gesture yields his crown to Cardinal Pandulph, fulfilling Peter's prophecy. Pandulph, now allied with John, presses Lewis to withdraw his forces, but the Dauphin refuses, and the battle goes on, the defecting nobles returning to support their King. Soon afterward John is poisoned, supposedly by a monk, and dies a lingering death in the orchard at Swinstead Abbey. Cardinal Pandulph finally arranges a truce between England and France, Prince Henry, John's son, is named King, and Faulconbridge pledges him his allegiance.

Richard II (ca. 1593/96). First of the eight historical plays dealing with the conflict between the houses of York and Lancaster. Richard II (r. 1377–1399), son of Edward the Black Prince and grandson of Edward III, ascended the throne at the age of ten. The government of England was vested in his uncles, John of Gaunt, Duke

Morris Carnovsky playing King Lear in a 1965 production. [The American Shakespeare Festival Theatre, Stratford, Conn.]

Gérard Philipe in the title role *Richard II*. Paris, Théâtre National Populaire, 1954. [French Cultural Services]

Scenes from *King John:* (left) Philip Davidson as Salisbury and Carol Condon as Constance; (right) Dennis Smith as Lewis and Jose Carillo as Cardinal Pandulph. Oregon Shakespearean Festival, 1969. [Carolyn Mason Jones, Oregon Shakespearean Festival Association, Ashland, Ore.]

berland and his fiery son Henry Percy, called Hotspur. When Richard returns from Ireland, he finds himself virtually powerless, deserted even by York, who has turned his troops over to Bolingbroke. Richard seeks refuge at Flint Castle, where he is found by Bolingbroke and brought to London. He is forced to abdicate and sign a humiliating confession enumerating his crimes. Bolingbroke is proclaimed King Henry IV and orders Richard's imprisonment in the Tower of London and later at Pomfret Castle, where he is brutally murdered by Sir Pierce of Exton, a faithful servant of Bolingbroke. Henry denounces the crime and resolves to do penance by a pilgrimage to the Holy Land.

Henry IV: Part I (1597/98). Drama concerned with the troubles following the deposition and murder of Richard II in 1400. Henry IV, son of John of Gaunt and formerly known as Bolingbroke, has resolved to do penance, by a pilgrimage to the Holy Land, for the murder of Richard, whose throne he has usurped. But faced with rebellion in Scotland and Wales, he postpones the pilgrimage. The Scottish rebels are defeated by the energetic Hotspur (Henry Percy), son of the Earl of Northumberland, who refuses to relinquish his prisoners to the King until Henry ransoms his brother-in-law Edmund Mortimer, who has been captured by Welsh forces under Owen Glendower. When Henry refuses, Hotspur forms an alliance with his father, his uncle, and Glendower, aiming to enthrone Mortimer, whom the childless Richard II had named as his successor. Sovereign powers would be divided among themselves.

Henry's son, the Prince of Wales (Prince Hal), appears to lack Hotspur's manly virtues and has aban-

doned the responsibilities of his position in favor of disreputable companions Sir John Falstaff and his friends Poins, Peto, and Bardolph, frequenters of the Boar's Head Tavern. In one of their pranks Hal induces Falstaff and the others to commit a robbery, and then, disguised and accompanied by Poins, he attacks the robbers and carries off their booty. Later, when Falstaff tells the story, he exaggerates both his own efforts to resist, and the number of his assailants, and, when Hal reveals who they were, Falstaff pretends he was but "a coward on instinct" and could not kill the heir apparent. Hal is summoned to appear before the King. Hearing of Hotspur's move, he takes the field in defense of Henry, having commissioned Falstaff to lead a company of infantry. Hotspur, though deserted at the last moment by his father and Glendower, recklessly enters into battle at Shrewsbury with a seriously depleted force, regardless of the fact that Henry has offered pardon to the rebels. During the fighting Hal kills Hotspur. With the defeat of Hotspur's forces, Henry divides his own: he and Hal leave to fight Glendower and Mortimer, while Prince John, his younger son, is sent to engage the armies of Northumberland and the Archbishop of York.

Henry IV: Part II (ca. 1597/98). This drama covers the last decade (1403–1413) of Henry's reign. Northumberland, learning of his son's death, determines to unite his forces with those of the Archbishop of York and his followers, Hastings and Mowbray, in order to meet Prince John's advancing armies in Yorkshire. However, his wife and Hotspur's widow prevail upon Northumberland to take refuge in Scotland until his allies have proved themselves. King Henry, dispirited and ill, abandons his Welsh campaign and returns to London with Prince Hal. At the home of his friend Justice Shallow, Falstaff, whom Hal has commissioned to raise soldiers for Prince John's army, makes money by allowing his healthier and wealthier recruits to buy themselves out of his service. While preparing for battle, the Archbishop, Mowbray, and Hastings meet the emissaries of Prince John, who promises that their grievances will be redressed if they will disband their armies. They accept this offer in good faith, but John immediately arrests them and orders his own forces to fall upon their disorganized troops. Meanwhile, in London, King Henry is on the point of death. Hal enters his chamber, sees the King asleep in his bed, and places the crown on his own head; when Henry awakens, he assumes that Hal must be eager for his death, an illusion that is dispelled only after prolonged pleading by Hal and the Earl of Warwick. The King, after advising Hal to forestall further civil war by engaging his nobles in foreign campaigns, dies. Falstaff receives word of the King's death and hastens to London to see his friend Prince Hal crowned, promising all his companions riches and favors. But the Prince, now Henry V, sternly admonishes the old reprobate, banishing him from his presence. He then leaves to convene Parliament, raising Prince John's hopes for an invasion of France.

Henry V (ca. 1598/99). Often considered the third play of a trilogy chronicling the growth of Prince Hal into

Monique Chaumette and Jean Vilar in a 1948 French production of *Richard II*. [Italian Cultural Institute]

Eric Berry as Falstaff in *Henry IV: Part I*, 1962. [The American Shakespeare Festival Theatre, Stratford, Conn.]

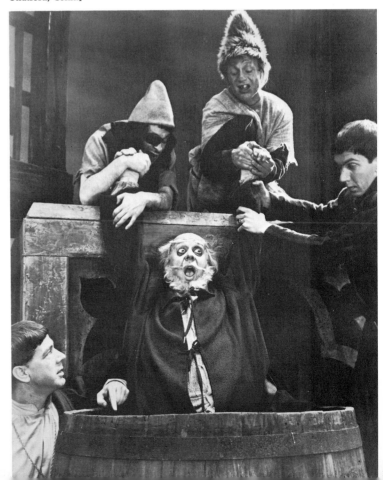

Scenes from a 1969 production of *Henry V:* (top) the peace settlement, witnessed by the dead of Agincourt; (bottom) Len Cariou in the title role wooing Roberta Maxwell as Princess Katherine. [The American · Shakespeare Festival Theatre, Stratford, Conn.]

the great King Henry V (r. 1413–1422). Henry has claimed certain dukedoms in France, and now the Archbishop of Canterbury, to divert attention from a proposed law confiscating inherited lands from the church, convinces the young monarch that he has moral as well as legal rights to the crown of France. In reply to Henry's demands for the throne, the Dauphin of France sends a scornful gift of tennis balls, which infuriates Henry, who raises an army to invade France. Sir John Falstaff has just died, depressed by Prince Hal's rejection of him (*Henry IV: Part II*), and his friends Pistol, Nym, and Bardolph dejectedly join the new expedition, following their King across the English Channel. Having landed in France, Henry, after a hard-fought siege, captures the town of Harfleur and makes his way farther into France. Although his army, a motley assortment of English, Irish, Scots, and Welsh, is dangerously weakened by sickness and privation, Henry leads it across the Somme to Agincourt, where it is confronted by a vastly superior French force. King Charles of France, confident of victory, sends his herald, Montjoy, to demand the English surrender, but he is turned away by Henry. On the eve of battle the French knights joke about their tattered enemy and eagerly await the dawn. In the English camp Henry wanders in disguise among his soldiers, talks with them, and ruminates on the coming conflict and the heavy responsibilities of kingship. The following morning he leads his army into battle and defeats the French, who send Montjoy to accept the conditions for peace which include the hand of Katharine, King Charles's beautiful daughter. Henry's subsequent wooing of Princess Katharine is more a matter of form than passion, although mutual affection draws them closer, and their marriage seals his right of succession to the French throne, ensuring that his future son, the infant king Henry VI, will be crowned King of France and England.

Henry VI: Part I (ca. 1589/91). First part of a trilogy dealing with the political chaos in England resulting from the death of Henry V when his son Henry VI was nine months old. The new King's uncles, the Dukes of Gloucester and Bedford, were regents for England and France, respectively. Their power was contested within their own Lancastrian faction by John Beaufort, Duke of Somerset, and within the house of York by Richard, Duke of York. Thus Shakespeare sets the stage for the Wars of the Roses.

The play opens with the funeral of Henry V. England is bordering upon anarchy. Henry Beaufort, Bishop of Winchester, challenges the power of the Duke of Gloucester, Protector of the Realm during the infancy of Henry VI; and brawling between supporters of the two men breaks out in the streets of London. The English forces in France, ill equipped and poorly supported, are defeated at Orléans and Rouen by French troops inspired by Joan la Pucelle ("Maiden" or "Virgin"; Joan of Arc), whom Shakespeare depicts as a lewd, diabolical witch; only the resourcefulness and determination of their leader, Lord Talbot, has prevented a rout. In London, at the Temple Garden, Richard Plantagenet asks his supporters to pluck white roses as a sign of their belief in

him, and Somerset (of the Lancastrian faction) calls on his to pluck red roses. Edmund Mortimer, Earl of March, whom Hotspur had sought to enthrone (in *Henry IV: Part I*), assures his nephew Richard that he is the rightful heir to the dukedom of York and thus to Richard II and the throne. In Parliament Henry VI, now a youth, grants him his title, and as the Duke of York he accompanies Henry to Paris for his coronation as King of France. There Henry exhorts Somerset and York to abandon their quarrel, appoints York regent of France, and asks them to supply the English forces with men and horses. Their mutual enmity, however, precipitates the defeat of the English at Bordeaux, where Talbot dies brokenhearted over the body of his son. Though Henry is betrothed to the daughter of the Earl of Armagnac, he is persuaded by the treacherous Earl of Suffolk to renounce the betrothal and to marry Margaret of Anjou, with whom Suffolk is himself in love and through whom he hopes to win control over the King and the country.

Henry VI: Part II (ca. 1590/92). Second part of the trilogy dealing with the rivalry for the English throne, which begins with the marriage of Henry VI to Margaret of Anjou. Henry's bride, arriving at the English court, delights the young King with her beauty. But the Lord Protector, Gloucester, and the Earls of Warwick and Salisbury are still smarting under the humiliating terms of the marriage arranged by Suffolk, by which Henry handed over hard-won territories in France to Margaret's father. The Lancastrians, as predicted by Suffolk, soon find an ally in the new Queen, who wants to gain control over her gentle, religious husband. Realizing that the faithful Gloucester may be an obstacle, she and Henry

Lester Rawlins (left) and Philip Bosco in a 1963 production of *Henry V*. [The American Shakespeare Festival Theatre, Stratford, Conn.]

Cardinal Beaufort, Bishop of Winchester, succeed in having Gloucester's wife accused of witchcraft and exiled—a scheme in which they are aided by the Duke of York, who has designs on the throne. They convince the gullible Henry that Gloucester himself is dangerous, and he is put in prison, where the Cardinal and Suffolk have him murdered. Popular reaction to this crime results in the banishment of Suffolk, who is killed by pirates off the Kentish coast. The Cardinal, taken ill, dies unrepentant.

After convincing Warwick and Salisbury of his lawful right to the throne, the Duke of York leaves to quell an Irish rebellion, but before going he incites the notorious rebel Jack Cade to foment an insurrection among the people. Cade's success is short-lived, for his mob, urged on by Lord Clifford, turns on him and forces him to flee; he is later killed in a fight. York, returning from Ireland, marches on London and, meeting the King on the way, demands the removal of his old enemy Somerset, whom Henry sends temporarily to the Tower of London. Later York claims the throne, and the long-smoldering antagonism between the houses of York and Lancaster finally erupts in battle at St. Albans, where Somerset is killed. York, supported by his sons Edward and the hunchback Richard, is victorious over the royal forces, and he hurries to reach Parliament before the King.

Henry VI: Part III (ca. 1590/91). Final play in the trilogy. After the Battle of St. Albans, the King and Queen arrive at Parliament to find York in control, supported by his family and the Earl of Warwick ("the Kingmaker"). Henry, dismayed, surrenders his son's birthright to the crown in return for York's loyalty during his lifetime. He then makes York Protector of the Realm and Warwick Chancellor. Infuriated, Queen Margaret raises an army and defeats the York faction in battle near Wakefield. After humiliating York by crowning him with a paper crown, she stabs him to death.

Warwick, rallying his forces, joins York's sons Edward and Richard and with the half-hearted support of the King, who still bears great affection for Margaret, drives her from England. She takes refuge in France with her son Prince Edward, knighted Prince of Wales. Henry is sent to Scotland, Edward of York is crowned king (Edward IV), and his brothers Richard and George are named respectively Duke of Gloucester and Duke of Clarence. Henry returns to England and is imprisoned in the Tower of London. Meanwhile, Warwick goes to France to arrange a marriage between the new King, Edward IV, and the sister-in-law of Lewis (Louis) XI. He finds Queen Margaret trying to enlist Lewis's aid in restoring Henry VI to the throne.

In the meantime, Edward marries Lady Elizabeth Grey. Furious, Warwick joins the armies of Lewis and Margaret and finds an unexpected ally in York's third son, George, now Duke of Clarence. Edward is temporarily overthrown, and Henry VI is restored to the throne. Edward, having escaped from imprisonment with the help of Richard, Duke of Gloucester, raises an army in Burgundy and returning to England, marches on

Richard III, with Douglas Watson in the title role, 1964. [The American Shakespeare Festival Theatre, Stratford, Conn.]

London, regains the crown, and defeats Warwick's forces. Warwick, from whom the Duke of Clarence has defected, dies in battle. Edward next triumphs over Margaret's armies at Tewkesbury; Richard, Duke of Gloucester, murders Henry VI in the Tower; and the three York brothers dispose of Margaret's son, the Prince of Wales. So Edward's path is cleared of opposition, but the play ends with Richard the hunchback hinting at his own ambition to wear the crown.

Richard III (ca. 1592/93). Henry VI has been murdered by the hunchbacked Richard, Duke of Gloucester, whose brother ascended the throne as Edward IV. Richard now embarks on a ruthless, diabolical campaign to secure the throne for himself.

To eliminate his brother George, Duke of Clarence, from the line of succession, Richard revives a prophecy made to the suspicious Edward that he would be disinherited by an heir whose name begins with "G." This results in the imprisonment of Clarence and his eventual murder, secretly arranged by Richard. Then, over the corpse of Henry VI, Richard wins a promise of marriage from Lady Anne, widow of Henry's son, the Prince of Wales, in whose death he has also had a hand; and, on the death of the ailing Edward IV, he has Edward's two young sons lodged in the Tower. Richard, realizing that the loyal Lord Hastings will not support him, accuses him of treason and has him beheaded. Persuaded by the eloquent Duke of Buckingham, who has now veered to Richard's side, the citizens of London offer Richard the crown, which he accepts after feigning reluctance. At last his hopes are fulfilled; but as Richard III he is uneasy with Edward's sons still alive and arranges their murder. Meanwhile, Henry Tudor, the Lancastrian Earl of Richmond, lands at Milford Haven in Wales with an army to challenge Richard's claim to the throne, and the English nobility, including Buckingham, who now realizes his precarious position, supports him. Richard meets the invading armies at Bosworth Field, where, after a night made hideous by ghosts of his victims, he is killed by Richmond, who then ascends the throne as Henry VII and marries Elizabeth of York, daughter of Edward IV, ending the Wars of the Roses.

Henry VIII (1612). The Tudors have established a firm hold on the English throne. Henry VIII, son of Henry VII and Elizabeth of York, is now the reigning monarch. In this drama Shakespeare investigates the struggle for power preceding Henry VIII's break with the Church of Rome.

Thomas Cardinal Wolsey, Archbishop of York and Lord Chancellor of England, possessed of an overbearing ambition for power and even for the papal throne, has made treacherous agreements with Emperor Charles V to undermine the recent Anglo-French treaty. The Duke of Buckingham, aware of Wolsey's treachery, is an obstacle in his path to power. The Cardinal has him arrested, discredited by bribed witnesses, convicted of plotting

Henry's overthrow, and executed. Wolsey next attacks Henry's Queen, Katharine, who has interceded for Buckingham and has persuaded the King to repeal some of Wolsey's oppressive taxes. Insinuating to Henry that his marriage to Katharine is illegal, since she was his dead brother's wife, Wolsey proposes a divorce, hoping then to persuade Henry to marry the French king's sister. Henry is receptive to the idea, because he is increasingly concerned over Katharine's inability to produce a surviving male heir. At the trial to decide the validity of the marriage, Katharine appears in her own defense, denouncing the treachery that has brought her to this end. Then, at a masked ball given by Wolsey, Henry falls in love with the Protestant Anne Bullen (Boleyn) and plans to marry her. Wolsey, disturbed by the idea of a Protestant alliance, sends a secret message to Rome to delay Henry's separation, but the letter, together with an inventory of Wolsey's vast wealth, falls into the King's hands. Henry impetuously confiscates Wolsey's property and has him arrested for high treason, but the Cardinal never reaches trial; he dies on the way to London at an abbey in Leicester. Henry then orders Cranmer, Archbishop of Canterbury, to enact his divorce, and Anne Bullen, whom Henry has secretly married, is crowned Queen of England. Cranmer, censured by a group of jealous noblemen, is accused of heresy by Stephen Gar-

Henry VIII, with (l. to r.) Walter Hampden playing Cardinal Wolsey, Victor Jory as King Henry, and Eva Le Gallienne as Queen Katharine. New York, International Theatre, 1946. [Photograph by Vandamm. Theatre Collection, The New York Public Library at Lincoln Center, Astor, Lenox and Tilden Foundations]

diner, Bishop of Winchester. Trusting Cranmer, Henry gives him official protection, reprimands the accusing council for treating him unfairly, and names him godfather of the child born to Anne, the princess Elizabeth.

COMEDIES

The Comedy of Errors (ca. 1591/94). Deals with the confused events of one day in the ancient town of Ephesus in Asia Minor and based on *The Twin Menaechmi* by Plautus. An aged Syracusan merchant, Aegeon, is arrested and, unable to pay the ransom demanded of Syracusans who enter Ephesus, is condemned to death by Duke Solinus. But he wins the duke's sympathy by telling his story. Years ago he had been shipwrecked with his wife Aemilia, their identical twin sons, and two infant slaves, also identical twins. When they were rescued, the parents, each with one son and one slave, were separated, and Aegeon had never again seen his wife or the two children. Antipholus, the son brought up in Syracuse by Aegeon, has been searching for his brother and his mother, and for five years Aegeon has been looking for him, coming eventually to Ephesus. After hearing Aegeon's story, the duke grants the old merchant one day's respite to raise his ransom.

The Taming of the Shrew, with Susan Chapple as Bianca and Mary McMurray as Kate. [Neptune Theatre, Halifax, Nova Scotia]

Scene from a 1963 production of *The Comedy of Errors,* with Douglas Watson as Antipholus (on litter). [The American Shakespeare Festival Theatre, Stratford, Conn.]

Without Aegeon's knowledge, Antipholus of Syracuse has recently arrived in Ephesus with his slave Dromio; he does not know that his twin, Antipholus of Ephesus (who is married to the shrewish Adriana), and his slave, Dromio of Ephesus, are also living in the city. None of these characters knows of the presence of the others, so that with the two sets of twins wandering the streets a series of mistaken identities ensues. Antipholus of Syracuse enjoys a pleasant dinner with Adriana, who believes him to be her husband, but makes overtures to her sister Luciana. Antipholus of Ephesus is barred from his own home because Adriana wishes to be left undisturbed with her "husband," and he seeks solace with a courtesan, to whom he gives gifts intended for his wife. A gold chain ordered by Antipholus of Ephesus finds its way into his brother's hands, and Antipholus of Ephesus, who has not yet received the chain, is imprisoned after a charge of nonpayment has been brought by the goldsmith. Antipholus of Syracuse and his Dromio, thinking everyone in the city is mad, decide to leave Ephesus but, pursued by the irate goldsmith, they take refuge in a priory. The confusion is resolved when Ae-

geon, on his way to his execution because he has not been able to raise his ransom money, is recognized by the Syracusans and the abbess of the priory, who is the lost Aemilia. The two sets of twins embrace, mother and father are reunited, Antipholus of Ephesus pays Aegeon's ransom, and the errors are explained.

The Taming of the Shrew (ca. 1593/94). In a boisterous induction (or prologue) a lord finds a tinker, Christopher Sly, asleep in front of an alehouse and has him carried to the most luxurious chamber in his manor. When he awakens, the Lord, by displaying rich clothes, fawning servants, and a "wife" (the Lord's page in disguise), convinces him that he is a wealthy nobleman who has recovered from a long fit of madness.

To amuse this "noble," a company of players performs a comedy, "The Taming of the Shrew," in which Baptista, a rich Paduan merchant, has two marriageable daughters, Katharina, a viper-tongued shrew, and her sister Bianca, gentle and lovable. Baptista proclaims that Bianca shall not marry until after her sister, which leaves Bianca's suitors in a quandary. One of them, Lucentio, sees her by dint of disguising himself as a tutor of languages. Another, Hortensio, has a ne'er-do-well friend, Petruchio, who is willing to accept any bride with a large dowry and announces that he will woo and wed Katharina. He asks Baptista for Katharina's hand, and the merchant is happy to consent. In Petruchio the wild Katharina meets her match. He declares that he finds her "most pleasing," and his uproarious behavior at their wedding is the first step in a merciless campaign for "taming" his strong-willed wife. On their way home he contrives to have her horse throw her in the mud; when they arrive, he starves her on the pretext that the food is ill prepared; he sends her new wardrobe back to the tailor; and he prevents her from sleeping by complaining about the bed. Katharina is so cowed by all this that she finally does whatever Petruchio tells her, even agreeing with him when he says the moon is the sun.

In the meantime, Lucentio has won Bianca's hand, and Hortensio has proposed to a rich widow. At the triple wedding feast, the newly married men bet on whose wife is most obedient to her husband, and Petruchio produces a humbled and obedient Katharina, who lectures both the other brides on their conjugal duties.

The Two Gentlemen of Verona (ca. 1594/95). Valentine, an open and honorable man, and Proteus, in whom there is a streak of inconstancy, have been friends since boyhood but are separated by Valentine's departure to seek his fortune at the Duke's court in Milan. Proteus's father Antonio, unaware that his son is in love with a Veronese lady, Julia, makes him follow Valentine to educate himself by traveling. Before Proteus and Julia are parted, they are secretly betrothed and exchange rings. Arriving in Milan, Proteus finds Valentine in love with the desirable Silvia, who reciprocates his love. But her father, the Duke of Milan, insisting on her marriage to the wealthy but stupid Thurio, locks her in a tower, from which Valentine plans to rescue her. He confides in Proteus who has succumbed, like himself, to Silvia's charms, breaking his vows to Julia. After betraying Val-

An **Italian production of** *The Taming of the Shrew*, **with Renzo Ricci and Laura Adani.** [Italian Cultural Institute]

James Dunn's production of *The Taming of the Shrew* starred Mark Rasmussen (left) as "the gunslinger Petruchio," Reynold Acevedo as "his Mexican sidekick Grumio," and Alice Rorvik as a "blue-jeaned, whip-snapping Kate." [Photography courtesy of Cannery Theatre, San Francisco]

entine's plan to the Duke, who foils his attempt to rescue Silvia and banishes him, Proteus, pretending to help the gullible Thurio, proceeds to woo Silvia himself. Meanwhile, when Julia, anxious about Proteus, arrives in Milan disguised as a page, she discovers his treachery. Unrecognized by him, she obeys his command to bear to Silvia the very ring she herself gave him as a token of her love. Meanwhile, Valentine, captured by a band of forest outlaws, becomes their leader. Silvia escapes from Milan with the aid of the chivalrous Sir Eglamour and, pursued by her father, Thurio, Proteus, and his "page," joins her lover. In the forest, Proteus's treachery is exposed when Valentine overhears him trying to force his attentions upon Silvia, but the noble Valentine forgives his friend's betrayal. The page, now recognized as Julia,

Nina Foch (left) as Kate and Barbara Lord as Bianca in *The Taming of the Shrew*. New York, Phoenix Theatre, 1957. [The American Shakespeare Festival Theatre, Stratford, Conn. Photograph by Friedman-Abeles]

is reunited with the penitent Proteus. The Duke allows his daughter's betrothal to Valentine and agrees to pardon the outlaws, who are willing to serve him loyally.

Love's Labour's Lost (ca. 1593/95). King Ferdinand of Navarre decides to turn his court into "a little Academe" for intellectual and spiritual pursuits. He and three of his lords, Berowne, Longaville, and Dumain, make a pact to lead an ascetic life in pursuit of scholarship and to give up the company of women for three years, a resolution that the witty Berowne prophesies they will be unable to keep. Their only recreation is to be conversation with Costard, a clown, and Don Armado, a verbose and "fantastical" Spaniard. The pact is threatened by the arrival of the Princess of France on a mission for her father, accompanied by three ladies-in-waiting, Rosaline, Maria, and Katharine. Although the pact does not allow the ladies to lodge within the palace walls, Ferdinand soon succumbs to the Princess' charms and his three lords to those of her ladies. Costard is caught with a country wench, Jaquenetta, and since everyone at court is under the same vow of abstinence, he is placed in the custody of Armado, who is himself enamored of Jaquenetta and gives the clown a love letter to deliver to her. Berowne gives him a letter, too, for Rosaline, but the letters are mixed up and presented to the wrong girls. The secret passions of the King and each of the courtiers are discovered when each overhears another reading poems composed to his lady. Berowne is claiming that he is the only one to keep his vow when Costard and Jaquenetta appear with the letter he had written to Rosaline. Admitting their loves and convinced by Berowne that love is a part of knowledge, they give themselves up to masques, revels, and courting. The three men disguise themselves as Muscovites, but the three ladies, learning of this, disguise themselves too and mislead their suitors into wooing the wrong girls. The King and his three lords eventually admit their absurdities, and there follows an entertainment, a classic pageant of the Nine Worthies, provided by a schoolmaster, a curate, Costard, Armado, and his page Moth. In the midst of this, the news arrives that the Princess' father has died. Before leaving, the four ladies make the four men promise to abjure all worldly pleasures for a year, but after that all four pairs of lovers will be reunited.

A Midsummer Night's Dream (ca. 1595/96). Theseus, Duke of Athens, is preparing to wed Hippolyta, Queen of the Amazons. His orders for his wedding celebrations inspire a group of rustic artisans to perform a homemade tragedy, which they plan to rehearse in a nearby wood. Meanwhile, two young Athenian lovers, Hermia and Lysander, take refuge in the wood when Hermia's father insists on her marriage to another youth, Demetrius. They mistakenly confide their elopement plans to Hermia's friend Helena, who is in love with Demetrius. In an effort to win his gratitude, she tells Demetrius of the elopement and then follows in his pursuit of the fugitives.

The forest is teeming with fairies who have come from India for the Duke's wedding. The fairy King, Oberon, having quarreled with his Queen, Titania, sends

Joseph Vernon as Thurio in *The Two Gentlemen of Verona.* [Theatre Collection, The New York Public Library at Lincoln Center, Astor, Lenox and Tilden Foundations]

to finance his courtship of Portia of Belmont, heiress to an enormous fortune. However, Antonio's money is invested in merchant ships and he is forced to borrow the sum from Shylock, a Jewish moneylender. Seeing an opportunity to revenge himself for Christian insults, Shylock declines interest on the loan and, as though in jest, says he will require instead a pound of Antonio's flesh if the money is not repaid by a certain date. At Belmont there are three suitors for Portia's hand, including Bassanio. When they are asked which of three caskets, gold, silver, or lead, contains her picture, Bassanio is the only one to give the right answers, and they become engaged. But this happiness is dispelled when a messenger arrives with news that Antonio's ships have been lost at sea and that Shylock, his resolve hardened by the elopement of his daughter with a Christian, is determined to sue for Antonio's pound of flesh. After marrying Portia, Bassanio hurries to Antonio's aid, having sent gold to Venice to pay the debt. Portia follows, disguised as a lawyer, Doctor Balthasar of Rome, and appears in court, where Shylock, having refused Bassanio's gold, presses his claim for Antonio's flesh despite Portia's plea for mercy. Shylock is about to exact payment when Portia warns him that the agreement calls for flesh only and that on pain of death he must not shed a drop of blood or take a fraction more or less than a pound. Defeated, his plea dismissed, Shylock is forced, as a penalty for plotting against the life of a Venetian, to give half his possessions

Puck, a sprite, to find a magic flower whose juice "on sleeping eyelids laid" will cause the sleeper to fall in love with the first creature he sees on waking. Oberon intends to make Titania ridiculous by using the juice on her. But when he sees Demetrius curtly rejecting Helena, he orders Puck to put the juice on the eyes of Demetrius too. By mistake Puck pours the juice on the sleeping Lysander, who awakens and instantly enamored of Helena, pursues her through the woods. To put matters right, Oberon performs the same service for Demetrius, who falls in love with Helena. With the arrival of Hermia the four lovers are plunged into a series of misunderstandings that are resolved only when Puck removes the spell from Lysander. While the rustic workmen are rehearsing their play, Puck, amused by their clumsy efforts, slips an ass's head on Bottom, the stupid weaver and self-assured star of the troupe, which makes his companions run away in terror; but Titania, now also under the flower's spell, falls in love with him. Oberon, having made her look ridiculous, restores Titania to her former state. The four lovers, now truly matched, are invited by the Duke to return to Athens for a triple wedding, for which the celebrations include a comically bad performance by Bottom and his companions of their play *The Most Lamentable Comedy and Most Cruel Death of Pyramus and Thisbe.*

The Merchant of Venice (ca. 1596/97). Bassanio, a spendthrift Venetian, asks his friend Antonio for a loan

Lawrence Pressman (left) as Berowne and William Hickey as Costard in *Love's Labour's Lost,* 1968. [The American Shakespeare Festival Theatre, Stratford, Conn.]

Scenes from the 1971 Oregon Shakespearean
Festival production of *A Midsummer Night's Dream*.
[Carolyn Mason Jones, Oregon Shakespearean
Festival Association, Ashland, Ore.]

to Antonio and half to the state. Antonio refuses his share but insists on Shylock's leaving his fortune to his daughter and on his becoming a Christian. Reunited with Bassanio at Belmont, Portia reveals that she was Doctor Balthasar and informs Antonio that three of his ships have arrived safely.

Much Ado about Nothing (ca. 1598/99). Don Pedro, Prince of Arragon, after quelling a rebellion led by his bastard brother Don John, pardons him and permits him to join his retinue on a visit to Leonato, governor of Messina. With them are two young lords, Benedick and Claudio, who have distinguished themselves in Don Pedro's campaign. In Messina, Benedick, a confirmed bachelor, resumes a long-standing battle of words with Leonato's niece Beatrice ("Lady Tongue"), and Claudio falls in love with Leonato's daughter Hero. Don Pedro offers to woo Hero by proxy for his young friend, but Don John, smarting for revenge, almost succeeds in convincing Claudio that Don Pedro has designs on Hero. This suspicion is removed by the success of Don Pedro in his matchmaking on Claudio's behalf. He then devises a plot of make Beatrice and Benedick fall in love. At the same time Don John makes a new attempt to slander the innocent Hero by arranging that Don Pedro and Claudio witness what looks like a tryst between Hero and a lover (it is really between Hero's gentlewoman and John's follower Borachio). This time Don John's ruse succeeds,

Katharine Hepburn playing Portia in *The Merchant of Venice*, 1957. [The American Shakespeare Festival Theatre, Stratford, Conn.]

The Merchant of Venice, with Morris Carnovsky (foreground) as Shylock and Barbara Baxley (center) as Portia, 1967. [The American Shakespeare Festival Theatre, Stratford, Conn.]

and the joyous atmosphere is dissipated by Claudio's denunciation of Hero during the wedding ceremony.

The company splits into two camps, with Beatrice and Benedick defending Hero's honor against the allegations of Claudio and Don Pedro. On advice from kindly Friar Francis, Leonato announces that Hero has died of a broken heart, and tragedy seems imminent when Beatrice urges Benedick to challenge the astounded Claudio to a duel. The constable, Dogberry, and the nightwatchmen, who have overheard the drunken Borachio boasting about his deception, eventually expose the plot of Leonato. Chastened, Claudio does penance by marrying, as he thinks, a hitherto unseen and unknown niece of Leonato, only to discover afterward that he is married to his own Hero. Beatrice and Benedick resume their verbal fencing in the old spirit, and finally they too marry.

The Merry Wives of Windsor (ca. 1598/99). Sir John Falstaff, a decrepit old knight who fancies he can still be attractive to women, woos two married women, Mistress Page and Mistress Ford, having designs on their husbands' money. He writes a love letter to each of them, then asks his friends Pistol and Nym to act as go-betweens for him. When they refuse, Falstaff dismisses them peremptorily and has his page Robin deliver the notes, which the ladies immediately compare. Amused

Morris Carnovsky and Dina Doronne as Shylock and Jessica in *The Merchant of Venice,* 1957. [The American Shakespeare Festival Theatre, Stratford, Conn.]

Much Ado about Nothing, with (foreground) Roberta Maxwell as Hero and Robert Foxworth as Claudio and (l. to r., rear) Wyman Pendleton, William Glover, Len Cariou, and Charles Cioffi, 1969. [The American Shakespeare Festival Theatre, Stratford, Conn.]

Philip Bosco and Frank G. Converse as Benedick and Claudio in *Much Ado about Nothing*, 1964. [The American Shakespeare Festival Theatre, Stratford, Conn.]

tion. Mistress Quickly arranges for him to meet the two ladies in Windsor Park late at night. Dressed as Herne, the hunter, and wearing a buck's head, the old knight is tormented by a host of urchins and fairies who are actually Mistress Quickly, Pistol, and a band of boys in costume. Slender and Dr. Caius, who have each arranged to elope with Anne, mistakenly steal away with two "fairies," who both turn out to be boys. Fenton and Anne manage to elude the company and are married.

As You Like It (1599/1600). The rightful Duke, his position and estates usurped by his younger brother Frederick, now lives in the Forest of Arden with a band of loyal followers, but his daughter Rosalind remains at Frederick's court as a companion to his daughter Celia. Rosalind is attracted to Orlando, a youth who defeats Frederick's wrestler. When he discovers that Orlando is the son of an old friend of the Duke, Frederick vents his annoyance by banishing Rosalind from court. Celia insists on following her, and together with Frederick's jester Touchstone they go to the Forest of Arden. Orlando has meanwhile been forced by the hatred of his elder brother Oliver, one of Frederick's courtiers, to take refuge in the same woods.

The fugitives join the outlawed Duke and his followers, who are leading a contented life in the forest. Rosalind, who is disguised as a boy (Ganymede), finds some

and annoyed, they plan revenge on the knavish Falstaff. They send him encouraging messages, arranging for Falstaff to meet Mistress Ford when her husband is away. Pistol and Nym, offended by the way they were discharged, retaliate by warning the respective husbands. Master Page is confident that his wife is faithful, but Master Ford is jealous and decides to spy on his wife. Disguised as "Master Brook," he tells Falstaff that he is in love with Mistress Ford and asks him to be his accomplice in courting her. Falstaff informs him that he is after Ford's money, and, having already planned a rendezvous with the lady, he will be happy to help Brook win her. At the same time Page's daughter Anne is being wooed by three suitors: Slender, an absurd and clumsy gentleman, her father's choice; Dr. Caius, a Frenchman lost in the maze of the English language, the choice of her mother; and Fenton, a sensible young man, Anne's own choice. All three confide in a Mistress Quickly and pay her to act as their go-between. Falstaff keeps his assignation with the mischievous Mistress Ford, who encourages his ridiculous advances until her husband arrives with officers of the law. Abandoning all dignity, Falstaff escapes in a laundry basket while Ford searches for him in vain. A second tryst results in another narrow escape. The husbands, now in their wives' confidence, collaborate with them to effect Falstaff's final humilia-

Gina Malo (left), Charles Coburn, and Jessie Royce Landis in a Theatre Guild production of *The Merry Wives of Windsor*, on tour in 1946. [Photograph by Vandamm. Theatre Collection, The New York Public Library at Lincoln Center, Astor, Lenox and Tilden Foundations]

Sada Thompson as Mistress Quickly and Richard Easton as Pistol in *The Merry Wives of Windsor*, 1959. [The American Shakespeare Festival Theatre, Stratford, Conn.]

his Cesario. Olivia soon becomes enchanted with this handsome youth, and sends him a ring through her melancholy steward Malvolio. In the subplot, the narrow-minded and pompous Malvolio antagonizes Olivia's bibulous uncle Sir Toby Belch, who with Olivia's maid Maria, a clown, Feste, and an absurd knight, Sir Andrew Aguecheek (also a suitor for Olivia's hand), plans to ridicule the egotistical steward. Malvolio receives a love letter, supposedly from Olivia directing him to perform a number of ludicrous actions. Following instructions, he appears before the astounded Olivia, who, believing him to be mad, has him shut up in a dark room. Viola's brother Sebastian has meanwhile arrived on the scene. Mistaken for Cesario, he becomes involved in a comic duel with Sir Andrew, who considers Cesario his rival. Olivia, mistaking Sebastian for her beloved "page," insists on marrying the astonished but willing young man. On learning of the marriage, Duke Orsino sorrowfully denounces Cesario, who disclaims all knowledge of the event. The confusion of identities is cleared up by the appearance of Sebastian, who reveals that "Cesario" is Viola. Orsino then becomes engaged to Viola and Sir Toby to Maria; Malvolio, now released, vows vengeance on the whole pack of them.

All's Well That Ends Well (1602/03). Helena, daughter of a former court physician, is the ward of the Countess of Rousillon, with whose son Bertram she is in love. Bertram, unaware of her love, departs for the French

verses written to her by the lovesick Orlando. Without realizing that "Ganymede" is Rosalind, he confides to "him" his love for her. To test his devotion, Rosalind offers to cure him of his lovesickness if he will woo her as though she were Rosalind, which he does. Oliver, sent by Frederick to find Orlando, is reconciled with him when Orlando saves his life. Then, when he meets Celia, Oliver falls in love with her, and they plan to marry the next day. At the wedding feast "Ganymede" reveals her identity, and a multiple marriage follows. During the festivities the news arrives that Frederick has reformed and, having decided to take religious vows, has restored all lands to his brother the Duke.

A subplot concerns the comic love affair of Touchstone and Audrey, a country girl, and a sardonic commentary on the action is made at intervals by the melancholy courtier Jaques.

Twelfth Night, or What You Will (1599/1600). Viola, a wellborn young woman, is shipwrecked on the coast of Illyria and separated from her twin brother Sebastian, whom she believes drowned. Disguised as a page named Cesario, she enters the service of Duke Orsino, who is languishing with unrequited love for the countess Olivia. Viola wins the duke's confidence and becomes his emissary in the courtship, but she falls in love with him while he, without realizing it, develops a strong affection for

Diana Van Der Vlis as Rosalind and Marian Hailey as Celia in a 1968 production of *As You Like It*. [The American Shakespeare Festival Theatre, Stratford, Conn.]

Carrie Nye portraying Celia in *As You Like It*, 1961. [The American Shakespeare Festival Theatre, Stratford, Conn.]

court, leaving Helena disconsolate. When questioned by the countess, Helena reveals her love, and the countess encourages her to win Bertram. Helena journeys to the court in order to attend the King, who suffers from a disease said to be incurable. She offers one of her father's remedies, cures him within two days, and is granted as a reward her choice of the King's unmarried courtiers. She chooses Bertram, but he rejects her because she is lowborn. However, the King is adamant, and they are married. Bertram immediately departs, with his knavish follower Parolles, to join the army of the Duke of Florence, sending his virgin bride back to his mother. Later he tells her in a letter that he will not recognize her as his wife until she has obtained a ring that he habitually wears and until she has presented him with a child, both apparently impossible since he vows never to return to France. Helena, after starting on a pilgrimage to Italy, allows a report of her death to be circulated. Disguised in her pilgrim's robes, she arrives in Florence, where she learns of Bertram's designs on Diana, daughter of a widow with whom she is lodged. With the widow's help Helena takes Diana's place in a midnight tryst with Bertram. He unwittingly presents her with his ring, and Helena gives him a ring bestowed on her by the King of France. Bertram returns to the French court, where the King, noticing the ring he had given Helena, accuses him of causing her death. In an intricate sequence of revelations Helena appears and tells Bertram that his two con-

Patrick Hines and James Valentine as Sir Toby Belch and Sir Andrew Aguecheek in *Twelfth Night*, 1968. [The American Shakespeare Festival Theatre, Stratford, Conn.]

Granville Van Dusen as Duke Orsino and Helen Carey as Viola in *Twelfth Night,* Minneapolis, 1968. [The Guthrie Theater Company]

ditions have been fulfilled: she has obtained his ring and is carrying his child. Bertram asks her pardon and, impressed by her cleverness and devotion, is reconciled to their marriage.

Measure for Measure (ca. 1603/04?). Duke Vincentio, realizing that Vienna has become corrupt, largely through his failure to enforce the city's laws, announces that he will depart on a visit to Poland and leave the management of his city in the care of a deputy, the cold-blooded, puritanical Angelo. Angelo begins to enforce the law by condemning young Claudio to death for fornication with Juliet, his fiancée. Desperate, Claudio sends for his sister Isabella, a novice in a convent, to intercede with Angelo on his behalf. Despite her eloquent pleas Angelo remains resolute. But she has aroused his lust, and at their second interview Angelo promises to save Claudio if she will give herself to him. Without Angelo's knowledge, the duke has returned to the city disguised as a friar. Overhearing Claudio begging Isabella to consent to Angelo's demands, he suggests she should arrange to meet Angelo but send in her place Angelo's former betrothed, Mariana, who has been living in seclusion since he cast her off. The meeting takes place as planned, but Angelo does not cancel Claudio's execution. The duke manages to substitute the head of another prisoner for that of Claudio, and this

leads both Angelo and Isabella to believe that he is dead. The duke now returns in his own person and at the city gates listens to Isabella's accusations against Angelo. Pretending not to believe her, he sends her to prison and orders someone to arrest the friar who has been seen with her. On reappearing as the friar, he criticizes the government of Vienna and the behavior of the duke. His hood is accidentally torn off, and his identity is revealed. Angelo is ordered to marry Mariana and then to be executed, as was Claudio, "measure for measure," but the pleas of Isabella and Mariana persuade him to let Angelo stay alive; Claudio comes forward and marries Juliet, while Duke Vincentio takes Isabella's hand in marriage.

Pericles, Prince of Tyre (1608/09). The medieval poet Gower, acting as chorus, tells the story of Pericles, Prince of Tyre, a wanderer in the eastern Mediterranean of the ancient world. The young Pericles, a suitor of the King of Antioch's beautiful daughter, is required to solve a riddle, the answer to which reveals the truth about the King's incestuous relations with his daughter. When Pericles answers correctly, the King decides to kill him, and, pursued by assassins, he must leave even his own land of Tyre. He carries a shipload of provisions to the starving citizens of Tarsus and remains for a time as the guest of Cleon, the Governor. On another voyage, he is shipwrecked on the coast of Pentapolis; his bravery in a tournament there wins the love and hand of Thaisa,

Scene from *Twelfth Night,* with (l. to r.) Jim Baker as Sir Toby Belch, Theodore Pejovich as Feste, and Scott Porter as Sir Andrew Aguecheek, in an Oregon Shakespearean Festival production, 1969. [Carolyn Mason Jones, Oregon Shakespearean Festival Association, Ashland, Ore.]

Larry Gates (foreground) in *All's Well That Ends Well*, 1959. [The American Shakespeare Festival Theatre, Stratford, Conn.]

daughter of King Simonides. Learning that the nobles of Tyre believe him to be dead, he sets sail for Tyre with his bride. During a storm Thaisa appears to die in childbirth, and the superstitious sailors demand that her body be cast overboard to calm the tempest. Pericles sadly complies, but the chest in which she is placed is washed up on the shore of Ephesus, where Cerimon, a skilled physician, revives her. She becomes a priestess of Diana.

Pericles takes the baby, Marina, to Tarsus, where for fourteen years she is brought up by Pericles's friend Cleon and his wife Dionyza. Her beauty inflames the jealousy of Dionyza, who plans to have her killed. The attempt is thwarted when Marina is abducted by a band of pirates who sell her to a brothel at Mytilene. She succeeds in preserving her virtue and even reforms Lysimachus, Governor of Mytilene, who goes to the brothel in disguise. Pericles eventually goes to Tarsus to fetch Marina but is told that she is dead. Deeply grieved, he throws off his royal robes, dons rags, and leaves Tarsus. Returning to Tyre, his ship is driven by winds to Mytilene; Lysimachus comes aboard and, noticing Pericles's despair, sends for Marina to entertain him with song and dance. Pericles, questioning her, discovers her to be his daughter. In a dream he is then told by Diana to go to her temple at Ephesus and describe the loss of his wife. He finds Thaisa there, the family is reunited, and Pericles succeeds his father-in-law as King of Pentapolis.

The Winter's Tale (1610/11). Polixenes, King of Bohemia, has been visiting his boyhood friend Leontes, King of Sicilia, but when asked to stay on a little longer, he refuses. When Hermione, Leontes' wife, makes the same request, he consents. As a result, Leontes at once becomes obsessed with the idea that Hermione is unfaithful to him. So great is his jealousy that he orders his counselor Camillo to poison Polixenes. When Camillo warns Polixenes and they escape together to Bohemia, Leontes takes their flight as confirmation of his previous suspicions. He publicly reviles his wife and has her cast into prison, where she gives birth to a daughter; her attendant Paulina shows the infant to Leontes, who furiously disowns the baby as Polixenes's bastard and secretly orders Paulina's husband Antigonus to take her away and abandon her. Even when the oracle at Delphi confirms Hermione's innocence, Leontes remains obdurate; but, with the death of his son and a report that Hermione too is dead, he repents and goes into mourning.

Antigonus meanwhile leaves the infant on the coast of Bohemia, together with tokens that eventually establish her identity and instructions that she be named Perdita. Soon after, he is killed by a bear and his ship is wrecked in a storm, so that no report reaches Sicilia. Perdita is found by an old Shepherd and his clownish son,

New York Shakespeare Festival production of *Measure for Measure*, with Shepperd Strudwick (left), 1966. [Friedman-Abeles]

A modern dress-version of *Pericles* directed by Toby Robertson was offered by New York's Jean Cocteau Repertory in 1980. Shown are (l. to r.) John T. Bower, Harris Berlinsky, and Andrew MacCracken. [Photograph by Gerry Goodstein]

with whom she remains as daughter of the family for sixteen years, growing into a young woman of such beauty and grace that Prince Florizel, Polixenes's son, happening to meet her, falls in love with her and decides to marry her. His father, who opposes the match, spies upon them during a pastoral festival and then, revealing himself, forbids their betrothal. But Florizel is determined; with the help of Camillo, who orders the roguish peddler Autolycus to change clothes with Florizel, the couple escape on a ship to Sicilia, but not before Autolycus has, with the help of his new finery, duped the Shepherd and his son into boarding the same ship that is carrying the two lovers. Polixenes follows them to Sicilia, where he is reconciled with Leontes and learns the truth about Perdita. Paulina takes the company into her chapel and shows the grieving Leontes a statue of the Queen, which before his astonished eyes comes to life and turns out to be the real Hermione, who has lived in seclusion all these years.

The Tempest (1611). For twelve years before the play begins, the sorcerer Prospero and his daughter Miranda have been marooned on a desert island. Once Duke of Milan, Prospero had allowed his obsession with necromancy to dominate his life, so that his treacherous brother Antonio, with the aid of Alonso, King of Naples, had usurped his title and set him and Miranda adrift in a boat. Prospero's faithful counselor Gonzalo had secretly provided him with books on magic and food. Now they live on the island attended by spirits under Prospero's control; the only other inhabitant of the island is Caliban, a savage, deformed creature. As the play begins, a ship bearing Prospero's old enemies passes the island, and raising a tempest he wrecks the vessel. Among the shipwrecked are Antonio, Gonzalo, Alonso with his son Ferdinand, and Alonso's brother Sebastian, who all land safely but are scattered over the island. Ferdinand and Miranda fall in love. Antonio plots with Sebastian to murder Alonso and Gonzalo. Meanwhile, the recalcitrant Caliban plots with Alonso's jester Trinculo and butler Stephano to murder Prospero and take control of the island. The spirit Ariel, Prospero's servant, discovers both plots and reveals them to his master. After the celebrations for the betrothal of Ferdinand and Miranda, a masque performed by spirits and nymphs, Caliban and his plotters are punished by spirits in the shape of dogs. Then Prospero, summoning the nobles through Ariel's magical music, reveals his identity, forces Antonio to restore his dukedom, and foils the plot against Alonso,

Ken Ruta (standing) and Mark Wheeler in *The Tempest.* San Francisco, Geary Theatre, 1970–1971 season. [Courtesy American Conservatory Theatre, San Francisco, Calif. Photograph by Hank Kranzler]

who is overjoyed to find his son alive and delighted by Miranda. Renouncing his occult powers, Prospero gives a final command to Ariel to ensure a calm voyage for the travelers' return home.

TRAGEDIES

Titus Andronicus (1584/93). Melodramatic tragedy in which Titus Andronicus, having led the Romans to victory over the Goths, is offered the imperial crown, which he declines, supporting the claim of Saturninus, the former Emperor's eldest son, and promises him the hand of his daughter Lavinia. However, Bassianus, younger brother of Saturninus, abducts her, aided by Titus's sons, one of whom Titus kills when the boy blocks his pursuit of Lavinia. Saturninus now chooses to marry Tamora, captured Queen of the Goths, who despises Titus because he has killed one of her sons. Tamora influences Saturninus's jealousy of Titus's popularity with the people and his anger at losing Lavinia. Both continue to feign friendship for him, attending a hunt Titus has arranged. When Tamora and her lover, the Moor Aaron, are discovered during the hunt by Bassianus and Lavinia, Tamora gives orders for them to be silenced. Her sons kill Bassianus, throwing his remains in a pit, and rape Lavinia, before cutting off her hands and tongue. Then Titus's sons Martius and Quintus, drawn to the camouflaged pit by Aaron, stumble into it. When Saturninus is brought to witness the scene, the brothers are accused of Bassianus's murder.

Later, in Rome, Titus pleads for Martius and Quintus, and Aaron promises that if Titus will chop off his hand and send it to the Emperor, they will be spared. Titus complies, but his hand is returned with the heads of his executed sons. Vowing revenge, Titus orders another son, Lucius, banished for trying to rescue his brothers, to form an army among the Goths. Lavinia manages to explain her mutilation by writing the names of Tamora's sons in the sand on the floor. Titus now feigns madness in order to expose the criminals. Meanwhile, Tamora has secretly given birth to a black child and, fearing it will be discovered by Saturninus, sends it to Aaron, who kills all witnesses and returns a white child to take its place. He then escapes to the Goths with his own baby. Lucius now advances on the city with his army of Goths, and Tamora arranges a peace conference, hoping to trick him. Presuming that Titus is demented, she disguises herself as Revenge and taunts him before going to the conference. However, she returns to a banquet served by Titus, only to find that her sons have been killed and their bones ground into the food. Titus first kills Tamora and then, to end her misery, Lavinia; Saturninus kills Titus; and Lucius kills Saturninus. From a balcony the saddened Lucius then tells the people the evil story. He is proclaimed Emperor. Aaron, who has been found among the Goths and brought back by Lucius, is condemned to a lingering death by starvation.

Romeo and Juliet (1591/96). Tragedy of young love set in Renaissance Verona, where a long-standing feud between two houses, the Capulets and the Montagues, provides the violent milieu in which the ill-fated lovers

Scene from *Romeo and Juliet,* with (l. to r.) Eulalie Noble as Lady Montague, Larry Gates as Montague, and Dino Narizzano as Benvolio, 1959. [The American Shakespeare Festival Theatre, Stratford, Conn.]

that Juliet is dead; brokenhearted, he returns to Verona. In the Capulets' burial vault Romeo encounters Paris, who, mistaking him for a grave robber, challenges him. In the ensuing fight Paris is killed. Romeo takes poison and dies at Juliet's side. Friar Laurence arrives as Juliet awakens, asking for her husband. She discovers Romeo's corpse, and stabs herself with his dagger. Montague and Capulet arrive on the scene and are sadly reconciled over the bodies of their children.

Julius Caesar (1599/1600). Tragedy set during the last days of the Roman Republic and the beginning of the empire. Although Marcus Brutus is the tragic hero, Julius Caesar, living and dead, dominates the play.

In 45 B.C., Caesar, having routed the sons of the Roman general Pompey, who were warring against Rome, returns in triumph. The people rejoice, but certain officials deplore Caesar's growing political ambition. At the feast of Lupercal, Mark Antony, Caesar's chief supporter, offers him the throne, which he refuses, but several patricians, including Marcus Brutus, Caesar's friend, fear he will yet make himself king. Under the leadership of Cassius, who envies Caesar, a plot to kill him is hatched. Brutus, whom the populace reveres, is wooed by the conspirators and, believing he is acting for the good of Rome, joins them.

Despite warnings and ill omens, on the Ides of March, 44 B.C., Caesar is lured to the Capitol and there stabbed to death by the conspirators, Brutus dealing him the final blow. Antony, spared on Brutus's advice, pretends to submit to them and is given permission to de-

are destroyed. The feud has so disrupted the life of the city that the Prince has threatened both families with death if their conflict continues. However, Romeo, Montague's son, and his friends Benvolio and Mercutio, prankishly go to Capulet's masked ball to help cure Romeo of a sentimental infatuation. At the ball Romeo and Juliet, Capulet's daughter, meet and fall in love. During the ball Capulet's nephew, the hot-tempered Tybalt, discovers Romeo's identity, but Capulet prevents him from challenging the uninvited guest.

Later that night, Romeo, unable to sleep, steals into Capulet's garden, where he overhears Juliet, from her balcony, confess her love for him to the stars. After exchanging passionate declarations of love, they decide to marry in secret. The next day, with the help of Juliet's nurse, they are married by Friar Laurence, Romeo's adviser, who hopes the union will heal the feud between the Capulets and the Montagues. After the wedding Romeo and his friends encounter Tybalt, who challenges him. Forced to avenge a friend's death, Romeo kills Tybalt, for which he is banished. After spending his wedding night with Juliet, he flees to Mantua. Meanwhile Juliet's parents are arranging her wedding to Paris, a nobleman. Desperate, Juliet seeks advice from Friar Laurence, who gives her a drug that will make her seem to be dead; she will then be placed in the Capulet tomb, from which Romeo will later steal her away. Juliet follows instructions, but the plan miscarries. The friar's letter to Romeo fails to reach him. Instead, Romeo hears

Roger Kozol as Romeo, Patrick Hines as Friar Laurence, and Carolyn Norton as Juliet in *Romeo and Juliet,* 1969. [Carolyn Mason Jones, Oregon Shakespearean Festival Association, Ashland, Ore.]

Romeo and Juliet, with (l. to r.) Grace Hampton as Lady Capulet, Gordon Burby as Capulet, Jane Cowl as Juliet, and Jessie Ralph as the Nurse. New York, Henry Miller's Theatre, 1923. [Theatre Collection, The New York Public Library at Lincoln Center, Astor, Lenox and Tilden Foundations]

liver Caesar's funeral oration. Brutus first assures the crowd that Caesar's murder was in Rome's interest; then Antony, with subtle but passionate rhetoric, incites the mob to seek vengeance for Caesar's murder, and the conspirators are forced to leave Rome. Antony now joins Octavius Caesar and Aemilius Lepidus in a triumvirate, and Antony combines forces with Octavius against the conspirators.

At Sardis, meanwhile, Brutus accuses Cassius of withholding funds. A reconciliation follows their quarrel, and Cassius allows Brutus to persuade him, against his better judgment, to meet the enemy in battle. That night Caesar's ghost appears to Brutus and tells him they will meet at Philippi. There, during a battle in which Brutus is at first successful against Octavius's forces, Cassius is hard-pressed by Antony. Unaware of Brutus's victory and believing that he is being overtaken, Cassius orders his servant to kill him. Subsequently, Brutus is defeated and commands his servant to hold his sword while he runs upon it, saying as he does so, "Caesar, now be still . . . ." When Antony and Octavius come upon the body of Brutus, they praise him as the only honest man among the conspirators, having done what he did for

what he thought was the good of Rome and not for personal gain.

Hamlet (1600/01). Renaissance revenge tragedy based on a medieval Danish tale. The complex and puzzling personality of Hamlet, Prince of Denmark, forms the heart of the play. On the death of his father, King Hamlet, young Hamlet returns to Elsinore from his studies at Wittenberg. Within two months his mother, the queen, marries his uncle Claudius and they ascend the throne. Though grief-stricken and appalled by his mother's "incestuous" remarriage, Hamlet remains silent, acquiescing to Claudius's and Gertrude's request that he remain at Elsinore. His friend Horatio reports that he and two guards have several times seen the ghost of Hamlet's father on the battlements. Hamlet joins their watch that night and confronts the ghost, who reveals that Claudius killed him, though without the Queen's knowledge. Hamlet swears to avenge the murder and bring peace to his father's troubled spirit. He decides to feign madness in order to observe Claudius and seek verification of the ghost's story.

Before these events, Hamlet has wooed Ophelia, daughter of Polonius, Lord Chamberlain to Claudius.

Douglas Watson as Brutus and Barbara Colby as Portia in *Julius Caesar*, 1966. [The American Shakespeare Festival Theatre, Stratford, Conn.]

Since Polonius has advised Ophelia to repel Hamlet's advances, he concludes that her rejection of him has unbalanced Hamlet. Claudius, however, is more skeptical, and he summons two of Hamlet's friends, Rosencrantz and Guildenstern, to spy out the secret of his malady, but in this they fail. Meanwhile, Hamlet devises a plan to make the King's guilty conscience betray him. He instructs a company of strolling players to enact a play about a murder similar to that of his father. During the performance Claudius reacts violently to the play, revealing his guilt to Hamlet, who is elated. He later finds Claudius alone in prayer but hesitates to kill him for fear that Claudius's contrite soul will go to heaven. Instead, Hamlet denounces his mother's untimely affection for Claudius. Discovering that someone is hidden behind a curtain and believing it to be Claudius, Hamlet stabs through the curtain and kills the prying Polonius. Claudius dispatches Hamlet to England escorted by Rosencrantz and Guildenstern, who carry orders to have him executed there. But Hamlet escapes at sea, substituting instructions to the English King to have Rosencrantz and Guildenstern put to death, and returns. Heartbroken by Hamlet's abandonment of her and by her father's death, Ophelia goes mad and drowns herself. Her brother Laertes has returned from France to avenge the death of his father and is persuaded by Claudius to lure Hamlet into a friendly fencing match during which he will kill Hamlet with a poisoned foil.

John Ramsey (left) plays Cassius and Allen Hamilton, Brutus in *Julius Caesar*, Minneapolis, 1969. [The Guthrie Theater Company]

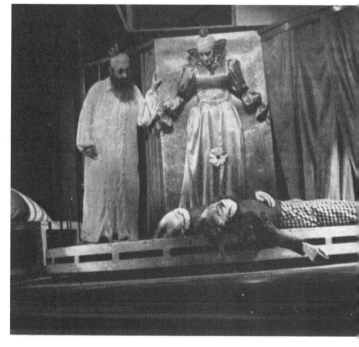

A 1930s Prague production of *Hamlet* inspired by a 1932 Marxist interpretation originally staged in Moscow and subsequently banned. Claudius and Gertrude view the bodies of Rosencrantz and Guildenstern. [*Theatre in Action*]

Hamlet, with Leslie Howard in the title role and Joseph Holland as Horatio. New York, Imperial Theatre, 1936. [Photograph by Vandamm. Theatre Collection, The New York Public Library at Lincoln Center, Astor, Lenox and Tilden Foundations]

During the match Laertes and Hamlet are both fatally wounded. At the same time, Gertrude unwittingly drinks some poisoned wine that Claudius has prepared for Hamlet. Before he dies, Laertes reveals the truth to Hamlet about the poisoned foil and begs Hamlet's forgiveness; Hamlet then kills Claudius. After Hamlet himself dies, Fortinbras, Prince of Norway, arrives in Denmark. Restoring order to the troubled kingdom, he proclaims his right to the Danish throne and orders ceremonial obsequies to honor Hamlet.

Troilus and Cressida (ca. 1598/1603). Story of Troilus and Cressida, set within the larger story of the Trojan War. During a truce in the eighth year of their campaign against Troy the Greek generals meet to discuss strategy. Agamemnon, their commander, is disturbed by the growing disunity in the Greek ranks, caused by lack of morale among their leaders: Achilles' arrogance and laziness, the subversive influence of his friend Patroclus, the angry outbursts of Ajax, and the railing of his servant Thersites. When a challenge is brought from Hector, eldest son of Priam, King of Troy, to any Greek who will meet him in single combat, the Greeks, realizing that the challenge is directed at Achilles, arrange a lottery in

Fritz Weaver as Hamlet in 1958. [The American Shakespeare Festival Theatre, Stratford, Conn.]

Scene from a Norwegian production of *Hamlet*. Oslo, National Theatre, 1956. [Royal Norwegian Embassy Information Service]

Donald Madden as Hamlet and Patricia Falkenhain as Queen Gertrude in a 1961 Phoenix Theatre production. [Courtesy of Phoenix Theatre. Photograph by Henry Grossman]

Alfred Drake (left) as Iago and Earle Hyman in the title role of a 1957 production of *Othello*. [The American Shakespeare Festival Theatre, Stratford, Conn.]

which Ajax will be chosen, hoping to humiliate Achilles, who reacts by moodily declining to join them in the field the following day. Greek terms for peace—payment of an indemnity and the return of Helen, King Menelaus's wife who had been abducted by Priam's son Paris—are rejected by the Trojans, despite the protests of Hector. Meanwhile, Troilus, Priam's youngest son, has fallen in love with Cressida, daughter of Calchas, a Trojan priest who has joined the Greeks, and her uncle Pandarus arranges a meeting for them. The young couple swear mutual devotion. But Calchas has a Trojan prisoner exchanged for his daughter, and Cressida is led off to the Greek camp by Diomedes just as the fight between Hector and Ajax proves abortive: Hector refuses to harm Ajax because they are kinsmen. The Greeks and Trojans then feast together, and Troilus is told that Diomedes is in love with Cressida. From a hiding place he discovers that she has already deceived him with Diomedes. During the following day's skirmish Troilus looks for his rival while Menelaus looks for Paris, but neither is successful. Hector enters the fray despite the warnings of the prophetess Cassandra, Priam's daughter, and kills Patroclus, causing the enraged and grief-stricken Achilles to shake off his moodiness and join the battle. Finding Hector at rest, Achilles dishonorably kills him and then drags his body about the field tied to his horse's tail. The Trojans withdraw to mourn, and Pandarus is left behind, musing on his dubious trade.

Othello (1602/03). Tragedy set in Renaissance Italy, in which a noble, uncomplicated, and apparently rational man, Othello the Moor, is destroyed by jealousy. A general serving the Venetian state, he unwittingly arouses the jealousy of Iago, his ensign, who had expected promotion, by instead promoting Cassio, who, Iago claims, has little experience.

Othello has secretly married Desdemona, daughter of Brabantio, a Venetian senator. To make mischief, Iago informs her father of the elopement but uses his dupe Roderigo, a rejected suitor of Desdemona, to mask his own involvement. Brabantio accuses Othello of bewitching his daughter but it becomes clear that she chose him of her own free will.

Suddenly, Othello is sent by the senate to defend Cyprus against the Turks. There Othello presides as Governor, the Turks having been destroyed in a storm at sea. Iago, who accompanies him, now sets out to convince Othello that Desdemona has been unfaithful to him with Cassio. After making Cassio drunk and causing him to lose his rank for disorderly conduct, he persuades him to ask Desdemona to intercede on his behalf. By the cunning manipulation of people and circumstances, by hints and innuendo, and by capitalizing on his own reputation for honesty, Iago gradually makes Othello believe Desdemona to be unfaithful. After gaining possession of a handkerchief given to her by Othello, and planting it in Cassio's room, Iago convinces Othello of her duplicity and Cassio's guilt.

Under Iago's spell Othello succumbs to jealousy, decides to kill Desdemona, and agrees to Iago's killing Cassio. Iago deputes the task to Roderigo, but Cassio is only

James Earl Jones (left) as Othello and Anthony Zerbe as Iago in *Othello*, 1971. [Center Theatre Group, Mark Taper Forum, Los Angeles, Calif.]

French production of *Othello*, with (l. to r.) Leopold Biberti, Eléonore Hirt, and Aimé Clariond, Théâtre Marigny, Paris. [French Cultural Services]

wounded, and to avoid being exposed Iago kills Roderigo. Meanwhile, Othello, refusing to believe Desdemona's protestations of innocence, smothers her in her bed. Emilia, Iago's wife and Desdemona's waiting woman, realizes her husband's villainy and reveals the truth to Othello. Iago murders Emilia, and Othello tries to kill him but fails and stabs himself, kissing Desdemona as he dies. Cassio, who has succeeded Othello as Governor of Cyprus, orders Iago to be tortured and then executed.

Timon of Athens (1604/05). Timon, a wealthy Athenian "free-hearted gentleman," lavishly entertains multitudes of acquaintances but has only three true friends: Alcibiades, an impecunious general; Apemantus, a cynical philosopher who advises him against "false hearts"; and Flavius, his faithful steward. Told that his undiscriminating prodigality has led to bankruptcy, Timon asks for loans from those he has helped financially. But, one by one, they desert him. Lucullus pretends to be away from home, Lucius complains that he has no funds, and Sempronius feigns anger at being the last to be asked. The disappointed Timon invites his perfidious friends to a banquet at which he places beautiful covered dishes before them. They contain nothing but warm water, which he dashes in their faces. He then abandons his mansion for a hermit's cave near the sea. Meanwhile, Alcibiades, asking mercy for a condemned soldier, is banished by the senate. Angry, he rallies his troops and marches on Athens. Finding Timon, now a poor misanthrope, Alcibiades offers his old friend what money he can from his small resources. But Timon has, while digging for roots, discovered a buried treasure. Learning that Alcibiades is about to avenge himself on the Athens he now hates, Timon dispenses money to the troops, not out of friendship, he assures Alcibiades, but out of hatred. Timon drives away the old philosopher Apemantus, who rails at his friend for abandoning society, telling him that nature can be just as cruel. Two thieves who try to steal his treasure are encouraged by him to go on stealing, and he sends them away with gold. Even Flavius, convincing his master of his love, is given a large sum and asked to leave. Two senators come to tell Timon that they regret the great wrongs done him. When they offer him money and position to return, he scornfully refuses. Alcibiades, arriving in Athens with his troops, negotiates a settlement, promising vengeance only upon his and Timon's enemies. But Timon has died, still hating men, and been buried near the sea.

King Lear (ca. 1605/06). Tragedy set in pre-Christian Britain. The elderly King Lear of Britain decides to abdicate and divide his kingdom among his three daughters, with whom he will live alternately. During the ceremony of the land distribution, Lear announces that the extent of his gift to each will depend upon her affection for him. His hypocritical elder daughters Goneril and Regan make extravagant promises of love, but his youngest, the virtuous Cordelia, unable to express her deep affection, says only that she loves him as a daughter should. Angered by what he interprets as indifference, Lear disowns her, but the King of France is still willing to marry

King Lear, **with (l. to r.) Janis Young, Clement Fowler, and Rene Auberjonois in the title role, Pittsburgh, 1965. [Courtesy of American Conservatory Theatre, San Francisco, Calif.]**

her, while Lear's devoted courtier, the Earl of Kent, defends her. For this he is banished. Meanwhile, the old Earl of Gloucester is deceived by his ambitious bastard Edmund into believing that his legitimate son Edgar is planning to murder him. He disowns Edgar and raises Edmund to his estate.

Lear soon discovers that his trust in Goneril and Regan is misplaced. Their cruelty is limitless. When they refuse him shelter from a storm unless he will submit to their authority, he goes out into the night, accompanied only by his faithful fool and his servant, the loyal Kent in disguise. The three find refuge in a hovel occupied by the fugitive Edgar, also disguised, and at this point Lear goes mad. Later, Kent, learning that Goneril and Regan are planning to murder Lear, arranges with Gloucester's help to convey him to Dover, where Cordelia has landed with the French Army.

Meanwhile, Edmund advances himself by betraying his father, who has secretly helped Lear. Gloucester is seized by the two sisters, blinded by Cornwall, Regan's husband, and cast out. Witnessing this barbarity, a servant mortally wounds Cornwall. Edgar, still disguised, finds his blind father wandering on a heath and leads him to Dover. Cordelia finds Lear and tenderly nurses him back to sanity and to an awakened sense of humanity. Goneril and Regan compete for the love of Edmund, who has become the leader of Cornwall's forces and with whom Albany, Goneril's weak but honorable husband, reluctantly joins forces against the invading French.

The Britons defeat the French in battle, and Cordelia and Lear become Edmund's prisoners. He secretly orders their execution. Jealous of the advantage Regan's widowhood gives her with Edmund, Goneril poisons her sister only to kill herself moments later when Albany discovers her adultery. Edgar reveals himself to Gloucester, who then dies happy in the knowledge that his son is safe.

Edgar challenges and defeats Edmund, who, as he dies, confesses that he has ordered the death of Lear and Cordelia. Edgar is too late to save Cordelia, whose dead body is brought in by Lear before he too dies. Edgar and Albany survive to restore the kingdom.

Macbeth (ca. 1605/06). Macbeth and Banquo, generals in the service of King Duncan of Scotland who have just suppressed a rebellion led by the Thane of Cawdor, encounter three witches on a heath. The witches hail Macbeth as Thane of Cawdor and prophesy that he will become king and that Banquo will beget kings. Soon after, emissaries arrive from the King to confer upon Macbeth the vanquished Cawdor's title, which makes Macbeth realize that he could make the rest of the prophecy come true. Learning on his return home that the King will spend a night at his castle, he acquiesces to his strong-willed wife's plot: she drugs the King's guards, leaves their daggers ready for her husband to use, and he kills Duncan. When the murder is discovered, Macbeth kills the guards, pretending to think them responsible for it. Fearing for their own lives, Duncan's sons Malcolm and Donalbain leave the country. Consequently they are suspected of their father's murder and Macbeth,

Scene from an Italian production of *Macbeth*, with Irma Gramatica and Ruggero Ruggeri. [Italian Cultural Institute]

next in line, is proclaimed King.

Worried by the witches' prophecy that Banquo's descendants will be kings, Macbeth invites him and his son Fleance to a banquet but arranges for murderers to intercept and kill them. Just before the festivities the assassins report that Banquo is dead but that Fleance has escaped. Greeting his guests, Macbeth sees the ghost of Banquo and calls out, almost revealing his guilt; Lady Macbeth makes excuses for him and quickly dismisses the group. Macbeth again consults the witches, who assure him that none "of woman born" shall harm him, that he shall be safe until Birnam Wood comes to Dunsinane, but that he should beware of Macduff. Returning to Dunsinane and learning that Macduff, a powerful lord, has left Scotland to join Malcolm and the army he is raising in England, Macbeth orders the murder of Lady Macduff and her children. Malcolm's army, led by Macduff and camouflaged with boughs from Birnam Wood, now moves against Macbeth, who is horrified that the prophecy seems to be fulfilling itself. Lady Macbeth, deranged by guilt, dies, and Macbeth is killed in battle by Macduff, whose Caesarean birth was an unnatural one, being "from his mother's womb untimely ripp'd." The prophecy has been fulfilled, and Malcolm is proclaimed King of Scotland.

"this false soul of Egypt," Antony turns on her. Frightened, Cleopatra escapes to her monument and sends Antony word of her suicide; soon regretting her message, she sends another, but the message that she is alive comes too late. Antony has fallen upon his sword and, dying, is carried into her presence. When she learns that Octavius is planning a triumphal return to Rome with her marching behind him to be reviled by the rabble, she commits suicide by means of deadly asps, smuggled to her by a countryman.

Coriolanus (1607/10). Tragedy set in ancient Rome, where a struggle for power is being waged between plebeians and patricians. The citizens, suffering from shortage of food, rebel against their patrician leaders, in particular against Caius Marcius, a brilliant general and a rigorous upholder of the virtues and values of his class. Marcius, filled by his mother Volumnia with such pride that he cannot compromise his aristocratic principles, hates the common people, and they in turn hate him. Despite his opposition to the plebeians' demands, the senate allows five tribunes to represent them, including Junius Brutus and Sicinius Velutus, demagogues who despise Marcius. His friend Menenius Agrippa, who is popular with the plebeians, tries to mediate between him and the people, but his efforts are cut short by news of impending war: the Volscians, a neighboring people led

Josef Sommer in *Coriolanus,* 1965. [The American Shakespeare Festival Theatre, Stratford, Conn.]

Katharine Cornell as Cleopatra and Kent Smith as Enobarbus in *Anthony and Cleopatra.* New York, Martin Beck Theatre, 1947. [Photograph by Vandamm. Theatre Collection, The New York Public Library at Lincoln Center, Astor, Lenox and Tilden Foundations]

Antony and Cleopatra (1606/07). Octavius Caesar, Lepidus, and Mark Antony rule the Roman Empire as an uneasy triumvirate. Their relations are strained by Antony's prolonged stay in Egypt, the result of his infatuation with Cleopatra, Queen of Egypt. With news that his wife Fulvia is dead and that the triumvirate is threatened by Sextus Pompeius, son of Pompey the Great, Antony at last leaves Egypt and returns to Rome. To cement his new alliance with Octavius, Antony agrees to marry his sister Octavia. When she hears of this, Cleopatra flies into a rage but immediately begins plotting to win back Antony. Campaigning in Athens, Antony hears that Octavius has imprisoned Lepidus and has attacked Pompeius, breaking their recent treaty. Hoping to mollify Octavius, Antony sends Octavia to Rome, but his subsequent return to Egypt intensifies Octavius's intention to gain sole control of the empire; he marches against Antony, who decides to battle him at sea, depending on Cleopatra's unreliable navy which lets him down.

Octavius presses on and Antony again meets him, this time by land. All goes well for Antony until Cleopatra, seeing that Octavius will probably be victorious, withdraws her forces, causing Antony's defeat. Blaming by Tullus Aufidius, plan to march on Rome. Marcius and the other generals go to stop the Volscians.

At the Battle of Corioli, Marcius's bravery inspires his troops, and they defeat the enemy. Disdaining both praise and spoils, he is given the honored title "Coriolanus." On his return to Rome, the senate nominates him as a candidate for consul. To win this office, Coriolanus reluctantly follows the custom that the candidate must display his wounds and gain the crowd's support in a public ceremony, and he wins scattered approval. Later, however, Sicinius and Brutus, representing the common people, refuse to endorse his appointment and persuade the mob not to vote for him. His friends persuade him that he should try to mollify the citizens, but goaded by the tribunes, he loses his temper, publicly denounces the people, and is banished.

Cursing Rome, Coriolanus joins Aufidius, who again plans to attack the city. Together they march on Rome. Before the gates of the city, Coriolanus appears deaf to appeals by his friends; but not to an appeal by his mother to his nobility and patriotism. He withdraws his troops to Corioli, where the jealous Aufidius denounces him as a traitor. During the confusion that follows, the mob, urged on by Aufidius, stabs Coriolanus to death; and then Aufidius, filled with remorse, vows to honor his memory.

Cymbeline (1609/10). Cymbeline, King of Britain, urged on by his evil second wife, has agreed to the marriage of his daughter Imogen to Cloten, his wife's son. But Imogen has secretly married Posthumus Leonatus, whom Cymbeline banishes. Posthumus goes to Rome and there accepts a wager with the evil Iachimo, who says that he can make Imogen into an unfaithful wife. Arriving in Britain, Iachimo talks to her and realizes that she will never betray Posthumus. Through trickery, he steals into her room hidden in a trunk, takes a bracelet given her by Posthumus, and returns to Rome, winning the bet and Posthumus's diamond ring, which was a gift from Imogen. In despair Posthumus sends his servant Pisanio to kill Imogen, giving him a letter containing false instructions for her to meet him at Milford Haven, in Wales. But Pisanio, convinced that his master has been misled, helps Imogen to escape.

Dressed as a page calling herself Fidele, Imogen sets out for Rome to find Posthumus but loses her way in the Welsh hills. She is sheltered there by Belarius, a British lord who, to avenge his unjust banishment by Cymbeline twenty years before, had kidnapped the king's infant sons, Imogen's brothers, Arviragus and Guiderius. Meanwhile, Imogen's absence has been discovered by Cloten, whose pursuit is misdirected by the faithful Pisanio's use of Posthumus's false letter. Disguised as Posthumus, Cloten encounters Belarius and the brothers in the hills, provokes Guiderius, and is killed by him. Meanwhile, Imogen takes a drug, thinking it a restorative, but it makes her appear to be dead.

The brothers leave her body in the forest beside Cloten's, and when she awakens, believing the corpse to be Posthumus, she faints. When she recovers, she is found by Lucius, commander of the Roman legions who are

A 1965 production od *Coriolanus*, with (l. to r.) Frederic Warriner, Rex Everhart, and Patrick Hines. [The American Shakespeare Festival Theatre, Stratford, Conn.]

invading Britain because of Cymbeline's failure to pay the tribute due to the emperor Augustus. With the Roman forces come Iachimo and Posthumus. Posthumus, disguised as a British peasant, joins the British Army, which, led by Belarius and the two princes, routs the Romans. But, hoping to die, Posthumus then claims to be a Roman and is taken prisoner. With other prisoners, including Lucius, Iachimo, and the disguised Imogen, he is brought to Cymbeline's tent. Seeing her ring on Iachimo's finger, Imogen demands an explanation. Iachimo confesses, Imogen reveals herself and is reunited with Posthumus. Belarius and the brothers are reinstated, and peace is made with Rome.

Plays

Eighteen of Shakespeare's plays were printed in early editions, called "quartos," before their publication in ths First Folio (1623), the earliest collected edition of his plays. Several of these quarto editions are said to be mangled versions of the original manuscripts, either reported from memory by actors ("memorial reconstruction") or transcribed from stenographic notes taken by an agent of the printer during the course of a performance ("stenographic report"). These corrupt versions are termed "bad quartos" and are so designated below. Although the division of plays into acts was not unknown in Shakespeare's time, only three bad-quarto editions were divided like this before the First Folio. Even in this carefully edited edition six plays remained undivided. *See* FOLIO; QUARTO in glossary.

Since it is assumed that Shakespeare's plays were performed soon after they were written, only the date of production or the best estimate of that date is given. While the chronology below is based on a consensus of scholarly material, it is necessarily approximate and may differ in certain particulars from the chronology of individual scholars.

"Q" followed by a numeral refers to the number of the quarto. "F1" refers to the First Folio, a text based upon either a promptbook version (a copy of the play taken from the author's manuscript for use on the stage), the original, uncorrected manuscript itself ("foul papers"), or the corrected copy submitted to the acting company ("fair copy"). In the listing of sources, "Halle" refers to Edward Halle's *The Union of the Two Noble and Illustrious Families of Lancaster and York* (1547, 1548); "Holinshed" to

Raphael Holinshed's *The Chronicles of England, Scotland and Ireland* (1577, 1587); and "Plutarch" to Sir Thomas North's *The Lives of the Noble Grecians and Romans* (1579; *New Lives*, 1595, 1603), a translation of Jacques Amyot's French version (1559/1565) of Plutarch's *Parallel Lives*.

See STATIONERS' REGISTER in glossary.

1. *Henry VI: Part I*. History, 5 acts. Published 1623 (F1). Produced ca. 1589/91. Earliest recorded production: London, Rose Theatre (Strange's Men), Mar. 3, 1592 (if the *Harry VI* performed was Shakespeare's play). Shakespeare may have collaborated on the play or reworked an earlier version. Sources: Halle and Holinshed.

2. *Henry VI: Part II*. History, 5 acts. Stationers' Register: Mar. 12, 1594. Published 1594 (Q1, bad); 1600 (Q2, bad); 1619 (Q3, bad); F1. Each of the quartos is titled *The First Part of the Contention Betwixt the Two Famous Houses of Yorke and Lancaster*. Produced ca. 1590/92. No recorded production during Shakespeare's lifetime. Sources: Halle and Holinshed.

3. *Henry VI: Part III*. History, 5 acts. Stationers' Register: Apr. 19, 1602. Published 1595 (Q1, bad); 1600 (Q2, bad); 1619 (Q3, *Henry VI: Part II and Part III* combined); F1. Q1 and Q2 were printed under the title *The True Tragedies of Richard Duke of York, and the Death of Good King Henry the Sixt*. The combined bad quartos of Parts II and III were printed in 1619 under the title *The Whole Contention Betweene the Two Famous Houses, Lancaster and Yorke*. Produced ca. 1590/91; known to have been performed before September, 1592. No recorded production during Shakespeare's lifetime. Sources: Halle and Holinshed.

4. *Richard III*. Tragedy, 5 acts. Stationers' Register: Oct. 20, 1597. Published 1597 (Q1, abridged); 1598 (Q2); 1602 (Q3); 1605 (Q4); 1612 (Q5); 1622 (Q6); F1 (based on Q6 with material from Q3). Produced ca. 1592/93. Earliest recorded production: London, Rose Theatre (Sussex's Men), Dec. 30, 1593 (if the *Buckingham* performed was Shakespeare's play). Sources: Halle and Holinshed.

5. *Titus Andronicus*. Tragedy, 5 acts. Stationers' Register: Feb. 6, 1594. Published 1594 (Q1); 1600 (Q2); 1611 (Q3); F1 (based on Q3 with additions). Produced 1584/93 (possibly ca. 1592). A *Titus and Vespacia* was performed by Strange's Men on Apr. 11, 1592. The title page of Q1 refers to performances by Pembroke's Men, who were disbanded in the summer of 1593. Earliest recorded production: London, Rose Theatre (Sussex's Men), January, 1594. Chief sources: Seneca's *Thyestes* and *Thoades*; Ovid's *Metamorphoses* (I, i).

6. *The Comedy of Errors*. Comedy, 5 acts. Published 1623 (F1). Produced ca. 1591/94. Earliest recorded production: London, Gray's Inn, Dec. 28, 1594. Source: Plautus's *Menaechmi*.

7. *The Taming of the Shrew*. Comedy, 5 acts. Stationers' Register: May 2, 1594? Published 1623 (F1). Produced ca. 1593/94. Early records create considerable confusion between Shakespeare's play and the anonymous *The Taming of a Shrew* (wr. ca. 1589, pub. 1594). One of the two (referred to as *The Taming of a Shrew*) was performed in Newington on June 13, 1594. The two plays are so similar that the anonymous one may be either a source or a corrupt text of Shakespeare's. Source: No direct source, but there is some material from George Gascoigne's *Supposes*.

8. *The Two Gentlemen of Verona*. Comedy, 5 acts. Published 1623 (F1). Produced ca. 1594/95. No recorded production during Shakespeare's lifetime. Source: Bartholomew Yonge's translation (wr. 1582, pub. 1598) of Jorge de Montemayor's *La Diana enamorada* (1559?).

9. *Love's Labour's Lost*. Comedy, 5 acts. Stationers' Register: Jan. 22, 1607. Published 1598 (Q1); F1. Produced ca. 1593/95. Earliest recorded production: At court, ca. Dec. 25, 1597. Source: No known source; apparently the play is original.

10. *Romeo and Juliet*. Tragedy, 5 acts. Stationers' Register: Jan. 22, 1607. Published 1597 (Q1, bad); 1599 (Q2); 1609 (Q3); n.d. (Q4); 1637 (Q5); F1 (based on Q3). Produced 1591/96 (probably ca. 1595/96). The title page of the first quarto refers to performances by Lord Hunsdon's Men. No recorded production during Shakespeare's lifetime. Source: Arthur Brooke's poem *The Tragical History of Romeus and Juliet* (1562), adapted from Pierre Boaistuau's French version (1559) of Matteo Bandello's novella *Romeo e Giulietta*, included in *Le novelle di Bandello*.

11. *Richard II*. Tragedy, 5 acts. Stationers' Register: Aug. 29, 1597. Published 1597 (Q1); 1598 (Q2); 1598 (Q3); 1608 (Q4); 1615 (Q5); F1 (based on Q3 and Q5). Produced ca. 1593/96. Earliest recorded production: London, home of Sir Edward Hoby, Canon Row, Dec. 9, 1595 (if the *K. Richard* performed was Shakespeare's play). Source: Holinshed.

12. *A Midsummer Night's Dream*. Comedy, 5 acts. Stationers' Register: Oct. 8, 1600. Published 1600 (Q1); 1619 (Q2); F1 (based partly on Q2). Produced ca. 1595/96. Earliest recorded production: At court, Jan. 1, 1604 (if the *Play of Robin Goode-Fellow* performed was Shakespeare's play). Source: No particular source.

13. *King John*. History (*The Life and Death of King John*), 5 acts. Published 1623 (F1). Produced ca. 1596/97 (or possibly even before 1590). No recorded production during Shakespeare's lifetime. Source: Anonymous play *The Troublesome Raigne of John King of England*, Parts I and II (pub. 1591).

14. *The Merchant of Venice*. Comedy, 5 acts. Stationers' Register: July 22, 1598. Published 1600 (Q1); 1619 (Q2); F1 (based on Q1). Produced ca.

1596/97. Earliest recorded production: At court (King's Men), Feb. 10, 1605. Source: No known source, although there are many parallel situations in other works.

15. *Henry IV: Part I*. History, 5 acts. Stationers' Register: Feb. 25, 1598. Published 1598 (Q1); 1599 (Q2); 1604 (Q3); 1608 (Q4); 1613 (Q5); 1622 (Q6); F1 (based on Q5). Produced 1597/98. Earliest recorded production: Lord Chamberlain's Men, Mar. 6, 1600. Sources: Holinshed and the anonymous play *The Famous Victories of Henry V* (wr. 1588, pub. 1598).

16. *Henry IV: Part II*. History, 5 acts. Stationers' Register: Aug. 23, 1600. Published 1600 (Q1); F1 (based on Q1 with additions and deletions). Produced ca. 1597/98. Earliest recorded production: At court, 1612. Sources: Same as *Henry IV: Part I*.

17. *Much Ado about Nothing*. Comedy, 5 acts. Stationers' Register: Aug. 4, 1600. Published 1600 (Q1); F1 (based on Q1). Produced ca. 1598/99. Earliest recorded production: At court, 1612. Sources: François de Belleforest's French translation (1559) of Bandello's *Novelle* (No. 22; 1554); Sir John Harington's translation (1591) of Ludovico Ariosto's *Orlando furioso* (V; 1532); and Edmund Spenser's *The Faerie Queene* (II, iv; 1591).

18. *Henry V*. History, 5 acts. Stationers' Register: Aug. 4, 1600. Published 1600 (Q1, bad); 1602 (Q2, bad); 1619 (Q3, bad); F1. Produced ca. 1598/99. Earliest recorded production: At court (King's Men), Jan. 7, 1605. Sources: Same as *Henry IV: Part I*.

19. *The Merry Wives of Windsor*. Comedy, 5 acts. Stationers' Register: Jan. 18, 1602. Published 1602 (Q1, bad); 1619 (Q2, bad); F1. Produced ca. 1598/99. Earliest recorded production: London, Whitehall (King's Men), Nov. 4, 1604. Source: No known source; apparently the play is original.

20. *Julius Caesar*. Tragedy, 5 acts. Published 1623 (F1). Produced 1599/1600. Earliest recorded production: London, Globe Theatre (?), Sept. 21, 1599. Source: Plutarch.

21. *As You Like It*. Comedy, 5 acts. Stationers' Register: Aug. 4, 1600. Published 1623 (F1). Produced 1599/1600. Earliest recorded production: Wilton House, Wiltshire (King's Men), Dec. 2, 1603 (reported performance based on a lost letter). Source: Thomas Lodge's *Rosalynde, or Euphues' Golden Legacy* (1590).

22. *Twelfth Night, or What You Will*. Comedy, 5 acts. Published 1623 (F1). Produced 1599/1600. Earliest recorded production: London, Whitehall, Jan. 5, 1601 (?); Middle Temple, Feb. 2, 1602. Source: Part of Barnabe Riche's *Farewell to Military Profession* (1581), which is based on Belleforest's translation (1571) of Bandello's *Novelle* (II, 36; 1554), in turn based on the Sienese comedy *Gl'ingannati* (1531).

23. *Hamlet*. Tragedy, 5 acts. Stationers' Register: July 26, 1602. Published 1603 (Q1, bad); 1604 (Q2); 1611 (Q3); n.d. (Q4); F1 (based in part on Q2). Produced 1600/01. Earliest recorded production: "Lately acted" by July, 1602; Cambridge and Oxford, 1603. Sources: Belleforest's translation (1576) of Saxo Grammaticus's *Historia danica* (1514); lost *Ur-Hamlet* (1594) or either Thomas Kyd or Shakespeare.

24. *Troilus and Cressida*. History (so called in the first quarto; redesignated "tragedy" in the First Folio), 5 acts. Stationers' Register: Feb. 7, 1603. Published 1609 (Q1, first state); 1609 (Q1, second state); F1. Produced London, Globe Theatre (?; Lord Chamberlain's Men), ca. 1598/1603 (probably 1601/02). References to production are indefinite and somewhat contradictory. No recorded production during Shakespeare's lifetime. Chief sources: Geoffrey Chaucer's *Troilus and Criseyde* (ca. 1385); William Caxton's *Recuyell of the Historyes of Troye* (1474/75); George Chapman's translation of *Seven Books of the Iliad*

25. *All's Well That Ends Well*. Comedy, 5 acts. Published 1623 (F1). Produced 1602/03. No recorded production during Shakespeare's lifetime. Source: William Painter's translation, published in his *The Palace of Pleasure* (1566), of the tale "Giglietta di Nerbona" from Giovanni Boccaccio's *The Decameron* (III, ix; 1353).

26. *Othello*. Tragedy, 5 acts. Published 1622 (Q1); F1. Produced 1602/03. Earliest recorded production: London, Whitehall (King's Men), Nov. 1, 1604. Source: Giambattista Giraldi Cinthio's *Hecatommithi* (III, vii; 1565).

27. *Measure for Measure*. Comedy, 5 acts. Published 1623 (F1). Produced ca. 1603/04? Earliest recorded production: At court (King's Men), Dec. 26, 1604. Source: George Whetstone's play *Promos and Cassandra* (1578), based on Giraldi Cinthio's *Hecatommithi* (VIII, v; 1565).

28. *Timon of Athens*. Tragedy (*Life of Timon of Athens*), 5 acts. Published 1623 (F1). Produced 1604/05. No recorded production during Shakespeare's lifetime. Source: Plutarch; Lucian's *Timon, the Misanthrope*; anonymous play *Timon* (wr. ca. 1585); Painter's *The Palace of Pleasure* (1566).

29. *King Lear*. Tragedy, 5 acts. Stationers' Register: Nov. 26, 1607. Published 1608 (Q1, bad); 1619 (Q2, bad); F1 (based in part on Q1). Produced ca. 1605/06. Earliest recorded production: London, Whitehall, Dec. 26, 1606. Sources: Holinshed; Spenser's *Faerie Queene* (II,x); *The Mirror for Magistrates* (1559); anonymous play *King Leir* (wr. ca. 1594, pub. 1605).

30. *Macbeth*. Tragedy, 5 acts. Published 1623 (F1). Produced ca. 1605/06 (perhaps 1601/02). Earliest recorded production: London, Globe Theatre, Apr. 20, 1611. Source: Holinshed.

31. *Antony and Cleopatra*. Tragedy, 5 acts. Stationers' Register: May

20, 1608. Published 1623 (F1). Produced 1606/07. No recorded production during Shakespeare's lifetime. Source: Plutarch.

32. *Coriolanus.* Tragedy, 5 acts. Published 1623 (F1). Produced 1607/10. No recorded production during Shakespeare's lifetime. Chief source: Plutarch.

33. *Pericles, Prince of Tyre.* Comedy ("play"), 5 acts. Stationers' Register: May 20, 1608. Published 1609 (Q1, bad); 1609 (Q2); 1611 (Q3); 1619 (Q4); 1630 (Q5); 1635 (Q6); not in F1 or F2; F3 (1664; based on Q6). Produced 1608/09. A performance was reported between Jan. 5, 1606, and Nov. 23, 1608. Earliest recorded production: Christmas, 1609. Sources: John Gower's *Confessio amantis* (1393); Laurence Twine's *The Pattern of Painful Adventures* (wr. before 1576).

34. *Cymbeline.* Tragedy, 5 acts. Published 1623 (F1). Produced 1609/10. A performance was reported before Sept. 12, 1611. No recorded production during Shakespeare's lifetime. Sources: Holinshed; Boccaccio's *The Decameron* (II, ix; 1353); possibly the anonymous play *The Rare Triumphs of Love and Fortune* (1589).

35. *The Winter's Tale.* Comedy, 5 acts. Published 1623 (F1). Produced 1610/11. Earliest recorded production: London, Globe Theatre, May 15, 1611. Source: Robert Greene's *Pandosto, or The Triumph of Time* (1588).

36. *The Tempest.* Comedy, 5 acts. Published 1623 (F1). Produced 1611. Earliest recorded production: London, Whitehall (King's Men), Nov. 1, 1611. Sources: No known source for the plot, although there were many sources for the material on the shipwreck and the island in contemporary travelers' accounts of the Americas.

37. *Henry VIII.* History, 5 acts. Published 1623 (F1). Produced 1612. Earliest recorded production: London, Globe Theatre, June 29, 1613 (the day the theatre was burned down). Sources: Holinshed; John Foxe's *The Book of Martyrs* (1563); possibly Samuel Rowley's play *When You See Me, You Know Me, or The Famous Chronicle of King Henry VIII* (ca. 1604). Shakespeare may have collaborated on this play, possibly with John Fletcher.

38. (With John Fletcher). *The Two Noble Kinsmen.* Comedy, 5 acts. Stationers' Register: Apr. 8, 1634. Published 1634 (Q1); 1679 (F2 of the plays of Beaumont and Fletcher); not in Shakespeare's F1. Produced ca. 1613/14. No recorded production during Shakespeare's lifetime. Source: Chaucer's "The Knight's Tale" from *The Canterbury Tales.* Authorship: Although some scholars reject either Shakespeare or Fletcher, most agree that the two were collaborators (as stated on the title page of Q1). Shakespeare may have written Act I, scenes i and ii; Act III, scene i; and Act V, scenes i and iii.

EDITIONS

There are so many editions of Shakespeare that the following list includes only the most important.

Comedies, Histories and Tragedies, First Folio, ed. by J. Heming and H. Condell, London, 1623 (the Second, Third, and Fourth Folios, editors unknown, were based on the First and were published in 1632, 1663, and 1685 respectively); *Works,* ed. by N. Rowe, 6 vols., London, 1709 (Alexander Pope's 6-volume edition, 1725, is based upon Rowe); *Works,* ed. by L. Theobald, 7 vols., London, 1733 (Thomas Hanmer's 6-volume edition, 1744, is based on Theobald, as is William Warburton's 8-volume edition, 1747); *Comedies, Histories and Tragedies,* ed. by E. Capell, 10 vols., London, 1768; *Plays,* ed. by G. Steevens, 10 vols., London, 1773; *Plays and Poems,* ed. by E. Malone, 10 vols., London, 1790; *Plays,* ed. by S. Johnson, 8 vols., London, 1765, Philadelphia, 1795–1796 (based on Warburton); *Plays,* ed. by I. Reed, 1st variorum ed., London, 1803 (based on the texts of Johnson and Steevens; the 2d variorum ed., 1813, was a reprint of the 1st); *Plays and Poems,* ed. by J. Boswell, 3d variorum ed., London, 1821 (based on Malone's text); *Works,* ed. by W. G. Clark and W. A. Wright, Globe ed., 1 vol., London, 1864; *Works,* ed. by W. G. Clark, J. Glover, and W. A. Wright, Cambridge ed., 9 vols., Cambridge, England, 1863–1866; *Works,* ed. by H. H. Furness et al., new variorum ed., vols. 1–14, 21–25, Philadelphia, 1871–   ; *The Arden Shakespeare,* ed. by W. J. Craig and R. H. Case, 17 vols. London, 1899–1924; *Yale Shakespeare,* ed. by W. L. Cross and C. F. Tucker Brooke, 40 vols., New Haven, Conn., and Oxford, 1917–1927; *The New Arden Shakespeare,* ed. by U. Ellis-Fermor, H. F. Brooks, and H. Jenkins, 37 vols., London and Cambridge, Mass. 1951-   ; *Works,* ed. by A. Quiller-Couch and J. D. Wilson, new Cambridge ed., Cambridge, England, 1921–1963.

CRITICISM

General Studies

J. Hunter, *New Illustrations of the Life, Studies, and Writings of Shakespeare,* 2 vols., London, 1844–1845; T. Kenny, *The Life and Genius of Shakespeare,* London, 1864; H. N. Hudson, *Shakespeare: His Life, Art, and Characters,* 2 vols., Boston, 1872; E. Dowden, *Shakespeare,* New York, 1888; A. C. Swinburne, *A Study of Shakespeare,* new ed., London, 1909; H. N. MacCracken, F. E. Pierce, and W. H. Durham, *An Introduction to Shakespeare,* New York, 1910; O. Smeaton, *Shakespeare; His Life and Work,* London, 1912; W. A. Neilson and A. H. Thorndike, *The Facts about Shakespeare,*

New York, 1913; G. L. Kittredge, *Shakspere,* Cambridge, Mass., 1916; A. E. G. Lamborn and G. B. Harrison, *Shakespeare: The Man and His Stage,* New York, 1923; C. F. T. Brooke, *Shakespeare of Stratford,* New Haven, Conn., 1926; J. Bailey, *Shakespeare,* London, 1929; E. K. Chambers, *William Shakespeare: A Study of Facts and Problems,* 2 vols., London, 1930; J. W. Mackail, *The Approach to Shakespeare,* Oxford, 1930; C. L. de Chambrun, *Shakespeare Rediscovered,* New York, 1938; E. I. Fripps, *Shakespeare, Man and Artist,* 2 vols., Oxford, 1938; R. Wilson, *The Approach to Shakespeare,* London, 1938; H. Spencer, *The Art and Life of William Shakespeare,* New York, 1940; I. Brown, *Shakespeare,* London, 1949; M. Chute, *Shakespeare of London,* New York, 1949; C. Norman, *The Playmaker of Avon,* New York, 1949; M. Van Doren, *Shakespeare,* Garden City, N.Y., 1949; M. Chute, *An Introduction to Shakespeare,* New York, 1951; G. I. Duthie, *Shakespeare,* London, 1951; H. Craig, *Introduction to Shakespeare,* Glenview, Ill., 1952; D. Ogburn and C. Ogburn, Jr., *This Star of England: Shakespeare, Man of the Renaissance,* New York, 1952; M. M. Reese, *Shakespeare: His World and His Work,* New York, 1953; G. B. Harrison, *Introducing Shakespeare,* rev. ed., Baltimore, 1954; T. M. Parrott, *William Shakespeare,* rev. ed., New York, 1955; D. A. Traversi, *An Approach to Shakespeare,* Garden City, N.Y., 1956; I. Brown, *William Shakespeare,* London, 1958; H. M. Burton, *Shakespeare and His Plays,* New York, 1958; E. K. Chambers, *Shakespeare: A Survey,* new ed., New York, 1958; J. Paris, *Shakespeare,* New York, 1960; F. E. Halliday, *Shakespeare,* New York, 1961; A. Nicoll, *Shakespeare,* reprint, London, 1961; I. Noble, *William Shakespeare,* New York, 1961; C. Norman, *So Worthy a Friend: William Shakespeare,* New York, 1961; W. Raleigh, *Shakespeare,* New York, 1961; E. Sitwell, *A Notebook on William Shakespeare,* Boston, 1961; P. Alexander, *Shakespeare's Life and Art,* New York, 1962; J. Drinkwater, *Shakespeare,* New York, 1962; E. E. C. Ludowyk, *Understanding Shakespeare,* New York, 1962; C. J. Sisson, *Shakespeare,* London, 1962; P. Alexander, *Shakespeare,* New York and London, 1964; *ibid., Introductions to Shakespeare,* New York, 1964; A. Fluchère, *Shakespeare,* New York, 1964; W. J. Grace, *Approaching Shakespeare,* New York, 1964; K. R. Srinivasa Iyengar, *Shakespeare: His World and His Art,* New York, 1964; J. Masefield, *William Shakespeare,* Greenwich, Conn., 1964; J. M. Murry, *Shakespeare,* reprint, London, 1965; J. S. Smart, *Shakespeare: Truth and Tradition,* London and New York, 1966; A. Cullum, *Shake Hands with Shakespeare,* Englewood Cliffs, N.J., 1968; R. M. Frye, *Shakespeare,* Boston, 1969; S. Schoenbaum, *William Shakespeare: A Documentary Life,* Oxford, 1975.

The Man and His Philosophy

Shakespeare the Man

1. *Biography.* N. Rowe, *Some Account of the Life, &c, of Mr. William Shakespear,* London, 1714; A. Skottowe, *The Life of Shakespeare; Enquiries into the Originality of His Dramatic Plots and Characters; and Essays on the Ancient Theatres and Theatrical Usages,* 2 vols., London, 1824; C. Knight, *William Shakspere: A Biography,* London, 1843; J. O. Halliwell-Phillipps, *Outlines of the Life of Shakespeare,* 9th ed., London, 1890; C. C. Stopes, *Shakespeare's Family, Being a Record of the Ancestors and Descendants of William Shakespeare, with Some Account of the Ardens,* New York, 1901; C. I. Elton, *William Shakespeare, His Family and Friends,* ed. by A. H. Thompson, London, 1904; J. Q. Adams, *A Life of William Shakespeare,* Boston, 1925; S. Lee, *A Life of William Shakespeare,* new ed., New York, 1931; E. K. Chambers and C. Williams, *A Short Life of Shakespeare, with the Sources,* London, 1933; O. Baker, *In Shakespeare's Warwickshire and the Unknown Years,* London, 1937; F. E. Schelling, *Shakespeare Biography and Other Papers, Chiefly Elizabethan,* Philadelphia, 1937; A. Gray, *Shakespeare's Son-in-law, John Hall,* Cambridge, Mass. 1939; J. Isaacs, *Shakespeare's Earliest Years in the Theatre,* London, 1953; E. B. Everitt, *The Young Shakespeare: Studies in Documentary Evidence,* New York, 1954; A. Keen and R. Lubbock, *The Annotator: The Pursuit of an Elizabethan Reader of Halle's "Chronicle" Involving Some Surmises about the Early Life of William Shakespeare,* London, 1954; F. E. Halliday, *Shakespeare: A Pictorial Biography,* rev. ed., New York, 1955; G. E. Dawson, *The Life of William Shakespeare,* New York, 1958; G. B. Harrison, *Shakespeare at Work, 1592–1603,* Ann Arbor, Mich., 1958; R. A. Sisson, *The Young Shakespeare,* New York, 1959; J. D. Wilson, *The Essential Shakespeare: A Biographical Adventure,* New York, 1952, 1960; G. E. Bentley, *Shakespeare: A Biographical Handbook,* New Haven, Conn., 1961; M. Eccles, *Shakespeare in Warwickshire,* Madison, Wis., 1961; D. Macardle, *Shakespeare, Man and Boy,* ed. by G. Bott, London, 1961; H. Pearson, *A Life of Shakespeare, with an Anthology of Shakespeare's Poetry,* New York, 1961; H. Buckmaster, *All the Living: A Novel of One Year in the Life of William Shakespeare,* New York, 1962; I. Brown, *How Shakespeare Spent the Day,* New York, 1963; F. E. Halliday, *The Life of Shakespeare,* Baltimore, 1963; P. Quenell, *Shakespeare: A Biography,* Cleveland, 1963; M. M. Reese, *William Shakespeare: A Biography,* New York, 1963; A. L. Rowse, *William Shakespeare: A Biography,* New York, 1963; H. Joseph, *Shakespeare's Son-in-law: John Hall, Man and Physician,* New York, 1964; W. J. Rolfe, *Shakespeare the Boy,* reprint, New York, 1965.

2. *Environment.* N. Drake, *Shakespeare and His Times,* 2 vols., London, 1817; W. Winter, *Shakespeare's England,* New York, 1893; C. C. Stopes,

Shakespeare's Warwickshire Contemporaries, Stratford on Avon, 1897; *id., Shakespeare's Environment*, London, 1918; E. I. Fripps, *Shakespeare's Stratford*, Oxford, 1928; *id., Shakespeare's Haunts near Stratford*, Oxford, 1929; J. D. Wilson, *Life in Shakespeare's England*, Baltimore, 1944; F. E. Halliday, *Shakespeare in His Age*, New York, 1956; *The Age of Shakespeare*, ed. by B. Ford, Baltimore, 1960; I. Brown, *Shakespeare in His Time*, London, 1960; W. Raleigh et al., *Shakespeare's England: An Account of the Life and Manners of His Age*, reprint, 2 vols., London, 1962; *Shakespeare's World*, ed. by J. Sutherland and J. Hurstfield, New York, 1964; F. A. Yates, *John Florio: The Life of an Italian in Shakespeare's England*, New York, 1967.

3. *Psychology*. D. Masson, *Shakespeare Personally*, ed. by R. Masson, London, 1914; H. G. McCurdy, *The Personality of Shakespeare: A Venture in Psychological Method*, New Haven, Conn., 1953; E. A. Armstrong, *Shakespeare's Imagination: A Study of the Psychology of Association and Inspiration*, Lincoln, Nebr., 1963; N. Holland, *The Shakespearean Imagination*, New York, 1964; *id., Psychoanalysis and Shakespeare*, New York, 1966.

Shakespeare's Philosophy of Life

1. *General Studies*. D. S. Bacon, *The Philosophy of the Plays of Shakspere Unfolded*, London, 1857; K. J. Spalding, *The Philosophy of Shakespeare*, New York, 1953; W. C. Curry, *Shakespeare's Philosophical Patterns*, reprint, Baton Rouge, La., 1959; W. Kaufmann, *From Shakespeare to Existentialism*, Garden City, N.Y., 1960; L. S. Champion, *Shakespeare's Tragic Perspective*, Athens, Ga., 1976.

2. *Concept of Justice*. C. J. Sisson, *Shakespeare's Tragic Justice*, London, 1963; J. M. O'Malley, *Justice in Shakespeare: Three English Kings in the Light of Thomistic Thought*, New York, 1964; G. S. Ghurye, *Shakespeare on Conscience and Justice*, Bombay, 1965.

3. *Human Condition*. G. Bush, *Shakespeare and the Natural Condition*, Cambridge, Mass., 1956; T. Spencer, *Shakespeare and the Nature of Man*, New York, 1961; *The Ages of Man*, ed. by G. Rylands, London, 1939, New York, 1963; M. Aronson, *Psyche and Symbol in Shakespeare*, Bloomington and London, 1972.

4. *Theories of Learning*. P. Whalley, *An Enquiry into the Learning of Shakespeare*, London, 1748; R. Farmer, *Essay on the Learning of Shakespeare*, Cambridge, England, 1767; V. K. Whitaker, *Shakespeare's Use of Learning: An Inquiry into the Growth of His Mind and Art*, San Marino, Calif., 1953; D. G. James, *The Dream of Learning: An Essay on the Advancement of Learning, Hamlet, and King Lear*, New York, 1961.

5. *Concept of Love*. J. Vyvyan, *Shakespeare and the Rose of Love*, New York, 1960.

6. *Moral Code*. R. G. Moulton, *The Moral System of Shakespeare*, New York, 1903; J. A. Bastiaenen, *The Moral Tone of Jacobean and Caroline Drama*, Amsterdam, 1930; E. Partridge, *Shakespeare's Bawdy: A Literary and Psychological Essay*, rev. ed., New York, 1955, 1960; J. Vyvyan, *The Shakespearean Ethic*, New York, 1960; A. Harbage, *As They Liked It*, New York, 1947, 1961.

7. *Political Beliefs*. A. Thaler, *Shakespeare and Democracy*, Knoxville, Tenn., 1941; A. Bloom and H. V. Jaffa, *Shakespeare's Politics*, New York, 1964.

8. *Concept of the Rational Intellect*. E. R. Hunter, *Shakspere and Common Sense*, North Quincy, Mass., 1954; T. Hawkes, *Shakespeare and the Reason*, New York, 1964.

9. *Religious Beliefs*. T. Carter, *Shakespeare, Puritan and Recusant*, Edinburgh and London, 1897; H. S. Bowden, *The Religion of Shakespeare*, London, 1899; W. Burgess, *The Bible in Shakespeare*, New York, 1903; E. M. Howse, *Spiritual Values in Shakespeare*, Nashville, Tenn., 1955; R. Stevenson, *Shakespeare's Religious Frontier*, The Hague, 1958; J. A. Bryant, Jr., *Hippolyta's View: Some Christian Aspects of Shakespeare's Plays*, Lexington, Ky., 1960; R. M. Frye, *Shakespeare and Christian Doctrine*, Princeton, N.J., 1963; G. W. Knight, *Shakespeare and Religion*, New York, 1967; R. W. S. Mendl, *Revelation in Shakespeare*, London, 1967; H. R. Coursen, *Christian Ritual and the World of Shakespeare's Tragedies*, Lewisburg, Pa., 1976.

10. *Miscellaneous Studies*. C. B. Watson, *Shakespeare and the Renaissance Concept of Honor*, Princeton, N.J., 1960; T. F. Driver, *The Sense of History in Greek and Shakespearean Drama*, New York, 1961; J. Vyvyan, *Shakespeare and Platonic Beauty*, New York, 1961; G. Kozintsev, *Shakespeare: Time and Conscience*, New York, 1966.

The Dramatist

General Studies

R. G. Moulton, *Shakespeare as a Dramatic Artist*, 3d rev. ed., New York, 1906; A. H. Thorndike, *Shakespeare's Theatre*, New York, 1916; R. G. Noyes, *The Thespian Mirror*, Providence, 1953; L. B. Wright, *Shakespeare's Theatre and the Dramatic Tradition*, Ithaca, N.Y., 1958; W. Rosen, *Shakespeare and the Craft of Tragedy*, Cambridge, Mass., 1960; U. Ellis-Fermor, *Shakespeare the Dramatist*, ed. by K. Muir, New York, 1961; A. Righter, *Shakespeare and the Idea of the Play*, London, 1962; E. E. Stoll, *Art and Artifice in Shakespeare*, reprint, New York, 1962; J. Arthos, *The Art of Shakespeare*, New York, 1964; T. R. Lounsbury, *Shakespeare as a Dramatic Artist, with an Account of His Reputation at Various Periods*, reprint, New York, 1965; P. Edwards, *Shakespeare and the Confines of Art*, New York,

1968; J. R. Brown, *Shakespeare's Dramatic Style*, London, 1970; W. Clemen, *Shakespeare's Dramatic Art*, London, 1972; R. L. Colie, *Shakespeare's Living Art*, Princeton, 1974.

Literary and Dramatic Sources

1. *General Studies*. *Shakespeare's Library: A Collection of the Plays, Romances, Novels, Poems, and Histories Employed by Shakespeare in the Composition of His Works*, ed. by J. P. Collier and W. C. Hazlitt, 6 vols., London, 1875; H. R. D. Anders, *Shakespeare's Books*, Berlin, 1904; F. S. Boas, *Shakespeare and His Predecessors*, London, 1904; G. C. Taylor, *Shakespeare's Debt to Montaigne*, New York, 1925; E. C. Pettet, *Shakespeare and the Romance Tradition*, London, 1949; K. J. Holzknecht, *The Background of Shakespeare's Plays*, Lancaster, Tex., 1950; T. W. Baldwin, *On the Literary Genetics of Shakespere's Plays, 1592–1594*, Urbana, Ill., 1959; K. Muir, *Shakespeare's Sources*, vol. I, *Comedies and Tragedies*, rev. ed., London, 1961; S. Lanier, *Shakespeare and His Forerunners*, new ed., ed. by K. Malone, Baltimore, 1965; A. H. Thorndike, *The Influence of Beaumont and Fletcher on Shakespeare*, reprint, New York, 1965; A. V. Griffin, *Sources of Ten Shakespearean Plays*, New York, 1966; J. E. Hawkins, *Shakespeare's Derived Imagery*, New York, 1966; *Narrative and Dramatic Sources of Shakespeare*, ed. by G. B. Bullough, 6 vols., New York, 1957–1966; J. Satin, *Shakespeare and His Sources*, New York, 1966; T. F. Thiselton-Dyer, *Folk-lore of Shakespeare*, New York, 1966; S. Guttman, *Foreign Sources of Shakespeare's Works: An Annotated Bibliography of the Commentary Written on This Subject Between 1904 and 1940*, New York, 1967.

2. *Classical Sources*. P. Stapfer, *Shakespeare and Classical Antiquity*, New York, 1880; *Shakespeare's Plutarch*, ed. by C. F. T. Brooke, 2 vols., Oxford, 1909; J. A. K. Thompson, *Shakespeare and the Classics*, New York, 1952; T. W. Baldwin, *William Shakespeare's Small Latine and Lesse Greeke*, reprint, 2 vols., Urbana, Ill., 1956; E. Schanzer, *Shakespeare's Appian: A Selection from the Tudor Translation of Appian's Civil Wars*, Liverpool, 1956; *Shakespeare's Ovid, Being Arthur Golding's Translation of the Metamorphoses*, ed. by W. H. D. Rouse, Carbondale, Ill., 1961; M. H. Shackford, *Shakespeare, Sophocles: Dramatic Themes and Modes*, New York, 1963; C. G. Smith, *Shakespeare's Proverb Lore: His Use of the Sententiae of Leonard Culman and Publilius Syrus*, Cambridge, Mass., 1963; T. J. B. Spencer, *Shakespeare's Plutarch*, Baltimore, 1964; R. A. Brower, *Hero and Saint: Shakespeare and the Graeco-Roman Tradition*, Oxford, 1971.

3. *Holinshed*. W. G. Boswell-Stone, *Shakspere's Holinshed*, London, 1907; *Holinshed's Chronicle as Used in Shakespeare's Plays*, ed. by A. Nicoll and J. Nicoll, New York, 1959; *Shakespeare's Holinshed*, ed. by R. Hosley, New York, 1968.

4. *Sources for Specific Plays*. *Greene's "Pandosto," or "Dorastus and Fawnia," Being the Original of Shakespeare's "Winter's Tale,"* ed. by P. G. Thomas, Oxford, 1907; *Brooke's Romeus and Juliet, Being the Original of Shakespeare's Romeo and Juliet*, ed. by J. J. Munro, London, 1908; *The Chronicle History of King Leir, the Original of Shakespeare's King Lear*, ed. by S. Lee, London, 1909; *Rich's Apolonius and Silla, an Original of Shakespeare's Twelfth Night*, ed. by M. Luce, London, 1912; K. Malone, *The Literary History of Hamlet: I. The Early Tradition*, Heidelberg, 1923; C. T. Prouty, *The Sources of Much Ado about Nothing: A Critical Study, Together with the Text of Peter Beverley's Ariodanto and Ieneura*, New Haven, Conn., 1950; I. Gollancz, *The Sources of Hamlet, with an Essay on the Legend*, New York, 1967.

5. *Influence of the Audience*. R. S. Bridges, *The Influence of the Audience on Shakespeare's Drama*, London, 1927; A. C. Sprague, *Shakespeare and the Audience*, New York, 1935; A. Harbage, *Shakespeare's Audience*, New York, 1961; M. Holmes, *Shakespeare's Public: Touchstone of His Genius*, London, 1964.

6. *Shakespeare and the Elizabethans*. B. Wendell, *William Shakespeare: A Study in Elizabethan Literature*, New York, 1894; R. L. Anderson, *Elizabethan Psychology and Shakespeare's Plays*, New York, 1927; S. L. Bethell, *Shakespeare and the Popular Dramatic Tradition*, London, 1944; A. Harbage, *Shakespeare and the Rival Traditions*, New York, 1952; H. Fluchère, *Shakespeare and the Elizabethans*, New York, 1956; W. Schrickx, *Shakespeare's Early Contemporaries: The Background of the Harvey-Nashe Polemic and Love's Labours Lost*, Antwerp, 1956; I. Ribner, *The English History Play in the Age of Shakespeare*, Princeton, N.J., 1957; M. C. Bradbrook, *Shakespeare and Elizabethan Poetry*, London, 1961; *id., Elizabethan Stage Conditions: A Study of Their Place in the Interpretation of Shakespeare's Plays*, reprint, New York, 1962; M. Joseph, *Rhetoric in Shakespeare's Time*, New York, 1962; W. H. Rogers, *Shakespeare and English History*, Totowa, N.J., 1966; T. Eagleton, *Shakespeare and Society: Critical Studies in Shakespearean Drama*, New York, 1967; M. C. Bradbrook, *The Living Monument: Shakespeare and the Theatre of His Time*, Cambridge, 1976.

7. *Dramatic Evolution*. G. P. Baker, *The Development of Shakespeare as a Dramatist*, New York, 1907; F. O'Connor, *Shakespeare's Progress*, Cleveland, 1960, 1962; N. Frye, *A Natural Perspective: The Development of Shakespearean Comedy and Romance*, New York, 1965; R. A. Foakes, *Shakespeare: from the Dark Comedies to the Last Plays*, London, 1971.

8. *Technical Habits*. A. Quiller-Couch, *Shakespeare's Workmanship*, London, 1918; W. J. Lawrence, *Shakespeare's Workshop*, Oxford, 1928.

9.*Dramatic Structure*. D. J. Snider, *System of Shakespeare's Dramas*, St. Louis, 1877; H. T. Price, *Construction in Shakespeare*, Ann Arbor, Mich., 1951; H. S. Wilson, *On the Design of Shakespearean Tragedy*, Toronto, 1957; T. W. Baldwin, *Shakespeare's Five-act Structure: Shakespeare's Early Plays on the Background of Renaissance Theories of Five-act Structure from 1470*, new ed., Urbana, Ill., 1963

Character and Character Studies.

1. *General Studies*. J. W. Draper, *The Humors and Shakespeare's Characters*, Durham, N.C., 1945; L. L. Schücking, *Character Problems in Shakespeare's Plays: A Guide to Better Understanding of the Dramatist*, reprint, New York, 1959; A. Sewell, *Character and Society in Shakespeare*, London, 1961; L. Kirschbaum, *Character and Characterization in Shakespeare*, Detroit, 1962; H. M. V. Matthews, *Character and Symbol in Shakespeare's Plays*, London, 1962; J. I. M. Stewart, *Character and Motive in Shakespeare*, London, 1965.

2. *Types of Characters*. W. Richardson, *A Philosophical Analysis and Illustration of Some of Shakespeare's Remarkable Characters*, 4th ed., Philadelphia, 1788; T. Whately, *Remarks on Some of the Characters of Shakespeare*, 2d ed., Oxford, 1808; J. C. Bucknill, *The Mad Folk of Shakespeare*, New York, 1867; H. Faucit, *On Some of Shakespeare's Female Characters*, new ed., London, 1887; G. W. Phillips, *Lord Burghley in Shakespeare: Falstaff, Sly and Others*, London, 1936; E. E. Stoll, *Shakespeare's Young Lovers*, London, 1937; R. H. Goldsmith, *Wise Fools in Shakespeare*, East Lansing, Mich., 1955; H. Plutzik, *Horatio*, New York, 1961; W. Hazlitt, *Characters of Shakespeare's Plays*, new ed., New York, 1962; J. Palmer, *Political and Comic Characters of Shakespeare*, new ed., New York, 1962; J. B. Priestley, *English Comic Characters*, New York, 1963.

3. *Comic Characters*. (a) *Falstaff*. M. Morgann, *An Essay on the Dramatic Character of Sir John Falstaff*, London, 1777; W. Richardson, *Essays on Shakespeare's Dramatic Character of Sir John Falstaff, and on His Imitation of Female Characters*, London, 1788; J. O. Halliwell-Phillipps, *On the Character of Sir John Falstaff*, London, 1841; A. H. Tolman, *Falstaff and Other Shakespearean Topics*, New York, 1925; H. B. Charlton, *Falstaff*, Manchester, England, 1935; J. D. Wilson, *The Fortunes of Falstaff*, London, 1953; A. G. Davis, *Merry Jack Falstaff*, Jamaica, N.Y., 1968. (b) *Shylock*. B. Grebanier, *The Truth about Shylock*, New York, 1962; H. Sinsheimer, *Shylock: The History of a Character*, new ed., New York, 1963. (c) *Characters in A Midsummer Night's Dream*. K. M. Briggs, *The Anatomy of Puck*, London, 1959; L. Zukofsky, *Bottom: On Shakespeare*, 2 vols., Austin, Tex., 1963.

4. *Heroes and Heroines*. B. Coles, *Shakespeare's Four Giants: Hamlet, Macbeth, Othello, Lear*, Rindge, N.H., 1957; L. B. Campbell, *Shakespeare's Tragic Heroes, Slaves of Passion*, New York, 1959; L. Simpson, *Secondary Heroes of Shakespeare and Others*, New York, 1960; M. N. Proser, *The Heroic Image in Five Shakespearean Tragedies*, Princeton, N.J., 1965; W. Lewis, *The Lion and the Fox: The Role of the Hero in the Plays of Shakespeare*, New York, 1966.

5. *Villains*. A. Goll, *Criminal Types in Shakespeare*, tr. by Mrs. Charles Weekes, London, 1909; C. N. Coe, *Shakespeare's Villains*, New York, 1957; B. Spivack, *Shakespeare and the Allegory of Evil: The History of a Metaphor in Relation to His Major Villains*, New York, 1958; C. N. Coe, *Demi-devils: The Characters of Shakespeare's Villains*, New York, 1963.

6. *Populace*. F. Tupper, *Shakespearean Mob*, New York, 1938; B. Stirling, *The Populace in Shakespeare*, New York, 1949.

Use of Language. M. L. Arnold, *The Soliloquies of Shakespeare*, New York, 1911; C. F. E. Spurgeon, *Leading Motifs in the Imagery of Shakespeare's Tragedies*, London, 1930; U. Ellis-Fermor, *Some Recent Research in Shakespeare's Imagery*, Oxford, 1937; F. P. Wilson, *Shakespeare and the Diction of Common Life*, Oxford, 1941; M. B. Kennedy, *The Oration in Shakespeare*, Chapel Hill, N. C., 1942; M. Joseph, *Shakespeare's Use of the Arts of Language*, New York, 1947; G. Rylands, *Shakespeare's Poetic Energy*, London, 1951; G. D. Willcock, *Language and Poetry in Shakespeare's Early Plays*, New York, 1954; M. M. Mahood, *Shakespeare's Wordplay*, London, 1957; C. F. E. Spurgeon, *Shakespeare's Imagery and What it Tells Us*, Boston, 1958; W. Clemen, *The Development of Shakespeare's Imagery*, New York, 1962; P. A. Jorgensen, *Redeeming Shakespeare's Words*, Berkeley, Calif., 1962; M. Crane, *Shakespeare's Prose*, Chicago, 1951, 1963; W. Clemen, *Shakespeare's Soliloquies*, London, 1964; I. B. Evans, *The Language of Shakespeare's Plays*, 3d ed., New York, 1964; F. E. Halliday, *The Poetry of Shakespeare's Plays*, New York, 1964; F. Berry, *The Shakespeare Inset: Word and Picture*, London, 1965; D. A. Stauffer, *Shakespeare's World of Images: The Development of His Moral Ideas*, Bloomington, Ind., 1966; B. Vickers, *The Artistry of Shakespeare's Prose*, New York, 1968; G. L. Brook, *The Language of Shakespeare*, London, 1976. E. A. M. Colman, *The Dramatic Use of Bawdy in Shakespeare*, London, 1974.

Use of Music. C. Wilson, *Shakespeare and Music*, London, 1922; F. Bridge, *Shakespearean Music in the Plays and Early Operas*, New York, 1923; R. Noble, *Shakespeare's Use of Song*, London and New York, 1923; J. J. Wey, *Musical Allusion and Song as Part of the Structure of Meaning in Shakespeare's Plays*, Washington, 1957; J. H. Long, *Shakespeare's Use of Music*, 2 vols., Gainesville, Fla., 1955–1961; F. W. Sternfeld, *Music in Shakespearean Tragedy*, London, 1963; E. W. Naylor, *Shakespeare and Music*, 2d ed., New York, 1965; P. J. Seng, *Vocal Songs in the Plays of Shakespeare*, Cambridge, Mass., 1967.

Use of Mythology. A. T. Nutt, *Fairy Mythology of Shakespeare*, New York, 1900; M. W. Latham, *Elizabethan Fairies, the Fairies of Folklore and the Fairies of Shakespeare*, Detroit, 1930.

Use of the Stage. W. Winter, *Shakespeare on the Stage*, 3 vols., London, 1911–1916; W. R. Davies, *Shakespeare's Boy Actors*, New York, 1939; A. V. Griffin, *Pageantry on the Shakespearean Stage*, New Haven, Conn., 1951.

Influence. J.-J. Jusserand, *Shakespeare in France under the Ancient Regime*, New York, 1889; L. Collison-Morley, *Shakespeare in Italy*, Stratford on Avon, 1916; D. J. McGinn, *Shakespeare's Influence on the Drama of His Age*, New York, 1938; D. M. McKeithan, *The Debt to Shakespeare in the Beaumont-and-Fletcher Plays*, Austin, Tex., 1938; P. Cruttwell, *The Shakespearean Moment and Its Place in the Poetry of the Seventeenth Century*, New York, 1955, 1960; *Shakespeare in Europe*, ed. by O. Lewinter, Cleveland, 1963; C. D. Narasimhaiah, *Shakespeare Came to India*, Bombay, 1964; E. Capell, *School of Shakespeare*, new ed., 3 vols., New York, 1966; D. L. Frost, *The School of Shakespeare: The Influence of Shakespeare on English Drama 1600–42*, Cambridge, England, 1968; G. Wickham, *Shakespeare's Dramatic Heritage*, New York, 1968.

The Plays

Comedies and Romances

1. *General Studies*. H. B. Charlton, *The Dark Comedies of Shakespeare*, New York, 1937; id., *Shakespeare's Comedies: The Consummation*, New York, 1937; S. C. Sengupta, *Shakespearean Comedy*, Calcutta, 1951; C. N. Desai, *Shakespearean Comedy*, Indore, 1952; E. M. W. Tillyard, *The Nature of Comedy and Shakespeare*, London, 1958; B. Evans, *Shakespeare's Comedies*, New York, 1960; H. B. Charlton, *Shakespearian Comedy*, reprint, New York, 1961; J. R. Brown, *Shakespeare and His Comedies*, 2d ed., London, 1962; M. Lascelles, *Shakespeare's Comic Insight*, New York, 1962; T. M. Parrott, *Shakespearean Comedy*, reprint, New York, 1962; R. G. Hunter, *Shakespeare and the Comedy of Forgiveness*, New York, 1965; *Shakespeare: The Comedies, a Collection of Critical Essays*, ed. by K. Muir, Englewood Cliffs, N.J., 1965; *Shakespeare's Comedies: An Anthology of Modern Criticism*, ed. by L. Lerner, Baltimore, 1967; R. T. Berry, *Shakespeare's Comedies: Explorations in Form*, Princeton, 1972; A. Leggatt, *Shakespeare's Comedy of Love*, London, 1974; L. Salinga, *Shakespeare and the Tradition of Comedy*, Cambridge, 1974.

2. *Chronology*. C. K. Hunter, *William Shakespeare: The Late Comedies—A Midsummer Night's Dream, Much Ado about Nothing, As You Like It, Twelfth Night*, London and New York, 1962; D. Traversi, *William Shakespeare: The Early Comedies—The Comedy of Errors, The Taming of the Shrew, The Two Gentlemen of Verona, Love's Labour's Lost, The Merchant of Venice*, London and New York, 1964; *Shakespeare's Early Comedies*, ed. by E. M. W. Tillyard and S. Tillyard, London, 1965; B. O. Bonazza, *Shakespeare's Early Comedies: A Structural Analysis*, The Hague, 1966.

3. *Types of Comedies*. (a) *Happy Comedies*. C. L. Barber, *Shakespeare's Festive Comedy: A Study of Dramatic Form and Its Relation to Social Custom*, Princeton, N.J., 1959; J. D. Wilson, *Shakespeare's Happy Comedies*, Evanston, Ill., 1963. (b) *Problem Comedies*. W. W. Lawrence, *Shakespeare's Problem Comedies*, New York, 1960; R. Ornstein, ed., *Discussions of Shakespeare's Problem Comedies*, Boston, 1961. (c) *Romantic Comedies*. P. G. Phialas, *Shakespeare's Romantic Comedies*, Chapel Hill, N.C., 1966; H. Weil, *Discussions of Shakespeare's Romantic Comedy*, Boston, 1966.

4. *Individual Comedies*. (a) *All's Well That Ends Well*. J. G. Price, *The Unfortunate Comedy: A Study of All's Well That Ends Well and Its Critics*, Toronto, 1968. (b) *As You Like It. Twentieth Century Interpretations of As You Like It*, ed. by J. Halio, Englewood Cliffs, N.J., 1968. (c)*The Comedy of Errors*. T. W. Baldwin, *On the Compositional Genetics of the Comedy of Errors*, Urbana, Ill., 1965. (d) *Love's Labour's Lost*. R. Taylor, *The Date of Love's Labour's Lost*, New York, 1932. (e) *Love's Labour's Won*. A. H. Tolman, *What Has Become of Shakespeare's Play "Love's Labour's Won"?*, Chicago, 1902; T. W. Baldwin, *Shakespeare's Love's Labor's Won: New Evidence from the Account Book of an Elizabethan Bookseller*, Carbondale, Ill., 1957. (f) *Measure for Measure*. R. W. Chambers, *The Jacobean Shakespeare and Measure for Measure*, Oxford, 1937; M. Lascelles, *Shakespeare's Measure for Measure*, new ed., London, 1953; J. W. Bennett, *Measure for Measure as Royal Entertainment*, New York, 1966; D. L. Stevenson, *The Achievement of Shakespeare's Measure for Measure*, Ithaca, N. Y., 1966. (g) *The Merchant of Venice: A Concise Bibliography*, New York, 1941. (h) *The Merry Wives of Windsor*. J. E. V. Crofts, *Shakespeare and the Post Horses: A New Study of the Merry Wives of Windsor*, London, 1937; W. Green, *Shakespeare's Merry Wives of Windsor*, Princeton, N. J. 1962. (i) *A Midsummer Night's Dream*. D. P. Young, *Something of Great Constancy: The Art of a Midsummer Night's Dream*, New Haven, Conn., 1966. (j) *The Tempest*. J. D. Wilson, *The Meaning of the Tempest*, Newcastle, 1936; R. G. Howarth, *Shakespeare's Tempest*, rev. ed., Sydney, 1947. (k) *Twelfth Night*. J. W. Draper, *The Twelfth Night of Shakespeare's Audience*, Palo Alto, Calif., 1950; J. L. Hotson, *The First Night of Twelfth Night*, London, 1954; B. Hardy, *Twelfth Night*, London, 1962; C. Leech, *Twelfth Night and Shakespearian Comedy*, Toronto, 1965; *Twentieth Century Interpretations of Twelfth Night*, ed. by W. King, Englewood Cliffs, N. J., 1968. (l) *The Winter's Tale*. S. L. Bethell, *The Winter's Tale: A Study*, London, 1947; J. A. Williams, *The Natural Work of Art: The Experience of Romance in Shakespeare's Winter's Tale*, Cambridge, Mass., 1967.

History and Chronicle Plays

1. *General Studies.* T. P. Courtenay, *Commentaries on the Historical Plays of Shakespeare*, 2 vols., London, 1840, 1861; P. Alexander and A. W. Pollard, *Shakespeare's Henry VI and Richard III*, New York, 1929; *Mirror for Magistrates*, ed. by L. B. Campbell, New York, 1938; M. B. Mroz, *Divine Vengeance: A Study in the Philosophical Backgrounds of the Revenge Motif as It Appears in Shakespeare's Chronicle History Plays*, Washington 1941; D. A. Traversi, *Shakespeare: From Richard II to Henry V.*, Stanford, Calif., 1957; Z. Stříbrný, *Shakespearovy historické hry.* Prague, 1959; M. Reese, *The Cease of Majesty: A Study of Shakespeare's History Plays*, New York, 1961; L. C. Knights, *William Shakespeare: The Histories—Richard III, King John, Richard II, Henry V*, London, 1962; C. Leech, *William Shakespeare: The Chronicles—Henry VI, Henry IV, The Merry Wives of Windsor, Henry VIII*, London, 1962; L. B. Campbell, *Shakespeare's Histories: Mirrors of Elizabethan Policy*, 2d ed., San Marino, Calif., 1963; R. J. Dorius, *Discussions of Shakespeare's Histories: Richard II to Henry V.*, Boston, 1964; S. C. Sengupta, *Shakespeare's Historical Plays*, London, 1964; E. M. W. Tillyard, *Shakespeare's History Plays*, 2d ed., New York, 1964; *Shakespeare: The Histories, a Collection of Critical Essays*, ed. by E. M. Waith, Englewood Cliffs, N.J. 1965; J. Winny, *Player King: A Study of Shakespeare's Later History Plays*, New York, 1968; W. A. Armstrong, ed., *Shakespeare's Histories: an Anthology of Modern Criticism*, Harmondsworth, 1972.

2. *Individual Plays.* (a) *Richard III.* S. Thomas, *The Antic Hamlet and Richard III*, New York, 1943; P. M. Kendall, *Richard the Third*, London, 1955; W. Clemen, *Commentary on Shakespeare's Richard III*, tr. by J. Bonheim, New York, 1968. (b) *Henry IV, Henry V, and Henry VI: Parts I, II, III.* H. T. Price, *The Text of Henry V*, Newcastle under Lyme, 1920; M. Doran, *Henry VI, Parts II and III: Their Relation to the Contention and the True Tragedy*, Iowa City, Iowa, 1928; C. T. Prouty, *The Contention and Shakespeare's 2 Henry VI: A Comparative Study*, New Haven, Conn., 1954; H. Jenkins, *The Structural Problems in Shakespeare's Henry the Fourth*, London, 1956; *Twentieth Century Interpretations of Henry V*, ed. by R. Berman, Englewood Cliffs, N.J., 1968; *Twentieth Century Interpretations of Henry IV, Part 2*, ed. by D. Young, New York, 1968.

Tragedies

1. *General Studies.* T. Rymer, *A Short View of Tragedy*, London, 1693; H. Baker, *Induction to Tragedy*, New York, 1939; A. Hollowell, *Shakespeare's Use of Comic Materials in Tragedy: A Survey of Criticism*, Chapel Hill, N.C., 1940; A. H. R. Fairchild, *Shakespeare and the Tragic Theme*, Columbia, Mo., 1944; H. B. Charlton, *Shakespearean Tragedy*, Cambridge, England, 1948; H. V. D. Dyson, *The Emergence of Shakespeare's Tragedy*, London, 1950; W. Farnham, *Shakespeare's Tragic Frontier*, Berkeley, Calif., 1950; J. V. Cunningham, *Woe or Wonder: The Emotional Effect of Shakespearean Tragedy*, Denver, 1951; A. C. Bradley, *Shakespearean Tragedy*, New York, 1956; F. M. Dickey, *Not Wisely But Too Well: Shakespeare's Love Tragedies*, San Marino, Calif., 1957; P. N. Siegel, *Shakespearean Tragedy and the Elizabethan Compromise*, New York, 1957; B. Stirling, *Unity in Shakespearean Tragedy: The Interplay of Theme and Character*, New York, 1957; I. Ribner, *Patterns in Shakespearian Tragedy*, New York, 1960; G. B. Harrison, *Shakespeare's Tragedies*, New York, 1961; G. W. Knight, *The Imperial Theme: Further Interpretations of Shakespeare's Tragedies, Including the Roman Plays*, 3d ed., London, 1961; R. Speaight, *Nature in Shakespearean Tragedy*, New York, 1955, 1962; J. Holloway, *The Story of the Night: Studies in Shakespeare's Major Tragedies*, Lincoln, Nebr., 1963; *Shakespeare: The Tragedies*, ed. by A. Harbage, Englewood Cliffs, N.J., 1964; L. D. Lerner, ed., *Shakespeare's Tragedies: A Selection of Modern Criticism*, London, 1964; G. W. Knight, *The Wheel of Fire: Interpretations of Shakespearian Tragedy, with Three New Essays*, 4th ed., rev. and enl., London, 1965; C. Leech, ed., *Shakespeare: The Tragedies*, Chicago and Toronto, 1965; R. B. Sharma, *Essays on Shakespearean Tragedy*, Mystic, Conn., 1965; V. K. Whitaker, *Mirror Up to Nature: The Technique of Shakespeare's Tragedies*, San Marino, Calif., 1965; T. McFarland, *Tragic Meaning in Shakespeare*, New York, 1966; K. Muir, *William Shakespeare: The Great Tragedies—Hamlet, Othello, King Lear, Macbeth*, London, 1966; N. Frye, *Fools of Time: Studies in Shakespearean Tragedy*, Toronto, 1967; H. A. Mason, *Shakespeare's Tragedies of Love*, London, 1970; J. L. Barroll, *Artificial Persons: the Formation of Character in the Tragedies of Shakespeare*, Columbia, S.C., 1974.

2. *Roman Tragedies.* M. W. MacCallum, *Shakespeare's Roman Plays and Their Background*, London, 1910; M. Charney, *Shakespeare's Roman Plays: The Function of Imagery in the Drama*, Cambridge, Mass., 1961; T. J. B. Spencer, *William Shakespeare: The Roman Plays—Titus Andronicus, Julius Caesar, Antony and Cleopatra, Coriolanus*, London, 1963; D. A. Traversi, *Shakespeare: The Roman Plays*, Stanford, Calif., 1963; *Discussions of Shakespeare's Roman Plays*, ed. by M. Charney, Boston, 1964.

3. *Individual Plays.* (a) *Antony and Cleopatra.* L. Mills, *The Tragedies of Shakespeare's Antony and Cleopatra*, Bloomington, Ind., 1964; J. Markels, *Pillar of the World: Antony and Cleopatra in Shakespeare's Development*, Columbus, Ohio, 1968. (b) *Coriolanus.* M. C. Felhoelter, *Proverbialism in Coriolanus*, Washington, 1960. (c) *Hamlet.* J. Corbin, *The Elizabethan Hamlet*, London, 1895; G. Murray, *Hamlet and Orestes*, Oxford, 1914; J. M. Robertson, *The Problem of Hamlet*, London, 1919; E. E. Stoll, *Hamlet*, Minneapolis, 1919; E. Jones, *A Psychoanalytic Study of Hamlet*, London, 1922; A.

S. Cairncross, *The Problem of Hamlet: A Solution*, London, 1936; W. Farnham, *Hamlet: The Medieval Heritage of Elizabethan Tragedy*, Berkeley, Calif., 1936; A. A. Raven, *A Hamlet Bibliography and Reference Guide 1877–1935*, Chicago, 1936; C. S. Lewis, *Hamlet: The Prince or the Poem?*, London, 1942; S. Thomas, *The Antic Hamlet and Richard III*, New York, 1943; R. Walker, *The Time Is Out of Joint: A Study of Hamlet*, London, 1948; R. Flatter, *Hamlet's Father*, New Haven, Conn., 1949; M. Hubner, *Shakespeare's Hamlet*, New York, 1950; P. MacKaye, *The Mystery of Hamlet, King of Denmark; or, What We Will: A Tetralogy with Prelude and Postlude, in Prologue to the Tragicall Historie of Hamlet, Prince of Denmarke, by William Shakespeare*, New York, 1950; *Readings on the Character of Hamlet, 1661–1947*, ed. by C. C. H. Williamson, London, 1950; D. S. Savage, *Hamlet and the Pirates*, London, 1950; B. L. Joseph, *Conscience and the King: A Study of Hamlet*, London, 1953; E. Jones, *Hamlet and Oedipus*, New York, 1954; P. Alexander, *Hamlet, Father and Son*, London, 1955; A. Wormhoudt, *Hamlet's Mouse Trap: A Psychoanalytical Study of the Drama*, New York, 1956; P. S. Conklin, *A History of Hamlet Criticism, 1601–1821*, New York, 1957; J. D. Wilson, *What Happens in Hamlet*, London, 1957; H. Levin, *The Question of Hamlet*, New York, 1959; *Discussions of Hamlet*, ed. by J. C. Levenson, Boston, 1960; *Hamlet: Enter Critic*, ed. by C. Sacks and E. Whan, New York, 1960; L. C. Knights, *An Approach to Hamlet*, Stanford, Calif., 1960; R. E. Leavenworth, *Interpreting Hamlet: Materials for Analysis*, San Francisco, 1960; W. Babcock, *Hamlet: A Tragedy of Errors*, West Lafayette, Ind., 1961; C. Devlin, *Hamlet's Divinity and Other Essays*, Carbondale, Ill., 1963; K. Muir, *Shakespeare: Hamlet*, London, 1963; H. Braddy, *Hamlet's Wounded Name*, El Paso, 1964; M. Holmes, *The Guns of Elsinore: A New Approach to Hamlet*, London, 1964; S. de Madariaga, *On Hamlet*, 2d ed., New York, 1964; G. R. Elliott, *Scourge and Minister: A Study of Hamlet as a Tragedy of Revengefulness and Justice*, reprint, Durham, N.C., 1965; J. W. Draper, *The Hamlet of Shakespeare's Audience*, New York, 1966; L. L. Schücking, *The Meaning of Hamlet*, tr. by G. Rawson, New York, 1966; C. M. Lewis, *Genesis of Hamlet*, Port Washington, N.Y., 1967; E. Prosser, *Hamlet and Revenge*, Stanford, Calif., 1967; W. C. Sanford, *Theater as Metaphor in Hamlet*, Cambridge, Mass., 1967; *Twentieth Century Interpretations of Hamlet*, ed. by S. Bevington, Englewood Cliffs, N.J., 1968. (d) *Julius Caesar.* A. Bonjour, *The Structure of Julius Caesar*, Liverpool, 1958; *Shakespeare's Julius Caesar*, ed. by J. Markels, New York, 1961. (e) *King Lear.* S. A. Tannenbaum, *Shakespeare's King Lear: A Concise Bibliography*, New York, 1940; E. Muir, *The Politics of King Lear*, Glasgow, 1947; J. M. Lothian, *King Lear: A Tragic Reading of Life*, Toronto, 1949; J. F. Danby, *Shakespeare's Doctrine of Nature: A Study of King Lear*, London, 1959; *The King Lear Perplex*, ed. by H. Bonheim, Belmont, Calif., 1960; N. Brooke, *Shakespeare: King Lear*, London, 1963; R. B. Heilman, *This Great Stage: Image and Structure in King Lear*, reprint, Seattle, 1963; M. Mack, *King Lear in Our Time*, Berkeley, Calif., 1965; W. R. Elton, *King Lear and the Gods*, San Marino, Calif., 1966; P. A. Jorgensen, *Lear's Self-discovery*, Berkeley, Calif., 1967; S. L. Goldberg, *An Essay on King Lear*, Cambridge, 1974. (f) *Macbeth.* W. C. Curry, *Demonic Metaphysics of Macbeth*, New York, 1933; L. C. Knights, *How Many Children Had Lady Macbeth?*, Cambridge, England, 1933; S. A. Tannenbaum, *Shakespeare's Macbeth: A Concise Bibliography*, New York, 1939; R. Walker, *The Time Is Free: A Study of Macbeth*, London, 1949; H. N. Paul, *The Royal Play of Macbeth*, Philadelphia, 1950; J. R. Brown, *Shakespeare: Macbeth*, London, 1963; J. W. McCutchan, *Macbeth*, New York, 1963; J. L. Halio, *Approaches to Macbeth*, Belmont, Calif., 1966; R. W. Dent, *Macbeth*, Dubuque, Iowa, 1969. (g) *Othello.* E. E. Stoll, *Othello: An Historical and Comparative Study*, Minneapolis, 1915; S. A. Tannenbaum, *Shakespeare's Othello: A Concise Bibliography*, New York, 1943; G. R. Elliott, *Flaming Minister: A Study of Othello as Tragedy of Love and Hate*, Durham, N.C., 1953; R. B. Heilman, *Magic in the Web: Action and Language in Othello*, Lexington, Ky., 1956; L. F. Dean, *A Casebook on Othello*, New York, 1961; E. Jones, *Othello's Countrymen: The African in English Renaissance Drama*, Oxford, 1965; P. A. Jorgensen, *Othello*, New York, 1965; J. W. Draper, *The Othello of Shakespeare's Audience*, New York, 1966. (h) *Romeo and Juliet.* H. B. Charlton, *Romeo and Juliet as an Experimental Tragedy*, London, 1939; O. H. Moore, *The Legend of Romeo and Juliet*, Columbus, Ohio, 1950; S. A. Tannenbaum and D. R. Tannenbaum, *Shakespeare's Romeo and Juliet: A Concise Bibliography*, New York, 1950; R. O. Evans, *The Osier Cage: Rhetorical Devices in Romeo and Juliet*, Lexington, Ky., 1966; R. Hosley, *Romeo and Juliet*, Dubuque, Iowa, 1969. (i) *Timon of Athens.* T. M. Parrott, *The Problem of Timon of Athens*, London, 1923; F. Butler, *Strange Critical Fortunes of Shakespeare's Timon of Athens*, Ames, Iowa, 1965; M. C. Bradbrook, *The Tragic Pageant of Timon of Athens*, Cambridge, England, 1966. (j) *Troilus and Cressida.* S. A. Tannenbaum and D. R. Tannenbaum, *Shakespeare's Troilus and Cressida: A Concise Bibliography*, New York, 1943; R. K. Presson, *Shakespeare's Troilus and Cressida and the Legends of Troy*, Madison, Wis., 1953; O. J. Campbell, *Comicall Satyre and Shakespeare's Troilus and Cressida*, San Marino, Calif., 1959; R. Kimbrough, *Shakespeare's Troilus and Cressida and Its Setting*, Cambridge, Mass., 1964.

Chronology

1. *Early Plays.* *Early Shakespeare*, ed. by J. R. Brown and B. Harris, New York, 1961; A. C. Hamilton, *Early Shakespeare*, San Marino, Calif.,

1967; J. Arthos, *Shakespeare: The Early Writings*, London, 1972.

2. *Late Plays*. D. Traversi, *Shakespeare: The Last Phase*, Stanford, Calif., 1955; F. Kermode, *Shakespeare: The Final Plays*, London, 1963; G. W. Knight, *The Crown of Life: Essays in Interpretation of Shakespeare's Final Plays*, New York, 1964; D. R. C. Marsh, *The Recurring Miracle: A Study of Cymbeline and the Last Plays*, Durban, 1964; E. M. W. Tillyard, *Shakespeare's Last Plays*, 6th ed., New York, 1964; *Later Shakespeare*, ed. by J. R. Brown and B. Harris, Stratford on Avon, 1967; W. Farnham, *Shakespeare's Tragic Frontier: The World of His Final Tragedies*, Oxford, 1973; F. Yates, *Shakespeare's Last Plays*, London, 1979.

3. *Problem Plays*. P. Ure, *William Shakespeare: The Problem Plays—Troilus and Cressida, All's Well That Ends Well, Measure for Measure, Timon of Athens*, London and New York, 1961; E. Schanzer, *The Problem Plays of Shakespeare: A Study of Julius Caesar, Measure for Measure, Antony and Cleopatra*, New York, 1963; E. M. W. Tillyard, *Shakespeare's Problem Plays*, reprint, Toronto, 1964; W. B. Toole, *Shakespeare's Problem Plays: Studies in Form and Meaning*, New York, 1966.

CRITICISM

General Studies

1. *Book-length Studies*. J. Upton, *Critical Observations on Shakespeare*, new ed., London, 1748; C. Lennox, *Shakespear Illustrated*, London, 1753–1754; R. G. White, *Shakespeare's Scholar: Being Historical and Critical Studies of His Text, Characters, and Commentators; with an Examination of Mr. Collier's Folio of 1623*, New York, 1854; A. A. Smirnov, *Shakespeare: A Marxist Interpretation*, tr. by S. Volochova et al., 3d ed., rev., New York, 1936; H. Craig, *An Interpretation of Shakespeare*, London, 1948; A. Gilbert, *The Principles and Practice of Criticism: Othello, The Merry Wives, Hamlet*, Detroit, 1959; H. C. Goddard, *The Meaning of Shakespeare*, 2 vols., Chicago, 1960; L. C. Knights, *Some Shakespearean Themes*, Stanford, Calif., 1960; W. H. Blumenthal, *Paging William Shakespeare: A Critical Challenge*, New Hyde Park, N.Y., 1961; E. Dowden, *Shakespeare: A Critical Study of His Mind and Art*, 3d ed., New York, 1962; G. Brandes, *William Shakespeare: A Critical Study*, tr. by W. Archer and D. White, 2 vols., New York, 1963; E. W. Talbert, *Elizabethan Drama and Shakespeare's Early Plays: An Essay in Historical Criticism*, Chapel Hill, N.C., 1963; M. Weitz, *Hamlet and the Philosophy of Literary Criticism*, Chicago, 1964; D. Horowitz, *Shakespeare: An Existentialist View*, New York, 1965; L. C. Knights, *Further Explorations*, Stanford, Calif., 1965; A. B. Harbage, *Conceptions of Shakespeare*, Cambridge, Mass., 1966; W. Whiter, *A Specimen of a Commentary on Shakespeare*, ed. by A. Over and M. Bell, 2d rev. ed., New York, 1967; S. Burckhardt, *Shakespearean Meanings*, Princeton, N.J., 1968.

2. *Critical Anthologies*. *Shakespeare Criticism: A Selection, 1623–1840*, ed. by D. N. Smith, London, 1916; *Shakespeare Criticism, 1919–1935*, ed. by A. Ridler, London, 1936; *Shakespeare's Criticism: 1919–1935*, ed. by A. Bradby, London, 1936; *Joseph Quincy Adams Memorial Studies*, ed. by J. G. McManaway et al., Washington, 1948; *Talking of Shakespeare*, ed. by J. Garrett, London, 1954; *More Talking of Shakespeare*, ed. by J. Garrett, New York, 1960; *New Readings in Shakespeare*, ed. by C. J. Sisson, 2 vols., Birmingham, Ala., 1961; A. P. Rossiter, *Angel with Horns, and Other Shakespeare Lectures*, ed. by G. Storey, London and New York, 1961; *Eighteenth Century Essays on Shakespeare*, ed. by D. N. Smith, reprint, New York, 1962; *Essays on Shakespeare and Elizabethan Drama in Honor of Hardin Craig*, ed. by R. Hosley, Columbia, Mo., 1962; *Shakespearean Studies*, ed. by B. Matthews and A. H. Thorndike, new ed., New York, 1962; *Shakespeare Criticism, 1935–1960*, ed by A. Ridler, London, 1963; *Approaches to Shakespeare*, ed. by N. Rabkin, New York, 1964; *Shakespeare 1564–1964: A Collection of Modern Essays by Various Hands*, ed. by E. A. Bloom, Providence, 1964; *Shakespeare's Critics from Jonson to Auden: A Medley of Judgments*, ed. by A. M. Eastman and G. B. Harrison, Ann Arbor, Mich., 1964; *Studies in Shakespeare: British Academy Lectures*, ed. by G. W. Chapman, Princeton, N.J., 1965; *Essays on Shakespeare*, ed. by G. R. Smith, University Park, Pa., 1965; *Four Centuries of Shakespeare Criticism*, ed. by F. Kermode, New York, 1965; *Pacific Coast Studies in Shakespeare*, ed. by W. F. McNair and T. Greenfield, Eugene, Oreg., 1966; *Shakespeare: Modern Essays in Criticism*, ed. by L. F. Dean, rev. ed., New York, 1967.

History of Criticism

1. *History*. C. F. Johnson, *Shakespeare and His Critics*, New York, 1909; G. C. D. Odell, *Shakespeare from Betterton to Irving*, 2 vols., London, 1920; C. H. Herford, *A Sketch of Recent Shakespearean Investigation 1893–1923*, London, 1923; D. N. Smith, *Shakespeare in the 18th Century*, Oxford, 1928; A. Ralli, *A History of Shakespearean Criticism*, 2 vols., New York, 1932; H. S. Robinson, *English Shakespearian Criticism in the Eighteenth Century*, Long Island City, N.Y., 1932; A. V. R. Westfall, *American Shakespearean Criticism, 1607–1865*, New York, 1939; F. E. Halliday, *Shakespeare and His Criticis*, reprint New York, 1963; L. Mander, *His Exits and His Entrances: The Story of Shakespeare's Reputation*, Philadelphia, 1963; P. N. Siegel, *His Infinite Variety: Major Shakespearean Criticism since Johnson*, Philadelphia, 1964; A. M. Eastman, *A Short History of Shakespeare Criticism*, New York, 1968. B. Vickers, ed., *Shakespeare The Critical Heritage Vol . 1*.

1623–1692, Vol 2. 1693–1733, Vol 3. 1733–1752, Vol. 4. 1753–1765, Vol. 5. 1765–1774, London 1974–1979.

2. *Idolatry*. N. Drake, *Memorials of Shakespeare, or Sketches of His Character and Genius by Various Writers*, London, 1828; C. M. Ingleby, *Shakespeare's Centurie of Prayse*, London, 1874; *A Book of Homage to Shakespeare*, ed. by I. Gollancz, Oxford, 1916; F. E. Halliday, *The Cult of Shakespeare*, New York, 1957; T. J. B. Spencer, *The Tyranny of Shakespeare*, New York, 1959; R. W. Babcock, *The Genesis of Shakespeare Idolatry, 1766–1799: A Study in English Criticism of the Late Eighteenth Century*, reprint, New York, 1964; H. Schueller, *The Persistence of Shakespeare Idolatry*, Detroit, 1964.

Special Problems

1. *Authorship*. (a) *Authorship Controversy*. (i) *General Studies*. N. Holmes, *The Authorship of Shakespeare*, New York, 1866; G. G. Greenwood, *The Shakespeare Problem Restated*, London, 1908; J. T. Baxter, *The Greatest of Literary Problems: The Authorship of the Shakespeare Works*, Boston, 1915; A. Feuillerat, *The Composition of Shakespeare's Plays: Authorship, Chronology*, New Haven, Conn., 1953; W. F. Friedman and E. S. Friedman, *The Shakespearean Ciphers Examined: An Analysis of Cryptographic Systems Used as Evidence that Some Author Other than William Shakespeare Wrote the Plays Commonly Attributed to Him*, New York, 1957; R. C. Churchill, *Shakespeare and His Betters: A History and a Criticism of the Attempts Which Have Been Made to Prove that Shakespeare's Works Were Written by Others*, Bloomington, Ind., 1959; H. N. Gibson, *The Shakespeare Claimants*, New York, 1962; J. G. McManaway, *The Authorship of Shakespeare*, Washington, 1962; C. Ogburn, Jr., and D. Ogburn, *Shakespeare: The Man behind the Name*, New York, 1962; *Shakespeare and His Rivals: A Casebook on the Authorship Controversy*, ed. by G. McMichael and E. M. Glenn, New York, 1962; W. H. Blumenthal, *Who Knew Shakespeare?*, Park Forest, Ill., 1964. (ii) *Edward de Vere*. J. T. Looney, *"Shakespeare" Identified in Edward de Vere, the 17th Earl of Oxford*, London, 1920; P. Allen, *The Case for Edward de Vere, 17th Earl of Oxford, as "William Shakespeare,"* London, 1930. (iii) *Sir Francis Bacon*. I. Donnelly, *The Great Cryptogram: Francis Bacon's Cipher in the So-called Shakespeare Plays*, 2 vols., New York, 1888; A. Lang, *Shakespeare, Bacon, and the Great Unknown*, London, 1912; J. M. Robertson, *The Baconian Heresy: A Confutation*, London, 1913; A. B. Cornwall, *Francis the First: Unacknowledged King of Great Britain and Ireland Known to the World as Sir Francis Bacon, Man of Mystery and Cipher*, Birmingham, 1936; F. L. Woodward, *Bacon and the Cipher Story*, Chicago, 1947. (iv) *Others*. L. Hotson, *I, William Shakespeare, Do Appoint Thomas Russell, Esquire . . .*, London, 1937; A. Brooks, *Will Shakespeare and the Dyer's Hand*, New York, 1943; C. Hoffman, *The Murder of the Man Who Was Shakespeare*, New York, 1961. (b) *Apocryphal Plays and Collaboration*. R. G. White, *Essay on the Authorship of the Three Parts of Henry the Sixth*, Cambridge, Mass., 1859; *Shakespeare's Doubtful Plays*, ed. by A.F. Hopkinson, 3 vols., London, 1891–1895; *The Shakespeare Apocrypha*, ed. by C. F. T. Brooke, Oxford, 1908; E. H. Wright, *The Authorship of Timon of Athens*, New York, 1910; B. Maxwell, *Studies in the Shakespeare Apocrypha*, New York, 1956; K. Muir, *Shakespeare as Collaborator*, New York, 1960; A. C. Partridge, *The Problem of Henry VIII Reopened: Some Linguistic Criteria for the Two Apparent Styles in the Play*, New York, 1963; P. D. Bertram, *Shakespeare and the Two Noble Kinsmen*, New Brunswick, N.J., 1965; A. W. Pollard, *Shakespeare's Hand in the Play of Sir Thomas More, and Shakespeare's Fight with the Pirates*, Cambridge, England, 1967.

2. *Textual Problems and Early Editions*. (a) *General Studies*. J. P. Collier, *Notes and Emendations to Shakespeare from Early Manuscripts*, New York, 1853; T. R. Lounsbury, *The Text of Shakespeare: Its History from the Publication of the Quartos and Folios Down to and Including the Publication of the Editions of Pope and Theobald*. New York, 1906; A. W. Pollard, *Shakespeare Folios and Quartos*, London, 1909; id., *Shakespeare's Fight with the Pirates and the Problems of the Transmission of His Text*, Cambridge, England, 1920; S. A. Tannenbaum, *Problems in Shakespeare's Penmanship*, New York, 1927; W. W. Greg, *Principles of Emendation in Shakespeare*, Oxford, 1928; L. Kirschbaum, *Shakespeare and the Stationers*, Columbus, Ohio, 1955; W. W. Greg, *The Editorial Problem in Shakespeare: A Survey of the Foundations of the Text*, 3d ed., New York, 1962; E. A. J. Honigmann, *The Stability of Shakespeare's Text*, London, 1965; J. M. Nosworthy, *Shakespeare's Occasional Plays: Their Origin and Transmission*, London, 1965; F. Bowers, *On Editing Shakespeare and the Elizabethan Dramatists*, Charlottesville, 1966. (b) *First Folio*. R. C. Rhodes, *Shakespeare's First Folio*, Oxford, 1923; M. H. Spielmann et al., *Studies in the First Folio*, Oxford, 1924; A. Walker, *Textual Problems of the First Folio: Richard III, King Lear, Troilus and Cressida, 2 Henry IV, Hamlet, Othello*, New York, 1953; W. W. Greg, *The Shakespeare First Folio: Its Bibliographical and Textual History*, New York, 1955; J. W. Shroeder, *The Great Folio of 1623: Shakespeare's Plays in the Printing House*, Hamden, Conn., 1956; C. Hinman, *The Printing and Proofreading of the First Folio of Shakespeare*, 2 vols., New York, 1963; T. W. Baldwin, *On Act and Scene Division in the Shakespeare First Folio*, Carbondale, Ill., 1965. (c) *Quartos*. H. C. Bartlett and A. W. Pollard, *A Census of Shakespeare's Plays in Quarto, 1594–1709*, New Haven, Conn., 1916; H. L. Ford, *Shakespeare 1700–1740: A Collation of the Editions and Separate Plays*, New York, 1935; M. W. Black and M. A. Shaaber, *Shakespeare's Seventeenth-century Editors, 1623–1685*, New York, 1937; A. Hart, *Stolen and Surreptitious Copies: A*

Comparative Study of Shakespeare's Bad Quartos, Melbourne and London, 1942; H. Craig, A New Look at Shakespeare's Quartos, Stanford, Calif., 1961; J. D. Gordon, Bard and the Book: Editions of Shakespeare in the Seventeenth Century, New York, 1964; R. E. Burkhart, Shakespeare's Bad Quartos, The Hague and Paris, 1975. (d) Individual Plays. (i) All's Well That Ends Well. A. E. Thiselton, Some Textual Notes on All's Well That Ends Well, London, 1900. (ii) Hamlet. H. de Groot, Hamlet: Its Textual History, Amsterdam, 1923; B. A. P. Van Dam, The Text of Shakespeare's Hamlet, London, 1924; G. I. Duthie, The "Bad" Quarto of Hamlet: A Critical Study, Cambridge, England, 1941; A. B. Weiner, Hamlet: The First Quarto, 1603, New York, 1962; J. D. Wilson, The Manuscript of Shakespeare's Hamlet and the Problems of Its Transmission, 2 vols., London, 1963. (iii) King Lear. M. Doran, The Text of King Lear, Stanford, Calif., 1931; B. A. P. Van Dam, The Text of Shakespeare's Lear, ed. by H. de Vocht, Louvain, 1935; W. W. Greg, The Variants in the First Quarto of King Lear, London, 1940; L. Kirschbaum, The True Text of King Lear, Baltimore, 1945; G. I. Duthie, Elizabethan Shorthand and the First Quarto of King Lear, Oxford, 1950. (iv) Measure for Measure. A. E. Thiselton, Some Textual Notes on Measure for Measure, London, 1901. (v) The Merry Wives of Windsor. W. Bracy, The Merry Wives of Windsor: The History and Transmission of Shakespeare's Text, Columbia, Mo., 1952; H. Parsons, Emendations to Three of Shakespeare's Plays: The Merry Wives of Windsor, Love's Labour's Lost, The Comedy of Errors, London, 1953. (vi) Richard III. O. L. Patrick, The Textual History of Richard III, Stanford, Calif., 1936; J. K. Walton, The Copy for the Folio Text of Richard III, Auckland, 1955. (vii) Romeo and Juliet. H. R. Hoppe, The Bad Quarto of Romeo and Juliet: A Bibliographical and Textual Study, Ithaca, N.Y., 1948.

3. Linguistics. (a) Grammar. E. A. Abbott, Shakespearean Grammar, New York, 1966. (b) Phonetics. H. Kökeritz, Shakespeare's Pronunciation, New Haven, Conn., 1953; W. Vietor, A Shakespeare Phonology: With a Rime Index to the Poems as a Pronouncing Vocabulary, reprint, New York, 1963. (c) Poetics. M. A. Bayfield, A Study of Shakespeare's Versification with an Inquiry into the Trustworthiness of the Early Texts . . . Including a Revised Text of Antony and Cleopatra, Cambridge, England, 1920; F. W. Ness, The Use of Rhyme in Shakespeare's Plays, New Haven, Conn., 1941; R. A. Fraser, Shakespeare's Poetics in Relation to King Lear, Nashville, 1966; D. L. Sipe, Shakespeare's Metrics, New Haven, Conn., 1968. (d) Punctuation. P. Simpson, Shakespearean Punctuation, Oxford, 1911; T. J. Cobden-Sanderson, Shakesperian Punctuation, New York, 1912; P. Alexander, Shakespeare's Punctuation, London, 1945. (e) Spelling. A. C. Partridge, Orthography in Shakespeare and Elizabethan Drama, Lincoln, Nebr., 1964. (f) Vocabulary. E. Ekwall, Shakspere's Vocabulary, Uppsala, 1903; H. M. Hulme, Explorations in Shakspeare's Language: Some Problems of Lexical Meaning in the Dramatic Text, New York, 1963.

4. Shakespeare and Other Authors. (a) Authors' Comments on Shakespeare. (i) Coleridge. Coleridge's Shakespeare Criticism, Mass., 1930; S. T. Coleridge, Lectures and Notes on Shakespeare and Other Dramatists, ed. by S. Coleridge, London, 1931; Coleridge's Writings on Shakespeare, ed. by T. Hawkes, New York, 1959; S. T. Coleridge, Shakespearean Criticism, rev. ed., 2 vols., New York, 1960. (ii) Emerson. W. M. Wynkoop, Three Children of the Universe: Emerson's View of Shakespeare, Bacon, and Milton, New York, 1966; (iii) Johnson. Johnson on Shakespeare, ed. by W. Raleigh, New York and London, 1908; A. Sherbo, Samuel Johnson, Editor of Shakespeare, Urbana, Ill., 1956; Samuel Johnson on Shakespeare, ed. by W. K. Wimsatt, Jr., New York, 1960; Johnson on Shakespeare, ed. by A. Sherbo, 2 vols., New Haven, Conn., 1965. (iv) Keats. C. F. E. Spurgeon, Keats' Shakespeare, New York, 1928. (v) Pope. J. E. Butt, Pope's Taste in Shakespeare, New York, 1936. (vi) Shaw. Shaw on Shakespeare: An Anthology of Bernard Shaw's Writings on the Plays and Productions of Shakespeare, ed. by E. Wilson, New York, 1961. (vii) Whitman. C. J. Furness, Walt Whitman's Estimate of Shakespeare, New York, 1932. (b) Shakespeare Compared with Other Authors. (i) Jonson. G. E. Bentley, Shakespeare and Jonson: Their Reputations in the Seventeenth Century Compared, 2 vols., Chicago, 1945, 1 vol., Chicago, 1965. (ii) Marlowe. H. Röhrman, Marlowe and Shakespeare: A Thematic Exposition of Some of Their Plays, Arnhem, 1952; F. P. Wilson, Marlowe and the Early Shakespeare, London, 1953; E. M. Waith, The Herculean Hero in Marlowe, Chapman, Shakespeare and Dryden, New York, 1962; J. H. Sims, Dramatic Uses of Biblical Allusions in Marlowe and Shakespeare, Gainesville, Fla., 1966; W. Sanders, The Dramatist and the Received Idea: Studies in the Plays of Marlowe and Shakespeare, Cambridge, England, 1968. (iii) Milton. O. J. Campbell, Studies in Shakespeare, Milton and Donne, New York, 1925; S. T. Coleridge, Seven Lectures on Shakespeare and Milton, new ed., New York, 1968. (iv) Spenser. A. F. Potts, Shakespeare and the Faerie Queene, Ithaca, N.Y., 1958; W. B. C. Watkins, Shakespeare and Spenser, Princeton, N.J., 1966. (v) Tolstoy. G. W. Knight, Shakespeare and Tolstoy, New York, 1934. (vi) Voltaire. T. Besterman, Shakespeare and Voltaire, New York, 1965; T. R. Lounsbury, Shakespeare and Voltaire, new ed., New York, 1968. (vii) The Greeks. E. Montagu, An Essay on the Writings and Genius of Shakespeare Compared with the Greek and French Dramatic Poets, 3d ed., London, 1772; L. Campbell, Tragic Drama in Aeschylus, Sophocles, and Shakespeare, New York, 1904; H. D. F. Kitto, Form and Meaning in Drama: A Study of Six Greek Plays and of Hamlet, London, 1957; D. Grene, Reality and the Heroic Pattern: Last Plays of Ibsen, Shakespeare, and Sophocles, Chicago, 1967. (viii) Others. B. Croce,

Ariosto, Shakespeare and Corneille, tr. by D. Ainslie, London, 1920; A. Chevrillon, Three Studies in English Literature: Kipling, Galsworthy, and Shakespeare, Port Washington, N.Y., 1923; E. E. Stoll, From Shakespeare to Joyce, Garden City, N.Y., 1944; A. Thaler, Shakespeare and Sir Philip Sidney: The Influence of the Defense of Poetry, Oxford, 1947; J. F. Danby, Poets on Fortune's Hill: Studies in Sidney, Shakespeare, Beaumont, and Fletcher, London, 1952; K. Muir, Last Periods of Shakespeare, Racine, Ibsen, Detroit, 1961; E. E. Stoll, Shakespeare and Other Masters, reprint, New York, 1962; W. Kaiser, Praisers of Folly: Erasmus, Shakespeare, Rabelais, Cambridge, Mass., 1963; M. Weitz, Philosophy in Literature: Shakespeare, Voltaire, Tolstoy, Proust, Detroit, 1963; R. F. Fleissner, Dickens and Shakespeare, New York, 1965; J. R. Northam, Dividing Worlds: Shakespeare's The Tempest and Ibsen's Rosmersholm, New York, 1965; G. W. Knight, Byron and Shakespeare, New York, 1966; J. M. Robertson, Montaigne and Shakespeare, and other Essays on Cognate Subjects, reprint of 2d ed., New York, 1968. F. Kermode, Shakespeare. Spenser. Donne, London, 1971; M. M. Badawi, Coleridge: Critic of Shakespeare, Cambridge, 1973.

5. Shakespeare's Knowledge of Other Professions. P. S. Clarkson and C. T. Warren, Law of Property in Shakespeare and the Elizabethan Drama, Baltimore, 1942; A. Duff Cooper, Sergeant Shakespeare, London and Toronto, 1949; P. A. Jorgensen. Shakespeare's Military World, Berkeley, Calif., 1956; R. R. Simpson, Shakespeare and Medicine, Baltimore, 1959; N. Coghill, Shakespeare's Professional Skills, London, 1964; G. W. Keeton, Shakespeare's Legal and Political Background, New York, 1967.

6. Shakespeare's Contemporary Relevance. M. Webster, Shakespeare Today, Chester Springs, Pa., 1957; The Living Shakespeare, ed. by R. Gittings, London, 1960; Shakespeare in a Changing World, ed. by A. Kettle, London, 1964; J. Kott, Shakespeare Our Contemporary, Garden City, N.Y., 1964; A. Thaler, Shakespeare and Our World, Knoxville, 1966; P. N. Siegal, Shakespeare in His Time and Ours, Notre Dame, 1968.

7. Miscellaneous Studies. G. R. French, Shakespeareana Genealogica, London, 1869; Shakspere Allusion-Books, ed. by C. M. Ingleby, London, 1874; J. A. R. Marriott, English History in Shakespeare, London, 1918; C. Still, Shakespeare's Mystery Play, London, 1921; B. B. Kaiser, Shakespearean Oracles, Boston, 1923; F. C. Kolbe, Shakespeare's Way, London, 1930; L. Hotson, Shakespeare versus Shallow, London, 1931; C. J. Sisson, The Mythical Sorrows of Shakespeare, Oxford, 1934; O. J. Campbell, Shakespeare's Satire, London, 1943; J. H. De Groot, The Shakespeares and "the Old Faith," New York, 1946; C. W. Scott-Giles, Shakespeare's Heraldry, London, 1950; A. Nicoll, Co-operation in Shakespeare Scholarship, London, 1952; G. W. Knight, Sovereign Flower, New York, 1958; R. B. Sharpe, Irony in the Drama, Chapel Hill, N.C., 1959; G. W. Knight, The Shakespearian Tempest, with a Chart of Shakespeare's Dramatic Universe, 3d ed., New York, 1960; W. I. D. Scott, Shakespeare's Melancholics, London, 1962; W. Talbert, The Problem of Order: Elizabethan Political Commonplaces and an Example of Shakespeare's Art, Chapel Hill, N.C., 1962; A. F. Falconer, Shakespeare and the Sea, London, 1964; H. Green, Shakespeare and the Emblem Writers, New York, 1964; N. Webb and J. F. Webb, Will Shakespeare and His America, New York, 1964; J. E. Harting, The Birds of Shakespeare; or, The Ornithology of Shakespeare Critically Examined, Explained and Illustrated, reprint, Chicago, 1965; J. Kirsch, Shakespeare's Royal Self, New York, 1966; N. Rabkin, Shakespeare and the Common Understanding, New York, 1967; J. Arthos, Shakespeare's Use of Dreams and Vision, London, 1977; R. T. Berry, On Directing Shakespeare: Interviews with Contemporary Directors, London, 1977.

Reference Materials

Bibliographies
W. Ebisch and L. L. Schücking, A Shakespeare Bibliography, Oxford, 1931; W. Jaggard, Shakespeare Bibliography: A Dictionary of Every Known Issue of the Writings of the Poet and of Recorded Opinion Thereon in the English Language, New York, 1959; G. R. Smith, A Classified Shakespeare Bibliography, 1936–1958, University Park, Pa., 1963; W. Ebisch and L. L. Schücking, Supplement for the Years 1930–1935 to a Shakespeare Bibliography, new ed. New York, 1964; R. Berman, A Reader's Guide to Shakespeare's Plays: A Discursive Bibliography, Chicago, 1965.

Dictionaries and Glossaries
C. Mackay, Glossary of Obscure Words and Phrases in the Writings of Shakespeare and His Contemporaries, Detroit, 1887; E. H. Sugden, Topographical Dictionary to the Works of Shakespeare and His Fellow Dramatist, New York, 1925; C. T. Onions, A Shakespeare Glossary, 2d ed., New York, 1958; H. Kökeritz, Shakespeare's Names: A Pronouncing Dictionary, New Haven, Conn., 1959; A. F. Falconer, A Glossary of Shakespeare's Sea and Naval Terms, London, 1965; F. G. Stokes, Dictionary of the Characters and Proper Names in the Works of Shakespeare, New York and Magnolia, Mass., 1968; J. Foster, A Shakespeare Word-book, reprint, New York, 1969.

Indexes and Concordances
S. Ayscough, An Index to the Remarkable Passages and Words Made Use of by Shakespeare, London, 1790; M. C. Clarke, The Complete Concordance to Shakespeare, rev. ed., London, 1870; C. Clarke and M. C. Clarke, The Shakespeare Key, 2 vols., New York, 1879; J. Bartlett, A Complete Concordance of Shakespeare, new ed., New York, 1960; An Index to "The Elizabethan Stage" and "William Shakespeare" by Sir Edmund Chambers, ed. by B. White,

reprint, New York, 1964; M. Spevack, *Complete and Systematic Concordance to the Works of Shakespeare*, 6 vols., New York, 1968—.

Running Commentaries
M. R. Ridley, *William Shakespeare: A Commentary*, New York, 1936; H. Granville-Barker and G. B. Harrison, *A Companion to Shakespeare Studies*, New York, 1955; T. M. Parrott, *William Shakespeare; A Handbook*, rev. ed., New York, 1955; A. E. Baker, *A Shakespeare Commentary*, 2 vols., New York, 1958; A. Harbage, *William Shakespeare: A Reader's Guide*, New York, 1963; F. E. Halliday, *A Shakespeare Companion,.1564–1964*, rev. ed., New York, 1964.

Miscellaneous Reading Aids
E. Capell, *Notes and Various Readings to Shakespeare*, 3 vols., London, 1779–1783; W. J. Lawrence, *Speeding Up Shakespeare*, New York, 1937; M. R. Ridley, *On Reading Shakespeare*, London, 1940; B. Deutsch, *The Reader's Shakespeare*, New York, 1946; G. Sanders, *Shakespeare Primer*, London, 1951; F. E. Halliday, *The Enjoyment of Shakespeare*, London, 1959; C. B. Purdom, *What Happens in Shakespeare*, London, 1963; W. Vietor, *A Shakespeare Reader: In the Old Spelling with a Phonetic Transcription*, new ed., New York, 1963; J. Wain, *The Living World of Shakespeare: A Playgoer's Guide*, New York, 1964; L. B. Wright, *Shakespeare for Everyman*, New York, 1964; *The Reader's Encyclopedia of Shakespeare*, ed. by O. J. Campbell and E. G. Quinn, New York, 1966; S. Usherwood; *Shakespeare Play by Play*, New York, 1967; J. Bate, *How to Find Out about Shakespeare*, Oxford, 1968; M. Charney, *How to Read Shakespeare*, New York, 1971.

Shakespeare on Film

With the coming of sound, film became eminently suitable for interpreting Shakespeare. Like Elizabethan drama the motion picture could present a dramatic narrative with as many scenes as the writer or director desired. In addition, during the silent era film had evolved a rich visual imagery quite comparable with the achievements of the best dramatic poetry.

Nevertheless, film does have a tendency to reproduce an *illusion* of reality which is far removed, not just from Shakespeare's poetry, but from the entire emblematic tradition of English stagecraft to which he belonged. Consequently, the main problem for any adaptor of Shakespeare to the screen was how to create an appropriate "space" or "environment" within which the poetry and conventions of Shakespeare's theatre could be assimilated.

The first sound version of Shakespeare in *Hollywood Review of 1929* (M.G.M., 1929) simply ignored the problem. This was not surprising as the sequence involved Norma Shearer and John Gilbert, first playing the balcony scene from *Romeo and Juliet* straight, then, with the balcony at ground level, parodying the exchanges between the lovers. More interesting was John Barrymore's lurid rendition of the opening soliloquy from *Richard III* in *Show of Shows* (Warner Bros., 1929). In order to encompass his larger than life performance, the designers created a setting based on the Doré illustrations for Dante's *Inferno*. Richard appears to be standing silhouetted against a fiery background on a mound of corpses, a significant anticipation of later more sophisticated attempts to link design with Shakespeare's imagery.

The first full-length Shakespearan sound film, however, was Samuel Taylor's *The Taming of the Shrew* (Pickford Corporation, 1929) with Douglas Fairbanks and Mary Pickford. The film is remarkably successful in creating a thoroughly believable Renaissance environment. William Cameron Menzies and Laurence Irving designed the magnificent interior of a medieval church for the wedding scene and a banqueting hall dominated by three adroitly placed arches. Taylor and his designers also devised a splendidly effective framing device for the main action: a pull-back broken by dissolves from a Punch and Judy show to reveal the bustle of Padua's main square.

Unfortunately, Taylor's script made little or no attempt to come to terms with the verse. The cast speak, for the most part, a kind of doggerel Shakespeare that includes some appalling misreadings ("cholera" for "choler," for example). Although the set pieces like the wedding and the final banquet are well handled, the action between the principles seems woefully under rehearsed. One confrontation between Katherine and Petruchio becomes a matter of who can crack his or her whip most effectively, and when Fairbanks carries her from the church, Mary Pickford virtually has to climb over his shoulder. Only in the last half, when the encumbrance of dialogue has been shed, do they recapture the grace and fluidity of their silent performances. Admittedly, these final sequences, with Katherine laying out her husband with a joint stool·after he has ripped their nuptial bed to pieces, become in effect a taming of Petruchio, but similar devices have appeared in the theatre.

A few years later, in 1933, some color tests were shot of John Barrymore as Hamlet. They included the Prince's soliloquy over the praying Claudius and Hamlet's encounter with the ghost. While the tests provide an invaluable record of Barrymore's interpretation of Hamlet, they also reveal that (at least on the screen) the part was, by then, beyond him. His hands are so swollen that he is barely able to handle the sword in the prayer scene, and when, on the battlements, he exits to follow the ghost, his gait is visibly uncertain. The settings are obviously theatrical, and the camera records the action in a series of medium shots.

Consequently, it was not until 1935 that another full-length version of Shakespeare was attempted: Max Reinhardt and William Dieterle's *A Midsummer Night's Dream* (Warner Bros., 1935). It was based on Reinhardt's stage productions of the play which had been performed the year before in locales as diverse as the Greek Theatre at the University of California, the San Francisco Opera House, and the Hollywood Bowl. But while many devices from these and other productions of the play, such as the use of "fog" to achieve transitions and the candlelight procession at the end, were incorporated into the film, *A Midsummer Night's Dream* remains one of the most *cinematic* translations of Shakespeare ever made. This was partly because Reinhardt's own concept of "total theatre," in which lighting, design, and performance were completely integrated, was in itself filmic. But, in addition, this approach was compatible with the development at Warner Brothers of the musical, a genre that, with its exploitation of different levels of reality, is formally very close to Elizabethan drama. As a result of this fortunate combination, the sequences in the forest become a kind of sinister ballet built around antitheses of light and darkness underscoring the awesome power of the fairies. The shape of these scenes is dominated by Eric Korngold's arrangement of the Mendelssohn inci-

Max Reinhardt's conception of "total theatre" found filmic
expression in his 1935 version of *A Midsummer Night's
Dream.* In the stills shown here, (above) Victor Jory is
Oberon, and (below) James Cagney as Bottom announces
the performance of a play to Hippolyta (Jean Muir) and
Theseus (Ian Hunter). [Film Archive, National Library of
Australia]

dental music. Not only were the ballet sequences and editing carefully timed to the score, but certain passages were actually set to music. The forest set, sprayed with aluminum, to create an incandescent effect, and photography through various kinds of spangled gauzes create a superb visual equivalent of the play's imagery of magic and enchantment, all of which seems to be based on the lines describing the fairies dancing in "spangled starlight sheen." Here Reinhardt and Deiterle anticipated many recent commentaries on the play that emphasize the sinister undertones of Oberon's power and the dark underside of the work as a whole.

The cast, made up mainly of Warner Brothers contract players including Dick Powell as Lysander, Olivia de Havilland as Hermia, Victor Jory as Oberon, a thirteen-year-old Mickey Rooney as Puck, Joe E. Brown as Flute, and James Cagney as Bottom, are surprisingly good. Certainly the text had to be cut extensively to accommodate their vocal limitations, but Reinhardt's legendary ability to get players to incorporate their own mannerisms into a role enabled these screen actors to be at once supremely themselves and also to give sensitive interpretations of Shakespeare's characters.

A Midsummer Night's Dream's skillful exploitation of musical conventions makes the world of the film, like the play world of Shakespeare's original, exist as a self-contained dramatic illusion that the audience knows is fantasy but accepts on its own terms. Although this version is by no means a translation of the full complexity of the play, the assimilation by the preexisting cinematic form of the musical creates a remarkably successful equivalent of the overall effect of Shakespeare's stagecraft and ma-

Leslie Howard and Norma Shearer in George Cukor's film version of *Romeo and Juliet*. [*From Quasimodo to Scarlett O'Hara*, Frederick Ungar Publishing Co.]

Mickey Rooney as Puck in Max Reinhardt's film adaptation of *A Midsummer Night's Dream*. [*From Quasimodo to Scarlett O'Hara*, Frederick Ungar Publishing Co.]

nipulation of theatrical illusion.

The next film version of Shakespeare, made at M.G.M. in 1936, also assimilated the dramatist's work to a preexisting cinematic genre. While the idea of adapting *Romeo and Juliet* to the screen at first seemed to have been undertaken to enable the production head, Irving Thalberg, to cast his wife, Norma Shearer, in one of the title roles, it was not such a radical departure for M.G.M. The studio had a long history of adapting classics to the screen (*Anna Karenina*, *A Tale of Two Cities*, and *David Copperfield*). Overlapping this genre was a cycle of period melodramas, such as *Queen Christina* and *Flesh and the Devil*, characterized by elaborate sets, soft-focus photography, stylized acting, and semipoetic dialogue. At their best, although flawed by poor dialogue or titles, these films were often visually very sophisticated. A film such as *Queen Christina* employs recurring images and symbols in ways very similar to Shakespearean poetry. Consequently, it was only a very short step to the filming of Shakespeare itself, especially when most stage productions in the thirties were performed in front of sets very similar to those employed in period films.

For *Romeo and Juliet*, however, designers Cedric Gibbons and Oliver Messel and director George Cukor fur-

Laurence Olivier in the title role of his 1944 film
Henry V wins the hand of Princess Katharine after
the victory at Agincourt. [Museum of Modern Art/
Film Stills Archive]

ther distance the action by employing a skillful framing
device of a tapestry that comes to life for the prologue,
followed by a track into a portrait of Verona that dissolves into the establishing shot of the first sequence.
The sets, based in part on Renaissance paintings of the
period, are sufficiently artificial to create a disjunction
between the world of the film and everyday reality, so
that the poetry of the original becomes not just acceptable but required. As a result, both Leslie Howard and
Norma Shearer were able to give believable, if stylized,
performances in the title roles. Although at forty-two
Howard was far too old for the part, Cukor and Howard
redesigned the role so that his Romeo is at the outset
half aware that his infatuation with Rosaline is self-indulgence. After meeting Juliet, he abandons his affectations and visibly grows in stature so that his suicide becomes a tragic waste. Although Norma Shearer's
dialogue is cut far more than Howard's, because she
lacked the breath control of an experienced Shakespearean actress, she still gives one of the finest interpretations of a classical role in the history of the cinema. Ini-

tially she is highly stylized, partly because girlishness
from a woman of thirty-seven would be absurd but also
as a response to the formality of the text itself. Later
Shearer succeeds in portraying a totally convincing
growth to womanhood and in the death scene responds
to the implied sensuality of the verse to make the suicide
explicitly erotic, her face registering an almost masochis-
tic combination of pleasure and pain as she stabs herself.

If Shearer and Howard make a necessarily serious
pair of lovers, John Barrymore is an exuberantly comic
Mercutio, mouthing the bawdy wit with gusto, yet suggesting beneath the frivolity a sensitivity and genuine affection for Romeo that blazes into a wickedly dangerous
anger in the duel scene.

But perhaps Cukor's greatest achievement was in
getting the whole cast to adopt a simple, unaffected style
of verse speaking that was completely believable in the
context Gibbons and Messel devised for the film. According to Cukor, cameraman Ray Rennahan devised a
series of links between the film's visual imagery and
Shakespeare's poetry that acts as both illumination and

enrichment of the text. The most striking of these is where Romeo's comment that Juliet's beauty makes the "vault a feasting presence full of light" is given visual expression by having the bier lit by four enormous candles.

In the same year as *Romeo and Juliet* was released in the United States (1936), Paul Czinner completed a film version of *As You Like It* in Great Britain. It was a fairly straightforward adaptation of the play, employing rather obvious theatrical settings. The direction was static, and although Laurence Olivier and Sophie Stewart give splendidly cinematic performances as Orlando and Celia, Elizabeth Bergner is an appalling Rosalind, speaking the verse in a whining, German-accented English.

Up to this point the best film versions of Shakespeare were those that assimilated the plays to equivalent cinematic genres. The man who confronted the full implications of the emblematic tradition of stagecraft to which Shakespeare belonged and who devised new forms to translate the conventions of the Elizabethan theatre into film was Laurence Olivier. When, in 1944, he came to make *Henry V*, he systematically contrasted Technicolor deep-focus shots in the reconstruction of the performance in the Globe with schematic "closed" compositions based on the illuminations in *Les Très Riches Heures* of the Duc de Berry. Consequently, while the sequences in Elizabethan London appear "realistic," the main action in Henry V's England, set in designer Roger Furse's painted landscapes and out of proportion castles, symbolizes medieval life rather than re-creating "the thing itself." The film world, like the play world of the Elizabethan theatre, becomes a self-contained dramatic illusion that the sudience is fully aware is an illusion even while watching it. In effect, the relationship between the viewer and the action on the screen is almost identical to that depicted in the reconstruction of the performance in the Globe. For all intents and purposes, Olivier made an Elizabethan movie.

A further dimension of meaning is added by the superbly executed battle scenes. The sequence is, of course, not an accurate reconstruction of Agincourt. Rather, it is a pageant that symbolizes the historical conflict, and, with its simple, direct compositions, emphasizes the defeat of a superior force by the outnumbered English and also represents Britain in 1944, about to yet again invade France.

Equally as important an achievement is Olivier's use of camera movement to re-create some of the effects of Elizabethan acting. For him the Shakespearean climax "is a fine gesture and a loud voice." Consequently for the "Once more into the breach" and "St. Crispin's Day" speeches the camera tracks back, its movement reflecting the structure of the verse. Olivier also found a more effective way to treat soliloquies than to have them spoken aloud to no one in particular as had been the case previously. Henry's meditations before Agincourt are delivered as a voice-over as the camera moves into a closeup.

Because of the stylized décor and skillful manipulation of the camera, the film was able to encompass more overtly "theatrical" performances than had Cukor's *Ro-*

meo and Juliet. Both Esmond Knight as a fiery Fluellan and Robert Newton's rascally Pistol are very much larger than life. However, Olivier's Henry, Leo Genn's sympathetic Constable, and Harcourt Williams's feeble-minded French king all adopted a middle style that was neither cinematic nor theatrical but, in the context provided, totally convincing. Indeed, it was Olivier's appealing impersonation of the hero king that was largely responsible for the film's popular success.

If the image of the Elizabethan theatre dominates *Henry V*, Olivier's next Shakespearean film, *Hamlet* (Great Britain, 1948), is almost aggressively cinematic. What influenced its director most was the deep-focus work by Welles and Gregg Toland in *Citizen Kane*. For all this, *Hamlet* is far from being naturalistic. Certainly the acting is more "low key" than in *Henry V*. Also, Olivier further develops his innovation of having the soliloquies as voice-overs, using frenetic camera movement to underscore the conflict in "To be or not to be" and a superbly executed tracking shot intercut with extreme close-ups for "O that this too too solid flesh t'would melt."

Nevertheless, Roger Furse's sets were designed as "abstractions" within which each piece of furniture became an object of increased significance. In addition, the compositions in depth permitted by Desmond Dickinson's black-and-white deep-focus photography meant that the action of the play was translated in terms very similar to those used on a thrust stage. Compositions in depth exploiting the foreground and background of the frame as well as triangular groupings were employed. And in the graveyard scene, with Horatio and Hamlet in the foreground and the funeral procession deep in the shot, the composition almost duplicates the kind of grouping that would have been employed on the Elizabethan stage.

But for all this, Olivier's *Hamlet* does present a somewhat distorted version of the play. Apart from the rearrangement of continuity whereby the film opens with the Prince's funeral (an idea borrowed from Sir Robert Helpmann's ballet) with the rest of the action appearing in the form of an extended flashback, Olivier focuses on Hamlet's Oedipal fixation on his mother as the "explanation" for his irresolution. This interpretation is as questionable as the view that *Hamlet* is the "tragedy of a man who cannot make up his mind," as Olivier informs us in the opening narration. Nevertheless, given these limitations, the film is very successful. Basil Sydney makes a sensual, anguished Claudius and Eileen Herlie a seductive Gertrude, while Jean Simmons, in her only Shakespearean performance to date, gives Ophelia a wit and intelligence in the early scenes that serves to make her later insanity all the more moving. But inevitably, it is Olivier's virile tormented Hamlet that dominates the film—a performance that with its expert blend of naturalism and theatricality is a triumph of classical screen acting.

While in the direction of *Hamlet* Olivier was concerned above all to make an effective film, with *Richard III* (Great Britain, 1955) he further developed the cinematic theatricality of *Henry V*. Instead of the false perspectives of the earlier film, Furse devised representational settings within

Laurence Olivier in the title role of his 1948 *Hamlet* informs the Queen (Eileen Herlie) that he has "that within which passeth show; These but the trappings and the suits of woe." [J. Arthur Rank Organisation Ltd.]

which the cast could move laterally toward camera and audience. Consequently, not only was it possible to re-create the relationships between performer and spectator that existed in the Elizabethan theatre, but the actual movements on the platform could, in part, be duplicated. In these sets Olivier's Richard is able to treat the camera virtually as the second person in the room, confiding as directly in the cinema audience as did Burbage (for whom the part was written) in the spectators in the Globe. Throughout Richard dominates the foreground like a malignant chorus, predicting the ends of all those who stand between him and the crown. So completely do the settings conform to the essentials of the Elizabethan playhouses that Olivier is even able to retain much of the "look who comes here" dialogue designed to bring a newly entered character to the end of the platform.

Although the text was cut and rearranged for the film, the play is not distorted as was the case with *Hamlet*. Even the introduction of a silent Jane Shore (Pamela Brown) and having Richard hacked to pieces by the troops instead of being killed by Richmond in single combat are perfectly in keeping with the basic impulses of the play.

Olivier planned to direct yet another Shakespearean film, a version of *Macbeth*, but the death of Sir Alexander Korda caused the collapse of the project. Nevertheless, Olivier's achievement in these films cannot be overestimated. With his dual loyalty to the theatre and film he devised and adapted the cinematic forms necessary to encompass the full implications of the emblematic tradition of stagecraft to which Shakespeare's plays rightly belong.

Even though Olivier may have borrowed from *Citizen Kane* for *Hamlet*, Orson Welles's own approach to filming Shakespeare proved to be very different. Even when he directed for the stage the famous "voodoo" *Macbeth*—a production set in nineteenth-century Haiti with an all-black cast—and *Julius Caesar*, Welles was compelled to remake the plays in his own image. For him adapting Shakespeare is a means of personal expression, and the reason that his film versions have proved to be so artistically successful is that Welles's own preoccupations are very similar to those of the tragedies. Like Shakespeare he is concerned with the fall of towering central figures like Kane, Quinlan (in *Touch of Evil*), and Arkadin (in *Mr. Arkadin*) and also with the disparity between what a man is and what he does. Consequently, Welles's film adaptations of Shakespeare tend to be a series of variations and amplifications of the themes and imagery of the originals.

A good example of this is Welles's first Shakespearean film, *Macbeth*. It was made at Republic in 1948 on a fourteen-day shooting schedule and released in a truncated form shorn of twenty-one minutes with a soundtrack that in some prints verged on the unintelligible. However, now that the film has been restored to something closer to Welles's original intentions by one of the archivists at U.C.L.A., Robert Gitt, it is clear that *Macbeth* embodies an oversimplified but fundamentally valid interpretation of the original. For Welles, Macbeth has

been rehearsing the murder in his mind for years and is now appalled that the Weird Sisters' prophecies have unleashed his "black and deep" desires for the crown. To convey this interpretation Welles drastically reshaped the dialogue so that the early exchanges between Macbeth and Lady Macbeth are dominated by an unspoken commitment to Duncan's murder. Of course, this approach is quite compatible with a full text, and Welles can be criticized for making rearrangements that are really unnecessary.

Not that Welles is insensitive to the motifs and themes of Shakespeare's dramatic poetry. The settings of slate gray suggesting weather-beaten rock with backguards in the shape of twenty-eight-feet-high cliffs reach beyond the letter of the text to create a visual equivalent of the atmosphere created by the play's imagery. The deep shadows filling great expanses of the frame come to represent the evil to which Macbeth has yielded, while the labyrinthine caverns in which his monstrous figure wanders in the final sequences of the film become a projection of the hero's tortured consciousness. Throughout, the action is recorded in expertly choreographed long takes that often make their own pointed comment on the action. When Macbeth after the murder speaks of his "hangman's hands," the camera is placed so that the extended hands seem gigantic and monstrous—a superb visual equivalent of the hand-and-eye imagery of the original, wherein the eye represents reason and the hand

Laurence Olivier is the ruthless king and Claire Bloom is the unfortunate Lady Anne, now his queen, in this 1955 British film version of *Richard III*. [Museum of Modern Art/Film Stills Archive]

the animal. Later, when Macbeth waits uneasily for the discovery of Duncan's body, an almost imperceptible tilt of the camera brings the entrance to the king's chamber on the upper level into the frame. Consequently, Macbeth's attempts during the exchanges with Lennox to avoid looking at the archway become a focusing device sharpening our awareness of the equivocations in the dialogue.

For all this, it would be idle to pretend that the rushed shooting schedule and hasty preparation have not left their mark. Some of the costumes are appalling, and many of the visuals have a ragged appearance that it is difficult to imagine Welles's passing in other circumstances. Nevertheless, the full version demonstrates that Welles and Jeannette Nolan give powerful performances in the principle roles, especially now that the original tracks have been restored and it is possible to appreciate their sensitive verse speaking. Particularly fine is Nolan's sleepwalking scene and Welles's rendition of the "tomorrow and tomorrow" soliloquy.

Welles's next Shakespearean film was a much more ambitious project, a film version of *Othello*, shot between 1949 and 1952 in locations as widely separated as Mogador, Morocco, and Venice. Several times his financing collapsed and the cast was dismissed only to be reassembled in yet another location in the Mediterranean. Yet in spite of all the financial difficulties and the problem of marrying footage from locations hundreds of miles apart, Welles was able to create a visual poem embodying a series of themes and variations on the motifs of the original.

Welles's treatment of this material, however, is very different from the style he adopted for *Macbeth*. Individual takes only last a few minutes, and his handling of the editing irresistibly recalls the methods and theories of Eisenstein. Many of the visuals reflect the influence of the Russian director, especially Welles's use of spears and pennons that seems at times to have come straight out of *Alexander Nevsky*.

Nonetheless, there are some important distinctions. Welles in *Othello* invariably works in deep focus; Eisenstein rarely did. Also Welles's editing is much more austere and disciplined. Whereas the Russian would build an elaborate montage around a visual idea, Welles's concern is the dramatic narrative. If anything can be said to have influenced the rhythms of the film, it is probably Verdi's *Otello* (a comparison Welles made himself in an interview). The editing has an austerity and tension comparable with Toscanini's interpretation of Verdi's score, and in the "Be sure you prove my love a whore" sequence, shot in the teeth of a westerly gale on the castle battlements in Morocco, the way Othello's outbursts are linked aurally and visually with the sea crashing against the cliff is very similar to the emphatic chords of Verdi's musical treatment of the same scene.

What dominates Welles's treatment of *Othello* is the perversion of the Moor's vision as a result of his yielding to jealousy. This is underscored by the powerful precredits sequence showing Othello and Desdemona's funeral processions. Here the military imagery first appears, and

also the dominant motif of the film, the cage into which Iago is thrust as the cortege passes. The basis of this symbol seems to have been the net in which Iago dreams of enmeshing "them all." Before each stage of Iago's conspiracy, Welles introduces a shot of the cage hanging from the battlements. There is also a linking series of bar or lattice images. Othello is covered by a pattern of bars when Iago's insinuations begin to evoke his doubts, and for the "I'd be happier in the general camp" speech the camera remains outside the armory viewing the Moor through the bars.

Ultimately, Desdemona's chamber becomes a prison for both her and Othello. She is observed before the murder through the gratings of the window, and, after the revelation of Iago's duplicity, Othello gazes through an enormous barred archway as he realizes that his lieutenant's evil has been transferred to him.

Unlike Olivier—on stage and in the 1965 film record of the National Theatre production—who had Othello throw away the crucifix around his neck when he dedicates himself to vengeance, Welles preserves the Christian context of the Moor's actions. Iago dedicates himself to "wronged Othello's service" before a statue of the Madonna and child while Othello himself, in a series of carefully designed icons as he pulls aside the curtains of Desdemona's bed, becomes a dangerously ambivalent crucifix at once tormented and menacing.

Unlike *Macbeth*, the performances in *Othello* are uniformly excellent. Fay Compton is a splendidly tiresome Emilia, and although Suzanne Cloutier as Desdemona had to be revoiced by an English actress, she functions effectively as a symbol of virtue and forgiveness. Michael MacLiammoir based his conception of Iago on an impotence that for Welles was to be "the keystone of the actor's approach," but as the part developed this came to embrace a much wider range of malevolence. What finally emerged is an incisive portrayal of a vindictive neurotic dedicated to malice and destruction almost as a vocation. Welles too is particularly impressive. At the outset, he is authoritative and virile; later he degenerates into a tormented haunted figure reduced to spying on his wife as she undresses.

Throughout, *Othello* remains true to the basic impulses and themes of the original yet functions as an independent artistic achievement of exceptional richness and complexity.

It was not until 1960 that Welles began to plan another Shakespearean film. This time he returned to the project that first caused him to go to Hollywood, the attempt to produce a version of the second tetralogy first staged unsuccessfully as *Five Kings*. Actually the script for *Chimes at Midnight*, or *Falstaff*, finally released as a Spanish-Swiss coproduction in 1966, is an immense improvement on the stage adaptation, which was far too long and included some appalling rewrites of Shakespeare. Wisely Welles took as his basis the design of *Henry IV, Part I*, the best structured of the plays, and interpolated sequences involving Doll Tearsheet, Pistol, and Shallow from *Part II*. Hotspur's scenes were abridged and the political maneuvering from the later play omitted altogether. The final movement of the film is based on a selection of scenes from *Part II* portraying Hal's reconciliation with his father and rejection of Falstaff. To overcome the problem of the Prince's double reformation in *Part I* and *Part II*, Welles introduces a wordless sequence in which the King overhears Falstaff's claim to have killed Hotspur and, believing that his son had slain his rival dishonorably, remains estranged from him.

Inevitably, this arrangement thrusts into the foreground the triangular relationship between Hal, his father, and Falstaff. For each of these conflicting characters and attitudes Welles creates an individual "space," or environment, that is adhered to throughout the work. In doing this the film strikes a delicate balance. On the one hand, the depersonalization associated with the office of ruler portrayed in the plays is fully re-created in the film. Henry IV (Sir John Gielgud) is shown against backgrounds of stone, stark, bare corridors, and spears and shields. When he rebukes the rebellious Worcester, a shaft of white blurs his features, his authority emphasized by a series of low-angle setups and the light glinting on the crown. On the other hand, Welles's treatment of the rebels emphasizes the need for a strong ruler. Hotspur's frantic pacings, recorded in a series of tight pans and swift cuts, embody his anarchic energy and hysteria. And even if the sequence when he receives the famous letter in his bath, placed in a room filled with weapons and armor, is intentionally hilarious, there is no denying Hotspur's irresponsibility.

A similar balance is achieved in Welles's treatment of the tavern scenes. The film's Boar's Head is a massive oak-beamed structure that markedly contrasts with the austerity of the royal palace. Welles's Falstaff is witty and charming, "the most supremely good man in all literature," and obviously provides Hal with the affection denied him by his more aloof father. Even the robbery at Gadshill, with Falstaff nimbly running between the trees, dropping the bags of money in his haste, is treated as infinitely less harmful than Hotspur's pursuit of honor. Moreover, the magnificent downward pan, showing people dancing in the inn just before the final parting of Hal and Falstaff, portrays a richness of community life and pleasure that the world of affairs could never approach.

Nevertheless, Welles does not gloss over the squalor of tavern life and Falstaff's behavior. Jeanne Moreau's Doll Tearsheet is authentically melancholy and diseased. The inn obviously doubles as a brothel, and the recruiting scene in Gloucestershire set against a background of pouring rain, muddy roads, and a squalid, leaky farmhouse in which Falstaff "misuses the kings press" is as distasteful a sequence as Welles has given us.

In this context it is possible to portray the rejection of Falstaff as a cruel necessity and as an inevitable consequence of Hal's credible psychological and emotional development. Because everything has been directed by Welles in the light of this final rejection, the film is dominated by the atmosphere of melancholy that exists mainly in *Henry IV, Part II*. Even the Battle of Shrews-bury, an occasion for heroic endeavor in the original, appropriately becomes a grim struggle for survival as men at arms writhe in the mud and the cavalry gallop frantically across the frame.

In spite of the condensation of the originals, *Chimes at Midnight* is at once an original creation and a remarkably perceptive interpretation of Shakespeare's last cycle of history plays. The film's structure creates a cinematic equivalent of the "diamond-cut diamond" effects of the plays whereby the world of the tavern comments on the world of policy and vice versa. Welles himself is a warmly sympathetic Falstaff, at once witty and vulnerable, while Sir John Gielgud's stylized intensity as Henry IV is enhanced by the director's superb exploitation of the settings. Keith Baxter, too, makes an engagingly credible Hal. Particularly impressive is his almost mystic authority in the unbearably moving rejection scene.

By any standards Welles's achievements in adapting Shakespeare to the screen are extraordinary. All are highly individual works of considerable merit as filmcraft. What is only now being recognized is that for all their textual licentiousness the films are remarkably faithful to the basic impulses and themes of the original plays.

Orson Welles's inspiration lies behind yet another adaptation of Shakespeare, M.G.M.'s version of *Julius Caesar* directed by Joseph L. Mankiewicz and released in 1953. According to the film's producer, John Houseman—Welles's collaborator on the famous "Fascist" modern-dress production of the play—the use of black-and-white stock was designed to evoke memories of the newsreel coverage of the dictator's rallies in the 1930.

However, with the exception of one overhead shot of Caesar's procession which echoes Hitler's entrances in Leni Riefenstahl's film of the 1934 Nuremberg rally, *Triumph of the Will*, the recycled *Quo Vadis* sets and the influence of Metro's design department predominate throughout. In many ways the look of the film is that of a conventional period picture of the 1950s. What makes *Julius Caesar* visually interesting is that Mankiewicz and cameraman Joseph Ruttenberg underscored many of the points made in the dialogue. Just before Cassius speaks the lines "Why man he doth bestride the narrow world/ like a colossus . . ." he is observed dwarfed by a massive statue of Caesar. Subtle tracking shots follow Brutus's restless pacings in his orchard, the movement of the frame corresponding to the rhythm of the verse. And when Brutus refers to Caesar scorning "the base degrees by which he did ascend," there is a cut to a slightly higher angle of vision. Also for Mark Antony's soliloquy over the dead body of Caesar, Mankiewicz follows Olivier's practice by cutting to a long shot for the climax of the speech "Cry havoc and let slip the dogs of war," which Marlon Brando almost screams. The editing too is carefully matched to the rhythms of the verse, and very few reaction shots are used because the editor was rightly reluctant to interrupt the line and cadence of a speech.

Inevitably with such a literary approach, the performances proved to be crucial. Dominating the film is James Mason's haunting performance as Brutus—tellingly contrasted with Gielgud's febrile Cassius—passionate and incisive in the early sequences, and gradually disintegrating in the second half as he moves toward his impulsive suicide. Veteran actor Louis Calhern superbly portrayed the ambivalence that is at the heart of Shakespeare's conception of Caesar, simultaneously projecting competence and efficiency with an arrogance and vanity that could degenerate into tyranny. But possibly the film's most remarkable performance comes from Marlon Brando as Mark Antony. The physical magnetism he possessed in the 1950s enables him to suggest the character's exuberant past while concentrating on Mark Antony's more sinister Machiavellian qualities. Even his light voice and hoarseness in the Forum scene make believable the claim that he is "a plain blunt man."

Although somewhat staider than its producer intended, *Julius Caesar* is one of the finest of the "faithful" versions of Shakespeare. The fine verse speaking by all the principals and the way the compositions and editing complement the dramatic values inherent in the dialogue make it as impressive now as it appeared in 1953.

The idea of filming Shakespeare more or less faithfully pioneered by Cukor's *Romeo and Juliet* and the Houseman-Mankiewicz *Julius Caesar* saw an interesting revival in the 1960s. It began with George Schaefer's *Macbeth*, released in 1960 with Maurice Evans and Judith Anderson in the principal roles. The film was shot in color on location in Scotland and in castle sets designed by Edward Carrick (Gordon Craig's son). There was little or no attempt to employ the resources of film to comment on the action or dialogue, and the sharp, bright colors of the costumes and the photography detract from the play's imagery of blood and darkness. Neither Maurice Evans as Macbeth nor Judith Anderson as Lady Macbeth was able to repeat their stage successes in the roles. She was merely a grotesque virago, he a pallid weakling. Also the idea of having Macbeth simply dream his second encounter with the witches is a gross distortion, as the emphasis in the original is on yet another commitment to evil.

Much more interesting was Peter Hall's version of *A Midsummer Night's Dream* released for American television in 1969. In contrast to the Reinhardt/Dieterle version, Hall chose to emphasize the English qualities of the woodland setting. Consequently Oberon became an Elizabethan squire, the worker players his tenants, and the lovers rural gallants and ladies. The sequences in the forest were shot during a period of bad weather because, as Hall put it, "the 'Dream' is quite clearly a play about an English summer that has gone wrong [because] . . . the King and Queen of the fairies . . . are quarreling and their quarrels have upset the balance of nature." For Hall the spirits were not etheral but "erotic, physical, down to earth." This is an interesting conception well grounded in the text. Unfortunately the execution was seriously flawed. Although the verse is spoken superbly by a cast including Diana Rigg, Judi Dench, Barbara Jefford, and Derek Godfrey, the framing of individual shots

arbitrarily isolates individual characters when dynamic interaction is required. In addition, the editing tends to cut across the rhythms and structure of the verse. Still, devices such as having Titania and Oberon's quarrels take place all over the forest and Peter Suschitzky's color photography, emphasizing the fairies' green, earthen hues, fully embody Hall's conception.

The same year also saw the release of yet another version of *Julius Caesar*, directed by Stuart Burge for Canadian producer Peter Snell. It proved to be an unmitigated disaster. Burge completely failed to relate camera movement and composition to the dramatic conflicts inherent in the text. In the crucial funeral sequence the speakers are placed to the left of the Panavision frame while the mob fills the remainder of the rectangle. But so incoherent are Burge's groupings that it becomes difficult to pick out the speakers in medium shot and impossible in the long shots. The director's handling of the more intimate scenes is little better. In the first exchange between Brutus and Cassius, he so overloads the sequence with extraneous "business" that the contrast between Brutus's caution and Cassius's energy disappears altogether. Even the murder, surely a gift to any director, becomes in his hands a protracted, distasteful ritual. Caesar staggers from conspirator to conspirator, the camera waving absurdly in a travesty of the then fashionable hand-held techniques so that the victim seems to be passively submitting to the violence with something akin to masochism—all of which distorts a whole area of meaning in the play. Stylizing the assassination so that it becomes a ritual *itself* instead of a brutal act that Brutus endeavors to *transform* into a ritual makes nonsense of Antony's line retained in the film—"Villains you did not so when your vile daggers/Hacked one another in the sides of Caesar."

The performances too are generally unconvincing. The usually reliable Jason Robards, Jr., is appallingly wooden as Brutus, speaking the verse in a flat monotone that ignores emphasis, meaning, and word music alike, while Richard Johnson is a competent but pallid Cassius. Although Sir John Gielgud is predictably assured as Caesar, the arrogance and vanity that make Brutus's decision to join the conspiracy at least understandable elude the veteran Shakespearean actor entirely. Only Charlton Heston's sheer physical presence enables him to rise above the general chaos and construct a believable interpretation of Mark Antony. He not only conveys the character's genuine affection for Caesar but also portrays the calculation and ambition together with the beginnings of the hubris that is eventually to destroy him.

Not quite as technically incompetent but equally unsatisfactory is Peter Brook's *King Lear*, released in 1971. For this version he adopted a similar approach to that of his famous stage production, even using some of the same performers—Paul Scofield as Lear and Irene Worth as Goneril. Both versions took as their starting point Jan Kott's ideas in *Shakespeare Our Contemporary*, which compare Shakespeare's play to Beckett's *Endgame*. To create a world of arbitrary cruelty, Brook makes Goneril and

Regan appear as reasonable as possible in the early scenes so that their later cruelty will seem unmotivated and part of the general absurdity of life. The more sympathetic characters—Cordelia, Edgar, and Albany—are weakened and the carefully wrought redemptive pattern of the original deliberately obscured. Shakespeare's rich, intricate poetry is spoken in a slow monotone so that whole stretches of the film are frankly boring. The Danish locations are quite appropriate to this conception, the barren, misty countryside complementing Brook's sterile interpretation of the tragedy.

Paralleling these film versions of Shakespeare have been a number of attempts simply to record important productions. The first of these was Bill Colleron's filming in Electronovision of Sir John Gielgud's New York production of *Hamlet* with Richard Burton in the role of the Prince in 1964. At the time it was hoped that the process could make first-class theatre available to wider audiences, but this was precluded by the curious foreshortening in some shots and the generally smudgy quality of the images. Nevertheless, Colleron's strategically placed fifteen cameras give adequate coverage of the live performance, and the production as a whole is well served by his sparing use of closeups. Consequently, for all its deficiencies the film provides an invaluable record of both Gielgud's production, staged against a starkly severe set in what were basically rehearsal clothes, and Burton's passionate, down-to-earth Hamlet.

Far more successful was Stuart Burge's record of John Dexter's National Theatre production of *Othello*, with Laurence Olivier in the title role, that was released in 1965. For this Burge had Jocelyn Herbert's stage sets reproduced in the studio, and much of the action was shot in sequence recorded by three wide-screen Panavision cameras, Regrettably the distinguished cast that included Frank Finlay as Iago and Maggie Smith as Desdemona just repeated their stage performances. Olivier's famous interpretation of Othello is particularly ill served by this approach. Often his performance, which was, reportedly, overpowering in the theatre, appears simply grotesque. On the other hand, Frank Finlay' subtle playing of Iago is enhanced by the intimacy of the camera. In addition, Geoffrey Unsworth's splendid low-key color photography makes this "record" far more generally accessible than Colleron's ill-fated venture.

The following year (1966) Frank Dunlop filmed his Edinburgh Festival production of *The Winter's Tale*. It featured Laurence Harvey (Leontes), Jane Asher (Perdita), and Moira Redmond (Hermione), and the whole action takes place on a single all-purpose set. Directed without imagination and flawed by an impossibly heavy-handed performance by Laurence Harvey, the film is very nearly unwatchable.

Perhaps the most successful translation of a stage production, however, is Tony Richardson's film version of his Roundhouse production of *Hamlet*, released in 1969. He wisely made no attempt to reproduce the open staging of the original version. Instead he blacked out the background and filmed the action with a hand-held camera in sustained closeups. In spite of the obvious lim-

itations of such a technique, the camera is still able to function cinematically by following the dramatic focus of any sequence by either holding the key figure in closeup or tightly framing two or three head shots. The background is suggested by flames of torches, a rich jewel in Claudius's ear, and, in one memorable sequence, a four-poster in which the King and Gertrude hold court functions as a symbol of their sensuality and corruption. Occasionally a tapestry is put to good use, such as when the Queen's description of Ophelia's suicide is backed by an elaborate pattern of embroidered flowers.

Inevitably the burden of such a film is carried by performance. Nicol Williamson portrays Hamlet as a mature, bearded scholar, incisive in speech and abrasive in manner. His verse speaking is aggressively modern, riding over the word music but imposing a cadence that exposes the meaning of the lines. Anthony Hopkins's Claudius makes a worthy adversary, combining facile charm and easy assurance with guilt-ridden eyes, while Marianne Faithful is a haunted and haunting Ophelia. In spite of this emphasis on performance, the film moves at a headlong pace. Partly this is because of Richardson's careful control of acting tempo but also because he has stripped away the detail from each scene so that only the essence of the play's movement remains.

At the same time as these attempts were being made to do justice to something approximating a full text of the plays, Franco Zeffirelli's very free cinematic translations of *The Taming of the Shrew* (U.S.A.-Italy, 1966) and *Romeo and Juliet* (Great Britain-Italy, 1968) appeared. These films solved the problem of finding an appropriate space for the action of the plays by reproducing the style of the paintings of the period. This approach was of course not completely original. M.G.M.'s designers had copied details from Renaissance and medieval art for the costumes of the 1936 *Romeo and Juliet*, and Roger Furse had used medieval illuminations as the basis for the design of his *Henry V* sets. But the most thoroughgoing application of this "pictorial" approach had been undertaken by Renato Castellani for his version of *Romeo and Juliet* in 1954. Not only were the costumes based on fifteenth-century portraits, but the actual composition of the shots and the set design were modeled on the work of artists such as Veneziano, Raphael, and Luca della Robbia. Consequently the film was made up of a series of exquisite tableaux (superbly photographed by Robert Krasker) that, although somewhat static, provided a very effective frame for the action. Unfortunately Castellani failed either to adapt the play satisfactorily or give the performers adequate direction. The dialogue was often so fragmented that it simply did not make sense, while Laurence Harvey's overprecious Romeo made nonsense of the character's reckless passion, and in spite of the fact that the inexperienced Susan Shentall made an engagingly direct Juliet, as drama the film failed abysmally.

But the approach through the art of the Renaissance has much to recommend it, and Zeffirelli's two versions of Shakespeare have benefited enormously from design, lighting, and composition based on the style of fifteenth-

and sixteenth-century painting. A good example of this is his treatment of the opening of *The Taming of the Shrew*. The problem Zeffirelli confronted here was that Shakespeare had deliberately distanced the brutality of the original wife-taming story by making it part of a play within a play. Wisely the Italian director made no attempt to film the introduction in which this situation is established because it depended for its effects on the conventions of the Elizabethan theatre. Instead he filmed a precredits sequence showing Lucentio (Michael York) riding across a highly artificial landscape and then into the streets of Padua to what appears to be a solemn university religious service which is suddenly transformed into an end of term festival. The fairytale quality of the "countryside," together with Oswald Morris's misted color photography in the style of fifteenth-century painting, function as a reminder that the film is indeed an illusion of reality, not reality itself. Furthermore, the switch from apparent solemnity to revelry, as well as the grotesque masks of the festival, anticipates the interchange of identities that is the basis of the main action.

The adaptation, for all its apparent freedom, is remarkably faithful to the essence of the original. Dialogue may be fragmented and lines allowed to overlap, but this reflects the vigorous colloquial quality of the play's prose and poetry. For the film's centerpiece, the wooing scene between Petruchio and Katherine, Zeffirelli devised a pattern of *visual* slapstick to correspond to the *verbal* slapstick of the original. This included a lunatic chase across rooftops into a storehouse, with Katherine vainly piling bales on a trapdoor to repel her unwelcome suitor and Petruchio swinging onto a balcony and bursting straight through a conveniently weakened wall, all of which culminates in a wrestling match between the brawling pair in a sea of wool.

Throughout, the bustling town life of Padua becomes in effect a character in the film. The Panavision screen is filled with swirling groups of extras, and the often hectic action is recorded in a series of fluid tracking shots with the camera held for the most part at eye level. Performances too are particularly effective. Michael Horden makes a corrupt, dithering Baptista, while Natasha Pyne is an elegantly superior Bianca. But the film's commercial success was ensured by the casting of Richard Burton and Elizabeth Taylor as Petruchio and Katherine. As it turned out, they are both very impressive. Burton makes Petruchio a roaring lout, and if this oversimplifies Shakespeare's more subtle portrait, there is no denying the performance's effectiveness. By contrast Elizabeth Taylor attempted a more complex interpretation of Katherine but was hampered, especially in the final speech, by her limited vocal range. Nevertheless she not unexpectedly threw herself into the brawls with gusto and deftly suggested the loneliness and pain that was, for her, the origin of Katherine's belligerence. Even given these qualifications, *The Taming of the Shrew* proved to be a particularly successful cinematic equivalent of the original that was faithful both to Shakespeare and the film medium itself.

For his next Shakespearean film, *Romeo and Juliet*,

Zeffirelli adopted a slightly different approach. He still borrowed freely from artistic sources and employed elaborately designed sets for the ballroom, crypt, and main square of Verona. But these were expertly matched with extensive location shooting in often remote parts of Italy where the architecture appropriate to the film's mid-fifteenth-century setting still exists. The result is a less consciously artificial style than had been employed for the earlier film. Hand-held shots proliferate, camera movement is less fluid, and the zoom is employed more freely. Nevertheless Zeffirelli exploited design to create a pattern of imagery complementing the dramatic narrative. Initially there is a wide range of colors—especially reds, russets, yellows, and blues. But as the tragedy approaches its climax, whites, blacks, and blues—all "cold" colors—dominate the visuals.

All of this works extremely well. The design of the film strikes a nice balance between realism and artificiality. It is with the handling of the love story itself that Zeffirelli runs into difficulty. Certainly it was a worthwhile experiment to cast in the title roles two attractive fifteen- and seventeen-year-old unknowns, Olivia Hussey and Leonard Whiting, especially when far too often in stage productions the lovers are impersonated by performers of embarrassing maturity. However, instead of requiring his young performers to portray Shakespeare's very Renaissance couple—who may be young and impulsive yet quite adept at playing the stately game of love—to stress the historical parallel between Shakespeare's lovers and the problems of youth in the 1960s, Zeffirelli directed Hussey and Whiting to portray the lovers as though they were modern teenagers. In addition, the play's formal structure was fragmented so that the tragic resolution comes about because of adolescent rashness and the brutal feud between the two families. There exists in the film no equivalent to Juliet's growth to womanhood, surely one of the play's most impressive achievements, and while Leonard Whiting does attempt to show something of Romeo's development, Zeffirelli's drastic cutting deprives him of the opportunity to explore this aspect of the character. To make matters worse, in some drastic reediting after the premiere at the Royal Command Performance, Zeffirelli removed any reference to Rosaline and Juliet's reception of the news of Tybalt's death. As a result, Romeo's appearance at the Capulet's ball seems completely unmotivated and Juliet's character drastically simplified.

The film, however, does contain some valuable fragmentary illuminations of the original. The balcony scene delightfully explores the humorous undertones of the verse. Juliet becomes almost comically alarmed at the question "Wilt thou leave me so unsatisfied?" while Romeo exuberantly dangles from one hand in a tree near Juliet's balcony as he realizes his love is returned. In addition, the languorous rhythms of the lovers' nude dawn farewell are an impressive visual equivalent of the eroticism in the poetry of Juliet's "Gallop apace thy fiery footed steeds" soliloquy. And although the imagery has on the whole been given short shrift in this film, when in the tomb we are able to see through Romeo's eyes the decomposing bodies of the dead Capulets, which reinforces the lines where he virtually becomes jealous of death's sway over his beloved. All this demonstrates just what a fine version of *Romeo and Juliet* Zeffirelli might have made had he not sought to make specious contemporary parallels and translated the full complexity of the original instead of a few fragments.

The adaptations of Shakespeare have not of course been confined to English-speaking countries. One of the most extraordinary and successful versions of *Macbeth*, *Throne of Blood*, was made by Akira Kurosawa in Japan in 1957 (released in the West in 1960). Essentially it assimilated the Macbeth story into a combination of the Japanese Nō play and the samurai film. There was no attempt to translate the original text: instead Kurosawa employed a stylized prose, and when verse was introduced it was linked to the traditional style of Nō songs. The plot follows the events of the play very closely except that at the end Washinju (Macbeth) is slaughtered by his own men. Visually the film is very spare. Kurosawa purposely restricted himself to shooting in carefully composed medium shots, employing only simple wipes and cuts and avoiding any fades or dissolves. *See* Nō.

The effect is to create an emphasis on the retributive elements in Shakespeare's tragedy. Everything is fated, part of a rigid cycle of murder and consequences. As a result Washinju lacks some of the grandeur of Shake-

speare's original. Nevertheless Toshiro Mifune movingly re-creates the character's torment and anguish while remaining throughout highly stylized in movement and gesture. Even more limited is Kurosawa's treatment of Lady Macbeth. If anything, Tsuzie Yamada, who plays the role, is even more stylized than Mifune. She moves heel to toe like a Nō actor, her face is made up to suggest the Nō mask, and the hand-washing sequence is pure Nō drama. Throughout she is portrayed as the most limited, the most driven, and the most completely evil of the characters. In many ways *The Throne of Blood* is an isolated masterpiece. It spawned no cycle of Japanese Shakespeare even though its complexity and richness does testify to the dramatist's ability to continue to inspire great works of art.

By contrast there exists a long tradition of Shakespearean production and filmmaking in Russia. Admittedly some of the early attempts to film Shakespeare verged on the ludicrous. Sergai Yutkivitch's *Othello* (U.S.S.R., 1955) incorporates such heavy-handed effects as Iago's making clawing motions through fishnets hung out on the beach during the temptation scene and Othello's hair turning white after the murder. More successful was Jakow Frid's *Twelfth Night* (U.S.S.R., 1955), which was acted with considerable verve but reduced Sir Toby Belch and Sir Andrew Aguecheek to caricatures and seriously distorted Malvolio's role in the comedy.

Toshiro Mifune as Washinju (Macbeth) kills the old king's guards in *Throne of Blood,* **Akira Kurosawa's 1957 film adaptation of** *Macbeth.* **[Photograph courtesy of Quality Films Australia]**

By far the most successful Russian director of Shakespeare to date has been Gregori Kozintsev. Not only has he had a distinguished career as a filmmaker reaching back to the silent era, but he also has directed Shakespeare very successfully on the stage. Kozintsev's first Shakespearean film, *Hamlet*, was not completed until 1964. Initially his approach seemed to be very similar to that adopted by Houseman and Mankiewcz for *Julius Caesar*. Much of the film's imagery either emerges from, or directly reinforces, the poetry of the original. The emphasis on bars throughout Hamlet's scenes with Ophelia combined with the massive drawbridge moat and portcullis that appear at key moments in the film all reinforce the Prince's claim that "Denmark's a prison." Similarly the appearance on the wall of Polonius's quarters of a portrait of Claudius underscores the King's statement that "The head is not more native to the heart/The hand more instrumental to the mouth/Than is the throne of Denmark to thy father." Even the juxtaposition of Claudius with an equestrian portrayal of himself as he confronts Laertes's rebellion reinforces the King's increased stature already apparent in the dialogue.

But for all this, the film as a whole oscillates between this kind of literary or interpretative treatment and a more imaginative cinematic translation. Before commencing work on the film, Kozintsev commented: "Hamlet is not only a play but also a novel. . . . The breadth of its outlook on an epoch and its depth of psychological research are fixed into a combination that defines novel. The same thing is implicit in the nature of the film." It is when Kozintsev endeavors to realize the psychological and physical dimension of a novel that the film becomes an independent work of its creator's imagination, employing Shakespeare's play as inspiration. The sea motif, for example, obviously derives from Hamlet's famous soliloquy in which he speaks of taking "arms against a sea of troubles," but in the film the sea has a much wider range of meaning. To quote from Kozintsev's diary, "Sea waves crashing against the bastions, ceaseless movement, the change of tides, the howling of chaos and again the silent endless surface of glass." All of which goes beyond the image in Hamlet's soliloquy which is a metaphor of *internal* conflict.

A further extension of the original is provided by Kozintsev's treatment of the court. Instead of the echoing empty corridors of the Olivier film, Hamlet is surrounded by watchful courtiers as we hear in a voice-over the equivalent of "O that this too too solid flesh t'would melt." Ophelia also is treated in a way significantly different from the original. She is conceived as "a sweet girl half a child whom they turn into a doll—a mechanical plaything with artificial movements." This doll motif is introduced on Ophelia's first appearance as she is being given a dancing lesson. After Polonius's death she claws mechanically at the "prison" of a mourning corset. Finally she claws off the mourning garments, escaping into the freedom of madness. Much of this is clearly based on Shakespeare's portrait but is still a quite distinct conception relying for its effectiveness on a variety of visual effects difficult if not impossible to reproduce on the stage. It ignores Ophelia's sexuality, which is clearly indicated in the songs, and deft intelligence she displays in her exchanges with Laertes. Much of this is clearly influenced by Boris Pasternak's translation of the original, which also omits this aspect of Ophelia's character, preferring to portray her in terms of a long-established Russian tradition as a fragile innocent destroyed by events she cannot control.

Kozintsev also follows Pasternak in emphasizing Hamlet's political rebellion against a corrupt regime. This is in part undermined by Kozintsev's treatment of the duel. In an attempt to break free from the conventional *Hamlet* and Olivier's film (an important influence throughout), he makes the confrontation between Hamlet and Laertes take place in the context of what amounts to a private fencing match. However, the logic of the play and the director's portrayal of a corrupt Elsinore demands that Claudius be exposed in front of the whole court. To have him perish in what amounts to a private scuffle deprives the film of a satisfying climax. Nevertheless Kozintsev's film remains a considerable achievement that successfully blends the approaches of Orson Welles and George Cukor. Consequently *Hamlet* is at once a perceptive interpretation and an impressive original creation.

Just before he died in 1973 Kozintsev completed yet another Shakespearean film, a version of *King Lear* (Russia-Lenin Film, 1970). His approach to this project was very similar to that of *Hamlet*. Once again he desires to create the density and texture of a novel so that characters are carefully portrayed as having a full existence extending beyond the confines of the events portrayed in the film. Throughout, the family squabble is treated in terms of its social and political implications. Lear's descent into poverty is constantly mirrored in the real condition of the King's poorest subjects, and Edgar gets the idea for his Poor Tom impersonation from a genuine mad beggar who passes him on the heath.

Unlike Brook, Kozintsev follows carefully the order of events in the text. His visuals, as well, which counterpoint panoramic views of the "feudal" countryside with intimate sequences such as Lear's trying of his ungrateful daughters in a genuine poorhouse, embody the original's movement between scenes of personal anguish and passages exploring the wider implications of the events of the play. In many ways Kozintsev's *Lear* is much more an interpretation of the original than was his *Hamlet*, and if the emphasis on the inequalities of feudal power is essentially socialist in inspiration, this understandable bias forms the basis of a valuable insight into the original.

With Kozintsev's death it was assumed that there would not be any more Russian versions of Shakespeare for some time. However, in 1973 Samson Samsonav produced a delightfully irreverent treatment of *Much Ado About Nothing*. Like the Reinhardt/Dieterle *A Midsummer Night's Dream* it is a very free translation of the original. All the misunderstandings and eavesdroppings take place during the masked ball, often with hectic musical numbers. This is very successful. Musicals, as *Kiss Me Kate* has demonstrated, always had a close affinity with

Gertrude (Eliya Radzin-Szilkonis) pleads with her son (Innokenti-Smoktunovsky) in this 1964 film version of *Hamlet* by the Russian director Gregori Kozintsev. [Photograph courtesy of Quality Films Australia]

Shakespearean comedy, and evoking the form in this way makes the superficially absurd misunderstandings of the plot quite believable. Even the film's emphasis on the Hero-Claudio plot probably has an Elizabethan precedent.

The main weakness of the film is that with all the movement, fast cutting, and zoom shots, not enough time has been devoted to establishing the characters and situations, so that at times not only is the plot unintelligible to anyone not familiar with the original, but many of the play's serious undertones are simply ignored.

During recent years in the West there have been some film versions of Shakespeare that seem to be at the least eccentric and at worst aberrant. In 1976 Celestino Coronado produced in Great Britain an abbreviated (67 minutes) treatment of *Hamlet*. Essentially this was a mosaic of excerpts from the play performed in illuminated areas of dark space by actors in stylized costumes. The Prince is portrayed literally as a split personality, impersonated by two actors, Anthony and David Meyer, who are nonidentical twins. Even stranger is Derek Jarman's *The Tempest* (Great Britain, 1979), which uses less than forty lines of the original text and suggests that the entire action of the play is Prospero's dream. This might have formed the basis of an interesting film, but Jarman's

treatment ranges from the disgusting—Caliban swallowing raw eggs—to the incoherent—a masque climaxed by the cast singing "Stormy Weather" that is both tedious and confused.

Two films made during the 1970s testify to the cinema's continuing ability to translate Shakespeare effectively. Roman Polanski's *Macbeth* (Great Britain-U.S.A., 1971) may have achieved a great deal of notoriety because of its nude sleepwalking scene and graphic depiction of the violence of the play, but is on the whole a fairly straightforward adaptation of Shakespeare's tragedy to the preexisting cinematic genre of the horror film. This not unexpectedly proved to be very successful. Polanski's emphasis on the supernatural seemed completely appropriate in the "medieval" context created for the film, while the depiction of the violence was based on Shakespeare's descriptions. Macbeth (Jon Finch) became something of an upwardly mobile young executive pushed into the murder by his wife's subtle taunts. According to Finch, Polanski was anxious to avoid the conventional portentous Lady Macbeth and instead directed Francesca Annis to play the temptation scene as though she were trying to embarrass Macbeth into committing the murder.

Certainly much of the grandeur disappears in this

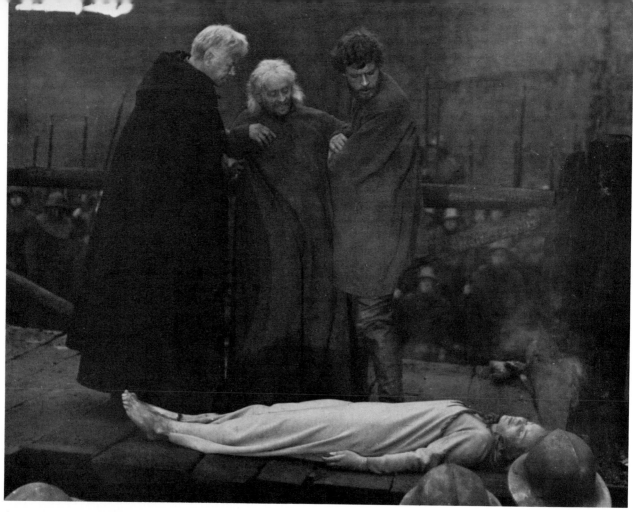

Gregori Kozintsev's final Shakespearean film was his 1970 version of *King Lear*. Here, Lear (Yuri Yarret) is confronted with Cordelia's body. [Photograph courtesy of Quality Films Australia]

interpretation, and the lurid portrayal of the violence detracts from the *moral* horror in the original. But Finch is particularly effective in portraying Macbeth's scenes of despair, and the film does create a believable cinematic equivalent to Shakespeare's portrayal of a land stained by blood guilt. Only the film's insistence that the pattern is about to repeat itself (borrowed from Orson Welles's "voodoo" *Macbeth*) can be regarded as a serious distortion.

Less accomplished technically but truer to Shakespeare's intentions was Charlton Heston's version of *Antony and Cleopatra* (U.S.A.-Spain, 1972). Like Polanski, Heston assimilated the play into a cinematic genre, this time the epic, which he believed would help convey the contrasts between Egypt and Rome that lie at the heart of Shakespeare's conception. Unfortunately restrictions on the budget prevented the settings from fully realizing these contrasts. Like Welles's *Macbeth*, the film contains some ragged visuals attributable to the painfully inadequate shooting schedule. Nevertheless Heston does manage some pointed amplifications and enrichments of the text. There is a telling visualization of one of Shakespeare's descriptions when he appears as Antony clad in a white caftan, his face made up with rouge and lipstick,

a string of pearls around his neck. Later Antony's first meeting with Octavius is intercut with a gladatorial combat, prefiguring their subsequent conflict.

Heston's script is also particularly adroit at assimilating some of the minor characters and rearranging passages so that their impact in the context of the film is maximized. One of his most striking innovations is to have Enobarbus's description of Cleopatra actually motivate Antony's return to Egypt. In Heston's version Antony is eavesdropping on the conversation and then and there decides to return to "where [his] pleasure lies." The script also solved one of the play's most difficult staging problems. Instead of using a pulley to hoist the dying Antony into Cleopatra's monument (a small pyramid in ths film), Heston has Antony get a death lock on the queen's trailing mantle and use this to hoist himself up to the entrance.

In spite of this the film is seriously flawed by Hildegarde Neil's Cleopatra. Although physically ideal for the part and delightful in the early scenes where she teases the besotted Antony, she lacks the vocal and emotional range necessary to make the climax work. Nevertheless Heston himself makes a very fine Antony, suggesting the character's self-indulgence without ever detracting from his heroic stature, and he receives excellent support from Eric Porter as Enobarbus and John Castle as Octavius.

What *Antony and Cleopatra* demonstrates, with all its flaws, is that the cinema can still encompass both cinematic translations of Shakespeare and films that simply complement the dramatic values in the text. Heston's adaptation at its best is able to do both, and even though it may not equal Welles's and Olivier's achievements in this area, it still is infinitely preferable to some of the more ponderous BBC Television versions and the aberrations of Jarman and Coronado.

NEIL MCDONALD

Shamir, Moshe   (1921–   )

Hebrew playwright and novelist. Born in the town of Safed, the seat of Jewish mysticism, Shamir was raised in Tel Aviv, where he graduated from high school and later studied literature and drama at the University of Tel Aviv and Bar Ilan University. In his youth Shamir was a leading member of the left-wing Hashomer Hatzair youth organization, joined a kibbutz, and during the War of Independence fought in the ranks of Palmach, the striking arm of the Jewish Defense Forces.

Though primarily a novelist, Shamir is a prolific playwright. His first play (1948), adapted by him and director Joseph Millo from his novel *He Walked in the Fields* (*Hoo Halakh be'Sadot*), was a milestone in Hebrew drama by virtue of being the first play to depict the new generation of Israelis, born or raised in the country. Shamir's subsequent plays dealt with the present reality of Israel, but in 1955 he turned to history with his *The War of the Children of Light* (*Milhemet Benei Or*). The hero of the drama, King David, is shown in a negative light, as a despot using his royal power for personal aims. In his later plays Shamir returned to contemporary problems, mainly the loss of idealism in Israeli society.

After the Six-Day War of 1967 Shamir joined the Greater Israel Movement which advocated the annexation of the occupied territories, and in 1976 he was elected to the Knesset. In 1979 he was one of the founders of the extreme right-wing Renascence (Ha'Tehiyah) Party. *See* HEBREW DRAMA.   MENDEL KOHANSKY

CRITICISM

M. Kohansky, *The Hebrew Theatre*, Jerusalem, 1969; G. Abramson, *Modern Hebrew Drama*, London, 1979.

Shaw, George Bernard   (1856–1950)

British dramatist. George Bernard Shaw was born in Dublin, Ireland, on July 26, 1856, the last of three children; his two older sisters were Lucy and Agnes. His parents, George Carr and Lucinda Elizabeth Gurly Shaw, were Protestants in a city that was predominantly Catholic. They were also "well born" but without corresponding financial means, members of a class Shaw described as "shabby genteel." Even when the older Shaw went into business, he clung to the supposed superiority of a wholesaler and forbade his son to play with the son of a retailer.

Although Shaw left school at the age of fourteen, he had a remarkable informal education. He made frequent visits to the Dublin National Gallery and was a voracious reader. He was also an avid theatregoer, attending all kinds of plays from melodramas to Shakespearean tragedies. His intimate knowledge of music resulted largely from the fact that his mother was a talented singer and befriended by George Vandeleur Lee, the Dublin conductor and voice trainer who for some time lived in the Shaw household and who, when he moved to London in 1873, was soon followed by Mrs. Shaw.

At fifteen, Shaw took a job as office boy in an estate agent's office, where he learned about slum rental practices. He later utilized this knowledge in his first play, *Widowers' Houses* (wr. 1885–1892). Although he rose to the position of cashier, he left in 1876 and went to London, where he moved into his mother's house. It was there that he began his career as a writer. His early work consists of five novels that publishers rejected: *Immaturity* (1879); *The Irrational Knot* (1880); *Love among the Artists* (1881), which first appeared in serial form in Mrs. Annie

With *The War of the Children of Light*, the playwright turned from contemporary to historical subject matter. [*Theatre in Israel*]

George Bernard Shaw. [Theatre Collection, The New York Public Library at Lincoln Center, Astor, Lenox and Tilden Foundations]

Shaw in later years. [Theatre Collection, The New York Public Library at Lincoln Center, Astor, Lenox and Tilden Foundations]

Besant's monthly, *Our Corner; Cashel Byron's Profession* (1882); and *An Unsocial Socialist* (1883), first published in the socialist magazine *Today.* The novels contain characteristics distinctly Shavian: unconventional viewpoints, articulate characters, and inimitable wit.

In 1884 Shaw, by this time a teetotaler, a nonsmoker, and a vegetarian, had been converted to socialism by a process that began with a lecture in 1882 by Henry George, author of *Progress and Poverty,* continued with a reading of Karl Marx's *Das Kapital* (in French), and culminated in membership in the newly formed Fabian Society. He joined in 1884 at the society's second meeting (the first had taken place in 1883). Shaw was among the leaders of an influential group that included Sidney and Beatrice Webb. For the Fabians he wrote several essays on socialism, edited other essays, and did an enormous amount of committee work. Shavian socialism, linked with the Fabian Society, underlies all his subsequent works.

During this period, Shaw was both a journalist and a prominent public speaker for the cause of socialism. In addition, he reviewed books and wrote art criticism for the *Pall Mall Gazette* (1885), reviewed music for the *Star* from 1888 to 1890 (under the name Corno di Bassetto, "basset horn") and the *World* from 1890 to 1894, and served as theatre critic for the *Saturday Review,* edited by Frank Harris, from 1895 to 1898. As critic, he attacked the well-made play (coining the term "Sardoodledom" after Sardou, a major writer of such plays) and pseudo-social plays (notably those of Pinero) that were really sentimental romances. He condemned Henry Irving and other actor-managers for emasculating Shakespeare's plays and for ignoring Ibsen's. Believing that the production of Ibsen's plays would spearhead a new theatre movement, Shaw published *The Quintessence of Ibsenism* (1891), which had originated as a lecture to the Fabian Society. He also wrote a major study of Wagner's *The Ring of the Nibelungs* entitled *The Perfect Wagnerite* (1898).

See IBSEN, HENRIK; *See also* WELL-MADE PLAY in glossary.

In 1891, J. T. Grein, a Dutchman, founded the Independent Theatre in London, hoping to produce native English plays. In response to Grein's call for English dramatists, Shaw reworked a play he had started with his friend and fellow critic William Archer. The result was *Widowers' Houses* (1892), a play that focused on slum landlordism. Conservative critics labeled it a sordid propaganda piece filled with loathsome characters who were distortions of life. Liberal critics, however, rallied to it.

In 1898 Shaw married wealthy Charlotte Payne-Townshend. The same year two volumes of his plays appeared under the title *Plays: Unpleasant and Pleasant,* this at a time when it was hard to persuade publishers that the public would buy plays. Shaw's substitution of simple narrative descriptions for technical stage directions was an important innovation. The first volume contained the "unpleasant" plays—*Widowers' Houses, The Philanderer,* and *Mrs. Warren's Profession,* about prostitution— plays to acquaint the audience with unpleasant facts about contemporary society. The "pleasant" plays— *Arms and the Man, Candida, The Man of Destiny,* and *You Never Can Tell*—dealt with what Shaw called "romantic follies."

Shaw's initial theatrical success was in the United States and Germany. Richard Mansfield produced *Arms and the Man* in New York in 1894, and *The Devil's Disciple* in 1897. Arnold Daly's production of *Candida* in New York was one of the hits of the 1903 season and it secured Shaw's reputation as a major playwright.

In London the next year, Shaw, J. E. Vedrenne, and Harley Granville-Barker leased the Royal Court Theatre. Shaw had found his actor in Granville-Barker, and his actress, too, in Lillah McCarthy. Under Shaw's direction Granville-Barker played Marchbanks in *Candida,* Tanner in *Man and Superman* (1905), Cusins in *Major Barbara* (1905), and Dubedat in *The Doctor's Dilemma* (1906). Vedrenne watched finances. The Vedrenne-Barker seasons at the Court, ending in 1907, began Shaw's rise to fame in England.

During this time, Shaw was a member of the South St. Pancras Council, but failed to get himself elected to the London County Council in 1904. Later he wrote a frank and unconventional treatise on British culpability for World War I entitled "Commonsense about the War," published in the *New Statesman.* It made him unpopular, but despite his chagrin at what he thought to be England's folly, he backed its cause and was invited to visit the front. In 1925 when he won the Nobel Prize for Literature he gave the prize money to help set up the Anglo-Swedish Literary Foundation. Tours with Mrs. Shaw in the 1930s took him to the U.S.S.R. (1931) and around the world.

Shaw had been a motion-picture fan since the days of the silent film. Hollywood producers tried to tempt him to sell screen rights to his plays, but he refused to do so unless he could control the final product. He wrote several screenplays that have been filmed: the cathedral scene from *Saint Joan* (1927), *How He Lied to Her Husband*

(1931), *Arms and the Man* (1932), *Pygmalion* (adapted by W. P. Lipscomb, Cecil Lewis, and Ian Dalrymple, 1938), *Major Barbara* (1941), and *Caesar and Cleopatra* (1945). The screenplay of *Saint Joan* which he wrote in 1936 was not filmed. Otto Preminger's movie version of this play utilized a screen version by Graham Greene.

Until the day of his death, on November 2, 1950, Shaw continued to write plays, books, prefaces, essays on socialism, and religious treatises. He died at Ayot St. Lawrence, Hertfordshire, at the age of ninety-four.

WORK

Concerned with politics and society, Shaw set out not only to write plays but to demonstrate the superiority of socialism to capitalism. His brilliant, incisive wit camouflaged his moral purpose: to lay bare the multiple errors of the current social order with its inhumanity, wastefulness, and inefficiency. Shaw made important progress towards popularizing the reformist critical intelligence; and in this way he set his political mark on future generations. His wit and his superb sense of language and verbal structuring were crucial in keeping his plays from becoming mere propaganda pieces. In addition, Shaw was able to expound his notions in his highly readable prefaces. Following Ibsen's lead, Shaw regarded romantic stage conventions as evasions of reality; accidents and artifacts of elaborate plotting, catastrophes, and romantic lies appear in his dramatic world only to be exposed as absurd or irrelevant. He wanted a "classical" drama, which he defined as one in which the dramatist "can present a dramatic hero as a man whose passions are those which have produced the philosophy, the poetry, the art, and the stagecraft of the world, and not merely those who have produced its weddings, coroners' inquests, and executions." Thus his themes deal with the clash within each character, the battle between characters, or the battle between a protagonist and religion, manners, customs, and the politics and mores of his time. His characters are extremely witty, sophisticated, and vivid—like their creator—highly articulate about themselves and their situations.

He called his plays "problem plays" (serious plays as opposed to frivolous plays) and judged their worth by their social utility. To Shaw, poets such as Shakespeare, who understood society and its complications but wrote in a less topical vein, were less significant than those who canvassed social change. "*A Doll's House*," said Shaw, "will be as flat as ditchwater when *A Midsummer Night's Dream* will still be as fresh as paint; but it will have done more work in the world; and that is enough for the highest genius."

His first produced play, *Widowers' Houses* (1892), condemning the society that permits the existence of slum landlords, is realistic. He utilized dramatic conventions for the purpose of making unconventional points. *Pygmalion* (1913) demonstrates the superficiality of class differences: Henry Higgins, a professor of phonetics, transforms Eliza Doolittle, a cockney flower girl, into a lady within six months by changing her speech, her patterns of behavior, and her perception of reality. Based on

the Greek legend of Pygmalion, an artist who creates a statue which comes to life and then falls in love with it, the play is a "romance" utilizing conventional devices, but the heroine, Shaw informs us, most assuredly does not marry the hero.

Although Shaw was not an atheist, as is generally believed, he rejected organized Christianity and its tenets in favor of the Nietzschean faith in a Life Force and Creative Evolution that he described in *Man and Superman* (1905), a modern version of Don Juan. Women, said Shaw, create life and are therefore part of the Life Force. Man, too, is part of that Life Force: motivated by another force within himself, the force of intellect, he is compelled to create something greater than himself (the Superman) and a world better than his world.

Other plays challenge the church and all it stands for. *The Devil's Disciple* (1897) depicts a man who has turned his back on religion as evolved under the Puritan tyranny of the old tribal idol Jehovah, as well as on romance and prophets, legal and social; but when put to the test, he is willing to lay down his life for a minister out of the necessity of his own nature and the cause of life. In *Androcles and the Lion* (1913), Shaw took the conventional Christian-martyr play and used it to dramatize a variety of religious experiences. The play illustrates the idea that the Romans (the solid citizens of today) persecuted early Christians because they were nonconformists, unwilling to subscribe to the traditional religion of their time. Ten years later, in *Saint Joan* (1923), Shaw presented the cases for both the nonconformists and the supporters of established religion. Generally held to be one of his two or three finest works, *Saint Joan* describes the clash between Joan, whose perception goes beyond conventional religious authority, and that authority which is obliged to destroy her because of the threat she poses. The horror of the play is that Joan is killed by good men.

Beyond the religious and social themes in *Saint Joan*, the character of Joan—a mystic, a martyr, and finally a saint—reveals the strong female, the fountainhead from whom the action typical of Shavian drama frequently flows. The title character in *Mrs. Warren's Profession* (wr. 1893, prod. 1902) is such a strong-willed woman. Formerly a prostitute and now the owner of several brothels, she is neither contrite nor repentant, for she realizes that her profession is her only means of maintaining her independence and self-respect. Instead of blaming Mrs. Warren, Shaw castigates the social system that makes her profession necessary. Another willful female is the subject of the well-constructed *Candida* (1897), a play that centers on a confrontation between the apparent common sense of a mature husband and the romanticism of a young poet. In this version of Ibsen's *A Doll's House*, Candida, unlike Nora, is not a doll; she has known the truth of her marriage all along: that her husband, Morell, is weaker and in many ways more romantic than the young poet Marchbanks, whose acute perception makes him the stronger.

Shaw describes a very different kind of marriage in *You Never Can Tell* (1899), in which the emancipated mother and conservative Victorian father, estranged for many years, battle over the custody of their maturing children, who have been raised abroad according to their mother's modern idea, which on their return to England they discover to be out of date. In *Misalliance* (1910), the sudden appearance of another emancipated woman, Lina Szczepanowska, who crashes through the roof in an airplane, disrupts a stuffy Victorian household but finally resolves the romantic entanglements and alleviates the boredom of its members.

Shaw's definitive words on women, sex, and marriage come in *Man and Superman* (1905). His philosophy of the chase, whose "stern biological purpose" demands that women pursue men because of the need to have children, is expounded with humor, but Shaw was in earnest. Structurally, the play consists of the framework of a Victorian farce and an insert, *Don Juan in Hell*, usually performed separately, which discusses at length Shaw's interpretation of the Life Force. When John Tanner, the protagonist, is finally caught by Ann Whitefield, his Everywoman, he accepts his biological destiny as the instrument of creation but refuses to accept the romantic idea of a wedding as a cause for joy and congratulations: marriage must take place, but only for the purpose of procreation in the hope that eventually a superman will be born.

A member of the Fabian Society, which believed in evolutionary socialism, Shaw wrote several important plays that project his socialist beliefs. In *Major Barbara* (1905), he maintained through Andrew Undershaft, a millionaire munitions manufacturer, that poverty is the worst of all crimes. Undershaft makes his daughter Barbara, a major in the Salvation Army, realize that she "can't talk religion to a man with bodily hunger in his eyes." *The Doctor's Dilemma* (1906) examines the self-serving conspiracy that all professions become under laissez-faire conditions. Its protagonist must decide whether to save the life of an undeniably wicked man of genius or that of a good humble general practitioner who tries to do his best for his patients. He chooses the right man but for the wrong reason, and in doing so indicates the practical remedy for the problem: a national health service in which doctors will be paid to keep people alive. Shaw proposed another national institution, a national theatre, in *The Dark Lady of the Sonnets* (1910), a witty one-act piece about a chance encounter between Shakespeare and Queen Elizabeth. He showed his pessimism about parliamentary democracy in *The Apple Cart* (1929), a fantasy set in a future where the main threat to the public good is a giant corporation, Breakages Limited, which in fact controls the government.

In *Arms and the Man* (1894), his first successful play, Shaw dealt with war. Using the form of the romantic military drama, he attacked the romantic attitude, showing how fatally easy it is to concentrate on the color and glamour of war while neglecting its barbarism. He exposed the amateurism of the glory-hunting soldier through the behavior of a Swiss mercenary, a professional in the business not for the sake of patriotism but for a job. To the British public of the 1890s, taking the romance out of war meant a denial of the existence of courage, patriotism, and faith in the empire.

In *Caesar and Cleopatra* (wr. 1898, prod. 1906), Shaw's aim was to write a part for Sir Johnston Forbes-Robertson, whom he regarded as the great classic actor of the day. In doing so he contradicted Shakespeare's idea of Caesar. Shaw's Caesar is the wisest man in the world, whose relationship with Cleopatra is primarily that of a teacher.

World War I marked a crucial change in Shaw's thinking. The impact of the war drew forth a new note of despair in *Heartbreak House* (wr. 1913/19, prod. 1920), which depicts, in a Chekhovian manner, a deteriorating society about to crumble. *Back to Methuselah* (1922) reflects Shaw's conclusion that the only resolution of man's sorry state rests in his theory of creative evolution: only if man can evolve to superman, strong enough to resist his own destructive forces, can his problems be solved and civilization be saved. The five-part play covers the course of biological history, from Genesis to Revelation, and takes many hours to perform. In the last part Shaw shows his "long livers" attempting to achieve Shavian perfection by becoming pure thought in a utopia where some of his favorite schemes for the ideal socialist state have become common usage. His postwar disillusionment is even more evident in *Too True to Be Good* (1932), in which a clergyman who has become a burglar because of the shock of the war realizes that it is necessary to continue to preach even though he has nothing left to say.

Bernard Shaw dealt with many themes, countless comic and serious situations, and numerous brilliant ideas, many of them taken from Nietzsche. He wrote for more than half a century, a social gadfly with wit, charm, and the perceptive eye of an eclectic genius. "I have had no heroic adventures. Things have not happened to me, on the contrary, it is I who have happened to them, and all my happenings have taken the form of books and plays. Read them or spectate them and you have my whole story."

Widowers' Houses (wr. 1885–1892, prod. 1892). Shaw's first produced play, revolutionary in relation to other plays of the Victorian theatre. When Harry Trench, a sturdy young doctor of twenty-four, discovers that the fortune of his fiancée, Blanche Sartorius, derives from her father's cruel exploitation of the poor, he makes the expected Victorian gesture of refusing such ill-gotten wealth. Blanche, however, refuses to live a life of penurious love. It is Sartorius who finally convinces Trench of the necessity, even the justice, of his practices. Trench's ultimate conversion takes place, however, when he learns that his own income is equally tainted, coming from the same source as that of Sartorius. Reversing his original disdain, he returns to Blanche.

The Philanderer (wr. 1893, prod. 1905). Comedy about a Don Juan-like character named Charteris, whom women find irresistible. He has resigned himself to this, though it does interfere in his own first genuine love affair. Trying to rid himself of his former woman, Julia, in order to marry Grace, he loses both. To his relief, Julia, in a feminine fit of pique, consents to marry the foolish Dr. Paramore, while Grace, the "new woman," refuses his proposal because her love will put her too much in his power. The comedy places Charteris's predicament in the context of a clash between the old order, as represented by the fathers of the two ladies, and the new, as described by Ibsen, who is their idol. Much of the play takes place in the Ibsen Club, wherein the members must conform to rules based on Ibsen's notions of "unwomanly women and unmanly men."

Mrs. Warren's Profession (wr. 1893, prod. 1902). Vivie Warren, an emancipated, intelligent, and self-sufficient young woman, is spending her postuniversity holiday with her mother and her mother's friends Sir George Crofts and Praed, an architect. Frank, a young man in love with her, lives nearby. Vivie is astounded to learn, first, that her mother rose from poverty to her present affluence through prostitution and, second, that she is now part owner and operator of a chain of European brothels. Sir George has been her mother's partner all these years, and Frank's father, Rev. Samuel Gardner, was once one of her mother's clients, bringing up the possibility, quickly dispelled, that Frank and Vivie are half-brother and sister.

Mrs. Warren cogently justifies her life with an attack on the hypocrisy of a society which rewards vice and oppresses virtue, saying that poverty and the society which fosters poverty are the real villains; that life in a brothel is preferable to life in a nineteenth-century fac-

Lynn Fontanne and Alfred Lunt as Raina and Bluntschli in the Theatre Guild production of *Arms and the Man*. New York, Guild Theatre, 1925. [Theatre Collection, The New York Public Library at Lincoln Center, Astor, Lenox and Tilden Foundations]

Scene from a French production of *Arms and the Man*, Théâtre Gramont, Paris. [French Cultural Services]

tory. Vivie, respecting her mother's courage, accepts her past but not her present. She cuts herself off from her mother and, rejecting all suitors, throws herself into the independent life of a career woman, for which she is qualified by her mathematical gifts and her education.

Arms and the Man (1894). Romantic comedy set in Bulgaria. After a disastrous battle, Bluntschli, a retreating Swiss mercenary serving in the Serbian Army, takes refuge in the bedroom of Raina, the daughter of a pretentious Bulgarian family. A practical and experienced campaigner who carries chocolates into battle instead of bullets, Bluntschli manages to undermine Raina's romantic notions of war and heroism. These ideas are personified in her fiancé Sergius, the Byronic Bulgarian officer who won the battle as a result of his heroic folly and a quirk of fate. Returning to Raina's home after peace has been signed, Bluntschli helps the incompetent Sergius and Raina's father, Major Petkoff, to demobilize their regiments. Sergius declares he is going to marry Louka, the servant girl, whereupon Bluntschli declares himself a suitor for Raina's hand. Her parents are hesitant, as he is a poor soldier and she is accustomed to a lavish (by Bulgarian standards) style of living. Bluntschli, however, reveals himself heir to a fortune, and all ends happily.

Candida (1897). Drama about a love triangle between the vigorous, upright Morell, a Christian Socialist pastor; the fragile, eighteen-year-old Marchbanks, a dreamer and poet given to flashes of insight; and Candida, Morell's calm, efficient, and wise wife, who handles her husband with love and understanding. Although staunchly bourgeois in her attitudes, she is touched by

Robert Harris as Marchbanks and Katharine Cornell as Candida. New York, Empire Theatre, 1937. [Photograph by Vandamm. Theatre Collection, The New York Public Library at Lincoln Center, Astor, Lenox and Tilden Foundations]

A 1971 production of *Candida,* with (l. to r.) Walter Rhodes, Polly Holliday, and James Sutorius. [Asolo State Theatre Company, Sarasota, Fla.]

the adulation of Marchbanks, who is determined to deliver her from her prosaic existence. Morell, unnerved by the poet's accusations of lack of understanding, is further disturbed when Marchbanks reveals that Candida may in fact love him and insists that Candida resolve the triangle by choosing one of them. Candida asks what each has to offer her: Morell offers his strength, honesty, ability, and dignity; Marchbanks his weakness, desolation, and heart's need. Candida then announces her choice to be the weaker of the two, whom Morell does not immediately recognize as himself. Candida explains their mutual love and the need that Morell has for her, and Marchbanks leaves, rising above mere romance and philistine domesticity to the heroic world of the creative imagination.

The Man of Destiny (1897). One-act comedy set in May, 1796, is an Italian inn where the young Napoleon is spending the evening. A young Frenchwoman has succeeded in beguiling an empty-headed lieutenant and pilfering some dispatches and letters that he was to deliver to Napoleon. The theft is made in an effort to retrieve an incriminating love letter that was written, Napoleon subsequently discovers, by his own wife. The dialogue between Napoleon and the lady is spiced with observations on war, generals, genius, and chivalry, ending in a prolonged attack on the English ruthlessness that masquerades as high-minded patriotism and manly principle.

You Never Can Tell (1899). Comedy in which the members of a fatherless family return to England after years in Madeira, where they have been living under the tutelage of their emancipated mother, a celebrated suffragette and writer, Mrs. Lanfrey Clandon. The elder daughter, Gloria, a "modern woman" cut from her mother's cloth, believes herself free from female frailties and immune to masculine attractions. Nevertheless, she succumbs to the advances of Valentine, a penniless dentist and "Duellist of Sex," much to the amusement of her twin brother and sister, Phil and Dolly, and the consternation of her mother. Meanwhile, the twins have invited to lunch Fergus Crampton, unaware that he is their father, Mrs. Clandon's abandoned husband. Thoroughly old-fashioned in his views on women and children, he is horrified to discover how his own have grown up and determines to seek custody of the twins and assume responsibility for their proper education. The problems of the family are brought up before Bohun, a barrister who is the son of a remarkably tactful waiter. He soon bullies everyone into "a friendly arrangement." The question of legal custody can be abandoned since the twins will soon reach maturity, and Gloria decides to accept Valentine's proposal despite all warnings about his philandering nature.

The Devil's Disciple (1897). Comedy set in Websterbridge, N.H., during the American Revolution. Richard Dudgeon, reacting against his puritanical mother, has abjured Christianity and claims to be a follower of the devil. Called home at his father's death, Dudgeon finds

William Paterson and Carol Mayo Jenkins in *The Devil's Disciple.* San Francisco, Geary Theatre, 1968–1969 season. [Courtesy of American Conservatory Theatre, San Francisco, Calif. Photograph by Hank Kranzler]

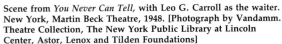

Scene from *You Never Can Tell,* with Leo G. Carroll as the waiter. New York, Martin Beck Theatre, 1948. [Photograph by Vandamm. Theatre Collection, The New York Public Library at Lincoln Center, Astor, Lenox and Tilden Foundations]

The Devil's Disciple, with Maurice Evans (left), Victor Jory, and Marsha Hunt. New York, City Center of Music and Drama, 1940. [Theatre Collection, The New York Public Library at Lincoln Center, Astor, Lenox and Tilden Foundations]

himself heir to the family property and legal guardian of his illegitimate niece; he is a thorn in the side of his pompous relatives. Meanwhile, the British, following their custom of hanging a leading citizen in every town through which they pass, are on their way to arrest Pastor Anderson, whom Dudgeon is visiting. Anderson, however, is called away from his home moments before the British arrive, and they seize Dudgeon, believing him to be the pastor. Dudgeon remains mute about the mistake, and Judith, Anderson's wife, believes he has done so out of love for her. In fact, Dudgeon continues the masquerade out of compassion; he cannot let harm come to another. But Judith, nagged by the thought that her husband has made a cowardly withdrawal and romantically attracted by the selfless performance of Dudgeon, frantically informs the British general, Burgoyne, that the prisoner is not her husband. Despite this, Dudgeon is to be hanged. Meanwhile, Burgoyne's troops are in a strategically untenable position. The American officer who arrives to discuss terms for the British withdrawal saves Dudgeon's life by revealing that he is Pastor Anderson. In his hour of trial, Anderson discovers that he is a man of war rather than of peace, and he begins a new life as a captain of the United States Militia. Dick, also discovering his true vocation, takes Anderson's place as pastor of the church.

Caesar and Cleopatra (wr. 1898, prod. 1906). Caesar, seeking Pompey after the Battle of Pharsalus, pursues him to Egypt. There he discovers Cleopatra hiding from the Romans between the great paws of a Sphinx and begins to teach her how to be a queen. He places her on the throne, to rule jointly with her brother Ptolemy, whose faction had driven her out of Alexandria. There he sets about collecting back taxes. Indignant, the Egyptians remind him that they had Pompey murdered for his sake. Caesar is horrified, but remembering early follies of his own, he pardons the murder. The Egyptians, however, reject his political settlement, and Pothinus, Ptolemy's intriguing guardian, further reminds Caesar that his army holds only the palace, beach, and harbor and is vastly outnumbered by Achillas, Ptolemy's general, and his so-called Roman army of occupation. While Achillas and the Egyptian army are diverted by the accidental burning of the great library of Alexandria, Caesar attempts to seize the lighthouse controlling the harbor. Shortly after Cleopatra joins him he returns to the palace, where Pothinus is now a hostage, and awaits reinforcements. Five months later he is still waiting. Meanwhile, as Pothinus perceives, Caesar has educated the charming but barbaric Cleopatra into a woman of insight and capability. Cleopatra loves and respects Caesar but also intends to rule Egypt alone when he leaves. Infuriated by her knowing superiority, Pothinus apprises Caesar of her intentions. To revenge herself, Cleopatra orders her maid Ftatateeta to kill Pothinus and thus brings on a riot of the populace that threatens to destroy them all. Fortunately, a relieving army is announced and Caesar goes out to conquer, but not before he has reprimanded Cleopatra and all his followers for their self-righteous adherence to the law of vengeance. He bears no grudges however, and on his later departure from Egypt he rewards his followers generously, leaving the government in their charge, though he nearly forgets to say goodbye to Cleopatra. In compensation, as he embarks for Rome and his death, he promises Cleopatra "a gift from Rome," in the person of Mark Antony.

Captain Brassbound's Conversion (1900). Comedy in which Sir Howard Hallam and his sister-in-law Lady Cicely, arriving in the Moroccan seaport Mogador, engage Captain Brassbound and his crew to escort them on a trip to the interior. Brassbound, a saturnine type who rules his men by force, takes the visitors to an ancient castle in the hills, where he informs them that he is Hallam's long-lost nephew, about to avenge himself for Hallam's injustices to his mother by turning his uncle over to Moslem tribesmen who will kill him. Gradually, however, Lady Cicely charms the fierce Brassbound and reduces his crew to adoring subservience. As she is about to turn her charm on the Moslems who have come to claim the infidels, a rescue party arrives. Brassbound is led away in custody and brought before a court of inquiry. Lady Cicely once again practices her wiles and saves his life, whereupon Brassbound, stunned, proposes to her. Mesmerized by his appeal, Lady Cicely is about to accept him when they are shocked to their senses by the sound of gunfire from Brassbound's ship, the crew's signal that they are ready to leave. Brassbound and Lady Cicely part, relieved, Lady Cicely happy to have escaped the confines of marriage and Brassbound to have stumbled on the secret of command: selflessness and an understanding of the folly of revenge.

Arthur Treacher (left), Cedric Hardwicke, and Lilli Palmer in *Caesar and Cleopatra*. New York, National Theatre, 1949. [Photograph by Vandamm. Theatre Collection, The New York Public Library at Lincoln Center, Astor, Lenox and Tilden Foundations]

The Admirable Bashville, or Constancy Unrewarded (1903). Blank-verse satire based on Shaw's novel *Cashel Byron's Profession*. Cashel Byron, a prizefighter, falls in love with Lydia Carew and discovers that she is an aristocrat. When Cashel visits Lydia, he is tripped up by her agile butler Bashville, who secretly loves his mistress. Cashel takes Lydia to see him fight a man named Paradise; the match ends in a general melee involving Zulu chieftains. Later, when he is being sought by the police for illegal prizefighting, Cashel's actress mother appears and he is revealed to be the son of a nobleman. Cashel then marries Lydia and, making the best of things, engages Bashville as his pugilistic protégé. "Fate," he says, "drives us all to find our chiefest good/ In what we can, and not in what we would."

Man and Superman (1905). Philosophical comedy in which John Tanner, Shaw's witty incarnation of Don Juan Tenorio, is appointed one of the two guardians of Ann Whitefield. Tanner is a young revolutionary, a man of passionate moral beliefs who tries to govern his life by

Scene from *Man and Superman*, with Paul Shenar and DeAnn Mears. San Francisco, Geary Theatre, 1966. [Courtesy of American Conservatory Theatre, San Francisco, Calif. Photograph by Hank Kranzler]

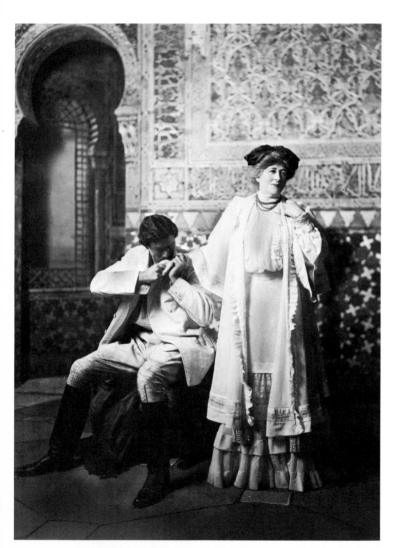

James Carew and Ellen Terry in *Captain Brassbound's Conversion*. New York, Empire Theatre, 1907. [Culver Pictures]

pure reason, in defiance of the dominant conventions of society. Unlike Tanner, Ann's other guardian, Roebuck Ramsden, is an old-guard liberal, in Tanner's eyes a prig and hypocrite. Each man objects to the other as guardian to Ann but accedes to the wishes of her father, unaware that Ann had requested their guardianship in an elaborate plan to make Tanner her husband, even though she is pursued by Octavius Robinson, Tanner's friend. At their first encounter, while the four are discussing the will, they receive the news that Octavius's sister Violet is pregnant and will not name her husband. Ramsden and Octavius are shocked, but Tanner praises her for her bravery. Presently an American, Hector Malone, Jr., comes to call on Violet. Left alone, they embrace and make plans to conceal their marriage, which has already taken place, until they elicit his father's approval.

Tanner soon discovers that Ann has designs on him, and he flees to the Spanish Sierra Nevada with his chauffeur, Henry Straker. There he and Straker are captured by a band of brigands whose leader, Mendoza, had taken up a life of crime after being repudiated by a lost love, Straker's sister. While captive, Tanner has a dream that takes the form of *Don Juan in Hell*, a play-within-the-play. In it, Tanner, Ann, Ramsden, and Mendoza take the roles of Don Juan, the passionate moralist, Doña Ana de Ulloa, the universal female, Don Gonzalo, the man of pleasure disguised as a statue, and the Devil. In a quasi-platonic dialogue, these characters discuss the state of the world. Don Gonzalo, bored with heaven where he says people behave as proper Englishmen, doing only what is expected of them, has arrived in hell. There he encounters Don Juan, who is expounding to Doña Ana, Gonzalo's daughter, his concept of heaven. In heaven, he says, one can find reality in the life of pure reason, while hell is all illusion, the citadel of romantics. Intelligence and reason (the Life Force in men) have enhanced the slow but purposive evolution of the species (the purpose of the Life Force in women), adding new dimension to life; reason directs the Life Force which resides in woman and with that Life Force will create the Superman. The Devil scoffs, retorting that man's intelligence has thus far created only war and destruction. Ana says that although man's intelligence can make him brave and noble, nevertheless women bear the responsible task of the species—to procreate. Don Juan, agreeing that the Life Force abides in women, points out that they use men only for the purpose of procreation. Romanticism, he says, led him to beauty and thence to women, whose Life Force drove him to seek them out; but they tried to romanticize their main purpose, the creation of children. Although the Devil provides the meaningless pleasures of romanticism, Don Juan eschews this course and decides to go to heaven so that he can develop an intellect better able to direct the Life Force. As Juan leaves, Ana looks for the superman. Learning that he has not yet been created, she proceeds to seek a mate to father the superman.

Mendoza and Tanner awaken from their dream to find that Ann has led a search party directly to them. Later, at a villa in Granada, Hector's father, a self-made man, appears, having intercepted a note written by Violet for Hector. Against a marriage to a middle-class girl, Mr. Malone is nevertheless persuaded by Violet that his son needs both of them, and he relents. Meanwhile, Octavius proposes to Ann once again and she refuses, continuing her campaign to catch Tanner. Eventually Tanner proposes, fully aware that in doing so he is yielding to the Life Force embodied in Ann, the Everywoman.

John Bull's Other Island (1904). Philosophical comedy in which Shaw focuses upon three characters: Broadbent, who is John Bull incarnate, a romantic English capitalist liberal who serves mammon with idealistic rhetoric; Larry Doyle, a cynical, realistic Irishman who is Broadbent's partner; and Peter Keegan, an unfrocked priest whose dream of turning Ireland into a heaven on earth he calls "the dream of a madman." Together Broadbent and Doyle go to Rosscullen, Ireland, where Broadbent takes charge of property for a land development syndicate, becomes a candidate for Parliament, and, to Larry Doyle's intense relief, wins the girl who for eighteen years had been waiting for Larry's return. Meanwhile, Keegan, unhappy with the world as it is and equally unhappy with the world as Broadbent would have it, proclaims his estrangement from it. In fact, the prosperity brought about by Broadbent will be both beneficial and harmful to Rosscullen, though, as Keegan realizes, it will be immensely profitable to the syndicate of which Broadbent and Doyle are stockholders. Throughout the play it is the masterful Englishman who, assuming that he will inherit the earth, does so.

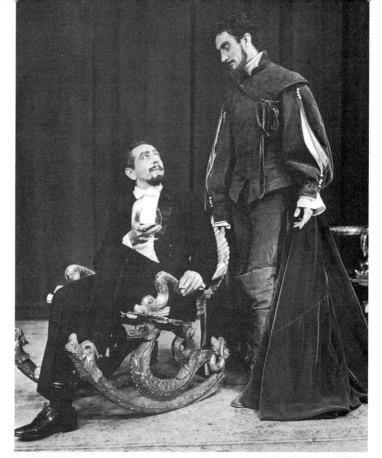

Two scenes from *Man and Superman*: (above) with Paul Sparer (left) and Ellis Rabb; (below) with Nancy Marchand and Ellis Rabb. New York, Phoenix Theatre, 1964. [Courtesy of Phoenix Theatre]

How He Lied to Her Husband (1904). One-act farce that in many ways parodies *Candida.* It concerns a husband-wife-lover triangle, although the lover here is a pugilist poet rather than a weak one as in *Candida.* Aurora Bompas, upset because she has lost some poems addressed to her by Henry Apjohn, her young lover, correctly fears that they are now in the hands of her husband Teddy. Refusing Henry's proposal that she divorce Teddy and flee with him, Aurora persuades him to tell her husband that the poems were written about another Aurora. Reluctantly, Henry assures Teddy that the verses were addressed to another Aurora, whereupon the husband angrily attacks Henry for failing to appreciate his wife. Peace is restored only when Henry admits his love; Teddy decides that the poems must be published.

This play was written for Harley Granville-Barker, who had made his reputation as Marchbanks. When first produced and published, it contained several references to *Candida;* the poet and the wife, for example, fall in love when they see a performance of *Candida.*

Major Barbara (1905). Social satire in three acts. With one daughter, Barbara, engaged to Adolphus Cusins, a professor of Greek, and the other, Sarah, to Charles, a young man-about-town, Lady Britomart asks her estranged husband, Andrew Undershaft, an armaments millionaire, to help support the young people af-

Scene from a Theatre Guild revival of *Major Barbara,* with (l. to r.) Percy Waram, Elliot Cabot, and Winifred Lenihan in the title role. New York, Guild Theatre, 1928. [Photograph by Vandamm. Theatre Collection, The New York Public Library at Lincoln Center, Astor, Lenox and Tilden Foundations]

Polly Holliday (left), Albert Stratton, and Virginia North in a 1967 production of *Major Barbara.* [Asolo State Theatre Company, Sarasota, Fla.]

ter their marriages. Their son Stephen is morally offended by his father's "tainted" source of wealth and is horrified to learn that it has supported the whole family for years. Stephen, however, is spared the shame of having to succeed his father in the business by a peculiar tradition, that the foundry is willed to a foundling by each succeeding generation. Undershaft's children are fascinated by their father when he finally meets them, and Barbara, an idealistic major in the Salvation Army, invites him to visit her mission. He agrees on condition that she will visit his foundry town.

When Undershaft appears at the mission, Barbara is shocked to discover that the Salvation Army is willing to accept a large donation of her father's "tainted" money. Desolate, Barbara removes her badge, pins it on her father, who she believes has "bought" the army, and leaves. Then, on visiting the foundry town, she finds that, in contrast to the army's thieving, lying, and indigent charges, Undershaft's workers are happy, healthy, and well fed. Undershaft has by this time persuaded Barbara's fiancé Cusins that poverty is more immoral than the manufacture of munitions. He then names Cusins, acceptable as a foundling on a legal technicality, as his heir. Barbara, who is challenged to save souls without the aid of bread as a bribe, prepares to tackle those of Undershaft's foundry workers.

Passion, Poison, and Petrifaction; or The Fatal Gazogene (1905). Burlesque in one act. Fitztollemache, Lady Magnesia's husband, attempts to murder Adolphus, her lover, by poisoning the contents of a soda siphon (a gazogene). As Adolphus writhes in agony after drinking the poisoned soda water, a celestial choir sings "Won't You Come Home, Bill Bailey?" Fitz is suddenly seized by a remorse. Quicklime is the only antidote and, in an attempt to save him, Adolphus is fed chips from the plaster ceiling and pieces of a bust of Lady Magnesia. The plaster, however, hardens when swallowed, and Adolphus becomes a dead "statue."

The Doctor's Dilemma (1906). "Tragedy" satirizing the medical profession. When Jennifer Dubedat learns of Dr. Colenso Ridgeon's miraculous cure for tuberculosis, she appeals to him to care for her artist husband Louis. Because Ridgeon would have to drop a patient if he took Louis's case he wants to observe Louis and have his colleagues also observe him in order to decide whether he is worth saving. Ridgeon therefore invites the couple to a dinner with several doctors. The party that gathers at a luxurious hotel includes Cutler Walpole, a fanatic on blood poisoning who favors surgery as a cure; Sir Ralph Bloomfield Bonington, "B. B.," a smug and radiant quack obsessed with cure by vaccination; Schutzmacher, who has amassed wealth by adding the words "cure guaran-

The Doctor's Dilemma, with Nancy Wickwire, John Cromwell (standing), and Ed Flanders. Minneapolis, 1966. [The Guthrie Theater Company]

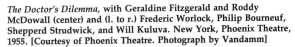

The Doctor's Dilemma, with Geraldine Fitzgerald and Roddy McDowall (center) and (l. to r.) Frederic Worlock, Philip Bourneuf, Shepperd Strudwick, and Will Kuluva. New York, Phoenix Theatre, 1955. [Courtesy of Phoenix Theatre. Photograph by Vandamm]

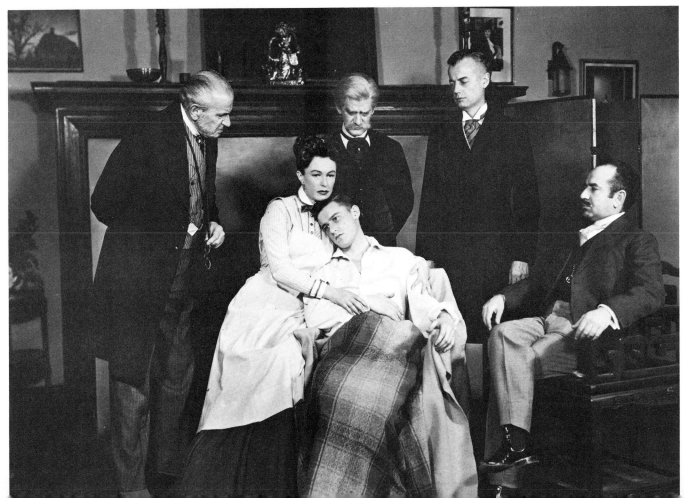

Scene from a French production of *The Shewing-Up of Blanco Posnet*. [French Cultural Services]

She begs them to encourage him. When he comes out, he does everything but make the speech and finally leaves in a huff. His wife, who takes his place, expresses the hope that the audience will enjoy themselves and will return.

Getting Married (1908). Full-length comedy in one act that takes place on the day that Edith Bridgenorth, the bishop's daughter, is to marry Cecil Sykes. When Edith reads a pamphlet telling her of the legal rights she will lose by marrying and Sykes reads another explaining the legal responsibilities he must assume, each wants to call off the wedding. At the same time various members of the two families reveal their own dissatisfaction with marriage and divorce laws, and they all try to frame a marriage contract to suit their needs. This precipitates arguments about marriage, celibacy, divorce, monogamy, and related matters. The effort to draw up a satisfactory contract fails, and the young couple, putting their faith in each other and an insurance policy, slip out and get married on their own.

The Shewing-Up of Blanco Posnet (1909). Religious tract in the form of a melodrama of the old West, subtitled *A Sermon in Crude Melodrama.* Blanco Posnet is on trial for stealing the sheriff's horse. Blanco says he can-

teed'' to his shingle; Blenkinsop, a mediocre doctor who grows increasingly poorer treating indigents; and Sir Patrick, an old cynic who casts a cold eye on physicians. Louis Dubedat, worshiped by Jennifer, proves a talented and charming man. Only after the couple's departure do the doctors discover that he has extracted money from all but Schutzmacher, and that he is also married to the hotel maid.

Unconcerned by the discovery of his rascally behavior, Louis maintains that he added charm to the maid's dull life and that the creation of art is more important than lost money. When Blenkinsop reveals that he too has tuberculosis, Ridgeon must choose between the two, and the choice is complicated by the fact that he now loves Jennifer and feels Louis to be morally reprehensible. He chooses to treat Blenkinsop and cures him, while Dubedat, under the ministrations of ''B.B.,'' dies within three days. But before he does so, Louis, on his deathbed, levels a few parting shots at Ridgeon, urges his wife to remarry, and commends his soul to Beauty. At a posthumous exhibit of Louis's paintings, Ridgeon at last confesses his love and his knowledge of Dubedat's character to Jennifer. But Jennifer now despises him for having caused Dubedat's death and has already remarried, as Louis had urged. She reveals, moreover, that a match between her and Ridgeon would have been impossible in any case since she considers him an elderly man.

The Interlude at the Playhouse (1907). Playlet dramatizing the opening of a new London theatre, the Playhouse. The actor-manager's wife appears before the audience, explaining that her husband is to make a speech.

Dorothy Gish and Hugh Buckler in a Theatre Guild production of *Getting Married.* New York, Guild Theatre, 1931. [Photograph by Vandamm. Theatre Collection, The New York Public Library at Lincoln Center, Astor, Lenox and Tilden Foundations]

Carol Williard and Macon McCalman in a 1970 production of *Misalliance.* [Asolo State Theatre Company, Sarasota, Fla.]

not be convicted unless they can find a witness who saw him with the horse. The town prostitute is brought in and testifies she saw him with the animal. Blanco is about to be convicted when a woman who is brought in explains that the horse was given to her because she needed it to take her child to a doctor. A man gave her the horse, she says, but she swears it was not Blanco. The prostitute insists on her story until she takes the stand. Then she suddenly recants, and Blanco is freed.

Press Cuttings (1909). Comedy sketch in which Prime Minister Balsquith goes to consult with General Mitchener on current problems such as the question of women's rights. Mrs. Banger and Lady Corinthia Fanshawe, members of the Anti-Suffragette League, try to convince him that women do not want the vote but rather the right to military service, for, they claim, the strong men in history were really women in disguise. This persuades General Mitchener to support the ideas of the suffragettes. Mrs. Banger announces she will marry General Sandstone and be the power behind the army; but Sandstone resigns, making Mitchener next in line to head the army. Then, to thwart any plan Mrs. Banger has to marry him, General Mitchener proposes to his charwoman, Mrs. Farrell, a most efficient person. Balsquith agrees to form a platonic alliance with Lady Corinthia.

The Fascinating Foundling (wr. 1909, prod. 1928). Comedy in which Horace Brabazon, a ward of the court, comes to the office of the Lord Chancellor and demands a wife. Soon after, a foundling, Anastasia Vulliamy, asks the Lord Chancellor for a husband. When Horace returns, she proposes. He accepts when she tells him that she is a foundling and has no relatives to bother them.

The Glimpse of Reality (wr. 1909, prod. 1927). Tragedietta in which Squarcio has agreed to kill Count Ferruccio in order to obtain a dowry for his daughter Giulia so that she can marry Sandro. Instead, the three decide that it will be more profitable for Squarcio and Sandro to become the count's bodyguards. Their payment for protective services will become Giulia's dowry.

Misalliance (1990). Long one-act comedy subtitled *Debate in One Sitting* (the subtitle was subsequently removed). In the garden room of a well-appointed Edwardian home, Mr. Tarleton, a wealthy manufacturer of underwear, holds court. His son has returned for a vacation with a friend, and his daughter Hypatia is entertaining her fiancé Bentley Summerhays, the neurotic son of Tarleton's best friend, who is also present. The group, settling down to a philosophical discussion to which Tarleton and his friend Summerhays are not attuned, is interrupted when an aircraft comes crashing through the conservatory roof bearing Lina Szczepanowska, a Polish aviatrix, and Joey Percival, college friend of Summerhays. With their arrival, the excitement begins: the men, first the old, then the young, make advances to Lina, who rejects them all; Hypatia immodestly chases Joey through the heather; and a serious young man, appearing armed with a pistol, threatens to shoot Tarleton because of the wrongs done his mother during her affair with Tarleton. The would-be assassin is brought to submission by Mrs. Tarleton and is disarmed by Lina; Hypatia finally catches Joey and, rejecting Bentley, forces her father to "buy the brute" to be her husband in order to protect her good name; and Lina, insulted by Tarleton's son's offer to make her an "honest woman," takes off in her airplane, carrying with her the puny young Bentley Summerhays, of whom she will make a man.

The Dark Lady of the Sonnets (1910). Comedy written to help raise funds for a National Theatre. Shake-

Patricia Falkenhain and Frederic Warriner in *The Dark Lady of the Sonnets.* New York, Phoenix Theatre, 1961. [Courtesy of Phoenix Theatre. Photograph by Henry Grossman]

Androcles and the Lion. New York, Phoenix Theatre, 1961. [Courtesy of Phoenix Theatre. Photograph by Henry Grossman]

Ernest Truex as Androcles and June Duprez as Lavinia in *Androcles and the Lion.* New York, International Theatre, 1946. [Photograph by Vandamm. Theatre Collection, The New York Public Library at Lincoln Center, Astor, Lenox and Tilden Foundations]

speare, waiting for his dark lady, meets Queen Elizabeth. Not recognizing her, he attempts to make love to her. When he discovers her identity, he pleads with the Queen to establish a National Theatre for him. She demurs, saying that the time is not yet right but that perhaps it will be in another 300 years. During the play conversation among the minor characters provides Shakespeare with some of his immortal lines.

Fanny's First Play (1911). Comedy in which Count O'Dowda, an Anglophobe who prefers Venice to London, refuses to recognize the vulgarities of the nineteenth century. Nevertheless, he sends his sheltered daughter Fanny to England to be educated. For her birthday, Fanny asks her father to stage a private showing of a play she has written, to invite the drama critics, but to conceal her authorship. The count expects the play to resemble the Italian and French fantasies of the seventeenth and eighteenth centuries; instead, it concerns a lively suffragette who falls in love with a footman (really the younger son of a duke) and her former fiancé, who is engaged to a good-natured prostitute. After the performance the critics demand to know the author, for without knowing who wrote it they cannot tell if it is good or bad. One critic thinks it is Pinero's work, another Granville-Barker's, a third Shaw's. Only Trotter (modeled on A. B. Walkley, the well-known critic of *The Times*) realizes that Fanny is the author and that the misadventures of the heroine are Fanny's own escapades.

Androcles and the Lion (1913). Fable, in a prologue and two acts, combining low comedy with the serious portrayal of human dignity. Androcles, a Christian, flees from Rome with his wife Megaera to avoid persecution. In a forest they come upon a lion in distress. Androcles removes a painful thorn from the beast's paw, and they become friends. Subsequently, Androcles is captured by the Emperor's soldiers and taken to Rome to be sent into the arena at the Colosseum with some Christians, who, he finds react to their predicament in differing ways: Ferrovius, formerly a ferocious fighter, is determined to subdue his ferocity and to turn the other cheek meekly; Lavinia, a beautiful Roman aristocrat, maintains her integrity and independence of thought, refusing a Roman captain's offer of freedom because she is determined to die in the Christian faith; Spintho hopes to atone for a life of debauchery and depravity, assuming that martyrdom settles all scores; and Androcles can love only animals, like St. Francis. When all the men except Androcles, who is too meek, are sent into the arena to fight the gladiators, Ferrovius, despite his resolve to turn the other cheek, kills them all and is awarded a crown of laurels by the Emperor, who then pardons all the Christians. However, at least one Christian must be thrown to a lion in order to satisfy the populace, and Androcles is chosen. When the lion appears, it recognizes him as the man who removed the thorn. They embrace and waltz around the arena, and Androcles is granted his freedom.

Overruled (1912). Comedy involving two married couples. In the sitting room of a hotel, Mr. Lunn and Mrs. Juno declare their love for each other. Hearing Mr. Juno's voice, they hide. Mr. Juno enters with Mrs. Lunn, and a similar scene ensues. The first couple returns and an argument on right, wrong, and morality follows. The dinner gong puts a temporary end to their bickering, and all four go in to dinner, Mr. Lunn escorting Mrs. Juno and Mr. Juno escorting Mrs. Lunn.

Beauty's Duty (wr. 1913). Playlet in which a husband reports his wife's philosophy of love to his solicitor. Since she believes she can improve men through love (she has a special talent for making men fall in love with her), she thinks it her duty to do so. When the solicitor's clerk announces a beautiful woman with whom he says he has fallen in love, the husband explains that it is only his wife practicing her charms again.

Pygmalion (1913). ''Romance'' in which Henry Higgins, a professor of phonetics, bets his friend, Colonel Pickering, that he will be able to pass off a flower girl, Eliza Doolittle, as a duchess within six months simply by changing her speech. Higgins takes Eliza into his home, and a period of intensive training begins. In the allotted time Eliza passes the test, after a catastrophic trial run in which Freddy Eynsford Hill becomes infatuated with her. Higgins wins his bet at the Ambassador's garden party. He and Pickering are delighted with themselves, but Eliza is disgruntled because her part in the triumph is ignored. Higgins has raised her above her class and supplied her with the manner, speech, and accomplishments of a lady, but she is now unfit for either class. After she has taken refuge with his mother, Higgins, realizing that Eliza has become indispensable to him, asks

Two scenes from *Pygmalion:* **(left) with Cecil Humphreys, Melville Cooper, and Raymond Massey as Colonel Pickering, Alfred Doolittle, and Henry Higgins; (right) with Gertrude Lawrence as Eliza Doolittle. New York, Barrymore Theatre, 1945. [Photograph by Vandamm. Theatre Collection, The New York Public Library at Lincoln Center, Astor, Lenox and Tilden Foundations]**

Julie Andrews as Eliza Doolittle and Rex Harrison as Henry Higgins in *My Fair Lady,* the musical by Alan Jay Lerner and Frederick Loewe based on *Pygmalion.* New York, Mark Hellinger Theatre, 1956. [Friedman-Abeles]

her to return and live with him and Pickering as three bachelors, but she refuses if she is only to be taken for granted. She wants kindness and consideration from him, but he insists that this is contrary to his nature. He asks her to do some errands, but she refuses and walks out of his life: she will marry Freddy and use what she has learnt from Higgins by setting up as a rival teacher.

Great Catherine [*(Whom Glory Still Adores), 1913*]. Comedy in which Edstaston, a young English captain in St. Petersburg seeking an audience with Empress Catherine, is disconcerted to find her attracted to him. After running away he tells his fiancée, Claire, that they must leave. But he is apprehended and brought back to Catherine, who tortures him by tickling him. Claire comes to the rescue, and Catherine gives them permission to depart. Edstaston's parting advice to Catherine is that she should remarry and raise children, as he and Claire intend to do.

The Music Cure (1914). Comedy, subtitled *Piece of Utter Nonsense,* about young Lord Reginald Fitzambey, who, while recovering from a nervous breakdown, is still so nervous that he screams at the sound of a piano. His mother hires the famous pianist Strega Thundridge to help him recuperate with her masterful playing. He tries to stop Strega, but she is stronger than he. Realizing that Strega is his superior and seeing himself in a feminine role in marriage, he asks her to marry him and take care of him, for he needs a dominant woman. She realizes that she needs a husband completely dependent on her, and seeing herself in the masculine role, accepts his proposal.

The Inca of Perusalem (1916). "Almost historical comedietta" centering on Ermyntrude, daughter of an archdeacon who cannot support her lavish tastes. She gets a position as maid to a frail and frightened princess who is to marry a son of the Inca. When the Inca's envoy arrives, Ermyntrude offers to meet him, correctly assuming that the envoy will be the Inca himself. He proposes to Ermyntrude, but she refuses because he has been bankrupted by the war he is waging and losing. However, she agrees to join him for tea.

O'Flaherty V.C. (1917). Comedy about Private O'Flaherty, who is awarded the Victoria Cross and returns home on leave to enlist recruits. As soon as he arrives, his mother berates him for fighting in the British Army, and his sweetheart urges him to return to the front and get himself wounded so as to claim a larger pension. O'Flaherty concludes that he will be glad to get back to the serenity of the front.

Augustus Does His Bit (1917). Farce in which Lord Augustus Highcastle has been warned that a lady spy is trying to steal a secret list of Britain's antiaircraft emplacements. When a lady arrives to warn him that the spy is her sister-in-law, his attention is diverted and she herself absconds with the list. But as soon as she reaches the street, she turns back. She had bet Augustus's brother "Blueloo" that she could secure the document. She now calls "Blueloo" at the War Office to say she has won the bet. Only then does Augustus discover that the document has been taken.

Annajanska, the Bolshevik Empress (1918). "Revolutionary romancelet" set in the country of Beotia, where a revolution is in progress. To the chagrin of the Commander in Chief, the grand Duchess Annajanska supports the rebels. She wins over the Commander in Chief by explaining that she must always belong to the ruling class, even if it means her becoming a Bolshevik empress.

Heartbreak House (wr. 1913/19, prod. 1920). Drama subtitled *A Fantasia in the Russian Manner on English Themes,* often compared to *The Cherry Orchard* by Anton Chekhov, dealing as it does with an effete society on the brink of disaster. In the home of an eccentric retired sea captain, Shotover, a bizarre collection of characters assembles: Mangan, a ridiculous industrial mogul whose fortune is based on unscrupulous dealings; Ellie Dunn, a young and pretty girl who intends to marry him for security's sake; her ineffectual, idealistic father, Mazzini Dunn; Shotover's second daughter, Lady Utterword, an Englishwoman whose husband is a colonial governor; her brother-in-law Randall, a witty and useless boulevardier; and a burglar. Already living in the house are Shotover's first daughter, Hesione, and her husband Hector Hushabye, a dashing and romantic liar who has been courting Ellie under another name.

The shifting relationships of these characters provide the background for a series of arguments, both social and psychological, on subjects ranging from Shotover's semi-mysticism to the battle of the sexes, with gibes at business, government, and conventional morality. Ellie is stripped of her romantic illusions but discovers the inadequacy of cynical realism. She decides to marry not Mangan but Shotover. The play ends with the explosion of bombs, indicating the apocalypse of World War I.

Back to Methuselah (1922). Shaw's "modern Bible" in five parts.

I: *In the Beginning.* In 4004 B.C. Adam and Eve in the Garden of Eden learn, through the discovery of a fawn with its neck broken, the fact of death. Although dismayed at the possibility that they and their kind shall cease to exist, they are equally horrified at the idea of living forever. Under the tutorship of the Serpent, who reveals that death can be conquered through birth, they choose a lifetime of 1,000 years. Life itself will continue through their progeny. "A few centuries later" they reject Cain, who glories in war and dangerous living, and Eve ponders the strange creatures she has spawned. She wonders what the future holds, since the actions of ministers of death like Cain ensure that her grandchildren will suffer death before they can attain wisdom.

II: *The Gospel of the Brothers Barnabas.* In 1920 in a house near London, two brothers, Conrad and Franklyn Barnabas, are visited by two Liberal politicians who seek their support in the coming elections. The brothers, however, think the politicians' notions irrelevant and propose their own program, based on the idea that man must find a way to live for 300 years. Until now, they say, leaders have died just as they were beginning to acquire wisdom, and as a consequence civilization is on the brink of ruin. The politicians are soon disillusioned

Scene from the Theatre Guild production of *Back to Methuselah.* **New York, Garrick Theatre, 1922. [Photograph by Vandamm. Theatre Collection, The New York Public Library at Lincoln Center, Astor, Lenox and Tilden Foundations]**

when they find that the brothers have no elixir for longevity but simply say that man must will his own long life in order to save the world. The politicians leave, believing that the Barnabas brothers have been joking.

III: *The Thing Happens.* In A.D. 2170, much to the discomfort of British statesmen who resemble characters appearing earlier in the play, two eminent public figures, Archbishop Haslam and Mrs. Lutestring, Domestic Minister, are discovered to be more than 200 years old. They have concealed the fact, fearing discrimination in a nation of "short livers" who, needing advisers, have called upon the African and Chinese races. In the interim, these advisers have come to rule the country, and Englishmen have come to prefer their leadership. Now, realizing that the improvement of mankind rests with them, the archbishop and Mrs. Lutestring decide to marry and produce long-lived children.

IV: *Tragedy of an Elderly Gentleman.* The "long livers" are thriving in A.D. 3000 in a community located in what was once Ireland, isolated from the rest of the confused world, still made up of "short livers." The long livers have become oracles and are acting as custodians of wisdom and advice for the rest of mankind. When an elderly gentleman arrives from Baghdad with the party of his son-in-law, who is the Prime Minister (he has come to consult the oracle), he is turned over to a young woman named Zoo, since he is unable to communicate with the older long livers. After the oracle has advised the Prime Minister to "Go home, poor fool," the elderly gentleman begs to be allowed to stay. Warned that he will die from discouragement if he stays, he chooses that death over despair. Then when the oracle gazes at him, he falls dead.

V: *As Far As Thought Can Reach.* The cycle is completed in A.D. 31,920. Infants are now born fully developed from eggs into a sort of Grecian utopia of art, music, and dance. Still immature, they scoff at the ancients who wander among them. A festival day finds the youths celebrating the creation, by their greatest artist Marcellus, of artificial human beings. Although the achievement is enormous, the resulting beings are hideous; they are vain, vulgar, and pompous, they argue incessantly, and they eventually kill Pygmalion, the man who helped Marcellus create them. Finally they themselves die of discouragement. The ancients, wise with the experience of centuries, then discover their failure, that they are not immortal, being subject to the death of their bodies. They aim at a world populated only by pure intelligence and will. No bodies will exist, only thought, and thus life will be eternal.

Jitta's Atonement (1923). Purporting to be a translation of Siegfried Trebitsch's *Frau Gittas Sühne,* Shaw's play deviates from the original considerably: it alters the motivations and attitudes of the characters and changes the ending. Jitta, wife of Alfred Lenkheim, a university professor, has had an affair with Bruno Haldenstedt, her husband's colleague, an affair that ends when Bruno dies of a heart attack. Before his death he has told Jitta that a book he had written must be published in Alfred's name. Alfred, a Shavian realist, refuses to allow this, condemning the book as trash. Jitta then tells him of their affair and says that Bruno wished Alfred to win fame from the book as Bruno's atonement for having stolen her love.

Meanwhile, Bruno's widow Agnes and his daughter Edith have learned that a woman was with Bruno when he died, and they are determined to find her—Agnes to revile her, and Edith, who hates her mother, to glorify the woman who must have meant so much to her father. Jitta persuades Agnes to forget the mysterious woman, but she later confesses to Edith that she was Bruno's mistress. Finally Alfred agrees to act as editor of Bruno's manuscript, which Bruno's widow hopes will provide her with an income. Realizing that his anger over the affair cannot last forever, Alfred persuades Jitta that they should evolve a *modus vivendi.*

Saint Joan (1923). Chronicle play in six scenes and an epilogue in which Joan of Arc, the young girl who led France to victory over the English, emerges as an unlettered country girl gifted with masterful will and innate intelligence. Shaw has removed all overt elements of the supernatural and romantic; her visions and miracles are associated with the intuitive nature of her apprehension of reality and her historical mission. Joan persuades the Dauphin to give her command of the forces at Orléans so that she can lead the army against the English and expel them from France. With the help of sound strategy and the spirit she brings to the French forces, she is victorious. In the English camp the Earl of Warwick says the Maid must be captured and tried by the Inquisition, which will then turn her over to him to be burned as a sorceress.

Meanwhile, Joan crowns the Dauphin King of France and urges continuation of the war. He explains to her what would happen if she were captured, that neither he nor the church would come to her aid. Joan persists, is caught by the English, and is tried for heresy by a French court of the Inquisition, which sentences her to be burned at the stake.

In the epilogue, King Charles dreams that Joan's name has been cleared of the charge of witchcraft. (Charles did, in fact, have her name cleared.) Also in his

Dame Sybil Thorndike in *Saint Joan.* The setting is by Charles Ricketts, who believed that the multilevel stage helped actors achieve naturalness of performance and delivery. [*Theatre Arts Monthly.* Photograph by Bertram Park]

Repertory Theatre of Lincoln Center production of *Saint Joan,* with Diana Sands (center) in the title role. New York, Vivian Beaumont Theatre, 1968. [Photograph by Martha Swope]

dream appears a man of the future, a twentieth-century man who announces Joan's canonization. The characters in the play all appear and praise her. But when she asks whether she should return to earth as the person she was when men were unable to face her saintliness, the answer is ''No,'' as they quickly exit. Alone, Joan asks, ''O God that madest this beautiful earth, when will it be ready to receive Thy saints? How long, O Lord, how long?''

The Apple Cart (1929). Political comedy about constitutional monarchy in Britain. King Magnus is given an ultimatum by his Cabinet that will in effect reduce him to the status of a puppet monarch by limiting his sovereign rights and powers. He tries to persuade the Cabinet members to withdraw the ultimatum by reminding them that they need him to serve as a scapegoat for their mistakes and to protect long-term values and interests from democratic whims and the self-interest of the moment. Their common adversary, in fact, is the Breakages Limited corporation—capitalism—which, although neither will admit it, runs the country. The Cabinet persists, however, and demands that he sign the ultimatum. Granted a period of reflection, he uses it to disport himself with his mistress, take tea with his wife, and receive the American Ambassador, who announces that the United States, having revoked the Declaration of Independence, wishes to rejoin the British Empire. Magnus objects to this on the ground that England would then become, in effect, another American state.

When the Cabinet returns for his decision, Magnus announces that he has decided to abdicate in his son's favor, dissolve Parliament, and call for a general election.

Then, no longer prohibited by his regal status, he will run for the House of Commons and eventually become a Cabinet minister himself, replacing the present Prime Minister. Horrified, the Prime Minister withdraws the ultimatum, and the *status quo* remains undisturbed.

Too True to Be Good (1932). Comedy in which a young society lady, Miss Mopply (Mopsy), living the life of a hypochondriac under her mother's influence, is being treated for measles. Sweetie, a chambermaid, poses as a night nurse to help Popsy, a burglar, steal Mopsy's pearls. Mopsy joins them to evade her mother, staging a mock kidnaping. All three agree to share the proceeds from necklace and ransom. A fake report that Mopsy is held by brigands in a Middle Eastern country prompts the formation of a British expeditionary force nominally led by Colonel Tallboys but really guided by the extraordinary Private Meek, a character modeled on Lawrence of Arabia.

Mopsy enters the headquarters as a native servant to Sweetie, who poses as Countess Valbrioni. The burglar, Popsy, awaits them under his true identity, the Hon. Aubrey Bagot, stepbrother of the real countess. Assuming command, Meek easily drives off a native attack. Mrs. Mopply arrives in search of her daughter, whose disguise has been penetrated. Mopsy is reconciled with her mother, but on a basis of friendship and independence rather than one of family bonds. Sweetie is to marry a sergeant. Aubrey is determined to preach, although he has no message to offer.

Village Wooing (1934). Comedy in which Author A. and Passenger Z meet on a world cruise. He, trying to write, ignores her; but she, determined to win him, engages him in conversation. Later he comes to the village shop where she works, and although he does not remember her, she persuades him to buy the shop and keep her on. She tells him that she intends to marry him and finally persuades him that he wants to marry her.

On the Rocks (1933). Political comedy. Sir Arthur Chavender, the British Prime Minister, is nearing a breakdown from overwork. Lady Chavender persuades him to go to a rest home under the care of a lady doctor, whose diagnosis of his condition is that he is dying of an acute lack of mental exercise. Her cure is for him to learn to think. Upon his return to politics, he makes a speech in which he proposes some revolutionary changes that will solve the nation's economic crisis. Representatives of every stratum of English society approve of a different single area of change while objecting to all the others. As a result, the program is acceptable to no one. Sir Arthur decides that the country needs a strong man who can command loyalty while enforcing solutions. Since he is not that man, he retires from public life.

The Simpleton of the Unexpected Isles (1935). Allegory about Judgment Day. At a tropical port in the British Empire an emigration officer and a young woman without a passport leave his office to tour the town. They meet a native priest and priestess, Pra and Prola, and then two tourists, Colonial Governor Sir Charles and Lady Farwaters. The six decide to live together in order to conduct an experiment in eugenics. Four children representing Love, Pride, Heroism, and Empire are born: two girls, Maya and Vashti, and two boys, Janga and

The world premiere of *The Apple Cart* took place in Poland. Shown are Maria Przybylko-Potocka and Kazimierz Junosza Stepowski. [*Theatre in Modern Poland*]

Kanchin. Twenty years later a young English clergyman, Iddy (short for Idiot) Hammingtap, arrives and marries Maya and Vashti. An angel appears to announce Judgment Day, explaining that those judged socially useless will disappear; only the socially useful will remain. The four children, who talk in slogans, disappear, and reports from London describe wholesale disappearances. All but Pra and Prola go offstage; in all probability it is they alone of the family who survive.

The Six of Calais (1934). Comedy set in the city of Calais, which after a year's siege surrenders to Edward III. In retaliation for its stubbornness, Edward plans to hang six of the city's burgesses. All are resigned to their fate except Piers de Rosty, who inveighs against the King. Queen Philippa cajoles Edward into pardoning the men, but Piers continues his abuse, to the delight of the King and the outrage of the Queen.

The Millionairess (1936). Comedy about the problems posed by an excess of wealth, the inequities brought about by money, and the ruthlessness of those who possess it. Epifania Fitzfassenden, heiress to £30 million and bored with her sportsman husband Alastair, visits Julius Sagamore, whom she wishes to employ as her solicitor to draw up a will. She will leave her fortune to her husband so that he will then have the means to ruin himself. Sagamore dissuades her from her intended suicide. At this point they are interrupted by the appearance of Alastair and his mistress Patricia Smith and, moments later, of Adrian Blenderland, Epifania's sybaritic companion. Accusations of infidelity are exchanged and the two couples depart, Epifania with Adrian and Patricia with Alastair, all having hired Sagamore as their lawyer in the divorce proceedings.

Adrian and Epifania are next seen at a small ramshackle country inn, where after an inferior meal they fall to arguing about money and pleasure. When Adrian presumes to insult the memory of Epifania's father, whom she idolizes, by calling him a bore, she uses her skill in wrestling and batters him unmercifully. It is after Adrian is taken off to a hospital, that Epifania meets the Doctor, a gentle middle-aged Egyptian residing at the inn. Feigning injuries, Epifania tries to hold his interest, but he resists, and she decides that she must marry him. He reveals, however, that he has to fulfill his mother's deathbed wish, that the woman he marries must prove herself first by going out into the world with only 200 piastres and earning her living unaided for six months. Coincidentally, Epifania's father also voiced a deathbed wish, that her intended be given £150 which in six months he must turn into £50,000.

Six months pass, and Epifania and the Doctor meet again in what was once the ramshackle country inn but is now, owing to her ruthlessly helping hand, a fashionable, well-appointed hotel. Epifania has kept her promise; in fact, she has emerged from her experience as a wage earner richer than ever. The Doctor, however, has spent all his money on the poor widow of his former teacher. Nevertheless, by Epifania's circuitous reasoning, she determines that money accumulated from an unpatented discovery made by the Doctor and his teacher

Violet Kemble Cooper and Tom Powers in *The Apple Cart*. New York, Martin Beck Theatre. [Photograph by Vandamm. Theatre Collection, The New York Public Library at Lincoln Center, Astor, Lenox and Tilden Foundations]

qualifies the Doctor as having fulfilled her father's stipulations for a suitable husband. Both having met the requirements of their dead parents, they can now marry.

In an alternative ending, to be played "in countries with Communist sympathies," Epifania entertains thoughts of going to Russia to use her managerial skills for the benefit of both the people and her own status. ("In Russia I shall have such authority! Such scope for my natural powers!") But the Doctor decides they should create a Soviet republic in the British Empire; agreeing, Epifania counters that in order to start the necessary repopulation of the empire, they must marry.

Cymbeline Refinished (1937). Comedy that supplies an alternative ending for Shakespeare's play, eliminating the Queen's death and confession, Posthumus's allegorical dream, and Cymbeline's identification of Guiderius by a birthmark. In this version, Imogen, reunited with Posthumus, is annoyed that he tried to have her killed; and neither of Cymbeline's long-lost sons wants to be king.

Geneva (1938). Fantasy on political themes. At the Geneva office of the International Committee for Intellectual Cooperation of the League of Nations, several com-

Scene from the first New York production of *Too True to Be Good,* with (l. to r.) Hugh Sinclair, Beatrice Lillie, Ernest Cossart, Hope Williams, and Leo G. Carroll. Guild Theatre, 1932. [Photograph by Vandamm. Theatre Collection, The New York Public Library at Lincoln Center, Astor, Lenox and Tilden Foundations]

plaints are made, one by a Jew who has been robbed and driven from his country. Begonia Brown, the Committee's secretary, writes letters to the International Court of Justice in The Hague, calling on it to take action. As a result of the complaints, three dictators—Signore Bombardone (Mussolini), the Battler (Hitler), and General Flanco de Fortinbras (Franco)—are summoned to the Court to answer for their actions. During the hearings Battler's troops invade Ruritania, but Bombardone and Flanco refuse to support him. Sir Orpheus Midlander, British Foreign Secretary, declares that England will fight him. After astronomers report that the orbit of the earth is jumping to its next quantum and it is expected that icecaps will cover the earth, the report is revealed to be inaccurate. The hearings, having exposed the three dictators to the court of world opinion, come to an end.

"In Good King Charles's Golden Days" (1939). Comedy about an imaginary meeting between Charles II of England; Isaac Newton; George Fox, founder of the Society of Friends (commonly called Quakers); Sir Godfrey Kneller, the portrait painter; Charles's brother James; three of Charles's mistresses, Nell Gwyn, Lady Castlemaine, and Mrs. Carwell; and Charles's Queen, Catherine of Braganza. Their conversations display opposing points of view on art, science, and religion. Also discussed are the matters of the organized church and per-

sonal revelation, government by force versus government by personal power and government by vested authority, the diminution of rule by vested authority, marital relations, the continual outmoding of science by its own discoveries, and attitudes toward women and the stage.

Buoyant Billions (1948). Comedy in which Junius Smith, son of wealthy upperclass parents, announces to his father that he intends to become a World Betterer. His father agrees to send him to Panama, where Junius meets the remarkable Clementina Buoyant. She, having escaped the commonplaces of civilization, spends her time charming snakes and alligators by playing a soprano saxophone. Junius promptly falls in love and pursues her to England, to the home of her billionaire father Bill Buoyant. Junius declares his love for her money. Her father, impressed by this straightforwardness, advises Clementina to accept, which she does, much to Junius's surprise.

Farfetched Fables (1950). Comedy consisting of six fables. The first fable begins with an announcement that the atomic bomb has been outlawed. In the second, the invention of a poison gas lighter than air makes war once again possible. Following this, the small surviving population is divided according to intellectual spheres, people learn to live on air, and individuals are reproduced in laboratories. The final fable shows a class of the future in which children learn by asking questions of the teacher.

Why She Would Not (wr. 1950). Unfinished comedietta in which Henry Bossborn rescues Serafina White from a robber and her father gives him a job in his factory. Two years later Bossborn controls the factory. He asks Serafina to marry him, but she refuses, presumably because he always gets his own way and would ruin her life.

PLAYS

The Royal Court Theatre, cited below, is frequently referred to as the Court Theatre.

1. *Passion Play*. Play, 2 acts; verse. Written 1878.

2. *Un Petit Drame*. Skit, 1 act. Written 1884. Published 1959.

3. *Widowers' Houses*. Original didactic realistic play. Written 1885–1892. Published 1893, 1898. Produced London, Royalty Theatre, Dec. 9, 1892.

4. *The Philanderer*. Topical comedy of the early 1890s, 4 acts. Written 1893. Published 1898. Produced London, Cripplegate Institute, Feb. 20, 1905; Court Theatre, Feb. 5, 1907.

5. *Mrs. Warren's Profession*. 4 acts. Written 1893. Published 1898. Produced London, New Lyric Club, Jan. 5, 1902.

6. *Arms and the Man*. Romantic comedy, 3 acts. Written 1894. Published 1898. Produced London, Avenue Theatre, Apr. 21, 1894.

7. *Candida*. Mystery (this subtitle was subsequently removed by Shaw), 3 acts. Written 1895. Published 1898. Produced Aberdeen, Her Majesty's Theatre, July 30, 1897; London, Strand Theatre, July 1, 1900.

8. *The Man of Destiny*. Trifle, 1 act. Written 1895. Published 1898. Produced Croydon, Grand Theatre, July 1, 1897; London, Comedy Theatre, Mar. 29, 1901.

9. *You Never Can Tell*. Pleasant play, 4 acts. Written 1896. Published 1898. Produced London, Royalty Theatre, Nov. 26, 1899; Strand Theatre, June 4, 1907.

10. *The Devil's Disciple*. Melodrama, 3 acts. Written 1897. Published 1901. Produced Bayswater, Bijou Theatre, Apr. 17, 1897; Albany, N. Y., Hermanus Bleecker Hall, Oct. 1, 1897; Kennington, Princess of Wales's Theatre, Sept. 26, 1899.

11. *The Gadfly: or The Son of the Cardinal*. Play. Produced Bayswater, Bijou Theatre, Mar. 31, 1898.

12. *Caesar and Cleopatra*. History, 4 acts. Written 1898. Published 1901. Produced Berlin, Mar. 31, 1906 (in German); New York, New Amsterdam Theatre, Oct. 30, 1906; Leeds, Grand Theatre, Sept. 16, 1907.

13. *Captain Brassbound's Conversion*. Adventure, 3 acts. Written 1899. Published 1901. Produced London, Strand Theatre, Dec. 16, 1900.

14. *The Admirable Bashville, or Constancy Unrewarded*. Play, 3 acts; verse. Written 1901. Published 1909. Produced London, Imperial Theatre, June 7, 1903. Based on Shaw's novel *Cashel Byron's Profession*.

15. *Man and Superman*. A comedy and a philosophy, 4 acts (usually produced without Act III, which is presented separately as *Don Juan in Hell*). Written 1903. Published 1903. Produced London, Court Theatre, May 23, 1905.

16. *Don Juan in Hell*. Act III of *Man and Superman*, usually produced separately. Written 1903. Published 1903. Produced London, Royal Court Theatre, Jan. 4, 1907.

17. *John Bull's Other Island*. Play, 4 acts. Written 1904. Published 1907. Produced London, Royal Court Theatre, Nov. 1, 1904.

18. *How He Lied to Her Husband*. Play, 1 act. Written 1904. Published 1907. Produced New York, Berkeley Lyceum, Sept. 26, 1904; London, Royal Court Theatre, Feb. 28, 1905.

19. *Major Barbara*. Play, 3 acts. Written 1905. Published 1907. Produced London, Royal Court Theatre, Nov. 28, 1905.

20. *Passion, Poison, and Petrifaction; or The Fatal Gazogene*. Brief tragedy for barns and booths, 1 act. Written 1905. Published 1905. Produced London, Regent's Park, July 15, 1905.

21. *The Doctor's Dilemma*. Tragedy, 4 acts and epilogue. Written 1906. Published 1911. Produced London, Royal Court Theatre, Nov. 20, 1906.

22. *The Interlude at the Playhouse*. Playlet, 1 scene. Written 1907. Published 1907. Produced London, Playhouse, Jan. 28, 1907.

23. *Getting Married*. Disquisitory play, 1 long act. Written 1908. Published 1911. Produced London, Haymarket Theatre, May 12, 1908.

24. *The Shewing-Up of Blanco Posnet*. Sermon in crude melodrama, 1 act. Written 1909. Published 1911. Produced Dublin, Abbey Theatre, Aug. 25, 1909; London, Aldwych Theatre, Dec. 5, 1909.

25. *Press Cuttings*. Topical sketch compiled from the editorial and correspondence columns of the daily press during the woman's war in 1909, 1 long act. Written 1909. Published 1909. Produced London, Royal Court Theatre, July 9, 1909.

26. *Fascinating Foundling*. Disgrace to the author, 1 act. Written 1909. Published 1926. Produced London, Arts Theatre Club, Jan. 28, 1928.

27. *The Glimpse of Reality*. Tragedietta, 1 act. Written 1909. Published 1926. Produced Glasgow, Fellowship Hall, Oct. 8, 1927; London, Arts Theatre Club, Nov. 20, 1927.

28. *Misalliance*. Debate in one sitting (no act divisions). Written 1910. Published 1914. Produced London, Duke of York's Theatre, Feb. 23, 1910.

29. *The Dark Lady of the Sonnets*. Interlude, 1 act. Written 1910. Published 1914. Produced London, Haymarket Theatre, Nov. 24, 1910.

30. *Fanny's First Play*. Easy play for a little theatre; introduction, 3 acts, and epilogue. Written 1911. Published 1914. Produced London, Little Theatre, Apr. 19, 1911.

31. *Androcles and the Lion*. Fable play, prologue and 2 acts. Written 1912. Published 1916. Produced Berlin, 1912 (in German); London, St. James's Theatre, Sept. 1, 1913.

32. *Overruled*. Demonstration, 1 act. Written 1912. Published 1916. Produced London, Duke of York's Theatre, Oct. 14, 1912.

33. *Beauty's Duty*. Playlet, 1 scene. Written 1913. Published 1932.

34. *Pygmalion*. Romance, 5 acts. Written 1912/13. Published 1914, 1916. Produced Vienna, Hofburgtheater, Oct. 16, 1913 (in German); London, His Majesty's Theatre, April 11, 1914.

35. *Great Catherine (Whom Glory Still Adores)*. A thumbnail sketch of Russian court life during the eighteenth century, 4 scenes. Written 1913. Published 1919. Produced London, Vaudeville Theatre, Nov. 18, 1913.

36. *The Music Cure*. Piece of utter nonsense, 1 act. Written 1913. Published 1926. Produced London, Little Theatre, Jan. 28, 1914.

37. *O'Flaherty V.C.* A recruiting pamphlet, reminiscence of 1915. Written 1915. Published 1919. Produced Belgium, on the western front, Feb. 17, 1917; New York, Thirty-ninth Street Theatre, June 21, 1920.

38. *The Inca of Perusalem*. An almost historical comedietta, prologue and 1 act. Written 1916. Published 1919. Produced Birmingham Repertory Theatre, Oct. 7, 1916.

39. *Augustus Does His Bit*. A true-to-life farce, unofficial dramatic tract on war saving and cognate topics; 1 act. Written 1916. Published 1919. Produced London, Royal Court Theatre, Jan. 21, 1917.

40. *Macbeth Skit*. Play. Written 1916. Published *Educational Theatre Journal*, 1967, with introduction by B. F. Dukore.

41. *Annajanska, the Bolshevik Empress*. Revolutionary romancelet, 1 act. Written 1917. Published 1919. Produced London, Coliseum, Jan. 21, 1918.

42. *Heartbreak House*. Fantasia in the Russian manner on English themes, 3 acts. Written 1913/19. Published 1919. Produced New York, Garrick Theatre, Nov. 10, 1920; London, Royal Court Theatre, Oct. 18, 1921.

43. *Back to Methuselah*. Metabiological pentateuch, 5 parts (I: *In the Beginning*; II: *The Gospel of the Brothers Barnabas*; III: *The Thing Happens*; IV: *Tragedy of an Elderly Gentleman*; V: *As Far as Thought Can Reach*). Written 1918/20. Published 1921. Produced New York, Garrick Theatre, Feb. 27, 1922; Birmingham Repertory Theatre, Oct. 9, 1923; London, Royal Court Theatre, Feb. 18, 1924.

44. *A Glimpse of the Domesticity of Franklin Barnabas*. Play, written as Act II of *Back to Methuselah*. Written 1920. Published 1932. Produced New York, 1960.

45. *Jitta's Atonement*. Play, 3 acts. Written 1922. Published 1926. Produced Washington, Shubert-Garrick Theatre, Jan. 8, 1923; London, Grand Theatre, Jan. 26, 1925. Translation of Siegfried Trebitsch's *Frau Gittas Sühne*.

46. *Saint Joan*. Chronicle play, 6 scenes and epilogue. Written 1923. Published 1924. Produced New York, Garrick Theatre, Dec. 28, 1923; London, New Theatre, Mar. 26, 1924.

47. *The Apple Cart*. Political extravaganza, 3 acts. Written 1929. Published 1930. Produced Warsaw, Teatr Polski, June 14, 1929 (in Polish); Malvern Festival Theatre, Aug. 19, 1929.

48. *Too True to Be Good*. Political extravaganza, 3 acts. Written 1931. Produced Boston, Colonial Theatre, Feb. 29, 1932, New York, Guild Theatre, Apr. 4, 1932; Malvern, Festival Theatre, Aug. 6, 1932; London, New Theatre, Sept. 13, 1932.

49. *How These Doctors Love One Another!* Playlet, 1 scene. Written 1931. Published 1932.

50. *Village Wooing*. Comedietta for two voices, 3 conversations. Written 1933. Produced Dallas, Little Theatre Company, Apr. 16, 1934; Tunbridge Wells Repertory Players, May 1, 1934.

51. *On the Rocks*. Political comedy, 2 acts. Written 1933. Produced London, Winter Garden Theatre, Nov. 25, 1933.

52. *The Simpleton of the Unexpected Isles*. Vision of judgment, prologue and 2 acts. Written 1934. Produced New York, Guild Theatre, Feb. 18, 1935; Malvern, Festival Theatre, July 29, 1935.

53. *The Six of Calais.* Medieval war story, 1 act. Written 1934. Produced London, Regent's Park Open-air Theatre, July 17, 1934.

54. *The Millionairess.* Jonsonian comedy, 4 acts. Written 1935. Produced Vienna, Akademietheater, Jan. 4, 1936 (in German); Melbourne, King's Theatre, Mar. 7, 1936; Bexhill, De La Warre Pavilion, Nov. 17, 1936.

55. *Arthur and the Acetone.* Playlet, 3 acts. Written 1936. Published 1936.

56. *Cymbeline Refinished.* Variation on Shakespeare's Act V ending, 1 act; verse. Written 1937. Published 1938. Produced Swiss Cottage, London, Embassy Theatre, Nov. 16, 1937.

57. *Geneva.* Fancied page of history (another political extravaganza), 4 acts. Written 1938. Produced Malvern, Festival Theatre, Aug. 1, 1938; London, Saville Theatre, Nov. 22, 1938.

58. *"In Good King Charles's Golden Days."* History lesson (a true history that never happened), 2 acts. Written 1939. Produced Malvern, Festival Theatre, Aug. 12, 1939; London, Streatham Hill Theatre, Apr. 15, 1940.

59. *The British Party System.* Playlet, 1 scene. Written 1944.

60. *Buoyant Billions.* Comedy of no manners, 4 acts. Published 1947. Produced Zurich, Schauspielhaus, Oct. 21, 1948, under the title *Zu viel Geld (Too Much Money)*; Malvern, Festival Theatre, Aug. 13, 1949.

61. *Farfetched Fables.* Six fables. Written 1948. Published 1949. Produced London, Watergate Theatre, Sept. 6, 1950; Newcastle, People's Theatre, Jan. 13, 1951.

62. *Shakes versus Shav.* Puppet play, 1 scene; verse. Written 1949. Produced Malvern.

63. *Why She Would Not.* Incomplete comedietta, 5 scenes. Written 1950.

EDITIONS

Collections

Saint Joan, Major Barbara, and Androcles and the Lion, New York, 1956; *Selected Plays and Other Writings,* ed. by W. Irvine, New York, 1956; *Four Plays by Shaw,* New York, 1957; *Seven One-act Plays,* Baltimore, 1958; *Plays,* New York, 1960; *The Shorter Plays of Bernard Shaw,* New York, 1960; *Ten Short Plays,* New York, 1960; *Plays Unpleasant,* Baltimore, 1961; *The Theatre of Bernard Shaw,* ed. by A. S. Downer, 2 vols., New York, 1961; *Four Plays by Bernard Shaw,* New York, 1965; *Selected One-act Plays,* 2 vols., Baltimore, 1965; *Pygmalion, and Other Plays,* New York, 1967.

Individual Plays

Androcles and the Lion. Published in *Cavalcade of Comedy,* New York, 1953.

Arms and the Man. Published in *Eight Great Comedies,* ed. by S. Barnet et al., New York, 1958.

Caesar and Cleopatra. Published in *Modern Drama,* ed. by E. J. Lovell and W. W. Pratt, Boston, 1963.

Candida. Published in *Studies in Drama,* ed. by B. O. Bonazza and E. Roy, New York, 1963.

The Devil's Disciple. Published in *Contemporary Drama,* ed. by S. A. Clayes and D. G. Spencer, New York, 1962.

The Doctor's Dilemma. Published in *Representative Modern Plays, British,* ed. by R. Warnock, Chicago, 1953.

Don Juan in Hell. Published in *From Beowulf to Modern British Writers,* ed. by J. Ball, New York, 1959.

Getting Married. Published in *Makers of the Modern Theater,* ed. by B. Ulanov, New York, 1961.

John Bull's Other Island. Published in *The Genius of the Irish Theater,* ed. by S. Barnet et al., New York, 1960.

Major Barbara. Published in *Masters of Modern Drama,* ed. by H. M. Block and R. G. Shedd, New York, 1962.

Man and Superman. Published in *Introduction to Drama,* ed. by R. C. Roby and B. Ulanov, New York, 1962.

The Man of Destiny. Published in *Comedy,* ed. by M. Felheim, New York, 1962.

Mrs. Warren's Profession. Published in *Six Great Modern Plays,* New York, 1956.

Pygmalion. Published in *Nine Great Plays, from Aeschylus to Eliot,* ed. by L. F. Dean, rev. ed., New York, 1956.

Saint Joan. Published in *The Theatre Guild Anthology,* New York, 1936.

The Shewing-Up of Blanco Posnet. Published in *An Introduction to Literature,* ed. by S. Barnet et al., Boston, 1961.

The Six of Calais. Published in *Drama: The Modern Genres,* ed. by R. G. Hogan and S. E. Molin, New York, 1962.

CRITICISM

H. Jackson, *Bernard Shaw,* London, 1907; A. Henderson, *George Bernard Shaw: His Life and Works,* London, 1911; C. F. Armstrong, *Shakespeare to Shaw,* London, 1913; J. L. Palmer, *George Bernard Shaw: Harlequin or Patriot?,* New York, 1915; R. Burton, *Bernard Shaw: The Man and the Mask,* New York, 1916; A. F. Hamon, *The Twentieth Century Molière: Bernard Shaw,* tr. by E. and C. Paul, New York, 1916; H. Skinpole, *Bernard Shaw: The Man and His Work,* London, 1918; J. G. Huneker, *Iconoclasts,* New York, 1919; H. C. Duffin, *The Quintessence of Bernard Shaw,* London, 1920; G. Norwood, *Euripides and Shaw, with Other Essays,* Boston and London, 1921; E. B. Shanks, *Bernard Shaw,* London, 1924; J. S. Collis, *Shaw,* New York, 1925; C. L. Broad and V. M. Broad, *Dictionary to the Plays and Novels of Bernard Shaw,* London, 1929; E. C. Wagenknecht, *A Guide to Bernard Shaw,* New York, 1929; M. Ellehauge, *The Position of Bernard Shaw in European Drama and Philosophy,* Copenhagen, 1931; F. Harris, *Bernard Shaw,* New York, 1931; A. Henderson, *Bernard Shaw, Playboy and Prophet,* London, 1932; R. F. Rattray, *Bernard Shaw: A Chronicle and an Introduction,* London, 1934; S. C. Sen Gupta, *The Art of Bernard Shaw,* London, 1936; J. P. Hackett, *Shaw: George versus Bernard,* New York, 1937; R. H. Sherard, *Bernard Shaw, Frank Harris & Oscar Wilde,* New York, 1937; E. Strauss, *Bernard Shaw: Art and Socialism,* London, 1942; J. M. Brown, *Seeing Things,* New York, 1946; S. Winsten, ed., *G.B.S. 90: Aspects of Bernard Shaw's Life and Work,* London, 1946; W. Clarke, *George Bernard Shaw: An Appreciation and Interpretation,* Altrincham, England, 1948; E. Wilson, *The Triple Thinkers,* rev. and enl. ed., New York 1948; M. D. Colbourne, *The Real Bernard Shaw,* London, 1949; C. E. M. Joad, *Shaw,* London, 1949; A. M. Laing, ed., *In Praise of Bernard Shaw,* London, 1949; S. Winsten, *Days with Bernard Shaw,* New York, 1949; E. Fuller, *George Bernard Shaw,* New York, 1950; A. West, *"A Good Man Fallen among Fabians,"* London, 1950; D. MacCarthy, *Shaw,* London, 1951; A. C. Ward, *Bernard Shaw,* London, 1951; S. Winsten, *Shaw's Corner,* London, 1952; I. J.C. Brown, *Shaw in His Time,* London, 1955; G. K. Chesterton, *George Bernard Shaw,* New York, 1956; St. J. G. Ervine, *Bernard Shaw: His Life, Work, and Friends,* London and New York, 1956; A. Henderson, *George Bernard Shaw: Man of the Century,* Washington, 1957; L. Kronenberger, ed., *George Bernard Shaw: A Critical Survey,* Cleveland, 1957; J. B. Kaye, *Bernard Shaw and the Nineteenth-century Tradition,* Norman, Okla., 1958; P. Kozelka, *A Glossary to the Plays of Bernard Shaw,* New York, 1959; A. Chappelow, ed., *Shaw the Villager and Human Being: A Biographical Symposium,* New York, 1962; R. M. Ohmann, *Shaw: The Style and the Man,* Middletown, Conn., 1962; M. Shenfield, *George Bernard Shaw: A Pictorial Biography,* London, 1962; S. S. Stanton, ed., *A Casebook on Candida,* New York, 1962; C. G. L. Du Cann, *The Loves of George Bernard Shaw,* New York, 1963; L. Langner, *G. B. S. and the Lunatic,* New York, 1963; M. Meisel, *Shaw and the Nineteenth-century Theater,* Princeton, N. J., 1963; H. Pearson, *George Bernard Shaw: His Life and Personality,* New York, 1963; C. B. Purdom, *A Guide to the Plays of Bernard Shaw,* New York, 1963; S. Weintraub, *Private Shaw and Public Shaw: A Dual Portrait of Lawrence of Arabia and G. B. S.,* New York, 1963; A. Williamson, *Bernard Shaw: Man and Writer,* New York, 1963; H. E. Woodbridge, *George Bernard Shaw: Creative Artist,* Carbondale, Ill., 1963; B. C. Rosset, *Shaw of Dublin: The Formative Years,* University Park, Pa., 1964; B. B. Watson, *A Shavian Guide to the Intelligent Woman,* New York, 1964; D. P. Costello, *The Serpent's Eye,* Notre Dame, Ind., 1965; R. J. Kaufmann, ed., *G. B. Shaw: A Collection of Critical Essays,* Englewood Cliffs, N.J., 1965; G. A. Pilecki, *Shaw's Geneva,* The Hague, 1965; J. P. Smith, *The Unrepentant Pilgrim: A Study of the Development of Bernard Shaw,* Boston, 1965; A. H. Nethercot, *Men and Supermen: The Shavian Portrait Gallery,* 2d ed., New York, 1966; J. O'Donovan, *Shaw and the Charlatan Genius,* Chester Springs, Pa., 1966; E. R. Bentley, *Bernard Shaw,* 2d British ed., London, 1967; H. Fromm, *Bernard Shaw and the Theater in the Nineties,* Lawrence, Kans., 1967; F. Mayne, *The Wit and Satire of Bernard Shaw,* London, 1967; O. E. Coolidge, *George Bernard Shaw,* Boston, 1968; B. F. Dukore, ed., *Saint Joan: A Screenplay by Bernard Shaw,* Seattle, 1968; W. Irvine, *The Universe of G. B. S.,* New York, 1968; C. A. Carpenter, *Bernard Shaw & the Art of Destroying Ideals: The Early Plays,* Madison, Wis., 1969; A. Chappelow, *Shaw, "the Chucker-out,"* London, 1969; L. Crompton, *Shaw the Dramatist,* Lincoln, Nebr., 1969; L. Crompton, *Shaw the Dramatist,* Lincoln, Nebr., 1969; J. A. Mills, *Language and Laughter: Comic Diction in the Plays of George Bernard Shaw,* Tucson, 1969; B. F. Dukore, *Bernard Shaw, Director,* Seattle, 1970; R. Zimbardo, ed., *Twentieth Century Interpretations of Major Barbara,* New York, 1970; B. F. Dukore, *Bernard Shaw, Director,* London, 1971.

Shaw, Irwin (1913–)

American novelist, screenwriter, and playwright. His social and humanitarian commitment has resulted in consistently powerful works. Shaw's one-act drama-fantasy, *Bury the Dead* (1936), is a poignant and haunting denunciation of war in which the fallen soldiers of all nations refuse to be buried despite the pleading of their loved ones. *Siege* (1937), set during the Spanish Civil War, deals with the conversion of a pacifist to militancy. *The Gentle People* (1939) demonstrates how otherwise peaceful

Scene from *Bury the Dead*. New York, Ethel Barrymore Theatre, 1936. [Theatre Collection, The New York Public Library at Lincoln Center, Astor, Lenox and Tilden Foundations]

Sam Jaffe (left), Sylvia Sidney, and Elia Kazan in *The Gentle People*. New York, Belasco Theatre, 1939. [Theatre Collection, The New York Public Library at Lincoln Center]

men take matters into their own hands when it becomes necessary: two fishermen, beset by a ruthless extortionist, lure him into a boat and throw him overboard. Among other plays by Shaw are *Quiet City* (1939), *Sons and Soldiers* (1944), *The Assassin* (1945), *The Survivors* (1948, with Peter Viertel), and *Children from their Games* (1963). *Patate* (1958) was an adaptation of a comedy by the popular French playwright Marcel Achard.

[GAUTAM DASGUPTA]

Sheldon, Edward Brewster (1886–1946)

American playwright. He was one of the first graduates of George Pierce Baker's 47 Workshop at Harvard University. Earlier, as a student at Harvard, Sheldon had organized the Harvard Drama Club. His first success, which came when he was only twenty-two, was *Salvation Nell* (1908), a sentimental and emotional story of low life in the big city with undertones of stark realism. Nell, a barmaid and fallen woman, achieves moral and spiritual purity through the Salvation Army. *Salvation Nell* established Sheldon's reputation as a realist. The next year, his *The Nigger* (1909), which deals with a racist governor of a Southern state who discovers that he has Negro blood, caused a controversy. The moral courage and newfound tolerance of the governor are matched by his fiancée, a white Southern girl. *The Boss* (1911) is a drama about machine politics with the then-novel thesis that a seemingly hopeless marriage can be made to work. *See* BAKER, GEORGE PIERCE.

Sheldon's most popular play was *Romance* (1913), in which a young clergyman tells his grandfather that he wants to marry an actress. The grandfather tries to dissuade him by relating a similar situation in his own life, but the young man stands firm and the grandfather acquiesces. *Romance* was one of the first plays to use flashbacks, and most of the action takes place in the past. Because of a paralyzing illness, Sheldon wrote most of his later plays in collaboration, including the romance *Bewitched* (1924) with Sidney Howard, the racial melodrama *Lulu Belle* (1926) with Charles MacArthur, and

Edward Brewster Sheldon. [New York Public Library]

Dishonored Lady (1930) with Margaret Ayer Barnes. He also collaborated with her on the completion of *The Age of Innocence* (1928), based on Edith Wharton's novel. Other plays include such romances as *The Princess Zim-Zim* (1911), *The High Road* (1912), and *The Garden of Paradise* (1914), an adaptation of H. C. Andersen's story "The Little Mermaid." *See* HOWARD, SIDNEY; MACARTHUR, CHARLES.

The Boss (1911). Social drama in four acts, set in a port city such as Buffalo. "Shindy Mike" Regan has swindled and intimidated the workers of his district, the Fourth Ward, gained control of grain contracts, and forced the collapse of the socially prominent Griswolds, who head a competing firm. He offers them a merger on condition that Emily Griswold marry him. Mr. Griswold refuses the offer, but Emily agrees to a marriage in name only, realizing that the Griswolds' collapse will also cause the collapse of the Fourth Ward's workers, for whom she has been doing charitable work. Emily's brother, seeking revenge, unionizes the workers; they now demand a minimum wage, a ten-hour day, and the right to spend their pay in their own bar rather than in Regan's. Regan retaliates by bringing in strikebreakers and destroying the competing bar. When Emily's brother is assaulted during a Fourth Ward speech, Regan is accused of the attack and arrested. His growing love for Emily humanizes him, however, and he deeds her all the mortgages of the Fourth Ward, thus making her its boss. When his henchman confesses to the assault on Emily's brother and the latter is out of danger, Regan offers to free Emily of their marriage. But his reformation has won her love. Produced Detroit, Garrick Theatre, January 9, 1911.

[GAUTAM DASGUPTA]

Shelley, Percy Bysshe   (1792–1822)

English poet and dramatist. He was one of the leading figures of the Romantic movement. Although his genius was predominantly lyrical and although he had little interest in the stage, he succeeded in writing *The Cenci* (pub. 1819, prod. 1886), which despite its manifest faults is one of the most impressive poetic dramas of the time. His other works are dramatic poems. *Prometheus Unbound* (pub. 1820) is an almost mystical statement of the Romantic theme of revolt and freedom, couched in the classical Promethean myth. *Hellas* (1822), another lyrical drama, deals with a confrontation between tyrant and revolutionary, who find redemption from their continual conflict in metaphysics and idealism. Of lesser importance is the burlesque *Oedipus Tyrannus, or Swellfoot the Tyrant* (pub. 1820).

The Cenci (1819). Tragedy based on the crimes of Count Francesco Cenci, a sixteenth-century Roman nobleman. Cenci, a monstrous and brutal man, takes pleasure in seeing people suffer. His daughter Beatrice, whom he has treated cruelly, has sent a petition to the Pope through her former fiancé, Count Orsini, begging for relief from the punishment dealt by her father. Meanwhile, Cenci arranges a banquet in celebration of the death of two of his sons. Beatrice, her petition undelivered, begs the guests to protect her, her stepmother, and her remaining two brothers from the cruelty of her father. But Cenci tells them she is insane, and they depart, leaving him to threaten his daughter with rape.

William Courtenary and Doris Keane in *Romance*.
[Private collection]

Percy Bysshe Shelley. [New York Public Library Picture Collection]

This crime having been committed, Beatrice is now willing to join her brothers, her stepmother, and Orsini in a plot to assassinate her father. The first plan fails, but finally they devise one which they carry through. Afterwards they are convicted of his murder and sentenced to death.

Shen Jing (1553–1610)

Chinese playwright. Born in Wujiang in present Jiangsu province, Shen Jing was a brilliant child. He obtained his doctorate (*jinshi*) in 1574 at an unusually early age. His was a rich, well-established mandarin family, and he himself embarked upon a career in government. After holding moderately responsible posts in central government organs, he was demoted in 1586 for objecting to the promotion of an imperial consort. Two years later he was made an assistant provincial examiner for the Peking region, but soon retired and at thirty-six years of age withdrew to live in rural reclusion and to devote himself to song and playwrighting. He and a fellow villager, Gu Dadian (fl. 1568), both kept musical entertainers, and he spent much of his time directing actors in performances of plays. A number of late Ming dramatists who followed his principles of playwrighting and his approach to song composition are termed the Wujiang school of playwrights. *See* CHINESE THEATRE.

Shen wrote seventeen *chuanqi* plays, all initially performed in his private theatre. Seven plays and song fragments of two others survive. He also wrote adaptations of Tang Xianzu's *Purple Hairpin* and *Peony Pavilion*, though neither of his versions has survived. Of his own plays only *Brigand Knight of Honor (Yi-xia ji)* gained lasting popularity. He did, however, have a great deal of influence on theatre through his works on play songs and prosody, one of which has remained a major standard for southern songs in the *qu* genre. He was a critic of the playwright Tang Xianzu and in many ways diametrically opposed to him, particularly as regards theatrical music. Whereas Tang was free and innovatory, Shen was an adherent par excellence of the traditional rule. A contemporary summed up the contrast as follows: "Tang Xianzu approaches eccentricity, and Shen approaches timid reticence. Could Shen's try square and ruler but be wielded with Tang's genius, what a union of two perfections that would be!" *See* TANG XIANZU.

WILLIAM DOLBY

Shepard, Sam (1943–)

American playwright. He is often considered the most original and important voice to grow through the Off Off Broadway theatre movement of the late 1960s and the 1970s. Employing such contemporary American mythology as rock-and-roll stars, science fiction monsters, cowboys, and movie stars, Shepard creates freewheeling comedies and disturbing dramas in which myth and reality clash. Between 1966 and 1979 Shepard accumulated an unprecedented ten Obie Awards for Distinguished Drama, and, additionally, a 1980 Obie for Sustained Achievement. His *Buried Child* (1979) won the Pulitzer Prize for drama.

Raised on a California farm, Shepard initially studied agriculture at San Antonio Junior College. After a brief tour with a small repertory company, he came to New York in 1963 as an actor. To his earlier careers as a stablehand, sheep shearer, and orange picker, Shepard added busboy, waiter, musician, and, increasingly, writer. His one-act plays *Cowboys* and *Rock Garden* were produced at Theatre Genesis at St. Marks in the Bouwerie Church on October 16, 1964. By February, 1965, Shepard plays were included in an Off Broadway New Playwrights Series at the Cherry Lane Theatre. Little more than a year later *Chicago, Icarus' Mother,* and *Red Cross* had been produced, each winning Shepard an Obie Award for Off Broadway Drama. Shepard was produced by the noted La Mama Theatre and in other Off Off Broadway situations, but his bizarre comedy, *La Turista,* produced in New York in 1967 and in London two years later, provided wider audiences with their first taste of Shepard. His attempts to retain and enlarge this audience can be seen in his screenplay for Michelangelo Antonioni's first American film, *Zabriskie Point* (1968), and his sprawling rock-and-roll play *Operation Sidewinder* (1970), which was produced by the "establishment" Repertory Theatre of Lincoln Center. But the screenplay for the film was largely unused, and the play, an apocalyptic vision of a secret military project in the American west, was a failure. Despite the New York success of *Mad Dog Blues* (1971)—perhaps most representative of his early work—Shepard moved to England, living in Hampstead with his wife for four years. There he wrote several plays that were successes on both sides of the Atlantic. *The Tooth of Crime* (1972) shows the confrontation of two rock stars—an up-and-coming performer and another past his peak—in terms of a verbal shootout between two gunslinging outlaws. *Geography of a Horse Dreamer* (1974) is a fable about a cowboy who is able to dream the winners of horse races but who finds his talents disappearing when gangsters try to exploit them. The debasing of creativity is also the theme of Shepard's 1976 musical mystery play, *Suicide in B-Flat,* and his comedy about Hollywood screenwriting, *Angel City* (1976). The following year Shepard created his satiric tragedy, *Curse of the Starving Class,* in which a starved, disintegrating family ultimately consumes itself. *True West* (1980) focuses on the competitive power play between brothers who constantly challenge each other as they attempt to collaborate on a screenplay. Shepard has occasionally acted in films, appearing as the doomed farmer in Terence Malick's *Days of Heaven* (1978) and with Ellen Burstyn and Eva Le Gallienne in *Resurrection* (1980).

The Mad Dog Blues (1971). Kosmo and his sidekick Yahoodi are having visions: of music and drugs, of power and wealth. Marlene Dietrich vamps Yahoodi while Kosmo is seduced by Mae West. Yahoodi's appetite for riches is whetted by Captain Kidd, who suggests that Yahoodi and Marlene help him recover his treasure. Mae West convinces Kosmo to tail his friend and steal the treasure. They set off in pursuit, accompanied by a burned-out cowboy named Waco. The two groups sail across the sea, travel through the jungle, and subdue the

The 1979 production of *Buried Child,* with Richard Hamilton (left).
[Martha Swope]

island natives. Marlene Dietrich wrestles with the Ghost Girl of the treasure, who later falls in love with Waco (Marlene having fallen in love with Paul Bunyan). Ya-hoodi claims the treasure after shooting Captain Kidd, only to have Kosmo steal it from him. However, the treasure is then stolen from Kosmo by Mae West and Jesse James, who later discover the sacks contain only bottle caps. The entire cast joins in singing the final song. Produced New York, Theatre Genesis, March 4, 1971.

The Tooth of Crime (1972). Hoss, a rock-and-roll outlaw, is warned by his chart reader Star Man that this is a dangerous time for him to go for the gold (record). But Hoss feels nervous about his supremacy and desperately wants to score a hit. He fears that someday soon some young punk will ride up the charts (with a bullet), looking to take Hoss out. Hoss confronts his worst fears in Crow, a dark dude who speaks in a violent, unfamiliar language. Crow takes Hoss out in three rounds, but Hoss makes his final statement of his own supremacy: he shoots himself through the mouth. Crow takes over Hoss's territory—for the moment. Produced New York, Performing Garage, March 7, 1973.

Buried Child (1978). Vince arrives unannounced at the Illinois farmhouse of his grandparents Dodge and Halie after six years of separation from his family. He has brought his girl friend Shelly to meet them. But his family proves to be a bizarre group of strangers who barely know who he is. In trying to make sense of the situation, Shelly uncovers the secrets of incest and infan-ticide—the murdered child is unearthed—which have destroyed these people. Startled by these unexpected realities, she flees, leaving Vince behind. Produced San Francisco, Magic Theatre, July 27, 1978.

TERRY MILLER

Sheridan, Richard Brinsley (1751–1816)

Anglo-Irish politician, theatrical manager, and dramatist. He was born in Dublin on October 30, 1751, the third son of Thomas Sheridan, an actor, and Frances Sheridan, a dramatist. The family moved to London in 1760, never

Richard Brinsley Sheridan. [Walter Hampden Memorial Library at The Players, New York]

to return to Dublin. After some private tutoring, the boy attended Harrow School from 1762 to 1768. During the next seven years he continued his studies under private instruction, published some translations, wrote a farce, *Jupiter,* and fought two duels in defense of Elizabeth Ann Linley (1754–1792), whom he married in 1773.

With the production of *The Rivals* in 1775 his reputation was assured. Two other plays, *St. Patrick's Day* and *The Duenna,* were produced the same year. In June, 1776, with his father-in-law, the composer Thomas Linley, and a Dr. Ford, he bought Garrick's share of Drury Lane Theatre; they bought the other half two years later. Sheridan was active in the management of the theatre, which was his principal source of income for the rest of his life. He was responsible for its extensive alterations in 1791 and its rebuilding after fire destroyed it in 1809. Meanwhile, he continued to write. *The School for Scandal* appeared in 1777, and *The Critic* two years later.

The second phase of Sheridan's career began in 1780, when, with help from his influential friend Charles James Fox and some judicious bribery, common in that era, he was elected to Parliament as the member for Stafford. From then on he contributed only one more play to the theatre, an adaptation of a play by Kotzebue, his popular German contemporary. *See* KOTZEBUE, AUGUST VON.

As a protégé and staunch supporter of Fox, Sheridan prospered in his political career, and held a number of responsible positions in the government. He was a popular figure in Parliament, noted for his sharp wit, easy humor, and eloquence. Only portions of his greatest speeches, some of which lasted for days, survive, but he is generally recognized as one of the greatest orators at a time when English oratory was at its zenith.

Sheridan served in Parliament until 1812, but after the death of Fox (1806), his influence diminished. His later years were not happy. After the death of his wife in 1792, he incurred heavy gambling debts. These, coupled with the heavy expense of twice rebuilding the Drury Lane Theatre, all but ruined him. After he lost his parliamentary immunity in 1812, his creditors descended upon him, and his last years were grim. He died in London on July 7, 1816, and was interred in Westminster Abbey.

WORK

Sheridan, who produced his last major play at the age of twenty-eight, realized the futility of his efforts to restore a comedy of wit to a theatre engulfed by bourgeois drama. His constant shortage of money led him in his management of the Drury Lane to place emphasis on spectacle and pantomime, playing down to this new audience, which was predominantly middle-class. *See* BOURGEOIS DRAMA in glossary.

By 1760 the secure aristocratic audiences of the Restoration no longer existed. Working against the strong current of middle class moralizing, Sheridan and his notable contemporary Goldsmith tried to reinject drama with wit and humor. (Beaumarchais, a contemporary, waged an analogous and equally unsuccessful struggle against the bourgeois sentimentalism of the French

John Gilbert as Sir Anthony Absolute in *The Rivals.* [Brander Matthews Dramatic Museum, Columbia University]

stage.) *See* BEAUMARCHAIS, PIERRE DE; GOLDSMITH, OLIVER.

Sheridan's first play, *The Rivals* (1775), for all its lively wit, spotlights the distance from the easy libertinism of Restoration dramatists. Because of miscasting, this brilliant play was badly received, but corrections were made, and it soon gained the popularity it deserved. Its success probably prompted Sheridan to try farce for his next venture, an insignificant two-act piece entitled *St. Patrick's Day, or The Scheming Lieutenant* (1775). Within a few months he produced *The Duenna* (1775), a comic opera that demonstrates his versatility in its charming lyrics and sparkling dialogue but contains little else remarkable. In 1777 Sheridan presented an adaptation of Vanbrugh's *The Relapse* as *A Trip to Scarborough.* The same year saw the production of one of the quintessential comic masterworks, *The School for Scandal.* It was followed by another masterpiece, *The Critic, or A Tragedy Rehearsed* (1779), a satire on contemporary tragedy with its burlesque play-within-a-play. Except for a translation of Kotzebue's *Pizarro,* made in 1799, Sheridan quit the English stage, which had to wait almost a century before Shaw and Wilde retrieved the comic spirit. *See* VANBRUGH, JOHN.

The Rivals (1775). Comedy in which the sentimentally romantic Lydia Languish, wanting to marry for love and into poverty, is in love with "Ensign Beverly," who is in fact the aristocratic Captain Jack Absolute. Well un-

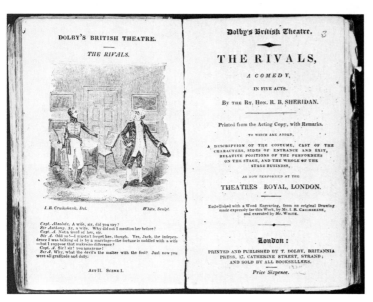

The Rivals, published in *Dolby's British Theatre.* [American Heritage]

derstanding the perversity of her nature, he has wooed her in disguised penury. The two meet and exchange letters despite the watchfulness of Lydia's aunt Mrs. Malaprop, who is determined to marry her to Bob Acres, a dull rural squire. When Jack's father Sir Anthony Absolute arrives, he suggests a match between Jack and Lydia, which makes Mrs. Malaprop immediately drop

Acres. When Sir Anthony tells Jack that he has found a wife for him, Jack, unaware of the lady's identity, objects, and they quarrel. But as soon as Jack learns of his father's choice, he plays the penitent and promises to marry Lydia. He proceeds to charm Mrs. Malaprop, who introduces him to Lydia. So he has to convince her that he is Beverly, passing himself off as Jack Absolute in order to gain access to her aunt's house. Soon Lydia discovers his identity and, offended by the affront to her romantic illusions, rejects him.

Meanwhile, Acres, whose sense of honor has been inflamed by Sir Lucius O'Trigger, a belligerent Irishman, sends a challenge to Beverly through his friend Jack. Sir Lucius, who has been corresponding with his beloved "Delia" (whom he takes to be Lydia but really is Mrs. Malaprop), challenges Jack. Finally, at the dueling place the confusions are resolved; Lydia accepts Jack, Lucius rejects Mrs. Malaprop, and Acres retires in haste from the field. In a subplot Jack's friend Faulkland, a young man who finds in every innocent action of Julia, his steadfast beloved, a reason for doubting her love, is finally united with her.

Mrs. Malaprop's comic abuses of the language have been named "malapropisms": "Sure, if I reprehend any thing in this world it is the use of my oracular tongue and a nice derangement of epitaphs" (III, iii).

The Duenna (1775). Comic opera in three acts, presenting the light and frothy world of a highly Anglicized Seville. Songs and arias course through this charming tale of young love in conflict with parental decrees.

Frances Reid, Mary Boland, and Haila Stoddard (l. to r.) in *The Rivals.* New York, Shubert Theatre, 1942. [Photograph by Vandamm. Theatre Collection, The New York Public Library at Lincoln Center, Astor, Lenox and Tilden Foundations]

John Gielgud (left), Ralph Richardson, and Geraldine McEwan in *The School for Scandal.* New York, Majestic Theatre, 1962. [Culver Pictures]

Donna Louisa is in love with Don Antonio, but her strict and bungling father has promised her to Isaac, a vain and clumsy Portuguese Jew. Changing places with her duenna, a lustful harridan, Donna Louisa not only contrives her own wedding to her beloved but also unites Don Ferdinand, her brother, with his melancholy sweetheart Donna Clara. Masquerades, mistaken identities, and intrigue nearly lead to tragedy, but the outcome is never seriously in doubt. Isaac, greedy for fortune, needs little coaxing to accept the homely duenna as Donna Louisa and discovers too late that he has been duped and tied forever to a formidable vixen.

The School for Scandal (1777). Five-act comedy of intrigue in which Sir Peter Teazle, an aging nobleman, marries a young country girl and brings her to London, where she soon succumbs to extravagance and the sophisticated mores of Lady Sneerwell's malicious clique. Lady Sneerwell, in league with Joseph Surface, begins circulating rumors about Lady Teazle's infidelity with Charles, Joseph's brother, who is likely to receive a considerable fortune from Sir Oliver, their uncle, and who is engaged to Teazle's ward Maria. Joseph has designs on his brother's superior position, while Lady Sneerwell wants Charles's love as well as his impending wealth. Sir Oliver now returns after a long absence to test the characters of his two nephews. Pretending to be a

usurer, he goes to the prodigal Charles, who during an evening's gaiety cheerfully auctions off his ancestral portraits. He refuses to part with Sir Oliver's portrait, however, which touches his uncle, who finds him "exactly like his father." Sir Oliver is further influenced by the discovery that a good part of Charles's money is going to a needy relative.

Meanwhile, Sir Peter, hearing rumors of an affair between his wife and Charles, arrives at Joseph's rooms when he is on the point of seducing Lady Teazle, who quickly retreats behind a screen. Teazle urges Joseph to draw Charles out, discloses his generous financial settlement upon Lady Teazle, and begins a discussion of Joseph's suit for Maria, which had been unknown to her. When a servant announces that Charles has come to pay a visit, Teazle persuades Joseph to "test" his brother while Teazle hides in a closet. Charles's candid protestations of innocence persuade Sir Peter to emerge from hiding and beg his pardon. Joseph, informed by a servant of Lady Sneerwell's approach, dashes out to prevent her arrival and returns to find Lady Teazle discovered. Moved by her husband's generosity, Lady Teazle refuses to support Joseph's lying explanations, tells the truth, and leaves. Joseph completes his ruination by pretending poverty to pleas for aid from a Mr. Stanly, who is really Sir Oliver in disguise. Charles then gains both money and Maria, and Lady Teazle has learned her lesson in Sneerwell's slanderous school.

The Critic, or a Tragedy Rehearsed (1779). Burlesque satirizing the absurdities of eighteenth-century theatre. In the first act, Mr. Dangle, an amateur critic, is visited by Sneer, a shrewd but malicious wit, Sir Fretful Plagiary, a pompous dramatic parasite who solicits but cannot abide criticism, and Puff, who has written a tragedy that is to be rehearsed that morning.

The next two acts show the rehearsal, attended and commented upon by Dangle, Sneer, and author Puff. The tragedy, called *The Spanish Armada*, is about the love of an English girl, Tilburina, for Don Ferolo Whiskerandos, whose death leads her to madness and drowning. This is followed by a dumb show of the naval battle. This brief tragedy ridicules most of the conventions of the would-be poetic drama: the absurd methods of giving information to the audience, the inflated declamations, the mellifluous speeches inappropriately put into the mouths of servants and attendants, the sudden "recognitions" that unexpectedly alter the course of the action, and the contrived mad scenes.

PLAYS

All were first produced in London. Unless otherwise noted, all are in prose.

    1. *The Rivals.* Comedy, 5 acts. Published 1775. Produced Theatre Royal, Covent Garden, Jan. 17, 1775.

    2. *St. Patrick's Day, or The Scheming Lieutenant.* Farce, 2 acts. Published 1788. Produced Theatre Royal, Covent Garden, May 2, 1775.

    3. *The Duenna.* Comic opera, 3 acts. Published 1776. Produced Theatre Royal, Covent Garden, Nov. 21, 1775.

    4. (Adaptation). *A Trip to Scarborough.* Comedy, 5 acts. Published 1781. Produced Theatre Royal, Drury Lane, Feb. 24, 1777. Based on Vanbrugh's *The Relapse.*

    5. *The School for Scandal.* Comedy, 5 acts. Produced Theatre Royal, Drury Lane, May 8, 1777.

    6. *The Camp.* Musical Entertainment. Published 1795. Produced Theatre Royal, Drury Lane, Oct. 15, 1778.

    7. *The Critic, or A Tragedy Rehearsed.* Dramatic piece (burlesque), 3 acts; prose and verse. Published 1781. Produced Theatre Royal, Drury Lane, Oct. 30, 1779.

    8. *The Glorious First of June.* Entertainment. Published 1794. Produced Theatre Royal, Drury Lane, Feb. 7, 1794.

    9. *Cape St. Vincent.* Entertainment. Published 1797. Produced Theatre Royal, Drury Lane, March 1797.

    10. (Adaptation). *Pizarro.* Tragedy, 5 acts. Published 1799. Produced Theatre Royal, Drury Lane, May 24, 1799. Based on Kotzebue's *Die Spanier in Peru* (1794).

EDITIONS

Collections
Plays and Poems, ed. by R. C. Rhodes, 3 vols., New York, 1928; *Plays,* ed. by L. Gibbs, New York, 1956; *Richard Brinsley Sheridan (Six Plays),* ed. by L. Kronenberger, New York, 1957; *Complete Plays,* London, 1963.
Individual Plays
    The Critic, or A Tragedy Rehearsed. Published in *Comedy,* ed. by M. Felheim, New York, 1962.
    The Duenna. Published in *Types of English Drama, 1660–1780,* ed. by D. H. Stevens, Boston, 1923.
    The Rivals. Published in *Masterpieces of the Drama,* ed. by A. W. Allison et al., New York, 1957.
    The School for Scandal. In *Introducing the Drama,* ed. by J. Gassner and M. Sweetkind, New York, 1963.

CRITICISM

T. Moore, *Memoirs of the Life of the Rt. Hon. Richard Brinsley Sheridan,* new ed., 2 vols., New York, 1858; W. F. Rae, *Wilkes, Sheridan, Fox,* London, 1874; P. H. Fitzgerald, *The Lives of the Sheridans,* 2 vols., London, 1886; L. C. Sanders, *Life of Richard Brinsley Sheridan,* London, 1890; W. F. Rae, *Sheridan: A Biography,* 2 vols., London, 1896; M. Oliphant, *Sheridan,* new ed., New York, 1901; W. S. Sichel, *Sheridan, from New and Original Material,* 2 vols., London, 1909; E. B. Watson, *Sheridan to Robertson,* Cambridge, Mass., 1926; N. W. Sawyer, *The Comedy of Manners from Sheridan to Maugham,* Philadelphia, 1931; W. A. Darlington, *Sheridan,* New York, 1933; R. C. Rhodes, *Harlequin Sheridan: The Man and the Legends,* Oxford, 1933; R. Snider, *Satire in the Comedies of Congreve, Sheridan, Wilde, and Coward,* Orono, Me., 1937; K. Foss, *Here Lies Richard Brinsley Sheridan,* London, 1939; A. Glasgow, *Sheridan of Drury Lane,* New York, 1940; L. Gibbs, *Sheridan,* London, 1947; G. Sinko, *Sheridan and Kotzebue: A Comparative Essay,* Wroclaw, 1949; O. Sherwin, *Uncorking Old Sherry: The Life and Times of Richard Brinsley Sheridan,* New York, 1960; M. Bingham, *Sheridan: The Track of a Comet,* London, 1972; J. Loftis, *Sheridan and the Drama of Georgian England,* Oxford, 1976.

Sherriff, R[obert] C[edric]   (1896–1975)

English novelist, screenwriter, and dramatist. His remarkably realistic and antiheroic treatment of men under the stress of combat made his *Journey's End* (1928) one of the most influential war dramas of modern times; it catapulted its unknown author to international fame and fortune. In it realism of atmosphere and characterization is tinged with mysticism in the face of imminent death. Sherriff collaborated with Jeanne de Casalis in writing *St Helena* (1936), a compelling drama about the final ignominious years of Napoleon.

Sherriff's later career was focused on the British motion-picture industry; but 1953 saw *The White Carnation,* a playful excursion into the occult and the spirit world in which a returning ghost runs afoul of earthly law, and 1961, *The Long Sunset,* a play first produced as a radio play in 1955, about the Roman occupation of Britain. He also wrote *Badger's Green* (1930), *Windfall* (1933), *Home at Seven* (1950), *The Telescope* (1959), and *A Shred of Evidence* (1960).

Journey's End (1928). Drama dealing with the life shared by British military officers at the front during World War I. Captain Stanhope, aged twenty-one, has taken to drink to steady his battered nerves, acquired af-

Scene from *Journey's End,* with (l. to r.) Henry Wenman, Colin Keith-Johnston, and Jack Hawkins. New York, Henry Miller's Theatre, 1929.
[Photograph by Vandamm. Theatre Collection, The New York Public Library at Lincoln Center, Astor, Lenox and Tilden Foundations]

ter three years' service on the front lines; he refuses to leave his men, however, until he has led them in an attack. Raleigh, a school friend and the brother of Stanhope's girl friend, joins the company. Stanhope is bitterly conscious of his drinking because he knows it will destroy Raleigh's heroic image of him. But his friend Osborne, known as Uncle, reassures him. It is not long before Osborne is killed on a special mission to capture a German prisoner. Then, during the attack for which they have been waiting, Raleigh is wounded in the spine and dies in Stanhope's dugout. The play ends with the future of all the officers in doubt. Produced London, Stage Society, December 29, 1928; Savoy Theatre, January 1, 1929.

[RONALD HAYMAN]

Sherwood, Robert E. (1896–1955)

American dramatist. Robert Emmet Sherwood was born in New Rochelle, N.Y., on April 4, 1896. He was a descendant of the Irish hero Robert Emmet. His father, Arthur Murray Sherwood, was a successful investment broker, and his mother, the former Rosina Emmet, was an artist. He was educated at Milton Academy and then at Harvard University (1914–1917), where he was an active member of the Hasty Pudding Club and editor of the *Lampoon.* His participation in the editing of a famous burlesque of *Vanity Fair* later led to a position on that magazine.

In 1917, during World War I, Sherwood enlisted in the Canadian Black Watch and was sent to France, where he was gassed and wounded in both legs. His experiences in the war led to the pacifist views that were to be reflected in many of his plays. After the war he worked briefly for *Vanity Fair,* directed *Barnum Was Right,* a play written for the Hasty Pudding Club while he was an undergraduate, and in 1920 took a position with the humor magazine *Life* as a motion-picture critic and associate editor. In 1922 he married Mary Brandon, whom he divorced in 1934.

By 1923 Sherwood was recognized as one of the country's leading film critics, and in 1924 he became editor of *Life,* a position he lost in 1928 because of his antiprohibition and anti-Hoover views. Meanwhile, in 1927, his first professionally produced play, *The Road to Rome,* was a huge success on Broadway. Not until his sixth play, *Reunion in Vienna* in 1931, was he to have another triumph. Beginning in 1935 he wrote a series of five successful plays, three of which were awarded Pulitzer Prizes: *Idiot's Delight,* in 1936; *Abe Lincoln in Illinois,* in 1939, and *There Shall Be No Night,* in 1941.

In 1935, shortly after his divorce, he married Madeline Hurlock Connelly, the former wife of dramatist Marc Connelly. At this time he was active in the Dramatists Guild, an organization that aimed at protecting member playwrights from unscrupulous managers and unfair cinema contracts. He also became a founding member of the Playwrights' Company, a production company formed by leading playwrights to produce their own plays without having to depend on commercial producers. In 1936 he wrote *The Ghost Goes West,* the first of a

Robert E. Sherwood. [Theatre Collection, The New York Public Library at Lincoln Center, Astor, Lenox and Tilden Foundations]

number of film scenarios leading eventually to an Academy Award for *The Best Years of Our Lives* (1946).

By 1940, with the production of *There Shall Be No Night,* Sherwood's pacifist views showed a change as a result of the spread of totalitarianism. For more than a decade he had been a close friend and adviser of Franklin D. Roosevelt and one of his major speech writers. In 1940 he was named special assistant to the Secretary of War and president of the American National Theater and Academy, formed by an act of Congress in 1935 to foster the advancement of theatre in the United States. With the entry of the United States into World War II, Sherwood became Director of the Overseas Branch of the Office of War Information, responsible for the flow of information to the people of the captive nations. When the war ended, he resumed playwriting and also wrote the massive *Roosevelt and Hopkins* (1948), a historical volume that received many awards, including his fourth Pulitzer Prize. In 1953 he began writing for television, but with little success. Sherwood died in New York on November 14, 1955.

WORK

Owing to his multifaceted career, Sherwood wrote only fifteen plays, including two adaptations and some collaborations. Despite this fairly small body of work he was one of the leading Americans to reach dramatic maturity in the 1930s. Although Sherwood was politically a liberal, his plays have little of the social comment and none of the proletarian fervor typical of other plays of the period. He was a pacifist, yet never doctrinaire; when, in 1939, Nazi Germany was terrorizing Western Europe, he wrote *There Shall Be No Night* (1940), advocating the need to fight aggression. His plays reveal an enlightened moderation toward attitudes and activities that do not impinge upon other individuals. Thus he exhibits a tolerant attitude toward sex and attacks social rigidity, militarism, and totalitarianism. Most of his sympathetic characters are romantic individualists willing to accept the realities of any situation.

His first professional play was *The Road to Rome* (1927), a tongue-in-cheek account of Hannibal's attack on Rome and the influence of Amytis, the woman behind him; through Amytis, the play defends pacifism and satirizes the smug self-satisfaction of Rome, symbolic of the United States in the 1920s. The plays that followed were far less successful. *The Love Nest* (1927), adapted from a story by Ring Lardner, is an ineffective comedy of the breakup of a Hollywood marriage. *The Queen's Husband* (1928) is the story of the henpecked king of a small country who manages, in a crisis, to avoid a revolution and reclaim his authority from his wife and a dictatorial general. *Waterloo Bridge* (1930) tells a sentimental tale of the regeneration of a prostitute through the love of a nice young man. *This Is New York* (1930) pits the philistine intolerance of Midwestern American respectability against the casual morality and personal honesty of New York, deciding in favor of the latter. *Reunion in Vienna* (1931), a comedy written in the spirit and style of contemporary Austria, points a satirical finger at the faddist popularity of psychoanalysis in Vienna resulting from the studies of Freud and Jung. In 1933 *Acropolis,* equating the death struggles of ancient Greece with the contemporary crisis in Europe, was produced in London, where it failed; it was never brought to New York. Sher-

Jane Cowl (left) in *The Road to Rome*. New York, Playhouse Theatre, 1927. [Theatre Collection, The New York Public Library at Lincoln Center, Astor, Lenox and Tilden Foundations]

Lynn Fontanne, Alfred Lunt, and Minor Watson (l. to r.) in *Reunion in Vienna*. New York, Martin Beck Theatre, 1931. [Photograph by Vandamm. Theatre Collection, The New York Public Library at Lincoln Center, Astor, Lenox and Tilden Foundations]

wood's next plays, beginning with *The Petrified Forest* (1935), a drama about vanishing idealism, were all successes, as were the three Pulitzer Prize-winners: *Idiot's Delight* (1936), which brings together in its varied characters many of the elements that started World War II; *Abe Lincoln in Illinois* (1938), a portrait of the doubt-ridden young Lincoln; and *There Shall Be No Night,* inspired by the invasion of Finland by Soviet forces in 1939.

Sherwood's last three plays, spread over a period of ten years, are undistinguished. *The Rugged Path* (1945) is the drama of a man who goes to war merely as a way of escaping the crude values of his civilian life. It was followed by *Miss Liberty* (1949), a musical with music and lyrics by Irving Berlin, which revolves around a circulation war between the publishers of two large newspapers in New York City. The posthumously produced *Small War on Murray Hill* (1957) is a comedy of the American Revolution, in which a segment of the American Army escapes from New York because the attentions of British General Howe have been otherwise occupied by an attractive American lady.

The Road to Rome (1927). Ingeniously comic combination of history, sex, and pacifism concerning Hannibal's attack on Rome, written in the idiom of the 1920s. Amytis, an individualistic, art-loving Athenian woman, is married to a self-important Roman senator who has

Humphrey Bogart as Duke Mantee and Leslie Howard as Alan Squier in *The Petrified Forest*. New York, Broadhurst Theatre, 1935. [Photograph by Vandamm. Theatre Collection, The New York Public Library at Lincoln Center, Astor, Lenox and Tilden Foundations]

been authorized to quell the Carthaginian invasion. When Hannibal defeats the Roman Army and stands before the gates of the unprotected city, Amytis, pretending to flee, makes her way to his camp. Once there, she plants doubts in the general's mind about his reasons for conquering Rome and at the same time seduces him. Hannibal loses all taste for military victory, restores Amytis to her husband, and withdraws his army from Italy.

Reunion in Vienna (1931). Comedy set in republican Austria of 1930, where nostalgia for the glitter of the deposed Hapsburg monarchy remains and where faddists come to experience the new psychiatry. The beautiful Elena, once the mistress of Archduke Rudolf Maximilian and now happily married to the psychiatrist Anton Krug, attends a clandestine party in honor of the Hapsburgs, where she again falls under Rudolf's spell. Even her husband is impressed by the scintillating duke and promises to help him escape from Austria. To do so he must leave

Elena and the duke alone for the night, with the inevitable result. The following day Rudolf departs, leaving Elena to resume her role as a dutiful wife, just as Austria faces its future as a proper republic.

The Petrified Forest (1935). Drama dealing with the obsolescence of all who do not conform to the smug, materialistic norms of American society, in this case, a young intellectual and an escaped criminal. The penniless intellectual, Alan Squier, arrives at the Black Mesa filling station and lunchroom in a desolate area of eastern Arizona. Black Mesa is run by the aging pioneer Gramp Maple, assisted by his dull son Jason and Jason's daughter Gabby, a vital girl who dreams of joining her mother in France. Gabby and Squier fall in love. When Duke Mantee, a notorious escaped killer, arrives, he makes hostages of everyone present. His individuality and occasional humanity are portrayed more favorably than is the crude blood lust of his pursuers. So that Gabby may go to France, Squier makes her the beneficiary of his in-

Lynn Fontanne (center) in *Idiot's Delight.*
[Library of Congress]

surance policy and persuades Mantee to kill him. Mantee does so and then flees into the night to an almost-certain death. Both individualists have thus been destroyed, and only Gabby, their budding successor, remains.

Idiot's Delight (1936). Drama with comic and musical elements, pacifist in tone, taking place in an Italian resort near the Swiss border just before the outbreak of World War II. Included among those trapped in the hotel are Harry Van, an American song-and-dance man, with his chorus girls; Achilles Weber, a munitions manufacturer, and his mistress Irene, who pretends to be a Russian countess; and Quillery, a French pacifist. Although all of them hate war, none can prevent it. When war comes, each except Weber takes refuge in his own nation's position; Weber supplies munitions impartially to all belligerents. Quillery, who protests against the Fascists, is taken away by the Italians to be shot. Irene is deserted by Weber after she has denounced his militarism. She is left alone with Harry, with whom she had had a brief affair. After having seen his girls safely over the border, Harry returns to Irene, and as the bombs fall around them, he launches into a jazz version of "Onward, Christian Soldiers."

Abe Lincoln in Illinois (1938). Drama spanning thirty years of Abraham Lincoln's life, from his early twenties

There Shall Be No Night, with (l. to r.) Alfred Lunt, Richard Whorf, Lynn Fontanne, Elisabeth Fraser, Sydney Greenstreet, and Montgomery Clift. New York, Alvin Theatre, 1940. [Photograph by Vandamm. Theatre Collection, The New York Public Library at Lincoln Center, Astor, Lenox and Tilden Foundations]

Frank Andrews (left) as Mentor Graham and Raymond Massey as Abraham Lincoln in *Abe Lincoln in Illinois*. New York, Plymouth Theatre, 1938. [Theatre Collection, The New York Public Library at Lincoln Center, Astor, Lenox and Tilden Foundations]

to his election as President, focusing on his integrity, humility, and loyalty to early pathways. The play begins with Lincoln as postmaster in New Salem, Ill., and follows his election to the state assembly and his years as a lawyer in Springfield. There he meets and proposes to wealthy, ambitious Mary Todd, only to jilt her on their wedding day. They are later married, but because of Mary's drive and will for power they drift apart. Lincoln's presidential aspirations, rooted in a desire to preserve the Union, conflict with the naked ambition of his wife, which leads to their final estrangement. After debates with Douglas, Lincoln is elected President and departs for Washington. In the end, despite his popularity, he is a lonely man bound in duty to his wife and country.

There Shall Be No Night (1940). Drama dealing with the plight of an eminent Finnish neurologist when his country is overrun by Soviet troops. When the play begins, Dr. Kaarolo Valkonen, whose loyalties are international rather than national, has been awarded the Nobel Prize. With the start of the Russian invasion, however, he realizes that his pacifist beliefs are useless in the face of the present danger and the growing Nazi menace.

Valkonen goes off to tend the wounded at the front, and his son Erik joins the army. Miranda, Erik's pregnant wife, is sent to America. Valkonen and Erik are both killed, and Miranda is left to carry on as best she can.

[GAUTAM DASGUPTA]

PLAYS

Unless otherwise noted, the plays were first performed in New York.

1. *The Road to Rome*. Comedy, 3 acts. Published 1927. Produced Playhouse, Jan. 31, 1927.
2. (Adaptation). *The Love Nest*. Comedy, 3 acts. Produced Comedy Theater Dec. 22, 1927. Based on Ring Lardner's story of the same name (1926).
3. *The Queen's Husband*. Play, 3 acts. Published 1928. Produced Playhouse, Jan. 25, 1928.
4. *Waterloo Bridge*. Drama, 2 acts. Published 1930. Produced Fulton Theatre, Jan. 6, 1930.
5. *This Is New York*. Comedy, 3 acts. Published 1931. Produced Plymouth Theatre, Nov. 28, 1930.
6. *Reunion in Vienna*. Comedy, 3 acts. Published 1932. Produced Martin Beck Theatre, Nov. 16, 1931.
7. *Acropolis*. Play, 3 acts. Produced London, Lyric Theatre, Nov. 23, 1933.
8. *The Petrified Forest*. Drama, 2 acts. Published 1935. Produced Broadhurst Theatre, Jan. 7, 1935.
9. *Idiot's Delight*. Comedy, 3 acts. Published 1936. Produced Shubert Theatre, Mar. 24, 1936.
10. (Adaptation). *Tovarich*. Comedy, 2 acts. Written 1936. Published 1936. Produced Plymouth Theatre, Oct. 15, 1936. Based on Jacques Deval's comic play of the same name (1933).
11. *Abe Lincoln in Illinois*. Drama, 3 acts. Published 1939. Produced Plymouth Theatre, Oct. 15, 1938.
12. *There Shall Be No Night*. Drama, 3 acts. Published 1940. Produced Alvin Theatre, Apr. 29, 1940.
13. *The Rugged Path*. Drama, 2 acts. Produced Plymouth Theatre, Nov. 10, 1945.
14. *Miss Liberty*. Musical comedy, 2 acts. Produced Imperial Theatre, July 15, 1949. Music and lyrics: Irving Berlin.
15. *Small War on Murray Hill*. Comedy, 2 acts. Published 1957. Produced Ethel Barrymore Theatre, Jan. 3, 1957.

Sherwood also finished Philip Barry's *Second Threshold* (1951), left incomplete at the author's death.

EDITIONS

Abe Lincoln in Illinois. Published in *The Dramatic Experience*, ed. by J. Bierman et al., Englewood Cliffs, N.J., 1958.

Idiot's Delight. Published in *Famous American Plays of the 1930s*, ed. by H. Clurman, New York, 1959.

The Petrified Forest. Published in *Sixteen Famous American Plays*, ed. by B. A. Cerf and V. H. Cartmell, Garden City, N.Y., 1941.

Reunion in Vienna. Published in *The Theatre Guild Anthology*, New York, 1936.

There Shall Be No Night. Published in *British and American Plays, 1830–1945*, ed. by W. H. Durham and J. W. Dodds, New York, 1947.

CRITICISM

R. B. Shuman, *Robert Emmet Sherwood*, New York, 1964; J. M. Brown, *The Worlds of Robert E. Sherwood*, New York, 1965; W. J. Meserve, *Robert E. Sherwood: Reluctant Moralist*, New York, 1970.

Shiels, George (1886–1949)

Irish dramatist. He was born in County Antrim on June 24, 1886. Shiels wrote the typical realistic Abbey Theatre play of the 1930s and 1940s, rivaling O'Casey in popularity. As a youth he emigrated to Canada, but after seven years there he was in a railway accident which crippled him for life. He returned to Ballymoney and wrote short stories and articles for the local papers before he turned to writing plays. His early plays were written for the Ulster Theatre, but after the Abbey accepted *Bedmates* (1921) he began to write mainly for the Dublin theatre.

Shiels's second Abbey production, *Insurance Money*

(1921), was followed by *Paul Twyning* (Oct. 3, 1922), *First Aid* (Dec. 26, 1923), *The Retrievers* (May 12, 1924), *Professor Tim* (Sept. 14, 1925), *Cartney and Kevney* (Nov. 29, 1927), *Mountain Dew* (Mar. 5, 1929), his very popular comedy *The New Gossoon* (Apr. 19, 1930), *Grogan and the Ferret* (Nov. 13, 1933), *The Passing Day* (Apr. 13, 1936), *The Jailbird* (Oct. 12, 1936), *Quin's Secret* (Mar. 29, 1937), a revision of *Cartney and Kevney* (Nov. 8, 1937), *Neal Maquade* (Jan. 17, 1938), *Give Him a House* (Oct. 30, 1939), the long running *The Rugged Path* (Aug. 5, 1940), its sequel *The Summit* (Feb. 10, 1941), *The Fort Field* (Apr. 13, 1942), *The New Regime* (Mar. 6, 1944), *Tenants at Will* (Sept. 10, 1945), *The Old Broom* (Mar. 25, 1946), and *The Caretakers* (Feb. 16, 1948). He also wrote several other plays that were performed in Ulster, such as *The Tame Drudge, Tully's Experts, Border Wine,* and *Moodie in Manitoba.*

After he died in Ballymoney on September 19, 1949, several manuscripts were found among his effects, the best of which was *Slave Drivers.* Shiels saw only one of his plays, an Abbey performance in Belfast of *Professor Tim,* which he witnessed from the wings. Fellow playwright T. C. Murray, although he met Shiels only once, sent him firsthand accounts of the openings of all his plays. Most were comedies; all were simple and warmhearted. *See* MURRAY, T. C.

The New Gossoon (1930). Comedy set in Northern Ireland. Luke Cary, a "new" gossoon (boy), having courted Sally Hamil incessantly, now prefers zooming around the countryside on his motorbike. Sally decides she is too good for him, and his mother, tired of his impudence, announces she is leaving and giving him the farm. Luke finally comes to his senses when an irate father threatens to kill him for trifling with his daughter. Saved by Sally, Luke decides she is the woman for him. Mrs. Cary promises to buy them a farm, and Sally promises to make Luke behave.

CAROL GELDERMAN

Shirley, James   (1596–1666)

English poet and dramatist. Shirley was baptized in London on September 7, 1596. He attended the Merchant Taylors' School and then entered St. John's College, Oxford, but left for St. Catherine's College, Cambridge, where he received his B.A. degree in about 1617. Apparently he took holy orders and became a clergyman in or near St. Albans, Hertfordshire. He married Elizabeth Gilmet on June 1, 1618. By 1621 he was headmaster of St. Albans Grammar School. In 1624 or 1625 he was converted to Roman Catholicism, resigned his position, and moved to London, where his first-known play, *The School of Compliment,* was performed in 1625.

Shirley quickly became a favorite of the court and enjoyed its patronage. When the plague closed London theatres in 1636, he moved to Dublin, where he wrote for John Ogilby's theatre. He returned to London in 1640 and joined the King's Company, for which he wrote five or six plays.

The outbreak of the civil war ended his prolific career as a playwright. He fought on the Royalist side under the Earl of Newcastle until 1644, then retired to London and resumed teaching. In 1646 he published some poetry. After the Restoration (1660) many of his plays were successfully revived, but he produced no new ones.

The Great Fire of London in 1666 destroyed Shirley's home, and with his second wife, Frances, he fled to St. Giles-in-the-Fields. They suffered injuries, and both died two months later. They were buried in the graveyard of St. Giles on October 29, 1666.

WORK

James Shirley is indebted to John Fletcher, frequently treating similar subject matter, situations, and characters, but Shirley's ingenuity enabled him to construct a formidable body of effective masques, comedies, tragicomedies, and tragedies. *See* FLETCHER, JOHN. *See also* MASQUE; TRAGICOMEDY in glossary.

Among his masques are the extravagant *The Triumph of Peace* (1634), with scenery designed by Inigo Jones, for presentation to the King and Queen and the four Inns of Court; and *The Triumph of Beauty* (pub. 1646), with a comic portion based on parts of Shakespeare's *A Midsummer Night's Dream.*

Shirley's elegant and witty comedies of manners are invariably more complicated than Fletcher's plays; their antiromanticism, derivative from Jonson, looks forward to Restoration drama. *The Witty Fair One* (1628) depicts Shirley's favorite character, the gay, forthright girl, fond of men but not foolish; *Hyde Park* (1632) brings horses onto the stage, one of the spectacular theatrical devices that became characteristic of Shirley; and *The Lady of Pleasure* (1635) brilliantly contrasts extravagance and liberality, license and gaiety. *See* JONSON, BEN.

The tragicomedies include *The Young Admiral* (1633), *The Duke's Mistress* (1636), a neglected-wife play, and *The Doubtful Heir* (ca. 1638), an example of Shirley's skill in handling the intricate theatrical devices developed by Fletcher: disguise and discovery; suspense through impending tragedy, and reversals in fortune, bringing an apparently inevitable tragic theme to a happy conclusion.

The best of the tragedies are *The Traitor* (1631) and *The Cardinal* (1641). *The Traitor,* immensely complex, deals with the murder of the Duke of Florence by his friend and cousin, the assassin Lorenzo, Shirley's one brilliant characterization. *The Cardinal,* an exciting tragedy of triple revenge, recalls Webster's *The Duchess of Malfi.* Although lacking the power of Webster's play, it has structural cohesiveness and considerable impact. *See* WEBSTER, JOHN.

Hyde Park (1632). Comedy of manners concerning the amours and adventures of two fashionable London ladies, Mistress Bonavent and Mistress Carol. Mistress Bonavent, having had no word from her traveling merchant husband for seven years, considers it time to remarry and does so; Mistress Carol, a manhater, sadistically dangles several suitors on a string, playing one against another. Mistress Bonavent's husband returns in disguise and breaks up the new marriage, which has not yet been consummated. Mistress Carol succumbs finally to one of her suitors, but only after he threatens to castrate himself.

A third lady, Julietta, the sister of Mistress Carol's successful suitor, is tested by her jealous fiancé, by leaving her alone with a reckless lord who thinks her wanton. Her chastity and virtue reform the lord, and he replaces the fiancé in her affections.

The Lady of Pleasure (1635). Comedy which has elements in common with Sheridan's *The School for Scandal* (1777). Sir Thomas Bornwell's extravagant wife Aretina has persuaded her conservative husband to leave the quiet country for the city's fashionably expensive life. Aretina's extravagance alarms Bornwell, who, to break her of her newly acquired habits, pretends to become converted to her lavish ways and outdoes her in wasteful spending until they seem to be on the brink of ruin. This treatment finally instills some sense of thrift in Aretina. *See* SHERIDAN, RICHARD BRINSLEY.

The comedy is replete with scandalmongering secondary characters, extended scenes of raillery involving such profligates as the Masters Kickshaw and Littleworth, and salacious goings-on instigated by the procuress Madam Decoy and directed against the virtuous and intelligent Celestina, Lady Bellamour.

The Cardinal (1641). Melodramatic tragedy centering on the Cardinal, the Machiavellian power behind the throne of Navarre. The Cardinal, unscrupulous and ambitious, wishes to force Duchess Rosaura into marriage with his nephew General Columbo. Rosaura, who is in love with Count D'Alvarez, succeeds temporarily in foiling the Cardinal's plan, but Columbo returns from the wars and murders the count during the performance of a play staged in honor of Rosaura's marriage to him. Then Rosaura becomes the Cardinal's ward and to protect herself feigns madness. After attempting to rape her, the Cardinal resorts to poisoning her, but she does not die; he is in turn wounded by one of Rosaura's champions, General Hernando. Believing that he is on his deathbed, the Cardinal still dissembles: pretending to forgive Rosaura, he toasts her with the poisonous drink that has been prepared for her. She, however, is tricked into drinking what she believes to be an antidote but is, in fact, a deadlier poison than the potion she took originally. They die together.

PLAYS

Unless otherwise noted, the plays were first performed in London. "Licensed" refers to the date a play was licensed for production in London. *See* STATIONERS' REGISTER in glossary.

1. *The School of Compliment.* Comedy, 5 acts. Published 1631. Produced Phoenix Theatre, 1625 (licensed Feb. 11, 1625, as *Love Tricks with Compliments*).
2. *The Maid's Revenge.* Tragedy, 5 acts. Published 1639. Produced Phoenix Theatre (Queen's Men), 1626 (licensed Feb. 9, 1626).
3. *The Wedding.* Comedy, 5 acts. Published 1629. Produced Phoenix Theatre (Queen's Men), 1626?
4. *The Brothers.* Comedy, 5 acts. Published 1652. Produced Blackfriars, 1626 (licensed Nov. 4, 1626).
5. *The Witty Fair One.* Comedy, 5 acts. Published 1633. Produced Phoenix Theatre, 1628 (licensed Oct. 3, 1628).
6. *The Grateful Servant.* Comedy, 5 acts. Published 1630. Produced Phoenix Theatre (Queen's Men), 1629 (licensed Nov. 3, 1629).
7. *The Traitor.* Tragedy, 5 acts. Published 1635. Produced Phoenix Theatre (Queen's Men), 1631 (licensed May 4, 1631).
8. *The Humourous Courtier.* Comedy, 5 acts. Published 1640. Produced Phoenix Theatre, 1631 (licensed May 17, 1631, as *The Duke*).
9. *Love's Cruelty.* Tragedy, 5 acts. Published 1640. Produced Phoenix Theatre (Queen's Men), 1631 (licensed Nov. 14, 1631).
10. *The Changes, or Love in a Maze.* Comedy, 5 acts. Published 1632 (Stationers' Register, Feb. 9, 1632). Produced Phoenix Theatre, Salisbury Court (King's Revels), 1631 (licensed Jan. 10, 1632).
11. *Hyde Park.* Comedy, 5 acts. Published 1637. Produced Phoenix Theatre (Queen's Men), 1632 (licensed Apr. 10, 1632).
12. *The Ball.* Comedy, 5 acts. Published 1639. Produced Phoenix Theatre (Queen's Men), 1632 (licensed Nov. 16, 1632).
13. *The Bird in a Cage.* Comedy, 5 acts. Published 1633 (Stationers' Register, Mar. 19, 1633). Produced Phoenix Theatre, 1632/33? (licensed Jan. 21, 1633, as *The Beauties*).
14. *The Young Admiral.* Tragicomedy, 5 acts. Published 1637. Produced Phoenix Theatre (Queen's Men), 1633 (licensed July 3, 1633).
15. *The Gamester.* Comedy, 5 acts. Published 1637. Produced Phoenix Theatre (Queen's Men), 1633 (licensed Nov. 11, 1633).
16. *The Triumph of Peace.* Masque. Published 1634. Produced Inns of Court, Feb. 3 and 13, 1634. Scenery: Inigo Jones.
17. *The Example.* Comedy, 5 acts. Published 1637. Produced Phoenix Theatre (Queen's Men), 1634 (licensed June 24, 1634).
18. *The Opportunity.* Comedy, 5 acts. Published 1640. Produced Phoenix Theatre (Queen's Men), 1634 (licensed Nov. 29, 1634).
19. *The Coronation.* Comedy, 5 acts. Published 1640. Produced Phoenix Theatre (Queen's Men), 1635 (licensed Feb. 6, 1635).
20. (With George Chapman). *Chabot, Admiral of France.* Tragedy, 5 acts. Written 1621/22(?), revised 1635. Published 1639. Produced Phoenix Theatre (Queen's Men), 1635 (licensed Apr. 29, 1635).
21. *The Lady of Pleasure.* Comedy, 5 acts. Published 1637. Produced Phoenix Theatre (Queen's Men), 1635 (licensed Oct. 15, 1635).
22. *The Duke's Mistress.* Tragicomedy, 5 acts. Published 1638. Produced Phoenix Theatre (Queen's Men), 1636 (licensed Jan. 18, 1636).
23. *The Royal Master.* Comedy, 5 acts. Published 1638. Produced Dublin, New Theatre, 1637; London, 1638 (licensed Mar. 13, 1638).
24. *The Doubtful Heir.* Tragicomedy, 5 acts. Published 1652. Produced Dublin, New Theatre, ca. 1638; London, Globe Theatre (King's Men), 1640 (licensed June 1, 1640, as *Rosania*).
25. *St. Patrick for Ireland.* Drama, 5 acts. Published 1640. Produced Dublin, New Theatre, 1639?
26. *The Gentleman of Venice.* Tragicomedy, 5 acts. Published 1655. Produced Phoenix Theatre, Salisbury Court (Queen's Men), 1639 (licensed October, 1639).
27. *The Politician.* Tragedy, 5 acts. Published 1655. Produced Phoenix Theatre, Salisbury Court (Queen's Men), ca. 1639?
28. *The Constant Maid.* Comedy, 5 acts. Published 1640. Produced Dublin, New Theatre, 1636/40?
29. *The Imposture.* Tragicomedy, 5 acts. Published 1652. Produced Blackfriars, 1640 (licensed Nov. 10, 1640).
30. *The Cardinal.* Tragedy, 5 acts. Published 1652. Produced Blackfriars, 1641 (licensed Nov. 25, 1641).
31. *The Sisters.* Comedy, 5 acts. Published 1652. Produced Blackfriars, 1642 (licensed Apr. 26, 1642).
32. *The Court Secret.* Tragicomedy, 5 acts. Written 1642. Published 1653.
33. *The Triumph of Beauty.* Masque. Published 1646. Privately performed on an unknown date.
34. *Cupid and Death.* Masque. Published 1659. Produced Mar. 26, 1653.
35. *Honoria and Mammon.* Moral allegory, 5 acts. Published 1658.

EDITIONS

Collections
Dramatic Works and Poems, ed. by W. Gifford and A. Dyce, 6 vols., London, 1833.

Individual Plays
The Cardinal. Published in *The English Drama: An Anthology,. 900–1642*, ed. by E. W. Parks and R. C. Beatty, New York, 1935.

The Lady of Pleasure. Published in *Six Caroline Plays*, ed. by A. S. Knowland, London, 1962.

The Royal Master. Published in *Representative English Comedies*, ed. by C. M. Gayley, vol. 3, New York, 1903–1936.

The Traitor. Published in *Shakespeare and His Fellow Dramatists*, ed. by E. H. C. Oliphant, vol. 2, New York, 1929.

The Wedding. Published in *Six Caroline Plays*, ed. by A. S. Knowland, London, 1962.

CRITICISM

J. Schipper, *James Shirley: Sein Leben und seine Werke*, Vienna, 1911; R. S. Forsythe, *The Relations of Shirley's Plays to the Elizabethan Drama*, New York, 1914; H. T. Parlin, *A Study in Shirley's Comedies of London Life*, Austin, Tex., 1914; A. H. Nason, *James Shirley: Dramatist: A Biographical and*

Critical Study, New York, 1915; S. J. Radtke, *James Shirley: His Catholic Philosophy of Life*, Washington, 1929.

Sholem Aleichem (1859–1916)

Yiddish-, Hebrew-, and Russian-language humorist, novelist, and dramatist; pseudonym of Sholem Rabinowitz. He may be the most beloved of all Yiddish writers and has been called "the Jewish Mark Twain." His literary output embraces 300 short stories, 5 novels, and more than a dozen plays, all written in the racy, picturesque idiom of his contemporaries. One of his most famous plays, *Tevye the Milkman* (*Tevye der Milcheker*, wr. 1915, prod. 1919), about Jewish life in a small Eastern European village, was based upon his Tevye stories, as was the Broadway musical *Fiddler on the Roof*.

Born in Russia, Sholem Aleichem as a youngster learned Biblical Hebrew and precise idiomatic Russian; he habitually saw the humorous side of situations, liked to mimic his elders, and invented amusements for his playmates. In 1900, with a successful business career behind him, he decided to devote himself to literature. He began writing in Yiddish, Hebrew, and Russian, but Yiddish proved his most viable linguistic instrument, particularly for the short story. His plays and monologues have been criticized as lacking dramatic power and depth, but they are nonetheless vivid, humorous, and lyrical.

His most popular play, *Two Hundred Thousand*, also known as *The Great Gain* (*Das groise Gevins*; wr. 1915, prod. 1922), has been widely acclaimed as one of the finest comedies written for the Yiddish stage. Other plays by Sholem Aleichem are *The Doctor*, translated into English by Isaac Goldberg as *She Must Marry a Doctor* (*Der Doktor*, 1887), a broad comedy about a matchmaker; *The Divorce* (*Der Get*; wr. 1887, prod. 1924); *Mazel Tov* (wr. 1899; prod. 1904); *Agents* (*Agenten*; wr. 1904, prod. 1916); *Scattered and Dispersed* (*Tzerzeit und tzershpreit*, 1905); *The Scoundrel* (*Der Ausvurf*, 1906); *The Treasure*, also known as *The Golddigger* (*Die Goldgreber*, 1908); *God Willing, a Broom Can Fire* (*Az Gott vil, shist a Bezem*, 1908); *King of Pic* (*Konig Pic*, 1910); and *Hard to Be a Jew* (*Shver tzu zein a Yid*, 1920), which is based on his novel *The Bloody Joke* (wr. 1912 about the ritual-murder trial of Mendel Beilis in Kiev, which a half century later was to be the basis of Bernard Malamud's novel *The Fixer* (1966). *See* YIDDISH DRAMA.

Tevye the Milkman (*Tevye der Milcheker*, 1915). Tevye, an aging milkman and part-time philosopher, lives with his wife, Golde, and his young daughter, Chava. Their oldest daughter, Tzeitel, has married a sickly tailor and moved away from home, though she visits occasionally. Chava has fallen in love with a local Christian boy, who plies her with books and love poetry. Unknown to Tevye, Chava and her lover have been meeting secretly, and, while she knows full well that it will break her father's heart, she runs away to marry her Christian lover. Tevye becomes enraged and decides that Chava is no longer his daughter, in fact, that she never existed. Several years pass, and the Jews are forced by the authorities to leave their homes, Tevye and his fam-ily among them. By this time both Golde and Tzeitel's husband are dead, and Tevye prepares to remove himself, Tzeitel and her two young children. Before their departure, however, Chava returns, contrite and repentant, and she and Tevye are reconciled.

[IRVING SAPOSNIK]

Shvarts, Yevgeny Lvovich (1896–1958)

Soviet Russian dramatist. Shvarts was born in Kazan on October 21, 1896, the son of a Jewish physician, and spent his childhood moving through southern Russia in the days before the Revolution. As a law student in Rostov-on-Don, he joined P. K. Veysbrem's theatre workshop as an actor (1917–1922), traveling with this amateur troupe to Leningrad in 1921, where he was to live the rest of his life. He began writing as a newspaper columnist and a provider of skits for amateur theatricals, then becoming a contributing editor to the children's magazines *The Hedgehog* (*Yozh*) and *The Siskin* (*Chizh*) and working on the staff of Samuil Marshak's Children's Literature Publishing House. In this period Shvarts was also closely associated with the writers' groups the Serapion Brothers and the Oberyuty; he shared their interest in magic and nonsense, the dense interconnection of dreams and reality. This mingling of the fantastic and the everyday appears in his first produced play, *Underwood* (*Undervud*, 1929), in which a typewriter is stolen by a witch and recovered by a plucky orphan girl; like many of his dramas, it was first staged at the Leningrad Theatre of the Young Spectator and then entered the standard repertoire of childrens' theatres all over Russia.

The anitformalist attacks on writers in the 1930s compelled Shvarts to adopt a more realistic style; *The Treasure* (*Klad*, 1933), *Brother and Sister* (*Brat i sestra*, 1937) and *Our Hospitality* (*Nashe Gostepriimstvo*, 1939) are undistinguished examples. At the same time he was developing a genre he would make peculiarly his own, the political fairy tale, in which a folkloric story is the frame for an ambiguous, richly textured allegory. His first such attempt, *The Naked King* (*Goliy Korol*; wr. 1934, prod. 1960), with its obvious satire of Nazi doctrine, was kept off the stage for diplomatic reasons; his next fairy-tale plays, *Little Red Riding Hood* (*Krasnaya shapochka*, 1937) and *The Snow Queen* (*Snezhnaya korolyeva*, 1939), though more simply children's entertainments, interwove revue elements with the naive tone of the original stories.

Shvarts's masterpieces were written in conjunction with the German invasion of Russia. *The Shadow* (*Ten'*, 1940) and *The Dragon* (*Drakon*, 1944), plays which pit the individual against corrupting and life-destroying societies, did not receive their best productions until the early 1960s, however, when his friend Nikolay Akimov revived them at the Leningrad Comedy Theatre. During the siege of Leningrad, Shvarts remained in that city, writing propaganda plays as his contribution to the war effort because he had been rejected by the Home Guard. After the war, when *The Dragon* was denied production, he turned to writing for the puppet theatre, the clown Arkady Raykin, and motion pictures. His best-known films were *Cinderella* (*Zolushka*, 1947) and *Don Quixote*

(1957), based on Mikhail Bulgakov's stage adaptation of Cervantes' novel. His last fairy-tale plays for grownups were *Two Maples* (*Dva klyona*, 1954), solidly grounded in Russian folklore, and *An Ordinary Miracle* (*Obyknovennoye chudo*, 1956), a play about a worldly-wise magician that has been compared to *The Tempest*. The middle-aged sorcerer and his practical wife are reflections of the retired Shvarts himself and his second wife who lived out their last years in a writers' community in Komarovo. A man of great sociability and quiet charm, loved by all who knew him, he died on January 15, 1958.

WORK

The fantasy elements in Shvarts's earlier plays such as *Underwood* (*Undervud*, 1929), a detective story, and *The Treasure* (*Klad*, 1933), an adventure story about a geological expedition, were appropriate to children's literature; in them, the villains tend to be easily bested or reclaimed by clear-sighted, earthy children. But with Stalinist repression of the arts and the German invasion of Russia, Shvarts's work grew darker and more complex. His propaganda plays, *Our Hospitality*, a spy-drama, and *One Night* (*Odna noch*, 1941), about the bombing of Leningrad, are crude and have never been produced; *Distant Region* (*Dalyokiy kray*, 1942), concerning the evacuation of Leningrad's children, was more successful. But his fame rests on his "fairy tales for grownups," in which well-known nursery fables embody serious considerations of human responsibility, freedom, and social abuse. The first of these, *The Naked King*, based on Hans Christian Andersen—as were *The Snow Queen* and *The Shadow*—was, Shvarts declared, not a concealment but a disclosure of the truth, an Aesopian means of speaking one's mind out loud. The fatuous king and his punctilious court satirize the early years of Hitler's regime and Nazi tenets of anti-Semitism and sterilization, and the play ends with a full-scale class revolution led by the swineherd. A more widely applicable political message appears in *The Shadow*, with its sinister opposition of Death and Life; here, the Student fails to effect a change in the people who turn incorrigibly toward corrupt authority. This theme is struck even louder in *The Dragon*, which represents any totalitarianism; even after Sir Lancelot has managed to defeat it, despite the nonparticipation of the townsfolk whom the dragon oppressed, the dragon's policies are carried out by the time-serving mayor. Shvarts' postwar dramas are more lyrical and elegiac. Baba-Yaga, the witch in *Two Maples*, seems merely trivial in comparison to the heroine, Vasilisa the Worker; and in *An Ordinary Miracle*, a romance is entangled and disentangled by a magician who eventually recognizes the existence of a power higher than his own.

Shvarts's plays are unique: the blend of political shrewdness and childlike naiveté, profound understanding of human behavior and high-spirited whimsy, poetic nuance, and earthy colloquialisms make the Shvartsian tone unmistakable. He is particularly good at creating animal characters who combine human characteristics with their own bestial attributes, and villains who are at once malevolent and trivial. His plays are never bare-

The stage adaptation of Hans Christian Andersen's fairy tale *The Snow Queen* in a 1971 production. [Sovfoto]

boned allegories, but complex webs of truth and fantasy; the objects of his satire are never local or narrow, but relevant to every society. His heroes, even when impotent, are sensitive and courageous and preserve their faith in mankind's potential.

The Naked King (*Goliy Korol*; wr. 1934; prod. 1960). Fairy-tale play in two acts, based on three stories of Hans Christian Andersen. In a Germanic kingdom everything is militarized, from the ladies-in-waiting to the useless soldiery. The swineherd Heinrich is in love with the Princess Henrietta, about to be wed to the country's ruler, and he decides to expose the King for the fool he is, to prevent the wedding. He and his friend Christian pose as weavers who claim to weave a wondrous wedding costume invisible to fools and time-servers. The befooled King, unwilling to admit he cannot see the cloth, parades in his underwear and is routed by a little boy crying, "Papa, he's got nothing on!" This provokes an uprising and the King is ousted.

The Shadow (*Ten'*, 1940). Fairy-tale play in three acts, based on a story by Hans Christian Andersen. A student visits a southern country, where the Princess is bound to marry an honest man; when he identifies a girl on the balcony opposite his room as the Princess in disguise, he suggests that his Shadow follow and woo her. The reporter Cesare Borgia and the innkeeper Pietro, fearful that a virtuous king will destroy the old, corrupt regime, win over the Shadow and use the singer Julia July to seduce the Student and bear false witness against him. Betrayed by his own shadow, the Student is beheaded but his Shadow dies with him; the Student is revived by the Water of Life, which is effective only on

A 1960 Moscow production of *The Shadow*, based on a
tale by Hans Christian Andersen. [Theatre of Comedy,
Moscow]

good people, marries the innkeeper's daughter Annun-
ziata, his true love, and leaves the country, which remains unregenerate in its corruption.

The Dragon (*Drakon*, 1944). Fairy-tale play in three
acts. The knight Lancelot arrives to rid a town of a
dragon which has ruled it for four hundred years and
has demanded a maiden as annual tribute; he is shocked
to discover that the townspeople are totally submissive
to the dragon and refuse to aid the knight. Assisted by
a cat, a donkey, and the gypsies whom the dragon had
driven out, Sir Lancelot defeats him but is left for dead.
The mayor and his son Henry take over, using a bureaucratic form of the dragon's tyranny, but on the day of
Henry's marriage to Elsa, the rescued maiden, Lancelot
reappears. He determines to wed Elsa and remain in the
town to extirpate dragonlike vestiges in all the townsfolk.

Two Maples (*Dva klyona*, 1954). The two sons of
Vasilisa the Worker have been turned into maple trees
by the witch Baba Yaga. She wins the favor of the vain
cat Kotofey Ivanovich and a dog and a bear who work
for the witch, and with their help she accomplishes the
impossible tasks Baba Yaga sets. The witch's power is
destroyed and the sons set free.

LAURENCE SENELICK

PLAYS

1. [Untitled. Adventures of a bandit in the early Soviet regime.]
Written ca. 1927. Unpublished.
2. *Undervud* (*Underwood*). Children's play. Written 1928. Published
1930. Produced Leningrad, Children's Theatre of the Young Spectator,
1929.
3. *Telefonnaya trubka* (*The Telephone Receiver*). Written ca. 1930. Unpublished.
4. *Ostrov "K"* (*K Island*). Written ca. 1930. Unpublished.
5. *Pustyaki* (*Nonsense*). Puppet play. Written 1932. Published 1932.
Produced Leningrad, Demmeni Theatre, 1932.
6. *Klad* (*The Treasure*). Written 1933. Published 1960. Produced Leningrad Theatre of the Young Spectator, 1933.
7. *Priklyucheniya Gogenshtaufena* (*The Adventures of Hohenstaufen*).
Written 1934. Published 1934.
8. *Goliy korol* (*The Naked King*)*. Written 1934. Published 1960. Pro-

duced Moscow, Sovremennik Theatre, 1960.
9. *Brat i sestra* (*Brother and Sister*). Written 1935–1936. Published
1936. Produced Leningrad, Theatre of the Young Spectator, 1937.
10. *Krasnaya shapochka* (*Little Red Riding Hood*). Written 1937. Produced Leningrad Theatre of the Young Spectator, 1937.
11. *Snezhnaya korolyeva* (*The Snow Queen*). Written 1938. Published
1960. Produced New Theatre of the Young Spectator, Leningrad, 1939.
12. *Kukolnyy gorod* (*Puppet Town*). Puppet play. Written 1939. Published 1959. Produced Leningrad, Demmeni Theatre, 1939.
13. *Skazka o poteryannom vremeni* (*Fairy Tale about Lost Time*). Puppet
play. Written 1939. Produced Leningrad, Demmeni Theatre, 1940.
14. *Nashe gostepriimstvo* (*Our Hospitality*). Written 1939. Published
1939.
15. *Ten'* (*The Shadow*)*. Fairy-tale play. Written 1940. Published 1960.
Produced Leningrad, Comedy Theatre, 1940, 1960.
16. (With Nikolay Akimov.) *Pod lipami Berlina* (*Under the Lindens of
Berlin*). Propaganda play. Written 1941. Produced Leningrad, Comedy
Theatre, 1942.
17. *Odna noch* (*One Night*). One-act play. Written 1941.
18. *Dalyokiy kray* (*Distant Region*). Children's play. Written 1942. Published 1950.
19. *Drakon* (*The Dragon*)*. Fairy-tale play. Written 1943. Published
1960. Produced Leningrad, Comedy Theatre, 1944, 1962.
20. *Skazka o khrabrom soldate* (*Fairy-tale of the Brave Soldier*). Puppet
play. Written 1946.
21. *Odin god* (*One Year*). Comedy. Written 1947.
22. *Zolushka* (*Cinderella*). Screenplay. Written 1947. Produced Lenfilm, 1947.
23. *Volshebniki, ili Sto druzey* (*Magicians, or The Hundred Friends*).
Puppet play. Written 1948.
24. *Povest' o molodykh suprugakh* (*Tale of the Newlyweds*). Written
1949. Published 1960. Produced Leningrad, Comedy Theatre, 1957. Revised version of *Odna noch*.
25. *Dva klyona* (*Two Maples*)*. Fairy-tale play. Written 1953. Published
1960. Produced Leningrad, Theatre of the Young Spectator, 1954.
26. *Tsar Vodokrut* (*King Whirlpool*). Screenplay. Written 1953. Published 1962.
27. *Obyknovennoye chudo* (*An Ordinary Miracle*). Fairy-tale play. Written 1954. Published 1960. Produced Leningrad, Comedy Theatre, 1956.
28. *Don Kikhote* (*Don Quixote*). Screenplay. Written 1957. Produced
Lenfilm 1957. Based on Mikhail Bulgakov's play *Don Quijote*.
29. *Kain XVIII* (*Cain XVIII*). Screenplay. Written 1957. Produced Lenfilm 1963. Finished by Nikolay Erdman.

EDITIONS

Collections
Kukolnyy gorod. Pyesy dlya teatra kukol, Leningrad-Moscow, 1959; *Skazki.
Povesti. Pyesy*, Leningrad, 1960; *Pyesy i kinostsenarii*, Moscow-Leningrad,
1962; *Three Plays*, ed. by A. Pyman, Oxford, 1972.
Individual Plays
The Dragon. Tr. by E. R. Hapgood, New York, 1963; published in
Three Soviet Plays, ed. by M. Glenny, tr. by M. Hayward, Harmond-
sworth and Baltimore, n.d.
The Naked King. Published in *Contemporary Russian Drama*, tr. by
F. D. Reeve, New York, 1968.
The Naked King. The Shadow. The Dragon. Tr. by E. Fen, London, 1979.
The Shadow. Published in *Anthology of Russian Plays*, vol. 2, tr. by
F. D. Reeve, New York, 1963.
The Two Maples. Published in *Russian Plays for Young Audiences*, ed.
and tr. by M. Morton, Rowayton, Conn., 1979.

CRITICISM

N. Akimov, "Pamyati Evgeniya Shvartsa," *Teatr*, 2, 1958; S. Dreyden,
". . . i kukolnykh del mastyor," *Zvezda*, 2, 1959; S. Tsimbal, *Evgeniy
Shvarts. Kritiko-biograficheskiy ocherk*, Leningrad, 1961; *My znali Evgeniya
Shvartsa*, Leningrad-Moscow, 1966; I. N. Corten, "Evgeny Lvovich
Shvarts: A Biographical Sketch and Bibliography," *Russian Literature Tri-
quarterly* 16, 1979.

Sigrid, Jean (1920–)

Belgian playwright, translator, and drama critic. Jean
Sigrid was born in Brussels. Although Sigrid's first six
plays, written between 1949 and 1959, tend to be banal
drawing-room dramas, a stunning transformation occurs
in his subsequent dramaturgy. These later plays, albeit
on widely diverse subjects, gain a resonance that is at
once more deeply personal and more widely universal
than his earlier works.

Jean Sigrid.
[Photograph by
Katina Avgouloupis]

Whether a witty reworking of the Caesar and Cleo-patra story, *What's New, Aruspice?* (*Quoi de neuf, Aruspice?*, 1970); the story of a wealthy family whose lives are disrupted by the Nazi occupation, *The Sound of Your Steps* (*Le bruit de tes pas*, 1976); or a Maeterlinckian mystery play, *Knife Angel* (*L'ange couteau*, 1980), in which Death insidiously enters into the lives of a family celebrating a wedding, Sigrid's later plays are permeated with a sense of loss, menace, and existential doubt. They typically involve intended meetings that are never realized and unintended meetings that seem predestined in retrospect. His best-known work is *The Hitchhiker* (*L'auto-stoppeur*, 1977), a Pinteresque domestic drama.

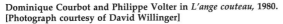

Dominique Courbot and Philippe Volter in *L'ange couteau*, 1980.
[Photograph courtesy of David Willinger]

Cecile Brany and Claude Etienne in *L'auto-stoppeur*, as presented by the Rideau du Bruxelles in 1977. [Photograph courtesy of David Willinger]

Other plays by Sigrid are: *Family Jewels* (*Bijoux de famille*, 1949), *Kind Acts* (*Les beaux gestes*, 1950), *Man with the Branch* (*L'homme à la branche*, 1951), *Pity for Violet* (*Pitié pour Violette*, 1953), *The Huge Birdhouse* (*La grande volière*, 1959), *The Knights* (*Les cavaliers*, 1959), *Death of a Mouse* (*Mort d'une souris*, 1966), and *The Swordfish* (*L'espadon*, 1977).

The Hitchhiker (*L'auto-stoppeur*, 1977). A school-teacher, Henry, while taking his customary morning drive, is tricked by a young girl, Leila, who steals his car and leaves him with her baby. Leila eventually turns up at Henry's home and asks that he accept her baby into his family. He initially refuses, but when his wife Mona returns from an extended business trip, she finds Leila and the baby firmly ensconced. Leila comes to tyrannize the household, leaving the baby in the care of Mona and Henry's daughter, Nadia. A complication occurs when Henry also takes in Wim, a Dutch hitchhiker, who then has relations with Henry's wife and his daughter. After Wim taunts Nadia by comparing her features to her mothers', Nadia stabs him with a knife. When Wim recovers, Henry sends him packing; the girl, Leila, has already left. Mona is about to go off on another business trip when Henry announces that he plans to take his customary morning drive.

DAVID WILLINGER

Silva, Antônio José da (1705–1739)

Brazilian dramatist; alias O Judeu. He was born in Rio de Janeiro on May 8, 1705, the youngest son of the lawyer and poet João Mendes da Silva and Lourença Coutinho, who was of Jewish descent. At the age of eight Antônio José da Silva accompanied his parents to Lisbon, where his mother was summoned before the tribunal of the Inquisition in their systematic purge of the so-called *cristãos novos* ("new Christians," or converts). Antônio José graduated in theological studies at the University of Coimbra. He made a brief visit to Rio de Janeiro in 1726, and on August 8 of that year he was denounced to the Inquisition and arrested. He was tortured during his imprisonment, but he was released in October after publicly repudiating the Jewish faith.

His career as a dramatist dates from 1733, and his comic operas gained him wide popularity in Lisbon, where he was generally known as Dr. Judeu. He married a first cousin, Leonor Maria de Carvalho, in 1734 or 1735, and their daughter Lourença, named after her paternal grandmother, was born in 1736. On October 5, 1736, Antônio José was arrested once more by order of the Inquisition. The next two years in prison marked a period of bitter humiliations and sufferings. He was finally sentenced to death as an impenitent lapsed Christian and burned at the stake in Lisbon on October 18, 1739.

WORK

Although educated in Portugal and generally identified with the evolution of Portuguese drama, the fact that Antônio José da Silva was born in Rio de Janeiro entitles him to a place in any history of Brazilian theatre. Antônio José da Silva became an instant success with his first comic opera, *The Life of the Great Don Quixote from La Mancha (Vida do grande D. Quixote de la Mancha),* which opened at the Pátio da Comedia in Lisbon's Bairro Alto in October 1733. The production was entrusted to a company headed by the distinguished Spanish comedian Antônio Rodríguez.

Successive comic operas reflected the current popularity of *opera buffa* imported from Italy. Introducing puppets and marionettes into his operas, Antônio José da Silva used these devices to satirize Lisbon society. The comic situations he invented and the social types he depicted could scarcely be more remote from his native Brazil, although some critics insist that the lyricism in his writing betrays his tropical origins. Most critics, however, refute this argument and see his comic operas as unmistakably European in inspiration and style and wholly within the traditions established by dramatists like Gil Vicente and Molière. His comic operas, such as *The Enchantments of Medea (Os encantos de Medéia,* 1735) and *The Labyrinth of Crete (Labirinto de Creto,* 1736), fully illustrate the author's natural gift for comic invention.

Comedy and satire were Antônio José da Silva's weapon against the hostilities and injustices of the epoch. The famous Teatro do Bairro Alto in Lisbon soon became a platform where the author could entertain audiences while expressing his contempt for a society of poseurs and sycophants. His comic operas were based on plots fraught with intrigues and misunderstandings. The pace is lively and sustained, and the witty dialogue betrays a penchant for baroque eloquence. The presence of an all-knowing *gracioso* or *graciosa* (comic role) untangles the complicated threads of the plots, a familiar convention of the period. *The Wars of Alecrim and Manjerona (Guerras do Alecrim e Manjerona,* 1737) is generally considered to be the outstanding example of Antônio José da Silva's sparkling humor. This spirited caricature of Carnival revelers and their antics constitutes a veritable landmark in the history of comedy written in Portuguese.

GIOVANNI PONTIERO

EDITIONS

Teatro cômico português, 2 vols., Lisbon, 1744; *Teatro de Antônio José (O Judeu),* ed. by J. Ribeiro, 4 vols., Rio de Janeiro, 1910–1911; *Obras,* ed. by J. Pérez, 2 vols., São Paulo, 1945; *Obras completas de Antônio José da Silva,* vol. 1, with a preface by J. Pereira Tavares, Lisbon, 1957.

CRITICISM

M. de Oliveira Lima, "Antônio José, o Judeu," in *Aspectos da literatura colonial brasileira,* Leipzig, 1896, pp. 109–128; C. de Abreu, "Antônio José, o Judeu," in *Ensaios e estudos,* 2d ser., Rio de Janeiro, 1931, pp. 47–69; J. L. de Azevedo, *Novas epanáforas,* Lisbon, 1932; C. Juca Filho, *Antônio José, o Judeu,* Rio de Janeiro, 1940; C.–H. Frèches, "Introduction au théâtre du Judeu," in *Bulletin d'histoire du théâtre portugais,* Lisbon, I/1 (1950), pp. 51–52, II/1 (1950), pp. 73–79, and "Antônio José da Silva et les marionettes," IV/2 (1954); C.–H. Frèches, "Une Source de l'Opéra Vida do Grande D. Quixote de la Mancha e do Gordo Sancho Pança" in *Bulletin des etudes portugaises,* no. 22, Lisbon, 1960.

Simon, [Marvin] Neil (1927–)

American dramatist. His comedies of middle-class American life and values have made him one of the most commercially successful writers of the twentieth century. The son of a New York City garment salesman, Simon graduated from DeWitt Clinton High School in 1943. After briefly studying engineering at New York University and serving in the Army Air Force Reserve, he went to work in the mailroom of Warner Brothers' New York office, where his older brother Danny wrote publicity. Veteran comedy writer Goodman Ace gave the brothers an overnight writing assignment in 1947, to test their abilities. The sketch they turned in proved so successful that they were hired as staff comedy writers on the Robert Q. Lewis program on CBS. For nine years they wrote material for radio and television programs starring Phil Silvers, Tallulah Bankhead, Jackie Gleason, and Red Buttons.

In 1952, and again in 1953, the Simon brothers wrote sketches for summer camp revues, and several of these sketches briefly made it to Broadway in *Catch a Star*

Neil Simon.
[Theatre
Collection, The
New York Public
Library at Lincoln
Center, Astor,
Lenox and Tilden
Foundations]

(1955). The Simon brothers collaborated for the last time in Leonard Sillman's *New Faces of 1956;* Danny then began a successful career as a television director.

Neil Simon returned to television on his own, writing for Sid Caesar, Gary Moore, and Phil Silvers's *Sgt. Bilko* show ("You'll Never Get Rich"). On a five-week writing assignment on the West Coast for Jerry Lewis, Simon finished his work so quickly that he used most of his time to begin writing his first full-length play. *Come Blow Your Horn* appropriated Simon's experiences in portraying a young man leaving his parents in the Bronx and moving into his brother's Manhattan bachelor apartment. After many dropped options and false starts, the play premiered at the Bucks County Playhouse in New Hope, Pennsylvania, in August, 1960, and was successfully presented on Broadway the following year.

In the next twenty years, Simon averaged very nearly one Broadway production a year. In collaboration with composer Cy Coleman and lyricist Carolyn Leigh, he wrote the musical farce *Little Me* (1962), based on Patrick Dennis's memoire of the fictional Hollywood star Belle Poitrine. Simon's comedy of posthoneymoon nest building, *Barefoot in the Park,* which featured Elizabeth Ashley and Robert Redford as the newlyweds, opened in October, 1963, and ran for 1,532 performances.

With *Barefoot in the Park* still running, Simon opened *The Odd Couple* in March, 1965. This hit comedy of mismatched, middle-aged male roommates later became both a successful film and a long-running television sitcom. These two Broadway comedies were joined by the musical *Sweet Charity* (1966), an adaptation of Federico Fellini's 1957 film, *Nights of Cabiria,* and by *The Star-Spangled Girl* (1966), a comedy of romantic entanglements involving two magazine publishers of social criticism and the all-American girl-next-door. With the December, 1966, opening of *The Star-Spangled Girl,* Neil Simon became the first author to have four simultaneously running Broadway shows since Avery Hopwood's similar achievement in 1920.

Unhappy with the 1963 screenplay of *Come Blow Your Horn,* Simon fashioned his own screenplay for a film version of *Barefoot in the Park* (1967), which featured Robert Redford and Jane Fonda and established Simon as a "bankable" film name. Simon returned to Broadway with *Plaza Suite* (1968), three one-act comedies unified by their common setting, a suite in New York's Plaza Hotel. It was followed that same year by his third musical, *Promises, Promises,* an adaptation of the Billy Wilder–I. A. L. Diamond film *The Apartment.* With an able assist from composer Burt Bacharach and lyricist Hal David, *Promises, Promises* also passed the 1,000-performance mark. Next came *Last of the Red Hot Lovers* (1969), in which a middle-aged restaurateur makes three attempts to initiate an extra-marital affair. The comedy proved a popular hit and suggested that Simon could deal with subject matter of greater depth. However, *The Gingerbread Lady* (1970), a departure from comedy-farce, backfired. It portrays a cabaret singer's attempts to defeat her alcoholism. Out-of-town response to the play was sufficiently negative to threaten a Boston closing, a thought unprecedented in Neil Simon's hit-after-hit career. Prior to the Broadway opening, Simon wrote a new third act in which the singer no longer succumbs to her addiction but instead achieves an uneasy truce with herself and a reconciliation with her daughter. Although punctuated with characteristic Simon wit, even the new version did not succeed.

Simon fared better with *The Prisoner of Second Avenue* (1977), a bitter satire of urban life. Another success, *The Sunshine Boys* (1972), depicted the bittersweet reunion of two vaudeville partners who have not spoken for twelve years. Simon next adapted several stories by Anton

Scene from *Barefoot in the Park,* with Robert Redford and Mildred Natwick. New York, Biltmore Theatre, 1963. [Friedman-Abeles]

George C. Scott and Maureen Stapleton in *Plaza Suite*. New York, Plymouth Theatre, 1968. [Friedman-Abeles]

Art Carney (left) and Walter Matthau in *The Odd Couple*. New York, Plymouth Theatre, 1965. [Friedman-Abeles]

Chekhov to form the 1973 comedy with music *The Good Doctor,* and adapted the Biblical story of Job as the suburban comedy-drama *God's Favorite* (1974). Neither play proved successful.

After the death of his wife in 1973, Simon married actress Marsha Mason, but felt torn between his devotion to his first wife's memory and his new life. This crisis formed the basis of his acclaimed 1977 play *Chapter Two,* which both amused and moved Broadway audiences for two years.

Chapter Two was preceded by Simon's *California Suite,* (1976), four short comedies set in the Beverly Hills Hotel, a Los Angeles companion piece to *Plaza Suite.* Simon had moved to California a year earlier, and in these pieces he successfully caught the tone of his new hometown. His fourth musical, *They're Playing Our Song* (1979), a romance between a composer and a lyricist, proved a popular success and ran nearly three years on Broadway. Neither *I Ought to Be in Pictures* (1980), a father-daughter reunion/confrontation, nor *Fools* (1981), a fable set in a Russian village, proved popular, and a 1982 reworking of *Little Me* also failed. But Neil Simon's failures have been few, and none has sullied his deserved reputation as a masterful writer of comedy.

Many of Simon's plays have been filmed, and most

of these screenplays were of Simon's authorship. Additionally, Simon has written original screenplays for *The Out-of-Towners*, *The Heartbreak Kid*, *Murder by Death*, *The Goodbye Girl*, *The Cheap Detective*, *Seems Like Old Times*, and *Only When I Laugh* (a reworking of the themes of *The Gingerbread Lady*).

Barefoot in the Park (1963). Comedy. An up-and-coming lawyer, Paul, loves his wife, Corie, but his sense of practicality clashes with her romantic blindness. (For example, he is not pleased that their fifth-floor walk-up apartment, though heavy on charm, lacks basic amenities.) After a brief visit from Corie's widowed (and out-of-breath) mother, the newlyweds meet Mr. Velasco, an eccentric neighbor. Corie decides to spice up her mother's life by introducing them to each other. Initially, the attempt fails and only points up the temperamental differences between Paul and Corie, who begin feuding. However, Corie's mother eventually finds that she and Mr. Velasco have things in common after all. Corie decides to give Paul the "space" he needs. Drunk for the first time in his life, he demonstrates his willingness to loosen up by going for a walk on the outside ledge of the window. As Corie frantically coaxes him back to her, the curtain falls. Produced New York, Biltmore Theatre, October 23, 1963.

The Odd Couple (1965). Comedy. Oscar's Friday night poker party is interrupted by the news that Felix, one of the regulars, has left his wife after sending her a suicide telegram. When Felix arrives, his every move is interpreted as a suicide attempt. Oscar calms him and suggests he move in with him. But Felix is a hyper-allergic fanatic for organization and cleanliness, while Oscar is a cigar-smoking, compulsive slob. The characteristics that drove each of them to leave their wives soon have them at each other's throats. Oscar tries to loosen up Felix by inviting the neighboring Pigeon sisters to dinner. But the party is a disaster, and the next day Oscar throws Felix out, only to be stricken with guilt. Felix returns for his clothes, announcing he's moving in with the Pigeon sisters. The rift in their friendship has been repaired, and as the poker game resumes, Oscar cautions his pals to use the ashtrays. Produced New York, Plymouth Theatre, March 10, 1965.

The Sunshine Boys (1972). Comedy. Ben Silverman, a young agent, is engaged by CBS to reunite his uncle, Willie Clark, with Al Lewis, Clark's former vaudeville partner, for a television tribute to comedy. But Willie is suspicious, still hurt over Al's retirement eleven years earlier which had left Willie abandoned and unemployed. When the Sunshine Boys meet to rehearse their famous Doctor sketch, their personal crotchets and faulty memories result in a quarrel and Al storms out. At the dress rehearsal, the two comics get through most of their routine before they resume their feud. Al leaves again, and in a rage, Willie collapses. Two weeks later, as Willie is recovering from his heart attack, Ben brings Al to Wil-

Scene from the original production of *The Prisoner of Second Avenue*, with Vincent Gardenia and Peter Falk (right). [Martha Swope]

lie's bedside. The two old men are reconciled only to discover that their respective relatives have decided they should live in the same Actor's Home. Produced New York, Broadhurst Theatre, December 20, 1972.

TERRY MILLER

PLAYS

All plays were first performed in New York unless otherwise indicated.

1. *Catch a Star*. Musical revue. Produced Plymouth Theatre, Sept. 6, 1955. Sketches with Danny Simon.
2. *New Faces of 1956*. Musical revue. Produced Ethel Barrymore Theatre, June 14, 1956. Sketches with Danny Simon.
3. *Come Blow Your Horn*. Comedy in 3 acts. Published 1963. Produced Bucks County Playhouse, New Hope, Pa., August, 1960; Brooks Atkinson Theatre, Feb. 22, 1961.
4. *Little Me*. Musical comedy in 2 acts. Music: Cy Coleman, lyrics: Carolyn Leigh. Adapted from Patrick Dennis's satire, "Little Me" (1961). Produced Lunt-Fontanne Theatre, Nov. 17, 1962.
5. *Barefoot in the Park*. Comedy in 3 acts. Published 1964. Produced Biltmore Theatre, Oct. 23, 1963.
6. *The Odd Couple*. Comedy in 3 acts. Published 1966. Produced Plymouth Theatre, Mar. 10, 1965.
7. *Sweet Charity*. Musical comedy in 2 acts. Music: Cy Coleman, lyrics: Dorothy Fields. Adapted from the film *Nights of Cabiria* (1957) by Federico Fellini, Tullio Pinelli, and Ennio Flaiano. Published 1966. Produced Palace Theatre, Jan. 29, 1966.
8. *The Star-Spangled Girl*. Comedy in 3 acts. Published 1967. Produced Plymouth Theatre, Dec. 21, 1966.
9. *Plaza Suite*. 3 one-act comedies, *Visitor from Mamaroneck*, *Visitor from Hollywood*, *Visitor from Forest Hills*. Published 1969. Produced Plymouth Theatre, Feb. 14, 1968.
10. *Promises, Promises*. Musical comedy in 2 acts. Music: Burt Bacharach, lyrics: Hal David. Adapted from the film *The Apartment* (1960) by Billy Wilder and I. A. L. Diamond. Produced Shubert Theatre, Dec. 1, 1968.
11. *Last of the Red Hot Lovers*. Comedy in 3 acts. Published 1970. Produced Eugene O'Neill Theatre, Dec. 28, 1969.
12. *The Gingerbread Lady*. Play in 3 acts. Published 1971. Produced Plymouth Theatre, Dec. 13, 1970.
13. *The Prisoner of Second Avenue*. Comedy in 2 acts. Published 1972. Produced Eugene O'Neill Theatre, Nov. 11, 1971.
14. *The Sunshine Boys*. Comedy in 2 acts. Published 1973. Produced Broadhurst Theatre, Dec. 20, 1972.
15. *The Good Doctor*. Comedy with music in 11 scenes. Music: Peter Link, lyrics: Neil Simon. Adapted from and suggested by stories by Anton Chekhov. Published 1974. Produced Eugene O'Neill Theatre, Nov. 27, 1973.
16. *God's Favorite*. Comedy in 2 acts. Published 1975. Produced Eugene O'Neill Theatre, Dec. 11, 1974.
17. *California Suite*. 4 playlets, *Visitor from New York*, *Visitor from Philadelphia*, *Visitor from London*, *Visitor from Chicago*. Published 1977. Produced Eugene O'Neill Theatre, June 10, 1976.
18. *Chapter Two*. Play in 2 acts. Published 1978. Produced Imperial Theatre, Dec. 4, 1977.
19. *They're Playing Our Song*. Musical comedy in 2 acts. Music: Marvin Hamlisch, lyrics: Carole Bayer Sager. Published 1980. Produced Imperial Theatre, Feb. 11, 1979.
20. *I Ought to Be in Pictures*. Comedy in 2 acts. Published 1981. Produced Eugene O'Neill Theatre, Apr. 3, 1980.
21. *Fools*. Comedy in 2 acts. Published 1982. Produced Eugene O'Neill Theatre, Apr. 6, 1981.
22. *Little Me*. Musical comedy in two acts. Music: Cy Coleman, lyrics: Carolyn Leigh; revision of their 1962 musical comedy. Produced Eugene O'Neill Theatre, Jan. 21, 1982.

EDITIONS

The Comedy of Neil Simon (includes *Come Blow Your Horn*, *Barefoot in the Park*, *The Odd Couple*, *Plaza Suite*, *The Star-Spangled Girl*, *Promises, Promises*, and *Last of the Red Hot Lovers*), Random House, 1974; *The Comedy of Neil Simon, Volume 2* (includes *Little Me*, *The Gingerbread Lady*, *The Prisoner of Second Avenue*, *The Sunshine Boys*, *The Good Doctor*, *God's Favorite*, *California Suite*, and *Chapter Two*), Random House, 1979.

Simonov, Konstantin Mikhailovich (1915–1979)

Soviet novelist, poet, dramatist, and short-story writer. Konstantin (Kiril) Mikhailovich Simonov was born in Petrograd on November 15, 1915 (N.S.). From 1930 to 1935

he worked as a turner, and his early poetry appeared on the walls of the factory where he was employed. In 1934 he entered the Gorky Literary Institute, an adjunct of the Soviet Writers' Union. By the time he completed the course, in 1938, he had become known as one of the better new poets and had published his first collection of poems, *Real People* (*Nastoyashchiye lyudi*, 1938). At this time he wrote mostly on love, as in the poem *Five Pages* (*Pyat stranits*, 1938) and his first play, *The Story of a Love* (*Istoriya odnoy lyubvi*, pub. 1940); and on historical-patriotic subjects, as in the long poems *Suvorov* (1939) and *The Battle on the Ice* (*Ledovoye poboishche*, 1938), about Alexander Nevski's triumph over the Teutonic Knights.

After the German attack on the Soviet Union in World War II, on June 24, 1941, Simonov left for the front, where he spent the greater part of the war with the Russian armies as correspondent for *Krasnaya Zvezda* and *Pravda*. The popular essays and short stories describing his war experiences were collected in *From the Black Sea to the Barents Sea* (*Ot Chernogo do Barentsova morya*, 1944). But his best works from this period are the long poem *You Remember, Alosha, the Roads of Smolensk . . .* (*Ty pomnish, Alyosha, dorogi Smolenshchiny . . .*, 1942), full of deep love and grief for Russia; the play *The Russian People* (*Russkiye lyudi*, wr. 1941/42); and his novel *Days and Nights* (*Dni i nochi*, 1944), which received the 1946 Stalin Prize and is a personal, stirring account of the siege of Stalingrad. He was awarded the Order of the Red Banner and other medals for his reporting of the battles of Khalkhin Gol, Stalingrad, Odessa, and Moscow.

After 1946 Simonov, like all Soviet writers, was faced with strict political control, and his election as a secretary of the Soviet Writers' Union added further obligations. His writings of the late 1940s dealt wih typical postwar political themes, anti-Westernism and anticosmopolitanism, as in the novels *Smoke of the Fatherland* (*Dym otechestva*, 1947) and *Comrades in Arms* (*Tovarishchi po oruzhiyu*, 1952) and the collection of poems *Friends and Foes* (*Druzya i vragi*, 1948), which received the 1949 Stalin Prize.

After Stalin's death Simonov became less rigid about adhering to party-approved themes. As editor in chief of the literary magazine *Novy Mir* from 1954 to 1957, he published several liberal works (though he rejected Pasternak's *Dr. Zhivago*), including Vladimir Dudintsev's *Not by Bread Alone* (1956), which cost him his editorship. In 1958 Simonov was sent by *Pravda* on an assignment to Soviet Central Asia, and for two years he lived in Tashkent.

He belonged to the group of "moderate" writers in the Soviet Union. Although he believed in a writer's freedom to choose his own themes and techniques and supported a few of the programs proposed by the liberal writers, he remained a member of the Communist party. In the 1960s he returned to the themes of the war years, as in his memoir-novel *The Living and the Dead* (*Zhivye i myortvye*, 1960) and its sequel, *Soldiers Are Not Born* (*Soldatami ne rozhdayutsya*, 1964), which describe some of the repressive measures and the suspicion that pervaded the front because of Stalin's secret police. He also published a collection of short stories written between 1941 and 1963 under the title *There, Where We Had Been* (*Tam, gde my byvali*, 1964), all dealing with experiences, people, and memories connected with the war.

WORK

Simonov's career as a dramatist began with *The Story of a Love* (pub. 1940), which depicts a love triangle. Before and during Soviet participation in World War II, Simonov became vastly popular by describing the personal aspects of human life in a romantic and sympathetic style. His plays of this period are weak in plot but strong on atmosphere and general lyricism, and act as guides to conduct. In *A Fellow from Our Town* (*Paren iz nashego goroda*, wr. 1940/41), which received the 1942 Stalin Prize, the hero Lukonin, an average Soviet youth, displays bravery and patriotism by fighting as a volunteer in Manchuria and Spain; *The Russian People* (wr. 1941/42), which received the 1943 Stalin Prize and is his best play, portrays the emotional intensity, sacrifice, and bravery of the Russian people during the war. *Wait for Me* (*Zhdi menya*, wr. 1943) is based on his very popular war poem of the same name, but it is a mediocre play that was soon forgotten. Simonov was not able in later works to equal the popularity of his war literature.

After the war, when descriptions of Russian suffering and patriotism were considered an "ideological mistake," Simonov wrote *Under the Chestnut Trees of Prague* (*Pod kashtanami Pragi*, 1945), which warned unwary Communists that a proper Czech burgher might really be a fascist enemy. In his November, 1946, address to an All-Union Conference of Theatre Leaders and Playwrights, Simonov declared that "a playwright must be a politician," and thus he, like other Soviet writers who chose to write during the next seven years of Zhdanovism, had to make his literary products strictly party-minded. The two plays written under this policy employed the required anti-Western themes. In *The Russian Question* (*Russky vopros*, pub. 1946), which received the 1947 Stalin Prize and which initiated the literature of the Zhdanov period, an American correspondent who has been commissioned to write an anti-Soviet book is too honest to follow the orders of his capitalist boss and consequently loses his job, fiancée, and friends. *The Foreign Shadow* (*Chuzhaya ten*, pub. 1949), which received the 1950 Stalin Prize, tells of a Soviet scientist who discovers a vital vaccine beneficial to mankind; in the hands of American scientists it is distorted into a weapon for future chemical warfare. From the early 1950s to the present time Simonov has worked almost exclusively on his prose and poetry with the exception of one drama, *The Fourth* (*Chetvyorty*, wr. 1961), which shows the considerable influence of his postwar travels.

A Fellow from Our Town (*Paren iz nashego goroda*, wr. 1940/41). Drama portraying the typical young Soviet citizen of the 1940s. Sergey Lukonin is initially an unimportant small-town schoolteacher given to boasting and foolhardiness. When a skirmish with the Japanese on the Manchurian border threatens to turn into war, in order

to prepare himself to help defend the motherland he enrolls in a school teaching tank warfare. There he is reprimanded for his impulsiveness and immature judgment; yet when the war breaks out, he develops into an excellent commander. His wife also proves to be a worthy citizen. His brother-in-law, initially a pacifist, acts heroically as a wartime surgeon but is killed by the enemy.

The Russian People (*Russkiye lyudi*, wr. 1941/42). Drama glorifying the idealism, stamina, and abnegation of the Russian people and set on the southern front in World War II. Across the river from a town most of which has fallen to the Germans, the Russians are holding out, waiting for the Red Army to arrive. Their captain, Sofonov, sends Valya, the girl he loves, on a dangerous mission and does not lose heart even when the Germans murder his mother out of sheer bloodlust. Globa, a doctor who has led a dashing life, now sacrifices himself with humility and leaves on a mission from which he knows he will not return. The threat of death only intensifies the Russians' love of life, and on the eve of their destruction they dream of future freedom. They feel that their lot is glorious compared with that of the fearful and suspicious Germans or that of the Russian traitor who, by submitting to the German order and displaying joy at the news of his son's death, loses all humanity. Finally, the Red Army enters the town singing and rescues the Russian heroes.   [LAURENCE SENELICK]

PLAYS

1. *Istoriya odnoy lyubvi* (*The Story of a Love.*). Drama. Published 1940.
2. *Paren iz nashego goroda* (*A Fellow from Our Town*). Drama, 3 acts, 9 scenes. Written 1940/41. Published 1941.
3. *Russkiye lyudi** (*The Russian People*). Drama, 3 acts, 9 scenes. Written 1941/42. Published 1941.
4. *Zhdi menya* (*Wait for Me*). Drama, 3 acts, 8 scenes. Written 1943. Published 1943.
5. *Tak i budet* (*Thus It Will Be*). Drama, 3 acts, 6 scenes. Written 1944.
6. *Pod kashtanami Pragi* (*Under the Chestnut Trees of Prague*). Drama, 4 acts, 5 scenes. Published 1946. Produced 1945.
7. *Russky vopros* (*The Russian Question*). Drama, 3 acts, 7 scenes. Published 1946.
8. *Chuzhaya ten* (*The Foreign Shadow*). Drama, 4 acts, 6 scenes. Published 1949.
9. *Dobroye imya* (*The Good Name*). Comedy. Published 1953.
10. *Chetvyorty* (*The Fourth*). Drama. Written 1961.

EDITIONS

Collections
Stikhi, pyesy, rasskazy, Moscow, 1949; *Sochineniya K. Simonova*, 3 vols., Moscow, 1952–1953; *Pyesy K. Simonova*, Moscow, 1954.
Individual Plays
The Russian People (*The Russians*). Published in *Four Soviet War Plays*, tr. by G. Shelley and T. Guthrie, London, 1944; *Seven Soviet Plays*, ed. by H. W. L. Dana and tr. by C. Odets, New York, 1946.
The Whole World Over. T. Schnee, tr., New York, 1949.

CRITICISM

L. Lazarev, *Dramaturgiya Konstantina M. Simonova*, Moscow, 1952.

Simpson, N. F. (1919–   )

British teacher and dramatist. His work, although akin to that of Ionesco is also closely linked to the English nonsense tradition. His first play, *A Resounding Tinkle*, produced in 1957, was then shortened from two acts to one and presented at the Royal Court Theatre in a double bill with another of his one-act plays, *The Hole* (1958). In the former there are a number of unrelated actions that, as the character representing the author explains, each member of the audience is free to interpret as he wishes, thereby constructing his own play. *The Hole*, based on a conversation between two women, shows the husband of one striving to be a nonconformist while the other's husband strives for conformity. Simpson's second full-length play, to date his most successful, is *One Way Pendulum*, first produced in 1959. A surrealist comedy, it concerns a young man who divides his time between homicide and teaching weighing machines to sing Handel's "Hallelujah Chorus." A homemade courtroom, built by his father as a replica of one at the Old Bailey, is the scene of his trial for murder. *Three* (1961) was a presentation of three one-act plays by John Mortimer, Harold Pinter, and Simpson. Simpson's contribution was *The Form*, a humorous statement of the futility of words. *The Cresta Run* was produced in 1965. His more recent work has not had the impact of his first three plays.

CRITICISM

J. R. Taylor, *Anger and After*, London, 1962.

Şinasi, İbrahim (1826–1871)

Turkish journalist, poet, and dramatist. The son of a well-to-do Istanbul family, Şinasi received, in 1849, a government scholarship which allowed him to spend five years in Paris, where he formed links with French literary circles and became especially friendly with the poet Alphonse de Lamartine (1790–1869). On his return to Turkey, he devoted his energy to publishing and became one of the leading spirits of the Tanzimat literature, which introduced Western literary ideas to Turkey. In 1859 he produced his first work, an anthology of poems in the classical style, and also published an anthology of translations from the French classics, mainly Racine and LaFontaine. With a friend Şinasi began publication of the first privately owned Turkish newspaper, *Tercüman-i Ahval (Interpreter of Opinions)*, but soon left to start his own paper, *Tasvir-i Efkâr (Representation of Opinions)*. Among

İbrahim Şinasi.
[Metin And Collection]

his employees was the young poet Namık Kemal, who was to become his most important disciple (*see* NAMIK KEMAL). Şinasi eventually returned to Paris, where he remained until 1870, devoting himself entirely to the study of literature and work on an Ottoman dictionary.

A pioneer in introducing Western concepts to Turkey, he attained influence out of proportion to his original creative work. Though there had been obscure attempts at Western-style playwriting before him, his *The Poet's Marriage (Bir Şair Evlenmesi, 1859)* is generally considered an important step toward establishing a Turkish national dramatic literature. A one-act farce, it ridicules the Muslim custom of making marriage contracts through intermediaries. A young poet is in love with a girl whose family attempts to take advantage of the fact that a groom may not see his bride's face until after the marriage contract to trick him into wedding an ugly older sister. With the help of friends who bribe the priest, the poet is eventually united with the girl of his choice. The play was apparently commissioned for the newly completed court theatre of the Dolmabahçe Palace, but there is no evidence that it was actually ever performed there.

METIN AND

Skelton, John (ca. 1460–1529)

English poet. He is best known for his trenchant satirical verse written in a vigorous kind of doggerel—a style that bears his name, "Skeltonic verse." Of his four known dramatic compositions, the sole survivor is *Magnificence*, which, although it must have been written between 1513 and 1523, was not published until 1530. A morality play, it chronicles the downfall of the title figure after he rejects the successive counsels of Liberty, Felicity, Measure, and other worthies, surrendering instead to Fancy, Counterfeit, and allied seducers. Plagued by Adversity, Poverty, and similar ills, Magnificence is finally rescued by Redress, Perseverance, and their cohorts. *See* MORALITY PLAY in glossary.

Sklar, George (1908–)

American dramatist. He is noted for his plays on proletarian themes. His best play is *Stevedore* (1934), a plea for racial equality written with Paul Peters. Among his other plays are *Parade* (1935), also with Peters; *Life and Death of an American* (1939); and two plays with Albert Maltz, *Merry-Go-Round* (1932) and *Peace on Earth* (1933). Sklar collaborated with Vera Caspary on the dramatization of her mystery novel *Laura* (1946). In 1966, Sklar returned to the theater after an absence of many years with *And People All Around*, a play inspired by the brutal killing of three civil rights workers in Mississippi in 1964.

[GAUTAM DASGUPTA]

Skourtis, Yeorgos (1940–)

Greek playwright. Born in Athens, he had little formal education, but graduated instead from what he refers to as the "university of life." Among other things, he has been a baker, waiter, construction worker, taxi driver, elevator operator, and publicity man.

Skourtis is a major representative of the new Greek

theatre that emerged in the 1960s and flourished in the 1970s. Mixing a clear sense of realism in his characterizations and dialogue with absurd or exaggerated situations, he has created a series of works that speak directly to Greek audiences of their problems. Skourtis shows a firm grasp of the economic elements that govern life, but does not, however, reduce his plays to political debates. His dramas are infused with a rich sense of Greek *laiki* ("popular") culture. He draws heavily on the lively demotic spoken language, popular and folk music, and the Greek sense of humor. Besides his full-length plays, he has written more than a dozen one-act plays, short stories, and has translated Shakespeare and other works, including Aristophanes's *The Knights* (from the ancient Greek), which was presented in a *laiki* spirit by Karolos Koun's Art Theatre at Epidauros during the summer of 1979.

His first play, *The Nannies (I Dadathes)* was produced by the Art Theatre in 1970. Social realism and a sense of absurdity are captured in a story of two poor "common men," Peter and Paul (names suggesting the two Apostles), who work as "nannies" for the "lady" of a bourgeois household who happens to be dead, but whose corpse remains on stage. Dramatically and sympathetically, Skourtis depicts the bitterness and humanity of these two homeless Greeks, who are neither strong enough to revolt against the "dead" weight of the Greek bourgeois ruling class nor mindless enough to live within the household peacefully. In 1979 the play was made into a film directed by Nikos Zopatinos.

His second play, *The Musicians (I Mousiki,* 1972), continues Skourtis's concern for the common man and the Greek popular tradition, but without the presence of the bourgeois or ruling class. The musicians are three street musicians, two men and a woman, who are poor except for their music. They have no names, rather they call themselves by the names of their instruments. Flute has a conscience, a memory of stories and sayings from his Mama, a concern for the Greek popular musical heritage, and a need to work for group ends—namely the formation of an orchestra, a task that is never completed in the play. Banjo is Flute's opposite in almost every way: he looks out for himself alone, prefers modern music to the Greek folk tunes, claims Spoons as his woman, and feels he has lost all sense of identity and purpose. Spoons, an ex-prostitute who has become an alcoholic, can sing Greek folk tunes beautifully when inspired by Flute. She is caught between the two men and the two views they represent toward life and Greek culture. Banjo (a foreign instrument to begin with) discovers his true name, Dionysos, and strikes out on his own. Spoons remains with Flute, who has told them, "We will lose the future if we don't go back to find our roots." In the end he sets out with Spoons and other musicians who join them with the goal of forming an "orchestra" still in mind.

In this play the role of the "dead" mother is the reverse of the lady of the house in *The Nannies,* where she represents a useless weight from the past to be cast off. In *The Musicians,* Flute's mother turns out to have been

The Nannies, as produced by Karolos Koun's Art Theatre in 1979. [Photograph courtesy of Andrew Horton]

a singer of Greek folk tunes who was beaten to death while singing a traditional ballad *(Saranda Palikaria).* The music for the play, which was composed and directed by Yannis Markopoulos, a Cretan who has devoted his career to injecting the rich traditional Greek music into contemporary Greek *laiki* music, serves to reinforce Skourtis's basic themes. But while such plays are firmly rooted in Greek situations, the simplicity of the drama and the powerful characterizations that blend humor and pathos remind us of Samuel Beckett's more starkly universal representations.

Skourtis is "didactic" in the sense of wishing to convey the human condition in a clearly Greek reality. His views have been expressed most vividly in a one-act play, *Dialogue with a Writer,* in which a critic and a writer work toward a final agreement on the needs of a modern playwright to express his times, but more specifically through his own culture, not by imitating Ionesco, Pinter, Albee, Brecht or others. Skourtis strongly believes that the theatre and all the arts develop according to the economics (financial and cultural) of a society. Serious drama, for Skourtis, becomes "political" theatre, not as party politics or as an imitation of Brechtian theatre, but as an expression of human and social historical reality. The "critic" ends the one-act dialogue saying: "Finally, political theatre means: to handle the specific problems of your country, for the people of your country with the sensibility and contemporary artistic expression and roots of your country."

This is Skourtis's creed and the conviction of a number of contemporary Greek playwrights. His next play, *Karaghiozis Almost a Vizier (Karaghiozis para ligo Veziris),* was a joyous celebration of the hero of Greek shadow theatre presented by the actors (Yeorgos Lazanis as Karaghiozis) as if it were a shadow play come to life.

His other produced plays include *The Noose* (*Thileia*, 1974); *Strike* (*Apergia*, 1975), a Brechtian work concerning a strike in a foreign factory by poor workers from a variety of countries; *Kommendia* (*Kommendia*, 1974); and *Bits and Pieces* (1977). He has also contributed to several successful *epitheorises*, such as *National Comedy* (*Ethniki Comodea*, 1975) and, with Costas Mourselas, *Where Is the Bus Going?* (*Pou Paei to Leoforeo*, 1979).

ANDREW HORTON

Slade, Bernard (1930–   )

Canadian playwright. He is best known for his comedy *Same Time, Next Year*. Slade was born in St. Catharines, Ontario, was educated in England, and now lives in Los Angeles. He began his dramatic career as an actor in Canadian amateur and summer-stock theatre, started his own theatre in Vineland, and later worked as a script writer for the Canadian Broadcasting Corporation. While living in Canada, Slade wrote two stage plays, *Simon Says Get Married* (1961), produced by the Crest Theatre in Toronto, and *A Very Close Family* (1962), produced by the Manitoba Theatre Centre in Winnipeg; neither has been published. After moving to California in 1964, Slade wrote situation comedies for television—creating "The Partridge Family," "The Flying Nun," "Love on a Rooftop," "Bridget Loves Bernie," "The Girl With Something Extra," and "Mr. Deeds Goes to Town"—as well as writing scripts for other series.

Same Time, Next Year opened in Boston in 1975 and went on from there to Broadway. It is a neatly constructed two-person play, each of its six scenes depicting an annual motel tryst between George and Doris, thus presenting the development of a relationship which begins as casual, if guilt-ridden, adultery in 1951 but which deepens and adapts as the couple progress through their times together over the next twenty-five years. On the whole, shifts between frequently risqué comic sequences and sentiment are adroitly handled, and the playwright makes good use of a situation in which the protagonists have known each other over a prolonged period of time but must still rediscover the other's personality at each encounter. Time elapsed between scenes also provides opportunities for pointed and sometimes poignant comment on changing attitudes and values through the fifties, sixties, and seventies. *Same Time, Next Year* has been enormously successful; it played on Broadway for over three years, has been given over fifty productions around the world, and has been presented as a film starring Alan Alda and Ellen Burstyn.

Slade's next play, *Tribute* (1978), was less enthusiastically received, although still a commercial success. More ambitious and serious than the earlier play, *Tribute* attempts to justify the apparently trivial life of its protagonist, Scottie Templeton, a glad-handing public relations man and failed screenwriter who is loved for his sense of humor and irreverence by the numerous friends who have organized the tribute, the evening of reminiscence and celebration which provides the frame for the play as a whole. Scottie's charm has been resisted, however, by his son, Jud, a serious young man whose tastes run more to books and art museums than to his father's vaudeville routines and golden-hearted party girls. Learning that he is dying of cancer, Scottie, in the main action of the play, makes a last attempt to reach his own son and "to teach him how to have fun." The mixture of one-liners and sentimentality is not as surely handled as the similar combination in *Same Time, Next Year*, and *Tribute* frequently falls victim to mawkishness, particularly during the unconvincing reconciliation between father and son. *Romantic Comedy* was seen briefly on Broadway in 1979, and *Special Occasions* (1982) proved to be a critical and commercial failure.

CHRIS JOHNSON

Słowacki, Juliusz (1809–1849)

Polish romantic poet and dramatist. Juliusz Słowacki was born on September 4, 1809, in Krzemieniec. Having graduated from the Law Faculty of the University of Vilna in 1829, he worked in the Treasury Department at Warsaw until the insurrection of 1830, when he served the revolutionary government as diplomatic courier to London. After receiving news of the insurrection's failure, he settled in Paris, where his first published work, *Poems* (*Poezje*, 2 vols., 1832), appeared. A falling-out with Adam Mickiewicz, who was also living in Paris, caused him to move to Geneva in December, 1832. *See* MICKIEWICZ, ADAM.

While Słowacki was in Switzerland, his third volume of *Poezje* (1833) was published in Paris, and he wrote *Kordian* (pub. 1834), his most important drama. In 1836 he moved to Italy. The same year he made a trip to Greece and the Middle East, which inspired new poetic endeavors: *A Journey to the Holy Land* (*Podróż do Ziemi świętej*, 1839); *Agamemnon's Grave* (*Grób Agamemnona*, 1840); *Hymn* (1839); and the symbolic prose poem *Anhelli* (1838), about national and individual suffering and sacrifice. This theme was continued in *Three Poems* (*Trzy poemata*, 1839) and *The Poem of Piast Dantyszek about Hell* (*Poemat Piasta Dantyszka w piekle*, 1839). In 1838 Słowacki

Juliusz Słowacki.
[Agencja Autorska, Warsaw]

returned to Paris, where he spent the remainder of his life and finally won the acclaim of the Polish *émigré* community with his long satirical Byronic poem *Beniowski* (1841).

His last creative period, influenced by his short and disillusioning association with Andrzej Towiański's circle, a mystical Slavophile-oriented group, produced a transcendental philosophical treatise, *Genesis from the Spirit* (*Genezis z ducha*, 1844), and many dramas and poems, including *Reply to the Psalms of the Future* (*Odpowiedź na psalmy przyszłości*, 1846), which refutes Krasiński's solution to Poland's problems; and *King Spirit* (*Król Duch*, 1847), his last and greatest work. *See* KRASIŃSKI, ZYGMUNT.

Słowacki returned to Prussian Poland to participate in the revolutionary activities of 1848. In danger of arrest, he went back to Paris, where he died of tuberculosis on April 3, 1849, leaving a literary corpus that includes 253 works of poetry and 25 dramas, some never completed. On June 28, 1927, his body was transferred from Paris to the royal vaults of the Wawel Castle in Cracow.

WORK

Słowacki was the precursor of modern Polish drama and the main influence on the writers of the later Young Poland group, a neoromantic and symbolist movement. Using rich imagery, symbolism, mysticism, fantasy, and imaginative neologisms, his themes revolve around Poland's history, national soul, and relation to the cosmos. His style is romantic; his form, dramatic verse; his linguistic construction, subtle, lyrical, and complex. *See* SYMBOLISM in glossary.

Słowacki's dramatic work falls into four periods. The early period exhibits strong classical influence, as in the tragedy *Mindowe* (pub. 1832, prod. 1869) and in *Maria Stuart* (pub. 1832, prod. 1862), which also shows some Shakespearean influence.

Kordian (pub. 1834, prod. 1899) exemplifies Słowacki's Swiss period, in which he attempts to extract from Polish history the true "Polish idea" in order to regenerate the Polish spirit. He criticizes his generation, symbolized by Kordian, for its readiness to die heroically but pointlessly. *Balladyna* (wr. 1834, prod. 1862) also expresses a fatalistic view of Polish uprisings. The unfinished drama *Horsztyński* (wr. 1835, prod. 1879) introduces a tormented Polish-style Hamlet in the setting of the Russo-Polish campaign of 1792.

The Parisian period includes two important historical tragedies, *Mazeppa* (*Mazepa*; pub. 1840, prod. 1847), which, using the method of Victor Hugo, shows the inhumanity resulting from the Polish gentry's preoccupation with honor; and *Lilla Weneda* (pub. 1840, prod. 1869), whose heroine symbolizes a perishing nation. *Fantazy* (wr. 1843, prod. 1867), Słowacki's only play with a contemporary background, is a semicomical satire exploring the hypocritical romantic posturing of the Polish gentry.

Słowacki's last period is influenced by his philosophy as explained in *Genesis from the Spirit* (1844), that is,

the metempsychosis of the human spirit to higher forms and the existence of King Spirits, whether nations or individuals to guide this process. Examples of these mystical spirits are seen in the historical tragedies *Father Marek* (*Ksiądz Marek*; pub. 1843, prod. 1901), set immediately before the first Polish partition, and *The Constant Prince* (*Książę niezłomny*; pub. 1844, prod. 1874), which explores the value of suffering, both showing the influence of Calderón; *Agesilaus* (*Agezylausz*; wr. 1844, prod. 1927), dramatizing the efforts of King Agesilaus to regain Sparta's former splendor; and *Prince Michael of Tver* (*Książę Michał Twerski*, wr. 1845) a five-scene fragment of a play showing a destructive "spirit" in the person of the bloodthirsty Uzbek Khan. In *The Silver Dream of Salomea* (*Sen srebrny Salomei*; pub. 1844, prod. 1900), a visionary drama of the eighteenth-century Ukrainian uprising, Słowacki experiments with mystical demonology. His philosophy culminated in *Samuel Zborowski* (wr. 1845, prod. 1927), a fantasy drama in which Polish historical problems are transposed to the cosmic plane and the dichotomies between order and freedom, crime and punishment, are explored in depth. Słowacki's plays were all staged posthumously.

Kordian (pub. 1834, prod. 1899). Poetic tragedy, showing the influence of Shakespeare, in which a generation of idealists is symbolized by the hero, Kordian. In the beginning, fifteen-year-old Kordian agonizes over the tormented state of both his soul and Poland. He considers several courses of action, including one described

Kordian, produced at the Teatr Polski, Wrocław. [Agencja Autorska, Warsaw]

Kordian as staged at the Teatre Polski Wrocław.
[Agencja Autorska, Warsaw]

Scene from *Balladyna*. Szczecin, Teatr Polski, 1965.
[Agencja Autorska, Warsaw]

by Grzegorz, his servant and a veteran of the Napoleonic Wars, as traditionally Polish: to die fighting for a cause. Recognizing that he is unable to act heroically, Kordian chooses to die and vainly attempts suicide.

In search of knowledge of himself and life, Kordian now travels to England, Italy, and Switzerland. Atop Mont Blanc he decides to return to Poland and fight for national independence. Meanwhile, in Warsaw the Czar is preparing for his coronation as King of Poland. Kordian, having become a leader of patriotic conspirators, volunteers to kill the royal family. En route to the Czar's chamber, however, he is paralyzed by imagination and fear and is presently discovered unconscious at the Czar's doorstep. Kordian is then interned in a madhouse, where he debates the value of patriotic self-sacrifice with an imaginary Faustus. Grand Duke Constantine, sympathetic to the Poles, wants Kordian pardoned, but the Czar refuses to rescind the death sentence until the Duke, desperate, relinquishes his sword. An aide races to the place of execution with the pardon but arrives too late.

Balladyna (wr. 1834, prod. 1862). Drama based on an early legend and expressing fatalism about Polish uprisings. Goplana, Lake Gopła's nymph, desiring Grabiec, Balladyna's lover, wants to eliminate her rival. Thus she orders her imp Chochlik to enchant Count Kirkor and lead him to Balladyna's hut. Under Chochlik's magic, Kirkor falls in love with both Balladyna and her sister Alina. Their mother suggests that whoever picks the greatest number of berries become the bride. Balladyna, unsuccessful, kills Alina and is cursed with a permanent bloodstain on her forehead. Nevertheless, Balladyna marries Kirkor, who soon thereafter leaves on a campaign to overthrow the usurper of the Polish throne.

During Kirkor's absence, a banquet given by Balladyna, Grabiec, and Kostryn, the head of Kirkor's castle guards, who had become Balladyna's lover and partner in the killing of a messenger sent by Kirkor, is interrupted by Balladyna's mother, who accuses her daughter of ingratitude and maltreatment. She is declared insane and ejected by Balladyna. News is then received from Kirkor that he has killed the usurper and is now seeking the missing crown. Balladyna and Kostryn retrieve the crown from Grabiec, who had received it as a gift from Goplana, and go with an army to Gniezno, where they defeat and kill Kirkor.

Goplana is exiled for interfering with human affairs, and Balladyna becomes the ruler of Poland. During her coronation she poisons Kostryn. Shortly afterward, sitting in a court of justice, Balladyna hears a complaint against a cruel daughter by her blind mother who is ignorant of the Queen's identity. The mother, unwilling to reveal the evil daughter's name but required by law to do so, is put on the rack and dies. Faced with the demand of the Chancellor to pronounce judgment on the evil daughter, Balladyna decrees death and is instantly struck and killed by lightning.

Lilla Weneda (pub. 1840, prod. 1869). Drama based on an early legend. Derwid, king of the Wenedians, and his sons are captured by the armies of Lech, king of the Lechites. Lech's ruthless wife Gwinona has Derwid blinded and tortured. Lilla, Derwid's daughter, arrives in the Lechite camp to rescue her family; she frees her brothers but not Derwid and his enchanted harp. Thrice Lilla saves Derwid from a horrible death. Discovering that her son has been captured by the Wenedians, Gwinona frees Derwid in exchange for Prince Lechon but keeps the harp as a hostage. Concurrently, the Wenedians decide to exchange Lechon for Derwid.

Unaware that Lilla and Derwid are en route and receiving a false report of their deaths, Roza, Derwid's oldest daughter, kills Lechon. The Wenedians are despondent when Derwid arrives without the harp, for only its magic song can ensure victory. Lilla returns to trick Gwinona and retrieve the harp. Gwinona, however, realizing that her son is dead, kills Lilla and then goes into battle. The Wenedians are losing when they receive a box, supposedly containing the harp. Opening it, Derwid discovers Lilla's body and kills himself in despair. Thus the Wenedians are vanquished. Gwinona is killed by the ashes of the cremated bodies of Derwid and Lilla. Derwid's sons also die, and only Roza remains.

[DANIEL GEROULD]

PLAYS

All the plays were written in verse.

1. *Mindowe Król Litewski* (*Mindowe, King of Lithuania*). Historical Tableau, 5 acts. Written 1829. Published 1832. Produced Cracow, Teatr Miejski, Apr. 17, 1869.

2. *Maria Stuart**. Play, 5 acts. Published 1832. Produced Lvov, Teatr Skarbka, Jan. 27, 1862.

3. *Kordian*. Play, prologue and 3 acts. Published 1834. Produced Cracow, Teatr Miejski, Nov. 25, 1899.

4. *Balladyna**. Tragedy, 5 acts. Written 1834. Published 1839. Produced Lvov, Teatr Skarbka, Mar. 7, 1862.

5. *Horsztyński*. Play, 5 acts. Written 1835. Published 1866. Produced Cracow, Teatr Miejski, Mar. 29, 1879.

6. *Beatryks Cenci*. Tragedy, 5 acts. Written 1839. Published 1866. Produced Poznań, Teatr Polski, Jan. 11, 1872.

7. *Lilla Weneda**. Tragedy, prologue and 5 acts. Published 1840. Produced Lvov, June 24, 1863.

8. *Mazepa** (*Mazeppa*). Tragedy, 5 acts. Published 1840. Produced Budapest, Nemzeti Színház, Dec. 13, 1847; Cracow, Teatr Miejski, June 5, 1851.

9. *Krak*. Fragment. Play, 1 act (4 scenes). Written 1840. Published 1866. Produced Cracow, Apr. 3, 1909.

10. *Beniowski*. Fragment. Play, 2 acts and 2 scenes of Act III. Written 1840. Published 1866. Produced Łódź, Teatr Polski, Nov. 4, 1909.

11. *Fantazy.** Play, 5 acts. Written 1841. Published 1866. Produced Stanisławów, Teatr Stanisławów, May 9, 1867, as *Niepoprawni* (*The Incorrigibles*).

12. *Jan Kazimierz*. Fragment. Play, 1 act (6 scenes). Written 1841. Published 1866. Produced Czestochowa Mar. 18, 1909.

13. *Krytyka krytyki literary* (*Criticism of Literary Criticism*). Fragment. Play. Published 1891. Produced Warsaw, Teatr Artystów Cricot, Apr. 10, 1939.

14. *Wallenrod*. Fragment. Play, 2 acts and 1 scene of Act III. Written 1841. Published 1866. Produced Łódź Nov. 4, 1909.

15. *Złota czaszka* (*The Golden Skull*). Play, 2 acts. Written 1842. Published 1866. Produced Cracow, Teatr Miejski, Aug. 26, 1899.

16. *Ksiądz Marek* (*Father Marek*). Dramatic poem, 3 acts. Published 1843. Produced Cracow, Teatr Miejski, Nov. 29, 1901.

17. *Sen srebrny Salomei* (*The Silver Dream of Salomea*). Dramatic romance, 5 acts. Published 1844. Produced Cracow, Teatr Miejski, Mar. 24, 1900.

18. *Książę niezłomny* (*The Constant Prince*). Tragedy, 3 acts. Published 1844. Produced Cracow, Teatr Miejski, Oct. 17, 1874. Adaptation of Calderón's play.

19. *Agezylausz* (*Agesilaus*). Play, 3 acts. Written 1844. Published 1884. Produced Warsaw, Teatr Narodowy, Sept. 30, 1927, as *Król Agis* (*King Agis*).

20. *Walter Stadion*. Fragment. Play, 3 scenes. Written 1844. Published 1866.

21. *Książę Michał Twerski (Prince Michael of Tver)*. Fragment. Play, 5 scenes. Written 1844. Published 1909.

22. *Zawisza Czarny (Zawisza the Black)*. Fragments. Play; first version, 21 scenes (1844); second version, 7 scenes (1845). Published 1889. Produced Lvov, Teatr Miejski, June 28, 1910.

23. *Samuel Zborowski*. Play, 5 acts. Written 1845. Published 1928. Produced Łódź, Teatr Miejski, Sept. 7, 1911; Warsaw, Teatr Polski, June 24, 1927.

24. *Makbet (Macbeth)*. Fragment. Play, 1 act (3 scenes). Written 1846. Published 1909. Adaptation of Shakespeare's *Macbeth*.

25. *Dziady (Forefathers' Eve)*. Fragment Play. Published 1909. Written 1846.

26. *Góry się oztocity, szafiry mórz ciemnieją (The Mountains Grew Golden, the Sapphire of the Seas Turns Dark)*. Fragment. Play. Written and published 1847.

27. *Syn ziemi (Son of the Earth)*. Fragment. Play. Written 1848. Published 1883.

28. *Król i wódz (The King and the Commander)*. Fragment. Play, 2 scenes. Written 1847. Published 1909.

EDITIONS

Dzieta, ed. by J. Krzyżanowski, 14 vols., Warsaw, 1952.

CRITICISM

J. Kleiner, *Studia o Słowackim*, Lvov, 1910; *Juliusz Słowacki 1809–1849. The Century Volume*, ed. by W. Folkierski, M. Giergielewicz, and S. Stroński; London, 1951; *Juliusz Słowacki*, ed. by M. Bezan and Z. Lewinówna, Warsaw, 1959; S. Treugutt, *Juliusz Słowacki, Romantic Poet*, Warsaw, 1959; E. Sawrymowicz, *Kalendarz życia i twórczości Juliusza Słowackiego*, Wrocław, 1960.

Smith, Dodie (1896–)

British actress, novelist, and dramatist. Miss Smith began her theatrical career as an actress in 1915. Although she wrote plays early in her career, her first professionally

Lillian Gish and Jack Hawkins in *Dear Octopus*. New York, Broadhurst Theatre, 1939. [Photograph by Vandamm. Theatre Collection, The New York Public Library at Lincoln Center]

Call It a Day, with (l. to r.) Philip Merivale, Jeanne Dante, John Buckmaster, and Gladys Cooper. New York, Morosco Theatre, 1936. [Photograph by Vandamm. Theatre Collection, The New York Public Library at Lincoln Center, Astor, Lenox and Tilden Foundations]

staged play, *Autumn Crocus*, was not produced until 1931. It enjoyed immediate success and was followed by *Service* (1932), *Touch Wood* (1934), and *Call It a Day* (1935), all of which were written under the pseudonym C. L. Anthony. Other notable plays include *Bonnet over the Windmill* (1937); *Dear Octopus* (1938); *Lovers and Friends* (1943); *Letter from Paris* (1952); *I Capture the Castle* (1954), adapted from her novel of the same name; *These People, Those Books* (1958); and *Amateur Means Lover* (1961). The first part of her autobiography, *Look Back with Love*, was published in 1971.

Smoček, Ladislav (1932–)

Czech playwright and theatre director. Smoček was a cofounder of the Drama Club, an important experimental stage in Prague. Although he is most famous for absurdist plays, he started his career as playwright with a neo-naturalist one-acter, *Picnic (Piknik,* 1965). The play, inspired by the war fiction of Norman Mailer, describes a patrol of American soldiers lost in enemy territory on an island in the South Pacific. There is no political-allegorical interest in his play; the situation serves Smoček merely as a background for a psychological study of man's conduct under extreme stress.

Following the general trend of Czech drama of the mid-1960s, Smoček's subsequent three plays are nonrepresentational. *The Strange Afternoon of Dr. Zvonko Burke (Podivné odpoledne doktora Zvonka Burkeho,* 1966) is a tragicomic nonrealistic portrayal of a superannuated bachelor who is to be evicted from the rented room in which he had been residing for twenty years. The transformation of a peace-loving, kindhearted individual into a raving maniac is achieved by means of grotesque hyperbole. The play, which lays out the relationship between the id and the superego, also contains some sociopolitical implications. Smoček uses more purely farcical elements than can be found in other absurdist dramas in Czechoslovakia and elsewhere in the West. The humor is typically Czech—robust and unadorned. *The Maze (Bludiště,* 1966) is a more conventional absurdist drama. The action takes place in front of an entrance to a maze in an amusement park. Those who enter the maze never return. The drama portrays the horror and fascination the unknown exerts on a curious but reluctant visitor who is finally driven into the maze by the guard. The play is generally interpreted as a political allegory on the Communist social system, but more general metaphysical implications are detectable as well. Smoček's drama *Cosmic Spring* (*Kosmické jaro*, 1969) is a somber, brooding, and deliberately obscure work describing a group of individuals passing their time in a condemned house. Its pervasive mood of doom, destruction and claustrophobic anxiety attains symbolic dimensions. The play contains veiled references to the ill-fated "Springtime of Prague," but its ambiguous, provocatively elusive design defies one-sided interpretations.

Smoček is one of the more successful Czech playwrights who has been capable of interweaving the topical and the timeless in his work. He is a great master of language, which he uses for striking dramatic effects, and his intermingling of patterns from various linguistic strata is particularly effective. His plays were written specifically for his company and are extremely difficult to produce outside their original ambience.

PAUL I. TRENSKY

Sobol, Yehoshua   (1939–   )

Israeli playwright. Born in Tel Aviv, Sobol spent his childhood on a farm, joined a kibbutz, and was a member of a left-wing youth organization. After leaving the kibbutz, he went to Paris, where he studied philosophy at the Sorbonne and worked as a journalist during the time of the students' revolt there. Back in Israel, Sobol joined the staff of the Haifa Municipal Theatre, wrote a number of documentaries, and in 1972 adapted Thornton Wilder's *Our Town*.

Sobol's first original play, *New Year's Eve 1972* (*Sylvester 1972*, 1974), was built around a confrontation of two generations. The generation of founders is represented by a senile man who spends his time compiling a scrapbook of old newspaper clippings and carrying on ideological discussions with comrades long dead, while the spokesman for the new generation, those born in Israel, is his son, a footloose wanderer leading an aimless existence. He is a bitter young man who blames the generation of his father for all the ills besetting the country.

The action of Sobol's *Joker* (1975) takes place during the 1973 Yom Kippur War, in a bunker where a band of hardened veterans of several wars conspire to send an eager young recruit to a certain death. In *The Night of the Twentieth* (*Leil ha'Esrim*, 1975), Sobol explores the social and psychological motivations of the pioneers who came to Palestine from Europe in 1921. His most ambitious project, a trilogy entitled *The House of Kaplan* (*Bet Kaplan*, 1978–1979), was planned as an Israeli version of the *Oresteia*, tracing the story of three generations of Israelis. Unlike Sobol's previous plays, the trilogy was not well received by the critics, who maintained that the playwright overreached himself and overestimated the weight of his material.

In 1978–1979 Sobol wrote and coauthored satirical revues which attacked the government and the military establishment. *See* HEBREW DRAMA.

MENDEL KOHANSKY

EDITIONS

The Night of the Twentieth. English translation published by the Institute for the Translation of Hebrew Literature Ltd., 1978.

Solís y Rivadeneyra, Antonio de   (1610–1686)

Spanish historian (author of the famous *Historia de la conquista de México*, 1684), poet, and dramatist. He was born in Alcalá de Henares in October, 1610, and died in Madrid on April 19, 1686. His nine extant *comedias* (pub. 1681) show the influence of Calderón. Although Solís contributed little of substance to theatrical literature, he was a stylist who excelled in sophisticated satirical comedy and caricature of manners. Situations and atmosphere in his plays tend to be artificial and contrived, but character motivation, on which Solís concentrated his irony and humor, is often realistic, as in, for example, *One Fool Makes a Hundred* (*Un bobo hace ciento*). Other plays are *Love à la Mode* (*El amor al uso*), the comedy of manners adapted by Thomas Corneille as *L'amour à la mode*; *The Little Gypsy Girl of Madrid* (*La gitanilla de Madrid*), based on the novella by Cervantes; and *Doctor Carlino* (*El doctor Carlino*). *See* CALDERÓN DE LA BARCA, PEDRO.

Love à la Mode (*El amor al uso*). Comedy in which Don Gaspar has been courting Doña Isabel and Doña Clara. Clara, who is also being courted by Don Diego, Isabel's brother, has been promised to Don García, who loves Isabel. Gaspar arranges an assignation with both ladies at the same time. He goes first to Isabel but, finding García there, goes to Clara, only to discover Diego hiding in the garden. The following day all the lovers

Antonio de Solís y Rivadeneyra. [Biblioteca Nacional, Madrid]

find themselves in Clara's house; and when the confusion is straightened out, Gaspar is engaged to Clara and García is free to wed Isabel.

[ANDRÉS FRANCO]

EDITIONS

Biblioteca de Autores Españoles, 94, Madrid, 1858, new edition, 1951; *Amor y obligación*, ed. by E. Juliá, Madrid, 1930.

CRITICISM

D. E. Martell, *The Dramas of D. Antonio Solís y Rivadeneyra*, Philadelphia, 1902; J. H. Parker, "The Versificación of the *Comedias* of Antonio de Solís y Rivadeneyra," *Hispanic Review* 17 (1949): 308–315.

Sologub, Fyodor (1863–1927)

Russian poet, novelist, short-story writer, and dramatist; pseudonym of Fyodor Kuzmich Teternikov. His first works, a volume of poems, a collection of short stories, and the novel *Bad Dreams (Tyazholye sny)*, were published in 1896. A modernist and a decadent poet, an important pioneer of Russian symbolism, he won immediate recognition with the publication of his masterpiece, the novel *The Petty Demon (Melky bes*; wr. 1892/1901, pub. 1907), which is now considered a classic. *See* SYMBOLISM in glossary.

His plays, like his other writings, exhibit sensuous despair, tortuous sexuality, and a preoccupation with the idea of liberation by death. Necromantic phantoms and other morbid elements abound: life is a conflict between dream and reality, from whose oppressive futility one can escape only by seeking miracles, demonology, and deification. Believing the poet to be the prime mover in the theatre, Sologub sought to emphasize the beauty of nature despite its chaos. He considered choral dancing an integral part of drama and expected actors to serve as automata whose slow and graceful movements and calm recital would display his poetry. His most notable dramas are *The Triumph of Death (Pobeda smerti ,*1907), based on a medieval legend and using powerful poetry and rich images to express the idea that love comes to its highest fulfillment in death; *Gift of the Wise Bees (Dar mudrykh pchyol,* 1907), in which a Greek myth is reshaped to illustrate love's fulfillment in death and escape through necromancy; and *Vanka the Steward and Jehan the Page (Vanka klyuchnik i pazh Zhean,* 1909), in which a vassal's seduction of his lady is shown alternately as it would take place in medieval Russia and in the France of the troubadours.

Other representative but less popular plays produced for limited audiences by avant-garde directors include *Hostages of Life (Zalozhniki zhizni,* 1912), produced by Vsevolod Meyerhold; *Nocturnal Dances (Nochnye plyaski,* 1909), an allegorical and fairy tale piece produced by Yevreinov; *Love over an Abyss (Lyubov nad bezdnami,* pub. 1914), in which the protagonists are merely He, She, an Earthly Man, a servant, and ladies in yellow, red, and green; and *The Guard of the Great Czar (Strazh velikogo tsarya,* pub. 1922), set in decadent-style exotic surroundings. *See* MEYERHOLD, VSEVOLOD EMILYEVICH; YEVREINOV, NIKOLAY NIKOLAYEVICH.

The Triumph of Death *(Pobeda smerti,* 1907). Pageant-like drama, set in medieval times and based on the leg-

end of King Clovis, who puts Algista to death. Algista's bleeding body comes to life, appears before the King, and intones: "Take me as Thou wilt, alive or dead. . . . My blood is upon the moist earth, and my voice is in the magic moon. My eyes shine brighter than the diamonds of thy diadem. Here I am all life and all death!" Then, by magic, she turns Clovis and his court to stone, and the chorus proclaims: "Love conquers by Death, for Love and Death are One!"

Gift of the Wise Bees *(Dar mudrykh pchyol,* 1907). Drama based on the Greek myth of Laodamia. When Laodamia's lover is killed in the Trojan War, leaving her heartbroken, Aphrodite asks the sculptor Lysippus to re-create him in wax, the gift of the wise bees. Laodamia is overjoyed and caresses the facsimile as though it were alive. But her father seizes the wax statue and casts it into the fire. As it begins to melt, Laodamia sinks lifeless to the ground, while the chorus sings the praises of Aphrodite.

Vanka the Steward and Jehan the Page *(Vanka klyuchnik i pazh Zhean,* 1909). Comedy ironically showing how the same immorality pervades all societies. Alternating scenes, the play shows medieval Russia in harsh, gaudy colors, and medieval France in pastel shades. In both plots, the noblewoman is seduced by a young servant. In the French episode, the wily page is aided by the wife's complicity. In the Russian episode, the steward, smelling of manure, practically rapes the mistress. In both versions, the seducers are spared final punishment. Jehan, thanks to the lady's intercession, gets off with a beating and exile; Vankan substitutes a beggar at his execution.

[LAURENCE SENELICK]

EDITIONS

Sobranie sochineniy, 9 vols., St. Petersburg, 1913; *The Triumph of Death,* tr. by J. Cournos, Chicago, 1916.

CRITICISM

A. Gornfeld, "F. Sologub," in *Russkaya literatura XX veka,* ed. by S. Vengerov, II, Moscow, 1915; J. Cournos, "Feodor Sologub," *Fortnightly Review,* September 1915; Z. Gippius, "Sologub," in *Zhivye litsa,* Prague, 1925; G. Chulkov, "Fedor Sologub," in *Gody stranstviy,* Moscow, 1930; A. Field, "The Theatre of Two Wills: Sologub's Plays," *Slavonic and East European Review,* December 1962; D. Gerould, "Sologub and the Theatre," *The Drama Review* 76, December 1977.

Solórzano, Carlos (1922–   )

Guatemalan born playwright who has lived and worked in Mexico. Critics consider Carlos Solórzano's best play the historical *Beatriz the Unlucky (Beatriz la sin ventura,* 1955), which concerns the life of Doña Beatriz, wife of the conquistador Alvarado, who ruled after her husband's death and signed all state papers "Beatriz the Unlucky." She is thought to have been the first woman to have ruled in an American country.

Solórzano adapted the Spanish *auto* to the modern stage in plays such as his popular *Hands of God (Las Manos de Dios,* 1956), in which another Beatriz, instigated by the devil, decides to steal jewelry from church statues, i.e., the hands of God, after she and her husband are defrauded of their land by the "Big Boss in Town."

In 1959 he published three one-act plays under the collective title *Tres actos.* The first of these was *Puppets*

(*Los fantoches*, 1958), which he called a "mimeo-drama for marionettes." An allegory on free will, it is set in the workshop of a maker of the giant effigies of Judas burned on Holy Saturday. Free will is also the theme of *The Crucified One* (*El crucificado*, 1958), which has as its protagonist a poor villager chosen to play the role of Jesus in the annual Easter reenactment of the Way of the Cross. The character identifies so thoroughly with his role that he is killed by his drunken fellow-actors.

The Wizard (*El hechicero*, 1954), a drama about Merlin the Magician, was enthusiastically received by Mexican critics for its dramatic presentation of man's destiny.

WILLIS KNAPP JONES and JUDITH A. WEISS

Sophocles　(ca. 496–406 B.C.)

Greek tragic dramatist. He was born in Colonus, a village just outside Athens, about 496 B.C. According to the only surviving ancient biography, his father was Sophillus, a maker of armor. Lamprus, the most distinguished musician of his day, was his music teacher, and he is said to have studied tragedy under Aeschylus. In 480 B.C., on the occasion of the victory of the Greeks over the Persians at Salamis, he was selected to lead a chorus of boys who performed a paean in celebration. *See* AESCHYLUS.

Although it is not known when he first exhibited at the dramatic festival, he gained his first victory in 468 B.C., defeating Aeschylus. The number of victories ascribed to Sophocles varies with the source: an inscription from the third century B.C. credits him with eighteen; Suidas, in the tenth century A.D., says he won twenty-four times; and the ancient *Life*, which also states that he won many second prizes but never placed third, records twenty victories. According to Suidas, he wrote 123 plays in all, while the *Life*, citing Aristophanes of Byzantium, gives the number as 130, of which 17 were considered spurious; 7 complete plays have survived, as have the titles or fragments of more than 90 others. Of his minor poems nothing remains.

Sophocles played a distinguished role in the public life of Athens, serving in 443–442 B.C. as Hellenotamias, chairman of the board that collected tribute from Athens's subject allies in the Delian League, and in 440 B.C. being elected one of the ten strategoi (generals and admirals) in the war against the revolting Samians (he may have been elected a second time). According to the *Life*, he served on numerous embassies to foreign states, though he refused to leave Athens to visit the courts of kings in spite of pressing invitations. In Athens he founded the Thiasos of the Muses, a society for the advancement of music and literature.

The amiability of his character is reflected in *The Frogs* of Aristophanes, in which Aeschylus and Euripides contend for the throne of tragedy in Hades, with Sophocles sitting by, ready to challenge Euripides if he should win; Aeschylus himself had offered the throne to Sophocles, but he had declined it, "courteous in Hades, as he had been on Earth." Renowned for piety, he is said to have been priest of the hero Alcon. For having discharged certain functions in connection with the worship of Aesculapius, he himself received heroic honors after

Bust of Sophocles. [Goethe House]

death. *See* ARISTOPHANES; EURIPIDES.

According to tradition, he was the first poet to eschew acting in his plays, possibly because of his weak voice. Yet he is said to have performed admirably on the lyre in his *Thamyras* and to have played the game of ball with grace in his *Nausicaa*.

Sophocles's wife was Nicostrata, by whom he had a son, the tragic poet Iophon. Somewhat late in life he formed a liaison with a certain Theoris, by whom he had a son called Ariston. Of three other sons mentioned by Suidas, nothing is known. Sophocles died in Athens in 406 B.C., a few months after the death of Euripides and just before the end of the Peloponnesian War. He was buried in his family's tomb near Athens, and over the spot a figure of a siren was erected.

One of the most widely celebrated legends concerning Sophocles is the charge that at ninety he was too senile to manage his own affairs. To prove his sanity he cited a portion of *Oedipus at Colonus* (*Oidipous epi Kolōnōi*), which he had recently composed, and is supposed to have said to his accusers, "If I am Sophocles I am no dotard, and if I dote I am not Sophocles." According to Plato, he welcomed old age as an escape from the sensual passions. Pericles, Plutarch tells us, rebuked Sophocles's love of pleasure and thought him a bad general though a good poet. It was also said that his appointment as a general was due to the political wisdom shown in his *Antigone* (*Antigonē*, ca. 442/441 B.C.).

Local legend connected Sophocles with the gods. He is supposed to have "entertained" Aesculapius in his house and to have had the power of charming baleful winds into stillness. The god Dionysus is said to have appeared in person to the Spartan commander Lysander on the occasion of Sophocles's death, charging him to permit the Athenians to bury their poet (in fact, in 406 B.C. Lysander was at sea, and the Spartans did not lay siege to Athens until 405).

Various legends about Sophocles's death are recorded in the *Life*: that he choked from eating grapes sent him by the actor Callippides at the time of Anthesteria (a flower festival that fell in February); that, when reading the *Antigone* aloud, he killed himself by trying to deliver a long sentence without taking a breath; and that his death was due to excessive joy at the success of *Antigone* in the competition.

WORK

Sophocles was above all else the great artist-craftsman of tragedy whose works most influenced Aristotle in his description of tragedy in *The Poetics*. His innovations in the genre were far-reaching. He introduced a third actor; increased the size of the chorus to fifteen from Aeschylus's twelve, while reducing its involvement in the action; invented scene painting, according to Aristotle; and broke with the custom of writing trilogies for the Dionysian festivals by creating individual works that were self-contained. With the introduction of a third actor, the greatest interest centered on the persons taking part in the action rather than on the static chorus, which was no longer a dramatic necessity. Yet Sophocles wrote for the chorus, which often relfected upon the action, some of the most beautiful of his odes. *See* CHORUS in glossary.

A master of dialogue, Sophocles used a variety of meters to create variations of tone and emotion. In scenes in which characters confront each other one-on-one (Oedipus and Tiresias in *Oedipus the King*, for example), the brisk economy of the lines not only makes the conflict of characters more evident, but intensifies the realism of the issues as well. Often characters—Odysseus in the *Philoctetes* (*Philoktētēs*, 409? B.C.), Creon in *Oedipus at Colonus* (ca. 404/401 B.C.)—recall the style and tempo of the Sophist rhetoric popular in this period. Although maxims and aphorisms abound, they are characteristically appropriate within the context of the play and its personae, and the language is rich in transmutations of ordinary forms, metaphors, unusual constructions, and coinages.

Structurally, the plays fall into two categories, those divided into two parts, the accomplishment of the fate of the hero and the development of the consequences of that fate; and those that develop a single plot throughout. Of the former, *Ajax* (*Aias*, ca. 450/447 B.C.), *Antigone* (ca. 442/441 B.C.), and *The Women of Trachis* (*Trakhiniai*, ca. 440? B.C.) are exemplary. Sophocles's other plays fall into the latter category; nothing in them is irrelevant—each incident relates to what has preceded it and to what follows it, and each is essential to the unfolding of plot and character. And, in fact, it is the characters, moving from action to inevitable action, that hold the final interest in Sophoclean drama: they are noble yet not faultless; confronted with unendurable suffering, disproportionate to any fault in themselves, they are not diminished. Sophocles's tragic vision touches the extremes of the human condition. He is more cynical than Aeschylus about the justice of divine will ("Say what you will, the greatest boon is not to be," says the chorus in *Oedipus at Colonus*); and yet more than the other tragic poets we know he maintains an unflinching faith in man's capacity to confront, accept, and live with his fate (consider the choral ode in *Antigone*, "Wonders are many on earth: and the greatest of these is man"). His characters are real to us because of their complexity and because of Sophocles's refusal to reduce them to symbolic caricatures. Oedipus, for example, blinded and disgraced, remains noble because of his acceptance of his unwittingly fulfilled fate, the despair and defiance of his self-blinding (which was not part of the prophecy), and the touching love for his daughters he displays in the final scene.

Ajax is a striking play that takes its plot from Homer but which goes far beyond a Homeric concept of heroism and honorable death to consider the absurd brevity of life, the uncertainty of any wordly title, and the need for compassion. Although it is Ajax's suicide that is the tragic event of the play (there are six other suicides in Sophocles's surviving plays), the drama is equally concerned with Odysseus as a compassionate figure who recognizes the need to accept his enemy. Athena's line, "One single day can overthrow or raise up anything human (1. 131)," is indicative of Sophocles's awareness of the fragility of human life.

Antigone, the tragedy most appealing to moderns, especially in times of authoritarian rule, and one that has been reworked, for example, by Brecht and Anouilh, is concerned with the clash of two orders, man-made law and divinely ordained law. Creon symbolizes the need for civic order, the supremacy of reason; Antigone represents the rule of heart over head, of intuition fed by faith in the supervening right of divine ordinances. On still another level the drama reflects the classic conflict between the state and the individual. Sophocles maintains the tension between the two points of view; yet sympathy remains with Antigone. The balance is never marred, however; Sophocles is not a partisan: Creon speaks in favor of firmness at the helm of government, and Antigone displays violent enthusiasm and overassertive heroism; both are seen dispassionately. It is indicative of Sophocles's skill that we come to feel sympathy for Creon, the man who condemned Antigone. *See* ANOUILH, JEAN; BRECHT, BERTOLT.

This mood also permeates *Philoctetes*, a much greater play, in which characters of divergent sensibilities converge. There is a magical quality to the island, "sea-girt Lemnos," which brings to mind the spirit of *The Tempest*; in the verses dedicated to sleep, the great "balm of all ill," one thinks of Shakespeare. A powerful relationship develops between the wounded and deserted old hero Philoctetes and Achilles' orphaned son Neoptolemus, and in the act of trying to kidnap Philoctetes and steal his magic bow, Neoptolemus comes to understand that Philoctetes must henceforth be both his father and his comrade in war. *See* SHAKESPEARE, WILLIAM.

In *Electra* (*Ēlektra*, 409? B.C.), Sophocles focuses his attention on the heroine, whom he humanizes. Though fixed on heroic vengeance, Electra walks in a domestic atmosphere that augments the effect of her overwhelming pain and suffering.

The Women of Trachis is the only one of the extant plays to deal at length with the love of a man and a woman. Its genius lies particularly in the depiction of the character of Deianira, a heroine whose Greek spirit is ex-

A production of *Ajax* at Epidaurus. [Royal Consulate General of Greece]

emplified by her words to the hesitant informer of her husband's infidelity: "Do not cheat me of the truth, for not to know would be the greater hurt."

Oedipus the King (*Oidipous Tyrannos*, ca. 430/426 B.C) is unparalleled in the history of the drama. Considered by Aristotle to be a model tragedy, it has the economy of language, the tightly knit construction, and the implacably building tension and suspense that have become touchstones of the genre. In the sequel, *Oedipus at Colonus* (though *Antigone*, written before either Oedipus play, follows both in terms of the chronology of the myth), a towering work of Sophocles's last years (produced posthumously), the mystical and religious tone of the final scenes, permeated as they are by a sense of infinite wisdom and peace, recalls again the vision of the later Shakespeare. The blinded Oedipus is a reconciling figure among the contending Thebans; the harmony he brings arises out of the strength of a spirit that has suffered beyond imagining. Theseus, King of Athens, emerges as a fascinating "double" Oedipus who is chosen to keep the mysteries of Oedipus's ascension because he alone, through suffering and rank, best understands the exiled king. With such a triumphant victory over misfortune and death, Sophocles pushed serious drama past the earlier perimeters of "tragedy." The chorus's final words epitomize the Sophoclean acceptance of existence and death: ". . . cease lamentation, for these things stand as they must, and ought."

A fragment of a satyr play, *Trackers* (*Ichneutae*, ca. 460 B.C.), consists of some 400 vigorous and ribald lines. Called the first detective drama of recorded history, it depicts the chorus trying to recover Apollo's stolen cattle and finding Hermes to be the culprit. *See* SATYR PLAY in glossary.

Taking the rough-hewn, monumental Aeschylean tragedy, to which he was heir, and the stories provided by Homer in the Trojan cycle, Sophocles added his own lyrical polish and a formal structure of unsurpassed excellence. Out of this amalgam were created some of the finest tragedies known in the history of drama. Through the centuries, by ancient and modern critics alike, Sophocles has been likened to Homer. Yet although he drew most of his stories from the epic poet's works, Sophocles expressed his own vision of a non-Homeric world in which, as Jan Kott has suggested, "the gods are silent" and man must learn from the knowledge of his own suffering.

Ajax (*Aias*, ca 450/447 B.C). Tragedy about the humiliation and death of Ajax, a Greek hero of the Trojan War. Following the death of Achilles, Odysseus and Ajax compete for the dead hero's armor. After Odysseus wins the contest, Ajax reacts with fury. Overcome by a madness induced by Athena, he comes upon a herd of cattle and, thinking that the beasts are Greek chieftains, slaughters them.

As the play opens, Athena mercilessly shows the

mad Ajax to his enemy Odysseus. Ajax boasts of his glorious victories over the "Greeks" that he has just slain; Odysseus turns away in pity and horror. When Ajax becomes lucid again, he weighs the consequences of his foolish action: that the Greeks plan to arrest him and bring him to trial. The full dimension of his plight is revealed when his retinue, a chorus of Salaminian sailors, begs him to defend his right to Achilles' armor and when his concubine Tecmessa pleads with him not to take his own life in shame and defiance. After bequeathing his shield and other arms to his infant son Eurysaces and enjoining him to become a brave man, Ajax departs to die. But he reappears, seemingly penitent, saying that he must go alone to the seashore to cleanse his wounds. There, after invoking the Furies to pursue his enemies in the Greek camp, he falls on his sword and dies. Teucer, Ajax's brother, arrives and asks permission to bury him. He is opposed by Menelaus and Agamemnon, but permission is finally granted on the advice of Odysseus, who has learned generosity from his enemy's fate.

Antigone (*Antigonē*, ca. 442/441 B.C). Tragedy dealing with the conflict between secular and divine law in King Creon's refusal to permit the burial of Polynices; the third of the Theban plays. It takes place before the palace in Thebes on the morning after the defeat of the Argives, who had come to place Polynices on the throne formerly occupied by his father Oedipus. Creon, his uncle, now

Scene from *Antigone,* as performed at the Epidaurus Festival. [Greek National Tourist Office]

Renée Faure and Jean Marchat in a French production of *Antigone.* Paris, Comédie-Française, 1959. [French Cultural Services]

King of Thebes, issues an edict that no one shall bury Polynices on pain of death. Antigone, Polynices' sister, performs the rite of burial against the advice of her sister Ismene and is consequently called before Creon. She insists that his edict cannot annul the unwritten laws of heaven. The King, disregarding the admonition of his son Haemon, who is betrothed to Antigone, orders her to the cave of death. The prophet Tiresias warns him that the gods are angered by the uncovering of Polynices' corpse by Creon's soldiers. Urged by a chorus of Theban elders, Creon relents and hastens to rebury Polynices. He then orders the release of Antigone, but she has hanged herself. On discovering this, Haemon stabs himself and dies beside her body. His mother Eurydice, hearing of his death, also commits suicide, and the play ends with Creon in inconsolable grief.

The Women of Trachis (*Trakhiniai; Trachiniae,* ca. 440? B.C.). Tragedy about the death of Heracles. Deianira, the loyal wife of the hero Heracles, lives in exile with her children in Trachis, where she awaits the return of her husband from his last labor. His appearance is preceded by a group of women captured in Oechalia, among them the princess Iole, with whom, Deianira discovers, Heracles is infatuated. Although Deianira has always forgiven her husband's infidelities, she cannot bring herself to shelter Iole in her home. She determines to win back Heracles's affection with the gift of a robe anointed with a potion given her long ago by a centaur, unaware that the potion is poisonous. When Heracles dons the robe, the poison begins to eat away his flesh. Deianira, cursed by her son Hyllus for her deed, commits suicide. Heracles then appears in his death agony. He orders the unwilling Hyllus to build a funeral pyre for him on Mount Oeta, exacts a promise from Hyllus to marry Iole, and is carried off to his death, still violent, lordly, and indomitable.

Oedipus the King (*Oidipous Tyrannos; Oedipus Tyrannus*, ca. 430/426 B.C.). Although perhaps the most famous of Greek plays, this play was adjudged second at the Great Dionysia to a lost play by Philocles. Oedipus unknowingly has fulfilled a prophecy of the Delphic oracle before the opening action of the play that he would kill his father, Laius, King of Thebes, and marry his mother, Jocasta.

As the play begins, Jocasta's brother Creon has returned from Delphi with news that the plague in Thebes has been inflicted on the city for harboring the murderer of Laius. Oedipus determines to find the murderer, but when he is informed by the blind seer Tiresias that he, Oedipus, is the man, he flies into a rage and accuses Tiresias and Creon of plotting his overthrow. Jocasta reassures Oedipus, telling him that the oracle erred in predicting Laius's death since witnesses have reported that he was slain by thieves at the intersection of three roads. Furthermore, her son had been abandoned on a mountainside at birth and could not have killed Laius. But Oedipus remembers that long ago he received an identical prediction from the oracle. Since he believed Polybus

Oedipus the King, **performed by the State Theatre of Northern Greece.** [Greek National Tourist Office]

was his father, he was convinced of the fallibility of the oracle. The messenger states, however, that Oedipus was not Polybus's son and that he himself received the child from a Theban shepherd and brought him to Corinth.

The chorus's joy is cut short when the shepherd is found and confesses that the child was indeed Laius's son. Horrified, Oedipus follows Jocasta, who has already rushed into the palace, where she hangs herself. Oedipus, overcome, blinds himself with her golden brooches. Leaving the palace, he encounters Creon, who has been named King, and asks that he be banished. Sorrowfully

The Women of Trachis **at Epidaurus.** [Royal Consulate General of Greece]

Two scenes from an Epidaurus production of *Oedipus at Colonus.*
[Above: Greek National Tourist Office; below: Royal Consulate
General of Greece]

taking leave of his daughters Ismene and Antigone,
whom he entrusts to Creon's care, Oedipus departs.

Electra (*Ēlektra*, 409? B.C.). Tragedy motivated by
Electra's hatred for her mother Clytemnestra and her
mother's lover Aegisthus, now King of Mycenae. Aegisthus had become King after he and Clytemnestra murdered Agamemnon, Electra's father, on his return from
the Trojan War. Electra desires revenge for Agamemnon's death, for her mother's ill will, for her sister's
timid passivity, and for Aegisthus's stern sovereignty.
She places all hope for vengeance on her brother Orestes. But Orestes' old servant appears and announces
his master's death in a chariot race. Electra, unaware that
this is only a ruse of Orestes to throw Clytemnestra and
Aegisthus off guard, becomes maddened with grief until
Orestes arrives and reveals himself. Forthwith, he slays
his mother and Aegisthus. The chorus praises him, declaring that by his bold deed he has ended the sufferings
of his family, the accursed house of Atreus.

Philoctetes (*Philoktētēs*, 409? B.C.). Philoctetes, one of
the chieftains journeying to Troy, had been bitten by a
snake. The noxious odor of his wound, which refused to
heal, caused the Greeks to leave him on the island of
Lemnos with his bow and arrows, a legacy from Heracles. In the tenth year of the Trojan War the Greeks learn
that Troy can be taken only with the help of Philoctetes
and his bow. Therefore, Odysseus and Neoptolemus are
sent to Lemnos to bring Philoctetes to Troy; Odysseus is
Philoctetes' most hated enemy, but Neoptolemus,
Achilles' young son, is unknown to him.

The play opens in a desolate spot on the island, facing the cliff in which is the cave of Philoctetes. After Odysseus convinces Neoptolemus to join in a plot to gain possession of the bow, Neoptolemus proceeds to win the confidence of Philoctetes by telling him that he will take him back to Greece. Meanwhile, Odysseus keeps in the background. The bow is finally secured, and Philoctetes, believing he is to be returned to Greece, is ready to leave for the ship. But first Neoptolemus tells him of the ruse: that they plan to take him to Troy. Philoctetes' rage and reproaches induce Neoptolemus to restore the weapon despite Odysseus's opposition and to promise Philoctetes a passage home. At the last moment Heracles appears and commands Philoctetes to go to Troy, where his wound will heal, and where, with Neoptolemus, he will kill Paris and win the war. Philoctetes heeds the voice of Heracles and departs for Troy.

Oedipus at Colonus (*Oidipous epi Kolōnōi; Oedipus Coloneus*, ca. 404/401 B.C.). The middle tragedy of Sophocles's Theban plays, but the last one he wrote, dramatizing the last hours of Oedipus, former King of Thebes. At Colonus, Oedipus is wandering with his daughter Antigone in a grove sacred to the Furies, where he realizes that he has found his final resting place, as predicted years ago by Apollo's oracle. However, at Colonus fresh evils beset Oedipus and his family. Ismene, his other daughter, arrives, to announce that although her brothers Eteocles and Polynices had agreed that their uncle Creon should inherit the throne of Thebes, a lust for power has seized Eteocles and he has banished his brother. As a result, Polynices has journeyed to Argos to persuade its leaders to make war on Thebes. Meanwhile, an oracle has told Creon that he must ensure that Oedipus die near Thebes lest his burial be unlucky for the outcome of the war.

Ismene's tidings enrage her father, but he is appeased by the graciousness of Theseus, King of Athens, who offers him and his daughters sanctuary. Creon appears and is confronted by the furious Oedipus, from whom he abducts both Ismene and Antigone. After Theseus's cavalry has rescued the sisters, Polynices arrives, beseeching his father's blessing, necessary for victory over Thebes. Oedipus angrily refuses and sends Polynices off to the fatal campaign of which Aeschylus wrote in *The Seven Against Thebes*. Suddenly the grove of the Furies is filled with thunder and lightning, and Oedipus, knowing that his death is at hand, asks Theseus to be his only witness. They go off, and a messenger reports Oedipus's mysterious disappearance into the earth, where his spirit will continue to bless Athens. Now Ismene and Antigone are left alone to return to Thebes in mourning.

[ANDREW HORTON]

PLAYS

The dating of Sophocles's plays is extremely uncertain. However, with the possible exception of No. 3, the chronology below is probably correct. In each instance the first title given is a transliteration from the Greek; the first in parentheses is the Latin designation.

1. *Aias** (*Ajax*). Ca. 450/447 B.C.
2. *Antigonē** (*Antigone*). Ca. 442/441 B.C.
3. *Trakhiniai** (*Trachiniae; The Women of Trachis*). Ca. 440? B.C.
4. *Oidipous Tyrannos** (*Oedipus Tyrannus; Oedipus the King*). Ca. 430/426 B.C.
5. *Ēlektra** (*Electra*). 409? B.C.
6. *Philoktētēs** (*Philoctetes*). 409? B.C.
7. *Oidipous epi Kolōnōi** (*Oedipus Coloneus; Oedipus at Colonus*), Ca. 404/401 B.C.

EDITIONS

Collections

Sophocles: The Text of the Plays, ed. by R. C. Jebb, Cambridge, England, 1897; *Sophocles: The Plays and Fragments*, tr. by R. C. Jebb, 7 vols., Cambridge, England, 1892–1900; *Tragedies*, tr. by F. Starr, 2 vols., Loeb Classical Library, Nos. 20 and 21, New York, 1912–1913; *The Complete Greek Drama*, ed. by W. J. Oates and E. O'Neill and tr. by R. Trevelyan et al., vol. 1, New York, 1938; *Great Books of the Western World*, ed. by R. M. Hutchins and tr. by R. C. Jebb, vol. 5, New York, 1952; *The Complete Greek Tragedies*, ed. by D. Grene and R. Lattimore and tr. by J. Moore et al., vol. 2, Chicago, 1959.

Also published in *Greek Dramas*, ed. by B. Perrin and tr. by R. C. Jebb and T. Francklin, New York, 1900; *Attic Tragedies*, tr. by R. Whitelaw, Boston, 1927; *Ten Greek Plays*, tr. by R. Whitelaw and G. Murray, New York, 1930; *Fifteen Greek Plays Translated into English*, tr. by R. Whitelaw, L. Campbell, and G. Murray, New York, 1943; *Greek Literature in Translation*, ed. by W. J. Oates and C. T. Murphy and tr. by R. C. Jebb, New York, 1944; *Plays of the Greek Dramatists*, tr. by G. Young, New York, 1946; *Greek Plays in Modern Translation*, ed. by D. Fitts and tr. by W. B. Yeats et al., New York, 1947; *An Anthology of Greek Drama*, ed. by C. A. Robinson, Jr., and tr. by R. Whitelaw and D. Grene, 1st ser., New York, 1949; *An Anthology of World Literature*, ed. by P. M. Buck, Jr., and H. S. Alberson and tr. by E. Plumptre, 3d ed., New York, 1951; *An Anthology of Greek Drama*, ed. by C. A. Robinson, Jr., and tr. by E. Plumptre and J. Workman, 2d ser., New York, 1954; *Greek Drama for Everyman*, ed. and tr. by F. L. Lucas, London, 1954; *The Spring of Civilization: Periclean Athens*, ed. by C. A. Robinson, Jr., and tr. by R. Whitelaw et al., New York, 1954; *Masterworks of World Literature*, ed. by E. M. Everett et al., rev. ed., vol. 1, New York, 1955; *Ten Greek Plays in Contemporary Translations*, ed. by L. R. Lind and tr. by S. O'Sheel et al., Boston, 1957; *The Theban Plays*, tr. by E. F. Watling, Baltimore, 1959; *Greek Tragedies*, ed. by D. Grene and R. Lattimore, vols. 1–3, Chicago, 1960; *Four Plays by Sophocles*, ed. by T. H. Banks, New York, 1966; *The Theban Saga*, ed. by C. A. Robinson, Jr., New York, 1966; *Oedipus and Drama*, ed. by M. Kallich, A. MacLeish, and G. Schoenbohm, New York, 1968; *Sophocles: Complete Plays*, ed. by M. Hadas, New York, n.d.; *Masterpieces of Classical Drama*, ed. by R. W. Corrigan, New York, n.d.

Individual Plays

Ajax. W. B. Stanford, ed., New York, 1963.

Antigone. R. C. Jebb, ed., Cambridge, England, 1902; also published in *The Classics, Greek and Latin*, ed. by M. M. Miller and tr. by T. Francklin, vol. 7, New York, 1909–1910; *The Genius of the Greek Drama*, tr. by C. E. Robinson, London and New York, 1921; *The Progress of Drama, Through the Centuries*, ed. by R. M. Stauffer and tr. by A. Way, New York, 1927; *A Treasury of the Theatre*, ed. by B. Mantle and J. Gassner and tr. by R. C. Jebb, rev. ed., vol. 2, New York, 1940; *Our Heritage of World Literature*, ed. by S. Thompson and J. Gassner and tr. by E. Plumptre, rev. ed., New York, 1942; *Ten Plays*, ed. by M. W. Bloomfield and R. C. Elliott and tr. by E. F. Watling, New York, 1951; *Classics in Translation*, ed. by P. MacKendrick and H. M. Howe and tr. by M. Neufeld, vol. 1, Madison, Wis., 1952; *Literature: An Introduction*, ed. by H. S. Summers and E. Whan and tr. by D. Fitts and R. Fitzgerald, New York, 1960; M. Townsend, tr., New York, 1962; *Introducing the Drama*, ed. by J. Gassner and M. Sweetkind and tr. by J. Gassner, New York, 1963; R. E. Braun, tr., New York, 1973.

Electra. G. Kaibel, ed., Leipzig, 1896; R. C. Jebb, ed., Cambridge, England, 1908; also published in *Chief Patterns of World Drama*, ed. by W. S. Clark II and tr. by E. Plumptre, Boston, 1946.

Oedipus at Colonus. R. C. Jebb, ed., Cambridge, England, 1900; R. Fitzgerald, tr., London, 1957; also published in *Poetic Drama*, ed. by A. Kreymborg and tr. by G. Young, New York, 1941; P. Arnott, ed. & tr., New York, 1975.

Oedipus the King. R. C. Jebb, ed., reprint, Cambridge, England, 1933; also published in *Types of World Tragedy*, ed. by R. M. Smith and tr. by E. Plumptre, New York, 1928; *Four Famous Greek Plays*, ed. by P. N. Landis and tr. by F. Starr, New York, 1929; *Greek and Roman Classics in Translation*, ed. by C. T. Murphy et al. and tr. by R. C. Jebb, New York, 1947; *Greek Literature in Translation*, ed. by G. Howe and G. A. Harrer and tr. by R. Whitelaw, New York, 1948; *A Book of Dramas*, ed. by B. Carpenter and tr. by G. Murray, rev. ed., New York, 1949; *The Book of the Play*, ed. by H. R. Walley and tr. by C. Mendell, New York, 1950; *A Treasury of the Theatre*, ed. and tr. by J. Gassner, rev. ed., vol. 1, New York, 1951; *Eight Great Tragedies*, ed. by S. Barnet et al. and tr. by J. Sheppard, New York, 1957; B. M. W. Knox, tr., New York, 1959; *Readings for Enjoyment*, ed. by E. R. Davis and W. C. Hummel and tr. by A. Cook, Englewood Cliffs, N.J., 1959; *Four Greek Plays*, ed. by D. Fitts and tr. by D. Fitts and R.

Fitzgerald, New York, 1960; *Greek Tragedies*, vol. I, tr. by D. Grene, 1960, rpt., Chicago, 1962; *Introduction to Drama*, ed. by R. C. Roby and B. Ulanov and tr. by W. B. Yeats, New York, 1962; *Introduction to Literature*, ed. by L. G. Locke et al. and tr. by D. Grene, 4th ed., New York, 1962; *Oedipus The King*, tr. by T. Gould, Englewood Cliffs, N.J., 1970; *Sophocles and Oedipus*, ed. and tr. by P. Vellacott, Ann Arbor, 1971; S. Berg and D. Clay, tr., New York, 1978.

    Philoctetes. R. C. Jebb, ed., Cambridge, England, 1898; also published in *Six Greek Plays in Modern Translation*, ed. by D. Fitts and tr. by A. Chase, New York, 1955.

    The Women of Trachis. R. C. Jebb, ed., Cambridge, England, 1892; E. Pound, tr., New York, 1957; R. Torrance, tr., Boston, 1966.

CRITICISM

H. F. Genthe, *Index Commentationium Sophoclearum*, New York, 1874; L. Campbell, *Tragic Drama in Aeschylus, Sophocles, and Shakespeare*, London, 1904; F. R. Earp, *The Style of Sophocles*, Cambridge, England, 1944; C. M. Bowra, *Sophoclean Tragedy*, 2d. ed., Oxford, 1947; R. Goheen, *The Imagery of Sophocles' Antigone*, Princeton, N.J., 1951; A. J. A. Waldock, *Sophocles, the Dramatist*, Cambridge, England, 1951; C. H. Whitman, *Sophocles: A Study of Heroic Humanism*, Cambridge, Mass., 1951; J. C. Opstelten, *Sophocles and Greek Pessimism*, tr. by J. A. Ross, Amsterdam, 1952; F. J. H. Letters, *The Life and Work of Sophocles*, London and New York, 1953; V. Ehrenberg, *Sophocles and Pericles*, Oxford, 1954; P. Mullahy, *Oedipus, Myth and Complex*, New York, 1955; S. M. Adams, *Sophocles, the Playwright*, Toronto, 1957; B. M. W. Knox, *Oedipus at Thebes*, New Haven, Conn., 1957; G. M. Kirkwood, *A Study of Sophoclean Drama*, Ithaca, N.Y., 1958; M. H. Shackford, *Shakespeare, Sophocles: Dramatic Themes and Modes*, New Haven, Conn., 1960; I. Velikovsky, *Oedipus and Akhnaton*, Garden City, 1960; A. S. Cook, ed., *Oedipus Rex: A Mirror for Greek Drama*, Belmont, Calif., 1963; J. T. Sheppard, *Aeschylus and Sophocles: Their Work and Influence*, New York, 1963; B. M. W. Knox, *The Heroic Temper: Studies in Sophoclean Tragedy*, Berkeley, Calif., 1964; T. M. Woodward, ed., *Sophocles: A Collection of Critical Essays*, Englewood Cliffs, N.J., 1966; D. Grene, *Reality and the Heroic Pattern: Last Plays of Ibsen, Shakespeare, and Sophocles*, Chicago, 1967; A. Cameron, *The Identity of Oedipus the King: Five Essays on the Oedipus Tyrannus*, New York, 1968; A. A. Long, *Language and Thought in Sophocles*, New York, 1968; W. N. Bates, *Sophocles, Poet and Dramatist*, reprint, New York, 1969; T. B. L. Webster, *An Introduction to Sophocles*, 2d ed., London, 1969; P. Vellacott, *Sophocles and Oedipus*, Ann Arbor, 1971.

Sorge, Reinhard Johannes   (1892–1916)

First German expressionist playwright. In his best-known "transition" play, *The Beggar* (*Der Bettler*; wr. 1912, prod. 1917), the seeds of all his subsequent achievements were implanted. This play brought subjectivism to the stage. Sorge's other early dramas are *Odysseus* (1910), dedicated to Nietzsche and reminiscent of Kokoschka's bizarre visions; *Prometheus* (1911), a dramatic sketch rich in poetic beauty, projecting the totality of human yearning and calling for regeneration through the "superman"; and *Antichrist* (1911), portraying Christ as the prophet of eternal life and Nietzsche (Judas) as the prophet of eternal renewal. *See* EXPRESSIONISM in glossary.

In the winter of 1912 Sorge experienced a sudden, possibly Kierkegaard-inspired enlightenment that converted him from Nietzschean philosophy to mystic Catholicism, making art for him thenceforth a medium for evangelism. His next work, *Judgment upon Zarathustra* (*Gericht über Zarathustra*, wr. 1912), also translated as *A Vision*, constitutes at once a repudiation of Nietzsche and an affirmation of the oneness of all men. Written later the same year, the one-act play *Guntwar, the School of a Prophet* (*Guntwar, die Schule eines Propheten*), pursuing the same idea of "being one with everybody, being truly common," rejects individualism and the personality cult and deals with the proselytizing efforts of a convert to convert his friend. After Sorge's adoption of Catholicism,

his style changed and became impersonal and objective, as evidenced by three Christmas mystery plays: *Mary's Conception—Mary's Visitation* (*Maria Empfängnis—Maria Heimsuchung*), *Christ's Birth* (*Christi Geburt*), and *The Presentation of Christ in the Temple* (*Darstellung Jesus—Wiederfinden im Tempel*). These were published in 1915 under the collective title *Metanoeite*. In *King David* (*König David*; wr. 1914, pub. posthumously), Sorge presents David as a forerunner of Christ. Among other plays are *Mystic Colloquies* (*Mystische Zwiegespräche*; wr. 1914, pub. 1922); *Christ's Victory* (*Der Sieg des Christos*; wr. 1914, pub. 1924); and *The Unknown* (*Das Unbekannte*), found after his death.

The Beggar (*Der Bettler*; wr. 1912, prod. 1917). Five-act expressionist drama of a poet's spiritual pilgrimage. A romantic young poet, introduced by his friend to a patron, refuses the latter's offer of a trip to observe life, stubbornly maintaining that he prefers a theatre in which to observe his own works. His friend, annoyed by this tactlessness, departs. Begged by his insane father to release him from the agony of life, the poet finally puts poison in his father's wine. But glasses are switched, and both his father and his mother drink the poison and die. Haunted by images of the grave, the poet then dreams of his beloved standing before a seaside cottage, of spring and peace. He turns back to city life and works, frustrated, as a journalist but is wrenched from this career by war. Then, returning to his writing, he dreams of youth and love and despairs of ever recapturing them in words. When he refuses to abandon writing, his friend forsakes him, but his beloved returns. She forswears her former life and offers her illegitimate child for adoption in order to give the poet his own child, born of their love.

[PETER JELAVICH]

Southeast Asian Theatre

The theatre of Southeast Asia, encompassing the mainland states of Burma, Thailand, Laos, Kampuchea (formerly Cambodia), and Vietnam as well as the peninsular and island countries of Malaysia, Indonesia, and the Philippines, was viewed until some two decades ago as an adjunct of the theatre of India and to a lesser extent of China. "Greater India" was the term frequently used by archaeologists, art historians, and theatre scholars before World War II to characterize the culture of Southeast Asia. There seemed to be much to justify this perspective. Wherever these early investigators ventured in Southeast Asia, they came upon one or more than one expression of the following aspects of Indian culture and religion: Brahmanism particularly of the Shaivite cult, Hinayana Buddhism; dramatic versions of the Hindu epics, *Ramayana* and *Mahabaratha*; tales of the birth of Buddha, known as *Jataka*; and the Indian style of dancing, not to mention a host of Indian-type musical instruments. Penetrating below the surface, however, recent researches have uncovered wide and firmly set transformations and localizations of these Indian borrowings. What had prevented the earlier scholars from viewing Southeast Asian theatre on its own terms was the predominantly oral nature of traditional genres in the region. Presentations of shadow theatre, dance dramas, and music had for many centuries been transmitted orally from generation to generation. Furthermore, apart from some shadow play guides and dance manuals, Southeast Asia has not produced a comprehensive written work like the Indian *Natyasastra* that might illuminate its theatrical theories and practices. (Curiously enough, the *Natyasastra* is not even known in Southeast Asia.) By looking beyond the confines of the written word, scholars today are beginning to regard the aesthetics of traditional Southeast Asian theatre as centered on performance as opposed to literature, thus confirming that any description of the traditional theatre of the region must begin and end with a consideration of how and in what contexts traditional plays are performed. In view of the contemporary Western quest for performance-oriented theatres, it is not surprising that American and European scholars and theatre practitioners have been turning to Southeast Asia for source material and inspiration. *See* INDIAN THEATRE.

SHADOW THEATRE

The performance of the flat leather puppets, known as *wayang kulit* in Indonesia and Malaysia and *nang* in Thailand and Kampuchea, is at once the most basic and sophisticated of the theatre arts of Southeast Asia. In fact, the technique of casting dramatic shadows on a performance screen is so deceptively simple that a protracted, scholarly search for its origins either in India and China or in an indigenous arena has so far proved to be largely futile. *Mewayang* or "performing *wayang*" is mentioned in a stone inscription issued by King Balitung of central Java in A.D. 907. We cannot, however, be absolutely certain that this performance "for the gods" entitled *Bimaya Kumara*, referring perhaps to the heroic Bima of the Mahabaratha stories, was in fact *wayang kulit*. But by the eleventh and twelfth centuries, shadow theatre performances are noted on numerous occasions in Javanese court literature. Some scholars, both Thai and Javanese, speculate that from Java *wayang kulit* was taken to Thailand, where it was first recorded in writing in the Palatine Law enacted by King Boromatrailoka in 1458.

All that is needed to make an elementary shadow theatre is the manipulation of puppets between a light source and a white, preferably cloth screen, regardless of whether the puppets are wooden like the *wayang klithik* of central Java, made of cardboard such as the *carillo* of the Philippines, or the more common and widely used leather variety. Yet this method of performance and its network of interweaving rituals reflects, if it has not engendered, the basic aesthetics that can be observed in traditional Southeast Asian theatre. Numerous variations in technique and repertory have been spawned by this genre. Java, probably the oldest and certainly the richest of the shadow theatre regions, is alone responsible for more than two dozen forms, ranging from the ancient *wayang purwa* to the modern *wayang suluh,* developed in 1947 to extol the heroic deeds of the Indonesian independance fighters. Collectively Javanese shadow theatre

Shadow theatre demonstration in New York. [The Asia Society, Performing Arts Department]

is an extraordinary reflection of the island's mythic and legendary history.

Nevertheless two performing styles are sufficiently different from each other to warrant separate categorization. The use of large leather puppets to depict a composite tableau with one or more characters, somewhat akin to the Mysore shadow theatre of India, is found only in mainland Southeast Asia. Accompanied by narrator-singers and an ensemble of musicians playing percussion-dominated instruments, the Nang Yai and Nang Sbek puppeteers of Thailand and Kampuchea respectively literally dance with their puppets behind and in front of the screen. They thus raise a multiplicity of sensations because as Jacques Brunet, the French expert on traditional Kampuchean theatre, has described the Nang Sbek performance of Kampuchea: "When the dancers pass round the screen, the hides are seen as shadows together with the dancers. It is important to point out that the spectacle is represented not only by the hides in movement, but also by the dancers themselves, the dancers and the figures forming an indissociable whole in the same way as when a dancer of the Royal Ballet [of Kampuchea] puts on her mask which has a function equivalant to that of the leather figure." Unfortunately the performance of the *nang yai* and the *nang sbek* is not a vital tradition today. Instead the performance of small puppets with single characters handled by a lone performer called the *dalang* is the dominant and most deeply rooted shadow theatre style of peninsular and insular Southeast Asia. Practitioners of this form of puppetry are also found in southern and northeastern Thailand (where it is called *nang tallung*) and among the Kampucheans (who have named it *Ayang*, a word presumably derived from the Malay *wayang*).

Whatever the tradition, the similarities in the structure of shadow theatre performances appear to be greater than the differences. Often, too, the plays are created from a commonly shared fund of stories, most particularly from the Hindu *Ramayana* (ca. 200 B.C.–A.D. 200). The other important Indian tale of relevance to Southeast Asia, the *Mahabaratha* (ca. 400 B.C.–A.D. 400), is only performed in Indonesia (especially Java, where *dalangs*, until very recently, primarily told the *Mahabaratha* stories of the battling cousins, the Pandawas and the Kurowas) and among the Javanese immigrants of Batu Pahat in Malaysia. Even if the source of the stories is Indian, the Southeast Asian shadow theatre performers have transformed them into local tales with distinctly local settings. As James R. Brandon has noted, Rama, the hero of the *Ramayana* and the reincarnation of the Indian god Vishnu, has in the hands of the Thai masters of the performance (or *nai-nang*) become a Thai prince, wearing Thai royal dress and displaying Thai aristocratic manners. In accordance with the prevailing Buddhist cosmology of the country, Rama is regarded as one of the previous lives of the Lord Buddha. In a similar fashion, the Islamic *dalangs* of Indonesia and Malaysia perceive Rama to be a descendant of Adam and a child of Allah. The Javanese *dalangs* have so thoroughly assimilated the *Ramayana* and the *Mahabaratha* into their local mythology that the geneology of their ancient kingship directly links Rama and the five Pandawa brothers with their historical kings. In an entirely invented episode entitled *Reincarnation of Rama* (*Wahyu Purba Sejati*), the divine rights of kingship are explicitly handed down from Rama to

Performer in a demonstration of the masked dance-drama of Korea. [The Asia Society, Performing Arts Department]

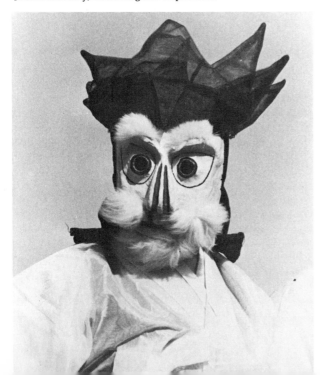

Kresna and Arjuna of the Pandawa party.

Furthermore, of the many cycles of Rama stories, the Southeast Asian performers appear to be mainly concerned with the spectacular story of the kidnapping of Sita, Rama's wife, by the demon-god Rawanna and her subsequent rescue by her husband, his brother Laksamana, and their loyal Simian army led by Sugriwa and the fabulous white monkey Hanuman, who in some versions is thought to be Rama's son. *Tales of King Rawanna* (*Cerita Maharaja Wana*) is what the Kelantanese *dalangs* of Malaysia call their performance version of the Rama stories, and among Thai practitioners Hanuman is so prominent a figure in their plots that their *Ramayana* is sometimes referred to as "the monkey story." Javanese *dalangs*, on the other hand, tend to dwell lovingly on the Pandawa's exile in Amarta, viewed in their plays (*lakon*) as a golden period of youthful adventure and romance, whereas the Indian versions barely mention this episode in the trials and tribulations of Yudhistra, Arjuna, Bima, Nakula, and Sadewa.

Clownish god-servants, creatures of a purely local imagination, such as Semar and his sons in the Javanese repertory and Pak Dogol and Wak Long of Kelantan are ubiquitous in the *dalangs'* performances. They hark back perhaps to indigenous and animistic godheads that had been superseded by the imported Indian ones. One of the most popular *wayang purwa* plays, *Petruk Becomes King* (*Petruk Jadi Raja*) is entirely devoted to the antics of the tall, long-nosed, mischievous Petruk, the son of Semar. When the fool assumes kingship, the world is turned topsy-turvy and through the experience of this extraordinary event the audience is temporarily relieved of the everyday effects of authority upon their lives. Cakil, a smallish demon of the forest, is also absolutely unknown to the Indian narrators of the epics, but he never fails to appear in the Javanese *wayang purwa* only to fall victim to the superior fighting skills of Arjuna. As A. L. Becker of the University of Michigan has put it: "Cakil dies, but not forever; he will be killed over and over again in each *wayang*." Not only localizations, but also spin-offs from the Indian epics, known as *cerita carangan* in Java and *cerita ranting* in Kelantan, attest to the *dalang's* inventiveness and paramount preoccupation with theatre as they satisfy their audiences' taste for novelty. Since many of the *dalangs* and *nai-nang* have worked with oral sources, it is not surprising that their versions of the Indian epics differ not only among themselves but also from the locally written ones.

The Southeast Asian shadow theatre then preeminently illuminates the complex and multifaceted art of the *dalang*. He is a puppeteer (often making his own puppets), actor, singer, story-teller, dramatist, leader of the musical ensemble, and shaman. (Female *dalangs* are rare, if they exist al all.) As puppeteer he manipulates puppets of various shapes and sizes with consummate skill and ingenuity. Depending on the regional tradition of the *dalang*, one arm or two arms of the puppet might be articulated, although the loquacious clowns, sages, and commoners are invariably endowed with moveable mouths as well. Manipulation of a whole puppet is, however, more varied than that of the specific parts of the body alone. A whole puppet can deftly be moved forward or backward, tilted, raised or abruptly lowered from a height, or even released completely from the hand and quickly retrieved before it falls. Aggressive characters like Hanuman and Cakil shake furiously in their anger and arrogance, leaping and dipping suddenly, much to the delight of the audience. By varying the distance between the puppet, or parts of it, and the screen, the *dalang* creates an exciting diversity of shadow forms and actions small or large, sharp or diffuse, or he can produce a "dissolve" by swiftly removing the figure from the screen. Disguises, such as that assumed by Rawanna as he comes to Sita supplicating hermitlike for alms before he rudely grabs her, are executed in the flick of an eye. More than any others, battle scenes call for the greatest expertise and adroitness, for often during combat two worlds collide—for instance, the realm of raw, uncontrolled passion exemplified by Cakil contrasted with Arjuna's refined, dispassionate parries. Even the position of the screen affects the nature of the shadows. The slightly inclined Balinese and Kelantanese screens produce rather more lively shadows than the upright screen of the somewhat formal Javanese *wayang purwa*.

Many, though not all, traditional *dalangs* make their own puppets. During each stage of the process of puppet-making the *dalang* is governed by tradition, not only with respect to technique, but also as regards the aesthetic aspects of iconography and iconometry. The final product in Java, for example, reflects the operation of a code decipherable to an initiated audience, although the intricacy and elegance of the figure is entirely a matter of individual artistry. Beginning with well-cured cow or buffalo hide, the *dalang* first carves out the outline of the figure. He then makes incisions for the facial features, clothing, jewelry, coiffure, weaponry, and other decorative and symbolic motifs. Next he attaches sticks (of buffalo horn or bamboo) for handling the puppets. One of the sticks ending on a sharp point extends down the middle of the piece, so that during performance it may be stuck to one of two banana trunks at the base of the screen. The conventional manner of painting the puppets renders the leather opaque and the shadows almost colorless. ("Modern" *dalangs* in some areas, like Kelantan, prefer thinner hide or even celluloid and plastic which they paint to achieve brightly—traditionalists would say luridly—colored shadows.) Even if the colors of the shadow are finally muted, they nevertheless serve a symbolic function, particularly in central Java, where color symbolism and other features of the puppet, such as the angle of the head, shape of the eye and nose, clothing, ornamentation, and stance, have been formalized into a veritable language which knowing Javanese audiences can "read."

Two broad and opposite types of puppets which define the difference between "refined" and "coarse" nature (*alus* and *kasar*) sum up the aesthetics permeating Indonesian culture. Albeit with differing cultural contexts and symbols, this aesthetic is adhered to in much

of traditional Southeast Asian theatre. Yudhistra, the oldest of the Pandawa brothers with his sharply slit "almond" eyes, thin nose, golden and aesthete body, narrow foot stance, and generally self-effacing demeanor is the quintessential Javanese *alus* character. In contrast, an ogre type representing the crude barbarian from overseas (*orang sebrangan*), is shown in tempestuous red with an outsized body, round eyes, bulbous nose, wide foot stance, and a haughty and overbearing pose. Between these two extremes there are a host of character types so subtly shaded from one another that together they emerge as a comprehensive picture of human nature as viewed by the Javanese. Major characters have more than one puppet representing them or, more properly, their age, mood, and emotions. The tapestry of Javanese character types also contains some surprises. Even if a heroic Pandawa, Bima is revealed as a primarily aggressive personality with a menacing claw as a weapon. Only his bowed head accords with the cultured poise of his brothers, demonstrating that *alus* does not necessarily negate arrogance. On the right side of the screen, sometimes referred to as the "good" side, the Pandawas and their followers are arrayed, while the Kurowas and their cohorts stand to the left. The right/good and the left/evil polarity, like that of *alus/kasar*, is not entirely consistent or predictable during performance. Even so, through an intimate knowledge of the complex code Javanese audiences know most of the famous characters by sight. If a particular personage is unknown to them, they can still guess the figure's role and status by the codified features of the puppet.

One puppet stands entirely on its own, but is seen throughout the performance in various guises. This is the bell-shaped "tree of life," or *kayon* or *gunungan*, as it is known in Java, or *pohon beringin*, as the Kelantanese abstract figure is called. While no two *kayon* are exactly alike, the Javanese is more representational, usually featuring serpents on a tree and a gate "guarded" by two garuda birds, while above it, there are ogres, an ox, a tiger, or a lion. The *kayon* acts as a curtain, beginning and ending a play and also marking the end of a scene. One of the most versatile of the puppets, it is also used as a palace, forest, boat, tomb, or other element of the scene. During the turmoil (or *gara-gara*) scene in the Javanese *wayang purwa*, the *kayon* is furled across the screen to herald the fury of the turbulence besetting the world.

The *dalang* as actor speaks the dialogue of all the puppets during the performance. He does not attempt to give a "realistic" portrayal of the characters, but instead seeks to grasp and convey their essence. In truth there is very little that is "realistic" about the shadow theatre world of gods, kings, princes, sages, clowns, and monkeys. *Wayang* plots as described by A. L. Becker in his discussion of the Javanese *wayang purwa*, are "built upon coincidences . . . In the lakon form many stories are occuring simultaneously. At some point in the performance these separate plots coincide, then go their separate ways. That is, *lakon* plots are not linear, Aristotelian plots, with clear beginning, middle and end—involve-

Indonesian *wayang golek* puppet. [Stadtmuseum, Munich]

and culture represented by ancient literary accounts of their heroes. One of the best-loved of the stories, *The Meditation of Arjuna (Arjuna Wiwaha)* (narrating how the Pandawa hero presses on with his meditation, or *semadi*, in spite of the many temptations before him, and as a reward for his fortitude acquires the powerful bow *pasopati*) had been written down in 1030 by Mpu Kanwa.

Before a performance, a Javanese *dalang* will refer to perhaps one or two pages of notes containing a scenerio of the play. But his performance might last all night, from about nine in the evening to about six in the morning. This all-night (*malam suntuk*) event is divided into three phases, or *patet*, taking their terminology from the mode struck by the gamelan ensemble during the performance. Each *patet*, lasting roughly three hours, is a combination of three scene types: an audience scene (*jejer*), a journey (*adegan*), and a battle (*perang*). For instance, the first phase, or *patet nem*, opens with a king receiving his court. Following upon and involving the revelations of this audience, a journey into the forest occurs. In the wilderness, the travelers encounter ogres by sheer coincidence, and a battle ensues. The hero of the play is not introduced until the beginning of the second *patet* called *sanga*, and then too, only after his servants and the clowns have had their hour. Furthermore, no plot is very new since even the most inventive ones are made up of episodes from other plots and because its outcome is predictable and known to the audience; for in the final *patet*, or *manjura*, the hero must always triumph, even if temporarily, and restore equilibrium to the cosmos.

The plot and the drama it creates does not begin or even end a shadow theatre performance. During the ritual preceding the play the *dalang* reveals his role as a magico-religious leader, or shaman. (Strictly speaking, the performance "begins" with the playing of the introductory music which, among other things, serves to draw the audience to the performance area.) When chanting the magical invocations, or *mantra*, to "open" the stage, the *dalang* becomes a medium through whom communication with the spirit world is conducted. In the broad meaning of the shaman in theatre suggested by Richard Schechner of New York University, the *dalang* might be seen as a ceremonial and educational leader who "actualizes" past time and place for his audience, in other words, bringing the "there and then" to the "here and now." In the shadow theatres of Kelantan, Thailand, and Kampuchea yet another ritual, quite apart from the *mantra*, must be fulfilled before the main play can begin. *Wayang kelantan*, for instance, always stages the short episode about the gods of the bow and arrow (or *Dewa-Dewa Panah*), a performance which is presided over by the apprentice *dalang* (or *dalang muda*). Thai and Kampuchean shadow theatres open their performances with a dramatization of a tale concerning a white and a black monkey. This ritual has the function of a prologue and also helps set the mood for the experience of "actualization." During a special type of performance or ceremonial called *Berjamu* in Kelantan, when the spirits of the puppets are propitiated or, more specifically, recalled (*panggil balik*), the *dalang* not only invites the spirits to

ment, climax, denouement—although they have often been interpreted that way. They are intricately cyclical. . . ." Whether the structure of performance is formal and tight as in Java or loose and casual as in Bali and Kelantan, *dalangs* resist delineating a plot in a causal and linear progression of events. Instead, the plot is revealed, indeed imbedded, in a series of ritualistic events and actions. Guided by traditional constraints which tell him what is fitting and what is not, the *dalang* as dramatist, "constructs" a play out of basic units of these occurrences. *Dalangs* have been known to "build" a play on the spot at the request or with the help of the sponsor of the performance. His musicians are not perturbed by the unexpected twists and turns of the novel tale because they too follow a fixed structure of performance and tight constraints. While they might not "rehearse" a play, in the Western sense of the word, the members of the musical ensemble, along with the *dalang*, are always "prepared" for a performance, whatever the *lakon*.

Perhaps the most literate of the shadow theatre practitioners, the Javanese *dalang* also lives in a society the "here and now" but also feasts them. Performing the *berjamu* at dawn without a screen, the *dalang* in a trance assumes the character of each of the puppets he feeds. In Central Java another daytime ceremonial enacting the exorcist play *The Birth of Kala* is performed. Like the Kelantanese Berjamu, this performance is also directed to an unseen spirit audience, because even though a lamp and a screen are used, the shadows in broad daylight can hardly be seen by mortals. Javanese believe that this ritual is valid only if performed by a venerable and spiritually powerful *dalang*.

In normal circumstances, performances are held at night, and more often than not they celebrate rites of passage such as births and marriages, or circumcision (if the area is Moslem), or give thanks for a boon granted by the gods. Those celebrating the occasion often sponsor the performance and their relatives, friends, and neighbors make up the audience. On such occasions shadow theatre is more than just a performance, it is a social and religious event, eliciting the atmosphere of a community ritual. Performances in southern Thailand and Kelantan are also staged during festivals and fairs, often before paying audiences; in fact, in the latter region shadow theatre has become a commercial enterprise operated by local entrepreneurs, who hire troupes, fence off the performing area, and charge admission. More recently, government agencies, such as Radio Republic Indonesia, have begun to finance performances in order to ensure the continued well-being of the performers and their art form.

Be it for the sake of community, commerce, or art, the chanting of the mantra, whether heard or not heard by the audience, begins the performance for the *dalang*. The dalang names the spirits, their origins and their abodes, and asks for their beneficence or at least their neutrality during the performance. No two *dalangs* chant the same *mantra*, but it is often considered essential in the traditional performances of Southeast Asia to name the denizens of the four points of the compass, the spirits of water, earth, fire, wind and the rice fields, and depending on the religious orientation of the *dalang* and his society, the imported Hindu and/or Buddhist gods or Allah are also invoked. Secret *mantras* are often chanted, but in a whisper. Kelantanese *dalangs* whisper or breathe upon the major puppet characters, including Pak Dogol. Magic therefore, as the anthropologist B. Malinowski explains, "is in the breath and the breath the magic."

By this time the audience would have gathered. The audience that attends a shadow theatre performance is neither formal nor single-focused in behavior. Most of the audience in Bali, Kelantan, and South Thailand view the performance from the shadow side of the screen, but from time to time, a few will go "backstage" to peer at the musicians and the puppet events from the *dalang's* side. Many more in central Java prefer to watch the *dalang* and the musicians rather than the shadows, especially if the performance takes place in an enclosed auditorium, which is often arranged so that a large majority of the audience sits behind the performers. Therefore, during the performance many realities operate and act

upon each other—the musicians, the *dalang*, the puppets, and the shadows—to create the event for the audience. Other realities not directly related to the performers may also impinge on the audience and the performance, namely the members of the audience, who are sometimes viewed with as much clarity and concreteness as the performance itself. If it is a village performance, the children invariably sit on the ground and fall asleep on and off throughout the performance. But when the comic and battle scenes appear on the screen, they are fully alert, and indeed they can have their fill of battle, especially at the end of the play. During the last *patet* of the Javanese *wayang purwa*, single combat scenes burst upon the screen, climaxed by the "flower battle" (*bunga*) exhibiting the exquisitely stylized fighting style of the hero. In Kelantan, Rama will eventually defeat Rawanna and rescue Sita, but the death of the demon-god is seldom shown on the screen. Rawanna is, after all, a god who accrued his legendary powers and near invulnerability as a result of an exemplary and strenuous period of meditation. It is therefore believed by many Kelantanese *dalangs* that the display of the demon's death will bring disaster upon those who create the exhibition or watch it.

The adults in the audience mostly stand and comment on the performance, talk among themselves, or flirt. (A shadow theatre performance as a community gathering is, of course, one of the main occasions for courtship.) Some among the audience can always be seen in the snack or coffee shops nearby. In Bali, as those who have visited the island never fail to testify, the mangy and irreverent dogs are as much part of the performance as anything else. By their various activities the audience creates the space for the performance, thereby shaping the actual environment for shadow theatre. No member of the audience sees all of the performance. It is too long—either about three to four hours or nine for an all-night affair—for an intense and con-

Javanese shadow theatre. [The Asia Society, Performing Arts Department]

centrated viewing. Also the story is known and shared by all as part of their communal history. Therefore, not the play but the performance is the center of the event, and even during the performance, the attention of the audience is selective. This attitude of "selective inattention," to use the felicitous phrase coined by Richard Schechner, is a common feature of Southeast Asian traditional theatre. (The musicians, too, sometimes chat among themselves and smoke, and occasionally they peep at the audience without ever losing their concentration or sense of preparedness. Only the *dalang*, it appears, gives full attention to the whole performance.) Different people in the audience are absorbed by different things in the performance. The elders might be moved by the philosophical and mystical moments and the *dalang's* poetic flights. Mostly set in their phraseology and exclusive to *wayang*, descriptions of kings and kingdoms and of supernatural heroes provoke a high-flown and grandly hyperbolic poetic language from the dalang. Repetitions, distortions, or purely invented words are frequent, especially in *wayang Kelantan*, and help produce a precious realm for the audience. Like those used by the other "technicians of the sacred," as Jerome Rothenberg called his book, the linguistic devices of the *dalang* "unite the user (with what Malinowski calls "the coefficient of wierdness") with the beings and things he's trying to influence and connect with, for a sharing of power, preparation of life beyond his own. . . ." Naturally the most poignant and sublime moments of poetry are occasioned by songs, which are employed to enhance a narrative or convey an emotional mood. In the Javanese *wayang purwa*, the lyrics are more or less fixed, and the dalang by himself or accompanied by a chorus of female and male singers produces an elaborately polyphonic sound. Greater improvisation with respect to the lyrics is exercised in the Kelantanese *wayang kulit*, where the *dalang*, singing alone, begins with a standard opening and then improvises according to his resourcefulness and mood (*angin*). (In common with many other Malay words, *angin*, literally meaning "wind," encompasses a constellation of meanings beyond that of mood, including, for instance, the sense that some people have *angin*, or "propensity" for wayang. Expressed casually or with great seriousness and solemnity, *angin* is, above all, a state of experience between consciousness and trance, and at peak moments produces an ineffable harmony between "awareness and action".) The music of the dream sphere is also characterized by set tunes which are played on the appearance of certain characters, thereby fixing the pace and the rhythm for the *dalang* to adopt when manipulating those puppets. These fixed and standard components are guided to their beginning and their end under the direction of the *dalang*, who uses a variety of linguistic and sound techniques to cue his musicians.

Among the characters whose appearance is eagerly awaited by all members of the audience, regardless of age and sex, the clowns are in first place. In every wayang a portion of the performance is completely given over to the humor of the clowns. During the all-night Javanese *wayang purwa* the clowns appear at about midnight to begin the second *patet* with the *gara-gara* scene, in which the resolute meditation of the soon-to-be-seen hero causes havoc and turmoil in the world. For about an hour, the hero's servants, or *panakawans*—that is, Semar and his sons—Petruk, Gareng, and Bagong—sing, dance, and feast the audience with humor. The episode involving the clowns in Java and elsewhere is by far the most improvised and spontaneous of the whole performance and severely tests the stamina and inventiveness of the *dalang*. *Dalangs* adapt the clowns' humor to the proclivities of their audience, sometimes even shortening or lengthening their stay on the screen in response to the crowd's fancy. The clowns perform a variety of functions during a performance. They might be servants of a noble personage, usually the hero of the play, whom they frequently rescue from many difficult and awkward situations, but they are also powerful local gods. In Bali the god-servants, or *parakans*, also act as translators for the audience, interpreting in everyday Balinese the high *Kawi* (or Old Javanese) spoken by the nobility. In their role as intermediaries the *parakans* and the clowns of shadow theatre in general are reminiscent of the clown, or *vidusaka*, of Indian theatre. Apart from their language which is highly colloquial, the clowns take many other liberties denied to the other characters. They come out of the play, alienating the audience from the story and the dream world of the *wayang*. By talking directly to them about the social issues of the day, they force the members of the audience to reflect, for a while at least, upon their present and ordinary concerns. Truly epitomizing the turbulence of the *gara-gara*, the clowns turn things upside down as they indulge in anachronisms or, more importantly, parody the high and the mighty; but all is done within an unhazardous framework of performance. The clowns therefore can be said to create a "liminal zone," which according to the anthropologist Victor Turner is "a moment when those being moved in accordance with a cultural script are liberated from normative demands; when they are, indeed, between and betwixt successive lodgements in jural political systems." The experience of liminality afforded by the clowns of shadow theatre provokes "reflexivity," in other words the capability "to stand aside not only from one's personal social position but from all social positions."

In the Javanese *wayang purwa*, when the battles are fought and won, Bima does a victory dance. The all-night performance often closes with the dance of the doll, or *golek*, puppet. These events help produce a resonance after the play is over. Indeed, as the Mangkunogoro VII of Surakarta, Java, has explained, *golek* is "associated with the verb 'golekki' (or to search)"—that is, "the search in one's consciousness for the inner value of the *lakon*." The performers also cool off from the heat of the performance by quickly dismantling the set and gathering and packing up the instruments and other stage paraphernalia. The puppets "cool off" when they are put to sleep in the box. In Bali they are put to rest with a prayer lest the contending parties fight with each other in the box.

An Indonesian demon's mask used in a *barong* dance. It is carved of wood and decorated with gilt animal hide. [Deutsches Ledermuseum, Offenbach am Main]

DANCE DRAMA

Most likely the masked dance drama known as *khon,* which was nurtured in the royal courts of Thailand during the Ayuthia period (1350–1767), was developed from *nang yai,* the central Thai shadow theatre. The hand and finger gestures of the originally all-male *khon* performers, who were first written about in the reign of King Boro Matrailoka (1448–1488), were presumably borrowed from the Indian mode of dancing, but the torso and foot movements show a strong kinship with those executed by the dancing puppeteers of *nang yai.* The sideways motion of the *khon* dancers and their dancing in profile also argue a close relationship between puppet and human theatre. Furthermore, the structure of the *khon* performance, centered upon an episodic framework referred to as *chud* (a shadow theatre term meaning "set of puppets) and much of the *khon* repertory of plays based on the *Ramayana* are almost indistinguishable from *nang yai.* During important festivals and fairs *nang yai* and *khon* were performed on the same grounds, sometimes even side by side, thus displaying twin aspects of a common style. The ritualistic beginnings of the *khon* have been recorded by the noted Thai theatre scholar Mattani Rutnin, who suggests that the *khon* was originally staged by court officials as a religious performance known as *chak nak dukdamban,* in which two rival parties, gods and ogres, engaged in a kind of tug-of-war with a serpent. Apparently this was an enactment of the ancient Hindu myth where the pulling of the serpent (*naga*) churned the

ocean to produce the fountain of impartiality.

The Thai aristocracy also created an exclusively female dance drama. As in many other Southeast Asian palace theatres, the social segregation practiced between the sexes in the Thai courts was also reflected in its dance dramas until the "modernization" of the country in the early years of the twentieth century. "Drama of women in the palace," or *lakon nai,* which acquired its stories from the Javanese *Panji* tales, with women playing both male and female roles, emerged into full bloom during the reign of King Boromokot (1733–1755). Despite his short tenure, King Rama II (1809–1824) completed the comprehensive version of the Panji cycle of stories containing 20,000 verses, which in length almost rivals the Indian *Ramayana.* Beginning with King Rama II's reign the adventures of Prince Panji, called Inao in Thailand, came to inspire the *lakon nai* repertory.

A similar relationship between shadow and human theatre can be found in the courts of central Java, the home of the dance drama called *wayang wong,* or "human puppets." Although Javanese court dances, including the ritualistic *srimpi* and *bedoyo* and the masked dance, *topeng,* are known to have existed since the end of the sixteenth century, the pedigree of the fully realized *wayang wong* is traced from the mid-eighteenth century. King Haemengkubuwana I is credited with the creation of the Javanese *wayang wong,* complete with lyrical dialogue and telling *Ramayana* and *Mahabaratha* stories. Eventually, following the Dutch-enforced division of central Java into two principalities during the eighteenth century two styles of dance and music representing the courts of Jogjakarta and Surakarta appeared. This led to the shaping of two styles of *wayang wong*, even if the differences between them can only be appreciated by a trained observer.

When performed in the Jogjakarta court, for example, *wayang wong* is staged in the *pendapa*, a polyfunctional hall used for meetings, for ceremonies such as weddings and funerals, and for performances. Whereas the court shadow theatre is performed in a hall behind, the square and walless *pendapa*, delineated by a central frame of four main pillars and twelve or more surrounding areas, is the principal arena for dance drama. According to Sudarsono, the Indonesian dance scholar and the director of his country's dance academy (ASTI), only two entrances and exits were traditionally employed for *wayang wong* in spite of the fact that the hall could accommodate many more. Such self-denial underlines the influence of *wayang purwa* on the scenography of *wayang wong*. Just like the puppets, *wayang wong* dancers often strike profilelike stances; also, much of the wayang wong choreography, running along flat and straight lines, smacks of shadow theatre.

Wayang wong is also to be found in the Indonesian island of Bali, by far the most prolific of the theatre regions of Southeast Asia. But whereas the Javanese version is an exposition of courtly elegance and precision, the Balinese *wayang wong*, catering to the tastes of its own audience, is a village art staged on dusty ground. All but the refined (or *alus*) characters wear masks in the Balinese *wayang wong*, which unlike the Javanese example has little dance and is very dependent on the poetic recitation of long passages to present its *Ramayana* stories. By way of contrast, in the Balinese *topeng*, or masked dance drama, the chief characters who act out the imperialistic adventures of Gadjah Madah, the Prime Minister of the Hindu-Javanese Kingdom of Majapahit (1293–ca. 1520), only dance and their attendants speak for them. In many masked dance dramas of Southeast Asia, most notably the Thai *khon*, the performer is invariably separated from his dialogue and the task of expressing the dancer's thought is assigned to a team of singer-narrators. The result is that the audience is coerced into focusing its attention on a number of temporal and spatial elements during one event in the performance. This tradition of employing intermediaries becomes a fine art in the popular Balinese dance drama called *ardja*. Whereas the *ardja* protagonists of the Balinese *Mahabaratha* dramas, for instance, are confined to their other worldly roles, their attendants, using a resourceful variety of vocal, mime, and dance devices, freely step in and out of their characters and the play. They precede their masters in entrances, parody their Javanese court style of dancing, make topical jokes, and comment on the current Balinese scene; in effect, they intercede between the mythic world of the play and the contemporary world of the audience.

Dance is also powerfully evident in the *barong*, a dance drama evoking the ritual and unresolved encounter between the positive powers of the lionlike figure Barong and the malevolent witch Rangda. Near the end of the play young men wielding *keris* (daggers) attempt to destroy Rangda, but are instead entranced by the witch into turning their daggers against themselves, thus beginning the famous *keris* dance of Bali. The dancers are shielded from harming themselves by the magical force of Barong, who chases off Rangda, but not for all time, as the witch will return to plague the village once again. The *barong* dance drama is often staged in response to a disturbance in the equilibrium of Balinese society. In the early 1970s, for example, when youthful hordes of Americans and Europeans "invaded" the southwest Balinese beach at Kuta, the *barong* play was performed in the streets for several nights each week.

Yet another puppet theatre tradition in Southeast Asia appears to have played a crucial role in the making of dance drama. Although Burma does not have a shadow play tradition, its marionette theatre has a long history. Until the middle of the eighteenth century, however, the string puppets were primarily used for the entertainment of children. But after Burma sacked the Thai capital in 1767, Thai-derived *Ramayana* and *Jataka* (or Buddhist birth) tales began to be dramatized by marionette performers. And when itinerant (or *zat pwe*) performers wished to incorporate Jataka stories into their repertory late in the nineteenth century, they turned to the marionette theatre for guidance.

The influence of shadow theatre is but one of the factors that has contributed to a remarkable coincidence in the character of Southeast Asian dance dramas. By smaller or larger degrees, a common adherence to the Indian style of dancing and, most significant of all, frequent exchange and borrowing between the countries over many centuries, especially during the precolonial era, account for a recognizable dance image in Southeast Asia. In Thailand the 66 prescribed dance movements, or *tha ram*, reconstructed in the first, second, and third regions of the Ratonokosin period (1782–1850) are a less complex and somewhat altered version of the 108 Indian *mudras* which collectively operate as an "alphabet" of dancing on the subcontinent. Peninsular and insular Southeast Asian countries also rely on some of the Indian gestures to convey action and express moods and emotions, but not to the extent of exposing a strict and symbolic code of meaning. Even though China's borders have loomed over most of mainland Southeast Asia, the imprint of the Chinese dance culture is much less widespread. Through its plays, costumes, and dance movement conventions, Chinese opera clearly influenced Vietnam's *hat boi*, or sung drama with gesture or pose, which first appeared in the thirteenth century. Popular theatres such as the Kampuchean *lakon bassac* and the Vietnamese *cai luong*, initiated in the early decades of the twentieth century, also owe a debt to Chinese stories, music, and dance, but that is about the extent to which Chinese dance is directly related to the formation of dance drama in Southeast Asia. *See* CHINESE THEATRE.

So much cross-fertilization has occurred in the performing arts of Southeast Asia that it would be foolhardy to locate the origins of any one genre without the support of concrete data. The intermittent wars plaguing precolonial mainland Southeast Asia between the thirteenth and eighteenth centuries have played their dubious role in instilling an almost identical style of continental dancing and dance dramas. These wars, which often led to the capture of the highly prized royal dance troupes by the victors, were partially responsible for the decline of the Kampuchean Kingdom of Angkor in the fifteenth century. The Thai-Burmese struggles were climaxed by the Rangoon victory of 1767. Therefore, the question of who first created the identifiable Thai-Kampuchean dance mode can only be answered chauvinistically.

The noticeable similarities between southern Thailand's *lakon jatri* (referred to by most Thais as *nora jatri* or simply *nora*, short for *Manora*, its most frequently performed play) and the *Mak Yong* of Kelantan in Malaysia stem from close sociopolitical relations between the two areas. (Kelantan and the other northwestern and northeastern states of peninsular Malaysia were under Thai suzerainty until the British brought them under imperial control in 1909.) The *Ramayana* might have been confined to the Brahmanic-oriented courts of Thailand, but the *nora* performers, thought to be the oldest of the Thai dance-drama practitioners, staged Buddhist Jataka tales. By so doing, they mirrored the popularity among the Thai peasantry of the egalitarian Theravada Buddhism introduced to the Thai peoples between the fifth and the tenth centuries. The *nora* plays, however, are not dependent on the 507 Jatakas of the sacred *Tripitaka* collection of the Buddhist canon; instead the *nora* performers produced dramatic versions of the Panyasa Jataka tales, which, drawing from local Thai legends, represent Thai heroes as incarnations of Buddha in his previous lives. *Manora*, for example, enacts the love of the beautiful bird-maiden Manora for the earthly prince Suton. The adventures of Sang Thong, the golden-conch prince, and Prince Rothasen, who is tutored in magical lore by ogres, are some of the other Panyasa Jataka stories often performed by *nora* troupes. The Sang Thong tale, known as *Anak Raja Gondang* in Kelantan, is also part of the repertory of some dozen plays of *Mak Yong*, whose origins, according to recent scholarship, are traceable to the Kelantanese exorcist ritual performance called *main petri*. Beginning about the middle of the nineteenth century, *Mak Yong* blossomed into a sophisticated court dance drama and flourished under the patronage of the sultans of Kelantan. As a result of the coinciding impact of deeper British involvement in Kelantan's affairs and the world depression of the 1930s, the economic resources of the sultan diminished and *Mak Yong* performers were forced out of the palace to seek out a precarious living among the general populace. Today *Mak Yong* is almost entirely dependent on the support of government and private agencies for its survival.

Not only between regions, but also within each country, interchange has been so penetrating that distinctions between theatre genres, such as between folk and court performances, must be made with caution. *Lakon jatri*, for example, evidently influenced the Bang-

Masked performer of the Topeng Dance Theatre of Bali. [The Asia Society, Performing Arts Department]

kok-based commercial theatre called *lakon nok*, which in turn helped shape the court's *lakon nai*.

Whether they be folk or court performers, Southeast Asian dancers, much like their puppet counterparts, tend to lean toward the ground as they dance, unlike western dancers who convey an upward élan in their dancing and attempt to defy gravity. There are regional variations in Southeast Asia to be sure—among them, the mainland Southeast Asian dancers' practice of lifting one foot behind their body and the gesture of touching the thumb and index fingers. Farther south, particularly in Java and Bali, the half-crouching position of the female dancers is characteristic. Nevertheless, most of the dance practitioners of Southeast Asia have crystallized an array of distinct movements involving sitting, kneeling, and crouching to express their attachment to the earth. In "The Salutation to the Spiked-Fiddle" (*Mengadap Rebab*), which begins each *Mak Yong* performance, the corps of dancers executes a complicated arabesque of hand and finger gestures while gently swaying on the ground. Even when upright, the quintessential pliant-knees attitude of both Indian and Southeast Asian dancers emphasizes the powerful pull of the earth. When playing refined and heroic characters, who are the epitome of self-will and containment, male and female dancers assume a severely narrow stance and travel through a series of tightly defined spaces with intricate and controlled movements and gestures. In keeping with their shy and self-effacing personality, the heroines' eyes are often cast downward and their faces are impassive. In this regard the Balinese dancer is an exception. A *legong* dance-drama performer, for instance, might have an ethereal look in common with her Southeast Asian skin, but her eyes are as vividly dramatic and flirtatious as her Indian counterparts. Larger spaces, however, are covered by proud and/or aggressive characters. The broad steps of a Rawanna, the ogre-god of the *Ramayana* stories, are raised high above the ground, but he too will eventually come down to earth before resuming his beligerent course across the stage. Skipping, hopping, whirling, and rotating movements are rare in all but some of the animal and trance dances and a few of the folk performances of Southeast Asia.

Dancing is only one of the events presented in a Southeast Asian dance drama. Narrative and dialogue, sung or spoken, music and mime are also exploited in a manner reminiscent of shadow theatre to produce a theatre of multilayered and multifocused sensations. The relationship between the various elements is often highly structured—in some cases strictly codified—but there is still sufficient latitude for improvisation and individual creativity. Most court-derived theatres for instance share a common sensibility for a neat and meticulous design. Three principal types of dancing and their functions have been described by Mattaani Rutnin for *khon* and *lakon*, one of the most complex and codified of the Southeast

Dancers of Bali. [The Asia Society, Performing Arts Department]

Asian dance dramas. For example, little or no improvisation is allowed for the pattern of dance movements known as *ram na phat*, or "dancing to set musical tunes." Generations old and strictly prescribed, *ram na phat* gestures illustrate particular actions like walking, running, exiting, flying, and assuming a disguise. Some of the danced events of *ram na phat* are entirely ritualistic, such as the mandatory *wai*, or paying homage to the dance teacher. One of the most exquisite is the ritual of courtship, where before reclining, the code for lovemaking, the couple propitiates the Buddha or other deities to ensure protection while they are "asleep." The second type of dancing, called *ram chai bot*, or "dancing by using the text," involves the interpretation of poetic narration. Only certain words of the passage are selected for dancing, and during this dance event the dancer can exercise freedom in choosing the words to be danced. In the meanwhile, the precise meaning of the passage is known to the audience if they give attention to the context of the play. This kind of interpretive dancing during which the dancer executes *ti bot* or the act of "smashing the text" can vary according to the dancer's individual choice and creative abilities. A particularly inspired interpretation, distinguished by a refined and profound rendition of the chosen words, is thought to be *ti bot taek* or the act of "smashing the text to pieces." Finally, *khon* and *lakon* practitioners have also revised a constellation of generalized dance movements which connect one dance phrase with another, fill the gaps when the chief characters are not dancing, or give support to them when they are. Large groupings of dancers on stage culminating in tableaus are as striking in Thai dance-dramas as they are in many of the other dance theatres of Southeast Asia.

Their strong and largely uninterrupted tradition of dance-dramas has helped the Thais to construct a national style of theatre in recent years. As currently performed in the National Theatre, the Bangkok-centered dance-drama, the product of three decades of reconstruction and experimentation following the Second World War, is an eclectic synthesis of the main performing arts of Thailand with *khon* and *lakon* as its backbone and guiding principle.

In its own way, the aesthetics of the Javanese *wayang wong* are just as definitive and demanding as the court-inspired *khon* and *lakon*. It was not enough for the traditional Jogjanese dancers merely to have talent; they were also expected to be spiritually and psychologically prepared for performance before the sultan and his entourage. The seventeenth-century dance manual, *Joged Mataram*, gives us a hint of the preparations demanded of a court performer. The dancer, it tells us, must have concentration, an ability to control expression according to the character being performed, and "a strong and immoveable will," and must be "full of personal dignity." Indeed, the delineation of characters, or more precisely character types, seems to be a paramount concern of *wayang wong* aestheticians. The level of the limbs, moving into subtle shifts beginning from a very narrow stance, and the symmetry and asymmetry of the arms,

Dancers of the Burmese National Theatre. [The Asia Society, Performing Arts Department]

are considered vital in the definition of character types. Sudarsono has categorized nine principal dance techniques, which are, in effect, descriptions of the nine chief character types found in the *Mahabaratha* and *Ramayana* stories of the *wayang wong*. Collectively and in their carefully nuanced variations, the dance attitudes expose a highly developed sensitivity for defining and describing human archetypes. A recognizable dance style has been invented for a refined female character, or *nggurdha*, and male character types are cataloged, for example, as follows: refined and humble (*impur*), refined and proud (*kagok kinantang*), strong and humble (*kambeng*), strong and proud (*kalang kinantang*), strong and refined (*kagok impur*), and so on. In addition, twelve different dance techniques govern minor characters, including giants, sages, gods, animals, and, not least, the humorous god-servants (*panakawan*) whose dance mode is called *merak gigel*, or "dancing peacock." Dance movements taking on the names of trees, animals, and other entities of nature express behavior and denote action onstage. There is also a finely differentiated series of dance movements encapsulating the peculiarities of the Javanese style of dancing, one of the most famous of which is the *wedhi kengser*, or "sand movement," which describes the feet as the dancer moves sideways without ever lifting them from the ground, thereby capturing the motion of "sand blown by the wind."

Although wayang wong moved out of the "protective" cover of the courts late in the nineteenth and early in the twentieth century, its basic choreography has prevailed even if with occasional incongruous consequences. The arena type of staging practiced in the courts, or *kraton*, necessitating the repetition of a dance phrase directed at audiences on at least three sides of the *pendapa*, appeared slow, langorous, and even tedious when transferred to the imported Western proscenium stage adopted by the commercial *wayang wong* troupes. Dance events conveying a strong aura of ritual have also been modified in response to the demands of the new staging for new audiences. Competition from the fast-moving rhythms of the media of the technological world, such as cinema and television, has hastened the transformation of wayang wong from a ritualistic performance lasting one to four days in the *kraton* to a secular evening of two to three hours. New dance dramas "unencumbered" by dialogue called *sendratari* have also appeared on the Indonesian stage since the 1960s. More recently young choreographers have created experimental dance dramas, or *creasi baru*, based on some of the profoundly ritualistic dances, such as *srimpi* and *bedoyo*. These are no longer *wayang wong* as practiced in the courts of central Java; in fact, in most of Southeast Asia it would be difficult to find "purely" traditional dance drama. But new creations and reconstructions of old ones derive their inspiration from traditional choreography and at the same time explore new structures and aesthetics to fit new contexts.

TRADITIONAL MUSIC

Most of the traditional music of Southeast Asia is intimately connected with theatre. Until some of the region's musical practitioners began to emulate Western practices in recent decades, music was rarely played for its own sake as autonomous orchestral, chamber, or solo concert performances. Instead, music accompanied and, indeed, was one of the basic elements of puppet theatre, dance drama, dance, narrative performance, and singing traditions. The Javanese gamelan musical mode (*patet*) informs the mood and sets the pace and rhythm of shadow theatre (wayang kulit). More or less fixed musical pieces are associated with specific actions, characters, and stage movements in much of Southeast Asian traditional theatre.

One of the earliest glimpses into Indonesian music, afforded by the reliefs decorating the walls of the ninth-century central Javanese monument in Borobodur dedicated to the Buddha, reveals the symbiotic relationship between dance and music. There we encounter, for example, four mixed couples apparently dancing to the accompaniment of what has been identified as a wooden xylophone called *gambang kayu*, which even today is an important member of the Javanese gamelan ensemble. Another relief features dancing drummers together with a flute and two cymbal players. Percussion instruments, in fact, are as prominent in early Southeast Asian records of music as they are today in the region's traditional theatre performances. Among the group of percussion instruments, the sets of tuned knobbed gongs—a clear example of which is sculptured in a twelfth-century Thommanon temple gable in Kampuchea (Cambodia)—are so predominant that one ethnomusicologist has used the term "gong-chime" to characterize traditional Southeast Asian music.

Two of the best studied of the gong-chime traditions, namely the Indonesian gamelan and the Thai *pi-phat*, not only provide us with a basic understanding of the musical cultures of these two countries, but also clarify some of the fundamental unities that prevail in traditional Southeast Asian music. Melody is the primary motivating force in Southeast Asia in music, as opposed to the mainstream of the Western musical tradition, which is essentially preoccupied with the exploration of harmonic progression and counterpoint. (Nor for that matter is Indian musical theory of very great help in the comprehension of Southeast Asian music, although Indian instruments or modifications of them are plentiful in almost all countries of the region.) Once a nuclear or main melody is stated, the musicians in a Southeast Asian ensemble—dictated, of course, by the idiom of their instruments—simultaneously undertake simple or elaborate and ornamental interpretations of it. Music in Southeast Asia is therefore made up of layers of simultaneous sounds and is often described as being stratified in a polyphonic fashion. At certain points, however, the layers of sounds will converge, only to diverge yet again. This relentless exercise of converging and diverging is anchored upon a formal structure mapped out by instruments acting as time-markers. Drums of various sizes and shapes, often playing in an interlocking style, lay the rhythmic foundations of the music.

Musical traditions do not exist in a vacuum; on the contrary they reflect and, in turn, are reflected by the society from which they arise. This is the common-sense proposition that led the ethnomusicologist Judith Becker to investigate the connection between Javanese musical theory and practice and Javanese society. The chain linking the two processes was found in the compelling operations of cyclicality and coincidence. Judith Becker arrived at the term "gongan" to refer to the cyclical recurrence of temporal/melodic units, which are begun, as they are ended, by the large, suspended, deep-sounding gong called *gong ageng*. The basic unit is governed by the principle of binary subdivision, and depending on the length of the gongan—some as simple as two beats and others as complex as 1,024 beats—these subdivisions occur once or more. Higher levels of subdivision are registered by other relatively smaller knobbed gongs—the *kenong*, *kethuk*, and *kempul*—which function as time-markers. In this way several subcycles are created, of which the most primary is called "kenongan" since it is ended by the *kenong*, a set of largish, inverted knobbed gongs resting on crossed cords above wooden resonators. Javanese music is driven "forward" by these small and large coincidences, during which all the instruments, including the time-markers and those engaged in the polyphonic demonstration of melody, converge or coincide at a single pitch. The five-toned (*slendro*) and the seven-toned (*pelog*) scales are the two used in the Javanese gamelan, the former being more popular than the latter. In large ensembles, which may have as many as 75 instruments, both scales are represented, and the musicians move comfortably from one to the other when it is necessary to do so.

Several aspects of Javanese society are also bound to the workings of cyclicality and coincidence. The Javanese express time, for example, in terms of several recurring cycles occurring simultaneously. By combining their five-day market week and the Western and Muslim seven-day week, the Javanese achieve thirty-five separate days in a cycle forming their month. Instead of being fixed, a "month" is defined as the length of time between any one day and its next appearance thirty-five days later. Every thirty-five days the cycles coincide, and this coincidence is invested with special meaning by the Javanese, as is the significance attached to several old gamelan pieces dominated by the operations of musical coincidence. Performed exclusively on ritual occasions, for weddings, and for shadow theatre, some of these pieces, estimated to have existed before A.D. 1000, are the only ones played by gamelan sets owned by the Javanese aristocracy. According to Javanese legend, Lord Siva himself (known as Batara Guru in Java) presented *Monggang*, one of the oldest of the gamelan pieces, to the Javanese people. The archaic *sempak*, *srepegan*, and *ayak-ayak* are indispensable to the old and ritualistic central Javanese shadow theatre (*wayang purwa*). Apart from the sacred pieces, the Javanese gamelan repertoire also comprises "great" pieces, which are very long and thought to be too exacting for contemporary performance. Contrary to Javanese belief, Judith Becker contends that it is not their difficulty but more their tediousness, resulting from an undeviating concentration on

Balinese dancers Suarti and Suarni in a New York demonstration performance. [The Asia Society, Performing Arts Department]

coincidence at the expense of melodic interpretation, that discourages present-day musicians from performing the "great" pieces.

Notions of cyclicality and coincidence also appear to guide the traditional Balinese. Personal names are mostly eschewed in Bali in favor of birth-order names. But the given names only stretch up to four generations after which the naming procedure is recycled, thereby setting up coincidences of names. Kumpi, for instance, is the name of both a great grandfather and a great grandchild. Even if cycles and coincidences rule the social and cultural system of Bali, the Balinese fondness for invention and novelty, albeit expressed within the safe and secure confines of tradition, has caused their music to take on a somewhat different texture from that of the Javanese. As in the current loud or soft-style Javanese gamelan, the old Balinese ensemble, or *gamelan gong*, articulates the nuclear melody, or *pokok*, through the *saron*, a xylophone with metal keys on a wooden resonator. In the relatively new *kebyar* ensemble, the nuclear melody is the responsibility of the *gangsa*, a xylophone with thin metal keys resting on cords over a bamboo resonator, an instrument that does not exist in traditional Javanese gamelan. Ac-

tually there are two *gangsa*, one tuned slightly different from the other, and when the same keys on the two metallophones are struck, a flutter provoked by the beats shimmers through. The existence of many beats produced by several paired instruments is what gives the Balinese gamelan its well-known electric quality.

Another peculiarly Balinese instrument is the set of inverted knobbed gongs called *trompong* found in the gamelan gong ensemble. While it has the same function of elaborating on the nuclear melody as the Javanese *bonang*, the *trompong* is unique for two reasons. First, unlike the two-rowed knobbed *bonang* gongs, the trompong has only one row of gongs; secondly, as played with two long wooden mallets, it exhibits the virtuosity of the musician, who virtually performs a dance with his flashing hand movements. Rather more complex variations on the nuclear melody are introduced by two quartets of metallophones called *penyachah* and *kantilan*. Because they are tuned an octave apart from each other, the *penyachah* and *kantilan* can either produce patterns of interlocking sounds, or if each pair of the quartet supplies half the melody, alternative pitches will ensue. The Javanese stringed instruments—the zither plucked with the thumbnails (*celempung*), the two-stringed spiked fiddle (*rebab*), and the flute (*suling*), serviced for the soft-style gamelan—have found no place in the singularly metallic-sounding gamelan of the Balinese.

"Gamelan Melayu" is the name used to refer to the Malaysian gamelan ensemble connected with "Joget Gamelan", a dance initiated in the nineteenth-century courts of the sultans of Pahang and Trengganu. Except for the absence of the gender-type instruments, or xylophones with metal keys suspended by strings over individual tubular resonators, the Gamelan Melayu, though much smaller than the standard Javanese and Balinese gamelan ensemble, has the necessary strategic instruments to give coherence to gamelan music. Originally the Malay palace gamelan may have had the five-toned (*slendro*) scale prevailing in Java, but in contemporary practice its *slendro* scale has been so altered that the Gamelan Melayu, with its combination of only seven instruments, appears unique unto itself. Whatever the character of its music, however, the Gamelan Melayu presents us with a supreme example of a demanding relationship between dance and music. Each and every musical phrase and even accent in Joget Gamelan is neatly and precisely tied to a specific dance phrase and accent, and this relentless coincidence epitomizes a most complete union between music and dance. Of the two main types of music in the Philippines, designated "Western" and "Malaysian" by the Filipino ethnomusicologist Jose Maceda, the "*Kulintang*" ensemble of the southern part of the islands is clearly related to the Indonesian gamelan. Polyphonic stratification also distinguishes the music of the Kulintang, with the important difference that rhythm rather than melody is the dominating energy of the Filipino ensemble. Rhythm is also the main concern of the Chinese-type flat bronze gong ensembles found among some Luzon mountain tribes, further highlighting the primacy of rhythm in a number of non-Christian musical traditions of the Philippines.

The Javanese and Balinese gamelan enjoy a wide currency in their society's traditional theatres because they participate in a variety of performance genres. The same, however, cannot be said of the Thai *pi-phat*, whose association with theatre is mostly restricted to court-derived forms of dance drama and shadow plays. But from the structural viewpoint, particularly as regards the role of melody and rhythm, the Thai *pi-phat*, along with the gong-chime cultures of Burma and Kampuchea, is very similar to the Indonesian gamelan. Since traditional Thai music, like all Southeast Asian music, has been transmitted orally, tracing the origins and evolution of the Thai *pi-phat* would be impossible, except to say that as performed today it was most probably derived from the court music of the Bangkok period of the nineteenth and twentieth centuries. The main melody of the Thai *pi-phat* ensemble, which can have six to fourteen musicians, is played in a fast rhythmic style by a sixteen-gong kettle set called *khong wong yai*. This instrument is also used for slight, though standard, ornamentations on the main melody, while greater variations are furnished by the wood and metal xylophones. *Ranat Ek*, a wood xylophone, is thought to be something of a leader of the ensemble because it launches the introduction and registers changes in tempo. The metal xylophone, *ranat Ek Lek*, has the responsibility of doubling the leader's efforts. Time is marked and kept on an even keel by the Chinese-looking cymbals, or *ching*. Only one gong, assigned the task of subdividing the musical structure in a binary manner, is sometimes present in the Thai ensemble. Since the diminutive ching and the lone gong note the form of the musical piece, they perform functions similar to the time-markers in the large Javanese gamelan. The cylindrical woodwind instrument with a bulging middle, or *pi nai*, the only nonpercussive component of the pi-phat, requires its player to practically "swallow" the reed constructed of four pieces of dried palm leaves, then expand his cheeks, and finally force the saved breath through the vibrators.

Neither the *pi-phat* nor any of the other mainland Southeast Asian percussion ensembles have metal xylophones like the Indonesian gender capable of sustaining long tones, with the result that mainland music tends to be sharp and incisive. Also, while the tuning systems of Thailand, Burma, and Kampuchea adhere to a seven-tone scale, the music is actually made around a core of five tones.

Beyond the confines of court-influenced theatre, string-centered ensembles creating softer music are more widely used in Thailand. This is not the case in Burma, where perhaps because of the impact of itinerant city performing troupes, percussion ensembles have a stronger foundation. The name of the Burmese ensemble *saing waing* originates from its musically and visually unusual set of 21-tone drums hung on a decorated circular screen. The musician playing the set of drums is partially concealed, and such visual effects, including markings and ornamentations, are a common feature in traditional Southeast Asian musical ensembles. The Burmese harp, or *saung kauk*, recalling an ancient past and at present accompanying singing, is also unique to Southeast Asia. Bowed lutes of several kinds are abundant in mainland Southeast Asia, but one of the most intriguing lute traditions is found in the *Mak Yong* dance drama of Kelantan, bordering on Thailand. During a *Mak Yong* duet between a singer and three-stringed spike fiddle and interlocking drums, two gongs and eventually a chorus of singer-dancers contribute what the ethnomusicologist William P. Malm of the University of Michigan has described as "their own mellismatic versions of the tune. The resultant massive proliferation of pitches and lines seems to be a unique form of disphony even in the context of mid-twentieth-century European choral experiments." The *saw duang*, known as *cai-nhi* in Vietnam, a two-stringed cylindrical lute, is reminiscent of the Chinese *hu ch'in*. There are many instances of Chinese musical influence on Southeast Asia, but none of the countries manifest this influence more than Vietnam, where almost all the musical ensembles are derivations of their northern neighbor's.

Western influence in all areas of music is relatively recent as compared with India, China, or even the Middle East. In spite of their late arrival, Western musical instruments and musical practices threaten to take center stage in the musical performances of Southeast Asia or, at the least, to cause radical alteration of many of the indigenous musical traditions. National pride in many countries of Southeast Asia, in reaction for example to the visible rise of local rock groups, has salvaged a few of the threatened species through financial aid and other institutional support. Ethnomusicologists, like Judith Becker, are confident that at least in Java, where gamelan has deep and resilient roots in the society, tradition will prevail. Optimism has also been expressed for the future of traditional music of the innovating Balinese, but in the rest of Southeast Asia the issue of the eventual consequence of Western impact is still very open.

MODERN THEATRE

The function and relevance of Western influence in modern Southeast Asian theatre are also being rigorously questioned. Just twenty years ago the aesthetics informing most modern plays and performances in the region were so imitative of those of the conventional theatre of Europe and America that the "modern" in Southeast Asian theatre was very nearly synonymous with "Western." Writing in 1967, James R. Brandon described Western-inspired and word-dominated modern theatre as "nonpopular" and therefore found sufficient cause to dismiss it with a few cursory remarks in his influential book *Theatre in Southeast Asia*. Actually, the leading modern playwrights of Southeast Asia—Usmar Ismail, Utuy Tatang Sontani, and Mottinggo Boesje of Indonesia, Nick Joaquin of the Philippines, and Mustapha Kamil Yassin and Usman Awang of Malaysia—have generated greater interest and excitement than Brandon has suggested, in some instances even beyond their natural coterie of Western-oriented intelligentsia in their countries. Compared with traditional theatre, with which they deliberately broke rank, their audiences were indeed small and selective. Even so, their engagement with themes involving conflicts between generations, between tradition and modernity, and on occasion, as in Malaysia, between races exposed some of the most important issues of their time. Furthermore, their emulation of Western methods of writing and performing plays accorded them recognition and respect, if not mass appeal, as one of a group of cultural and literary arbiters of "progress" in their recently independent societies.

Their dramas were never as popular, however, as the professional urban-based commercial theatre that emerged around the turn of this century, at a time when almost all of Southeast Asia had been colonized by the Western powers. The first to reflect a substantial and sustained Western influence in Southeast Asian theatre were the performers of *zat pwe* (Burma), *likay* (Thailand), *lakon bassac* (Kampuchea), *cai luong* (Vietnam), *bangsawan* (Malaysia), *ketoprak, ludruk,* and later *lenong* (Indonesia), and *zarzuella* (Philippines), all of whom were discriminating in their approach to Western theatre. Even as they adopted some of the Western methods of production, such as the proscenium stage and wing-and-drop sce-

Members of the Burmese National Theatre in a performance at Carnegie Hall during the 1975–1976 New York theatre season. [The Asia Society, Performing Arts Department]

nery, borrowed Western musical instruments, and incorporated Western stories culled from such diverse sources as Shakespeare and Hollywood movies into their eminently eclectic repertory of stories drawn of local, Indian, Chinese, and Arab tales, they continued to appeal to the traditional tastes of their audiences by heightening the multifarious excitations of song, music, dance, mime, and comic turns. By and large, while their theatres afforded great latitude for improvisation, they seldom deviated from their devotion to the traditional structures of performance. Before World War II many of these theatres were among the most popular forms of entertainment in the cities of Southeast Asia; since then, however, only a few have survived the onslaught of cinema and television.

In at least one sense modern Southeast Asian theatre appears to have come full circle. Once again, as in the first decades of the twentieth century, an eclectic merger between traditional and Western performance styles is beginning to be preferred over an excessive preoccupation with Western theatre. Significantly, many of the contemporary playwrights of Southeast Asia—for example, W. S. Rendra, Arifin C. Noer, and Putu Wijaya of Indonesia, Syed Alwi and Noordin Hassan of Malaysia, and those clustered around the Philippine Educational Theatre Association (PETA)—have often chosen popular and folk theatre as their points of entry into the arena of traditional performance. Such choices call attention to their egalitarian inclinations, just as they reveal the fact that these forms provide ready access to tradition. This self-conscious return to tradition is designed to "decolonize" modern Southeast Asian theatre; or, to put it more positively, the present search for indigenous roots is impelled by the need to construct a local identity in theatre. And to the extent that some of the contemporary Southeast Asian playwrights have been influenced by Antonin Artaud, Bertolt Brecht, and Jerzy Grotowski, all three of whom have touted one or another traditional Asian performance genre as a living example of a performance-centered theatrical universe, they have come to the new path partly through the West. Putu Wijaya and the Malaysian playwright Dinsman have also added generous helpings from the European absurdist philosophies and theatre styles into their mixture. One of the most successful alliances between a traditional performing genre and a modern story is W. S. Rendra's *The Struggle of the Naga Tribe* (*Kisah Perjuangan Suku Naga*, 1975). The play tenaciously clings to the *wayang purwa* performance of central Java as its guiding framework as it uncovers the political economy of the Third World. Plays like Rendra's hint at a viable and efficacious model for a future modern theatre in Southeast Asia.

See DINSMAN; NOER, ARIFIN C.; NOORDIN HASSAN; RENDRA, W. S.; SYED ALWI; WIJAYA, PUTU.

KRISHEN JIT

CRITICISM

B. De Zoete and W. Spies, *Dance and Drama in Bali*, London, 1938; J. R. Brandon, *Theatre in Southeast Asia*, Cambridge, Mass., 1967; C. Holt, *Art in Indonesia: Continuities and Change*, Ithaca, 1967; J. Rothenberg, *Technicians of the Sacred: A Range of Poetries from Africa, America, Asia and Oceania*, Garden City, N.Y., 1969; J. R. Brandon, *On Thrones of Gold: Three Javanese Shadow Plays*, Cambridge, Mass., 1970; P. L. A. Sweeney, *The Ramayana and the Malay Shadow Play*, Kuala Lumpur, 1972; V. Turner, *Dramas, Fields and Metaphors: Symbolic Action in Human Society*, Ithaca, 1974; T. O. Mohd., ed., *Traditional Drama and Music of Southeast Asia*, Kuala Lumpur, 1974; Sudarsono, *Java and Bali: Two Centres of the Development of Traditional Dance Drama in Indonesia*, Jogjakarta, 1974; M. Rutnin, *The Siamese Theatre: Collection of Reprints from Journals of Siam Society*, Bangkok, 1975; D. Morton, *The Traditional Music of Thailand*, Berkeley, 1976; J. Becker, *Traditional Music in Modern Java*, Honolulu, 1976; W. P. Malm, *Music Cultures of the Pacific, the Near East, and Asia*, 2d ed., Englewood Cliffs, N.J., 1977; A. L. Becker and A. A. Yanoongan, eds., *The Imagination of Reality: Essays in Southeast Asian Coherence Systems*, New Jersey, 1979.

Soya, Carl Erik Martin (1896–)

Danish novelist and playwright. The son of C. M. Soya Jensen, a well-known painter and teacher, he was raised in a middle-class environment, and his works reflect his complete rejection of its values and taboos. Though his output as a novelist and essayist has been considerable, his first love has always been the theatre.

Soya's first important play, *The Parasites* (*Parasitterne*), was written in 1926. Though accepted by the Royal Theatre the following year, it was not performed on that stage until 1945. In the interval, however, this somewhat lurid drama in which the youthful dramatist expressed his indignation with social parasites was produced by the Sociale Teater in 1931. The year before the Royal Theatre had accepted and successfully produced what has sometimes been considered his best play, *The*

Carl Erik Martin Soya. [Danish Information Office]

Laughing Maid (*Den leende Jomfru*, 1930), which focuses on life in a Danish boarding house. In *My Top Hat* (*Min høje Hat*, 1939) Soya mischievously depicts himself as one of the main characters—Professor Spoya—who temporarily transforms the dreary lives of a middle-class family by allowing them to experience their dreams in reality.

Soya is probably at his best as a social satirist. In *The New Play of Everyman* (*Det nye Spil om enhver*, 1938), for example, a man convicted of tendencies toward a variety of dishonest behaviors is exonerated when the blame is shifted to the failure of science and religion to show him how to live a moral life. As a result of experiences during World War II, when Soya was twice interned by the Nazis and eventually had to flee to Sweden, his drama took on a more philosophical and moralistic coloring. In the years 1940–1948 he wrote *Blindman's Bluff* (*Blindebuk*), a tetralogy consisting of three tragedies and one satyr piece: *Fragments of a Pattern* (*Brudstykker af et Mønster*, 1940), *Two Threads* (*To Tråde*, 1943), *30 Years Respite* (*30 Års Henstand*, 1944), and *Free Choice* (*Frit Valg*, 1948). Soya described *Two Threads* as "a play in two plays" because it has two separate plots which merge only at the very end. The parts of the tetralogy are completely independent and do not tell a continuous story; however, they share a common theme: the influence of random incidents on life.

Though Soya's artistic production has been prolific, the quality of his work has varied enormously. Noteworthy among his later plays are *After* (*Efter*, 1947), dealing with life in postwar Denmark, and *Lion with Corset* (*Løve med Korset*, 1950), an antiwar satire. In 1947 *Fragments of a Pattern* was filmed as *The Soldier and Jenny* (*Soldaten og Jenny*), and the following year *After* was filmed as *Three Years After* (*3 År efter*).

PLAYS

1. *Parasitterne* (*The Parasites*). Play, 5 acts. Written 1926. Published 1929. Produced Det Sociale Teatre, 1931.

2. *Den leende Jomfru (The Laughing Maid)*. Play, 5 acts. Produced Det Kongelige Teater (The Royal Theatre), Jan. 4, 1930.

3. *Lord Nelson laegger Fiegenbladet (Lord Nelson Puts Aside the Fig Leaf)*. Historic play, 2 vols. Published 1934. Produced Casinos Little Theatre, 1937.

4. *Hvem er jeg (Who Am I)*. Comedy. Published 1932. Produced Det Ny Teater (The New Theatre), Mar. 1, 1932.

5. *Det nye Spil om Enhver (The New Play of Everyman)*. Verse play, 1 act. Written, 1938.

6. *Min høje Hat (My Top Hat)* Surrealistic play, 2 parts. Written, 1939.

7. *Blindebuk (Blindman's Buff)*. Tetralogy. (1) *Brudstykker af et Mønster (Fragments of a Pattern)*. Play, 6 parts. Published 1940. Produced Folketeatret, Sept. 29, 1940. Filmed under the title *Soldaten og Jenny (The Soldier and Jenny)*, 1947. (2) *To Tråde (Two Threads)*. Play, 5 parts. Published 1943, Produced Det Kongelige Teater (The Royal Theatre), Nov. 24, 1943. (3) *30 Års Henstand (30 Year's Respite)*. Play, 4 parts. Published 1944. Produced Apr. 1, 1944. (4) *Frit Valg (Free Choice)*. Play 2 parts. Published 1948. Produced Det Ny Teater (The New Theatre), Sept. 16, 1949.

8. *Umbabumba*. An anti-Nazi satire, 5 acts. Produced Det Ny Teater (The New Theatre), Nov. 28, 1935.

9. *Chas*. Satire on sports heroes, 2 acts. Produced Det Kongelige Teater (The Royal Theatre), May 12, 1938.

10. *Efter (After)*. Play, 4 acts. Published 1947. Produced Folketeatret, Nov. 4, 1947. Filmed under the title *3 År efter (Three Years After)*, 1948.

11. *Løve med Korset (Lion with Corset)*. Experimental drama, 1 act. Published 1950.

12. *Afdøde Jonson (The Late Jonson)* and *Bare en Tagsten (Just a Roof Tile)*. Two comedies. Published 1966.

13. *Vraggods (Wreckage)*. Play, 4 acts. Published 1965.

EDITIONS

Lion with Corset. Published in *Five Modern Scandinavian Plays*, vol. 11, New York, 1971.

Two Threads. Published in *Contemporary Danish Plays*, ed. by E. Bredsdorff, London, 1970.

CRITICISM

O. Lundbo, *Soya*, Danish Author Biographies, no. 4, 1944; J. Claudi, *Contemporary Danish Authors*, 1952, p. 128–131; P. M. Mitchell, *A History of Danish Literature*, New York, 1958.

Soyfer, Jura (1912–1939)

Austrian poet, journalist, and dramatist. He was born December 12, 1912, in Kharkov, of wealthy Russian parents, who became refugees in the wake of the Bolshevik Revolution and settled in Vienna in 1921. Already fluent in French, as well as Russian, Jura quickly learned the German of his new home and adopted it as his literary language.

Witnessing the steady erosion of democratic government during the 1920s and the Austrian drift to fascism, Soyfer became a dedicated exponent of a political idealism based on humanist values. In the Realgymnasium he began to write antifascist poems, prose pieces, and reviews for the high school Socialist organization, as well as songs and sketches for the party's political cabaret. By 1931 he was contributing regularly to *Arbeiter Zeitung*, the official organ of the Social Democratic party, using poems that were satirical thrusts at local happenings to attack Hitlerism in Germany as well as the arbitrary verdicts passing for justice in Austria at the time. He chided the middle class for its tolerance of right wing extremists, while it sought to restrain the Socialists from arming. The humanism pervasive in his writing took the form often of a naive pleading for justice and peace.

In February 1934, when the Austrian Fascists executed nine Socialist leaders and the Socialist party was liquidated, Soyfer joined a Communist underground. His Marxist view led him to condemn the capitalist system, especially its predilection for fascist methods and its disregard of the needs and dreams of working people. After the *Arbeiter Zeitung* was outlawed in 1934, Soyfer wrote for the *Wiener Tag*, recording his continuing dismay at the worsening political climate. In theatre and film reviews he criticized the establishment theatre in Vienna for its emphasis on escapist entertainment and judged writers by their social relevance, vaunting instead the political courage and artistic experiments in the small cabaret theatres, which sprang up in coffeehouses and basements. To circumvent the restraints of increasing political authoritarianism and the need for an official license, these minitheatres limited their seating capacity to forty-nine, thus hoping to evade censorship. They evolved a new dramatic form, based on a model conceived by Rudolf Weys, a Viennese cabaret writer. Soyfer became the most gifted practitioner of this new form, in which the unconnected individual acts that had typically comprised cabaret entertainment became the frame for a longer middle piece (*Mittelstück*), which was actually a 50-minute play with a socially or politically relevant theme.

Although Soyfer's criticism of the Dollfuss-Schuschnigg regime in his cabaret pieces was camouflaged, Soyfer's hostility was well known to authorities. In November 1937 he was arrested and jailed for three months without a trial, being released in the general amnesty for political prisoners which Hitler dictated to Schuschnigg in February 1938. When the Germans invaded Austria in March of that year, Jura at last tried to flee—on skis. He was arrested in a mountain hut on the Swiss border and imprisoned at Dachau. Even there under the strains of prison camp life, he continued his political writing. One of his poems, *Dachau-Lied*, was set to music by a fellow-prisoner and became known among the prisoners in the camp and later among German and Austrian emigrants to England. In the autumn of 1938 Soyfer was transferred to Buchenwald, where he died of typhoid fever, the night of February 15–16, 1939. He was less than twenty-seven years old.

WORK

Like other beleaguered writers caught in the social and political upheavals of the 1930s in Europe, Soyfer wrote on the run at coffeehouse tables and later secretly in prison camps. Much of his work for cabaret theatres was lost; what survives was smuggled out of the country hidden in suitcase linings, stiffly laundered shirts, and book bindings. Friends painstakingly gathered and collated scattered manuscripts only after the war.

All of Soyfer's writing reflects the day-to-day deepening of political crisis in Europe. His newspaper accounts of a trip through pre-Hitler Germany in 1932, ominously identifying Oldenbourg as the likely capital of the Third Reich, describes its provincial inhabitants as typical of the petit bourgeois who were the most fervent supporters of Hitler. In the satirical poems, which were often directly topical and always critical of the current political situation, Soyfer relied on puns, parody, and cliche to ridicule the system. Later he refined his poetic technique in the protest songs he wrote for political meetings. In the poems he inserted into his plays he achieved lyricism as well as political irony. His journalistic pieces, his poems, and his plays reveal his pro-Soviet sympathies and his idealistic faith that the working class could somehow unite to defeat Nazism. Like Ödön von Horvath, and using an unmasking technique similar to that in Horvath's novel *The Eternal Babbit* (*Der ewige Spiesser*, pub. 1930), Soyfer wrote of his generation, especially the plight of the young, pointing out the ideology and the stultifying social assumptions determining their frame of mind. In an ambitious political novel, *Thus Died a Party* (*So starb eine Partei*), only fragments of which were ever published, Soyfer analyzed the reasons for the Socialist defeat in 1934. Another striking affinity to Horvath in the novel is Soyfer's focus on the latent aggression and mental obtuseness of the Austrian middle class as predisposing them to accept political manipulation. See HORVATH, ÖDÖN VON.

Soyfer's earliest dramatic pieces were written for presentation at holiday celebrations at Socialist Party meetings. They reveal his political commitment to the working class, his repudiation of exploitation and complacency. In them Soyfer uses the conventions of medieval morality plays, nineteenth-century popular Viennese theatre, and even religious ritual. His characters are allegorical. Of course, fascist reprisals after 1934 curtailed all such communal criticism of the regime. By 1937 Soyfer was writing his social philosophy into his theatre and film reviews. Opposed to the establishment culture of Vienna, he supported the little theatres, idealistically championing intellectual challenge rather than escapist entertainment for the working class. Unfortunately, the audiences for his own cabaret pieces were intellectuals, not workers. Although his plays are powerful testimonials against oppression, they escape the sterile didacticism of most propagandist drama. The four extant *Mittelstücke* intersperse the realism of disillusioned social comment with scenes of fantasy, lyricism, and pure comedy in the tradition of Raimund and Nestroy (*see* NESTROY, JOHANN; RAIMUND, FERDINAND). Soyfer skillfully uses the nuances of Viennese dialect. Like Horvath he unmasks, through a corrupted speech, mean or naïve purposes and unconscious attitudes. At the same time he delicately uncovers the modest aspirations of his characters. His plays are short and do not fit traditional categories, but they are viable artistically and dramatically. Above all, they are significant, comprising a record of a writer's personal warnings against the coming holocaust and a moving articulation of the humanist vision of a gifted and clear-eyed being who is courageous enough to sustain the worst of times.

The End of the World (*Weltuntergang*) was performed in the summer of 1936, just before the *Anschluss* which wiped out Austrian independence. A farce, full of buffoonery, with an apocalyptic theme as well as title, the play, in a series of comic episodes, opposes the helplessness of ordinary people to the cynical covetousness of the rich and powerful. Both groups are so myopically self-absorbed that they fail to protect themselves against the threat of imminent world destruction, of which they are warned by Professor Peep. The satire, which pokes fun at representative people and nations and ends in a Hollywood lampoon, strikes at Soyfer's favorite targets: the shortsightedness of the capitalist, too intent on profits, and the confused passivity of the powerless, too distracted by necessity, to grasp their plight. The analogy to Austrian politics is only slightly blurred by the amusing frame scenes set in outer space. In scene one the Sun, the Moon, and the planets wittily discuss the earth, agreeing it must be destroyed because of the human beings plaguing it. In the final scene eleven the comet delegated to the apocalyptic task confesses he could not do the deed, for he fell in love with the human world. The play ends in a stirring *Song of the World* celebrating the beauty and health that will ultimately triumph despite human misery and folly.

The same optimism saves the race in *Eddie Lechner's Trip to Paradise* (*Der Lechner-Edi schaut ins Paradies*; prod. 1936, pub. 1947, 1962), a parable of the desperate search of a young unemployed worker to destroy the machine he blames for his joblessness. When the machine also turns out to be displaced because the workers can no longer buy the shoes it manufactures, the two set off on a journey backward through time to affix the blame. Eddie entreats Galvani, Galileo, and other representative men of science and human progress not to finish their inventions. Each claims his feat was made inevitable by some preceding one. Eddie and the machine end up at the very gates of Paradise, but it is too late. Paradise is full employment in a huge, busy factory. The Adam and Eve models have already been cast. Eddie plaintively sings *The Gruesome Ballad of Paradise*, and finds out that he himself and all ordinary people must take responsibility for the race.

Astoria (1937) is bitterer, more ironic, and often more richly comic. Two hapless vagabonds, as craftily foolish and funny as Beckett's Gogo and Didi in *Waiting for Godot*, are hoping a policeman will arrest them, so that they will be warm and safe for the winter. When Hiccup, the central character, is alone, fantastic things begin to happen. A kind policeman refuses to arrest him, and a millionairess, Countess Gwendolyn Buckleburg-Marasquino, née Cash, gives him a lift in her American limousine. She has been shopping for a country to give her senile husband as a birthday present. Hiccup offers himself. He will pose as a citizen of the mythical country she has presumably bought, trusting in the pretentious gullibility of social climbers to carry off the hoax. It works. The cream of London society fawn on Gwendolyn's husband, who is posing as the mythical country's foreign minister. He bestows imaginary honors to silence suspicions. Unhappily the poor are also swindled. They pay bounty on the promise of jobs, dreaming of emigration to a paradisiacal land of full employment, an environment they picture as a duplicate of the set for a Hollywood extravaganza. Soyfer's satire not only savages the rich, but castigates the capitalist state for its exploitation and also exposes the stupid manipulability of the masses.

Just as Astoria was a thinly disguised name for Austria, so Vineta, the title of Soyfer's last play, represents Vienna. Comedy and song are banished from the nightmarish atmosphere of this surrealist play, based on a north German legend of a city that sank to the bottom of the sea after a tidal wave. In Soyfer's play, an old sailor named Johnny garrulously recounts his oft-told adventure in the drowned city when he was a young diver. When something went wrong with his oxygen line, he blacked out and awoke to find himself in the cathedral square of a medieval city called Vineta, where the inhabitants are ageless, outside time, and historyless. They lack memory and will. Their behavior is mechanical and their conversations consist of memorized phrases as incoherent as the lesson book sentences of Ionesco's characters in *The Bald Soprano*. They wait stolidly for boats that never come, for the rich to give them soup. They feel neither hate nor love, and even in the trenches their soldiers do not know who the enemy is. They have ceased to question or to yearn. The political analogy hides behind the legend here, suggesting the intensified restrictiveness of the fascist government in Austria, its stultifying effects on the citizens. Certainly Soyfer intended a last-ditch outcry against the doom in store for the stagnating Viennese society. He was not heeded. The play was first performed in September 1937. In November Soyfer was jailed. In March German troops overran Austria.

VIOLET B. KETELS

CRITICISM

L. Askin, "Die Auferstehung des Jura Soyfer," afterward to *Astoria, Der Lechner-Edi schaut ins Paradies; Zwei Satiren*, Eisenstadt, 1974; K. Budzinski, *Die Muse mit der scharfen Zunge: Vom Cabaret zum Kabarette*, Munich, 1961; H. Gruel, *Bretter, die Zeit bedeuten: Die Kulturgeschichte des Kabaretts*, Cologne, 1967; F. Herrmann, "*Jura Soyfer: Die Anfänge eines volksverbundenen österreichischen Dichters*," dissertation, University of Vienna, 1949; H. Jarka, intr. to *The Legacy of Jura Soyfer*, Montreal, 1977; W. Neugebauer, *Bauvolk der Kommenden Welt: Geschichte der sozialistichen Jugendbewegung in Österreich*, Vienna, 1975; R. Weys, *Literatur—am Naschmarkt: Kulturgeschichte der Wiener Kleinkunst in Kostproben*, Vienna, 1970; R. Weys, *Cabaret und Kabarett in Wien*, Vienna, 1970; R. Weys, *Wien bleibt Wien und das geschicht ihm ganz recht*, Vienna, 1974.

Soyinka, Wole (1934–   )

Nigerian playwright. He was the first to establish an international reputation. Also a poet, novelist, critic, and director, Soyinka currently holds a chair of comparative literature at the University of Ife.

Born in Western Nigeria of Egba and Ijebu parents, he was educated at Government College, Ibadan, a school with a strong tradition of drama. Following a two-year preliminary arts course at University College, Ibadan, he went to England and studied at Leeds University (1954–1958). During this period he wrote his first plays: *The House of Banigeji* (1956), *The Lion and the Jewel* (1957), and *The Swamp Dwellers* (1957), which was staged at a London student drama festival in 1958.

Soyinka was a member of the Writers Group organized by George Devine and William Gaskill at the Royal Court Theatre, and his one-act play *The Invention* was tried out there in November 1959. Returning to Nigeria early in 1960, he obtained a research fellowship in drama at the University of Ibadan. While acting in a production of Brecht's *The Good Woman of Setzuan* at the Arts Theatre, Ibadan, he completed *The Trials of Brother Jero*, which was staged in April 1960, and *The Dance of the Forests*, which was done during the Nigerian independence celebrations in October 1960.

In 1960 Soyinka founded the Masks Company, and from 1962 to 1967 he held lectureships at the University of Ife's Ibadan campus and the University of Lagos. This period saw the productions of his satirical revues *The Republican* (1964) and *Before the Blackout* (1965). Other plays of this period include *The Road*, produced in London for the 1965 Commonwealth Arts Festival, and *Kongi's Harvest* (1966), one of his major works.

Soyinka's stormy career as a political activist began in 1962 with a lampoon of Dr. Majekodunmi, premier of the Western Region. In December 1965 he was tried and acquitted on charges of having substituted his own recorded speech for an election victory broadcast by the Western Region's premier, Akintola. Two years later he criticized the futility of the impending Civil War, and his attempts to arrange peace with Biafran leaders led to a two-year prison term for illegal dealing with the enemy. The horrors of this sentence are related in his autobiography, *The Man Died* (1973). On his release in 1969 he returned to the directorship of the School of Drama at Ibadan, but resigned in 1972 after disturbances on campus led to the shooting of several students. He then went to France, where he played the role of Patrice Lumumba in Joan Littlewood's production of Conor Cruise O'Brien's *Murderous Angels*. In 1973 he adapted Euripides's *The Bacchae* for the National Theatre, London. Before returning to Nigeria he also edited the magazine *Ch'Indaba* (formerly *Transition*).

The Swamp Dwellers, Soyinka's first published play, signaled his compassionate concern for his countrymen who were caught up in radical changes and were also constant victims of natural disasters. In it the son of a village barber is sent to the city to look for his brother. Rejected by the latter, who has lost all sense of family ties, the son returns home, where his father has at razor point forced a greedy priest to confess that he had stolen the people's cattle by pretending to sacrifice them to the serpent of the swamp. The priest goes into exile, taking with him a blind beggar driven from the north by a famine caused by drought.

Soyinka's civil war experiences dampened his sense of humor and the delight he had previously found even in villains like the priest in *The Swamps Dwellers*. In *Madmen and Specialists* (1971) Dr. Bero prostitutes his healing knowledge to the cause of destruction. He kills his father, who by feeding warmongers human flesh has tried to make them aware of the horrors for which they are responsible. Dr. Bero's sister's escape from the holocaust is the only ray of hope at the end of this savage and baffling play. Soyinka covered similar experiences in his novel *Season of Anomy* (1973).

In an effort to relieve his anguish and reconnect with practical theatre, Soyinka turned to more traditional forms and themes in *Death and the King's Horseman* (1975). In this drama he focused on a Yoruba tradition which demanded that when a king died his horseman should follow him into death to protect him on his journey. The practice was still being followed in 1946, when a British official interfered with this ritual suicide and the king's horseman was exposed to community scorn. The king's son, newly returned from studying abroad, committed suicide in his place.

After a disappointing premiere in Soyinka's own theatre at the University of Ife, the play's potential was revealed in a production directed by Soyinka at the Goodman Theater, Chicago, in October, 1979. The same production was later successfully transferred to the Kennedy Center in Washington, D.C.

The Lion and the Jewel (1959). Lakunle, a Europeanized village schoolboy, falls in love with Sidi, the village belle, and hopes to wed her without paying the bride price. Her head turned by a photograph of herself in a geographic magazine, Sidi falls easy prey to the lecherous Chief Baroka, whom she mistakenly believes to be impotent. Lakunle is now sure that the fallen woman will wed him for nothing, but she elects to be one of the chief's wives instead.

The Trials of Brother Jero (1960). A farce in which Jeraboam, a self-proclaimed prophet, maintains his hold on his following, the Holy Rollers of Lagos Bar Beach, by denying them their wishes. Unfortunately, he loses his power when he grants one disciple's longstanding wish to beat his wife, who had camped outside the prophet's door in hope of making him pay his debts. A gullible member of the federal parliament who has come to the beach to practice his oratory is tricked into testifying to Brother Jero's ascension into heaven. Soyinka returned to the same character in a later play, *Jero's Metamorphosis* (1973), in which Jero reacts to the competition of the "Bar Beach Show"—the public execution of convicted thieves after the civil war—by offering his religious services.

A Dance of the Forests (1960). An ambitious and enigmatic play, it failed to win the approval of the committee that had commissioned it for the Nigerian independence celebrations. In a daring break with tradition the playwright offers a tribal celebration to which the gods send not orators who praise the heroic past but "the Restless Dead," who complain of their terrible sufferings. Soyinka's later writings have clarified the play's intention, but it has had no subsequent production because of the demands it makes both on the audience and on theatrical technique; however, many critics consider the play a magnificent creation of youthful ambition—Soyinka's *Peer Gynt*.

The Strong Breed (1964). A drama focusing on the plight of the educated in a backwoods society. Eman, to escape his inherited duty to expiate his community's sins in a cruel ceremony, becomes a teacher in another community. The latter has the even more savage custom of driving away social misfits and leaving them to die of starvation. Finding that his year's victim is to be an idiot boy whom he has befriended, Eman resists and himself becomes the victim.

The Road (1965). The Professor, a charlatan, uses his eloquence to manipulate the thugs and misfits who inhabit the weird underworld of a truck parking lot. The carnage on Nigerian roads was something of which Soyinka had direct experience when he commuted daily between Lagos and Ibadan for rehearsals of *A Dance of the Forests* five years earlier. The same theme appears in poems and other plays.

Kongi's Harvest (1965). Written for the Festival of Negro Arts at Dakar, it was criticized as unsuitable for a celebration of African unity, and even Soyinka had doubts when its satirical target, Ghana's Kwame Nkrumah, fell from power shortly before the play opened. Kongi, like Nkrumah, is the prophet of a political creed which he dictates to his advisers from his high mountain retreat. Kongi's attempts to secure the homage of the traditional ruler, King Danlola, at the New Yam Festival, result in his own downfall.

A musical comedy which draws upon all the resources of popular theatre, this is one of the most accessible of Soyinka's plays. Though the specific political references may be lost on foreign audiences, the antics of despots are universal. The zany behavior of Kongi and his Carpenters Brigade is presented against a musical background that mixes African chants and drumming with strains of "The British Grenadiers." The results are similar in their appeal to Charlie Chaplin's *The Great Dictator* or the outrageous world of Gilbert and Sullivan's *The Mikado*.   GEOFFREY AXWORTHY

EDITIONS

Collections
Collected Plays, vol. 1 (*A Dance of the Forests, The Swamp Dwellers, The Strong Breed, The Road, The Bacchae of Euripides*), London, 1974; *Collected Plays,* vol. 2 (*The Lion and the Jewel, Kongi's Harvest, The Trials of Brother Jero, Jero's Matamorphosis, Madmen and Specialists*), London, 1978.
Individual Plays
Death and the King's Horseman, London, 1975.

CRITICISM

Ian Watson, "Soyinka's 'Dance of the Forests'," *Transition,* no. 27, 1966; Gerald Moore, *Wole Soyinka,* London, 1971; Oyin Ogunba, "Traditional Content of the Plays of Wole Soyinka," *African Literature Today,* nos. 4–5, 1970; Eldred Jones, *The Writing of Wole Soyinka,* London, 1973; James Gibbs, *Critical Perspectives on Wole Soyinka,* Washington, D.C., 1978.

Spanish Drama

In Spain as elsewhere the beginnings of the drama must be sought in the Middle Ages; however, the subject of dramatic activity in medieval Spain, unlike other European countries, is controversial, at least as regards Castile, the region which would eventually dominate the rest on the country.

MEDIEVAL PERIOD

Whereas Castile excelled in most literary genres, its achievements in the drama, to judge by the almost complete dearth of extant texts, appears to have been minimal: a few brief examples of liturgical plays in Latin, a vernacular religious work of the late twelfth century, and then a total void until some three centuries later, when Gómez Manrique wrote a short Christmas play and several other quasi-dramatic pieces. The last decade of the fifteenth century marks a turning point, when we can begin to perceive a constant flow of plays, commencing with Juan del Encina and Lucas Fernández, who continued writing well into the next century.

The scarcity of texts from the medieval epoch is especially surprising when compared with the richness of drama in the Siglo de Oro, or Golden Age, an admittedly rather imprecise term used to designate a brilliant period in Spanish cultural history embracing most of the sixteenth and seventeenth centuries (*see* SIGLO DE ORO in glossary). Even more perplexing is the comparison with Catalonia (including the territories of Valencia and the Balaeric Islands), where there is ample evidence of a flourishing dramatic tradition. In contrast to Castile, many texts from medieval Catalonia have survived, both Latin and vernacular, as well as abundant documentary material. The almost total absence of texts outside Catalonia has led some scholars to conjecture that drama was extremely weak in the rest of the peninsula. On the other hand, there are those who maintain that the texts have been lost, pointing to epic and lyric poetry as genres formerly considered to have had little or no development in medieval Castile, a notion since disproved.

According to the most widely accepted theory, the serious drama of the Middle Ages originated with Latin tropes, or brief illustrative scenes, performed in church from about the tenth century onward and associated with the liturgy for Christmas, Epiphany, and Easter. Examples of this early liturgical drama are rare in Castile but plentiful in Catalonia. By the fourteenth century it had developed into long, elaborately staged cycles of "mystery plays" in England and France, but no evidence of such an evolution has been found in Spain. When "mysteries" eventually appeared in the Levantine provinces in the late fifteenth and the sixteenth centuries, they still had not developed beyond isolated pieces in honor of a saint or of a festival, such as the Assumption. The most notable example is the *Mystery of Elche (Misterio de Elche)*, still performed in that town every August. Recent scholarship offers a plausible explanation for the abundance of liturgical drama in Catalonia and its scarcity in the western part of the peninsula: at the crucial period Catalonia was under strong French influence, while Castile had come under the influence of the Cluniac monks, an order founded in France but not particularly interested in the development of the drama.

Despite this remarkable lack of texts, it is in Castile, curiously enough, that we find one of the earliest extant plays in a modern language, *Play of the Three Kings (Auto de los Reyes Magos)*. Probably written late in the twelfth century, the surviving fragment (147 lines) reveals an impressive level of dramatic craftmanship. It has been established with a fair degree of certainty that the *auto* derived from French sources; its anonymous author was most likely a Gascon priest who had settled in Toledo. While some critics view the *auto* as proof of a flourishing tradition of vernacular religious drama, others tend to play down its significance, dismissing the work as a for-

A miniature page from an early-twelfth-century *Biblia Sacra* from Avila shows scenes from the life of Jesus that figure in early drama. At top is pictured Judas's kiss; in the center, the Crucifixion; below, the descent from the cross. [National Library, Madrid]

eign import. Whether this type of drama was extensively cultivated or not between the twelfth and fifteenth centuries remains a matter of speculation. *See* LITURGICAL DRAMA in glossary.

Outside Catalonia there is a lapse of some three hundred years before the next extant example of a vernacular play in Spain. During this long span there are references in legislative documents to dramatic performances. For example, in the thirteenth-century code of laws known as the *Siete partidas*, Alfonso X (1252–1284) eluded to religious plays as regular occurrences at his court in Toledo and warned the clergy against participating in popular entertainments, *juegos de escarnio* ("mocking games"), which were not to be tolerated in church. Popular entertainments included mime, minstrel performances, puppet shows, and burlesque ceremonies. Dramatic rituals, whether religious or profane, accompanied by song and dance, seem to have been very common in medieval Spain. To this tradition belong ecclesiastical celebrations, such as the feast of Corpus Christi, marked by outdoor processions and pageants. Court and aristocratic festivities (for example, increasingly elaborate tournaments in which mock battles were staged or equally elaborate banquets featuring mumming) must be added to this list of activities; though neither full-fledged drama nor evidence for the existence of drama, they provided elements which could be exploited by playwrights. It is important to note that dramatic features are to be found not only in popular and court entertainments but also in literary texts, such as debate poems, the earliest of which date from the thirteenth century. There is reason to believe that some debate poems from the fifteenth century and other semidramatic compositions in dialogue form may have been staged.

The medieval phase of the Spanish drama comes to a close in the second half of the fifteenth century, when speculation as to the existence of drama is replaced by the concrete evidence of extant texts. The first known Spanish dramatist and the last to belong to the medieval tradition was the aristocrat Gómez Manrique (ca. 1412–ca. 1490), whose *Nativity Play (Representación del Nacimiento de Nuestro Señor)* was composed between 1467 and 1481 to be performed by nuns at a convent where his sister was abbess. He also wrote three other short pieces, two of them secular, all probably intended for reading rather than performance.

Celestina (Maureen Mileski) frightens the servant Lucretia (Kathleen Turco) in an attempt to gain entrance to the house of the beautiful Melibea in this 1979 San Francisco production of Fernando de Rojas's *La Celestina*. [Photograph courtesy of the Stagegroup Theatre]

The last decades of the fifteenth century brought the transition from the Middle Ages to the Renaissance. Events of enormous importance shaped Spanish history during those years: the consolidation of political power in an absolute monarchy, the setting up of the Inquisition (a body whose primary function was to become increasingly political), the recapture of the Moorish kingdom of Granada to complete national unification, the expulsion of the Jews, and the discovery of America. Spain was preparing to enter a period of international expansion and to assume her future role as champion of the Counter Reformation in the religious wars of the sixteenth century. Orthodoxy would eventually become synonymous with allegiance to the State; religious and intellectual dissent would be suppressed. The nobility, however, was never forced to relinquish its social and economic power. An alliance was formed between the aristocracy and the crown which would endure until modern times. As a result of the affirmation of a seignorial system, the middle class was stifled, and the vast bulk of the population reduced to virtual sefdom. Confident that the flow of precious metals from the New World would never cease, the Spaniards failed to develop their commerce and industry. Unable to perceive the need to adjust to a new economic order, the Spanish ruling classes were condemning the nation to centuries of social and economic stagnation.

During the sixteenth century Spain became the most powerful country on earth but then swiftly declined to a second-class status from which she was never fully to recover. This hegemony in world affairs was accompanied by a splendid flowering of its culture and by the installation of Castilian (that is, Spanish) as an international tongue. During its Golden Age of arts and letters Spain gave birth to the modern novel, to some of the greatest lyric poetry ever written, and to a truly national theatre comparable to the best Europe could offer in the sixteenth and seventeenth centuries. (Spanish literature in this period was almost entirely Castilian. Basque was without a literature. Galician, after flourishing for a while as a language of lyric poets, had gone into eclipse. Catalan, with an even richer literary tradition than Galician, had begun to yield to Castilian even before national unification.) Intellectual and aesthetic production did not achieve full maturity until after 1600, when the decline of Spain as a world power was already evident. In fact, the Golden Age of Spanish culture, and particularly that of theatre, extended beyond 1640, at which time Spain's military and political decline appeared irreversible. Two events associated with the history of the drama could well serve to establish the boundaries of this extraordinarily fertile period: The publication of *La Celestina* in 1499 and the death of Calderón de la Barca in 1681. *See* CATALAN DRAMA; ENCINA, JUAN DEL; MANRIQUE, GÓMEZ.

THE GOLDEN AGE: FROM THE EARLY RENAISSANCE TO CERVANTES

Second only to *Don Quixote* among Spanish masterpieces and universally recognized as the most powerful work in European literature of the fifteenth century, *La Celestina*

(*The Spanish Bawd* is its traditional English title) appeared just as that century was drawing to a close. It has been attributed to Fernando de Rojas (d. 1541), a converted Jew about whose life very little is known. Written in dialogue form, it was originally divided into sixteen acts. A longer, twenty-one act version was published in 1502. In either form it is unactable as it stands, though there have been numerous adaptations for the stage.

In some final verses which accompany the edition of 1500, the *corrector,* or printer's editor, states that the work is intended for reading aloud and instructs the reader in how to proceed to obtain the best results. Because *La Celestina* defies classification according to modern concepts of genre, critics have applied to it such designations as "dramatic novel" and "dialogue novel." It has been argued that it is a hybrid work (part novel and part drama), that it is "ageneric," and that it forms a new genre, the "celestinesque." A very convincing case has been made in recent years for viewing it as an example of "humanistic comedy," a medieval tradition developed in the schools, which consisted of composing plays in Latin or the vernacular, utilizing Roman authors (Plautus and Terence) as models. These plays flourished in the fourteenth century and even more in the fifteenth. They were not written to be staged, since it was then believed that Roman plays were recited rather than acted.

Restricting ourselves to the major figures of the Spanish stage before Lope de Vega, we find that Juan del Encina, Lucas Fernández, and Bartolomé de Torres Naharro all wrote plays deriving from *La Celestina*. It is interesting to note that one of Lope de Vega's finest literary achievements is *Dorothea* (*La Dorotea,* pub. 1632), a sequel to Rojas's work and classified by the author as "prose action" (*acción en prosa*) not intended for performance. In addition to its influence on individual writers, *La Celestina* was important because it established a precedent by employing a subplot and by combining the elevated tragic style with that of comedy. In spite of these substantial contributions, however, Spanish drama did not develop in the direction signaled by *La Celestina,* and the work remained, as far as the theatre was concerned, a relatively isolated masterpiece which did not give rise to any school or tradition. Had the great masters of the Golden Age drama of the seventeenth century taken fuller advantage of the legacy of *La Celestina,* they would have produced plays in which character was not subordinated to action; in short, they might have written the type of drama associated with Shakespeare.

The two great Spanish dramatic art forms, the *comedia* and the *auto sacramental,* gradually emerged as a result of continuous experimentation during the sixteenth century (*see* AUTO SACRAMENTAL; COMEDIA in glossary). Contact with Renaissance Italy was responsible for transforming Spanish theatre, though at a slower pace than poetry. The initiator and progenitor of modern drama was Juan del Encina (1468–1530?), the author of some fifteen eclogues intended for private staging and the first Spanish dramatist to have his plays printed (1496). Comic peasants figure largely in some of these charades meant to amuse Encina's patron, the Duke of Alba, and

Rojas's *La Celestina* as staged by Pierre Achard in a decor by Władysław Daszewski in Łodz in 1947. [*Theatre in Modern Poland*]

the ducal household. While some of his early pieces follow traditional patterns of medieval religious drama, others are secular and reveal a Renaissance outlook. In 1513, during a visit to Rome, Encina wrote his most ambitious play, *Eclogue of Plácida and Vitoriano* (*Egloga de Plácida y Vitoriano*), an Italianate pastoral play which was performed there. Divided into thirteen scenes, it has sentimental and even tragic pretensions. But like his other Italianate eclogues, *Plácida and Vitoriano* (banned by the Inquisition in 1559, presumably because of its suicide theme) remains episodic in structure and lyrical rather than dramatic in tone. Encina's main legacy to later secular drama was the stock character of the comic shepherd, expressing himself in a stylized form of the subdialect of Leonese spoken in the Salamanca countryside and known as *sayagués*.

Encina had several disciples among his contemporaries. Although not in the same category as the others, Lucas Fernández (1474?–1542) deserves to be remembered for his amorous comedies, which are not devoid of innovations, and especially for his *Passion Play (Auto de la Pasión)*, the first conversion play of the Golden Age drama and a notable predecessor of the seventeenth-century *comedias de santos* ("saint plays"). The second dramatist who was to benefit from Encina's creation of the modern Spanish drama was the enormously talented Gil Vicente (ca. 1465–1537?), one of the bilingual Portuguese writers of the sixteenth century (*see* VICENTE, GIL). Dramatist to the Portuguese court, he composed some plays in Spanish, some in Portuguese, and others in a mixture of both. Though he did not evolve any distinct dramatic form, he surpassed both Encina and Fernández in scope and technique.

The fourth member of this outstanding first-generation of Iberian dramatists, Bartolomé de Torres Naharro (ca. 1485–ca. 1520), wrote most of his plays in Italy. His collected plays, published in 1517 under the title *Propal-*

ladia, came much closer to the modern concept of drama than anything previously written in Spanish. Instead of short pieces in dialogue form there now appeared real stage action for the first time. For the evolution of dramatic writing in Spain during the first half of the sixteenth century, Encina was by far the most influential playwright of his generation, but for the later development of the Spanish drama Torres Naharro was perhaps more important than Encina. The Italianization of the drama may be considered to have begun with Encina, but it became a serious movement when Torres Naharro wrote the first of his five-act plays, probably the *Comedia Seraphina* (1508–1509). Sometimes described as the founder of Spanish romantic comedy, he was also Spain's first dramatic theorist. At this early stage in the development of the Spanish theatre Torres Naharro already rejected (in the preface to his *Propalladia*) the basis of classical drama. It should be pointed out that the *Propalladia* was banned in 1559, but an expurgated version was published in Madrid in 1573, which the young Lope de Vega must have read.

Religious theatre still flourished, and *autos*, or one-act plays on the type of Encina's early eclogues, continued to appear, albeit with new refinements. The best of the religious dramatists of the first half of the sixteenth century was Diego de Badajoz (d. ca. 1550). He significantly modified the traditional pastoral eclogue, substituting universalized characters for the conventional shepherds, developing the use of allegory even in the plays which he wrote for occasions other than Corpus Christi, and greatly increasing anticlerical satire in the drama. His deployment of allegory makes him a precursor of the *auto sacramental* of Calderón. Other more ambitious authors copied the technique of Renaissance drama from Torres Naharro, and so the first full-length religious plays came to be written. Plays like *Tragedy of Josephine* (*Tragedia Josefina*, pub. in 1535), by Micael de Carvajal (ca. 1480–ca. 1530), represent the beginnings of an important current in Spanish drama: the full-length dramatization of the life of a saint or biblical character.

Encina and his disciples, like their Italian contemporaries, wrote for private patrons. Their plays were performed in the palaces of kings, nobles, or cardinals and were not destined for the general public. About the middle of the sixteenth century new developments occurred as Italian professional actors began to appear in Spain. In addition to the romantic type of comedy, with its by now usually intricate and sensational plot, there also came from Italy a reinvigoration of the mime tradition in the form of the *commedia dell'arte*. This kind of drama not only influenced public taste, but it must certainly have been witnessed frequently by Lope de Vega, who learned much from it about plot and dramatic technique. *See* COMMEDIA DELL'ARTE in glossary.

The first known Spanish professional actor was the playwright Lope de Rueda (ca. 1510–1565), who flourished from about 1540 onward, performing in inn yards and patios under contract to local town councils or in the houses of the wealthy. Unlike previous drama, Rueda's plays were in prose and divided into six to ten scenes.

He also wrote *pasos*, short one-act interludes of knockabout farce, noted today for their mastery of popular language but owing much of their success in the author's time to the skill of his actors at playing such parts. His *comedias* are drawn from Italian sources. Rueda's career marks the establishment of acting as a full-time profession in Spain. Beginning in the 1560s public theatres (sponsored by charitable brotherhoods) came into existence in Madrid, Seville, Valencia, and other cities, thus creating a continuous demand for plays and assuring employment for players.

Another important occurrence which should not be overlooked was the banning of many printed plays in Spain (among them those of Torres Naharro) by the Toledan Index of 1559. The exact reasons for prohibiting most of them remains uncertain, but the Index must have forced playwrights after 1559 to write with much more attention to doctrine and decorum than previously. The repressive spirit of the Counter Reformation was beginning to invade all aspects of Spanish culture, compelling artists and thinkers to conform, at least outwardly, to the accepted ideology and moral standards of what Spain was becoming: a theocracy in which dissent was not tolerated.

Religious drama in the second half of the sixteenth century continued along the two lines of development previously indicated. Some hundred of the *autos* of the period are contained in a collection preserved in the Biblioteca Nacional de Madrid and usually known as the *Códice de autos viejos*. From the point of view of dramatic development the collection is especially noteworthy in that it reveals the increasing popularity of allegory and the *farsa sacramental*, a form which would eventually evolve into the *auto sacramental*. In the domain of the full-length play, popular *comedias de santos*, often written to celebrate the feast day of a local patron saint, are found in increasing numbers; but there also appears a learned type of play foreshadowed by the classical tendencies in Carvajal's *Tragedy of Josephine*, owing to a link with the school drama. Academic institutions throughout Renaissance Europe were now cultivating a learned, or humanistic, theatre directly influenced by that of the ancients as part of their educational activities. At first they were always in Latin, but this gradually gave way to the vernacular. Since by late in the sixteenth century the Jesuits were the most important body of teachers throughout Europe, not surprisingly much of the school drama originated in Jesuit colleges and used religious subject matter. It should be remembered that all the great dramatists of the Golden Age would have witnessed performances of this type of play in the course of their formal education, and some may even have taken part in them. School drama must be regarded as an important contributing factor in the formation of the *comedia* and the *auto sacramental*.

Another influence on the later theatre was classical tragedy, a mode which made its appearance in Spain hesitatingly and late. It was not until the 1570s that a school of deliberately classicizing Spanish tragedians came into existence. The group included Jerónimo

Bermúdez (1530?–1599), Andrés de Artieda (1544–1613), Cristóbal de Virués (1550–1609), Lupercio Leonardo de Argensola (1559–1613), and Gabriel Lobo Lasso de la Vega (1559–1625). The Spanish school was given impetus by a Portuguese dramatist, Antonio Ferreira (1528–1569), who in a play of 1558 *(A Castro)* on Portugal's national tragic heroine, Inés de Castro, started a new tradition among peninsular classicizing tragedians, of writing dramas not only on classical and mythological subjects but also on peninsular history. The chief stylistic source for these authors was not Greek tragedy but Seneca, the great model of all the Renaissance and seventeenth-century schools of tragedy. Seneca's strain of horror, violence, and bloodshed was strong in the Spanish tragedians, as it was in Thomas Kyd and the Elizabethans. It was to persist in later Spanish drama after Aristotelian forms were swept aside. It was the one clear legacy of the ancient theatre to the *comedia.*

One of Lope de Vegas's most notable predecessors, Juan de la Cueva (1550?–1610), wrote his fourteen tragedies and comedies for the early public theatres of Seville, where they were performed in 1579–1581. A disappointing dramatist, he nonetheless helped steer Spanish tragedy away from classical forms and give it a more national cast. He appears to have been one of the first playwrights to introduce Spanish history and legend into the drama, treating his themes with great freedom. He initiated, in fact, one of the great traditions of the Golden Age—that of dramatizing popular national history drawn from chronicles and ballad cycles and of treating it in such ways as to produce not only emotional but also didactic effects. *The Challenge of Zamora (El reto de Zamora),* for instance, most poignantly dramatizes King Sancho II of Castile's siege of Zamora, a well-known ballad subject. In addition, he reduced the number of acts to four, and wrote only in verse. Even more important, his plays might have been political allegories alluding to current affairs. If so, Cueva was the first of many dramatists who appear to have used the theatre of the Golden Age for treating themes with concealed political implications—a practice that would be revived in the eighteenth century and then again during the Franco regime.

Another active dramatist of Cueva's time was Miguel de Cervantes (1547–1616), who in the prologue to his *Eight Plays and Eight Interludes (Ocho comedias y ocho entremeses,* 1615) says he wrote some twenty or thirty plays for the Madrid stage in the 1580s, claiming that he reduced Cueva's four acts to three and was the first to put abstract allegorical and moral figures on the secular stage. Cervantes began as a supporter of the classical theatre. Only two of his early plays survive. One of them, *The Siege of Numantia (El cerco de Numancia),* has been praised as the finest tragedy written in Spanish. His later plays, never performed, were composed in the new style of Lope de Vega, classical canons having been modified in accordance with the now prevailing practice. But the author of *Don Quixote* never really mastered the art of writing full-length plays. Cervantes the playwright is at his best in his one-act comic *entremeses,* direct descen-

Pedro de Urdemalas, a picaresque play by Miguel de Cervantes, as produced by Madrid's Teatro Español. [Consulate General of Spain]

dents of the *pasos* of Lope de Rueda and undoubtedly the culmination of the mime tradition in Spain *(see* ENTREMÉS in glossary). Had Cervantes achieved greater success as a dramatist, the seventeenth-century Spanish theatre might have become broader based than it did under Lope de Vega's influence. It might also have moved in the direction of a more character-oriented dramaturgy, with less emphasis on complicated plots and accelerated action. *See* CERVANTES, MIGUEL DE; CUEVA, JUAN DE LA; ENCINA, JUAN DEL; ROJAS, FERNANDO DE; RUEDA, LOPE DE; TORRES NAHARRO, BARTOLOMÉ DE.

THE GOLDEN AGE: FROM LOPE DE VEGA TO CALDERÓN

The Spanish theatre of the Golden Age was dominated by two writers of genius, Lope Félix de Vega Carpio (1562–1635), more commonly known as Lope de Vega, and Pedro Calderón de la Barca (1600–1681). To the former belongs the distinction of having created the dramatic formula for the seventeenth-century *comedia.* It was this formula, originally devised by Lope de Vega at the end of the sixteenth century, that enabled Spanish playwrights to turn out the great supply of plays that the theatres consumed. When Lope made his appearance as playwright, the time was ripe for the creation of a new drama. Drawing on the experiments of other dramatists who were moving toward the form, Lope perfected it and gave it authority, but not before overcoming the resistance of those who defended the classical theatre. Though aspects of the formula were considerably modified by Calderón and by the emergence of a court theatre in the 1630s, the original Lopean formula continued to guide Spanish playwrights even into the eighteenth century. The Spanish word for "play" is *comedia,* with no distinction between plays having happy or sad endings. Applied to the seventeenth century, however, the term *comedia* refers specifically to the type of full-length play

The Dog in the Manger by Lope de Vega Carpio, as given in Paris with Jean-Louis Barrault and Madeleine Renaud. [French Cultural Services]

written by Lope de Vega and his followers from about 1580 to 1700. It constitutes the largest distinctive corpus of national drama in existence.

In short, Lope's formula signified the more or less absolute rejection of the neoclassical canons of dramaturgy. The *comedia* has the following formal characteristics:

1. It is always in three acts rather than the five prescribed by neoclassical theory.

2. It is written in verse but employs a well-developed polymetric system, in contrast to the Alexandrine of French classical drama and the Shakespearean iambic pentameter.

3. There is no strict separation of comedy and tragedy. While the majority of plays are pure comedy, the remainder have some comic relief and a very few are real tragedies. The term "tragicomedy" has been applied, not inappropriately, to some of the plays. Regardless of whether a play is conceived as comedy or tragedy, there is one *gracioso* character, the comic servant who is a humorous parody of his master in some ways and a complete contrast in others. The down-to-earth philosophy of the servant serves as a counterpoint to the elevated ideas of the master. It should be noted that the *gracioso* is descended from the comic rustics found in the early Renaissance drama of Juan del Encina and his disciples.

4. It dispenses with the neoclassical unities of time, place, and action, particularly the first two. This freedom

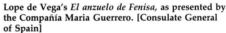

Lope de Vega's *El anzuelo de Fenisa,* as presented by the Compañía Maria Guerrero. [Consulate General of Spain]

from the constraining effects of the unities allows the dramatist to shift the action rapidly from one location to another and to present an entire lifetime in a concentrated synthesis. *See* UNITIES in glossary.

5. The main plot is normally accompanied by a comic or serious subplot that is not irrelevant to it (which had often been the case in the sixteenth century).

The *comedia* has sometimes been criticized as superficial because it lacks profound character portrayal. The charge is unfair. The *comedia* subordinates character to action and individualism to social tradition. The characters represent typical Spaniards in their social roles and milieu. This is what the *comedia* is all about. It is centered not on the exploration of the individual soul, but on the comportment of men in society. Character tends to be revealed in the *comedia* by means of dialogue and action rather than soliloquy. Before the time of Calderón, characters given to philosophizing or reflection are rarely encountered in Spanish drama.

The average *comedia* is marked by rapid dialogue, lightness of touch, and swift-moving action, often sensational, involving physical violence and complicated plots and subplots, all of which made for exceptional theatricality. The *comedia de capa y espada*, ("cloak and sword drama"), with its abundant use of intrigue, deceptions, concealments, mistaken identities, supernatural occurrences, and other romantic ingredients, was perhaps the most popular type of play, comparable in its appeal to modern adventure films or certain television programs. Many of the *comedias*, including a good number by Lope de Vega, are simply potboilers. Others, however, deal with serious, even transcendental matters, usually without precluding comic moments. The masterpieces of the *comedia* fall into this category.

Eclectic in structure and content, the *comedia* takes its plots from multiple sources, the most frequent being Spanish history, legend, and literature, as well as from other modern literatures (particularly the Italian *novelle*). While classical material is rarely utilized, at least before the time of Calderón, the Bible and hagiographic literature are always fertile sources of inspiration. In addition to these historical, literary, and religious sources, the *comedia* also draws upon aspects of contemporary life in all its social manifestations, from the courtly to the picaresque.

Within this common artistic framework there exist a great variety of plays: heroic, religious, philosophical, pastoral, and cloak and sword, as well as the abundant production of *autos sacramentales* and *entremeses*, two forms intimately related to the *comedia*. The inventiveness of the *comedia* was such that foreign dramatists of the seventeenth century borrowed freely from its repertoire. Corneille, Molière, Dryden, and Wycherley, to name only major figures of the seventeenth-century European stage, were all indebted to the Spanish *comedia*.

The great motifs of the Golden Age are religion (understood as orthodox Roman Catholicism), honor (*honra*: honor experienced in its social dimensions, not self-esteem), love (always seen in relation to marriage), and patriotism (expressed as loyalty to the concept of monar-

Late-seventeenth-century scene design for a play by Pedro Calderón de la Barca. [National Library, Madrid]

chy). Despite the wide diversity of plots, every *comedia* revolves around one or more of these basic themes, none of which is ever questioned, with the possible exception of honor when carried to unreasonable extremes. The aesthetic freedom (relative freedom, of course, since departure from the Lopean formula was unacceptable) enjoyed by the playwrights is in sharp contrast to the rigid

Serge Reggiani and Maria Casarès in Calderón's *Devotion to the Cross*, as presented in 1953 at the Deuxième Festival d'Art Dramatique, Paris. [French Cultural Services]

An open-air Swiss performance of Calderón's *The Great Theatre of the World,* an *auto sacramental* in which humanity is called before the sovereign Stage Manager. [Consulate General of Spain]

ideological patterns to which they must subscribe. It seems safe to say that this unquestioning submission to authority creates a distance between much of the Golden Age drama and the modern sensibility. It is on these grounds, and not because of an alleged superficiality, that the *comedia* may be legitimately criticized.

Golden Age plays were not written to provoke a critical reaction in the spectator; on the contrary, their purpose was to confirm and reinforce his beliefs. Some, of course, were composed solely to give pleasure—the cape and sword plays would fall into this category—and to provide a form of escapism for the audience; however, most included a didactic component. Ideas were therefore usually important in the plays of this period, sometimes extremely so.

It is customary to divide the drama of the Golden Age into two schools or cycles. Lope's most talented disciples are usually considered to be Guillén de Castro y Bellvis (1567–1631), Antonio Mira de Amescua (1574?–1644), Luis Vélez de Guevara (1579–1644), Juan Ruiz de Alarcón (1581–1639), and Gabriel Téllez (1584–1628), better known as Tirso de Molina, after Lope de Vega and Calderón the outstanding seventeenth-century Spanish dramatist. Among the other playwrights of the school of Lope are Juan Pérez de Montalván (1602?–1638) and Luis de Belmonte y Bermúdez (1587–1650?), as well as José de Valdivieso (1560?–1638) and Luis Quiñones de Benavente (1589?–1651), both of

whom owe their fame to dramatic forms other than the *comedia.* Calderón's greatest disciples are Agustín de Moreto y Cabaña (1618–1669) and Francisco de Rojas Zorrilla (1607–1648). Other noteworthy members of the school of Calderón are Alvaro Cubillo de Aragón (1596?–1661), Antonio de Solís y Rivadeneyra (1610–1686), Antonio Coello y Ochoa (1611–1652), Juan Bautista Diamante (1625–1687), and Francisco Antonio de Bances y López Candamo (1662–1704), the last important dramatist of the seventeenth century. The majority of these playwrights, including Lope, Calderón, and Tirso de Molina, were ordained members of the church, though some of them did not become priests until late in life. Given the ideological implications of much seventeenth-century Spanish theatre, the predominance of clergymen among the dramatists does not appear to have been a mere coincidence.

The most remarkable feature of the playwrights of Lope's school is the closeness with which they generally followed the master's formula. This situation was due in part to the fact that the Lopean formula had by this time established certain roles in which actors and actresses specialized, thereby forcing dramatists to provide parts suitable to the players' specialized talents. In addition, individual companies tended to concentrate on given types of plays, so that dramatists also had to take that into account. A third contributing factor was the public, which, having grown used to a formula, would not readily accept innovations. Playwriting did not, however, remain static. While the *comedia* was gradually developing greater dramatic unity—most of the plays written before about 1610 are carelessly and loosely constructed—the *auto scaramental* was similarly undergoing a notable evolution during Lope's lifetime. Borrowing material and techniques from the *comedia,* this characteristically Spanish manifestation of liturgical drama had been in the process of development since the previous century. Allegorical in form and doctrinal in content, its function was always to illustrate the meaning of the Eucharist. Specifically designed for performance in the street as part of the popular religious festivities and processions held on the feast of Corpus Christi, it became increasingly more effective and sophisticated artistically as the seventeenth century progressed. Though Lope, Mira de Amescua, and Tirso de Molina also cultivated the *auto sacramental,* the most significant contributions to the development of the genre before Calderón were made by a less famous writer, the religious poet José de Valdivieso. Certain minor dramatic forms, too, evolved notably, in particular the *entremés,* which attained in the hands of Quiñones de Benavente a level of brillance unmatched since Cervantes.

Rediscovered by European romanticism, Calderón has long been regarded as Spain's foremost playwright. If Lope de Vega created the formula for the *comedia,* it was Calderón who refined it, making possible plays of greater universal appeal. Calderón did not limit himself to the *comedia* but was also responsible for developing a new type of *auto sacramental*—longer and more complex and spectacular than any previously written. So adept

The early deeds of Spain's legendary hero are the focus of Guillén de Castro y Bellvís's *Las mocedades del Cid,* shown above in a production by the Teatro Español de Madrid. [Consulate General of Spain]

did he become in this form, that from 1649 onward the only *autos sacramentales* presented were by Calderón.

By the 1620s rudimentary staging procedures had begun to give way to stage machinery and props even in the *corrales* (the municipally owned public theatres established in uncovered rectangular courtyards overlooked by the backs of houses, whose rear windows served as boxes for the affluent members of the audience). Calderón's work underwent important changes as the result of the establishment of a permanent court theatre in Philip IV's new Buen Retiro palace, completed in 1632. Plays written for this theatre stressed spectacular visual effects achieved by means of complicated stage machinery and lavish sets. These new conditions were reflected not only in Calderón's *comedias,* but also in the fact that in the last decades of his career he composed works for the court theatre—court performances were held at various palaces in and near Madrid—in which singing and instrumental music played a large part. Before advancing on, in 1660, to write full-fledged operas, he produced a number of *zarzuelas,* a characteristically Spanish genre, partly sung, partly spoken, derived from the Italian lyric theatre. This form was in fact named after the royal palace of the Zarzuela located just outside of Madrid. *See* ZARZUELA in glossary.

In general, the Calderonian school differs from the Lopean in several aspects. First, the Calderonians show a marked predilection for the use of richly rhetorical imagery and expressive devices in their dramatic poetry, especially in descriptive and emotional speeches. This dazzling poetic style, called *culturanismo,* is associated with the great Baroque poet Luis de Góngora (1561-1627). Secondly, the Calderonians' plot construction is usually more careful and polished than that of the more spontaneous playwrights of the early seventeenth century. Contributing factors to this greater stylistic improvement appear to have been the publication of a number of treatises emphasizing the importance of careful plot construction and the fact that from the 1630s onward many dramatists tended to write more frequently for the court theatre than for the *corrales.* The real focal points of dramatic activity during the Calderonian period were the court theatres in Madrid and in the royal palaces outside the capital. A third distinguishing feature between the two schools is that the Calderonians often rewrote earlier plays—sometimes their own, but mostly works by Lope and his disciples—to satisfy the new aesthetic canons of the theatre, as well as to convey new moral and political ideas to their audiences. These remolded plays, or *refundiciones,* were considered perfectly legitimate in the seventeenth century.

Another noteworthy feature of the Calderonian school is its greater preoccupation with the classical principle of decorum. This represented a concession to those opponents of the *comedia,* who denounced it on aesthetic and moral grounds. The *comedia* now became more acceptable to both classicists and moralists (the Jesuits had been among its harshest critics). On the one hand,

Tirso de Molina's *Don Gil de las calzas verdes*, Compañía de Teatro de Carmen Bernardos. [Consulate General of Spain]

drama underwent a subtle classicizing and, on the other, was transformed more and more into an instrument of morality. A final distinguishing feature is that many of the plays of the Calderonian school are more intellectual than emotional in their effects as compared with those written by the earlier dramatists.

See BANCES Y LÓPEZ CANDAMO, FRANCISCO ANTONIO DE; CALDERÓN DE LA BARCA, PEDRO; CASTRO Y BELLVIS, GUILLÉN DE; COELLO Y OCHOA, ANTONIO; CUBILLO DE ARAGÓN, ÁLVARO; DIAMANTE, JUAN BAUTISTA; HOZ Y MOTA, JUAN CARLO DE LA; MIRA DE AMESCUA, ANTONIO; MOLINA, TIRSO DE; MORETO Y CABAÑA, AGUSTÍN DE; PÉREZ DE MONTALVÁN, JUAN; QUIÑONES DE BENAVENTE, LUIS; ROJAS, FERNANDO DE; ROJAS ZORRILLA, FRANCISCO DE; RUIZ DE ALARCÓN, JUAN; SOLÍS Y RIVADENEYRA, ANTONIO; TIMONEDA, JUAN DE; VALDIVIESO, JOSÉ DE; VEGA CARPIO, LOPE DE; VÉLEZ DE GUEVARA, LUIS.

A 1963 production of Agustín de Moreto y Cabaña's *El lindo Don Diego*, a comedy about a fop. [Consulate General of Spain]

The death of Calderón in 1681 signaled the end of an era. The creative impulse in Spanish culture had become exhausted. Theatrical activity by no means came to a halt in the eighteenth century; it simply experienced a disastrous decline in quality. In the first half of the eighteenth century two playwrights of modest talent, Antonio de Zamora (1660?–1728) and José de Cañizares (1675–1750), both very popular in their time, continued to adhere to seventeenth-century patterns, for the most part rehashing plays of the Golden Age. Spectacular effects rather than dramatic content characterize most of the plays which had the widest appeal in eighteenth-century Spain.

This same passion for spectacular effects explains the popularity attained in the second half of the century by two types of plays, the *comedia de magia* ("magic play") and the martial extravaganzas known as *comedias heroicas* ("heroic plays"), *dramas de batallas* ("battle plays"), or *comedias militares* ("military plays"). The *comedia de magia* was in effect a magic show, with all sorts of marvelous events taking place before the astonished eyes of the spectators. The second group of plays called for the staging of battles, as well as marches and countermarches, all accompanied by music (also employed in the *comedia de magia*), frequent scene changes, and twisting plots. The extremes to which some playwrights would go to satisfy the public's taste for spectacle knew no bounds. One such author was the now all but forgotten Luciano Francisco Comella (1775–1812), whom Leandro Fernández de Moratín seems to have been attacking in *The New Play, or the Café* (*La comedia nueva, o el café*, 1792).

With the advent of the Bourbon dynasty in 1700 new attitudes began to manifest themselves in literature and in public life. French court influence was in part responsible for the reemergence of the classicist tradition, which had never been entirely submerged in the Golden Age. The first important neoclassical theorist to appear was Ignacio de Luzán (1702–1754), whose *Poética* was published in 1737. In matters regarding theatre he was an inflexible advocate of the neoclassical rules, accepting on theoretical grounds of verisimilitude the unities of time and space. Condemning the *tragicomedia* as a monstrous aberration unknown among the ancients, he insisted on the absolute separation of comedy and tragedy. Luzán's *Poética* gave rise to a fierce controversy between defenders of the national Golden Age traditions and other neoclassical theorists who condemned the *comedia* in far harsher terms than Luzán. In 1765, taking advantage of the official support they enjoyed at the time, the advocates of neoclassicism were successful in securing the prohibition of the *autos sacramentales*, a genre which they deemed had become a debased spectacle devoid of any religious significance. But despite this victory the theatre remained dominated by *comedias de magia* and plays with similar appeal, reworkings of Golden Age dramas, and French translations. There were, however, attempts by a number of prominent writers to acclimatize the classical tragedy, many of them employing Spanish themes. The only work of this type which can be considered in any way successful is *Rachel* (*Raquel*, 1778), by Vicente García de la Huerta, which combines continuous echoes of Golden Age theatre with neoclassical principles.

The cultivators of classical tragedy in the eighteenth century were men who identified with the Enlightenment, intellectuals who were in favor of social and moral reforms. They viewed theatre as an ideal instrument for propagating their ideas and "educating the masses." However, most of these authors were not professional playwrights, and their lack of dramatic talent and ability could not be compensated by precepts and good intentions.

Far more successful than the neoclassical attempts at tragedy were the *sainetes* of Ramón de la Cruz (1731–1794), short sketches in verse reflecting the popular life of Madrid. With their emphasis on the picturesque and the vivid spoken language of the marketplace, streets, and taverns, the *sainete*, with its roots in the Golden Age *entremés*, constitutes the favorite theatre fare of the general public in the second half of the eighteenth century. *See* SAINETE in glossary.

After 1773 official support for tragedies declined, although they continued to be written. By the early years of the nineteenth century, tragedy had acquired a more or less established form, which would endure until the arrival of romanticism in Spain. However, few if any of the plays written during this period could be classified as authentic tragedies. Another sign of the evolving public taste was the diminishing popularity of the *refundiciones*, or reworking of Golden Age plays, although they never completely lost their appeal. Interestingly, in the closing years of the eighteenth century and in the beginning of the nineteenth, a number of Golden Age plays were adapted in accordance with neoclassical standards. The last decades of the eighteenth century also witnessed the appearance of the sentimental drama, or *comédie larmoyante*, a genre common in other European countries. The most celebrated Spanish example of this form—more celebrated because of the importance of its author than because of any intrinsic merits of the play itself—was *The Honest Delinquent* (*El delincuente honrado*), written in 1773 by one of the most distinguished representatives of the Spanish Enlightenment, Gaspar Melchor de Jovellanos (1744–1811).

While neoclassical tragedy never really imposed itself on the Spanish stage in a decisive manner, neoclassical comedy found an outstanding dramatist in Leandro Fernández de Moratín (1760–1828), whose *When a Girl Says Yes* (*El sí de las niñas*), completed in 1801 but not performed until 1806, is beyond a shadow of a doubt the best play written in Spain since Calderón's time. A minor masterpiece, it was also the greatest theatrical success of its era. The son of a pioneer of neoclassical drama, Nicolás Fernández de Moratín (1737–1780), the younger Moratín, wrote only five plays, in which the dominant theme was criticism of the practice of arranging marriages against the wishes of the parties involved. He thus opened up the theatre to the presentation of serious sub-

jects relevant to contemporary society. Despite his limited output—Moratín did not earn his living as a dramatist—he set the pattern for a type of play which would prevail in the Spanish theatre for a substantial portion of the nineteenth century. The basic components of the Moratinian *comedia* of manners were: a certain elasticity as regards the classical unities, emphasis on the spoken word, a minimum of plot, a predominance of character portrayal over action, and the elimination of spectacular stage effects. Moratín, who also translated Molière and Shakespeare, did more to bring Spanish theatre in line with European traditions than all the other Spanish dramatists of the eighteenth century combined.

Neoclassical plays, both comedy and tragedy, were often vehicles for transmitting the progressive ideas of the Enlightenment. In the last decades of the eighteenth century it is obvious that theatre was developing a middle-class orientation. Even those dramatists catering to the least exigent sector of the public were making an effort to deal with the broader questions of hierarchical society, a preoccupation that was central to the Enlightenment.

See CAÑIZARES, JOSÉ DE; CRUZ, RAMÓN DE LA; FERNÁNDEZ DE MORATÍN, LEANDRO; FERNÁNDEZ DE MORATÍN, NICOLÁS; GARCÍA DE LA HUERTA, VICENTE ANTONIO; ZAMORA, ANTONIO DE.

NINETEENTH CENTURY

After the resounding success of Leandro Fernández de Moratín's *When a Girl Says Yes* in 1806, the Spanish theatre marked time for several decades until the advent of

El sí de las niñas by Leandro Fernández de Moratín, presented by Teatro Español. [Consulate General of Spain]

José Zorrilla's *Don Juan Tenorio*, as staged by Madrid's Compañía Titular del Teatro Español in 1968. [Consulate General of Spain]

romanticism in the middle 1830s. Moratín, whose influence would outlast romanticism, remained the most prestigious figure; however, he had no immediate disciples of any real importance. A few praiseworthy if futile attempts were made to write neoclassical tragedy by some writers, including two who were destined to play key roles in the history of the romantic theatre, Francisco Martínez de la Rosa (1787–1862) and Angel de Saavedra (1791–1865). The public still favored *refundiciones* of the Golden Age drama or the absurd monstrosities which Moratín had satirized in *The New Play, or the Café*. Neoclassical comedies (including Moratín's), bourgeois sentimental drama, opera, and above all translations from the French also flourished.

The arrival of romanticism was long overdue in Spain. The romantic movement had already peaked in England, France, and Germany when it was introduced by the returning émigré writers who had been forced to seek exile abroad in 1823 as the result of the repressive policies of Ferdinand VII. No doubt the weakness and short duration of Spanish romanticism were due in some measure to its late appearance, which never allowed it to grow roots. With a few notable exceptions—Mariano José de Larra, for example—the country proclaimed abroad as essentially romantic had to import its romanticism. Adopting the form of historical drama, the romantic theatre reached back to Spain's past for thematic material: to the *Romancero*, its national legacy of heroic balladry inherited from the Middle Ages, and to the

Golden Age theatre, still being staged in a steady stream of *refundiciones*. Like the *comedia* of the seventeenth century, it disregarded the neoclassical rules, completely ignoring the three unities, mixing tragic and comic ingredients (however, the *gracioso*, or comic servant who was a humorous parody of his master, was eliminated), and normally employing polymetric versification, though sometimes it combined prose and verse. It retained a preference for improbable and complicated plots, as well as an emphasis on the concept of honor, while striving for spectacular theatrical effects. Written in sonorous and often colorful language, the typical Spanish romantic drama was also characterized by a passionate tone, emphatic gestures, rapid movement, and facile theaticality—all calculated to arouse the spectator's emotions.

When romanticism finally reached Spain, its battleground was the theatre, as had also been the case in France and to some extent in Germany. Francisco Martínez de la Rosa (1787–1862), a writer with impeccable neoclassical credentials, turned to romanticism during his exile in France. There he composed two historical dramas. The first, *Aben Humeya*, was written and produced in French in 1830 and not staged in Madrid, in its Spanish version, until 1836. The second, *The Venice Conspiracy (La conspiración de Venecia)*, also written in 1830, was performed in 1834, making it the first romantic or quasi-romantic play to be staged in Spain. For all their romantic atmosphere and exotic effects, neither of these dramas (both in prose) is romantic in spirit. That same year, just a few months after the successful performance of *The Venice Conspiracy*, Mariano José de Larra (1809–1837), the ill-fated satirist who was to owe his fame to his mordant critical essays and not to the theatre, attempted romantic drama with *Macías*, a disappointing play only partially committed to the new form. Its influence, however, on two later romantic dramas, *The Troubadour* and particularly *The Lovers of Teruel*, give it the status of a seminal work. Full-fledged romantic drama began in 1835 with *Don Alvaro or the Force of Destiny (Don Álvaro o la fuerza del sino)*, by Angel de Saavedra (1791–1865), later Duque de Rivas. The theme of *Don Álvaro*, the triumph of fate over love, was the basic theme of all major Spanish romantic dramas. Not an initial box-office success, it was to become a great favorite much later thanks to the celebrated actor Rafael Vico (1842–1888), who included it in his repertory. *The Troubadour (El trovador)*, by Antonio García Gutiérrez (1812–1884), premiered in 1836, was a huge immediate success and became the longest-running (twenty-five performances) Spanish romantic drama. The following year Juan Eugenio de Hartzenbusch (1806–1880) launched his theatrical career auspiciously with *The Lovers of Teruel (Los amantes de Teruel)*, which was also warmly received. *Don Juan Tenorio* (1844), a mediocre version of the Don Juan legend by José Zorrilla (1817–1893), was the last significant romantic drama, and for very peculiar reasons it has continued to be performed every year to coincide with the celebration of All Souls' Day. Modern critics generally agree that Spain did not produce great romantic drama. Even the just-mentioned "masterpieces" are considered little more than period pieces lacking structural coherence and characterization.

By the middle of the 1840s romanticism had about run its course, although the historical drama would continue to retain its appeal. In the same way that all the leading romantic playwrights wavered between a commitment to romantic drama and neoclassical forms, both tragedy and comedy, a similar aesthetic ambivalence is visible in the work of several playwrights of lesser stature. Two especially worthy of mention are Antonio Gil y Zárate (1793–1861) and the Cuban poet Gertrudis Gómez de Avellaneda (1814–1873), whose plays, in particular her two biblical tragedies, *Saul (Saúl, 1846)* and *Balthazar (Baltasar, 1858)*, are among the most distinguished of the lackluster transition period extending from 1845 to the rise of the *alta comedia*, or high comedy, in the middle 1850s.

Throughout the years when romanticism reigned supreme, the popularity of Moratinian comedies never completely declined either with dramatists or with the public. The romantic dramatists regularly produced them during the intervals when they were not writing historical dramas. Three dramatists, however, were especially responsible for the continuity of the genre throughout the romantic period and even contributed to its further development: the Mexican-born Manuel Eduardo de Gorostiza (1789–1851), Manuel Bretón de los Herreros (1796–1873), and Ventura de la Vega (1807–1865). The

latter's *A Man of the World (El hombre de mundo, 1845)* is considered the link between the neoclassic comedy in the Moratinian style and the *alta comedia* which was to follow.

The emergence of the *alta comedia* ("bourgeois realist drama" would perhaps be the most appropriate rendition of the term) coincides with and is a reflection of the position of dominance attained by the Spanish middle class in the second half of the nineteenth century. Moralistic in outlook, sentimental in approach, and didactic in purpose, the *alta comedia* aspired to present serious problems of contemporary society in a realistic manner. In actual practice, however, it was neither realist nor profound in its social commentary. Its settings were invariably upper class, from whose conventional mores and traditionally Catholic viewpoint its authors never deviate. Elegantly dressed characters lecture to us in verse on the superiority of spiritual values over the materialistic concept of life. For almost twenty-five years, the "pseudo-realist" dramas of the *alta comedia* enjoyed great favor with Spanish audiences, which since the eighteenth century had ceased to represent a cross section of society.

The acknowledged masters of the *alta comedia* were Adelardo López de Ayala (1828–1879) and Manuel Tamayo y Baus (1829–1898). The finest dramatic achievement of the period, Tamayo's *A New Drama (Un drama nuevo, 1867)*, does not belong to the *alta comedia* species; instead, it is a well-constructed historical drama, in prose, set in Shakespeare's time and making effective use of the "play within a play" device. Like most Spanish dramatists of his day Tamayo was equally attracted to the neoclassical and romantic traditions of dramaturgy, and cultivated a variety of genres: *alta comedia*, historical drama, light comedy, tragedy, and the ever popular *zarzuela*, all interspersed with innumerable adaptations ranging from Schiller to the most ephemeral titles of the contemporary French stage. Tamayo's eclectic approach to playwriting was the rule rather than the exception among his contemporaries. This confirms that the Spanish theatre of the post-romantic era, despite the timid renovation attempts of Ayala and Tamayo in the *alta comedia*, was still lacking a clear orientation. In all fairness, it should be pointed out that the situation of the theatre in the rest of Western Europe was not so different at the time.

In the slow evolution of the Spanish theatre of the second half of the nineteenth century toward modern realism, one particular dramatist, too often ignored or hastily dismissed, merits special mention: Enrique Gaspar (1842–1902), who strongly defended the prose medium against those playwrights who continued to use verse (prose had been almost completely displaced by verse in the theatre since the romantic period). In dramas such as *The Frock Coat (La levita, 1868)* and *The Stomach (El estómago, 1874)*, both of which criticized aspects of the bourgeoise mentality, he was already moving beyond the conventional *alta comedia* of the Tamayo and Ayala type, not only in terms of an increased social awareness, but also as regards the modernization of dialogue.

This promising advance in the direction of realism spearheaded by Gaspar was brought to an abrupt halt by the sudden and unexpected appearance in the mid-1870s of José Echegaray (1832–1916), the dramatist who was to dominate the Spanish stage for the remainder of the century with an extravagant formula of his own concoction. Written in stilted verse or bombastic prose, Echegaray's plays are totally dependent on the author's ability to exploit grotesquely improbable theatrical plots. While most of the time he was content to serve up warmed-over Calderonian concepts of duty and honor to nostalgic middle-class audiences with aristocratic ideals, on several occasions he attempted to write social drama of ideas, always with dismal artistic results but great box-office success. The award of the Nobel Prize to him in 1904 was energetically protested by the leading members of the "generation of 1898"—a term used to designate the group of rebellious young writers who were to revitalize Spanish literature and thought in the first decades of the twentieth century.

Echegaray was not without followers, though each attempted to strike out in his own direction. In overwrit-

Julie Opp and William Faversham in *The World and His Wife,* an adaptation by Charles Frederic Nirdlinger of José Echegaray's *The Great Galeoto.* New York, Daly Theatre, 1908. [Theatre Collection, The New York Public Library at Lincoln Center, Astor, Lenox and Tilden Foundations]

ten dramas which purported to be realistic, Eugenio Sellés (1844–1926) and Leopoldo Cano (1844–1934) combined Echegaray's melodramatic style with the French *pièce à thése* ("thesis play"). Sellés treated the question of adultery and divorce from the traditional Spanish viewpoint in *The Gordian Knot* (*El nudo gordiano,* 1878), while *The Avengers* (*Las vengadoras,* 1884) was a not very successful effort to portray the class of "fallen women," as Alexandre Dumas *fils* had done some thirty years earlier in *The Demimonde* (1855). Cano, in whom social preoccupations are often expressed in very one-sided fashion, is chiefly remembered for *The Passion Flower* (*La Pasionaria,* 1883), also with the theme of "fallen woman." (This drama should not be confused with Benavente's famous play of the same title in English.) New ground was broken by the Catalán dramatist José Feliú y Codina (1847–1897), who exploited the possibilities of regional rural settings of the traditional theme of honor and revenge, notably in *Dolores* (*La Dolores,* 1892), paving the way for Benavente's rural dramas in the twentieth century.

Joaquín Dicenta (1863–1917), by far the most important of Echegaray's disciples, scored a triumphant success with *Juan José* (1895), a curious blending of the drama of social protest, or "proletariat drama" as it later came to be designated, and the persistent Spanish preoccupation with honor. The characters are motivated not by class consciousness as in true social drama but, rather, by personal conflicts. Dicenta brought new dignity to proletarian characters in drama, but he did not endow them with a new mentality. They continued to behave like the punctilious heroes of another era. Nevertheless, *Juan José* remains a landmark in the history of the Spanish drama of social protest, a genre which rapidly degenerated into dramatized political tracts with a revolutionary message, and which was not to be effectively revived as a legitimate art form until the second half of the twentieth century.

While European theatre had already entered or was about to enter a phase of development that would radically transform drama in the next century, Echegaray and his followers monopolized the serious theatre in Spain. Also extremely popular was the *género chico,* a term used to designate two forms of light theatrical entertainment: the traditional *sainete,* with its colorful and humorous treatment of lower-class life, now often accompanied by music; and the *zarzuela,* a genre which had become a more popular art form after the end of the eighteenth century, when the bourgeois audience began to abandon it in favor of Italian opera. As a result of these changing conditions, full-length *zarzuelas,* generally in three acts and lasting approximately two and a half hours, eventually gave way to the shorter, *género chico.* Both the *sainete* and the *zarzuela* had enjoyed a tremendous revival in the second half of the nineteenth century, largely because of the development of *costumbrismo,* an artistic phenomenon anticipated by the *entremeses* of Ramón de la Cruz in the midst of the eighteenth-century attempts to impose neoclassical drama in Spain. *Costumbrismo* consisted of the depiction of Spanish regional traits (usually those of the Madrilenians and Andalusians), with stress on picturesque detail and comic anecdote. (*Costumbrismo* could also be employed with far more serious intentions, as in the essays of Larra or many of the realist novels of the second half of the nineteenth century. Political satire is sometimes found in the *género chico* pieces, both *sainetes* and *zarzuelas*.) The extraordinary appeal of the *género chico* led to the establishment of *teatros por horas*, theatres specializing in staging this type of fare at popular prices. Meeting the endless demand for new works—a situation reminiscent of Lope de Vega's time—brought forth legions of authors. The number of *sainetes* and *zarzuelas* turned out during the course of a half century is estimated to have been in the thousands. Many were collaborations, also a quite common practice in the Golden Age, owing to the economics of the Spanish theatre. While several writers who will be mentioned later managed during the first two decades of the twentieth century to temporarily rescue the prose *sainete* from an accelerating process of debasement, the *sainete lírico*, written in verse and set to music, and the *zarzuela* disappeared, to be replaced by vaudeville and variety shows. The outstanding author associated with the *género chico* during the last twenty-five years of the nineteenth century was Ricardo de la Vega (1839–1910), who like Moratín before him had inherited the theatrical vocation of his father, Ventura de la Vega. Other popular cultivators of the *género chico* of the same period were Javier de Burgos (1842–1902), Tomás Luceno (1844–1931), Miguel Ramos Carrión (1845?–1915), and Vital Aza (1851–1912).

The fundamental feature of the Spanish theatre in the second half of the nineteenth century was the struggle between a lingering romantic tradition (historical drama, verse plays, Echegaray and his school) and the urge to move forward. As the century drew to a close it was apparent to many intellectuals that Spanish drama, in sharp contrast to the novel (dormant since the seventeenth century but splendidly resurrected in the second half of the nineteenth), was in a state of stagnation.

While realism in the theatre (especially the bourgeois drama of French vintage) was elsewhere being challenged by new dramatic theories, in Spain it had barely made any inroads. The undiminished interest in more or less old-style historical drama, the growing popularity of an increasingly decadent *género chico*, the passion which the middle and wealthy classes had developed for the Italian opera, the anachronistic phenomenon of the Echegaray type of melodrama, and the unceasing flow of second-rate, often outdated French plays in translation constituted a formidable barrier to any possibility of renovating the Spanish stage.

Perhaps the underlying problem was, as Miguel de Unamuno (1864–1936) pointed out in a famous essay of 1896, that the Spanish theatre had ceased to be a public institution and was now a private enterprise. With the exception of the *género chico*, the theatre catered almost exclusively to one segment of the population. Its primary purpose was profit rather than culture. Even Madrid's municipally owned Teatro Español was operated on a commercial basis. This unhealthy situation was further aggravated by the fact that theatrical activity was centered almost entirely in Madrid, with Barcelona occupying a very secondary position. Theatre in the provinces was limited to occasional performances by companies on tour, usually between seasons in Madrid.

Among the writers disturbed by the prevailing conditions in the theatre was Benito Pérez Galdós (1843–1920), who turned to the drama (his original literary vocation) after having already established himself as Spain's greatest modern novelist. In 1892 he staged a theatrical version of his dialogue novel *Reality (Realidad)*, which had appeared in 1889. Encouraged by the moderate success of the play, he went on to produce about twenty original dramas and adaptations of his own novels during the next twenty-six years, although most of his works for the theatre were written between 1892 and 1910. He had at least four striking successes, two of which, *Electra* (1901) and *The Grandfather* (*El abuelo*, 1904), rank among the most significant works of modern Spanish drama. Combining realism with symbolism (a trend very much in evidence on the European stage at the time), Galdós hoped to infuse the theatre with new vitality by bringing to it psychological veracity, observation, and above all intellectual depth. A liberal and progressive thinker, Pérez Galdós was unable to change the course of the Spanish drama, though he did exercise some influence on other playwrights (Arniches, for example, and perhaps even Benavente). Handicapped by a lack of technical ability, he also had to deal with audiences which for the most part were reluctant to accept his aesthetic innovations and ideological outlook; that he managed to have his plays performed at all was due to his enormous prestige as a novelist.

See BRETÓN DE LOS HERREROS, MANUEL; DICENTA Y BENEDICTO, JOAQUÍN; ECHEGARAY, JOSÉ; GARCÍA GUTIÉRREZ, ANTONIO; GASPAR, ENRIQUE; HARTZENBUSCH Y MARTÍNEZ, JUAN EUGENIO DE; LARRA Y SÁNCHEZ DE CASTRO, MARIANO JOSÉ; LOPEZ DE AYALA Y HERRERA, ADELARDO; MARTÍNEZ DE LA ROSA, FRANCISCO; NUÑEZ DE ARCE, GASPAR; PÉREZ GALDÓS, BENITO; SAAVEDRA, ANGEL DE; TAMAYO Y BAUS, MANUEL; UNAMUNO, MIGUEL DE.

THE TWENTIETH CENTURY: FROM BENAVENTE TO THE SPANISH CIVIL WAR

The Spanish theatre has experienced some renewal in the twentieth century, though it has rarely attained the high level of poetry or the novel, as only those authors willing to cater to the tastes of the public could hope to prosper. Instead of advancing along the lines proposed by Pérez Galdós, the drama followed other paths of development, the most successful of which was determined by Jacinto Benavente (1866–1954), the playwright who was to dominate the Spanish stage for more than half a century. Even though he rescued the theatre from the excesses of Echegaray, the success of Benavente's formula also produced less positive results: legitimate theatre in Spain was to remain outside the mainstream of the most significant European developments, indifferent to the works of such international figures as Ibsen, Chekhov, Strindberg, Maeterlinck, Hauptmann, Shaw, and Pirandello. In the area of production and scenic design, naturalism became the prevailing mode, and the Spanish stage remained unaffected by the experimental work of Stanislavsky, Meyerhold, Craig, Appia, Reinhardt, and Piscator. The plays written by those authors who tended to monopolize the theatre throughout the period, ending with the outbreak of the Spanish Civil War in July 1936, lacked any lasting merit. The most interesting works being written were seldom successfully performed; many of them never even reached the stage. The Spanish theatre of Benavente's heyday was characterized by what one critic, G. G. Brown, has described as "the great vitality and impregnable bourgeois vulgarity of the commercial stage." As a result, a succession of incredibly fecund dramatists kept churning out plays designed to satisfy a public similar to that which had applauded Echegaray: upper middle class, predominately female, and middle-aged. The lower classes soon abandoned the theatre altogether and in due time turned to the cinema for entertainment.

After the poor reception given his first play, *Another's Nest* (*El nido ajeno*, 1894), Benavente learned to temper his criticism of bourgeois society. By the end of the century, he had mastered a formula for satires which would offend no one. His more than one hundred and fifty original plays (an average of almost three per year, not including another dozen or so translations and adaptations, as well as numerous miscellaneous writings) employed a great variety of dramatic forms. His typical pieces were drawing-room comedies, with little action and no melodrama. His immediate models seem to have been Oscar Wilde and Arthur Wing Pinero among the

A sketch of Gregorio Martínez Sierra by Bagaria. [National Library, Madrid]

British playwrights and Maurice Donnay and Georges de Porto-Riche among the French. Benavente, who received the Nobel Prize in 1922, actually succeeded in imposing the nineteenth-century bourgeois *alta comedia* on the contemporary Spanish stage. He is best known abroad, however, for *The Bonds of Interest* (*Los intereses creados*, 1907), a comedy of intrigue combining elements from the *commedia dell'arte* tradition with others from the Spanish Golden Age drama, and *The Passion Flower* (*La malquerida*, 1913), a somewhat melodramatic rural drama of incest. His reputation among critics has greatly declined; and with the exception of *The Bonds of Interest* and *The Passion Flower*, his works are seldom performed.

Among those playwrights who constituted what was considered the school of Benavente, two were especially successful. Completely forgotten now but held in high esteem in his time, Manuel Linares Rivas (1878–1938) was an impassioned advocate of "modern" bourgeois ideas in thesis dramas in which the influence of Echegaray's manner was still present. He won fame and fortune with plays such as *The Claw* (*La garra*, 1914), a defense of divorce against clerical obscurantism. Equally forgotten, Gregorio Martínez Sierra (1881–1947) enjoyed great prestiege in Spain and abroad during the first quarter of the century. His plays, which evidence his wife's collaboration, were noted for their sentimentality. In *The Cradle Song* (*Canción de cuna*, 1911), his most famous drama, he timidly approached the theme of frustrated maternal instincts in nuns. More significant than his playwriting was his work as director of Madrid's Eslava Theatre, where during his tenure (1917–1925) he staged, whenever possible, plays by important contemporary foreign authors and promising Spanish dramatists who were not yet established (Martínez Sierra gave Federico García Lorca the opportunity to have his first drama

Playwright Jacinto Benavente as Crispín in his *Los intereses creados*. [Italian Cultural Institute]

performed). Under Martínez Sierra the Eslava Theatre became, in a limited way, Madrid's first important experimental theatre.

The same audiences which flocked to the plays of Benavente and his followers also bestowed their approval on two distinctly different types of theatre, the *costumbrista* comedy and the so-called *teatro poético*, or verse drama. The *costumbrista* theatre derived from that heterogeneous form of popular entertainment known as the *género chico*, which had reached its heights in the last decades of the previous century. In some two hundred plays, which included *sainetes*, *zarzuelas*, and full-length comedies, the brothers Serafín and Joaquín Álvarez Quintero (1871–1938 and 1873–1944) presented a sentimental, charming, and thoroughly false vision of their native Andalusia, the most backward and underdeveloped of all the regions of Spain. The *género chico* usually concentrated on portraying the happy life of Madrid's idle poor. This is the world which attracted Carlos Arniches (1866–1943), himself a bourgeois *madrileño*. Like the Alvarez Quinteros, he began his theatrical career as an author of musical pieces, but he evolved toward a dramaturgy in which social criticism was to play a significant role. The Madrid populace of his *sainetes*, formerly merely picturesque types humorously portrayed, became the subject of his compassion. At the same time, degraded, grotesque characters foreshadowing Valle Inclán's *esperpento* technique began to appear in his longer plays, commencing with *The Young Lady from Trévelez* (*La señorita de Trévelez*, 1916), a *tragedia grotesca* ("grotesque tragedy") using black humor to denounce social evils. Arniches was not a revolutionary, and after about 1925 he returned to less aggressive forms of playwriting, once more content to be a purveyor of lightweight entertainment. The public's appetite for such fare had not decreased, which explained the enormous success of Pedro Muñoz Seca (1881–1936), a name associated with the coarse humor of the *astracán*, a degraded form of the *género chico*. Though the Quinteros and Muñoz Seca have faded into oblivion, there has been a revival of interest in Arniches. In the summer of 1980 there were three productions of Arniches's works in Madrid, two of them officially sponsored by the municipality.

The third type of theatre which appealed to the public of this period was verse drama, whose resurgence on the Spanish stage stemmed initially from the successful presentation of the historical play *The Daughters of the Cid* (*Las hijas del Cid*, 1908) by Eduardo Marquina (1879–1946). Though Marquina was to remain the most popular exponent of verse drama, he was soon joined by other dramatists, among them Francisco Villaespesa (1877–1936), who achieved considerable success with rhymed plays of extravagant passion in exotic settings. His *The Fortress of the Pearls* (*El alcázar de las perlas*, 1911) and *Aben Humeya* (1914), for example, were superficial attempts to recreate the atmosphere of Moorish Spain. Like Marquina, Villaespesa has been associated with *modernismo*. A reaction to realism and naturalism, this turn of the century literary movement produced a litera-

The last days of the Spanish occupation of The Netherlands are evoked in Eduardo Marquina's *En Flandres se ha puesto el sol*, shown here in a production by the Compañía Lope de Vega. [Consulate General of Spain]

ture characterized by the ethereal, and the exotic. It primarily affected poetry, for which it opened up a brilliant world of forms, sounds, and rhythms.

In 1921 Luis Fernández Ardavín (1891–   ) established himself as one of the more successful authors of verse drama with *The Lady in Ermine* (*La dama del armiño*), set in the Toledo of El Greco. During the same decade two poets of indisputable merit, Antonio and Manuel Machado (1875–1939 and 1874–1947), motivated by financial considerations, turned to the theatre and collaborated on a series of verse dramas which added nothing to the literary reputation of either. The *teatro poético* flourished in Spain between 1910 and 1930, gradually diminishing thereafter. Despite the fact that the genre was already on the wane, José María Pemán (1898–   ) managed to exploit it successfully in such historical dramas as *The Divine Saint* (*El divino impaciente*, 1933) and *Cisneros* (1934), both of which expressed the views of the Catholic right. Pemán, along with Marquina and Ardavín, is one of the few authors who continued cultivating the *teatro poético* after the 1930s.

In a country heading for a social cataclysm these dramatists, oblivious of reality, entertained themselves and their public with idealized, ahistorical recreations of the nation's past. While they attempted to revive the tradition of seventeenth-century Spanish drama, it was obvious that they were closer to the romantic theatre than to that of the Siglo de Oro. Verse drama on historical subjects was, in effect, a pastiche based on another pastiche. A number of writers whose place in the history of the contemporary Spanish theatre will be discussed below—Valle-Inclán, García Lorca, Alberti, and Miguel Hernández—also wrote verse drama at some point in their careers. In fact, their efforts in this form are far more interesting than those by the conventional *teatro poético* dramatists.

The Spanish theatre of the period under consideration would only be of sociological interest were it not for a number of original writers who attempted to elevate the level of the drama but invariably found the path blocked by the insurmountable barriers of public taste. The poet Federico García Lorca was to be a notable exception in that he managed to achieve popular success without compromising his artistic principles. Though Benavente, Martínez Sierra, the Alvarez Quintero brothers, and Marquina unfortunately continue to be routinely regarded abroad as Spain's foremost twentieth-century dramatists (along with García Lorca, of course), it is now generally recognized that the most significant drama written in Spain during the two decades preceding the proclamation of the Spanish Republic in 1931 was usually denied access to the stage. The Spanish theatre was not receptive to experiment and innovations. Whenever Valle-Inclán, Unamuno, Azorín, Grau, or Gómez de la Serna managed to have one of their plays performed, most of the critics and the major portion of the public tended to reject it.

The men of the "generation of 1898," that loose-knit group of writers vitally concerned with the historical plight of their country and who played a key role in the rebirth of Spanish literature, were all dissatisfied with the state of the drama. Even Benavente, whose inclusion as part of that movement is debatable, began as a reformer of the stage. Three of his contemporaries—Valle-Inclán, Unamuno, and Azorín—were much more intransigent in their attitude toward the theatre.

Until recently even admirers of Ramón del Valle-In-

clán (1866–1936) tended to consider his unorthodox plays as literary works meant to be read rather than staged. Not until the early 1960s, some twenty-five years after his death, did he begin to be seen as a major dramatist.

The reappraisal of Valle-Inclán's dramaturgy was set in motion by the successful Madrid revival of *Divine Words (Divinas palabras)*, a tragicomedy set in rural Galicia and composed in 1920. Though it had originally been staged in 1934, the full impact of the work was not felt until almost four decades later. The richness of the author's plastic conception of the theatre, the extraordinary display of verbal brilliance, and the intensity of passions generated by instinctive human existence brought to mind Fernando de Rojas's fifteenth-century masterpiece, *La Celestina*.

Whatever doubts that remained regarding Valle-Inclán's mastery of the dramatic form were definitively dispelled in 1963, when *Bohemian Lights (Luces de bohemia)*, another major work dating from 1920, was performed for the first time, not in Spain, but in Paris by the company of Jean Vilar under the direction of Georges Wilson. Even though he still has not attained the international reputation achieved by García Lorca, his plays are now regularly performed in Spain and his influence on contemporary Spanish dramatists has been considerable.

Though Valle-Inclán's theatre is undeniably difficult, he was not helped by the fact that his plays required a

Almost five decades after his death, Ramón María del Valle-Inclán's "literary" plays are being widely produced. *Romance de lobos*, staged by the Compañía María Guerrero, is part of a rural trilogy.
[Consulate General of Spain]

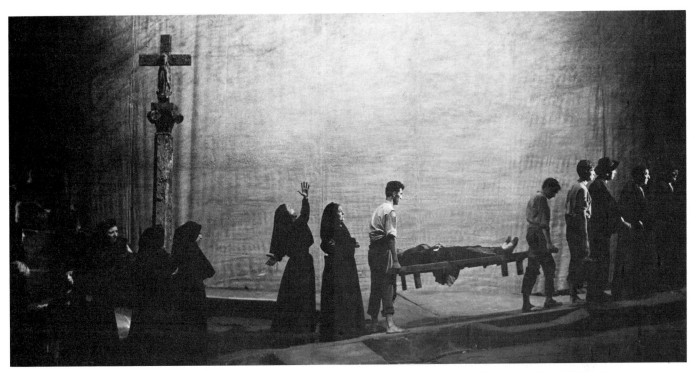

Scene from the Compañía Lope de Vega production of Valle-Inclán's *Divinas palabras*. [Consulate General of Spain]

far more sophisticated level of theatrical production (both technically and from the acting point of view) than the Spanish stage of his time was capable of providing. In addition, the satirical irreverence of his plays caused some of them to be proscribed during the Franco regime (1939–1975). *Bohemian Lights*, Valle-Inclán's first *esperpento*, was not allowed to be performed in Spain until 1972, and then only after certain portions of the text were deleted, while his second experiment with this new mode, *The Horns of Don Friolera (Los cuernos de Don Friolera)*, written in 1921, was barred from the Spanish stage until after the end of Franco's dictatorship, as it was considered offensive to the military establishment. The rediscovery of Valle-Inclán is undoubtedly the most important event in the history of the contemporary Spanish theatre.

Valle-Inclán's theatrical creativity reached its peak in the years following World War I, when expressionism and other avant-garde movements were manifested in all the arts. It was then that he created the *esperpento*, one of the most original attempts in our century to explore the dramatic possibilities of the grotesque. Like Unamuno, Valle-Inclán had a tragic sense of life, but it was inspired more by the calamities of Spanish society than by religious or metaphysical considerations. Though his *esperpentos* focus on exclusively Spanish subjects, his place in modern European drama seems assured. It has been demonstrated that he anticipated Brecht's technique of artistic distance, the theatre of the absurd, and Artaud's theatre of cruelty. Miguel de Unamuno (1864–1936) never fully mastered the art of play-writing,

but his theatre is far more worthy of attention than that of many more successful dramatists. Like Valle-Inclán, he made no concessions to public taste. Whereas the former was a man of the theatre—Valle-Inclán had done some acting early in his career, had married an actress, and had moved in theatrical circles—for Unamuno drama was essentially literature. Regardless of the deficiencies in his technique, Unamuno anticipated some important modern tendencies in dramaturgy, among them the employment of a bare stage, the restoration of monologue (a practice abandoned in the nineteenth century),

Scene from Miguel de Unamuno's *El otro*. [Italian Cultural Institute]

A Hundred Years Old by Serafín and Joaquín Álvarez Quintero, with Otis Skinner (seated). New York, Lyceum Theatre, 1929. [Photograph by Vandamm. Theatre Collection, The New York Public Library at Lincoln Center, Astor, Lenox and Tilden Foundations]

and the re-creation of classical myths in a modern setting. An advocate of the need to restore the tragic dimension to drama, he was also a precursor of the existentialist theatre of Jean-Paul Sartre, Albert Camus, and Gabriel Marcel. As early as 1898, when he wrote his first play, *The Sphinx (La esfinge)*, Unamuno had hoped to fuse Calderonian symbolism with Ibsen's intellectual drama and to thereby orient the Spanish theatre in a significant European direction compatible with Spain's own dramatic tradition. He was unable to do so, however, and the only time he experienced anything approaching a success in the theatre was in 1932, shortly after the establishment of the Republic, when *The Other (El otro)*, a drama written 1926, was performed in Madrid and later in Buenos Aires. Several of his plays were staged professionally in the 1960s and 1970s with inconclusive results. While most critics maintain that Unamuno's plays are merely dialogue versions of the themes of his novels and essays, the two genres to which he owes his universal reputation, many remain convinced of their theatrical viability. *See* ARTAUD, ANTONIN; BRECHT, BERTOLT. *See also* THEATRE OF THE ABSURD in glossary.

The case of Azorín, the pen name used by José Martínez Ruiz (1873–1967), is quite different. Aside from a recent television performance of *The Unseen (Lo invisi-*

ble, 1928), no attempt has been made to revive his works, most of which was written between 1926 and 1930. Though he did succeed in having a number of his works performed, his dramaturgy failed to impress either the public or the critics, including the more discriminating ones. To provoke change in the theatre, he incorporated elements of the contemporary European stage—Pirandello, Lenormand, Maeterlinck, Cocteau, and Evreinov—but he was unable to create convincing dramas. His anguished meditations on the themes of time, happiness, and death resulted in a static, essentially undramatic theatre notwithstanding its literary qualities. Azorín's experiments in playwriting were important because another prestigious figure of the "generation of 1898" had joined Valle-Inclán and Unamuno in their battle to revitalize the theatre. A similar intention had motivated Ramón Gómez de la Serna (1888–1963) to return to playwriting. A precocious author, almost all of his works for the theatre were written before he reached his twenty-fourth birthday. Discouraged by the prevailing conditions in the theatre, he had resigned himself to composing dramas which were not intended for performance. Between 1909 and 1912 he published seventeen plays, most of them short pieces. He did not attempt the dramatic form again until 1929, when *The Semi-Beings (Los medios seres)* was staged in Madrid and received with mixed reactions. An avant-garde farce dealing with the human condition, its most notable feature was the presentation of characters who appear onstage split vertically in two, with one segment visible and the other blacked out. Though not a masterpiece by any means, the play was another sign of rebellion against the provincialism of the Spanish stage and its outmoded conventions.

Among the more unfortunate casualties of the Spanish theatre in the early decades of this century was Jacinto Grau (1877–1958), a thoroughly professional dramatist who, having been rejected in his own country, had the bittersweet satisfaction of seeing some of his plays succeed abroad. Grau experimented with different theatrical forms during his career, always determined to rescue Spanish drama from the decadence into which it had sunk. An ardent admirer of Unamuno, he shared the latter's aversion to naturalism, as well as that author's conviction that it was necessary to restore to drama the tragic grandeur and passion so noticeably lacking in the bourgeois theatre. Abandoning earlier attempts to write tragedy—*The Prodigal Son (El hijo pródigo)*, written in 1917 and staged the following year, was the culmination of his efforts in that direction—Grau wrote and published in 1921 his most famous play: *Mr. Pygmalion (El señor de Pigmalión)*. A tragicomic farce bearing a certain thematic resemblance to Pirandello's *Six Characters in Search of an Author*, it was actually inspired by Unamuno's novel *Mist (Niebla*, 1915). Grau's play deals with the relation between an artist and the characters he invents, as well as the robotlike existence of modern man in a dehumanized world of his own creation. It was finally performed in Madrid in 1928, but only after having been staged in Paris in 1923 by Charles Dullin (with

Dullin himself and Antonin Artaud in key roles), by Karel Čapek in Prague two years later, and by Pirandello in Rome in 1926. Because he was hampered throughout his career (in Spain as well as in Argentina, where he lived in exile following the defeat of the Spanish Republic) by his reputation as an author with little box-office appeal, a number of his plays were never staged. Though he is often self-consciously "literary" in his treatment of traditional themes, he surely deserved a better fate.

During the brief existence of the Second Republic (1931–1936) the Spanish theatre, thanks in part to government encouragement of cultural activities, began to show signs of receptivity to change. The pioneering efforts of Valle Inclán, Unamuno, and Grau were about to bear fruit in a new generation of playwrights also committed to the task of renovation. The initiative was taken by Federico García Lorca (1898–1936), whose murder at the hands of Fascist assassins at the start of the Civil War helped bring him international recognition. Even though he had already written several plays, Lorca did not devote himself seriously to the theatre until the early days of the Republic, when he helped found La Barraca. This government-subsidized theatre composed mainly of university students and unpaid amateurs, was created to tour the country and perform plays from the Golden Age repertory before audiences with no access to theatre. Lorca's activities with La Barraca served as a catalyst for his own work as a playwright. During the few years of life left to him, he was to restore to the Spanish drama those elements which had long been missing and which Unamuno deemed essential: tragedy, intensity, and passion.

Alejandro Casona's *La barca sin pescador.* **Madrid, Teatro Bellas Artes, 1963. [New York Public Library Picture Collection]**

As a playwright, Lorca is perhaps best known for his rural dramas, which reflect a tragic side of Andalusian life (in sharp contrast to the quaint and rosy picture found in the superficial comedies of the Álvarez Quintero brothers), with its archaic system of values and its rigid class structures. It was not his intention to write didactic drama, but he was, in effect, calling attention to those repressive aspects of Spanish society—still basically agrarian and feudal—in which natural instincts were subordinated to outmoded social codes or material interests, with women as the principal victims. Essentially a poet, he was still experimenting and searching for an adequate dramatic formula at the time of his murder. Even in his last play, *The House of Bernarda Alba (La casa de Bernada Alba)* completed a few weeks before his death but not performed until 1945 (in Buenos Aires), despite his desire to move in the direction of documentary realism ("*documental fotográfico*" is the term he employed) and the consequent elimination of verse dialogue, the poet very often predominates over the dramatist. Interestingly enough, his most daring experiments in the theatrical medium, his surrealistic plays—*The Audience (El público)* and *When Five Years Pass (Así que pasen cinco años)*, written in 1930 and 1931, respectively were not performed during his lifetime. There were limits to the innovations the traditional public was willing to tolerate.

Alejandro Casona (1908–1965), as Alejandro Rodríguez Alvarez preferred to be known, headed a theatrical company similar to Lorca's La Barraca, the Teatro del Pueblo (People's Theatre), also subsidized by the Ministry of Education. In addition to opening up the theatre to audiences previously excluded, these projects made possible the performance of plays which otherwise would not have found a place on the commercial stage. Moreover, they set a precedent for the university theatre groups formed after the Civil War and the even more important "independent theatre" movement which was to emerge in the late 1960s. A decidedly more modest talent than García Lorca, Casona had already established a reputation as a promising young playwright prior to the outbreak of the Civil War with *The Stranded Mermaid (La sirena varada;* wr. 1929, prod. 1934) and *Our Natacha (Nuestra Natacha,* 1936), a mildly reformist play in its social implications. Both works reveal Casona's tendency to create a world in which fantasy transforms reality into something more pleasant. A staunch supporter of the Republic, he was forced to seek exile in Argentina, where he continued to write successfully for the stage, an activity which did not interfere with his work as a director. Casona later publicly admitted his ideological "errors" and was allowed to return to Spain in 1962. He was received with open arms as a repentant *rojo*, or "Red" (the term used by the Right to designate those who had sided with the Republic), and from the moment of his arrival until his death three years later he enjoyed extraordinary popularity with bourgeois audiences. Dissident intellectuals, however, lost no time in branding his theatre evasionist and irrelevant to the problems of a country living under a dictatorship.

In addition to García Lorca, two other writers who

had already established themselves as poets turned their attention to the theatre: Rafael Alberti (1902–) and Miguel Hernández (1910–1942). From the point of view of the drama, the more important of the two is Alberti, whose first play, *The Uninhabited Man (El hombre deshabitado),* completed in 1930 and staged the following year, was a notable success. An allegorical *auto* in the Calderonian tradition, it had, however, nothing in common ideologically with the seventeenth-century religious drama. The theme of original sin and paradise lost is presented from a thoroughly modern perspective. Alberti's next work, *Fermín Galán* (1931), a political drama dealing with a real event from recent history, caused such a furor that the safety curtain had to be lowered to protect the actors from the irate spectators. Actively committed to the Republican cause, he managed to flee Spain just as the Civil War was ending. He continued to write highly imaginative dramas which were staged abroad, but his theatre was banned in Spain all during the Franco era. Alberti's dramaturgy has followed two principal directions: poetic theatre and political theatre. *The Monster (El adefesio,* 1944), based like Lorca's *The House of Bernarda Alba,* on observation of an Andalusian family and written partly in verse, stands out among his poetic dramas, while *Night and War in the Prado Museum (Noches de guerra en el Museo del Prado,* 1956) is perhaps the finest play written on the Spanish Civil War.

Since Alberti's return to Spain in 1977, both works have been performed there, with critics and public divided along ideological lines. Like Alberti, Miguel Hernández had also become a Communist. In 1933, while still in his Catholic period, he had attempted a modern *auto sacramental,* but his most notable contribution to the Spanish theatre was *The Bravest Farmer (El labrador de más aire,* 1937), inspired by Lope de Vega's rural dramas. The theme of social justice is treated from a revolutionary perspective. While crude and simplistic in the formulation of its thesis—the intention of the work was to stir up emotions on the Republican side—this verse play has exquisite lyrical moments, attaining levels not even remotely matched by any of the cultivators of the bourgeois *teatro poético.* Hernández's untimely death was a loss not only for poetry but also for dramatic literature.

Another dramatist of considerable interest whose efforts to renovate the theatre were cut short by the Civil War was Max Aub (1903–1972). He and Alberti are the two outstanding playwrights of the Spanish theatre in exile. Unlike Alberti, however, Aub died before his plays could be performed in postwar Spain. An avant-garde dramatist prior to 1936 (his first experimental plays date from the early 1920s), he wrote his most important works in Mexico, where he began his life anew. Aub was an extremely prolific novelist, essayist, and dramatist. Most of the plays he composed outside Spain form part of a great chronicle, or epic, of modern man: the Spanish Civil War, World War II, concentration camps, anti-semitic persecution, exile, the Cold War, and scientifically organized terror. The majority of his dramas have never been performed, and it remains to be seen whether Aub will finally find his rightful place on the Spanish stage.

See Alberti, Rafael; Álvarez Quintero, Serafín and Joaquín; Arniches y Barrera, Carlos; Aub, Max; Benavente, Jacinto; Casona, Alejandro; García Lorca, Federico; Grau Delgado, Jacinto; Linares Rives y Astrey, Manuel; Martínez Sierra, Gregorio; Muñoz Seca, Pedro; Péman y Pemartín, José María; Unamuno, Miguel de; Valle-Inclán, Ramón María del; Villaespesa, Francisco.

The Twentieth Century: From 1939 to the Present

The Spanish Civil War, which raged from 1936 to 1938, resulted in the overthrow of the democratic Republic established in 1931 and the imposition of a dictatorship that would endure until 1975. Before the outcome of the struggle was finally decided in favor of the so-called Nationalists led by Generalissimo Francisco Franco, over a half million people had been killed. Fashioned on fascist models—Hitler and Mussolini had ensured Franco's victory—the new regime, which reunited church and state, set out to eradicate any trace of unorthodox religious, political or philosophical thought from the nation's cultural life. A rigid system of censorship was instituted and continued to function throughout the duration of a dictatorship that was to last thirty-six years.

No artistic medium was more severely repressed than the theatre. Any work deemed detrimental to the prevailing political, social, or moral order was banned outright or, at best, authorized only in censored and distorted versions. Equally restrictive was the censorship which writers imposed on themselves. The fear of subversive ideas from abroad was reflected in the government's reluctance to allow performances of plays by the major contemporary foreign dramatists, a situation which did not change substantially until late in the 1960s. However, if serious international theatre was not encouraged, official censorship was only partly to blame. The task of the censors was made easier by the existence of a bourgeois public comfortable only with plays that reaffirmed its class values and did not depart from tra-

Federico García Lorca. [National Library, Madrid]

A Greek production of García Lorca's *Doña Rosita the Spinster,* with Anna Synodinous in the title role. [Greek National Tourist Office]

ditional forms. There was nothing new in this, and even now that government censorship has been abolished, the vast majority of the plays performed on the commercial stage reflect a similar mentality.

As a result of the Civil War, the Spanish theatre entered one of the bleakest periods in its long history. The efforts at renewal which had begun to take effect during the brief existence of the Republic came to an abrupt end. The writers most strongly committed to the idea of reforming the theatre were either dead or in exile. Two notable dramatists who produced all their theatre in exile were Pedro Salinas (1892–1951), a poet of the same brilliant generation that included García Lorca and Alberti, and José Ricardo Morales (1915–   ), whose work has only recently become known in Spain. (A number of Galician and Catalan writers shared the same fate.) All in all, the country's finest writers, foremost stage directors, scenic designers, and performers were also in exile. Most of them settled in Latin America, as did the majority of exiled writers, where they were able to resume their activities. The leading Spanish actress of her day, Margarita Xirgu, established herself in Argentina and, with the collaboration of other exiles, brought to Latin American audiences a vastly superior Spanish theatre than that which was being presented in Spain in the decade following the Civil War.

The Spanish stage of the 1940s (particularly up to 1945) was distinguished by the wretched quality of its fare: escapist trivialities, historical plays exulting the glories of a bygone age, pseudo-folkloric spectacles and the ever popular *revistas,* or musical reviews, and modern melodramas expressing the ideology of those who had won the Civil War. Benavente, ever more tired and reactionary, returned to the stage and between 1939 and his death in 1954, produced some thirty-five new plays, few of which can compare with those of his early period. The names of Marquina (this loyal defender of traditionalist Spain died in 1946) and the Alvarez Quintero brothers (Serafín had died in 1938, but Joaquín, who lived on until 1944, continued signing the plays which he was now writing alone as if his brother had not ceased to exist) reappeared on the theatre billboards. The only relief from this fare was provided by occasional Golden Age productions, a few experimental university-affiliated groups, and the comic theatre of Enrique Jardiel Poncela (1902–1952) and Miguel Mihura Santos (1905–1977).

The work of these two dramatists continues to generate interest, and the Madrid public has seen several successful revivals of their plays. Starting with his first comedy, *A Sleepless Spring Night* (*Una noche de primavera sin sueño,* 1927), and continuing until well after the Civil War, Jardiel Poncela envisioned himself as an experimental dramatist who could contribute to the revitalization of the Spanish theatre. Unfortunately, his plays do not go beyond attempts to adapt traditional bourgeois comedy to certain experimental tendencies in the modern theatre. Spanish audiences after the war were so narrow-minded in their tastes that they did not approve of even these minimal innovations. Mihura was to reach his peak as a humorist in *Three Top Hats* (*Tres sombreros de copa*), a play written in 1932, but which had to wait until 1952 to reach the stage and then only thanks to a university experimental group. While the piece has been linked with the theatre of the absurd, particularly in its use of language, it stops just short of entering the basically tragic world of true absurdist farce. Though Mihura went on to enjoy great success in the postwar theatre, he was

A scene from Miguel Mihura Santos's *Tres sombreros de copa,* a play with absurdist overtones that had to wait twenty years before being produced. [Consulate General of Spain]

forced to make concessions and the quality of his work declined as the years passed.

Benavente, who earlier in the century had spawned a school of followers, now saw another generation of playwrights successfully adopt his formula. The first wave of neo-Benaventian dramatists includes (along with the previously mentioned José María Pemán) Juan Ignacio Luca de Tena (1897–   ), Joaquín Calvo-Sotelo (1905–   ), Edgar Neville (1899–   ), José López Rubio (1903–   ), and Victor Ruiz Iriarte (1912–   ). With the exception of the latter, they had all had one or more plays performed before the war and were now ready to take the place of Benavente, Marquina, and the Álvarez Quinteros in the bourgeois theatre. Intent on pleasing their middle-class public, they tended to cultivate the drama of ideas (the ideological content was, of course, conservative) and escapist comedies (impeccably constructed), two complementary forms sometimes present in a work by a single author (Pemán or Calvo-Sotelo, for example). The neo-Benaventian style prospered throughout the 1950s, and has continued to survive up to the present in the works of such playwrights as Juan Antonio de Laiglesia (1917–   ), Jaime Salom (1925–   ), and to an extent Alfonso Paso (1926–1977) and Antonio Gala (1936–   ).

The other type of theatre which has remained extremely popular with bourgeois audiences is the comedy associated with the deteriorating tradition of Jardiel Poncela and Mihura. After the death of Jardiel Poncela in 1952, Mihura was left the undisputed master of the comic style in playwriting. Two of his collaborators, Antonio de Lara (1898–   ), more commonly known as Tono, and Alvaro de Laiglesia (1918–   ), also ingratiated themselves with the postwar public. Other dramatists who have successfully exploited the humoristic theatre are Carlos Llopis (1912–1971), Jaime de Armiñán (1927–   ), and Juan J. Antonio Millán (1936–   ), as well as the recently deceased Alfonso Paso, the most prolific Spanish playwright since Benavente and the bourgeois public's favorite author throughout most of the 1950s and 1960s. The brand of comedy cultivated by the imitators of Jardiel Poncela and Mihura has been described as the modern version of that debased form of the *género chico* known as the *astracán*, though the present-day dramatists perhaps employ a more intellectual humor than their prewar predecessors (Muñoz Seca, for example). The possible evolution of the humoristic theatre had come to a halt in the experiments of Jardiel Poncela and Mihura. The serious humoristic dimension would only be restored to the Spanish theatre by Fernando Arrabal and the new avant-garde playwrights, but it was to be a different type of humor than that with which the bourgeois public was familiar—corrosive, irreverent, black humor.

The first sign of a theatre that dared suggest that postwar Spain was not the best of all possible worlds was the performance in 1949 of *Story of a Stairway (Historia de una escalera)*, a drama in the naturalist tradition

Best known for his work in the naturalist tradition, Antonio Buero Vallejo is also the author of *La detonación,* a two-part fantasy presented in 1977 by Madrid's Teatro Bellas Artes. [Photograph courtesy of Andrés Franco]

Un soñador para un pueblo by Buero Vallejo, as presented by the Compañía Lope de Vega. [Consulate General of Spain]

of Elmer Rice's *Street Scene* (1929). The author, Antonio Buero Vallejo (1916–   ), was a former Republican soldier who had been imprisoned for seven years. The success of the play allowed Buero to devote himself to restoring a measure of seriousness and dignity to the Spanish theatre. Though the author was expressing the point of view of those who had lost the Civil War, he did so in a stark, obliquely critical manner which the censors were usually willing to tolerate. Inspired by Buero's example, other dramatists began to probe contemporary social problems from a critical perspective, giving rise in the 1950s to social realism in the theatre. Known as the "realist generation," the group included Alfonso Sastre (1926–   ), Lauro Olmo (1923–   ), José Martín Recuerda (1925–   ), José María Rodríguez Méndez (1925–   ), and Carlos Muñiz (1927–   ). The only one who became known outside Spain was Sastre, whose *Condemned Squad* (*Escuadra hacia la muerte*, 1953), an antimilitaristic play which implicitly criticized authoritarianism, was presented by a university group and immediately banned. It ranks as one of the landmarks of the postwar Spanish theatre for its efforts to rise above bourgeois mediocrity.

Though Franco had won the Civil War, by the early 1950s it was clear that he had lost the cultural battle. The new generation of intellectuals, which had not taken part in the war, identified with the opposition. The realist dramatists coincided ideologically in their denunciation of contemporary Spanish society. Even though at first most of them sought artistic inspiration in the naturalistic style of *Story of a Stairway*, it would not be the only path they followed: Muñiz evolved in the direction of neoexpressionism; Rodríguez Méndez advanced toward the grotesque farce of the Valle Inclán tradition; Martín

Recuerda has continued to explore the depths of a tragic Andalusia in a manner which combines the legacy of Valle Inclán with that of García Lorca; and Olmo has not only experimented with Brechtian techniques, but in his last works he has approached the allegorical forms favored by the avant-garde dramatists. Sastre, whose first attempts at drama in the 1940s reveal an uncommitted avant-garde orientation with existentialist overtones, would eventually move beyond social realism, and concentrate on transcending the Brechtian antinomy between tragedy and epic *See* EPIC THEATRE in glossary.

Like their avant-garde counterparts, the dramatists of the "realist generation" were all influenced by Valle Inclán, though in the former this influence affects primarily the language, while in the latter it is to be found chiefly in the characterization and situations. Late in the 1950s and the early 1960s Buero Vallejo and the other dissident dramatists of the realist school achieved a series of important stage successes: Buero Vallejo with *A Dreamer for a People* (*Un soñador para un pueblo*, 1958), *Las Meninas* (1960), and *The Concert at Saint Ovide* (*El concierto de San Ovidio*, 1962); Sastre with *Death Thrust* (*La cornada*, 1960) and *In the Net* (*En la red*, 1961); Muñiz with *The Inkwell* (*El tintero*, 1961); Rodríguez Méndez with *The Innocents of the Moncloa* (*Los inocentes de la Moncloa*, 1961); Olmo with *The Shirt* (*La camisa*, 1962); and Martín Recuerda with *The Savages in Puente San Gil* (*Las salvajes en*

Ana Kleiber by Alfonso Sastre, as presented by the Théâtre Hébertot in Paris in 1961 with Françoise Spira in the title role. Pierre Tabard was Alfredo. [French Cultural Services]

Puente San Gil, 1963). For a brief time it appeared that the prospects for the drama were becoming more positive, but the tightening up of censorship and the subsequent reaction of the impresarios who were afraid to risk financial loss by staging potentially troublesome plays brought the renovation process to a halt. Only Buero Vallejo continued to have his plays performed (though no longer in government-owned theatres), no doubt because of his prestige and the more tempered nature of his criticism.

While the names of the dramatists of the "realist generation" disappeared almost completely from the theatre billboards after 1962 (only after Franco's death did some of them reappear, as in the case of Martín Recuerda with a play that was a major success), that decade was to see Alfonso Paso become the most performed Spanish playwright of the postwar period. From 1962 to 1965 he was forced to share his popularity with Alejandro Casona, the prodigal son who was now back in the fold.

A large percentage of the plays staged in Spain are translations and adaptations. Though most of these works of foreign origin tend to be lightweight comedies (usually French or English), beginning in the late 1960s a number of works from the most nonconformist segment of the modern world drama were allowed to be performed: Brecht, Sartre, Genet, Pinter, Beckett, Weiss, Albee, Mrozek, Behan, O'Casey, Wesker, and others. The Spanish government was now interested in projecting a liberal image abroad and this explains a tolerance which was, however, extended only to foreign authors and those Spanish dramatists now sadly dead: García Lorca and Valle Inclán.

During the late 1960s an avant-garde movement began to manifest itself in the Spanish theatre. There had been earlier indications that a new sensibility was starting to develop in the drama, but it was not until after 1968 that these innovative trends, due in large measure to influences from abroad as well as from the rediscovery of Valle Inclán, showed signs of crystallization. A comparable reaction against the prevailing tenets of social realism had already taken place in the novel and in poetry. Generally referred to as the "New Spanish Theatre" (*Nuevo teatro español*), the phenomenon has brought forth some gifted playwrights whose work had been suppressed during the Franco years. This vanguard movement has also been marked by the emergence of some excellent experimental groups which constitute the Independent Theatre, a loosely formed alliance of young actors and directors seeking an alternative to the commercial stage. One would expect the Independent Theatre to support the avant-garde dramatists, but this has been the exception rather than the rule. Despite the political repression exerted by the Franco dictatorship, Spanish avant-garde drama, always sharply satirical on social and political issues, has managed to survive extremely difficult conditions, and new plays are constantly being written, albeit seldom performed.

Works by several of the avant-garde dramatists have been successfully staged in Madrid and elsewhere in Spain since the end of Franco's rule. Though these writers continue to occupy a marginal place in the Spanish theatre, they have been receiving growing recognition as one of the most exciting and fertile elements of contemporary Spanish culture. A number of their works have been published in the United States, both in translation and in Spanish, and some were first performed here.

The new Spanish avant-garde dramatists do not share the vision of the world normally associated with the theatre of the absurd, although their debt to it is undeniable. The fundamental difference between the absurdist dramas of French or English origin and those

Scene from *Los esclavos* by Antonio Martínez Ballesteros, as presented in Toledo in 1971. [Consulate General of Spain]

written in Spain is that the former tend to be pessimistic, while the latter on the whole are not. Whereas Beckett, Ionesco, or Pinter produce plays with metaphysical overtones, the Spaniards, closer in spirit to the avant-garde dramatists writing in German (Friedrich Dürrenmatt, Max Frisch, Wolfgang Hildescheimer, etc.), normally focus on social and political issues, with the human condition as a subordinate theme. Although the plays of the avant-garde dramatists spring from the realities of Spanish life, the problems they denounce are universal. This distinguishes their work from that of Buero Vallejo and the dramatists of the "realist generation," whose work never fully broke with the naturalistic style and was more often of local than universal interest. Combining allegory and fantasy, the plays of the avant-garde dramatists are usually not set in any specific time or place. Though it can be argued that this device was intended to deceive the censors, it is also true that it has been a common feature of all avant-garde drama. Broadly stated, the principal themes which reappear in their plays are alienation and the exploitative, deceptively repressive character of contemporary society. Despite the fact that theirs is not a flight from reality, but rather an attempt to probe it more deeply, they still encounter opposition from several influential critics who continue to view realism in traditional terms.

Censorship is now, for all intents and purposes, a thing of the past; yet these dramatists (once classified as "underground" because performance or publication of their plays was prohibited) still are faced with serious obstacles. There exists in Spain (perhaps to a greater extent than elsewhere) a theatre "establishment" comprised of successful authors, critics, actors, directors, and impresarios, all of whom share common interests. This group determines what plays will be performed not only in private theatres but in state-operated or state-subsidized theatres as well. It was precisely in reaction to this situation that the Independent Theatre came into being (its chief source of inspiration was Off-Off Broadway). Unfortunately for the avant-garde dramatists, the Independent Theatre groups are generally inclined to reject "authored" texts in favor of collective works.

Noteworthy among the older dramatists (born before the Civil War and contemporaries of the "realist generation") of the avant-garde movement are Luis Riaza (1925–   ), José Ruibal (1925–   ), and Miguel Romero Esteo (1930–   ), three of the most original writers of the contemporary Spanish theatre. Mention should be made as well of Francisco Nieva (1927–   ), also a noted stage designer; Juan Antonio Castro (1927–1980), whose career was tragically cut short just as he was beginning to establish himself in the theatre; and two playwrights who, along with Ruibal, were the first representatives of the "New Spanish Theatre" to be translated and to be published in the United States: José María Bellido (1921–   ) and Antonio Martínez Ballesteros (1929–   ). Luis Matilla (1939–   ), Manuel Martínez Mediero (1939–   ), Angel García Pintado (1940–   ), Eduardo Quiles (1940–   ), and Jerónimo López Mozo (1942–   )stand out among the younger dramatists.

Playwright José Ruibal (left) and director Alfred G. Brooks on the set of the former's *The Man and the Fly,* which had its world premiere at the State University of New York at Binghamton in November, 1971. [Photograph by Chris Focht]

Fernando Arrabal (1932–   ) is Spain's best-known living dramatist. Widely translated and performed internationally, he belongs to a second wave of Spanish artists and intellectuals who chose exile rather live in the repressive atmosphere of Franco's Spain. Barred from returning to his native country and completely proscribed after a mock trial in 1967, Arrabal had never been professionally performed in Spain until 1977. Arrabal is undoubtedly one of the forerunners of the avant-garde movement in the Spanish theatre, but he left Spain in the middle 1950s and was absorbed into the French theatre with respect to production and publication. He is another example of a writer who will perhaps never be fully recovered by the Spanish theatre, even though

In 1974 Miguel Romero Esteo's *Pasodoble* was presented in Madrid as part of the First International Theatre Festival. [Photograph courtesy of Ditirambo, Teatro Estudio]

Luis Matilla's *El observador,* as produced by the Puerto Rican Traveling Theatre, New York, in 1980.

Spanish and not French is his language of expression. (In recent years Arrabal has admitted that he writes his plays in Spanish, then translates them into French, with the aid of his wife, a native of France and professor of Spanish. That he kept this fact hidden for so long seems to have been part of a scheme designed to make it easier for him to gain international recognition.)

Since Franco's death and the subsequent establishment in 1977 of a democratic constitutional monarchy, the Spanish theatre has been in a disoriented state. The elimination of censorship resulted in a proliferation of pornographic and semipornographic comedies. (Spain under Franco had been subjected to nearly forty years of sexual as well as political and intellectual repression.) For several years following Franco's death, total nudity seemed to be the formula for assuring a play's success. This trend began to subside in 1978. While the Madrid stage was in the midst of a severe economics crisis, the 1978 season also saw the emergence of a new theatre of the ultra-Right. Threatened by major changes all around them, the nostalgic admirers of the dictatorship now turned to the stage for the purpose of propagating their ideology. Such a ploy was unnecessary when Franco was alive. Two playwrights, Eloy Herrera and Antonio D. Olano, have been the chief beneficiaries of the discontent with which the more reactionary sectors of Spanish society have greeted the new democracy. Unlike the ideologically conservative plays of the Franco era, the theatre of the neo-Fascist movement is explicitly antidemocratic. It owes its success not only to the surviving *franquista* elements but also to the opposition or apprehension felt by many ordinary, apolitical Spaniards toward the disintegration of the family, liberalization within the Catholic Church, abortion, divorce, homosexuality, pornography, separatism, terrorism, a rising delinquency problem, the use of drugs among young people, and other related matters which are now surfacing in this transitional period in Spanish history. To make matters worse, the economy is weak, with unemployment on the

increase, uncontrolled inflation, and a mounting burden of foreign debt. Democracy has not created these problems, but the theatre of the ultra-Rightists, with its simplistic approach to complex realities, would have us believe otherwise.

One potentially positive development has been the creation of the National Dramatic Center *(Centro Dramático Nacional),* a government-financed institution charged with presenting works from the traditional Spanish repertory and contemporary world theatre, as well as plays by new Spanish authors (both Luis Matilla and Luis Riaza have enjoyed commercial production thanks to this program). Permanent regional theatres have been established in various cities, and a system of state subsidies for independent groups is now in effect. The results of these measures still leave much to be desired. Theatrical activities continue to be controlled by a relatively small clique, even more powerful than before, since some members of the clique are now functionaries in the state bureaucracy; most of the new dramatists see few real possibilities for having their plays performed on a regular basis; and the Independent Theatre is in a desperate situation. Two factors seem to be the primary causes of its decline: first, it no longer fulfills the same political function as during the time of Franco's dictatorship, when to participate in or to witness an Independent Theatre performance had unmistakable political implications; secondly, with the creation of permanent regional theatres, many groups are no longer willing to go on tour, an essential feature of the Independent Theatre from its very inception. *See* ARRABAL, FERNANDO; BELLIDO CORMENZANA, JOSÉ MARÍA; BUERO VALLEJO, ANTONIO; CALVO-SOTELO, JOAQUÍN; GALA, ANTONIO; GIMÉNEZ ARNAU Y GRAN, JOSÉ MARÍA; JARDIEL PONCELA, ENRIQUE; LAIGLESIA, JUAN ANTONIO DE; LAIGLESIA GONZÁLEZ LABARGA, ÁLAVARO DE; LÓPEZ RUBIO, JOSÉ; LUCA DE TENA, JUAN; MARTIN RECUERDA, JOSÉ; MARTÍNEZ

Fernando Arrabal (second from left) with the director and cast of *Inquisición* following its opening in Barcelona in September, 1980. Also appearing were (l. to r.) Carmen Sansa, director A. Berenguer, Alfonso Guirado, and Juan Borras. [Photograph courtesy of Andrés Franco]

BALLESTEROS, ANTONIO; MATILLA, LUIS; MIHURA SANTOS, MIGUEL; MUÑIZ, CARLOS; NEVILLE, EDGAR; NIEVA, FRANCISCO; OLMO, LAURO; PASO GIL, ALFONSO; RIAZA, LUIS; RODRÍGUEZ MÉNDEZ, JOSÉ MARÍA; ROMERO ESTEO, MIGUEL; RUIBAL, JOSÉ; RUIZ IRIARTE, VICTOR; SASTRE, ALFONSO.

This survey has been necessarily limited to the Spanish theatre written in Castilian for the obvious reason that Castilian is, of the several languages spoken in that country, the one with the widest universal projection. It should be pointed out, however, that since the second half of the nineteenth century regional literatures and cultures have experienced a strong revival in Spain. This has been especially true of Catalonia, where the vernacular language had reached great heights in the Middle Ages, a period in which it could boast of such figures as Ausias March (1397–1459), Ramon Muntaner (1265–1336), Joanot Martorell (ca. 1410–1468), and Jaume Roig (ca. 1400–1478). Starting with the romantic movement up to the present, Catalan literature has exhibited an extraordinary vigor. In drama it has since then produced such notable authors as Ángel Guimerà (1845–1924), Ignasi Iglésias (1871–1929), Josep M. de Sagarra (1894–1961), Salvador Espriu (1913–   ), Joan Brossa (1919–   ), and Manuel de Pedrolo (1918–   ). Among the numerous younger Catalan dramatists, Josep Benet i Jornet (1940–   ) seems to be the most talented. While the Catalan theatre of today is in many respects comparable to the Spanish theatre written in Castilian, the superiority of the Catalans as regards production and staging is generally acknowledged. Unfortunately, it is a theatre written in a language of only regional scope (even translations into Castilian are nonexistent or hard to come by). *See* CATALAN DRAMA; GUIMERÀ, ÁNGEL.

Stimulated by the awakening of nationalist sentiments, the Galician theatre has recently been showing signs of vitality. The origins of the phenomenon can be traced back, as in the case of Catalonia, to the last century. However, for reasons that cannot be gone into here, the indigenous cultural movement in Galicia has lacked the strength of its Catalan counterpart. The present vitality of the Galician theatre is still more of an aspiration than a reality. It should be noted that the greatest dramatist to have come from Galicia, Valle Inclán, wrote in Castilian, as does the contemporary avant-garde playwright José Ruibal, who hails from the same region. The most distinguished figure of the Galician theatre was Alfonso Rodríguez Castelao (1886—1950).

ANDRÉS FRANCO

CRITICISM

This list is limited to general works. In the case of anthologies and collections of texts, only those volumes which contain plays by a number of dramatists are listed. Bibliographies for particular authors are supplied at the end of the individual author articles.

General

Historia general de las literaturas hispánicas, ed. by G. Díaz Plaja, 5 vols., Barcelona, 1949–1956 (contains individual monographs on the theatre of each period); *A Literary History of Spain*, ed. by R. O. Jones, 8 vols., London, 1971–1973 (individual volumes by leading British Hispanists); R. E. Chandler and K. Schwartz, *A New History of Spanish Literature*, Baton Rouge, La., 1961; E. González López, *Historia de la literatura española*, 2

vols., New York, 1962–1965; M. de Montolíu, *Manual de historia de la literatura castellana*, Barcelona, 1957; A. del Río, *Historia de la literatura española*, rev. ed., 2 vols., New York, 1963; *Diccionario de la literatura española*, ed. by G. Bleiberg, and J. Marías, 3d ed., Madrid, 1964; J. Simón Díaz, *Manual de bibliografía de la literatura española*, 2nd ed., Barcelona, 1966; A. Valbuena Prat, *Historia de la literatura española*, 8th ed., 4 vols., Barcelona, 1968; J. L. Alborg, *Historia de la literatura española*, 4 vols. to date, Madrid, 1970– ; J. Hurtado and A. González-Palencia, *Historia de la literatura española*, Madrid, 1943; *Historia de la literatura española*, ed. by J. M. Díez Borque, 3 vols., Madrid, 1974–1975 (contains individual monographs on the theatre of each period); R. S. Rudder, *The Literature of Spain in English Translation*, New York, 1975.

General Bibliographies

C. A. de la Barrera y Leirado, *Catálogo bibliográfico del teatro antiguo español desde los orígenes hasta mediados del siglo XVIII*, 1860 (repr. Madrid, 1969); E. Cotarelo y Mori, *Bibliografía de la controversias sobre la licitud del teatro en España*, Madrid, 1904; R. A. O'Brien, *Spanish Plays in English Translation: An Annotated Bibliography*, New York, 1963; W. T. McCready, *Bibliografía temática de estudios sobre el teatro español antiguo*, Toronto, 1966 (includes studies published between 1850 and 1950); L. S. Thompson, *A Bibliography of Spanish Plays on Microcards*, Hamden, Conn., 1968; L. T. Valdivielso, *España: Bibliografía de un teatro "silenciado,"* Society of Spanish and Spanish-American Studies, 1979 (an annotated bibliography of the contemporary Spanish avant-garde drama with biographical material and commentaries on each play); R. L. Grismer, *Bibliography of the Drama of Spain and Spanish America*, 2 vols., Minneapolis, n.d.

Bulletin of the Comediantes includes biographical notes in each of its numbers; *PMLA* issues an annual bibliography; and *The Year's Work in Modern Language Studies* includes an indispensable critical bibliography.

Critical Studies

A. Histories of Spanish Theatre

A. Valbuena Prat, *Literatura dramática española*, 1930 (rept. Barcelona, 1950); A. Valbuena Prat, *Historia del teatro español*, Barcelona, 1956; J. H. Parker, *Breve historia del teatro español*, Mexico City, 1957; C. V. Aubrun, *Histoire de Théâtre espagnol*, Paris, 1965; F. Ruiz Ramón, *Historia del teatro español*, 3d ed., 2 vols., Madrid, 1977–1979.

B. Middle Ages and Golden Age

H. Mérimée, *L'Art dramatique à Valencia*, Toulouse, 1913; W. S. Jack, *The Early "Entremés" in Spain: The Rise of a Dramatic Form*, Philadelphia, 1923; *Dramatic Theory in Spain: Extracts from Literature before and during the Golden Age*, ed. by H. J. Chaytor, Cambridge, 1925; J. Meredith, *Introito and Loa in the Spanish Drama of the Sixteenth Century*, Philadelphia, 1928; W. H. Shoemaker, *The Multiple Stage in Spain during the Fifteenth and Sixteenth Centuries*, 1935 (repr. Westport, Conn., 1973); R. L. Grismer, *The Influence of Plautus in Spain before Lope de Vega*, New York, 1944; J. García Soriano, *El teatro universitario y humanístico en España*, Toledo, 1945; A. A. Parker, *The Approach to the Spanish Drama of the Golden Age*, Diamante Series VI, London, 1957; R. B. Donavan, *Liturgical Drama in Medieval Spain*, Toronto, 1958; J.–L. Fleckniakoska, *La formation de l'"auto" religieux en Espagne avant Calderón (1550–1635)*, Paris, 1961; N. D. Shergold and J. F. Varey, *"Los autos sacramentales en Madrid en la época de Calderón (1637–1681),"* Estudios y documentos, Madrid, 1961; H. A. Rennert, *The Spanish Stage in the Time of Lope de Vega*, 2nd ed., New York, 1963; E. Asensio, *Itinerario del entremés desde Lope de Rueda a Quiñones de Benavente*, Madrid, 1965; C. V. Aubrun, *La comédie espagnole (1600–1680)*, Paris, 1965; N. Salomon, *Recherches sur le thème paysan dans la "comedia" au temps du Lope de Vega*, Bordeaux, 1965; A. A. Beyersterveldt, *Repercussions du souci de la pureté sur la conception de l'honneur dans la "Comedia Nueva" espagnole*, Leiden, 1966; J. P. W. Crawford, *Spanish Drama before Lope de Vega*, 3d rev. ed. Philadelphia, 1967; N. D. Shergold, *A History of the Spanish Stage from Medieval Times until the End of the Seventeenth Century*, Oxford, 1967; B. W. Wardropper, *Introducción al teatro religioso del Siglo de Oro*, rev. ed., Salamanca, 1967; E. Carilla, *El teatro español en la Edad de Oro (Escenarios y representaciones)*, Buenos Aires, 1968; A. Hermenegildo, *La tragedia en el Renacimiento español*, Madrid, 1968; E. W. Hesse, *Análisis e interpretación de la comedia*, Madrid, 1968; H. López Morales, *Tradición y creación en los orígenes del teatro castellano*, Madrid, 1968; O. Arróniz, *La influencia italiana en el nacimiento de la comedia española*, Madrid, 1969; M. Wilson, *Spanish Drama of the Golden Age*, Oxford, 1969; F. Sánchez Escribano, and F. Porqueras Mayo, *Preceptiva dramática española del Renacimiento y el Barroco*, 2d ed., Madrid, 1971; J. Varey and N. D. Shergold, *Teatros y comedias en Madird: Estudio y documentos*, 4 vols., London, 1971–1979 (vol. I, 1600–1650; vol II, 1651–1665; vol III, 1666–1687; vol. IV, 1687–1699); E. M. Wilson and D. Moir, *The Golden Age Drama (1492–1700)*, London, 1971 (vol. 3 of *A Literary History of Spain*, ed. by R. O. Jones); E. W. Hesse, *La comedia y sus intérpretes*, Madrid, 1972; J. A. Maravall, *Teatro y literatura en la sociedad barroca*, Madrid, 1972; J.–L. Fleckniakoska, *La loa*, Madrid, 1975; J. M. Díez Borque, *Sociología de la comedia española del siglo XVII*, Madrid, 1976; J. G. Weiger, *The Valencian Dramatists of Spain's Golden Age*, Boston, 1976; O. Arrón, *Teatro y escena-*

rios del Siglo de Oro, Madrid, 1977; J. M. Díez Borque, *Sociedad y teatro en la España de Lope de Vega*, Barcelona, 1978; B. W. Wardropper, "La comedia española del Siglo de Oro," in *Teoría de la comedia: La comedia española del Siglo de Oro* (comprising essays by E. Olson and B. W. Wardropper), Barcelona, 1978; J. G. Weiger, *Hacia la comedia: De los valencianos a Lope de Vega*, Madrid, 1978.

C. Eighteenth and Nineteenth Centuries

J. Yxart, *El arte escénico en España*, 2 vols., Barcelona, 1894–1896; E. A. Peers, *History of the Romantic Movement in Spain*, 2 vols., Cambridge, Mass., 1940; J. Deleito y Peñuela, *Origen y apogeo del género chico*, Madrid, 1949; J. H. Peake, *Social Drama in Nineteenth Century Spain*, Chapel Hill, N.C., 1964; J. Campos, *Teatro y sociedad en Madrid (1780–1820)*, Madrid, 1969; R. Andioc, *Sur la querelle du théâtre au temps de Leandro Fernández de Moratín*, Bordeaux, 1970; J. A. Cook, *Neo-Classic Drama in Spain: Theory and Practice*, Dallas, Tex., 1970; I. L. McClelland, *Spanish Drama of Pathos (1750–1808)*, Liverpool, Eng., 1970; A. Goenaga and J. P. Maguna, *Teatro español del siglo XIX, Análisis de obras*, New York, 1971; R. Andioc, *Teatro y sociedad en el Madrid del siglo XVIII*, Madrid, 1976; J. L. P. Kosove, *The "Comedia Lacrimosa" and Spanish Romanticism (1773–1865)*, London, 1978.

D. Twentieth Century

H. Gregerson, *Ibsen in Spain*, Cambridge, Mass., 1936; N. González Ruiz, *La cultura española en los últimos veinte años: El teatro*, Madrid, 1949; G. Torrente Ballester, *Teatro español contemporáneo*, Madrid, 1957; A. Marquerie, *Veinte años de teatro en España*, Madrid, 1959; F. García Pavón, *Teatro social en España (1895–1962)*, Madrid, 1962; J. Rof Carballo et al., *El teatro de humor en España*, Madrid, 1966; W. Giuliano, *Buero Vallejo, Sastre y el teatro de su tiempo*, New York, 1971; J. Monleón, *Treinta años de teatro de la derecha*, Barcelona, 1971; G. E. Wellwarth, *Spanish Underground Drama*, University Park, Pa., and London, 1972 (Spanish ed. with a prologue and notes by A. Miralles, Madrid, 1978); L. García Lorenzo, *El teatro español hoy*, Barcelona, 1975; M. P. Holt, *The Contemporary Spanish Theater (1949–1972)*, Boston, 1975; A. Amorós, M. Mayoral, and F. Nieva, *Análisis de cinco comedias (Teatro español de la postguerra)*, Madrid, 1977; A. Miralles, *Nuevo teatro español: una alternativa social*, Madrid, 1977; C. Oliva, *Cuatro dramaturgos realistas: Sus contradicciones estéticas*, Murcia, 1978 (studies on Carlos Muñiz, Lauro Olmo, José María Rodriguez Méndez, and José Martín Recuerda); C. Oliva, *Disidentes de la generación realista*, Murcia, 1979.

Journals and reviews specializing in contemporary Spanish theatre are *Primer Acto*, *Yorick*, *Pipirijaina*, and *Estreno*.

Anthologies and Collections

A. Spanish

Dramáticos contemporáneos a Lope de Vega, ed. by R. de Romanos Mesonero, 2 vols., *Biblioteca de Autores Españoles*, XLII and XLV, Madrid, 1857–1858 (texts are unreliable); *Dramáticos posteriores a Lope de Vega*, ed. by R. de Romanos Mesonero, 2 vols., *Biblioteca de Autores Españoles*, XLVII and XLIX, Madrid, 1858–1859 (texts not always reliable); *Colección de autos, farsas y coloquios del siglo XVI*, ed. by L. Rouanet, 4 vols., Macon, Georgia, 1901; *Colección de entremeses, loas bailes, jácaras y mojigangas, desde fines del siglo XVI a mediados del XVIII*, ed. by E. Cotarelo y Mori, 2 vols., Madrid, 1911; *Teatro español del siglo XVI*, ed. by U. Cronan, vol. I, Madrid, 1913; *Ten Spanish Farces*, ed. by G. T. Northrup, Boston, 1922 (a selection of *pasos* and *entreméses*, with notes and critical material in English); *Poetas dramáticos valencianos*, ed. by E. Juliá Martínez, 2 vols., Madrid, 1929; *Nineteenth Century Spanish Plays*, ed. by L. E. Brett, New York, 1935 (notes and critical material in English); *El teatro español: Historia y antología (desde el siglo XIV al XIX)*, ed. by F. C. Sainz de Robles, 7 vols., Madrid, 1942–1943; Yearly anthologies of five or six representative plays of every theatrical season of 1949–1950 to 1970–1971, ed. by F. C. Sainz de Robles, Madrid; *Piezas maestras del teatro teológico español*, ed. by N. González Ruiz, 2 vols., Madrid, 1946; *Antología del teatro medieval*, ed. by R. Benítez Claros, Mendoza, 1951; *Autos sacramentales eucarísticos*, ed. by A. Sanvisens, Barcelona, 1952; *El teatro anterior a Lope de Vega*, ed. by E. W. Hesse, Madrid, 1971; *Autos, comedias y farsas de la Biblioteca Nacional*, ed. by J. García Morales, 2 vols., Madrid, 1962–1964; *El género chico: Antología de textos completos*, ed. by A. Valencia, Madrid, 1962; *Teatro medieval*, ed. by F. Lázaro Carreter, 2d ed., Madrid, 1965 (texts in modern Spanish); *Teatro inquieto español*, ed. by A. del Hoyo and A. Espina, Madrid, 1967 (plays by Unamuno, Azorín, Grau, Gómez de la Serna, García Lorca, and Aub); *Teatro romántico: Antología*, ed. by J. Alcina Franch, Barcelona, 1968; *Diez comedias del Siglo de Oro*, ed. by J. Martel and H. Alpern, 2nd ed., New York, 1968 (with notes and critical material in English); *Ramillete de entremeses y bailes (siglo XVII)*, ed. by H. E. Bergman, Madrid, 1970; *Teatro español del Siglo de Oro*, ed. by B. W. Wardropper, New York, 1970 (notes and criticism in English); *El teatro anterior a Lope de Vega*, ed. by E. W. Hesse and J. O. Valencia, Madrid, 1971; *Spanish Drama of the Golden Age: Twelve Plays*, ed. by R. R. MacCurdy, New York, 1971 (notes and critical material in English); *Teatro español del siglo XVIII. Antología*, ed. by J. L. Johnson, Barcelona, 1972; *Selección de comedias del Siglo de Oro español*, ed. by A. V. Ebersole, Valencia, 1973; *Teatro español contemporáneo*, ed. by E. Larraz, Paris, 1973 (three short plays by Martínez Ballesteros, Matilla, and Ruibal, with selected materials on the

contemporary Spanish theatre); *Años difíciles: Tres testimonios del teatro español contemporáneo*, ed. by R. Salvat, Barcelona, 1977 (plays by Buero Vallejo, Olmo, and Gala); *Teatro español contemporáneo*, ed. by J. W. Zdenek and G. I. Castillo-Feliú, 2 vols., Mexico City, 1977; *Contemporary Spanish Theatre: Seven One-Act Plays*, ed. by P. W. O'Connor and A. M. Pasquariello, New York, 1980 (plays by contemporary avant-garde authors, with notes and critical material in English).

Annotated texts with critical introductions in Spanish are available in the following collections: Clásicos Castellanos, Clásicos Castalia, Textos Hispánicos Modernos (Labor), Clásicos Ebro, and Letras Hispánicas (Cátedra).

B. English

Masterpieces of Modern Spanish Drama, ed. by B: H. Clark, New York, 1928 (Echegaray, Pérez Galdós, and Guimerá); *The Classic Theatre*, vol. 1: *Six Spanish Plays*, ed. by E. Bentley, New York, 1959; *Spanish Drama*, ed. by A. Flores, New York, 1962 (Lope de Rueda, Cervantas, Lope de Vega, Tirso de Molina, Ruiz de Alarcón, Calderón, Moratín, Echegaray, Benavente, and Lorca); *Eight Spanish Plays of the Golden Age*, ed. by W. Starkie, New York, 1964; *Masterpieces of Modern Spanish Theatre*, ed. by R. W. Corrigan, New York, 1967 (Benavente, Martínez Sierra, García Lorca, Buero Vallejo, and Sastre); *Modern Spanish Theatre*, ed. by M. Benedikt and G. E. Wellwarth, New York, 1969 (Mihura, Casona, Olmo, Arrabal, Bellido, Alberti, García Lorca, and Valle-Inclán); *The Modern Spanish Stage: Four Plays*, ed. by M. Holt, New York, 1970 (Buero Vallejo, Sastre, López Rubio, and Casona); *The New Wave Spanish Drama*, ed. by G. E. Wellwarth, New York, 1970 (coverage of Sastre, Ruibal, Bellido, and Martínez Ballesteros); *New Generation Spanish Drama*, ed. by G. E. Wellwarth, Montreal, 1976 (Quiles, Matilla, Rellán, and López Mozo); *3 Catalan Dramatists*, ed. by G. E. Wallwarth, Montreal, 1976 (Pedrolo, Benet i Jordi, and Teixidor).

Addenda

A. General Surveys and Studies on Various Periods

A. F. Schack, *Historia de la literatura y del arte dramático en España*, 5 vols., Madrid, 1885–1887; J. Casalduero, *Estudios sobre el teatro español*, Madrid, 1962; F. Ruiz Ramón, *Estudios sobre teatro español clásico y contemporáneo*, Madrid, 1978.

B. Middle Ages and Golden Age

W. Sturdevant, *The Misterio de los Reyes Magos: Its Position in the Development of the Medieval Legend of the Three Kings*, Baltimore, Paris, 1927; C. D. Ley, *El Gracioso en el teatro de la Península (siglos XVI–XVII)*, Madrid, 1954; C. Ortigoza Vieyra, *Los móviles de la "Comedia" en Lope, Alarcón, Tirso, Moreto, Rojas, Calderón*, Mexico City, 1954; C. Bravo Villasante, *La mujer vestida de hombre en el teatro español (siglos XVI–XVIII)*, Madrid, 1955; J. de J. Prades, *Teoría de los personajes de la comedia nueva*, Madrid, 1963; E. Orozco Díaz, *El teatro y la teatralidad del barroco*, Barcelona, 1969; J. A. García Baquero, *Aproximaciones al teatro clásico español*, Seville, 1973; M. Newels, *Los géneros dramáticos en las poéticas del Siglo de Oro*, London, 1974; R. L. Fiore, *Drama and Ethos*, Lexington, Ky., 1975; E. W. Hesse, *Interpretando la comedia*, Madrid, 1977; *Perspectivas de la comedia*, ed. by A. V. Ebersole, Valencia, 1978; R. R. MacCurdy, *The Tragic Fall: Don Alvaro de Luna and Other Favorites in Spanish Golden Age Drama*, Chapel Hill, N.C., 1978.

C. Eighteenth Century

I. M. Cid de Sirgado, *Afrancesados y neoclásicos (su deslinde en el teatro español del siglo XVIII)*, Madrid, 1973; J. Caro Baroja, *Teatro popular y magia*, Madrid, 1974.

Supplementary Bibliography on the Comedia

A. G. Reichenberger, "The Uniqueness of the *Comedia*," *Hispanic Review* XXVII (1959), pp. 303–313; E. Bentley, "The Universality of the *Comedia*," *Hispanic Review* XXXVIII (1970), pp. 147–162, and in the same issue, Reichenberger's "The *Comedia*: Universality or Uniqueness?," pp. 163–173; G. E. Wade, "The Interpretation of the *Comedia*," *Bulletin of the Comediantes* XI (1959), pp. 1–6; C. A. Jones, "Some Ways of Looking at Spanish Golden Age Comedy," *Homenaje a William A. Fitcher: Estudios sobre el teatro antiguo español y otros ensayos*, ed. by A. D. Kossoff and J. Amor y Vázquez, Madrid, 1971, pp. 329–339.

Speroni, Sperone (1500–1588)

Italian man of letters and dramatist. His varied literary activity included the verse tragedy *Canace* (1542). The play, which is conceived, in imitation of the ancients, in the "horrible" mode of the time, concerns the incestuous love of Canace for Macareus and their violent deaths at the hands of their father Aeolus. The work generated a polemical battle over the rules of neoclassical tragedy in Italy, and a number of contemporary critics condemned the work for its inadequate fulfillment of Aristotelian theatrical precepts.   [PETER BONDANELLA]

Spewack, Samuel (1899–1971) and Bella (Cohen) (1899–)

American husband-and-wife team of screenwriters and playwrights. Their collaboration produced a series of popular comedies and farces, the most notable of which is *Boy Meets Girl* (1935), a hilarious lampoon of the Hol-

Samuel Spewack, Bella Spewack, Dorothy Hall, and George Abbott (l. to r.). [Theatre Collection, The New York Public Library at Lincoln Center, Astor, Lenox and Tilden Foundations]

lywood mystique, about a fading movie star who is supplied by a team of enterprising writers with an illegitimate baby as a costar. With Cole Porter, who wrote the music, they wrote *Kiss Me Kate* (1948), one of the most popular musical comedies of the modern stage, a blend of Shakespeare's *Taming of the Shrew* and the amorous difficulties of Broadway show people. In the comedy *My Three Angels* (1953), based on *La Cuisine des Anges* by Albert Husson, a trio of convicts in a French penal colony come to the aid of a shopkeeper and his daughter. Among the Spewacks' other plays are *The Solitaire Man* (1926), *Poppa* (1928), *The War Song* (with George Jessel, 1928), *Clear All Wires* (1932), *Spring Song* (1934), and *Miss Swan Expects* (1939). Among the plays Mr. Spewack wrote on his own were his popular *Under the Sycamore Tree* (1952) and *Once There Was a Russian* (1961), which was revised as the musical *Pleasures and Palaces* (1965). *See* MUSICAL COMEDY. [GAUTAM DASGUPTA]

Squarzina, Luigi (1922–)

Italian director and dramatist. He was born in Leghorn on February 18, 1922. After completing his law studies in 1945, he attended the Accademia Nazionale d'Arte Drammatica and received a diploma in theatrical direction. From that time on he devoted himself to the theatre as a playwright, director, translator, and critic.

From the beginning Squarzina showed himself particularly alert to contemporary theatrical trends, especially those inaugurated in the United States. Among the first plays directed by him were productions of Arthur Miller's *All My Sons* and Sidney Kingsley's *Detective Story*. He wrote his first play *The Indifferent Ones* (*Gli indifferenti*, 1948), an adaptation of Alberto Moravia's novel of the same name, in collaboration with the novelist. It was followed by *Universal Exposition* (*L'esposizione universale*; wr. 1949, prod. 1955), which was awarded the Gramsci Prize. Produced in Poland, it has yet to be staged in Italy, where it is known only in its published version and through two public readings.

Squarzina was awarded a scholarship to the Yale

Ron Hastings, David Renton, and David Murray (l. to r.) in *My Three Angels*. **Halifax, Nova Scotia, Neptune Theatre, 1968.**

Luigi Squarzina. [Federico Arborio Mella, Milan]

Drama School in 1951 and spent the following year in the United States. On his return to Italy, he produced his first popular success, *The Three-quarter Moon (Tre quarti di luna)*, which was awarded the St. Vincent Prize. He has continued to combine his activities as a playwright and a director, though his fame as a director has tended to obscure his reputation as a dramatist, especially in recent years. As codirector of the Teatro Stabile di Genoa, from 1962 until 1976 (when he moved to direct the Teatro di Roma), Squarzina became known for his innovative productions of Brecht (whom he championed in Italy), Pirandello, and Goldoni (both of whom he revived on the contemporary Italian stage). For radio, Squarzina has written *The Pantograph (Il pantografo,* wr. 1958) and *Near and Difficult (Vicino e difficile,* wr. 1960), and he has contributed articles on theatre history to numerous magazines. Among his many translations into Italian are those of Shakespeare's *Hamlet,* Maxwell Anderson's *Anne of the Thousand Days,* and Robert Anderson's *Tea and Sympathy.* In 1948 he married the actress Zora Piazza.

WORK

Squarzina's reputation as a dramatist is based largely on his skill in presenting personal dramas against the panorama of Italy's crucial years under fascism and during the immediate post-World War II period. His first play, *The Indifferent Ones* (1948), an adaptation of Alberto Moravia's novel, set the intellectual tone of his theatre in its presentation of a middle-class family whose moral sense is paralyzed by the Fascist environment in which it lives. The play was only a partial success because the dialogue, stripped of the morbid and sensual atmosphere provided by the novelist, proved insufficiently dramatic. The plays that followed reflect the great influence of the author's parallel career as a director and often give evidence that many of the incidents were suggested to him by his vision of their effect as dramatic spectacle.

In 1949 he wrote the prizewinning *Universal Exposition* (1955), which presents the plight of homeless refugees who, in the days immediately following the war, have occupied the buildings of Mussolini's incomplete Universal Exposition of Rome. In spite of armed resistance, they are eventually forced to leave when a ruthless speculator decides to acquire the fairgrounds from the government.

The Three-quarter Moon (1953), set in Romagna on the eve of the Fascist march on Rome, is an attack on a system of education that discourages and suppresses the free development of new ideas. It was followed by *Her Part of History (La sua parte di storia,* 1958), which assails modern civilization for its tendency to treat human beings as mere statistics. A young American woman doctor, attached to a medical mission fighting poliomyelitis in a poverty-stricken community, so identifies herself with the poor around her that she finds herself morally responsible for the lynching of a postman who has been stealing remittances from immigrants abroad. She is prevented, however, by the publicity-minded mission from proclaiming her guilt and is forced to participate in the "humanity of numbers."

Critics generally consider *The Girl from Romagna (Romagnola,* 1959) Squarzina's major play. Written in 1957 and awarded the Marzotto Prize two years before its actual production, the drama presents a tragic love story against a tapestry of historical events in Romagna during the last fifteen years of Fascist rule. Its thirty episodes and large cast emphasize Squarzina's tendency to stage scenes of mass social action, and the use of songs and music of a popular nature points up the influence of Brecht's epic theatre. Italian rightists were angered by the political message of the play, which often occasioned angry demonstrations. *See* EPIC THEATRE in glossary.

A number of Squarzina's plays have been designed for radio and identified as "tales for sounds and voices." In 1962 he published a "dialogue" entitled *An Entomological Epilogue, or The Incommunicability of Beings (Un epilogo entomologico, ovvero L'incommunicabilità degli esseri).* After years of feverish activity as one of Italy's most respected directors and interpreters of the works of others, Squarzina has of late returned to writing for the theatre. Reflecting the contemporary Italian obsession with political themes and recent social history, he has produced several documentary dramas. *Five Days at the Port (Cinque giorni al porto,* 1969) employs historical sources to examine the general strike of 1900 in Genoa which represents an important milestone in the rise of the labor movement. *Rosa Luxemburg (Rosa Luxemburg,* 1976) presents a dramatization of the well-known German revolutionary. Both works are more important as barometers of the thematic concerns of contemporary Italian theatre than as lasting contributions to Italy's dramatic literature.

The Three-quarter Moon (*Tre quarti di luna,* 1953). Drama in which Enrico, a university student, is found dead, having apparently fallen from the balcony of his apartment. His sister Elisa, unwilling to believe his death accidental, decides to conduct a private inquiry. With the help of her brother's close friend Mauro, she slowly uncovers the possibility of Enrico's suicide. Finally, the two discover that just before his death Enrico had a discussion with Piana, his dean, regarding his thesis, which the latter had severely criticized. Confronting Piana, they force him to confess that he had disapproved of Enrico's thesis because it differed from his own theory and therefore might have prevented him from obtaining an important post promised by the Fascist authorities. Now seemingly repentant, he asks how he can make reparation, but Mauro, recognizing the inherent evil of Piana's expediency, kills him with the letter opener that is the ironic symbol of his mission as an educator.

The Girl from Romagna (*Romagnola,* 1959). Set in the Romagna countryside before and during World War II, the play concerns the resistance of the peasants and small landholders to Fascist control. Into this setting comes Cecilia, a Fascist idealist whose mission it is to win over the peasants. She and Michele, a young peasant with a gift for painting, embark on an idyllic affair, traveling to the seashore and other Fascist spas as Cecilia attempts to gain acceptance of Michele as a peasant artist. As the young lovers prosper, World War II begins, and in brief scenes the audience learns of the Albanian and African campaigns, the beginning of Italy's defeat, and, finally, of the partisan attacks and reprisals. Michele volunteers for service and is sent to Sicily, but after the Allied invasion he escapes and, thoroughly convinced of the evils of fascism, returns north, where he joins a partisan group and marries a young girl whose family has been killed. Cecilia, believing Michele dead, has married the powerful Count Gardenghi, an old admirer. When she learns that Michele lives, however, she kills the count and journeys to Rome to join Michele. On discovering that Michele is married, she falsely denounces him to the Fascists for the murder of the count. Michele is arrested and shot, and Cecilia is eventually killed by the partisans in reprisal. Before her death, however, she learns that Michele had always loved her and had forgiven her betrayal.

[PETER BONDANELLA]

PLAYS

1. (With Alberto Moravia). *Gli indifferenti (The Indifferent Ones)*. Play. Published 1947. Produced Rome, Teatro Quirino, April, 1948. Based on Moravia's novel (1929).

2. *L'esposizione universale (Universal Exposition)*. Play. Written 1949. Published 1959. Produced Katowice, Poland, Nov. 30, 1955.

3. *Tre quarti di luna (The Three-quarter Moon)*. Play. Published 1959. Produced Rome, Teatro Valle, Mar. 3, 1953.

4. *La sua parte di storia (Her Part of History)*. Play. Written 1955. Published 1959. Produced Vienna, Volkstheater, October, 1958.

5. *Romagnola (The Girl from Romagna)*. Play. Written 1957. Published 1959. Produced Rome, Teatro Valle, Feb. 6, 1959.

6. *Il pantografo (The Pantograph)*. Play. Written 1958. Published 1959. Produced 1959.

7. *Vicino e difficile (Near and Difficult)*. Play. Written 1960. Published 1962.

8. *Un epilogo entomologico, ovvero L'incommunicabilità degli esseri (An Entomological Epilogue, or The Incommunicability of Beings)*. Dialogue. Published 1962.

9. *Cinque giorni al porto (Five Days at the Port)*. Play. Published 1969. Produced Genoa, Teatro Stabile di Genoa, Apr. 1, 1969.

10. *Rosa Luxemburg (Rosa Luxemburg)*. Play. Produced Genoa, Teatro Stabile di Genoa, Feb. 17, 1976.

EDITIONS

Teatro, Bari, 1959; *Cinque giorni al porto*, Genoa, 1969.

Šrámek, Fráňa (1877–1952)

Czech poet, prose writer, and dramatist. His plays are impressionistic in technique, with emphasis on atmosphere and character. Avoiding complex social situations, he focuses on individual psychology. His most successful play, *Summer (Léto, 1915)*, is an excellent portrayal of youthful sensuality. *Moon over the River (Měsíc nad řekou, 1922)* is a bittersweet comedy that uses the theme of a reunion of a graduating class in a small provincial town for the portrayal of human hopes and failures.

PAUL I. TRENSKY

Stallings, Laurence (1894–1968)

American librettist, author, scriptwriter, and dramatist. He is best known for *What Price Glory?* (1924), a play, written with Maxwell Anderson, that grew out of Stallings's World War I experiences. Among his other plays are *First Flight* (1925) and *The Buccaneer* (1925), also in collaboration with Anderson; the book and lyrics for *Deep River* (1926); *Rainbow* (1928), with Oscar Hammerstein II; the stage adaptation of Ernest Hemingway's novel *A Farewell to Arms* (1930); *Virginia* (1937), with Owen Davis; and *The Streets Are Guarded* (1944), a play set in the Pacific in World War II. His work for the screen includes *Old Ironsides* (1926), *So Red the Rose* (1935), *Northwest Passage* (1940), and *She Wore a Yellow Ribbon* (1949). *See* ANDERSON, MAXWELL; DAVIS, OWEN.

[GAUTAM DASGUPTA]

Stanislavsky, Konstantin (1863–1938)

The most universally known of Russian actors, directors, and teachers. Stanislavsky was born Konstantin Sergeyevich Alekseyev in Moscow, on January 15, 1863, the son of a rich textile manufacturer whose circle included many well-to-do patrons of the arts. On his mother's side, he was descended from the French actress Varley. He first began performing as an amateur in 1877, and the homegrown shows burgeoned into a club, "The Alekseyev Circle," for the staging of farces and operettas. Stanislavsky, who adopted this Polish pseudonym in 1885, played dozens of musical roles including Nanki-Poo in *The Mikado*. Like most amateurs, he began by imitating famous professional stars but soon grew tired of the clichés that resulted. In 1887 he married Mariya Petrovna Perevoshchikova, who, under the stage name Lilina, became an excellent actress in her own right.

Stanislavsky's penchant for self-criticism and his growing belief that an actor should educate his public in liberal sentiments and refined feelings led him in 1888 to found, along with three collaborators, The Art and Literature Society, where he played such leading roles as Pushkin's Don Juan and Shakespeare's Othello. He had all the personal attributes of a good leading man—great height, a handsome, expressive face, a musical voice, and graceful movements—and as he rapidly gained fame, he played opposite a number of popular actresses on their tours. His first directorial attempt was Lyov Tolstoy's *Fruits of Enlightenment* (1891), which brought him

Stanislavsky in two favorite Chekhov roles: (left) Gaev in *The Cherry Orchard* and (right) Vershinin in *The Three Sisters*.]*Moscow Art Theatre Plays*]

to the favorable attention of the playwright and acting teacher Vladimir Nemirovich-Danchenko. In this period, his most daring innovations were made in staging Hauptmann's *Hannele's Ascension* and Erckmann-Chatrian's *The Polish Jew.*

In 1897 he and Nemirovich-Danchenko founded the Moscow Art and Publicly Accessible Theatre, staffed by amateurs of the Literature Society and students of the Moscow Conservatory. Soon renamed the Moscow Art Theatre, or MXT (abbreviation of Cyrillic characters), it was intended to develop a socially responsible repertory, to foster ensemble acting of high dedication, and to serve the interests of the theatre as a high art. The influence of the Meiningen Troupe, with its authentic re-creations of the past and its carefully organized crowd scenes, could be detected in the Art Theatre's opening production, Aleksey Tolstoy's *Tsar Fyodor Ioannovich* (1898), which endeavored to re-create the historical past with verisimilitude. After an uneven first season, the company attained success with a revival of Anton Chekhov's *The Seagull,* in which Stanislavsky made clever use of lighting, sound effects, picturesque staging, and naturalistic acting to evoke a lyrical ethos and cast a romantic glamor over the fecklessness of the intellectual class. Chekhov, who regularly complained that Stanislavsky misinterpreted him and missed the comedy in his plays, became the favored author of the Moscow Art Theatre, which created the premieres of *Uncle Vanya, Three Sisters,* and *The Cherry Orchard.* Similar successes were produced by Gorky's *The Lower Middle Class* and *The Lower Depths.*

Stanislavsky's achievement lay in the integration of every element in the production to create a "mood," and this included the individual performances of the actors, in a mode of psychological naturalism. It worked for Chekhov and Gorky but was less effective when he tried to stage Maeterlinck, Gogol, Turgenev, Shakespeare, and Ibsen, and Stanislavsky made many attempts to broaden the stylistic base of the MXT without abandoning his basic principles. He invited Gordon Craig to direct and design *Hamlet* (1909–1912) and Aleksandr Benois to do the same with plays of Molière and Goldoni (1913–1914); he encouraged his student Vsevolod Meyerhold to experiment with Maeterlinck in a studio which he then refused to open; and he explored nonrealistic styles in staging the plays of Leonid Andreyev and Aleksandr Blok. But each of these excursions proved a dead end, and he kept returning to an enriched psychological realism.

As an actor Stanislavsky was immensely popular, especially as Doctor Stockmann in Ibsen's *An Enemy of the People,* Argan in Molière's *The Imaginary Invalid,* and Astrov in Chekhov's *Uncle Vanya,* roles which displayed considerable comic flair. But he kept seeking new means of freeing the actor's imagination and bringing him closer to the truth; and in collaboration with Leopold Sulerzhitsky in 1912 he opened the Moscow Art Theatre's First Studio, to conduct experiments with students on his "system," which was viewed with suspicion by the older members of the acting company. The studio's production of *Twelfth Night* (1917) proved to be the MXT's first major success after the Revolution.

An upper-middle-class liberal with the nineteenth-century mind of a romantic positivist, Stanislavsky was disoriented by the new world effected by the October Revolution, and he tried to avoid its consequences by turning to opera work at the Bolshoy Theatre, supervising a number of experimental studios, and taking the MXT on a tour of Europe and the United States in 1922–1924. The repertory of these tours was the somewhat outdated one of the theatre's first successes, which gave the impression that Stanislavsky's work was wholly naturalistic, while the ensemble playing and cohesive productions made a deep impression on theatre practitioners in Paris, Berlin, and New York. In the United States Stanislavsky wrote, for publicity purposes, an autobiography, *My Life in Art,* an inspiring if anecdotal work, which was rewritten in many important aspects when he returned to the Soviet Union.

Stanislavsky's worsening health caused his retirement as an actor in the late 1920s, but his directing displayed a new flair for highly colored, almost grotesque productions such as Ostrovsky's *The Ardent Heart* (1926) and Beaumarchais' *Marriage of Figaro* (1927). The government demand that the MXT present more Soviet drama was not to Stanislavsky's aesthetic tastes, and while such successes as Mikhail Bulgakov's *Days of the Turbins* and Vsevolod Ivanov's *Armored Train 14-69* were put on by younger members of the directing staff, Stanislavsky withdrew to his home, from which he supervised productions, rehearsed actors and opera singers, and compiled his notes on acting technique. His last work as a director was on Molière's *Tartuffe* (1935), and in 1936 he was created a People's Artist of the USSR. In 1937 he completed the first part of his book *The Actor's Work on Himself (Rabota aktyora na soboy)* and began the second part. He died in Moscow on August 7, 1938.

Stanislavsky's influence as a teacher of acting is possibly the single most important factor in twentieth-century acting technique. Spread by expatriate members of the MXT company like Mikhail Chekhov, Richard Boleslavsky, and Tamara Daykharkanova, his system became the basis for most actor's training in Eastern Europe and the United States up to the 1970s and influenced the kinds of plays being written there. The system centered around the *perezhivaniye,* or "inner experience," of the actor, who was to follow a consistent line of action throughout the play, with attention to a main objective, while rapt in a circle of concentration. The most famous of his bywords is "The Magic If," whereby the actor generates a belief in the fictional character's feelings. In latter years Stanislavsky emphasized the importance of the precise physical action to externalize these inner feelings, but such offshoots as the Method, as taught at the Actors' Studio in New York, have preferred to explore his comments on emotional memory and the actor's ego.

See Moscow Art Theatre.

Laurence Senelick.

WORKS

My Life in Art, Boston, 1924; *An Actor Prepares*, tr. by E. R. Hapgood, New York, 1936; *Building a Character*, tr. by E. R. Hapgood, New York, 1949; *Stat'i, rechi, besedy, pis'ma*, Moscow, 1953; *Sobranie sochineniy*, 8 vols., Moscow, 1954–1961; *Stanislavsky's Legacy*, tr. by E. R. Hapgood, New York, 1958; *Stanislavsky on the Art of the Stage*, tr. by D. Magarshack, New York, 1961; *Creating a Role*, tr. by E. R. Hapgood, New York, 1961.

CRITICISM

Russian.
N. E. Efros, *K.S. Stanislavskiy (opyt kharakteristic)*, St. Petersburg, 1918; V. Volkenshteyn, *Stanislavskiy*, Leningrad, 1927; V. Toporkov, *Stanislavskiy na repetitsii*, Moscow, 1950; N. Gorchakov, *Rezhissyorskie uroki K. S. Stanislavskogo*, Moscow, 1950, 1952; *K. S. Stanislavskiy. Materialy, pis'ma, issledovaniya*, Moscow, 1955; V. Prokofiev, *V sporakh o Stanislavskom*, Moscow, 1962; N. Vinogradov, *Zhizn' i tvorchestvo K. S. Stanislavskogo. Letopis'*, 4 vols., Moscow, 1971–1976; E. Polyakova, *Stanislavsky—aktyor*, Moscow, 1972. M. N. Stroeva, *Rezhissyorskie iskanija Stanislavskogo*, 2 vols., Moscow, 1973–77; E. Polyakova, *Stanislavskiy*, Moscow, 1977.

English.
O. M. Sayler, *Inside the Moscow Art Theatre*, New York, 1925; *Stanislavsky Produces Othello*, tr. by H. Nowack, London, 1948; D. Magarshack, *Stanislavsky, a Life*, New York, 1951; *The Seagull Produced by Stanislavsky*, tr. by D. Magarshack, London, 1952; N. M. Gorchakov, *Stanislavsky Directs*, tr. by M Goldina, New York, 1954; *Stanislavsky in America*, ed. by E. Munk, New York, 1965; P. I. Rumyantsev, *Stanislavsky on Opera*, New York, 1976; V. Toporkov, *Stanislavsky in Rehearsal*, tr. by C. Edwards, New York, 1980.

Steele, Richard (1672–1729)

English essayist, dramatist, and politician. Sir Richard Steele was born in March, 1672, in Dublin, the son of Richard Steele, a lawyer. Orphaned before the age of six, he was cared for by an uncle, Henry Gascoigne, private

Frances Abington in Act III of *The Conscious Lovers*. [Theatre Collection, The New York Public Library at Lincoln Center, Astor, Lenox and Tilden Foundations]

Richard Steele. [Theatre Collection, The New York Public Library at Lincoln Center, Astor, Lenox and Tilden Foundations]

secretary to the 1st Duke of Ormonde.

In 1684 Steele entered Charterhouse and, in 1689, Oxford University. A few years later he left Oxford to become a gentleman trooper in the service of the grandson and heir of the 1st Duke of Ormonde bringing upon himself the displeasure of Gascoigne and eventual disinheritance. In 1694, after dedicating an elegy on Queen Mary to Lord Cutts, he was removed to Cutts's Coldstream regiment and became his secretary. By 1700 he had been promoted to a captaincy, and in 1702 he transferred to Lord Lucas's regiment. When Steele injured a fellow officer in a duel, he developed the hatred of dueling that was to be apparent in many of his writings. Meanwhile, his first comedy, *The Funeral, or Grief A-la-mode*, was produced in 1701, followed by *The Lying Lover, or The Ladies' Friendship* in 1703. Steele's avowed purpose, to expound on good breeding and virtuous behavior with wit and good humor, was in the first instance received with favor but in the second was "damned for its piety."

In 1705 Steele married Mrs. Margaret (Ford) Stretch, a wealthy widow many years his senior. That year *The Tender Husband, or The Accomplished Fools* was produced with great success. Mrs. Steele died the following year, during which her husband was gentleman waiter to Prince George of Denmark. In 1707 Steele married Mary Scurlock, the "dear Prue" of his letters, whom he loved despite his infidelities, at least one of which produced an illegitimate daughter.

The year of his second marriage, Steele was appointed gazetteer of the *Gazette*, the official government newspaper, but Robert Harley, the Secretary of State whom Steele had satirized, dismissed him from this position in October, 1710. Steele's career as an essayist began when he founded the *Tatler* in 1709 under the pseudonym Isaac Bickerstaff. He accepted many contributions from Joseph Addison, whom he had met at Charterhouse and with whom he had a long friendship. *See* ADDISON, JOSEPH.

The last issue of the *Tatler* (No. 271) appeared in 1711. Steele then entered into a partnership with Addison and produced 555 numbers of the *Spectator*, 236 of which were written by Steele alone. Other papers he published include the *Guardian* (1713–1715), the *English-man* (1713–1714), and the *Lover* (1714). In addition, he published several short-lived periodicals.

An ardent and outspoken Whig, Steele became a member of Parliament in 1713 for Stockbridge, Hampshire. But on March 18, 1714, he was expelled from the House of Commons after printing *The Crisis*, a pamphlet in favor of the house of Hanover. When George I was crowned, Steele's star began to rise, and among other lucrative appointments, he received that of supervisor of the Drury Lane Theatre. In 1715, the year he was knighted, he was elected member of Parliament for Boroughbridge, Yorkshire. After a few good years of lecturing, writing, and re-election to Parliament for Wendover, Buckinghamshire, his fortunes began to decline. His wife died in 1718, and soon afterwards he broke with Addison. In 1722, after a seventeen-year absence from the theatre, Steele saw his *The Conscious Lovers* produced and acclaimed.

Despite all his sources of income, financial imprudence led him deeply into debt. He retired to his wife's estate in Wales and died in Carmarthen on September 1, 1729.

WORK

Esteemed as an essayist and as the founder of the famous periodicals the *Tatler* and (with Addison) the *Spectator*, Steele was also a comic playwright of some merit. Although his pious moralizing often blunts the comic thrust of the plays, such sentimentality accurately reflects contemporary middle-class attitudes. Steele is recognized as the first writer of this new form, although it was not until later that sentimental comedy became popular. Steele's plays, despite their moral sincerity, teach little, as they never directly confront the truth about social conditions or the nature of man. But they are well constructed, the comic situations are neatly managed, and the characters are skillfully developed. *The Funeral, or Grief A-la-mode* (1701), burdened by sententious moralizing, succeeded because of the enlivening diversion of its cruder passages. The story turns on old Lord Brumpton's disinheritance of his son at the instigation of his greedy young wife, who wants the estate for herself. After the supposed death of Brumpton, a comic interlude ensues between the undertaker and his hired mourners, whom he exhorts to look sadder and act more dismal. In *The Lying Lover, or The Ladies' Friendship* (1703), which Steele adapted from Pierre Corneille's *The Liar*, young Bookwit and his friend Latine pose as a soldier and his footman in order to woo Penelope and Victoria. Steele's moralizing so far outweighs the comic effects that the play did not succeed with the Drury Lane audience. *The Tender Husband, or The Accomplished Fools* (1705) concerns Clerimont's successful efforts to subdue his domineering wife. A delightful subplot offsets the sentimental outbursts. *The Conscious Lovers* (1722) proved to be Steele's greatest success. According to tradition, it was submitted to Colley Cibber, manager of the Drury Lane, who persuaded Steele to lengthen the scenes between the ser-

vants Tom and Phillis; these amusing scenes remain among the best in Steele's plays. *See* SENTIMENTAL COMEDY in glossary.

The Conscious Lovers (1722). Comedy in which Bevil, an unfashionably clean-cut and honorable young gentleman, is engaged, at the behest of his father Sir John, to Lucinda, with whom his friend Myrtle is deeply in love. Bevil is in love with Indiana, a young lady whom he met in Toulon and has brought to England with the intention of marrying her, provided his father agrees. Both Bevil and Lucinda admit their aversion to their marriage. Myrtle, however, jealously misunderstanding the exchange of letters, challenges his friend to a duel. Bevil refuses to fight and voices Steele's distaste for what he considered an insufferable custom. Then, when Indiana is revealed to be Lucinda's long-lost half sister, the complications are untangled and the two couples are united with the blessings of Sir John.

PLAYS

All were first performed in London.

1. *The Funeral, or Grief A-la-mode*. Comedy, 5 acts. Published 1702. Produced Drury Lane Theatre, ca. December, 1701.

2. *The Lying Lover, or The Ladies' Friendship*. Comedy, 5 acts. Published 1704. Produced Drury Lane Theatre, Dec. 2, 1703. Based on Pierre Corneille's *Le menteur* (1643).

3. *The Tender Husband, or The Accomplished Fools*. Comedy, 5 acts. Published 1705. Produced Drury Lane Theatre, Apr. 23, 1705. Based on Molière's *Le sicilien* (1667).

4. *The Conscious Lovers*. Comedy, 5 acts. Published 1723. Produced Drury Lane Theatre, ca. Nov. 7, 1722.

EDITIONS

Dramatick Works, London, 1723; *Dramatic Works*, London, 1761.

The Conscious Lovers. Published in *Eighteenth-century Plays*, intro. by R. Quintana, New York, 1952.

CRITICISM

H. R. Montgomery, *Memoirs of the Life and Writings of Sir Richard Steele*, 2 vols., Edinburgh, 1865; A. Dobson, *Richard Steele*, New York, 1886; G. A. Aitkin, *The Life of Richard Steele*, 2 vols., London, 1889; W. Connely, *Sir Richard Steele*, New York and London, 1934; J. C. Loftis, *Steele at Drury Lane*, Berkeley, Calif., 1952; C. Winton, *Captain Steele: The Early Career of Richard Steele*, Baltimore, 1964.

Steinbeck, John [Ernst] (1902–1968)

American novelist, essayist, and playwright. His drama *Of Mice and Men* (1937), based on his own novel, is generally considered an American classic (it was staged by

John Steinbeck. [Theatre Collection, The New York Public Library at Lincoln Center, Astor, Lenox and Tilden Foundations]

Broderick Crawford (left) as Lennie and Wallace Ford as George in *Of Mice and Men*. New York, Music Box Theatre, 1937. [Photograph by Vandamm. Theatre Collection, The New York Public Library at Lincoln Center, Astor, Lenox and Tilden Foundations]

George S. Kaufman). In a setting of western ranch hands, the play deals with the deep and moving relationship between an itinerant worker and his powerful but simpleminded friend, whose childlike mentality brings about his own death. Less successful was *The Moon Is Down* (1942), set in Nazi-occupied Europe. *Burning Bright* (1950), described by the author as a "play-novelette," employs an interesting technique whereby the action is continuous but the settings and the characters' professions change for each act. It relates the story of a sterile man's desire for children. Steinbeck wrote a number of screenplays, including *Viva Zapata!* (1952).

Of Mice and Men (1937). Drama dealing with the lives of two itinerant farm workers, George, good-natured and intelligent, and Lennie, a feebleminded giant of great strength. They share a dream of owning their own farm, a possibility that seems almost in reach when Lennie's fondness for stroking soft things destroys it. Their boss's daughter-in-law, who has been flirting with Lennie, invites him to touch her hair, and in the excitement aroused in doing so he inadvertently kills her. A mob sets out to lynch him, but George, finding Lennie first, mercifully kills him to protect him from its vengeance. Produced New York, Music Box Theatre, November 23, 1937.   [GAUTAM DASGUPTA]

Sternheim, Carl (1878–1942)

German critic, novelist, and satirical dramatist. He was born on April 1, 1878, in Leipzig, the son of a Jewish banker. He spent his early childhood in Hannover, where his father owned the newspaper *Hannoversches Tageblatt* and served as its theatre critic. In 1884 the family moved to Berlin; there, in close proximity to an uncle who ran the Belle-Alliance Theatre, his interest in the drama was nurtured. By the age of fifteen Sternheim had written his first play, *The Iron Cross (Das eiserne Kreuz)*, which has never been performed. Between 1897 and 1901 he studied philosophy, literature, and history at the Universities of Munich, Leipzig, Göttingen, and Freiburg. After graduating, Sternheim married and had a son, but

he was divorced within five years. He then married Thea Bauer, the stage designer, and settled for five years in a large house near Munich. There, in collaboration with the critic Franz Blei, he founded the literary magazine *Hyperion*. After writing two important plays, *Ulrich and Brigitte (Ulrich und Brigitte*, wr. 1907) and *Don Juan* (wr. 1909), he achieved his first theatrical success with a comedy entitled *The Underpants (Die Hose*, wr. 1909/10), the first part of a trilogy, which was produced by Max Reinhardt. By 1926 he had written almost a score of plays, ten of which, dealing with the corrupt and intellectually dishonest bourgeoisie of the time, were published in the collection *Views of the Heroic Life of the Bourgeois (Aus dem bürgerlichen Heldenleben*, 1922). During this period he also wrote two well-known critical essays, *Berlin, or The Right Milieu (Berlin, oder Juste Milieu*, 1920) and *Tasso, or The Art of the Right Milieu (Tasso, oder Kunst des juste Milieu*, 1921); and two novels, *Europa* (1920) and *Fairfax* (1921), both of which are examples of expressionist prose. He achieved his greatest popularity in 1929, when the composer Dohnányi produced the opera *The Tenor*, based on the text of Sternheim's most successful comedy, *Citizen Schippel (Bürger Schippel*, wr. 1911/12). His last major success came in 1926 with *The School at Uznach or The New Matter-of-factness (Die Schule von Uznach oder Neue Sächlichkeit). See* EXPRESSIONISM in glossary.

In 1927 Sternheim divorced his second wife. He later married the actress Pamela Wedekind, the daughter of the dramatist Frank Wedekind. Gradually the rate of his creative output slackened, and with time and age he became increasingly restless and nervous. After Hitler came to power in 1933, Sternheim left Germany and wandered extensively through Europe before settling in Brussels, where he lived in enforced retirement until his death on November 3, 1942. *See* WEDEKIND, FRANK.

WORK

The majority of Sternheim's plays, including his best work, are devoted to a satirical examination of the German bourgeoisie. Far less blatant and frenetic than his

Carl Sternheim. [Hermann Luchterhand Verlag]

Theo Lingen as Professor Krull in *Die Kassette*. Munich, Bayerisches Staatsschauspiel, 1961. [Goethe house]

predecessor Wedekind, Sternheim chose to ridicule rather than excoriate. While his dramatic style anticipated that of the expressionists, he avoided their tendency toward exaggerated characterization: bourgeois traits themselves, if properly presented, were damning enough. Nor did Sternheim offer theories for social reform. He had little admiration for the upper classes, and he saw the lower classes as only too eager to adopt bourgeois values. Consequently his work has been alternately condemned as cynical and hailed as free of all contaminating illusion. Sternheim's stated aim was, by means of artistic expression, to reconcile morality and reason, which he found to be in perpetual conflict. The form of his expression is itself unusual. His plays have a staccato effect marked by crispness of form and rapidity of expression. The language is deliberately free of all lyricism and pared to the bare essentials of speech.

Sternheim's reputation (he was considered the foremost playwright of his time) rests largely on five plays: the double-edged *Citizen Schippel* (1913), a devastating attack on bourgeois and proletarian alike; the satirical trilogy chronicling the rise of the Maske family, *The Underpants* (1911), *The Snob* (*Der Snob*, 1914), and *1913* (wr. 1913/14, prod. 1919); and *The Strongbox* (*Die Kassette*, 1911). Others of particular interest are *Tabula rasa* (wr. 1915, prod. 1919), in which the Socialist Herr Ständer shamelessly exploits his party, comrades, and family in order to attain individual freedom in the form of a pen-

sion and then abandons them; *Oscar Wilde* (wr. 1925), which reflects Sternheim's view of woman as a secondary sex that is incomprehensible to man; three short plays collectively entitled *The Adventurer* (*Der Abenteurer*, pub. 1922), which present a remarkably antierotic view of the exploits of Casanova; a skillful adaptation from Diderot entitled *The Mask of Virtue* (*Die Marquise von Arcis*, wr. 1918); and *The School at Uznach or The New Matter-of-factness* (1926), set in a progressive Swiss girls' school and describing the pursuit of the principal's son by four modern, aggressive, and emancipated young women. Sternheim's other plays, some of which are adaptations or imitations of existing dramatic models, fall far short of his best work and are of little interest.

The Underpants; A Pair of Drawers (*Die Hose*, 1911). First play of a satiric trilogy, in which the middle-class world of Theobald Maske is shattered by the news that his wife's underpants have fallen down during the Kaiser's parade. Passionate advances are made to the wife following this embarrassing incident, but the wily husband turns passion to profit, taking two of his wife's admirers in as roomers. Meanwhile, his wife plots with her romantic neighbor Gertrude, a young spinster, to arrange an affair with one of the roomers, a young nobleman. But Theobald appears, manages cleverly to divert the suitor's thoughts, and disappears on a drunken spree with the nobleman. Later, when he meets Gertrude on her way to his wife with a new pair of bloomers, Theobald promptly seduces her. As the passionate roomer moves on to other conquests and is supplanted by a new tenant, Theobald happily reckons his profits on the nobleman's forfeited lease and announces to his wife that they can now afford to have a child.

The Strongbox (*Die Kassette*, 1911). Expressionist drama satirizing the obsessive materialism of the bourgeoisie. Professor Heinrich Krull returns home from a blissful honeymoon with Fanny, his second wife, to find himself caught between the connivings of Fanny and his spinster aunt. The aunt uses her wealth, 140,000 marks contained in a strongbox, as a means of asserting her authority over him, although it is revealed that she has already willed her money to the church. Krull's happiness dissolves into an obsession to secure the contents of the strongbox. His daydreams of elaborate schemes for investment after he has stolen the strongbox drive the passionate Fanny into the arms of Silkenbrand, a dilettantish woman chaser who has already seduced Krull's daughter into marrying him. When Silkenbrand, finally attracted by the contents of the strongbox, joins forces with Krull, Fanny is left waiting at her bedroom door.

Citizen Schippel (*Bürger Schippel*, 1913). Comedy satirizing the snobbery of the proletarian Paul Schippel and the hypocrisy of the bourgeois Hicketier. The latter, head of the local male chorus, loses through sudden death his tenor Naumann, who has also been his sister Thekla's fiancé. Eager to win the Prince's laurel wreath at the annual singing contest, Hicketier has no choice but to ask Schippel, the only comparable tenor in town, to fill the vacancy. Schippel is initially overjoyed at this opportunity for social advancement, but the resentment and hatred he has accumulated over the years prompt him to accept only on condition that Thekla marry him. Hicketier agrees to this condition, but meanwhile Thekla has been compromised in a romance with the Prince. On learning this, Schippel, who has now adopted middle-class virtue, rejects her. When Thekla becomes engaged to Krey, another member of the choir, Schippel warns him about her "dark past." Krey challenges him to a duel, from which Schippel, a coward by nature, emerges the winner and a full-fledged *Bürger*.

The Snob (*Der Snob*, 1914). Satirical comedy, the second in a trilogy depicting the bourgeois mentality of the Maske family. Having become newly wealthy, Christian Maske seeks social prestige through marriage to Marianne, an impoverished nobleman's daughter. After breaking off relations with his mistress, to whom he is greatly indebted, and repaying her devotion in money, Christian sends his socially unacceptable parents (the Maskes of *The Underpants*) abroad. But his father reappears unexpectedly when Christian is entertaining Graf Palen, Marianne's father. In the ensuing conversation Christian learns that his humble origin does not change the nobleman's opinion of him, provided he identifies himself with the nobility. After the wedding Christian boasts to Marianne that he is a self-made man; but failing to impress her, he eventually conquers her by telling her that he is the illegitimate son of a count.

1913 (wr. 1913/14, prod. 1919). Last satire in the Maske family trilogy, so charged with tension that Sternheim ends it in pantomime. Christian Maske, shrewd and unscrupulous, having attained the status of baron and the power of a great industrialist, discovers that he has a worthy rival in his daughter Sofie. Her rapacity and cynicism have led her to the brink of destroying her father by arranging arms shipments to the Netherlands, shipments which he, expecting war and subsequent larger German contracts, has rejected. She circumvents Catholic competition by capitalizing on her Protestantism, but the craving for power in the seventy-year-old Maske explodes violently, and he is converted to Catholicism in order to frustrate his daughter's schemes. He cannot carry out his plans, however, for he suddenly dies of a heart attack. As the news of Maske's death reaches them, his other two daughters, whose empty lives are centered on the world of fashion, freeze like puppets. Wearing careless negligees, they parade their hypocritical sorrow in front of the corpse, a tacit, spectral symbol of capitalism, as the wind blows through the window. With Maske's death, the quest for material values is ended, and the family is left with nothing of value.

[PETER JELAVICH]

**Gustav Gründgens
in *Der Snob*,
Berlin, 1946.**
[Goethe House]

PLAYS

1. *Das eiserne Kreuz* (*The Iron Cross*). Play. Written 1893.
2. *Der Heiland* (*The Savior*). Comedy. Written 1898.
3. *Judas Ischarioth* (*Judas Iscariot*). Tragedy. Written 1901.
4. *Fanale!* Play. Written 1901.
5. *Auf Krugdorf*. Play. Produced 1902.
6. *Perleberg*. Comedy. Produced Frankfurt am Main, 1917. First unpublished version: *Mihlow* (1903).
7. *Vom König und der Königin* (*About the King and the Queen*). Play. Written 1905.
8. *Ulrich und Brigitte* (*Ulrich and Brigitte*). Play. Written 1907.
9. *Don Juan*. Tragedy. Written 1909. Produced Berlin, 1910. Early version of *Der Abenteurer*.
10. *Die Hose** (*The Underpants; A Pair of Drawers*). Comedy, 4 acts. Written 1909/10. Published 1911. Produced Berlin, Kammerspiele des Deutsches Theater (Max Reinhardt), Feb. 15, 1911, as *Der Riese* (*The Giant*). First play of the Maske family trilogy.
11. *Die Kassette* (*The Strongbox*). Comedy, 5 acts. Written 1910/11. Published 1912. Produced Berlin, Deutsches Theater, Nov. 24, 1911.
12. *Bürger Schippel* (*Citizen Schippel*). Comedy, 5 acts. Written 1911/12. Published 1913. Produced Berlin, Kammerspiele, Mar. 5, 1913.
13. *Der Snob** (*The Snob; A Place in the World*). Comedy, 3 acts. Written 1913. Published 1914. Produced Berlin, Kammerspiele, Feb. 2, 1914. Second play of the Maske family trilogy.
14. *Der Kandidat* (*The Candidate*). Comedy. Published 1914. Produced Vienna, Volksbühne, 1915. Based on Gustave Flaubert's play *Le candidat*.
15. *1913*. Drama, 3 acts. Written 1913/14. Published 1915. Produced Frankfurt am Main, Schauspielhaus, Jan. 23, 1919. Third play of the Maske family trilogy.
16. *Das leidende Weib* (*The Suffering Woman*). Play. Published 1915. Produced in closed production, 1916. Based on Friedrich von Klinger's play of the same title.
17. *Tabula rasa*. Drama, 3 acts. Written 1915. Published 1916. Produced Berlin, Kleines Theater, Jan. 25, 1919.
18. *Der Scharmante* (*The Charming One*). Comedy. Written 1915. Produced Vienna, 1915. Based on Guy de Maupassant.
19. *Der Geizige* (*The Miser*). Comedy. Written 1916. Produced Berlin, 1917. Based on Molière's play *L'avare*.
20. *Die Marquise von Arcis** (*The Mask of Virtue*). Play. Written 1918. Published 1919. Based on a play by Denis Diderot.
21. *Der entfesselte Zeitgenosse* (*The Unchained Contemporary*). Comedy. Written 1920. Produced Darmstadt, 1921.
22. *Manon Lescaut*. Play. Written 1921. Produced Berlin, 1921. Based on the novel by Abbé Prévost.
23. *Das Fossil* (*The Fossil*). Drama, 3 acts. Written 1921/22. Published 1925. Produced Hamburg, Kammerspiele, Nov. 6, 1923.
24. *Der Nebbich*. Comedy. Written 1922. Produced Darmstadt, 1922.
25. *Der Abenteurer* (*The Adventurer*). Comedy. Published 1922. New version of *Don Juan*.
26. *Oscar Wilde*. Tragedy. Written 1925. Produced Berlin, Deutsches Theater.
27. *Die Schule von Uznach oder Neue Sächlichkeit* (*The School at Uznach or The New Matter-of-factness*). Comedy. Written 1926. Produced Hamburg, Cologne, and Mannheim, 1926.
28. *Die Väter oder Knockout* (*The Fathers or Knockout*). Comedy. Written 1928.
29. *Die Königin* (*The Queen*). Play. Produced Görlitz, 1929.
30. *John Pierpont Morgan*. Play. Written 1930. Published 1930.
31. *Aut Caesar aut nihil*. Comedy. Written 1930. Published 1930.

EDITIONS

Collections
Dramen, ed. by W. Emrich, Berlin, 1963; *Gesamtwerk*, ed. by W. Emrich, Neuwied am Rhein, 10 vols., 1963–1976; *Scenes from the Heroic Life of the Middle Classes*, tr. by M. A. L. Brown, London, 1970.
Individual Plays
The Mask of Virtue. Published in *Famous Plays of 1935*, tr. by A. Dukes, London, 1935.

The Snob. Published in *From the Modern Repertoire,* ed. and tr. by E. R. Bentley, ser. 1, Bloomington, Ind., 1949–1956.

The Underpants. Published in *The Modern Theatre,* ed. and tr. by E. R. Bentley, vol. 6, Garden City, N.Y., 1955–1960.

CRITICISM

G. Manfred, *Sternheim und seine besten Bühnenwerke,* 1923; F. Eisenlohr, *Carl Sternheim,* Munich, 1926; F. Blei, *Über Wedekind, Sternheim und das Theater,* Munich, 1951; H. Karasek, *Carl Sternheim,* Velber bei Hannover, 1965; W. Wendler, *Carl Sternheim,* Frankfurt am Main, 1966; W. G. Sebald, *Carl Sternheim: Kritiker und Opfer der wilhelminischen Ära,* Stuttgart, 1969; J. Schönert, ed., *Carl Sternheims Dramen: Zur Textanalyse, Ideologiekritik und Rezeptionsgeschichte,* Heidelberg, 1975.

Stevenson, William   (d. 1575)

English lecturer and dramatist. He is believed to be the "Mr. S., Master of Art," named as the author on the title page of *Gammer Gurton's Needle,* which was produced at Christ's College, Cambridge, between 1552 and 1563. Although some scholars have attributed the play to John Still (1543?–1608), bishop of Bath and Wells, Stevenson's presence as a fellow of Christ's College at the time of its production and his involvement in the dramatic productions of the college point to his authorship. The play, a lively farce reflecting Elizabethan country life, is divided into five acts and written in verse. The author reproduced the atmosphere of village life by his use of country dialect and realistic, homespun characters.

Gammer Gurton's Needle (1552/1563). Farce in which the loss of Gammer Gurton's mending needle quickly develops into a village crisis. Owing to the mischievous plotting of Diccon, the beggar who is responsible for suggesting that the needle has been stolen when, in fact, it was lost while the old woman was mending the leather breeches of her handyman Hodge, Gammer Gurton and the alewife Dame Chat are at odds with one another. Other characters involved in the story are the absurd curate Dr. Rat, whose head is broken for his interference; Master Bailey, the bailiff; and Gib, a cat. When Master Bailey arrives, Diccon brazenly confesses to the trick; Bailey imposes a good-natured penalty on the beggar, and the unlucky Hodge discovers the missing needle inside his breeches.

Stodola, Ivan   (1888–1977)

Slovak playwright. Stodola was a physician and later in life a high-ranking official of the Czechoslovak Ministry of Health. His career as playwright was closely related to the foundation of the Slovak National Theatre after World War I. Prior to that, plays in Slovakia were performed only by amateur groups, which influenced many playwrights to write mostly literary dramas. Stodola was the first Slovak playwright who fully understood the mechanism of the theatre, and he was a skillful craftsman.

The center of gravity of Stodola's work lies in his satirical comedies. In *Our Minister* (*Náš pán ministr,* 1926) Stodola ridicules people's fascination with impressive-sounding official titles and positions that due to historical changes have lost their meaning. *A Tea Party with the Senator* (*Čaj u pana senátora,* 1929) describes the rise of an insignificant individual to political prominence thanks to

the folly and narrow-mindedness of society. A much more bitter satire is Stodola's most successful play *Jožko Pučík and His Career* (*Jožko Pučík a jeho kariéra,* 1931). Set in the milieu of a charitable organization, it exposes the cynical abuse of peoples' trust and humanitarian feelings. Unlike the rather traditional earlier plays, *Banking House Khuvich & Comp.* (1935), set in the United States, bears some resemblance to the dramatic hyperboles of Brecht. Besides comedies, Stodola wrote social dramas, such as *The Shepherd's Wife* (*Bačova žena,* 1928) and *The Last Symphony* (*Posledná symfonia,* 1930), as well as the historical plays *King Svatopluk* (*Král Svatopluk,* 1931) and *Marina Havranová* (1941).   PAUL I. TRENSKY

Stoppard, Tom   (1937–   )

Born in Czechoslovakia on July 3, 1937, Tom Stoppard was the son of Eugene Straussler, a doctor employed by a shoe manufacturing company. In 1939 the family moved to Singapore, and in 1942 the mother evacuated with her two sons to India before the Japanese invasion, in which her husband was killed. She became the manager of a shoe shop, and in 1946 she married Kenneth Stoppard, who was serving in the British Army. Returning to England with his newly acquired family, he worked in the machine tool business.

After being educated in a Nottinghamshire prep school and a Yorkshire public school, Tom became a journalist in Bristol, working for the *Western Daily Press* and the *Bristol Evening World* as news reporter, feature writer, theatre critic, film critic, and gossip columnist. Six years of regular employment and two years as a freelance writer were followed by an appointment as drama critic to the London-based magazine *Scene.* He published some short stories, and was commissioned to write two short plays and five episodes of a serial for the BBC's Radio 4. In 1964 he wrote *Rosencrantz and Guildenstern Meet King Lear,* a one-act play in verse. A revised version, *Rosencrantz and Guildenstern Are Dead,* was produced by Oxford students at the Edinburgh Festival in 1966 and at the National Theatre in 1967. His subsequent full-length plays include *Jumpers* (1972), *Travesties* (1974), and *Night and Day* (1978).

Tom Stoppard.
[Courtesy of
Fraser & Dunlop
(Scripts) Ltd.]

Tom Stoppard's first marriage was to José Ingle in 1965, and in 1972 he married Dr. Miriam Moore-Robinson.

WORK

Many of Stoppard's best plays have been launched like satellites out of other plays. *Rosencrantz and Guildenstern Are Dead* drags two minor Shakespearean characters into the foreground while demoting Hamlet to a small supporting role. *Travesties* might have been written in the margin of Oscar Wilde's *The Importance of Being Earnest* if there had been enough blank space on the pages of the edition Stoppard owned. *The Real Inspector Hound* (1968) is an affectionate parody of the murder mystery, with two drama critics starting on the periphery and becoming progressively ensnared in the action.

The two strongest influences on his plays have been Beckett and T. S. Eliot. Without the example of *Waiting for Godot* Stoppard would never have arrived at the idea of making inaction into action. Like Vladimir and Estragon, Rosencrantz and Guildenstern do nothing but wait. As courtiers it is their role to attend on the prince. It is not a play in which the actors can be called on to improvise, but the impression it gives is that the characters do nothing but improvise ways of passing the time. (Implied ontological question: do any of us ever do anything else?) And like Eliot's Prufrock, who has no ambition to be Prince Hamlet, Rosencrantz and Guildenstern are content to be of use, politic, cautious, and deferential.

Much of Shakespeare's dialogue is interpolated into Stoppard's play, and the shifts from Elizabethan blank verse to modern prose are disconcertingly vertiginous. The change of style seems to bring a change of values with it. (Implied moral question: what have we lost in abandoning the heroic?)

In other plays Stoppard has experimented with different ways of changing perspective. In the 1966 radio play *If You're Glad I'll Be Frank*, Gladys, who provides the voice of the Post Office's speaking clock, complains that "the scale you live by" is upset when you look down from a great height, "reducing the life-size to nothing." In the 1967 radio play *Albert's Bridge*, Albert is happy only when he is painting a very high bridge: from this viewpoint the urban chaos looks orderly. Seen from

Brian Murry (left) and John Wood were the luckless protagonists in the Broadway production of *Rosencrantz and Guildenstern Are Dead*. [Martha Swope]

Royal Shakespeare Company production of *Travesties* with John Hurt (left) as Tristan Tzara and John Wood as Henry Carr. [Photograph by Sophie Baker]

above, "The idea of society is just about tenable." In both *Jumpers* (1972) and in an earlier television play, *Another Moon Called Earth* (1967), a woman is driven almost insane by the intrusion of astronauts on the surface of the moon. Why should they have the right to look from a lunar standpoint at human life on earth?

Like John Donne's poems, Stoppard's plays are full of relationships between things that commonsense would never have brought together. Sometimes the connections depend on the multiple meanings of a single word like "jumpers," which is made to link gymnastics with philosophical leaps. Sometimes the connections depend on history: commonsense would never have brought Lenin, James Joyce, and Tristan Tzara together in Zurich, and it is characteristic of Stoppard to make them all subsidiary characters in a drama that revolves around an insignificant English diplomat, Henry Carr.

Until 1978 Stoppard prided himself on having the courage of his lack of political conviction, but the television play *Professional Foul* (1978), the extravaganza for actors and orchestra, *Every Good Boy Deserves Favour* (1977), and the stage play *Night and Day* (1978) all react strongly against the left-wing conformism that has become so fashionable among the younger British playwrights. The television play hits out against repression in Iron Curtain countries, the extravaganza mocks at the Soviet habit of imprisoning dissidents among the insane in asylums, and the stage play argues strongly against the idea of a closed shop in journalism. It is also one of the few British stage plays of the seventies to show a trade unionist in an unfavorable light.

Stoppard has written no original plays for the stage since *Night and Day*, but his translations and adaptations have approximated more and more closely to the condition of creative writing. His first two translations—of

Mrozek's *Tango* (1960) and Lorca's *The House of Bernarda Alba* (1973)—stuck fairly closely to the original script, but *The Undiscovered Country* moved uninhibitedly away from Schnitzler's *Das weite Land*. *On the Razzle* was based on *Einen Jux will er sich machen*, but, as Stoppard said in a program note, "I abandoned quite early on the onus of conveying Nestroy intact into English."

Rosencrantz and Guildenstern Are Dead (1966). Taking *Hamlet* as a point of departure and repeatedly returning to incorporate slabs of it into the dialogue, Stoppard effectively equates Shakespeare's text with destiny, implicitly raising the question of free will in the new slabs of twentieth-century prose that are laid neatly in between the long passages of quotation. How much initiative or freedom of maneuver do attendant lords have? Their game playing, their philosophical speculations, their arguments, their half-hearted attempts at rescuing their dignity and asserting themselves are rather like the pathetic fluttering of a brilliantly colored butterfly with its feet and its insect body inextricably caught in the web of text. They can no more evade the death that Shakespeare has ordained for them than any of us can evade the death that the human condition has ordained for us. And like them, we exist on the edge of great events we cannot control.

Shakespeare, who shows little interest in Rosencrantz and Guildenstern, provides proportionately little information about them; Stoppard, refusing to invent their past experiences, leaves us in equal ignorance about what has shaped them, but he focuses sympathetically on their ignorance and their impotence. As he says, he sees them less as henchmen than as bewildered innocents. The two questions are: How did they pass the time when they were given so little to do? And when they were given something, did they have any alternative—not being heroes—to doing it?

The Real Inspector Hound (1968). What *The Real Inspector Hound* has in common with *Rosencrantz and Guildenstern* is the central structural device: in oscillating between one style of dialogue and another, both are oscillating between one play and another, but Stoppard ingeniously welds the two plays together. As the author of both plays in *The Real Inspector Hound*, he can create an even tighter interrelationship between the two levels of unreality, contriving, on both, plentiful opportunities for parody. Like Rosencrantz and Guildenstern, the two theatre critics watching the thriller start off as passive spectators, privileged to comment and mock from the sidelines, so Stoppard can guy their affectations and their jargon. Interwoven with their conversation is a hilarious display of coincidences, clichés, and complications such as might almost be found in a murder play. The charwoman who feeds background information to the audience by the way she answers the telephone, the suave stranger, the ingenue in tennis clothes, the demonstratively casual policemen—with apparent effortlessness Stoppard brings them all in, making neatly comic points about each.

Jumpers (1972). More ambitiously constructed than any of his previous plays, and more elaborately serio-comic, *Jumpers* makes a materialistic new university serve as a microcosm for a materialistic new society, while the professor of moral philosophy, a theist in a godless world, seems almost heroic in continuing with his unfashionable idealism. Once again a murder mystery is woven into the plot, adding to the tension without detracting from the high-spirited comedy. Almost as if he were nervous of not offering the audience enough, Stoppard incorporates songs from the retired pop singer rather improbably married to the moral philosopher, a striptease performed by a secretary dangling from a chandelier, and acrobatics performed by a pyramid of athletes. The storyline would have been quite strong enough for him to manage without these diversions, but they do no damage to it.

Travesties (1974). Set in Zurich in 1918, when Lenin, James Joyce, and Tristan Tzara were living there, the play questions the relationship between artistic revolution and political revolution. We meet the elderly Henry Carr, who erroneously remembers himself as having been British Consul in Zurich at the time, and all the events from the past are presented through the distorting mirror of his memory. The real Henry Carr played Algernon in the amateur production of *The Importance of Being Earnest* for which James Joyce, cofounder of the amateur society, acted as business manager; Stoppard's play aptly runs parallel to Wilde's, using Tzara as Ernest and introducing a Gwendolyn and a Cecily—Carr's younger sister and a librarian in the Zurich public library.

Night and Day (1978). A war of secession is about to break out in an African state which was formerly a British colony, but the main conflict in the play is between two journalists, a seasonal unionist and an inexperienced idealist, who believes, as Stoppard does, that trade union pressure for a closed shop in journalism is endangering the freedom of the British press. They meet at the house of a businessman who owns a telex and whose wife has spent one night in a London hotel with the unionist. She now prefers the younger man, and is broadly in agreement with his ideas, but the machinations of the unionist, who is anxious to scoop an interview with the black president of the country and to have his young rival out of the way while he does so, lead to his death.

RONALD HAYMAN

PLAYS

1. *A Walk on the Water*. Stage play (see 7) adapted for television. Produced ITV, February, 1964.

2. *The Gamblers*. Play. Produced by the Drama Department of Bristol University, 1965.

3. *Rosencrantz and Guildenstern Are Dead*. Play, 3 acts. Published 1967. Produced by the Oxford Theatre Group at the Edinburgh Festival, August, 1966, and by the National Theatre in April, 1967.

4. *A Separate Peace*. Play. Published 1969. Produced BBC, August, 1966.

5. *Teeth*. Play. Produced BBC, February, 1967.

6. *Another Moon Called Earth*. Play. Produced BBC, June, 1967.

7. *Enter a Free Man*. Play, 2 acts. Published 1968. Produced March, 1968.

8. *The Real Inspector Hound*. Play, 1 act. Published 1968. Produced June, 1968.

9. *Neutral Ground*. Play. Produced Thames Television, December, 1968.

10. *The Engagement*. Play. Produced NBC, March, 1970.

11. *After Magritte.* Play. Published 1971. Produced April, 1970.
12. *Dogg's Our Pet.* Play, 1 act. Published 1976. Produced December, 1971.
13. *Jumpers.* Play, 2 acts and a coda. Published 1972. Produced January, 1972.
14. *Travesties.* Play, 2 acts. Published 1975. Produced June, 1974.
15. *Dirty Linen* and *New-Found-Land.* Play. Published 1976. Produced April, 1976.
16. *Every Good Boy Deserves Favour.* Play with music. Produced July, 1977.
17. *Professional Foul.* Play. Produced BBC, October, 1977.
18. *Night and Day.* Play, 2 acts. Published 1978. Produced 1978.

CRITICISM

R. Hayman, *Tom Stoppard*, London and New York, 1977 (3d ed. 1979).

Storey, David (1933–   )

English playwright. Born in Wakefield, the son of a miner, David Storey went on from the local art school to the Slade School in London. He has been a professional rugby football player and has published several novels including *This Sporting Life* (1960), *Radcliffe* (1963), *A Temporary Life* (1973), and *Saville* (1976). Some of his plays are by-products of his novels. *The Contractor* (1969) grew out of *Radcliffe*, while *Life Class* (1974) is a variant on an incident in *A Temporary Life.*

The first play, *The Restoration of Arnold Middleton* (wr. 1959; prod. 1966), tells the story of a provincial schoolmaster driven to the verge of madness. *In Celebration* (1969) deals with a family reunion in the house of a miner whose work seems to have more significance for him than any of his educated sons (teacher, solicitor,

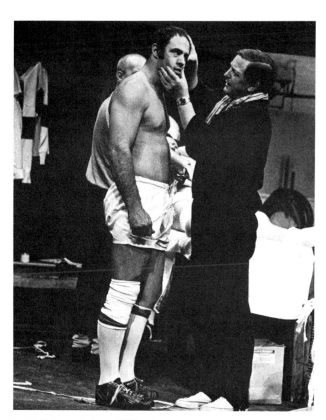

David Daker and Don McKillop in a scene from *The Changing Room*. [Royal Court Theatre. Photograph by John Haynes]

publicist) can find in theirs. The main event, the dinner party to celebrate the fortieth wedding anniversary, occurs offstage in an interval, and similarly in *The Contractor* (1969) the central incident in the plot is squeezed out of the action. We see a marquee being erected for a wedding breakfast, which is eaten during the interval after the second act. The action of the play revolves around desultory conversations between representatives of different age groups, social strata, and attitudes to society.

Home (1970) moves further away from realism. Set in a mental home, it takes its color from conversations between two male and two female inmates. The rhythm and the tone Storey creates for them determine the play, which gains its resonance from its audience in its sense of dislocation.

The Changing Room (1971) is more realistic, portraying rugby football players in their changing room before and after a match. The wooden benches, clothes pegs, clothes, and towels seem to contribute almost as much as the dialogue to the substance of the play, while the male bodies in progressive stages of dressing and undressing provide a spectacle which is fully exploited theatrically, but not pornographically.

RONALD HAYMAN

CRITICISM

J. R. Taylor, *The Second Wave*, 1971; R. Hayman, *British Theatre since 1955*, London and New York, 1979.

Strindberg, August (1849–1912)

Swedish novelist, poet, and dramatist. He was born on January 22, 1849, in the Riddarholm district of Stockholm. His father, Carl Oscar Strindberg, was a shipping agent who could boast a trace of aristocratic blood but relatively little business success, and his mother, Ulrika Eleonora Norling, was a tailor's daughter who had been a domestic servant before becoming Carl Oscar's mistress. August, the fourth of their eleven children, was the first to be born in wedlock.

That Strindberg identified with his mother's proletarian background is evident in the title of his autobiographical novel, *The Son of a Servant* ((*Tjänstekvinnans son*, 1886), but he was also his father's son, proud and fastidious, with aristocratic, antidemocratic inclinations. This was only one of the many paradoxes in his life. He professed to be a skeptic, and occasionally an atheist; yet religion was a lifetime preoccupation. He often used Biblical images to express the special nature of his destiny. A contentious, tormented, compulsive, and lonely man, he saw himself as an Ishmael cast into the desert or as a Jacob wrestling with God. He was an artist of prodigious energy (his collected works number fifty-five volumes), who made innovative contributions to a variety of literary genres—drama, poetry, biography, the novel, the short story, and the essay. Nevertheless, for long periods in his life he insisted that art was a useless occupation. Dismissed by some critics as a strident misogynist, it was his fate to seek an impossible ideal: a mate who would be both mother and lover, intellectual comrade and dedicated domestic.

August Strindberg.
[Swedish
Information
Service]

As a child he was precocious but hypersensitive, and in later years he still felt the pain caused by the cruelties and injustices that he said he had suffered at home and in school. He regarded his father as fair-minded but strict and aloof. He was very attached to his mother, and her death when he was thirteen years old was traumatic for him. Matters became worse when his father remarried within a year. Shocked by his father's action, the adolescent boy soon became hostile to his stepmother. She, in turn it seemed, scorned his intellectual ambitions. In his studies he was now discovering science; he devoured books on chemistry and physics, aspiring to become an inventor. But the time of sexual awakening proved difficult for him, as his pietistic family background had taught him to associate sexuality with impurity and sinfulness. He plunged into his childhood faith to save his soul from damnation, but finding no solace in it, he turned instead to the liberalism of Theodore Parker, the American Unitarian and social reformer.

With the aid of a small inheritance from his mother, he entered the University of Uppsala in 1867; but instead of the free and glorious search for truth he had expected, he found an academic formalism that struck him as rigid and meaningless. He stayed for one semester, and after a brief and unpleasant period of teaching, he was hired to tutor the children of Dr. Axel Lamm, a physician who encouraged him to study medicine. His failure to pass the preliminary examination in chemistry ended these hopes.

By now Strindberg was interested in becoming an actor. After working for a short time as a supernumerary at the Royal Dramatic Theatre, he auditioned for a regular position in the acting company. When he was turned down and advised to enroll in the theatre's acting school, his humiliation and disappointment were so great that he attempted suicide by means of opium. He tried to regain his self-respect by writing a comedy, *A Name-day Gift* (*En namnsdagsgåva*, now lost), which he submitted to the Royal Dramatic Theatre. It was rejected, as were two other plays written in the autumn of 1869: *The Freethinker* (*Fritänkaren*), another comedy, and *Hermione*, a verse tragedy. The theatre director, however, was encouraging; he advised Strindberg to return to the University of Uppsala and prepare for a writing career.

Returning to Uppsala in the spring of 1870, he helped found the Runa Förbundet (Runa Society), a student group devoted to Nordic folklore and literary pursuits. Soon he was the group's literary leader, a position affirmed in 1870 when the Royal Dramatic Theatre produced his play *In Rome* (*I Rom,* 1870). He then began to write in earnest and received encouragement from King Charles XV in the form of a small stipend, which shortly after was abruptly terminated. In 1872, having completed a senior candidacy essay on Danish playwright Adam Oehlenschläger's *Earl Hakon*, Strindberg left Uppsala to work as a newspaperman in Stockholm. *See* OEHLENSCHLÄGER, ADAM.

It was at this time, when he was twenty-three years old, that Strindberg wrote *Master Olof (Mäster Olof)*, a historical drama so powerful and unconventional that the Royal Dramatic Theatre would have nothing to do with it. The director declared that Strindberg had rendered commonplace several of the great heroes of Swedish history and had handled them with too much familiarity. He suggested drastic revisions, including a properly respectful attitude, and the rewriting of the play in verse. Distressed but anxious to please, Strindberg labored over an inferior verse version of the play, which he did not complete until 1876.

From 1872 to 1874 he earned a bare subsistence as a journalist, often obtaining a job because of his writing talent, only to forfeit it because of his unorthodox and original insights. His journalistic experience may have helped give his writing style a spontaneity that has remained as fresh today as when the plays were first written.

In 1874 he became an assistant librarian at the Royal Library, a position that for the first time gave him economic stability and status, although he had still to teach to supplement his salary. At the library he studied Chinese so that he could catalogue the library's collection of Chinese manuscripts.

The following year was a fateful one. The strong-willed young man, fully aware of his intellectual power and inbued with a keen sense of sexual superiority, met the first of the three women who became his wives, all antagonists in excruciating marital contests. Siri von Essen, a member of the Swedish aristocracy in Finland, was the wife of Baron Carl Gustav Wrangel when Strindberg first met her. In 1876 Siri divorced Wrangel, became Strindberg's mistress, and embarked on an acting career. She became pregnant and married Strindberg on December 30, 1877. A child born in January 1878 survived only several hours. Although the couple had three more children, two girls and a boy, Strindberg never lost the sense of guilt he felt over the death of his first child.

During this period Strindberg began to enjoy a modest success as an author of fiction. In 1879 he published *The Red Room (Röda rummet)*, a satirical novel inspired by Balzac and Dickens which dealt with the reactionism and opportunism that pervaded Swedish political, cultural, and religious institutions. The resulting furor established Strindberg as a leading, if controversial, Scandinavian author. His new status enabled him to persuade the Royal Dramatic Theatre to produce his original prose version of *Master Olof*. The enthusiastic reception it received in 1881 spurred him to intense activity, and he rapidly produced works of almost every literary genre.

The original ideas he expressed in these works continued to bring him into conflict with nearly all segments of the establishment. *The Swedish People (Svenska folket,* 1882), a history of Sweden emphasizing its cultural and folk traditions, earned him the enmity of scholars for whom the glory of Sweden's history resided in its kings and their exploits.

This rejection as well as attacks by literary critics irritated Strindberg immensely. He retaliated with *The New Kingdom (Det nya riket,* 1882), a savagely satirical story collection in which he singled out for ridicule prominent noblemen, bankers, publishers, and institutions such as the Swedish Academy and the Royal Dramatic Theatre. The resentment provoked by *The Red Room* was mild compared with the hostility that greeted *The New Kingdom.* Haunted by feelings of guilt and anxiety, Strindberg was close to nervous collapse. In 1883 he left Sweden and took his family to Grèz, a colony of Scandinavian expatriates near Fontainebleau in France. There he was welcomed by Bjørnstjerne Bjørnson and the Norwegian novelist Jonas Lie (*see* BJØRNSON, BJØRNSTJERNE). Shortly after his arrival in France, his first volume of verse, *Poems (Dikter)*, was published in Sweden. In its own way it was as innovative as *The Red Room,* bringing to Swedish poetry a fresh realism that paved the way for a lyrical renaissance in the 1890s.

The autumn of 1884 marked another fateful turning point in Strindberg's life: the first volume of a two-volume story collection, *Married (Giftas),* appeared and caused a major sensation. Written in a candid, racy style, the stories depicted various kinds of domestic problems. Because of a sarcastic reference to the sacrament, both author and publisher were indicted on a charge of blasphemy. At first Strindberg wanted to avoid the furor by remaining in Switzerland, but then, persuaded by his friends, he returned to Sweden for the trial and was acquitted.

The effects of the trial on his marriage were disastrous. It could not have been easy for Siri, who felt that she had abandoned a promising stage career in Sweden, to move about the Continent with three small children and a restless, increasingly paranoid husband. After the trial her husband suspected her of being part of an international league of women who were persecuting him. Eventually he made public his suspicions in an outrageously indiscreet but brilliant autobiographical novel, *A Madman's Defense* (first published in a rather free German translation after several years' delay as *Die Beichte eines Thoren,* in 1893). The original manuscript was found only recently among the papers left by the Norwegian painter Edvard Munch. In addition to its inherent literary value, it is a valuable source book, containing incidents and character relationships that Strindberg used again in his so-called naturalistic plays written in 1887 and 1888.

Even as his marital and financial problems worsened, Strindberg's interests widened, particularly in philosophy, psychology, and theatrical experimentation. He corresponded with Friedrich Nietzsche, became an admirer of Edgar Allan Poe, and a follower, albeit skeptical, of Emile Zola's naturalistic movement (*see* ZOLA, EMILE). In Strindberg's hands the "slice of life" (*tranche de vie*) realism of the French naturalists became broader in scope, more deeply probing into dramatic character and conflict. In fact, "naturalism" is really a misnomer when applied to plays like *Comrades (Kamraterna;* wr. 1881, prod. 1905). *The Father (Fadren,* 1887), *Miss Julie (Fröken Julie,* wr. 1888), and *Creditors (Fordringsägare,* wr. 1888). In these four plays, which share the source material of *A Madman's Defense,* jealousy, hatred, and lust so distort the situations and characterizations that the effects produced often seem more unreal than real; yet each of them (particularly *The Father* and *Miss Julie*) evokes a harrowing and authentic sense of reality. These works established Strindberg as an international dramatist of the first rank. Unfortunately, few of his plays were produced, and even those brought in little income.

In Paris, Strindberg had been impressed by André Antoine's Théâtre Libre. Having decided to open a Scandinavian counterpart in Denmark, he began to write a series of short plays that would be appropriate for such a theatre. *Miss Julie* opened his Scandinavian Experimental Theatre in Copenhagen in 1889, but after one performance Strindberg had to abandon the project as hopeless.

He returned to Stockholm in 1889 an unhappy man and continued to write satirical and naturalistic one-act plays for an experimental theatre, which remained his persistent dream. Meanwhile his personal affairs had become stormy and complex; his marriage ended in 1891 with vicious mutual recriminations. Strindberg was in dire poverty, and late in 1892 friends provided him with funds to move to Berlin, where he met Frida Uhl, an Austrian journalist. They were married in May 1893, but the new marriage was in trouble from the start. They had one child—a daughter—but were separated in 1894 and divorced in 1897.

The years between 1892 and 1897 were desperate for Strindberg. Deeply depressed, he abandoned writing for his early love, scientific experimentation. Characteristically, he eschewed the conventional. He became an alchemist, with dreams of upsetting the international market for gold, and a serious student of the occult, sensing mysterious signs and portents everywhere. All the while, his physical and mental health was deteriorating.

From 1894 to 1896 he experienced five psychotic episodes that are commonly referred to as his "inferno crisis." Most of this period was spent in Paris, where he was a pitiful figure, believing himself persecuted by corrective spirits which he called "the Powers." His shabby appearance shocked friends, whom he never forgave for their charitable efforts to raise money on his behalf.

Finally, in the fall of 1896, Strindberg managed to rouse himself from his state of near-insanity. He concluded that he was being punished for his arrogance and defiance of God. Readings in Swedenborg, Pythagoras, Origen, and Schopenhauer convinced him that he had to learn resignation. Earthly life became endurable for him only when he was able to interpret it as a special kind of hell, "a half-reality, a bad dream," in which one was punished for sins committed in another life and from which one would one day awaken with the comforting knowledge that all the "evil one had done [was] only a dream."

From then on, much of his work was to have a mystical and religious cast. After a short stay in Austria, he returned to Sweden and settled in the southern university town of Lund where he wrote the central portion of *Inferno*, a book which gives a frightening picture of his mental derangement, but also demonstrates the author's ability to re-create, in prose remarkable for its clarity and precision, the adventures of a man on the verge of lunacy. Strindberg was once more using his own tormented life as source material. There are, in fact, strong indications that he had at times willingly used himself as a guinea pig in psychological experimentation. Nevertheless, his inferno crisis must be taken seriously. It brought him back to religion, not to the pietism of his childhood, but to a syncretist faith and a mystical belief that transcendental powers were operative and expressed themselves in the most everyday happenings. Nothing was left to chance and coincidence; everything could be explained and understood through a system of correspondence or symbolic manifestations by supraterrestrial spirits.

His new religious faith had so improved his health that by 1898, when he had moved back to Stockholm, his mind was clear and he had a new zest for life. A successful revival of *Master Olof* encouraged him to resume playwriting after six unproductive years. From 1898 to 1909 he created thirty-six plays.

In 1898 he wrote the first two parts of *To Damascus* (*Till Damaskus, första delen* and *andra delen*) and *Advent* (*Advent, ett mysterium*). The following year, after writing *Crime and Crime* (*Brott och brott*), he turned once again to historical drama with *The Saga of the Folkungs* (*Folkungasagan*), *Gustav Vasa*, and *Erik XIV*; he also began *Gustav Adolf*.

In 1900, while searching for an actress to play the role of the lady in *To Damascus, I,* he attended a performance of *A Midsummer Night's Dream*, in which Harriet Bosse, a young Norwegian actress playing the role of Puck, attracted his attention. For her he wrote *Easter* (*Påsk*) and *The Crown Bride* (*Kronbruden*), the latter showing his growing interest in Maeterlinck (*see* MAETERLINCK, MAURICE). Soon he was again in love, and on May 6, 1901, the fifty-two-year-old dramatist and the twenty-three-year-old actress were married in Stockholm. They had one daughter, but before long Strindberg's jealousy and excessive protectiveness clashed with his young wife's adventurous disposition. Several times she fled from home, and in 1904 they were divorced.

During the marriage Strindberg had begun or completed work on a dozen plays, but afterward he wrote none for four years. He returned to the public eye in 1907 with a satirical novel, *Black Banners* (*Svarta fanor*), and the production of *A Dream Play* (*Ett drömspel*, wr. 1902) by the Swedish Theatre. Strindberg now joined forces with the young director August Falck to found the Intimate Theatre. In a matter of months they had assembled an enthusiastic company, created a theatre seating 161 persons in a remodeled store, and produced the first of five chamber plays which Strindberg was to write especially for the company.

In the summer of 1908 Strindberg moved into a new modern house with electricity and elevator, to which he gave the name "the Blue Tower." There he lived until his death from stomach cancer in May 1912 and wrote, among other things, his last play, *The Great Highway* (*Stora landsvägen*, wr. 1909), a station, or pilgrimage, drama. In 1909 the Intimate Theatre closed its doors. The audience reaction to Strindberg's last plays had been one of bewilderment at their unorthodox form and "expressionistic" conception of character.

Strindberg remained an active writer to the end of his life. The last years were much taken up by what became known as "the Strindberg feud"—a newspaper and magazine debate in which the author attacked such diverse topics as the Swedish Academy (of which he never became a member), the cult of Charles XII, the Olympic Games, the monarchy, and religious intolerance. The undaunted spirit behind these articles made Strindberg's name a household word in Sweden, feared among the upper classes and revered among young students and radicals.

In an essay entitled "The Poet's Children," written toward the end of his life, Strindberg emphasized the anonymity of the artist, suggesting that "the writer should have no grave and his ashes should be strewn before the wind and he should live only through his works, if these possess any vitality." When Strindberg died, his countrymen did not, however, pay much attention to his suggestion. Instead of being a quiet anonymous affair, his funeral attracted large groups of students, workers, and notables from various walks of life, who followed the procession to a simple grave at the New Church Cemetery—a route popularly known as "the great highway," also the title of Strindberg's last play.

WORK

Strindberg shares with Ibsen the distinction of having most influenced the development of drama in the twentieth century. Although both men overcame the deadening limitations of the dominant form of their day, the well-made play (*pièce bien faite*), Strindberg's search for new, more expressive forms was more far-reaching than Ibsen's and had more profound implications for subsequent dramatic practice. If Ibsen vitalized the well-made play by turning it into a subtle poetic instrument for the expression of psychological and philosophical speculation, Strindberg wrenched it beyond recognition by emphasizing the grotesque and irrational, by mirroring more starkly the turbulent despair that tortures modern man. Sean O'Casey said that "Strindberg shakes flame from the living planets and the fixed stars," and Eugene O'Neill called him "the precursor of all the modernity in our present theater." *See* IBSEN, HENRIK. *See also* WELL-MADE PLAY in glossary.

Strindberg has come down in history as one of the most autobiographical of writers, who crowded his plays with his own life experiences. A highly self-conscious artist, he searched for form as a means of giving structure and meaning to his own tumultuous existence. The result was a surprising number of highly original, independent works of art. The torments in his life—the broken marriages, the chronic financial problems, the stormy literary and political controversies, and, above all, the solitude that brought both anguish and inspiration—were transformed and objectified into brilliantly revealing images of alienation and anxiety.

Although drama was only one of Strindberg's literary outlets, the sheer bulk of his dramatic works is impressive: forty-seven full-length plays, twelve short plays, and four dramatic fragments. Even more impressive is the broad range of styles and genres that he mastered. It is tempting to categorize the different styles he employed as either realistic-naturalistic or nonrealistic, but the contours are often blurred. The so-called naturalistic plays are jarringly larger than life, and the nonrealistic plays are grounded in commonplace details that evoke a strange atmosphere of "half reality."

The plays can, however, be grouped by genre, although some overlap. There are plays set in a contemporary milieu, including the relatively realistic *Miss Julie* (1889) and the expressionistic *Ghost Sonata (Spöksonaten,* 1908). There are period plays, ranging from the cycle of twelve plays that present a chronicle of Swedish history from the late thirteenth to the late eighteenth century to plays that take place in ancient Greece, Iceland and Sweden in the Middle Ages, and Germany during the Reformation. There are fantasy plays with settings appropriate to fairy tales and folk ballads, such as *Swanwhite (Svanevit;* wr. 1901, prod. 1908) and *The Crown Bride (Kronbruden;* wr. 1900, prod. 1906). And there are pilgrimage plays, from *Lucky Per's Journey (Lycko-Pers resa,* 1883), inspired by *Peer Gynt,* to the unique masterpieces *To Damascus* (wr. 1898–1901) and *A Dream Play* (wr. 1902, prod. 1907).

It is significant that Strindberg chose the pilgrimage as the structural form for several of his finest works, for in a sense almost everything he wrote was part of an endless quest for the sources and meaning of his suffering. He found the chief source quite early: the feeling of love-hate at the core of all relations between men and women. But it was not until after the religious experiences of his "inferno crisis" that he found meaning in this destructive force. By then he had learned to accept certain of life's injustices as inevitable and even necessary. He looked upon himself as a vicarious sufferer, who because of his sensitivity experienced more pain than others. But he was never totally reconciled to the human condition; at best, the love between a man and a woman was "supreme joy in the greatest suffering," and living was endurable only because of the hope of an afterlife in which the spirit was released from the body.

Strindberg's work as a playwright was spasmodic and confined to four periods: 1869–1882, 1886–1892, 1898–1903, and 1907–1909. The plays of the first period were largely derivative efforts in a variety of dramatic forms showing influences from Shakespeare, Goethe, Oehlenschläger, Bjørnson, and Ibsen. It was a time when Strindberg's literary career was ascending and his private life stable and satisfactory. Marital problems receive attention in several of the plays, but there was no emphasis as yet on the deep-rooted conflict between the sexes that would dominate the later works.

The subject matter of the early plays reflects the concerns of an idealistic and sensitive young writer fighting both his family's opposition to his artistic ambitions and his own uncertainty about his talent. The lost manuscript *A Name-day Gift* apparently dealt with a young man's efforts to become reconciled with his father through his stepmother. *In Rome* (1870), a one-act verse comedy, is a fictional treatment of the period in the life of the Danish sculptor Bertel Thorvaldsen (1768/70–1844) when he reached the decision to become an artist rather than yield to his father's demand that he choose a more practical occupation. *The Outlaw (Den fredlöse,* 1871), a one-act tragedy, also deals with family conflict. It is set, like many popular plays of the day (such as Bjørnson's *Between the Battles,* which Strindberg used as a model), in the age of the Vikings.

Scene from a 1968 production of *The Father.* [Swedish Information Service]

Two of the early plays touch on social and political themes that Strindberg treated more comprehensively in the satirical prose works *The Red Room* and *The New Kingdom*; in the four-act comedy *In the Year 1848* (*Anno fyrtioåtta*, wr. 1877?), which contains some of the same character relationships later used in *The Red Room*; and in *Lucky Per's Journey*, the first of the pilgrimage dramas. Ironically, considering Strindberg's own plight, one of the lessons Lucky Per learns from his adventures is the danger of being too outspoken about society's failings.

Two other plays of the first period were written to help advance Siri von Essen's acting career. Critics have speculated that the first of these, *The Secret of the Guild* (*Gillets hemlighet*, 1880), shows the influence of Ibsen's *The Pretenders*. Strindberg believed that his play had influenced Ibsen's *The Master Builder*. The second play, *Herr Bengt's Wife* (*Herr Bengts hustru*, 1882), a five-act drama set in Sweden during the Protestant Reformation, deals with marital discord, but not rancorously, as the quarreling couple reconcile after the wife learns that the romance of marriage must be tempered by a respect for ordinary domestic problems.

The most important of the early plays is *Master Olof* (prose version, wr. 1872, prod. 1881; verse version, wr. 1876, prod. 1890), the first work in the cycle about Swedish rulers. Strindberg's achievements in these dramas, ranging in style from the realism of the well-made play to expressionism, make him one of the most significant writers of chronicle plays since Shakespeare, whose influence he acknowledged. Going against the tradition of his day, Strindberg created multidimensional individuals instead of patriotic cutouts, characters whose development is not only central to the plays but also a revealing counterpoint to the march of historical events.

In *Master Olof*, set during the Reformation, the title character, a religious leader, has made common cause with his monarch, Gustav Vasa, to break the Vatican's hold over Sweden's affairs. The two become enemies, however, when Olof criticizes the King for appearing to care more about centralizing political power than converting the country to Lutheranism. Like Luther, Olof is eventually forced to compromise with temporal power. Strindberg heightens the dramatic impact of the compromise by introducing an apocryphal character, Gert Bookprinter, a religious fanatic who tests Olof's idealism by involving him in a futile plot against the King and goes to his death accusing the penitent and humiliated Olof of being a renegade.

A profoundly different Strindberg returned to playwriting in 1886 after a four-year absence. His deteriorating marriage, added to his growing interest in hypnosis, the power of suggestion, and Nietzsche's theory of human existence as a series of struggles between stronger and weaker wills, led Strindberg to conceive of the battle of the sexes primarily as psychological warfare—a "battle of brains" between a superior male intellect and an inferior but, through its cunning, often victorious female intellect. Study of French literary thought had brought to his attention Emile Zola's naturalism, which insisted on painfully scientific objectivity in the depiction of life and society. From this base Strindberg developed his own brand of naturalism by cutting away all the verbiage and incident required for realistic authenticity and concentrating solely on moments of crisis and catastrophe. *See* NATURALISM in glossary.

It was in his so-called naturalistic plays that Strindberg began the practice that was to earn him notoriety as a reactionary misogynist: investing a female character with grim symbolic meaning in her role as wife, mother, or daughter. As wife she is a kind of vampire; jealous of her husband's accomplishments, she saps his creative energies until his talent dries up or his will is conquered. As mother she deprives her children of sustenance and love and poisons their minds against their father. As daughter she is likely to side with her mother in any family dispute. There are vampire wives in *Comrades* (wr. 1888, prod. 1905) and *Creditors* (1899). In *Comrades* Bertha lies to her husband Axel and tries to cheat him not only out of money but also out of his reputation as an artist; when his patience runs out, he orders her to leave his house. Adolf in *Creditors* is not so fortunate. His wife, Tekla, has devoured his courage and will, and when he overhears her talking intimately with her first husband, he suffers a fatal attack of epilepsy.

Two one-act plays, part of a group that Strindberg patterned after the French *quart d'heure* plays, stress the dangerous influence of bad mothers. *Facing Death* (*Inför döden*, 1893) concerns a widower whose daughters have been turned against him by their mother, and *Motherlove* (*Moderskärlek*, 1894) is about a former prostitute who refuses to allow her daughter to see or accept help from her natural father. The motif of the devouring mother recurs in such later plays as *The Pelican* (*Pelikanen*, 1907) and *The Ghost Sonata* (1908), in which women destroy the young by withholding food.

As strident and uneven as Strindberg's work was at this time, he produced two plays, *The Father* (1887) and *Miss Julie*, which masterfully exploit the love-hate theme. *The Father* reveals the full range of Strindberg's expectations and disappointments in woman as wife, daughter, and mother. Laura uses the power of suggestion to drive her husband, the Captain, insane by encouraging him to believe that he is not the father of their daughter Bertha. When the Captain turns to Bertha for support, she remains loyal to her mother. His anguish is soothed for a time by his old nurse, who mothers and comforts him, but she does so only to distract him as she lures him into a straitjacket. Zola was complimentary about *The Father*, but he had reservations. He felt that the characterization was excessively abstract and that the action was too abbreviated and lacked proper psychological motivation. Ironically, these supposed shortcomings give the play a dramatic power, however primitive, that Zola never achieved in his doctrinaire naturalistic dramas.

In *Miss Julie* Strindberg demonstrates that he can adhere faithfully to naturalistic effects that strain the limits of verisimilitude. Brilliantly distilled in the brief and tragic Midsummer Eve affair between the Count's daughter, Miss Julie, and her father's valet, Jean, is the essence of Strindberg's interpretation of the love-hate bond: an inevitable and hopeless rhythm of mutual attraction and repulsion from courtship to consummation to bitter disillusionment. Raised to compete with men at riding, hunting, and farming by a masculinely aggressive mother, Miss Julie is ill-prepared to accept the traditional female sex role. It is symptomatic of Strindberg's patriarchal viewpoint that her upbringing is seen as a violation of her biological nature, which in turn destroys her sense of social identity and psychological equilibrium. Her attitude toward the physical act of love is an ambivalent mixture of longing and disgust, like that of Blanche DeBois in Tennessee Williams's *A Streetcar Named Desire* (which bears a strong resemblance to Strindberg's play) and, in fact, like that of the sexually insecure Strindberg himself. *See* WILLIAMS, TENNESSEE.

Strindberg showed that he could also deal comically with a love triangle in the one-act *Playing with Fire* (*Leka med elden*, 1893). A husband discourages his wife's lover with a device perhaps borrowed from Sardou's *Let's Get a Divorce:* he offers to give his wife up if her lover will agree to marry her. *See* SARDOU, VICTORIEN.

The remaining plays of the group Strindberg wrote before the traumatic inferno years are a mixed lot. Several of the short pieces, such as *Debit and Credit* (*Debet och kredit;* wr. 1892, prod. 1900) and *The First Warning* (*Första varningen*, 1893), are strained and obvious, and the insignificant four-act comedy *The People of Hemsö* (*Hemsöborna*, 1889) is an attempt to exploit in dramatic form the success of his novel of the same name. More noteworthy are two effective short plays involving "battles of brains," *Pariah* (*Paria*, 1889) and *The Stronger* (*Den starkare*, 1889), and two long plays that reflect the sadness and bitterness Strindberg felt when the divorce court granted his wife the custody of their three children. Thus in the touching first scene of the sprawling pilgrimage play *The Keys of the Kingdom of Heaven* (*Himmelrikets nycklar;* wr. 1892, prod. 1929), a father stands before three tiny empty beds and mourns the terrible loss of his children to the plague. The setting for the powerful one-act *The Bone* (*Bandet;* wr. 1892, prod. 1902) is a divorce trial that results in a man and wife losing custody of their child when the court decides that they are both unfit to raise him.

In the "naturalistic" plays Strindberg's apparent intention had been to reveal the brutalizing effects of sexual love as unsparingly as possible. His motto could be Laura's statement in *The Father:* "Life between the sexes is strife." But after the inferno crisis the love-hate theme takes on another dimension. Preoccupied with religious ideas, particularly Swedenborgian mysticism, Strindberg pictures earthly life as a hell in which one seeks to expiate sins committed in another existence. To make the pain of guilt and atonement especially exquisite, Providence has provided Eumenides-like "powers," or "chastising spirits," who use love-hate as a means for getting men and women to torture each other. Strindberg still saw women as instrumental in men's misfortunes, but they are now agents operating within a larger than human schema rather than willful and unscrupulous hetaeras whose drive is the destruction of the male. The Cap-

tain and his wife in *The Dance of Death* (*Dödsdansen;* wr. 1900, prod. 1905) are not only equally malicious but, like galley slaves chained together, equally pitiful. The Lady in *To Damascus* points out that although it was Eve who introduced sin into the world, it was another woman, Mary, who brought expiation.

The remarkable pilgrimage play trilogy *To Damascus*, the work with which Strindberg returned to playwriting in 1898, is an inventory of revolutionary dramatic innovations. The Stranger and the Lady (a composite portrait of Strindberg's three wives) travel through the real-life landscape of the inferno crisis: the seaside resort where Strindberg and Frida Uhl spent their honeymoon, her relations' home in Austria, and the hospital in Paris where he was confined. They endure the torments of marital hell, learning that love is "a one-season plant that blossoms during the engagement, goes to seed in marriage, and then bends toward the earth to wither and die."

Afflicted by what psychologists today would probably call free-floating anxiety, the Stranger is on a desperate journey in search of salvation, atonement, and reconciliation, a journey made analogous to Saul's conversion and transformation into St. Paul on the road to Damascus. As Strindberg himself did during the inferno, the Stranger suffers frightful and inexplicable spiritual and psychological experiences that make him wonder if he is on the brink of insanity. Some of the people he meets are his doubles, and others appear and disappear for no apparent reason. Affluent guests at a sumptuous banquet mysteriously change places with people dressed in rags, and the banquet hall becomes a cheap tavern.

Despite its perplexities and incongruities, *To Damascus* has a special logic and reality that made it a watershed for twentieth-century drama. Proceeding from the premise that earthly life is "a half-reality, a bad

Scene from *Comrades*. Stockholm, Nya Theatre, 1941.
[Drottningholms Teatermuseum]

dream,'' Strindberg created a fictional world that is as improbable but as meaningful as a dream, thus paving the way for movements such as surrealism, expressionism, and the theatre of the absurd. See EXPRESSIONISM; THEATRE OF THE ABSURD in glossary.

All the plays Strindberg wrote after 1898 were elaborations on one or more of the themes suggested in *To Damascus*, the implications of the cycle of guilt and atonement and the special hell of conjugal love; and his stylistic experiments were part of a continuing search for viable alternatives to traditional dramatic concepts of characterization and logical, sequential action. Of special significance was the introduction of a farcical note into the battle of the sexes. The marital squabbles in *The Dance of Death* are as vicious as those in *The Father*, but the touches of gallows humor in the later play produce a strangely touching, softening effect. When Edgar dies of a stroke at the end of the second part of the play, Alice expresses regret: she will miss their violent battles. Strindberg's eloquent image of the bond of human love as a chain that holds both partners captive in a cruel, absurd, but strangely satisfying relationship prefigures the work of Beckett, Ionesco, Genet, and Albee. See ALBEE, EDWARD; BECKETT, SAMUEL; GENET, JEAN; IONESCO, EUGÈNE.

The chronicle-play form, a large canvas on which to illustrate how Providence intervened in the destinies of men and nations to punish sin, especially the sin of hubris, ''which the gods hate above everything else,'' was particularly appropriate for the theme of guilt and atonement. The King in *Gustav Vasa* (1899), Strindberg's masterpiece in the chronicle genre, has his mettle tested and his arrogance subdued; and in *Erik XIV* (1899) Vasa's eccentric, Hamlet-like son is punished for his godlessness. King Magnus's sufferings in *The Saga of the Folkungs* (1901) are of a different order: he must do penance for crimes committed by his entire clan. Similarly, the title character in *Gustav Adolf* (1903) must suffer for the ''blood guilt'' he inherited from his father. Strindberg intended to illustrate through the fates of Magnus and Gustav Adolf his interpretation of the doctrine of *satisfactio vicaria*, which suggests that though the innocent may suffer, their suffering can be redemptive, expiating the sins of others.

The later chronicle plays are not so deeply imbued with the atonement theme as the earlier works, and in them, as Strindberg narrowed his focus to psychological studies of the individual monarchs, the historical backgrounds are less important. The central character in *Charles XII* (*Karl XII*, 1902), a ruler who was a romantic hero to his countrymen at the end of the nineteenth century, is depicted by Strindberg in an unfavorable light as ''the nation's destroyer''; the brilliant and controversial daughter of Gustav Adolf appears in *Queen Christina* (*Kristina*; wr. 1901, prod. 1908) as a ''half-woman,'' raised improperly like Miss Julie and never allowed to develop normally; and *Gustav III* (wr. 1902, prod. 1916) is an interesting study of the mercurial and effeminate monarch who brought the Enlightenment to Sweden. Each of these plays has provided virtuoso roles for prominent actors, particularly in Sweden and Germany.

Strindberg was less successful in dealing with the history of other nations. *The Nightingale of Wittenberg* (*Näktergalen i Wittenberg*; wr. 1903, prod. 1914) is a series of stiff cardboard tableaux from the life of Luther; and the trilogy known in short as *Moses-Socrates-Christ* (wr. 1903, prod. 1922) is thinly realized and unconvincing.

Satisfactio vicaria plays an important role in *Easter* (1901), in which the mystical Eleonora, the daughter of a man imprisoned for embezzlement, convinces her family that they must all expiate the father's sin. Strindberg planned a sequel to *Easter* in which Eleonora was to have endured ''all the suffering of mankind and the pain of existence,'' but the plan was realized in a different setting in *A Dream Play*, the pilgrimage play destined to be one of the masterpieces of twentieth-century drama.

In *A Dream Play*, as in *The Father*, Strindberg explored the symbolic nature of the multiple role woman is called upon to play, but his treatment of the theme is vastly different. Sent down to earth by her father, the Vedic-Hindu god of sky and storms, to investigate whether the lamentations of mankind are justified, Indra's daughter marries and has a child, thus learning at first hand the bitterness of conjugal love. Again and again during her journey she is moved to remark compassionately that ''mankind is to be pitied.'' Strindberg never found a more poignant or more lyrically imaginative expression for the love-hate theme than in this brilliant play.

In the Author's Note to *A Dream Play* Strindberg referred to *To Damascus* as his ''former dream play,'' and there are similarities between the two works: each play is an attempt to approximate ''the disconnected but apparently logical form of a dream,'' and each contains characters who undergo the terrifying experience of having their most persistent fears and nightmarish fantasies materialize before their eyes. But the flow of the action from scene to scene in *A Dream Play* is more cohesive, if not more comprehensible, because of devices such as the cupboard door in one scene that becomes a stage door in the next and a cabinet door in the scene following, all the while retaining a mysterious cloverleaf opening. Furthermore, *A Dream Play* is devoid of the self-pitying autobiographical references that mar *To Damascus*. Ironically, Strindberg had become both more objective and more ambiguous; there are elements in *A Dream Play* that will forever remain puzzling. But it is unimportant whether the linear development of the plot is meaningful; the significance of the play is in the powerful cumulative effect of the kaleidoscopic dream images of human suffering.

Strindberg was displeased with the literal treatment given the play in its premiere in 1907. Nevertheless, for many years this approach prevailed, involving elaborately constructed sets or graphic projections to represent the many locations specifically and concretely. The results have often tended to make the play seem cumbersome and pretentious. Ingmar Bergman's 1970 production took a different turn by treating the work as an intimate chamber play with simple, suggestive scenery.

The variety of genres with which Strindberg experimented in his final years was amazing, but no more so than the ingenuity he showed in adapting the guilt-and-atonement theme to fit different contexts. In the fascinating, dark "boulevard" drama *Crime and Crime* (1900), a Parisian playwright wishing to escape from his family responsibilities suffers remorse when his small daughter dies. In *Advent* (wr. 1898, prod. 1915), one of several plays dealing with the Swedenborgian concept that crime is its own punishment, an evil judge and his wife are brought to the anteroom of hell, a grotesque scene reminiscent of Hieronymus Bosch's landscapes and Ebenezer Scrooge's nightmares. The central character in the folk-play fantasy *The Crown Bride*, a young woman who plotted with a witch to drown her illegitimate baby, expiates her sin by sacrificing her life, thus ending a feud between her lover's family and her own.

Grouped with *To Damascus* and *A Dream Play* as the most important plays of the final period are the four chamber plays (all written in 1907). Taking his inspiration from Max Reinhardt's Kammerspiel-Haus experiments, Strindberg stated his goal as "The concept of chamber music transferred to drama. The intimate approach, the significant theme, the painstaking treatment." But the strongest influence on the style of the chamber plays was probably his own occultist experiences.

During the inferno crisis, Strindberg had developed a special sensitivity for the hidden meanings contained in random sights and sounds, detecting in them messages or directives sent by "the powers." His desire to find expressive dramatic form for these mysterious phenomena led him to take an interest in symbolism, particularly in the work of Maurice Maeterlinck, whose statements about "the tragic in daily life" crystallized his own thinking about the dark truths that lay concealed behind apparently ordinary or harmless facades.

In the chamber plays the image of false facades applies to people as well as to houses. In *The Burned House* (*Brända tomten*, 1907), the destruction of a building leads to the revelation that a supposedly respectable family who lived there was actually made up of thieves and smugglers who secreted contraband in walls and closets. And the proper-looking tenants and guests in the house in *The Ghost Sonata* (*Spöksonaten*, 1908) have been involved in fraud, intrigue, and murder. Even the exposer of this corruption, old man Hummel, is himself exposed and punished for his sins.

The development of Strindberg's style from *Comrades* to *The Ghost Sonata* might be called a journey from simile toward metaphor. The vampirelike figures of the earlier plays are replaced in *The Ghost Sonata* by more literal vampires: Hummel, the "slave trader" and "stealer of souls," and the Cook, who boils all the nourishment from the food she serves and drinks it herself. With this play Strindberg paved the way for surrealist drama and anticipated the expressionist movement of the 1920s.

The flashes of savage misanthropy that mark references to the love-hate theme in the plays and novels of Strindberg's final years reflect a lifetime of bitterness, but there are other references sometimes melancholy and elegiac, sometimes sentimental, that reveal an understanding born of both resignation and self-pity. In the fantasy-play fragment *The Dutchman* (*Holländaren*; wr. 1902, prod. 1923), the shipmaster, so often disappointed many times in a futile search for love, finally recognizes that he can be reconciled with life only through suffering, not through finding a faithful woman. Significantly, however, Strindberg was compelled to temper resignation with a Promethean defiance. The Hunter in his last play, the monodramalike pilgrimage play *The Great Highway* (1910), is an old hermit who is weary of being a scapegoat, an Abasuerus, and for his epitaph chooses to be called Ishmael:

Who fought a battle with God
And did not stop fighting until laid low.

Plays in Contemporary Settings

The Freethinker (*Fritänkaren*, wr. 1869). A young man, Karl, is torn between the dictates of his conscience and an oppressive and hypocritical social code. Choosing the first alternatives, he proclaims his contempt for society and announces his intention to emigrate to America.

The Father (*Fadren*, 1887). Tragedy. The Captain, a cavalry officer, scientist, and freethinker, lives surrounded by women: his wife Laura, their daughter Bertha, his old nurse Margaret, his mother-in-law, and a governess. The Captain wants to send his daughter away for her education, but Laura is determined to keep her at home. To get her way, she insinuates that Bertha may not be the Captain's child and therefore not legally under his control. By creating an atmosphere of suspicion, in which she is unwittingly abetted by the family doctor, Laura succeeds in forcing her husband to question his own sanity. Driven to distraction by uncertainty and by Laura's machinations, he loses his temper, is put into a straitjacket by his nurse, then suffers a stroke and dies.

Comrades (*Kamraterna*; wr. 1888, prod. 1905). Drama set in Paris late in the nineteenth century. Axel and his wife, Bertha, are artists and "comrades" of equal status in the household, but Bertha resents Axel's superiority as an artist. When she hears that one of her paintings is accepted for exhibition and his is rejected, she becomes superior and domineering, while Axel, who had switched the paintings so that she would get the credit for his work, becomes completely disenchanted with her. Finally, after attempting to mortify him at a party celebrating her apparent triumph, Bertha learns the truth and begs Axel for forgiveness. Now at last she really loves him, but he no longer loves her and sends her away. His new mistress arrives as Bertha leaves, and Axel tells his wife: "At a café I want comrades, but at home I want a wife."

Miss Julie (*Fröken Julie*, 1889). Drama in one act set on a country estate in late-nineteenth-century Sweden. On Midsummer Eve, while her father, the Count, is away, Miss Julie dismays the servants by joining in their festivities. She focuses her attentions on the valet, Jean, who at first repels her advances but then tells her that he has been in love with her since their childhood. They are drinking together in the kitchen where Jean's fiancée, the maid Christine, is asleep in a chair, when other servants come to look for Jean. To avoid scandal the two go to his room, where Miss Julie gives herself to Jean. Now they agree that they must leave the country immediately. But once the sexual spell is gone, the social and psychological barriers, reinforced by Christine's moralistic judgments, make their flight plans untenable. Distraught, Julie asks Jean what he would do in her position; in response he points to a razor which he has put on the kitchen table. The ringing of the service bell announces the Count's return, and Jean's arrogance disappears. Miss Julie, enraptured by the thought of freeing herself from her agony by committing suicide, flees from the kitchen with the razor in her hand, while Jean reassumes his role as a subservient menial.

Creditors (*Fordringsägare*, 1889). One-act drama in which Gustav, concealing his identity, befriends Adolf, the husband of his former wife, Tekla. Gustav convinces Adolf that Tekla has devoured his creativity as an artist, his talent, and his manhood. Later, Adolf overhears a conversation between Gustav and Tekla in which she scorns Adolf and agrees to carry on an affair with Gustav. Adolf dies from the shock of the betrayal.

The Stronger (*Den starkare*, 1889). One-scene drama in which Mrs. X and Miss Y, both actresses, meet accidentally in a women's café in Stockholm. Mrs. X chatters away about her children, her husband, and her admiration for Miss Y. As she talks, she begins to realize that Miss Y, who never utters a word, has been having an affair with her husband and that her husband's attraction to Miss Y's idiosyncrasies has caused him to make his wife imitate them. Yet Mrs. X believes that she is the stronger, for Miss Y has given but received nothing in

Eva Dahlbeck and Olof Wildgren in *Creditors*. Stockholm, Royal Dramatic Theatre, 1957. [Drottningholms Teatermuseum]

return, and what she has given has served only to bind Mr. X closer to his wife.

Pariah (*Paria*, 1889). One-act drama involving two men: X, who once involuntarily killed a man and has never been punished; and Y, a forger who has been in prison. These facts come out in a "battle of brains," during which Y tries to blackmail X. The latter, a man of intelligence who is free of base motives, uses his superior mind to expose his companion as a stupid common criminal and sends him away.

Simoom (*Samum*, 1890). One-act drama in which an Arab girl avenges the death of her lover by destroying a French soldier. Exhausted and confused after a lengthy struggle through the simoom, the violent, searing African wind, the soldier falls into the hands of the Arab girl, who proceeds to play upon his fantasies and hallucinations. She skillfully fills his mind with doubts and fears until he loses the will to live and dies.

Debit and Credit (*Debet och kredit*; wr. 1892, prod. 1900). One-act play in which Axel, a scientist, suffers the drawbacks of success. When he returns home from an African expedition, he finds himself surrounded by friends and relatives who demand payment for past favors. Axel satisfies the "beasts of prey" by granting them their material demands, and then he walks out.

The First Warning (*Första varningen*, 1893). Originally titled *The First Tooth* (*Första tanden*). One-act comedy in which a husband, weary of being humiliated by his flirtatious wife and wishing that she would age quickly and become toothless and unattractive, cancels his plans to leave her after she shows signs of jealousy and tells him that she has marred her appearance by breaking a tooth.

Facing Death (*Inför döden*, 1893). One-act drama centering on M. Durand, a wretched old widower who is forced to rent rooms in his house. His three ungrateful daughters, turned against him by their mother, scorn and betray him and make his life miserable by denying him food and begrudging him even the simple pleasure of smoking his pipe. Unable to carry his burdens any longer, Durand sets fire to the house and ends his life by taking poison.

Motherlove (*Moderskärlek*, 1894). One-act drama in which a rapacious former prostitute refuses to allow her twenty-year-old daughter to see her natural father despite the fact that the mother is supported by her daughter's earnings as an actress. When the daughter learns the truth about her mother's past, she becomes disillusioned and cynical, but the insensitive mother interprets even this as a sign of acquiescence.

Playing with Fire (*Leka med elden*, 1893). One-act comedy set in a country villa and focusing on the triangular relationship of Knut, his wife Kerstin, and her lover Axel. When Knut discovers that Kerstin and Axel are strongly drawn to each other, he agrees to give up his wife if Axel will marry her. The gesture causes Axel to lose his passion for Kerstin; he leaves hastily, and life at the villa returns to normal.

The Bond (*Bandet*; wr. 1892, prod. 1902). One-act tragedy set in a courtroom where the divorce proceedings of a baron and a baroness take place. They have agreed on a settlement that would give the baroness custody of their young son. But because it is up to the court to decide who deserves the child, the husband and wife are forced to attack each other savagely, and they succeed so well in besmirching each other that the judge finds neither fit to raise a child. The couple intend to appeal to higher courts, knowing that their fierce hatred will bind them together and compel them to attempt to destroy each other for the rest of their lives.

Crime and Crime (*Brott och brott*, 1900). Drama set in Paris late in the nineteenth century. Maurice, a young playwright on the threshold of success in the Parisian theatre, promises to marry his mistress Jeanne, mother of his five-year-old daughter Marion. On the day of the opening performance of his play, Maurice meets his friend's mistress, Henriette. He and Henriette are immediately attracted to each other and become lovers. They think of running away together, but Maurice says his daughter holds him back. Henriette wishes the child were dead; Maurice agrees that this would simplify things.

The next morning the child is found dead, and Maurice and Henriette are suspected of murder. Although innocent of the crime, each feels guilty for having wished the child dead. Shunned by their friends, they fling accusations and insults at each other, and their love turns into hate. Finally it is determined that the child died of a rare disease. Exonerated, Henriette goes to live with her mother. Maurice visits his friend the Abbé, who points out that, though Maurice may be innocent legally, "we are responsible for our thoughts, our words, and our desires."

Easter (*Påsk*, 1901). Passion play in three acts taking place on Maundy Thursday, Good Friday, and Easter Eve. Elis Heyst, a schoolteacher, carries a heavy burden: his father is in prison for embezzling trust funds, his young sister Eleonora is in a mental hospital, and he and his family are awaiting a creditor to take house and furniture. Eleonora, an angelic, Christ-like mystic, escapes from the hospital and returns home. By her faith in the redemptive power of suffering she helps the family to bear its shame. On Good Friday the Heysts fear that they are on the brink of ruin, but Easter Eve brings them hope: the creditor forgives the father's debts; and there are signs that the winter ice has begun to thaw, heralding the coming of spring.

The Dance of Death, I (*Dödsdansen, första delen*; wr. 1900, prod. 1905). First of a two-part drama, set late in the nineteenth century on an island off the coast of Sweden, in the home of Edgar, an artillery captain, and his wife Alice. For twenty-five years, Edgar and Alice have been tormenting each other. Edgar has insisted that the couple live as virtual hermits, and their home has become a prison. Alice's only means of contact with the outside world is a telegraph key she has secretly learned to operate. During a visit from Alice's cousin Kurt, who has just been appointed officer to the island, Edgar has a heart attack. His wife is delighted and hopes that he will die soon. She deliberately adds to his suffering by flirting with the bewildered Kurt. Only after Edgar at-

Anders Ek and Ingrid Thulin in *Miss Julie*. [Swedish Information Service]

tacks her with his saber do they declare a weary truce.

The Dance of Death, II (*Dödsdansen, andra delen*; wr. 1900, prod. 1905). Second part of a two-part drama. The ailing Edgar plots to dominate those around him, particularly his wife's cousin Kurt, whom he discredits and undermines. His daughter Judith is in love with Kurt's son Allan, but Edgar has other plans for the spirited girl: he wants her to marry a colonel from his old regiment. Judith takes matters into her own hands, breaks the engagement with the colonel, and follows Allan to the military post where he is stationed. The shock is too much for Edgar, who suffers a stroke; to the accompaniment of taunts from his exultant wife, he finally dies, but not before spitting in her face. She concludes that she must have loved as well as hated him and hopes that his soul will rest in peace.

Storm Weather (*Oväder*, 1907). Chamber play in which the peaceful existence of the Gentleman, a retired government official, is threatened. Outside a storm is brewing, and he thinks of his young second wife, Gerda, whom he left five years earlier. After a marriage in which he felt more sinned against than sinner, his life had become uncomplicated and sterile, colored only by a few selected memories. Recently, however, Gerda and her second husband, the wastrel Fischer, have moved into the flat above his, and the Gentleman learns with satisfaction that Fischer has just deserted her. He refuses to become involved in "other people's affairs" and after a bitter scene declines to aid the helpless woman, leaving the matter in the hands of his understanding brother, the Consul. Gerda goes to live with her mother. The storm passes, cleansing the sultry air of the city. The Gentleman decides to move away from his dull, bourgeois apartment and away from his memories as well.

(Above) *Motherlove.* Stockholm, Blanche Theatre, 1931. (Left) *The Bond.* Stockholm, Royal Theatre, 1928. (Bottom) *Playing with Fire.* Stockholm, Blanche Theatre, 1922. [Drottningholms Teatermuseum]

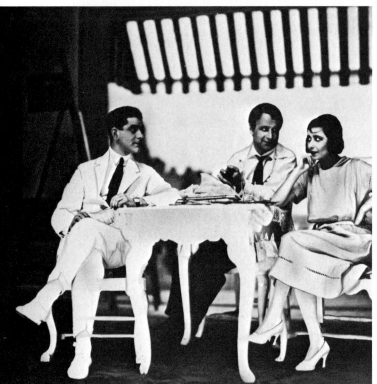

The Burned House (*Brända tomten,* 1907). Chamber play set in a neighborhood known as the Swamp, which contains a house that belonged to the Dyer. In the Swamp the lives of all the families are interwoven. The Dyer's brother, the Stranger, world traveler and perceptive observer of life, comes to revisit the scene of his childhood after thirty years in America. Out of the relics and mementos rescued from the fire he reconstructs his own memories and those of his brother. He takes part in an investigation of the fire, believed to have been set by a student who had been rooming with the Dyer and his family. Relentlessly the Stranger exposes one buried truth after another. Each forgotten event of years ago becomes a thread in a design fashioned by the World Weaveress and apparent only in retrospect. The illusions of the past are stripped away, displaying the evil and the hypocrisy of family and neighbors. The student is proved innocent, and the Stranger leaves, disgusted by the revelations.

The Ghost Sonata (*Spöksonaten,* 1908). Chamber play in three scenes. In a square outside a fashionable house, the Student talks with a milkmaid seen only by him. He meets an old man, Hummel. When Hummel learns that the Student is a Sunday child (which gives him supernatural powers) and that he is the son of an old acquaintance, he offers to introduce him to the inhabitants of the house. These include the Colonel; his wife, the Mummy; their fragile daughter, the Young Lady, who lives in the Hyacinth Room; and a cook who draws off and saves for herself all the nourishment from the food served in the house. All the characters are bound together by marriages, affairs, and betrayals. Hummel and the Student enter the Colonel's apartment for a ghost supper. The old man exposes the crimes of the house and says that the Young Lady in the Hyacinth Room is actually his daughter, whereupon the Mummy reveals Hummel's sordid past. He goes to hang himself, and a death screen is put around him. In the Hyacinth Room scene the Student and the Young Lady are attracted to each other, but the girl asks for his patience; she wants a period of testing before they can be wed. She tells the Student that the cook is a vampire, and this prompts him to describe the horrors that appearances hide. At the same time, life seeps out of the girl.

The Pelican (*Pelikanen,* 1907). Chamber play. A miserly, selfish, and cruel mother mistreats her son and her daughter. In her greed she has denied the children as well as her recently deceased husband warmth and nourishment, devouring the rich food alone in the kitchen and leaving dried morsels for the others. The husband has left a letter to the children telling them of the mother's deeds. Furthermore, the daughter discovers that her husband has been her mother's lover. Daughter and son plan revenge. They make the mother eat her own thin gruel; then the son sets the house on fire, forcing her to throw herself out of the window. As the flames and smoke encircle the two children, they embrace in their first moment of happiness and warmth.

Period Plays

Hermione (wr. 1870). Blank-verse tragedy dealing with the conquest of Athens by Philip of Macedon. Despite the efforts of the orator Demosthenes, the Athenians' will to resist is disintegrating. Against a background of intrigue and cowardice, Hermione sets out to kill Philip but instead falls in love with him. When Criton, her father, learns that she has betrayed her people, he kills her and commits suicide.

In Rome (*I Rom,* 1870). One-act play in verse that describes a crucial incident in the life of the great Icelandic-Danish sculptor Bertel Thorvaldsen (1768/70–1844). About to abandon his artistic career in despair, Thorvaldsen is saved by the providential appearance of a wealthy patron, Thomas Hope, who commissions a marble statue of Jason, thus enabling Thorvaldsen to continue his work.

The Outlaw (*Den fredlöse,* 1871). One-act tragedy set in Iceland. The arrogant Viking Thorfinn can neither reject the Nordic gods in whom he no longer believes nor accept the conversion of his daughter Gunlöd to Christianity. When he is saved from a storm at sea, he will not thank the gods and insists that he received help from no one but himself. Finally, having been declared an outlaw by the Icelandic Althing (Parliament), he is fatally wounded in combat, but before he dies, he is forced to face the truth about his mortality and is reconciled with his family.

The Secret of the Guild (*Gillets hemlighet,* 1880). Drama set in Sweden during the early 1400s. The worthy Sten and the unworthy Jacques both aspire to the post of master builder of the Cathedral of Uppsala. Concealing his ignorance of the secret of the guild, the mystical master plan embodying the "idea" of the cathedral, Jacques receives the appointment. When the tower he builds collapses, Sten replaces him and reveals the secret: one must follow the design of the cross and have faith in its meaning.

Herr Bengt's Wife (*Herr Bengts hustru,* 1882). Drama set in Sweden during the Reformation, describing the plight of a haughty aristocrat, Lady Margit, who refuses to face the realities of life. Her husband, Herr Bengt, is forced to mortgage his estate without his wife's knowledge and she becomes disillusioned, rejecting him in favor of friends who ultimately betray her. She tries to commit suicide, and when her life is saved, she becomes reconciled with her husband and with the rigors of human existence.

Through the Wilderness to the Promised Land, or Moses (*Genom öknar till arvland, eller Moses;* wr. 1903, prod. 1922). Twenty-one tableaux depicting the life of Moses; first part of the *Moses-Socrates-Christ* trilogy. The story closely follows the Old Testament version of Moses' life, with great emphasis on the Hebraic reliance on law and order and on the belief in one God who is both stern and just.

Hellas, or Socrates (*Hellas, eller Sokrates;* wr. 1903, prod. 1922). Nineteen tableaux showing famous Greeks

Benkt-Åke Benktsson in *Easter.* Malmö, Civic Theatre, 1955. [French Cultural Services]

The Dance of Death, with (l. to r.) Nancy Wickwire, Philip Kerr, and Robert Jackson, Minneapolis, 1966. [The Guthrie Theater Company]

discussing the nature of the universe; second part of the *Moses-Socrates-Christ* trilogy. Socrates experiences marital difficulties, and the play ends with his death.

The Lamb and the Wild Beast, or Christ (*Lammet och vilddjuret, eller Kristus;* wr. 1903, prod. 1922). Fifteen tableaux including scenes from the New Testament and from the power struggle in Rome between Caligula, Claudius, and Nero; last part of the *Moses-Socrates-Christ* trilogy. The play ends with the death of Nero and the imminent victory of the Christians.

Swedish History Plays

The arrangement of the following synopses follows the chronology of historical events rather than order of composition.

Earl Birger of Bjälbo (*Bjälbo-Jarlen,* 1909). Drama portraying the last years of Earl Birger, founder of Stockholm and first ruler of the Folkung dynasty. In the mid-thirteenth century Earl Birger has succeeded in bringing peace to the country, yet he has been unable to settle the discord in his own family. He wants to become King in

A 1964 production of *Storm Weather.* [Swedish Information Service]

place of his frivolous son Waldemar, who is having an affair with his sister-in-law. Ivar Jonsson Blå, a prominent lord, advises Birger to marry Mechtild of Denmark, ostensibly to increase his power in the kingdom but actually to thwart his aspirations. The earl tries to turn his other sons against Waldemar and gain their support. He reveals to his second son, Prince Magnus, the King's incestuous relationship and promises him succession if he, the earl, becomes King. But Magnus, with the help of Ivar Blå, schemes to capture the throne on his own and acts resolutely, releasing the secular priests from celibacy and refusing Birger's new wife entry into the capital. The earl finds himself powerless in his struggle with the daring Magnus and goes into retirement.

The Saga of the Folkungs (*Folkungasagan,* 1901). Tragedy set in fourteenth-century Sweden and focusing on the downfall of King Magnus Eriksson, the last of the reigning Folkungs. The sensitive, generous King is surrounded by intrigues. A madwoman reveals that his mother and her lover are planning to usurp his power and that his wife is betraying him. All the corruption and disloyalty, she predicts, will lead to great horrors. Birgitta, a fanatic seeker of political and religious influence, gives her approval when a bishop excommunicates Magnus, who does penance by carrying a cross through the streets of Stockholm. The madwoman's prediction comes true: Magnus watches as his heir dies of the plague. Resigned to his fate, Magnus awaits the combined armies of the rebellious lords and his German nephew, who will succeed him.

Engelbrekt (1901)). Drama about Engelbrekt, a Swedish national hero who, in 1434, led a victorious rebellion against the union of Sweden, Norway, and Denmark. The middle-aged Engelbrekt, a former mineowner and farmer, is an idealist, and at first he is loyal to the union. He begins to see its weaknesses, however, through conversations with the nationalistic Erik Puke and through witnessing the degrading spectacle of a banquet where Swedes are humiliated by the Danish bailiff Jens Eriksen. A series of personal tragedies intervenes: his wife, a Dane, deserts him and returns to her native country; he is wounded in battle by his son Karl; and his daughter falls in love with the son of Måns Natt-och-dag, his bitter enemy. Engelbrekt, however, takes up arms against the union, the King, and defectors from the Swedish cause. After victory has been achieved and the Swedes decide to elect a regent independent of the union, Engelbrekt's pride leads him to believe that he will be chosen. But he is bypassed and is shortly afterward murdered by Måns Natt-och-dag.

The Last of the Knights (*Siste riddaren,* 1909). Drama in five acts about the regency of Sten Sture (1512–1520). The play begins with the election as regent of the nineteen-year-old Sten Sture, leader of the Swedish nationalists, instead of Erik Trolle, a prominent supporter of the union of Sweden, Denmark, and Norway. Sture tries to reconcile old differences and even consents to the election of Gustav Trolle, Erik's son, as Archbishop of Sweden. But Gustav Trolle has ambitions of his own. After accepting the archbishopric, he rebuffs Sture, refuses to recognize his right to rule, and barricades himself in his fortress at Stäke. Wishing to avoid a conflict, Sture sends his emissary, Gustav Vasa, to reason with the Archbishop. When Trolle and Vasa cannot agree, Sture storms Stäke, captures Trolle, and then, stubbornly true to the chivalric code, pardons him.

Using this incident as an excuse, the Danish King, Christian II, invades Sweden and blockades Stockholm. Unable to capture the city, Christian invites Sture on board his ship for a conference. Fearing a trap, Gustav Vasa and five others go in Sture's place and are taken hostage. The siege continues; Sture is killed in battle and, after a heroic but futile defense of the city led by his wife Kristina, the land falls to the Danes and Archbishop Trolle.

The Regent (*Riksföreståndaren*, 1911). Drama concerning the overthrow of Danish rule in Sweden by Gustav Vasa and his assumption of the Swedish throne. Gustav Trolle, the Archbishop of Sweden who, together with the King of Denmark, Christian II, was responsible for the Stockholm bloodbath in 1520, holds Vasa's mother and sister hostage in an attempt to stop the advance of Vasa's army. Vasa tries to rescue his mother and sister in a surprise raid but succeeds only in carrying off the young son of Sten Sture, the deceased regent. Tormented by defections, his own conscience, and the hatred of those around him, Trolle nearly goes insane. Gustav Vasa overcomes, at least for the time being, the opposition of Bishop Brask, who fears for the future of the church in the hands of the secular Vasa. Vasa is elected regent and then King, despite protests from those who see him as a crude though talented upstart. The play closes with Vasa's royal entry into Stockholm. The joyous celebration is darkened by the news that Vasa's mother and sister are dead, but this is somewhat offset by a message announcing that Christian II of Denmark has been deposed.

Master Olof (*Mäster Olof*; wr. 1872, prod. 1881). Drama in five acts depicting the introduction of the Lutheran Reformation into Catholic Sweden at the beginning of the sixteenth century. Master Olof, a monk who teaches in a cathedral school, is convinced that he must free Sweden from the Church of Rome. In order to do this he enters the service of King Gustav Vasa, founder of the modern Swedish state. Inspired by growing support, Olof defies the church by tearing up a proclamation of his excommunication, preaching a Lutheran sermon in the Great Church of Stockholm, and becoming affianced to Kristina over the objections of his devoutly Catholic mother. When the King refuses to pursue to completion all the goals of the Reformation, Olof joins a plot to assassinate him. The plot is revealed, and Olof is tried and condemned to death but offered mercy if he recants. He finally does, and he swears allegiance to the king.

Gustav Vasa (1899). Play in five acts describing the final attempt of King Gustav Vasa, who liberated Sweden from Danish influence, to strengthen and unite the kingdom by quelling a rebellion of southern lords from Småland in 1543 and 1544. The King expects the allegiance of the proud yeomen in the northern mining

The Pelican, **Stockholm, 1968. [Swedish Information Service]**

Gösta Ekman and Tora Teje in *Herr Bengt's Wife.* **Stockholm, Swedish Theatre, 1920. [Drottningholms Teatermuseum]**

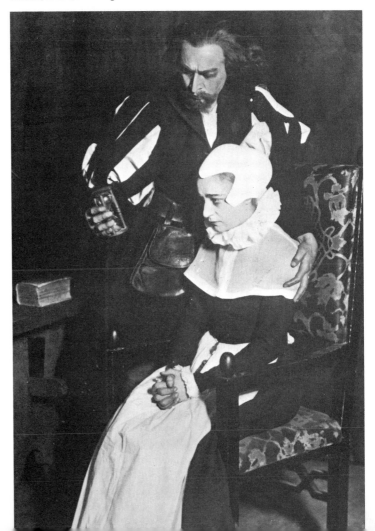

province of Dalecarlia, men who have never fully submitted to the King although they helped him win his first victories. Now that they are being summoned by Gustav for questioning and punishment, the Dalesmen try to decide where their loyalties lie. A revolt in Småland led by Nils Dacke threatens the King politically and spiritually, and he is prepared to abdicate when he learns that the rebels have approached the gates of Stockholm and that the 2,000 Dalesmen camped outside the city have yet to declare themselves. But then a group of Dalesmen pledge their loyalty to the Crown and assure the chastened and grateful King that they will give him the help he needs.

Erik XIV (1899). Drama about King Erik of Sweden, son of Gustav Vasa. The newly crowned King Erik is handsome, dashing, and intelligent, but he is emotionally unstable and has a volatile temper bordering at times on madness. Göran Persson, his loyal and intimate friend, aids him in his struggle with his ambitious stepbrothers, the dukes John and Charles, and with the rebellious Sture family. Persson is a resourceful statesman, but his efforts to reinforce the King's position are thwarted time and again by Erik's impulsive actions. After Erik orders the slaughter of the Stures while in a blind rage, the dukes decide to overthrow him and to share the throne.

Further complicating Erik's life is his unrealistic desire to marry Queen Elizabeth of England. Rebuffed, he returns to his commoner mistress Karin Månsdotter and makes her his Queen. Their wedding banquet is turned into a travesty as Erik invites beggars and harlots to the table. Days later, his stepbrothers begin a rebellion and capture the throne; Erik and Göran Persson are taken prisoner, and Erik's younger brother is declared King John III.

Gustav Adolf (1903). Monumental play, with more than fifty characters and sixteen scenes, set during the

Anders de Wahl in *The Last of the Knights.* Stockholm, Royal Dramatic Theatre, 1909. [Drottningholms Teatermuseum]

Thirty Years' War, in the last two years (1630–1632) of the reign of King Gustav II Adolf of Sweden. Germany, ravaged by the war, is in a state of chaos, waiting for help from the Swedish monarch, who has promised to restore order and give the persecuted German Protestants religious freedom. Gustav Adolf, a devout Lutheran, considers his mission a crusade. During the battles in Germany, which reveal the brutality and futility of the war, the King becomes tolerant of other faiths. Having secured religious freedom for the Protestants through his victory at Breitenfeld, Gustav Adolf turns his mission into an effort to unite Germany and win the imperial crown. He is torn between his desire for greater power and his role of deliverer from oppression. Just before his victory, having caused misery and suffering to the Germany he wanted to save, Gustav Adolf dies in the battle of Lützen. At his funeral he is hailed as a great liberator and hero.

Queen Christina (*Kristina;* wr. 1901, prod. 1908). Drama that describes the last years of the reign of the Swedish Queen. Christina is a capricious, strong-willed woman who presides over a court divided into factions. She is surrounded by courtiers vying for her favor, lovers, would-be lovers, ex-lovers, and the "old guard" of generals and administrators who served her father, the great Gustav Adolf. At a memorial service for her father, the Queen receives a copy of a pamphlet censuring her for her disastrous foreign policy and her immoral private life. She has the distributors of the pamphlet arrested and, in a gesture of defiance, restores her ex-lover Magnus de la Gardie to favor and initiates an affair with a young lieutenant, Klas Tott. Meanwhile, conditions within the kingdom are deteriorating despite the efforts of the able old chancellor Count Axel Oxenstjerna. The

Anders de Wahl in the title role of *Erik XIV.* Stockholm, Royal Dramatic Theatre, 1929. [Swedish Information Service]

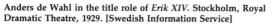

trial of the pamphlet distributors rouses the anger of the people, and riots break out as the Queen plans an extravagant banquet and ballet. Her cousin Karl Gustav, whom she has named heir apparent, tries to persuade her to marry him, but she finds the idea of marriage repugnant. However, the romantic love of Tott, who worships and idealizes her, awakens a tenderness in her, and she falls in love for the first time in her life. Thus moved, and under pressure from her ministers, she decides to abdicate. Only then does Tott see her as a woman rather than a goddess, and he abandons her. Now, deserted by most of her friends and sycophants, Christina shows signs of becoming a sympathetic and truly regal woman.

Charles XII (*Karl XII*, 1902). Expressionistic drama set in Sweden and Norway. Charles XII, King of Sweden, is at the end of his reign (1697–1718). His egotism and despotic nature have brought Sweden to the brink of disaster; military defeats have swept away his European conquests and almost cost him the Swedish mainland. The country is impoverished.

The play begins when the defeated Charles returns to Sweden. He immediately sets out to improve his financial condition with the help of the unscrupulous Baron Görtz. Meanwhile, the wives of captive soldiers and other petitioners assemble in the street before his door, hoping for an audience, but Charles refuses to receive them. To regain his lost honor he needs a war. Despite the financial collapse for which he and Görtz are responsible, Charles decides on a desperate campaign against Norway, and after a brief quarrel with his sister Ulrika Eleanora, he makes his final preparations. He enlists the aid of the great scientist and mystic Emanuel Swedenborg and marches into Norway, laying siege to the fortress of Fredriksten. Confronted with the certainty that his world is crumbling, he falls into a stupor of despair and is killed by a stray bullet.

Gustav III (wr. 1902, prod. 1916). Drama of intrigue set in the eighteenth-century Sweden of King Gustav III, the monarch whose assassination inspired Giuseppe Verdi's *The Masked Ball*. The King immerses the court in pomp and theatrics in an attempt to carry on the heroic tradition of the two Gustavs who preceded him and to make his own reputation equal to theirs. An enlightened monarch, he has a flair for historical gestures and witty verbal play, but he tends to be arrogant, vacillating, and superficial. Although he has given the commons power in their dealings with the lords and guaranteed a limited freedom of the press, he is faced with the problems of a corrupt government and with adversaries who want to liquidate him. Gustav manipulates those around him as if they were actors in a play; yet he cannot be sure that he controls them. He appears at a meeting of conspirators plotting against him, engages in a sharp duel of words, and invites his enemies to a banquet. The struggle between Gustav and the conspirators is presented in a series of moves and countermoves, and the play ends with the King narrowly escaping murder.

Fantasy Plays

Advent (*Advent, ett mysterium*; wr. 1898, prod. 1915).

Five-act mystery play which in allegorical terms describes the cruelty and avarice of a judge and his wife, who live in an illusory world of coquetry and frivolity. By self-deception the two succeed in ignoring a host of supernatural admonitions, among them a dance attended by corpses. The judge and his wife eventually find themselves in a "Waiting Room," a nightmarish limbo where their redemption is to begin when they see a vision of the first Christmas.

Casper's Shrove Tuesday (*Kaspers fet-tisdag*, 1901). One-act Lenten Punch-and-Judy show. The director of a puppet show instructs his wife to guard a wooden box containing his subjects while he goes to buy some paint. He wants to freshen them up in honor of the approaching First of May. But she leaves the box unattended, and from it emerge Casper (an aged man), his wife, a Mexican, an officer, and a creditor. The group performs a sketch with songs. When they have finished, the director returns, starts to paint them, and thanks them for playing their roles.

The Crown Bride (*Kronbruden*; wr. 1900, prod. 1906). Folk play set in the Swedish countryside. Kersti, a peasant girl, having given birth to a child by her future husband Mats, has the baby killed by a half-human, half-

Anders Ek and Birgitta Valberg in *Charles XII*. [Swedish Information Service]

supernatural midwife so that she can wear the virgin's bridal crown on her wedding day. Her deed is soon exposed, aggravating a feud between the families of the couple. Kersti, redeemed by her faith in the forgiveness of God, drowns in the cleansing waters of the spring thaw, and the feud is settled.

Swanwhite (*Svanevit;* wr. 1901, prod. 1908). Swanwhite's father, the Duke, promises her that while he is away in battle a handsome, chaste prince will be sent from her fiancé the King to teach her the ways of the court. Swanwhite's cruel stepmother tries to prevent the two from seeing each other, but they do meet and fall in love. Using evil forces, the stepmother causes the Prince's death by drowning. Swanwhite summons her father home, and he sentences the stepmother to death. When Swanwhite begs the Duke to be merciful, her stepmother repents and brings the Prince back to life.

The Black Glove (*Svarta handsken,* 1909). Lyrical fantasy in five acts. The lady of a great mansion, who adores her child but is cruel to her husband and her servants, becomes incensed when she finds that her best ring is missing. She accuses her servant Ellen of theft, but Ellen swears she is innocent. Father Christmas and a Christmas angel meet and decide to take the child from the young mother to teach her that she cannot love just one person and hate everyone else. After she has learned her lesson, they will return the child as a Christmas pres-

Scene from *To Damascus*. [Swedish Information Service]

ent. They decide also to help an old man who, having left his wife and child, has devoted sixty years to a study of the mystery of life and now longs to end his philosophical search and die. Father Christmas answers his prayers by giving him a black glove, which he in turn gives to Ellen, who finds the lost ring inside it. The old man, pleased to see that he has done something to help others, falls asleep and dies. When Ellen tells her mistress the story of the old man, the young woman realizes he was her lost father. Ellen then gives her the ring, and the young woman, falling to her knees, begs forgiveness for her hateful accusations. On Christmas the young woman finds her lost child.

Pilgrimage Plays

Lucky Per's Journey (*Lycko-Pers resa,* 1883). Fifteen-year-old Per, accompanied by the loving and sensible Lisa, makes a journey with the help of a magic ring. He learns that every pleasure and happiness of life is also a source of suffering and discontent: flatterers and leeches accompany wealth; intrigue and ingratitude attend social reform; tradition and position make senseless demands on the powerful; and nature itself is cruel and terrifying. At the end of the journey Per knows that he must abandon feelings of self-love and vanity to find deliverance through life's greatest gift, love, which no magic ring can bestow.

The Keys of the Kingdom of Heaven, or St. Peter Wanders on Earth (*Himmelrikets nycklar, eller Sankte Per vandrar på jorden;* wr. 1892, prod. 1929). Verse play about a blacksmith grieving for his three children who died of plague. He sets off on a quest for the kingdom of heaven when a doddering St. Peter, who has come to him for a new set of keys, cannot remember the way back to the gates of heaven and requests his help. They are joined by a physician who guides them through fantastic landscapes. On the way they meet, among others, a Don Quixote, grown fat and practical, accompanied by an emaciated, idealistic Sancho Panza, and a Lady Macbeth married to Bluebeard. The pilgrimage ends in frustration and disappointment as St. Peter dies of fatigue. The physician advises the blacksmith: "Build now again a heaven of your own on earth but trust not all who rattle with its keys."

To Damascus, I (*Till Damaskus, första delen,* 1900). Drama that opens Strindberg's trilogy *To Damascus.* The Stranger, a famous author who has abandoned wife and children, meets a Lady as he is about to walk into a post office to see if his royalties have arrived. The Stranger feels attracted to the Lady; she is moved by his sadness and wants to protect him. At her home he recognizes her husband, the Physician, as the person who in school was punished for a crime committed by the Stranger and who consequently lost his faith in human justice. He also sees a madman, who is called by the Stranger's childhood nickname, Caesar. The Lady leaves her husband and goes off with the Stranger. Soon, however, their romance is overshadowed by his depression and their abject poverty. As outcasts they reach a house in the mountains where the Lady's mother and grandfather live. Reluctantly they shelter the couple. Urged on by her mother, the Lady breaks a promise she had made to the Stranger: she reads his latest book. The result is a rupture in their relationship. He leaves, falls down a cliff, and is taken to an insane asylum which he is told is a hospital. There he meets people who resemble those he knew in the past, and the Confessor reads him a curse from the Book of Deuteronomy. He returns to the house in the mountains, but the Lady has gone. When they are reunited, the Stranger dreams that his first wife has married the Physician. He visits the Physician and finds him planning a wedding. Then he returns to the post office and receives the money that earlier would have eased his suffering.

To Damascus, II (*Till Damaskus, andra delen;* wr. 1898, prod. 1916). Second drama in Strindberg's trilogy. As husband and wife, the Stranger and the Lady torment each other relentlessly. There are separations and threats of divorce. The Lady has become cunning and spiteful, and he takes revenge by speaking about his first wife. They have some hope that the child the Lady is expecting will save the marriage, although the Lady's mother hints that it is not the Stranger's. The couple is visited by Caesar, a madman, and the Physician, the Lady's former husband, who went mad after his wife's desertion and is now in the madman's custody. The Stranger, after experimenting with alchemy, believes he has finally succeeded in making gold. He goes to a banquet he thinks is in honor of his discovery, but it turns out to be a prank played on him by a society of alcoholics. He is expected to pay the expenses, but, not being able to do so, he lands in jail. On his way home after his release, the Stranger suffers a severe blow when he sees the children of his first marriage pass without recognizing him. At home he is repelled by the sight of the newborn child. He asks the Lady why they ever met, and she replies that it was to torture each other. Now that he has liberated her from her husband, she says, he has become enchained to evil. Delivered into the hands of a Confessor, who was once engaged to the Lady but devoted his life to God when she left him, the Stranger leaves to do penance in a monastery.

To Damascus, III (*Till Damaskus, tredje delen;* wr. 1901, prod. 1916). The last drama in Strindberg's trilogy depicts the main character's road to salvation. The Confessor takes the Stranger to a river. Beyond the river there are mountains and a monastery where he can turn away from his sufferings and toward faith. Before going to the retreat the Stranger wants to say farewell to his world. He meets his beloved daughter Sylvia, who has lost her innocence. Then the Lady, dressed in mourning for her own dead child, greets him and begs for sympathy. Once they have crossed the river, the Stranger discovers that he has suffered seven years in vain for Maia, his mistress and the nurse of his first child, who he thought had lived in poverty because he had not paid her wages. He confesses to the Lady that all his life he has been searching for the love his mother did not give him: "I sought an Ariel, and I found a Caliban." A pilgrim, formerly Caesar the madman, tells how his ingratitude has robbed him of his sanity. The Tempter appears

Scene from *A Dream Play*. [Swedish Information Service]

and takes the Stranger to see the trial of a man who shot his fiancée because she rejected him. The blame falls successively on the young man, the fiancée, the Tempter, Eve, and the serpent until it becomes apparent that everyone is in some way guilty and the trial is discontinued. The Stranger makes his last attempt at a rewarding human relationship when he and the Lady try once more to live together as man and wife, but their love proves ephemeral and the Lady leaves. The Stranger and his first wife discuss the failure of their marriage and their mutual antagonism. Finally the Stranger allows the Confessor to lead him to the monastery. There he is shown a gallery of portraits of famous men each having two heads, symbols of human contradiction. A mother with a child in her arms passes the Stranger just as he is to be buried and resurrected to bear the name Brother John; the child, about to be baptized, initiates the recurrence of the cycle.

A Dream Play (*Ett drömspel;* wr. 1902, prod. 1907). Pilgrimage play in fourteen scenes. The daughter of the Vedic god Indra descends to earth to experience human life. She moves through a phantasmagoric world where "time and space do not exist." Buildings grow like plants, a lifetime is contracted into a few moments, identities are changed, and the sum of human misery and suffering is exposed with startling clarity. Everyone she meets is either oppressed or an oppressor; only the Poet seems somewhat free from the vicissitudes of life. Nowhere can she find solace from the pain of being human, and so she abandons her earthly form with the conviction that "mankind is to be pitied" and the promise that she will carry man's complaints to her father.

The Great Highway (*Stora landsvägen*, 1910). Strindberg's last drama, in seven scenes set in the Sweden of the early twentieth century. The central character is a wandering hunter, a pariah who sees too much, feels too deeply, and speaks too honestly. A former preacher, he once offered himself as scapegoat for the sins of his town and thus of all mankind. For the last time he descends to the world of men from the clean, pure air of the alpine peaks that symbolize his quest for spiritual fulfillment. Among others, he encounters Hiroshima, a bitter, disillusioned Japanese craving self-destruction. Having reaffirmed his conviction that "the beautiful does not exist in this life, cannot be made reality down here—where the ideals are not practiced," he leaves the company of men forever and climbs to his final resting place under "a white and icy blanket."

BIRGITTA STEENE

PLAYS

Unless otherwise noted, the plays are in prose and were first performed in Stockholm.

1. *Fritänkaren* (*The Freethinker*). Dramatic sketch, 3 sections. Written 1869. Published 1870.

2. *Hermione*. Tragedy, 5 acts; verse. Written 1870. Published 1871.

3. *Det sjunkande Hellas* (*Greece in Decline*). Tragedy, 3 acts; verse. Written 1870. Published 1960. Early version of *Hermione*.

4. *I Rom* (*In Rome*). Dramatic situation, 1 act; verse. Written 1870. Published 1870. Produced Royal Dramatic Theatre, Sept. 13, 1870.

5. *Den fredlöse** (*The Outlaw*). Tragedy, 1 act. Written 1871. Published 1876. Produced Royal Dramatic Theatre, Oct. 16, 1871.

6. *Mäster Olof** (*Master Olof*). Historical play, 5 acts. Written 1872. Published 1881. Produced Nya Theatre, Dec. 30, 1881.

7. *Mäster Olof* (*Master Olof*). Historical play, 5 acts; verse. Written 1876. Published 1878. Produced Royal Dramatic Theatre, Mar. 15, 1890.

8. *Efterspel* (*Epilogue*). Play. Written 1877. Produced Göteborg, Lorensberg Theatre, Jan. 10, 1920.

9. *Anno fyrtioåtta* (*In the Year 1848*). Comedy, 4 acts. Written 1877? Published 1881.

10. *Gillets hemlighet* (*The Secret of the Guild*). Comedy, 4 acts. Written 1880. Published 1880. Produced Royal Dramatic Theatre, May 3, 1880.

11. *Lycko-Pers resa** (*Lucky Per's Journey*). Pilgrimage play, 5 acts. Written 1882. Published 1883. Produced Nya Theatre, Dec. 22, 1883.

12. *Herr Bengts hustru* (*Herr Bengt's Wife*). Period play, 5 acts. Written 1882. Published 1882. Produced Nya Theatre, Nov. 25, 1882.

13. *Marodörer* (*Marauders*). Play. Published 1886. Earlier version of *Kamraterna* by Strindberg alone.

14. *Fadren** (*The Father*). Tragedy, 3 acts. Written 1887. Published 1887. Produced Copenhagen, Casino Theatre, Nov. 14, 1887; Stockholm, Nya Theatre, Jan. 12, 1888.

15. (With Axel Lundegård.) *Kamraterna** (*Comrades*). Comedy, 4 acts. Written 1888. Published 1888. Produced Vienna, Lustspieltheater, October, 1905; Stockholm, Intimate Theater, May 17, 1910.

16. *Fröken Julie** (*Miss Julie*). Naturalistic tragedy, 1 act. Written 1888. Published 1888. Produced Copenhagen, Studentersamfundet, Mar. 14, 1889; Stockholm, Folk Theatre, Dec. 13, 1906.

17. *Fordringsägare** (*Creditors*). Tragicomedy, 1 act. Written 1888. Published 1890. Produced Copenhagen, Dagmar Theatre, Mar. 9, 1889; Stockholm, Swedish Theatre, Mar. 25, 1890.

18. *Hemsöborna* (*The People of Hemsö*). Comedy, 4 acts. Written 1889. Published 1905 (Germany), 1914 (Sweden). Produced Djurgårdsteatern, May 29, 1889.

19. *Den starkare** (*The Stronger*). Play, 1 scene. Written 1889. Published 1890. Produced Copenhagen, Dagmar Theatre, Mar. 9, 1889; Stockholm, Intimate Theatre, Dec. 5, 1907.

20. *Paria** (*Pariah*). Play, 1 act. Written 1889. Published 1890. Produced Copenhagen, Dagmar Theatre, May 9, 1889; Stockholm, Intimate Theatre, Feb. 11, 1908.

21. *Samum** (*Simoom*). Play, 1 act. Written 1889. Published 1890. Produced Swedish Theatre, Mar. 25, 1890.

22. *Himmelrikets nycklar, eller Sankte Per vandrar på jorden* (*The Keys of the Kingdom of Heaven, or St. Peter Wanders on Earth.*). Pilgrimage play, 5 acts; verse. Written 1892. Published 1892. Produced Radio Theatre, Oct. 17, 1929.

23. *Debet och kredit** (*Debit and Credit*). Play, 1 act. Written 1892. Published 1893. Produced Berlin, Residenztheater, May, 1900; Stockholm, Royal Dramatic Theatre, Aug. 31, 1915.

24. *Första varningen** (*The First Warning*). Comedy, 1 act. Written 1892. Published 1893. Produced Berlin, Residenztheater, Jan. 22, 1893; Stockholm, Intimate Theatre, Sept. 14, 1910. Original title: *The First Tooth* (*Första tanden*).

25. *Inför döden** (*Facing Death*). Tragedy, 1 act. Written 1892. Published 1893. Produced Berlin, Residenztheater, Jan. 22, 1893; Stockholm, Intimate Theatre, Mar. 5, 1910.

26. *Moderskärlek** (*Motherlove*). Play, 1 act. Written 1892. Published 1893. Produced Germany, 1894; Uppsala Theatre, fall, 1909.

27. *Leka med elden**(*Playing with Fire*). Comedy, 1 act. Written 1892. Published 1893 (Germany), 1897 (Sweden). Produced Berlin, Lessingtheater, December, 1893; Stockholm, National Restaurant (in their large room), May 3, 1907.

28. *Bandet** (*The Bond*). Tragedy, 1 act. Written 1892. Published 1893 (Germany), 1897 (Sweden). Produced Berlin, Kleines Theater, Mar. 11, 1902; Stockholm, Intimate Theatre, Jan. 31, 1908.

29. *Till Damaskus, första delen** (*To Damascus, I*). Pilgrimage play, 7 scenes. Written 1898. Published 1898. Produced Royal Dramatic Theatre, Nov. 19, 1900.

30. *Till Damaskus, andra delen** (*To Damascus, II*). Pilgrimage play, 4 acts. Written 1898. Published 1898. Produced Munich, Kammerspiele, June 6, 1916; Göteborg, Lorensberg Theatre, Dec. 9, 1924.

31. *Advent, ett mysterium** (*Advent*). Tragic fantasy, 5 acts. Written 1898. Published 1899. Produced Munich, Kammerspiele, Dec. 23, 1915; Stockholm, Royal Dramatic Theatre, Jan. 22, 1926.

32. *Brott och brott** (*Crime and Crime*). Comedy, 4 acts. Written 1899. Published 1899. Produced Stockholm, Royal Dramatic Theatre, Feb. 26, 1900.

33. *Folkungasagan** (*The Saga of the Folkungs*). Historical play, 5 acts. Written 1899. Produced Swedish Theatre, Jan. 25, 1901.

34. *Gustav Vasa**. Historical play, 5 acts. Written 1899. Published 1899. Produced Swedish Theatre, Oct. 17, 1899.

35. *Erik XIV**. Historical play, 4 acts. Written 1899. Published 1899. Produced Swedish Theatre, Nov. 30, 1899.

36. *Gustav Adolf**. Historical play, 5 acts. Written 1900. Published 1900. Produced Berlin, Berliner Theater, December, 1903; Stockholm, Cirkus, June 4, 1912.

37. *Midsommar* (*Midsummer*). Serious comedy, 6 tableaux. Written 1900. Published 1901. Produced Swedish Theatre, Apr. 17, 1901.

38. *Kaspers fet-tisdag* (*Casper's Shrove Tuesday*). Lenten Punch-and-Judy show, 1 act. Written 1900. Published 1915. Produced Royal Dramatic Theatre, Apr. 16, 1901.

39. *Påsk** (*Easter*). Drama, 3 acts. Written 1900. Published 1901. Produced Frankfurt am Main, Schauspielhaus, March, 1901; Stockholm, Royal Dramatic Theatre, Apr. 4, 1901.

40. *Dödsdansen, första delen** (*The Dance of Death, I*). Drama, 2 acts. Written 1900. Published 1901. Produced Cologne, Residenztheater, September, 1905; Stockholm, Intimate Theatre, Sept. 8, 1909.

41. *Dödsdansen, andra delen** (*The Dance of Death, II*). Drama, 2 acts. Written 1900. Published 1901. Produced Cologne, Residenztheater, September, 1905; Stockholm, Intimate Theatre, Oct. 1, 1909.

42. *Kronbruden** (*The Crown Bride*). Fantasy folk drama, 6 sections. Written 1900. Published 1902. Produced Helsingfors, Swedish Theatre, Apr. 24, 1906; Stockholm, Swedish Theatre, Sept. 14, 1907.

43. *Svanevit** (*Swanwhite*). Fantasy play, 3 acts. Written 1901. Published 1902. Produced Helsingfors, Swedish Theatre, Apr. 8, 1908; Stockholm, Intimate Theatre, Oct. 30, 1908.

44. *Till Damaskus, tredje delen** (*To Damascus, III*). Pilgrimage play, 4 acts. Written 1901. Published 1904. Produced Munich, Kammerspiele, June 6, 1916.

45. *Karl XII** (*Charles XII*). Historical play, 5 acts. Written 1901. Published 1901. Produced Royal Dramatic Theatre, Feb. 13, 1902.

46. *Engelbrekt**. Historical play, 4 acts. Written 1901. Published 1901. Produced Swedish Theatre, Dec. 3, 1901.

47. *Kristina** (*Queen Christina*). Historical play, 4 acts. Written 1901. Published 1901. Produced Intimate Theatre, Mar. 27, 1908.

48. *Ett drömspel** (*A Dream Play*). Pilgrimage play, 14 scenes. Written 1902. Published 1902. Produced Swedish Theatre, Apr. 17, 1907.

49. *Gustav III**. Historical play, 4 acts. Written 1902. Published 1903. Produced New Intimate Theatre, Jan. 25, 1916.

50. *Holländaren* (*The Dutchman*). Dramatic fragment, 4 sections. Written 1902. Published 1918. Produced Göteborg, Lorensberg Theatre, Apr. 5, 1923.

51. *Näktergalen i Wittenberg* (*The Nightingale of Wittenberg*). Period play, 4 scenes. Written 1903. Published 1904. Produced Berlin, Deutsches Künstlertheater, fall, 1914; Stockholm, Swedish Theatre, Jan. 26, 1917.

52. *Genom öknar till arvland, eller Moses* (*Through the Wilderness to the Promised Land, or Moses*). Period play, 21 tableaux. Written 1903. Published 1918. Produced Hannover, Stadttheater, 1922.

53. *Hellas, eller Sokrates* (*Hellas, or Socrates*). Period play, 19 tableaux. Written 1903. Published 1918. Produced Hannover, Stadttheater, 1922; Stockholm, Dramatikerstudien, May 13, 1942.

54. *Lammet och vilddjuret, eller Kristus (The Lamb and the Wild Beast, or Christ)*. Period play, 15 tableaux from Christ to Nero; 3 divisions. Written 1903. Published 1918. Produced Hannover, Stadttheater, 1922.

55. *Ováder* (Storm Weather)*. Chamber play, 3 scenes. Written 1907. Published 1907. Produced Intimate Theatre, Dec. 30, 1907.

56. *Brända tomten* (The Burned House)*. Chamber play, 2 scenes. Written 1907. Published 1907. Produced Intimate Theatre, Dec. 5, 1907.

57. *Spöksonaten* (The Ghost Sonata)*. Chamber play, 3 scenes. Written 1907. Published 1907. Produced Intimate Theatre, Jan. 21, 1908.

58. *Toten-Insel* (The Isle of the Dead)*. Dramatic fragment, 1 scene. Written 1907. Published 1918.

59. *Pelikanen* (The Pelican)*. Chamber play, 3 scenes. Written 1907. Published 1907. Produced Intimate Theatre, Nov. 26, 1907.

60. *Siste riddaren* (The Last of the Knights)*. Historical play, 5 acts. Written 1908. Published 1909. Produced Royal Dramatic Theatre, Jan. 22, 1909.

61. *Riksföreståndaren* (The Regent)*. Historical play, 5 acts. Written 1908. Published 1909. Produced Royal Dramatic Theatre, Jan. 31, 1911.

62. *Bjälbo-Jarlen* (Earl Birger of Bjälbo)*. Historical play, 5 acts. Written 1908. Published 1908. Produced Swedish Theatre, Mar. 26, 1909.

63. *Abu Casems tofflor (Abu Casem's Slippers)*. Fantasy play, 5 acts. Written 1908. Published 1908. Produced Gåvle, Dec. 28, 1908.

64. *Svarta handsken (The Black Glove)*. Fantasy play, 5 acts. Written 1909. Published 1909. Produced on tour, 1909; Stockholm, New Intimate Theatre, Dec. 26, 1911.

65. *Stora landsvägen* (The Great Highway)*. Pilgrimage play; verse. Written 1909. Published 1909. Produced Intimate Theatre, Feb. 19, 1910.

EDITIONS

Swedish

The standard (but incomplete) edition is *Strindbergs Samlade Skrifter*, ed. by J. Landquist, 55 vols., Stockholm, 1912–1920. A new definitive edition is in preparation.

English

Except for some early plays, all of Strindberg's dramas have been translated, appearing in numerous volumes of more than one play as well as in separate editions, anthologies, and periodicals. The most important are listed below.

Two early editions are still of value, despite the inadequacy of the translations, because they contain material that is unavailable elsewhere: *Plays*, tr. by E. and W. Oland, 3 vols., Boston, 1912–1914; and *Plays*, tr. by E. Bjorkman, 4 vols., New York, 1912–1916. A selection of the Bjorkman translations was reprinted as *Eight Famous Plays*, New York, 1950.

The Anglo-Swedish Literary Foundation sponsored a series published in London: *Easter and Other Plays*, 1929; *Lucky Peter's Travels and Other Plays*, 1930; *Master Olof and Other Plays*, 1931; and *To Damascus*, 1939 (also New York, 1960).

E. Sprigge's translations are represented in *Six Plays*, Garden City, N. Y., 1956; *Five Plays*, Garden City, N.Y., 1960; *Plays*, Chicago, 1962; and *Twelve Plays*, London, 1963.

Other recent editions are *Seven Plays*, tr. by A. Paulson, New York, 1960; *The Chamber Plays*, introd. by E. Sprinchorn, New York, 1962; *Plays*, tr. by M. Meyer, vol. 1, New York, 1964; and *Eight Expressionist Plays*, tr. by A. Paulson, New York, 1965.

W. Johnson has recently completed his translation of Strindberg's dramatic oeuvre, including all the Swedish history plays. The volumes are published by the University of Washington Press, Seattle: *Queen Christina, Charles XII*, and *Gustav III*, 1955; *The Last of the Knights, Earl Birger of Bjälbo*, and *The Regent*, 1956; *Gustav Adolf*, 1957; *The Vasa Trilogy*, 1959; *Engelbrekt* and *The Saga of the Folkungs*, 1959; *A Dream Play* and *Four Chamber Plays*, 1973; *Dramas of Testimony*, 1975; *Plays of Confession and Therapy*, 1979.

CRITICISM

Swedish

E. Hedén, *Strindberg: En ledtråd vid studiet av hans verk*, 2d ed., Stockholm, 1926; M. Lamm, *Strindbergs dramer*, 2 vols., Stockholm, 1924–1926; M. Lamm, *August Strindberg*, 2 vols., Stockholm, 1940–1942; G. Ollén, *Strindbergs dramatik*, rev. ed., Stockholm, 1961; H. G. Carlson, *Strindberg och myterna*, Stockholm, 1979; O. Lagercrantz, *Strindberg*, Stockholm, 1980.

English

J. Bulman, *Strindberg and Shakespeare*, London, 1933; B.M.E. Mortensen and B. Downs, *Strindberg: An Introduction to His Life and Work*, Cambridge, England, 1949; E. Sprigge, *The Strange Life of August Strindberg*, London, New York, 1949; A. Gustafson, "Strindberg and the Realistic Breakthrough," in *A History of Swedish Literature*, Minneapolis, 1961; B. G. Madsen, *Strindberg's Naturalistic Theatre*, Copenhagen, Seattle, 1962; W. Johnson, *Strindberg and the Historical Drama*, Seattle, 1963; C.E.W.L. Dahlstrom, *Strindberg's Dramatic Expressionism*, Ann Arbor, Mich., 1930, New York, 1965; M. Valency, *The Flower and the Castle*, New York, 1963, 1966; R. Brustein, *The Theatre of Revolt*, Boston, 1964; M. Lamm, *August*

Strindberg, tr. and ed. by H. G. Carlson, New York, 1971; *Strindberg*, ed. by O. Reinert, Englewood Cliffs, N.J., 1971; B. Steene, *The Greatest Fire: A Study of August Strindberg*, Carbondale, Ill., 1972, Stockholm, 1982; W. Johnson, *August Strindberg*, Boston, 1978.

Stroupežnický, Ladislav   (1850–1892)

Czech playwright. A representative of the realistic movement, Stroupežnický began his career writing historical tragedies, but he soon turned to comedy. His most important plays are *The Little Devil of Zvíkov* (*Zvíkovský rarášek*, 1883), *The Master's Wife* (*Paní mincmistrová*, 1886), and *Our Proud Peasants* (*Naši furijanti*, 1887). The last play, a humorous portrayal of Czech village life, uses colloquial language with dialectical elements; it was an important turning point in the development of the Czech drama at the end of the nineteenth century. *At the Valdstein Mine* (*Na Valdštejnské šachtě*, 1893) is an Ibsenite social drama.

[PAUL I. TRENSKY]

Suassuna, Ariano   (1927–   )

Brazilian poet and dramatist. He was born in João Pessoa, Paraíba, on June 16, 1927, to João Urbano Pessoa de Vasconcelos Suassuna and Cássia Dantas Vilar. Ariano graduated from the faculty of law at the University of Recife in 1946. As professor of drama at the University of Recife, Suassuna also helped to found the Teatro do Estudante de Pernambuco, the theatre group for which he wrote his first plays. In 1967 he became a founding member of the Federal Arts Council. In 1969 he was appointed director of the Center for Cultural Activities at the Federal University of Pernambuco. He is professor of aesthetics both in the arts faculty of the University of Recife and in the city's Catholic University. He also lectures on the theory of drama in the School of Fine Arts at Recife University.

WORK

The plays of Ariano Suassuna, with their natural, straightforward style, are dominated by popular and religious elements reminiscent of medieval drama in Europe. Reviving the primitive legends of the Brazilian Northeast, Suassuna discovers a wealth of suitable material for the genre; but in matters of form he acknowledges his debt to European tradition. His *auto sacramentals*, such as *Segismundo or The Desolate Arch* (*Segismundo ou o arco desolado*, 1952), have been validly compared with Calderón's *Life Is a Dream* (*La vida es sueño*, 1673). *See* CALDERÓN DE LA BARCA, PEDRO. *See also* AUTO SACRAMENTAL in glossary.

With consummate skill Suassuna fuses popular native elements with elaborate and erudite techniques. Colorful, everyday speech forms are ingeniously combined with refined expressions so that what might have been purely regional suddenly becomes universal. The superstitious character of folklore achieves a new depth and complexity in Suassuna's religious plays. His work is enhanced by a note of satire and gentle malice that corresponds to the psychology of the provincial types he depicts.

Suassuna's *Auto of John of the Cross* (*Auto de João da Cruz*, 1950) is wholly characteristic of his vision of the universe insofar as it establishes a sharp conflict between good and evil. Man wavers between the forces of light and darkness. Human frailty is the archenemy but sincere repentance insures salvation in the end. The difficulties and pitfalls of earthly existence are ultimately resolved by the divine ordinances of forgiveness and grace.

This spiritual world, with its orthodox Christianity and unswerving faith, is best seen in his acknowledged masterpiece, *Auto of Our Lady of Mercy* (*Auto da Compadecida*), first performed at Recife's Teatro Santa Isabel on September 11, 1956. It epitomizes an authentic popular theatre inspired in the traditional beliefs and cults of provincial communities untouched by the sophistications of contemporary society. Suassuna's next play, *The Suspect Marriage* (*O casamento suspeitoso*, 1957), is generally considered to be less successful. Here the popular elements so skillfully handled in Suassuna's major play degenerate into caricature, and the text suffers from a dispersive prolixity.

He regains his form in another play written that same year, *The Saint and The Sow* (*O santo e a porca*, 1957), a comedy based on the theme of the miser with shades of Plautus and Molière; however, Suassuna creates his own characters and forges his own techniques. A series of misunderstandings sustain the farce, but the author's preoccupation with the play's moral aspects results in some unconvincing distortions. In final analysis, the inherent dichotomy in the miser's nature is not entirely resolved.

Auto of Our Lady of Mercy (*Auto da Compadecida*, 1955). A circus clown (alias the author) presents the play—the tale of man's salvation through God's divine mercy. The first two scenes have all the characteristics of popular farce: musical instruments that resuscitate the dead; dogs buried with solemn Latin rites; characters who declare their astuteness but are deceived at every turn; and João Grilo, the picaresque hero whose wits have been sharpened by hunger and privation.

At the end of the second scene all the characters in the play die—bishops, peasants, priests, and bandits. The Day of Judgment has arrived, presided over by a mulatto Jesus Christ and a maternal warmhearted Virgin Mother. This central scene permits Suassuna to voice his own interpretation of Roman Catholic theology and Christian morality. The day of justice and victory, in which the powerful and corrupt are castigated, has arrived for the humble and honest. The outlaw who has lost his way in life is pardoned more readily than the hypocritical clergyman who has sold out his integrity to temporal power.

The most original feature of this arbitrary vision of Divine Providence is the importance attributed to the joyful atmosphere of heaven—a lively and animated place where souls can rejoice to their hearts' content. By contrast, the Devil and his victims are enmeshed in eternal discontent, tortured by the sadness of evil itself. Jesus Christ (alias Manuel) is vigorous and cheerful and completely relaxed in the company of the rustic, ingenuous *sertanejos* of the hinterland, whose simplicity he approves and understands. João Grilo and the Virgin Mother exchange their views on theological issues, which they interpret with the heart rather than the mind. The closing scenes constitute a remarkable fusion of farcical humor and religious fervor. The sham values of the world are finally exposed, and João Grilo's intervention wins forgiveness for his former enemies on earth. Restored to life, João Grilo voices the play's final message that life is the greatest gift of all, whatever man's condition.

GIOVANNI PONTIERO

PLAYS

1. *Uma mulher vestida de sol* (*A Woman Clothed in Sunshine*, 1947). Published 1964.
2. *Cantam as harpas de Sião* (*The Harps of Siam Sing*, 1948).
3. *Os homens de barro* (*The Clay Men*, 1959).
4. *Auto de João da Cruz* (*Auto of John of the Cross*, 1950).
5. *Segismundo ou o arco desolado* (*Segismundo or the Desolate Arch*, 1952).
6. *O castigo da soberba* (*The Proud Woman's Punishment*, 1953). Published 1960.
7. *O rico avarento* (*The Rich Miser*, 1954).
8. *Auto da Compadecida* (*Auto of Our Lady of Mercy*, 1955). Published 1959. English translation by D. F. Ratcliff, Berkeley, Los Angeles, 1963; also translated into French, German, Spanish, and Polish.
9. *O casamento suspeitoso* (*The Suspect Wedding*, 1957).
10. *O santo e a porca* (*The Saint and the Sow*, 1957). Published 1964.
11. *O homem da vaca e o poder da fortuna* (*The Man with a Cow and the Power of Fate*, 1958).
12. *A pena e a lei* (*Punishment and the Law*, 1959).
13. *Farsa da boa preguiça* (*The Farce of Happy Indolence*, 1960).
14. *A caseira e a Catarina* (*The Housekeeper and Catharine*, 1962).

CRITICISM

A. Houaiss, *Crítica Avulsa*, Ser. 1, no. 23, Salvador, Bahia, 1960; S. Magaldi, *Panorama do teatro brasileiro*, São Paulo, 1962, pp. 220–228; J. Pontes, *O teatro moderno em Pernambuco*, São Paulo, 1966; W. Martins and S. Menton, *Teatro brasileiro contemporâneo*, New York, 1966.

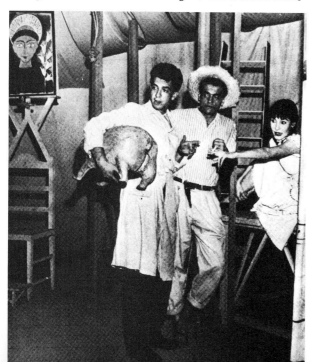

The Saint and the Sow, directed by Zbigniew Ziembinski in 1958 and starring Cacilda Becker and Walmor Chagas. [Archives IDART-PMSP]

Sudermann, Hermann (1857–1928)

German novelist and dramatist. He was born on September 30, 1857, in Matziken, East Prussia. His family, de-

Hermann
Sudermann.
[Walter Hampden
Memorial Library
at The Players,
New York]

scended from an old line of Dutch Mennonites, were intent on maintaining the puritan morals of their faith. Beset by financial difficulties, his parents were obliged to apprentice young Hermann, at fourteen years of age, to a chemist. But the position soon became intolerable to the boy, and he was permitted to return to school. It was at this time, when scornful schoolmates would treat him condescendingly for having worked, that he first became aware of social injustice and gradually developed a socialist orientation. After finishing the course of study at the Realgymnasium in Elbing, he attended the University of Königsberg and then the University of Berlin. While studying journalism there, he earned a meager living as tutor to the children of the writer Hans von Hopfen. Beginning as editor of the *Deutsches Reichsblatt*, he soon turned to short-story writing, publishing a first collection entitled *At Twilight* (*Im Zwielicht*, 1886), followed by the novels *Dame Care* (*Fran Sorge*, 1887), *The Siblings* (*Geschwister*, 1888), and *Regina* (*Der Katzensteg*, 1890). In 1889 the play *Honor* (*Die Ehre*) finally earned him success.

In 1891 Sudermann married a widow with three children, but after six weeks he left for Paris on the first of a series of trips that were to keep him from his family. Thereafter he seldom acted as a responsible paterfamilias, and his amorous escapades throughout Europe were common knowledge. Driven now by the success of *Honor,* he wrote a series of plays that rapidly added to his fame, especially the well-known *Magda* (*Heimat*, 1893), regarded as the *Camille* of the 1890s. The superb acting opportunities offered by this play contributed to its renown: Helena Modjeska, Sarah Bernhardt, Eleanora Duse, and Mrs. Pat Campbell all played the leading role. Sudermann soon began to manifest symptoms of megalomania. In his essay *The Brutalization of Theatre Reviewing* (*Die Verrohung der Theaterkritik*, 1902), he attacked the critics Alfred Kerr and Maximilian Harden, who had written unfavorable accounts of his work. From then on his career as a dramatist suffered. Returning to the novel, he created a number of works which have survived in German literature while his dramas are all but forgotten. Among Sudermann's best-known novels are *The Song of Songs* (*Das hohe Lied*, 1908), *It Was* (*Es war*,

1893), *The Mad Professor* (*Der tolle Professor*, 1926), *The Wife of Steffen Tromholt* (*Die Frau des Steffen Tromholt*, 1927), and *The Dance of Youth* (*Perzelchen*, 1928). A collection of short stories, *Lithuanian Stories* (*Litauische Geschichten*, 1917), is considered his best work. He died on November 22, 1928, in Berlin.

Work

Sudermann's reputation as a dramatist rests upon his extraordinary ability to exploit the new theatrical ideas and themes of his time in such a way as to appeal to the tastes of the audiences who attended commercial theatres. Like Pinero in England and Echegaray in Spain, he was a transitional figure whose plays bore an external resemblance to those of Ibsen and Hauptmann. In fact, after the successful production of his first play, *Honor* (1889), he was hailed as one of the foremost realists and, for a time, became Hauptmann's immediate rival. *See* ECHEGARAY, JOSÉ; HAUPTMANN, GERHART; IBSEN, HENRIK; PINERO, ARTHUR.

However, his fame declined rather rapidly because his plays were far from achieving the depth and power of Hauptmann's drama; they were in substance as well as in dramatic technique far more traditional. In short, whereas Sudermann toyed with the new ideas, he generally managed to discredit or modify them by providing a resolution that reinforced the traditional values and postures of society. Despite this, the great popularity of his plays helped prepare audiences for the more serious works of naturalism. In this and in his considerable talent for dramatic construction and stage effects lies Sudermann's importance. *See* NATURALISM in glossary.

Sudermann was principally interested in the question of honor, the distinction between honorable behavior and the facade of reputation, and his subjects were frequently chosen from the Prussian *Junker* class for which honor was a major preoccupation.

This question is central to his four best-known plays: *Honor*, *Magda* (1893), *St. John's Fire* (*Johannisfeuer*, 1900), and *The Joy of Living* (*Es lebe das Leben!*, 1902). Similar to these are *The Vale of Content* (*Das Glück im Winkel*, 1895), in which a wife who longs to be free to join her former lover discovers her love for her husband when he offers her freedom; *A Man and His End* (*Sodoms Ende*, 1890), in which an artist becomes entangled in the decadent society he despises and is destroyed; and the one-act *Freddie* (*Fritzchen*, 1896), an ironic portrait of a young lieutenant on the eve of a duel in which he will most certainly be killed.

Having already lost much of his popularity around the turn of the century, Sudermann was even less successful with those of the plays that were written after World War I because the superficiality of his themes and his concern for theatrical effects were totally foreign to the new expressionistic movement. *See* EXPRESSIONISM in glossary.

Honor (*Die Ehre*, 1889). Four-act drama, set in Prussian Berlin, that contrasts two kinds of "honor," that of the rich and that of the poor. Owing to the generosity of his patron, Councillor Mühlingk, Robert Heinecke is educated abroad and his family is given a home on the lower-class alley behind Mühlingk's palatial home. Returning from India after almost ten years in Mühlingk's service, Robert now finds his family crude, vulgar, and avaricious, bartering his sister's body to Mühlingk's son Kurt for material gain. Although in love with Lenore, his employer's daughter, Robert feels that he and his family are beneath her, and he "honorably" rejects her. Then he insists that Kurt marry his sister. But his family, who need money more than honor, accept a bribe from Mühlingk in return for not pressing the question of marriage. Fortunately Count Trast, Robert's wise friend, reimburses Mühlingk to restore Robert's sense of honor and then persuades Robert to leave his family by promising him his business. He thus makes it possible for Robert to marry Lenore, who is just as revolted by the crudity of the rich as Robert is by the crudity of the poor.

Magda (*Heimat*, 1893). Four-act drama, literally translated as *Home*, set in provincial Germany in the late nineteenth century. After refusing to marry a pastor chosen for her by her austere father, a retired colonel, Magda leaves home for the free life of Berlin, where she eventually becomes an opera star and bears a child out of wedlock. Some years later, abandoned by her lover, she returns home for a music festival. Her father discovers that her past affair was with a local councillor, with whom he tries to force her into marriage. The councillor, afraid of scandal, agrees to the wedding on condition that the existence of the child be kept secret. When Magda rejects his proposal, her father, fearing family disgrace, threatens to kill her and himself unless she agrees. He reaches for his gun, but before he can shoot, he is seized by a stroke and dies.

St. John's Fire (*Johannisfeuer*, 1900). Drama that unfolds in the Prussia of the 1860s, where classes were rig-

idly defined. Lacking a home and family of their own, Georg von Hartwig, son of a profligate father, and Marike, foundling daughter of a ragged gypsy thief, have been lovingly raised in the home of Herr Brauer, Georg's uncle. Marike, prevented by her status from encouraging Georg's love for her, buries her feelings and plunges selflessly into the preparations for Georg's wedding to Gertrud, Brauer's daughter. But on the holiday of St. John's Eve, Georg and Marike succumb to their hidden passion as the festival fires burn low. Class distinctions reassert themselves the next morning, when the festival is over: Georg marries Gertrud, and the hapless Marike prepares to leave the Brauer home.

The Joy of Living (*Es lebe das Leben!*, 1902). Five-act drama of adultery taking place in political circles of the aristocracy. After a passionate love affair that dates back twenty years, Richard von Volkerlingk and Beata von Gellinghausen have decided to remain platonic friends in order to avoid bringing scandal to their families. Beata uses her husband's influence to promote Richard's political ambitions, their two families remain close, and their children become engaged to each other. However, when Richard, at the climax of his political career, runs for election, a blackmailer threatens to disclose his affair with Beata. Richard thwarts the blackmail by revealing the truth to Beata's husband. Then, to prevent Richard from taking his own life, Beata, knowing that her death will be attributed to a weak heart, poisons herself, having first arranged the marriage of their children.

[PETER JELAVICH]

PLAYS

1. *Die Ehre** (*Honor*). Drama, 4 acts. Published 1889. Produced Berlin, Lessingtheater, Nov. 27, 1889.

2. *Sodoms Ende* (*A Man and His End*). Drama, 5 acts. Published 1891. Produced Berlin, Lessingtheater, Nov. 5, 1890.

3. *Heimat** (*Magda*). Drama, 4 acts; prose. Published 1893. Produced Berlin, Lessingtheater, Jan. 7, 1893.

4. *Die Schmetterlingsschlacht* (*The Battle of the Butterflies*). Comedy, 4 acts. Published 1895. Produced Berlin, Lessingtheater; Vienna, Burgtheater, Oct. 6, 1894.

5. *Das Glück im Winkel* (*The Vale of Content*). Drama, 3 acts. Published 1896. Produced Vienna, Burgtheater, Nov. 11, 1895.

The following three plays (Nos. 6, 7, and 8) form the trilogy *Morituri* (*Those Who Are about to Die*).

6. *Teja*. Drama, 1 act. Published 1896. Produced Berlin, Deutsches Theater; Vienna, Burgtheater, Oct. 3, 1896.

7. *Fritzchen* (*Freddie*). Drama, 1 act. Published 1896. Produced Berlin. Deutsches Theater; Vienna, Burgtheater, Oct. 3, 1896.

8. *Das ewig Männliche* (*The Eternal Masculine*). Drama, 1 act. Published 1896. Produced Berlin, Deutsches Theater; Vienna, Burgtheater, Oct. 3, 1896.

9. *Johannes* (*John the Baptist*). Tragedy, 5 acts. Published 1898. Produced Berlin, Deutsches Theater; Dresden, Königliches Hoftheater, Jan. 15, 1898.

10. *Die drei Reiherfedern* (*The Three Heron Feathers*). Dramatic poem, 5 acts; verse. Published 1899. Produced Berlin, Deutsches Theater; Dresden, Königliches Hoftheater; Stuttgart, Königliches Hoftheater, Jan. 21, 1899.

11. *Johannisfeuer** (*St. John's Fire*). Drama, 4 acts; prose. Published 1900. Produced Berlin, Lessingtheater, Oct. 5, 1900.

12. *Es lebe das Leben!** (*The Joy of Living*). Drama, 5 acts. Published 1902. Produced Berlin, Deutsches Theater, Feb. 1, 1902.

13. *Der Sturmgeselle Sokrates* (*The Storm Companion Socrates*). Comedy, 4 acts. Published 1903. Produced Berlin, Lessingtheater, Oct. 3, 1903.

14. *Stein unter Steinen* (*A Stone among Stones*). Drama, 4 acts; prose. Published 1905. Produced Berlin, Lessingtheater, Oct. 8, 1905.

15. *Das Blumenboot* (*The Flower Boat*). Drama, 4 acts. Published 1906. Produced St. Petersburg, Alexandrinsky Theatre, Mar. 25, 1906; Berlin, Lessingtheater, Oct. 5, 1906.

Magda, with Sarah Bernhardt in the title role. New York, Daly Theatre, 1895. [Theatre Collection, The New York Public Library at Lincoln Center, Astor, Lenox and Tilden Foundations]

The following three plays (Nos. 16, 17, and 18) form the trilogy *Rosen (The Roses)*.

16. *Margot*. Drama, 1 act. Produced Vienna, Burgtheater, Oct. 3, 1907.

17. *Der letzte Besuch (The Last Visit)*. Drama, 1 act. Produced Vienna, Burgtheater, Oct. 3, 1907.

18. *Die ferne Prinzessin (The Faraway Princess)*. Drama, 1 act. Produced Vienna, Burgtheater, Oct. 3, 1907.

19. *Lichtbänder (Bands of Light)*. Drama, 1 act. Produced Stuttgart, Königliches Interimstheater, Oct. 26, 1907.

20. *Strandkinder (Children of the Beach)*. Drama, 4 acts. Published 1910. Produced Berlin, Königliches Schauspielhaus, Dec. 21, 1909.

21. *Der Bettler von Syrakus (The Beggar of Syracuse)*. Tragedy, 5 acts. Published 1911. Produced Berlin, Königliches Schauspielhaus, Oct. 19, 1911.

22. *Der gute Ruf (The Good Reputation)*. Drama, 4 acts. Published 1913. Produced Berlin, Deutsches Theater; Munich, Königliches Hoftheater, Jan. 7, 1913.

23. *Die Lobgesänge des Claudian (Claudian's Songs of Praise)*. Drama, 5 acts. Published 1914. Produced Hamburg, Deutsches Schauspielhaus, Jan. 20, 1914.

The following three plays (Nos. 24, 25, and 26) form the trilogy *Die entgötterte Welt: Szenische Bilder aus einer kranken Zeit (The World Without God: Scenic Tableaux from a Sick Age)*.

24. *Die Freundin (The Woman Friend)*. Drama. Produced Berlin, Lessingtheater, and Munich Schauspielhaus, Jan. 28, 1916, as *Die gutgeschnittene Ecke*; Berlin Residenztheater, Feb. 1, 1919, as *Das höhere Leben*.

25. *Die gutgeschnittene Ecke (The Well cut Corner)*. Tragicomedy. Produced Berlin, Lessingtheater, and Munich Schauspielhaus, Jan. 28, 1916, as *Die gutgeschnittene Ecke*; Berlin Residenztheater, Feb. 1, 1919, as *Das höhere Leben*.

26. *Das höhere Leben (The Higher Life)*. Comedy, 4 acts. Produced Berlin, Lessingtheater, and Munich Schauspielhaus, Jan. 28, 1916, as *Die gutgeschnittene Ecke*; Berlin Residenztheater, Feb. 1, 1919, as *Das höhere Leben*.

27. *Regina*. Dramatization of Sudermann's novel *Der Katzensteg*, 5 acts. Produced Berlin, Theater an der Königgrätzerstrasse, Sept. 27, 1919.

28. *Die Raschhoffs (The Raschhoffs)*. Play. Published 1919. Produced Königsberg, Neues Schauspielhaus, Oct. 18, 1919.

The following three plays (Nos. 29, 30, and 31) form the trilogy *Das deutsche Schicksal (The German Fate)*.

29. *Notruf (Emergency Call)*. Drama, 5 acts. Published 1920/21.

30. *Heilige Zeit (Holy Time)*. Scenic tableaux, 4 acts.

31. *Opfer (The Sacrifice)*. Drama, 4 acts.

32. *Wie die Träumenden (As the Dreaming)*. Drama, prologue and 4 acts. Published 1922; Republished 1932, as *Die Entscheidung der Lissa Hart*.

33. *Der Hasenfellhändler (The Dealer in Hare Skins)*. Drama, 4 acts. Published 1927.

EDITIONS

Collections
Dramatische Werke, 6 vols., Stuttgart, 1923.
Individual Plays
John the Baptist. Published in *German Classics of the Nineteenth and Twentieth Centuries*, ed. by K. Francke and tr. by B. Marshall, vol. 17, New York, 1913–1914.
Magda. Published in *Contemporary Drama: European Plays*, ed. by E. B. Watson and B. Pressey and tr. by C. Winslow, vol. 2, New York, 1931–1934.
St. John's Fire (The Fires of St. John). Published in *Representative Continental Dramas, Revolutionary and Transitional*, ed. by M. J. Moses and tr. by C. Swickard, Boston, 1924.
The Vale of Content. Published in *Chief Contemporary Dramatists*, ed. by T. H. Dickinson and tr. by W. Leonard, 1st ser., Boston, 1915.

CRITICISM

W. Kawerau, *Hermann Sudermann*, Magdeburg and Leipzig, 1897; H. Schoen, *Hermann Sudermann*, Paris, 1904; K. Knortz, *Sudermanns Dramen*, Halle, 1908; H. S. Cannon, *Sudermann's Treatment of Verse*, Tübingen, 1922; K. Busse, *Hermann Sudermann: Sein Werk und sein Wesen*, Stuttgart, 1927; *Hermann Sudermann*, ed. by T. Duglor, Troisdorf, 1958.

Sukhovo-Kobylin, Aleksandr Vasilyevich (1817–1903)

Russian philosopher and dramatist. He was born into the Russian nobility in Voskresensky on September 17, 1817. He studied at the University of Moscow from 1834 to 1838 and then traveled for several years. The murder of his French mistress in 1850 led to his arrest and impris-

onment. Intricate judicial proceedings went on for seven years. While in jail, in 1854, Sukhovo-Kobylin wrote his comedy, *Krechinsky's Wedding (Svadba Krechinskogo)*. The first play of a trilogy later published under the title *Tableaux of the Past (Kartiny proshedshego*, 1869), it was successfully produced at the Maly Theatre, in Moscow, in 1855. Sukhovo-Kobylin was acquitted in 1857, and his painful experience with the corrupt Russian judicial system became the basis for his second play, *The Case (Delo*, wr. 1862). This was so brutal an indictment of Russian bureaucracy that the unabridged version was not produced until the 1917 Revolution. In 1868 Sukhovo-Kobylin finished his third and last play, *The Death of Tarelkin (Smert Tarelkina)*, a macabre farce.

Sukhovo-Kobylin devoted the latter part of his life to metaphysics and, in 1902, was elected honorary member of the literature branch of the Russian Academy of Sciences. On March 11, 1903, he died in Beaulieu, France.

WORK

Sukhovo-Kobylin's principal interest was philosophy (in addition to writing his own philosophical treatises, he made translations into Russian of Hegel's works), but in his dramatic trilogy *Tableaux of the Past* (pub. 1869) he created first-rate realistic-grotesque drama. Although connected, the plays—*Krechinsky's Wedding* (1855), *The Case* (wr. 1862), and *The Death of Tarelkin* (wr. 1869)—are marked by differences in approach and tone. The first is deft, psychological, and tightly constructed; its "hero," who bears a resemblance to Gogol's Khlestakov, is characterized with brilliant irony and humor. *The Case*, based on the playwright's experiences with the judicial system, details the destruction of a man by the irrational forces of Russian bureaucracy, a theme closely allied to Kafka's in *The Trial*. Here, the satire is harsh and the humor sardonic. *The Death of Tarelkin* describes the conflict between two archvillains, Varravin and Tarelkin, who seek to destroy each other. The humor is dark, macabre, and grotesque; the play assumes qualities of the surrealistic and fantastic. Sukhovo-Kobylin very skillfully used the Gogolian grotesque to portray the unreal quality of life in late-nineteenth-century Russia. *See* GOGOL, NIKOLAY VASILYEVICH.

The basic dynamic principle of each play is to embroil its hero—Krechinsky, Muromsky, or Tarelkin—deeper and deeper in difficulties; as the dilemma intensifies, the pace increases, the language becomes more brutal, and the incidents more physicalized. Just as each individual play accelerates in this way, so the tone of each within the trilogy grows more caustic and unrelentingly cynical. By the end, the relatively normal human beings of *Krechinsky's Wedding* are replaced by "vampires" and automata. Sukhovo-Kobylin is not merely a satirist of red tape, but a forerunner of the existentialists and the playwrights of the absurd.

Krechinsky's Wedding (Svadba Krechinskogo, 1855). Satirical comedy, first of a trilogy, in which an elegant rogue, Mikhail Krechinsky, in order to recoup his squandered fortune becomes engaged to Lidochka, the impressionable daughter of a wealthy provincial landowner,

A Russian production of *The Death of Tarelkin*. [Theatre Collection, The New York Public Library at Lincoln Center, Astor, Lenox and Tilden Foundations]

ceased neighbor, Kopylov, and then to blackmail Varravin for the rest of his life. Thus, he arranges his own funeral. Varravin, suspecting fraud, disguises himself and goes to Tarelkin's home in search of his papers. There, under the guise of Kopylov, Tarelkin is entertaining the scoundrel Rasplyuyev. Discovering Tarelkin's wig and dentures in a drawer, Varravin confirms the swindle. He then convinces Rasplyuyev that Tarelkin is actually a vampire and that he, Rasplyuyev, will receive a high reward provided he follows orders. Tarelkin is taken into custody and is tortured by thirst (because any liquid would make a vampire invincible), and proceedings against him are begun. Finally, weakened by the torture, Tarelkin returns the papers to Varravin, who magnanimously allows him to leave with Kopylov's identity papers.

[LAURENCE SENELICK]

PLAYS

The three plays form the trilogy *Kartiny proshedshego* (*Tableaux of the Past*, pub. 1869).

1. *Svadba Krechinskogo** (*Krechinsky's Wedding*). Comedy, 3 acts. Written 1852/54. Published 1856. Produced Moscow, Maly Theatre, Nov. 28, 1855; St. Petersburg, Alexandrinsky Theatre, October, 1856. First play in trilogy.

2. *Delo* (*The Case*). Drama, 3 acts. Written 1862. Published 1869. Produced, in censored, cut version, Moscow, Maly Theatre, Aug. 31, 1882, as *Otzhitoye vremya* (*Bygone Times*). Second play in trilogy.

3. *Smert Tarelkina* (*The Death of Tarelkin*). Drama, 3 acts. Written 1869. Published 1869. Produced in censored, cut version, St. Petersburg, Theatre of the Literary and Artistic Society of St. Petersburg, Sept. 15, 1900, as *Vesyolye Rasplyuyevskiye dni* (*The Gay Rasplyuyev Days*). Third play in trilogy.

EDITIONS

Trilogiya, Moscow-Leningrad, 1927; *Krechinsky's Wedding*, tr. by R. Magidoff, Ann Arbor, 1961; *Trilogiya A. V. Sukhovo-Kobylina*, ed. by K. L. Rudnitskiy, Moscow, 1966; *The Trilogy of Alexander Sukhovo-Kobylin*, tr. by H. B. Segal, New York, 1969.

CRITICISM

A. V. Sukhovo-Kobylin: Zhizn, lichnosti i tvorchestvo, Moscow-Leningrad, 1927; V. Shakhnovsky, *Teatralnaya sudba trilogii Sukhovo-Kobylina*, Moscow-Leningrad, 1927; L. Grossman, *Teatr Sukhovo-Kobylina*, Moscow-Leningrad, 1940; N. Brodyanska, "Sukhovo-Kobylin," in *Slavonic Review* (1947); K. L. Rudnitsky, *A. V. Sukhovo-Kobylin. Ocherk zhizni i tvorchestva*, Moscow, 1957; I. Kleyner, *Dramaturgiya Sukhovo-Kobylina*, Moscow, 1961.

Sumarokov, Aleksey Petrovich (1717–1777)

Russian dramatist. Considered the first genuine Russian playwright, he was born in Finland to an impoverished family of the old nobility, and in 1731 was enrolled in the Cadet School, where he studied history, philosophy, political economy, and philology. His first play, *Khorev*, a neoclassical tragedy, was performed by the students of the Cadet School in 1747; its enormous success on account of its theme—the subject's obligations to the monarchy—and its historical subject matter confirmed him in his theatrical interests. Between 1747 and 1771 he wrote nine tragedies and twelve comedies; at first these were played by the amateur Cadets, under Sumarokov's direction. But in 1756 he was appointed director of the first Russian professional permanent public theatre, which he had helped to organize in St. Petersburg, and in 1759 founded the journal *Trudolyubivaya pchyola* (*The Industrious Bee*), which disseminated mildly liberal views. Besides his playwriting, his activities at the theatre in-

Pyotr Muromsky. Although Muromsky has misgivings at first, Krechinsky wins him over and a date is set for the wedding. So pressing are Krechinsky's financial problems, however, that he cannot wait until the marriage; he borrows Lidochka's diamond pin, claiming that he needs it to win a bet, and sends his scoundrel friend Ivan Rasplyuyev to "pawn" it, first substituting a worthless imitation. Nelkin, a friend of Muromsky and also a suitor of Lidochka, has been observing these machinations, and during a dinner party for Lidochka at Krechinsky's flat he demands that Krechinsky produce the diamond. When Krechinsky triumphantly does so, Nelkin retires in confusion. Now the pawnbroker, who has discovered the substitution, arrives with police and Krechinsky is unmasked. He is saved from prison by Lidochka, who impulsively hands over the genuine pin and rushes from the room in tears.

The Case (*Delo*, wr. 1862). Second play of the trilogy, a drama of caustic satire and unrelieved despair, which details the destruction of a helpless landowner and his daughter by a bureaucratic legal system. Lidochka has been accused of abetting a swindle through an amorous relationship with Krechinsky, and Muromsky becomes entangled in drawn-out judicial proceedings in order to clear her. Lidochka is innocent, and Muromsky refuses to be blackmailed by greedy and dishonest officials. He spends most of his fortune trying to extricate himself and his daughter from the "case." Finally he obtains an interview with Councilor Varravin and his subordinate Tarelkin, who agree between themselves to strip Muromsky of all he owns. Varravin demands an impossibly high bribe in return for his cooperation. Muromsky refuses to pay and goes to the Prince, who turns a deaf ear. Varravin then extorts Muromsky's remaining money, and the old man dies defeated. Now penniless, Lidochka, against whom there was no real case, vanishes into oblivion.

The Death of Tarelkin (*Smert Tarelkina*, 1869). In the last play of the trilogy, the two predatory conspirators from *The Case* turn against one another in a grotesque life-and-death struggle. Tarelkin has stolen some compromising papers from Varravin and has contrived an ingenious way of starting a new life without creditors and without work. He plans to assume the identity of a decluded staging plays, coaching the actors, and supervising the scene designs. But his quarrelsome nature led to his dismissal in 1761; he lost interest in drama and sank into alcoholism and paranoia.

In general, Sumarokov followed the dictates of French neoclassicism, subscribing to the unities, a five-act structure, Alexandrine verse, and stage decorum. His best tragedies are *Khorev* (1747), in which the theme of love versus duty is played out by the title-character and the Princess Osnelda; *Hamlet* (1748), a version of Shakespeare's play based on French translations, which suppresses the ghost and increases the love interest; and *Dimitry the Pretender*, (*Dimitriy Samozvanets*, 1771), based on the same historical events as Pushkin's *Boris Godunov* was to be. Sumarokov was the first Russian playwright to draw on national history, but his characters, no matter what their source, speak and act like abstract versions of Racine's heroes. However, he reduced the role of the confidant, allowing the characters' reason to conflict with their passion, thus creating a modicum of self-revelation. *See* CONFIDANT; NEOCLASSICISM; UNITIES in glossary.

His comedies cleave closely to the French comedy of character, very much in the tradition of Molière. The best examples are *Tresotinius* (1750), *The Guardian* (*Oepkun*, 1765) and *The Imaginary Cuckold* (*Rogonosets po voobrazheniyu*, 1772), which were regarded as old-fashioned by the end of his lifetime. But despite his deficiencies, Sumarokov opened the way for a native school of drama, and *Dimitriy Samozvanets* held the stage well into the 1820s. *See* MOLIÈRE.

LAURENCE SENELICK

EDITIONS

Polnoe sobranie vsekh sochineniy v stikhakh i proze, 10 vols., 2d ed., Moscow 1781–1787; *Demetrius the Impostor*, London, 1806; *Izbrannye proizvedeniya*, Moscow, 1957; *Dimitrii the Impostor*, in *The Literature of Eighteenth-Century Russia*, ed. and tr. by H. B. Segel, vol. 2, New York, 1967; *Selected Tragedies of A. P. Sumarokov*, tr. by R. and R. Fortune, Evanston, 1970.

CRITICISM

D. M. Lang, "Sumarokov's 'Hamlet," *Modern Language Review* XLIII, 1 (Jan. 1948); "Boileau and Sumarokov," *Modern Language Review* XLIII, 4 (Oct. 1948); P. N. Berkov, *A. P. Sumarokov*, Leningrad-Moscow, 1949; E. Vetter, *Studien zu Sumarokov*, Berlin, 1961.

Supervielle, Jules (1884–1960)

French poet, short-story writer, novelist, and dramatist of both French and Uruguayan citizenship. He completed his studies in France before returning to South America, where he married. Back in France, during the post-World War I period he established his reputation with some remarkable short stories and poems that are generally associated with the surrealist school but are permeated by South American imagery and greatly influenced by Spanish literary techniques. His novels include *Man of the Pampa* (*L'homme de la pampa*, 1923) and *The Man Who Stole Children* (*Le voleur d'enfants*, 1926), both of which have South American protagonists. Supervielle turned to the theatre in his late forties with *Beauty in the Forest* (*La belle au bois*; prod. 1931, rev. 1947, 1953), in which many of the characters from Charles Perrault's immortal fairy tales appear. Beauty and Bluebeard, whose

Scene from *Robinson,* Théâtre de l'Oeuvre, Paris. [French Cultural Services]

love is threatened by the latter's "lower instincts," are plunged into a protective sleep and awakened in the twentieth century by an idiotic Prince Charming. Because legendary characters cannot survive in a mechanized civilization, Beauty refuses the prince and chooses eternal magic sleep with Bluebeard, the man she really loves. *Adam* (1930), revised in 1934 as *The First Family (La première famille)*, is a farce in which the father of us all is shown as a ladies' man who invents wine as a compensation for fidelity. *Bolivar* (1936) is a historical spectacle that tends to emphasize the Liberator's love life rather than his military and political involvements. Darius Milhaud, who wrote the incidental music for this poetic pageant (originally intended as a film scenario), used the play as the basis for his 1954 opera of the same name. *Robinson* (prod. 1948, rev. 1952) is an extension of the story of Defoe's shipwrecked hero. His youthfulness miraculously preserved, Robinson returns to England and marries the daughter of a woman he once loved. *Shéhérazade* (1948) borrows many of the characters from *The Thousand and One Nights* and calls for spectacular scenic effects—a flying palace, among others—difficult to achieve on the stage. It was originally presented outdoors in the courtyard of the Palace of the Popes in Avignon.

Supervielle's plays are poetic fantasies that often include verse passages and songs, but his 1949 adaptation of his novel *The Man Who Stole Children* comes close to being a straight drama and is considered by some critics to be his most successful theatre work. Middle-aged and childless, Colonel Bigua steals unwanted children. He falls in love with one of his charges, but she runs off with a young boy. Bigua attempts suicide but learns to accept old age gracefully when the girl, abandoned by her lover after the birth of a child, returns to find shelter with her former protector. *The Consequences of a Race (Les suites d'une course*, 1959) is a verse farce in which a young man is transformed into a horse.

In addition to his original plays, Supervielle translated Shakespeare's *As You Like It* (1934), *The Tempest* (1955), and *A Midsummer Night's Dream* (1959).

[JOSEPH E. GARREAU]

Sutherland, Efua (1930–)

Ghanaian playwright and theatre pioneer. Sutherland, who has played a key role in modern Ghanaian theatre, founded the Experimental Theatre Players in Accra in 1958, the first year of Ghana's independence. In 1960 she opened the Ghana Drama Studio, the first purposely built modern African theatre, featuring an open courtyard with a covered stage on one side. The Drama Studio provided the essential workshop for the creation of a new Ghanaian theatre.

In 1962 she joined the staff of the New School of Music and Drama, headed by the distinguished Ghanaian musicologist J. W. C. Nketia. She continued to present her company at the downtown Drama Studio rather than on the remote campus of the University at Legon, which had relatively poor theatre facilities. During the regime of Kwame Nkrumah the emphasis in Ghanaian theater was on national traditions, bringing arts to the people, new writing expressive of social duties, and theatre for young people. Culture became an important, state-controlled element of national prestige abroad. (The dance troupe founded in 1960 to perform Saka Acquaye's dance drama *Obadzeng* was immediately dispatched to Moscow by President Nkrumah.)

Sutherland's published plays demonstrate this change of emphasis. *Edufa* (1957) is a free poetic rendering in Ghanaian terms of Euripides's *Alcestis* and adapts the theme of the faithful wife who offers her life to save her husband from death. Sutherland's most important play, *Foriwa* (1967), expressed the spirit of national reawakening in the person of Labaron, a young graduate who brings new hope to a neglected Ghanaian town and to Foriwa, the Queen's beautiful daughter. He does this by demonstrating the potential of self-help, the importance of action rather than words.

Sutherland's writing is only a small part of her total contribution to the Ghanaian cultural scene, which has by no means been limited to the city. Her most cherished project was the creation of a popular village theatre based on the African storytelling tradition. These stories are widely used in drama education. Sutherland's *Marriage for Anansewa* (1975) tells how the cunning spider Ananse tried to make money by demanding a bride price for his daughter from several suitors at once.

GEOFFREY AXWORTHY

Sütő, András (1927–)

Transylvanian Hungarian playwright and writer. András Sütő pursued higher studies at Nagyenyed (now Aiud, Rumania) and Kolozsvár (now Cluj, Rumania), and was editor of a number of Transylvanian Hungarian papers. He has received two Rumanian State Prizes, and is a member of the Presidium of the Rumanian Writers' Association and the Communist Party of Rumania.

Sütő's development as a playwright was slow. During the 1950s and early 1960s he wrote stereotyped "socialist realist" plays about class struggle in the countryside and idyllic rural existence under "socialism." Not until *Pompás Gedeon* (1967) did he start blending critical anecdotizing with formal expressions of the grotesque. Four plays written during the 1970s made Sütő an internationally recognized playwright. They deal with loss of illusions, beliefs, ideals, and human ties. *The Whitsunday of a Horse Dealer* (*Egy lócsiszár virágvasárnapja*, ca. 1973) is based on Heinrich von Kleist's classic novel *Michael Kohlhaas*. The protagonist believes in divine and human justice—and is abandoned by both. He dies convinced that the order of the human world must change before true justice can be achieved. *Star on the Stake* (*Csillag a máglyán*, ca. 1974) represents the conflict between the religious leader John Calvin and his friend Servet. It is an allegory of the paradoxes of revolutions and other radical social movements. Servet appears as a poet and dreamer, symbolizing a force moving onward to ultimate aims, whereas Calvin, a radical in comparison with Luther, himself finds it necessary to turn to rationalism and assert the status quo threatened by his onetime friend.

In *Cain and Abel* (*Káin és Ábel*), originally published under the title *A Drama in Three Shrieks of Woe* (*Dráma három jajkiáltásban*, 1978), and in *The Wedding of Susa* (*A szúzai menyegző*, 1980), Sütő's dramatic and philosophical scope takes on wider and more symbolic dimensions than in the historical plays. The Biblical drama starts years after the expulsion, when the equilibrium of man and the world no longer exists. This makes Cain defy the capricious Creator and his senseless law. His counterpoint is Abel, the perfect subject, timid citizen, and prototype of the modern mass man. He questions nothing but blindly fulfills God's most extravagant demands to secure his own survival. In Sütő's interpretation Cain kills Abel when his brother is ready to sacrifice to God "the one dearest to him." Abel interprets this to mean Arabella, the woman God gave him and whom both brothers love. Ironically, God's will is carried out by the fratricide, since what was dearest to Abel was actually his own life.

While *Cain and Abel* continues the dilemma presented by Imre Madách in his *Tragedy of Man*, more pertinent to violence-ridden modern history and to the tribulations of Sütő's 2 to 3 million Hungarian kinsmen in Rumania is *The Wedding of Susa* (see MADÁCH, IMRE). The historical background—the conquest of Persia by Alexander the Great—is just an excuse to give shape to an allegory. The Macedonians are shown as the incarnation of timeless neophytism as they impose their newly adopted Hellenic civilization on the conquered Persians with ruthless arrogance. The drama is a not very optimistic plea for respecting the right of all nations and cultures to existence.

Sütő's dramas have been staged in a number of European countries. He is regarded as the greatest Hungarian playwright living outside the present borders of Hungary.

GEORGE BISZTRAY

1. (With Zoltán Hajdu). *Mezítlábas menyasszony (Barefoot Bride)*. Comedy. Written 1950.

2. *Fecskeszárnyú szemöldök (Swallow-Winged Eyebrow)*. Comedy, 1 act. Written 1958.

3. *Esküvő a kastélyban (Wedding in the Castle)*. Written 1960.

4. *Szerelem, ne siess! (Don't Hurry, Love!)*. Comedy. Written 1961.

5. *Tékozló szerelem (Lavish Love)*. Written 1963.

6. *Pompás Gedeon*. Written 1967. Hungarian production Kaposvár, Csiky Gergely Színház, 1972.

7. *Egy lócsiszár virágvasárnapja (The Whitsunday of a Horse Dealer)*. Drama, 3 acts. Based on Heinrich von Kleist's *Michael Kolhaas*. Published 1975. Hungarian production Kaposvár, Csiky Gergely Színház, 1974.

8. *Csillag a máglyán (Star on the Stake)*. Drama, 3 acts. Hungarian production Budapest, Madách Színház, 1975.

9. *Káin és Ábel (Cain and Abel)*. Published under the title *Dráma három jajkiáltásban (A Drama in Three Shrieks of Woe)*, 1978. Hungarian production Budapest, Nemzeti Színház, 1978.

10. *Vidám sirató egy bolyongó porszemért (Cheerful Lament for a Rambling Speck of Dust)*. Hungarian production Szeged, Szegedi Nemzeti Színház Kisszínháza, 1978.

11. *A szúzai menyegző (The Wedding of Susa)*. Published 1980.

L. Kántor and G. Láng, *Romániai magyar irodalom 1944–1970*, Bucharest, 1973, p. 241; Mész Lászlóné, *Mai magyar drámák*, Budapest, 1980, pp. 96–143.

Sutro, Alfred   (1863–1933)

British dramatist. In his day he was one of the most popular writers of the well-made play. He was proficient in light comedy as well as drama and through a career that spanned three decades turned out many commercial successes. Sutro appears to have been influenced by the styles of Henry Arthur Jones and Arthur Wing Pinero, although his was a lesser talent. His first big success was

Alfred Sutro.
[Walter Hampden
Memorial Library
at The Players,
New York]

The Walls of Jericho (1904), written after a number of earlier plays. Among his works are *Carrots* (1900); *The Perfect Lover* (1905); *The Fascinating Mr. Vanderveldt* (1906); *John Glayde's Honour* (1907); *The Perplexed Husband* (1911), which combines drama and burlesque in dealing with the feminist movement; *The Two Virtues* (1914); and *The Laughing Lady* (1922). Sutro also translated several of Maeterlinck's works into English. *See* WELL-MADE PLAY. in glossary.

J. R. Taylor, *The Rise and Fall of the "Well-Made Play*," London, 1967.

Svevo, Italo   (1861–1928)

Italian novelist and playwright from Trieste; pseudonym of Ettore Schmitz. He has come to be recognized as one of the most original writers of the twentieth century. With a number of short stories and three major novels—*A Life (Una vita*, 1893), *As a Man Grows Older (Senilità*, 1898), and *The Confessions of Zeno (La coscienza di Zeno*, 1923)—Svevo was instrumental in turning the course of Italian fiction from the naturalism of the nineteenth century toward new narrative forms and themes concerned with psychological introspection and literary experimentation. First acclaimed abroad by Valéry Larbaud and James Joyce, Svevo developed a reputation as a prose stylist that is now secure. His contribution to Italian theatre is less impressive but by no means minimal. Nor was his interest in theatre only a passing fancy, for recent examination of his posthumous manuscripts and extant correspondence proves that he actually began his literary career as a playwright and only later moved to prose. Between 1880 and 1928, Svevo worked on some thirteen dramatic pieces, including plays of one, two, three, and four acts. In general, they do not reflect the innovative qualities characteristic of his fiction and are closer in tone to the middle-class drama of the period. One play of a single act, *Inferiority (Inferiorità*, 1921) is considered an excellent example of Svevo's introduction of psychoanalytical themes (the inferiority complex) into Italian drama and has been revived on Italian television and radio in recent years. It is the story of a practical joke played by two noblemen on a man with the assistance of a servant; it ends absurdly and tragically with the death of the man at his servant's hands. Other less successful works include *Fragmentary Trio (Terzetto spezzato*, ca. 1890), the only theatrical work by Svevo performed during his lifetime (1927); *The Theories of Count Alberto (Le theorie del Conte*, ca. 1880), a two-act play which reflects Svevo's interest in Darwin; and the unfinished four-act work *With the Golden Pen (Con la penna d'oro*, 1926), which recent criticism has termed a possible precursor of the contemporary antiplay.

PETER BONDANELLA

Commedie, ed. by U. Apollonio, Milan, 1960; "Inferiority," tr. by P. N. Furbank, in *Essays on Italo Svevo*, ed. by T. F. Staley, Tulsa, 1969.

P. N. Furbank, *Italo Svevo: The Man and the Writer*, Berkeley, 1966; O. Ragusa, "'The Light Is Split in the Prism . . .': The Unfinished Play, *Con la penna d'oro*," in *Essays on Italo Svevo*, ed. by T. F. Staley, Tulsa, 1969; B. Weiss, "Svevo's *Inferiorità*," *Modern Fiction Studies* 18 (1972), 45–52.

Swedish Drama

In the opening scene of August Strindberg's historical drama *Master Olof*, the title figure, Swedish Lutheran reformer Olaus Petri (1493–1552), is rehearsing a play, *Tobiae Comedia*, wih his pupils. This play, allegedly written by Petri in 1550, is a typical example of the so-called school drama, a form of didactic religious play that represents one of the earliest known types of drama in Sweden.

SCHOOL DRAMA

The early school drama, performed by alumni at the cathedral schools or at the University of Uppsala (founded 1477), was an offshoot of the medieval liturgical play found all over Western Europe. Its origin was the religious cult, and its purpose was to represent visually and dramatically stories and episodes from the Bible. In Sweden, as elsewhere, two central events of the Christian year, Easter and Christmas, formed the core of this religious drama. Historical evidence tells us that ritualistic plays depicting the Resurrection and the Epiphany survived into the seventeenth century, though not without creating a certain amount of controversy. *See* LITURGICAL DRAMA in glossary.

With the Reformation of 1521, when King Gustav Vasa broke with the church of Rome and established the Lutheran state church in Sweden, many early church dramas—all, of course, Roman Catholic in origin—were forbidden, especially those pertaining to the worship of saints. But also burial rituals enacted at Easter and processions impersonating the Magi visiting the newborn Christ at Christmas were banished from the churches. In 1575 a royal decree stated that no plays with characters representing the Trinity were to be performed, and in 1594, during a visit of the Catholic King Sigismund of Poland, a popular uprising occurred when Catholic priests buried a picture of Christ to be lifted out of a replica of Christ's tomb on Easter morning.

The Protestant antagonism toward religious drama with roots in Catholic rituals prompted the author of the aforementioned *Tobiae Comedia* to write a preface in which he tried to justify his "comedy" with a reference to his wise ancestors' use of such plays to instruct the common people about Christian morality: "Our forefathers had done the same in this country as in other countries since the coming of Christianity, with songs, rhymes and comedies about holy men." But to mark their break with earlier liturgical plays, *Tobiae Comedia* and other school dramas, which were first performed in Latin and later in Swedish, simply added Protestant ideas to the existing religious plot. Thus Petri's didactic *comedia* treats one of the favorite themes of Lutheran teaching: the necessity of marriage.

In addition to the didactic school drama, two other remnants of early medieval drama survived the Reformation—namely the allegorical morality play and the Epiphany "star procession." No Swedish religious allegory or morality play is extant in manuscript form, however, from before the seventeenth century. In 1681 Sveno Dalius's (1604–1693) *The Choice (Valet-Skänck)* found its way into print. The play treats the same subject as the well-known drama of *Everyman*.

Epiphany plays enjoyed a longer life than any other form of medieval drama in Sweden. Originally performed by the priests, who impersonated the Magi as they walked in a procession up the aisle of the church and halted before a crib at the altar rail, the Epiphany drama was eventually taken over by the students in the Latin schools, who at Christmastime would march from house to house clad in white and wearing high paper caps. Remnants of the Epiphany performance, which eventually included the characters of Herod and a boy angel, may survive in the boy star processions that often accompany St. Lucia (December 13) and Christmas celebrations in Sweden today.

The church play and the subsequent school drama were performed in a given place or town. But an ambulatory secular theatre also existed in Sweden during the Middle Ages. These itinerant players performed farces that chiefly emanated from the Shrovetide celebrations. This season of merrymaking produced a Swedish version of the German *Fastnachtsspiel*, or Carnival play. But despite their popularity, very few of the medieval farces have survived in Sweden. An extant example from the sixteenth century is *A Merry Comedy about Doctor Simon (Een Lustigh Comedia om Doctor Simon)*. The plot revolves around a farming couple who engage in a domestic squabble over a pair of trousers, the emblem of household power. Matriarchy is established in the end as the beaten husband must concede his role as head of the house and resign himself to the fact that his wife—whose nickname is Doctor Simon—will now wear the pants. *See* FARCE in glossary.

In Scandinavia, roving performers had a long history which antedated the arrival of the Carnival farce. Snorre Sturlusson (1178–1241), author of the Icelandic *Younger Edda*, tells us in the saga of King Huglek, from about 1210, that the king had actors, harp players, and fiddlers at his court. Ambulatory actors also participated in celebrations on more solemn occasions. In 1455, when King Knutsson's daughter took her vows as a nun in the cloister of Wadstena, itinerant performers participated in procession. Little by little, however, this type of popular theatre—a precursor of the circus—lost its status and fell into disrepute. At the beginning of the sixteenth century Gustav Vasa declared that anyone who housed "magicians, jesters, and other rovers" without permission from the local sheriff would have to pay a stiff fine.

SIXTEENTH CENTURY

With the arrival of humanism in the sixteenth century, Swedish school drama developed in a profoundly secular direction. The Renaissance movement created a new interest in the Latin language and eventually also a keen curiosity about classical Roman drama. It became part of the educational structure of humanism to set up literary models: Cicero for letter writing, Vergil for the epic, Seneca for tragedy, and Plautus and Terence for comedy. Swedish disciples of the humanist Philip Melanchton (1497–1560) claimed that next to the Bible there could be no more useful source of study than the classical tragedies. A Swedish church ordinance of 1572 urged schoolmasters to train their pupils in acting of classical comedies and tragedies "so that both those who play and those who watch may be instructed and improved." In 1620 King Gustav II Adolf was advised by his bishops that the best way to improve learning in Sweden was to have the students enact classical plays directed by teachers of rhetoric.

In Swedish schools Terence soon became the preferred classical writer of comedy for study and performance. His six plays were read closely, and at the end of the school term the pupils, called *djäknar*, would perform one of them to show the authorities that they had acquired a command of Latin. But before too long a group of church people referred to as the *ramister* began to object to the pagan content of Terence's plays. As a result many Swedish schoolmasters wrote new comedies with Terence as their model, using many of his phrases and a good deal of his plots. Such Terence imitations became extremely popular and were later translated in Swedish, probably to amuse parents and relatives who did not know Latin.

SEVENTEENTH CENTURY

By the early seventeenth century dramatic performances flourished in the schools in the provinces. In the town of Södertälje, south of Stockholm, schoolmaster Jacobus Petri Rondeletius (1580?–1662) wrote a tragicomedy, *Judas Redivivus* (1614), which was performed by his students. It is a morality play based on the story of Judas Iscariot, but with burlesque comic interludes derived from the Carnival play.

A further step toward the complete secularization of Swedish drama was taken when school pedagogues began to abandon the moralistic tone of the Swedish Terence-inspired comedies for translations of comedies performed by ambulatory players on the Continent and designed primarily for entertainment. An early example is *An Amusing Comedy by the Name of Thisbe* (*Een lustigh comaedia vidh nampn Tisbe*) by Magnus Olai Asteropherus (d. 1647). Dating from 1609 or 1610, Asteropherus's work is based on Ovid's famous tale of Pyramus and Thisbe, and it seems to have had continental forerunners. Another immensely popular play of the same period is *Disa* (1611), subtitled "a merry comedy about the wise and renowned Queen of Sweden Lady Disa," by Johannes Messenius (1579–1636), a professor at the University of Uppsala, who would be a strong contender for the title "father of Swedish drama." His ambition was to depict the entire history of his country in a series of fifty plays that would be performed by his students. Only a half dozen of these plays based on Scandinavian sagas and legends were completed; however, Messenius had initiated the creation of a nationalistic drama—a genre that would be revived from time to time by Swedish playwrights, most notably August Strindberg, who devoted several years to the composition of a cycle of plays concerning Swedish history.

Little by little the performance of Swedish school dramas developed from pedagogical exercises—at first based on Bible stories and Luther's catechism and, later, imitations of classical comedy—into important civic events, apparently often subsidized by town councils. School dramas also found their way to the court of Sweden. The sons of Gustav Vasa shared none of their father's reservations about theatrical performances. At the wedding of Prince Johan in 1612 a production of Messenius's play *Signill* was part of the celebrations at the palace in Stockholm. As the arena for humanist dramas expanded, Swedish playwrights, following the example of their continental counterparts, began to incorporate music and dance into their works. Songs and dances often not only opened or closed each act but were also part of the dramatic action.

With this trend toward pageantry and spectacle, it was only natural that theatrical activity should gradually shift from civic performances by school students to performances by professional acting companies and visiting troupes who catered to the lavish tastes of the royal house and the court. Queen Christina, who reigned from 1644 to 1654, followed the practice of Renaissance courts elsewhere in creating stunning *ballets de cour*, musical and dance celebrations that sometimes went on for days and even weeks. Significantly, whereas Queen Christina only once invited the student players at the University of Uppsala to perform at her court, she involved some of Sweden's most prominent writers in her ballets, called *upptåg* in Swedish. Thus Georg Stiernhielm (1598–1672), remembered in literary history as the father of Swedish verse, wrote texts for three musical ballets, the best entitled *The Imprisoned Cupid* (*Then fångne Cupido*, 1649). The dramatic action depicts a contest between Cupid (assisted by his mother, Venus) and Diana, goddess of chastity, who succeeds in making Cupid her prisoner. Queen Christina herself played the role of Diana. The piece shows a distinct tendency toward the flamboyant taste of baroque literature.

In 1665 Urban Hjärne (1641–1724), Sweden's Seneca, presented his tragedy *Rosimunda* in Uppsala. The drama is an adaptation of a tragedy written in Latin by the Dutchman Zevecotius, to which Hjärne's real contribution is the dramatic verse form. Instead of writing in the Germanic *knittel* verse of Swedish school dramas, Hjärne introduced a dactylic verse, with dialogue composed in unrhymed verse and occasionally in hexameters and alexandrines. Like its model, Seneca's gory tragedy, *Rosimunda* is extremely bloody: the villain Alboin has murdered Cunimund and married his daughter Rosimunda, whom he forces to drink out of her father's skull, whereupon she murders him. As in Seneca, the ghosts of the murdered ones appear onstage.

The development towards a concept of drama as a secular and aesthetic art form received new impetus in Sweden during the seventeenth and eighteenth centuries through the performances of an increasing number of troupes of strolling players from the Continent. Mostly German and Dutch, these groups of wandering actors performed a variety of tragedies and comedies, often drastically adapted to itinerant conditions. Hjärne's *Rosimunda* probably reveals an influence from such eclectic presentations by strolling players in the interruption of the strictly serious action of Seneca's tragedy by a number of comic interludes.

The visiting strolling players, who often performed in the marketplace, and the sojourn of foreign acting troupes invited by the Swedish court, served as a challenge to existing Swedish ensembles and sometimes jeopardized the existence of newly established ones. The university town of Uppsala deserves special mention because of its long history of dramatic activity dating back to school drama. A particular factor in making Uppsala a center of dramatic activity was the sixteenth-century quarrel between two of its most prominent professors, Johannes Rudbeckius (1585–1646) and Johannes Messenius, both of whom utilized the dramatic genre to carry on their feud. Rudbeckius tried to enlist support among his students by having them perform classical Latin comedies, while Messenius tried to win disciples by engaging them in productions of his own dramas written in Swedish. After Messenius was moved to Stockholm, dramatic activity among the Uppsala students deteriorated until the administration complained that "the students shamed the academy with their *actions.*"

In 1682 a new troupe was formed in Uppsala, which performed at the castle in town as well as in the Lion's Den (Lejonkulan) and the Bollhuset Theatre in the Stockholm Palace. Named The Swedish Theatre (Dän Swänska Theatern), the Uppsala troupe was a genuine native repertory theatre which performed plays written by some of its members. Among these were *Disa* (1687) by Johan Celsius (1660–1710); a Senecan tragedy, *Darius* (1688), by Isak Björk (1660?–1700); and three tragedies by anonymous authors: *Troas, Hippolytus,* and *Philomena.* The troupe lasted until the death of its main supporter, Count Erik Lindschöld, in 1691.

In 1697 the Stockholm Palace burned to the ground, destroying "the Comedy House in the Lion's Den." In the same year King Charles XI died at the age of forty-two and all theatres were closed for a period of national mourning. Foreign acting ensembles left the country. Two years later, however, the Swedish government invited a French troupe led by Claude Rosidor to establish itself permanently in Stockholm and perform plays by Molière, Corneille, and Racine. This initiative had been taken by the court architect Nicodemus Tessin the Younger (1654–1728), who designed a new theatre for the troupe in the Wrangel Palace, which, however, was to be only partly completed. The extensive wars during the reign of Charles XII led to national bankruptcy, and in 1706 the Rosidor troupe had to head homeward with empty pockets as the Swedish government was unable to pay their salaries.

EIGHTEENTH CENTURY

For several decades after the departure of the Rosidor troupe, dramatic and theatrical activity in the Swedish capital was low-keyed while the country, no longer a political power, was recovering from the devastating warfare with Russia and other European countries. But in 1737 a group of students and aristocratic civil servants gained access to the Bollhuset, the palace theatre in Stockholm. Before an enthusiastic crowd they performed the anonymous *Tobiae Historia* (not to be confused with Olaus Petri's *Tobiae Comedia*), an event that led to the formation of the Royal Swedish Stage (Kongliga Svenska Skådeplatsen), which opened officially in October of the same year with a production of an original five-act comedy, *The Swedish Fop (Svenska Sprätthöken),* 1737, by Carl Gyllenborg (1669–1746).

Probably inspired by the Danish playwright Ludvig Holberg's play *Erasmus Montanus* (1731), Gyllenborg's comedy revolves around the snobbery of a young Swedish count who, upon returning from France, refuses to acknowledge the Swedish language and his nation's customs. He is saved from the ostracizing consequences of his attitude by a young girl who promises to marry him on the condition that he abandon his follies and become a loyal Swede. *See* HOLBERG, LUDVIG.

The leadership of the Royal Swedish Stage was soon turned over to a French actor, Charles Langlois. Twice weekly his troupe presented a varied repertory, ranging from tragedies to burlesque afterpieces and harlequinades. Among the native tragedies first performed by Langlois' ensemble were *The Tragedy of Snow White* (*Fröken Snöhwits Tragaedia,* 1731) by Erik Wrangel (1686–1765) and *Brynilda* (1738) by Olof von Dalin (1708–1763). Among the noteworthy comedies were *The Jealous Man* (*Den afwundsiuke,* 1738) by Dalin and *Mrs. Rank-Sick* (*Fru Rangsjuk,* 1738) by R. G. Modées (1698–1752).

The fate of a theatre like the Royal Swedish Stage depended very much on the attitude of the reigning monarch. The aging King Frederick (r. 1720–1751) appreciated other pleasures more than the theatre, while Lovisa Ulrika, wife of Fredrik's successor, Adolf Fredrik (r. 1751–1771), scorned the dramatic efforts of Langlois' company. After a single visit to the theatre, she vowed never to return. A few years later (1753) Langlois was sent packing together with his Swedish actors, to be replaced by a new French troupe which performed in French.

One of Langlois' Swedish performers, Petter Stenborg (1719–1781), formed his own company and was granted permission to perform in the Swedish capital provided he could find a suitable theatre. Stenborg's theatre continued to exist for many decades, but by the beginning of the reign of King Gustav III in 1771 it had fallen into disrepute.

The ascendance of Gustav III to the Swedish throne marked not only a new beginning for Stenborg's theatre troupe but also a new era for Swedish drama. Gustav (1746–1792), who was also an actor and playwright, had a particular passion for the stage, and during his reign (1771–1792) theatre activity in Sweden outdazzled that of most other European countries. His assassination during a masquerade ball at the Opera (which he had founded) in Stockholm was curiously symbolic in implication: for Gustav politics and theatrical activity merged; for him the Royal Swedish Opera had as much reality as the Swedish parliament.

Gustav's mother, Lovisa Ulrika, sister of Frederick the Great of Prussia, had established the Drottningholm Court Theatre in 1744, after having been disgusted by the "vulgarities" of Langlois' Royal Swedish Stage. It was at Drottningholm, Lovisa Ulrika's summer residence, that her son Gustav made his debut as an actor when he participated at the age of six in a children's pageant. After a fire in 1762 the Drottningholm theatre had to be completely rebuilt. In its rococo auditorium Gustav III ushered in a new era in the Swedish theatre. Today it remains the best-preserved example of an eighteenth-century court theatre in Europe.

Among Gustav's actions on the theatrical scene was the foundation of the Royal Swedish Opera, which was housed in the restored theatre in Bollhuset. The Opera opened in 1773 with *Thetis and Pelée (Thetis och Pelée)*, written by the King and Johan Wellander (1735–1783). To encourage the performance of plays in Swedish, the Improvement Society for the Swedish Language was formed, and from time to time the Stenborg troupe, now under the auspices of the court, performed Swedish language plays on the opera stage in Bollhuset.

In 1782, when the Opera moved to a new location in Stockholm, a Swedish literary journalist Adolf Ristell (1750–1812?) requested use of the former opera house for the performance of Swedish dramas, tragedies, and comedies. In 1787 Ristell formed a Swedish acting ensemble under the name Swedish Dramatic Theatre (Svenska Dramatiska Teatern). A year later Ristell had to leave the capital because of bankruptcy, whereupon his theater came under the king's protection and received the right to call itself the Royal Swedish Dramatic Theatre. In the meantime Stenborg's theatre, having changed its name to the Swedish Comic Theatre, was performing vaudevilles, operas comiques, and parodies. In 1799 this theatre merged with the Royal Dramatic.

In the last quarter of the eighteenth century Swedish drama developed almost exclusively in the direction of French neoclassical tragedy. The continuing French influence is not difficult to explain, for in 1781 Gustav III had invited to Sweden yet another French troupe, whose members came from the Comédie-Française. This company, directed by J. M. Monvel, performed French plays twice a week at the Drottningholm Court Theatre. Among the Swedish plays modeled on French neoclassical drama which continued to be performed were *Torilla* (1738) by Erik Wrangel, *Ingeborg* (1739) by Olof Celsius (1716–1794) and Olof von Dalin's *Brynilda*—all of which maintain the three unities and are full of the "nobles et douces sentiments" that the age of Louis XIV had been fond of glorifying.

The influence of French neoclassical drama lasted throughout the eighteenth century. Its design was followed as late as 1799 by G. G. Adlerbeth (1751–1818) in his tragedy *Ingiald Illråda*. Gustav's own dramas were patterned after Voltaire's tragedies, many of which had been translated into Swedish. In *Gustav Adolf's Noble Courage* (*Gustav Adolfs ädelmod*, 1782), the King borrowed the plot intrigue from Voltaire's *Charlot ou la comtesse de Givry*. Just as Voltaire's works for the theatre were tendentious plays in which he propagated his religious and political ideas, Gustav's dramas exhibit similar didacticism. In his *Frigga* (1786), set in pagan times, he presents the heathen god Woden as wise but treacherous and condemns, in the spirit of contemporary deism, the morbid human sacrifices of a pagan era.

Gustav III envisioned the creation of a Swedish political theatre which would glorify Sweden's history and its royal houses. He began by outlining a three-act drama entitled *Birger Jarl*, which was put into verse by Carl Gyllenborg in 1774. The King wrote another half dozen

plays together with writers whom he commissioned to help him realize his ideas. Many of these dramas were performed under the indefatigable supervision of the King in his eighteenth-century court theatre at Gripsholm Castle on the Lake Malar.

The dramatic form that exerted the most profound impact on the Swedish theatre world during the reign of Gustav III was opera. Gustav's most successful works were written for this art form, even though he does not seem to have been very musical. Opera fascinated him for its pageantry and decor; in his mind the opera was not very different from the Swedish court ballets (*upptåg*) of the sixteenth century. His *Thetis and Pelée*, written with Johan Wellander, is a veritable *coup de théâtre* filled with storms, phantoms, and spectacular descents to the stage. Gustav participated in the planning of entire play or opera productions; therefore, most of the Swedish operas written during the Gustavian era carry the baroque stamp of Gustav's imagination. The most successful of these was *Gustav Wasa* (1786), in many ways the superb achievement of the Gustavian theatre. Referred to as a lyrical tragedy, *Gustav Wasa* was based on a scenario by the King which had been put into verse by the Swedish poet and literary critic Johan Kellgren (1751–1795). The staging was designed by Louis Jean Desprez (1743–1804), whom Gustav III had met in Italy and brought to Sweden. Splendid battle scenes between Swedish and Danish troops aroused the patriotism of the audience. In *Gustav Wasa*, the King succeeded in fusing his ambitions for a political theatre with his love of the spectacular.

In 1793, a year after Gustav's death, the Konlige Mindre Teatern (Royal Smaller Theatre), also known as the Arsenal Theatre, opened in a building housing the arsenal in Stockholm. Its first production was Gustav III's last dramatic work, *The Jealous Neapolitan (Den svartsjuke neopolitanaren)*, written in 1789. Set in medieval times, it is symptomatic of the end of a period in Swedish drama during which the French influence had been dominant. From then on, "Gothic" dramas from Germany and, to a lesser extent, England would furnish the dramatic models.

In 1781, however, a Swedish historical play, *Erik XIV*, by the poet Bengt Lidner (1757–1793), had foreshadowed the demise of neoclassical drama in Sweden. Though written in Paris, Lidner's *Erik XIV* shows greater affinity with Shakespeare than with Corneille, Voltaire, and Racine. Although a minor motif in *Erik XIV* is the clash between duty and love (the dominant theme in Corneille's plays), the central action of Lidner's drama concerns not heroes but characters torn by sentimental passion. His title figure is more father than king, and he explains his bloody deeds in a tone of romantic rationalization: "I was more unhappy than cruel and criminal." Lidner's *Erik XIV*, like later Romantic drama, was inspired by the pathos in Shakespeare rather than the stylized restraint in French neoclassical drama. The play is set in dungeons where murders are enacted before the eyes of the spectator, where people go mad, and where in the end only the villain, Johan III, is left alive on the stage until the play's Fortinbras appears in the figure of

Duke Charles, later to restore order in Sweden as King Charles IX.

The emerging bourgeois drama, originating in France and England, attempted to portray the middle class, rather than the nobility, and tended to be both moralistic and *larmoyante* ("tearful"). It had been introduced to the Swedish public by the Stenborg troupe in 1768, when the company performed the British jeweller George Lillo's bourgeois tragedy *The London Merchant. See* LILLO, GEORGE. *See also* BOURGEOIS DRAMA in glossary.

But Lillo's real contender on the Swedish stage was the German playwright August von Kotzebue, whose prolific production of melodramas focusing on abducted virgins, disguised gypsies, and Gothic ruins reached some two hundred plays. Between 1791 and 1794 Kotzebue was the preferred author of both the Royal Dramatic Theatre and the Arsenal Theatre in Stockholm. Swedish imitations of Kotzebue's tearjerkers were produced by Carl Johan Lindegren (1770–1815) in such sentimental dramas as *The Blind Lover (Den blinde älskaren)* and *The Reconciled Father (Den försonade fadern)*, both written in 1795. These early bourgeois melodramas were so popular that Lindegren was made secretary of the Royal Dramatic Theatre in 1796. By now, the controlled artifice of the baroque theatre was giving way to the unabashed sensationalism and histrionics of gothicism. *See* KOTZEBUE, AUGUST VON.

By the end of the eighteenth century Swedish playwrights were no longer writing dramas for scholastic performance or for court spectacles. With the establishment of several new theatres in Stockholm—some private, like the Munkbroteatern, and some under the auspices of the crown—the middle-class audience became more and more important. Stage equipment became more sophisticated, perhaps because of the predilection of Gothic drama for thunderous happenings on stage.

NINETEENTH CENTURY

The death of Gustav III brought, however, not only the end of neoclassicism but also a harsher climate for the theatres in the Swedish capital. Gustav's successor, Gustav IV Adolf, soon closed several stages, including the private Munksbroteatern and the Royal Opera. Ironically, Swedish drama moved at the same time in the direction of the romantic closet drama—the long verse play meant for reading rather than staging (*see* CLOSET DRAMA in glossary). Although Sweden did not produce romantic playwrights of the stature of Goethe, Schiller, and Lessing in Germany or Adam Oehlenschläger in Denmark, Swedish poets of the early nineteenth century excelled in a particualr genre, the *sagospel* (fairy-tale play), which must be deemed a remarkable literary if not a stage-conscious achievement.

Referred to as "the arabesque of poetry," the *sagospel* defied prosaic reality for the world of myth and legend. Its origin has been traced to the Italian playwright Carlo Gozzi's *fiabes*—that is, dramatized folktales incorporating commedia dell' arte figures—and to the work of German author Ludwig Tieck, who followed in Gozzi's footsteps, (*see* GOZZI, CARLO). But Shakespeare's later plays were also a source of inspiration. Shakespeare had his break-through on the Swedish stage at the end of the eighteenth and the beginning of the nineteenth century. At first it was the "Gothic" element in Shakespeare that appealed to Swedish audiences. But the poet Amadeus Atterbom (1790–1855), who became the foremost creator of the *sagospel*, was less attracted to the great tragedies and more affected by *Cymbeline, The Winter's Tale* and *The Tempest*. Especially *Cymbeline* seems to have inspired Atterbom's *Bluebird (Fågel Blå)*, on which he worked from 1811 to 1835 but without finishing more than one third of it. Both Shakespeare's drama and Atterbom's *sagospel* use the same fairy-tale motifs: the evil stepmother, her ugly and stupid daughter, the beautiful and lovely stepdaughter, the kind but ineffectual king, and the young prince. In both works the authors succeed in combining dream and reality, fairy tale and realism. Like Shakespeare, Atterbom used blank verse.

Bluebird is based on a genuine folktale—an Old French *lai* written down in 1710 by one of the folktale collector Charles Perrault's successors, Madame d'Aulny, and translated into Swedish in the eighteenth century. Into this folktale Atterbom projects many of his romantic ideals. Inspired by the religious mysticism that accompanied the romantic movement, Atterbom divides his characters into two categories: the good and the evil, the idealists and the materialists. His play is a contest between these two moral and philosophical points of view. The play's central figure, however, is the magician Deolatus, in whom Atterbom draws a portrait of the romantic poet. He is a restless northerner attracted to exotic southern countries—the drama is set on the island of Cyprus—and a dreamer who lives in the world of fantasy. When challenged by his friend Cyprianus, a realist, Dealotus replies that the world of the imagination is the only real world.

The *sagospel* is a poetic and declamatory form of drama suited to the reflective mind of the romantic poet. Other samples of the genre in Swedish literature are Atterbom's *The Island of Bliss (Lycksalighetens ö,* 1824–1827) and two plays by Johan Stagnelius (1792–1823), *Sigurd Ring* and *Visbur* (printed posthumously 1824–1826), which can be described as romantic attempts at writing Greek tragedy with a chorus, seers, and messengers, as well as heroes suffering from *hubris*, while retaining the folktale elements of old ballads and sagas.

Victor Hugo's *Hernani* (1830) impressed Swedish writers, and the play was translated and performed in Stockholm in 1833. Hugo's fascination with the criminal mind made an impact on the Swedish author Carl Jonas Love Almqvist (1793–1866). Stagnelius had earlier introduced the subject in his closet drama *The Knight's Tower (Riddartornet,* printed posthumously 1824), in which he treated the motif of incest, juxtaposing it to the innocent world of virginity.

In 1834 Almqvist published two dramas in the Spanish spirit of *Hernani*. One, *Ramido Marinesco*, treats the Don Juan theme; the other, *Signora Luna* depicts a blind, saintlike Spanish woman's return to earthly life. The latter play is controlled by the same kind of tragic coincidence that permeates Hugo's dramatic works (*see* HUGO, VICTOR). The following year (1835) Almqvist wrote *Isido-*

ros of Tadmor (*Isidoros av Tadmor*) and a sequel, *Marjam*. The two plays dramatize the conversion of two Hellenic men to Christianity. He was no doubt the most original dramatist in Sweden in the first half of the nineteenth century, but his plays were read as closet dramas only. None of Almqvist's works reached the stage until director Alf Sjöberg adapted his novels *Amorina* for the Royal Dramatic Theatre in 1951 and *The Queen's Jewel* (*Drottningens juvelsmycke*) in 1957.

The Swedish stage continued to decline in the early part of the nineteenth century. After the Arsenal Theatre burned down in 1825, the only remaining theatre in Stockholm was the Royal Opera. But in 1842 Anders Lindeberg opened a private theatre, New Theatre (Nya Teatern) with ambitions of presenting classical and recent drama. Subsequently other small theatres sprang up, most of which produced plays in translation. The most frequently performed dramatists were Schiller, Hugo, and Scribe. By the time August Strindberg arrived on the scene in the 1870s, Scribe had become the dominant playwright on the Swedish stage. Works by native dramatists were relatively rare in Stockholm theatres in the mid-nineteenth century though Lindeberg inaugurated his New Theatre with a Swedish tragedy, *Agne* (1812), by Per Henrik Ling (1776–1829), better known as the originator of Swedish gymnastics.

Ling's drama was typical of the prevailing native genre on the Swedish stage at the time—the historical play glorifying the Nordic past. Influenced by Schiller and Oehlenschläger, a small group of second-rate playwrights produced formula dramas about Sweden's past rulers and heroes. Using the folk legends collected by A. A. Afzelius (1785–1871) and Anders Fryxell (1795–1881), these playwrights attempted to string together a series of anecdotes into dramatic action. As most of the title characters of these historical dramas had long lived on in the popular imagination, the playwright could count on a built-in interest in them among the public. The plays bear the stamp of post-romantic patriotism. Their purpose seems to have been not only entertainment but also the apotheosis of Sweden's past leaders. Samples of this type of drama are *Erik XIV* (*Erik den fjortonde*, 1827) and *Birger and His Family* (*Birger och hans ätt*, 1837) by Bernhard von Beskow (1796–1868); *Dagvard Frey* (1877) by Edvard Bäckström (1841–1886); *Erik XIV* (*Erik den fjortonde*, 1846) by Johan Börjesson (1790–1866); *Engelbrekt and his Dalecarlians* (*Engelbrekt och hans dalkarlar*, 1846) by August Blanche (1811–1868); *Regina von Emmeritz* by Zacharias Topelius (1818–1898) and *Daniel Hjort* by Julius Wecksell (1838–1907), both from the 1860s and both emanating from Swedish Finland; and *The Wedding at Ulfåsa* (*Bröllopet på Ulfåsa*, 1865) by Frans Hedberg (1838–1908)—which became one of the most popular Swedish plays of the nineteenth century.

In addition to the serious historical dramas, some popular comedies were written and produced, such as *The People in Wermland* (*Vermländingarne*, 1846) by F. A. Dahlgren (1816–1895) and *A Traveling Theatre Company* (*Ett resande teatersällskap*, 1848), by August Blanche (successfully revived on Swedish television in 1978).

It would be no exaggeration to claim that when Au-

gust Strindberg came upon the scene, the Swedish theatre was in dire need of a talented, original playwright. Throughout the nineteenth century the stage had attracted mostly hack writers, while prominent literary people wrote poetry, novels, or closet dramas. When trying their hand at drama, they frequently produced their weakest works. For instance, the only play by the poet Johan Ludvig Runeberg (1804–1877), a five-act drama entitled *The Kings on Salamis* (*Kungarne på Salamis*, 1847), does not measure up to any of the epic and lyrical poems that made him Swedish-speaking Finland's greatest writer.

August Strindberg made his debut during a period that is usually referred to in Scandinavian literary history as "the modern breakthrough" (1870–1890). New philosophical and political ideas were in the offing. The Danish novelist J. P. Jacobsen (1847–1885) translated Charles Darwin's *The Origin of the Species* in the years 1871–1873. Parliamentary reform in Sweden in 1866 paved the way for a popular change in political representation. The working-class newspaper *Social-Demokraten* began publishing in 1885. Three years earlier students at Uppsala had formed a new radical club called Verdandi, to which many young future writers belonged. Feminists asserted their demands for independence and equal rights, encouraged by such topical Norwegian plays as Bjørnstjerne Bjørnson's *A Gauntlet* (*En handske*, 1883) and Henrik Ibsen's *A Doll's House* (*Ett dukkehjem*, 1879). Economically Sweden was undergoing a change with an upsurge of business activity in the wake of industrialization. Although the demographic shift from the rural areas to the cities was much slower than in England or on the Continent, the urban middle class, composed of business people and civil servants, was increasing. The first all-literate Swedish generation was now reaching adulthood after the compulsory school reform of 1850.

Strindberg lived in a tumultuous era of reform and change, a fitting social complement to his own fiery and restless temperament. His literary breakthrough came in 1879 with his novel *The Red Room* which bespeaks his

Anne-Marie Kuster was Julie and Michael Degen was Jean in Ingmar Bergman's adaptation of August Strindberg's *Miss Julie*, produced in Munich in 1981 as part of the Bergman Project, a trilogy including a new version of Henrik Ibsen's *A Doll's House* and a stage adaptation of Bergman's film *Scenes from a Marriage*. [Photograph by Jean-Marie Bottequin]

impatience and disillusionment with contemporary society. By then, however, Strindberg had ten years of frustration in the theatre behind him. It began in 1869, when as a twenty-year-old student, he tried his luck at acting. Interrupting his studies at Uppsala, he sought admission to the Royal Dramatic Theatre with a performance of the role of Karl Moor in Schiller's *The Robbers (Die Räuber)*. Advised by the director to settle for less, Strindberg finally chose the part of Härved Boson in F. Hedberg's *The Wedding at Ulvåsa*, a work that hardly impressed him. In his autobiographical novel *Son of a Servant* (*Tjänstekvinnans son*, 1886) he recalls: "Johan [August] read it at home and just about fainted. That was no role. It dealt with nothing. He [the character] just quarreled a couple of times with his brother-in-law, and then he embraced his wife."

Strindberg's acting career was short, but it challenged him to write for the theatre. In 1870 he made his debut as playwright with the one-act drama *In Rome (I Rom)*, which was staged on a double bill with *The Icon (Madonnabilden)* by the Norwegian artist Lorentz Dietrichsen (1834–1917). Strindberg's work made little impression, but in 1872 he stirred up a controversy in theatre circles when he delivered the prose version of his historical play *Master Olof*. *See* STRINDBERG, AUGUST.

Rather typically, hot-tempered Strindberg had stormed into the most conservative theatre fortress he could find, but the hegemony of the Royal Dramatic Theatre was already being challenged by more modern acting establishments. Four years prior to Strindberg's unsuccessful attempt to have his *Master Olof* accepted, the New Theatre, the largest private theatre in Stockholm, had opened its doors with the world premiere of Bjørnson's *A Bankruptcy* (*En fallit*, 1874). Five years later, after various transactions and economic ups and downs, the New Theatre gained considerable respect in the Swedish capital with a five-hour production of Goethe's *Faust*. In January 1881 Strindberg decided to send his revised (verse) version of *Master Olof* to the head of the New Theatre, Ludvig Josephson, who promptly gave him an enthusiastic reply: "For years I have not read a drama that has made such an overwhelming impression on me. I frankly declare that it must have been a most shortsighted, nonartistic, false and un-Swedish stage management to have declined to accept this piece for production."

Shortly afterwards *Master Olof* was performed at the

Strindberg's *The Pelican* as produced in Stockholm, 1968, with Marie Göranzon, Börje Ahlstedt, and Göran Graffman. [Swedish Information Service]

Scene from Ingmar Bergman's production of the first two parts of Strindberg's trilogy *To Damascus*. [Swedish Information Service]

New Theatre with August Lindberg, later famous as actor and theatre manager, in the title role. Lindberg moved to Finland in 1882 but returned to Sweden for guest appearances. It was he who introduced Ibsen's "infamous" *Ghosts* (1881) to Scandinavian audiences, with performances at both the New Theatre and the Royal Dramatic. His visit was symptomatic of a growing interest in theatre in the Swedish capital, which resulted in invitations to internationally famous companies and actors. Thus the Meininger troupe visited Stockholm in 1888 (*see* MEININGEN), and in the following years a succession of glittering stage personalities appeared in the Swedish capital, including Eleonora Duse, Constant Coquelin, Betty Hennings, and Ida Aalberg. New private theatres began to spring up, most of them catering to vaudeville audiences.

While Ibsen and Bjørnson continued to be staged in Stockholm, its native son August Strindberg had to seek production elsewhere. Both *The Father* (*Fadren*, 1887) and *Miss Julie* (*Fröken Julie*, 1888) were first staged outside Sweden—the former in Copenhagen, the latter in André Antoine's Théâtre Libre in Paris. It was only on his return to Sweden after years of exile and psychic upheavals that Strindberg became a regularly performed playwright in Stockholm, beginning with the world premiere of his historical drama *Erik XIV* in 1899. His version of the flute-playing king and son of Gustav Vasa, whose tragic life had been the subject of more dramatization attempts by Swedish playwrights than the life of any other royal personage, can be said to bridge the gap between traditionalist and modern Swedish drama.

Revealing—as in his entire oeuvre of historical dramas—as nationalistic an ambition as that of Johannes Messenius three centuries earlier, Strindberg's *Erik XIV* displays the author's irreverent free spirit vis-à-vis his country's past. Like Shakespeare, Strindberg is not afraid to telescope time and historical events to gain dramatic stringency, and he does not hesitate to add anachronisms to his dramatic plot. Thus his Erik is a "characterless character" (the term Strindberg used in the preface to *Miss Julie* to describe the modern fragmented soul), whose psyche is torn by the same conflicts as those that ravage his contemporary characters. In a discussion of the historical drama Strindberg contested his Swedish predecessors over the centuries by deemphasizing the heroic aspect of his royal characters and focusing on their human qualities: "Even in the historical drama, the purely human is of major interest, and history the background: the inner struggle of souls awakens more sympathy than the combat of soldiers or the storming of walls; love and hate, and torn family ties, more than treaties and speeches from the throne."

TWENTIETH CENTURY

From an international perspective Strindberg's historical dramas are less significant than his naturalistic tragedies and his dream plays. Especially the latter have had a seminal impact on modern drama, but their full significance was never realized during Strindberg's lifetime, not only because the public was often puzzled by their fusion of dream and reality, but also because modern stagecraft had not yet caught up with Strindberg's vision. Not until Pär Lagerkvist (1889–1974) published his crucial essay *Modern Theatre: Points of View and Attack* in 1918 did the full meaning of Strindberg's post-inferno production begin to be understood in Sweden. *See* LAGERKVIST, PÄR.

Lagerkvist's essay appeared during a period of theatrical revival for the drama, reaction against the Ibsenite fourth-wall play, and intense interest in the spatial and visual expansiveness of the stage. German expressionist playwrights after World War I acknowledged Strindberg as their master. Playwrights like Maxim Gorky and Eugene O'Neill praised him for his dramatic intensity and innovative spirit. Strindberg became the only truly international dramatist that Sweden had ever had.

A year before Lagerkvist published his "Strindbergian manifesto," the German director Max Reinhardt visited Stockholm with a production of Strindberg's *The Ghost Sonata*. This was in fact Reinhardt's third visit to the Swedish capital, each of them stirring up critical controversy in the local press, for neither the reviewers nor the public were quite ready to accept Reinhardt's dictum that the theatre was not an after-dinner entertainment or a moral and literary institution, but art for its own sake:

Gösta Ekman in Pär Lagerkvist's *The Hangman*. [Swedish Information Service]

"The theatre belongs to the theatre. . . Its fantastic richness of color, its limitless resources and variations, the blend of sound, words, color, line and rhythm create the basis from which its profoundest effect stems."

Reinhardt returned to Stockholm in 1920 with Strindberg's *The Pelican*. By that time he had aroused the enthusiasm of two young directors, Per Lindberg (1890–1944) and Olof Molander (1892–1966), who were to carry on the Strindberg renaissance and Reinhardt's ideas into the 1940s. Molander, in turn, was to fire the imagination of teenaged Ingmar Bergman (1918–   ) as he watched productions of *A Dream Play* in 1935 and *The Ghost Sonata* in 1941.

In 1918 Per Lindberg moved to the newly opened Lorensberg Theatre in Gothenburg (Göteborg) on the west coast of Sweden. This theatre, with its modern turntable and cyclorama stage, had begun its repertory in 1916 with a Danish guest performance of Strindberg's *A Dream Play*, directed by Svend Gade. In the years to follow, Gothenburg's several theatres came to reflect both Strindberg's shifting relevance to the Swedes and a changing emphasis in stagecraft, from the visually stunning *mise-en-scene* of Gade's *A Dream Play* and Per Lindberg's and Knut Ström's *Gustav Vasa* (1919), *Creditors* (1920), *The Saga of the Folkungs* (1920), *Master Olof* (1920) and *To Damascus III* (1922) to the simple chamber play format of the production of *Pariah* with which director Mats Johansson opened a small theatre in Gothenburg's public library in 1967, charging only a token admission.

Especially as author of dream plays Strindberg has remained a living presence in twentieth-century Swedish theatre. It is no mere coincidence that Ingmar Bergman's lifelong commitment to the theatre as a director revolves around a series of mostly post-inferno Strindberg interpretations, from a student production of *The Pelican* at the University of Stockholm in 1942 to his staging of *The Bridal Crown* at the Malmö City Theatre in 1954 and of *A Dream Play* at the Royal Dramatic Theatre in 1970 and again at Munich's Residenz-Theater in 1977, not to men-

Bergman's production of Strindberg's *The Ghost Sonata* as given at the Malmö State Theatre in 1954, with Benkt Åke-Benktsson as Hummel and Folke Sudqvist as The Student. [Swedish Information Service]

Anders de Wahl in Hjalmar Bergman's *Swedenhielms*, Grand Theatre, Malmö. [Swedish Information Service]

tion his many radio and television productions, such as *Playing With Fire, Crimes and Crimes, Easter,* and *Storm Weather.*

Because of Strindberg's key position in the Swedish theatre, his works have inevitably influenced Swedish playwrights who have emerged since his death in 1912. Such dramas as Lagerkvist's one-act play *The Tunnel* (*Tunneln,* 1918), Stig Dagerman's modern morality play *The Condemned* (*Den dödsdömde,* 1947), Ingmar Bergman's *Moraliteter* (1948) and his radio play *The City* (*Staden,* 1950), and Lars Forssell's visionary dramatic recreations of Swedish history all reflect Strindberg's pervasive influence, while Werner Aspenström's sci-fi dramas *The Apes* (*Det eviga,* 1959) and *The Spiders* (*Spindlarna,* 1966) represent a more indirect offshoot of Strindbergian drama via the international absurdist theatre. *See* ASPENSTRÖM, WERNER; BERGMAN, INGMAR; DAGERMAN, STIG; FORSSELL, LARS.

The dynamic growth of theatre throughout Sweden since the 1920s has also helped maintain the close rapport between playwright and stage that is a legacy of Strindberg's time. Modern Swedish drama is to no small extent linked with specific stagecraft developments and a national decentralized theatre policy. The collaboration between August Falck and Strindberg at the Intimate Theatre in the period 1907–1910 found a parallel of sorts in the special attention that Per Lindberg gave Pär Lagerkvist's dramatic works in the 1920s and 1930s. To Lindberg, Lagerkvist's drama "is what drama was originally: a cultic action, a hypnotic festival for the moral edification of mankind." Lindberg wanted to establish Lagerkvist as "a son and a poet of the people" by making him

part of a folk theatre movement. This ambition reflects a timely encounter between two creative minds who were fired by the same stylistic trends in the post-World War I theatre.

Lagerkvist was no doubt spurred on in his dramaturgic efforts by Lindberg's understanding enthusiasm, while his works—*The Tunnel* (*Tunneln,* 1918), *The Man Who Lived His Life Over* (*Han som fick leva om sitt liv,* 1928), *The Hangman* (*Bödeln,* 1933), *Man without a Soul* (*Mannen utan själ,* 1936), *Victory in the Dark* (*Seger i mörkret,* 1939), and *Midsummer Dream in the Poorhouse* (*Midsommarnattsdröm i fattighuset,* 1941)—became the vehicle through which Lindberg could in part realize his own ambitions for a new *mise-en-scène* and theatrical vision. It is significant that after Lindberg's death in 1944, Lagerkvist wrote only one more drama, *The Philosopher's Stone* (*De vises sten),* which had a respectful but lukewarm reception at the Royal Dramatic Theatre in 1948.

The picture of contemporary Swedish drama would be incomplete if confined to the Strindbergian renaissance and its aftermath. A realistic provincial and topical drama has also been part of the post-Strindbergian scene. Hjalmar Bergman, Per Lindberg's brother-in-law, established himself as the author of modern classics in both the poetic Maeterlinckian vein, such as his *Marionette Plays* (*Marionettspel,* 1917), and the realistic small-town comedy genre, such as *Swedenhielms* (1923), *Markurell's of Wadköping* (*Markurells i Wadköping,* 1930), and *The Baron's Will* (*Hans nåds testamente,* 1930). Vilhelm Moberg wrote a large number of folk comedies and dramas, including *Widower Jarl* (*Änkeman Jarl,* 1939), *Eve of the Market* (*Marknadsafton,* 1929), and *Our Unborn Son* (*Vår ofödde son,* 1945), as well as plays intended to arouse public debate, such as *The Judge* (*Domaren,* 1957) and *The Fairy Tale Prince* (*Sagoprinsen,* 1962). *See* BERGMAN, HJALMAR; MOBERG, VILHELM.

The documentary realism and biting satire of Moberg's thesis plays live on in such works from the 1960s

Scene from the original 1967 production of Kent Andersson's *The Raft.* [Swedish Information Service]

and 1970s as *Chez Nous* (1977) by Per Olof Enquist and Anders Ehnmark (1931–); *The Raft* (*Flotten*, 1967) and *The Home* (*Hemmet*, 1967) by Kent Andersson and Bengt Bratt (1937–); *The Princesses at Haga* (*Sessorna på Haga*, 1976) by Suzanne Osten; *While Sweden Slept* (*Medan Sverige sov*, 1967) by Pi Lind (1936–); and *NJA (Nils Johan Andersson)* or *Norrbotten's Iron Works* (*Norrbottens Järnverk AB*, 1968) by the Fria Proteatern Ensemble, a group of actors who broke away from the Royal Dramatic Theatre in 1968. All these plays uncover scandals or dramatize current problems in Sweden in barely veiled fictional form. *See* ANDERSSON, KENT YNGVE; ENQUIST, PER OLOF; OSTEN, SUZANNE.

But beginning in the 1960s the Swedish docu-drama broadened its scope to include international topics in such plays as *Hammarskjöld and God* (1969) by Öyvind Fahlström (1928–1976); *We Are One Country* (*Vi är ett land*, 1971), dealing with Vietnam and a global conscience by Mats Ödéen (1937–); and the Narren (Jester) Theatre group's *The Girl in Havana* (*Flickan i Havanna*, 1971), based on its experiences during a visit to Cuba.

In 1972 a commission appointed by the Swedish government submitted a proposal for a new national *kulturpolitik*. Two years later the Swedish ministry of education presented to the Riksdag a bill which incorporated the main principles of the commission's report, namely that "cultural policy shall contribute to improvement of the social environment and to promotion of greater equality." Though couched in the political jargon of the late 1960s, the premises of the new cultural policy could be traced back to the ideals of the emerging *folkhem* thirty to forty years earlier. These ideals were given a new impetus and a new focus in the social-conscious 1960s, and they affected Swedish drama and theatre more than they did any other art form.

As has often been pointed out, the early Social-Democrat ideologues in Sweden paid much more than lip service to the educational and cultural prospects of the

Gee, Girls—Freedom Is Near by Suzanne Osten and Margareta Garpe. [Swedish Information Service]

The Home by Kent Andersson and Bengt Bratt, as produced in 1970 under the direction of Fred Hjelm. [Swedish Information Service]

working class. Even in the economically stringent 1930s, when problems of unemployment and breadwinning had to take precedence over cultural matters, the party's minister of culture, Artur Engberg, took the initiative of founding the National Touring Company (Riksteatern), an ambulatory state-subsidized theater designed to replace the defunct private touring companies and bring stagecraft of high quality to every corner of Sweden. Since then the *folkteater* concept has become firmly established in Swedish theatre policy. From the Riksteatern and also from Per Lindberg's somewhat different ambitions for a popular theatre in the *Grosspielhaus* tradition, the concept evolved in the 1960s into the creation of state-subsidized city theatres—blueprint copies of the Royal Dramatic Theatre—and a plethora of alternate theatres, today organized as the *Teatercentrum* and receiving state support too. Inevitably, artistic, cultural, and political interests have at times collided in the contemporary Swedish theatre world, but they have also frequently reinforced one other.

Since the 1940s the Swedish theatre has been, as Lionel Trilling once said of the English poet John Keats, both a barometer and a forecaster. For instance, during World War II, the Gothenburg (Göteborg) City Theatre became an outspoken component of the anti-Nazi position taken by intellectuals and journalists in that city. The theatre reflected one important aspect of the political climate locally, but also theatre critics throughout the country began to pay regular attention to the Gothenburg theatre scene.

The cabaret writer and performer Karl Gerhard (1891–1964), long associated with the theatre in Gothenburg, expressed his political views so strongly during World War II that words of protest were submitted from the German embassy in Sweden. But relatively few dramatic works dealing with current political events were written in Sweden at that time. However, beginning in the 1960s the group theatre concept, which included scriptwriting, began to emerge in the Gothenburg theatre and spread to a growing number of small independent theatre groups. In imaginative, often doctrinaire dramas produced by single playwrights or by theatre collectives, Swedish playwrighting today often helps articulate flaws in the welfare state, or global social problems not yet fully formulated in the mind of the general public. Current Swedish drama reflects, above all, a strong commitment to "agitprop" theatre.

BIRGITTA STEENE

CRITICISM

There is no book-length study in English dealing exclusively with Swedish drama, but F. and L. Marker's *Scandinavian Theatre*, Totowa, N.J., 1975, includes a good presentation of the subject in the larger Scandinavian context plus an extensive bibliography. For readers of German, V. Arpe's *Das schwedische Theater*, Stockholm, 1969, is recommended.

A. Gustafson's *A History of Swedish Literature*, Minneapolis, 1961, contains sections on Swedish drama. The Swedish Institute in Stockholm has published two pamphlets on Swedish drama and theatre: N. Brunius, G. O. Eriksson, and R. Rembe, *Swedish Theatre*, 1967, and H. Sjögren, *Stage and Society in Sweden*, 1979.

Brief introductions to specific plays and playwrights are to be found in numerous Strindberg anthologies in English and in the following U. S. editions of Nordic plays: *Masterpieces of the Modern Scandinavian Theatre*, ed. by R. W. Corrigan, New York, 1967; *Five Modern Scandinavian Plays*, New York, 1971; *Scandinavian Plays of the Twentieth Century*, vols. 1 and 2, ed. by A. Gustafson, New York, 1954; *Modern Nordic Plays: Sweden*, New York, 1973; "The Modern Theater in Sweden," *Tulane Drama Review*, VI, 1961; *New Theatre of Europe*, vol. 3, New York, 1968.

Swedish studies include the following: A. Beijer, *Teaterrecensioner, 1925–1949*, Stockholm, 1954; G. Bergman, *Svensk teater, Strukturförändringar och organisation 1900–1970*, Stockholm, 1970; A. Klemming, *Sveriges dramatiska litteratur tom 1875*, Stockholm, 1863–1879; G.H. Ljunggren, *Svenska dramat intill slutet av sjuttonhundratalet*, Lund, 1864; N. Personne, *Svenska teatern*, 8 vols., Stockholm, 1913–1927; A. Pettersson, *Studier i svenska skoldramat*, Göteborg, 1929; G. Wingren, *Svensk dramatisk litteratur under åren 1840–1913*, Uppsala, 1914.

Swiss Drama

Linguistically there is no Swiss drama; however, Switzerland, a country with four national languages corresponding roughly to four geographic areas, has produced drama. The language boundaries inside the country are also literary boundaries. In each linguistic area the development of drama has taken a separate course reflecting its culture and history. Under German-Swiss sovereignty until the Napoleonic Wars, a large section of the French part and the entire Italian part of the country had no political and only limited cultural autonomy; now both French-Swiss and Italian-Swiss authors suffer from being cut off politically from their respective language communities. German-Swiss writers, too, have difficulties to overcome. As their mother tongue is the dialect of the community or region they have grown up in, they have to learn High German in school; thus in their own cultural province they are truly bilingual. In the Grisons, politically autonomous for centuries and having a long theatre tradition, Romansh—Switzerland's fourth language—accessible only to a relatively small local population has been an isolating factor. Drama in Switzerland has been characterized by a curious alternation between comparatively short spans of intense dramatic productivity and periods, at times entire centuries, during which the stage has ceased to be an important focus of cultural life. Playwrights of international renown are few and far between; however Switzerland is rich in authentic popular spectacles, folkloristic manifestations, and masques.

MEDIEVAL DRAMA

German-Swiss drama has its origins in the sacred liturgy of the Middle Ages. By the thirteenth century, as a first step toward secularization of the theatre, religious plays—formerly given exclusively in Latin—began to appear in the vernacular. The oldest known religious drama entirely in German, *The Easter Play of Muri (Das Osterspiel von Muri)*, was written about 1250 in the Benedictine monastery of Muri and most likely performed simultaneously on a series of stages in small-town squares. The unknown author delights in portraying little realistic scenes and elaborates upon those parts of the action that from the point of view of the Easter liturgy are irrelevant, for instance, when a merchant praises his cold creams and cosmetics in the language of contemporary love lyrics.

The oldest known German Christmas play is also of Swiss origin. *The Play about the Childhood of Jesus (Das Spiel von der Kindheit Jesu)*, though written in St. Gallen in the latter half of the thirteenth century, shows the influence of *The Easter Play of Muri* and shares its stylistic heterogeneity: Benedictine hymns and Franciscan nativity plays as well as courtly discourse have left their imprint. In the late Middle Ages *The Last Judgment (Das Spiel vom jüngsten Gericht)*, written in the monastery of Rheinau, was frequently staged; its considerable popularity appears to have been a reflection of the contrite *memento mori* spirit of the waning Middle Ages.

SIXTEENTH CENTURY

Among the achievements of humanism·and the Reformation in Switzerland are about one hundred extant plays from the sixteenth century: polemical religious satires, humanist comedies, Biblical and morality plays, plays with patriotic or classical themes, Shrovetide plays, and plays combining these various dramatic forms. Educated citizens partook in the performances. In Lucerne the patriciate organized theatre festivals, and the best-known playwrights generally belonged to the upper middle class or the nobility and were otherwise prestigious in city affairs. The reformers of German-speaking Switzerland supported the theatre as an alternative pulpit and often relatively little attention was paid to sophisticated plot development as scene followed scene in a very loosely connected manner. Characters entered, presented their opinions on whatever the issue might be, and exited. Their portrayal was rudimentary, and even the more carefully drawn figures were types rather than psychologically complex individuals.

The first playwright of stature in the sixteenth century was Pamphilius Gengenbach (ca. 1480–1524/25) from Basel. A book printer by training, he came into contact with some of the leading humanists in Basel. Sebastian Brant's satirical poem *The Ship of Fools (Das Narrenschiff)*, printed in Basel in 1494, illustrated with woodcuts by Albrecht Dürer and a best seller at the time, significantly influenced the paratactic structure of Gengenbach's works. His Shrovetide play *The Ten Ages of This World (Die zehn Alter dieser Welt*, 1515), the first printed German language play, was performed in Basel in 1515 and soon became popular in other towns as well. Reminiscent of morality plays such as *Everyman* or *The Dance of Death*, in which Death calls upon various representatives of human society, Gengenbach's play introduces a hermit talking in turn to ten characters who portray themselves in their own sinfulness. Of them, only a centenarian has come to regret his sins. In his *Fools' Meadow* (*Die Gauchmatt*, 1521), Lady Venus lures foolish men such as the Husband, the Soldier, the Physician, the Old Dude, and the Peasant onto her meadow, where they are robbed and ridiculed by her seductive maid servants. In *Eaters of the Dead* (*Die Totenfresser*, 1521 or 1522) Gengenbach serves the Reformation by attacking priests for accumulating riches by reading requiems. Representatives of the clergy complain about Luther as responsible for their dwindling number of customers. In addition, peasants, noblemen, and beggars complain about exploitation and neglect by the clergy. The Devil finally declares the priests to be his very own children.

The most impressive playwright of the period, not to be equaled for several centuries, was Niklaus Manuel from Bern (1484–1530). A true Renaissance man, he was dedicated to painting in his early years. As field scribe he subsequently joined a Bernese contingent fighting on the French side during the Italian campaign. After the disastrous defeat of 1522, Niklaus Manuel returned to Bern and played a decisive role in its conversion to Protestantism. His literary output was restricted to roughly four years (1522–1526).

In his two Shrovetide plays, both performed with great success by fellow citizens in the streets of Bern in 1523, Manuel ridicules the secularized clergy. *Concerning the Pope and His Priests* (*Vom Papst und seiner Priesterschaft*) shows greater wit and virtuosity than Gengenbach's. In it, as a deceased rich peasant is carried from his house in a coffin, everyone belonging to the Church—from the Pope down to the Priest's Whore—is jubilant about the anticipated revenues. Christ's teachings are remote to the Pope, and the Swiss Guards declare their indifference toward the Savior and that poor beggar, "bald St. Peter." A Maltese knight pleading unsuccessfully for papal support in the fight against the Turks identifies the Pope with the Antichrist. Peter and Paul, greatly surprised that the prince they took for a Turkish pasha is in fact the Pope, also consider him Christ's opponent. Peasants complain about the fraudulent selling of indulgences, and the play closes with a prayer by one Doctor Schüchnit ("don't be shy"), an ardent supporter of the Reformation who believes in Christ alone and not in the Pope, that "mortal bag of refuse."

Manuel's second, much shorter Shrovetide play, *About the Difference between the Pope and Christ* (*Von Papsts und Christi Gegensatz*), consists of a simple dialogue between two peasants commenting on a street scene: on one side of the street there is Christ, with his crown of thorns, riding on a donkey, followed by beggars and cripples; on the other there is the Pope on horseback, in military attire and surrounded by his glamorous entourage. Manuel's plays, essentially social documents, nevertheless distinguish themselves by their powerfully ex-

pressive language and by their visual suggestiveness.

Not surprisingly, the earliest "patriotic" plays come from Switzerland. One of the oldest is *The Uri Play about William Tell* (*Das Urner Tellenspiel*), performed in Altdorf in 1512. The plot is unfolded in the naive and simple tone characteristic of ballads. Unlike other versions, it presents Tell as one of the three founders of the Swiss confederacy; it is he who recommends the gathering on the Rütli and, after the assassination of Gessler, urges the people to storm the Governor's castles.

Of Old and Young Confederates (*Von den alten und jungen Eidgenossen*), staged in Zurich on New Year's day of 1514, is the first German-language drama to deal with contemporary politics; the events of the preceding year are reviewed and critically evaluated, followed by advice for the future. The author, possibly Balthasar Spross, a Zurich teacher, celebrates political independence and autonomy, cautions against treaties with foreign powers, rejects the wanton life of the mercenary, and recommends quiet, God-fearing work at home. As in Manuel's play *About the Difference between the Pope and Christ*, the author does not develop his thoughts within a plot; rather, they emerge from conversations between foreign heroes on the one side (Scipio Africanus and Hannibal are among them) and old and young confederates on the other.

Heinrich Bullinger (1504–1574) is the author of a tragedy set in ancient Rome, *Lucretia and Brutus* (*Lucretia und Brutus*), performed in Basel in 1533. It shares the tendentiousness of all literature written in the pious circle of reformer Ulrich Zwingli. A plea for democratic and just rule, as well as for moral purity, the play attacks pensions and the mercenary system. Bullinger's careful style and presentation, clear plot development, and impressively nuanced character portrayal and striving for psychological depth of motivation—so rare at the time—

A sixteenth-century woodcut showing *Das Urner Tellenspiel*, which told the story of Wilhelm Tell.

all make him next to Niklaus Manuel the best playwright of the period. In the first act of *Lucretia and Brutus*, Bullinger juxtaposes vile tyranny and chaste virtue. Lucretia, wife of Collatinus, has been raped by Sextus Tarquinius, the depraved son of the violent despot Tarquinius; the young woman commits suicide in front of her father, her husband, and Brutus. The latter feels prompted to call upon the people to rise against the tyrant and expel him. The second act shows Brutus as judge, inexorable yet just, putting even his own sons to death for having supported the exiled Tarquinius.

Biblical themes outnumbered national and classical ones. Switzerland's oldest sixteenth-century Biblical play, written anonymously and performed in Zurich in 1529, is also one of the finest of its kind. *About the Rich Man and Poor Lazarus (Vom reichen Mann und armen Lazarus)* is in the tradition of the popular Everyman plays and dwells on the agony and fear of the dying rich man.

Another frequently treated theme was the parable of the prodigal son. One version is by Hans Salat (1498–1561), a fervent defender of Catholicism and a man who had led a wild, adventuresome life. *The Lost or Prodigal Son (Vom verlorenen oder güdigen Sohn*, 1537) is particularly noteworthy for an insertion in the tradition of the *novella*, recited at the banquet of the spendthrifts by the Speaker, who fulfills a function similar to that of the chorus in ancient drama. The son of a rich Venetian is a glutton and spendthrift. His dying father has a shield filled with gold attached to the ceiling of his mansion and tells his son to hang himself by the attached rope should he ever become destitute and depraved. This comes about soon enough, and as the son is tightening the noose, much to his surprise he is showered with gold. He recognizes his father's wisdom, comes to terms with himself, and becomes an honorable man.

Besides serious, openly didactic plays there were a host of others meant merely to entertain. Many lack true wit, as their comic effect frequently relies on little more than bawdy language. Others, like the Shrovetide play *Marcolfus* (1546) by Zacharias Bletz (1511–1570), a Lucerne patrician, are quite amusing. The theme goes back to an ancient Jewish tale, which had previously been treated as minstrel song, gnomic poem, and chapbook. Marcolf is a shrewd peasant and practical joker, a Till Eulenspiegel type. His blunt and cynical observations make him the winner in debates against the idealistic King Salomon; however, despite a series of irritating pranks—having eaten the king's cake he replaces it with cow dung—he manages to stay in the King's favor and even ends up getting a permanent place at court.

The artistic decline of drama began to set in before the middle of the sixteenth century. Plays became verbose, unbalanced concoctions; performances grew into daylong events demanding excessive props and unmanageable numbers of actors; and the spectacles themselves were frequently followed by lavish banquets and revelries. Many citizens began to have misgivings about such spectacles and the Protestant clergy in Zurich, initially so supportive of the theatre, called a halt to all performances. While not all cities in the reformed German-speaking part of Switzerland followed suit, the theater gradually lost its importance.

In the Catholic regions of Switzerland events took a different course. Lucerne, for instance, had a flourishing theater tradition that began late in the fifteenth century and culminated by the 1580s in *The Passion Play of Lucerne (Das Luzerner Passionsspiel)*, which was performed over two days and involved 271 actors on the first day alone. The play was performed on an enormous simultaneous stage on the Weinmarkt, which could hold as many as four thousand spectators. The city had its official theater directors, who edited the texts encompassing the Old and the New Testament, conducted rehearsals, and supervised the actual performance. In 1616, however, with the Counter Reformation in full sway, the citizens' play groups in Lucerne were disbanded, and the Jesuits took over, removing such spectacles from public squares and using them strictly for didactic purposes in their colleges. Their plays, which eventually became highly elaborate theatrical operations, were written in Latin and performed by lay students in Jesuit institutions.

SEVENTEENTH, EIGHTEENTH, AND NINETEENTH CENTURIES

The Grisons had a flourishing tradition of passion plays transmitted orally since the Middle Ages and written down only shortly before they ceased to be performed altogether by the end of the nineteenth century. Improvised dialogues revealed not only the spiritual and moral values but also the legal and political views of the people. Both *The Passion from Sumvitg (La Passiun da Sumvitg)* and *The Passion from Lumbrein (La Passiun da Lumbrein)* were colorful spectacles. The former reflects the passionately political life of the Grisons from the sixteenth to the eighteenth century; the passion of Christ takes place on home soil, and it is intertwined with local history. The famous Shrovetide play *The Judgment (Dertgira nauscha)*, which goes back to pagan rites in honor of vegetation demons, presents Squire Carnival and Lady Lenten appearing before the Judge in criminal court. The verdict orders Squire Carnival to leave the valley within ten days and to return no sooner than ten months later, and be-

Reconstruction model for the sixteenth-century *Das Luzerner Passionsspiel*, presented in the wine market of Lucerne. [Theater-Museum, Munich]

cause he offended Lady Lenten, he must empty his purse besides, so that the court and the people may merrily celebrate Carnival. *The Judgment* was probably last performed in 1764.

It was to take several centuries to overcome puritan sensibilities spurred by the Reformation in German-speaking Switzerland and to abolish the strict prohibition against theatrical performances in Calvinist Geneva, where even in the eighteenth century permission for a theatrical performance was difficult to obtain. Amazingly enough, *Macbeth* was given there in English in 1741, and *Romeo and Juliet* was printed in a German translation in Basel in 1758. Undoubtedly the rise of the bourgeoisie in the eighteenth century, especially after the French Revolution, helped to bring about new interest in the theatre. Both Gottfried Keller (1819–1890) and Conrad Ferdinand Meyer (1825–1898), Switzerland's outstanding representatives of bourgeois realism *(bürgerlicher realismus)* in fiction and poetry, considered drama a higher form of art than the narrative and felt that their not having written plays was a definite shortcoming. Keller's various attempts at writing plays did not get beyond the fragmentary stage. To be celebrated on his seventieth birthday (1889) as a great poet although he had never completed a single drama was to him a sign of the mediocrity of his times.

TWENTIETH CENTURY

In his *Letter to d'Alembert Concerning Theatrical Performances* (*Lettre à d'Alembert sur les spectacles*, 1758), Jean-Jacques Rousseau had opposed the introduction in Switzerland of the classical French theatre, suggesting instead the development and cultivation of performances in which the people in general could take part. Heinrich Pestalozzi, Madame de Staël, Gottfried Keller, and Richard Wagner, a refugee in Switzerland, all followed suit, each developing his own theory of communal festivities and spectacles for mass attendance. Historical festival plays with hundreds of walk-on parts were thus seen everywhere by the end of the nineteenth century. In 1908 in the countryside of Mézières, the Théâtre du Jorat, a folk theatre in the Rousseauan spirit, was established. In 1921 it produced *King David* (*Le Roi David*) and *Judith* by René Morax (1873–1963) and Arthur Honegger, the Swiss composer. Throughout the first half of the twentieth century numerous plays on religious or national topics were written and performed, many by lay theatres and many in open-air productions: *Tell* (1920) by Paul Schoeck (1882–1952); *The Manichaens* (*Die Manichäer*, 1916) and *The Fall of Antichrist* (*Der Sturz des Antichrist*, 1927) by the mystic Alfred Steffen (1884–1963); *Swiss Legend Plays* (*Schweizer Legendenspiele*, 1919), *The Red Swiss Woman* (*Die rot Schwizerin*, 1921), and for performance on a huge open-air stage, *Independence Day Pageant* (*Bundesfeierspiel*, 1941), all by Caesar von Arx (1895–1949); and *The Lucerne Passion Play* (*Das Luzerner Passionsspiel*, 1934) and a dialect version of Austrian playwright Hugo von Hofmannsthal's *Everyman* entitled *Jedema* (1940) by Oskar Eberle (1902–1956). Arthur Caflish (1893–1967) wrote Romansh festival plays, such as *The Two Travers* (*Il duos Travers*, 1945), performed with the participation of entire village populations in the 1950s. Also in Romansh, the Biblical plays of Gian Belsch (1913–   ) have been repeatedly performed by young lay actors with great success, and they appear to signal a literary and intellectual renaissance in the Grisons from the late 1940s on.

There are, however, also those playwrights who have shied away from communal theatre and religious spectacles. Josef Victor Widmann (1842–1911), although demonstrating imaginativeness and a pronounced sense for the stage in his early plays, needed years to break away from traditional models and to find his own style. His *Cockchafer Comedy* (*Maikäferkomödie*, 1897), influenced by Schopenhauer's philosophy, is considered his finest play and has been successfully revived in our own time in Zurich. In the play a new generation of cockchafers (large beetles), full of expectations and lust for life, of idealism as well as skepticism, is swarming out and experiencing all the joys and, even more so, all the sorrows of existence. Violence and death appear to have the last word on earth. Albeit resigned, their king professes the beauty of creation but also deplores the fact that earth is not nearly so good as it is beautiful.

Paul Haller (1882–1920), one of the few Swiss playwrights truly indebted to naturalism, wrote a brooding and heartwrenching verse play, *Marie and Robert* (*Marie und Robert*, 1916) about a young worker, Robert, who guiltily wishes for the death of Marie's husband. When the latter dies accidentally, Robert finds that his guilt prevents him from marrying Marie. The depressing and paralyzing atmosphere created in the play together with the portrayal of deep moral conflicts and the harshness of a proletarian destiny are all reflections of Haller's personal experiences. Written in dialect, *Marie and Robert* has remained accessible to German-Swiss audiences only.

The French-Swiss novelist and essayist Charles-Ferdinand Ramuz (1878–1946) collaborated with Igor Stravinsky on the libretto of the opera *The Soldier's Tale* (*L'Histoire du soldat*, 1920); for the Lucerne premiere the decor was by René Auberjonois and the direction by Ernest Ansermet. Caesar von Arx, who had established his reputation by writing legend and folk plays for lay actors, eventually began to adapt to the expectations and demands of metropolitan audiences and to write for the professional theatre. In *Opera Ball 13* (*Opernball 13*, 1932), for instance, he dramatized a notorious Austrian espionage case. With the Nazi takeover in Germany, however, the playwright, like many of his contemporaries, once again turned to national topics as part of what was known as the "spiritual defense of the country" (*geistige Landesverteidigung*). *The Betrayal at Novara* (*Der Verrat von Novara*, 1933) delves into the Swiss past—the ignominious betrayal of Ludovico Moro by his Swiss mercenaries in 1500. The plays of Caesar von Arx, though technically exemplary, tend to be less satisfactory in content and poetry. He owes much to the German expressionist Georg Kaiser, whom he helped support financially when the artist chose exile in Switzerland in 1938.

Anticipating literary trends of the 1950s to the 1970s, the socialist Jakob Bührer (1882–1978) was the first dram-

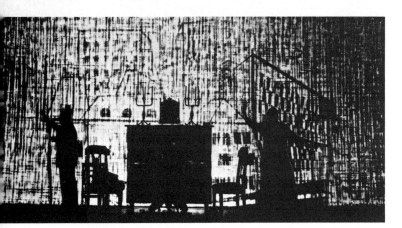

Max Frisch's *The Firebugs,* as staged in Poland in 1959 in a setting by Otto Axer. [*Theatre in Modern Poland*]

atist to write about Switzerland in an altogether new tone. His play *The Nation of Shepherds* (*Das Volk der Hirten*, 1914) is a dialect satire directed against his fellow citizens, challenging their complacent cultivation of patriotic legends. In *Marignano* (1918) Bührer expresses the conflicts and turmoils of a family that represents *in nuce* Switzerland during World War I: the father, a railroad engineer, is a staunch soldier, his son a pacifist, and the mother a would-be revolutionary; yet they all long for peace. In later plays, *Galileo Galilei* (1933) and *Pericles* (1940), he pleads for greater social justice. Most importantly, for the first time in several centuries, Bührer's work jolted Swiss drama out of its predominantly retrospective stance, so that it became once again a forum for public concerns—the place where the "state of the union" could be discussed and national self-analysis urged upon the audience. Bührer was very definitely a forerunner of another Swiss institution, the political cabaret, which with its acid commentaries on national and international events in the 1930s and 1940s constituted a form of "resistance" to Fascism.

After World War II, Swiss drama finally achieved international resonance with the plays of Max Frisch (1911–) and Friedrich Dürrenmatt (1921–). Their meteoric success is due to the fact that both of them are ingenious dramatists who transcended the provinciality that had so frequently been characteristic of Swiss theatre. In addition, they came to the fore at the very moment when Germany and Austria lost most of their playwrights, actors, and directors because of Nazi persecution. With intense censorship in German and Austrian theatres, the Schauspielhaus in Zurich became the only free German-speaking theatre, and overnight a host of internationally famed directors and actors became available to a hitherto provincial stage. At the Schauspielhaus some of Bertolt Brecht's greatest plays—*Mother Courage* (1941), *The Good Woman of Setzuan* (1943), and *Galileo* (1943)—had their world premieres.

Contemporaries and open to the experiments and achievements in modern theatre elsewhere, Max Frisch and Friedrich Dürrenmatt are, however, two very differ-

ent dramatists, expressing quite different concerns. Max Frisch's theatre was haunted at the beginning of his career by his impressions of World War II. His first play, *Now They Sing Again* (*Nun singen sie wieder*, 1945) is a requiem for the war victims in which the dead and the living join in a plea for peace. The malicious repetitiveness of history dogs the characters in *The Chinese Wall* (*Die chinesische Mauer*, 1946), as summed up in the Contemporary's words toward the end of the play, "the entire farce starts all over again." Frisch translates his concern with man's unwillingness to change and with the ensuing cyclical course of events into a non-Aristotelian form of theatre. In *Count Öderland* (*Graf Öderland*, 1951) place and space are no longer fixed, as the ambiguity of perspectives dissolves individual contours: the hero is split into dual figures with separate existences. Elsewhere Frisch has pointed out the problematic relationship between the individual and society. Time and again he shows individuals trapped by the fixed images others make of them or, alternatively, individuals create of themselves, as in *Don Juan or The Love of Geometry* (*Don Juan oder Die Liebe zur Geometrie*, 1953) and *Andorra* (1961). Frisch has refuted, on the one hand, the Greek concept of *moira* and, on the other, Brecht's didactic theatre, which dupes the audience into believing that events can take only one course—the one presented on stage. Instead, Frisch has created the theatre of permutation, either intimating that events can indeed take different courses, as in *The Firebugs* (*Biedermann und die Brandstifter*, 1953), or actually playing with biographical alternatives onstage, as in *Biography: A Play* (*Biografie: Ein Spiel*, 1967). *See* FRISCH, MAX.

Dürrenmatt appears to be less concerned with the troubled self; in fact, he questions modern man's right to take himself so seriously. He views the world as a monstrous, calamitous enigma that has to be accepted but to which there must be no surrender. His plays are cosmic in scope and eschatological in nature. They point back, in a

Friedrich Dürrenmatt's *Der Besuch der alten Dame.* [German Information Center]

parodistic vein, to the allegorical plays of the Middle Ages and the Reformation, but lack an all-comforting faith in ultimate order. With good reason, Dürrenmatt can be called heir to the early Bernese playwright Niklaus Manuel, but he is an heir who is "afflicted with the tumor of doubt." The Old Lady in *The Visit* (*Der Besuch der alten Dame*, 1956) is a perverted portrait of Lady World in the mystery plays; and Wolfgang Schwitter in *The Meteor* (*Der Meteor*, 1966) is an absurd latter-day Lazarus (*see* MYSTERY PLAY in glossary). Dürrenmatt's world is cruel and chaotic. In his plays—in contrast to Brecht's—the human condition cannot be changed, and as demonstrated in *The Physicists* (*Die Physiker*, 1961), not even thoughts can be revoked, even if it means the destruction of humanity. An amorphous world "about to fold like ours" can only be portrayed grotesquely in farces and tragicomedies; true tragedy of guilt and retribution has become obsolete in the twentieth century. Dürrenmatt has also rewritten and directed plays by Shakespeare, Goethe, and Strindberg. *See* DÜRRENMATT, FRIEDRICH.

While Frisch and Dürrenmatt continue to be actively involved in the theatre, a new generation of playwrights has come to the fore, many of them generously encouraged by the two "elder statesmen." The plays of Herbert Meier (1928–   ) have attracted considerable attention. Notable among them is *The Barge of Gawados* (*Die Barke von Gawados*, 1954), a lyrical play portraying a man in conflict between his love for a girl and his desire to avenge the murder of his father by killing her father in turn. As demonstrated in *Raven Plays* (*Rabenspiele*, 1971), for instance, Meier is master of a skill frequently lacking in German-Swiss drama: the formulation of good, fast dialogue.

Most of the contemporary playwrights have distinguished themselves first and foremost as poets or novelists, and their plays—good for reading—tend to suffer onstage. The novelist and university professor Adolf Muschg (1934–   ) is the author of *Rumpelstilz* (1968), a tragedy of lower middle-class life portraying a hypochondriac schoolteacher who is blind to the fact that his quiet and considerate wife is slowly dying of cancer, the very disease he fancies to have himself. In *Keller's Evening* (*Kellers Abend*, 1975), he dramatizes Gottfried Keller's last evening as a ne'er-do-well before assuming office as Secretary of the State of Zurich in 1861.

Otto F. Walter (1928–   ), also better known for his novels, is also author of the plays *Elio or A Merry Gathering* (*Elio oder Eine fröhliche Gesellschaft*, 1963) and *The Cat* (*Die Katze*, 1967). The theme of both plays is coping with the past. Reminiscent of Frisch, Walter is concerned with the "cursed stage that makes everything so unequivocal." In *Elio* he attempts to overcome this handicap through the device of recollection. A man escaped from prison shows up at the house of a middle-aged couple; the wife calls the fugitive Elio, the nickname she had given her husband many years earlier, and with the name the hopes and dreams of the past are brought back to life again.

Hugo Loetscher (1929–   ), Jürg Federspiel (1931–   ), Jürg Laederach (1945–   ), and Gertrud

Ruth Segal and Yosef Graber in a 1964 Haifa production of Dürrenmatt's *Frank the Fifth*. [*Theatre in Israel*]

Leutenegger (1948–   ), all better known for their prose, have also written plays in recent years.

In French-speaking Switzerland staunch regionalism has stood in the way of any unified effort among the major cities for the establishment of a theatrical center. There exists, however, an active tradition of festival plays, and Paris frequently serves the theatre. Small experimental theaters have sprung up as elsewhere in Switzerland, and they tend to be wide open to foreign influences. The best-known dramatist is Alfred Gehri (1895–1972), whose greatest success, *Sixth Floor* (*Sixième étage*, 1947), has been translated into twenty other languages and produced from Warsaw to Rio de Janeiro. Robert Pinget (1919–   ), resident in Paris from the 1940s and primarily known for his novels, has written several plays: *Dead Letter* (*Lettre morte*, 1959), *The Handle* (*La Manivelle*, 1960), and *Here or Elsewhere Archthingamagig: The Hypothesis* (*Ici ou ailleurs Architruc: l'hypothèse*, 1961). All of them recall the plays of Beckett and Ionesco, but they are rarely performed. Henri Debluë (1924–   ), Louis Gaulis (1932–   ), Bernard Liègme (1927–   ), and Walter Weideli (1927–   ) are also noteworthy.

Italian-speaking Switzerland has practically no theatrical tradition at all—a situation that is unlikely to change. The Ticino is cursed with political fragmentation and factionalism, and it has no significant cultural center and no real constituency for drama. There has been a tremendous influx of German speakers in Switzerland's "sun belt," most of whom do not acquire enough knowledge of Italian to develop interest in furthering a local stage. For the committed theatregoer Milan, with the Scala and the Piccolo Teatro, is only an hour away from Lugano. Finally, publication of works in Italy, where a broader public could be reached, has proved exceedingly difficult since authors from the Ticino are considered outsiders and usually not sufficiently trendy. Among the Italian-Swiss dramatists Reto Roedel (1898–   ) has been the most prolific.

Despite the isolated situation of Romansh, its literature and drama continue to live and to gain new adherents. Since the nineteenth century, historical dramas and comedies have been very popular. Among the modern Romansh playwrights Jon Semadeni (1910–   ) is the most noteworthy. In his plays contemporary issues are discussed in extremely refined dialogue. The hero in *Chispar Rentsch* (1946) is a young mountain farmer who renounces the temptations of the more lucrative hotel industry. *The Solar Eclipse* (*La s-chiürdüm dal sulai*, 1953) demonstrates that only through self-sacrifice can the free individual detach himself from totalitarian institutions such as the church or the state. Semadeni's juxtaposition of events and characters separated by centuries is reminiscent of techniques used by both Brecht and Frisch.

At present, Swiss hope for a new and significant playwright appears to lie with Hansjörg Schneider (1938–   ), who has written dynamic plays such as *Bread and Wine* (*Brod und Wein*, 1973) and *The Inventor or Bacon and Beans* (*Der Erfender oder Schpäck ond Bohne*, 1975); his powerful tragedy *Cowherds' Doll* (*Sennetuntschi*, 1972) is a Freudian reinterpretation of an ancient legend of the Swiss Alps.

Critics concerned with the future of drama in Switzerland all ask the same question: Despite all the new talent, will Max Frisch and Friedrich Dürrenmatt prove to have been grand exceptions in Switzerland's theatre history?

TAMARA S. EVANS

CRITICISM

J. Nadler, *Literaturgeschichte der deutschen Schweiz*, Leipzig, Zurich, 1932; A. Zäch, *Die Dichtung der deutschen Schweiz*, Zurich, 1951; C. Riess, *Sein oder Nichtsein*, Zurich, 1963; G. E. Wellwarth, *The Theater of Protest and Paradox*, New York, 1964; E. Catholy, *Fastnachtspiel*, Stuttgart, 1966; *Intellectual and Artistic Life in Switzerland*, P. Béguin, ed., Lausanne, Zurich, 1969; P. Demetz, *Postwar German Literature*, New York, 1970; *Die zeitgenössischen Literaturen der Schweiz*, M. Gesteiger, ed., Zurich, Munich, 1974; D. Fringeli, *Von Spitteler zu Muschg*, Basel, 1975.

Syed Alwi (1930–   )

Malaysian playwright, short-story writer, television producer, and filmmaker; full name, Syed Alwi bin Syed Hassan. Born in Pondok Tanjung near the town of Taiping on the west coast of peninsular Malaysia on March 29, 1930, Syed Alwi, like most Malays of his generation, got his early education in a Malay school near his village. His secondary education, however, was completed in the English-language schools of King Edward VII in Taiping and the Clifford in nearby Ipoh. Between 1953–1958 he was in the United States taking an A.B. degree in journalism and theatre from the University of Minnesota. After his return to Malaysia, Syed Alwi worked in Radio Malaysia (later Radio Television Malaysia) as a broadcaster, television producer, and until 1970 head of television drama. In the late 1960s, when he led the Malaysian Arts Theatre Group, Syed Alwi helped pioneer the writing and staging of local plays in the English language. Beginning in the 1970s all of his plays have been written and produced in Bahasa Malaysia, the national language of Malaysia, and as a result of this crucial decision, he has become significantly more prolific and innovative as a playwright, addressing himself to some of the most vital issues in the country in a style that allies modern and traditional theatre.

His comedy *Alang of a Thousand Actions (Alang Rentak Seribu)*, winner of the National Literary Award for Best Drama in 1973, is for the most part a conventionally realistic play depicting the clash that ensues between city and country values when a movie company appears in a village to make a film. But the characterization of Alang, the chief protagonist of the play, reflects a new sensibility arising perhaps from a profound change in the playwright's thinking following the racial riots in urban Malaysia on May 13, 1969. The supranaturalistic gestures of Alang, which seem to be efficaciously free of the confines of time and place, inject a mythic element into the play, urging values that might mediate the confrontation of tradition and modernity.

Syed Alwi won the National Literary Award again the following year with his play *Tok Perak* (wr. 1974; prod. 1975), the title of the play being the name of its chief character. *Tok Perak* was Malaysia's first intermedia play, presenting the stunning effects of both traditional and modern media—shadow theatre (*wayang kulit*), dance, sung poetry (*syair*), and films and slides. Through these means, the audience enters into the experiences of an old-style medicine man caught "betwixt and between" traditional medicine, which he represents, and modern technology. Simultaneously Tok Perak is also suspended midway between his craving for roots and family life and his lust for adventure and individual freedom.

Futuristic satire engaged Syed Alwi in his next play, *Happy Village* (*Desaria*; wr. 1975, prod. 1978), which bitterly predicts the end of creative excellence if artists submit themselves to bureacratic direction as they do unthinkingly in the futuristic village called Desaria. In his next play *Friends, Loved Ones and Countrymen* (*Rakan, Teman dan Para Bangsawan*; wr. 1979, prod. January 1980), Syed Alwi counsels the audience to confront the racial problems in the country unflinchingly and suggests that behind the personable patriotism and interracial fellowship of the four Malaysians in his play, there lurk inveterate devotees of Western values. Even as he has contended with large and seemingly abstract problems, particularly relating to the struggle between tradition and modernization, Syed Alwi has concretized these experiences into some of the most subtly textured plays produced in modern Malaysia. *See* SOUTHEAST ASIAN THEATRE.

KRISHEN JIT

Synge, John Millington (1871–1909)

Irish dramatist. Synge was born on April 16, 1871, in Newton Billas, Rathfarnham (now a Dublin suburb), to Kathleen Trail and John Hatch Synge, a barrister whose Anglo-Irish Protestant family had been in Ireland for several centuries. His father died when John was one year old, and the child was raised by his mother in an atmosphere permeated by an obsessive concern with religion and the penalties of sin. He attended a number of private schools, but his education was periodically interrupted by recurrent ill health.

In 1888 he entered Trinity College in Dublin, where he renounced his religious beliefs, became interested in

John
Millington
Synge.
[Irish Tourist
Board]

ancient Irish culture and language, and pursued his love of music and the violin. Otherwise Synge was an indifferent student. After taking his degree in 1892, he set out the following year for Germany to study the violin. For the next three years he attended schools in various German cities, traveled in Italy and France, made an abortive attempt at playwriting, and began the study of French authors.

By 1896 he had settled in Paris and matriculated at the Sorbonne. He might have continued indefinitely in this semiliterary life if he had not, on December 21, 1896, met William Butler Yeats—the single most important event in his literary life—and shortly thereafter the fiery Irish patriot Maud Gonne. For a time, early in 1897, he was associated with Miss Gonne's nationalistic, expatriate Irish League. *See* YEATS, WILLIAM BUTLER.

In mid-1897 he returned to Ireland, where he experienced his first attack of Hodgkin's disease, which was to be the cause of his death twelve years later. A successful operation caused the symptoms to remain relatively dormant until 1905. Early in 1898 he returned to Paris and renewed his friendship with Yeats, who, having read his current work, advised Synge to make contact with the common folk; he suggested the desolate Aran Islands off the Atlantic coast of Ireland, thus uncovering the wellspring of talent that until then had lain dormant.

Having taken Yeats's advice, Synge spent a month in the islands in the late spring of 1898 and returned each summer for the next four years. These trips were to have a great effect on his plays, but the immediate result was an imaginative journalistic account entitled *The Aran Islands* (1907). In June 1898 he returned from his first Aran sojourn to Coole Park, Lady Augusta Gregory's home in Galway, to be present at the initial planning sessions for the Irish Literary Theatre, which was to become the famed Abbey Theatre. Synge took no active part in the enterprise at this stage, for by this time he had begun to write in earnest. His articles and reviews appeared regularly in publications in Ireland and elsewhere. In 1901

he composed a florid three-act play that he submitted to Yeats and Lady Gregory. Although they rejected it, they encouraged him to continue writing plays. *See* GREGORY, LADY AUGUSTA.

The following year he wrote *In the Shadow of the Glen*. Its production in 1903 brought Synge instant notoriety when his portraits of Irish peasants were loudly denounced by militant Irish patriots as libelous. *Riders to the Sea*, produced in 1904, was more successful, but the applause was relatively mild for a work that many believe to be the finest short play in the English language. Synge's play *The Tinker's Wedding* (wr. 1903, prod. 1909) was considered too inflammatory even by the intrepid Yeats and was not produced during the author's lifetime.

By 1904 Synge was actively engaged in theatre work and participated in the formation of the Abbey Theatre, which opened on December 27 of that year. His *The Well of the Saints* was produced the following February, to the accompaniment of the patriotic hostility that was becoming customary at premieres of his plays.

Late in 1905 the Abbey Theatre lost a number of its more nationalistic members, and Synge, one of the three members of the board of directors (with Yeats and Lady Gregory), was forced to take an active role in the management of the company. One of the young actresses accepted into the reorganized, professionalized theatre was Molly Allgood, to whom Synge became deeply attached.

Despite his managerial commitments, Synge continued to write, and in January 1907 his *The Playboy of the Western World* provoked fierce opposition in Dublin, with near riots at some of the performances. Active violence also broke out when the play was presented in the United States. Nevertheless, from the very start *The Playboy of the Western World* was recognized as a dramatic masterpiece. *See* IRISH DRAMA.

At this time Synge's health was steadily declining, and he was to remain a semiconvalescent to the end of his life. He found the time and strength to draft (but not complete) *Deirdre of the Sorrows* and to make short trips to the Continent. In early 1909 he was forced to enter a nursing home in Dublin, where he died soon after, on March 24, 1909.

WORK

Although Synge wrote only six plays, two of them one-acters, he is nevertheless one of the finest dramatists, if not the finest, of the Irish theatre as well as an important figure in modern drama. His influence on Irish drama and literature has been particularly important, since his realistic assessments of Irish life and character have proved to be an effective force in opposing the tradition of the heroic myth.

If the artist is to read life truly he must be occupied with "the whole of life," Synge wrote Yeats. Only then can he provide "the nourishment, not very easy to define, on which our imaginations live." And that nourishment is found in the "strong things of life," rather than in the seedy problems of modern plays. But where can one find in this modern world the "strong things of life" that will make the drama the powerful nourishment it once was? Synge's wanderings among the hills of Wicklow, the wild wastes of Connemara, and the bare, gray islands of Aran provided the answer—the peasant folk of Ireland, a people in whom there still remained "a popular imagination that is fiery, and magnificent, and tender." In the preface to the *Playboy* Synge insisted that the vitality of modern drama depends upon a rich language that grows spontaneously out of the living reality of the folk imagination, "the rich joy found only in what is superb and wild in reality." Like Yeats, Synge was reacting against the naturalism of Zola and the didacticism of Ibsen.

The structure of Synge's dramas seems to flow directly and effortlessly from the characters; mechanics are so well hidden as to appear entirely natural. His gift for language is outstanding. The fluid, poetic prose, rich in colorful imagery drawn from the speech of the western counties and the Aran Islands, is unequaled in modern drama in English. It is a special form of dramatic expression forged from the union of poetry and the particular intonations of Ireland.

Synge's first play, the one-act *In the Shadow of the Glen*, shows his talent for naturalistic comedy. The development of a macabre but comic situation, in which a jealous husband pretends to be dead to trap his young wife with a lover, is treated realistically; yet there are flights of poetic language. This was followed by the one-act tragedy *Riders to the Sea*, one of the finest short plays ever written. Two lesser plays came next: *The Tinker's Wedding* (wr. 1903, prod. 1909), a broad comedy about the shenanigans of a group of itinerant ne'er-do-well tinkers and a mercenary priest; and *The Well of the Saints*, an ironic tale of an old couple who find strength in illusion and beauty in blindness.

Synge's comic masterpiece, *The Playboy of the Western World* (1907), is an imaginative treatment of a young man who becomes a hero by being forced to live up to the heroic lies he has told about himself. Although resented by Irish and Irish-American traditionalists, it is now

Scene from an Abbey Theatre production of *Riders to the Sea*. [Dermot Barry photograph]

widely acclaimed as one of the great comedies of Irish life.

Synge's last play, a tragedy entitled *Deirdre of the Sorrows* (1910), left complete but unrevised at his death, nevertheless contains the elevated language and realistic analysis of human relationships found in his other plays. It deals with Ireland's most famous legendary figure and represents a new departure for the dramatist. In abandoning contemporary Irish peasant culture for a traditional subject more suited to the school of the "Celtic twilight," Synge quite consciously tried to revitalize the moribund tradition of Irish historical drama.

In the Shadow of the Glen (1903). One-act comedy drama based on a folktale Synge had heard in the Aran Islands. In a remote and simple cottage in County Wicklow, Nora Burke sits before her husband's shrouded body and chats with the poetic Tramp, telling him of her prosaic existence and making plans to go off with him. Suddenly a sneeze is heard from the shroud, and the furious husband arises and chases her out of the house, presumably to join the Tramp and to fulfill her longing for poetry, romance, and nature.

Riders to the Sea (1904). One of the most celebrated one-act plays in dramatic literature. On an island off the west coast of Ireland, Maurya, bent with age and sorrow, has seen her husband's father, her husband, and five of her six sons killed by the sea. Now she is reluctant for her last remaining son, the headstrong, impetuous Bartley, to cross the rough seas to the mainland. Soon the news that she has almost expected comes: he has drowned. The long-suffering Maurya grieves over his body and the clothes of another son who was drowned only nine days earlier in the far north, saying "There isn't anything more the sea can do to me."

The Well of the Saints (1905). Synge's first attempt at the full three-act dramatic form. Set in "some lonely mountainous district in the east of Ireland one or more centuries ago," the story concerns Martin Doul and his wife Mary, blind beggars who have been benevolently deceived by the town's inhabitants into believing they are beautiful. Their sight is temporarily restored by the waters of a miraculous well administered by a saint. The harshness of reality and the realization of the townsfolk's deceit cause Mary and Martin to part, each to find a sep-

In the Shadow of the Glen, with (l. to r.) Eddie Golden, John Kavanagh, and Kathleen Barrington, Abbey Theatre, Dublin. [Dermot Barry photograph]

arate way in the world. But the cure is only temporary, and darkness descends once again. Mary and Martin, having found one another, now refuse the saint's offer of permanent sight, retreating forever into their blindness. The dream of perfection which is possible to the blind cannot be sustained in the world of reality.

The Tinker's Wedding (wr. 1903, prod. 1909). Two-act comedy with four characters that has never been performed in Ireland because of its irreverent portrayal of a country priest. The cleric is grasping, hypocritical, and thoroughly un-Christian in his dealings with a pair of disreputable young tinkers (gypsies) who wish to be officially married, though they have lived together for some time. The priest drives a hard bargain for the ceremony, and, failing to come to terms, the couple manhandle him. Terrified, the clergyman ends the play by calling down a Latin curse on their superstitious heads.

The Playboy of the Western World (1907). Christy Mahon, a cloddish, shy young farmer, appears at the local pub in a village on the wild coast of Mayo, bearing news that he has recently murdered his father with one blow of a spade while they were out digging potatoes. To his delighted astonishment he is hailed as a hero in the town, where he is a stranger, and begins to bask in the unexpected adulation. Thinking himself quite dashing, he becomes the object of amorous intentions from both the razor-tongued but desirable Pegeen Mike and the man-hungry Widow Quin. Inspired by his newly realized self-confidence and pride, Christy carries the day at the local sporting events and is about to claim Pegeen as his bride when his outraged father, Old Mahon, appears—bloody, unsteady, but very much alive. His arrival instantly transforms the much-admired Playboy into the butt of jokes and jeering and turns the disillusioned Pegeen against him. But Christy has had a taste of a new kind of existence, and unwilling to return to his former sniveling self, he downs his father a second time, apparently for good. But what had appeared to the townsfolk as a grandiose accomplishment from a distance becomes outrageous behavior when performed in their own backyard. When Christy is seized and bound by his erstwhile admirers, who now prepare to hang him, the indestructible Old Mahon crawls back again, still alive. A new

Sara Allgood, Barry Fitzgerald, and Arthur Shields in *The Playboy of the Western World*. [Irish Tourist Board]

Christy Mahon, master of the situation, returns with his father to their farm, causing Pegeen to lament: "Oh my grief, I've lost him surely! I've lost the only Playboy of the Western World!"

Deirdre of the Sorrows (1910). Tragedy based on the Irish legend of Deirdre, a beautiful young woman who has been claimed by the elderly King Conchubor of Ulster for his bride. The girl resists, telling him that she prefers to remain secluded in the wilderness with her old nurse Lavarcham. After a storm has brought the heroic Naisi and his brothers to her cottage, Deirdre and Naisi fall in love, are married, and fly far away from the wrath of the rejected Conchubor. Seven happy years have passed when the lovers are visited by Fergus, an emissary from the King, offering to allow them to live unmolested near the palace at Emain. Despite misgivings, they agree that they cannot hope to prolong their happiness in exile indefinitely and decide to accept the offer. As they are being welcomed by Conchubor, Naisi's brothers are slaughtered by the King's men and Naisi himself is killed while rushing to their defense. Then, when the King tries to persuade Deirdre to become his queen, Fergus announces that he has set Emain afire as punishment for Conchubor's treachery. Deirdre commits suicide, leaving Conchubor alone with the wreckage of his ambitions.

[CAROL GELDERMAN]

Maire Ni Domhaill and Eamon Kelly in *The Well of the Saints*, Abbey Theatre, Dublin. [Dermot Barry photograph]

PLAYS

1. *In the Shadow of the Glen.* Comedy, 1 act. Written 1902. Published 1904. Produced Dublin, Molesworth Hall, Oct. 8, 1903.
2. *Riders to the Sea.* Tragedy, 1 act. Written 1902. Published 1903. Produced Dublin, Molesworth Hall, Jan. 25, 1904.
3. *The Well of the Saints.* Parable, 3 acts. Written 1903. Published 1905. Produced Dublin, Abbey Theatre, Feb. 4, 1905.
4. *The Tinker's Wedding.* Comedy, 2 acts. Written 1903. Published 1908. Produced London, His Majesty's Theatre, Nov. 11, 1909.
5. *The Playboy of the Western World.* Comedy, 3 acts. Written 1906. Published 1907. Produced Dublin, Abbey Theatre, Jan. 26, 1907.
6. *Deirdre of the Sorrows.* Tragedy, 3 acts. Written 1909. Published 1910. Produced Dublin, Abbey Theatre, Jan. 13, 1910.

EDITIONS

Collected Works, vol. 1, *Poems,* ed. by R. Skelton, New York, London, 1962; vol. 2, *Prose,* ed. by A. Price, New York, London, 1966; vols. 3 and 4, *Plays,* ed. by A. Saddlemyer, New York, London, 1968.

CRITICISM

D. Greene and E. Stephens, *John Millington Synge, 1871–1909,* New York, 1959; A. Price, *Synge and Anglo-Irish Drama,* London, 1961; D. Gerstenberger, *John Millington Synge,* New York, 1964; D. Johnston, *John Millington Synge,* New York, 1965; A. Saddlemyer, *John Synge and Modern Comedy,* Chester Springs, Pa., 1968; R. Skelton, *The Writings of John Millington Synge,* Indianapolis, Ind., 1971; S. B. Bushrui, *Sunshine and the Moon's Delight: A Centenary Tribute to John Millington Synge,* 1972; P. Levitt, *John Millington Synge: A Bibliography of Published Criticism,* 1974.

Szakonyi, Károly (1931–)

Hungarian playwright and writer. After a try for a university diploma, Károly Szakonyi was a factory worker for ten years. His first publications appeared in 1958. Between 1963, when his first play appeared and was staged, and 1979, he was literary assistant of several theatres around the country. Since 1979 he has been a freelance. Szakonyi has received three cultural and literary prizes.

Hungarian Stalinism in the early 1950s and the revolution of 1956 greatly influenced Szakonyi's artistic development. His first drama, *Sophie, My Life* (*Életem, Zsóka,* 1963) was a penetrating analysis of the psychological and ethical corruption caused by political manipulation and tempting conformity. The writer Köves, the protagonist of the drama, epitomizes a new privileged, servile caste, hardly different from the discredited party protégés of earlier in the 1950s. In the course of the play Köves's disillusioned old-time friend commits suicide and the center of his existence, his lovely emancipated wife, walks out on him. Szakonyi's second drama, *Devil's Hill* (*Ördöghegy,* 1968) revolves around the same dilemma, but here the wife of the protagonist discovers that her husband erred when he thought that inaction and withdrawal were ethically the most correct means of avoiding corruption.

Telecast Breakdown (*Adáshiba,* 1970), Szakonyi's third play, has been translated into sixteen languages and staged in almost as many countries. The implied cultural criticism is equally pertinent to Western and Eastern European society and life-style. All through the play members of a suburban Hungarian family keep staring at an invisible television set—living, eating, celebrating, weeping and carrying on banal conversations under its spell. Nothing jolts their indifferent existence, even when it becomes obvious that their gentle new tenant is Jesus Christ. Even when he performs miracles similar to those in the Bible, the family is not surprised; the illusion and technology provided by television are considered even more dramatic "miracles."

The shallowness of modern existence and the inability of people to get in touch with their emotions or to establish human contacts are the themes of Szakonyi's more recent plays: *The Hongkong Wig* (*Hongkongi paróka,* 1973), *Until Doomsday* (*Ítéletnapig,* 1976), and *If You Stayed at Home* (*Ha itthon maradnál,* 1976). While the latter two one-act plays show similarities with the psychologically oriented absurdist allegories of Szakonyi's compatriot Miklós Hubay, the former comedy is a satire of snobbery and favoritism in present-day socialist Hungary (*see* HUBAY, MIKLÓS). The tongue-in-cheek question is which one of two equally incompetent careerists will get the coveted position in the Hungarian business commission in West Germany? *The Hongkong Wig,* in which stagehands repeatedly carry on private conversations with the actors, employs a number of experimental devices that are reminiscent of Luigi Pirandello's drama. Perceptively reflecting on the changes in Hungarian society, Szakonyi makes use of the theatre's potential but avoids mannerism.

GEORGE BISZTRAY

Károly Szakonyi.
[Photograph courtesy of George Bisztray]

PLAYS

1. *Életem, Zsóka (Sophie, My Life).* Drama, 2 acts. Published 1963. Produced Budapest, Ódry Színpad, 1963.
2. *Ördöghegy (Devil's Hill).* Drama. Published 1971. Produced Budapest, Madách Színház Kamaraszínháza, 1968.
3. *Adáshiba (Telecast Breakdown).* Comedy, 2 acts. Published 1971. Produced Budapest, Pesti Színház, 1970.
4. *Hongkongi paróka (The Hongkong Wig).* Comedy, 2 acts. Published 1976. Produced Miskolc, Miskolci Nemzeti Színház, 1973.
5. *Ha itthon maradnál (If You Stayed at Home).* Play, 1 act. Published 1976.
6. *Ítéletnapig (Until Doomsday).* Tragicomedy, 1 act. Published 1976. Produced Budapest, Ódry Színpad, 1978.
7. (With Tibor Gyurkovics). *De ki lesz a gyilkos? (But Who'll Be the Murderer?)* Produced Kecskemét, Katona József Színház, 1977.
8. *A hatodik napon (On the Sixth Day).* Produced Budapest, Madách Színház, 1978.

9. *Holt lelkek (Dead Souls)*. Comedy. Published 1979. Stage adaptation of N. V. Gogol's novel.

CRITICISM

P. Agárdi, "Szakonyi Károly első évtizede," *Kortárs*, no. 5, 1976.

Szigligeti, Ede (1814–1879)

Hungarian actor, director, and dramatist; pseudonym of József Szatmáry. He was Hungary's first professional playwright and the founder of Hungarian folk drama. The son of a Roman Catholic lawyer, he was born on March 8, 1814, in Nagyvárad (Oradea), Transylvania. His family wished him to become a priest; he wanted to study medicine. Financial difficulties solved the conflict; he became an engineer's assistant and then began studies in engineering. But contact with the stage soon brought out his real vocation, and he joined a theatre company in Buda in 1834. His father disowned him, requesting that he change his name.

In 1835 Szigligeti's first play, *Faked Contrivances (Megjátszott cselek)*, was performed, with little success. The same year he founded the Hungarian Dramatists' Society. In 1837 he joined the Hungarian Theatre of Pest, which became a state theatre in 1840 and was renamed the Hungarian National Theatre (Magyar Nemzeti Színhás). Szigligeti never left the company, serving it for forty years as resident playwright, director, secretary, and from 1873, managing director. Between 1837 and 1867, his plays comprised one-third of the company's repertory. In 1840 *Rose (Rózsa)* won its author the first of five first prizes he was to receive from the Hungarian Academy of Sciences. Popular acclaim soon followed with the great success of *The Deserter (Szökött katona)* in 1843. In 1845 he became a member of the Kisfaludy Society, and in 1849 his best-known comedy, *Liliomfi*, had its first performance. On December 27, 1872, a year before Szigligeti became managing director of the National Theatre, *Struensee*, his 104th play, opened with a gala performance.

Having married the young actress Franciska Sperling

**Ede Szigligeti.
[Interfoto MTI,
Budapest]**

early in life, Szigligeti had many children, some of whom became famous actors and actresses. He died in Budapest on January 19, 1879, at the age of sixty-four.

WORK

Szigligeti was first and foremost a working professional, able to produce several plays a year with consummate skill; he wrote, for the most part, with particular actors in mind, tailoring roles and situations to the needs and assets of the Hungarian National Theatre.

His major contribution to the Hungarian stage consisted in the creation of a national genre: the *népszinmü*, a form of folk theatre integrating music, singing, and dancing. He was the first Hungarian playwright to feature the people in his plays; his theatre displays a strong nationalist vein, although his first concern was always to entertain.

This incredibly prolific playwright wrote plays of every possible description: historical romantic dramas such as *The Deserter* (1843), in which a young blacksmith forced to join the military is sentenced to death for having taken too many absences without leave, and *Two Pistols (Két pisztoly,* 1844), which portrays a man turned highway robber in an attempt to rectify some of the legalized robbery tolerated by society; peripatetic comedies of light social satire, including *Liliomfi* (1849), Szigligeti's best-known play, in which he set down some of his own experiences through the misadventures of his hero, who turns to acting in order to escape an overly comfortable, predictable existence; historical tragedies, of which *The Pretender (A trónkereső,* 1868), a bitter comment on the dichotomy between power and morality, may well be the best; dramas of social protest such as *The Strike (A strike,* 1871), in which he came out in favor of striking workers against their capitalist exploiters; and of course folk plays, the most popular of these being *The Cowboy (Csikós,* 1847), which concerns a poor but noble cowboy who overcomes his jealousy toward a rich rival, thus foiling the intrigues of a ruthless schemer, and is able to marry the girl he loves.

The Cowboy *(Csikós,* 1847). Folk play in which András, a young cowboy, and Asztolf, a rich landowner, are both in love with Rózsi, the daughter of a poor peasant. Bence Ormodi, a lazy schemer, plans to take advantage of this situation in order to appropriate his cousin Asztolf's money. He hopes to make András so jealous that he will kill Asztolf, in which event Bence would inherit Asztolf's wealth. He tells András that Rózsi will allow Asztolf into her room that night and informs Asztolf that Rózsi expects him. The two men meet in front of Rózsi's house. At the last minute the suspicious András overcomes his jealousy and tells Asztolf that they may be victims of Bence's intrigues. His plot discovered, Bence kills Asztolf. András is suspected; then Rózsi's father is accused of the crime. Finally Bence, the real killer, is trapped by the peasants, and András is finally able to marry Rózsi.

Liliomfi (1849). Comedy of mistaken identity that opens as Professor Szilvási is traveling to Kolozsvár to bring home his foster daughter Mariska. Mariska is in

Engraving of a scene from *The Deserter*. [Goethe House]

love with an actor known as Liliomfi, but the professor has no intention of letting an actor into the family. In fact, however, Liliomfi is the professor's cousin living under a stage name. On the way home, the professor and Mariska stop at an inn, to which they are followed by Liliomfi and Szellemfi, a fellow actor. The waiter, Gyuri, recognizes Liliomfi, a former customer, and will keep the secret of Liliomfi's presence only if Liliomfi will help him gain the hand of the innkeeper's daughter. Szellemfi impersonates a rich suitor more to the liking of Professor Szilvási, but he behaves so scandalously that the innkeeper throws him out. A real suitor whom the professor prefers for Mariska arrives and surprisingly asks for the innkeeper's daughter. After many misunderstandings and mistaken identities, the comedy of errors is brought to an end by Gyuri's marriage to the innkeeper's daughter and–after he promises to give up the stage–Liliomfi's marriage to Mariska.

PLAYS

Unless otherwise noted, the plays were first performed in Budapest.

1. *Megjátszott cselek (Faked Contrivances)*. Social drama. Written 1834. Produced Budai Várszínház, 1835.

2. *Lidércek (Will-o'-the-wisps)*. Play with songs. Written 1834.

3. *Frangepán Erzsébet (Elisabeth Frangepán)*. Historical tragedy, 3 acts. Written 1835. Produced Budai Várszínház, 1835. Early version of *Cillei Fridrik*.

4. *Diénes, vagy a királyi ebéd (Dennis, or The Royal Treat)*. Historical tragedy, 5 acts. Published 1838. Produced Budai Várszínház, 1836. Early version of *Dávid*.

5. *Április bolondja (April's Fool)*. Comedy, 1 act. Published 1836. Produced Budai Várszínház, 1836.

6. *Gyászvitézek (Sorry Figures)*. Historical tragedy, 4 acts. Published 1838. Produced Pesti Magyar Színház, 1838.

7. *Vazul (Basil)*. Historical drama, 4 acts. Published 1838. Produced Pesti Magyar Színház, 1838.

8. *Pókaiak (The Pókai Brothers)*. Historical tragedy, 5 acts. Published 1838. Produced Pesti Magyar Színház, 1838.

9. *Aba (The Third Hungarian King)*. Historical tragedy, 5 acts. Published 1838. Produced Pesti Magyar Színház, 1838.

10. *Romilda*. Historical tragedy, 3 acts. Published 1839. Produced Pesti Magyar Színház, 1839.

11. *Rontó Pál (Paul Rontó)*. Musical comedy. Written 1839. Produced Pesti Magyar Színház, 1839. Based on József Gvadányi's story in verse.

12. *Micbán családja (The Micbán Family)*. Drama, 3 acts. Published 1840. Produced Magyar Nemzeti Színház, May 30, 1840.

13. *Rózsa (Rose)*. Comedy, 3 acts. Published 1840. Produced Magyar Nemzeti Színház, 1840.

14. *Cillei Fridrik (Frederick Cillei)*. Historical drama, 3 acts. Published 1841. New version of *Frangepán Erzsébet*.

15. *Ál Endre (King Andrew's Impostor)*. Historical drama, 4 acts. Published 1841. Produced Magyar Nemzeti Színház, 1841.

16. *Dávid (David)*. Play. Written 1841. Produced Magyar Nemzeti Színház, 1841. New version of *Diénes, vagy a királyi ebéd*.

17. *Trubadur (Troubadour)*. Historical tragedy. Written 1841. Published 1850. Produced Magyar Nemzeti Színház, 1841.

18. *Korona és kard (Crown and Sword)*. Historical tragedy, 5 acts. Published 1842. Produced Magyar Nemzeti Színház, 1842.

19. *Nagyidai cigányok (The Gypsies from Nagyida)*. Musical comedy. Written 1842. Produced Magyar Nemzeti Színház, 1842.

20. *Kinizsi*. Historical comedy, 3 acts. Published 1844. Produced Magyar Nemzeti Színház, 1843.

21. *Szökött katona (The Deserter)*. Folk play with songs and dance, 3 acts. Published 1844. Produced Magyar Nemzeti Színház, 1844.

22. *Két pisztoly (Two Pistols)*. Folk play with folk songs and folk dances, 3 acts. Published 1844. Produced Magyar Nemzeti Színház, 1844.

23. *Zsidó (The Jew)*. Folk play with songs, 4 acts. Published 1844. Produced Magyar Nemzeti Színház, 1844.

24. *Gerő (Lord Chief Justice)*. Historical drama, 4 acts; iambics. Published 1845. Produced Magyar Nemzeti Színház, 1844.

25. *Gritti*. Historical tragedy, 5 acts. Published 1846. Produced Magyar Nemzeti Színház, 1845.

26. *Debreceni ripők (The Rogue from Debrecen)*. Folk play. Written 1845. Produced Magyar Nemzeti Színház, 1845.

27. *Vándorszínészek (Touring Players)*. Comedy, 3 acts. Published 1845. Produced Magyar Nemzeti Színház, 1845.

28. *A rab (The Convict)*. Play with songs, 3 acts. Published 1846. Produced Magyar Nemzeti Színház, 1846.

29. *Egy szekrény rejtelmei (The Mysteries of a Closet)*. Play with songs, 3 acts. Published 1846. Produced Magyar Nemzeti Színház, 1846.

30. *Zách unokái (The Grandsons of Zách)*. Historical tragedy, 5 acts. Published 1847. Produced Magyar Nemzeti Színház, 1847.

31. *Paszkvill (Love and Family Intrigue)*. Comedy, 3 acts. Published 1847. Produced Magyar Nemzeti Színház, 1847.

32. *Mátyás fia (The Son of Matthias)*. Historical drama, 5 acts. Published 1847. Produced Magyar Nemzeti Színház, 1847.

33. *Egy színésznő (An Actress)*. Social drama. Written 1847. Produced Magyar Nemzeti Színház, 1847.

34. *Csikós (The Cowboy)*. Folk play with folk songs and folk dances, 3 acts. Published 1848. Produced Magyar Nemzeti Színház, Jan. 23, 1847.

35. *Renegát (Renegade)*. Historical tragedy. Written 1848. Produced Magyar Nemzeti Színház, 1848.

36. *II. Rákóczi Ferenc fogsága (Francis Rákóczi II in Captivity)*. Historical drama, 5 acts. Published 1875. Produced Magyar Nemzeti Színház, Nov. 4, 1848.

37. *Párbaj mint istenítélet (Trial by Combat)*. Folk play. Written 1848. Produced Magyar Nemzeti Színház, 1848.

38. *Liliomfi*. Comedy, 3 acts. Published 1849. Produced Magyar Nemzeti Színház, Dec. 21, 1849. A plagiarized version of *Liliomfi* is in circulation in German under the title *Umsonst*.

39. *Vid (Guy)*. Historical tragedy. Written 1850. Produced Magyar Nemzeti Színház, 1850.

40. *Házassági három parancs (The Three Commandments of Marriage)*. Comedy, 3 acts. Published 1879. Produced Magyar Nemzeti Színház, 1850.

41. *Fidubusz (Fidubus)*. Folk play. Written 1850. Produced Magyar Nemzeti Színház, 1850.

42. *Egri nő (Woman from Eger)*. Historical tragedy. Written 1851. Produced Magyar Nemzeti Színház, 1851.

43. *Andronik*. Historical tragedy. Written 1851. Produced Magyar Nemzeti Színház, 1851.

44. *Aggteleki barlang (The Cave of Aggtelek)*. Folk play. Written 1851. Produced Magyar Nemzeti Színház, 1851.

45. *Nagyapó (Grandpa)*. Folk play. Written 1851. Produced Magyar Nemzeti Színház, 1851. Music: Károly Doppler.

46. *III. Béla (Béla III)*. Historical tragedy. Written 1852. Produced Magyar Nemzeti Színház, 1852.

47. *IV. István (Stephen IV)*. Historical tragedy. Written 1852. Produced Magyar Nemzeti Színház, 1852.

48. *Arckép (Portrait)*. Social drama. Written 1852. Produced Magyar Nemzeti Színház, 1852.

49. *Lári-fári (Fiddle-dee-dee)*. Social comedy. Written 1853. Produced Magyar Nemzeti Színház, 1853.

50. *A cigány (The Gypsy)*. Folk play. Produced 1875. Produced Magyar Nemzeti Színház, 1853.

51. *Árgyil és Tündér Ilona (Árgyil and Ilona Tündér)*. Play, 3 acts. Writ-

ten 1853. Produced Magyar Nemzeti Színház, Apr. 16, 1853. Music: Doppler.

52. *Castor és Pollux (Castor and Pollux)*. Social comedy. Written 1854. Produced Magyar Nemzeti Színház, 1854.

53. *Diocletian*. Historical drama, 5 acts. Written 1855. Produced Magyar Nemzeti Színház, Sept. 19, 1855.

54. *Veszedelmes jóbarát (Dangerous Bosom Friend)*. Social comedy. Written 1855. Produced Magyar Nemzeti Színház, 1855.

55. *Pünkösdi királyné (Passing Glory)*. Folk play with music. Written 1855. Produced Magyar Nemzeti Színház, 1855.

56. *Csokonai szerelme (The Love of Csokonai)*. Musical comedy. Written 1855. Produced Magyar Nemzeti Színház, 1855.

57. *Dalos Pista*. Play with music. Published 1879. Produced Magyar Nemzeti Színház, 1856.

58. *Világ ura (Conqueror of the World)*. Historical drama, 5 acts. Published 1875. Produced Magyar Nemzeti Színház, 1856.

59. *Nevelő kerestetik (Tutor Wanted)*. Social comedy. Written 1856. Produced Magyar Nemzeti Színház, 1856.

60. *Pál fordulása (Sudden Change)*. Folk play. Written 1856. Produced Magyar Nemzeti Színház, 1856.

61. *Tizezer forint (Ten Thousand Forints)*. Folk play. Written 1856. Produced Magyar Nemzeti Színház, 1856.

62. *Béldi Pál (Paul Béldi)*. Tragedy, 5 acts. Produced Magyar Nemzeti Színház, 1857.

63. *Trücskök és prücskök (The Chirping of the Crickets)*. Historical comedy. Written 1857. Produced Magyar Nemzeti Színház, 1857.

64. *Petronella*. Social comedy. Written 1857. Produced Magyar Nemzeti Színház, 1857.

65. *Obsitos huszár (Veteran Hussar)*. Folk play. Written 1857. Produced Magyar Nemzeti Színház, 1857.

66. *A mama (The Mother)*. Comedy, 3 acts. Published 1863. Produced Magyar Nemzeti Színház, Apr. 26, 1858.

67. *Mátyás király lesz (Matthias Becomes King)*. Historical drama. Written 1858. Produced Magyar Nemzeti Színház, 1858.

68. *Fenn az ernyő, nincsen kas (Spending Spree)*. Comedy, 3 acts. Published 1863. Produced Magyar Nemzeti Színház, 1858.

69. *Zsigmond fogsága (Sigismund in Captivity)*. Historical drama. Written 1859. Produced Magyar Nemzeti Színház, 1859.

70. *Álmos*. Historical drama. Written 1859. Produced Magyar Nemzeti Színház, 1859.

71. *A műszeretők (Imitation Lovers)*. Historical comedy; verse. Written 1859. Produced Magyar Nemzeti Színház.

72. *A titkos iratok (The Secret Papers)*. Historical drama. Written 1860. Produced Magyar Nemzeti Színház, 1860.

73. *Az adósok börtöne (The Debtors' Prison)*. Social drama. Written 1860. Produced Magyar Nemzeti Színház, 1860.

74. *A molnár leány (The Miller's Daughter)*. Folk play. Written 1861. Produced Magyar Nemzeti Színház, 1861.

75. *Tinódi*. Historical play with music. Written 1861. Produced Magyar Nemzeti Színház, 1861.

76. *A trónvesztett (The Dethroned)*. Historical drama. Written 1861. Produced Magyar Nemzeti Színház, 1861.

77. *Laczkfi Imre (Emeric Laczkfi)*. Historical drama, 5 acts. Written 1862. Produced Magyar Nemzeti Színház, 1862. Early version of *Nadányi*.

78. *A nőuralom (Petticoat Government)*. Comedy, 3 acts. Published 1879. Produced Magyar Nemzeti Színház, 1862.

79. *Istenhegyi székely leány (The Transylvanian Girl from Istenhegy)*. Folk play. Written 1862. Produced Magyar Nemzeti Színház, 1862.

80. *A háromszéki leányok (The Girls from Háromszék)*. Folk play, 3 acts. Published 1875. Produced Magyar Nemzeti Színház, 1862. Based on Mór Jókai's story.

81. *A fogadott leány (The Adopted Girl)*. Musical comedy. Written 1862. Produced Magyar Nemzeti Színház, Nov. 16, 1862. Music: József Bognár.

82. *A debreceni biró (The Judge from Debrecen)*. Play. Written 1862. Produced Magyar Nemzeti Színház, 1862. Music: Gusztáv Böhm. Based on Jókai's story.

83. *A bujdosó kuruc (Insurrectionist in Hiding)*. Historical play. Written 1863. Produced Magyar Nemzeti Színház, Oct. 2, 1863. Music: Böhm.

84. *Az eladó leányok (The Marriageable Girls)*. Social comedy, 3 acts. Written 1863. Produced Magyar Nemzeti Színház, Jan. 16, 1863.

85. *A lelenc (The Waif)*. Folk play, 4 acts. Published 1879. Produced Magyar Nemzeti Színház, Nov. 20, 1863.

86. *Nadányi*. Historical drama, 5 acts. Written 1864. Produced Magyar Nemzeti Színház, Oct. 31, 1864. New version of *Laczkfi Imre*.

87. *A szerencse kereke (The Wheel of Fortune)*. Social drama. Written 1864. Produced Magyar Nemzeti Színház, 1864.

88. *A nagyratermett férfiu (Born to Greatness)*. Historical comedy. Written 1864. Produced Magyar Nemzeti Színház, 1864.

89. *A fény árnyai (The Shadows of Light)*. Drama, 5 acts. Published 1879. Produced Magyar Nemzeti Színház, Apr. 28, 1865.

90. *A próbakő (The Touchstone)*. Social comedy. Written 1866. Produced Magyar Nemzeti Színház, 1866.

91. *Szerencsés Imre (The King's Treasurer)*. Historical drama. Written 1867. Produced Magyar Nemzeti Színház, 1867.

92. *Az üldözött honvéd (The Pursued Soldier of the War of Independence)*. Historical drama. Written 1867. Produced Magyar Nemzeti Színház, Oct. 25, 1867.

93. *A halottak emléke (The Memory of the Deceased)*. Play. Written 1867. Produced Magyar Nemzeti Színház, Mar. 31, 1867.

94. *A trónkereső (The Pretender)*. Historical tragedy, 5 acts. Published 1868. Produced Magyar Nemzeti Színház, Nov. 13, 1868.

95. *A bajusz (The Moustache)*. Historical comedy. Written 1868. Produced Magyar Nemzeti Színház, Oct. 4, 1868.

96. *Kedv és hivatás (Desire and Calling)*. Social comedy. Written 1869. Produced Magyar Nemzeti Színház, Nov. 19, 1869.

97. *A szent korona (The Holy Crown)*. Play, 1 act. Written 1869.

98. *Uj világ (New World)*. Comedy, 3 acts. Published 1873. Produced Magyar Nemzeti Színház, Mar. 6, 1870.

99. *Ne fujd, ami nem éget (Don't Blow into the Flame)*. Social comedy. Written 1870. Produced Magyar Nemzeti Színház, Oct. 29, 1870.

100. *IV. Béla (Béla IV)*. Historical drama. Published 1870. Produced Magyar Nemzeti Színház, Jan. 20, 1877.

101. *Török János (Janos Török)*. Historical drama, 5 acts. Produced Magyar Nemzeti Színház, Jan. 20, 1871.

102. *Az udvari bolond (The Court Jester)*. Historical comedy. Published 1871. Produced Magyar Nemzeti Színház, Apr. 21, 1871.

103. (With Sándor Balázs). *A strike (The Strike)*. Folk play, 3 acts. Published 1872. Produced Magyar Nemzeti Színház, Oct. 29, 1871.

104. *Struensee*. Historical drama, 5 acts. Published 1871. Produced Magyar Nemzeti Színház, Dec. 27, 1871.

105. *Az amerikai (The American)*. Folk play. Published 1874. Produced Magyar Nemzeti Színház, Nov. 8, 1872.

106. *Valéria (Valerie)*. Historical drama, 5 acts. Published 1873. Produced Magyar Nemzeti Színház, Dec. 17, 1873.

107. *A várur és a szegényleány története (The Story of the Poor Girl and the Lord of the Castle)*. Play. Written 1874.

108. *Kényes Bertók*. Folk play with music. Written 1877. Produced Népszínház, Jan. 4, 1877.

109. *Perényiné (Mrs. Perényi)*. Drama, 2 acts. Produced Magyar Nemzeti Színház, Apr. 20, 1878.

110. *Kortesnő (The Lady Campaigner)*. Play.

EDITIONS

Sz'inművei, ed. by J. Bayer, 2 vols., Budapest, 1902–1904; *Sz'inművek*, ed. by S. Szalai, Budapest, 1960.

CRITICISM

P. Gyuīai, "Szigligeti és újabb színművei," *Dramaturgiai dolgozatok*, II, pp. 395–442, Budapest, 1908; L. Szentgyörgyi, *Szigligeti népszínművei*, Budapest, 1910; G. Czeiner, *Szigligeti társadalmi vígjátékai*, Budapest, 1932.